Basic Business Finance
TEXT AND CASES

Basic Business Finance
TEXT AND CASES

PEARSON HUNT, D.C.S.
Edmund Cogswell Converse Professor of Finance and Banking

CHARLES M. WILLIAMS, D.C.S.
George Gund Professor of Commercial Banking

GORDON DONALDSON, D.C.S.
Willard Prescott Smith Professor of Corporate Finance

All of the Graduate School of Business Administration
Harvard University

Fourth Edition

1971
RICHARD D. IRWIN, INC.
Homewood, Illinois   60430
IRWIN-DORSEY INTERNATIONAL, Arundel, Sussex BN18 9AB
IRWIN-DORSEY LIMITED, Georgetown, Ontario L7G 4B3

FOURTH EDITION

First Printing, August, 1971

Second Printing, February, 1972

Third Printing, June, 1973

Fourth Printing, December, 1973

Fifth Printing, February, 1974

Sixth Printing, July, 1974

Seventh Printing, December, 1974

Eighth Printing, May, 1975

Ninth Printing, November, 1975

Tenth Printing, March, 1976

Eleventh Printing, August, 1976

Case material of the Harvard Graduate School of Business Administration is made possible by the cooperation of business firms who
may wish to remain anonymous by having names, quantities, and
other identifying details disguised while basic relationships
are maintained. Cases are prepared as the basis for class
discussion rather than to illustrate either effective or
ineffective handling of administrative situations.

Library of Congress Catalog Card No. 71–158049

Printed in the United States of America

Preface

Although this book can serve as an introduction to the field of corporation finance, it is more properly named "basic" because it holds steadily to its focus on the decision-making financial officer within the firm.

Each section of a business organization works to further the organization's objectives. What distinguishes the sections is that each emphasizes a different component of the business problems that must be dealt with. The marketing man emphasizes the consumer, the production man the physical product, and so on. The financial man looks for and emphasizes the funds aspects of the organization's work.

It is the special province of financial work to procure, receive, and handle the funds of the firm in such a way as to increase the values obtained from the devotion of resources to the business.

The decision maker is not a theorist. Rather, it is the function of theory to serve him. The theorist is able to extract related components found in actual problems—and he performs a great service in doing so because he finds general principles that otherwise might be obscured. But business decisions are made for *specific* firms in *specific* circumstances. Rather than disassociating himself from these details, the decision maker must act with reference to them. The latest theories will help him only if he can obtain guidance toward the solution of the problem of the day.

We believe our book introduces the valuable contributions of theory in ways which permit the reader to learn to use them in the detailed environment in which decisions are actually made. Or, if the reader should choose to continue his studies of finance at the more abstract level, he will have the basic information about the real world that can keep him from making "simplifying assumptions" which lead to logical but inapplicable conclusions.

Every effort has been made to keep the book up to date in the factual area, in its recognition of developments in the theoretical area, and in the cases we have selected.

Several of the techniques and concepts introduced in past editions were novel at the time of first publication. We are gratified that some of them are now generally in use in the financial world. Readers familiar with past editions will find that, this time also, there are some novelties.

This book represents the work of many persons, and complete acknowledgment of all the contributions of a book now in the fourth edition is impossible. We would like to express here our appreciation of especially significant contributions.

First, we express our gratitude to the many professors who have given us the benefit of their experience with earlier editions of the book and their suggestions for its improvement. Surely this edition will be much enriched by modifications they have recommended.

Further, we want to thank those business leaders whose active cooperation made possible the preparation of case problems from actual situations. Unfortunately, they must remain anonymous.

Charles Moffett was of particular assistance to Professor Williams in the revision of Chapters 1–7 and 11–17, and John Heptonstall to Professor Hunt in the revision of Chapter 21. Assistant Professor Peter J. Barack of the Harvard Business School revised Chapters 26 and 29.

Sherry Frisk and Susan Robinson have been invaluable in the secretarial work on this edition. Eve Bamford was particularly helpful in the proofing and Josepha Perry was responsible for the indexing.

Along with the authors, who supervised the collection and writing of most of the cases, a number of faculty associates and research assistants at the Harvard Business School, present and past, played vital roles in the preparation of the case materials. We are grateful for their contributions.

The cases in this volume are copyrighted by the President and Fellows of Harvard College and are used with their permission.

Any error of commission or omission should be charged to the authors.

August, 1971   PEARSON HUNT
                                        CHARLES M. WILLIAMS
                                        GORDON DONALDSON

Contents

List of Cases   xv

Selected List of Tables, Charts, and Exhibits   xix

PART I. INTRODUCTION

1. Introduction   3

The Finance Function in Business. Organization to Carry Out the Finance Function in Business. The Design of This Book. The Substantive Plan of the Book. The Need for Funds: An Overall Look. Underlying Objectives of Resource Management. Alternative Ways to Improved Return on Investment. Different Routes to a Satisfactory Return on Investment. The Need for Pressures toward Effective Use of Assets.

PART II. THE MANAGEMENT OF ASSETS AND THE NEED FOR FUNDS

2. Inventory Management and the Need for Funds   21

A Focus on Manufacturers' Inventories. The Varied Makeup of Manufacturers' Inventories. What Determines the Amount of Funds Invested in Inventory? The Investment in Raw Materials. The Cash Flows Associated with Raw Material Inventories. Investment in Work-in-Process Inventory. Cash Flows Associated with Work in Process. The Investment in Finished Goods Inventories. Risks in Inventory Investment. Aids in the Analysis of the Investment in Inventory. Sharpen-

ing the Analysis of Inventory Position and Changes. The
Financial Officer's Role in Inventory Management.

3.   Receivables Management and the Need for Funds   42

Form of Receivables. Objectives in the Management of the
Investment in Receivables. Major Determinants of the Size of
the Investment in Receivables. The Work of the Credit Department. Sources of Credit Information. Evaluation of Credit
Risk. Policing the Collection of Outstanding Credits. Aids to
the Analysis of the Investment in Accounts Receivable. Accounting for Accounts Receivable. Cash Receipts from Receivables. The Trend toward Longer Collection Periods.

4.   Management of the Money Position   66

The Function of the Investment in Money Assets. Operational
Requirements for Cash. Reserves of Liquidity. Bank Relation-
ship Requirements. Intangible Values of a Strong Liquid
Position. "The Money Just Rolled In." Earning a Direct
Return. Short-Term Investment Policy Issues. An Example:
A.T.&T.'s Money Position. Approaches to More Effective
Management of the Money Position. Money Mobilization. The
Contribution of Improved Cash Flow Forecasting. Pinning
Down Needs for Protective Liquidity. Assessing Alternative
Methods of Providing Protective Liquidity. Aggressive Search
for More Productive Uses of Money Assets.

5.   Fixed Assets and the Need for Funds   86

Importance of the Investment in Fixed Assets. Distinctive
Aspects of the Investment in Fixed Assets. Major Funds Flows
Related to Fixed Assets. The Impact of Depreciation Account-
ing on Cash Outflows for Income Taxes. Business Investment
and Depreciation. Summary of Funds Flows Related to the
Ownership of Fixed Assets. The Total Business Outlay for
Fixed Assets in Recent Years. Aids in the Analysis of the
Investment in Fixed Assets.

PART III.   ANALYSIS OF PAST FINANCING AND FUTURE
            FUNDS NEEDS

6.   Interpreting Financial Statements   107

SOURCES AND USES OF FUNDS ANALYSIS. THE USE
OF RATIOS IN FINANCIAL ANALYSIS: Ratios in the
Measurement and Analysis of Profitability. Profits Compared
with Assets. Ratios as Measures of Asset Use. Ratios as Mea-

sures of Liquidity. The Source of Funds for the Business: Comparison of Borrowed Funds with Ownership Funds. Increasing the Usefulness of Ratio Analysis. Recognizing the Limitations of Ratio Analysis.

7. Forecasting Future Needs for Funds   127

Techniques of Forecasting the Need for Funds. The Cash Flow Forecast. The Essential Nature of the Projected Balance Sheet Method. Major Steps in Preparing the Projected Balance Sheet. Some Basic Problems in Effective Cash Forecasting. Long-Range Financial Forecasting.

PART IV.   CAPITAL BUDGETING

8. The Elements of the Investment Decision   145

THE NATURE OF BUSINESS INVESTMENT. MEASURING THE FINANCIAL IMPACT. BASIC QUANTITIES TO BE ESTIMATED: Initial and Later Investment. Terminal Values. The Change in the Operating Cash Flows. The Anticipated Length of Life. Effect of Tax Laws on Funds Flows. The Investment Standard or Opportunity Rate. BACKGROUND MATHEMATICS: The Procedure of Time Adjustment. The Behavior of Values over Time. Discounting an Annuity. Amortization of Loans.

9. Determining Investment Priorities: The Analytical
Framework   165

The Dynamics of Investment Choice. Ranking by the Internal Rate of Return Method. Ranking Projects by Present-Value Differentials. Assessing the Effects on Reported Income. The Use and Misuse of Payback. The Analysis of Variations in Risk.

10. Setting the Limits on Investment through *ROI* Standards   183

Why Limits? Defining the Corporate Cost of Capital: Individual Sources. The Average-Cost-of-Capital Standard. The Cost of Capital as an Investment Hurdle Rate. Some Valid Alternatives to the Cost-of-Capital Standard.

PART V.   SHORT-TERM SOURCES OF FUNDS

11. Spontaneous Sources of Credit   203

NORMAL TRADE CREDIT: Analyzing Changes in Trade Payables. ACCRUED EXPENSES. ACCRUED INCOME TAXES.

12.   The Effective Use of Bank Credit—I   209

IMPORTANCE OF BANK CREDIT TO BUSINESS. THE
STRUCTURE OF U.S. COMMERCIAL BANKING: Com-
mercial Banking as a Business. BANK LENDING STAN-
DARDS AND PROCEDURES: Basic Economics of Bank
Lending. Bank Credit Contrasted with Trade Credit. Contrast
between Owner's and Creditor's Return for Risk Taking.
Traditional Theories of Sound Commercial Bank Lending.
Differences between Banks and Bankers. General Procedures
in Making New Loans. Form of Loan. NEGOTIATING A
BANK LOAN: Paving the Way for Credit Applications.
Supporting the Loan Application.

13.   The Effective Use of Bank Credit—II   233

Key Characteristics of Bank Term Loans. The Development of
Bank Term Lending. CURRENT TERM LENDING PRAC-
TICE: Measures by Lenders to Restrict Risk. Distinctive
Aspects of the Credit Analysis. Repayment Provisions. Curb-
ing Risks through the Provisions of the Loan Agreement.
The Costs of Bank Term Loans. Term Loans from the Bor-
rower's Viewpoint. Advantages of Term Credit. Inherent
Disadvantages or Problems in the Use of Term Credit. NE-
GOTIATING   EFFECTIVE   TERM   LOAN   ARRANGE-
MENTS: Getting Ready for the Loan Negotiations. Top
Management's Role in Negotiating Term Credit. Appraisal
of Provisions and Selective Bargaining. Keeping a Good
Banking Relationship.

14.   Nonbank Sources of Short-Term Credit   249

The Commercial Paper Market as a Source of Short-Term
Funds. Finance Companies. The Use of Factoring. Private
Lenders. Customer Advances and Prepayments. Special Credit
from Suppliers. Credit Instruments Used Predominantly in
Foreign Trade: The Banker's Acceptance. State, Regional, or
Local Development Credit Corporations. U.S. Governmental
Sources of Short-Term Funds. Broad-Scale Government
Financing to Business under Depression Circumstances. Gov-
ernment Efforts to Fill Gaps in the Availability of Credit.
Financial Aids to Military Suppliers. Programs of Aid to
Especially Deserving Groups.

15.   The Effective Use of Security in Business Borrowing   267

Why Borrowers Offer Security to Lenders. Why Security Is
Valuable to the Lender. What Assets Make Good Security.

Establishing a Legally Valid Security Interest. BORROWING AGAINST RECEIVABLES: Discounting Notes Receivable. Borrowing against Accounts Receivable as Collateral. What Lenders Make Accounts Receivable Loans? Costs of Borrowing against Accounts Receivable. BORROWING AGAINST INVENTORY: What Inventory Makes Good Collateral? BORROWING AGAINST FIXED ASSETS: Borrowing against Equipment. Borrowing against Plant or Other Real Estate. BORROWING AGAINST SECURITIES AND LIFE INSURANCE. USE OF COMAKER, ENDORSEMENT, OR GUARANTY OF LOANS. SUBORDINATION OF CERTAIN DEBT CLAIMS TO OTHER OBLIGATIONS: Some Cautions Regarding the Giving of Security.

PART VI. THE SOURCE OF LONG-TERM CORPORATE CAPITAL

16. External Sources of Long-Term Capital   293

The Use of Long-Term External Capital in Perspective. The Volume of Funds Raised through Sale of New Securities. The External Sources of Funds for Purchase of Corporate Securities. Competing Demands for Savings. The Institutional Market for Corporate Securities. The Life Insurance Companies as Buyers of Corporate Securities. Property-Liability Insurance Companies. Private Pension Funds. Public Pension Funds. Investment Companies. The Commercial Banks. Mutual Savings Banks. Savings and Loan Associations. Religious, Educational, and Charitable Funds. Summary of the Institutional Market for Corporate Securities. The Noninstitutional Market for Corporate Securities.

17. Tapping the Sources of Long-Term Capital   315

Relation of the Markets for Outstanding Securities to the Distribution of New Issues. Major Types of New Offerings. The Role of Investment Bankers in Distribution of New Issues. Underwritten Public Issues—Negotiated Deals. Underwritten Issues under Competitive Bidding. Investment Bankers' Activities in Nonunderwritten Public Issues. Sale of New Issues to Existing Security Holders. The Investment Banker as Agent in Private Placements. Direct Sale of Common Stock to Employees, Suppliers, or Other Special Groups. Costs of Sale of New Security Issues. The Secondary Markets for Corporate Securities. The Over-the-Counter Markets. A Look at the Firms Doing Business in the Primary and Secondary

Security Markets. Secondary Offerings through Investment Bankers.

PART VII.   THE LONG-TERM CAPITAL STRUCTURE

18. The Basic Security Types   345

THE BOND: The Basic Promises. Sinking Funds. The Flow of Funds Related to the Bond. The Tax Implications of Debt Service. The Burden of Debt: Measures of Significance. Debt Ratios from the Balance Sheet. THE COMMON STOCK: The Flow of Funds Related to Common Stock and Its Measurement. Summary: Common Stock. THE PREFERRED STOCK: The Flow of Funds Related to Preferred Stock. Summary: The Preferred Stock. GENERAL SUMMARY.

19. The Use of Securities to Allocate Income, Risk, and Control   364

A Company's Capitalization. The Allocation of Income. Trading on the Equity. The Distribution of Risk—Priorities. Effects on the Cost of Capital. The Location of Control. Dilution and Control. Summary Grid.

20. Deciding on the Mix of Security Issues   385

Some Basic Premises. The Method of Analysis. Forecasting Operating Funds Flow. Forecasting Earnings. Forecasting the Capital Budget. The Funds Profile. Flows Related to Existing Financing. Meeting the Financial Specification. The Analysis of Risk in the Individual Company. The Question of Marketability. Timing the New Security Issue. Historical Behavior of Costs of Capital. The Need for Flexibility.

21. Reinvestment of Earnings and Dividend Policy   402

The Nature and Form of the Dividend. Taxation and Dividend Policy. Voting and Distributing the Dividend. The Concept of a Dividend Policy. Determining Dividend Policy. Dividend Policy under Capital Adequacy. Dividend Policy under Cash Inadequacy. The Dividend as Information. Dividends in Practice.

PART VIII.   THE BARGAIN FOR FUNDS

22. Leasing as an Alternative to Ownership   421

Examples of Leasing Arrangements. The Avoidance of Investment. Effect on Borrowing Capacity. The Question of Terminal

Values. Tax Advantage in Leasing. The Cost of the Arrangement. Ownership versus Leasing, an Example. Lease Obligations, Burden Coverage, and Debt Ratios. Summary.

23.   Modifications of the Distribution of Risk   434

Types of Protection. The Nature of Default. Technical Default. Sinking Funds. Preferred Stock. Control over Other Obligations. The Call Provision. Protection after Default: Priority.

24.   Modifications of the Distribution of Income and Control   452

Commitments to Fixed Payments. Convertibility. Warrants, Units. Contingent Payments. The Cumulative Preferred Dividend. Classified Common Stock. Dilution and the Position of Common Stock. Privileged Subscriptions: Rights. Stock Purchase Warrants. Modification of the Distribution of Control. Summary.

25.   Refinancing   471

Definitions. Refunding Bonds at Maturity. Refunding after Call. Recapitalization. Stock Splits. Stock Dividends. Conversion as a Means of Recapitalization. The Repurchase of Outstanding Common Shares.

26.   The Nature and Effects of Government Regulation on Long-Term Finance   488

FEDERAL REGULATION OF NEW ISSUES. FEDERAL REGULATION OF SECURITIES TRADING: Full Disclosure. Regulation of the Securities Markets. Prevention of Fraud and Manipulation. Credit Regulation. STATE REGULATION OF SECURITIES AND SECURITY TRADING. THE FUTURE REGULATORY PATTERN: SEC STUDIES AND INVESTIGATIONS. FEDERAL REGULATION OF CORPORATE FINANCIAL POLICY: Debt-Equity Balance. Cost of Financing. Preferred Stock. Shareholders and Voting Control. Financial Planning. SUMMARY.

PART IX.   FINANCING GROWTH AND DEVELOPMENT

27.   Financing the New Small-Scale Enterprise   517

Newness as a Financial Problem. The Related Problem of Smallness. The Sources of Funds for New Enterprise. Special

Assistance to Small Businesses. The Conservation of Scarce Funds. Summary and Conclusion.

28.   Growth through Merger or Acquisition: Financial Aspects   538

Internal versus External Growth. Definition of Terms. The Merger Movement. The Procedure of Mergers. Some Accounting Aspects of Business Combinations. The Conglomerate Phenomenon. Valuation. Kinds of Value. The Capitalized Earnings Approach. Asset Approaches to Valuation. Market Value Approach. Valuation in Practice.

PART X.   BUSINESS FAILURE

29.   Liquidation or Reorganization   563

Definitions. Statistics of Business Failure. The Causes of Business Failure. Insolvency without Bankruptcy. Bankruptcy without Liquidation: Chapters X and XI. Chapter XI Arrangements. Chapter X Reorganizations. Liquidation. Failure as a Management Problem.

Table A   932

Table B   933

Tax Table   934

Index of Cases   939

Index   941

List of Cases

PART II. THE MANAGEMENT OF ASSETS AND THE NEED FOR FUNDS

and

PART III. ANALYSIS OF PAST FINANCING AND FUTURE FUNDS NEEDS

The Case of the Unidentified Industries 585
　The influence of industry characteristics on financing patterns.

Shin Mitsubishi Financial 588
　Comparison of financial statements of a Japanese and a U.S. company.

American Motors Financial 594
　Comparison of financial ratios of four automobile manufacturers.

The O. M. Scott & Sons Company 599
　Financing dealers' inventories by means of trust receipts.

Union Paint and Varnish Company 614
　Evaluation of a request for heavy trade credit.

Inconco Corporation 624
　Revision of cash flow forecast to be more useful to corporation directors.

Big City Trust Company 630
　Analysis of financial statements to determine effect of growth in funds requirements and financing methods.

Sprague Machine Tool Company 635
　Estimating future needs and arranging bank credit.

Brown Marine Supply Company (1) 641
  Study of financial reports to discover reasons for cash shortage in a
  profitable company.

Brown Marine Supply Company (2) 647
  Monthly cash budget in a seasonal business.

The Estella Five-Year Plan 654
  Review of five year financial plans.

Illuminated Tubes Company 663
  Forecasting cash position and overall financial position in event of
  strike in customers' industry.

PART IV. CAPITAL BUDGETING

The Case of the Unidentified Investment Projects 667
  Ranking projects to determine desirability.

The Zenith Steel Company, Inc. 669
  Lease or buy a large computer.

Liberty Petroleum Company 679
  Use of cash flow estimates to determine offering price for an
  acquisition.

Molecular Compounds Corporation 689
  Possible change in cut-off criterion.

PART V. SHORT-TERM SOURCES OF FUNDS

Storkline Shops 698
  Financing rapid growth through short-term bank loans.

Plowman Poultry Farm 707
  Protection of increased loan to an aggressively expanding enterprise.

Long Beach Electronics Company, Inc. 716
  Bank's appraisal of request for additional short-term loan.

Custom Plastics, Inc. 725
  Evaluation of receivables as collateral for continued bank credit.

Digital Engineering Company 735
  Possible participation by a small bank in a multi-bank loan.

The Dunning Cabinet Company 743
  Financing plant expansion through a term loan.

Central Broadcasting Company 749
  Analysis of cash flow forecasts and a request for a bank term loan.

Ampro Europe 762
  Protective covenants for an overseas loan.

PART VII. THE LONG-TERM CAPITAL STRUCTURE

Shannon Corporation 775
  Choice between debt and equity for long-term financing.
Piedmont Garden Apartments 782
  The financing of residential real estate.
Nautilus, Inc. 793
  Analysis of alternate ways to finance rapidly growing firms.
SCM Corporation 807
  Desirability of resumption of cash dividends.

PART VIII. THE BARGAIN FOR FUNDS

The Prudential Insurance Company of America 815
  Selection of protective provisions.
Oren Weaving Company, Inc. 824
  Simplification of a complex financial structure.
Sun Stores, Inc. 833
  Convertible securities to raise equity.
Boxer Corporation 839
  Refunding preferred stock.
General Public Utilities Corporation 845
  Substitution of stock dividends for cash dividends.
Extone Chemicals, Inc. 857
  Purchase of own common stock.

PART IX. FINANCING GROWTH AND DEVELOPMENT

Upstate Canning Company, Inc. 870
  New enterprise: Analyzing the opportunity and arranging financing.
Head Ski Company, Inc. 877
  Pricing the first public offering of a growing business.
Wizard Corporation 893
  Negotiating an acquisition.
Norwest Construction Holdings, Limited 906
  Rapid growth through acquisitions.
Cerarts Company 918
  When and how to go public.

Selected List of Tables, Charts, and Exhibits

Table 1–1   Composite Balance Sheet, All U.S. Manufacturing Corporations, December 31, 1969   10

Table 1–2   Composite Balance Sheet, All U.S. Manufacturing Corporations   11

Chart 2–1   Investment in Inventory of Corporations in Selected Industry Groups, as a Percentage of Their Total Assets, for Companies with Accounting Periods Ended July, 1966–June, 1967   22

Table 2–1   Inventory Turnover, U.S. Manufacturing Corporations, 1969   23

Chart 2–2   Quarterly Inventories of All U.S. Manufacturing Corporations Compared with Quarterly Sales, 1964–69   26

Chart 2–3   Monthly Sales and Inventories of U.S. Manufacturers of Durable Goods, 1946–69   30

Chart 3–1   Investment in Notes and Accounts Receivable, Less Allowance for Bad Debts, of Active Corporations in Selected Industry Groups, as a Percentage of Their Total Assets, for Companies with Accounting Periods Ended July, 1966–June, 1967   43

Chart 3–2   Quarterly Accounts Receivable of All U.S. Manufacturing Corporations Compared with Quarterly Sales, 1956–Second Quarter, 1970   44

Exhibit 3–1   Key to Dun & Bradstreet Ratings   52

Exhibit 3–2   Symbols Used in Dun & Bradstreet *Reference Book*   53

Exhibit 3–3   Example of Business Information Report   55

Chart 3–3   Bad Debts Reported in Returns from All Active Corporations in Mining, Contract Construction, Manufacturing, Wholesale and Retail Trade, and Services   57

Chart 3–4   Bad Debts Reported in Returns from All Active Corporations in Mining, Construction, Manufacturing, Wholesale and Retail Trade, and Services, Expressed as a Percentage of Sales and of Receivables   58

Chart 4–1   Investments in Cash and U.S. Obligations of Active Corporations in Selected Industry Groups, as a Percentage of Their Total Assets, for Companies with Accounting Periods Ended July, 1966–June, 1967   67

Table 4–1   Summary Data on Short-Term Investment Media   76–77

Chart 4–2   Price of a 6% Coupon Bond to Yield 7% as a Function of Years to Maturity   78

Table 4–2   Liquid Assets/Current Liabilities, Very Large U.S. Corporations, 1961 and 1969   81

Chart 5–1   Investment in Net Capital Assets of Corporations in Selected Industry Groups, as a Percentage of Their Total Assets, for Companies with Accounting Periods Ended July, 1966–June, 1967   88–89

Table 5–1   Comparison of the Results of Straight-Line and 150% Declining Balance Methods of Allocating Depreciation of $200,000 Asset over 10 Years with No Salvage Value   97

Chart 5–2   Purchases of Plant and Equipment and Capital Consumption Allowances, Nonfinancial Corporations, 1946–69   98

Chart 5–3   Business Expenditures for New Plant and Equipment, 1947–69   100

Exhibit 6–1   Major Sources of Funds for American Business   108

Exhibit 6–2   Parkwood Homes, Inc. and Subsidiary, Consolidated Balance Sheet   109

Exhibit 6–3   Parkwood Homes, Inc. and Subsidiary, Statement of Consolidated Income and Retained Earnings   110

Exhibit 6–4   Parkwood Homes, Inc. and Subsidiary, Uses and Sources of Funds   113

Exhibit 6–5   Parkwood Homes, Inc. and Subsidiary, Uses and Sources of Funds   114

Table 7–1   Schedule of Cash Receipts from Sales   131

Table 7–2   Summary Schedule of Forecasted Cash Receipts   132

Table 7–3 Schedule of Planned Purchases and Payment for Purchases 133

Table 7–4 Summary Cash Payment Schedule 133

Table 7–5 Summary Schedule of Cash Flows 134

Table 7–6 Current Balance Sheet 138

Table 7–7 Projected Balance Sheet 139

Chart 8–1 The Basic Quantities of an Investment Analysis 151

Table 8–1 Summary of Investment 153

Table 8–2 Before- and After-Tax Funds Flows, from Proposed Investment in 9%, 10-Year Bond 155

Chart 8–2 Chart of After-Tax Funds Flows, Proposed Investment in 9%, 10-Year Bond 156

Table 8–3 Compound Amount of $1 158

Table 8–4 Present Value of $1 159

Chart 8–3 Effects of Time Adjustment: Single Sum 160

Table 8–5 Present Value of $1 Received Periodically for n Periods 161

Chart 8–4 Effects of Time Adjustment: Annuity 162

Table 9–1 Measuring the Benefit from a Computer Purchase vs. Lease Option: Internal Rate-of-Return Method 168

Table 9–2 Net Increase in Cash Flows of Table 9–1 Broken Down to Show Preservation of Investment and 10% Compound Rate of Return 171

Table 9–3 Comparison of Profitability Indexes of Two Investment Proposals 172

Table 9–4 Statement of Income from Proposed Purchase of Computer 174

Chart 9–1 Typical Curves of Probabilities 177

Table 10–1 Section of Bond Value Table Relating to 8% Bonds 186

Table 10–2 RCA Corporation Issue of 20-Year Sinking Fund Debentures 187

Table 10–3 Costing a Preferred Stock Issue 188

Table 10–4 Weighting from the Current Capital Structure, RCA Corporation 194

Table 12–1 Summary Balance Sheet, All U.S. Commercial Banks, June 30, 1970

Table 12–2 Loans of U.S. Commercial Banks on June 30, 1970 211

Table 12–3 Business Loans of Member Banks of the Federal Reserve System, October 5, 1955, by Business of Borrower ... 212

Table 12-4   Business Loans of Member Banks, 1957, by Size of Borrower ... 213

Table 12-5   Selected Income and Expense Data, 1969, All U.S. Insured Commercial Banks ... 217

Chart 12-1   Prime Bank Rate on Business Loans ... 218

Exhibit 12-1   Typical Promissory Note ... 228

Table 12-6   Relative Frequency of Various Reasons for Rejections of Small-Business Loan Applications ... 232

Table 13-1   Outstanding Term Loans to Business of Large Commercial Banks as of April 29, 1970 ... 235

Chart 14-1   Commercial Paper Outstanding at Year-End, 1918-70 ... 251

Chart 14-2   Selected Short-Term Money Rates, Monthly, 1951-70 ... 253

Table 15-1   Relation of Secured Loans to Total Business Loans of Member Banks, 1957, within Size-of-Borrower Groups ... 268

Table 15-2   Business Loans at Member Banks of Federal Reserve System, October 5, 1955 ... 277

Table 16-1   Sources and Uses of Funds, U.S. Corporations (Excluding Financial Corporations and Farms) ... 294

Table 16-2   Net Changes in Outstanding Corporate Securities ... 296

Table 16-3   Funds Raised by Major Sectors of the Economy ... 298

Table 16-4   The Financial Savings of U.S. Individuals, 1966-69 ... 301

Table 16-5   Distribution of Assets of U.S. Life Insurance Companies ... 302

Table 16-6   Sources and Uses of Funds, Life Insurance Companies, 1955, 1960, 1965-69 ... 304

Table 16-7   Distribution of Assets of Private Noninsured Pension Funds, December 31, 1969 ... 305

Chart 16-1   Estimated Aggregate Market Value of Investment Company Assets as of June 30 ... 308

Table 16-8   Distribution of Mutual Fund Assets at End of Years, 1960-69 ... 308

Table 16-9   Asset Holdings in Personal Trust Accounts Administered by Commercial Banks ... 309

Table 16-10   Dividends and Interest Received by Individuals in Various Income Groups, as Reported in Income Tax Returns for 1967 ... 314

Chart 17–1   Total New Issues of Corporate Bonds, Gross Proceeds   317

Table 17–1   Number of New Security Issues by Type of Transaction, 1935–49   319

Exhibit 17–1   Proposed Time Schedule and Assignment Sheet   324–26

Exhibit 17–2   Illustration of Invitation for Bids for a New Issue of Bonds   327

Table 17–2   Weighted Average Underwriting Spreads, as a Percentage of Gross Proceeds, on Underwritten Securities Registered with the Securities and Exchange Commission, 1951–53–55 and 1963–65   333

Table 17–3   Costs of Sale as Percentage of Proceeds (securities offered general public in selected years: 1951, 1953, 1955)   334

Table 17–4   Costs of Sale as Percentage of Proceeds (registered underwritten common stock offerings through rights to existing stockholders, 1963–65)   336

Table 17–5   Costs of Sale as Percentage of Proceeds (securities placed privately in selected years: 1951, 1953, 1955)   337

Table 17–6   Sales of Stocks on Registered Exchanges during 1969   339

Table 18–1   The Burden of Debt   351

Table 18–2   Ratios of Burden Coverage   352

Table 18–3   Debt and Equity Ratios from the Balance Sheet at December 31, 1969   354

Table 18–4   The Burden of Debt and Preferred Stock   362

Table 18–5   Ratios of Burden Coverage—Debt and Preferred Stock   362

Table 19–1   Westinghouse Electric Corporation, Condensed Consolidated Balance Sheet as of December 31, 1969   365

Chart 19–1   Effects of Trading on the Equity in Westinghouse Electric Corporation   368

Chart 19–2   Effect of Leverage on Rate of Return per Dollar of Equity Investment   371

Table 19–2   Calculation of Earnings per Share from E.B.I.T. for Alternate Financing Proposals   372

Chart 19–3   Effect of Leverage on Earnings per Common Share   373

Chart 19–4   Changes in Market Price of Three Securities, Weekly   376

Table 19–3   Summary Grid of Characteristics of Security Types Illustrated by Data on Westinghouse Electric Corporation, December 31, 1969   383

Table 20–1   Emphasizing Solvency   390

Table 20–2   Emphasizing Earnings   391

Chart 20–1   Indicators of Costs of Corporate Issues, 1946–65
              (after tax on debt instruments)   399

Chart 22–1   Relationships in a Typical Financial Lease   423

Chart 22–2   Accumulated after-Tax Cash Outflows in Bond versus
              Lease Methods of Financing an Investment of
              $225,000   429

Table 25–1   Comparison of Funds Flows, 1965–66   475

Table 27–1   Percentage Distribution by Employment Size of Com-
              pany of Total Business Population and of Sales and
              Receipts, 1958 and 1963   520

Table 27–2   Balance Sheet Percentages for Manufacturing Cor-
              porations with Assets under $1 Million and Assets of
              $1,000 Million and Over, End of Third Quarter, 1970   523

Table 27–3   Loan Levels of the Small Business Administration,
              1968–70   529

Chart 28–1   Mergers and Acquisitions in Manufacturing and
              Mining   541

Table 29–1   Total Industrial and Commercial Failures in the
              United States, 1955–70   565

Table 29–2   Why Businesses Fail—Year Ended December 31, 1969   567

Table 29–3   Bankruptcy Cases in the U.S. Courts, Fiscal Year 1968   581

PART I

INTRODUCTION

chapter 1

Introduction

In this introductory chapter of *Basic Business Finance: Text and Cases* we shall begin by describing the finance function in business. Having explained what this book is about, we then describe the design of the book—the point of view from which we approach the subject, the users for whom the book has been prepared, the needs we seek to meet through inclusion of both textual and case problem materials, the objectives of the text and of the cases, and how each should be used. Then we shall briefly outline the substantive plan of the book, that is, the major subject areas covered and the order of their presentation.

After this introduction to the book as a whole, we shall turn to an overall look at the needs for funds in business. The importance of using funds effectively and widely used methods of measuring the effectiveness with which funds are being employed are then considered.

The Finance Function in Business

This book is concerned with the finance function of business and how it can be carried out effectively. The finance function was once viewed simply as the task of providing the funds needed by the enterprise on the terms most favorable in the light of the objectives of the business. This long-held concept had the merit of highlighting a central core of the finance function—keeping the business supplied with enough funds to accomplish its objectives. Certainly, seeing to it that the business has the funds to support programs embarked upon is a basic part of the finance function. Getting the needed funds in the most suitable way and on the best terms possible also is clearly a central part of the finance job.

But the finance function is much broader than one of funds procurement or supply. It can and should contribute to the basic business objective of building values. Speaking broadly, values will be maximized only if the firm's resources are used effectively. Hence, the finance function is vitally concerned with the use of funds within the business, not just the supply of funds to the business.

Money seldom is available to the firm in unlimited quantities. In all cases, it has a cost. Evaluation of proposed projects that involve a need for funds should take into account the costs and other problems involved in getting these funds and balance these factors with the amount of added profits or other benefits expected to be achieved through use of the added funds. Moreover, the forecasted profits can seldom be regarded as assured; rather, most profit projections involve a significant degree of uncertainty. Consequently, the degree of uncertainty that should be attached to the achievement of the projected benefits also should be weighed in the decision whether to undertake the project.

To illustrate, let us assume that the production manager of a manufacturing firm is urging the construction of a new plant. This new plant, he predicts, will cut production costs and increase the firm's profits. Yet, to build the new plant will require a large outlay of cash and necessitate heavy borrowing. The financial aspects of the problem do not stop with a decision that the funds can be obtained or even with the decision that they can best be raised in a particular way—say, through an issue to the public of 20-year first-mortgage bonds. Instead, the financial considerations extend toward questions of whether the added profits from the new plant, in the light of the uncertainties involved, adequately compensate for the costs and risks involved in the borrowing. Further, are there alternative methods of getting the same or some of the profits at much less financial burden? Would, for instance, modernization of the existing plant at half the total cost and three quarters of the cost savings achieved by a new plant be a better alternative? Or could the funds required for the new plant be used to better advantage in research devoted to new products that could be produced efficiently with the existing facilities?

The concern of the financial function with the effective use of funds is most vivid in the case of proposed new projects that require funds, like the example above of the new plant. But it may be even more important to the firm that the funds tied up in its existing operations are being employed effectively. For example, action to free up funds by sale or liquidation of low-return divisions or product lines may contribute as much to the economic progress of the firm as careful policies and procedures of evaluating the cost/benefit relationship of new projects.

Altogether, it seems to us clear that the financial function cannot be separated out and divorced from broad consideration of the effective use of funds in the business.

The breadth of the financial function as we see it can be illustrated by noting the range of considerations involved in a seemingly narrow financial issue facing the board of directors: what dividends to declare on the common stock of the company. Certainly, in reaching a reasoned decision, the board will wish to take into account the financial needs of the business and the opportunities for using the funds that have been made available from profits in the business. But the board will also be concerned with such matters as the objectives and desires of the stockholders, the likely impact of alternative dividend decisions on the short-run and long-term market price of the stock, and the consequent effect of its own dividend action on the ability of the company to sell more common stock at a favorable price in the future.

Further, few firms enjoy financial positions so strong that planning can go forward on the assumption that any funds required can readily be obtained. Indeed, in a great many less affluent concerns the financial situation is such that the current and future operations of the business must be shaped to fit the funds available, rather than the reverse.

Even the relatively specialized or central-core aspects of the broad financial function—those related to supplying the needed funds—are not to be regarded as narrow or separated from the operations of the business, as we shall see in detail later in this book. The need for funds in a business is affected by every activity of the business and by virtually everything that happens to the business. In order to understand and meet its needs for funds efficiently and astutely, the financial officer must understand the business and keep in touch with all phases of its operations. Probably no other functional area of business is so intimately interrelated with other areas of the business as is the finance function. The successful financial man in business must be not only a "money man"; he must be a businessman of "wide-angled vision."

Organization to Carry Out the Finance Function in Business

The financial function, broadly considered, is much the same in its basic aspects in all businesses. The details of the function may differ widely, but the basic and important features of the job to be done are universal in nature. In larger firms many of the important aspects of the financial function are carried on by the top management of the company—the president, executive vice president, the board of directors, or top-management committees. The board of directors, with the advice of the president, treasurer, or other senior officers, may well make the final decision on such issues as building a new plant or liquidating a product line. Though final decisions on matters with strong financial implications may be taken by the board or by officers with overall responsibility in the firm, financial officers generally have an important opportunity and, indeed, responsibility, to contribute to good decision making on issues that cut across functional areas of the business. They should see to it that the financial implications of broad decisions are clearly brought out and are understood by those who must make the final decisions.

The ways in which enterprises organize to carry out the finance function differ widely. In very small concerns the head of the firm often assumes direct responsibility for marketing, production, finance, and still other functions. In medium and large concerns a separate financial department headed by an officer with a title such as treasurer may be assigned primary responsibility for the narrower funds supply aspects of the finance function. In some concerns responsibilities in the broad financial area are divided between a treasurer and a controller who, in addition to his usual duties as the chief accounting officer of the firm, may be assigned responsibility for such aspects of the finance function as financial forecasting and the appraisal of the effectiveness with which funds are used in various parts of the business. In many large concerns both the treasurer and the controller report to a chief financial officer who often has the title, vice president–finance. To minimize problems of terminology, we shall refer to the officer with primary responsibility for the financial function as the chief financial officer or simply the financial officer, be his literal title president, general manager, treasurer, or controller.

As is suggested by the nature of the finance function, the chief financial officer usually is one of the senior officers of the firm reporting directly to the president or executive vice president and is an important member of the "top-management team."

The Design of This Book

This book is written from the point of view of the chief financial officer in an operating business, a man with responsibilities for getting a job done well. His job involves participating in or making specific decisions and hence is oriented toward responsible recommendations and action rather than abstract theorizing. This viewpoint of the active businessman is in contrast with that of some finance textbooks which seem to be written more from the viewpoint of a detached observer and reporter of the business scene, or with other books written primarily from an investor's viewpoint. It is also in contrast with still other books on finance which are written more or less implicitly from a public or governmental policy point of view, such as that of a congressman heading a committee which has an interest in the financing of business.

The primary emphasis in the book is on financial decision making and administration in a going concern. When we deviate somewhat from our going-concern framework in the chapters dealing with business failure and the financing of new enterprises, the emphasis is on the special problems which management may face at either end of the life cycle of an individual business organization. Our general adherence to the point of view of internal management does not preclude our occasionally looking at business as might an outside analyst—investor, trade creditor, etc.

Since we take a point of view encompassing that of the chief financial officer, we are much concerned with what we term "the funds point of view." While, as we have emphasized, the chief financial officer, along with the president and other top officers, has a real concern for profits and the effective use of assets, typically he has the direct and primary responsibility for seeing to it that the firm does not run short of funds. The term *funds* is often used here and elsewhere synonymously with *cash* or *money*, but a more accurate and complete definition of *funds* would be *the means of payment*. Thus, the purchase of raw materials requires funds; but for a time, at least, credit supplied by the seller can take the place of cash as the medium by which ownership of the materials was accomplished. As the man responsible for seeing to it that the firm has the means of payment it desires, the chief financial officer appropriately is strongly oriented toward a funds point of view.

In this book, textual material and case problems are combined, on the premise that a basic course in finance should serve two major purposes. The text seeks primarily to inform—to provide the student with useful background information about the financing job in business. The case problems are designed to help the student to develop some skills in thinking through financial problems and in reaching sensible decisions for action in the context of specific situations.

To be more specific, one of the functions of the textual material is to supply background facts in key areas of our subject. For example, before introducing cases dealing with problems in raising funds, we describe the major suppliers of funds to business and the economic and operational conditions which govern the arrangements under which they make funds available to business. Particularly important sources of funds, such as the commercial banks, are treated at some length.

In addition, part of the text material is devoted to introducing techniques of analysis or interpretation of material that can be useful in handling the case problems or in business. For example, a chapter is devoted to discussion of techniques of forecasting future needs for funds and problems in their use.

Still other parts of the text go well beyond the task of painting a factual background or describing financial techniques and attempt to develop basic ideas on some important issues. We hope thereby to stimulate rather than close out student thinking on these issues. In most instances where we have put forward our own ideas on debatable subjects, the student will have a chance to test the usefulness of these concepts in dealing with related issues raised in the cases.

We should make clear, however, that we do not attempt in the text to supply the answers to the case problems that follow. Rather, we hope through the text to bring the student along to a point where he can comprehend the problems posed in the cases and work out sensible answers to these problems. In other words, we hope through the text to equip the student with useful tools for attacking the issues raised in the cases.

Since few students will have had previous training through case problems, some discussion of the case problems is appropriate. Most of the cases are descriptions of actual business problems faced by real firms. The names, and sometimes other nonvital facts, have usually been disguised to conceal the true identity of the firms—indeed, the use of a disguise has usually been a condition of permission by the firm for us to use the material. Usually, too, the actual facts of the business situation have been simplified somewhat by omission or alteration of peripheral aspects.

The case problems are much more than illustrations; typically they are "live" problems calling for solutions. Seldom is there one easy or "right" answer to the problem, but some actions clearly are better than others that might be suggested. Each student should think through the major alternative solutions and be prepared to defend under challenge his choice of course of action. The cases are designed to stimulate a maximum of both individual and group analysis and thinking—active participation —that goes well beyond mechanical assertion of principles or unthinking application of prescribed decision rules. Seldom have the authors had a really good case class discussion that did not produce some interesting facet or consideration that had not come up before in his own thinking or in earlier classes. The class session should be more joint faculty-student searches for the best working solutions than demonstrations of preestablished truths. It is with no apology that the authors acknowledge that their own ideas as to the best actions often have changed materially through successive discussions of the cases.

The Substantive Plan of the Book

It may be helpful to review briefly the major subject areas to be covered and indicate the order in which they are taken up in the book. We first are concerned with helping the student understand the nature of the need for funds in business. The nature and amount of funds needed to operate a business are grounded on the nature of its operations. We seek to help the student to see how operational decisions affect the need for funds and how changes in operations, such as changes in the policy of the firm toward granting credit to customers, affect the finances of business. Attention is directed, in turn, to the investment in inventory, in receivables, in cash and near-cash investments, and in fixed assets. Methods by which the financial officer can play a useful part in controlling the need for funds are also examined.

In Part III we discuss techniques of analyzing the past and current financing of the business as a means of understanding the past needs for funds and the way they have been met.

From a focus on understanding past needs, we then shift to the forecasting of future needs for funds. Techniques for organizing information on the future operations of the business into specific forecasts of funds needs are introduced and discussed.

Part IV is also concerned with methodology of analysis. Three chapters deal with the evaluation of major capital investment opportunities or "capital budgeting." Current analytical techniques for assessing likely project costs and benefits are described, including time adjustment of cash flows, the cost of capital funds, and opportunity cost considerations.

Having equipped (hopefully) the student with some working tools and concepts of analysis, we turn in Parts V and VI to the sources of funds for business and how they can be utilized effectively. Part V focuses on the use of short- and intermediate-term sources, while Part VI introduces the sources of long-term funds and describes the institutions and methods through which firms draw funds from the "capital markets." The underlying considerations of risk, income, and control are presented, and analytical approaches are offered for considering objectively the choices that must be made. At this stage the choices are presented in their simplest form so that the essential features will be more readily apparent.

Part VIII, dealing with the bargain for funds, turns attention to a number of the more important variations in long-term capital contracts and observes how modifications in the distribution of risk, income, and control evolve to meet the recognized needs of suppliers and users of capital. This section also includes chapters on leasing as an alternative to ownership, on refinancing, and on the nature and effects of government regulation. The objective of this last chapter is not only to describe the nature of present-day regulation, with special emphasis on the role of the Securities and Exchange Commission but, more importantly, to bring out the impact of such regulation on the financial practices and policies of individual business corporations.

The final sections of the book group a number of special aspects of business finance under the headings "Financing Growth and Development" and "Business Failure." The financial problems peculiar to the new, small-scale business are presented in some detail. Other chapters deal with valuation and other financial aspects of mergers and with the problems surrounding the firm during a period of serious financial difficulty, contrasting liquidation with the reconstruction of the corporate structure to permit a continuing business.

The Need for Funds: An Overall Look

"You've got to have money to make money." This business adage is a simple recognition that most enterprises require a continuing commitment of funds in order to operate. The typical manufacturer, for example, must have a plant and production equipment, maintain some stocks of goods, extend credit to its customers, and maintain a bank account. Table 1–1 shows the assets and liabilities of all U.S. manufacturing corporations at year-end 1969. Together, these corporations owned assets of almost $544 billion. The largest single asset category was physical facilities; plant and equipment net of depreciation reserves amounted to $215 billion, or

Table 1-1

Composite Balance Sheet, All U.S. Manufacturing Corporations,
December 31, 1969
(dollar figures in millions)

ASSETS	December 31, 1969	Percentage of Total
Cash.................................	$ 23,754	4.4%
U.S. government securities...............	6,783	1.2
Notes and accounts receivable............	96,538	17.8
Inventories..........................	126,229	23.2
Other current assets....................	19,776	3.6
Total current assets...............	$273,080	50.2%
Plant and equipment....................	405,351	
Less: Reserve for depreciation..........	190,060	
Plant and equipment, net................	215,291	39.6
Other noncurrent assets.................	55,342	10.2
Total assets....................	$543,712	100.0%

LIABILITIES		
Short-term bank loans....................	$ 24,604	4.5%
Trade accounts and notes payable.........	47,604	8.8
Accrued income taxes....................	11,593	2.1
Instalments on long-term debt due within 1 year........................	7,187	1.4
Other current liabilities..................	44,550	8.2
Total current liabilities.............	$135,538	25.0%
Long-term debt.........................	90,692	16.7
Other noncurrent liabilities...............	20,365	3.7
Total debt......................	$246,595	45.4%
Capital stock and capital surplus..........	101,876	18.7
Earned surplus and surplus reserves.......	195,241	35.9
Total stockholders' equity..........	$297,117	54.6%
Total liabilities..................	$543,712	100.0%

Source: U.S. Federal Trade Commission and Securities and Exchange Commission, *Quarterly Report for Manufacturing Corporations, Fourth Quarter, 1969* (Washington D.C.: U.S. Government Printing Office, 1970).

39.6% of total assets. The next most important investment was in inventories ($126.2 billion, or 23.2%) followed rather closely by receivables ($96.5 billion or 17.8%).

In understanding the financing of business, it is useful to think of the various assets as representing the investment of funds. Viewed in this light, the outstanding investment in inventory reported on the balance sheet represents funds absorbed or tied up in inventory on that date. If the inventories are built up, more funds are absorbed, or used, in maintaining this type of asset. If the inventories are reduced, funds are released for other uses. In many respects the analogy of a sponge is appropriate. An increase in inventory or other assets soaks up cash or funds; a squeezing-down of the inventory sponge frees cash for other uses.

The typical business commonly has a wide range of alternative or competing uses for its funds. A proposed buildup of raw material inventories may require an implicit choice of use of funds over alternative uses, such as purchase of new machines, increased advertising outlays, purchase of another concern, repayment of debt, or higher dividends to shareholders. At a single point of time the asset side of the balance sheet can be regarded as the reflection of a cumulative complex of the investment decisions of management. Similarly, the net changes in asset accounts between balance sheet dates reflect decisions implemented during the intervening period.

Table 1–2 shows the balance sheets of manufacturing corporations at the beginning and end of the decade of the 1960's—10 years which saw their total sales increase by 106%, from $337.8 billion in 1959 to $694.5 billion in 1969. During the decade their assets grew from $244 to $544 billion, or 122.4%.

Looking further at the asset changes during the decade, we see that

Table 1–2

Composite Balance Sheet, All U.S. Manufacturing Corporations
(dollar figures in millions)

	December 31, 1959*	December 31, 1969	Net Change	Percentage Change from 1959
ASSETS				
Cash	$ 15,298	$ 23,754	+ 8,456	+ 55.3%
U.S. government securities	14,411	6,783	− 7,628	− 52.9
Accounts and notes receivable	38,056	96,538	+ 58,482	+153.7
Inventories	57,922	126,229	+ 68,307	+117.9
Other current assets	5,311	19,776	+ 14,465	+272.4
Total current assets	$130,998	$273,080	+142,082	+108.5
Plant and equipment	180,134	405,351	+225,217	+125.0
Less: Reserve for depreciation	85,664	190,060	+104,396	+121.9
Net fixed assets	$ 94,471	$215,291	+120,820	+127.9
Other noncurrent assets	19,033	55,342	+ 36,309	+190.8
Total assets	$244,502	$543,712	+299,210	+122.4
LIABILITIES				
Short-term bank loans	$ 6,664	$ 24,604	+ 17,940	+269.2
Trade accounts and notes payable	20,019	47,604	+ 27,585	+137.8
Accrued income taxes	10,792	11,593	+ 801	+ 7.4
Instalments on long-term debt due within 1 year	1,871	7,187	+ 5,316	+284.1
Other current liabilities	12,873	44,550	+ 31,677	+246.1
Total current liabilities	$ 52,219	$135,538	+ 83,319	+159.6
Long-term debt	29,500	90,692	+ 61,192	+207.4
Other noncurrent liabilities	2,329	20,365	+ 18,036	+774.4
Total debt	$ 84,048	$246,595	+162,547	+193.4
Capital stock and capital surplus	65,269	101,876	+ 36,607	+ 56.1
Earned surplus and surplus reserves	95,184	195,241	+100,056	+105.1
Total stockholders' equity	$160,453	$297,117	+136,663	+ 85.2
Total liabilities	$244,502	$543,712	299,210	+122.4

* Except newspapers in 1959.
Source: U.S. Federal Trade Commission and Securities and Exchange Commission, *Quarterly Report for Manufacturing Corporations, Fourth Quarters, 1960 and 1969* (Washington, D.C.: U.S. Government Printing Office, 1961 and 1970).

the investment in every type of asset except the government securities was expanded significantly. Of the major types, the growth in receivables (credit extended customers) was especially rapid, up by $58.5 billion, or 153.7%. Some $7.6 billion was released for other uses by contraction of the investment in government securities.

Now let us turn to the liability side of the balance sheet, which shows the sources of the funds committed to the various asset uses. In Table 1–1 we can see that short-term creditors provided 25% of the 1969 total assets, long-term debt sources an additional 20.4%, and the stockholders $297.1 billion, or 54.6%, of the $543.7 billion total through their purchase of stock in these companies and by leaving profits in the business.

The funds required to increase the investment in one asset may be provided by the squeezing-down of the investment in another asset—for example, the added need for funds created by an inventory buildup might be met by drawing down the investment in cash. Alternatively, the needed funds might be secured by increasing a liability—for example, by added borrowing from banks. Or the use could be matched through the sale of more stock—or an increase in the stockholders' investment in the company through the reinvestment of earnings.

Table 1–2 reveals how manufacturers financed the $299.2 billion increase in their assets during the 1960's. Greater reliance was put on debt than ownership sources during the decade, in both absolute and relative terms. Both banks and trade creditors were important sources of short-term credit, increasing by 269.2% and 137.8% respectively. Long-term debt was expanded by $61.2 billion, or 207.4%. Total equity sources increased $136.7 billion, or 85.2%, primarily through surplus increases from earnings not paid out in dividends.

Organized and careful analysis of sources and uses of funds over a period of time, as reflected in balance sheet changes supplemented with material from income statements, can be a useful aid to understanding the needs of a business and how they have been met. In Chapter 6 we shall explain in some detail the technique of funds flow analysis—which is built around the construction of statements of sources and uses of funds. At this point, it will suffice if the student recognizes clearly that the various assets represent the use or investment of funds, that increases in these assets absorb or use funds, and that decreases in particular assets free or release funds.

Underlying Objectives of Resource Management

The basic reason for being of most business enterprises is to build maximum sustainable values for the owners. True, enlightened owners and managers recognize that the firm also has responsibilities to its customers, its employees, its community, and perhaps to the firm itself as a total organization. But the obligation of management to use the funds contributed to its care by the owners to the maximum advantage of the owners is the paramount one of the financial manager.

Wise choices in the use of funds (resources) and in the ways available sources of funds are drawn upon are central to the building of enterprise values. Generally, the objectives of wise funds allocation and value building are served if profit opportunities and performance are viewed in relation to the scale of resources or funds required to produce them. That is, a given amount of profit return should be evaluated in terms of the percentage profit return on the investment of funds involved. To illustrate, let us suppose that an entrepreneur has an opportunity to buy either of two businesses. Business A promises an annual profit of $24,000 but will require an investment of $240,000. Business B offers only a $20,000 annual return, but the investment needed is $140,000. If all other considerations were the same, surely the 14.3% prospective return on investment in firm B ($20,000/$140,000 = 14.3%) is more attractive than the 10% return ($24,000/$240,000) on investment in firm A.

The usefulness and validity of effort to maximize *return on investment* as an intermediate means to the end objective of building values is gaining increasing acceptance, and return on invested funds is also gaining acceptance as a prime measure of management's performance in handling the funds entrusted to its supervision. Note the choice of words, "a prime measure." We do not argue that other criteria have no relevance or validity or that achievement of a maximum return on investment necessarily will maximize values. Yet the increasing acceptance of return on investment (*ROI*) as a prime objective and measure of performance rests on solid grounds.

First, the return-on-investment objective inherently recognizes the value of capital—the fact that its owners could use their funds to advantage in other ventures—and that capital is seldom available for an enterprise in unlimited amount. Second, it puts a premium on economical use of capital in the firm. Third, use of this performance criterion and objective points to broad avenues for improvement of performance. Fourth, the *ROI* concept has a high degree of what might be termed "administrative feasibility." It is straightforward and can be understood throughout an organization. Moreover, it can be applied to the operations of subsidiaries, divisions, or other subgroupings within the firm.

Alternative Ways to Improved Return on Investment

Return on investment can usefully be calculated both in terms of the return on asset investment and also on that portion of the investment funds of the business that is supplied by the owners. Let us first concern ourselves with the return on total funds or asset investment.

The profit return on asset investment (*ROI*) can be simply and directly calculated as follows:

$$ROI = \frac{\text{Net Profit after Taxes}}{\text{Total Assets}}.$$

A more revealing method of calculating *ROI* breaks out two variables that lie behind the net profit figure, the amount of sales and the percentage of profit on sales. It also isolates the turnover of assets in sales. Under this "turnover" method, *ROI* is calculated as follows:

$$ROI = \frac{\text{Sales}}{\text{Assets}} \times \frac{\text{Net Profit}}{\text{Sales}}.$$

Let us illustrate. Firm X had total assets of $400,000, sales of $1,000,000, and net income after taxes of $40,000 in 1964. Application of the direct formula shows the *ROI* to be 10% ($40,000/$400,000).

Using the turnover formula approach we proceed:

$$ROI = \frac{\$1,000,000}{\$400,000} \times \frac{\$40,000}{\$1,000,000}$$

$$ROI = 2.5 \times 4\%$$

$$ROI = \underline{10\%}.$$

Now let us assume that firm X in the following year, 1965, increased sales to $1,200,000 and net income after taxes to $48,000. However, total assets were increased to $600,000. Using the direct formula we note that *ROI* dropped to 8% ($48,000/$600,000). Calculating by the turnover method, we derive the following:

$$ROI = \frac{\$1,200,000}{\$600,000} \times \frac{\$48,000}{\$1,200,000}$$

$$ROI = 2 \times 4\%$$

$$ROI = \underline{8\%}.$$

The turnover calculation highlights the fact that the profit return held constant at 4% and that it was the large increase in asset investment relative to sales (reflected in a decline in the turnover of assets in sales to 2 times) that was responsible for the lower *ROI*. If the management of firm X had been able to achieve the sales and profit increases on the old investment base of $400,000, it would have boosted the turnover rate to 3.0 and the return on asset investment to 12% (4% times 3.0).

It should be apparent that success in boosting return on asset investment can be achieved by progress along either of two broad avenues —by increasing the rate of profit on sales or by increasing investment turnover. Investment turnover, in turn, can be raised by increasing sales more than assets or by cutting assets more than sales are reduced. Put differently, increases in sales or profit returns on sales enhance return on investment only if the investment is held to a less than proportionate increase.

So far we have spoken only in terms of return on investment in total assets. The owners of the enterprise—the common stockholders if it is a corporation—may well have an especial concern with the return on the funds they have invested in the business. In calculating *return on owners' investment*, the investment base is the total of the common stock accounts (capital and surplus).

Let us illustrate with firms Y and Z and the following facts:

	Firm Y	Firm Z
Sales..................................	$1,000,000	$1,000,000
Net income before taxes and interest....	80,000	80,000
Interest................................	–0–	10,000
Net income before taxes.................	$ 80,000	$ 70,000
Taxes @ 50%.............................	40,000	35,000
Income after taxes......................	$ 40,000	$ 35,000
Total assets............................	$ 400,000	$ 400,000
Total debts.............................	–0–	$ 200,000
Owners' investment......................	$ 400,000	$ 200,000
ROI (total assets)......................	10%	8.75%
ROOI (return on owners' investment).....	10%	17.50%

Note that we have made the unlikely assumption that firm Y operates with no debts at all, in contrast to firm Z which has financed equally with debt and ownership. Sales and earnings were assumed equal except for the interest costs in firm Z, which were deducted before income taxes were calculated. The extra interest cost cut *ROI* down modestly, from 10% in firm Y to 8.75% in firm Z. But the lesser use of ownership funds in firm Z meant a sharply higher *ROI* in firm Z (17.5%) over the 10% figure for firm Y. In effect, firm Z borrowed at 5% ($10,000 interest ÷ $200,000) before taxes, and effectively 2½% after taxes, while it was able to earn 20% before interest and taxes on assets ($80,000/$400,000), and 8.75% after interest and taxes. These examples point up the fact that so long as the after-tax interest costs are less than the rate of return on asset investment, the rate of return on owners' investment can be increased by increasing the proportion of borrowed money to ownership funds. This is simply another way of saying that if assets can be made to earn more than the cost of borrowed money, financing through debt is profitable to the owners.

Balanced against the attractions of the opportunity for boosting return on owners' investment through increased use of debt are the added financial risks imposed by borrowing. If interest or agreed loan repayments cannot be met on schedule, creditors can force bankruptcy of the firm. And in liquidation or reorganization of the firm, creditors' claims must be met in full before the owners can recover any of their investment.

The decision as to the optimum balance in financing through debt and ownership funds is one of the most important financial decisions in most firms, and one discussed at length later in this book. Suffice it here to recognize the impact of the debt/ownership relationship on the return on owners' investment.

Different Routes to a Satisfactory Return on Investment

Widely varied approaches can lead to a gratifyingly high return on invested capital. Let us examine the results of several successful firms with quite different approaches. These approaches reflect industry characteristics.

First, let us look at The Gillette Company, which in 1969 showed a return of 14.7% on total assets at year-end and 26.4% on owners' investment, a figure more than double a median return figure of 11.3% computed for the 500 largest U.S. industrial companies. How were such striking results achieved? The answer lies primarily in a rate of profit on sales of 10.8%, a figure which compares with a 4.6% median for *Fortune*'s 500.[1] Coupled with an asset turnover of 1.37 (a little above the 1.28 average for all manufacturing corporations) and a turnover of ownership funds of 2.46 (average for all manufacturers of 2.34), this produced an unusually high return on owners' investment despite only moderate use of debt.

Safeway Stores, Incorporated, a national food retailer, in contrast earned only 1.3% on sales of $4.1 billion during 1969. However, Safeway achieved a turnover of assets of 5.19 and of ownership investment of 8.96! Consequently, the company was able to earn 6.92% on total assets and 11.9% on owners' investment.

Still another approach to a generally satisfactory return on ownership funds is illustrated by Commonwealth Edison Company, of Chicago. As in the case of most utilities which require massive facilities, the turnover of assets in sales (operating revenues) was low—only 0.27. Since, again like most utilities, much debt was employed, the 16.5% return on sales was enough to produce a return on owners' investment of 12.4%.

The Need for Pressures toward Effective Use of Assets

As our endorsement of the usefulness of the return-on-investment concept indicates, we believe that vigorous, well-thought-out, and continuing management effort to keep the firm's assets working hard and productively is essential to the success of the business. The financial officer can and should play a leading role in these efforts.

---

[1] "*Fortune*'s Directory of the 500 Largest Industrial Corporations," *Fortune*, Vol. 81 (May, 1970), p. 201.

This emphasis may appear misplaced or platitudinous without full recognition of the basic pressures that exist in most enterprises, and particularly in highly profitable ones, toward extravagant or indulgent use of resources. Some of these pressures stem from seemingly innate human qualities—the human animal is not by nature thrifty or wise in his use of resources. For example, all of us like to have the latest and best tools with which to work. And many, if not most, people tend to equate "bigger" with "better." Personal empire-building tendencies also seem almost innate. Further, the sheer convenience of abundant resources at hand is attractive—witness the number of financially pressed families who embrace the luxury and convenience of a second or even third family automobile. Participation in business—especially in a business owned by someone else—does not convert the human animal into a machine that grinds out economically rational decisions.

Even in enterprises whose management generally is imbued with concern for return on investment or similar goals stressing maximum productivity of resources, certain sources of pressure toward indulgent use of assets can be identified. One such is the common preoccupation of management personnel having specialized responsibilities with the gains from increased sales or cost cutting which can be achieved with more capital. Production managers are likely to be keenly aware of possibilities of greater output or of cutting production costs with added laborsaving equipment (larger equipment investment). An expensive shutdown due to exhaustion of raw material stocks provides an obvious push toward the carrying of greater stocks. The sales manager can be expected to be vigorous in exposing the potential for bigger sales through more generous credit extension (larger receivables) or through more complete stocks of goods for sale (larger finished goods inventory). Such added use of resources *may* appear to boost overall return on investment and be desirable. But too often, the partisans of such actions overlook or underemphasize important but less obvious operating costs involved in higher asset accumulation and the costs of the added capital investment required.

The carrying of added raw material stocks, for example, may well mean a need for greater storage facilities, higher property taxes, insurance, and other costs of protecting and caring for the stocks. Further, risks of loss through physical deterioration, obsolescence, or price declines may be significant and inadequately recognized. Similar operating costs and risks of loss are likely to be significant in the case of all other types of assets—with the exception perhaps of cash itself, and even cash is subject to the risks of loss of value through inflation.

The *net* gains, after full allowance for the added operating costs and risks of loss of values involved in added investment, must be compared with the costs or economic burden of the added investment. The objective, of course, should be one of balance—of ensuring that the savings or added revenues from more assets match or exceed the costs of the capital involved. The net return-on-investment concept basically is a device to see that the added assets "pay their way" and to point up the price in lower return on investment of less productive investment.

But even adherence to return-on-investment doctrines does not ensure adequate management recognition of the problems of raising the funds to finance the added investment. In large, prosperous firms the assumption that funds can readily be secured for any investment judged worthy may in fact be justified. But in a great many firms—particularly new, smaller, or less successful concerns—the problems in financing even obviously desirable investment may be formidable, often controlling. Here, management must balance the advantages of moves that call for more capital against the financial problems of getting the needed money. The interest of the financial officer here is immediate and direct. In such cases imaginative effort may reveal ways in which many, if not all, of the gains of proposals for added investment can be garnered with smaller or no added investment. *Often, the easiest and best way to raise funds is to avoid the need for them.*

PART II

THE MANAGEMENT OF ASSETS AND THE NEED FOR FUNDS

chapter 2

Inventory Management
and the Need for Funds

As we noted in Chapter 1, the need for funds to carry on a business typically stems from the need to invest in three major categories of working capital—inventories, receivables, and cash and temporary investments of cash—and in property, plant, and equipment. Decisions relating to investment in these asset categories shape the overall need for funds. In the next four chapters we focus in turn on each of these major uses of funds. In each case we identify the more important considerations that lie behind management decisions as to how large a commitment of funds should be maintained in that asset category. We next are concerned with how buildup or contraction of the commitment affects the funds flows of the firm and its overall financial needs and with techniques of analysis that are helpful in exposing the significance of changes in the pattern of asset use. Highlighted are distinctive problems in managing and controlling the investment of funds in each of the four major asset categories.

Once we have provided the student with some knowledge of what is behind the bare numbers of the asset (or use) side of the balance sheet, we can focus on techniques of analysis of past financing and of future funds needs. The background of the next four chapters should make it easier for the student confronting financial data to make the figures come alive and tell a meaningful story. In effect this background should help him to think more as a manager than as a figure technician.

The great bulk of business inventories represents goods carried for ultimate sale in the normal course of operations. The overall category also includes stocks of supplies—items that are not intended for sale directly but are needed to operate the business, such as coal for the heating plant, lubricants for machines, and paper for the office. The total value of supplies usually is of minor importance in the inventory total.

21

Chart 2–1

Investment in Inventory of Corporations in Selected Industry Groups, as a Percentage of Their Total Assets, for Companies with Accounting Periods Ended July, 1966–June, 1967

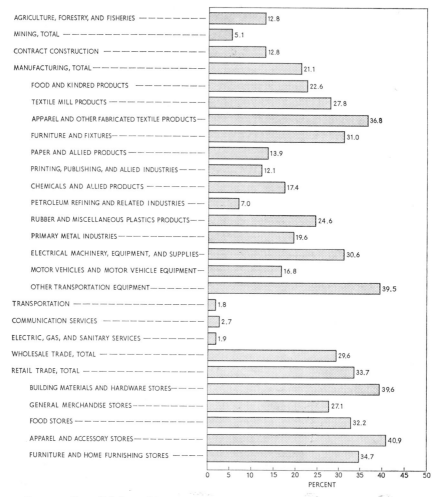

SOURCE OF DATA: U.S. Internal Revenue Service, *Statistics of Income—1966, Corporation Income Tax Returns* (Washington, D.C.: U.S. Government Printing Office, 1970), Table 2—"Balance Sheets and Income Statements, by Major Industry." The statistics were derived from a stratified sample of corporation income tax returns, blown up to sample class totals by use of "weighting factors." There were 855,890 returns of active corporations in the industries covered in this table.

Manufacturers, wholesalers, and retailers typically maintain a large investment in inventory, and its management is a highly important function. On December 31, 1969, U.S. manufacturers had $126.2 billion or 23.3% of their total assets tied up in inventory.[1] Inventory makes up about

[1] U.S. Federal Trade Commission and Securities and Exchange Commission, *Quarterly Financial Report for Manufacturing Corporations; Fourth Quarter, 1969* (Washington, D.C.: U.S. Government Printing Office, 1969).

Table 2–1

Inventory Turnover, U.S. Manufacturing Corporations, 1969
(dollar figures in millions)

	Net Sales	Year-End Inventories	Turnover Rate*
All manufacturing corporations........	$694,584	$126,229	5.5
Motor vehicles and equipment.........	59,900	10,093	5.9
Aircraft and parts...................	26,392	11,179	2.4
Electrical machinery, equipment, and supplies.....................	67,017	15,186	4.4
Other machinery....................	57,667	13,180	4.4
Other fabricated metal products........	35,236	6,374	5.5
Primary iron and steel...............	27,747	5,182	5.4
Primary nonferrous metals............	21,441	4,288	5.0
Stone, clay, and glass products........	17,485	2,371	7.4
Furniture and fixtures...............	7,978	1,217	6.6
Lumber and wood products, except furniture.........................	13,331	2,041	6.5
Instruments and related products......	16,440	3,671	4.5
Miscellaneous manufacturing, and ordnance.....................	9,756	1,905	5.1
Food and kindred products...........	92,950	11,883	7.8
Dairy products.....................	13,773	1,259	10.9
Bakery products....................	5,272	299	17.6
Alcoholic beverages.................	9,588	2,155	4.4
Tobacco manufactures...............	9,162	3,068	3.0
Textile mill products................	21,780	4,153	5.2
Apparel and other finished products....	22,687	3,776	6.0
Paper and allied products............	20,607	2,987	6.9
Printing and publishing..............	23,269	1,880	12.4
Basic chemicals....................	27,148	5,014	5.4
Drugs.............................	11,538	2,062	5.6
Petroleum refining..................	58,006	5,902	9.8
Rubber and miscellaneous plastics products........................	16,868	3,342	5.0
Leather and leather products.........	6,434	1,251	5.1

* Annual sales divided by year-end inventories.

30% of the total assets of wholesale firms and about 34% of retailers' assets.

The importance of the commitment of funds to inventory in relation to total assets in a number of selected industry groups is shown graphically in Chart 2–1. Note particularly how minor the inventory investment is to companies in the fields of transportation, communication, and electric power. Basically, these concerns sell a service or a commodity that cannot be stored. Thus, an electric power company sells power virtually as it generates it; its inventory consists almost entirely of fuel for generating plants and other items of supplies.

Another indication of the importance of investment in inventory is given in Table 2–1, which lists the relation of year-end inventories to annual sales in selected industry groups. Here again, differences appear among industries in the amounts of inventories held in stock in order to maintain sales. The turnover rates in the table range from 2.4 in aircraft and parts to 17.6 for bakery products.

A Focus on Manufacturers' Inventories

In this chapter we shall discuss aspects of inventory management of especial significance to the financial manager. We have chosen a focus on inventory management in manufacturing concerns. Manufacturing firms hold well over half of all business inventories. Moreover, the problems of managing manufacturing inventories are relatively complex. If they can be understood, the basic concepts involved can be applied to inventory problems in retailing and other fields. Further, most manufacturers' operations are subject to rapid change, and the dynamic quality of their inventory problems makes them a particularly interesting subject for study.

The Varied Makeup of Manufacturers' Inventories

Although the inventory investment often is shown on published balance sheets as a single figure, the total "inventory" of the typical manufacturing company is a composite of one minor (supplies) and three major types of inventory:

1. Raw materials.[2]
2. Work in process.
3. Finished goods.

Percentage of Total Inventory Investment

	All Manufacturers	Durable Goods Manufacturers	Nondurable Goods Manufacturers
Raw materials............	30.6%	27.6%	36.4%
Work in progress..........	36.4	46.9	15.8
Finished goods............	33.0	25.5	47.8
	100.0%	100.0%	100.0%

Each of the major categories of inventory differs significantly from the others, so that analysis of the inventory investment and its management can be most meaningful if each category is thought of as separate and distinct.

As can be seen from the breakdown of inventories at the end of 1969

---

[2] For simplicity of presentation, we shall use the term *raw materials* in a broad sense —that is, to include with basic materials all parts, subassemblies, and components purchased from other firms but not yet put into the manufacturer's own production processes.

(page 24), for manufacturers as a whole the three major categories are of somewhat similar magnitude.[3] Work in process is particularly important for durable goods producers. For nondurable goods manufacturers (textiles, food, gasoline, and the like), it is of much less consequence than raw materials or finished goods.

What Determines the Amount of Funds Invested in Inventory?

As noted earlier, Chart 2–1 makes apparent the wide difference from one manufacturing grouping to another of the inventory investment as a percentage of total assets. Another way of viewing the inventory investment is in relation to sales volume. U.S. manufacturers had inventories of $126.2 billion on December 31, 1969, while sales for the preceding quarter were $183.3 billion or approximately $2.04 billion a calendar day. Thus, the inventories amounted to approximately 62 days' sales. In Chart 2–2 the investment in inventory of U.S. manufacturers from 1952 to 1969 is plotted along with sales figures. A ratio scale is used to facilitate comparison of the movements in inventory and sales. The variation from the overall average figure among industry groups is great. At the end of 1969 manufacturers of aircraft and aircraft parts were carrying an inventory equal to 153 days' sales while manufacturers of bakery products had total inventory equal to only 20 days' sales. Doubtless the figures for individual firms within industry groups would show significant variations from the average figure for the industry.

Most established firms have arrived at a number of policy determinations affecting inventory. Important among these are judgments as to what levels of stocks are optimum under the circumstances. Often the target levels of inventory the firm works toward are expressed in terms of anticipated rate of usage or sales. Thus, a target level for raw materials might be set at 45 days' anticipated usage and that for finished stocks at, say, 30 days' anticipated sales. Shortly, we shall examine the more important considerations that managements are likely to weigh in fixing or modifying target levels. Basically, manufacturers could operate with almost no raw material or finished goods inventories and a work-in-process inventory representing only that minimum amount of goods necessarily tied up in the manufacturing process provided:

1. Purchased materials were continuously available from suppliers when and as needed and at stable prices.
2. Sales were stable over long periods or variations in sales were predictable with great accuracy well in advance.
3. Manufacturing operations could be counted upon to proceed precisely on schedule at all times.

---

[3] U.S. Department of Commerce, *Survey of Current Business*, April, 1970, p. S-6.

Chart 2–2

Quarterly Inventories of All U.S. Manufacturing Corporations* Compared with
Quarterly Sales, 1964–69
(vertical axis in ratio scale)

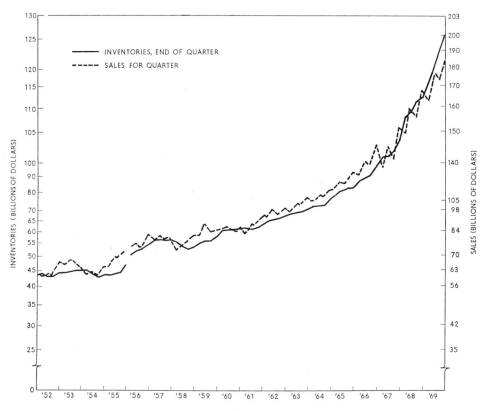

* Excluding newspapers except in 1969.
Source: U.S. Federal Trade Commission and U.S. Securities and Exchange Commission, *Quarterly Financial Report for Manufacturing Corporations, First Quarter, 1965–Fourth Quarter, 1969.*

4. Manufacturing schedules were subject to easy, cost-free adjustment so that output would mesh perfectly with changes in customer demand.

While some firms can enjoy one or more of the above conditions, few enjoy most or all. Hence, raw materials and finished stocks, and to a degree in-process stocks, serve a buffer or "change-absorbing" function. Thus, management faced with a sudden, unexpected decline in sales volume may elect to continue production at scheduled volumes and let the unsold products accumulate in finished goods inventory. If sales rebound, the additional costs of stop-and-go production involved in a shutdown will be avoided by this use of finished goods inventories to absorb the fluctuations in sales.

In other words, inventories are subject to unplanned as well as scheduled developments, and, at any particular point in time, actual inventory levels may be significantly above or below optimum or target levels.

This brief set of comments about inventory levels should suggest that the financial officer is only one of the men in top management concerned with the levels and fluctuation of the investment in inventories. Obviously, production officials, who are concerned with keeping the production operation going smoothly and at minimum costs, and sales executives, who are concerned with maximizing sales and full service to customers, are keenly concerned with inventory management practices and policies.

Now let us look more closely at the key considerations that shape management decisions relative to inventory levels of raw materials, work in process, and finished goods.

The Investment in Raw Materials

At any point in time, the investment in raw materials represents the sum of the dollar value of all materials, purchased components, subassemblies, or parts owned but not yet put into the productive process. The commitment of funds to raw material inventory swells with purchases and shrinks as materials are issued for entry into the productive process and are taken up in work-in-process inventory.

Virtually all manufacturing concerns must carry some stocks of raw materials. But what is judged enough—supplies for 1 day or 90—is very much a matter for management judgment in the light of a variety of considerations in the particular case. However, for manufacturing industry broadly, several considerations are likely to be important determinants of the level of raw material stocks:

1. The volume of "safety stocks" needed to protect against material shortages that interrupt production.
2. Considerations of economy in purchase.
3. The outlook for future movements in the price of the materials.
4. Anticipated volume of usage.
5. The efficiency of the procurement and inventory control functions.
6. The operating costs of carrying the stocks.
7. The costs and availability of funds for investment in inventory.

The management decision as to how large the safety stocks should be is an especially important one. The basic justification for safety stocks is that they serve a cost-cutting function by avoiding costly interruptions of production due to "stock-outs." Hence, judgment is required as to the likely cost-inflating or revenue-loss consequences of running out of material stocks. In some cases it may be feasible to utilize available substitute materials or to shift production for the time to other products with little strain or cost. Or the marketing situation may be such that the sales seemingly lost through temporary shutdowns may be simply postponed. In such cases it is feasible to operate with very much lower safety stocks than in the case of firms that might anticipate near-catastrophic results from production stoppages.

Also of basic importance to the determination of optimum safety stock levels are the *conditions of supply,* that is, the speed and reliability with which suppliers can be counted on to fill orders. If suppliers of a particular item are nearby and customarily carry sizable stocks on hand for immediate shipment, the user can safely carry very much smaller stocks of this item than of others requiring a long "procurement lead time." Thus, if a key component is available only on a made-to-order basis from a foreign manufacturer who customarily has heavy order backlogs, the time required for new orders to be filled may be very long indeed, and larger inventories of the item may be desirable.

In recent years New England manufacturers of silverware have been able to get overnight delivery of silver bullion from New York City suppliers who carry large stocks ready for immediate shipments. Consequently, many silverware manufacturers have concluded that 2 or 3 days' stock of silver provides reasonable assurance that operations will not be impeded. Similarly, a New York doughnut maker, whose main plant was located near flour mills, carried only a few days' supply of flour. The same manufacturer, however, who used large quantities of dried egg yolks imported from the Orient, carried several months' supply of egg yolks.

Threats from such events as an industrywide strike also affect inventory levels. For example, several times in recent decades when a strike of steelworkers was in prospect, users of steel built up large stocks against the threat of shortage.

Also, supplies of raw materials may be available only at certain times of the year. The steel mills in Cleveland, Ohio, or Gary, Indiana, which depend on iron ore from the Mesabi Range in Minnesota, find it necessary to build up huge piles of iron ore in the summer and fall in order to continue production through the winter, when ice on the Great Lakes prevents economical water transportation of the ore.

Considerations of purchase economy may affect stock levels. Purchasers of large lots frequently can command favorable prices from suppliers and lower transport costs. For example, small paint manufacturers often buy minor ingredients in economical carload lots, even though a carload may last them several months. This method of purchase is of particular importance to smaller concerns and to processors using small quantities of a wide variety of commodities or purchased parts.

The outlook for changes in the price of important materials may well influence stock levels. Unquestionably, some managements act on their anticipation of price movements, building up commitments when price increases are expected and trimming them when price declines are anticipated. When price trends have been in one direction for an extended period, manufacturers' inventory policies commonly reflect the trend. Thus, manufacturers in countries experiencing continuing inflation typically carry heavy stocks.

The efficiency of the procurement and inventory control functions in the firm can have a significant effect on raw material inventories, particularly when a great number of different items are carried. If management has full confidence in the accuracy of the stock records and the reliability of replenishment routines, it can work with leaner stocks than if such were not the case. In a number of firms the use of computers in inventory control has been credited with making possible operation with significantly lower levels of stock than would have been feasible under manual methods.[4] On the other hand, many firms have accumulated unintentionally heavy stocks simply because record keeping was so poor that no one knew the true state of inventories.

As suggested above, of major significance in the determination of optimum inventory levels are the operating costs of carrying raw material stocks. These include the costs of storage facilities, loss of value through physical deterioration, property taxes, insurance, and protection against theft.[5] Less obvious, but often of critical importance, particularly in the case of components of industrial products subject to rapid change in design, are the hazards and costs of obsolescence of particular inventory types. In a survey reported in *Purchasing Week*,[6] 70 firms gave their cal-

---

[4] The "economic order quantity" (EOQ) is one widely used method for setting order quantities which, when combined with procedures for setting appropriate safety allowances, determine the level of inventory. EOQ is based on the formula $EOQ = \sqrt{\dfrac{2DC}{PI}}$, where D = demand for the item during the period, C = purchasing cost per order, P = price paid per unit, and I = annual inventory carrying charge as a percentage of the average inventory value. Essentially, this method equates the procurement cost (ordering costs, quantity discounts, freight differentials, etc.) with the inventory carrying costs (interest, risk of price declines, obsolescence, depreciation, insurance, taxes, storage, etc.) as a function of expected demand.

More advanced inventory control techniques, based upon the use of computers employing more sophisticated mathematical models to obtain rules for operating inventory systems, have been developed in recent years and doubtless will be further refined.

[5] Inventory shortages have become a major element of cost, particularly in retailing. It is difficult to identify just how much of the shortage increases, very sharp in the late 1960's, were attributable to accounting errors (failure to record markdowns, etc.), how much to internal theft by employees, and how much to shoplifting. One source, Pinkerton's, Inc., a large security and investigative concern, attributed 26.8% of the shortages in stores surveyed to accounting errors, 27.3% to internal theft, and 45.9% to shoplifting. Merchandise losses per store ranged from a low of 0.8% to a high of 7.5%! Obviously, over time the high costs of the thievery, and of the security efforts to prevent it, will be passed on to the buying public.

On the same day as *The New York Times* report of the Pinkerton survey, February 22, 1971, Handy and Harmon, Inc., a precious-metals concern, announced a reward for information regarding the disappearance of $1.8 million of gold from the company's inventories.

[6] *Purchasing Week*, Vol. 7, No. 50 (December 14, 1964), p. 1.

culations of the cost of carrying inventories. The range was from 12%
to 33+% of the purchase price per year with 68% of the firms placing
their carrying costs between 18% and 27%. We should add that a figure
for "interest on investment" was included in the estimate of costs. Later
in this book, we devote close attention to just how capital costs should be
measured. Suffice it here for us to note that use of the rate of interest the
firm pays on borrowings as a measure of the firm's overall cost of capital
usually substantially understates the true cost of capital.

As we have suggested, inventory-level objectives very commonly are
set in terms of so many days of sales or, in the case of raw materials, of
anticipated usage in production. Once levels are set in these terms, fluctuations in anticipated and actual usage are responsible for much of the
change in inventory investment. The common tendency of purchased
materials inventories of durable goods manufacturers to move directly
with sales and new orders is illustrated in Chart 2–3. Also apparent is the
secular trend toward lower materials relative to sales.

So far, this discussion of inventory policies has appeared to assume
that funds are available to support whatever inventory investment is

Chart 2–3

Monthly Sales and Inventories of U.S. Manufacturers of Durable Goods, 1946–69
(billions of dollars)

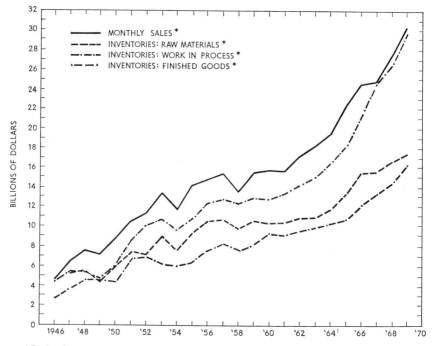

* Book value, seasonally adjusted, end of period.
SOURCE: *Economic Report of the President, 1970*, pp. 227, 228.

desired. In the case of many strongly financed firms, this is a valid assumption. But a great many firms do not enjoy unlimited access to capital, and heavy use of funds in inventories may well mean that other opportunities for effective use of funds must be forgone. In still other firms, financial resources are so limited and the problems of raising more funds so great that the need to minimize investment becomes the dominant consideration in inventory policies.

Thus far, we have talked of size of inventory primarily in terms of physical volume. The financial burden of these inventories, of course, is measured in dollars; a general rise in price heightens the dollar investment required to maintain a given volume of goods. True, a sustained price rise often increases profits as low-cost materials eventually are sold in the form of higher-priced finished goods.[7] But the added "inventory profits" left after income taxes usually are inadequate to provide funds needed to replenish stocks with the then higher-cost new materials. Conversely, a decline in prices may have the net effect of so reducing the dollar commitment to inventory that the cash account is swelled despite reduced profit inflows.

Clearly, the more obviously financial considerations—the costs of the funds tied up in raw material and the financial problems of raising those funds—are of keen significance in the determination of optimum raw material inventory levels. Since these apply equally to in-process and finished inventories, we shall defer comment on these aspects until later in this chapter.

The Cash Flows Associated with Raw Material Inventories

For purposes of financial planning, the financial officer is particularly concerned with the cash flows connected with inventory. From a cash flow standpoint the crucial dates connected with the purchase of raw materials are the dates by which the invoices for the materials must be paid. Typically, the business concern will not have to pay cash at the time of purchase. Instead, an account payable, due perhaps in 30 days, is created at the time of purchase. The cash outflows resulting from purchases of

---

[7] During the periods of significant price movements of important raw materials, the choice of accounting method employed to assign costs to particular batches of materials as they are moved from inventory into production may have a noteworthy effect on both the materials inventory figure on the balance sheet and the costs of materials in the income statement. Used most widely is FIFO, the first-in, first-out method. Under FIFO, for costing purposes materials are presumed to be used in the order of purchase. In a period of rising prices, the costs employed under FIFO will be less than the current costs of replacing the materials.

An alternative approach, which has been adopted by a number of firms, is LIFO, the last-in, first-out method. As the name implies, materials put into use are assigned the costs of the most recent purchases. In a period of rising prices, use of the LIFO method results in the reporting of higher costs, lower profits, and lower inventory values than if FIFO were used. On the other hand, in a period of declining prices, reported profits and inventory values will be higher under LIFO than under FIFO.

raw materials can be planned for by setting up a schedule of future payments. In the accompanying illustration, assume accounts payable were
$1,500 on December 31 and that purchase terms called for payment in 30
days:

	January	February	March	April	May	June
Expected raw material purchases............	$2,000	$4,000	$8,000	$7,000	$6,000	$2,000
Cash required to pay accounts payable— raw materials during month..............	1,500	2,000	4,000	8,000	7,000	6,000

No cash inflows occur when raw materials are put into production.
Instead, cash inflows come only when finished goods are sold for cash or,
if sales are on credit, when the related accounts receivable are collected
weeks or months later.

Investment in Work-in-Process Inventory

As the name suggests, this category of inventory comprises the goods
in the process of being manufactured. From an accounting viewpoint a
part of the investment in goods in process at any one time consists of the
original cost of the raw materials. Added to the material costs transferred
to the work-in-process account are the cost charges for wages and other
direct costs of manufacture applied to these raw materials, together with
an allocation of overhead costs such as heat, power, and plant supervision.
Thus, the balance sheet value assigned to work-in-process inventory at
any particular date is the summation of all costs assigned up to that date
to the partially completed products.

What are the main determinants of the amounts of funds locked up in
work-in-process inventory? To what extent is the size of the investment
dictated by the nature of the operations? And to what degree can managerial policies shape the size of the funds commitment?

The length of the complete productive process clearly has a major influence on the value of the inventory undergoing processing at any one
time. An extreme illustration is furnished by a canner of peaches. Less
than a day is normally required to pick, grade, process, can, label, and
package peaches. Naturally, the canner's work in process at any date will
be negligible in relation to annual sales. In contrast, consider the case of
a manufacturer of large aircraft. Production and assembly of the complicated aircraft typically will extend over many months; at any one time,
once production is well under way, the aircraft company will have accumulated a sizable investment in aircraft in all stages of completion,

from raw stampings of parts to aircraft undergoing final tests before being delivered.

Although technological considerations may largely dictate the length of time required for the production process, management policies usually can have significant influence on the process time and hence on the process inventory investment. In the case of durable goods manufacturing, an important decision area is the extent to which parts or subassembly items will be produced in long runs or in shorter runs closer to the time they are needed for assembly. For example, the aircraft manufacturer working on an order for 200 planes with staggered delivery dates might well try to cut production costs by making all of a particular part in one long production run, even though most of the 200 would not be needed for final assembly for many months. Thus, a decision as to the length of production runs for parts, at first thought to be purely a production problem, has decided implications as to the size of in-process inventories.

Actions that speed the production process increase output without proportionately increasing in-process stocks. Thus, adding second or third production shifts should boost output without proportionate boosts in inventories. Conversely, interruptions in the flow of work through the plant—such as would result from unexpected delays in the receipt by the aircraft firm of the engines for installation in the partially completed aircraft—inflate the tie-up of funds in inventories. Many new firms not yet skilled in production scheduling and control have encountered unexpected problems and delays in moving jobs through the plant and have in consequence tied up much larger amounts in in-process inventories than expected, with resulting serious financial problems.

The amount of costs incurred in the particular manufacturing process, often referred to as the "value added in manufacture," also affects the amount of funds converted to work in process. A very simple operation, even if extended over a long period—such as the aging of wines—requires little outlay.

The volume of production is also a major determinant of work in process. If other factors are equal, as production increases, the amount invested in work in process increases. And as volume of production operations is curtailed, the investment in in-process inventory drops. As we noted earlier in connection with raw material inventory, production generally is geared to anticipated sales. Hence, the amount of funds tied up in work in process might also be expected to fluctuate directly with sales expectations and perhaps somewhat less directly with actual sales levels.

The price levels of raw materials used, wages, and other items that enter into production costs also influence the dollar investment in in-process inventories.

Cash Flows Associated with Work in Process

As indicated above, the accounting for work in process involves accumulation of accounting charges for raw materials used and for various expenses of manufacture and overhead, including depreciation charges. The flow of funds out of the company in connection with manufacturing, of course, will not coincide in timing or in amount with these accounting charges. No checks are written or payments made when raw materials are moved from the company's storerooms into production. Rather, the cash payments associated with raw materials occur when the accounts payable generated by the raw material purchases are paid. Further, payment of manufacturing costs—such as those for wages and salaries—seldom takes place at the time when these obligations are incurred. One item of expense—depreciation—calls for no cash payment at all. In planning the outflow of cash to support manufacturing, then, it is necessary to determine which of the anticipated expenses will require payment and to schedule these payments according to the time when they will be made.

The Investment in Finished Goods Inventories

Finished goods inventories build up with additions from the production line and are cut down with sales. Finished goods inventories can be minimized if production can be geared only to firm orders in hand. By producing only to order, many manufacturers—particularly those of specialized machines—avoid finished goods inventory, other than of spare parts, almost entirely.

Most manufacturers find it advantageous or necessary to maintain stocks of finished goods ready for shipment when anticipated orders come in. Pressures to carry sizable stocks of finished goods may stem from considerations of production convenience and economy and/or of marketing effectiveness. Where demand for the products is in small or uneven increments, production for stock permits longer production runs and more even and efficient production scheduling. For example, the demand for skis is concentrated in the late fall and early winter. Ski manufacturers can achieve steady production through the year only by building up heavy stocks of finished skis in advance of the selling season.

Some manufacturers must produce for stock, because vital raw materials are available on a seasonal basis while customers' demand is spread throughout the year. The California canner of peaches, for example, must process the fruit when it ripens in July and build up a huge finished inventory if he is to meet orders spaced throughout the year.

Sales considerations may dictate an ability to fill orders without delay. In many lines, competition for sales necessitates maintenance of stocks near customers so that fast delivery can be promised. For example, a number of cement manufacturers have found it necessary to build silos near key market centers.

A number of firms with far-flung distribution systems have reported success in the use of mathematical models and electronic computers to work out distribution patterns and inventory locations and levels that best reconcile considerations of customer service, manufacturing and distribution costs, and inventory turnover.

In some industries, such as seasonal apparel, manufacturers have attempted over the years to force retailers to carry a larger part of the inventory burden—a burden in terms of space and risk as well as investment—with limited success. Of course, if the manufacturer is in a very strong position vis-à-vis the retailers, he may be able to force inventories on the dealers. Thus, Henry Ford in 1921 was seriously short of funds to meet bank loans; at the same time there were large stocks of unsold Fords at the plant. Mr. Ford simply shipped large numbers of unordered cars to his dealers with drafts calling for cash payment attached to the shipping papers. The dealers were forced to provide cash and accept the inventory burden or yield their dealerships. However, few manufacturers today possess either the commanding position or the willingness to take the risks of such action.

Optimum finished goods stock levels, like those of raw materials, are usually set in terms of so many days' or months' anticipated sales. Thus, over extended periods, finished goods inventories tend to move directly with sales volume.

But in the short run, finished stocks often vary inversely with sales. If sales fall below expectations and production is not cut back sharply, unsold goods pile up. Despite strenuous efforts to forecast sales accurately, a great many manufacturers (and retailers) are confronted with unexpected, and often inexplicable, declines in sales which pose poignant problems. Seldom can production be cut back or expanded rapidly without severe organizational strains and higher unit costs. If the sales drop proves short-lived, holding production steady and accepting temporarily swollen inventories may well maximize return on investment. But if sales stay off, inventories pile up, and even more drastic production cutbacks ultimately are needed to bring inventories into line with the reduced sales prospects. Many manufacturers have experienced severe cash stringency, sometimes leading to business failure, as a result of allowing too much of their funds to flow into finished goods for which timely orders failed to develop.

Unexpected sales spurts also present inventory management problems. Unless production and inventory levels are boosted, service to customers may suffer, and sales opportunities may be lost. But if production is boosted and the sales surge proves temporary, excess inventory results. The critical relationship of sales forecasting to effective inventory management can hardly be overemphasized. Increasing effort is being devoted by the managements of many companies to improve their "feel" for their customers and their intentions, and to respond rapidly and perceptively to shifts in demand. But the problem of anticipating changes in sales remains a difficult one—especially where a wide range of products is involved.[8]

The impact on cash of an inventory buildup or decline is usually a deferred one. The immediate cash flow impact of a sales decline and inventory buildup is minimal, as cash flows in from collection of the receivables from sales at the old high level. But the decline in sales means fewer new receivables, and a sharp drop in inflows occurs when the smaller volume of receivables comes due and is collected.

Risks in Inventory Investment

The decades since 1945 have been ones of general prosperity and broad commodity price increases. Nevertheless, there have been enough sharp drops in the prices of important commodities to remind businessmen that heavy inventory positions, particularly in standard commodities with free markets, expose their firms to risks of loss through sustained price declines. For example, the market price of cocoa, a basic material for candymakers, fell from a high of $0.500 in November, 1969, to a low of $0.2825 in May, 1970,[9] a decline of 43.5% in 5 months. Generally, the vulnerability to price declines has been greatest on standard raw materials and least on differentiated finished goods.

More significant in recent years have been the risks of inventory obsolescence. Changing customer tastes, as in high-style merchandise, may make finished goods, work in process, and even raw materials obsolete and therefore unsalable and nearly worthless. Nor is vulnerability to obsolescence restricted to luxury consumer goods. Changing needs of industrial customers, new production techniques, or product improvements by competitors may force changes in product specifications and design that cut the value of old-model stocks and of components or materials distinctive to the earlier models. An electronics firm responding to the *Purchasing Week* survey reported on page 29 estimated its annual cost of obsolescence on stored products at 10%. As the rate of technical change and product development shows evidence of acceleration, full sensitivity to the hazards of inventory obsolescence becomes more urgent.

---

[8] The problem of interpreting their own sales experience and of projecting their future sales is made more difficult for manufacturers by the possibility that changes in their own sales may be due to the accumulation or reduction of stocks of their products by distributors or retailers. Many firms have made major efforts to keep close tabs on the sales of their products to the ultimate consumer so as not to be misled by unsustainable increases or decreases in products in the distribution pipeline. The return by buyers of warranty cards represents a valuable source of information about retail sales of their products for many manufacturers.

[9] Quotations from *Survey of Current Business.*

Further, those numerous firms whose resources are limited must be particularly wary of the risks to their liquidity—indeed, their solvency—in tying up too much of their limited funds in hard-to-move inventories.

Aids in the Analysis of the Investment in Inventory

The financial and other officers of the company are seldom alone in their interest in the company's inventory investment. Because of the importance of this asset group to the financial condition of the concern, important stockholders, the credit analysts of commercial banks or other lenders, and the credit men of important suppliers are also interested in discovering and understanding significant movements in inventory or its turnover. Unless the "outside" analysts receive more information about inventories than is usually available from published financial statements, the degree of penetration of analysis and understanding they can hope to achieve is limited. This is particularly true if only annual statements are available and inventories are reported in a single lump sum. Yet some calculations can be made and often prove useful, especially in raising questions which may indicate the desirability of further inquiry.

The same general methods of analysis used by outside analysts, which we shall discuss below, can be pushed further and used with greater precision by the financial officer of the firm, who has full access to available sources of data. For example, while the outside observer must often work with a single inventory figure, the financial officer of the firm would have figures available for each major type, and indeed for each major item, of inventory and thus should be able to arrive at more meaningful conclusions. For example, a seemingly "in-line" total figure for inventory can mask serious imbalances between the stocks of particular products so that acute shortages and stock-outs are being experienced on some items while others are overstocked. Obviously, the greater availability of detail about stocks and sales increases the conclusiveness of judgment about inventory levels.

It is often helpful to determine whether changes in inventory investment are in line with changes in the volume of sales. As we have seen, the level of investment in inventory tends naturally and normally to vary directly with the volume of sales. Movements not in line with sales raise questions for further inquiry—for example, an increase in inventory levels substantially beyond that which might be expected from an increase in sales should stimulate the analyst to further investigation. Is the unexplained increase the result of a conscious policy shift to higher stock levels, of unintended accumulation of unsold stocks, of inventory speculation, or simply of stocking in anticipation of an almost certain surge of orders?

Among the more common ratios used to depict the relationship between inventories and sales are the following:

1. Inventories as a percentage of sales or of cost of sales.
2. Number of average days' sales in inventory.
3. Inventory turnover ratios.

Let us use the facts in the accompanying table concerning the XYZ Corporation to illustrate common methods of comparing inventories to sales.

	1968	1969	1970
Sales............................. ...		$880,000	$1,060,000
Cost of sales.................... ...		702,000	860,000
Inventories on December 31......	$270,000	274,000	462,000

Quick observation shows that inventories advanced sharply in 1970. But sales also were up. A comparison of inventory to sales in each year shows that inventory at year-end as a percentage of sales for the year increased sharply to 43.6%.

$$\frac{\text{Inventory, End of 1969}}{\text{Sales, 1969}} = \frac{\$274,000}{\$880,000} = 31.1\%.$$

$$\frac{\text{Inventory, End of 1970}}{\text{Sales, 1970}} = \frac{\$\ 462,000}{\$1,060,000} = 43.6\%.$$

A somewhat crisper measure of inventory relative to sales can be derived by converting inventories into *days' sales in inventory*. This figure is computed in two steps. First, a figure for an average day's sales is computed by dividing annual sales by 365. The figure for one day's sales is then divided into the inventory figures:

$$\frac{\text{1969 Sales}}{365} = \frac{\$880,000}{365} = \$2,411 \text{ Sales per Day, 1969.}$$

$$\frac{\text{December 31, 1969}}{\text{Sales per Day}}\ \frac{\text{Inventory}}{\ } = \frac{\$274,000}{\$\ 2,411} = 113.6 \text{ Days' Sales in Inventory, 1969,}$$

Compared with

$$\frac{\text{1970 Sales}}{365} = \frac{\$1,060,000}{365} = \$2,904 \text{ Sales per Day, 1970.}$$

$$\frac{\text{December 31, 1970}}{\text{Sales per Day}}\ \frac{\text{Inventory}}{\ } = \frac{\$462,000}{\$\ 2,904} = 159.1 \text{ Days' Sales in Inventory, 1970.}$$

It can be seen that the 1970 year-end inventory represented 159.1 days' sales at the 1970 rate, whereas the year-end 1969 inventory figure was 113.6 days' sales at the 1969 rate.

As the label suggests, turnover calculations portray the relationship between inventory levels and output (sales) in terms of the number of times the stocks are turned over in the period. Since "turnover" suggests physical movement of goods, and inventories are carried at cost rather than selling price, turnover usually is calculated by dividing inventory into cost of sales rather than sales.

$$\frac{\text{Cost of Sales, 1969}}{\text{December 31 Inventory at Cost}} = \frac{\$702,000}{\$274,000} = 2.56 \text{ times.}$$

$$\frac{\text{Cost of Sales, 1970}}{\text{December 31 Inventory at Cost}} = \frac{\$860,000}{\$462,000} = 1.86 \text{ times.}$$

Thus, the buildup of inventory in 1970 at a faster rate than sales is reflected in the drop in turnover at cost based on year-end inventories from 2.56 times in 1969 to 1.86 times in 1970.

Turnover figures based on sales at selling price can also be calculated (see Table 2–1 on page 23), but these do not measure physical turnover.

Some analysts prefer to use the average of beginning and ending inventories in computing turnover ratios. It can be argued that use of average inventory figures gives a more accurate "turnover" figure, but it also plays down the influence of the recent inventory figure, which is generally the item of particular interest to the analyst concerned with the "here and now" as a guide to future developments. Thus, turnover of *average* inventory in 1970 was 2.3 times [860,000/(462,000 + 274,000/2] and in 1969 was 2.6 times [702,000/(274,000 + 270,000/2)]. It will be noted that the average turnover figures, being an average of beginning and ending inventories, changed less widely (from 2.6 to 2.3 times) than did the ending inventory turnover figure (from 2.6 to 1.9).

Sharpening the Analysis of Inventory Position and Changes

As we noted earlier, internal management generally has very much more data at hand regarding inventory, sales, carrying costs, competitive pressures for generous stocks, risks of loss through obsolescence, etc., and funds availability than do outside analysts. The detailed information should facilitate analysis in many respects. First, as we have noted, full and detailed sales/inventory data permit a product by product or item by item evaluation of inventory/sales position. Assessments may also be made by division or other organization unit so that inventory policy and results can be identified with the management man responsible. For example, it might be found that the buildup of inventory in the XYZ Corporation was concentrated entirely in the finished inventory of one or two product lines in a single division of the corporation.

Data regarding the trend of sales within periods can be meaningful. If only annual sales and inventory data are available, important movements of sales and inventories within the year will not be discernible, and ratios drawn from annual sales totals may have limited value or be positively misleading. Certainly, our view of the 1970 year-end inventory position in XYZ Corporation would be very different if the annual sales of $1,060,-000 had been achieved according to pattern A rather than pattern B or C, in the accompanying table.

Quarterly Sales, 1970	Pattern A	Pattern B	Pattern C
First quarter..........	$ 175,000	$ 320,000	$ 265,000
Second quarter........	220,000	300,000	265,000
Third quarter.........	300,000	260,000	265,000
Fourth quarter........	365,000	180,000	265,000
	$1,060,000	$1,060,000	$1,060,000

Moreover, as we have implied, inventories are stocked to meet *future* sales. Thus, the outlook for future sales and management's capacity to accurately forecast future demand have keen relevance to the appropriateness of a specific inventory level.

In the case of firms that operate under essentially similar conditions, the comparisons of inventory/sales ratios of one company with those of its competitors may prove useful in calling attention to distinctive policies of the subject firm.[10] On the other hand, it is extremely difficult to apply value judgments on the basis of summary ratios, and intercompany comparisons will usually suggest more questions than answers. As one writer has put it, ratios such as those of turnover provide many clues but few conclusions.

The Financial Officer's Role in Inventory Management

Seldom is the financial officer the corporate officer most directly concerned with inventory policies. Usually, purchasing and production officers are more directly concerned with raw material policies, production officers with work in process, and production and sales officers with finished goods inventories. But it should be clear that inventory policies have a very direct and important impact on the financial needs of the firm. The financial officer can do a good job of anticipating changes in the need for funds only if he thoroughly understands the implications of changing inventory policies and positions. Where finances are a limiting factor, he should be prepared to help directly in shaping inventory policies that are consistent with the realities of the firm's financial position.

But the financial officer's role should be much more than that of an

---

[10] Among the sources of information on average inventory/sales and other ratios for different industries are the results of a continuing program of ratio analysis published periodically in *Dun's*. For example, ratios in the retailing field were published in the September, 1970, issue; for wholesalers in various lines in October, 1970; and for manufacturers in November, 1970.

informed observer—or monitor if funds are short. Good inventory management is good financial management. Levels should be under frequent or constant review. When inventory levels are set, the financial officer can help in applying pressure against practices that slow turnover and debase return. For example, in one outstanding firm the financial officer was instrumental in the establishment of a highly productive program of periodic "turnover audits" in which questions like the following are investigated:

1. Are we exercising full vigilance against imbalances of raw material and in-process inventory that limit the utility of overall stocks to that of the item in shortest supply?
2. Are we employing the shortest procurement lead-time assumptions and leanest stock levels consistent with safety, recognizing that complete safety has a prohibitive cost?
3. Do we keep the heat on uncompleted production items held in suspension to get them into salable condition?
4. Do we press hard enough to keep production schedules firm, so that unneeded materials and in-process inventories don't accumulate? Does purchasing get early notification of production schedule changes?
5. Do we move vigorously to dispose of goods that are obsolete, surplus, or for any other reason unusable for production?
6. Are we continually striving to shorten the production cycle? Are we careful to be sure that long production runs are worth the cost and risks of the extra inventory investment?
7. Is design engineering making maximum use of standard materials and components available from suppliers' shelves on short notice?
8. Are we quick enough to use special pricing to move extremely slow-selling finished items?
9. Are we doing all we can to flatten out seasonal sales patterns that bulk up inventories?

To firms short of funds, imagination in exposing, and full vigor in exploiting, opportunities to cut inventory investment can be highly rewarding in reduced capital requirements. The advice of one experienced businessman speaking to a group of small manufacturers, "When you need money, look to your inventories before you look for your banker," deserves more than a smile.

Even if funds are plentiful, the financial officer should be prepared to participate actively and helpfully in the formulation of inventory policies designed to speed turnover and maximize return on investment. Our discussion has indicated some of the key considerations in setting and trying to hold to inventory levels that represent the best reconciliation of profit and turnover objectives and that give appropriate emphasis to the impact on the need and availability of funds for inventory investment.

chapter 3

Receivables Management
and the Need for Funds

This chapter is primarily concerned with the management of receivables arising out of the sale of goods and services by business firms
on terms other than for cash. Since most business sales are made on credit
terms, the investment in receivables represents a major and continuing
commitment of funds for most business enterprises. The investment is
increased as new credit sales are recorded and is reduced as payments in
settlement of purchase obligations are received from customers or bad
debts are written off.

Many nonfinancial firms make loans to other entities or individuals.
Thus, a short-term investment in U.S. bonds by a business firm is, in
effect, a loan to the government. Such extensions of credit involve considerations that usually are very different from those involved in credit
to customers and will not be discussed in this chapter.

U.S. manufacturing corporations, which sell primarily to other firms
and almost entirely on credit terms, had $96.5 billion or 17.8% of their
total assets tied up in receivables on December 31, 1969. Almost all of
this represented *trade credit*—that is, credit extended from one business
firm to another arising out of the sale of goods or services. Wholesalers,
who also sell primarily on credit and to other businesses, on a recent date
had $21.2 billion or 34.6% of their total assets in receivables. Among
retailers, sales for cash are common. As many readers well know, most
retail food chains sell only for cash and avoid an investment in receivables
altogether. Nevertheless, recent data for all retailing corporations showed
a receivables investment of $18.4 billion or 25.0% of total assets.

Chart 3–1 portrays the importance of the investment in receivables in
relation to total assets in a number of industry groups. The range is wide
—note, for example, the great importance of receivables to construction
firms and the minor importance to public utilities.

Chart 3–1

Investment in Notes and Accounts Receivable, Less Allowance for Bad Debts, of Active Corporations in Selected Industry Groups, as a Percentage of Their Total Assets, for Companies with Accounting Periods Ended July, 1966–June. 1967

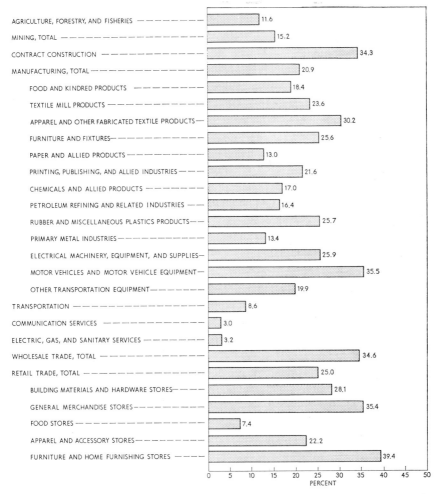

	PERCENT
AGRICULTURE, FORESTRY, AND FISHERIES	11.6
MINING, TOTAL	15.2
CONTRACT CONSTRUCTION	34.3
MANUFACTURING, TOTAL	20.9
FOOD AND KINDRED PRODUCTS	18.4
TEXTILE MILL PRODUCTS	23.6
APPAREL AND OTHER FABRICATED TEXTILE PRODUCTS	30.2
FURNITURE AND FIXTURES	25.6
PAPER AND ALLIED PRODUCTS	13.0
PRINTING, PUBLISHING, AND ALLIED INDUSTRIES	21.6
CHEMICALS AND ALLIED PRODUCTS	17.0
PETROLEUM REFINING AND RELATED INDUSTRIES	16.4
RUBBER AND MISCELLANEOUS PLASTICS PRODUCTS	25.7
PRIMARY METAL INDUSTRIES	13.4
ELECTRICAL MACHINERY, EQUIPMENT, AND SUPPLIES	25.9
MOTOR VEHICLES AND MOTOR VEHICLE EQUIPMENT	35.5
OTHER TRANSPORTATION EQUIPMENT	19.9
TRANSPORTATION	8.6
COMMUNICATION SERVICES	3.0
ELECTRIC, GAS, AND SANITARY SERVICES	3.2
WHOLESALE TRADE, TOTAL	34.6
RETAIL TRADE, TOTAL	25.0
BUILDING MATERIALS AND HARDWARE STORES	28.1
GENERAL MERCHANDISE STORES	35.4
FOOD STORES	7.4
APPAREL AND ACCESSORY STORES	22.2
FURNITURE AND HOME FURNISHING STORES	39.4

SOURCE OF DATA: U.S. Internal Revenue Service, *Statistics of Income—1966, Corporation Income Tax Returns* (Washington, D.C.: U.S. Government Printing Office, 1970), Table 2—"Balance Sheets and Income Statements, by Major Industry."

Chart 3–2 pictures the investment of manufacturing firms in receivables and also their sales over a period of years on a ratio scale. While much of the great growth in the commitment to receivables is explained by the growth in sales, a long-term tendency for collection periods to lengthen (that is, for receivables to increase faster than sales) is clearly discernible. If manufacturers during the last quarter of 1969 collected on sales as rapidly as they did in the last quarter of 1947, the investment in receivables could have been lower by over $42 billion—that is, $54 billion

Chart 3–2

Quarterly Accounts Receivable of All U.S. Manufacturing Corporations* Compared
with Quarterly Sales, 1956–Second Quarter, 1970
(in billions; vertical axis in ratio scale)

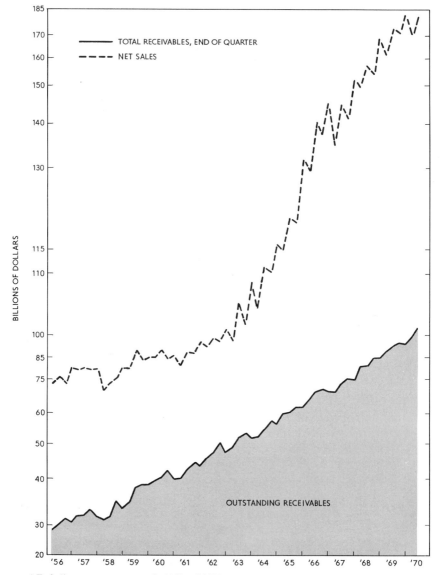

* Excluding newspapers except in 1969 and 1970.

instead of the actual figure of $96.5 billion. We shall comment further on the trend toward longer collection periods at the end of this chapter.

Form of Receivables

The bulk of credit sales are made on *open account*. That is, the seller keeps a simple book record of the obligations arising out of sales and does not ask his customers for formal acknowledgment of their debts or for signed promises to pay. In case of dispute the seller has the customer's order, copies of the sales invoice, and shipping papers as evidence of the validity of the debt.

In open-account selling there is no security behind the obligation. The seller enjoys no special rights to recover the goods he has sold if the account is not paid. Usually no interest is charged on open-account sales to business buyers.[1]

At one time, decades ago, it was the common practice of many business firms to ask their customers to sign unsecured *notes*, or written promises to pay by a stated date the amount of credit extended on routine credit sales. This practice was especially common in product lines customarily sold on long credit terms. The holder of an ordinary note receivable does not enjoy any priority of claim to payment over open-account creditors in the event of a debtor's bankruptcy and the subsequent liquidation of his assets for distribution to creditors. But the signed note does provide strong legal evidence of the validity of the debt; and written stipulation of a due date, together with the practice of note collection through banks, provides psychological pressures for prompt payment at maturity. Too, the mechanics of charging interest on notes are simple. Further, usually it is easier to use notes from customers than accounts receivable as security for bank loans. Despite these advantages, the use of notes in routine domestic trade credit by manufacturers and wholesalers has given way in the United States to the current practice of sale on open account.

In many countries sellers still ask their customers to sign a note or other form of written obligation. In Mexico, for example, many firms send along with shipping papers a form for signature by the customer by which he formally accepts the obligation to pay for the goods on stated terms. After it is signed, the acceptance form is returned to the seller.

Although most retail credit sales in the United States are also made on an open-account basis, "big-ticket items"—durable goods of considerable value, such as automobiles, television receivers, and refrigerators—commonly are offered for sale on terms that call for *instalment payments* extended over many months. Such sales are customarily made subject to

---

[1] It is common for retailers to charge interest, usually at the rate of 1.5% per month or 18% per annum, on overdue accounts or on revolving credits. In recent years, some businesses have adopted this practice on sales to other firms.

the terms of *conditional sales contracts*, which give the seller (or his assignee) the right to recover the merchandise if payments are not made as agreed upon in the contract. Usually, a significant cash payment, often 20% to 30% of the retail price, is required. And unlike the case in routine open-account credits, significant interest and other credit charges are added to the cash sales price.

The retailer may retain the instalment sales obligation. More commonly, instalment contracts are sold to banks or specialized sales finance companies. Some retailers, such as Sears, Roebuck and Company, have formed subsidiaries to hold and collect instalment credits. Some manufacturers, who have found easy credit vital to the ability of final users to buy their products, have established sales finance subsidiaries to buy the instalment "paper" of customers of their dealers. Thus, major farm equipment makers, such as Deere & Company, now finance not only the sale of equipment to dealers for inventory but the dealers' sales to farmers as well. Indeed, some farm equipment manufacturers also finance the resale by their dealers of other makes of used equipment acquired as trade-ins on new equipment.

In recent years an increasing number of manufacturers of industrial equipment also have found it necessary or desirable to offer instalment credit terms to their business customers. Most manufacturers of machine tools and of equipment for service industries, such as dry-cleaning equipment, for example, offer credit terms extending over as much as 3 to 4 years. A number have formed so-called *captive finance companies* to take over these credits or have arranged their resale to other finance companies. Usually, these credits are extended on conditional sales contracts. Since the instalment credit terms include substantial financing charges, companies whose finances are strong generally prefer to purchase equipment on the normal trade terms and open account.

Although some increase in export selling on an open-account basis has been reported in recent years, the great bulk of the sales to overseas customers is not on an open-account basis. Instead, a number of distinctive credit and financing instruments and practices have been developed in response to the special problems of international commercial transactions. Particularly important among the credit instruments of international trade are the *letter of credit* and the *banker's acceptance*. These will be discussed in Chapter 14.

Objectives in the Management of the Investment in Receivables

In the typical firm the financial officer has operating responsibility for the management of the investment in receivables. Reporting directly to him in most firms is the head of the credit department, which carries out the work of granting credit and supervising the collection of receivables. In addition to his role in overseeing the administration of credit, the financial officer is in a particularly strategic position to contribute to top-management decisions as to the best credit policies for the firm.

Unless the firm's own finances are closely limited, the basic objective of receivables management, like that of inventory management, should be maximizing return on investment. Policies which stress short credit terms, stringent credit standards, and highly aggressive policing of collections clearly should work to minimize bad-debt losses and the tie-up of funds in receivables. But such policies may well restrict sales and profit margins, so that despite the low receivables investment, rate of return on total investment of the firm is lower than that attainable with higher levels of sales, profits, and receivables. Conversely, extremely lenient or sloppy credit extension may well inflate receivables and bad debts without compensating increases in sales and profits. Clearly, the objective of receivables management should be the achievement of that balance which in the particular circumstances of the firm results in the combination of turnover and profit rates that maximizes the overall return on investment of the firm. Mutual understanding and close cooperation of the financial officer with sales executives are essential to full progress toward the objective.

We should recognize, however, that limited financial resources of the particular firm may force greater restraint in receivables than would be ideal from a return-on-investment viewpoint. If the availability of funds is restricted, their use in inventory, equipment, or other areas offering even higher return may dictate severe restraint on credit administration. Or if the financial position of the firm is so precarious that a major bad-debt loss would be disastrous, extreme caution in credit administration, though costly in forgone profit, may nevertheless be wise.

Now let us turn to a consideration of the major determinants of the size of the investment in receivables in the individual firm, with special attention to those particularly subject to management influence and control.

Major Determinants of the Size of the Investment in Receivables

Of particular importance in shaping the size of the firm's investment in receivables are the following factors:

1. The terms of credit granted customers deemed creditworthy.
2. The policies and practices of the firm in determining which customers are to be granted credit.
3. The paying practices of credit customers.
4. The rigor of the seller's collection policies and practice.
5. The degree of operating efficiency in the billing, record keeping, and adjustment functions.
6. The volume of credit sales.

Let us look briefly at each of these factors. In theory each firm is free to specify whatever *terms of sale* best suit its objectives and circumstances. It may sell only for cash on delivery in order to avoid tying up its funds in receivables and risking bad-debt losses, perhaps consciously conceding the added sales that might be achieved through selling on credit. Or it may use the extension of generous credit as an aggressive selling tool. One used-car retailer in Boston has advertised that he would sell cars to any customer "whose credit is good" on terms of "no down payment, 48 months to pay." Further, the seller is free to change his terms of sale when and as he likes.

In actual practice, competitive pressures tend to push the individual firm to offer credit terms at least as generous as those of most of its competitors. Over a long span of years, particular terms of sale have become traditional in many product lines. Buyers have come to expect these terms to such an extent that new suppliers joining an industry usually offer the "customary" terms of sale of the industry as the course of least resistance. Thus, manufacturers of machine tools often sell on terms of "2/10, net 30." This notation means that a discount of 2% is allowed if payment is made within 10 days of invoicing, and payment regardless of discount is expected within 30 days, although sometimes on an "E.O.M." basis, that is, within 30 days after the end of the month of sale. Terms on a few products are quite long; for example, loose diamonds usually are sold on terms of 6 to 9 months.[2]

A 1958 study of the terms of sales used by 1,600 firms in 145 manufacturing lines and 75 wholesale lines[3] brought out the prevalence of cash discounts. Sixty-five percent of the manufacturers and 93% of the wholesalers surveyed customarily extended prompt-payment discounts. The most common period within which payment was required to earn the cash discount was 10 days among manufacturers and the 10th day of the following month among wholesalers. If discounts were not earned, the period of credit most commonly specified under manufacturers' terms of sale was 30 days.

Most firms make their "customary terms" available to all customers whom they have judged worthy of this credit. Changes in the customary terms of sale generally are made only infrequently; in many firms and industries the customary terms have remained constant over decades. Evidence to support this view is afforded by two broad studies of changes in credit terms during the years from World War II to 1958.[4] Each study reported that only 16% of the firms studied had changed their formal terms of trade during these years. Moreover, among those changing, there were no pronounced trends toward tighter or more liberal terms.

---

[2] For a list of customary terms of sale for 160 types of products, see T. N. Beckman and R. S. Foster, *Credits and Collections: Management and Theory* (8th ed.; New York: McGraw-Hill Book Co., 1969), pp. 697–704.

[3] R. A. Foulke, *Current Trends in Terms of Sale* (New York: Dun & Bradstreet, Inc., 1959).

[4] Described in Martin H. Seiden, *The Quality of Trade Credit* (Occasional Paper 87 [New York: National Bureau of Economic Research, 1964]), pp. 42–43.

The constancy of formal terms, however, suggests a misleading degree of rigidity toward credit extension by sellers. While few respondents to formal studies have said that they grant special terms freely, it is clear that in many competitive fields suppliers do tacitly extend their terms by permitting selected customers to take much longer to pay than the formal terms allow. As one student concludes:

> . . . in practice credit standards are normally altered through a change in credit policy rather than through a change of terms. . . . Less than vigorous enforcement of the net period [the stated terms of credit] has particular advantages. It facilitates discriminatory price discounts and conceals price changes from competitors. As a result of its flexibility, selectivity, and low cost relative to formal price changes, credit policy is an important factor determining both the quantity and the quality of the trade credit outstanding.[5]

In particular industries, such as the textile industry during especially competitive periods, many firms, while announcing no changes from the traditional terms of sale of the industry, reportedly were granting special terms to so many of their customers that their formal terms had become more nominal than real.

At any rate, it should be clear that the credit terms granted customers are an important determinant of the size of the investment in receivables. If other factors are constant, the longer the credit terms offered, the larger will be the investment in receivables.

It is interesting to note that the outstanding receivables of U.S. manufacturers on June 30, 1970, represented some 51 days' sales at the rate of sales reported for the preceding quarter.

The policies and practices of the individual firm in deciding which of its customers should be granted its customary terms of credit also affect the size of its investment in receivables. The firm's customary credit terms typically are extended only to those customers which are adjudged acceptable credit risks. Terms of cash on order or on delivery, or shorter than usual credit terms, may be used for sales to "poor risks" or to concerns for which available information is insufficient to establish their creditworthiness for the amounts involved. Different firms apply different standards in appraising the creditworthiness of their customers. Speaking generally, the more liberal the standards used in extending credit, the larger will be the investment in receivables. Some firms modify their standards in granting credit with the sales outlook, taking greater risks of bad debts when demand is slack. Most firms, however, appear to change their standards infrequently and then only within relatively narrow limits. We shall have more to say at a later point in this chapter on how credit risks are evaluated and controlled.

The actual paying practices of customers also have an impact on total credit outstanding. As noted earlier, many firms offer customers a discount for early payments. Firms offering terms of 2/10, net 30 give their

---

[5] *Ibid.*, p. 43.

customers the option of taking discounts and paying within 10 days or forgoing the discount and waiting 30 days to pay. The choice exercised by the customers clearly affects the amount of credit outstanding. Further, as we have noted, even where inflexible terms are quoted, customers may take liberties with them. Customers who buy primarily from sellers offering, say, 30-day terms, often ignore shorter terms of minor suppliers and pay all bills on the same basis. In other cases important customers deliberately and habitually take extra time to settle their trade obligations. In such instances, rather than risk losing the valuable sales outlets, the sellers may allow their stated terms to be exceeded. Still other customers, financially hard pressed, may let their debts run as far overdue as their creditors will tolerate.

While many firms are careful to meet all their trade obligations when due, others appear all too willing to take advantage of tolerant suppliers. The closeness with which the supplier follows up on overdue accounts and the degree of pressure he brings for prompt payment have a material effect on the paying practices of many customers and hence on the level of outstanding receivables.

In many firms, a huge and never ending volume of paper work is involved in filling orders, invoicing for goods shipped, recording payments, and making adjustments for discounts, returned items, defective items, short shipments, and the like. Speed in getting out invoices and statements, accuracy which avoids the delays associated with correcting errors and reconciling records, procedures for prompt investigations and resolution of customer claims for merchandise adjustments, and procedures for rapid recording of payments received and deposit of the checks all can help materially in minimizing unproductive investment in receivables. In retailing, the effectiveness of such a seemingly minor clerical function as the maintenance of the customer address file can have a sharp impact on the receivables investment and the bad-debt experience.

The most important variable affecting the level of the receivables investment is the volume of credit sales. If the other variables we have discussed remain constant, the level of receivables may be expected to vary directly with changes in sales volume. As sales increase, receivables expand, absorbing funds. As sales fall off, the related receivables decline, releasing funds. Unless long credits are granted, the time lag between changes in sales volume and proportionate changes in receivables is short. This behavior is often forgotten by planners, in relation to both expansion and contraction.

Since the determinants of the investment in receivables other than sales volume typically do not change rapidly or drastically, most of the important short-term changes in the amount of outstanding receivables can be traced to changes in sales volume. Conversely, important variations in the outstanding receivables of firms whose sales volume has been constant must be attributed to changes in credit terms, in the standards for granting credit, in the paying practices of customers, or in the rigor with which collections are policed.

The Work of the Credit Department

Since the financial officer usually is responsible for the effective functioning of the *credit department*, it is appropriate that we review the key functions and major problem areas in the effective administration of trade credit.

The work of the credit department consists of three main activities. First, the department must gather and organize the information necessary for decisions on the granting of credit to particular customers. Second, it must police the collection of receivables to ensure that efforts are made to collect the debts when due. Finally, in the case of accounts which appear to have "gone bad," that is, accounts of customers who apparently cannot or do not intend to pay, it must determine and carry out appropriate efforts to collect the accounts and avoid loss.

Sources of Credit Information

Although the usual standards for extension of trade credit are not severe, prospective new customers seldom are automatically extended normal credit terms. Typically, before shipment of a sizable order to a new customer, the credit department conducts a quick investigation to determine whether the company is justified in extending its normal credit terms to the new customer. Usually, the investigation must be a rapid one lest the prospective sale be lost as a result of delays in clearing the credit.

In checking on the creditworthiness of the prospective customer, the credit department can take advantage of a widespread network of credit information for data other than those provided by the customer. Particularly valuable sources are *credit reporting organizations* which make a business of collecting and supplying credit information. The largest firm in this field, Dun & Bradstreet, Inc., operates on an international basis, but its files on U.S. firms are particularly comprehensive in coverage.

Subscribers to its services receive the Dun & Bradstreet *Reference Book*, published every 2 months, listing about 3 million manufacturing, wholesaling, and retailing firms. Approximately 70% of the listings are accompanied by an estimate of the financial strength of the firm and a composite *credit rating* assigned the firm by Dun & Bradstreet. The rating seeks to reflect and summarize the information assembled to throw light on the creditworthiness of the subject firm. The key to Dun & Bradstreet ratings is reproduced as Exhibit 3–1, and an illustrative page from the *Reference Book*, with explanations of the symbols used, as Exhibit 3–2.

Unrated firms are those for which insufficient information was available to justify a rating. The *Reference Book* also includes firms "for whom

Exhibit 3–1

Key to Dun & Bradstreet Ratings

UNITED STATES KEY TO RATINGS					
ESTIMATED FINANCIAL STRENGTH		COMPOSITE CREDIT APPRAISAL			
		HIGH	GOOD	FAIR	LIMITED
AA	Over $1,000,000	A1	1	1½	2
A+	$750,000 to $1,000,000	A1	1	1½	2
A	$500,000 to $ 750,000	A1	1	1½	2
B+	$300,000 to $ 500,000	1	1½	2	2½
B	$200,000 to $ 300,000	1	1½	2	2½
C+	$125,000 to $ 200,000	1	1½	2	2½
C	$ 75,000 to $ 125,000	1½	2	2½	3
D+	$ 50,000 to $ 75,000	1½	2	2½	3
D	$ 35,000 to $ 50,000	1½	2	2½	3
E	$ 20,000 to $ 35,000	2	2½	3	3½
F	$ 10,000 to $ 20,000	2½	3	3½	4
G	$ 5,000 to $ 10,000	3	3½	4	4½
H	$ 3,000 to $ 5,000	3	3½	4	4½
J	Up to $ 3,000	3	3½	4	4½

CLASSIFICATION AS TO BOTH ESTIMATED FINANCIAL STRENGTH AND CREDIT APPRAISAL

Financial Strength Bracket		EXPLANATION
1	$125,000 and Over	When only the numeral (1, 2, or 3) appears, it is an indication that the estimated financial strength, while not definitely classified, is presumed to be within the range of the ($) figures in the corresponding bracket and that a condition is believed to exist which warrants credit in keeping with that assumption.
2	20,000 to 125,000	
3	Up to 20,000	

NOT CLASSIFIED OR ABSENCE OF RATING

The absence of a rating, expressed by two hyphens (--), is not to be construed as unfavorable but signifies circumstances difficult to classify within condensed rating symbols and should suggest to the subscriber the advisability of obtaining additional information.

SEE REFERENCE BOOK FOR EXPLANATION OF ABSENCE OF A LISTING AND ADDITIONAL SYMBOLS USED IN REFERENCE BOOK

Dun & Bradstreet, Inc.

OFFICES IN PRINCIPAL CITIES OF THE UNITED STATES

CANADIAN KEY TO RATINGS					
ESTIMATED FINANCIAL STRENGTH		COMPOSITE CREDIT APPRAISAL			
		HIGH	GOOD	FAIR	LIMITED
3A	Over $1,000,000	1	2	3	4
2A	$750,000 to $1,000,000	1	2	3	4
1A	$500,000 to $ 750,000	1	2	3	4
BA	$300,000 to $ 500,000	1	2	3	4
BB	$200,000 to $ 300,000	1	2	3	4
CB	$125,000 to $ 200,000	1	2	3	4
CC	$ 75,000 to $ 125,000	1	2	3	4
DC	$ 50,000 to $ 75,000	1	2	3	4
DD	$ 35,000 to $ 50,000	1	2	3	4
EE	$ 20,000 to $ 35,000	1	2	3	4
FF	$ 10,000 to $ 20,000	1	2	3	4
GG	$ 5,000 to $ 10,000	1	2	3	4
HH	$ 3,000 to $ 5,000	1	2	3	4
JJ	Up to $ 3,000	1	2	3	4

CLASSIFICATION AS TO BOTH ESTIMATED FINANCIAL STRENGTH AND CREDIT APPRAISAL

Financial Strength Bracket		EXPLANATION
1	$125,000 and Over	When only the numeral (1, 2, or 3) appears, it is an indication that the estimated financial strength, while not definitely classified, is presumed to be within the range of the ($) figures in the corresponding bracket and that a condition is believed to exist which warrants credit in keeping with that assumption.
2	20,000 to 125,000	
3	Up to 20,000	

NOT CLASSIFIED OR ABSENCE OF RATING

The absence of a rating, expressed by two hyphens (--), is not to be construed as unfavorable but signifies circumstances difficult to classify within condensed rating symbols and should suggest to the subscriber the advisability of obtaining additional information.

SEE REFERENCE BOOK FOR EXPLANATION OF ABSENCE OF A LISTING AND ADDITIONAL SYMBOLS USED IN REFERENCE BOOK

Dun & Bradstreet, of Canada Ltd.

OFFICES IN PRINCIPAL CITIES OF CANADA

SOURCE: Dun & Bradstreet, Inc., *Reference Book.*

the information available disclosed financial weaknesses of hazardous proportions, an undue moral risk, litigation critical to the business, or other circumstances of similar import."[6]

The "high" rating indicates minimum credit risk. At the other end of the scale, "limited" is applied to firms with substantial and chronic deficiencies. A sampling of ratings undertaken in connection with the Seiden study showed the following distribution of 1,200 ratings drawn from the editions of July, 1950, and July, 1958:

Rating	1950	1958
High	17.5%	14.0%
Good	71.6	59.3
Fair	10.9	24.9
Limited	–0–	1.8
	100.0%	100.0%

SOURCE: Martin H. Seiden, *The Quality of Trade Credit.*

[6] Seiden, *op. cit.*, p. 66.

Exhibit 3–2

Symbols Used in Dun & Bradstreet *Reference Book*

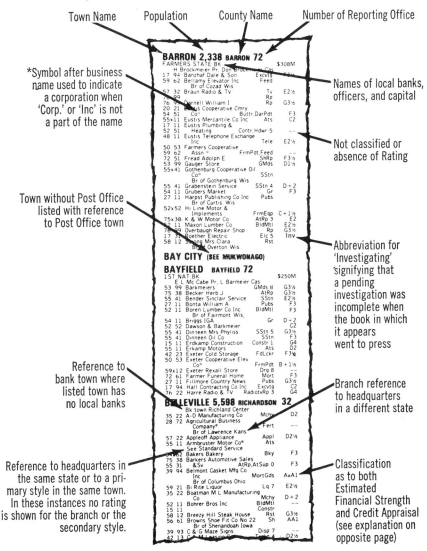

Town Name   Population   County Name   Number of Reporting Office

*Symbol after business name used to indicate a corporation when 'Corp.' or 'Inc' is not a part of the name

Names of local banks, officers, and capital

Not classified or absence of Rating

Town without Post Office listed with reference to Post Office town

Abbreviation for 'Investigating' signifying that a pending investigation was incomplete when the book in which it appears went to press

Reference to bank town where listed town has no local banks

Branch reference to headquarters in a different state

Reference to headquarters in the same state or to a primary style in the same town. In these instances no rating is shown for the branch or the secondary style.

Classification as to both Estimated Financial Strength and Credit Appraisal (see explanation on opposite page)

SOURCE: Dun & Bradstreet, Inc., *Subscriber's Manual.*

It is interesting to note the downward shift in quality ratings during the 8-year period, which was overall one of economic progress and prosperity. It should be pointed out, however, that the above distribution of ratings is by number of firms. Smaller and new firms dominate the limited and fair ratings. Large firms, which do a high percentage of total business, are mostly in the high category.

To the firm considering whether to ship an order to a new customer on normal terms, the credit ratings afford a handy, quick screening device. If the customer enjoys a good rating and the size of the order is reasonable in relation to his financial strength, the decision may well be to ship the order on normal terms but to proceed with a more complete investigation for future use.

If the customer is a concern of any size, the department can probably obtain, at moderate cost, a *credit report* from one of the credit reporting agencies. Dun & Bradstreet, for instance, usually is able to supply information about the background and experience of the principal executives of the concern, a summary of its history and methods of operation, notation of any bankruptcies or compromises with creditors on the part of the firm or its executives or owners in the past, and also income and balance sheet data. Further, the credit agency periodically conducts trade checks on concerns on which it maintains files. The agency investigates the collection experience of the major suppliers of the firm and summarizes this experience in the credit report, together with information on present credit outstanding, amount past due, recent high credits, and whether the concern usually pays on time. For an example of a credit report see Exhibit 3–3.

In addition to the large national credit information firms, a number of industry associations operate credit information services. Further, local mercantile credit agencies, dealing mainly in information about the credit standing of individuals, operate in almost every city. These are widely used by retail establishments whose potential sales to individual customers hardly justify extensive credit investigations of their own.

Commercial banks serve an important function in the exchange of credit information. Usually, the banks stand ready to help customers carry out credit investigations. If the subject of the credit investigation is not a customer of the bank, upon request the bank will commonly make inquiries of banks that are familiar with the subject's reputation and financial standing.

The company's own salesmen, who may well have visited the subject concern in getting the order, are sometimes helpful. However, sales personnel often are more concerned about the booking of the sale than the collection of the ensuing debt, and their information must be interpreted accordingly.

Where it appears necessary, the credit department can approach the prospective customer directly, either to discuss questionable aspects of the credit or to round out the file of information. In determining how much time and effort to devote to accumulation of credit information and its analysis, credit managers must balance the costs of added information against the benefits from the degree of improvement in the credit decisions that can be expected as a result of the more refined analysis. Usu-

Exhibit 3–3

Example of Business Information Report*

```
PLEASE NOTE WHETHER NAME, BUSINESS AND STREET ADDRESS CORRESPOND WITH YOUR INQUIRY
Dun & Bradstreet  BUSINESS INFORMATION REPORT  RATING
                                               UNCHANGED
```

SIC	D-U-N-S	©️ DUN & BRADSTREET, INC.	STARTED	RATING
34 61	803-4520	CD 13 APR 21 19-- N	1957	D 1½
	ARNOLD METAL PRODUCTS CO	METAL STAMPINGS		

53 S MAIN ST
DAWSON MICH   66666
TEL 215 999-0000

SUMMARY

SAMUEL B. ARNOLD	)	
GEORGE T. ARNOLD	) PARTNERS	

SUMMARY	
PAYMENTS	DISC PPT
SALES	$177,250
WORTH	$42,961
EMPLOYS	8
RECORD	CLEAR
CONDITION	SOUND
TREND	UP

PAYMENTS

HC	OWE	P DUE	TERMS	APR 19--	SOLD
3000	1500	1 10	30	Disc	Over 3 yrs
2500	1000	1 10	30	Disc	Over 3 yrs
2000	500	2 20	30	Disc	Old account
1000			30	Ppt	Over 3 yrs
500			30	Ppt	Over 3 yrs

FINANCE

On Apr 21 19-- S.B. Arnold, Partner, submitted statement Dec 31 19--

Cash	$	4,870	Accts Pay	$	6,121
Accts Rec		15,472	Notes Pay (Curr)		2,400
Mdse		14,619	Accruals		3,583
		------			------
Current		34,961	Current		12,104
Fixed Assets		22,840	Notes Pay (Def)		5,000
Other Assets		2,264	NET WORTH		42,961
		------			------
Total Assets		60,065	Total		60,065

19-- sales $177,250; gross profit $47,821; net profit $4,204. Fire insurance mdse $15,000; fixed assets $20,000. Annual rent $3,000. Signed Apr 21 19-- ARNOLD METAL PRODUCTS CO by Samuel B. Arnold, Partner Johnson Singer, CPA, Dawson

-----0-----

Sales and profits increased last year due to increased sub-contract work and this trend is reported continuing. New equipment was purchased last Sept for $8,000 financed by a bank loan secured by a lien on the equipment payable $200 per month. With increased capacity, the business has been able to handle a larger volume. Arnold stated that for the first two months of this year volume was $32,075 and operations continue profitable.

BANKING

Medium to high four figure balances are maintained locally. An equipment loan is outstanding and being retired as agreed.

HISTORY

Style registered Feb 1 1965 by partners. SAMUEL, born 1918, married. 1939 graduate of Lehigh University with B.S. degree in Mechanical Engineering. 1949-50 employed by Industrial Machine Corporation, Detroit, and 1950-56 production manager with Aerial Motors Inc., Detroit. Started this business in 1957. GEORGE, born 1940, single, son of Samuel. Graduated in 1963 from Dawson Institute of Technology. Served U.S. Air Force 1963-64. Admitted to partnership interest Feb 1965.

OPERATION

Manufactures light metal stampings for industrial concerns and also does some work on a sub-contract basis for aircraft manufacturers. Terms net 30. 12 accounts. Five production, two office employees, and one salesman. LOCATION: Rents one-story cinder block building with 5,000 square feet located in industrial section in normal condition. Housekeeping is good.
4-21 (803 77) PRA

* This is a fictitious example. Reproduced by permission of Dun & Bradstreet, Inc.

ally, the balance indicated is far short of the complete analysis that theoretically could be made.

We should note that the practice of providing credit and financial information and the institutional network for its dissemination in the United States and Canada far exceed those in other countries. Overall, the availability of reliable credit information facilitates credit extension and trade development. Although progress in the area in some other countries appears rapid, the room for further progress is great.

Reference might also be made to the network of information regarding individuals as well as businesses. Many credit organizations are prepared to report on individuals, their background, reputation, payment practices, and financial strength. Men must live with the record and reputation they have formed.

Evaluation of Credit Risk

Once the available sources of information have been utilized and a mass of data accumulated, the data must be interpreted and the credit decision made. In digesting the facts and reaching a credit decision, many financial officers more or less explicitly keep in mind as basic criteria the "Four C's of Credit—Capital, Capacity, Character, and Conditions." *Capital* obviously refers to the financial resources of the company, as indicated primarily by the balance sheets. *Capacity* has reference to the experience of the principals and the demonstrated ability of the concern to operate successfully, the latter to a good degree indicated by the profit record of the company. *Character* refers to the reputation of the owners and management for honesty and fair dealing. Information reflecting unfavorably on the integrity of the principals is especially important, because time and cost considerations limit the extent and thoroughness to which investigation can be pushed, and a clever rascal is likely to be able to present an outwardly attractive situation. The criterion *conditions* suggests the possibility of placing special limitations or restrictions on the extension of credit to doubtful accounts.[7]

In most companies a minor fraction of the credit accounts causes a very high percentage of the credit department's headaches. Chronically slow in paying but quick to claim faulty merchandise, these problem accounts dilute turnover and enrich correspondence files. The cost of credit mistakes is not measured by bad debts alone but by the trouble and expense of collection efforts and litigation in the case of accounts that ultimately are collectible.

As Chart 3–3 shows, the amount of corporate credit losses has been increasing rapidly in recent years. Chart 3–4 puts the losses in better perspective by expressing them as a percentage of sales and of outstanding receivables.

Analysis of bad-debt losses has shown that smaller firms have suffered a very much higher percentage of losses than have large firms. For example, Seiden's analysis of data from tax returns showed that bad-debt

---

[7] The term *conditions* is also used by some in a very different sense. Some use the term to stress the importance of the business conditions or level of prosperity of the customer's industry as a factor affecting his creditworthiness.

Chart 3–3

Bad Debts Reported in Returns from All Active Corporations in Mining, Contract Construction, Manufacturing, Wholesale and Retail Trade, and Services
(in millions)

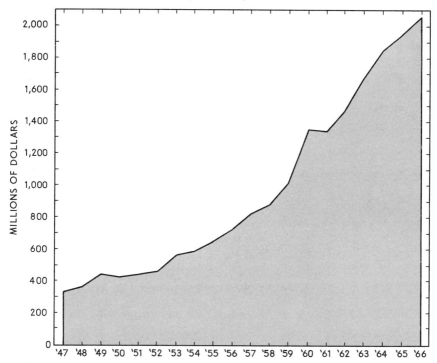

Sources of Data: 1947–59: Martin H. Seiden, *The Quality of Trade Credit*, Table 5, p. 16; 1960–66: U.S. Internal Revenue Service, *Statistics of Income: Corporation Income Tax Returns.*

losses of all manufacturing concerns from 1947 through 1957 averaged 0.81% of outstanding receivables. When the losses were analyzed by size of firm, the following results were obtained:

Small........................ 1.87%
Medium...................... 1.19
Large........................ 0.80
Giant........................ 0.37

It seldom is difficult for trained credit men, on the basis of information easily gathered, to spot those accounts—both new and already on the books—that are inherently high-risk accounts. The key problem in credit evaluation is to decide which of the admittedly higher-risk accounts are to be given credit, how much, and under what conditions. At one time the ability to avoid credit losses was widely regarded as the complete measure of the success of a credit manager. Measured by such standards, the credit manager had every incentive to turn down the credit requests of question-

Chart 3–4

Bad Debts Reported in Returns from All Active Corporations in Mining, Construction, Manufacturing, Wholesale and Retail Trade, and Services, Expressed as a Percentage of Sales and of Receivables

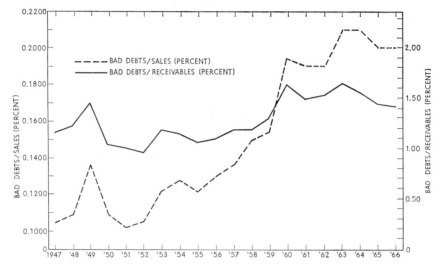

SOURCES: Data for 1947–59 from Martin H. Seiden, *The Quality of Trade Credit*, Table 6, p. 17; data for 1960–66 from U.S. Treasury Department, Internal Revenue Service, *Statistics of Income: Corporation Income Tax Returns.*

able customers. This concept of credit evaluation clearly is a gross over-simplification; the credit manager who maintains a credit policy so strict that credit losses never occur is properly suspected of turning away profitable business.

In deciding what credit risks to accept, the responsible officer should balance the risks of loss and the burdens involved in possibly tying up funds in slow-paying accounts against the value to the firm of the pro-spective sales involved. Commonly, the value of added business is high enough to justify a high degree of risk taking in trade credit. But just how the value of the added business should be calculated can be open to sharp differences of opinion. One approach is to value additional business simply in terms of the average profit rate on sales of the firm. Another approach measures the contribution of the added volume in terms of the excess of sales revenue over the additional costs that the company will incur in producing and selling the added goods. The added costs represent those costs that will change by virtue of the added volume—the cost of the materials going into the product, the additional labor necessary, added freight, added commissions paid on the sales, and so on. Not included will be costs such as depreciation and general and administrative expense, which are expected to remain fixed in amount despite this increase in volume. If the firm operates with a high level of fixed costs, and if it is operating below capacity, additional volume may be handled at limited "out-of-pocket" or additional expense, and the added profits to the firm from the additional business will be very much more than the average profit on sales of the firm.

An illustration should be helpful. Suppose prospective new customer A promises to buy $10,000 of goods a month, but his financial position is weak and he may take 60 days to pay, disregarding the regular 30-day term. Our firm is operating well below capacity, and if we do not supply new customer A, our competitor will. Our average profit is 10% of sales; however, inquiry reveals that the additional or out-of-pocket costs that will be created in producing and selling the added $10,000 a month will be only $6,000. Thus, our net income before taxes should increase by $4,000 a month, not $1,000, if we take on the account. In return for tying up and exposing to the risk of bad-debt loss an average of $20,000 (if the outstanding receivable balance is held to 60 days' sales), we can expect added net revenues of $4,000 a month or $48,000 a year. If the account were to stay active for only 6 months, the added marginal revenue from $60,000 in sales, which would be $24,000, would more than match complete loss of $20,000, the average balance in this account.

Once an initial credit to a new customer is approved, it is customary for the credit department to approve continued shipments to the customer, provided the shipment does not bring the outstanding balance due from the customer above a designated high limit established for that customer. Shipments on orders that would mean exceeding the high limit or credit line on the account are subject to review by the credit executives. Credit lines usually receive periodic routine review, often on an annual basis, and are revised only if important changes develop.

Policing the Collection of Outstanding Credits

The credit department also has the work of supervising or policing the accounts to see that customers are billed promptly and that slow-paying customers are reminded in effective fashion of their delinquency before it becomes serious. Books have been written on the art of gentle but effective "needling" of slow-paying customers so that prompt payment may be obtained without giving offense and jeopardizing future business.

In getting prompt payment of receivables, credit men are aided by the pressures stemming from the general recognition that failure to pay promptly will receive widespread publicity in trade circles and reflect adversely on the credit standing of the firm. Furthermore, for continuing customers the credit department has a more drastic weapon at hand: it can cut off future shipments on credit unless overdue accounts are given attention.

Once either supplier or customer has ceased active business, the pressure vanishes. The threat of unfavorable publicity is a minor one to customers in severe and well-publicized difficulty. It is also true that liquidators have had disappointing experiences in collecting the accounts receivable of bankrupt concerns.

Collection of inactive and long-overdue (or "sour") accounts involves difficult problems. In such circumstances normal pressures on the debtor to make payment are not likely to be effective, and bad-debt losses or excessive expense and effort in collection can be avoided only through skillful action. Initial efforts should be designed to discover the real reasons for the debtor's delinquency.

If the debtor appears able to pay, vigorous collection procedures are in order. If the account is small, often it is best to turn it over to a specialized collection agency. The collection agencies generally are paid a percentage —often as much as 30% to 50%—of the money they are able to collect. These agencies typically act with vigor, and they are set up to handle such operations with a minimum of expense.[8] Direct legal action by the seller in the case of small accounts often involves legal expense and managerial effort disproportionate to the amounts involved. This is especially true since persons seeking to avoid legal obligations frequently challenge quantities or qualities of the goods involved and do anything else they can to make the collection effort so tiresome that it will be abandoned.

In the case of important customers who freely acknowledge the debt but are in such financial difficulties that payment in full is difficult, somewhat different tactics are in order. If the creditor insists on his full legal rights and brings suit to collect the debt, he may only force the company into bankruptcy. When bankruptcy results, the affairs of the company are put in the hands of the courts, usually federal, for reorganization or liquidation under the supervision of court-appointed officials. If liquidation of the company results, the assets left after payment of the legal and administrative expenses of bankruptcy are divided among the creditors. Typically, the net proceeds from asset liquidation permit only a modest partial payment to trade creditors. Further, unless the sales outlet can be replaced, the future sales that might have been made to the customer are lost if he is forced out of business.

Consequently, it is often desirable for the creditor to seek a compromise settlement with an embarrassed customer that will get some payment yet permit the customer to stay in business. Unfortunately, if the customer

---

[8] The collection agencies are particularly involved with overdue consumers' obligations. One Chicago-based firm with 105 collection offices over the country reported its annual volume at an $130 million level at year-end 1970. The number of new accounts each month had reached 125,000. Department stores generally turned over uncollected accounts after carrying them for 6 months. Utilities submitted them 45 to 90 days after discontinuing service, and oil companies with credit cards turned over after 6 to 10 months. In more than 60% of the cases, the delinquent debtor had moved from the area. See *The New York Times* of December 26, 1970, p. 28, for a description of the operations of the Chicago firm.

has many other debts, as is typical, a compromise settlement may not be feasible unless other creditors will join in the compromise, since any unpaid creditor can demand its legal rights and throw the debtor into the courts. To help achieve such concerted action, standing creditors' committees in some industries and cities provide a continuing organization to bring the credit officers of the cooperating concerns together in particular cases as the need arises. Although compromise settlements are difficult to accomplish when many creditors are involved, such efforts have been relatively successful. In fact, experience dictates that a creditor should carefully investigate compromise settlement before it resorts to the more drastic use of full legal remedies, which often prove remedies in name only. Procedures of compromise and of bankruptcy are discussed in some detail in Chapter 29.

Aids to the Analysis of the Investment in Accounts Receivable

We have noted that the level of the investment in trade receivables can be expected to fluctuate in direct relationship with the volume of sales, provided sales terms and collection practices do not change. Naturally, credit officials, financial officers, and others associated with the finances of the concern are interested in detecting any tendency toward more lenient credit extension and potentially higher bad debts. These interested parties look carefully at the relationship of receivables to recent credit sales. The comparison of receivables to sales can take several forms. One comparison simply expresses outstanding receivables as a percentage of sales. Unless sales terms are unusually long, the existing receivables should be the product of recent sales. Consequently, persons within the firm, who have available recent monthly or quarterly sales data, relate reported receivables to these data. As an illustration consider the following data:

Sales fourth quarter, 1970...............	$1,890,000	
Accounts receivable, Dec. 31, 1970........		$967,200
Sales fourth quarter, 1969...............	1,200,000	
Accounts receivable, Dec. 31, 1969........		492,000

Let us assume in this case that the analyst is the financial officer, who knows that sales during each quarter were at a relatively even rate. It can be quickly determined that the 1970 receivables are 52% of the last quarter's sales (967,200/1,890,000 = 52%). Looking back to 1969, he can readily see that receivables then were only 41% of the preceding quarter's sales. Thus, the analyst can see that the large increase in receivables in 1970 is not simply the natural result of the growth in sales, and he is alerted to the need for further inquiry as to the reasons for the slowing of payments.

The relationship between sales and receivables is also expressed in terms of *average day's sales/outstanding* or *collection period*. Using the above data the average day's sales outstanding is calculated as follows:

$$\frac{\text{Sales in Last Quarter of 1970}}{90 \text{ Days}} = \frac{\$1,890,000}{90} = \$21,000 \, .$$

$$\frac{\text{Accounts Receivable, Dec. 31, 1970}}{\text{Average Day's Sales}} = \frac{\$967,200}{\$21,000} = 46.1 \text{ Days} \, .$$

The same method of calculation shows that the 1969 receivables equaled 36.9 days' sales at the 1969 rate of $13,333 a day. Comparison of 46.8 days' sales currently outstanding against 36.9 last year thus also reveals the apparent slow-up of receivables. The result in days' sales outstanding also permits comparison with stated terms of sale. If the company offers 30-day terms, it is apparent that these terms are being abused significantly.

Outside analysts often have only annual sales totals to compare with year-end receivables. If sales are steady through the year, the comparisons drawn from the data can be meaningful. But if sales fluctuate through the year, a comparison of year-end receivables with sales at the annual rate can be misleading. For example, if a firm sold on net 30-day terms and had monthly sales of $100,000 for January through November and $250,000 in December, it might well have receivables outstanding on December 31 of $250,000. Yet, in comparison with the annual sales of $1,350,000, or average monthly sales of $112,500, the $250,000 in receivables would appear unduly high.

Of course, if monthly sales are known to follow a consistent seasonal pattern year after year, the analyst can compare a year-end receivables/annual sales ratio with those of the same date in earlier years. The results should be comparable in relative if not absolute terms. Yet, as we have suggested earlier, receivables should be compared with recent sales data whenever such data can be obtained.

A useful management control device for review of the condition of receivables is the *aging schedule*. As the name suggests, this is a tabulation of receivables outstanding according to the length of time they have been outstanding. Each account, or a broad sample of accounts, is broken down according to the date of sale, and the results tabulated.

Let us suppose, for illustration, that two firms each have monthly sales of $700,000 on 30-day terms. Each has outstanding receivables of $1,000,-000. Aging produces the schedules shown in the accompanying table.

	Firm A		Firm B	
Outstanding less than 30 days....................	$ 700,000	70%	$ 700,000	70%
Outstanding 30–59 days......	280,000	28	150,000	15
Outstanding 60–89 days......	15,000	1.5	60,000	6
Outstanding 90+ days.......	5,000	0.5	90,000	9
	$1,000,000	100.0%	$1,000,000	100%

Without the aging schedule, the receivables position of the two firms appears the same. Certainly, receivable/sales ratios and the collection period are identical. But firm B may be encountering serious difficulty in collecting the $150,000 in long-overdue receivables, even though it has a number of customers who are more prompt in paying after 30 days than those of firm A. Thus, the aging schedule, by revealing any tendency for old accounts to accumulate, provides a useful supplement to the various receivables/sales ratios. Since the outstanding receivables are appraised in terms of the associated dates of sale, the tabulation automatically recognizes recent bulges or slumps in sales. Many financial officers have such schedules prepared in routine at periodic intervals, and commercial banks and other lenders to firms with important investments in receivables frequently ask for aging schedules.

Accounting for Accounts Receivable

The accounting for accounts receivable involves a large volume of record keeping, calling for rapid and accurate recording of sales and payments. The accounting theory, however, is simple. When a sale is made, the appropriate amount is added to an account kept for each customer and is thus included in the total of accounts receivable. As payments are received, the fact of payment is noted on each account, and the total of accounts receivables is decreased at the same time cash is increased.

Most concerns recognize the fact that some of their sales on credit will not be paid and set up an account called *Reserve for Bad Debts* or *Provision for Bad Debts*. An amount equal to the portion of sales which it is estimated will prove uncollectible is charged to income as Bad-Debt Expense, and an equal credit is made to the Reserve for Bad Debts. When it is determined that a particular account receivable will not be collected, it is taken off the books by reducing accounts receivable and the Reserve for Bad Debts by an equal amount. Many firms, in reporting their accounts receivable on the balance sheet, show "Accounts Receivable, net" —in other words, after subtraction of the Reserve for Bad Debts.

Cash Receipts from Receivables

In planning when and in what amounts cash will be received as a result of credit sales, the critical dates are the dates when receipts of payment for credit sales can be expected. Thus, forecasts of credit sales must be converted into estimated collections of accounts receivable in order to determine cash receipts from such sales. Usually, an average figure based on past experience is employed as a measure of the time lag between sales and collection of the related receivables. If the average collection experience has been 30 days, for instance, and there is no reason to anticipate a change in this figure, the receipts from future sales on credit can be scheduled a month behind the sales. Appropriate deductions should be made for bad debts if there is reason to believe they will prove significant.

In recent years the rapid growth of bank-sponsored credit cards has provided participating merchants, airlines, hotels, etc., a means for converting consumer receivables under the cards into cash. Generally, the bank will charge the merchant a fee (often 2% of the amount) for discounting the debt, and in addition will charge the cardholder interest if he does not pay within a stated time (commonly 20 days) after billing. To date, early 1971, most major department stores have chosen not to accept the bank or other general credit cards. Many issue their own cards.

For many years, factoring firms have made a business of buying business receivables from client firms. The practice will be discussed in Chapter 14.

The Trend toward Longer Collection Periods

Earlier we noted with interest the long-term trend made apparent in Chart 3–2 for receivables to grow faster than sales. By way of emphasis we pointed out that manufacturers would have had an investment of only $54 billion in receivables rather than the actual $96.5 billion on December 31, 1969, if they had collected for sales as rapidly in 1969 as in 1947. In terms of the collection period, the 1969 receivables represented almost 47.4 days' sales compared with 26.5 days in 1947.

The growth in receivables relative to sales is in striking contrast to the movement of inventory relative to sales. As noted in Chapter 2, the inventory/sales ratio has declined modestly.

Why have American manufacturers let receivables outpace sales? The discussion in this chapter on management policy toward receivables should suggest some likely explanations. Our listing of contributing factors could almost serve as a summary to this chapter. The factors include:

1. A long-term continuing shift in top-management policy objectives away from a dominant emphasis on minimizing credit losses toward one of maximizing overall firm profits. This latter emphasis balances the gains from more sales attributable to more accommodating credit policies against the larger investment in receivables and the higher credit losses that may be expected from less rigorous credit policies.

2. The fact that the larger suppliers typically have not found it difficult to meet the additional funds requirement stemming from the increased investment in receivables. In periods of tight money, such as 1970, many large corporate suppliers have found it easier to raise funds than their customers. Hence they are encouraged to help their customers through generous trade credit.

3. The existence through most postwar years of excess productive

capacity and the related fact that in many industries the incremental costs of producing and selling additional units was small. Thus, the profit reward for additional sales was high.

4. The fact that in many industries competition for sales by covert credit leniency was thought easier to administer selectively and less likely to bring quick competitive retaliation by other suppliers than would price cutting.

5. The general prosperity of recent decades, which has made managers bolder in assuming exposure to bad-debt losses. Thus, the rising volume of losses has been taken in stride by many managements.

chapter 4

Management of the Money Position

In earlier editions of this book, this chapter was titled "Management of Cash and Near-Cash Reserves and the Need for Funds." We have concluded that "Management of the Money Position" is more sharply descriptive of the work of controlling and utilizing effectively the liquid resources of the firm. *Money Position* is intended to encompass the cash position of the firm, investments that can readily be converted into cash, and indeed readily available sources of credit that can be drawn upon if and when needed. In many respects the financial officer's job in managing the cash position and in drawing upon or rebuilding short-term investment portfolios or credit lines is like that of the commercial bank officer charged with the day-to-day and hour-to-hour management of the bank's own cash and investment position—its "money position." Like the banker, the alert corporate financial officer wants to minimize unproductive cash balances, to invest temporarily excess cash advantageously, and to make the best possible arrangements for meeting both planned and unexpected demands on the company's cash. Although top management can be expected to have a keen interest in the liquidity of the firm and in the shaping of policies governing cash and near-cash accounts, the direct and immediate responsibility for management of the money position of the firm typically rests with the chief financial officer.

The commitment of funds to *cash* and *near-cash investments* (near-cash in the sense that they are readily marketable with little fear of loss) for American businesses generally is a significant one. Thus, U.S. manufacturing corporations on December 31, 1969, had $30.5 billion in cash and U.S. government securities, an amount almost 5.6% of their total resources. Since many firms invest surplus funds in securities other than those of the U.S. government, the above figures understate the totals committed to cash and liquid investment.

Chart 4–1 shows the percentage of total assets committed to cash and U.S. securities in a number of manufacturing industries and in a number of nonmanufacturing industry groups. Only in the cases of communication services and electric and gas utilities were the totals in cash and U.S. obligations relatively insignificant. It should be emphasized, however, that this chart presents industry averages in which the large companies have heavy weight. The figures for individual companies can and do vary

Chart 4–1

Investments in Cash and U.S. Obligations of Active Corporations in Selected Industry Groups, as a Percentage of Their Total Assets, for Companies with Accounting Periods Ended July, 1966–June, 1967

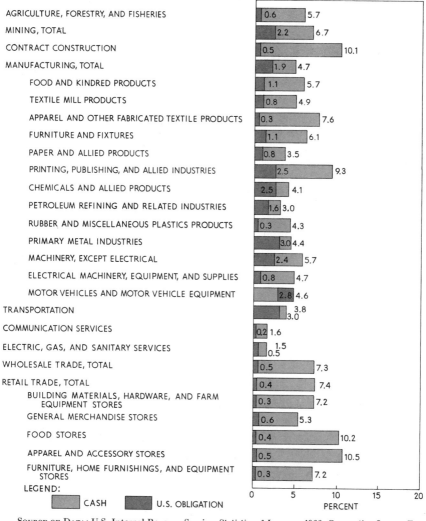

SOURCE OF DATA: U.S. Internal Revenue Service, *Statistics of Income—1966, Corporation Income Tax Returns* (Washington, D.C.: U.S. Government Printing Office, 1970), Table 2—"Balance Sheets and Income Statements, by Major Industry."

widely from the industry averages—more so generally than in the case of inventory and receivables. Many hard-pressed firms necessarily operate with a very lean money position. On the other hand, at year-end 1969, such a highly regarded company as General Motors Corporation had $1,824 million or 12.3% of its total resources in "money assets," and another, Standard Oil Company (New Jersey), had $1,276 million or 7.3%. Nor was a heavy money position restricted to the giants. American Metal Climax, Inc., a leading mining company, reported money assets of $139 million or 14.8% of total assets, while Dun & Bradstreet, Inc., reported money assets of almost $59.5 million or 31.9% of its total assets!

In the chapters just preceding, we stressed the importance of managerial efforts toward efficient employment of the funds committed to inventory and receivables. Moreover, we emphasized the potential contribution of the financial officer to policies and practices that speed asset turnover and maximize return on investment. Against this background, the relatively heavy money positions of the companies cited above might well raise such questions in the student's mind as these:

1. Isn't it as important to make economical use of money assets as of inventory and receivables? Should not financial officers practice what they preach?
2. What are the functions served by the money assets? What are the key determinants of the corporate investment in cash and near-cash?
3. What are the key considerations in the effective management of the money position?

The answer to the first question above must be a resounding affirmative. Money assets *are* susceptible to management; money has a real cost, and failure to utilize money assets efficiently will dilute return on investment —"lazy cash" is just as debilitating to a healthy return as sluggish inventories. Moreover, the financial officer does have a unique opportunity with those assets peculiarly under his dominion to demonstrate skill and drive in achieving judiciously economical use of these resources. As in the case of other assets, the end objective is not simply to minimize the investment in money assets. It is rather to achieve a level of investment that balances effectively considerations of cost of resources and return on investment on the one hand, and on the other the functions served by the money assets and the closely related tangible and intangible benefits of a strong money position.

Let us turn first to an examination of the functions served by the money assets or, put differently, the various reasons why companies carry such assets. Then in the light of these we shall look at the key guidelines to effective management of the money position.

Before going further, though, we should be clear as to what we include under the classification *money assets*. Basically, we include those assets that management itself regards as a part of, or an adjunct to, the cash position. Along with currency on hand and bank deposits (both *demand deposits*—checking accounts—and *time deposits*), we include those investments which management would not hesitate to liquidate as cash is needed and which in fact are held in a form that makes conversion into cash easy and at little risk of loss of principal. Investments in subsidiaries or in the common stock of concerns believed to represent rewarding, long-term capital gain opportunities would *not* be considered as money assets but rather as long-term investments.

Most companies now show marketable securities as a separate current asset just below the cash account on the balance sheet. Investments in subsidiaries or in stocks for appreciation objectives are normally shown separately and among the noncurrent assets.

The Function of the Investment in Money Assets

Why do well-managed companies, such as General Motors, carry huge amounts in money assets, which earn directly at most a return very low in relation to the rate of return on assets overall? In most firms the money assets serve a variety of needs or purposes. The more important of these functions can be usefully classified and summarized as follows:

1. Meet operational requirements.
2. Provide reserves of liquidity against:
   a) Routine net outflows of cash.
   b) Scheduled major outlays.
   c) Exploitation of possible opportunities for advantageous longer-term investment.
   d) Unexpected drains of cash.
3. Meet bank relationship requirements.
4. Enhance investment image and other such intangibles.
5. Serve as a reservoir for net inflows of cash pending the availability of better uses for the funds.
6. Earn directly.

Operational Requirements for Cash

Most firms find it convenient to keep on hand small amounts of petty cash for making the minor disbursements most conveniently made in cash. Retail firms and service establishments normally keep some currency on hand to make change on cash sales. But the cash account consists primarily of funds on deposit at commercial banks.

The operating needs of the firm for bank balances are sharply influenced by the balance between the *deposit collection float* it must sustain and the *check payment float* it enjoys.

At the time it deposits at its banks the cash and checks it has received from its customers, the firm adds these deposits to its "cash in banks" account. The bank, however, will not allow the depositing firm to draw on these funds until the bank has "collected" the amount of the checks deposited which were drawn on accounts in other banks. The time required for the bank to convert the checks into "collected funds" is called *deposit collection float*. For example, a New York manufacturer receives a check for $1,000 from a California customer, drawn on the customer's account at the Bank of America in San Francisco. The New York manufacturer deposits the check in his New York bank, the Irving Trust Company, on Monday, and it in turn deposits the check at the Federal Reserve Bank of New York for collection and *ultimate* credit to Irving Trust's own reserve account at the New York "Fed." The New York Fed will airmail the check to the Federal Reserve Bank of San Francisco, which will deduct the amount of the check from the deposit account with it of the Bank of America. The check is then turned over to the Bank of America, which in turn deducts the $1,000 from the account of the customer who wrote the check.

The Federal Reserve banks, which handle the mechanics of collection of most out-of-town checks, give depositing banks such as the Irving Trust unrestricted credit for the deposited funds only after an allowance of time for the check to be sent to San Francisco for collection. A set schedule of collection time is followed; normally the Fed makes funds available in one day for nearby cities and in two days for more distant points—a relatively quick schedule made possible only by the air shipment of checks. Thus, the deposit of $1,000 would be credited to Irving Trust's account at the Fed on Wednesday. Naturally, Irving Trust in the above example and other banks of deposit normally will not let depositing customers draw on uncollected funds that the bank itself cannot yet use. Hence, a part of the New York manufacturer's bank balance is effectively immobilized by being tied up in the process of check collection.

We might add that banks may choose not to make funds available for withdrawal even when nominally collected by the Federal Reserve because the checks may turn out uncollectible—because of improper preparation or, more importantly, because the writer of the check has insufficient funds on deposit to cover the check. The process of getting a bad check to the bank on which it was written and back to the bank where it was deposited may take several days. If the depositor's account is a good one, and the bank can count on him to make good on bad checks he has deposited, the bank may allow him to draw on deposited funds as soon as the scheduled 1 or 2 days' collection time has elapsed. Otherwise, it may well insist that the deposit balances created by checks on other banks should not be drawn upon until enough time has elapsed that it can be confident the deposited checks are good.

Payment float reflects the time interval between the time a payment check is written (and deducted by the firm from its bank balance on its books) and the time the check gets back to the bank it was written on and is deducted from the firm's deposit balance on the bank's books. The interval reflects the time the check was in the mails to the payee, the time the payee uses up in his routines of receipt, accounting, and deposit in his bank, and the time for the check to move physically back to the bank it was drawn on and be charged against the paying firm's deposit account.

Firms that buy large amounts from distant suppliers, yet sell largely for cash or to local customers who settle their accounts with checks on local banks, are likely to experience greater payment float than deposit collection float. They are able to supply the bank with sizable balances while showing little or no deposit balances on their own banks.

So far we have spoken as if the firm had a single bank account. Actually, firms with decentralized manufacturing or distribution facilities across the country—or around the globe—typically find it useful to keep deposit accounts with a number of banks, using some primarily as receiving or collection banks, others as major depositaries where major reserve accounts are held, and still others as paying banks—that is, for payroll check or other disbursement purposes.

In recent years American companies have made much progress in devising techniques to minimize the amounts necessarily tied up in operational requirements. We shall describe some of these later. Many firms appear to have cut operational requirements for cash near to an irreducible minimum—at least under existing banking practices.

Reserves of Liquidity

If the daily cash receipts almost exactly matched the daily outflow, the total cash balances would not have to be very large to meet the purely operational needs described above. Such even flows, however, seldom can be expected. Consequently, the cash account serves the added function of absorbing the normal ebbs and flows in funds through a business from day to day and week to week. For example, most department stores buy from suppliers whose terms call for payment around the 10th of each month, while their major receipts come in more evenly through the month. Unless they are to borrow for midmonth needs, routine cash balances must be sufficient to cover the heavy outflow around the 10th.

Liquid asset balances are also swelled by accumulation of funds in anticipation of major outlays for such items as planned expansion of inventories or receivables, dividend payments, income tax payments, debt retirement, and purchase of major items of equipment. Prudence may suggest that the funds for such purposes be raised well in advance of the scheduled payment date to ensure that payments can be met without strain. For example, if a major building program is to be financed through the sale of securities, the company may well prefer to sell the securities and have the funds in hand before firm contracts for the construction are let, even though the payments for the construction will not be required for many months or even years into the future.

Further, many managements like to keep "extra" cash on hand as an "opportunity fund" to permit rapid exploitation of attractive opportunities for investment that may present themselves—development of a research finding pointing up a new product possibility, an unexpected chance to buy another company, and the like.

An additional highly important function of the cash and near-cash accounts is that of providing a defensive or protective reserve against unexpected drains on liquidity. Interruptions in production or sales as a result of a strike, a transportation tie-up, or a fire in a major plant can rapidly deplete cash. A sudden decline in sales or an extremely bad year with heavy losses may create major cash drains at an unpropitious time for borrowing or for selling securities. Further, major adverse changes in the firm's competitive position may call for heavy expenditures at times when new capital is relatively unavailable. Moreover, the adverse developments setting up heavy cash needs may well be linked, so that the pressures on cash are multiple in nature. In uncertain times—and when is the future outlook entirely clear?—it is highly comforting to all those dependent on a business to know that it is "well heeled." To Benjamin Franklin is attributed the observation that in adversity a man can count on only three truly reliable friends: "a faithful dog, an old wife, and money in the bank."

Bank Relationship Requirements

Considerations of bank relationships have an important influence on the size of deposit balances maintained. While some banks are quite willing to provide their services on a cash-fee basis, most prefer to be compensated in the form of demand deposit balances. Deposits are vital to the banks; naturally, large and less active deposit accounts are especially valued. And to the firm the favorable regard and active support of its major banks can be valuable in a variety of ways. First, the banks are in a position to supply a variety of tangible services, such as the provision of credit information, beyond the routine ones of servicing deposit accounts. Second, the bankers, by virtue of their experience and wide contacts, often can render important intangible services such as the discovery of attractive merger opportunities or advice as how best to raise needed capital.

A third and particularly important consideration for many firms in recent years stems from the value of bank deposit balances as a form of insurance of continued access to bank credit, particularly during tight-money periods. In many recent years banks have had more attractive loan and investment opportunities than money to loan, and in some years of intensely tight money conditions, such as 1966 and again in

1969 and 1970, the demand for the available bank credit was so strong that severe rationing of credit was necessary. In such circumstances, the deposit balances the customer had carried with the bank provided a measure of his "call on the bank" for credit. It also influenced the terms of the loan; but when credit was particularly tight, the fact of availability of credit was more important to many firms than the terms. Treasurers that had treated their banks parsimoniously on balances found themselves being treated at arm's length when credit was rationed.

As the demand for their funds has grown, most larger banks have come to insist that a stated percentage of outstanding loans must be kept on deposit with the lending bank. These *supporting* or *compensating* balances usually are fixed at 15% or 20% of the credit. If the firm normally would carry a sizable account with the bank anyhow, the compensating balance requirement is more nominal than burdensome. If not, the balance requirement effectively increases the amount of credit needed and the cost of the usable funds.

Intangible Values of a Strong Liquid Position

In the past, many business executives believed that considerable prestige flowed from a demonstrably strong liquid position. Certainly, an illiquid position can adversely affect credit and other appraisals of the firm, and a strong money position may contribute to an image of strength and solidity with investors. But once an obviously strong position has been achieved, it is doubtful that further liquidity adds materially to prestige values. Indeed, overly abundant liquidity may suggest that management is unduly cautious or ineffective in developing more rewarding uses for the firm's financial resources.

"The Money Just Rolled In"

It should be recognized that the cash balance is to an extent a residual figure—the net result at any time of a multiplicity of inflows and outflows. If unforeseen or unexpectedly heavy inflows swell the account, redundant cash may be carried for a long time before decisions as to its use are made and implemented. Consequently, the level of a firm's cash at any particular time may be as much the result of happenstance as of conscious decision and plan.

Earning a Direct Return

Since 1933 banks have been forbidden to pay interest on demand deposits (checking accounts). During the late 1930's and the war years, short-term interest rates were very low, providing little incentive for corporate financial officers to invest the bank balances that were in excess of needs for operations and maintenance of banking relationships. However, as interest rates rose in the postwar period, financial officers of cash-heavy firms increasingly undertook to invest currently surplus cash in income-producing securities.

U.S. Treasury bills have been an especially popular vehicle of short-term investment. Weekly issues of Treasury bills of 3-month and 6-month maturities supply the market with a choice of maturities from 1 week to 26 weeks, and bills up to 1 year often are available. The Treasury bill market is extremely active and broad, so that trading costs are small and marketability unquestioned in large or small amounts. During 1970, market yields on 3-month Treasury bills ranged from a high of 8.12% to a low of 4.90%.[1]

U.S. government tax anticipation bills have been a popular means of reserving funds for tax payments. The Treasury issues these bills with a maturity a week later than the quarterly due dates for payment of income tax liabilities, but the bills have a "bonus feature" in that they can be used at par to pay tax bills.

Early in 1961 the First National City Bank of New York introduced a new money market instrument, the *negotiable certificate of deposit*. These "CD's" are receipts for deposits for a stated period of time and bear interest rates according to market demand at the date of issue. Maturities of less than a year are most common, but CD's are also issued for as much as 5 years. There is a market for these, so that they can be sold readily if the holder needs funds before the stated maturity. Sale of CD's by the banks permits the banks to compete for corporate cash that otherwise would have been invested in Treasury bills or other investment media.

The negotiable CD's quickly became a popular money market instrument. Smaller banks as well as large can compete for CD money, but the failure early in 1965 of two smaller banks, which had sold CD's to a number of corporate investors, emphasized that the CD's were only as safe as the issuing bank and that the small extra yield available from buying the CD's of lesser-known banks might not be worth much risk of loss. Consequently, the CD's of big, highly-regarded banks have been favored in the market.

Since 1933 the Federal Reserve Board has regulated the maximum interest rates banks could pay on time or savings deposits. In 1966 and again in 1969–70, market rates on other short-term investments rose above the ceiling rate, 6¼%, that banks legally could pay on large-denomination CD's. Consequently, as outstanding CD's matured, investors were encouraged to seek the higher rates available in the commercial paper or other unregulated markets. In consequence, the amounts of out-

---

[1] No interest as such is paid on bills. They are sold at a discount, the amount of which determines the yield on the face amount. Since the actual investment is less than the face amount by the amount of the discount, the true return on the amount invested is somewhat higher than the stated yield figure.

standing bank negotiable CD's dropped sharply—from $24.3 billion to $10.9 billion between December, 1968, and December, 1969. After the suspension of rate ceilings on some CD's and relaxation on other maturities in June, 1970, permitting the banks to pay competitive rates, demand for bank CD's reappeared.

Commercial paper—the short-term notes sold by finance companies and by sizable concerns of presumed strong financial standing—have become a popular form of short-term investment by cash-rich companies. The amounts of commercial paper outstanding have grown sharply in recent years, especially during the period when bank CD's were made uncompetitive. In fact, a number of bank holding companies sold commercial paper for the first time in 1969 and 1970.

The commercial paper market has offered investors the opportunity to arrange directly with issuers, primarily finance companies, the amounts and maturities desired and usually has afforded rates well above those available in Treasury bills.

Corporate treasurers have developed a number of other outlets for their short-term funds, several of which are described in summary form in Table 4–1.

Short-Term Investment Policy Issues

While the chief financial officer normally has the responsibility for managing the money position, generally the board of directors and top management have established policy guidelines that shape and constrain the investment policies and practices. Commonly, these investment policies are directly concerned with the balance to be struck between the objectives of maximum investment safety and maximum marketability on the one hand and the maximization of current income from investment on the other. Case studies of the policies of a number of individual firms have suggested that initial investment guidelines emphasized investment safety and marketability to a high degree. For example, many firms gave their financial officers authority only to invest in U.S. government securities of maturities of less than one year.

Over the years many companies have liberalized their investment policies in order to boost income. Available income yields on money market investments reflect a variety of shifting supply and demand factors including inherent vulnerability to loss. As we indicated earlier, securities of the U.S. government, which to American firms involve no bad-debt risk, enjoy exceptional marketability. The income available on U.S. Treasury bills normally provides a base for comparison of other rates available in short-term money market instruments.

The developing risk-taking spirit of corporate treasurers has been dampened periodically by well-publicized investment fiascos, which emphasized that even investments judged low risk were not risk free.

Table 4-1

Summary Data on Short-Term Investment Media

Short-Term Investment Media	Summary Description	Approximate Amount Outstanding 6/30/70	Marketability	Yield on 6/30/70 3 Month Maturities
U.S. Treasury bills	Direct obligations of U.S. government. Weekly sales of 3- and 6-month maturities so that bills maturing each week up to 6 months are available in secondary market. Treasury also sells 9-month and 1-year maturities on less frequent basis. Sold at a discount. Amount of discount determines investment return.	$76.2 billion	Extremely good secondary market	6.36%
Federal agency issues	Securities issued by agencies of U.S. government, such as Federal Home Loan Bank notes. A substantial percentage of total outstandings of agency securities are of maturities less than 1 year. Enjoy an investment standing close to that of direct obligations of U.S.	About $31 billion	Good secondary market	6.99
Negotiable bank certificates of deposit	Represent receipts for time deposits at commercial banks. Maturities and interest rates are negotiated directly by investors with issuing banks. Maturities most commonly under one year, but can be longer.	$14.1 billion	Good—for CD's of larger banks	8.00
Prime bankers' acceptances	Bills of exchange usually arising out of international trade transactions, which an "accepting" bank has effectively guaranteed. Bank's backing gives a strong quality standing. Maturities less than 1 year, commonly 90 days.	$4.0 billion held outside banks	Good secondary market	8.00

Commercial paper—prime industrial names	Unsecured notes of leading industrial firms, normally sold through a dealer. Issued on a discount basis. Maturities generally in 30–120-day range.	$9.3 billion	No reliable secondary market	8.38
Commercial paper—prime finance paper	Unsecured notes, generally placed directly by sales finance company issuers with investing firms. Usually sold on discount basis. Investor commonly can specify maturity desired in range of 5–270 days.	$23.0 billion	No reliable secondary market	7.75
Euro-dollars	U.S. dollar denominated time deposits or negotiable certificates of deposit at banks or branches outside the United States. Rates are free of regulation, but U.S. corporations can use only funds raised outside the United States to acquire these deposits.	Perhaps as much as $40 billion, but estimates vary widely.	Good for CD's—none for time deposits	8.81%
Short-term tax exempts	Temporary and preliminary notes of local housing authorities, which have quality rating like that of U.S. agencies, and tax and bond anticipation notes of states and municipalities, and other political subdivisions. Usually carry fixed interest rates and interest is exempt from federal income taxation.	Several billion	Fair secondary market	4.50 tax free

Notable among these shocks to yield-hungry investors were the failure in 1965 of the San Francisco National Bank, a relatively small bank that had aggressively gathered funds through CD's; a large Canadian finance company, Atlantic Acceptance Corporation, Ltd.,[2] also in 1965; and the relatively sudden bankruptcy in June, 1970, of the Penn Central Transportation Company, a huge railroad which had more than $87.5 million of commercial paper outstanding when it succumbed.

Policies regarding choice of appropriate maturities for portfolio investments also involve a reconciliation of the objectives of safety of

Chart 4–2

Price of a 6% Coupon Bond to Yield 7% as a Function of Years to Maturity

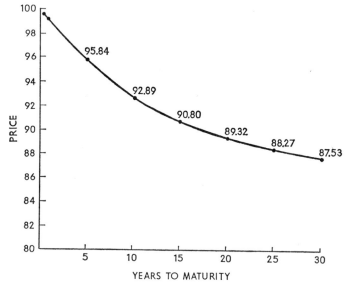

principal and maximum income. Generally, during postwar years, securities of intermediate or long maturity have offered investors higher yields than have very short maturities. Thus, in mid-1970, 3-month U.S. Treasury bills yielded 6.36%; 1-year U.S. securities, 6.9%; and 5-year U.S. bonds, 7.7%. When patterns like these prevail and these interest rates do not change, an investor likely to need cash in a year or two could earn more on his investment in the interim if he were to buy, say, 5-year bonds and sell these bonds when the cash was needed. However, if interest rates rise, the prices of outstanding securities will fall, and their sale will be possible only at a loss. The vulnerability to loss with rises in interest rates

---

[2] American corporate investors, including the Dow Chemical Company, National Lead Company, Minnesota Mining and Manufacturing Company, and The Ford Foundation, were reported to have held more than $50 million of the notes of Atlantic Acceptance when it failed.

increases as the maturity of the investment instrument lengthens. If interest rates move up from 6% to 7%, a 6% bond will decline to a price level at which buyers are offered a 7% return on the purchase price. If the maturity is short, the price decline to be expected if interest rates rise will be small—to only $995.20 for a $1,000 6-month bond. Yet, as Chart 4–2 demonstrates, a $1,000 bond with a 5-year maturity would drop very much more, to $958.40, while a 30-year bond would fall to $875.30. Thus, exposure to price risk due to interest rate increases is minimized by use of short maturities.

Despite evidence of relaxation in some companies from time to time in their customary policies of keying maturities to the dates of projected needs and/or staying within a year, most companies continue conservative policies on maturities. Indeed, overall, most appear to continue to regard income generation as a portfolio objective decidedly subordinate to liquidity and safety.

An Example: A.T.&T.'s Money Position

Many of the reasons for carrying sizable liquid reserves can be illustrated by reference to the American Telephone and Telegraph Company (A.T.&T.), a holding company for the operating telephone companies in the Bell System, which provide telephone service for most of the country. A.T.&T. carries a significant investment in cash and marketable securities. The total cash and marketable securities (primarily short-term U.S. government securities) account of the System on December 31, 1969, amounted to $848 million or 1.9% of total assets. Since the telephone companies are regulated utilities, their earnings are limited to a *fair return* on total capital employed in their businesses. To the extent that capital is tied up in cash and low-return temporary investments, the return on stockholders' investment may be diluted. Hence, the cost of carrying a sizable investment in cash and low-return securities is significant.

In considering the reasons why A.T.&T. has chosen to carry such liquid reserves, it should be understood that the parent company acts as a sort of central banker for the operating companies. Certain cash balances must be carried by the parent and the subsidiary companies with banks to compensate them for the activity in clearing checks and drafts and for other services. As bank balances build up above these levels, the excess is withdrawn and added to the central pool of funds with the parent company.

One of the functions of the central pool of funds is to provide funds needed for large payments anywhere in the System, most of which can be scheduled. They include quarterly dividend payments, interest payments on bonds, and payments of income and excise taxes, which are collected by the companies and turned over to the U.S. government at regular intervals. Large payments to contractors for new facilities can also be scheduled. Thus, the central pool covers uneven but predictable outflows of cash for the System.

The central pool of funds also serves as backup for commercial paper which the Operating Telephone Companies have been issuing since 1968. Bank lines of credit are the conventional backup for commercial paper issued by corporations and the Operating Companies have access to the central pool as a proxy for such bank lines of credit.

The central funds must also be prepared to meet on call unpredictable cash needs such as the funds needed to repair the damage from Hurricane Camille in 1969.

In addition, the Bell System in recent years has had to raise huge sums through almost continuous sale of new securities. An offering of 30-year A.T.&T. debentures in April, 1970, amounted to over $1.5 billion, accompanied by warrants, which, on their exercise, would raise a like amount of capital. This is the largest single offering in financial history, and the first time that the Bell System has marketed debt securities with warrants. The proceeds of such sales are held in the central fund until needed. System expansion to meet public need for service (the Bell System laid out $5.7 billion for its construction program in 1969) should not be subject to interruption through any demoralization of the capital markets, such as that in the 1969–70 period, which might interrupt the sale of new securities. While A.T.&T. would doubtless find it hard to "stay out of the market" for new funds for long periods, it is deemed advantageous to keep on hand enough funds so that new offerings could be deferred if such action seemed urgently desirable.

Finally, as a very large enterprise aware of its great public responsibilities, the Bell System wants to keep in a sound, reasonably liquid condition against the general uncertainties of the times, and in striking a balance between too much in money assets and too little, doubtless would prefer to have been on the safe rather than the sorry side of a theoretically perfect balance.

Approaches to More Effective Management of the Money Position

During recent years increasing management effort and attention has been devoted in many firms to the management of the money assets, and indeed to the entire liquidity position of the firm. Overall, the money assets of American corporations have been reduced relative to such items as current liabilities. This trend was spotlighted in a June 15, 1969, article in *Forbes* magazine, which we have used in constructing Table 4–2.

Good management of the money assets and total liquidity of the firm clearly involves much more than keeping excess cash fully invested. Even if surplus funds are kept invested continuously, the net after-tax return from even the less conservative money market instruments is modest—

probably less than 4%. Almost certainly the costs of capital to the firm are well above this figure, and the carrying of unnecessarily large money assets will dilute overall rate of return.

We suggest five major approaches to effective management of the money position, which have proved helpful in a number of firms:

1. Exploitation of techniques of money mobilization to reduce operating requirements for cash.
2. Major efforts to increase the precision and reliability of cash flow forecasting.
3. Maximum effort to define and quantify the liquidity reserve needs of the firm.
4. The development of explicit alternative sources of liquidity.
5. Aggressive search for more productive uses for surplus money assets.

Table 4–2

Liquid Assets/Current Liabilities, Very Large U.S. Corporations, 1961 and 1969

	Cash and Marketable Securities as Percentage of Current Liabilities	
	12/31/61	*12/31/69*
Standard Oil of N.J.	84%	34%
General Motors	119	55
Ford Motor	57	23
Texaco	94	31
Gulf Oil	138	45
Mobil Oil	53	42
IBM	203	95
Sears, Roebuck	99	6
U.S. Steel	85	26
Standard Oil of Calif.	56	23
General Electric	39	14
Standard Oil of Ind.	92	33
Chrysler	119	19
Shell Oil	54	40
I.T.&T.	51	22

Money Mobilization

Many firms have found that the operating needs for cash can be cut sharply through various devices of *money mobilization*. These aim at the reduction of funds tied up in the process of receiving and collecting checks and in the routines of transfer of bank balances to the points where they are most useful. In the absence of special effort, cash equal to several days' sales is likely to be tied up in the process of receiving check payments from far-flung customers and converting them into collected, and hence usable, bank balances.

With the aid of their banks, a number of firms have developed comprehensive programs to cut days off this process and free up the funds in the unnecessarily long process. For example, company X formerly asked its customers all over the country to mail their payments to the company headquarters in New York. The customers regarded their obligations to company X as settled when they put checks in the mail. Yet several days would normally elapse while the check was in the mail to New York, while company X's routines of receiving and accounting for the payment and getting the checks to its New York bank were accomplished, and while the New York bank converted the check into collected funds available for use by company X. In essence, an amount equal to several days' sales was tied up in the "collection pipeline."

Under a program designed to reduce this pipeline, company X opened accounts with a number of regional banks around the country, for instance, Los Angeles. Customers in southern California were asked to remit to company X at a post office lockbox in Los Angeles. Actually, company X's Los Angeles bank maintained the lockbox. The bank was authorized to open the incoming mail, deposit all checks for collection, and send a record of receipts airmail to company X in New York. Since most of the checks were drawn on Los Angeles or area banks, the collection period was very short, with same-day credit on many checks. Arrangements were made to transfer to company X's main depository bank in New York by wire[3] all collected balances beyond a modest amount designed to compensate the regional collecting bank for its services.

A variety of other programs of money mobilization have proved helpful in reducing operational requirements for cash. In the case of smaller firms with predominantly local sales, simple programs such as organized effort to cut the time utilized in office routines of processing incoming checks and getting them into the bank can be rewarding in freeing up otherwise unproductive cash. If under particular cash strain, small firms have often been known to pick up checks personally from their large local customers in order to be able to meet their own payment deadlines.

The Contribution of Improved Cash Flow Forecasting

In recent decades most well-run companies have sharply expanded their programs of cash flow forecasting. Building on study of past patterns of receipts and expenditures and learning from experience, many

---

[3] A private telegraph network between more than 200 larger banks permits telegraphic or "wire transfers" of funds between banks. Thus, a San Francisco investor could direct his San Francisco bank to transfer a given amount of funds to the credit of his broker's account at a New York bank and have the whole transaction carried out in a matter of minutes.

companies have achieved a degree of forecasting skill and precision once believed impossible. Such improved forecasting has led to improved money management in a variety of ways. First, money position managers are able to keep temporarily surplus funds more fully invested. Where large amounts are involved, the knowledge that it is safe to delay conversion of an investment into cash by a day or two or over a weekend can add materially to income. Second, once future needs are clearly outlined, alternative methods of meeting the outflows can be explored. Some companies, for example, have arranged with their major suppliers to set due dates on bills to coincide with the buying firm's forecasted periods of peak receipts. Other firms have changed their own collection terms in an effort to iron out the differences between patterns of inflow and outflow.

In other cases improved forecasting has shown that normal cash inflows will be adequate to cover major future outlays previously funded with a special reserve. Thus, many firms have gained sufficient confidence in their forecasting and money management techniques to abandon long-in-advance specific funding of major tax payments.

Of course, efforts to forecast cash needs involve some expense. However, we are confident that there is still room for substantial progress in cash forecasting in many companies, particularly smaller ones, which will permit closer management of money assets and more than justify the expense involved.

Pinning Down Needs for Protective Liquidity

A third approach to more effective utilization of money assets seeks to define as crisply as possible and to quantify the needs for liquidity reserves against various kinds of unplanned developments that might well require substantial amounts of cash. Almost every firm faces a great number of uncertainties and contingencies that might sponge up cash. Yet, to gain absolute protection against cash stringencies from the worst combination of the worst possibilities would require unthinkably large hoards of money assets. A compromise must be struck between the degree of protection afforded and the cost of holding reserves of protective liquidity. Holding money assets against possible needs has a real and, within limits, calculable cost. It is highly desirable to try to evaluate the protective benefits gained for these costs.

To try to quantify precisely the need for protection against uncertain developments is in some respects to seek "to unscrew the inscrutable." Yet many firms have had some success in gauging the need for protective liquidity. These efforts usually take the form of:

1. Explicit identification of the kinds of contingencies against which protection is desirable—a long strike, a recession, need to reequip major production units, etc.

2. Assessment of the probabilities or odds that each of these will develop within a given period in the future, such as 5 years.
3. Assessment of the probabilities that the developments creating cash drains will occur at the same time.
4. Assessment of the likely amount of the cash drain that will result if each of the contingencies develops. This requires pencil pushing with appropriate assumptions—in a number of cases careful projections have resulted in estimates of the amounts of net drain quite different from management's general impressions.

Assessing Alternative Methods of Providing Protective Liquidity

Once the efforts to identify and measure the potential unscheduled demands for cash have been made, alternative methods of meeting these needs should be canvassed and evaluated. Many U.S. firms—a very high percentage of those with heavy money positions—have unused borrowing capacity. Many managements regard this ability to borrow as a part of the overall money position of the firm and expect to draw on it to meet unscheduled needs if and when they develop. A strong argument can be made in favor of this approach over that of carrying sizable money assets as precautionary reserves. First and foremost, it can well be a more economical method of dealing with the possible needs, since funds are drawn down from lenders only as and when the possible needs actually develop. It may be years before a major unexpected need does develop. In the meantime, reliance on credit makes it possible to avoid holding low-yielding money assets as a protective reserve of liquidity. Moreover, if the unexpected need for cash proves short-lived, the loans can be repaid and the reserves of borrowing capacity restored.

Those managements that support policies of carrying large precautionary balances of money assets commonly stress the risk that funds may not be available from lenders when needed or else will be available only on unfavorable terms. Banks may be "loaned up" and unable to accommodate the firm's needs when they develop. Or the circumstances that created the need—such as a period of price cutting leading to heavy volume and very low profits or even losses—may damage the credit standing of the firm and make banks hesitant to meet its needs for credit when the needs are more intense. Negotiation of loans with insurance companies or the sale of bonds may be too slow a process to meet rapidly developing needs. Moreover, the need for funds might come at a time unpropitious for the sale of common stock. Altogether, they argue, carrying liquid reserves against possible needs is a useful form of insurance against having to make rushed and possibly unsatisfactory arrangements at unpropitious times. Moreover, in this view, invested money reserves do add something to income so that the "net cost of self-insurance" against embarrassing cash stringencies or having to make a bad deal is quite tolerable.

Many firms relying on borrowing power as a source of precautionary liquidity do take steps to help assure that loan funds will be available to them when and if needed. These may simply take the form of efforts to cultivate close relationships with a number of strong banks, perhaps by carrying larger deposit balances than otherwise necessary or desirable. In such cases the firm may test its credit standing by arranging lines of credit at several banks. As we shall explain in some detail later, the line of credit does not represent a firm commitment to lend on the part of the bank. However, for a fee of one quarter or one half of 1% of the unused credit, it may well be possible to arrange a definite standby loan commitment with bank or other lenders—if this is judged necessary.

On the whole, it seems to us that the management carrying unused reserves of liquid assets for long periods is properly suspect of striking an unnecessarily comfortable, conservative, and costly balance between risk avoidance and effective utilization of resources.

Aggressive Search for More Productive Uses of Money Assets

Now let us focus on the fifth of the suggested approaches to more effective use of money assets—the desirability of aggressive search for more productive uses for surplus money assets. In recent years many firms have experienced such a heavy inflow of cash from operations that unplanned accumulations of money assets have resulted. In these circumstances many firms have found that it took much time and effort to turn up attractive opportunities and to complete the necessary negotiations and arrangements for the investment. Rather than waiting until the funds come in to begin their search for outlets and thus facing a long delay in getting surplus funds into high-return use, many firms have organized for a continuous search for promising acquisitions, mergers, or other long-term uses for funds outside the usual ones generated internally.

Facing up to the fact that continued, vigorous, and organized search is likely to prove necessary if attractive outlets for available funds are to be kept in good supply will help many firms avoid the accumulation of a large pool of funds temporarily invested at low return pending more lucrative permanent investment.

chapter 5

Fixed Assets and the Need for Funds

In preceding chapters we have discussed the necessary commitment of funds in cash, inventories, and trade credit, pointing out the continuing nature of the basic investment of funds in these categories, despite the movement of individual items through the process of production and sale. In this chapter we turn to the investment of funds in assets where the permanent nature of the underlying need for funds is paralleled by the more enduring characteristics of the assets themselves.

The most important group of these assets is the *fixed assets,* also termed *capital assets.* To quote Kohler:

Included in the usual fixed-asset categories are land (from which the flow of services is seemingly permanent), buildings, building equipment, fixtures, machinery, tools (large and small), furniture, office devices, patterns, drawings, dies, and often containers. . . . The characteristic fixed asset has a limited life (land is the one important exception), and its cost, less estimated salvage, at the end of its useful life, is distributed over the periods it benefits by means of provisions for depreciation.[1]

Many businesses also have investments of consequence in *intangible assets,* which represent investments having no physical existence in themselves, but rather rights to enjoy some privilege. Examples are patents and investments in the securities of other companies. If the value of the intangible assets is expected to have a limited life, their cost usually is distributed by charges similar to depreciation, known as *amortization.*

---

[1] Eric L. Kohler, *A Dictionary for Accountants* (4th ed., Englewood Cliffs, N.J.: Prentice-Hall, Inc., 1970), p. 190.

Importance of the Investment in Fixed Assets

The technology of the industry in which a company operates largely determines the quantity of funds it must commit to fixed assets. While other factors influence the investment of individual firms in fixed assets, firms in the same industry generally tend to have a similar portion of their total assets in fixed assets. Thus, no electric utility company can avoid a heavy investment in generating and/or distributive facilities. Since these utilities have little need for inventories and only moderate receivables, it is not surprising to note from Chart 5–1 that fixed assets represent over four fifths of their total assets.

In the aggregate, U.S. manufacturers' investment in fixed assets was $215.3 billion, or 39.6%, of their total resources on December 31, 1969. Chart 5–1, which is based on earlier but more detailed data, shows the relative importance of fixed assets to manufacturers in various industry groups. As might be expected, primary metal manufacturers, such as the steelmakers, have a relatively high commitment in plant facilities. In contrast, note the low investment in fixed assets of apparel manufacturers. The technology of the garment industry is very simple compared to that of steelmaking. Much of the needed machinery, such as sewing machines, is relatively simple and inexpensive and is available on rental. Specialized buildings are not required, and the "loft space" available for rent in New York and other garment centers meets the needs of many manufacturers.

The reference to the garment industry has indicated another significant determinant of the required investment in fixed assets—the extent to which needed plant or equipment is available on reasonably satisfactory rental terms. Rental of office space is especially common, even among the largest and most affluent concerns. Of 129 new office buildings put into place in Manhattan (New York City) during the 1950's, only 28 were owner-occupied. Many retailers, and some manufacturers whose space needs are not distinctive, are able to meet their major building needs through rental. Certain leading manufacturers of office and plant equipment, notably International Business Machines Corporation and Xerox Corporation, have made their products available on rental terms. In recent years an increasing variety of productive equipment—from refrigerator trucks to automatic machine tools—has become widely available on a rental basis, both from equipment manufacturers and from specialized leasing firms. Long-term leasing of industrial and commercial plant also has come to represent a financial alternative to ownership and debt financing. Since most long-term leases deserve to be evaluated as a form of long-term financing, we shall discuss such leasing in the long-term financing section of this book.

Another determinant of fixed asset investment of particular importance to firms with limited finances is the degree to which the need for facilities, particularly highly specialized and expensive equipment, can be avoided

Chart 5-1

Investment in Net Capital Assets of Corporations in Selected Industry Groups, as a Percentage of Their Total Assets, for Companies with Accounting Periods Ended July, 1966–June, 1967

Industry Group	Percentage
AGRICULTURE, FORESTRY, AND FISHERIES	52.7
MINING, TOTAL	49.6
CONSTRUCTION	21.6
MANUFACTURING, TOTAL	34.3
FOOD AND KINDRED PRODUCTS	34.4
TEXTILE MILL PRODUCTS	31.0
APPAREL AND OTHER FABRIC PRODUCTS*	12.9
FURNITURE AND FIXTURES	24.0
PAPER AND ALLIED PRODUCTS	51.9
PRINTING, PUBLISHING, AND ALLIED INDUSTRIES	28.8
CHEMICALS AND ALLIED PRODUCTS	39.9
PETROLEUM REFINING AND RELATED INDUSTRIES	48.5
RUBBER AND MISCELLANEOUS PLASTICS PRODUCTS	30.5
PRIMARY METAL INDUSTRIES	45.8
ELECTRICAL MACHINERY, EQUIPMENT, AND SUPPLIES	21.2
MOTOR VEHICLES AND MOTOR VEHICLE EQUIPMENT	21.9

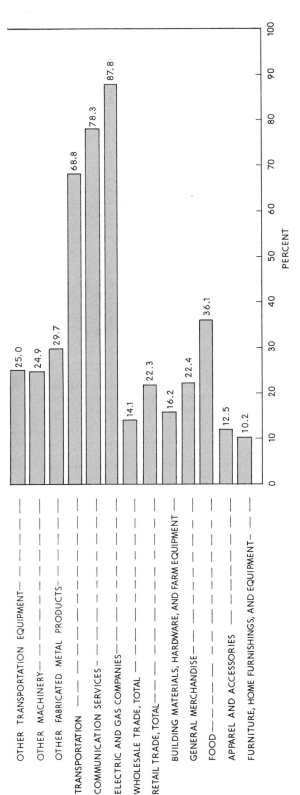

PERCENT

OTHER TRANSPORTATION EQUIPMENT — 25.0
OTHER MACHINERY — 24.9
OTHER FABRICATED METAL PRODUCTS — 29.7
TRANSPORTATION — 68.8
COMMUNICATION SERVICES — 78.3
ELECTRIC AND GAS COMPANIES — 87.8
WHOLESALE TRADE, TOTAL — 14.1
RETAIL TRADE, TOTAL — 22.3
BUILDING MATERIALS, HARDWARE, AND FARM EQUIPMENT — 16.2
GENERAL MERCHANDISE — 22.4
FOOD — 36.1
APPAREL AND ACCESSORIES — 12.5
FURNITURE, HOME FURNISHINGS, AND EQUIPMENT — 10.2

* Apparel and other finished products made from fabrics and similar materials.
† Total transportation, communication, electric, gas, and sanitary services.
SOURCE OF DATA: U.S. Treasury Department, Internal Revenue Service, *Statistics of Income, 1966: Corporation Income Tax Returns* (Washington, D.C.: U.S. Government Printing Office, 1970), Table 2—"Balance Sheets and Income Statements, by Major Industry."

through subcontracting of work or outside purchase of parts and components requiring special equipment. For example, if a machinery builder can arrange to have the electroplating of certain parts performed by an outside specialist in this work, he may be able to avoid otherwise necessary ownership of expensive and little-used plating equipment. Or the small wheat farmer may find it wiser to have his wheat harvested by custom combiners than to own a little-used combine. One of the less widely recognized strengths of American industry lies in the extent to which finished product manufacturers can rely on specialized manufacturers for particular parts or components. By virtue of their large volume as suppliers of their specialty items to many end-item manufacturers, these specialty manufacturers can make economic use of highly specialized and expensive equipment that would be burdensome if production of these items were widely diffused.

In some fields used equipment or old plant, available at prices that are far below those of new facilities, may be satisfactory. This is particularly likely to be true in areas where the rate of technological change in production methods has been moderate or slow. Their use can materially reduce the required investment in fixed assets, and firms with limited financial resources should carefully investigate the possibilities of buying used facilities before committing themselves to heavier investment in new fixed assets.

Distinctive Aspects of the Investment in Fixed Assets

In earlier chapters we have stressed the central importance in asset management of concern for overall return on investment, and there should be no need to belabor the point that these same considerations apply with equal force in fixed asset management. Indeed, certain distinctive aspects of investment in fixed assets make it especially important that new fixed assets be acquired only after searching consideration of the impact on investment return. First, proposed additions to fixed assets are commonly in sizable increments which can be considered deliberately and consciously as discrete proposals. Given reasonable foresight, it is usually possible to plan new acquisitions sufficiently far ahead that analysis of their desirability can be deliberate and appropriately organized.

Second, the purchase of plant and equipment (or their long-term lease) represents a financial commitment that will be binding over a period of years. If increases in inventory, receivables, or liquid reserves prove unwise, or if funds stringencies make it necessary, management often can act to cut back these investments and free the funds involved in a matter of weeks or months. But the typical fixed asset investment can be recovered only through operations over a period of years. Further, uncertainty of return, as well as time, is very much involved. For example, demand for the products to be made with a new machine may not develop as expected, so that operations do not return the investment in the form of added profits and coverage of depreciation. Or new methods of production may make the machine expected to have an economic life of 10 years obsolete in 3.

Third, the loss in forced sale of excess or obsolete equipment and facilities typically is great. For example, the automobile manufacturer faced with unsold stocks of an unsuccessful model can usually find economy-minded buyers for the unsold cars coming forward to buy the cars at reductions of 10% or 20%. Buyers for specialized productive equipment and facilities designed especially for manufacture of this model are likely to be found only at prices that are a small fraction of their book value—if at all. Thus, International Paper Company found it necessary to make an extraordinary charge to 1970 earnings of $39.6 million to cover losses on the closedowns of obsolete mills.[2]

In brief, investments in plant and equipment are inherently illiquid, that is, retrievable only over years and then only under conditions of uncertainty. Consequently, it is important that purchases of new plant or important items of equipment be made only after particularly careful consideration of the prospects of recovery of the investment from operations, with a profit return that is adequate in the light of the risks, the cost of the funds, and the effect on the financial position of the firm of tying up substantial amounts of funds for long periods.

In recent decades there has been a developing recognition of the importance of the points noted above and of the desirability of searching examination of proposals for new asset investment to ensure that they justify the use of capital and that the selection among available opportunities is a keen and discerning one. Many large firms have organized special departments for this work and are engaged in a restless search not only for new opportunities to invest but for better methods of assessing opportunities. In academic circles, interest in what has come to be known as "capital budgeting" has also flourished. The literature on the subject is growing in quantity, in complexity, and, overall, in quality.

To go into the techniques of evaluation of opportunities for fixed asset expansion at this point in our book would represent a diversion from the primary emphasis of these early chapters on the impact of varying asset management policies on the need for funds. Chapters 8, 9, and 10 will be devoted to various aspects of capital budgeting.

Major Funds Flows Related to Fixed Assets

From the cash flow viewpoint, the costs of fixed assets take on importance as the funds are actually expended by the firm. A major construction project may well require substantial payments during the period of

---

[2] *The Wall Street Journal*, February 10, 1971.

construction, perhaps as long as several years before any productive activity can be commenced. One of the authors has visited a new rubber plantation on the Amazon River where large expenditures for land clearance, dwellings for workers, and nursery plants were not expected to become productive for at least 10 years. Although this type of project is exceptionally long, the lead time for an ordinary factory building is often 2 years.

On the other hand, fixed assets may be acquired under a time payment contract where (usually after some initial expenditure for a *down payment*) the actual funds are expended during the use of assets. Again, if the use of fixed assets may be acquired by lease, there is no transfer of ownership, and the actual flows of funds take place during the period of use as the rent is paid. The first step in looking at a fixed asset project from a funds flow point of view is, therefore, to ask, "When must payments be made?"

Another flow of funds must also be considered. It is the net effect of inflows and outflows which occurs because the fixed assets have been acquired and put into operation, and can be referred to as *funds provided by operations*. In collecting information to permit the determination of this quantity, the analyst must be careful to choose only those flows of funds whose magnitudes change because the particular capital investment project has been undertaken. Such a search is sometimes easy, as when the project does not displace or compete with some existing operation. Sometimes, the determination is difficult. To illustrate the major cash flows in fixed asset investment, we shall now look at a simple project, a new motel to be added to an existing chain of motels.

Our motel will cost $200,000, and we estimate its useful life at 10 years.[3] In order to determine the funds that will be provided by operation of the motel, we estimate that all rentals—$40,000 annually—will be collected and that we shall incur and pay for the expenses listed below:

Rental income		$40,000
Expenses:		
Heat, lights, etc.	$10,500	
Repairs and maintenance	500	
Income and real estate taxes, and all other expenses	5,000	
Outflow for expenses		16,000
Funds provided by operations		$24,000

For the time being, we prefer not to explore the question of how income taxes are determined; the topic gets considerable attention later on. The table above shows that for the year in question, the net inflow of

---

[3] For simplicity we assume that there will be no salvage value at the end of the period.

funds from operations is $24,000. How should this quantity be considered by management? Does it constitute funds that can be used for any corporate purpose? Must a portion of it be regarded as tied to the particular investment in some way?

Any business operation that produces a net gain in funds does so throughout a period of time and not in a single sum at the end of the period. Thus, in our example the gain of $24,000 will be simply the cumulative result of the operations of the period. In the absence of special action to that end, the funds will not be segregated as they are received, and there will be no special box or bank account where they can be found at the end of the year. All we can say with assurance is that management will have at its disposal $24,000 more in funds than if the motel had not been in operation. Surely, the funds will be in liquid form immediately after receipt; and they may well be kept in such form, but not certainly. It all depends on how management decides to use the funds, and the possibilities cover all types of transactions.

Having looked at 1 year of operations, let us try to foresee what problems management will face at the end of the 10-year life of the motel. If one of the vital concerns of management is that of *preserving* the earning power of the investment in this motel, much more must be done than simply to try to regain the original investment of $200,000. Let us suppose that in looking forward to the 10th year of the life of this project, management estimates that the earning power of the motel can be extended for a new period of time by the expenditure of $100,000 for extensive alterations. It is then management's task to see to it that the needed funds are available in liquid form, either from accumulated funds provided by operations over the first 10 years, or from available credit, or otherwise. This same task, in different magnitude, would confront management if it found that rising prices made an investment of $275,000 necessary and desirable. It cannot be overemphasized that recovery of the cost of the original investment does not assure the availability or adequacy of funds to provide for its continuation or replacement.

The Impact of Depreciation Accounting on Cash Outflows for Income Taxes

As we shall emphasize, charges to income for depreciation do not in themselves affect the total inflow of cash from operations. However, the allowance of depreciation expense as a deduction from income subject to taxation does have an important effect on the outflows of cash necessary to satisfy tax requirements. For this reason, it is desirable that we devote attention to the accounting for depreciation for tax purposes. As an accountant views the $200,000 investment in the motel at the beginning of the 10-year period, he finds he must record an outflow of funds of that amount. Among the principal concerns of accounting is the determination of income, year by year (or more generally period by period), and for this purpose the expenditure of $200,000 is obviously not an expense to be charged wholly to the first year of the 10. The accountant, therefore, *capitalizes* the expenditure by "booking" $200,000 as fixed assets. There then ensues the procedure referred to by Kohler: "The characteristic fixed asset has a limited life . . . and its cost, less salvage, is distributed over the periods it benefits by means of provisions for depreciation."

A widely used method (known as the *straight-line method*) of providing for the depreciation of the $200,000 motel in 10 years would take one tenth of its cost as an expense each year, deducting $20,000 from the gross income (along with the other costs), and reducing the capitalized value of the fixed asset accordingly. If this were done, the income statement of our sample year of operations would become:

Rental income	$40,000
Expenditure of funds	16,000
Funds provided by operations	$24,000
Depreciation	20,000
Net profit	$ 4,000

While this income statement is decidedly more useful to those who are studying the profitability of the firm, especially from year to year, it must be emphasized that the charging of depreciation, itself, does nothing that alters by as much as 1 cent the amount of funds provided by operations. All that has happened (apart from the income tax effect discussed below) is that the $24,000 has been divided into two accounts, one called Depreciation and the other Net Profit.

Business income taxes in the United States are levied on net profits, so that all allowable expenses are deductible from gross revenues before the "net income subject to tax" is determined. Treasury regulations govern the admissibility of items as deductible expenses. Depreciation is one of the acceptable charges.

The consequence of any allowable expense is a reduction of the tax liability. Taking the annual depreciation of the motel as $20,000 and the income tax rate as 48%, there will be a reduction in net profits of $20,000 and therefore a decline in the tax liability of (0.48) $(\$20,000) = \$9,600$. In other words, the depreciation expense permits retaining $9,600 more net funds after taxes than would otherwise be possible. This is referred to as the *tax shield*, which is always the full amount of the deductible item multiplied by the applicable tax rate. How much this shield can be depends, of course, on the amount of depreciation permitted by the tax authorities to be used for tax purposes.

As we have explained, the amount of the annual expense item for depreciation derives from four key elements:

1. The cost of the item—$200,000 in our illustration.
2. The estimate of its economic life—10 years in our illustration.

3. Its salvage value once the economic life is over—estimated at zero in our illustration.

4. The pattern by which the total amount to be depreciated is spread over the years of economic life. So far, in our motel case, we have employed the straight-line method, that is, spread the $200,000 to be depreciated equally over the 10 years of estimated economic life.

Focusing now on the estimate of economic life, it is clear that the use by business of short life estimates will result in larger expense charges over a shorter period of years, and hence in lower income tax payments in these years, than if depreciation charges were spread over a longer period. It is not surprising that federal tax authorities have long been interested in seeing that the estimates of useful life used by taxpaying firms are not unreasonably short. In 1962 the Internal Revenue Service published a list of "guideline lives" for large classes of assets. For example, the guideline life of hotel buildings was put at 40 years, office equipment and fixtures at 10 years, automobiles at 3 years, and metal-working machinery at 12 years. The new guidelines were intended to conform to actual industry replacement experience; generally, they were significantly shorter than the earlier lives specified for a great number of individual items.

Basically, taxpayers may use these rates until and unless a test of their own replacement experience shows the guideline lives to be excessively short. Taxpayers are not required to use these life estimates, but they may well be called upon to justify their use of shorter ones. Treasury interest in the matter, however, extends only to the depreciation claimed in tax returns as a business expense deductible before determination of taxable income. Many thoroughly reputable companies go so far as to keep two sets of property records and charge depreciation for their own accounting purposes differently from the charge for purposes of accounting for income tax.[4]

Now let us turn to the matter of how the total amount to be depreciated is spread among the years of economic life and look at alternative approaches to the straight-line method. The tax laws in effect from time to time have authorized a variety of methods of allocating depreciation to particular years that have had the effect of permitting larger amounts of the total depreciation to be charged in the early years of useful life of newly acquired assets. Since the total charged as depreciation under any method cannot exceed the cost of the item to its owner, the new methods do not alter the total depreciation that can be charged off as a business

---

[4] Thus, the Carborundum Company commented in a note to the financial statements in its 1969 Annual Report: "Depreciation and amortization charged to income was $9,624,000 in 1969 and $8,206,000 in 1968. Depreciation is computed principally on the straight-line method for financial statement purposes while an accelerated method is used for tax purposes. Taxes on income applicable to the difference between tax and financial statement depreciation is included in other long-term liabilities."

expense, nor is the total life of the asset reduced. Thus, given constant tax rates, the ultimate total of tax liabilities is not reduced by shifts in the timing of depreciation deductions. By advancing the time when much of the depreciation can be taken as an expense, however, the new methods do permit the postponement of part of the tax liability and give the firm the use for a time of the funds that otherwise would have been paid in taxes at an earlier date.

The Tax Reform Act of 1969, which eliminated some methods previously authorized, provided that newly acquired commercial and industrial property may be depreciated for tax purposes by either the straight-line method, the 150% *declining balance* method, or any other consistent method which does not yield higher allowances in the first two thirds of life than the 150% declining balance method. Under the declining balance method a uniform rate, which may be as much as 150% of the straight-line rate, is applied to the undepreciated asset balance. In the case of an investment for a 10-year period, the annual rate would be 150% of the straight-line rate of 10%, or 15%; but the charge for each year would be determined from the application of the 15% rate to the declining book value of the asset. At any time during the life of the asset, a shift may be made to the straight-line method for the undepreciated balance. As an example, we give the computation of the depreciation charges for a $200,000 asset as a part of Table 5–1.

Business Investment and Depreciation

In this discussion of the funds flows related to fixed asset use, we have stressed the concept that the charging of depreciation does not in itself require or create funds but rather divides the flow of funds from operations into two parts, a net income portion and a portion measured by the amount of the depreciation charge. In order to calculate the funds flow from operations from the income statement, one simply adds to the net income figure the amount of depreciation charged as an expense. For this reason, it has become common in business usage to refer—loosely and erroneously, as we have indicated, but understandably—to "depreciation as a source of funds."

The importance of the depreciation component of the funds flow from operations has grown greatly in recent years. In 1969 total capital consumption allowances (depreciation and depletion) of U.S. nonfinancial corporations amounted to $48 billion, while increases in plant and equipment totaled $76.9 billion.[5] As Chart 5–2 shows, capital consumption allowances of corporations grew from $4.6 billion in 1946 to $17.0 billion by 1955 and to $48 billion in 1969.

The chart also depicts annual purchases of plant and equipment for the

---

[5] *Survey of Current Business*, November, 1970, p. 20.

Table 5–1

Comparison of the Results of Straight-Line and 150% Declining Balance Methods of Allocating Depreciation of $200,000 Asset over 10 Years with No Salvage Value

| | Straight-Line, 10% Rate | | | 150% Declining Balance Method | |
	Allowable Depreciation	Undepreciated Cost, Year-End		Allowable Depreciation	Undepreciated Cost, Year-End
At purchase......	......	$200,000	At purchase......	......	$200,000
First year......	$20,000	180,000	First year......	$30,000	170,000
Second year......	20,000	160,000	Second year......	25,500	144,500
Third year......	20,000	140,000	Third year......	21,675	122,825
Fourth year......	20,000	120,000	Fourth year......	18,424	104,401
Fifth year......	20,000	100,000	Fifth year......	17,400	87,001
Sixth year......	20,000	80,000	Sixth year......	17,400	69,601
Seventh year......	20,000	60,000	Seventh year......	17,400	52,201
Eighth year......	20,000	40,000	Eighth year......	17,400	34,801
Ninth year......	20,000	20,000	Ninth year......	17,400	17,401
Tenth year......	20,000	0	Tenth year......	17,401	0

corresponding years. If the size, quality, and cost of the total plant and equipment were to remain constant, and if depreciation charges proved thoroughly accurate, depreciation charges could be expected to match new-equipment outlays. It can be seen from the chart that such has not been the case in the postwar period. As the country and the economy have grown, corporate plant investment has grown in size and in complexity—

Chart 5–2

Purchases of Plant and Equipment and Capital Consumption Allowances,
Nonfinancial Corporations, 1946–69
(in billions)

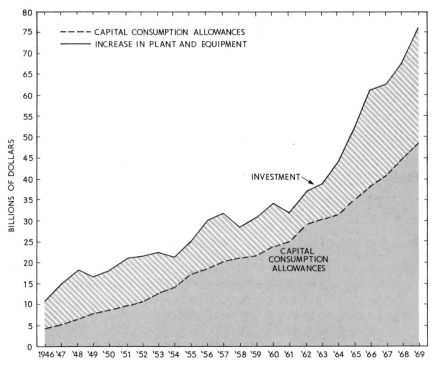

SOURCE: *Survey of Current Business*, November, 1970, p. 20.

compare the Boeing 747 aircraft with the DC–3—and costs of plant have increased. Consequently, depreciation charges based on the smaller, less complex, and cheaper fixed asset acquisitions of the past have fallen far short of current outlays. It can be seen that the gap between depreciation charges and new-plant outlays in the late 1950's and early 1960's narrowed. This was in part due to the rise of depreciation charges as the heavy postwar plant investment was reflected in the accounts and as more liberalized methods of computing depreciation for tax purposes were used. Also, the mix of new-asset outlays shifted somewhat toward machinery and equipment, which is subject to rather rapid depreciation, and away from buildings. In recent years the gap has widened again.

Summary of Funds Flows Related to the Ownership of Fixed Assets

Now, let us recapitulate our main points regarding the funds flows related to acquisition and ownership of fixed assets. In planning the outflows related to the acquisition of fixed assets, care should be taken to schedule the outflows in payment for the assets as they actually will be made, since their timing may differ materially from the time at which ownership of the assets is reflected in the accounting records of the firm. Further, funds inflows from operations are *not* reduced by the acknowledgment of depreciation as an expense appropriate for purposes of income determination. The amount of depreciation which can be taken as a deduction from taxable income does, however, have a significant effect on the timing of outflows required to satisfy income tax liabilities. So the firm's pattern of allowable depreciation deductions does affect its depreciation tax shield and hence the timing of its outflows for taxes.

Further, the tax-free recovery through operations of the original cost of fixed assets will not, in a period of rising costs, supply a sufficient inflow of funds, even if segregated and accumulated for the specific purpose, to pay for replacement of the assets with higher-cost physical equivalents. To maintain a constant level of physical facilities over a long period of rising costs, added funds are required to match the excess of replacement over original fixed asset costs.

Since American business has been adding to its stock of fixed assets, acquisition in the postwar years of fixed assets has represented a major use of funds and one well in excess of the operational inflows measured by depreciation. This has continued to be true despite the impact of liberalized tax laws governing the timing of tax-deductible depreciation charges.

The Total Business Outlay for Fixed Assets in Recent Years

The aggregate outlays of business for new fixed assets are great enough to have a major impact on the total demand for funds by business and hence on the conditions of the capital market faced by the individual firm needing external financing. Further, the volume of business spending on fixed assets both influences and is influenced by the overall level of the economy. Consequently, a brief review of aggregate business spending on fixed assets in recent years may be useful.

During the period from 1930 through 1941, the expenditures of American business on new plant and equipment were very low—just about equaling the use or depreciation of equipment and plant. During the war years, business expenditures on plant and equipment fell behind the

Chart 5–3

Business Expenditures for New Plant and Equipment, 1947–69*
(in billions)

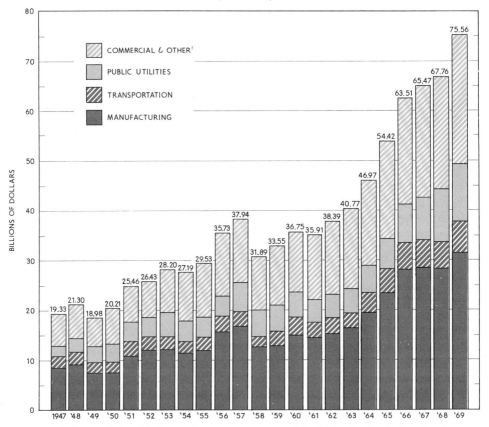

* Excludes agricultural business; real estate operators; medical, legal, educational, and cultural service; and nonprofit organizations. Includes both incorporated and unincorporated businesses. Covers expenditures on all items for which depreciation is charged, but not charges to current expenditures.
† Includes trade, service, finance, insurance, communications, construction, and mining.
Source: U.S. Department of Commerce, *Survey of Current Business*, January, 1970, p. 29, and April, 1970, p. S–2.

heavy use of physical facilities. For a period of 16 years the *net* investment of American business in fixed assets actually declined.

Since 1947, as is apparent from Chart 5–3, expenditures for plant and equipment have surged sharply upward. Total business outlays for new plant and equipment during the 23 years from 1947 through 1969 amounted to over $881 billion. Since, as we have noted, the outlay for new plant and equipment outran depreciation and retirements in each of the 23 years by a significant margin, the net investment in plant and equipment for business as a whole has increased substantially.

Several reasons appear to account for the increased outlays on plant.

The low rate of capital expenditures during 1930 to 1945, together with rapid technical development and heavy wartime usage, meant that much of the nation's facilities in 1946 were worn or obsolete. A second basic cause has been the rise in population under conditions of general prosperity, in which the effective demand of the population for goods and services has been great and rising. The development of new products— television, jet aircraft, diesel locomotives, synthetic fibers, air condition- ing, and the computer, to mention a few—and radical changes in others, such as the extension of dial telephoning, called for new or expanded facilities. Changes in productive processes and methods, such as the shift to oxygen furnaces in the steel industry, have been important. Further, the rise in labor wage rates and the periodic shortages of labor have accelerated a long-term trend toward greater use of laborsaving ma- chinery. Adding to the costs of new facilities has been a trend toward provision of improved working facilities—for example, air conditioning in plants, offices, and stores. Important also in adding to the dollar cost of new construction and equipment outlays has been the general rise in price levels since 1945 and especially sharp increases in wages in the construction industry.

Finally, it would be most inappropriate for authors of a book on finance to overlook the facilitating role of finance in making possible the huge outlays on plant and equipment. The fact that the necessary cash or credit needed to finance the outlays has been forthcoming on terms judged reasonable must be included among the major reasons for the postwar upsurge in business spending for plant and equipment.

Business spending for new fixed assets falls into one of two broad categories:

1. Expansion of capacity to produce existing or new products.
2. Replacement and modernization of facilities to cut costs or produce other benefits such as higher-quality output.

During certain boom years in the 1950's, spending for new capacity exceeded that for replacement and modernization. Thus, in 1957, 52% of all new spending planned by manufacturers was to increase capacity.[6] During the years from 1959 through 1965, manufacturers concentrated their new fixed asset investment on replacement and modernization, putting only about one third into expansion. This added about 4% each year to capacity.[7] Nevertheless, the overall rate of expansion of manufac- turing capacity since 1950 was enough to bring 1964 manufacturing capacity to a level more than twice that of December, 1950. Expansion was especially strong among manufacturers of nonautomotive transporta-

---

[6] McGraw-Hill Publishing Company, Inc., *Business Plans for New Plants and Equip- ment, 1957–1960* (10th Annual Survey [New York, 1957]), p. 7.

[7] McGraw-Hill Publishing Company, Inc., *Business Plans for New Plants and Equip- ment, 1965–1968* (18th Annual Survey [New York, 1965]), pp. 3–4.

tion equipment (aircraft, etc.) and chemicals and electrical machinery.

Plant and equipment expenditures by total business continued to rise sharply through 1966, slowed down in 1967 and 1968, and then resumed a strong rising trend. In 1969 manufacturers expected to devote 53% of their investment to expansion and 47% to replacement; and they planned to divide expenditures equally between the two during the next few years.[8] In early 1970 manufacturers began cutting back plans for expenditures on new plants and equipment, apparently because the manufacturing operating rate dropped between 1969 and 1970. Nonmanufacturing companies were stepping up plans in 1970 to account for about 60% of the capital spending pie. Manufacturers planned to devote 49% of their spending to expansion and 51% to replacement and modernization. Of the $82.3 billion business planned to spend in 1970, 20% was to go to buildings, 4% to motor vehicles, and 76% to machinery and equipment.[9]

Aids in the Analysis of the Investment in Fixed Assets

As we emphasized early in this chapter, commitments of funds to fixed assets typically are for long periods into the future and usually are difficult and costly to reverse. Often, they are in large increments. Consequently, it is important that the firm carefully establish and apply a valid pattern of analysis of the impact of proposed investments on the rate of return on the investment involved. The importance and inherent complexity of such analysis and selection among opportunities for fixed asset investment appear to us to justify the extended treatment of this subject which we undertake in Chapters 8, 9, and 10.

The impact of fixed asset outlays on the firm's financial needs and position also typically is major. Unduly heavy commitment of available resources to relatively illiquid fixed assets—even ones of promising long-term earning power—can precipitate major liquidity problems and, indeed, in extreme situations, make it impossible for the firm to meet maturing obligations. In Chapter 6, we shall consider some leading ratios used to measure liquidity and the impact of the firm's fixed asset investment on its liquidity, and Chapter 7 discusses the forecasting of cash needs.

At this point, it may well suffice to note that ratios similar to those applied to the investment in inventory and receivables can also usefully be applied to fixed assets. Thus, net fixed assets can be expressed as a percentage of total assets. Also, the turnover of net fixed assets in sales (sales/net fixed assets) is useful as a quick, if rough, index of the efficiency of use of fixed assets. Those firms which, by the nature of the

---

[8] McGraw-Hill Publishing Company, Inc., *Business Plans for New Plants and Equipment, 1969–1972* (22nd Annual Survey), p. 1.

[9] McGraw-Hill Publishing Company, Inc., *Business Plans for New Plants and Equipment, 1970–1973* (23rd Annual Survey), p. 1.

technology of their industry, can hope to achieve only low turnover of fixed assets, notably utilities, can achieve a satisfactory return for their shareholders only if a high rate of profit can be achieved on sales (or revenues) and/or relatively heavy use can be made of low-cost debt money. Firms, on the other hand, that can achieve a high turnover of fixed assets, such as retail food chains, may well be able to achieve a high return on assets with only a moderate rate of profit on sales.

PART **III**

ANALYSIS OF PAST FINANCING AND FUTURE FUNDS NEEDS

chapter 6

Interpreting Financial Statements

Our emphasis in recent chapters has been on uses of funds, as we looked in turn at the need for funds in inventory, receivables, and money assets and in plant and equipment. In this chapter we are concerned with how to draw meaning from the basic financial statements. To the uninitiated, balance sheets and income statements represent a confusing jumble of figures. But those skilled in drawing out their meaning can make the financial statements tell a revealing story of what has happened to the needs for financing and how these needs were met. Moreover, to the skilled analyst, the statements provide the raw material for judgments as to the financial condition of the subject firm.

In Chapter 7, the other chapter in Part III of this book, we shall shift attention from techniques of analysis of past developments and the current financial position, as mirrored in the financial statements, to a focus on future needs for funds. In Chapter 7 we introduce the major methods of forecasting funds requirements and discuss the main problems in doing an effective job of forecasting.

After considering investment opportunity analysis in Part IV, we turn in Part V to issues of where and how to raise needed funds.

While we shall delay a focus on sources of funds until Part IV, the chapters on interpreting financial statements and forecasting needs necessarily are concerned with the total finances of the firm—that is, with sources as well as uses of funds. Hence, we believe it desirable to provide at this point an overview of the major sources of funds for business. Exhibit 6–1 sets forth in highly capsuled form the more important sources of debt and ownership financing. The exhibit includes references to the pages in the book at which each major source is discussed in some detail. Students who may be confused as to the essential nature of particular sources of funds can refer to the appropriate pages for clarification.

Exhibit 6–1

Major Sources of Funds for American Business

Broad Classification of Sources	Instruments or Form in Which Funds Are Acquired	B.B.F. Page Reference	Major Suppliers of Funds	Classification by Length of Term
Spontaneous	Normal trade credit	203	Vendors selling to the firm	Short term
	Accrued expenses	206	Miscellaneous creditors	
	Accrued U.S. income taxes	207	U.S. government	
	Special credits from suppliers	258	Major vendors	
	Customer loans and advances	257	Major customers	
	Short-term bank loans	220	Commercial banks	
	Loans from specialized lending companies	253–56	Business finance companies, factors, sales finance companies	
	Commercial paper (short-term notes payable)	250	Nonfinancial corporations, banks and other financial institutions	
Negotiated	Term bank loans	233	Commercial banks	Intermediate term
	Term loans—directly placed with nonbank lenders	235	Insurance companies, pension funds, small-business investment companies	
	Long-term debt instruments (bonds, notes, debentures, mortgages)	346	Primarily insurance companies, pension funds, savings banks and other institutional investors, (to lesser extent) individual investors	Long term
	Preferred stock	358	Institutional investors, individual investors	
	Common stock	354	Individual investors, institutional investors	
Operational	Inflows from operations represented by retained earnings; noncash charges to earnings (depreciation, etc.)	294	Operations of the business	

Exhibit 6–2

PARKWOOD HOMES, INC. AND SUBSIDIARY
Consolidated Balance Sheet*

ASSETS	February 28, 1969	February 28, 1970
Current assets		
Cash..................................	$ 433,768	$ 75,244
Trade accounts receivable, net of reserve....	2,473,113	3,886,447
Inventories—at the lower of cost (first-in, first-out method) or market:		
Finished products.....................	27,424	64,367
Work in process......................	158,919	213,435
Materials and supplies................	750,373	1,123,747
	$ 936,716	$1,401,549
Prepaid insurance and other expenses......	54,903	63,661
Total current assets..................	$3,898,500	$5,426,901
Investments and other assets................	218,180	216,721
Property, plant, and equipment (at cost)		
Land...................................	119,749	154,749
Buildings..............................	976,489	1,412,985
Machinery and equipment................	1,035,202	1,658,671
	$2,131,440	$3,226,405
Less: Allowances for depreciation..........	(481,686)	(732,758)
	$1,649,754	$2,493,647
	$5,766,434	$8,137,269

LIABILITIES

	February 28, 1969	February 28, 1970
Current liabilities		
Notes payable to bank...................	$ 500,000	$ 600,000
Trade accounts payable.................	1,911,071	2,167,520
Federal income taxes....................	295,932	449,691
Accrued expenses.......................	403,342	641,229
Contributions to profit-sharing trust.......	41,250	56,250
Portion of long-term debt due within one year............................	43,198	48,157
Total current liabilities...............	$3,197,793	$3,962,847
Deferred federal income taxes..............	32,235	94,235
Long-term debt.........................	316,729	268,572
Stockholders' equity		
Common Stock, no par value— Authorized 3 million shares; Issued and Outstanding: 1970—810,000 shares; 1969—750,000 shares............	125,000	425,000
Capital surplus........................	75,000	571,436
Retained earnings......................	2,019,677	2,815,179
	$2,219,677	$3,811,615
	$5,766,434	$8,137,269

* Slightly condensed and with footnotes omitted.

Exhibit 6–3

PARKWOOD HOMES, INC. AND SUBSIDIARY
Statement of Consolidated Income
and Retained Earnings*

	February 28, 1969	February 28, 1970
Income		
Net sales.........................	$24,893,085	$33,517,770
Other income......................	41,410	85,395
	$24,934,495	$33,603,165
Cost and expenses (including provisions for depreciation: 1970—$268,777; 1969—$191,333)		
Cost of products sold.................	20,944,967	28,058,765
Selling, administrative and general expenses.......................	2,618,213	3,726,548
Profit sharing.....................	50,000	50,000
Interest..........................	25,246	54,782
Other expenses....................	32,307	45,568
	$23,670,733	$31,935,663
Income before income taxes..............	$ 1,263,762	$ 1,667,502
Federal income taxes.................	657,235	872,000
Net income.........................	$ 606,527	$ 795,502
Retained earnings at beginning of year.....	1,433,150	2,019,677
	$ 2,039,677	$ 2,815,179
Deduct cash dividends paid..............	(20,000)	....
Retained earnings at end of year.........	$ 2,019,677	$ 2,815,179
Per share of common stock		
Net income........................	$ 0.81	$ 1.00
Cash dividends paid.................	0.03	....

* Slightly condensed and with footnotes omitted.

Now let us turn to a consideration of techniques of interpretation or analysis of the basic financial statements. We shall be concerned here with generally useful techniques or tools of analysis and we shall illustrate their use on the financial statements normally available to persons outside the subject firm.

In business usage, the term *financial analysis* is applied to almost any kind of detailed inquiry into financial data. The specific nature of the financial inquiry or analysis undertaken will be shaped by the following factors:

1. The objective and the point of view of the analyst. A trade creditor considering what action to take on a long-overdue account may well focus his inquiry on the immediate financial condition of the subject firm and the liquid resources it has with which to meet maturing obligations. In contrast, a security analyst considering a purchase of common stock, after a quick check to see that the balance sheet offers no cause for alarm, tends to center his efforts on the profit results in an effort to gain clues as to the future profitability of the firm.

2. The degree of interest in the company and the need for depth of

inquiry. An insurance company considering a multimillion dollar loan to a new customer will be justified in devoting a great deal more time and effort to analysis of the company and its finances than will the credit department of a manufacturing firm making a routine annual review of the data on a small customer who has followed satisfactory payment practices. We know of one investment firm which permitted one of its security analysts to spend 6 months investigating the investment merits of a single company. (Happily his reports strongly recommended the purchase, and the stock has quadrupled in value; he is now a vice president, not an ex-employee.)

3. The amount and quality of the data available. Trade creditors in routine seldom are furnished more than summary financial statements, supplemented modestly by credit agency reports. The individual investor usually has little more than the financial information published in the annual report or in a prospectus. In contrast, the commercial banker considering a large loan is usually in a position to get from the company a great deal of additional information, such as breakdowns of inventory, aging schedules of receivables and payables, sales and production plans, and product line profitability estimates.

If a thorough analysis is desired and the full data needed are not available, or if the suspicion exists that the firm involved is trying to hide or confuse its real situation, the financial analyst must be a virtual detective in order to ferret out the full facts and piece together the story they tell.

Exhibits 6–2 and 6–3 reproduce the financial statements of Parkwood Homes, Inc., as presented in its fiscal year 1970 report. Parkwood manufactures mobile homes for sale through more than 1,000 dealers around the country. The financial data presented in its annual report typify those readily available to stockholders, trade creditors, and the public.

Analysts interested in Parkwood's progress during the year can make significant observations from a quick scanning of these financial statements. Readily apparent, for example, is the sizable increase in sales and in net profits. But the person equipped with basic techniques of financial analysis may use his skills to shape a much more meaningful picture of Parkwood's financing. With these tools he may follow more clearly the changes in Parkwood's financial needs during the year and how these needs were met. He may also better appraise Parkwood's financial position at year-end. In short, he may shape the data into a story of what happened.

Let us use Parkwood data as an illustration of the application of techniques of analysis and see what story develops. In so doing, it is well to be alert to the limitations of our data and to the danger of drawing unwarranted conclusions from the analysis. With the detailed information normally available to management, it would be possible to make a more complete and discerning analysis and to evaluate developments with keener insight and confidence than when we have only the summary financial statements with which to work.

By *funds* again is meant, of course, cash or other means of payment. Thus, as we have noted in Chapter 2, an increase in inventory absorbs or "uses" funds. If the increase in inventory was financed by increasing accounts payable, the use of funds was met, not with cash outflow, but with credit. The increase in a liability, accounts payable, served as a source of funds. Also, Chapter 5 discussed how funds are provided through operations.

SOURCES AND USES OF FUNDS ANALYSIS

Both the income statement and the balance sheets may be drawn upon in developing a *statement of funds flows*, also known as a *statement of sources and uses of funds*. Various formats are used in developing such statements. Suggested here is preparation of a statement for Parkwood in three steps.

1. Note from the income statement the net cash inflows from operations during the year.
2. Classify the net changes in the asset, liability and net worth accounts from the balance sheet at the beginning of the year and that at year-end.
3. Bring the statements of funds flows from operations and the balance sheet changes together into a statement of funds flow for the year. In so doing, any double-counting involved should be eliminated in bringing the material together.

Proceeding with step 1, it is noted from the Parkwood income statement in Exhibit 6–3 that net earnings for the year were $795,502. A footnote indicated that the noncash charge for depreciation in 1969 was $268,777. Thus, funds inflow from operations was $1,064,279. Although Parkwood paid no dividends in fiscal year 1970, it should be noted that this is unusual and that most companies make annual dividend payouts to their stockholders which will be recorded in their financial statements. The importance in noting such dividend payments is that they have the effect of reducing the amount of funds inflow available to management for use in the ongoing operations of the business.

The above funds flows from operations during fiscal year 1970 will, of course, be reflected in the balance sheet changes. Thus, the net income of the year not paid out in dividends of $795,502 (as noted above, Parkwood paid no dividends in fiscal year 1970) should increase the retained earnings balance by that amount. And the charge for depreciation should be reflected in the net fixed asset account. Double-counting should be avoided in these accounts when, in step 3, the funds flows from operations and those reflected in the balance sheet changes are brought together.

Now let us undertake step 2, classification of the net changes in the asset and liability and net worth accounts, according to whether each change represented an absorption or use of funds or alternatively a provision or source of funds. Listed in the use column are:

Increases in assets (*e.g.*, an increase in inventory).
Decreases in liabilities (*e.g.*, payment of a bank loan).
Decrease in net worth (*e.g.*, payment of dividends).

Conversely, the following changes provide funds and thus are sources:

Decreases in assets (*e.g.*, reduction of inventory).
Increases in liabilities (*e.g.*, increases in accounts payable).
Increases in net worth (*e.g.*, from sale of stock).

Using this approach, let us classify the net changes in the various Parkwood balance sheet accounts in fiscal 1970 as shown in Exhibit 6–4.

Step 3, next, brings together information about cash flows from operations and that drawn from balance sheet changes.

It was noted that the net income inflow from operations was $795,502 and that no dividends were paid out, resulting in an increase in retained

Exhibit 6–4

PARKWOOD HOMES, INC. AND SUBSIDIARY
Uses of Funds
(in thousands)

Increases in assets

Increase in accounts receivable, net......................		$1,413
Increase in inventories		
Finished products.............................	$ 37	
Work in process..............................	55	
Materials and supplies.........................	373	465
Increase in prepaid insurance and other expenses...........		9
Increase in total property, plant and equipment, net..........		842
Decreases in liabilities		
Decrease in long-term debt........................		48
Total uses................................		$2,777

Sources of Funds

Decreases in assets

Decrease in cash and marketable securities...............	$ 356
Increases in liabilities	
Increase in notes payable to bank....................	100
Increase in accounts payable.......................	256
Increase in accrued federal income taxes................	154
Increase in accrued expenses.......................	237
Increase in contribution to profit trust.................	15
Increase in long-term debt due within one year............	5
Increase in deferred federal income taxes...............	62
Increases in net worth	
Increase in common stock.........................	300
Increase in capital surplus........................	496
Increase in retained earnings......................	796
Total sources.............................	$2,777

earnings of $795,502. Ordinarily, when dividends are paid, a funds flow statement is more useful if it shows the net income as a source and the dividends as a use of funds, replacing the single figure for the net increase in retained earnings.

We should also bring into our summary of funds flows the figure for funds flow from operations-depreciation. In our tally of uses of funds we showed only the amounts of increase in the *net* property and equipment accounts. Thus, the net property increased $843,893 after deduction of the reserve for depreciation. It was noted earlier that depreciation expense amounted to $268,777, so that a similar amount must have been added to the reserve for depreciation during the year. Thus, if "funds provided from operations-depreciation" of $268,777 is shown as a source, we should add $268,777 to the $843,893 shown as an increase in the property accounts and label this $1,112,670 figure "outlay for new fixed assets."

Our statement of sources and uses, expanded by the items in italics now appears as shown in Exhibit 6–5.

Now let us draw on the sources and uses of funds statement and summarize in narrative form how Parkwood's needs for funds grew and how they were met. Would the paragraph below be an accurate and clear summary?

Exhibit 6–5

PARKWOOD HOMES, INC. AND SUBSIDIARY

A. Uses of Funds

Dividends paid		$ 0
Increase in accounts receivable, net		1,413
Increase in inventories:		
Finished products	$ 37	
Work in process	55	
Materials and supplies	373	465
Increase in prepaid insurance and other expenses		9
Outlays for property, plant, and equipment		1,113
Decrease in long-term debt		48
Total uses		$3,048

B. Sources of Funds

Funds provided by operations		
Net income	$796	
Depreciation charged without outlay	269	1,065
Decrease in cash and marketable securities		356
Increase in notes payable to bank		100
Increase in accounts payable		257
Increase in accrued federal income taxes		154
Increase in accrued expenses		237
Increase in contribution to profit trust		15
Increase in long-term debt due within one year		6
Increase in deferred federal income taxes		62
Sale of equity		796
Total sources		$3,048

Common stock + capital surplus

During fiscal year 1970 Parkwood experienced a major need for funds to match sharp increases in receivables and in all types of inventories, apparently keyed to Parkwood's large increase in sales. A modest paydown on their long-term debt also contributed to the need for funds. Extensive new plant facilities were acquired, and the outlays for plant and equipment overshadowed the much smaller operational inflows related to depreciation.

Several sources were drawn upon to finance the expansion of receivables, inventories, and facilities. The substantial net income, all retained in the business, met 26% of total needs. The combined increases in accounts payable, accrued expenses, and in the tax accrual stemming from higher earnings were a slightly less important source. Management also drew down Parkwood's cash balance by over 80%. Despite these actions, external funds were needed, and they not only took out an additional $100,000 in short-term bank loans but sold stock to the public in order to obtain the equity funds necessary to support the increased requirements for fixed assets and working capital. The company netted $796,436 of new funds from this sale of common stock.

But our opportunities for possibly useful analysis of Parkwood's financial data have by no means been exhausted by our review of funds flow management. We have done little to probe profits beyond noting their increase and the funds they have provided. Remaining unanswered are such relevant queries as: Was the profits increase due solely to higher volume of sales or were margins increased? Did management succeed in getting a higher gross margin over cost of goods sold? Did operating expenses increase in line with sales? How was profit return relative to total assets? To owners' investment? Nor have we explored the big increases in receivables and inventory to see whether they were in line with sales increases. Beyond noting the pulldown of liquid assets, we have not looked into the financial condition of the company as revealed by the latest balance sheet. Nor have we devoted attention to the developing capital structure of the firm and the extent to which it is relying on the use of debt relative to ownership funds. Exploitation of the opportunities for further analysis can be aided by purposeful ratio analysis.

But before we turn to a discussion of ratios and their application to the Parkwood data, some further general comments on funds flow analysis are appropriate.

Professional accountants making up source and use of funds statements for clients where full facts are available often undertake further refinement of the funds statement to remove from the tabulation any transactions which were merely "paper transactions" not actually involving any flows of funds. Seldom does the outside analyst have enough information on transactions of this sort to attempt such refinements in the source and use of funds statements he constructs.

The reader should appreciate the fact that the source and use of funds statement, as we have constructed it, and as it is generally prepared, does not attempt to picture all the flows of funds through a business during the period. Note that from the income statement, we picked up only *net* profits and the noncash expense depreciation. Left off the source side were the remainder of the sales dollars received, and the cash expenses paid during the year do not show up on the use side. Many other transactions within the year are not shown. For example, Parkwood might have borrowed from banks for short periods and repaid the loans several times during the year; these intraperiod flows would not show up in our statement, which deals primarily with *net* changes during the year.

While it is more thorough to bring all known flows during the period into the source and use statement, in practice published statements of sources and uses of funds seldom show more than does our revised one for Parkwood. The source and use statement often is put together in somewhat different form, though with essentially the same information. Other approaches are presented in the Ross Corporation and Inconco Corporation cases.

THE USE OF RATIOS IN FINANCIAL ANALYSIS

Ratios, discriminatingly calculated and wisely interpreted, can be useful tools of financial analysis. Ratios are simply a means of highlighting in arithmetical terms the relationships between figures drawn from financial statements. A great number of ratios can be computed from the basic financial statements—for example, the relationship of Parkwood's accrued expenses to its net investment in fixed assets can be readily calculated as 11.7% (376 ÷ 3,226). But does this relationship have any significance? None is apparent, so that the 11.7% figure is meaningless and its calculation distracting.

Ratios will be meaningful and useful, then, only to the extent that significant relationships exist between the figures selected for comparison through ratios. And as we earlier pointed out, the viewpoint and particular interests of the analyst will make some relationships of especial interest to him. The more commonly used ratios fall into one of three generic groupings according to their use. These main groups or families of ratios are:

1.   Measures of profitability.
2.   Measures of asset use.
3.   Measures of liquidity and the use of debt.

Let us identify and discuss these ratios in the practical context of their use in the analysis of the Parkwood data.

Ratios in the Measurement and Analysis of Profitability

SALES AND PROFIT COMPARISONS.   The absolute figures for profit take on more meaning when compared with sales. Widely used as a measure of profitability is the percentage ratio of net income after taxes to net sales—or to total income if income from sources other than sales is material and recurring. In Parkwood, the fiscal year 1970 net profit after taxes on sales was 2.37%, calculated as follows:

$$\frac{\text{Net Income after Taxes}}{\text{Net Sales}} = \frac{796}{33,518} = 2.37\% .$$

The corresponding ratio for fiscal year 1969 was 2.44%. Thus, it is apparent that increased profits in fiscal year 1970 were solely the result of higher sales; Parkwood had no success in taking down into net profit a higher percentage of total revenues from sales and, in fact, earned a slightly lower margin on its sales in 1969.

Since the burden of income taxation can vary from year to year, operational results often are measured in terms of net income before taxes compared with sales. In Parkwood, net profit before taxes was 4.9% of sales, again down slightly from 5.1% in fiscal year 1969.

SALES AND EXPENSE RATIOS. Management and those outside analysts particularly interested in profit performance and the control of expense commonly compute many expense/sales ratios. Outside analysts, who commonly have no breakdowns of expenses beyond the summary ones presented in published income statements, make frequent use of "100% statements"—that is, convert each of the expense and profit items in the income statement into percentages of total sales. The Parkwood income statement, in percentages, appears below:

	Fiscal Year 1969	Fiscal Year 1970
Total income............................	100 %	100 %
Cost of products sold....................	84.0	83.5
Gross profit...........................	16.0	16.5
Selling, administrative, and general expenses.............................	10.5	11.1
Operating profit.......................	5.5	5.4
Profit sharing, interest, and other expenses.............................	0.4	0.5
Income before income taxes..............	5.08	4.96
Federal income taxes....................	2.64	2.59
Net income............................	2.44	2.37

The percentage statement makes it apparent that Parkwood's profit percentage in fiscal year 1970 is due, not to a lower gross profit or *gross margin* percentage, but to expenses which increased faster than sales. These unfavorable factors were not offset by the lower tax burden. With its more complete information about various expense items, management can make a similar but much more detailed expense/profit analysis.

Profits Compared with Assets

In Chapter 1 we discussed measures of profitability which related the amount of profit to the funds employed in the business. We stressed the importance of return-on-investment ratios as gauges of the ability of managements to make effective use of the resources at their command.

Now let us relate the Parkwood profit results to the funds or resources employed in the business. Parkwood's return on overall assets in fiscal year 1970 is found to be 9.78%:

$$\frac{\text{Net Income after Taxes}}{\text{Total Assets, Year-End}} = 9.78\% .$$

The 9.78% return in fiscal year 1970 represents a slight decrease over the 1969 return of 10.54%.

We can also come to the same rate of return on assets figures by a two-step calculation employing return-on-sales and asset-turnover figures, as described in Chapter 1.

$$\frac{\text{Net Income}}{\text{Sales}} \times \frac{\text{Sales}}{\text{Assets}} = \text{Net Return on Assets} .$$

$$2.37 \quad \times \quad 4.12 \ = 9.76\% .$$

As we pointed out in Chapter 1, management can boost return on assets by either or both the routes of higher profit per dollar of sales or of higher turnover of assets in sales. The two-step calculation highlights the source of improvement, or in this case, of decline. Thus, comparison with Parkwood's 1969 results, as set forth below, shows that both a lower profit rate on sales (2.37 versus 2.44) and a lower turnover of assets in sales (4.12 times versus 4.32 times) contributed significantly to the overall lower return on assets.

$$\frac{607}{24{,}934} \times \frac{24{,}934}{5{,}766} = 2.43 \times 4.32 = 10.5\% \text{ in } 1969 .$$

Another measure of profitability of widespread use and keen significance, particularly to shareholders, relates total income after taxes to the total investment of the common shareholders as shown in the balance sheet. This return-on-owners'-investment ratio supplements the return-on-total-assets ratio. The return on owners' investment in Parkwood was 20.9% in 1970, down from 27.3% in 1969.

The 1970 figure of 20.9% was derived as follows:

$$\frac{\text{Net Income after Taxes}}{\text{Owners' Investment}} = \text{Rate of Return on Owners' Investment} .$$

The much higher return on ownership funds in Parkwood than on total assets (20.9% versus 9.78%) reflects the fact that creditors were the source of much of the funds used in the business. The degree to which the return on total assets and the return on owners' investment differ from one company to another will hinge on the relative mix of ownership and creditors' funds in the business. Thus, the figure for return on ownership funds reflects the financial policies of the firm as well as its effectiveness in employing the assets. In later chapters we shall be very much concerned with the considerations bearing on the choice of debt versus equity sources of funds.

The discerning student may have taken note of the fact that we used year-end figures for total assets and for owners' investment in calculating the return on total assets and on owners' investment. Some analysts prefer to use a figure representing an average of the figures at the beginning and end of the year for total assets and/or owners' investment. This, they argue with considerable logic, more accurately depicts the assets or ownership funds in actual use during the year against which to relate the earnings for that full year. In growing firms, use of average figures will result in a higher figure for return than use of the year-end figures. For example, the calculation below of Parkwood's return on average ownership funds in 1970 shows it to be 26.6% compared with the figure of 20.9% on year-end equity as calculated above.

$$\frac{\text{Net Income}}{\substack{\text{Average of Beginning} \\ \text{and Year-End Figures} \\ \text{for Owners' Investment}}} = \substack{\text{Return on Average Ownership} \\ \text{Investment during Year}}$$

$$\frac{796}{(2,220 + 3,812) - 2} = 26.6\% \ .$$

Ratios as Measures of Asset Use

In Chapter 2 we emphasized the significance of the relationship between inventories and sales and described key ratios used to depict this relationship. We suggest that the reader review this material. Now, let us apply the ratios discussed there to Parkwood. First, we can note that total year-end inventories as a percentage of sales rose from 3.76% of sales in 1969 to 4.18% in 1970. Similar checks on each type of inventory show that each increased at a rate greater than that of sales.

The same relationship can be expressed in terms of turnover (sales/inventory). Since inventories are usually carried at cost, a more precise measure of physical turnover can be obtained by dividing inventories into cost of sales rather than sales. As might be expected, turnover decreased from 22.4 times to 20.0 times.

In Chapter 3 we introduced some ratios useful in appraising the investment in receivables. The first of these simply expressed receivables as a percentage of sales. Parkwood's receivables were 9.9% of sales in 1969, 11.6% in 1970. Thus, like inventories, receivables went up faster than sales.

The growth in receivables relative to sales is brought out, perhaps more sharply, by calculation of "days' sales outstanding," or collection period.

It will be recalled that this ratio is calculated in two steps, the first being determination of an average day's sales:

$$\frac{\text{Annual Sales, 1970}}{365} = \frac{\$33,517,770}{365} = \$91,830 \; .$$

In the second step the average day's sales are divided into year-end receivables:

$$\frac{\text{Year-End Receivables, 1970}}{\text{Average Day's Sales}} = \frac{\$3,886,447}{\$91,830} = 42.3 \text{ days} \; .$$

The 42.3-day figure at the end of 1970 compares with a 36.3-day figure at the end of 1969.

The net investment in plant can also be compared with sales: Parkwood's net plant investment in 1970 was 7.44 of sales, up from 6.63 in 1969. In terms of turnover (sales/net plant), the moderate rates of 13.4 times and 15.1 times call attention to the volume of sales achieved by Parkwood on its increasing fixed asset investment.

Ratios as Measures of Liquidity

Several ratios are used as measures of liquidity—that is, they are concerned with short-term obligations and the assets that are more readily convertible into the means of payment. Outside analysts who lack detailed data about the anticipated cash flows of the business use the liquidity ratios as rough indices of the likely ability of the subject firm to meet its near-term obligations or of possible need to raise additional funds through borrowing or stock issues.

Perhaps the most widely used ratio is the *current ratio*, which is simply the current assets divided by the current liabilities. Using Parkwood's figures, we find the following:

$$\frac{\text{Current Assets, Year-End 1970}}{\text{Current Liabilities, Year-End 1970}} = \frac{\$5,427}{\$3,963} = 1.37 \; .$$

The 1970 ratio of 1.37 compares with that of 1.22 a year earlier. The increase in Parkwood's current ratio during fiscal year 1970, despite its sharp drop in cash, reflects the increase of receivables and inventory in its asset structure and the large inflow of retained earnings and new equity.

Despite its wide use—which suggests that analysts think it revealing— the current ratio is at best a very crude measure of the financial health of a firm and its ability to meet its debts. An example of the limited conclusiveness of the current ratio as a measure of debt-paying ability arises out of the fact that inventory is included in current assets. Actually, the inventory may be of limited salability, particularly in the short run. Consider the situation of a manufacturer of ice skates at the end of March with the following summary balance sheet and the strong current ratio of 3 to 1:

Cash................	$ 10,000	Current liabilities......	$100,000
Receivables............	10,000		
Inventory.............	280,000		
	$300,000		

This firm could still be in financial difficulty if the $100,000 of current liabilities were all due within a month, while inventory could be sold without severe loss only over a period of many months.

Recognized for what it is—a very rough and not necessarily conclusive indicator of liquidity—the current ratio can be useful in the absence of better information or as a small part of a more complete and discerning analysis. In the case of Parkwood, the slight increase in the current ratio from 1969 to 1970 does not call attention to any real rise in liquidity during the year.

The current ratio is also used by creditors as a measure of the extent that current asset values could shrink in liquidation of the firm and still be adequate for repayment of current creditors—fixed assets and long-term debts left aside. Thus, the current assets of a firm with a 4.0 current ratio could shrink to one fourth and still match the current debts.

Another widely used ratio is one called the *acid test* or the *net quick* ratio. This ratio is like the current ratio except that inventory and prepaid expenses are excluded. Using the 1970 Parkwood figures, we see the following results:

$$\frac{\text{Cash, Marketable Securities, and Receivables}}{\text{Current Liabilities}} = \frac{\$75 + \$3,886}{\$3,963} = 1.0.$$

The 1970 figure, 1.0, represents a slight increase from that of 1969, 0.91. Both figures indicated that Parkwood's cash and receivables, without reference to inventory, do not provide a safety margin to cover more than current liabilities.

A third ratio used to assess liquidity is one which compares the level of cash and near-cash accounts to average daily cash payments:

$$\frac{\text{Cash} + \text{Marketable Securities}}{\text{Average Daily Cash Payments}}.$$

Since no figures for daily outflows are available in the case of Parkwood, this ratio cannot be calculated by outsiders. Here again, speaking broadly, the ratio is open to "ifs, ands, and buts." A firm with strong, little-used lines of credit with banks or other creditors can well afford to operate with a lower cash balance relative to the size of its outflows than can a firm without such "credit backstops" in reserve for use if cash stringencies develop.

The accounts payable of firms whose purchase terms and payment practice do not change can be expected to fluctuate with the recent volume of purchases. Hence, a sharp rise in payables may simply reflect a bulge in purchases. A significant increase in *payables relative to purchases*, however, may well indicate developing financial stringency. Firms experiencing a shortage of funds face strong temptation to lean on their supplies by delaying payment of trade obligations. The tolerance of suppliers is not unlimited, however, and an increasing ratio of payables to purchases often is one of the first signs of a developing shortage of funds.

The level of payables can be usefully related to the volume of purchases in either of two ways:

1. Payables are expressed as a percentage of recent purchases. For example, if monthly purchases data are available, the outstanding payables become the numerator in a payables/purchases ratio.
2. Payables are expressed in terms of average day's purchases outstanding:

$$\frac{\text{Payables Outstanding}}{\text{Average Day's Purchases}} \cdot$$

Clearly, this figure will be more significant if average day's purchases are based on recent purchase figures. If they are so based, the resultant figure can be compared with the customary terms of sale of the major suppliers. For example, assume purchases in company X were running at a fairly even rate of $120,000 a month during the last quarter, and it was known that its suppliers were reluctant to have customers exceed their 30-day payment terms. Company X's outstanding accounts payable of $300,000 thus are found to represent 75 days' purchases.

$$\frac{\$120,000}{30} = \$4,000 \text{ Average Day's Purchases .}$$

$$\frac{\$300,000}{\$4,000} = \underline{75 \text{ Days .}}$$

In the light of the usual terms of 30 days, this 75-day figure suggests that company X has stretched the payment terms far beyond a sustainable level or else has arranged for special credit from suppliers.

If full data are available, an aging schedule of payables can be developed using an approach like that used in aging receivables (see Chapter 3).

In the Parkwood case, purchase data are not available, and so we cannot assess Parkwood payables in these terms.

The Source of Funds for the Business: Comparison of Borrowed Funds with Ownership Funds

Of much interest to many analysts is the relative use of debt and of ownership funds in the concern. A useful and simple way of depicting the extent of debt financing is to calculate the percentage of total assets provided by all creditors. As shown by the calculations below, in Parkwood, *debt as a percentage of total assets* decreased considerably in fiscal year 1970, reflecting particularly the increased equity from the sale of stock:

$$\frac{\text{Total Debts, 1970}}{\text{Total Assets, 1970}} = \frac{\$4,326}{\$8,137} = 53.2\% .$$

$$\frac{\text{Total Debts, 1969}}{\text{Total Assets, 1969}} = \frac{\$3,547}{\$5,766} = 61.5\% .$$

Also in wide use, particularly in the public utility and railroad industries, are ratios that focus on the relationship between equity and long-term debt. The total of long-term debt and total equity sources (*preferred stock, common stock, and surplus accounts*) is referred to as the *capitalization* of the firm. A commonly used ratio shows *long-term debt as a percentage of total capitalization*. Using Parkwood figures of 1970 we have:

$$\frac{\text{Long-Term Debt}}{\text{Total Capitalization}} = \frac{269}{269 + 3,812} = 6.6\% .$$

The 6.6% figure compares with one of 12.5% for 1969. Thus, this ratio indicates at least a temporary decline in the importance of long-term debt in the total long-term financing at Parkwood.

Another ratio used to summarize the relationship between total equity and total debt is the *equity-to-debt* ratio. Computing this ratio for Parkwood at year end, 1970, we show the following:

$$\frac{\text{Total Equity, 1970}}{\text{Total Debt, 1970}} = \frac{3,812}{4,326} = 0.88 .$$

The 1970 equity-to-debt ratio of 0.88 compares with one of 0.63 for year-end 1969. The rise in the ratio reflects the decreased reliance on debt in the total financing of Parkwood, which is also highlighted by the figures for total debt as a percentage of total assets.

Speaking generally from a creditor's viewpoint, the lower the percentage of debt financing to total assets the better. The creditor can regard the ownership funds as representing a buffer protecting him from loss. If, for example, debt is only 20% of total assets, the assets could shrink in liquidation to one fifth of the balance sheet values and still be sufficient to cover debt claims, since creditors are entitled to be paid out in full before the owners are entitled to anything. In contrast, if total debts amount to 90% of total assets, a shrinkage of more than 10% would leave the creditors "under water."

Of course, the amount of debt that the business can reasonably carry depends on many factors, to be discussed at length in a later chapter. A public utility with stable earnings and favorable prospects may safely finance a much larger percentage of its assets with debt than can, say, a manufacturer with a past record of erratic profitability who produces a single specialty product of uncertain long-term demand.

As we observed earlier, the conclusion that a particular ratio depicts a good or bad condition may rest with the analyst's viewpoint. One suspects that the holders of Parkwood's outstanding long-term debt might well prefer a slower expansion financed predominantly by retained earnings or equity issues to faster expansion with debt. Yet, to the common stockholders the alternative of more debt may well represent the most feasible means of financing desirable rapid expansion in the year ahead, now that they have bolstered their equity capital.

Increasing the Usefulness of Ratio Analysis

In our analysis of Parkwood, we have looked only at the balance sheets at the end of Parkwood's 1969 and 1970 fiscal years and at operating results for those two years. We could add depth to our analysis by extending it backward over a much longer span of years. The calculation of ratios for a span of years may bring to light important trends not apparent in analysis focused on short periods. Further, marked changes in the ratios from those characteristic of the past may signal important changes in industry conditions, or in management policies, deserving further investigation. Thus, data on the use of debt relative to equity financing over, say, a 10-year period would make clearer whether the drop in the debt percentage shown in 1970 was in line with a long-standing management policy of gradually reducing reliance on debt or a sharp departure from past debt policies. Similarly, the profit ratios for 1970 would take on more meaning against the background of profit ratios over a longer period.

It can also be helpful to compare the funds flow data and the ratios of the subject firm with those of competitors in the same industry. Many trade associations and other industry groups collect and publish data for firms in the industry, often classified by size or specialized activities within the industry. If the firms within industry groups operated along similar lines and under reasonably comparable conditions, comparison of the subject firm's ratios with industry ratios can add much to the analysis. It should be emphasized that deviations from typical industry ratios should not be judged as being undesirable per se. For example, the firm under study may show a much higher investment in receivables relative to sales than its competitors. At first thought, it might appear that the subject firm was guilty of dangerously lax credit policies. But in fact, the high ratio may be simply the reflection of a conscious management policy of competing for sales through especially liberal credit policies; and this policy might be paying off handsomely to the firm in the form of higher sales and profits, and even return on assets, than it otherwise would have achieved. In other words, deviations from "normal" may mean simply that the firm operates differently, not less effectively. Further, the ratios are drawn from the accounting data of the firm, and differences in accounting policies and practices between firms naturally limit complete comparability between their respective ratios.

In recent years the moves of many firms toward diversification into multiple-product lines that cut across traditional industry groupings has made more difficult comparison of these firms with industry indices. Indeed, a number of firms are sufficiently unique to defy close comparison with any other. However, it may still be possible for management of these concerns to make useful ratio comparisons among certain of their divisions or subsidiaries and of these units with ratios drawn from other firms in the industries in which these units operate.

Since this discussion is already an extended one, we shall concede in our analysis of Parkwood the advantages of depth of analysis that might have been gained through comparison with Parkwood ratios of earlier years or with industry ratios. Let us see what we can add from our admittedly limited ratio analysis to the interpretative comments on Parkwood's statements that were based only on the funds flow analysis. The reader is asked to compare the following with what he would regard as the major points from the analysis worthy of inclusion in a summary commentary. There is abundant room for differences in view as to the more significant points for comment and emphasis.

Parkwood's 1970 sales increased 34.6% over 1969; profits were up 31.1%. The lower profit increase reflected primarily an increase in Parkwood's operating expenses which overshadowed a small increase in gross margin and a slight decrease in Parkwood's effective tax rate.

Though turnover of inventories was high (20 times at cost), the small investment in inventory did increase faster than sales. Year-end receivables were up much more than sales, the collection period rising from 36.3 to 42.3 days. Inquiry here might well be warranted.

Turnover of plant in fiscal 1970 fell to 13.4 times from the 15.1 achieved in fiscal year 1969, reflecting the fact that fixed assets were increased even faster than sales in 1970.

Profit return on total assets at year-end declined from 10.54% to 9.78%, while return on shareholders' investment also fell from 27.3% in 1969 to 20.9%.

Reflecting the various financing procedures, liquidity ratios all showed slight improvements, but the acid-test ratio at the end of fiscal year 1970 was still a modest 1.0. Liquid assets were only 1.9% of current liabilities, down from 13.6%. A decrease in the percentage of debt to total assets from 61.5% to 53.2% reflected in large measure the funds raised by the issue of new shares in 1970.

The above summary of the results of the ratio analysis could well be integrated with the earlier comments drawn from the funds flow analysis for a more comprehensive single statement of the results of our financial analysis.

Recognizing the Limitations of Ratio Analysis

At several points in our discussion of ratio analysis we have counseled caution in the interpretation of ratios. Hasty or overconfident judgments as to the reasons for ratio changes may prove very wrong. For example, the increased collection period in Parkwood MIGHT reflect credit or collection difficulties. But other possible interpretations may, upon inquiry, prove the real explanation. For example, public school administrative agencies are notoriously slow in processing and paying bills. A shift in the mix of total sales toward more sales of trailers to schools as mobile or temporary classrooms could well explain the change. Or it might simply be due to very heavy sales in the weeks before the fiscal year-end. Ratios are mechanical tools of analysis; they never should be used standing alone as arbitrary standards of excellence. As aids to judgment, they can be helpful; as mechanical substitutes for thought and judgment, they can be worse than useless.

chapter **7**

Forecasting Future Needs for Funds

Virtually all financial managers do some sort of forecasting of the future needs for funds of their business. Yet, in many firms the forecasting is so limited in scope, haphazard, based on rules of thumb of dubious reliability, or on such a short-term basis that many of the potential gains from careful, organized planning of financial needs are lost. As a practical matter, the major issue connected with cash planning in most concerns is not whether any financial planning will be attempted but rather how far the managers should go in putting their funds forecasting into organized, systematic, and careful form.

Effective forecasting of funds needs, like any kind of forward planning, calls for organized effort, cooperation of the nonfinancial executives, and time and energy. The advantages to be gained must justify the effort involved. Actually, in the typical firm fully effective forecasting of financial needs is likely to pay off handsomely by:

1. Making possible the pretesting of the financial feasibility of various programs before moves are made that are difficult to retract.
2. Facilitating the raising of additional funds that may be required.
3. Inspiring confidence in the firm's management on the part of lenders or other sources of funds.
4. Providing a control device or checkpoints useful in exposing deviations from plans.
5. Improving the utilization of funds, particularly of cash balances.

Systematic financial forecasting pushed well into the future permits timely review by top management as to the advisability of projected plans and programs in the light of their probable impact on the company's finances. In most concerns the supply of available funds is not unlimited,

127

and the plans of the company must be shaped to fit the financial capabilities of the firm. Once the needs implicit in proposed programs are identified, those programs involving undue outlays can be cut back or reshaped before embarrassing commitments are made. An example of the unfortunate and unnecessary consequences of a cavalier approach is provided by the·experience of a medium-sized manufacturing concern known to the authors. This firm had expanded profitably over the years without particular cash stringencies to signal the need for careful cash planning. Rather casually, management undertook the construction of a new plant and office building, the expansion of civilian sales, and a large government manufacturing contract, all of which, it developed, called for heavy cash outlays at about the same time. Some of the needs for cash, such as the heavy cash outlays involved in moving to the new location, and the extent and timing of the other needs were not calculated or foreseen by top management. Consequently, a serious shortage of cash developed, which had to be met through hasty and improvised borrowing arrangements on highly disadvantageous terms. Very serious embarrassment was narrowly averted. To use a nautical analogy, careful cash planning would have pointed up the financial rocks and shoals ahead before the course of the business was firmly set. Further, in many cases where no major new programs calling for large cash outlays are planned, many diverse and individually small needs can combine to confront management with unexpected cash stringency.

When the cash forecasts indicate that programs desirable on balance will result in the need to raise additional funds, the advance warning gives the company time to turn around in planning and·executing programs to raise funds. Many methods of raising funds—sale of common stock, for example—normally require several months in consummation. Unanticipated cash stringencies leading to hasty crash-program efforts to find funds often result in the company's assuming loan repayment or other commitments it subsequently regrets.

Furthermore, advance discussion and planning of financial needs with lenders or other sources of money tend to inspire confidence that management is on top of its problems. For example, two young men promoting a new enterprise appeared at a commercial bank to discuss prospective loan needs of their business several months in the future. With them, they brought a full outline of their plans, with schedules showing financial needs under various alternative plans of action. The banker, who was more accustomed to seeing loan applicants only after financial needs had become immediate and urgent, was impressed and offered a substantial credit. The banker was even more impressed (and the young businessmen were almost equally surprised in view of the many variables involved) when their cash forecast for the program selected proved accurate almost to the dollar.

Cash forecasts can be valuable also as a control mechanism. Once plans are agreed upon and programs are under way, the forecasted levels of cash can serve as checkpoints against which actual results can be compared. Significant deviations from expected levels signal that the program is not moving along as it should and hence requires top-management attention and action, or the deviations may indicate that the plans were unrealistic and should be revised in the light of unforeseen or uncontrollable developments.

While cash forecasting is especially important for firms whose financial resources are limited, it can also be useful in affluent concerns by pointing up opportunities to use liquid funds more profitably. In one very large and liquid company, only a modicum of financial planning was done prior to a postwar management reorganization. The new financial management undertook a wide range of planning activities, including cash forecasting. The cash forecasts revealed that existing cash balances were unnecessarily high. Subsequent investment of unneeded cash in income-producing securities contributed income sufficient to more than cover the costs of a wide range of valuable planning activity.

Techniques of Forecasting the Need for Funds

Two different methods of forecasting future cash needs are widely used. These are the cash flow forecast method and the projected balance sheet method. Naturally, being forecasts of the same thing, they should show the same net results. In this chapter we shall explain the essential nature of each approach and outline for each method the basic procedures in building a forecast of cash needs. Each method will be illustrated by reference to a simple situation, but we do not wish to imply that a single format can be applied mechanically to any business situation. While the essentials of forecasting are broadly applicable, the details of the approach should be adapted to fit the distinctive circumstances of each business. The related case problems are relied upon to help the student apply the basic techniques to specific business situations. We suggest that the student review this chapter carefully after he has worked with the forecasting cases. The descriptive materials will have more meaning after the student has struggled with the specifics of the case problems.

The Cash Flow Forecast

The most basic and comprehensive method of predicting the amount and the time of future funds needs is through preparation of a *cash flow forecast* or, as it is often called, a *cash budget*. The cash flow forecast is a tabulation of the plans of the firm in terms of their impact on the receipts and expenditures of cash. The basic aim is simple—to predict when and in what quantity receipts of cash will come into the firm and when and in what quantity payments of cash will be made. It is not much of an oversimplification to think of the cash forecast as a timed prediction of additions to and deductions from the company's bank accounts.

All anticipated receipts of cash are taken into the cash forecast regardless of whether or not they represent income in the accounting sense. Included along with collection of cash from sales and receivables arising out of sales are cash receipts from such sources as sale of securities or sale of fixed assets. Similarly, the tabulation of payments should include, along with routine payments of accounts payable, wages, salaries, rents, etc., any planned payments of taxes, dividends, loan repayments, or outlays for equipment or buildings. Not included are those expense items which do not represent outlays of cash, such as the allowance for depreciation and the allowance for bad debts.

Usually, the financial planner is interested in revealing not only the total outflow and inflow over an extended period, such as a year, but also the timing of the cash flows within this period. In most cash forecasts, receipts and payments are broken down by months. If uneven inflow and outgo are anticipated within the monthly intervals, it may be necessary to break the forecast down into weekly or even daily periods if maximum needs are to be brought to light.

Some concerns vary the time period breakdown of the cash forecast according to how far into the future the forecast is projected. One concern, for example, has a program of cash flow forecasting that extends 5 years ahead. Estimates for the next month are broken down by days, for the following 11 months by months, for the next 12 months by quarters, and for the ensuing 3 years only by annual periods. This pattern is based on two arguments, the first being that highly detailed information as to timing is needed only for short periods ahead. The second is that the accuracy of the estimating decreases markedly as the forecasts are pushed out into the future and consequently that the distant forecasts are too uncertain to justify more than general planning for the needs suggested by them.

We have described the cash flow forecast as a tabulation of the plans of the business in terms of the effect of these plans on the cash account. As such, the results of the cash flow forecast will prove only as accurate and as reliable as the underlying planning on which the forecast is based. And as we have seen in earlier chapters, virtually all of the significant activities of the firm affect its flow of funds. Thus, for complete effectiveness in his work the forecaster of funds flows first needs comprehensive and accurate data on what the operations of the firm will likely be.

The task of assembling the background data for the cash flow forecast is much easier in those firms which operate under profit budgeting, whereby profit objectives are set for the firm and operations are planned to produce the desired results.

The profit budgets supply much of the background information needed for preparation of cash flow forecasts. The task of forecasting cash flows becomes one of translating these plans, which are stated primarily in terms of accounting income and expense, into cash flow terms, as described later in this chapter. Although the use of profit budgeting is growing, many firms still do not have a carefully organized profit budget program. Yet, cash flow planning, though on a less solid footing, may still be highly useful to them. Under such circumstances, what information must the financial officer assemble, and how can he organize it into a cash flow forecast?

Probably the most critical estimate in cash flow forecasting is the forecast of sales. Usually, sales represent the primary source of cash receipts. Further, the operations of the business requiring cash outlays are typically geared to the anticipated volume of sales. Particularly closely tied to sales are the purchases of materials and outlays directly related to manufacturing. In compiling sales forecast data, the financial officer must usually rely heavily on the active cooperation of the sales department. Ideally, the sales department will provide a sales forecast in terms of both physical units and dollar value, and this will be checked and approved by top management.

Let us assume, for purposes of illustration, the role of the financial officer of the Able Company in preparing a cash forecast for the first 6 months of the year. The best estimate we can get calls for sales of $200,000 per month in the first 3 months, $250,000 per month for April and May, and $300,000 in June. Ten percent of the sales are expected to be for cash, the remainder on credit terms. The experience of the firm indicates that the receivables arising out of sales will be collected approximately 1 month after sale. We anticipate that the outstanding receivables on December 31 will amount to $185,000 and that these will all be collected in January. No bad debts are expected. The sales forecast now can be converted into a schedule of cash receipts from sales, expressed in thousands of dollars, as in Table 7–1.

Table 7–1

	Jan.	Feb.	March	April	May	June	Total
Total sales..............	$200	$200	$200	$250	$250	$300	$1,400
Credit sales.............	180	180	180	225	225	270	1,260
Receipts from collection of accounts receivable............	185	180	180	180	225	225	1,175
Cash sales..............	20	20	20	25	25	30	140
Cash receipts—sales.....	$205	$200	$200	$205	$250	$255	$1,315

Note that the collection of the receivables is scheduled to lag 1 month behind the credit sales. Thus, the $225,000 credit sales of April are shown as cash receipts of May.

Now, let us take into account any anticipated receipts from sources other than sales. The only such cash receipts which are anticipated are from the planned sale for cash of used equipment no longer required, amounting to $40,000 in April and $30,000 in June. With this information, we are ready to put together a summary schedule of forecasted cash receipts (Table 7–2), expressed in thousands of dollars.

Table 7–2

	Jan.	Feb.	March	April	May	June	Total
Cash receipts—sales.....	$205	$200	$200	$205	$250	$255	$1,315
Proceeds from sale of used equipment.......	...	...	...	40	...	30	70
Total cash receipts........	$205	$200	$200	$245	$250	$285	$1,385

Now, let us turn to the forecast of cash payments. As we have noted, many of the operations of the company are geared to the sales forecast. It serves as the basis for the development of manufacturing schedules that will provide the products needed for sale and inventory. The production schedules indicate the timing and amount of labor, material, and additional equipment needed. On the basis of the material needs established by the production schedules, procurement officials can be expected to prepare schedules of planned purchases of materials and of equipment. A major step in building the forecast of payments is the conversion of the purchase schedules, employing appropriate assumptions as to the terms of sale that will be offered by suppliers, into a schedule of anticipated payments of the accounts payable arising out of these purchases. Any purchases for cash usually are best listed separately.

Let us assume that the purchase schedule drawn up in the Able Company calls for purchase of materials costing $70,000 in each of the first 3 months and $90,000 a month thereafter. All are to be purchased on 30-day payment terms, and the accounts payable will be paid promptly when due. The company is also planning to buy two major items of equipment costing $200,000 each, one for delivery in January and the second in June. Sixty-day terms are expected on these items. In addition, routine replacement of minor equipment items of $5,000 per month is expected, also purchased on 60-day terms. Miscellaneous cash purchases of $1,000 per month are also planned. The outstanding payables together with miscellaneous accrued expenses on December 31 are estimated at $110,000, all due in January.

With these data, we can schedule the planned purchases and, from this schedule, prepare a schedule of planned payment for purchases, expressed in thousands of dollars. See Table 7–3.

The wage costs established by the production program next are tabu-

Table 7–3

	Jan.	Feb.	March	April	May	June	Total
PLANNED PURCHASES							
Cash purchases....................	$ 1	$ 1	$ 1	$ 1	$ 1	$ 1	$ 6
Production materials..............	70	70	70	90	90	90	480
Replacement equipment...........	5	5	5	5	5	5	30
Special equipment................	200	...	...	...	...	200	400
PAYMENT FOR PURCHASES							
Trade payables outstanding on							
December 31...................	110	...	...	...	...	...	110
Cash purchases....................	1	1	1	1	1	1	6
Production materials..............	...	70	70	70	90	90	390
Replacement equipment...........	...	...	5	5	5	5	20
Special equipment................	...	...	200	...	...	...	200
Total.....................	$111	$71	$276	$76	$96	$ 96	$726

lated and brought into a summary schedule of payments when they are expected to be paid. Usually, wages are paid weekly so that the payments closely coincide with the incurring of wage expense. In our illustration, wage payments of $50,000 are scheduled for each of the 6 months. Other manufacturing costs, such as light and power, are estimated to require payments of $10,000 each month.

General and administrative expenses, such as rents, salaries, travel expense, and property taxes, should next be tabulated and included in the summary schedule of payments in the month of payment. The total of these is estimated to call for payments of $25,000 each month.

Income tax payments, scheduled repayment of existing loans, dividends, and other nonroutine items of significance are usually listed separately in the summary payments schedule. The only such payments anticipated in the Able Company are income tax payments of $20,000 in March and again in June, and a dividend payment of $40,000 in January.

Having satisfied ourselves that no prospective payments have been overlooked, we can now bring the anticipated payments together in Table 7–4 a summary schedule of payments.

Table 7–4

Summary Cash Payment Schedule

	Jan.	Feb.	March	April	May	June	Total
Payments for purchases.........	$111	$ 71	$276	$ 76	$ 96	$ 96	$ 726
Wages paid....................	50	50	50	50	50	50	300
Other manufacturing payments..	10	10	10	10	10	10	60
Payments of general and ad-							
ministrative expenses........	25	25	25	25	25	25	150
Payments of income taxes......	...	...	20	...	...	20	40
Dividend payments............	40	...	...	...	...	...	40
Total payments.........	$236	$156	$381	$161	$181	$201	$1,316

Now, let us bring together the summaries of payments and receipts and calculate the *net* cash inflows or outgoes for each month. An additional calculation of cumulative inflow, or outgo, should next be made. When matched with cash on hand at the beginning of the period, it is then possible to calculate the additional cash needed (or excess cash above minimum needs) to maintain the minimum cash balance desired. In Table 7–5, assume that cash on hand on December 31 amounted to $65,000 and that management wished to maintain a month-end cash balance no less than $50,000.

Table 7–5

Summary Schedule of Cash Flows
(in thousands)

	Jan.	Feb.	March	April	May	June	Total
Total receipts.................	$205	$200	$ 200	$245	$250	$285	$1,385
Total payments..............	236	156	381	161	181	201	1,316
Net inflow or outgo ( ).......	$(31)	$ 44	$(181)	$ 84	$ 69	$ 84	$ 69
Cumulative inflow or outgo ( ).	(31)	13	(168)	(84)	(15)	69	69
Beginning cash..............	65						65
Minimum cash..............	50						50
Funds above minimum needs or funds shortage ( ) end of month....................	(16)	28	(153)	(69)	0	84	84

It can be seen that a substantial shortage of cash is in prospect for March but that operations of the business should generate enough net cash inflow in April and May. Thus, the need for extra funds should last little more than 2 months. A brief analysis of the data reveals that the shortage is primarily attributable to the $200,000 equipment item scheduled for purchase in January and payment in March. Confronted with the forthcoming shortage of cash, management can plan to finance the needs by borrowing or other methods. Alternatively, it can reconsider the plans, perhaps postponing the $200,000 equipment purchase until March or April, in order to reduce the need for funds during this 6-month period.

We should emphasize again that those expenses which do not by their nature require cash outlay are not included in the cash forecast. Thus, we did not include the important expense item for manufacturers, depreciation, among the payments listed in our illustration. On the other hand, appropriately, we did include the payments for equipment purchased (except for the second purchase, for which payment was not due until July) and of dividends, even though they are not treated as expenses.

Our cash forecast illustration was based on a single set of plans for the business. Where alternative plans of operation are under consideration, it will often prove helpful to run cash forecasts based on each alternative plan. This permits the financial officer to determine the cash impact of each plan and to help top management decide on the best alternative in the light of this information.

The Essential Nature of the Projected Balance Sheet Method

The projected or *pro forma* balance sheet method of forecasting funds requirements is built around a forecast of the size of key balance sheet items at a selected date or dates in the future. Four major steps are involved in building a balance sheet forecast. The first involves forecast of the net investment required in each of the assets in order to carry out operations at the level planned on the date involved—say, a date 6 months ahead. Second, the liabilities that can be counted on without especial negotiation are listed. Third, the net worth on that date is estimated. The total of projected assets is then compared with the total sources of funds—debts and net worth. If the total of assets required exceeds the total for expected liabilities and net worth, the difference represents the additional sources that must be negotiated if operations and the buildup of assets to desired levels are to proceed as planned. Should the projected sources exceed the assets required, the excess presumably indicates the additional cash above the desired minimum level that will be on hand.

Put another way, in using the balance sheet approach, the forecaster is reasoning essentially as follows: To carry out our plans, certain predictable investment in assets is required. On the other hand, we can count on certain spontaneous sources of credit. The owners' investment in the business as of the future date can also be predicted. If our indicated sources fall short of meeting the desired investment in the various assets, the amount by which the sources must be expanded or asset investment held down is made apparent. If the expected sources more than cover the needed asset investment, a measure is provided of the cash cushion above minimum working balance needs or of cash available for uses beyond those envisioned in the original estimates.

Major Steps in Preparing the Projected Balance Sheet

With this general explanation of the approach in mind, let us now look more closely at each of the key steps in preparation of a projected balance sheet forecast. Let us assume that the subject firm has prepared fairly definite estimates of sales through to the date of the projected balance sheet and that in the light of the sales expectations, manufacturing and procurement schedules have been drawn up in some detail. Let us also assume that profits for the period have been budgeted.

A first item to be estimated is the anticipated investment in accounts receivable on the forecast date. As we have seen, a major determinant of the size of the receivables investment is the volume of sales. From past records of sales and receivables, the forecaster can determine what the relationship of receivables has been to sales in the past. The ratio suggested by past experience then should be adjusted in the light of any anticipated changes in credit terms, in the leniency with which credit will be granted, or in any other factor that might affect the receivables balance. The adjusted ratio then can be applied to the forecasted sales immediately preceding the forecast date.

Inventory needs can also be projected on the basis of "normal" inventory/sales relationships in the past. Alternatively, if purchase, production, and sales plans have been worked out in detail, the value of inventory that will be left on hand at the forecast date can be directly determined, using the approach: Beginning inventory plus purchases plus value added in manufacture less cost of goods sold equals value of inventory left on hand. All inventory values should be in terms of cost rather than selling prices.

The investment in fixed assets should next be forecasted. Planned purchases of new plant or equipment are added to the existing net investment in fixed assets, and planned depreciation is subtracted, in order to arrive at the estimated net investment in fixed assets on the forecast date.

Taking into account the considerations discussed in Chapter 4, the minimum cash balance that the firm would wish to carry is next determined.

Turning to the liability side of the balance sheet, the level of accounts payable on the forecast date must next be calculated. Based on the schedule of planned purchases, the assumed purchase terms, and the policy of the firm in meeting the due dates of trade payables, the purchases for which payment will not yet have been made on the forecast date can be tabulated and entered on the projected balance sheet as the anticipated accounts payable.

Accrued wages and other accrued expenses can also be calculated by reference to the production schedule, allowing for the usual lag between the incurring of the wage and other expense items and the required payment of the accrued expenses. Often it is useful to assume that these items are constant.

The amount of accrued income tax can be estimated directly if the probable profits and income tax rates are known. To the currently outstanding balance of accrued income taxes, the taxes accrued on income to be earned before the forecast date are added. Scheduled payments of taxes are then deducted to arrive at the amount of accrued taxes which will be outstanding on the forecast date.

Next, existing net worth must be adjusted for planned sales of stock, stock retirements, or any other such changes in prospect. Further, the addition to surplus from retained earnings (net profits after taxes less planned dividend payments) must be reckoned. The profits forecast is usually based on a projected income statement.

Let us suppose that when all the anticipated assets and all liability and net worth items are added up, the totals show \$1,200,000 for assets and \$1,050,000 for combined liabilities and net worth. Somehow, an additional \$150,000 must be secured from owners or creditors if the \$1.2 million level of assets is to be reached. Thus, the balancing figure, when planned assets exceed anticipated liabilities and net worth, represents the additional funds needed to permit the planned asset investment—or else the dollar extent by which the investment in assets must be reduced in order to bring it into line with available sources of funds.

On the other hand, if the sources exceed the assets needed, the excess presumably will accrue as cash above the required minimum amount.

It must be emphasized that the projected balance sheet method of forecasting depicts funds requirements as of the particular balance sheet date only. It does not show varying needs in the interim. In the case of companies whose needs fluctuate sharply from month to month, or seasonally, a forecast of needs based upon construction of a balance sheet as of a single distant date can be highly misleading. Maximum needs during a future period will be brought out only if the dates for projection of balance sheets are carefully selected so as to represent the balance sheet situation at times of maximum strain—that is, dates on which the combinations of heavy asset commitments and below normal liabilities and net worth are most severe.

Some forecasters, using the projected balance sheet approach, attempt to meet the problem of interim fluctuations by setting the minimum level of cash desired at a high enough level to take care of short-lived peak needs within the forecast periods. As indicated earlier, this can be a costly method of meeting peak and temporary needs.

Our outline of procedures useful in fashioning a projected balance sheet was based on the assumption that detailed plans for the business existed and were available to the forecaster—information of a sort that would have permitted preparation of a full-fledged cash flow forecast showing interim needs as well as those on the balance sheet date. But one of the attractions of the projected balance sheet approach is that it can be used (as a cash flow schedule cannot) to make rough—yet often highly useful—forecasts in situations where detailed forward plans of the sort necessary for cash flow forecasting do not exist.

Consider, for example, the following simplified problem. A program of sales expansion was being considered by the Baker Company. The owners of the company said they would be willing to advance any added funds needed to finance the expansion but asked whether they could look forward to the return of these additional advances within a year. Consequently, the question was raised: "If we double sales in the next year, what will be our need for additional funds at the end of one year?"

Let us see if we can answer the query by means of a projected balance sheet a year ahead. The current balance sheet was as shown in Table 7–6.

In the past year, sales had amounted to \$1.2 million and profits were

$60,000 after taxes. Production and sales were at a relatively even rate, and the sales at the doubled rate were also expected to be achieved evenly through the coming year. In the past, receivables and inventory had borne approximately the same relationship to sales as currently. Profits of 6% after taxes were expected on the new volume of $2.4 million. No dividends were planned. The Baker Company's productive facilities were adequate for the expanded volume, and new equipment to be purchased would about equal the depreciation to be charged during the year. Since detailed plans did not yet exist, other than for sales, we shall have to draw liberally on the relationships between the various assets and sales in the past as guidelines for estimating the needed investment in these assets at the doubled volume of sales.

Turning first to the estimate of receivables, we note that the current $120,000 figure represents approximately 10% of annual sales at the $1.2 million volume. In the absence of indications of change in this relation-

Table 7–6

Cash...................	$ 50,000	Trade payables..........	$120,000
Receivables.............	120,000	Accrued expenses........	90,000
Inventory..............	240,000	Net worth..............	600,000
Net fixed assets.........	400,000		
Total assets.......	$810,000	Total liabilities.....	$810,000

ship, we can estimate the receivables on $2.4 million sales at $240,000.

A similar approach to the inventory figure suggests a doubling of the current inventory to $480,000. Since the new acquisitions of fixed assets are expected to equal the depreciation to be charged, we can carry $400,000 forward as our net investment in fixed assets.

Now, let us assume that after consideration of all aspects of the problem, it is decided somewhat arbitrarily that $75,000 will provide an adequate minimum level of cash for the expanded operations.

Accounts payable in the past have fluctuated with the volume of purchases, which in turn have varied with sales. Similarly, accrued expenses have tended to vary with the level of production, which also has moved with sales. Consequently, we can forecast with some confidence a doubling of these items with a doubling of sales.

Net worth should increase by the amount of the profits after taxes, or $144,000, to a projected total of $744,000. Putting these estimates together, Table 7–7 shows the projected balance sheet.

Thus, we see that on the assumptions built into the above forecasted balance sheet, additional funds of $31,000 will be required a year hence to support operations at double the previous year's level of sales of $2.4 million. Although, as is true of any forecast, the estimate is only as reliable as the assumptions on which it was based, it does give an approximate answer to the owners' question which prompted this forecast. We can assure the owners that if operations proceed as we expect them to, they will need to keep only $31,000 in added investment in the firm for more than a year.

Upon reflection, it should be apparent that the balance sheet does not picture the maximum amount the owners will have to advance during the coming year if sales are to be built up to the $2.4 million annual volume at once. Receivables and inventory presumably will be doubled almost at once in line with the immediate doubling of sales. While trade payables and accrued expenses also can be expected to increase rapidly, the net worth account will only gradually be built up through retained earnings to the year-hence totals. Thus, the need for additional funds should peak

Table 7–7

Cash..................	$ 75,000	Trade payables.........	$ 240,000
Receivables............	240,000	Accrued liabilities.......	180,000
Inventory.............	480,000	Net worth.............	744,000
Net fixed assets........	400,000		
	$1,195,000		$1,164,000

Desired asset position...........	$1,195,000
Anticipated liabilities and net worth.......................	1,164,000
Additional funds needed.........	$ 31,000

at a high figure soon after the higher sales volume is reached. Our projected balance sheet as of a year ahead, though it supplies an answer to the specific question posed, definitely does *not* show the maximum amount the owners will have to advance the company in the interim months. A further balance sheet projection as of the anticipated date of maximum need or a monthly cash flow forecast would be necessary in order to establish this figure.

So far, we have spoken of the projected balance sheet method primarily as an alternative to the cash flow forecast approach. Actually, when a cash flow forecast has been made, it is a relatively simple matter to round out the forecast data by preparation of projected balance sheets also. If consistent assumptions are used in the two approaches, the cash flow forecast and projected balance sheets should yield similar estimates of cash as of corresponding dates.

Once projected balance sheets are constructed, it is easy to draw up projected statements of sources and uses of funds to accompany the balance sheet and operating statement projections.

Some Basic Problems in Effective Cash Forecasting

An important practical limitation to effective cash forecasting by either method, but especially to cash flow forecasting, is suggested by our earlier discussion. We refer to the fact that virtually all of the firm's operations affect its need for cash; and hence, in order to forecast cash needs closely, comprehensive and detailed planning data are required. Most of these data cover operational areas outside the direct responsibility of the financial officer. It is seldom hard for the financial officer to get his management associates to agree in theory that careful planning is important and desirable. But it often is more difficult, when day-to-day problems are clamoring for their attention, to get other department personnel to devote time and effort to the less obviously urgent task of planning well into the future. Unless top management appreciates the value of good forecasting and insists that planning is given appropriate attention throughout the organization, getting the necessary data on which to base his cash forecasts is likely to be a continuing problem for the financial officer.

Even if top management appreciates the need for careful planning and organizes to do a good job of it, the realistic forecaster knows that no matter how well he does his work, he cannot expect to prove exactly right in his forecasts. Most businesses operate in an atmosphere of change, and predictions of an inherently uncertain future necessarily are subject to error. Of course, the degree of predictability of the future varies among firms. Some are highly vulnerable to sharp fluctuations in sales or to disruptions of their plans owing to such events as strikes or the breakdown of key equipment. For example, firms whose sales are directly dependent on the vagaries of the weather have difficult cash forecasting assignments. Manufacturers of fertilizer being sold in areas where its use by farmers is sharply influenced by the season's rainfall face forecasting problems inherently more formidable than those of firms whose sales are made against firm orders placed long in advance of production.

Yet, even in those firms where the future is hard to predict, the choice is not one of planning or not planning. Rather, it is one of the degree to which the difficult job of planning is thought through and organized. And there is much that the firm whose future operations are inherently difficult to plan can do to make its forecasting as helpful as possible and to reduce management's problems of staying on top of the finances of the firm.

First, in the highly variable situation, it is particularly important that management recognize the likely margins of error inherent in its forecasts. So, at the least, management can avoid the hazards involved in attaching false connotations of accuracy in forecast data based on inherently tenuous assumptions.

Second, in situations where different assumptions as to key variables reasonably can be made, it may be helpful to prepare several different forecasts, each employing a different basic assumption as to the key variable. This, in effect, permits the financial officer to determine, "If this happens, then this will be the effect on cash . . . , etc." For example, a forecaster for the fertilizer concern referred to earlier might well run different forecasts using sales estimates based on normal, on heavy, and on sparse rainfall, and thus be forewarned as to the funds implications of each development. Along the same lines, some firms find it helpful to put together forecasts under combinations of assumptions that would picture likely minimum and maximum, as well as most probable, needs for the future period.

The computational problems of drawing up multiple projections that illumine the consequences of use of different assumptions as to key variables have been enormously reduced in many companies where computer programs have been developed for cash flow and/or balance sheet projections which permit the forecaster to manipulate the key variables. Obviously, it is important to evaluate the computer print-out results in the light of the key assumptions incorporated. As computer experts admonish, "Garbage input equals garbage output"; the computer makes calculations as programmed on the material put into the programs—it doesn't make magic.

Third, frequent revision of the forecasts as the future unfolds helps to keep them attuned to changing conditions and to provide as much advance notice as possible of developing changes in the need for funds. In the very dynamic firm the forecasts must be adjusted almost continuously if they are to be helpful in detailed financial planning.

Fourth, the organization of the firm and the way its finances are handled can be adjusted to fit the degree of variability of its future needs. For example, the firm subject to sudden, hard-to-predict cash outflows might well plan to carry a much larger cash balance than would be appropriate in a firm whose future needs were subject to more accurate prediction.

Further, experience with forecasting in the firm should lead to development of improved methods, both of preparation of forecasts and of their interpretation, which will reduce to a minimum the inherent margins of error. Learning by trial and error has its place in forecasting.

When forecasts of cash needs are prepared for use by top managers or outsiders such as bank lending officers, the forecaster should include with the forecast data a careful statement of the key assumptions upon which his forecasts were based. This gives the reviewer a better basis for understanding the figures and an opportunity to form his own judgments as to the validity of the key assumptions. Further, subsequent revisions of the forecasts based on differing assumptions can be more readily understood and appraised.

Long-Range Financial Forecasting

Just as financial management in the short term can be made far more effective by the practice of budgeting financial sources and needs, so in the long run it is desirable to have an estimate of the quantity and timing of funds movements. Of course, the farther into the future one looks, the less detail is seen, and the greater is the likely variance of the long-term estimate from the actual event. While it must be admitted that in a few cases the outlook is almost completely unpredictable (and a long-range forecast meaningless), in the majority of firms some meaningful specification can be made about the next few years.

There is every reason not to forecast in greater detail than the uncertainties of the situation permit. Early in World War II, one of the authors was shown a 3-year forecast, by months, of the detailed income statements and balance sheets of a company making military aircraft. It had been made with immense labor, and it was worthless, because everyone knew that the product was obsolescent and that any new product would have very different funds flow (as well as airflow) characteristics. A simple forecast, showing a few broad categories of inflow and outflow, was all that might usefully have been made.

On the other extreme, the electric and telephone utilities estimate their financial flows, and plan their expansion and its financing, 5, 10, and even 15 years ahead of actual construction. They are able to do so, of course, both because the demand for their product is related in a very stable way to the growth of production and population and also because (despite technological changes) the capital investment and other funds flow characteristics relative to volume are also stable.

A format for long-range financial forecasts found useful by many firms is one in which funds flows over the near future are tabulated in detail, the intermediate future is pictured in a more generalized way, and the long-term by even fewer categories. The short-term forecast often takes the form of a cash budget, while the longer term will be presented by pro forma funds flow statements with aggregate figures under such captions as: funds provided by operations, working capital changes, plant and equipment expenditures, tax payments, financial burden, and proceeds of new financing. Many of these items can be expected to have a steady ratio to sales, others are matters of contract or law, and the rest will reflect established policies concerning the security issues of the corporation.

PART IV

CAPITAL BUDGETING

chapter **8**

The Elements of the Investment Decision

THE NATURE OF BUSINESS INVESTMENT

The introductory chapters described the major categories of assets to which a business must commit its limited capital resources. The typical business, like an individual, finds many more opportunities to spend money than it has money to spend. Consequently, a primary need for decision making lies in the selection of the specific mix of investments through which, in combination with its human resources, the business will attempt to achieve its objectives.

The detailed plans for how the funds available during a given time period will be spent are normally divided into an *operating budget* and a *capital budget*. The operating budget includes expenditures for goods and services consumed during the fiscal year in the process of producing the income of that year. The capital budget includes expenditures the benefit of which is expected to be received over several income periods. From a practical standpoint, it is the set of choices involved in putting together a capital budget with which this and the succeeding two chapters are concerned. As we shall see, however, the analytical method developed to aid the decision process can be applied to any choice involving a change in the magnitude and timing of the income stream, and this could include a number of choices not normally found in a capital budget, such as the bond refunding described below.

To most businessmen the term *capital expenditure* or *capital budget* would call to mind the purchase of a major piece of equipment or the construction of a new plant or research facility. This means durable physical assets which will serve the business for many years. It implies a large lump-sum outlay at one point in time and a stream of savings or added earnings received for 5 or 10 or more years. In an accounting sense it means "capitalizing" the cost as an asset on the balance sheet and feeding it out to the income statement gradually by so-called depreciation charges over the expected useful life.

There are other kinds of expenditures, however, which, although very different in nature, involve precisely the same kind of financial analysis. For example, compare the purchase of a machine designed to automate a part of a production process and thereby save labor costs with an expenditure required to refund a bond issue—to replace an outstanding debt contract with another debt contract at a lower interest rate. In the year 1970, the act of bond refunding seems a wistful memory of years when interest rates were declining, thus presenting an opportunity to sell a new debt issue at a rate below the original offering. The recall of the original debt and repayment prior to maturity usually require a substantial premium over the face value of the debt: for example, a $100 bond might be refundable at $107. Thus there is a substantial initial outlay ($70 per bond) necessary to replace the original issue carrying, say, a 7% interest rate with a new one carrying, say, 6½%. Nevertheless, if the original interest charge has 15 years to run, the savings could be substantial.

In real terms the two investment proposals described above are very different. In financial terms they are identical in nature. Both involve a substantial outlay of capital now, the purpose of which is to lower costs and therefore increase net income for several years in the future. The analytical problem is how to find a logical framework for comparing a variety of similar proposals all differing in magnitude, timing, and certainty of the impact on funds flows.

While much of our discussion of this subject will be taken up with the analytical logic, it is important to bear in mind that in practice capital budgeting is also concerned with the organizational process by which a large business exercises its collective judgment on many competing uses for funds. Since many people are involved in producing and evaluating the various elements of a capital budget, there must be a system for delegating responsibility and for coordinating the total effort so that it produces a consistent and predictable result. If one were to describe a formal capital budgeting system in use in terms of the expenditure of time and energy by those responsible for it, one would have to say that the problems of logic—that is the intricacies of discounted cash flow—are minor in comparison with the unending problems of educating various layers of management to perform their appointed roles in gathering and processing the financial data upon which the final judgments will be made. Since investment decisions inherently involve risk, they include both subjective and objective elements. The delegation of judgment respecting the trade-off between risk and return for risk bearing is a particularly complex issue.

A final word of perspective before we plunge into the details of investment decision making concerns the relation between financial and nonfinancial considerations in business management. From a financial viewpoint it is convenient to assume that the ultimate purpose of a business enterprise is to create economic value and maximize profit. But a business is more than a money machine; it has a tangible role in society in producing a useful product or rendering an important service. Thus, while business policy may be phrased in part in terms of profit objectives, it is also phrased in terms of tangible goals related to its specific products and services and to the human organization that exists around these activities. In discussions of capital budgeting one often hears certain investments referred to as "mandatory" or "defensive" or "noneconomic," by which is meant that the management feels it must make the investment even though the financial benefit cannot be measured or appears to be unattractive. The compelling reasons are usually to be found in the nonfinancial goals of the business and in the simple fact that having chosen to be in the steel business, for example, you must survive in the steel business. This means doing the things necessary to the continuity of that business from month to month, including some investments which may cost a lot of money and produce a very low return. Of course, if there are many such low-return investments to be made, you may well wonder whether you want to stay in the steel business; but the option for a mature business organization to change industries usually takes considerable time to work out and is fraught with many uncertainties along the way. In the meantime the stream of capital requirements continues to flow.

Thus, while we shall be considering investment decisions on the assumption that choices can be made on the basis of financial benefit alone, we must keep in mind that in the real world the motivations and pressures to invest are more complex. As a result, the purity of the financial choice may be compromised.

MEASURING THE FINANCIAL IMPACT

The decision to commit a sum of money to a specialized business use has at the same time a negative and a positive effect. Given that the capital available to an individual business is finite, at least at a point in time, the decision to build a warehouse or buy a machine means that for a certain period of time those funds are denied to the many alternative uses which opportunities or events are urging on management. This is the negative implication. On the positive side the act of investment opens up the possibility of a stream of financial benefits resulting from the use of the asset in the form of increased income or decreased cost. Investment analysis is the process of measuring these expected benefits and relating them to the initial outlay needed to acquire them in such a way as to permit objective comparison with alternative opportunities.

There are two basic ways in which to measure the financial benefits of an investment. One of these is in terms of *incremental cash flow effects*. The analysis starts with the simple question: If we make this investment, what changes will take place in the cash outflows and cash inflows? To construct the analysis in terms of the impact on the corporate bank account gives the analysis a special managerial emphasis. This is so not only because these are terms readily understood by nonfinancial as well as financial management but also because the flow of real purchasing power is what will enable management to implement its future policy decisions.

Thus, the purchase of a $100,000 machine to automate some part of a production process means initially that there will be an outflow of $100,000 in cash when the check is written on the due date of purchase of the machine. When the machinery is installed and operating as intended, there will be a reduction in the work force so that the weekly wage payroll will be reduced by the amount formerly paid to the displaced workers. There will also be a reduction in related fringe benefit payments. Future cash outflows will also be reduced, since depreciation charges on the new machinery will reduce taxable income and therefore taxes payable. The decrease in future cash outflows for production is expected in time to substantially exceed the $100,000 originally paid. In the meantime, expendable funds are considerably reduced as a result of the decision.

A second way to measure the financial benefits is in terms of the *incremental effect* of the investment decision *on the value of the business*. This approach shifts the viewpoint to that of the shareholder and the worth of his investment. He wants to know whether an investment makes his shares more valuable and by how much. He wants the company to choose those investments that will have the maximum positive impact on value. Considered in terms of the accountants' measures of value as reflected in the balance sheet, the immediate effect of the purchase of a $100,000 machine for cash is nil: Cash decreases by $100,000, fixed assets increase by $100,000, and total assets are the same as before. In the accountants' view of value, the effects of the investment will emerge later through changes in the income statement, where net income measures the increase in value over units of time. Net income will be affected by changes in cost, not cash flow; that is, by changes in wage and other costs, changes in taxes, and most importantly by changes in depreciation charges. The changes in cost will follow accounting rules, which adjust the allocation of production expense to the income statement according to the flow of units sold. Thus, the controlling factor is the accountants' definition of net income and not the time when bills are actually paid.

Another important measure of value is the day-to-day judgment of the stock market. Here the dominant impact of the investment decision will be the way in which it may change expectations for net income or earnings per share—now and into the future.

As we get into the analysis of the capital budgeting process, we shall see that the basic quantities we are trying to measure and compare are cash flows and changes in net income. There are enough differences in viewpoint and measurement and timing to require us to look at both, though the preferred analysis nowadays is a cash flow analysis. The remaining parts of this chapter will be concerned with the specific data needed for a cash flow analysis and with the mechanics of relating flows that occur at different points in time. With the primary emphasis on cash flow, the reader will nevertheless be reminded from time to time of the need to look at the impact on near-term net income as well.

The first steps in the capital budgeting process require an estimate of the specific financial consequences of the individual investment expressed in a schedule of cash flows. Thus, if new assets are needed to establish the capacity to introduce a new product, there must be estimates both of the costs to buy, install, and put the assets into production and of the results of the selling, manufacturing, and other operations that will take place. All such estimates are uncertain, and some may be recognized to have wide margins of error.

In order to postpone questions of dealing with uncertainty, we have chosen as our example a possible use of funds through the purchase of a high-grade corporate bond. All of the procedures of capital budgeting can be brought to bear on such an investment opportunity. In fact, bond valuation, using time adjustment, has been a regular part of the work of investment analysts for many years. In recent years financial analysts have learned how to apply the same type of evaluation to the more complex and uncertain investment opportunities that exist outside the bond market, but there has been no change in the kinds of information needed or in the essential mathematics. Our choice of a possible purchase of a corporate bond is, therefore, a good example to use when introducing the basic procedures, and we shall use it as a project for the analysis known as capital budgeting.

Perhaps we should say to those of our readers who are already somewhat familiar with the subject that our presentation does not employ all the timesaving shortcuts familiar in practice. They add nothing to the quality of the results, and we have avoided them deliberately, in order to be sure that the structure of the logic of analysis is not concealed by any combination of steps that might easily confuse the inexperienced reader.

BASIC QUANTITIES TO BE ESTIMATED

A firm is assumed to have available to it at any time a number of alternative ways to invest its funds. These are termed *projects*, and the purpose of the capital budgeting procedure is to obtain an indication of the value each might contribute to the firm, so that the ones offering greater value can be chosen as the more desirable from the financial point of view.

Since this value indicator cannot be chosen without quantitative information, the first step in the work of capital budgeting is the projection of the amounts of cash flows, both in and out, related to the project, together with the time dimension of each flow. Such a schedule is referred to as a *schedule of cash flows*. Six quantities must be estimated to make up such a schedule. Three are in terms of quantity of money, two are in terms of time, and one is a rate of return.

1. The amount of the initial capital outlay necessary to acquire the project, and any later investment in the project.
2. The amount of cash (if any) that will be released when the investment is liquidated at the end of its productive life.
3. The net increase in future operating cash flows expected to result from this investment project—the stream of financial benefits.
4. The times at which the above inflows and outflows are expected to occur.
5. The expected productive life of the investment.
6. The rate-of-return standard by which this investment can be compared with alternative investments.

The first five of these elements of a cash flow analysis for a typical business investment are illustrated in Chart 8–1, showing their relationship to each other.

Initial and Later Investment

An *investment* takes place whenever an economic unit devotes some of its funds to the establishment of a project. By doing so, it removes resources from other possible uses and supplies them to the project in question. The amount that has been devoted to a project until the time it commences to receive net cash inflows from operations may be termed the *initial investment*.

We are not concerned here with the accountant's separation of "invested capital" from "expense." All movements of funds, no matter what their nature, having a net negative influence are part of the investment. Not only the cash outlays associated with the initial price of some property are needed, but also such items as installation costs for equipment must be included. Also (although frequently forgotten), there must be a determination of the addition to permanent working capital necessary to support the output of the new assets at the desired capacity. This may include, for example, the added inventory of materials in process related to a machine and the added accounts receivable related to an estimated increase in sales. In other words, any and all outlays necessary to produce the expected stream of benefits must be included.

Chart 8–1

The Basic Quantities of an Investment Analysis

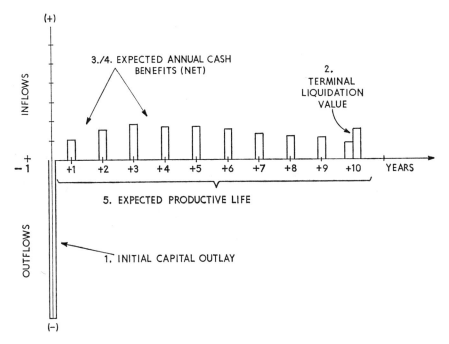

The desired figures are net of all related cash flows. If, say, a new machine has been intended as a replacement for an existing machine, certain variations in the calculation would occur. On the outlay side, changeover costs would be included. But there would probably be an inflow from the proceeds of disposing of the old machine.

Further investment in a project may take place later on, if a period of cash outflow occurs for any reason. Thus, if a particular division of a firm falls temporarily into a condition of seriously depressed sales volume resulting in net cash outflows, it can continue only by drawing funds away from alternative uses, and the process of investment is again taking place. It is important to search for all these later investments, because it is fundamental that a firm cannot enjoy income from a project until it is assured that all of the investment will be returned to it by the time the project ends. But at the moment it is the initial investment that concerns us.

Much of the detailed questioning we have just suggested is intended for use on projects that are less simple than our example of the purchase of a corporate bond. Yet, even in this case there are payments that make the net investment different from the quoted price.

Our project is the possibility of buying a 9% corporate bond, par

value $1,000, due in 10 years, at the market price of $1,043.50 to yield
$8\frac{5}{8}\%$. If this bond were purchased on the New York Stock Exchange, the
firm would make an initial investment of:

Market price....................	$1,043.50
Broker's fee....................	5.00
Delivery charge................	1.20
Total....................	$1,049.70

A corporate bond is a contract specifying that certain funds are to be
paid at certain times. It is the contractual specification that makes such
a project easier to deal with than a type of project where both time and
amount are uncertain. Here, the potential investor is assured of payments
of $90 a year (we assume their receipt at the end of each year of the
10-year period) and $1,000 at the end of the 10th year. The prospect of
this large payment at the end of the period leads us to write in general
terms about the problem of recovering invested capital.

Terminal Values

At the end of a project's productivity, the firm must have received and
retained for the purpose of reinvestment the amount of the funds that was
devoted to investment in the project. If this were not the case, and the
situation repeated itself, the firm would ultimately have no resources to
invest. Only after this return of capital has been provided for can one
speak of "income" from the project.

A firm looks for the recovery of its investment from two sources: (1)
the liquidation of the assets assigned to the project as they exist when
it ends, (2) the retention of enough of the proceeds from operations to
make up differences between final values and the amounts originally invested. Speaking of projects in general, one can say that nondepreciable
assets, such as elements of working capital, should preserve their value
during the project so that they can return funds equal to those invested in
them. Depreciable assets, especially special-purpose equipment, are usually liquidated for much less than cost. In a small number of cases, where
great appreciation in price can be anticipated (as might in a few instances
be expected of strategically located real estate or an investment in a
growth stock), the liquidation may not only return the initial investment
but contribute to the income. What the analyst must remember (many
forget) is that the exploration of *terminal value* or *residual value* must
never be omitted.

In the case of the bond, the terminal value is $1,000. Since the initial
investment was $1,049.70, we see that the depreciable portion of the
initial investment is $49.70. The facts concerning the investment may be
summarized as in Table 8–1.

Table 8–1

Time		Amount
Beginning........	Initial investment	$1,049.70
	Intermediate investment	none
End year 10......	Terminal value	1,000.00
By end year 10....	To be supplied from operations	$ 49.70

The Change in the Operating Cash Flows

As we have said, six quantities must be estimated to provide the basis for a time-adjusted cash flow analysis. The first, the amount of the capital investment required, and the second, its terminal value, were presented above, together with the needed time dimension. We now turn to the quantity resulting from the investment, namely, the change in the firm's operating cash flows.

It cannot be overemphasized that, as was the case for investment amounts, we are searching for the incremental change in cash—the difference between what the total cash received from the operations of the business would be if the change is not made and what cash the firm is expected to receive if the project is adopted. The desired number, it must be emphasized, is not an accounting figure, and it must not include any item which is not a cash movement. Also, we strongly recommend excluding at this stage any flows related to the financing that may be proposed to provide the needed investment. Financial devices can affect the final value put on a project, but value cannot be created by financial means if there is no value in the underlying project itself, and that is what we are now trying to estimate.

In the case of the projected investment in the corporate bond, the increase in cash flows is $90 a year for 10 years. This amount, however, is subject to income tax, and grave errors in capital budgeting can be committed if this factor is forgotten. We shall return to this point a few paragraphs further on.

The certainty and regularity of the estimate in this instance should not obscure the fact that the estimate of operating flows is difficult to make in most of the cases that require study. One proceeds from the great certainty associated with financial contracts, with their precise terms, through a variety of classes of projects where estimates are possible but uncertain.

Many investment projects cannot be expected to produce funds at an even rate over the length of life that it is reasonable to assume for their use. A project to introduce a new product is often slow in coming into profitability, if only because a growing market has been anticipated and the demand has yet to be experienced. A period of the collection of know-how, during which income is often reduced for some time, also often occurs in the early part of the project's life. A central period of profitability follows. Toward the close of its life a project can be expected to produce somewhat less than it did earlier, because of increased maintenance if nothing else. On the other hand, a project that revives the profitability of an existing operation, such as pumping an oil well where the natural flow has slowed, can be expected to show high net inflows at once, tapering off as time goes by. In the interests of financial analysis it is essential to attempt to describe irregularities and their timing, even though all must recognize that estimates of this kind are sure to be inaccurate.

Finally, there are some investment projects where one cannot set down an estimate of benefit in terms of the direct effect on cash flow. Some research work falls into this category, as well as the often-quoted example of the project to air-condition the factory lunchroom. Although in recent years new techniques have been devised to obtain useful quantitative estimates from some of these cases and the number of exceptions is therefore narrowing, some investment proposals will not permit the use of the procedures we are presenting here.

The Anticipated Length of Life

The fifth quantity to be estimated is the total time the project is expected to be productive. By the term *economic* or *productive life,* we refer to the period over which the equipment (or other investment) remains economically superior to alternative equipment that might be purchased for the same purpose—the period before it becomes obsolete. It is often difficult to estimate this time; yet, the effort must always be made, since the period of time within which a project must justify itself is extremely critical. An estimate based on the experience of persons who have spent considerable time in the business is often more useful than some technical estimate by either an engineer or a tax accountant.

Thus, there is uncertainty both in estimating income in years far removed from the time of making the forecast and in estimating the length of the economic life of productive assets. These combined uncertainties lead many firms to select for application as a general rule some term of years within which a project must justify itself—leaving possible gains in later years to be hoped for but not relied upon. Some analysts refer to this terminal date as a *horizon*—a happy choice of terms since we are dealing with operations requiring foresight.

Here again, experience is usually the ultimate guide. One can merely ask that those who have experience use it as carefully as possible. Too many managers use horizon times that are arbitrarily shorter than experience would seem to justify, as shown by the continued desirability of many projects years after the horizon has been passed or by the high terminal values at the horizon date. When this occurs, we have evidence

that decisions were based on erroneous assumptions. However, we expect
to find a horizon time often used in practice and to find it often an
arbitrary figure.

Effect of Tax Laws on Funds Flows

Few economic units enjoy freedom from taxation. In fact, the forces
of taxation are too large to ignore, and the analyst must recognize them,
giving particular attention to the options his firm faces that may permit
lessening the adverse effects of the tax claim on the project he is studying.
This may be a most complex matter. We chose the corporate bond in
order to stay as far as possible from such details, and we shall take the
simplest way out for the particular case. This chapter is already too
complex for us to do otherwise. Thus, we assume an unchanging income
tax rate of 48% and tabulate and chart the net funds flows in Table 8–2
and Chart 8–2.

Table 8–2

Before- and After-Tax Funds Flows,
from Proposed Investment in 9%, 10-Year Bond
(tax rate 48%)

	Time 0	Years 1–10		Year 10	
		B.T.	A.T.	B.T.	A.T.
Net investment.......	$1,049.70				
Annuity..............		$90.00	$46.80		
Principal............				$1,000.00	$1,023.85*

* Tax credit for capital loss added to principal: ($49.70)(0.48) = $23.85.

The Investment Standard or Opportunity Rate

The final quantity we need in order to begin the analysis is the rate-of-
return standard by which the individual project is to be judged. The
derivation of this standard—variously referred to as the *ROI* (*return-on-
investment*) criterion, *hurdle rate*, or *cutoff rate*—is a matter of considerable complexity, to which we will devote a whole chapter (Chapter
10). Among other things it must be related to the relative riskiness of
the project. The example we have chosen—the investment in a high-grade
corporate bond—is relatively safe, and the appropriate investment standard would therefore be lower than for some other alternatives. At this
point, we shall not try to specify the precise rate. Since we are talking
about a popular financial investment in a well-organized and continuous
market, the opportunity rate is probably very close to the actual yield on
the bond. For more specialized, unique corporate assets the rate on

Chart 8–2

Chart of After-Tax Funds Flows, Proposed Investment in 9%, 10-Year Bond

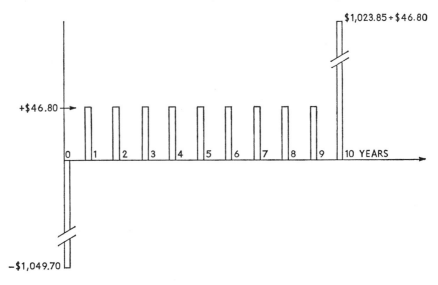

alternative investment opportunities of comparable risk could be quite different from the expected return on the proposed investment.

BACKGROUND MATHEMATICS

We have now accumulated, for the project to buy the corporate bond, the six estimates necessary to permit considering one project as an alternative to another. We need one more thing to answer the question: Does the investment promise more value to the firm than other ways to use the same funds? It is a procedure for relating quantities that occur at different points in time to a common point of reference. Here enter the mathematics of time adjustment; so we turn away from the example so far used to explain the mathematics required. We hope that even the reader with background in this technique will skim the following paragraphs, to refresh his memory and to see the order in which the procedures are introduced.

The Procedure of Time Adjustment

COMPOUNDING A SINGLE SUM. We first turn to *compounding*, that is, the growth in the value of funds invested to yield an income when the income received is not consumed but is itself retained and invested. This process is one with which most readers will be familiar from such well-advertised operations as savings accounts on which interest is compounded. We shall then be better able to understand *discounting,* which looks in the other direction along the time scale. Discounting is the procedure more often used in financial analysis.

Four quantities must be specified:

1. *The rate of return:* In the following exposition we shall use 4% and 10%, in order to see the changing results from using different rates.
2. *The frequency of compounding:* In the following examples (and throughout this chapter) annual compounding will be used.
3. *The amount of funds in question:* It is convenient to use the sum of $1 to develop the formulas, since if one knows how the values of this sum are affected by time, one can compute the values of any other sum by simple multiplication.
4. *The length of time from the chosen date:* This may be measured in days, weeks, etc., so that for the sake of generality, one refers to the *period* rather than to some specific unit of time. One warning is necessary here. The rate of return used must be stated consistently with the actual length of time period. Thus, 6% per year becomes 0.5% per month, and so on.

At present we are searching for an answer to the question: How much will a sum increase over a stated time interval if it is invested at the present time at compound interest?

The growing amount that will be found at later times from an investment at the present time is referred to as the *compound amount* (of a single sum). Interest is computed on the original sum and then added to the original sum at the end of the first period. The new and larger principal is then the base for the interest calculation in the second period, and so on. Jumping over the detailed mathematics, we can turn to almost any set of tables for business computations, among which we shall find values for the compound amount of a single sum invested at a given time. Table 8–3 is a portion of such a table. Note how the higher rate produces values that are increasingly greater than those obtained from the lower rate.

In Table 8–3 the present time is designated by a zero, and may be called "time zero." It can also be read "beginning of year one," with 1 designating "end of year one," 2 "end of year two," and so on.

DISCOUNTING A SINGLE SUM. The process of compounding discloses how the value of an investment made at the present time grows in later time. We now turn to discounting, a process that in financial analysis also looks at times following the present but asks a different question. Instead of asking, as in Table 8–3, "To what value would $1 invested today at 4% increase in 5 years?" discounting is designed to respond to the question: "Assuming invested funds earn 4% compound interest, what (smaller) amount would be required for investment today in order to accumulate to the amount of $1 in 5 years from now?"

Table 8–3

Compound Amount of $1

At the End of n Periods	Rate 4%	Rate 10%
n = 0	1.000	1.000
1	1.040	1.100
2	1.082	1.210
3	1.125	1.331
4	1.170	1.464
5	1.217	1.611

The answers to such questions are determined by using the reciprocals of the values in the table of compound amounts, for the reasons exemplified in the following instance. Let us use for our example four periods and 4%. Table 8–3 shows that if $1 is compounded for this time and rate, it will increase to $1.17. Therefore, to have only $1 at the end of four periods of compounding, we obviously need to invest less than $1, in proportion to the ratio of 1.00 to 1.17, as follows:

If an investment of: $\dfrac{1.000}{1.170}$
       will produce   in 4 years at 4%

Then an investment of: $\dfrac{x}{1.000}$
       which will produce   in 4 years at 4%
will be in the same proportion.

Thus: $\dfrac{1}{1.17} = \dfrac{x}{1} = 0.855$ (i.e., the reciprocal of 1.17).

The number so produced is known among financial analysts as the *present value* (at the selected time and rate), which if invested now at compound interest will produce $1 at a specified date in the future. The term *discounted value* is also used, although less frequently. Specifically, the investment of $0.855 at 4% compounded annually will produce $1 at the end of the fourth year.

Since discounted values are often used in financial calculations, a table of present values is provided in this book (Table A, at page 932). For convenience, we reproduce a portion of it in Table 8–4.

EXAMPLES OF COMPOUNDING AND DISCOUNTING. We now present two simple examples of how problems of compounding and discounting arise in business, and briefly indicate the nature of their solution.

EXAMPLE 1. A firm with a major debt maturity at the end of 2 years sets aside $500,000 for investment in tax-exempt bonds at 4% to help meet the maturity. How much will be available from this source when the debt matures?

The problem is one of compounding. The initial date is the present and the period is 2 years. From Table 8–3, we find 1.082 as the compound amount of $1 at 4%. Multiplying by $500,000 gives us $541,000, which is the sum that will be on hand.

EXAMPLE 2. A firm has granted a license to another firm to use one of its patented processes, upon a promise to pay $1 million 5 years in the future. The licensing firm now advises the licensee that it would prefer payment at present and that it is ready to negotiate a settlement. What price should the licensee suggest?

The problem is one of discounting, the difficulty being the selection of

Table 8–4

Present Value of $1
(reciprocals of Table 8–3)

Received n Periods Hence	Rate 4%	Rate 10%
n = 0	1.000	1.000
1	0.962	0.909
2	0.925	0.826
3	0.889	0.751
4	0.855	0.683
5	0.822	0.621

a rate. Suppose the licensee learns that the licensor could, as an alternative to making the settlement, borrow at 4%. Surely it would not accept a price computed at a higher rate. Using 4%, and Table 8–4, we find the discounted value of $1 to be received 5 years hence is $0.822. The suggested value for a settlement "on a 4% basis" is, then, $822,000.

EXAMPLE 3. A factor often given importance when a firm is deciding whether to own or lease land and buildings is the residual value of the property that the firm would own if it bought rather than leased. Suppose that a certain property now costing $1 million is expected to be worth $2 million (after allowance for taxes on the capital gain) at the end of 25 years. How much importance should this terminal value have on a decision now, when the company has the option to buy or to lease?

The problem is one of discounting. Let us assume that the firm averages 10% return (after taxes) on assets invested in the business. One way to obtain $2 million at the end of 25 years is by holding the real estate. An alternative way would be to invest some funds now and use them at 10% to produce $2 million.

A calculation is necessary to find what present investment at 10% will produce $2 million 25 years hence. From Table A, p. 932, we find that at 10% the present value of $1 to be received after 25 periods is 0.092. Multiplying by $2 million, we obtain $184,000. Thus, the desired value can be obtained either by using $184,000 in the business and allowing profits to compound, or by spending $1 million to buy the property. Obviously, the latter choice requires a much larger commitment of present funds to reach the desired results. It is therefore less valuable than the alternative opportunity that calls for $184,000 now.

The Behavior of Values over Time

Before we apply our newfound skill to make a time adjustment of the figures so far accumulated, let us pause to consider some generalizations about the behavior of values over time. Chart 8–3 has been designed to

Chart 8–3

Effects of Time Adjustment: Single Sum

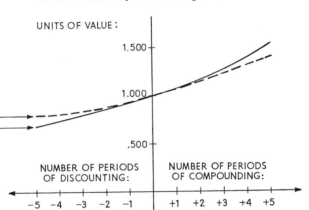

show the continuity of the mathematics of compounding and discounting. Time zero is represented in the center of the horizontal scale. The effects of compounding are shown to the right and of discounting are shown to the left. The basic relationships to be observed are simple but very important:

1. The value of a sum invested at any time grows as time passes.
2. The necessary investment to produce a future sum decreases as the time allowed to produce it is increased.
3. Both these effects are magnified as the rate of return increases.

Discounting an Annuity

We have now equipped ourselves with the mathematics necessary to bring the promised flows of our investment project to a common figure, the present value, but we can save time in this and later work by extending the analysis to consider the case of a series of equal sums received or paid over a number of periods. This situation occurs frequently in business and is illustrated by our earlier example of the interest received on a 10-year bond. It fits the definition of an *annuity:* A series of equal payments at fixed intervals.

When we introduced discounting, we said that the procedure answered the question: "What (smaller) amount would be required for investment today in order to accumulate (at a given interest rate) to the amount of *x* dollars *n* periods from now?" The parallel question for an annuity is to ask "What amount would be required for investment today in order to produce an annuity of *x* dollars per period over a specified number of periods in the future?"

The answer can be found by considering each payment separately and computing its individual present value. Let us take 4% and 5 years for the purposes of our example. Table 8–4 can be used. From it we see that:

It takes 0.822 to produce $1 in 5 years,
It takes 0.855 to produce $1 in 4 years,
It takes 0.889 to produce $1 in 3 years,
It takes 0.925 to produce $1 in 2 years,
It takes 0.962 to produce $1 in 1 year.
Total 4.453, value of annuity at period —5

This example shows how the desired present values of annuities can be obtained by accumulating values from the table of the present values of a single sum. Such a table has been included in this book as Table B at page 933; but for convenience, we reproduce a portion in Table 8–5.

Table 8–5

Present Value of $1 Received Periodically for *n* Periods

Number of Periods	Rate 4%	Rate 10%
0	0	0
1	0.962	0.909
2	1.886	1.736
3	2.775	2.487
4	3.630	3.170
5	4.452*	3.791

* The difference between this figure and 4.453, the value of the annuity given above, is due to rounding.

When we were dealing with the changing values of a single sum over time, we ended our explanation with a diagram. A similar one, Chart

8–4, can be presented for annuities, although the situation is more complex, so that the values get larger as one proceeds away from the present. This is because of the periodic payments of $1 that are involved. The reader will also note here, as in the simpler case, that changing the rate of return has considerable influence on the values, especially as time becomes more remote. In each instance the higher the rate, the greater the advantage to a person who invests funds to purchase the annuity. That is,

Chart 8–4

Effects of Time Adjustment: Annuity

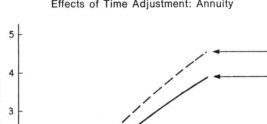

if 10% is applied, an annuity will cost less than if the 4% rate were applied.

EXAMPLES. As before, we conclude our explanation of the derivation of tables of present value for annuities with examples taken from business situations.

EXAMPLE 1. Analysis of a certain investment project indicates that it will produce $50,000 a year, before taxes, for 10 years. How much could the company justify investing in this project if other investments are available at 4%? At 10%?

The problem is the evaluation as of now of an annuity whose terminal date is 10 years from the present. Using Table B we find the present value factor of $1 a period for 10 periods to be 8.111 for 4%, and 6.145 for 10%. Multiplying each factor by $50,000, we find $405,550 for 4% and $307,250 for 10%. These are the sums that could be invested at the specified rates to produce $50,000 a year for 10 years.

EXAMPLE 2. Taking the figures as developed in Example 1, assume that the firm finds that $350,000 is required as an investment to establish the project. Since this number is more than the present value at 10%, the firm should not undertake the project if it has other opportunities on which 10% can be earned. The firm should, however, consider the project an excellent one if the alternative opportunities are offering 4% return.

Amortization of Loans

With increasing frequency in business practice, the terms of payment of long-term loans are designed so that the debtor makes a *level payment* of the same sum each time, the sum being large enough to cover the interest due and leave the necessary balance to be applied to the reduction of principal. The problem can be stated: Given the present value, the term of the arrangement, and the rate of interest, how does one arrive at the annuity?

The table of present values gives us the value of an annuity of $1 per year. For instance, at 10% for 5 years, the present value is 3.791. The following calculation derives the annuity that $1, invested now, will buy.

If an annuity of: $\dfrac{1.000}{3.791}$
has a present value of:

Then an annuity of: $\dfrac{x}{1.000}$
which has a present value of:
will be in the same proportion.

Thus, $\dfrac{1}{3.791} = \dfrac{x}{1} = 0.264$ (the reciprocal of 3.791) .

In other words, an investment of $1 today will buy an annuity of $0.264 for 5 years, assuming a 10% interest rate is applied. Knowing the specification of an annuity, you multiply by the factor in Table B to get the present value. Or, knowing the amount at hand, you divide by the factor in Table B to get the annuity.

We have already presented in Example 1 above an instance of the former operation. Here is an example of the latter.

EXAMPLE. A corporation borrows $5 million for 20 years at 6%. What is the level of payment that will pay principal and interest on an annual basis?

From Table B we find the present value of an annuity of $1 for 20 years at 6% to be 11.470. Dividing $5 million by 11.470, we obtain $435,920, the desired amount.

We have now reviewed the basic elements of an investment analysis and the arithmetic process by which we can relate these elements at a common point in time. We are ready to consider the central issues which management must cope with in discharging its responsibility for rational investment decisions.

chapter 9

Determining Investment Priorities: The Analytical Framework

The Dynamics of Investment Choice

Consider for a moment how investment proposals arise in the typical business enterprise. Contrary to the impression given by many financial articles and books, the production manager does not awake each morning with the thought: "How can I make a 15% return (after taxes) on investment today?" Rather, he wakes up with a set of practical problems relating to production targets, deadlines, cost standards, and technological difficulties; and he struggles to solve them. In the process, ideas emerge that suggest the purchase of a new machine, a change in the assembly line, an R&D program, or the construction of a new plant, all of which require money as well as time and effort and ingenuity.

With every manager busy at his assigned role and constantly turning up new ways to spend the company's capital, the result is a steady stream of needs, the scale of which is often substantially in excess of the flow of funds becoming available for investment. It is very important that we should be aware of this dynamic character of the problem. At any given time, there will be a set of investments on which a commitment has already been given, a set of specific proposals currently on the table and under review, a set of proposals half formed in the minds of management, and an as yet undefined set of proposals that the course of future events will certainly unfold. A vigorous management will make sure that this stream will continue, even though it may vary in magnitude from time to time.

The procedures of capital budgeting deal with this difficult, open-ended decision process by arbitrarily dividing the future into segments of time (planning periods) and reviewing only those alternatives which management believes can be effectively implemented during the next planning period. This finite set of proposals is then considered in the light of the funds expected to be available during that period.

The review process has two basic steps. The first is to determine the order of preference among the available proposals—a ranking or priority list by which the financial benefit of each is clearly and objectively identified. When funds are limited, choices may have to be made between what will be done and what will have to be left undone. The first order of business of this chapter will be a consideration of the basic procedures for ranking in common use today. These relate primarily to the discounting process described in the preceding chapter. There are also some simpler methods in use which we should know about.

It might appear that if we are provided with a reliable system of ranking alternatives, the job is done. All that is left is to determine the amount of available funds and approve proposals in order of descending financial benefit until the funds are exhausted. Some companies do in fact take this approach. But this implies that a business should invest all available funds regardless of the rate of return on the less desirable proposals, and this is an idea most of us would instinctively reject. There must be some level of expected return—15%, 10%, 5%—below which the company should retain the liquid funds on the assumption that the future will offer better alternatives than some of those now being considered.

Thus, the second major step in the investment review process is to determine an investment standard—a minimum acceptable rate of return which all proposals must meet. This standard is sometimes referred to as a *hurdle rate*, suggesting a level of performance that all proposals must clear in the race for approval. It is also referred to as a *cutoff rate*, meaning a level of return used to cut off part of the list of proposals, which are ranked in descending priority, and thus to separate the list into an "accept" and "reject" category. The determination of the investment hurdle rate is the subject of Chapter 10. We shall find it a difficult problem to resolve in terms that can be applied in practice with confidence.

Chapter 9 will also have something to say about a matter involved in both the ranking process and the setting of hurdle rates, namely, how to deal with varying degrees of risk or uncertainty as to the expected results. This, too, is an area of considerable conceptual and practical difficulty. Nevertheless, it is part of the real world and ways must be found for providing analytical guidelines that reconcile rationality and applicability. The theorist can retreat into a world of certainty; the practitioner cannot.

Ranking by the Internal Rate-of-Return Method

Several approaches may be taken in arriving at a ranking of investment proposals arranged in order of the financial benefit they are expected to produce. Some of these approaches make use of the mechanics of time adjustment discussed in the preceding chapter. We will consider these first, since they are regarded as being the most "rational," i.e., as having the best logic for relating the important variables. We will take up the less sophisticated approaches later and compare their strengths and weaknesses.

One of the widely used methods of ranking, which views the decision in terms of incremental cash flow effects and takes account of the timing of the changes, is known as the *internal rate-of-return* method. Given an investment expected to produce a stream of net cash benefits, this method responds to the question "What rate of discount would give the stream of future net cash benefits a combined present value equal to the present investment required to purchase the stream?" We can best explain the method by means of an example.

A real-world example is that of a company which, as part of its annual capital budgeting review, was considering whether to take advantage of the purchase option on its computer equipment. The equipment had been installed for some time and was currently under a rental contract. The general problem was how to compare this investment option with the many other investment proposals currently before the capital budgeting committee.

The question of purchase versus lease had a number of technical aspects, which we will not consider here. It is interesting to note that this proposal could be considered as a pure financial investment; that is, whether the computer was owned or leased made no difference to the actual operations of the computer installation and its team of employees. For many capital assets, use is necessarily tied to ownership, so that operating considerations become mixed with the purely financial or investment considerations in presenting the proposal. This was not the case here; the financial aspects were therefore clearly dominant.

Let us look at the details of the case in Table 9–1. The computer was judged to have a remaining economic life of 5 years, over which time rentals ranging from $690,000 to $760,000 were calculated in relation to expected usage. Purchase would eliminate these rental payments, but there would be some continuing outlays for tab equipment, maintenance, and insurance. There were also changes in taxes payable to be considered in line with expected changes in taxable income (see Table 9–4). The net cash flow effect of all this is shown on the line headed "Net Increase in Cash Flows" and ranges from $625,000 improvement in year 1 to $388,000 in year 5.

So, in simple financial terms a cash outlay of $2,033,000 now buys this stream of inflows in the future. In terms of absolute numbers this stream adds up to $2,548,000, but these are dollars in later years, which are not as valuable as today's dollars because today's dollars have a head start in producing future income. One method of comparing these amounts is to find the discount rate that gives the future savings a com-

Table 9–1

Measuring the Benefit from a Computer Purchase vs. Lease Option:
Internal Rate-of-Return Method
(dollar figures in thousands)

			Year			
	0	*1*	*2*	*3*	*4*	*5*
Total cost of purchase....	$2,033					
Outlay, continued rental........		$690	$710	$724	$745	$760
Costs under ownership						
Tab rental.................		$ 45	$ 28	$ 28	$ 28	$ 28
Maintenance...............		67	69	75	79	84
Insurance.................		7	7	7	7	7
Total.................		$119	$104	$110	$114	$119
Expected cash savings.........		$571	$606	$614	$631	$641
Change in taxes payable (from						
Table 9–4, alternative B)...		$ (54)	$ 32	$104	$180	$253
Net increase in cash flows.......		$625	$574	$510	$451	$388
		FACTORS FROM TABLE A (p. 932)				
P.V. at 10%.................	$1,974	0.909	0.826	0.751	0.683	0.621
P.V. at 8%..................	$2,071	.926	.857	.794	.735	.681
P.V. at 8.8%...............	*$2,033 (approx.)					

* The discount rate that gives a present value of $2,033 is obtained by extrapolation:

$$\frac{2{,}071 - 2{,}033}{2{,}071 - 1{,}974} \times 2\% = 0.8\% \text{ (approx.)} .$$

bined present value of $2,033,000—in other words, equates them to the
purchase price. This rate is found by trial-and-error calculations using
Table A. Starting arbitrarily with 10%, we find the present value to be too
low (see Table 9–1). Since the difference is not great, we next try a
slightly lower discount rate, 8%, and find the present value at that rate
above the purchase price. The rate which equates obviously lies between
8% and 10%. By extrapolation we calculate the desired discount rate
to be approximately 8.8%.

In the same manner all other competing proposals could be reduced
to the discount rate that equates their expected stream of benefits to the
initial outlay in each case, producing a ranking such as the following:

Project D:	Project A:	Project C:	Project E:	Project B:
16%	13%	8.8%	7%	6%

Thus, a confusing array of opportunities, which differ widely in operational function and in amounts and timing of outflows and inflows, is
readily compared in a familiar rate-of-return form. Our computer pro-

posal, Project C, is clearly number 3 on the list. If funds are not available for all, Projects D and A will be given precedence unless nonfinancial considerations for some reason dominate the choice.

The internal rate-of-return (IRR) method, sometimes referred to as the *implicit rate of interest* or the *discounted cash flow rate* (DCF), has wide practical appeal because rate-of-return standards are commonly expressed in percentage terms, and thus a feel for the relative "efficiency" of a project in its use of capital is quickly transmitted. However, writers on the subject have brought to our attention an inherent assumption of the IRR method which is open to question under some circumstances. The assumption is that all cash flows generated by the investment, including income on income (compounding), are reinvested for the rest of the project's economic life at the same internal rate. In our computer example all future flows were related to the present outlay by one rate—8.8%.

The assumption is innocent enough so long as the IRR of the individual project is close to the average or typical return realized by the company in its investment area. Reinvestment at that rate is a reasonable assumption. But suppose a particularly favorable project works out at an IRR of 25% whereas the average return is 10%. Then the assumption about all funds released being reinvested at 25% is highly unrealistic. Because of this problem with the method, most writers concerned with cleaning up the logic of capital budgeting recommend an alternative approach to time-adjusted comparisons. This approach is to rank projects in terms of their present value calculated from a common discount rate. We now turn to examine this method.

Ranking Projects by Present-Value Differentials

The new ingredient in the present-value approach is that we are provided with a standard discount rate to be used in all cases to find the present value of the future stream of benefits. For the moment we will not respond to the obvious question as to where that rate comes from. To provide a satisfactory answer would require an extensive digression. We will devote an entire chapter to this subject (Chapter 10) and will merely say here that the rate of discount is unique to each company and is its minimum acceptable return on investment—the so-called *hurdle* or *cutoff rate* referred to earlier in this chapter. Since this is the rate of return that the company expects to meet or exceed on all of its invested dollars, it is an appropriate discount rate to answer the objections raised with respect to the internal rate-of-return method.

Once the expected changes in cash flow have been worked out for a given investment project, the application of the present-value method is simple. If the returns happen to be the same from year to year, the annuity method of Table B can be used. If the benefits are uneven, then Table A is used, as in the case of the following figures reproduced from

Table 9–1. The computer purchase was expected to realize the following cash savings:

		Year		
1	2	3	4	5
$625,000	$574,000	$510,000	$451,000	$388,000

Assume that the company in question uses an investment hurdle rate for all proposals of 10% after taxes. The above amounts are then discounted at this rate to produce a combined present value of $1,974,000. Since we were told that it would cost $2,033,000 to acquire the computer, it is clear that this is not a desirable investment. We would be paying more for it than it is worth in present value of expected benefits. The hurdle rate indicates that the company is confident it could earn 10% or better in alternative uses of the money.

It might be helpful for some readers to be reminded as to just what the $1,974,000 of present value represents. Table 9–2 shows the details. It should be clear that even though the physical asset is assumed to be valueless after 5 years, the expected savings will preserve the financial investment *and* produce a compound rate of return of 10% (assuming that $1,974,000 and not $2,033,000 is invested). Each amount shown as the terminal value across Table 9–2 represents the original sum plus interest each year at the 10% rate compounded. Thus, it can be said that the present-value analysis makes adequate provision for depreciation of physical assets by assuming the preservation of the original investment in all its calculations.

As already indicated, the present-value method produces a number to be compared with the cost of the investment. If it exceeds the cost, the proposal is acceptable. While this calculation provides the information for an accept/reject decision, it does not enable us to rank proposals, since it is an absolute amount that is primarily a function of the size of the investment. In order to rank proposals, we need one more calculation, known as the *profitability index:* a ratio of the present value of the benefits to the original outlay.

Assume we are comparing two investment proposals having different original outlays, periods of savings or revenue, and patterns of savings or revenue. One, Project A in Table 9–3, costs $95,000 and is expected to have a useful life of 5 years and cash savings ranging from $15,000 to $40,000 per year. The other, Project B, is expected to cost $450,000 as the initial outlay, to have a useful life of 10 years, and to have annual cash benefits ranging from $40,000 to $175,000 per year. Initial inspection of this information gives no clear answer as to the preferred alternative.

Table 9-2

Net Increase in Cash Flows of Table 9–1 Broken Down to Show
Preservation of Investment and 10% Compound Rate of Return

Present Value	Year 1		Year 2		Year 3		Year 4		Year 5	
	Interest at 10%	Total Value	Interest at 10%	Total Value	Interest at 10%	Total Value	Interest at 10%	Total Value	Interest at 10%	Total Value
$ 568	$57	$625	$52	$574	$46	$510	$41	$451	$35	$388
474	48	522	42	464	37	410	32	353		
383	39	422	34	373	29	321				
308	31	339	27	292						
241	24	265								
$1,974										

Table 9–3

Comparison of Profitability Indexes of Two Investment Proposals

	Expected Flows		10%	Present Values	
	Project A	Project B	Factor	Project A	Project B
Initial outflow......	$ 95,000	$ 450,000		$ 95,000	$450,000
Future inflows:					
Year 1.........	$ 20,000	$ 40,000	0.909	$ 18,000	$ 36,000
2.........	35,000	125,000	.826	29,000	103,000
3.........	40,000	150,000	.751	30,000	113,000
4.........	40,000	175,000	.683	27,000	120,000
5.........	15,000	175,000	.621	9,000	109,000
6.........		150,000	.564		85,000
7.........		125,000	.513		64,000
8.........		100,000	.467		47,000
9.........		50,000	.424		21,000
10.........		50,000	.386		19,000
	$150,000	$1,140,000		$113,000	$717,000

Profitability index:

$$\text{Project A:} \frac{113,000}{95,000} = 1.19$$

$$\text{Project B:} \frac{717,000}{450,000} = 1.59$$

The first step in providing the answer is to reduce each stream of benefits to its present value by applying the corporate investment hurdle rate as the discount factor. Here we have used 10%. Project A is found to have a present value of $113,000 and Project B, a present value of $717,000. These amounts are then related to the initial investment in each case to produce a ratio: $113/95 = 1.19$ and $717/450 = 1.59$. These profitability indexes show the relative gain of each investment on a common basis of comparison. They show that Project B is clearly superior to Project A.

Assessing the Effects on Reported Income

So far we have stressed the ranking of investments in terms of cash flows. If used intelligently and consistently, the time-adjusted cash flow analysis should produce the best selection of alternatives aimed at maximum long-term growth in the value of the firm. However, management must also consider the near-term impact of investment decisions, particularly as they relate to the income statement. In the process of evaluating company and executive performance, the earnings per share for the current year and the years immediately following have a special significance, of which all chief executives are fully aware.

For any major increment of investment, therefore, management would be interested in a measure of the effect on earnings. Returning to the example of the proposed computer purchase, we can recalculate the results, this time in terms of the net change in reported income. Since the method of depreciation is critical here and since we are considering reported income, we will produce two sets of figures, one on a straight-line basis and one on an accelerated basis. The results are shown in Table 9–4.

The first thing to be seen in these results is that if the company was reporting earnings to the shareholders based on accelerated depreciation, this investment would actually reduce earnings in the first year by $54,000. This points up the possibility that an investment can have a substantial positive cash flow but a negative effect on income in a given year. After the first year the increment of earnings would be positive and would increase at a rapid rate from year to year. By contrast, if the company was reporting earnings on a straight-line basis, there would be increased earnings in every year as a result of the investment. (The assumption here is that the same method of depreciation is used for tax and public reporting.)

Other than to show that the impact on the income statement would be positive, these calculations are of little use for comparing one investment proposal with another. In the years before time adjustment came into wide usage (and even today), many companies developed a basis of comparison by averaging the expected net earnings over the useful life of the investment and calculating the average as a percentage of the dollars invested. In this case the average annual earnings (straight line) are $102,800, which is 5.1% of the original investment or a 10.1% return on the average investment—a more appropriate number, since the $102,800 is after allowance for depreciation.

This basis of ranking has the inherent weaknesses of an average as well as the arbitrariness of accounting conventions, but it stands on familiar ground—a comparison of an income statement number with a balance sheet number. As indicated, it is still in common use and is what many companies would mean when they refer to the average *ROI* on an investment proposal. From our viewpoint, it should be seen as a crude but useful supplement to the discounted cash flow method, because it checks on the relative merits of investments as they relate to the important matter of reported earnings. A check of this sort on first-year and average change in reported earnings is particularly important for major increments of investment where the change could be substantial.

The Use and Misuse of Payback

We have saved the simplest method of ranking to the last—the much maligned *payback criterion*. The payback period is a measure of the time it will take to recover the original investment from the resultant improve-

Table 9–4

Statement of Income from Proposed Purchase of Computer
(dollar figures in thousands)

	Year					
	0	1	2	3	4	5
Cost of purchase	$2,033					
Outlay, continued rental		$ 690	$710	$724	$745	$760
Expenses of ownership						
Tab rental		$ 45	$ 28	$ 28	$ 28	$ 28
Maintenance		67	69	75	79	84
Insurance		7	7	7	7	7
Subtotal		$119	$104	$110	$114	$119
Depreciation						
(A) Straight-line		$407	$406	$407	$406	$407
(B) Sum of digits		$678	$542	$407	$271	$136
Total expenses (A)		$ 526	$510	$517	$520	$526
(B)		$ 797	$646	$517	$385	$255
Net gain (loss) in taxable income (A)		$ 164	$200	$207	$225	$234
(B)		$(107)	$ 64	$207	$360	$505
Net change in after-tax income* (A)		$ 82	$100	$103	$112	$117
(B)		$ (54)	$ 32	$104	$180	$253

* Tax at 50%.

ment in cash flows from earnings or savings. Referring once again to the computer purchase option and Table 9–1, which shows the cash flows related to that choice, we can illustrate the idea of payback. The initial net cash outlay was $2,033,000. The net cash inflows by year were as shown in Table 9–2. We can see that if things work out as expected, the initial investment will be recovered sometime in the fourth year. The exact payback period by this method is $3 + 324/451 = 3.7$ years. All other proposals could be measured and ranked on the same basis. Businesses which use this method will have a minimum acceptable payback period, such as 3 years. This is the accept-reject criterion. The computer proposal would fail to meet the test of a payback period of 3 years.

It is apparent that what this criterion does is favor those projects

From Table 9–2:

Year	Annual Amount	Cumulative
1	$625,000	$ 625,000
2	574,000	1,199,000
3	510,000	1,709,000
4	451,000	2,160,000
5	388,000	2,548,000

which return the largest amounts in the early years relative to the initial outlay. This in itself is desirable, but the criterion is universally criticized by experts because it does not discriminate as to the timing of the flows and because it ignores the magnitude of the benefits lying beyond the payback period. These are serious criticisms. The payback criterion is not in fact a true measure of profitability.

It should be noted that the payback criterion has been in wide use; and although its popularity has declined relative to the time-adjusted methods, it is still in common practice. It is useful to consider why. Unquestionably familiarity, simplicity, and apparent objectivity are important practical reasons. Further, the primary criticisms suggested above are less significant if the comparisons of alternatives are among a family of investment opportunities having roughly the same economic life and profile of benefits. There is a rough similarity with the time-adjusted method in that both methods favor high cash flows in the early years. The expected cash flows in the years following the payback period undoubtedly enter the payback analysis in practice but as qualitative rather than quantitative data. It would be naïve to assume that a businessman would accept an investment proposal that promised to return the initial investment and nothing else.

However, with all these factors considered, the rational justification for a payback analysis probably lies more in the area of risk than of profitability analysis. An important qualification to the refinement of time-adjusted values is that many businesses cannot see with any degree of confidence more than a few years ahead. It is in the nature of some industries that there is a sharp decline in confidence in forecasts beyond a year or two. This is related to such real considerations as demand cycles, capital expenditure programs, and so on. Thus, there is a natural inclination to measure the time it will take for an investment to return the original outlay and to consider this period in relation to near-term expectations in which management has some confidence. The payback period is a crude measure of riskiness. The longer the period, the more exposure there is to events beyond the range of confident judgment. The payback standard can be considered as a rough measure of the horizon of confident judgment.

The Analysis of Variations in Risk

Up to this point in our discussion of investment analysis, we have assumed that the data base for the analysis invariably takes the form of a unique set of numbers relating to one set of assumptions about the future impact of the investment decision. The net cash flow for each interval of time is assumed to be a single number consistent with someone's best estimate of what the actual effects will be. This view of the problem appears to be consistent with general business practice, where it is the custom to deal with an uncertain future by reducing it to the most probable outcome.

It is apparent, however, that for any investment decision there are several, perhaps many, possible outcomes. This is the nature of business risk: that the investment of capital in a private enterprise system links the hope of a profit with the possibility of a loss. It is therefore more realistic to describe an investment decision in terms of a range of possible outcomes and to introduce the dimension of risk by examining the characteristics of that range. To illustrate, we can refer back to an earlier example. Project A in Table 9–3 had the following expected inflows resulting from a $95,000 investment:

Year 1	Year 2	Year 3	Year 4	Year 5
$20,000	$35,000	$40,000	$40,000	$15,000

The number used for the expected inflows of year one, $20,000, is an oversimplification of the possible effect of the investment in year one as evaluated by the management concerned. If questioned, it is likely that the management would confirm that it saw year one, not in terms of a certainty of exactly $20,000 in net cash inflow, but rather in terms of a range of possible net cash flows within which $20,000 represented the most probable result. A crude description of how management actually saw year one might be as follows:

Possible inflows, Year One (000).........	$5	$10	$20	$30	$35
Probability of Occurrence..............	.10	.25	.30	.25	.10

In the typical case the management is unlikely to have refined the probability distribution of outcomes even this far but might have in mind the upper and lower limits and the most probable value. However, in more abstract terms we can visualize the expectations for year one (and all other years) in the familiar terms of a curve of probabilities as in Chart 9–1.

Chart 9–1

Typical Curves of Probabilities

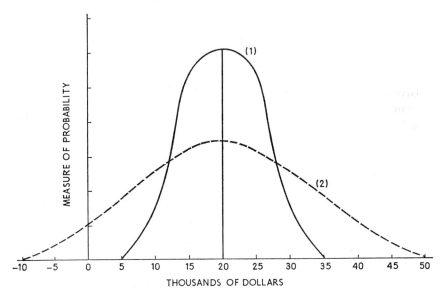

THOUSANDS OF DOLLARS

The normal curve (1) characterizes the figures we chose for illustration. If we had assumed other numbers, such as those suggested by the probability distribution (2), we could have seen immediately that this distribution has quite different risk characteristics. It suggests that the net inflow of the first year could be as high as $50,000, but it also suggests that the first year could produce a net outflow of $10,000. This is clearly a more risky expectation. Note, however, that both distributions have the same expected value of $20,000. This is the mean in each case, the average consisting of the value of each outcome weighted by its probability of occurrence.

Thus we can see that for a full evaluation of an investment proposal, including an assessment of the risk involved, we need not only a measure of central tendency (the mean, $20,000 in this case) but also a measure of the dispersion or distribution of other possible outcomes around that value. Given that the range of outcomes is distributed normally and that we have *adequate data for the analysis,* statistics provide this measure in the form of what is known as the *standard deviation.* The calculation of the standard deviation produces a number that gives a range around the mean within which a given percentage of the outcomes will fall. If, for example, the standard deviation in our example works out at $5,000, then $20,000 ± one standard deviation ($15,000–$25,000) is the range within which 67% of the outcomes are expected to fall. The higher the standard deviation, the wider the range necessary to capture 67% of the observations and therefore the higher the risk.

Since the standard deviation is expressed as an absolute number and since we may wish to compare alternatives having different means or expected values, it is customary to convert the standard deviation into a relative number by dividing it by the mean to which it is related. This ratio is known as the *coefficient of variation.* In the above case the coefficient of variation would be $5,000/$20,000 = 0.25.

Given a command of the relatively simple mathematics of calculating a mean, a standard deviation, and a coefficient of variation, it would appear that an objective measure of the riskiness of an investment proposal is within our grasp, permitting a ranking of projects in terms of both an index of profitability and risk. However, the problems of both the logic and the application in any life-size investment analysis are very great. The statistics rapidly become much more complex than we have indicated as soon as the analysis is extended to a time series of related outcomes and to a consideration of interrelated investments. The theory of statistics is equipped with a logical framework for such analysis, but a practical application would require considerable statistical expertise—a level well beyond the scope of this book to develop.[1]

However, the primary obstacle to extensive risk analysis as a practical tool of investment decision making lies in the data and not in the logic. Historical data on cost-revenue relationships upon which probability distributions can be built rarely exist in business. This is due primarily to the fact that truly repetitive experience is unusual, and change in the business and its environment is continuous and substantial. To most

---

[1] For a more extensive statement of the logic of risk analysis, see J. Fred Weston and Eugene F. Brigham, *Managerial Finance* (3d ed.; New York: Holt, Rinehart & Winston, Inc., 1969), chap. viii; or James C. Van Horne, *Financial Management and Policy* (Englewood Cliffs, N.J.: Prentice-Hall, Inc., 1968), chaps. iv and v.

businesses the product, the consumer, the competition, the management, the work force of today are significantly different from those of 10 years ago; and even 10 years is a short period over which to observe variations in such key variables as volume of production or sales.

Two solutions to the problem of inadequate data have been proposed and have had limited application. One solution is to substitute judgmental probabilities for historical probabilities. Managers whose experience makes them most familiar with the variable—say, the collection period on accounts receivable—are interviewed. They are asked to use their experience to assign probabilities—in this example to various collection periods between whatever boundaries they consider realistic, say, 30 to 90 days. The resultant probability distribution is an outcome of their perception of their own experience.

Although this approach has the appeal of uniting rigorous analysis to mature judgment, there are a number of practical problems to be faced. Experience may provide confident judgments about the upper and lower boundaries of the variable and a measure of central tendency, but a practicing businessman may become uncomfortable in efforts to refine his judgment beyond that point. Given an expectation that the data are more or less normally distributed around the mean, even this information can be the basis for a probability curve. However, refined applications of this information on risk may be unwarranted. There is likely to be resistance to the use of such data if the investment decisions in question are of major consequence and if the risk and return differences are small. On the other hand, if the risk and return differences are large, a full description of the probability curve may be unnecessary.

The other solution to the lack of historical data requires a more elaborate substitute in the form of a computer model of the variables in order to simulate the environment of experience. Given the ability to make sound judgments on the boundaries of future experience and on the relevant revenue-cost relationships over the range of assumptions, it is possible to explore with the computer model a wide range of possibilities outside the limits of past experience. Such data can be used to build up probability distributions for purposes of comparing risk.[2]

It is obvious that such a model requires a major input of research time, talent, and money and would not be undertaken unless the payoff in terms of risk analysis was considered to be substantial and, it is to be hoped, available for other applications. At the present time a few large companies are experimenting with this kind of information, but real applications are very few so far. As computer-assisted financial analysis becomes

[2] See David B. Hertz, "Risk Analysis in Capital Investment," *Harvard Business Review*, Vol. 42, No. 1 (January–February, 1964), pp. 95–106; and *idem*, "Investment Policies That Pay Off," *Harvard Business Review*, Vol. 46, No. 1 (January–February, 1968), pp. 96–108.

more widespread, the possibility for meaningful risk analysis along these lines will increase. Until then it is likely that the more rough-and-ready approaches to risk will prevail.

How do companies take risk into consideration in their investment analysis at the present time? Several approaches can be identified. These represent some attempt to give explicit attention to the problem where substantial differences in risk may exist among investment alternatives. Of course, many businesses give no evidence of risk analysis in their formal capital budgeting procedures. Undoubtedly, however, this factor would enter subjectively into the final decision whenever differences were apparent and substantial.

As we have already mentioned, although the payback period is essentially a crude measure of riskiness, it is widely used in decision analysis in practice. For companies that use a rate-of-return or time-adjusted analysis, the risk dimension usually enters through the hurdle or discount rate. Most businesses today use a single corporate hurdle rate, which is generally considered to be the company's cost of capital or some higher target chosen arbitrarily as an attainable level of profitability. The question of hurdle rates will be the subject of detailed discussion in the next chapter. The point to be made here is that an attempt to measure the cost of debt and equity capital will produce a number that reflects a market judgment of the overall or typical risk level of the business.

Thus, the cost-of-capital standard may be considered an appropriate standard for investments with risk characteristics similar to those currently reflected in the business. If, however, a proposal is a clear departure from the risk norms of the business, some adjustment of the standard would be in order. The problem is that the analysis merely provides one reference point for relating risk to return and suggests the direction of the adjustment but not its magnitude. That is left for purely subjective response by management.

Some companies carry the risk analysis one step further by having multiple hurdle rates reflecting different risk categories. One way this is done in a multidivision company is by division or product grouping. Thus, an integrated oil company might have four different investment hurdle rates for the exploration, refining, transportation, and marketing divisions. Exploration might be viewed as the most risky and have the highest hurdle rate, and transportation the least risky and have the lowest hurdle rate. The method by which multiple hurdle rates are established in practice does not appear to follow an explicit analytical line of reasoning. To say that it is arbitrary, however, should not be interpreted to mean that the system is devoid of rationality.

Another approach to a multiple hurdle rate system designed to handle differences in risk, cuts across product lines and is categorized in terms of the ability to predict the outcome of the investment based on experience or familiarity. Along these lines some companies have a three-rate system.

The lowest rate applies to replacement expenditures where the investment is designed to support an established sales volume for a familiar product and market. A higher rate is required for an investment in the expansion of sales volume in established products and markets. The ability to achieve or sustain the higher volume is in some doubt. The highest rate is reserved for new products where the experience factor is low or non-existent. Here again the basic rationale is apparent, but the derivation of the precise numbers is obscure.

These references to the efforts at a practical approach to risk differentials raise an issue central to the whole question of risk analysis. By now the reader will be well aware of the fact that the general framework for capital budgeting is based on an analysis of the incremental benefits derived from each separable investment proposal at the point in time when it is available for implementation. Thus, for example, someone decides that now would be a good time to buy a new drill press, and he undertakes to calculate the benefits in financial terms flowing from improved quality, greater capacity, reduced labor costs, and a faster rate of output.

It is natural to ask that the precise information on expected benefits be supplemented by information on the riskiness of these expected benefits. In the light of the obvious complexity of risk measurement on a large number of proposals, however, there is likely to be an effort to limit the number of proposals where risk measurement is subject to formal analysis. It is usual to focus only on the proposals that involve large sums of money and have a risk dimension that appears to be substantially different from the risk typical of the business. In fact, there is good reason to argue that risk analysis should not be centered around each individual investment proposal but rather should be in terms of identifiable income streams flowing from major investment centers (divisions, product lines, market areas). Thus, the risk associated with an investment in a special-purpose drill press would not be separable from all other investments in plant, equipment, and working capital required for a given product line from which a segment of corporate earning power is derived. Another way to say this is that careful risk analysis should be reserved for the financial changes resulting from major strategic choices in the use of corporate resources.

A final point to be made on this extremely complex and largely unresolved topic needs major emphasis. It is that any investment standard which purports to reflect the riskiness of a category of investments contains not only a judgment on the risk magnitude but also an expression of willingness to bear risk. The standard indicates the expected level of compensation which the individual or corporation demands before it is willing to assume the perceived risk. The willingness to bear risk is inherently subjective rather than objective and cannot be separated from the particular people charged with the investment decision.

Some writers on this subject suggest that these attitudes can be reduced to an objective form by defining a "utility function" for the people in question—a graph or equation that describes in generalized form their preferences for risk bearing as measured by risk-return trade-offs. This approach has theoretical significance. Ideally, we are referring here to the risk preferences of the shareholders. As a practical matter we must substitute the risk preferences of management acting on behalf of the general ownership group. However, even with this simplification we question the applicability of the concept. It is our opinion that few if any managements would be willing to submit critical investment choices to a mathematical formula which relates a utility or indifference curve to a measure of the risk of the project. Rather they would prefer to be presented with the best evidence on expected returns and risk magnitudes and to respond judgmentally to the individual proposal, leaving risk preferences implicit in the choice they make.

If at the end of this chapter the reader feels that he has been left without an objective tool with which to deal with the problems of risk differentials in the real world, he has come to the right conclusion. At present the gap between the theory and practice of risk analysis is too wide to close into a reliable generalized application. However, this is not discouraging vigorous efforts to make headway on a major dimension of investment decision making.

Setting the Limits on Investment through *ROI* Standards

Why Limits?

The popular fiction written about American Capitalism has produced the notion that anyone with a good idea for business investment can
find the funds necessary to place him on the road to another business
success story. The only limits are perceived to be native intelligence, drive,
and good ideas—better mousetraps. Of course, this just isn't so. There
are the limits placed by a scarcity of ability, initiative, and real innovation.
There are also limits placed on investment opportunity by a tough competitive environment, by a lack of managerial and organizational skill,
and, not least, by a lack of capital itself.

Those who have been raised on the classical economic theory of a continuous capital supply curve limited only by the price the user is willing to
pay for it may be surprised to find that the real world is different. The
typical business firm, which operates in terms of specific plans for finite
intervals of time, customarily sees the future in terms of a finite capital
supply: limited capacity to generate funds internally, limited borrowing
capacity with its bank or insurance company, limited capacity to raise
new equity as imposed by considerations of control or market value or
market conditions.

If this is so, it would seem that there should be no great problem of
deciding which investment proposals to proceed with this year. Given a
reliable procedure for ranking investment proposals in order of financial
benefit such as we have discussed in Chapter 9, it would seem obvious
that a company would start with the most beneficial and approve the list
down to the point where the current capital supply ran out. Assuming the

estimates of benefit were reliable, this would produce the maximum return on the capital provided.

Some companies follow this simple rationing procedure. However, other businesses, particularly the larger and more mature organizations, go to considerable lengths to devise return-on-investment (ROI) standards—minimum acceptable rates of return on new investments, which every proposal must meet in order to be considered at all. This suggests that there may be times when these companies do not invest all the capital to which they have access and hence have idle resources at least for a period of time. On the face of it, this practice of using investment "hurdle rates" would appear to prevent the company from maximizing its overall return on investment.

One obvious reason for having an ROI standard is to assure that new investments will at least cover the cost of the funds needed to finance them. As we shall see shortly, this can become a complex question; but no one would disagree with the idea of covering at least the out-of-pocket costs associated with the necessary financing arrangements. It is obvious that there will be no net gain from new investment if the incremental profit is offset by incremental interest or other capital charges.

Another reason for a specific standard relates to the uneven flow of investment opportunities and the year-to-year variation in potential return. Even though a set of investment proposals promised a return in excess of the cost of capital, defined in some way, management might still withhold approval for some of them if it believed that it could obtain full employment of capital at higher rates of return by waiting a while. The expected return on proposals submitted this year might be judged as below the potential of the industry and the company, and management might therefore be unwilling to make long-term capital commitments at this year's marginal return. An ROI standard could be an attempt to capture the judgment of top management as to what the company's normal potential for return was, and the standard would act as a means of distributing available resources over several budgeting periods so as to achieve full employment of capital at the best long-run return.

Another factor leading to the establishment of specific guidelines on ROI is the need in a large organization for a delegation of the decision process while at the same time achieving some consistency among the actions of many people. An ROI hurdle rate is a means by which top management communicates its expectations and assures a common effort to try to fulfill those expectations. Where all decisions are being made by one man or a small intimate committee, the need for a formal explicit standard is greatly diminished.

In this chapter we will explore some of the ways in which a business may go about the calculation of an ROI standard or hurdle rate. We will start with the widely accepted cost of capital concept.

Defining the Corporate Cost of Capital: Individual Sources

The normal approach to the calculation of a corporate cost of capital is to make estimates of the separate costs of the several primary sources from which the business may be expected to draw its funds in the future and then to bring these together in the form of a composite cost with each source weighted in some manner. We will take up first the calculation of the separate capital costs of debt and equity sources and consider the problem of a composite capital cost in the next section.

The principal types of cash costs associated with the acquisition of funds through financial contracts may be classified as follows:

a) Periodic payments to the contract holder in the form of interest, dividends, or rent.

b) Any payment to the distributor of the issue as compensation for his services in marketing the issue and for assuming the risks associated with a public offering. The distributor deducts from the price received from the investor an amount that he has agreed is adequate compensation and then remits the net proceeds to the company. The difference between the price to the investor and the price to the company is referred to as the *spread.*

c) Other costs incidental to the making of the contract which are paid by the issuing company, such as legal and printing costs.

d) Any payment to the contract holder at the retirement of an issue in excess of the amount originally provided by the investor. This *discount* applies only to securities that have a definite maturity, or which may be redeemed at the option of the company, and only when the issue is sold at a price less than the amount payable at retirement. This amount may be amortized over the life of the issue and considered as an addition to the periodic interest or dividend cost. According to similar reasoning, a security sold at a *premium* would involve a downward adjustment of the interest or dividend cost.

THE COST OF DEBT CAPITAL. The measurement of the annual cash obligation on bonds takes as its point of departure the fact that bonds must be repaid at a specific future date and that the amount originally received by the company is likely to differ from the amount repaid to the investor at maturity. Thus, for example, if we are considering a 15-year, 8% bond with a face value of $1,000, which brought the issuer $980 net, we must take into account not only the $80 annual interest payment but also the $20 that must be paid to the investor at the end of 15 years in addition to the $980 actually received and used by the company. As was shown in the previous chapter, these amounts can be tabulated with proper attention to time, and the "yield" or internal rate of return may be computed. Since a calculation of this sort with reference to bonds is needed many times a day by specialists in bond financing, *bond value tables* have been published to which one may make reference. The section of a bond value table applicable to the problem at hand is reproduced in Table 10–1. It will be seen that for an 8% 15-year bond which nets

Table 10–1

Section of Bond Value Table Relating to 8% Bonds

Yield to Maturity	14 Years	15 Years	16 Years
7⅝%	103.19	103.32	103.43
7¾	102.11	102.19	102.27
7⅞	101.05	101.09	101.13
8	100.00	100.00	100.00
8⅛	98.97	98.93	98.89
8¼	97.95	97.87	97.80
8⅜	96.94	96.83	96.73

the company $98 per $100 of bond, the actual cost lies between 8⅛% and 8¼%. A more precise figure may be gained by interpolation. It is 8.23%.

The difference between this calculation of the effective cost to the user of funds and the yield calculation of an investor may be noted. The bond above might have been sold by the underwriter to the investor at a premium—say, at $1,020. The difference of $40 was used to compensate the distributor and pay other costs. As far as the investor is concerned, the yield to him is less than 8%, since he must make allowance for the fact that he will not receive $1,020 at maturity but only $1,000. His effective return (from a yield table) at this price would be 7.77%. It will be apparent that the difference between the yield to the investor and the cost to the company results from the use of a portion of the proceeds to cover the costs of issue. And obviously, the yield to the investor is normally less than the cost to the issuer.

We may now proceed to consider an actual case of a recent bond issue, that of the RCA Corporation. On June 16, 1970, the company issued $75 million of 20-year sinking fund debentures with the details shown in Table 10–2.

Following the method of computation suggested above, we note that the company must pay $92.50 of interest per year for each $1,000 bond and, in addition, amortize over 20 years the amount of $10.08—the excess of the amount to be repaid over the net amount received on a $1,000 bond. The effective cost in this case is 9.348%. Since we are dealing with a bond, this represents a before-tax cost. On an after-tax basis, using a 50% tax rate the cost would be 4.675%.

Readers who are watchful of details will note that we have made no allowance for the effect of periodic retirement of the bond through sinking funds, although methods do exist for this refinement. The usual calculations for the cost of bonded debt are based on the assumption either that the bonds in question are not to be retired by sinking fund or (another way of saying the same thing) that sinking fund purchases and the ultimate maturity will be priced so as not to incur further costs or to create further income. For most purposes, the values given by the method presented in this chapter are sufficiently accurate.

Table 10–2

Total amount.............................		$75 million
Term......................................		20 years
a)	Coupon rate..........................	9.25%
	Price to public........................	100.000%
b)	Spread...............................	0.875%
	Proceeds to company..................	99.125%
c)	Other costs of issue...................	$100,000*
	Other costs as % of total issue...........	0.133%
	Net proceeds to company...............	98.992%
d)	Discount.............................	1.008%
	Maturity value.......................	100.000%

* Assumed.

It is significant to note that this bond issue was rated "A" by Moody's Investors Service, a designation widely regarded in the investment community as a key measure of quality. Ratings range from Aaa, the highest, down to C. In order to give the reader some idea of what these designations are intended to convey, we quote the following statements from *Moody's Industrial Manual*[1]:

Aaa—Bonds which are rated Aaa are judged to be of the best quality. They carry the smallest degree of investment risk and are generally referred to as "gilt edge." Interest payments are protected by a large or by an exceptionally stable margin and principal is secure. While the various protective elements are likely to change, such changes as can be visualized are most unlikely to impair the fundamentally strong position of such issues.

A—Bonds which are rated A possess many favorable investment attributes and are to be considered as higher medium-grade obligations. Factors giving security to principal and interest are considered adequate but elements may be present which suggest a susceptibility to impairment sometime in the future.

B—Bonds which are rated B generally lack characteristics of the desirable investment. Assurance of interest and principal payments or of maintenance of other terms of the contract over any long period of time may be small.

The most significant and visible effect of any given bond rating is on the interest rate attaching to that particular issue—the higher the rating,

---

[1] *Moody's Industrial Manual*, 1970, page vi.

the lower the cost of debt. The particular considerations that led Moody's to give the RCA bonds an A rating are not made public, but they undoubtedly reflect a judgment as to the future ability of the company to meet all the commitments of the contract on time and in full. A major consideration would be the anticipated size and stability of RCA's future earnings and cash flows related to the annual cash drain of the debt contract. This means that RCA will be expected to earn substantially more on its total invested capital than it commits itself to pay in interest and repayment of principal (the so-called "earnings coverage") in order to justify the confidence reflected in the rating and its related coupon rate.

A measure of what these perceived differences in quality do to cost can be seen by comparing the yield to the investor on the RCA bonds, 9.25%, with that of two other issues which came out at about the same time. Bethlehem Steel Corporation 30-year bonds rated Aa by Moody's were sold to yield 9.00% and Puget Sound Power & Light Company 30-year bonds rated Baa were sold to yield 9.559%.

THE COST OF PREFERRED STOCK. For many companies the two basic contractual forms under which external funds are raised are debt and common stock. However, some companies make use of preferred stock contracts from time to time, and this has been true of the company used here for illustrative purposes—RCA Corporation. We will make the assumption that the company does plan to use the preferred stock form in the future to a modest extent and further assume that it will be a straight (nonconvertible) preferred stock in order to avoid undesirable complexity at this point. We therefore need a method for costing a preferred stock so as to include it in our final overall cost of capital.

Unfortunately for our purposes, RCA has not issued a straight preferred stock in recent years, and we do not have up-to-date information on the costs which are likely to be associated with an issue in the near future. As the next best source of information, we can look at the current market performance of RCA's outstanding straight preferred issue and make some good guesses as to what a similar new issue would sell at today. The outstanding issue is RCA's $3.50 Cumulative First Preferred no par stock issued in 1936. This issue sold in 1970 at around $48.50; and the dividend rate was clearly out of line with the 1970 market. A review of recent preferred issues, primarily by public utilities, shows that preferred stocks with a dividend rate around 9% sold at or near par. We will use this as the starting point for costing a possible new issue (see Table 10–3).

Table 10–3

Amount.....................................		100,000 shares, per $100
a)	Cumulative dividend.........................	9.00%
	Price to the public...........................	$100.00
b)	Underwriter's spread.........................	$1.50
	Proceeds to company (from underwriter)........	$98.50
c)	Other costs of issue to company...............	$80,000.00
	Other costs as % of total issue................	0.80%
	Net proceeds to company.....................	$97.70

It will be seen that although the public would pay $100 per share if RCA were to issue a 9% preferred stock at this time, the company would receive net only $97.70. Thus the effective cost to the company for money obtained by this contractual form is:

$$\frac{\$9.00}{\$100 - (1.50 + .80)} = 9.21\% \ .$$

This cost is paid out in dividends, which are, of course, *after-tax* dollars and are to be compared with the interest costs of debt on a comparable after-tax basis. The after-tax cost of an RCA bond issue was calculated to be 4.675%.

THE COST OF COMMON EQUITY. It is the calculation of the cost of funds raised through common equity issues which is the stumbling block to an efficient and operational calculation of cost of capital. It is quite feasible to conceptualize how this cost should be measured—though there are substantial disagreements on approach—but it is another matter to translate this into a precise number for the individual firm.

The problem lies in the fact that the common stock, unlike the bond and the preferred stock, has neither a floor nor a ceiling on the benefit received by the stockholder. The benefit derived is a residual value subject to considerable uncertainty. There is no guarantee or promise of anything, except to treat all shareholders of a given class equally. Thus, "cost" as it relates to common stock, defined in the sense of what the business must do in order to attract new equity investment, is a matter of *stockholder expectations* with respect to the benefit they hope to derive. To shift the analysis from contractual commitments to market expectations introduces a whole new element of complexity and vagueness into the analysis.

Let us become more specific. Since the common shareholders are the residual beneficiaries, one can argue that the expected benefits are the earnings after taxes available to the common shareholder whether paid out or not. These earnings can be expressed as a rate of return on current market price (E/P), the so-called "earnings yield." Some companies think of cost of common equity in these terms. Others will argue that the only real benefit derived by the shareholder is dividends, and therefore it is the dividend yield which measures the cost.

However, a moment's reflection in the light of the market price trends of recent years shows the error of thinking of common equity cost in these oversimplified terms. With price-earnings ratios of successful, rapidly growing companies ranging up to 50 times earnings, earnings and dividend yields have been as low as 1% and 2%. It is perfectly clear that a cost of equity capital defined in these terms would be a totally unacceptable standard for new investment and completely contradictory to the actual performance of these companies.

A more meaningful line of reasoning recognizes the two basic forms in which the common shareholder receives his benefit. One of these is the dividend income received, and the other is capital gains realized on sale of the security, and we must take account of both expectations. The elements of the calculation are: (i) the current market price of the stock, (ii) an expected stream of dividend payments, (iii) an expected terminal value for the stock, hopefully higher than the current market price, (iv) a discount rate that equates the future benefits to the current market price. If we have (i), (ii) and (iii), we can calculate (iv), and this discount rate will be our cost of equity capital—the expected return that justifies investment at the current market price.

This relationship has been expressed numerically[2] as follows:

$$\text{Price} = \frac{\text{DIV }(1)}{(1+K)} + \frac{\text{DIV }(2)}{(1+K)^2} + \frac{\text{DIV }(3)}{(1+K)^3}$$
$$+ \cdots + \frac{\text{DIV }(N)}{(1+K)^N} + \frac{\text{Price }(N)}{(1+K)^N}.$$

In this equation K, the discount rate, is the shareholders' opportunity rate of return derived from expected returns on investments of comparable risk. In addition to this rate, the assumptions that must be worked out are the assumed growth rate in dividends and the factor or factors determining the terminal value in year N.

On the question of what determines future market values, volumes have been written and no clear consensus reached. One can, of course, make some crude assumptions. One can agree, for example, that the dominant consideration in market value is the expected growth rate in earnings per share (EPS). Given the expected growth rate in EPS and an assumed price-earnings ratio in year N we have a terminal value—but this assumes a great deal. *If* one makes the assumptions that the price-earnings ratio in year N will be the same as at present, that earnings per share will grow at a constant rate g, and that dividends will continue to be a constant percentage of earnings, then it can be shown that the equation expressed above can be reduced[3] to the simple form:

$$\text{Shareholders' Discount Rate} = \frac{\text{DIV}}{\text{Price}} + g.$$

This means that the cost of common equity is reduced to the expected dividend yield *plus* the expected growth rate in earnings per share which, according to previous assumptions, also equals the growth rate in market price and in dividends.

Although grossly oversimplified, this is an appealing concept of the cost of equity capital in that it reduces the considerations to two commonly observed variables which undoubtedly play a major role in determining

---

[2] William L. White, *Note on Cost of Capital*, available through the International Case Clearing House (Soldiers Field, Boston, Mass., 02163) as Case ICH 13F 114.

[3] *Ibid.*

market value in the real world. One can observe historical trends in these values and extrapolate them into the future. The problem is that the simplification does not fit the real world. Price-earnings ratios *do* change, as do dividend payouts and rates of growth in earnings per share. This makes the analysis considerably more complex. Investors have different investing horizons, and the expectations will be strongly influenced by the choice of the *N*th period chosen for terminal date.

Under these circumstances a precise mathematical formulation that attempts to capture all the nuances of the real world is a practical impossibility. As a practical matter, the best one can hope for in deriving a cost of equity capital is a crude approximation that gets at the two basic elements we have been discussing—dividends and capital gains. Since valid data on current shareholder expectations are beyond reach, a company can only fall back on historical performance and use this as the presumed basis of any current extrapolations of future performance.

To return to our example of RCA, the current market price of RCA common stock at the time of writing is $27. The dividend for 1970 is listed as $1, to provide a yield of 3.70%. The year 1970 is a poor time to be talking of capital gains, but we must assume recovery of the economy and the market within a reasonable period of time. Surely an uncertain 3.70% yield on common stock is no match for a certain 9.25% on RCA bonds unless substantial capital gains are in prospect for the longer run.

If we are considering an investment horizon of 5+ years, the trend of the last 5 years is relevant. A look at the record for the past 5 to 7 years shows up the problems one faces in this kind of analysis. For the years 1963 to 1968, the earnings per share grew appreciably from year to year. Then there was a leveling off in 1969. With the year 1970 just coming to an end, the record is not officially in, and it is unclear what the final results will be. However, press reports indicate that because of the business recession and a long strike, 1970 earnings will be substantially below 1969.

For purposes of illustration some quick assumptions can be made which in fact should be carefully researched. If we go back to the 5 years preceding 1969, we find that earnings per share grew at varying rates but averaged out at 15% per year. Those were years of continuous growth, which the experience of 1969 and 1970 shattered. As a consequence, the 15% growth rate is likely to be deflated by market experts. Let us assume arbitrarily that expectations for the next 5 years are adjusted downward to 10% and that it is this assumed growth rate in earnings which justifies the current market price of $27.

Making the simplifying assumption of constant payout and price-earnings ratio, we can return to our formula of DIV/Price $+ g$ and come up with the following cost of equity capital: $3.70\% + 10.00\% = 13.70\%$ on an after-tax basis. It should be noted that if we are talking about a new issue of common stock, the offering price will be somewhat under the assumed market price of $27. This, as in the case of the other securities mentioned earlier, will mean a modest increase in the cost of capital above 13.70%. The method having been illustrated earlier, we shall not bother to make that adjustment here.

On the assumption that these figures approximate the way current shareholders see the future of RCA at this point, then one must also assume that at a price of $27 the stock promises performance comparable to investment alternatives of similar risk characteristics. If this were not so, then the price would rise or fall, thereby adjusting the dividend yield and the price-earnings ratio to a level considered comparable to the security's risk class.

Before concluding these comments on the cost of common equity, we should note that the two forms of benefit derived from common stock have different tax status—dividends as regular income, and capital gains. Thus, the individual investor will not be indifferent as to the mix of benefit. The tax consideration tends to favor a higher proportion of capital gain. On the other hand, the dividend component may be considered the more assured benefit and this may tend to offset the tax factor to an unknown degree.

The Average-Cost-of-Capital Standard

Having considered the measurement of the separate costs of each major contractual form used in raising long-term capital, we are now ready to put them all together. The customary approach to an average cost of capital is a straightforward one: it is to sum the separate costs of debt, preferred stock, and common stock, each weighted by the proportions each source is expected to have in future financing. This is the approach we propose to follow.

However, before proceeding, the reader should know that there is a school of thought, primarily found in academic literature, which argues that the costs of separate debt and equity contracts for the same firm cannot be summed as suggested above because they are not independent of each other.[4]

Stated in very brief terms, the reasoning runs that changes in the proportions of debt change the riskiness of the equity component and therefore its cost. Thus, it is argued that the assumed advantages of leverage through increasing amounts of low-cost debt are negated by a rising cost of equity, that the adjustment is continuous, and that in fact, tax considerations aside, the cost of capital for the individual firm is independent of the debt equity proportions.[5] Tax considerations require

---

[4] See, for example: Wilbur G. Lewellen, *The Cost of Capital* (Belmont, Calif.: Wadsworth Publishing Co., Inc., 1969).

[5] *Ibid.*, p. 29.

qualification of this conclusion, however, because of differences between the tax position of a corporation and those of its shareholders.

This line of reasoning has considerable logical appeal. It is undoubtedly true that a firm cannot assume any debt level it wishes and disregard the potential impact on the price-earnings ratio for its common stock. Unquestionably, at some point the gains derived from lower-cost debt are eroded by the negative effect on market price of the common stock as the financial risk becomes "excessive" in the minds of investors. They will demand higher compensation for assuming this risk.

However, our observation of the stock market and of how businessmen perceive that market suggests that the adjustment for the financial risk of higher debt levels is not a smooth, continuous function as the theory defines it. There is, rather, a band of "acceptable" debt proportions for a given firm in a given industry or risk classification within which the market price of the common stock is relatively insensitive to change in the debt proportions. To put this somewhat differently, in practice there are many factors operating on market value at any given time, and the unique impact of a change in debt proportions within the band considered as normal is not observable. If this is correct, there is therefore an opportunity to benefit from leverage by raising the debt level to the upper limit tolerated by the market (tolerated without negative reaction in the price-earnings ratio). Such adjustments are undoubtedly a matter of "artistic judgment" on the part of those who are closest to the situation.

Thus, we conclude that, provided a company's planned debt levels are not noticeably out of line, we can in fact proceed to an aggregate cost of capital by summing the separate costs of debt, preferred stock, and common stock as previously calculated. If the planned debt level is clearly aggressive and well beyond current levels, some adjustment in the price-earnings ratios suggested by current market performance should be considered, though the extent of the adjustment cannot be objectively derived.

We therefore develop a cost of capital for our example of RCA Corporation using the formula:

$$\text{Cost of Capital} = C_D W_D + C_P W_P + C_C W_C,$$

where the C's stand for the separate capital costs, the W's for the proportions of each source in the capital structure, and the subscripts indicate the contractual form. It should be clear that the costs involved are intended to be representative of what is expected to obtain in the capital market for the company in question in the foreseeable future. Likewise, the weights to be attached to each cost are the proportions of each source expected to be used in future financing. These proportions are likely to be derived by management by first deciding how much additional senior securities should be used; the balance will then be supplied by new common equity.

In the absence of specific information on management's plans, the outside analyst must fall back on the guidelines suggested by the company's existing capital structure. This raises a question as to whether the proportions should be measured in terms of book or market values. Because market values of common equity can differ substantially from book values, the choice can materially affect the weights and therefore the average cost of capital. The primary argument for the use of book value weights is that debt-equity proportions are commonly defined by borrowers and lenders alike in book value terms.

On the other hand, we need to remember that the cost of capital is a standard designed to reflect the investors', and particularly the common shareholders', perceptions of risk and reward and it is through market values that the investor communicates his preferences including the matter of capital structure. The current market value placed on RCA common stock of $1,698 million (at $27 per share) when related to the total of debt and equity outstanding may be assumed to represent proportions acceptable to the investor in the future and in line with the current price-earnings ratio. Thus to be consistent with the basic investor orientation of the cost-of-capital concept we prefer to use market values for the weighting of the common equity cost. Summarizing for the RCA example, the weights from the current capital structure are as shown in Table 10–4.

Table 10–4

	Amount	Percent
Long-term debt................	$ 538,000,000*	24%
Preferred stock.................	13,000,000	1%
Common stock................	1,698,000,000	75%
	$2,249,000,000	100%

* Midyear estimate.

Obviously the amount of preferred stock is currently unimportant in the company's capital structure. In order to give this source some significance we will arbitrarily assume a proportion of 5% in the future and reduce the common stock to 71%. Thus the calculation of RCA's cost of capital would work out as follows (after tax):

$$\underset{Debt}{4.675(0.24)} + \underset{Preferred}{9.21(0.05)} + \underset{Common}{13.70(.71)} = 11.31\%$$

We have arrived at a precise number for RCA's cost of capital, but it is important to remember the considerable subjectivity involved in its calculation. We have made several assumptions about the future condition of the capital markets, about corporate financing strategy, and about shareholder attitudes and objectives, all of which could be seriously in error. As new information unfolds, it may be possible to adjust and refine the estimate. In spite of its limitations, however, it does identify the key components of the cost of capital and the principal variables affecting their magnitude. It is in focusing attention on these elements of cost that the calculation serves an important and practical purpose.

The Cost of Capital as an Investment Hurdle Rate

The concept of the cost of capital as *the* standard for choosing among new investment opportunities is universally accepted among financial theorists. The reasoning is clear and persuasive. The basic purpose of investment is to add to the value of the owners' equity. That value can be increased if, and only if, the incremental profit (net, before capital costs) realized on the new investment exceeds the cost of the capital necessary to obtain the added net income. The cost of capital provides the connecting link between financing decisions on the one hand and investing decisions on the other. As we shall see more clearly later in this book, financial policy with respect to debt, dividend policy, and new equity becomes embedded in the cost-of-capital calculation and sets the hurdle which new investment proposals must clear in order to gain approval for the commitment of the company's scarce financial resources. As we have seen, a key element of that standard is the shareholders' opportunity cost as reflected in the calculation of the cost of new equity capital.

One of the points of confusion arising in the real world derives from the fact that new inputs of external capital often come irregularly and from one source at a time. Thus, if the current financing happens to be by debt, because now is considered the right time to take advantage of lower interest rates or to avoid a depressed equity market, then some managers are inclined to use the direct interest costs as the hurdle rate for current investment proposals.

While it is literally true that revenues in excess of the new interest charges would produce an increment of profit in the short run, the consistent application of this approach would result in a fluctuating standard as the company alternated between debt and equity sources. Thus, some proposals would get by and others be rejected simply on an accident of timing due to shifts in the capital market conditions—or in expectations. More seriously, the large injection of equity capital that comes through retained earnings and which has no explicit out-of-pocket cost would be treated as if it were a cost-free source. The average-cost-of-capital concept, quite properly we believe, separates individual investments from the related individual financing and treats all investments as if financed by a package of debt and equity in proportions considered appropriate for the firm. This provides a relatively stable standard over time.

The reference to retained earnings raises a question about the cost-of-capital standard: Does it apply only to funds invested from external sources or does it apply to internally generated funds as well—retained earnings and depreciation? The answer is that the standard should apply to *all* funds from whatever source which are applied to all investments for which management has genuine freedom of choice. The funds available to a business are either debt capital or ownership capital, and every investment must meet the standard of interest charges and external investment alternatives. There is nothing that dictates the recommitment of earnings or of so-called depreciation funds to an unprofitable venture when there are better options elsewhere. To argue for low cost or no cost for retained earnings and depreciation funds is to argue for the perpetuation of a venture regardless of how unattractive it proves to be.

A final point on the use of the average cost of capital as the investment hurdle rate concerns the question of risk differentials. Risk as an aspect of investment decisions was discussed at some length in Chapter 9. It is apparent that investment opportunities can present a wide spectrum of risk. To apply one standard to all investment proposals where the forecast benefits have not been adjusted for risk would favor high-risk proposals and discriminate against low-risk proposals.

As we explained in Chapter 9, an objective and at the same time practical solution to the risk differential problem is one of the as yet unsolved aspects of financial management. We can say with confidence that the cost of capital, if properly calculated, contains the collective judgment of the stock market on the overall risk characteristics of the firm and in that sense provides an appropriate standard for new investment opportunities similar to existing investments. For opportunities that are clearly more risky than the current mix of investments, a premium over the cost of capital would be expected, and for those less risky a discount would be appropriate. Thus, the reference point (the cost of capital) and the direction of the adjustment may be clear but the magnitude uncertain.

As we suggested earlier in Chapter 9, the most fruitful direction for risk analysis aimed at identifying the risk premiums and discounts within a multiproduct company lies not in risk analysis by projects but in the analysis of the risk characteristics of whole divisions. When a company has only one central source of income—one income stream—the risk characteristics of the several investments necessary to preserve and expand that income stream are inextricably linked together and are reasonably well reflected in the cost-of-capital standard. Where a company has several separable income streams with distinctive risk characteristics, the composite cost-of-capital standard could be a misleading standard for any given division (income stream), and efforts should be directed toward learning more about these risk differentials.

Some Valid Alternatives to the Cost-of-Capital Standard

With unanimous academic endorsement of the cost of capital as the appropriate investment standard, it may come as a surprise to the inexperienced reader that its use in practice is by no means universal. It is always instructive to explore such differences between theory and practice. One obvious answer lies in the inherent complexity of the cost-of-capital notion once it has been extended beyond explicit out-of-pocket costs to include the notion of opportunity cost and shareholders' expectations. We have stressed the great difficulty if not the actual impossibility of applying the theory to real-world data with any degree of confidence.

But significant as it is, this is not the only reason to question the dominant role of the cost of capital in corporate investment decisions. The questioning goes back to the fundamental assumption of the cost-of-capital concept, namely, that the only purpose of business investment is to create value in the equity market. We know that in practice investment decisions are often prompted by a mix of objectives related to the continuity and growth of a real economic and organizational entity. Only one of these objectives is to create value for the shareholder. Other objectives imply other criteria, including quantitative criteria, which may become reflected in an investment standard.

Of course, theory can handle the real-world complexity of a mix of objectives by treating other considerations (for example, becoming a million-dollar or a billion-dollar company within 5 years) as constraints within which pure maximization of market value considerations are free to operate. We can still apply the cost-of-capital standard even though recognizing that some choices may be beyond its influence for "nonrational" reasons.

However, this is not the end of the problem of the cost-of-capital standard. Even granting that a cost of capital can be calculated in a meaningful way and that creating new equity value is a primary, if not the only, corporate objective, there are still other reasons why alternative standards have an important place alongside the cost of capital in business investment decisions. These reasons relate to the essential characteristics of an ongoing business and the management process.

It is clear from the formula for the cost of capital that the dominant variable is the opportunity cost of the shareholder—the measure of what the shareholder could earn on investment opportunities outside the firm having comparable risk characteristics. This is so because this component of cost has the highest value and is normally assigned the highest weighting. A strict application of this standard would prevent new investments that were less promising than these external alternatives even though funds were available. One can visualize a company in a depressed industry or with mediocre management which was unable to fully utilize all its available funds over an extended period of time. Rising liquidity would result. In such a case the ultimate event would be a distribution of these surplus funds through increased dividends, thus permitting the shareholders to reinvest in the more attractive external opportunities.

This logical extension of theory is perfectly consistent with the way in which a free capital market is supposed to work, but it runs afoul of practical considerations in the individual firm. If we look at the professionally managed corporation with a dispersed ownership, we see an organization with a strong instinct for self-preservation, and survival is generally interpreted to require growth. What self-respecting management is going to concede that it cannot find productive use for at least internally generated funds? What management is not going to argue that it is uneconomic to have the government tax away half or more of the dividend dollars before shareholders get a chance to invest them?

The natural extension of this line of reasoning is that the company itself should be finding the new investment alternatives, and if this means diversification outside traditional lines of business, then diversification should take place. No one asks the question whether the mediocre performance in traditional lines is a result of management, not the industry itself, and therefore whether the mediocrity may not be extended to the new products and markets as well. But setting incompetent management aside, the argument has validity and is borne out frequently in practice. Progressive diversification has been the pathway to success in many of our mature business firms today and they will go on evolving.

This being the case, it raises the question whether the standard should be the stockholders' opportunity cost *or the corporate opportunity cost.* If funds accumulate within a business because of a hurdle rate that is too high for traditional business opportunities, the relevant alternatives are not the stockholders' options, which are almost infinite, but the company's options. In other words, the relevant alternatives are a subset of the shareholders' alternatives and have the characteristics of being managed assets (as opposed to financial assets or securities) of a type which complements existing activities and which existing management feels competent to manage. Once identified, the potential returns on these investment opportunities can be evaluated and become the basis for a generalized corporate opportunity cost to complement the shareholder-oriented cost-of-capital standard.

In a multidivision company the corporate opportunity cost is intended to capture the external investment opportunities available through direct investment or acquisition. In addition, a meaningful standard for any one division is going to be the earnings performance of the other divisions as they compete for corporate resources. Thus, there will be an internal as well as an external corporate opportunity cost standard.

Both of these standards, as well as the conventional cost-of-capital standard, are addressed primarily to strategic investment decisions. They serve as guides to management in choosing those turning points in patterns of investment which can have a material effect on overall return and value. They are addressed primarily to the identification of alternative income streams related to new products or services, new markets, or new technologies rather than the choice between this machine or that one or buying versus leasing a warehouse.

In this sense these standards have certain practical limitations for what may be called nonstrategic, tactical, or short-run investment decisions. As a practical matter, businesses do not make strategic changes every week or quarter or every year. Even when the decision has been made, it takes time to reduce or liquidate one investment and replace it with another. In the meantime organizations require a continuing commitment to existing income streams in order to remain motivated and efficient.

If and when it becomes apparent that a product, market, or division is submarginal according to strategic opportunity cost standards, a business does not often have the luxury of instant disinvestment as the shareholder does. It must continue to make the most of that product or division until a change can be effected. Under such circumstances what could be done with the money elsewhere is rather academic. The more meaningful standards for performance in this interim period would be historical performance within the same company or the rate-of-return record of competitors in the same product or market. When the time comes when this investment activity can in fact be replaced, then the strategic investment standard becomes the relevant one.

The conclusion is that there are in fact several bases for meaningful investment standards, and the cost of capital needs to be set in this perspective. Standards must be related to objectives, to circumstances, and to the time frame. These observations do not lead to a rejection of the shareholder viewpoint, which is reflected in the cost of capital, but rather to the realization that this viewpoint must compete with other powerful considerations in the arena of corporate investment decisions.

PART V

SHORT-TERM SOURCES OF FUNDS

chapter 11

Spontaneous Sources of Credit

In preceding chapters we have discussed at length how continued investment in particular assets is a necessary feature of most business operations. Before we turn to further consideration of sources, we should recognize that successful business operations give rise not only to needs for funds but, happily, to certain significant sources of credit. In the normal course of profitable operations, three major sources of continuing credit tend to develop without special effort or negotiation. Together, these sources constitute a substantial offset to the gross need for funds in the business. Since they grow out of normal patterns of profitable operation without special effort or conscious decision on the part of owners or managers, they can be thought of as *spontaneous* or *self-generating sources* of credit. They reduce the amounts of funds that the managers must raise from other sources.

NORMAL TRADE CREDIT

The first and most important of these spontaneous sources is the trade credit normally provided by suppliers of the company. As we have seen, most raw materials, supplies, and other items purchased on a recurring basis are available on purchase terms which permit a delay in payment. The credit standards imposed by sellers, which buying firms must meet in order to get credit on their purchases, seldom are severe. Concerns whose purchases bear a reasonable relationship to their capital and scale of operations, and which can show some liquidity, seldom have difficulty in qualifying for the credit terms normally offered by suppliers.

For American business in general, trade credit represents a major source of funds. For all manufacturing companies, total trade credit was

$47.6 billion, or 8.8% of all assets, on December 31, 1969. In the case of manufacturers of apparel and related products, trade payables represented 19.2% of all assets.[1] In some companies, which buy on very generous credit terms, have a short and inexpensive manufacturing operation, and sell on short terms, the trade credit virtually finances their entire operations, making it possible for them to do a very large volume of business with a minimum of ownership funds and negotiated credits. For example, we learned of a manufacturer who insisted that he could finance his working capital needs for the manufacture of parachutes under a government contract on an investment of his own funds of only $17 for each $1,000 of annual sales. Making this possible was the combination of generous credit from suppliers, a simple and fast production operation, and fast collection from the government.

In the wholesale and retail fields, trade credit is relied on heavily. Tax data for a recent year showed that accounts payable were more than 25% of the total assets of wholesale firms and 17% of retailers' asset totals. In some other fields, trade credit is equally important. Thus, in the construction industry accounts payable were 25% of total assets.

Trade credit is a particularly important source of funds for smaller companies. Many financially weak small firms that find it difficult to negotiate loans from banks or other institutional lenders are able to qualify for trade credit. The importance of trade credit to smaller firms is evidenced by available data on manufacturing concerns. On December 31, 1969, manufacturing firms with assets under $1 million relied on trade credit to finance 17.7% of their total assets. In contrast, manufacturers with assets over $1 billion used trade credit to the extent of only 7.6% of their total assets.[2]

Normal credit terms offered by many suppliers leave purchasers the option of earning a discount by paying within a certain period or of having longer credit without the discount. Very common, for example, are terms of 2/10, net 30—that is, the buyer can deduct a 2% discount from payments made within 10 days, or he can take 30 days to pay without discount. Using the full 30 days is quite permissible under such terms, but the buyer pays a high price for the extra 20 days of credit. By taking the extra 20 days on a $1,000 purchase under such terms, the purchaser gets the use of $980 for an extra 20 days at the cost of the discount forgone of $20. In effect, the purchaser is paying 2.04% (20 ÷ 980) for the use of the $980 for 20 days, or one eighteenth of a year. In terms of annual interest, the cost of continued loss of the discount is almost 37% (2.04% times 18).

Some suppliers let their terms be regarded as somewhat nominal,

[1] Federal Trade Commission and Securities and Exchange Commission, *Quarterly Financial Report for Manufacturing Corporations Fourth Quarter, 1969* (Washington, D.C.: U.S. Government Printing Office, 1970).

[2] *Ibid.*

taking no action to speed collection until payments become well overdue. If the supplier's terms were nominally 2/10, net 30, but he actually permitted payment in 60 days, the buyer then gets credit for 50 extra days, or 50/365ths of a year, bringing the cost of discounts forgone in terms of annual rates down to 14.8%. Failure to take discounts is still expensive, even when nominal terms are stretched considerably.

Firms which are short of funds find it tempting to lean on their suppliers by delaying payment of trade debt well beyond due dates. Where loss of discounts is not involved, the extra credit taken at the expense of suppliers appears to be "cost-free" credit. Further, suppliers are likely to be the most indulgent of the firm's creditors, particularly if they are well financed and are earning a good profit on the sales to the firm. Some managers have become masterful tacticians in stretching their trade credit to an extent just short of the breaking point. Tactics used in making full use—or perhaps we should say "abuse"—of trade credit include "selective payment" of trade debts, a euphemism for testing and taking full advantage of the limits of indulgence of each major creditor, concentration of purchases with the most lenient suppliers, and periodic cleanup of overdue accounts on a rotating basis as a means of reducing pressures from suppliers. Many firms have been able to stay in business only through continuous heavy use of trade credit over many years.

As a general rule, taking of cash discounts wherever available, and prompt payment of trade debt when due, represent sound long-run business and financial practice. Not taking discounts is expensive. Too, as we indicated, the network of exchange of credit information is sufficiently well organized and extensive in this country that the payment record of firms becomes a matter of widespread knowledge. A record of promptly meeting all its obligations adds much to the general reputation of the firm. Further, the way the firm handles its obligations to trade creditors will have an impact on its ability to get credit from banks and other lenders. Also, in a sellers' market, where demand pushes hard on supply, "slow-pay" customers may find themselves at a real disadvantage in competing for scarce supplies. In the long run, the tangible and intangible benefits flowing from a record of prompt payment of trade obligations are impressive.

Analyzing Changes in Trade Payables

It should be apparent from the foregoing discussion that the three major determinants of the size of the accounts or notes payable are the terms offered by suppliers, the payment practices of the firm, and the volume of purchases. In most concerns the terms offered by suppliers and the firm's policy as to payment of trade debt do not change frequently. Consequently, the major element back of most changes in the level of trade payables is variation in the volume of recent purchases.

Although increases in the level of trade payables are likely to be the result simply of higher level of buying, they may reflect a shift in policy or practice toward "slow pay." Consequently, analysts typically seek to determine whether changes in the amount of payables outstanding are in line with changes in the volume of purchases. The methods by which payables are compared with purchases are similar to those by which receivables are compared with sales, as are the problems of interpreting the results of the comparison. One method of comparison is to express payables as a simple percentage of recent or annual purchases. A second is to convert outstanding payables into a figure of *days' purchases outstanding*. As was the case in computing days' sales outstanding, a single day's purchases are computed and divided into the outstanding payables. A third method of comparing purchases and payables is to compute the *turnover of payables* by dividing the payables, either year-end or average of beginning and ending payables, into total purchases for the period.

Each of the purchases/payables ratios should, when compared with similar ratios for earlier periods and with terms of purchase common for the type of goods purchased, bring to light tendencies toward slowing up or speeding up in payment. Of course, as was true of receivable/sales comparisons, it is most desirable to use *recent* purchase figures wherever they are available, since fluctuations in the level of purchases within an annual period will distort a comparison of annual purchases with the payables at the end of the year which relate to relatively recent purchases only.[3]

Analysts particularly interested in the condition of a firm's accounts payable sometime require an *aging schedule* of the payables. This schedule simply breaks down the payables according to the time they have been outstanding. An aging schedule serves to bring to light the existence and extent of overdue accounts.

In forecasting cash outflows of a concern, the dates when payments for purchases are due, rather than the dates of purchase themselves, are of key concern. Consequently, in planning cash outflows arising out of purchases, it is necessary to prepare a schedule of purchases and then, using time lags appropriate to the customary terms of purchase, to construct a schedule of required payments of trade payables.

ACCRUED EXPENSES

The typical concern is supplied with many services on a continuing basis, with the suppliers of such services not expecting payment immediately upon rendering the service. For example, it is common practice in

---

[3] In many cases no data on purchases may be available to the outside analyst. In such cases an analyst with some knowledge of the industry may be able to estimate the annual purchases from cost of sales and annual inventory figures. Assuming a constant rate of purchases, a highly approximate but possibly useful appraisal of the condition of the payables can be made.

many businesses to pay the labor force weekly, clerical and supervisory personnel twice a month, and executive personnel monthly. In the accounting sense, an expense is created when the services are rendered. But since payment is not made at once, a liability is created, usually termed an *accrued expense*. In effect, the company receives some credit from the wage earner and other suppliers of services. A related source of funds of some significance to important employers stems from established patterns of payment to the federal government of old-age benefit and income taxes which employers must withhold from employees' pay. The patterns permit a short time lag between the payroll deduction and the turnover of the funds to the government.

In the aggregate the credit represented by accrued expenses is of some significance. On December 31, 1969, all U.S. manufacturers reported "other current liabilities," which were chiefly accrued expenses, of $37.3 billion, or 6.9% of their total assets.[4]

Normally, there is little opportunity to postpone the outlays connected with accrued expenses. Thus, the volume of accruals tends to vary with the level of operations. However, if wages and salaries are a major item, the size of accrued expenses shown on the balance sheet will be affected by the date on which employees are paid in comparison with the date on which the balance sheet is computed. Just after payday, the amount will be small.

ACCRUED INCOME TAXES

Under our tax laws, corporations operating at a profit are required to share such profits with the federal government and in many cases with state governments. In accounting for federal income taxation, the claim of the government to a portion of accruing profits is usually recognized each time profits are calculated by adding an appropriate amount to a liability account variously termed *Accrued Income Taxes, Reserve for Income Taxes,* or *Provision for Income Taxes.* Although the government lays claim to a percentage of the profits as they are made, it does not require payment of the taxes due until after the time when the profits are earned and the liability for taxes is created. So long as a company continues to make profits and thus to incur an income tax liability, it will continue to have an outstanding liability to the government for taxes. As new tax obligations are recognized, these add to the liability, while periodic payments to the government to extinguish old tax debts reduce the total tax liability. Thus, the liability to the government represents, in effect, a continuing source of funds for profitable corporations.

Until 1951 the authorized time lag between receipt of income and required payment of taxes approximated 1 year. A series of revenue acts have cut into the authorized delay in payment to a point where corpora-

---

[4] Federal Trade Commission and Securities and Exchange Commission, *op. cit.*

tions are nearing a "pay as you earn" basis. A high percentage of the estimated taxes payable on current revenues must be paid by the 15th of the month after each quarter, and any remaining taxes are due by the 15th of the third month after the end of the tax year.

While the importance of the accrued taxes account as a source of funds has been trimmed, the income tax accrual of U.S. manufacturing corporations on December 31, 1969 totaled some $11.6 billion or 2.1% of their total assets.

So far, we have assumed that the individual corporation continues to make profits and to accrue a liability for new taxes during the year. What happens if a profitable concern ceases to be profitable and just breaks even? Clearly, it must pay off its liability for back taxes on schedule. But it is not adding to the Accrued Income Taxes account, since it is making no profits. The "spontaneous" source that it enjoyed while profitable disappears. So it not only loses the inflow of funds from net profits after taxes but must pay off its liability for back taxes. The squeeze on funds from a shift from profitable to break-even operations is thus a double-barreled one, as many concerns have learned to their sorrow.

If losses are realized, partially compensating relief may be obtained through application for refunds of taxes paid in earlier profitable years. Operating losses may be carried back 3 years, or forward for 5 years. If carried back, the losses reduce the taxable income of the previous years and the taxes due on that income. Provision is made for rapid processing of claims for the difference between the taxes actually paid and the taxes due on the income of the earlier year remaining after deduction of the loss carried back.

In planning cash outflows of corporations related to income taxation, the significant dates are the dates when tax payment must be made. The federal government is not an indulgent creditor, and it is wise to make the required payments strictly on schedule.

In the case of concerns organized as individual proprietorships or as partnerships, the business enterprise in the eyes of the law and of tax regulations normally has no entity apart from that of the proprietor or the partner-owners. Consequently, such businesses incur no income tax liability on their income. Instead, the individual owners are expected to report their share of the business earnings in their personal tax returns and to pay taxes on this income at the rates of personal income taxation applying to their income. Therefore, the income statements and balance sheets of individual proprietorships and partnerships make no provision for income tax obligations.

Provisions have also been made to permit certain small business corporations to elect to be treated like a partnership for tax purposes—that is, to have the income of the corporation taxed directly to its shareholders. In 1966, about 12.4% of all corporations filed returns under this option, but these were typically small and accounted for only about 3.9% of total corporate income.

chapter 12

The Effective Use of Bank Credit—I

Immediately following the attack on Pearl Harbor on December 7, 1941, Rear Admiral Yokoyama, the Japanese naval attaché in Washington, together with two naval officer associates, was interned at Hot Springs, Virginia. For several months there, they had full access to the American press and could add to their knowledge of America and the American Navy. When their diplomatic exchange ship arrived in Japan in August, 1942, they were met at dockside by an officer of the Naval General Staff and taken directly to headquarters. They were allowed to see no one and to read no Japanese newspapers. The idea was that they should use their fresh knowledge of America and the U.S. Navy to play the role of the U.S. leaders in an extended war game. In this game, Admiral Yokoyama was to conduct the war against Japan as he thought the American commanders should and would. Thus, through this and other measures the Japanese sought to know and understand their adversary and to forge their own plans in the light of this understanding.

Fortunately, the negotiations of businessmen are unlike the wars of nations, and the gains of one need not be at the expense of the other. Business relationships *can* be profitable and satisfactory from the viewpoint of *each* party—indeed, if they are to endure, the arrangements must be good ones from the standpoint of each concern involved. But effective business planning and negotiation, just as certainly as military planning, must be grounded in a basic understanding of the circumstances and thinking in the organizations with which a relationship is to be developed. The more that can be learned about how their managers operate, their aims, their procedures, the logics of their operations, and the human prejudices and irrationalities of their managers as well, the more likely it is that arrangements can be made that will meet their needs and situation and yet will be a "good deal" for the initiating firm.

This philosophy certainly is pertinent in the case of the businessman hoping to make good use of potential sources of credit. This chapter and the three that follow are intended to help the reader to gain a basic understanding of banks and other lenders to business, and their lending attitudes and practices.

IMPORTANCE OF BANK CREDIT TO BUSINESS

American business firms depend on their commercial banks for a wide range of important services. Carried on with such smooth routine that it is taken virtually for granted is the service of the banks in handling the mechanics of payment by check. A very high percentage of the nation's business transactions are settled by check, and the number of business checks handled annually by the banks runs into the billions—one informed estimate put the 1970 total at 23 billion. But in this chapter we are interested primarily in the banks as sources of credit for business and in the manner in which these sources can be tapped effectively by business concerns.

The commercial banks have long been a highly important source of credit to business. As Table 12–1 shows, loans are the major investment

Table 12–1

Summary Balance Sheet
All U.S. Commercial Banks
(June 30, 1970)

ASSETS	Total in Millions	Percentage of Total
Cash	$ 85,631	16.2%
U.S. government securities	51,569	9.7
Other securities	75,579	14.3
Loans	296,091	55.9
Other assets	20,809	3.9
Total assets	$529,679	100.0%
LIABILITIES		
Demand deposits	$227,413	42.9%
Time and savings deposits	205,016	38.7
Other liabilities	55,542	10.5
Capital	41,708	7.9
Total liabilities	$529,679	100.0%

SOURCE: *Federal Reserve Bulletin*, December, 1970.

outlet for commercial bank funds, and a substantial portion of total bank credit is extended to business. As Table 12–2 reveals, banks reported $107.6 billion of "commercial and industrial loans" outstanding on June 30, 1970, out of a $284.1 billion loan total. Further, a number of the loans reported under other categories, such as mortgage loans on commercial real estate, also represented credit to business units. The total of

"C.&I. loans" had more than doubled during the preceding decade, growing somewhat faster than the total of bank credit.

Two studies of bank lending at member banks of the Federal Reserve System provide particularly comprehensive evidence of the nature and breadth of bank lending to business. These were based on loans outstanding on October 5, 1955, and October 16, 1957. On the 1955 date, business firms had outstanding 1,317,000 loans from member banks. Since these banks accounted for some 86% of total commercial bank loans, the total of business loans from all U.S. banks on that date must have been more than 1.5 million. Table 12–3 shows the industry distri-

Table 12–2

Loans* of U.S. Commercial Banks on June 30, 1970
(in billions of dollars)

Commercial and industrial loans	$107.6
Agricultural loans	11.2
Loans to purchase or carry securities	7.4
Loans to financial institutions	16.7
Real estate loans	70.3
Loans to individuals to finance expenditures	63.9
Other loans	7.0
Total	$284.1

* Excludes federal funds sold of $10.9 billion.
Source: *Federal Reserve Bulletin*.

bution of the loans by number and by dollar amount. While the dollar amount of outstanding business loans at member banks by the early 1970's had grown to a figure more than three times the 1955 total, there is reason to believe that a current survey would show a broadly similar pattern. Since many firms borrow for short periods, the total number of businesses that look to the banks for credit during the year would be significantly larger than the number borrowing on a single date.

The *availability* of bank credit is of keen importance to a great many companies that may not borrow at all for extended periods. To these companies the banks serve as a "backstop" or reserve source of cash. As we have seen, it is often difficult for the businessman to forecast with precision or full confidence the amount of funds his business will need in the future. Many unpredictable events can create a need for cash. Yet it is not feasible for most businesses to carry large cash or liquid reserves against such possible needs. If the business has a good credit standing with its bank and knows it can borrow if unexpected needs develop, it can undertake larger-scale and more risky operations than would be feasible in the absence of the reserve of funds availability at the banks.

In the interests of undistorted perspective, we should recognize that bank credit is a much smaller source of funds for business than the spontaneous sources, notably trade credit. But for business generally, the

Table 12–3

Business Loans of Member Banks of the Federal Reserve System, October 5, 1955,
by Business of Borrower
(estimates of outstanding loans)

Business of Borrower	Amount of Loans		Number of Loans	
	In Millions of Dollars	Percentage Distribution	In Thousands	Percentage Distribution
All business...............	30,820	100.0	1,317	100.0
Manufacturing and mining, total.......	11,283	36.6	225	17.1
Food, liquor, and tobacco...........	1,838	6.0	36	2.7
Textiles, apparel, and leather.......	1,689	5.5	31	2.3
Metals and metal products.........	3,235	10.5	59	4.5
Petroleum, coal, chemicals, and rubber......................	2,646	8.6	28	2.2
Other..........................	1,875	6.1	72	5.4
Trade, total......................	6,539	21.2	517	39.2
Retail..........................	3,476	11.3	411	31.2
Wholesale.......................	2,312	7.5	96	7.3
Commodity dealers...............	751	2.4	9	0.7
Other, total......................	12,998	42.2	575	43.7
Sales finance companies...........	2,872	9.3	13	1.0
Transportation, communication, and other public utilities.............	2,906	9.4	44	3.4
Construction....................	1,691	5.5	105	7.9
Real estate.....................	2,405	7.8	76	5.7
Services........................	1,783	5.8	239	18.2
Other nonfinancial................	1,340	4.4	98	7.5

SOURCE; *Federal Reserve Bulletin*, April, 1956.

banks represent the dominant source of negotiated short-term credit. For
most smaller firms and a large percentage of medium-sized firms, bank
loans represent the paramount source of *negotiated* credit—long, intermediate, and short term. For very strong and larger firms that can sell bonds
in the capital markets, bank credit represents one of several important
sources of credit open to them.

There is abundant evidence of the particular importance of bank credit
to small business. As Table 12–4 (note that the figures relating to the
number of loans are in thousands) makes clear, almost a million of the
outstanding business loans of member banks in 1957 were to firms with
total assets of less than $250,000. For most such smaller businesses, the
banks are likely to be the only available source of negotiated credit. A
Department of Commerce study in the mid-1950's showed that bank
loans constituted nearly 80% of all negotiated credit for a broad sample
of established small and medium-sized firms. For newly established
firms in the sample, bank loans accounted for nearly 70% of all loans.[1]

---

[1] McHugh Loughlin and Jack N. Ciaccio, "Financing Small Business in the Postwar
Period," *Survey of Current Business*, November, 1955.

Table 12–4

Business Loans of Member Banks, 1957, by Size of Borrower

Size of Borrower (Total Assets, in Thousands of Dollars)	Amount of Loans		Number of Loans		Average Size of Loan (In Thousands of Dollars)
	Millions of Dollars	Per-centage Distribution	Thou-sands	Per-centage Distribution	
All borrowers.........	40,618	100.0	1,280.6	100.0	31.7
Less than 50..........	1,456	3.6	504.7	39.4	2.9
50–250..............	5,256	12.9	494.3	38.6	10.6
250–1,000............	6,302	15.5	157.6	12.3	40.0
1,000–5,000..........	6,775	16.7	48.2	3.8	140.5
5,000–25,000.........	5,912	14.6	13.3	1.0	445.7
25,000–100,000.......	4,893	12.0	5.4	0.4	901.6
100,000 or more.......	8,815	21.7	6.5	0.5	1,363.5
Not ascertained.......	1,207	3.0	50.7	4.0	23.8

SOURCE: *Federal Reserve Bulletin*, April, 1958, p. 396.

Several factors contribute to the especial importance of bank credit to smaller business. First, banks generally are actively interested in making small as well as large business loans. Usually, the borrowers are well known to their banks, and the costs of the credit investigation required are quite tolerable. Second, there are commercial banks in almost every town in the country, and local firms are likely to find their local bank interested in helping enterprises which contribute to the community's economy. Further, small businesses generally are less strongly capitalized and their internal sources of funds less adequate than in the case of large firms; many, if not most, are chronically short of funds. Apart from the relatively small number of "glamour firms" with outstanding prospects, smaller firms, and many of intermediate size, find the capital markets ill-suited and unreceptive to their needs. The inability to tap other institutional sources makes it especially important that the managers of small and intermediate-sized firms make effective use of the credit facilities of their commercial banks.

That bank credit is not restricted to established firms with demonstrated earning power is indicated by the fact that 107,000, or 8.4%, of the loans reported in the 1957 Federal Reserve study, were to businesses less than 2 years old. The bank loans outstanding to these new firms totaled almost $2 billion.

THE STRUCTURE OF U.S. COMMERCIAL BANKING

U.S. commercial banks are distinguished from the two other major deposit institutions—mutual savings banks and savings and loan institutions—by their ability to accept demand deposits subject to check as well as time and savings deposits. The savings accounts of mutual savings banks and the share accounts of savings and loan associations are invested predominantly in residential mortgage loans and in bonds. The savings institutions play an important role in the financing of home construction, but their lending to business outside the construction industry is very limited.

The deposit accounts of business firms are carried predominantly at commercial banks. While the commercial banks make home mortgage loans, they specialize in loans to business and to individuals. Unless reference to the contrary is made, hereafter when we speak of "banks," we refer to commercial banks.

The federal government and each of the states have enacted specialized legislation governing the operations of commercial banks. Further, banks are subject to continuing supervision of their activities by one or more public agencies. The regulations applicable to a particular bank are governed in part by its decision to incorporate as a *national* or as a *state bank*.

At the end of 1969 about one third of the nation's 13,661 commercial banks were incorporated as national banks and as such were subject to federal banking legislation. The 4,669 national banks, however, held well over half of the total bank assets. The remaining banks have chosen to incorporate under the laws of the states in which they are located.

Primary responsibility for supervision of national banks rests with the U.S. Comptroller of the Currency. The Comptroller has a sizable staff which reviews periodic reports from the banks and conducts field examinations of the banks' affairs. A team of examiners visits each national bank at least once a year to examine the condition of the bank and to check compliance with pertinent laws and regulations. The examiners give particular attention to the bank's investment in loans and securities. Responsibility for supervision of state banks typically rests with a state banking department whose examiners perform a function similar to that of the national bank examiners.

By law, all national banks must be members of the Federal Reserve System. State banks may apply for membership in the Federal Reserve System. To date, most of the state banks have not sought membership, but enough of the larger state banks have become members so that member banks hold 82% of all commercial bank assets. State banks joining the System become subject to Federal Reserve regulations and to supervision and examination by the System.

All national banks and 97% of the state commercial banks have a portion of their deposits guaranteed by an agency of the U.S. government, the Federal Deposit Insurance Corporation.[2] Since the FDIC assures depositors of the safety of their deposits (up to $20,000 in each account),

---

[2] At the end of 1969, 221 state commercial banks were not insured by the FDIC. These banks held less than 1% of total commercial bank deposits.

it naturally is interested in seeing that the bankers manage depositors' money with due regard for avoidance of loses or illiquid investments that would impair their ability to meet their deposit liabilities. The FDIC, too, has a staff of examiners.

A few of the detailed restrictions on bank lending are of general interest to business borrowers. For example, national banks are subject to a "legal limit" on the amount they can lend to a single borrower. Unsecured loans to one borrower may not exceed 10% of the bank's combined capital stock and surplus. This usually means a limit equal to about 0.5% of total assets. Most state banking laws also have provisions aimed at forcing diversification in loan portfolios, but the precise legal limit may well be different from that of a national bank in similar circumstances. Although the regulations governing specific banks may differ in detail, the similarities are more striking than the differences, and the typical business borrower is unlikely to be materially affected in his use of bank credit by the differences.

The most important point for the businessman to appreciate with respect to bank regulation and supervision is that the bankers operate under certain definite and vigorously enforced restrictions on their lending activity.

In terms of numbers, most of the nation's commercial banks operate as unit banks from a single office. Over the years, there has been vigorous and continuing debate in the United States as to whether it is wise public policy to permit individual banks to establish branches. The various states have come to different conclusions. At the end of 1970, 12 states, including Illinois, Texas, and Florida, virtually prohibited branch banking. On the other hand, 17 states, including California and Oregon, permitted statewide branch banking. The largest bank in the country, the Bank of America National Trust and Savings Association, operated from 955 offices in California cities and towns and 96 foreign offices in 1969. The remaining 21 states permitted some branch banking but restricted it to certain areas within the state.

Branch banking is more completely established in other countries than in the United States. Ten banks dominate the commercial banking business in Canada, as do five in England. A few large banks with many branches also characterize the commercial banking systems of Italy, Belgium, France, West Germany, and Japan.

Commercial Banking as a Business

So much has been written and said about the obligations of banks to their depositors, to their borrowing customers, to their communities, and to the general public that it is easy to overlook the basic fact that our commercial banks are also private businesses, owned by the stockholders, operating to make a profit for the stockholders. They are not charitable institutions or organizations operating exclusively, or even in large measure, for the public welfare as such.

It is true that most banks are operated in the interests of *long-run profitability* rather than for "the fast buck." Few bank shareholders invest in bank shares for quick speculative profit. Most managements identify the long-run interests of their banks with the prosperity of their customers and the long-term economic health of their communities. Further, few broad-minded bankers challenge the social need for substantially more supervision and regulation of bank affairs in the depositors' and the public interest than is appropriate for most other businesses. Nevertheless, *banking is a business*, with profit making the mainspring and basic objective of banking operations.

Banks have been aptly described as "dealers in debts." The basic features of the commercial banking business are relatively simple. When a commercial bank is started, the stockholders, by purchasing common stock, commit capital as a continuing investment in the business. Then the bank receives deposits. The deposits may be on a *checking* or *demand deposit* basis, subject to check and withdrawal on demand without notice. Banks also compete for interest-bearing time and savings deposits. In recent years the intensified competition for time and savings deposits as well as other rate-sensitive money market funds, at home and in the "Eurodollar" market overseas, has contributed to more rapid growth in these sources than in demand deposits. The growing burden of interest expense associated with the increased "money gathering" has put increasing pressure on the banks to invest the funds effectively and achieve a satisfactory "spread" over the money costs.

Deposits are debts of the bank; if it is to stay in business, the bank must be prepared to meet deposit withdrawals *at all times*. As can be seen from Table 12–1, depositors provided 81.6% of all commercial bank assets in mid-1970, other creditors 10.5%, and the owners 7.9%. Banks typically earn profits by investing a substantial amount of the deposited funds in interest-bearing loans to individuals and business firms or in income-producing securities. Obviously, the banks, in investing the deposit funds, should so invest them that ability to meet potential withdrawals is not jeopardized.

Table 12–5 shows how important the income from loans and investment in securities is to commercial banks generally. Interest from loans account for 69.9% of the total operating income of commercial banks in 1969. Interest on investments produced 18.7% of total revenues.

The income after taxes of commercial banks in 1969, which was $4,566 million, represented only 0.88% of average total assets held by the banks in that year. Yet, this was enough to represent a net return of 11.9% on the average investment of stockholders during 1968.

The rates charged on loans are influenced by a variety of factors. The

Table 12–5

Selected Income and Expense Data, 1969, All U.S. Insured Commercial Banks

	In Millions	Percentage of Operating Income
Interest on loans	$21,538	69.9%
Interest on securities	5,747	18.7
Service charges on deposit accounts	1,120	3.6
Other current earnings	2,402	7.8
Operating income	$30,807	100.0%
Employee costs	6,782	22.0
Interest paid	11,529	37.4
Other expenses	5,766	18.8
Operating expenses	$24,077	78.2%
Income before taxes and security gains and losses	6,730	21.8
Income taxes	2,164	7.0
Income before securities gains and losses	$ 4,566	14.8%
Dividends paid	$ 1,769	
Gross income on loans as % of loans	7.6%	
Income as % of average assets for 1969 ($516,325 million)	0.88%	
Income as % of average capital ($38,215 million)	11.9%	

rates charged by the large metropolitan banks, sometimes termed "money market banks," are more sensitive to changes in the supply and demand for credit than are the rates charged borrowers by smaller banks. Bank loan rates have generally been lower in the east and midwest areas than in the south, southwest and western areas.

Chart 12–1 shows the changes in the "prime rate" in recent years. This is the rate generally accepted by the larger banks throughout the country as the "going minimum" rate for short-term loans to larger firms of the strongest credit standing. The charges to other business borrowers generally represent adjustments upward from the prime rate.

BANK LENDING STANDARDS AND PROCEDURES

Basic Economics of Bank Lending

As emphasized earlier, commercial banks are in business to make money for their stockholders. Income from interest on loans is a major source of bank income. But it is *net* income from lending that counts—income after taking into account the added return on supporting balances required, any loan service charges or fees, *and* after appropriate allowance for losses and other costs of the lending operation. Naturally, in their effort to maximize their net profits, banks compare loan opportunities with other investment opportunities open to them. In recent years there has been an abundant supply of U.S. government bonds available to

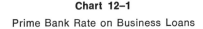

Chart 12–1

Prime Bank Rate on Business Loans

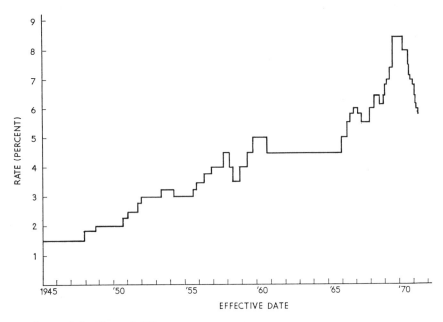

SOURCE: *Federal Reserve Bulletins.*

banks with cash to invest. It is appropriate for bankers to regard the government bonds as entirely free of risk of nonrepayment. In recent years banks have been able to earn 6% or more·on certain government bonds held to maturity. In appraising the risks and return from loans to private businesses, the bankers can appropriately ask that the amount of interest they can receive above the "risk-free" 6% at least compensate for the risk of default by the prospective borrower.[3] Theoretically, banks might appropriately consider making loans of any degree of risk, however great, by simply charging an interest rate high enough to compensate for the estimated risk of nonrepayment and return a profit on the business. In some cases, such a charge might run to 20%, 30%, or even 50%. Actually, for many years in this country, borrower attitudes, custom among bankers, and legal requirements have restricted the maximum interest rates banks charge. Before the tight-money years of the late 1960's, 6% or 7% operated as a psychological ceiling on the interest

---

[3] As a means of cementing close relationships with borrowers and of boosting deposit funds, many banks require borrowers to keep deposit balances with the bank. The amount of the "compensating balance" required is usually about 20% of the amount of the loan. To the extent that the required deposit balances would *not* have been maintained in any case, the compensating balance requirement may be regarded as indirectly boosting the rate of interest on the net funds actually made available to the borrower.

rates banks charged business borrowers.[4] Loan applications involving high risk were referred to other lending agencies which are in a position to charge rates more nearly commensurate with the high-risk appraisal.

Bank Credit Contrasted with Trade Credit

The gain to the bank from risk taking on a typical loan is in striking contrast to the gain to the typical manufacturer from risk taking in extending trade credit to a customer. Consider the following illustration. A manufacturer sells on 30-day credit terms to a particular customer. The customer's credit position has deteriorated, and the manufacturer must decide whether or not to grant him 30-day payment terms. Assume that the manufacturer is not selling at his full capacity and that the sales involved will be lost if he does not offer the 30-day credit terms. If the manufacturer sells $10,000 worth a month to this customer and collects the account receivable in 30 days, he will have just $10,000 at risk at any one time, assuming sales at an even rate. In a year he would turn over the $10,000 receivable 12 times, achieving sales of $120,000 while risking no more than $10,000 at any one time. If profit before taxes on the sales is 10%, a not uncommon figure, he will realize $12,000 profit on the $120,000 yearly sales (in addition to any contributions to the manufacturer's fixed costs) in return for his continuing risk of $10,000. On the other hand, if a banker loaned the shaky customer $10,000 at 7% interest for a year, he would get $700, less any cost associated with making the loan. If he could get 5% for his money in "risk-free" government bonds, the banker's return for risking $10,000 would be something less than $200 a year, in contrast to the $12,000 or more return of the manufacturer. Obviously, in his own economic interest the banker must take a very different view of the risk he is willing to undertake in the total relationship than should the manufacturer in his extension of trade credit.

Contrast between Owner's and Creditor's Return for Risk Taking

It is important also to appreciate the very significant difference in the gain from risk taking of a banker whose lending agreement provides only for a fixed and limited interest return for his risk taking[5] and the gain from risk taking of shareholding investors who, as owners, participate fully in the profits of the business. Consider, for example, the position of a banker asked to make a loan to a newly established business which

---

[4] Exceptions to this generalization do exist. For example, in the case of some loans repayable in instalments over a 2- or 3-year period, a 6% or 7% rate is applied to the full amount of the loan. Thus, the effective interest rate on the loan balances actually outstanding is much larger than the nominal rate. Also banks may add service charges related to loans to supplement the interest return.

[5] Some European banks have invested money in business enterprises on a common stock or ownership basis, but U.S. commercial banks generally have not.

appears highly risky but may be very profitable. If the business proves highly profitable, the bank will get its money back with only the fixed amount of interest as its reward for its courage and capital. The owners, on the other hand, in return for their capital ventured, will get all the profits after taxes of the venture, whether they are 10%, 20%, or even 100% per year. Viewed in this light, it is obvious that the limited and fixed return available to the bank does not justify its taking risks in providing capital that a partner or common stockholder participating fully in prospective profits might well regard as reasonable.[6]

Traditional Theories of Sound Commercial Bank Lending

As we have seen, commercial bankers must limit their risk taking to situations that promise an acceptable return after allowances for the risk of losses and the total relationship with the customer. The bankers also must have regard for investing the banks' funds in such a manner that the demands of depositors can be met at all times. What kind of business loans have bankers regarded as particularly appropriate to their needs and to the nature of their liabilities? Or put most simply, "What sort of loans are the bankers looking for?" Although some pragmatic modern bankers might snort in reply, "Anything we can make money on," over a very long span of years one type of loan has been regarded as especially suitable for commercial bank portfolios. This "ideal bank loan" is a short-term, inherently self-liquidating loan for productive or commercial purposes.[7] *Short-term* is usually interpreted to mean a few months, normally

---

[6] An experienced Canadian banker, Mr. A. B. Jamieson, writing in *Chartered Banking in Canada* (Toronto: Ryerson Press, 1953), makes this same point in these terms: "In many cases where a banker is approached for a loan, the financial position of the prospective borrower is such that what he really needs is more risk capital. When the banker points this out, perhaps the applicant's response is 'If I get someone to put money in my business, he will expect a proportionate share of the profits; if I get money from the bank, all it will cost is the interest on the loan.' With such an answer the banker can tell the applicant he is showing exactly why the loan should not be made. The bank does not share in the profits of the business; therefore, it should not put up money which might be lost if the business proves unsuccessful."

[7] Adam Smith, writing in 1776, set forth the arguments in favor of short-term, self-liquidating loans in the following terms:
"What a bank can with propriety advance to a merchant or undertaker of any kind, is not either the whole capital with which he trades, or even any considerable part of the capital; but that part of it only, which he would otherwise be obliged to keep by him unemployed, and in ready money for answering occasional demands. . . .
"When a bank discounts to a merchant a real bill of exchange drawn by a real creditor upon a real debtor, and which, as soon as it becomes due, is really paid by that debtor; it only advances to him a part of the value which he would otherwise be obliged to keep by him unemployed and in ready money for answering occasional demands. The payment of the bill, when it becomes due, replaces to the bank the value of what it had advanced, together with the interest. The coffers of the bank, so far as its dealings are confined to such customers, resemble a water pond, from which, though a stream is continually running out, yet another is continually running in, fully equal to that which runs out; so that, without any further care or attention, the pond keeps always equally or very near equally full. Little or no expense can ever be necessary for replenishing the coffers of such a bank. . . .

less than 6 and certainly less than 12. *Self-liquidating* indicates that the loan is for a purpose that will generate the funds for repayment in the normal course of the projected operations. Loans to support a seasonal buildup of inventory and receivables are generally of this type. Consider, for example, a fertilizer manufacturer whose sales are heavily concentrated in the spring and early summer months yet who wishes to mix and bag the fertilizer at an even rate through the year. The manufacturer will experience a heavy buildup of inventory in the winter months of slack sales. A bank loan in early winter to provide the funds for the seasonal inventory buildup would meet what is expected to be a temporary need. As the peak inventory is reduced through heavier sales in the spring months, accounts receivable will be increased. When these are collected, cash accumulation will permit repayment of the loan. In this example, then, if operations, sales, and collections proceed as expected, the loan to finance the temporary expansion of inventory and receivables can be regarded as self-liquidating.

The merchant's buildup of inventory for the heavy pre-Christmas sales season, the manufacturer's need to finance production of an unusually large order, and the needs of the farmer who buys cattle in the fall to "feed out" and fatten for sale to the packers in the spring represent other situations in which operations of the enterprise are expected to sponge up, then to release, funds. The short-term, inherently self-liquidating type of loan, which for ease of reference we shall hereafter refer to as "STISL"

". . . A bank cannot, consistently with its own interest, advance to a trader, the whole or even the greater part of the circulating capital with which he trades; because, though that capital is continually returning to him in the shape of money, and going from him in the same shape, yet the whole of the returns is too distant from the whole of the outgoings, and the sum of his repayments could not equal the sum of its advances within such moderate periods of time as suit the conveniency of a bank. Still less could a bank afford to advance him any considerable part of his fixed capital; of the capital which the undertaker of an iron forge, for example, employs in erecting his forge and smelting-house, his work-houses and warehouses, the dwelling-houses of his workmen, etc.; of the capital which the undertaker of a mine employs in sinking his shafts, in erecting engines for drawing out the water, in making roads and waggonways, etc.; of the capital which the person who undertakes to improve land employs in clearing, draining, enclosing, manuring and ploughing waste and uncultivated fields, in building farmhouses, with all their necessary appendages of stables, granaries, etc. The returns of the fixed capital are in almost all cases much slower than those of the circulating capital; and such expenses, even when laid out with the greatest prudence and judgment, very seldom return to the undertaker till after a period of many years, a period by far too distant to suit the conveniency of a bank. . . . [The] money which is borrowed, and which it is meant should not be repaid till after a period of several years, ought not to be borrowed of a bank, but ought to be borrowed upon bond or mortgage, of such private people as propose to live upon the interest of their money, without taking the trouble themselves to employ the capital; and who are upon that account willing to lend that capital to such people of good credit as are likely to keep it for several years." (Adam Smith, *An Inquiry into the Nature and Causes of the Wealth of Nations* [Modern Library; New York; Random House, Inc., 1937], pp. 288–92).

The attention of the authors was directed to this quotation by a similar reference by H. V. Prochnow in his book, *Term Loans and Theories of Bank Liquidity* (New York: Prentice-Hall, Inc., 1949).

loans, has several basic attractions as an outlet for commercial bank loan funds. First, the inherently self-liquidating aspect means not only that the borrower's need for bank funds is essentially temporary but also that the timing of the need derives from predictable patterns of the business operations. Once these needs are understood, the banker has a solid basis on which to establish sound loan repayment terms—"sound" in the sense that the terms fit a predictable pattern of developing, and then abating, need.

Second, the fact that STISL loan requests are to meet identifiable, understandable needs permits the banker to make a meaningful evaluation of the risks that the plans of the business will miscarry and that repayment will be jeopardized. Thus, in the case of the farmer's request for credit to finance his cattle-feeding program, the banker can weigh the risks of unfavorable movements in feed or cattle prices over a known, rather than indefinite, period of exposure.

Third, lending for needs of short duration also tends to reduce the inherent risk exposure of the bank, since risks and uncertainties tend to increase as the time horizon is extended.

Fourth, in lending only against predictably temporary needs the bank reduces the likelihood of becoming frozen into the financial structure of borrowing customers. In cases where the bank supplies capital to meet a long-continuing need, the bank loses mobility in its credit relationship with the borrower. Should the bank believe it necessary to insist on repayment, the borrower may have to make major dislocating changes in his pattern of operations in order to free up funds for loan repayment. Indeed, the borrower's needs for the funds may be so acute that the bank in self-interest may be forced to continue with a loan it would have preferred to terminate. Obviously, such *frozen-loan* situations are unsatisfactory to all involved.

Fifth, emphasis on STISL loans gives a high degree of theoretical liquidity to the bank's loan portfolio. The liquidity inherent in an STISL loan portfolio has long been regarded as consistent with and appropriate to the banks' deposit source of funds. However, in recent decades, U.S. bankers have tended to reassess downward the extent of the need for liquidity to be met through the loan portfolio. Moreover, the use of STISL loans provides real liquidity only to the extent the bank does not reloan the funds from loan repayment. Since the bank's lending is likely to be in large measure in response to the needs of valued customers, failure to respond to customers' loan demands can seriously damage the bank's long-term competitive position. Hence, in an environment in which good relations with borrowers are important, the STISL loan portfolio represents a last resort rather than a routinely utilizable source of liquidity against deposit declines.

In periods when customer demand for loans is heavy relative to the amount of funds available for lending, STISL loans have a further attraction. On a given amount of money to lend, the bankers are able to serve the intermittent needs of many more STISL loan customers than would be possible if the loans were to continuous borrowers.

Despite the attractions, theoretical and practical, of STISL business loans, in actual practice few U.S. banks have restricted their business lending to this type of loan.[8] One basic reason they have not is that the demand from business for STISL credit has seldom been sufficient to absorb fully the bank funds available for lending to business. Patterns of seasonality in production and sales still exist in some firms, but most have sought vigorously to iron out or offset peaks and valleys of activity; many have succeeded to a high degree, so that their primary need for funds is continuing in character rather than temporary. Banks have had to accommodate lending policies and practices to the need of a great many of their customers for more or other than STISL credit. This accommodation has taken three major forms.

A first form has been the long-standing practice of extending credit on nominally short terms (often 90 days), even though there was little prospect that the business borrower actually would be able to repay the loan at the stated maturity date. Both lending bank and borrower expected that the maturity would be extended by renewal of the note. In defense of the practice, bankers pointed out that the use of short maturities did afford the lending officer an opportunity to review the company's progress and situation before renewal and perhaps the occasion to insist on changes in the terms of the credit (i.e., the interest rate) or in the operations of the business. Also, many banks insisted that the borrower arrange his affairs so as to pay off, or clean up, the loan for a period each year in order to demonstrate that the bank loan did not represent permanent capital. In many cases the need for funds actually was continuous, and the cleanup was accomplished only by letting trade creditors go unpaid for a period or by "rotating the line," that is, shifting the borrowing to another bank for a time. Under a rotating-line arrangement, each bank could have the dubious satisfaction of showing a nominal cleanup of the loan on its books, and the borrower could finance a portion of his con-

---

[8] A study by the Federal Reserve Bank of Cleveland of loans in the Fourth Federal Reserve District (Ohio and parts of Pennsylvania, Kentucky, and West Virginia) provided impressive evidence of the extent of continuous bank borrowing through renewal of short-term loans. While only one third of the dollar amount of the notes outstanding of business borrowers were over a year old, nearly two thirds of the business loans were outstanding to business firms who were continuously in debt to the same bank for more than a year. Further, only 6% of the amount of notes were 5 years old or more, but 25% of the outstanding loan volume was to firms continuously in debt to the same bank for 5 years or longer! Details of this study are described in the *Monthly Business Review* of the Federal Reserve Bank of Cleveland, September, 1956.

The author of a more recent study of New York City bank loans to business estimated that nearly one half of the volume of nominally short-term loans represented credit continuously extended for more than a year ("Turnover of Business Loans at New York City Bankers," *Monthly Review* of the Federal Reserve Bank of New York, January, 1962).

tinuing needs at the banks. Such arrangements in which neither party means what it says about repayment incorporate a high potential for misunderstanding between bank and borrower. Moreover, the bank risks being frozen into the loan should its own needs for funds or deterioration of the credit make it desirable to terminate the loan. Nevertheless, many business loans continue to be made on this basis.

Banks have also been willing to provide extended or continuing credit to firms able to provide suitable security. Thus, most banks make 2- to 5-year loans secured by industrial equipment and longer loans against plant facilities or commercial real estate. Also, many loans are extended against the security of accounts receivable and/or inventory. Often these are made under *revolving credit arrangements* in which the notes may be of short maturities but the bank is committed to renewal over an extended period. The use of security is important not only in facilitating longer-term or continuing accommodation to business but also as a support to loan requests by firms that might otherwise not be able to qualify for bank credit. The use of security in business borrowing from banks and other lenders is sufficiently important and complex that we devote a separate chapter to the subject.

A third major accommodation of lending practice to business needs has taken the form of *term loans*, credits calling for repayment in instalments over a number of years, sometimes as much as 10, in which the bank looks to the cash flows from profitable operations over a span of years rather than to reduced needs as the source of loan repayment. While security commonly is not required, the company has to agree to a variety of protective covenants designed to help protect the banks' interests. Bank term lending has grown to great importance and is discussed at some length in the following chapter.

Differences between Banks and Bankers

So far, we have spoken of the lending policies and practices of commercial banks as a group and perhaps implied a uniformity of approach to lending. Actually, many factors condition the business loan practice of particular banks and bankers. Consequently, while there can be general agreement along the lines suggested above, there are important differences in the lending practices between banks and even between loaning officers in a single bank.

The following are some of the factors that make loan officers react differently toward similar loan opportunities.

1. The importance of business loans to the particular bank will influence the reaction. In recent decades, many banks have developed a very important volume of home mortgage loans and consumer instalment loans to cover purchases of automobiles or other such purposes. Where these alternative outlets for loan funds are large and profitable, the interest of

the bank in business loans may be very much less intense than that of other banks which depend more heavily on business borrowers.

2. The basic policies of banks toward risk taking differ. Some managements prefer to remain conservative, perhaps in a conscious concession of gross income to peace of mind.

3. Banks have different concepts of appropriate loyalty to borrowing customers. The onetime First National Bank of New York for many decades was famous for the care with which it entered into lending relationships with its customers. Once it decided to meet the needs of a customer, it was equally famous for standing by its customer in good times *and* bad. Other New York banks loaned more freely in good times but felt more at arm's length with their borrowers.

4. Differences in the nature of the deposit liabilities of banks create different liquidity needs. Lending policies of banks with a large number of inactive, stable deposits can differ from those of banks with a few very large but volatile deposits which may be quickly withdrawn. Also, if interest costs on savings or time deposits are high, the pressure for income may be especially great.

5. Banks tend to specialize in particular types of loans, developing experience and confidence in their ability to gauge risks in their specialties. For example, one New York bank has developed a particularly large business in shipping loans. Too, a textile manufacturer would be more likely to find credit in a North Carolina bank, while an oil producer would usually find a Dallas bank more interested in lending against security of oil production runs.

6. The amount of assets a particular bank already has invested in loans obviously affects its willingness to undertake new loans. As general credit conditions tightened during the 1950's, and again in the mid-1960's, many banks with substantial loan credit outstanding reviewed requests from new borrowers very severely, preferring to save some lending power to meet the possible additional credit needs of old customers.

7. As indicated earlier, legal regulations to which they are subject, such as the limitation of amounts that can be loaned to a single borrower to a fixed percentage of permanent capital, can make for differences between banks.

8. Perhaps most important are the twin facts that loans are made by men, not machines, and that the appraisal of the risks of most loans is in the last analysis a matter of personal judgment. No bank lending officer has a crystal ball that reveals the future to him. Within a single bank, individuals with different personality, experience, and status frequently form very different judgments on particular loan requests. A lending officer who has just had important loans for which he was responsible "go sour" and is wondering what to do about them is likely to look differently on a new loan request before him than would another more confident colleague.

General Procedures in Making New Loans

As we have said, there are many differences among banks and bankers in procedures and practices of lending. However, most banks follow a relatively similar procedure in considering an initial loan request from a prospective borrower. A first formal step consists of a request, often in letter form, by the prospective borrower for a loan of a stated amount. Let us assume that the president of a small manufacturing concern visits his bank and, after a discussion with a bank lending officer, writes asking for a loan. Immediately, the bank will undertake to accumulate information about the background, experience, business and personal reputation of the company and its management, its record with suppliers for prompt payment of its trade debts, the reasons the company needs the loan, sources of funds for repayment, its record as to profitability in past operations, and recent balance sheets detailing its assets and liabilities.

With the aid of specialized credit techniques, lending officers of the bank review the accumulated information and reach a decision whether and on what terms the proposed loan represents a good investment. In most banks the lending officers have authority to make loans within certain limitations of bank policy and according to their own experience and status. In the case of large or complicated loans, the loan officer typically arrives at a recommendation on the loan, but final decision on the request is made by a committee of officers and, in some cases, by the board of directors.

In many instances prospective borrowers do not need a bank loan immediately but would like to determine, perhaps many months in advance, what the viewpoint of the bank will be toward a subsequent request for a loan. In such cases most banks are willing to consider a request for a *line of credit* at the bank. The prospective borrower usually discusses with a loaning officer his anticipated needs for credit in advance of the need, and the request is considered in much the same fashion as if he were asking for an immediate loan. If the customer's situation is a strong one and the loan looks clearly attractive, the bank may decide to extend a line of credit to the customer. This represents an assurance by the bank that, barring major changes in the borrower's situation, the bank will be willing to lend up to a stated amount to the borrower. Once a line of credit has been opened, when the company wants the money the bank lending officers review the situation of the company primarily to determine that no major changes have in fact occurred. If not, the loan will be granted. While the line of credit is not a contract and does not absolutely guarantee the borrower that the loan will be forthcoming, it does serve to let him know how he stands with the bank. In many cases it permits the prospective borrower to embark on operations that will probably require bank credit with reasonable assurance that such credit will be forthcoming. Lines of credit are usually extended for periods of a year or less.

In recent years banks, in granting lines of credit, have become more explicit in their expectations as to deposit balances to "support the credit facility."

Recurring periods of credit stringency have stimulated many corporate officers to get firm commitments from their banks to lend in the future. A common fee for a firm commitment has been 0.50% per annum on the unused but available funds, and a deposit relationship is expected. Firm commitments have been most common from larger banks to sizable but generally not the very strongest companies.

A rough classification of the purposes of the potential borrower in seeking a definite commitment can be made.

1. Pinning down the arrangements for funding known needs in the future. Many borrowers for projects such as a new plant prefer to negotiate a loan agreement before embarking on the project but will need the cash only in increments over many months. The commitment fee covers the obligation of the bank to advance funds as needed. This kind of commitment is not new.

2. Hedging against unfavorable conditions in the long-term market. Companies planning to finance major projects may well plan to finance with a long-term debt issue yet prefer to delay the offering in hopes of lower interest rates and more favorable terms. A firm commitment from the bank to cover the needs in the interim reduces the risks in such bets on capital market conditions.

3. Insurance of funds availability against likely but uncertain needs, such as a planned corporate acquisition for cash which may or may not materialize.

4. Insurance of funds availability if unexpected needs develop. The intense credit stringency of 1969–70 caused some wary treasurers to develop precautionary commitments as a form of cheap insurance that they would in fact have bank credit available as a right in times when they might not otherwise have found it available. A rush for protective cover tends to intensify demand pressures in periods of stringency and could create self-fulfilling predictions of shortages.

Form of Loan

In a number of foreign countries, bank credit is extended in the form of authorized overdrafts; that is, the borrowing customer is permitted to overdraw his deposit balance at the bank up to an agreed-upon amount. Often there is no written evidence of the debt except the checks drawn on the account and the account itself, which serve as evidence of the debt. Interest is calculated periodically on the average amount of the overdraft. This arrangement is perhaps the simplest and in some respects the most logical of lending arrangements. In this country the deposit and the loan accounts of a borrowing customer are kept separately by the banks.[9]

---

[9] Many U.S. banks have adopted personal loan plans that have many features of authorized overdraft lending.

When a company borrows money, its authorized officers sign on its behalf a written agreement to repay, known as a *note*. The note, typically in the form shown in Exhibit 12–1, serves as evidence of the debt and states the terms of the credit extension. Except in the case of very large borrowings, it is customary to make the note for a term of at least 30 days, even though

Exhibit 12–1
Typical Promissory Note

$75,000.00 ....   Boston, Massachusetts, ...November 23..., 19 70.

..................................Ninety (90) days.......... after date,

for value received, the undersigned, which term wherever used herein shall mean all and each of the signers of this note jointly and severally,

promises to pay to NEW ENGLAND MERCHANTS NATIONAL BANK OF BOSTON, or order, at said bank, ...

Seventy-five thousand and 00/100 ─ Dollars.

At the option of the holder, this note shall become immediately due and payable without notice or demand upon the occurrence at any time of any of the following events of default: (1) default in the payment or performance of any other liability or obligation of the undersigned, or of any indorser or guarantor of any liability or obligation of the undersigned, to the holder; (2) if the undersigned or any indorser or guarantor hereof is a corporation, trust or partnership, the liquidation, termination or dissolution of any such organization or the appointment of a receiver for its property; (3) the institution by or against the undersigned or any indorser or guarantor hereof of any proceedings under the Bankruptcy Act or any other law in which the undersigned or any indorser or guarantor hereof is alleged to be insolvent or unable to pay their respective debts as they mature or the making by the undersigned or any indorser or guarantor hereof of an assignment for the benefit of creditors, or (4) the service upon the holder hereof of a writ in which the holder is named as trustee of the undersigned.

The undersigned agrees to pay upon default costs of collection including reasonable fees of an attorney.

No delay or omission on the part of the holder in exercising any right hereunder shall operate as a waiver of such right or of any other right of such holder, nor shall any delay, omission or waiver on any one occasion be deemed a bar to or waiver of the same or any other right on any future occasion. Every one of the undersigned and every indorser or guarantor of this note regardless of the time, order or place of signing waives presentment, demand, protest and notices of every kind and assents to any extension or postponement of the time of payment or any other indulgence, to any substitution, exchange or release of collateral if at any time there be available to the holder collateral for this note, and to the addition or release of any other party or person primarily or secondarily liable.

The proceeds of the loan represented by this note may be paid to any one of the undersigned.

All rights and obligations hereunder shall be governed by the law of the Commonwealth of Massachusetts and this note shall be deemed to be under seal.

Edgewater Manufacturing Company..........

No...........................   By: .... *[signature]*
                                                                                    Treasurer

the borrower may actually need the funds involved for only a few of the 30 days. From the borrower's point of view, such a note arrangement is obviously less flexible than the authorized overdraft approach.

The interest charged by the bank usually is deducted at the time the loan is made. Thus, on a $10,000, 3-month note at 6% per annum, interest of $150 would be deducted, $9,850 being deposited to the credit of the borrower. This is known as *discounting* the note. Under an optional form commonly used on notes of more than 1 year or on notes payable on demand, the full amount of the loan is advanced, with payment of the interest called for upon repayment of the principal amount of the loan.

If the repayment of the loan is to be secured by the borrower's pledge of valuable assets as specific security for the loan, in addition to the preparation of the note as evidence of the debt, preparation of documents conveying a security interest in the asset pledged will also be involved.

NEGOTIATING A BANK LOAN

The businessman who can be confident that he will never need bank credit is in a position to treat his bank relationship lightly. But the businessman who may need bank credit at some time in the future *can do much* to improve his chances of getting the necessary credit on favorable terms when it is needed.

The earlier discussion of the differences in lending practices among banks and bankers should suggest the wisdom (and the difficulty) of judicious selection of the bank with which to do business. Since it takes time to build the mutual understanding and confidence basic to a good banking relationship, unnecessary change should be avoided. If the firm may want to borrow from the bank, the likely reaction to future requests for credit should be a major factor in selection of a bank.

Paving the Way for Credit Applications

The work of building a favorable climate for loan requests should begin long before the credit is needed. Company officers should devote substantial effort to building up a background of information and goodwill with the bank. They should seek to know well the lending officers with whom they may deal, and to be known well and favorably by the lending officers, before they go into the bank with outstretched palms. Specifically, the banker should be told that credit might be asked in the future, so that he will accumulate a file of basic data on the company. At least annually, preferably quarterly, the bank should be furnished balance sheets and income data along with a verbal fill-in on the current operations and future outlook of the business. Projection of anticipated cash flows will be of special interest to the banker. Unfavorable information, as well as good news, should be discussed candidly. The banker should be urged to visit the company and to meet key officers. A loan officer familiar with a business over a period of years and confident that he has a complete picture of the company will be much more competent in working out a satisfactory loan arrangement, and certainly more comfortable in doing so, than in a situation completely new to him. Such knowledge promotes future confidence.

A further factor has become particularly important in recent years, when loan demands have increased faster than the deposits of many banks, particularly the large city banks which loan heavily to national corporations. We refer to the renewed interest of bankers in deposit balances. Concerns that have kept, and will maintain, sizable collected deposit balances with a bank will find that their requests for loans receive more favorable attention than those of equally creditworthy firms which have favored the bank with smaller deposits.

Supporting the Loan Application

Before applying for credit, the prospective borrower should attempt to analyze his own situation from the perspective and point of view of the bank lending officer. He should anticipate the banker's questions and have careful and convincing answers ready. While the detailed questions will vary with the situation, a number of the following will almost surely be raised:

1. Why has he left his former bank connection?
2. Why does the business need funds?
3. How much is needed?
4. How and when will the loan be repaid?
5. What are the possibilities that the plans of the company will miscarry?
6. If the plans miscarry, what will be the situation of the company, and how will it meet its commitment to the bank?
7. What is the background, character, and experience of the principal executives and/or owners of the business? This question will be particularly pointed and detailed in the case of the small company, where the success of the company is especially dependent upon only a few persons.
8. What is the record of profitability in the company?
9. What is the current financial position of the company?

In general, the better the evidence of careful planning, the more convincing will be the loan application. The banker must be confident that the managers of the borrowing company are and will stay "on top of their business."

Recent financial statements, preferably audited by a certified public accountant, should be submitted with loan requests. Highly desirable as supporting data are carefully prepared cash flow forecasts and projected balance sheets extending beyond the term of the loan requested. These projections should be invaluable in indicating the nature, timing, and amount of the need for funds and the cash inflows that will provide the means of repaying the loan—in other words, properly drawn, they provide ready answers to key questions in the banker's analysis. In those cases where the forecasts are based on tenuous assumptions, alternative forecasts on other assumptions may well be put before the banker so that he can fully understand the more important variables that will affect the borrower's funds requirements.

As bankers have developed familiarity with financial forecasts, many have developed, often out of bitter experience, a considerable degree of skepticism about the reliability of projections generally and skill in critically assessing the projections put before them. The applicant should be prepared to support in depth his estimates and assumptions.

Few bankers will be willing to finance operations or projects that do not promise to succeed. But there are few "sure things" in business, and risks of failure are present in some degree in almost all projects. Consequently, the answers to questions 5 and 6, above, are of particularly keen interest to the bank lender whose return for risk taking typically is small. In a very real sense the investment of the owners in the business serves as a protection or buffer against loss by the creditors should the venture fail. Naturally, the bank lender will be keenly interested in the size of this buffer in relation to the debts of the business and its adequacy to absorb the shrinkage in asset values from operations so unfavorable that failure of the firm results. Again, we can refer to classic and highly pertinent observations of the 18th-century writer, Adam Smith:

Traders and other undertakers may, no doubt, with great propriety, carry on a very considerable part of their projects with borrowed money. In justice to their creditors, however, their own capital ought, in this case, to be sufficient to ensure, if I may say so, the capital of those creditors; or to render it extremely improbable that those creditors should incur any loss, even though the success of the project should fall very much short of the expectation of the projectors.[10]

Just how much ownership capital the lender will deem enough to provide the desired protection is a matter of judgment in the light of the circumstances of the particular case. The greater the chances are of failure and of major shrinkage in the asset values should liquidation of the enterprise prove necessary, the greater, generally, will be the ownership capital the lender will require in relation to his and other debts of the enterprise. In virtually all instances the bank lender will give important attention to the size of the ownership investment relative to the borrowings on the enterprise.

In interviews with bankers representing more than 670 banks, members of a Federal Reserve System research group sought to determine the more important reasons for banker rejection of credit requests of small business firms. Each bank was asked to rate the relative frequency with which each of a list of reasons for rejection had occurred. Responses were in terms of "frequent, occasional, rare, or never." In Table 12–6 the percentage of all banks responding either "frequently" or "occasionally" to each of the reasons is presented.

---

[10] Smith, *op. cit.*, pp. 291–92.

Table 12–6

Relative Frequency of Various Reasons for Rejections
of Small-Business Loan Applications

Reasons for Loan Rejections Involving Small Business	Percentage of All Banks Citing Each Reason as "Relatively Important"
Reasons involving creditworthiness of borrower:	
1. Not enough owner's equity in business	93
2. Poor earnings record	85
3. Questionable management ability	84
4. Collateral of insufficient quality	73
5. Slow and past due in trade or loan payments	69
6. Inadequacy of borrower's accounting system	51
7. New firm with no established earnings record	48
8. Poor moral risk	41
9. Other reasons	6
Reasons involving bank's overall policies:	
1. Requested maturity too long	71
2. Applicant has no established deposit relationship with bank	49
3. Applicant will not establish deposit relationship with bank	36
4. Type of loan not handled by bank	33
5. Line of business not handled by bank	21
6. Loan portfolio for type of loan already full	19
7. Other reasons	4
Reasons involving federal or state banking laws or regulations:	
1. Loan too large for bank's legal loan limit	23
2. Other reasons	9

SOURCE: Federal Reserve System, *Financing Small Business* (Report to the Committees on Banking and Currency and the Select Committees on Small Business, U.S. Congress [Washington, D.C.: U.S. Government Printing Office, 1958]), Part II, Vol. III, p. 415.

chapter 13

The Effective Use of Bank Credit—II

In the preceding chapter we sought to explain the commercial banks' traditional preference for STISL–type business loans. At the same time we noted that banks have been willing, particularly in recent years, to meet other kinds of loan demand from business. Particularly important has been the development and growth of *term lending*, and in this chapter we focus attention on this form of bank credit. After first identifying the distinguishing characteristics of term credits, we shall briefly review the history and growth of term lending. We then describe recent term loan practice with an emphasis on the measures taken by lenders to control distinctive risks in this type of lending. Assuming the borrower's viewpoint, we next focus on the attractions and disadvantages of this form of financing. Further, we consider how borrowers best can negotiate suitable term credit and maintain good relationships with the lenders.

Key Characteristics of Bank Term Loans

Bank term loans have taken on several distinguishing characteristics. First, they are business loans with an original maturity of more than 1 year. Most bank term loans are written for a maximum term of 5 years or less. However, in recent years, a significant portion have carried maturities of from 5 to 10 years. A small percentage have had maturities over 10 years.

Second, repayment in periodic instalments typically is required. Although many term loans call for equal instalments each quarter or year, the schedule of repayment customarily is designed to fit the borrower's projected capacity to repay as well as the needs of the lender. So long as the borrower carries out his commitments under the loan agreement, the lender can require payment only in accordance with the specified maturity schedule. Should the borrower fail to comply with any important provision of the agreement, the agreement typically provides that the maturity of the loan is accelerated so that the lender(s) legally may demand payment of the full amount outstanding.

Third, as suggested above, the credit extension is based on a formal loan agreement that specifies the terms and conditions on which the credit is extended and will be administered, as well as various provisions regarding the financial conduct of the borrower. The protective covenants incorporated in the term loan agreement usually are a mixture of customary or "boilerplate" items and ones especially designed to fit the distinctive circumstances of the particular borrower.

Fourth, the terms of the loan are arrived at in direct negotiation between the borrower and the lending bank. In the case of large loans, several banks commonly participate in a single loan, with one bank serving as *agent* or *lead bank* in working up the terms of the loan agreement and in its subsequent administration. The direct contact makes it easy to accomplish modifications of the loan agreement that are mutually acceptable.

Additionally, it can be observed that the term loan typically is for other than a STISL–type need for funds. Commonly, the projected means of repayment are from operational cash flows over an extended period rather than from a lessened asset requirement.

The Development of Bank Term Lending

Banks became term lenders on a significant scale only after 1935. As we noted in the preceding chapter, banks long have made many loans on nominally short terms but which really represented *intermediate-term* credit (1 to 15 years) inasmuch as borrower and lender anticipated that the need for funds would continue and the loan would be renewed, not repaid at the stated maturity. But the deliberate and definite commitment of loan funds for a period of years represented a noteworthy departure from traditional theory and practice.

The new term arrangements fitted the needs and wants of many businesses for intermediate credit instead of, or in addition to, temporary accommodation. By 1946 one fifth by number and one third by amount of member bank loans to business were on a term basis.

The increasing difficulty experienced by a number of banks in recent years in being able to meet the avid loan demand of their customers has fostered a reluctance to build up their term loan portfolios. When bankers must ration credit among their creditworthy customers, they can use a given amount of funds for lending to satisfy the needs of a larger number of short-term than of long-term borrowers. Furthermore, bankers point out that if an undue proportion of loanable funds is tied up in term credits to strong, big firms, which could have borrowed through public issues of bonds, other borrowers, who possess no other sources of credit than their banks, are deprived of access to short-term funds. Nevertheless, it is difficult for the bankers to turn down term credit requests of highly valued customers, and data on the lending of large member banks, which accounted for about 70% of all bank loans to business, showed that term loans had grown by 1970 to about 40% of their total loans to business.

Table 13–1

Outstanding Term Loans to Business of Large Commercial Banks
as of April 29, 1970

Business of Borrower	Amount (In Millions)	Term Loans as Percentage of Total Bank Loans to Industry Group
Durable goods manufacturing		
Primary metals	$ 1,463	70.9%
Machinery	2,761	45.1
Transportation equipment	1,560	56.5
Other fabricated metal products	772	35.2
Other durable goods	1,178	44.7
Nondurable goods manufacturing		
Food, liquor, and tobacco	950	33.6
Textiles, apparel, and leather	709	27.7
Petroleum refining	1,254	79.0
Chemicals and rubber	1,831	63.7
Other nondurable goods	1,099	54.3
Mining, including crude petroleum and natural gas trade	3,590	83.8
Commodity dealers	77	7.8
Other wholesale	684	19.1
Retail	1,242	29.5
Transportation	4,199	77.0
Communication	445	32.4
Other public utilities	1,020	39.5
Construction	888	28.5
Services	2,962	43.6
All other domestic loans	1,183	24.6
Foreign commercial and industrial loans	1,614	73.7
Total loans	$31,481	39.9%

Source: *Federal Reserve Bulletin*, May, 1970.

Many of the largest banks in New York and other major cities have had as much as 60% of their loan portfolio in term loans.

An industry distribution of term loan borrowers in 1970 is shown in Table 13–1. Note the especial importance of term lending in the transportation field (especially the airlines), petroleum refining, and in mining.

CURRENT TERM LENDING PRACTICE

The commitment of loan funds directly to a borrower for a period of years has basic implications keenly important to the lender. Recognizing and understanding these implications helps much toward understanding key features of term-lending practice.

A basic fact that the lender must face in considering a loan for a period of years is the near certainty of major change in the situation and affairs of the borrower before the loan is repaid. Five or ten years is long enough in our dynamic and competitive economic environment for material developments to occur in the management of any borrowing enterprise, in its products, its markets, its competitive position, and in the general level of the economy in which it operates. Of course, lenders have always had to cope with change. But the extent, speed, and intensity of change in our present-day economy particularly complicates the job of working out lending arrangements that will stand up for years under rapidly shifting circumstances.

A related and rather obvious point is that risk increases with uncertainty and that uncertainty increases as the length of the loan commitment is extended. If term lending is to be extended beyond those few companies with particularly outstanding prospects and those seemingly invulnerable to unfavorable developments, while the risks in lending are to be held to proportions consistent with the interest income, lenders must exercise imagination, skill, and vigor in working out provisions that will minimize the risks inherent in the unpredictable but certainly changing future. Furthermore, once a term loan is made, the lender is firmly committed to that investment, since there is no secondary market for term loans corresponding to the active markets that exist for many bonds.

Measures by Lenders to Restrict Risk

During three decades of active term lending, lenders have developed a variety of measures to restrict the risks inherent in term credit. As in the case of all bargaining for funds, the final provisions of a credit reflect the bargaining strength of the parties as well as the objectives of each party. When credit was easy and the supply of funds for loan investment exceeded the demand, as was true of most years between 1935 and 1955, competitive pressures commonly forced concessions on the part of the lender that in periods of active loan demand and less avid competition for loans, as in the 1969–70 period, were successfully resisted. But regardless of what competing lenders might do, the intelligent lender must at all times keep his risk taking in line with his prospective rewards for risk taking.

Distinctive Aspects of the Credit Analysis

Since most term loans are for sizable amounts, as well as for considerable periods of time, the credit analysis of a typical term loan application is more comprehensive and thorough than for short-term credits. The industry in which the company operates and its vulnerability to downturn in business conditions is the subject of close scrutiny. Industries with a history of vulnerability to cyclical changes in demand are obviously less attractive than those which have stood up well under recession conditions.

Particular emphasis in the analysis is placed on the long-term profit and cash-generating prospects of the borrower's industry and of the company within the industry. Loan repayment over a period of years is highly dependent on profitable operations. The protection afforded by even a very strong asset position can be swept away by only a few years of heavy losses. Looked upon with favor are companies with a diversified line of products which have built-in protections against especially rigorous competition. Such protections include particularly strong quality features in their products, research effective in developing profitable new products, strong consumer brand loyalty, and fixed asset requirements great enough to discourage entry into the field by new competitors.

Term lenders place much stress on appraisal of the competitive effectiveness of the applicant's management. Certainly, an alert, able, and aggressive management is essential if even those companies most successful in the past are to make the adaptations necessary to keep ahead of competition in a dynamic economy. But as intangibles, the character and skill of management are not easy to measure and project into the future. For example, the past success of a particular company may be due largely to a top-management team that is nearing retirement, so that another generation of management, as yet not fully tested, may hold the key to the future. However, if the lending institution has had a long relationship with the would-be term borrower, its officers have had considerable opportunity to get a useful, if inconclusive, size-up of the caliber of those who will guide the borrower's affairs in the future. Put most simply, the question to be answered is: Are these the kind of men able to light on their feet if major problems knock them off balance? or Will these people do all right, come what may?

The emphasis on the outlook for profit and cash flow generation and the relative de-emphasis of balance sheet analysis does not mean that such items as the working capital position or the relationship of debt to ownership funds are ignored. It is more an implicit recognition that even though working capital is adequate for the apparent near-term needs of the company, and the debt/equity position is reasonable, the long-term maintenance of a healthy balance sheet must hinge on profitability, which not only provides funds for debt service but forms the basis for equity or other financing as needed.

As the length of term credit is extended, the analysis becomes closer to that of a reasonably conservative and astute common stock investor and less like that of the typical short-term creditor.

While larger term loans generally have been made on an unsecured basis, lenders commonly take security—typically equipment or land and buildings—in the case of smaller term loans.

Repayment Provisions

One of the main protections against risk built into term loans is the typical provision for instalment repayment beginning soon after the credit is extended. From the outset of the loan the borrower is forced to think of repayment and to plan for it as an integral part of his financing. Most lenders prefer to set repayment schedules that leave no large *balloon payment* at the final maturity date. Indeed, many see a need by the borrower for deferral of large amounts to the final maturity as a confession of weakness in the loan. While conditions at final maturity *may* be sufficiently favorable to permit refunding or extension of the unpaid amount, there is no assurance that this will be the case. There is evidence that the percentage of loans with balloon payments has increased in recent years; perhaps bankers have become somewhat more tolerant of the practice.

Provision for instalment repayment from cash provided by retained earnings compensates to some degree for the risks inherent in term loan commitments, inasmuch as the size of the loan is reduced as time goes on. At the same time as repayment is made from cash from retained profits, the ownership equity (in the form of earned surplus) increases, so that the debt/ownership relationship is improved both by reduction of the debt and by the retention, in a balance sheet sense, of the earnings in the business. Some have labeled term loans repaid out of profits as programs of *forced reinvestment of earnings*.

In judging ability to repay and in setting repayment schedules, bankers have been giving increasing attention to estimates of the net cash flows that likely will be available to *service the debt*, that is, to meet interest and principal payments. Gross cash inflows include net income plus noncash expenses such as depreciation, depletion, and amortization. From the gross figure for cash inflows are deducted anticipated outlays for new fixed assets, additional working capital needs, projected dividends, and other debt service. It is the *net* cash flow or *cash throwoff* on which term loan repayment properly can be programmed. Moreover, the net cash flow figure should be sufficiently greater than scheduled loan payments to provide a reasonable margin of safety. What will be needed for a reasonable margin varies with the circumstances. Clearly, the need for a margin of safety increases as the degree of stability and reliability of the projections decreases. As yet no rule of thumb as to what net cash flow coverage bankers should and do expect has won wide acceptance, but one banker recently put his judgment in these terms, "the amount [of net cash flow] available to service the loan should probably equal 150% to 200% of the amount required, depending on the stability of cash flow and the adequacy of working capital."[1]

Some lenders prefer to build repayment plans only on projected cash

---

[1] Dean E. Rogers, "An Approach to Analyzing Cash Flow for Term Loan Purposes," *Bulletin of Robert Morris Associates*, October, 1965.

throwoff from profits and to treat the projected excess of noncash charges over new asset outlays as providing only a contingent margin of safety should profits prove disappointing. Also regarded as a possibly helpful but not-to-be-counted-upon source of funds for loan repayment is the extra cash that might well be made available if sales declined and funds were released as inventories and receivables were reduced.

Of course, the ironical observation that "them what has gits" applies to loan repayment scheduling. In the case of companies with excellent prospects for large, continuing profits, which could afford fast repayment, the lender is less anxious to get his money back quickly and more prepared to accept the risks of a long loan with smaller repayments. Conversely, lenders are more anxious to keep short the term of loans to companies with more uncertain profit potentials, and shorter term means higher instalment payments. Speaking generally, effort is made to compensate for higher risk by shorter repayment schedules.

Not uncommon is a provision requiring repayment of a percentage of profits in addition to the fixed minimum instalment. This contingent requirement is common where the credit analysis suggests the likelihood of large but fluctuating profits. From the lender's viewpoint, it provides an opportunity for getting paid "while the getting's good" without embarrassing the borrower if profits prove only moderate.

Since profit and net cash flow forecasts are at best estimates, tailoring repayment to cash throwoff remains an art rather than a science.[2] The repayment schedule frequently is a major bargaining issue during the term loan negotiation, the borrower seeking the most lenient terms the lender is willing to supply.

Typically, provision for prepayment at the option of the borrower is also made in the term loan agreement. Commonly, prepayments are applied to reduce the principal in inverse order—that is, applied against the most distant instalment rather than the one next due, so that they are not a substitute for regular repayments. Usually, lenders insist on provisions calling for prepayment fees, but this is often a matter for bargaining.[3]

---

[2] One eminent banker explained his approach to scheduling term loan repayment in the following terms: "My own homely method, over a number of years of term lending, has been to arrive at the term of the loan backwards, which is, perhaps, the way I do a lot of things. Having been satisfied with the desirability of the amount of the loan requested, and then having satisfied myself from a cash flow sheet or forecast as to the actual annual cash throw-off or debt paying ability and having reduced that figure, perhaps arbitrarily, to provide some elbow room for the borrower in the event of unforeseen conditions, I then divide the amount of the loan by the figure thus obtained and the resultant figure is the number of years that the loan should run" (Hugh H. McGee, "Term Lending by Commercial Banks," *15th New England Bank Management Conference* [Boston: New England Council, 1945], October 11, 1945).

[3] In actual practice, many commercial banks waive the penalty payments on early repayments by customers with large deposit balances. Insurance companies have become increasingly insistent on significant prepayment premiums and on flat prohibitions of refunding the loan to take advantage of lower interest rates.

Curbing Risks through the Provisions of the Loan Agreement

The direct contact between the business borrower and the bank lender affords the banker an excellent opportunity to try to curb the risks he sees in the commitment by incorporating *protective provisions,* also called *conditions precedent,* in the loan agreement. For example, a rather standard provision in term loan agreements bars the corporate borrower from repurchasing outstanding common stock during the life of the loan. The borrower in turn has the opportunity to identify those proposed provisions he thinks might prove unduly restrictive or burdensome. The final terms should reconcile the conflicting needs and desires of each party in the light of their respective bargaining strengths. Because the issues involved in the negotiation of term loan covenants are conceptually similar to those involved in the fixing of terms in longer-term debt financing, we shall leave detailed discussion of protective covenants to a later chapter.

The Costs of Bank Term Loans

The costs of bank term borrowing are of both a direct and an indirect nature. The chief direct costs are the continuing cost of interest and the one-time costs associated with the negotiation of the loan. Except in large or complex situations, the costs of negotiation are small. If the bank engages special counsel to assist in the drafting of the loan agreement, it is customary for the borrower to pay for the bank's counsel as well as for its own. Beyond the legal expense, there is usually little direct cost of issue.

The interest rate on term loans commonly has been slightly higher (often 0.50%) above the rate the bank would charge the company on a STISL loan. Since a substantial percentage of total term credit is to strong and large borrowers, the average rate charged on term loans is not very far above the prime rate.

The wide fluctuation in bank interest rates has caused the widespread use of floating rates on term loans in recent years. Customarily, the interest rate on the loan is established as the prime rate plus, say 0.50%, so that the amount charged will fluctuate with the prime rate—and presumably the bank's costs of attracting deposits. Sometimes limits or "collars" are established on the extent of upward or downward movement of the interest rate, but most in recent years "float fully."

Some banks have developed special term loan programs for small businesses. Under such a program a bank might well loan a delicatessen $5,000 to cover the costs of rehabilitating the premises and installing new display cases, repayable monthly over a 3-year period. In these special programs, the stated interest rate commonly is applied to the face amount of the loan for the full life of the loan. If this rate were 8% on the $5,000 loan for 3 years, $1,200 interest would be charged (0.08 × $5,000 × 3).

Since the loan is to be repaid over the full period, the $1,200 represents 16% interest on the *average* loan balance outstanding ($2,500 × 16% × 3 years = $1,200).

It has become customary for banks to insist on a supporting or compensating balance requirement, generally 15% or 20% of the loan. To the extent that this requires the borrower to maintain a higher deposit balance than he would have in any case, the income forgone on the extra deposit funds can be regarded as an additional cost of the term loan.

Term Loans from the Borrower's Viewpoint

Now let us take advantage of the background material on bank term lending policies and practice to consider the attractions and shortcomings of bank term loans as a source of funds.

In the actual case, the attractiveness of term loan capital depends on the nature and intensity of the need and the alternative sources available. Most readers have heard of the reply of a careful man to the question, "How's your wife?" The reply was, "Compared with what?"

With what alternative sources of funds can bank term credit be compared? Most large, successful firms have a range of very real, though not directly comparable, alternative sources of debt financing open to them. Such firms could probably place a debt issue with much longer maturities directly with life insurance companies, which are very active buyers of corporate debt issues. Alternatively, they could sell publicly an issue of bonds or they might well be able to secure bank credit on short terms frequently renewed.

Many smaller firms that could qualify for bank term credit have available very limited alternative sources of intermediate credit. The alternative of a public sale of bonds, if it exists at all, is likely to be unattractive; the capital markets are not receptive to the bonds of smaller companies, and the issue costs and the interest rate would have to be high in order to attract buyers. A few life insurance companies and pension funds have been receptive to requests for intermediate credit of as little as $200,000. However, the costs of investigating, making, and administering loans of this size have tended to be a high percentage of the interest return on the investment, and for this and other reasons most insurance companies and pension funds are not much interested in issues below $500,000 or $1 million. Further, when mortgage loans or public bond issues at high rates have been plentiful, many insurance companies have sharply curtailed their private purchase activities. As we shall see in the following chapter, the Small Business Administration or small-business investment companies represent sources of intermediate capital for smaller firms that may be satisfactory, but in each instance some disadvantages attach to use of these sources.

Advantages of Term Credit

To most firms the big attraction of term loan credit is the contractual assurance of continued credit for an extended period so long as the terms of the credit are met. Armed with credit made available under terms explicitly spelled out in writing, the borrower can go forward with plans and projects for the use of the funds for a period corresponding with the duration of the credit. Usually, these plans involve investment of the funds in a continuing expansion of working capital or in plant and equipment that will "pay out" only over a period of years. In other words, term credit fits the nature of their need for funds.

Some borrowers who have been successful in financing medium-term needs with renewed, short-term borrowings are likely to overemphasize the restrictions of the term loan and to overlook the fact that the lender, as he considers each renewal of the short-term notes, has very much in mind certain minimum standards for continued credit, even though these standards may not be discussed with the borrower and renewal seems routine.[4] The requirements spelled out in the term loan are *not necessarily* more stringent than those the lender in fact requires upon renewal of a short-term credit. The lender may be short of funds and long on alternative loan opportunities at renewal time. And lender attitudes are not always constant or, indeed, fully logical; at least, the term loan agreement commits the lender to a definite, constant set of standards and requirements. The borrower can plan accordingly.

The direct negotiation implicit in the bank term loan has a number of advantages to the borrower. Term loans typically can be negotiated faster and at less expense than public issues of debt securities. The major inescapable *issue costs* of term loans are those of legal counsel. In the case of debt issues placed with insurance companies and pension funds, borrowers frequently employ the services of an investment banking firm as an adviser in planning the financing and as an agent in searching for the most suitable lender and in negotiating terms. The usual charge for such services—0.25% to 1.25% of the principal amount—is avoided in bank term borrowing where use of an intermediary is unusual. In term borrowing, disclosure of information is only to the lender(s), not to the general public; and the time and trouble of preparing the registration statement and prospectus necessary in larger public offerings also are avoided. Altogether, the mechanics involved in arranging a term loan are less than those of a typical public issue.

Many borrowers want to make firm arrangements for funds that they will not need in hand for some months or even years. Under such circumstances, funds raised from a public issue of securities before construction contracts are signed are likely to remain relatively unproductive for an extended period. As we have noted, term lenders, for a fee, perhaps 0.50%

---

[4] This is particularly true in other countries where American banks' efforts to introduce American style term lending has had uneven acceptance.

per annum on the committed but unused funds, will commonly permit the borrower to *take down* or draw against the loan in increments corresponding with his planned needs. This flexibility can mean significant interest savings for the borrower.

As we have indicated, to many firms that can qualify for term loans the alternative of a public issue of debt securities is not available. These firms are likely to find the costs of term credit very much lower than the cost of funds raised through sale of common or preferred stock. Many owners of smaller companies are extremely reluctant to concede the degree of control over the corporation that might well be involved in a major issue of common stock. The interference by the term lender with the control exercised by the borrower's management is restricted to that explicit in the loan agreement provisions so long as these are met. While it is not prudent, of course, for the borrower to count on the willingness of the lender to agree to any modification of the term loan the borrower might like, reasonable and appropriate changes can usually be made without problems.

One further advantage of term borrowing from banks, and indeed from insurance companies, has been particularly apparent during recent periods of heavy loan demand; that is, the fact that most term lenders look upon their borrowers—or at least the ones with whom their experience is favorable—as clients whose reasonable needs for money deserve precedence over those of new customers. Consequently, the borrower who has repaid on schedule has something of an inside track to funds needed in the future.

Inherent Disadvantages or Problems in the Use of Term Credit

Earlier we cited, as a basic attraction of borrowing under a term loan agreement, the contractual assurance of credit over the scheduled life of the loan. Yet, it follows clearly from our brief discussion of restrictive covenants typical of term loans that the assurance of credit is a *conditional* one, dependent upon the borrower's meeting fully the terms of the loan agreement throughout the life of the credit. The *accelerated maturity* feature of the loan agreement can be a severe penalty for acts of default by the borrower. Even if the lender does not avail himself of his rights to insist upon accelerated payment of the loan, the lender may well be able to insist upon new terms and restrictions that are very onerous from the borrower's point of view.[5] In effect, the defaulting borrower must "bargain while flat on his back"—an unenviable position.

---

[5] Some astute bankers who have read this chapter disagree with this emphasis. They argue that as a practical matter the strong legal position of the bank in the event of default is misleading and that in most cases, exercise of the bank's legal rights is less feasible than efforts to work out the difficulties over a long period. In such efforts, they insist, the cooperation of the borrower's management is almost essential. While recognizing the merits of the point, it seems to the authors only to temper somewhat the points in the text and not to invalidate them.

Consequently, the astute term borrower must appraise the proposed terms with care and foresight. If he plans carefully and bargains skillfully, the restrictions arrived at may be entirely reasonable and tolerable. But even though they are judged acceptable, it must be recognized that the restrictions do reduce the flexibility of management to some degree.

The major disadvantages of term borrowing, however, are those of any borrowing. Lenders expect debts to be repaid; the penalty for nonrepayment can be severe. Further, loan funds are not like water from an everflowing spring—the more a borrower draws on his ability to borrow, the lower is the reserve of additional borrowing power for future expected or unexpected needs. Debt money is "unfriendly money"; it repels other money, unless it is used so profitably as to attract additional equity investment.

The typical term loan involves only one or a few lenders. The term loan borrower is dealing with an informed, sophisticated lender, who can be expected to be vigorous in protecting his sizable investment. Compared with the creditors in the form of small investors who buy a widely distributed issue of bonds, the term lender is a fast-moving, informed creditor who has such a big stake in the credit that he can be expected to follow it carefully and to defend his right effectively.

While the bank term lender can usually be presumed to be an intelligent and reasonable creditor who will react sensibly to requests for modification of the loan agreement, it is important that the borrower recognize an inherent or potential conflict of interest between himself and the lender. Many possible modifications, which seem clearly desirable from the borrower's point of view, will not be attractive to the lender. Consider, for example, the situation of a borrower who sees opportunities for expansion into a new field that promises big profits but contains substantial risks. The borrower might well, in view of the profit outlook, be willing to assume the risks to him of more debt and hence want the banker to waive restrictions on further debt. But the term lender, who gains little from extra profits from expansion, may well refuse to increase his risks by permitting the expansion of debt.

Many borrowers find the maturities and repayment schedules preferred by the banks unduly restrictive as compared with the 15-year, 30-year, or even longer maturities that they can arrange by public sale of bonds or by a private sale of debt securities to insurance companies. Hence, many larger firms of good credit standing which can sell or place long-term bonds at a reasonable cost prefer such action to term borrowing from their banks. Often these firms turn to use of term credit when capital market conditions are not favorable to a long-term issue, in the expectation that the term loan will be *refunded*, that is, be repaid out of proceeds of a longer issue, when capital market conditions improve.

Concerns that have never come under the full disclosure requirements of the Securities and Exchange Commission and that have borrowed before only on a short-term basis may find irksome the relatively full investigation of a term lender. Certainly, the borrower should expect to have few secrets and should anticipate having any "skeletons in the corporate closet" exposed to the view of the lender. However, term lenders are accustomed to respecting the confidences of borrowers and can usually be counted upon to treat confidential data in proper fashion. And surely, the disclosure of facts to a single lending institution is much less distasteful to a reticent firm than would be the public disclosures involved in public offerings of bonds or other securities subject to the informational requirements of the SEC.

NEGOTIATING EFFECTIVE TERM LOAN ARRANGEMENTS

For most term borrowers, it is highly important that the term loan arrangements be negotiated effectively. What aids to successful term borrowing can be suggested? Our more important suggestions can be grouped under four headings:

1. Getting ready for the loan negotiation.
2. Top management's role in negotiating term credit.
3. Appraisal of provisions and selective bargaining.
4. Keeping a good banking relationship.

Getting Ready for the Loan Negotiations

Many of our comments in the preceding chapter on the importance of careful selection of the major bank or banks are particularly relevant if term credit is likely to be needed. Several considerations make highly desirable a long-established relationship with the bank or banks which will be asked for term credit. First, these banks will have had more opportunity to build up a depth of knowledge about, and confidence in, the firm. Second, there is a widespread prejudice among lenders against "shopped-around" loan proposals. Many lenders flatly refuse to consider a loan application—and to undergo trouble and expense in the process— if the borrower is engaged in serious discussion of the loan with even one other lender. In other words, custom dictates that the borrower select the lender with whom he wants to do business in advance of serious discussion and exhaust the possibilities of a satisfactory agreement with that firm before turning to other lenders.

As indicated earlier, in periods of tight money, lenders are more likely to accommodate old customers than new applicants to whom they owe no loyalty and with whom they have had no experience. The nature of the credit analysis described earlier further suggests the wisdom of building a good relationship with the most likely term lender well in advance of "putting on the touch." And finally, since the association of term borrower and lender may well become an intimate and extended one, it is well that compatibility be pretested as far as is feasible.

Top Management's Role in Negotiating Term Credit

While many financial matters are appropriately delegated to financial specialists, especially in larger firms, term borrowing seldom is one of them. The working-out of a credit arrangement that can stand up over a period of years calls for careful planning of a variety of aspects of the firm's operations. The more clearly the future needs of the business for facilities, for working capital, for dividends, etc., can be formulated, the more effectively can the plans for financing through term credit be brought into harmony with the overall plans and objectives of the firm.

Top management's responsibilities toward term lending are not limited, however, to formulation of the plans which are to serve as the basis for term borrowing that will fit in with those plans. For the desires of the would-be borrower must be reconciled with the needs and demands of the lender. Almost inevitably, the give-and-take of bargaining over specific provisions raises questions that can only be resolved by top management. For example, only top management and the board of directors should assume final responsibility for the reconciliation of dividend objectives with lender proposals for restricting dividend payout.

In brief, term borrowing is intertwined with many matters of significance to top management. Top-management understanding and participation in the planning and decision making that is a part of effective term loan negotiation are essential to term borrowing that serves, rather than stifles, management's objectives.

As we have noted, many firms who seek to tap insurance company credit—and to a very much smaller extent, bank term loan credit—enlist the advice and counsel of investment bankers in approaching lenders and in working out suitable terms. Legal counsel who are experienced in this area may also be of great assistance. But such advice should supplement rather than substitute for top-management understanding of term lending.

Appraisal of Provisions and Selective Bargaining

The shrewd borrower enters the bargaining conference in which the amount of the loan, the repayment terms, and the various restrictive covenants are to be worked out only after he has considered carefully the provisions the lender may propose and their probable impact on his company and its future operations. Once he has forearmed himself with knowledge of term-lending practice, the major limiting factor on the borrowing management's skill in appraising the terms is the extent and degree of accuracy of the future planning of the company. If plans for the future are vague and uncertain, skillful bargaining is difficult, if not impossible.

Particularly important to the borrower are the terms of repayment. Some firms are content with the haphazard approach of seeking credit as large and a repayment schedule as lenient as the lender's indulgence will grant. Yet, the borrower has as much (or more) to lose from too much borrowing as the lender. Moreover, he is in a much better position than the lender to appraise his own capacity to carry and repay debt, since he has a depth of internal experience and information bearing on the subject. Few subjects deserve more careful scrutiny and analysis. Speaking generally, the borrower should estimate as carefully as he can, through cash flow forecasting, his future cash throwoff from operations and borrow no more than can be repaid easily—allowing a comfortable margin between his forecasted means of repayment and the contractual repayments. The more uncertain or unreliable the forecast, the greater should be the planned margin of safety. If reasonable margins between the repayment demanded by the lender and the capacity to repay cannot be projected, serious doubt is thrown on the wisdom of borrowing, and curtailment or abandonment of the borrowing plans is suggested.

A key problem in the appraisal of the restrictive covenants is to separate those restrictions that may well prove burdensome from those with which compliance is painless—which require policies that the borrower would in ordinary business prudence follow anyway. Separating the onerous from the innocuous again requires forecasts over the life of the loan. A requirement that no dividends be paid during the life of the loan might not appear very objectionable if the company were owned by a few stockholders who had little need or desire for dividends. But should the company want to sell common stock to the public, dividend payments may be essential to the sale of the stock at a good price, and the provision barring dividends would become highly restrictive.

Of course, few borrowers can expect to have the bargaining go all their way. The secret of successful bargaining is to discover and concede those points which are important to the other party but represent relatively minor concessions to you, and vice versa.

The interest rate is a good illustration of a feature which is very important to the lender, yet of lesser significance to many borrowers. The range for bargaining on the interest rate proposed by the lender is usually small—one half of 1% or less. Since the lending institution lives largely on its interest income, the fraction of 1% is important to it. Yet, the cost to the borrower is reduced by the inclusion of interest as a business expense before calculation of income tax—hence the *net cost* is about halved for most companies. More importantly, the borrower typically expects to make 15% or more on the borrowed funds, so that availability of the credit and freedom from onerous restrictions commonly are much more vital than the difference in cost that would result from concentrating his bargaining power on the interest rate.

Keeping a Good Banking Relationship

A good banking relationship, like a good marriage, requires and is worth some cultivation. Well maintained, a good banking relationship should grow stronger over the years and become a priceless, if intangible, asset of the business.

Of course, loan arrangements are only part of the total relationship with the bank. Of great importance to the bank are the deposit balances maintained. Hence maintenance of an attractive collected deposit balance can be regarded as a key ingredient of a strong relationship with the bank.

Another ingredient of a good relationship is provided by continued diligence in meeting all commitments to the bank precisely and scrupulously and in spirit as well as in letter.

It is hard to overemphasize the importance of providing the lender with good and candid information about the company, not only at the outset of negotiations but throughout the loan as well. Since the lender has an important financial stake in the enterprise, his interest in timely notice of major developments affecting it—favorably and unfavorably—should be taken for granted and freely met. Moreover, the bank lending officers prefer to hear of major developments affecting the company promptly and from company officers. In the absence of confidence that they are in complete and continual contact with their borrowing customers, the bank officers must depend on the unreliable and often distorting services of the grapevine.

As suggested above, candor is extremely important in a continuing relationship. It is not very difficult for a glib person to sell a "bill of goods" to a banker once and perhaps twice, but the passage of time will help even an unsophisticated banker recognize a "phony" for what he is.

If modifications of the agreement are needed, as is so often the case, the borrower should give the lender as much notice as possible of the impending need for change and carefully work out appropriate modifications to propose. Similarly, as the borrower has unfavorable developments to report, he should have plans worked out to cope with these developments. While the lender wants to know of impending problems, he does not want them thrust in his lap for solution. Instead, he is entitled to evidence that the borrower is making constructive plans to overcome his own problems.

Yet, in the final analysis, there is no adequate substitute for effective performance—the meeting of commitments—as the foundation for a sound and viable borrower-lender relationship.

chapter 14

Nonbank Sources of
Short-Term Credit

In preceding chapters we have discussed the spontaneous sources of credit normally available to business in routine and the use of bank credit on a short- and intermediate-term basis. In this chapter we shall review the variety of other sources of short or intermediate credit available to business generally. The amount of credit provided to business firms by the other sources is much less than the total credit extended by the spontaneous sources and by commercial banks, but the total is significant, and to many firms these nonbank sources are of critical importance.

Because the nonbank or secondary sources are diverse and heterogeneous, this chapter will appear cut up and digressive. To help the reader keep his perspective as he is introduced in turn to different and less familiar sources, we list below the various sources we shall discuss.

1. The commercial paper market for the sale of unsecured notes.
2. Business finance companies.
3. Factoring firms.
4. Private lenders.
5. Customer advances.
6. Special credits from suppliers.
7. Credit arrangements primarily oriented to international trade.
8. State, regional, or local development credit corporations.
9. U.S. government sources of funds to meet particular needs:
    a) Depression relief.
    b) To fill gaps in private availability of funds.
    c) Special financial aids available to military suppliers.
    d) Special aids to groups adjudged especially deserving.

The Commercial Paper Market as a Source of Short-Term Funds

To several hundred concerns of strong credit standing, the commercial paper market has become an important source of short-term funds. *Commercial paper* refers to short-term promissory notes, generally unsecured, which are sold through commercial paper dealers or directly to investors. The investors in commercial paper include banks and other financial institutions; but in recent years, nonfinancial concerns with excess funds to invest on a short-term basis have been the major buyers of commercial paper.

Notes sold in the commercial paper market typically are written in denominations or multiples of $5,000 and with maturities of from 3 days to 9 months. Ninety-day maturities are particularly common. Some firms sell commercial paper on a continuing basis; others borrow through its sale only to meet seasonal and other temporary needs.

The setup and pattern of operation of the commercial paper market is such that it is at the disposal only of borrowers presumed to be of high credit standing. Issuers typically are sizable; the National Credit Office, a Dun & Bradstreet subsidiary that long has assigned credit quality ratings to commercial paper issuers, requires a minimum net worth of over $25 million for its "prime" rating. An article that appeared in May, 1970, expressed generally held views on the credit quality of commercial paper issuers.

The security of commercial paper is considered second only to that of U.S. Government obligations. The commercial paper market has historically experienced only minimum financial losses, with no loss reported for almost 35 years. This no-loss record reflects both the strong financial position of the companies that issue paper and the constant surveillance of dealers and agencies in assuring the integrity of the market.[1]

In the following month, June, 1970, the Penn Central Transportation Company, a "prime" issuer with more than $85 million of commercial paper outstanding, filed for reorganization under federal bankruptcy laws. Severe losses are in prospect for unsecured creditors, including the holders of its commercial paper. Despite the shocks to investor confidence from the Penn Central debacle and the well-publicized difficulties of other issuers, and some initial declines in overall volume, the commercial paper market continued to function on a very sizable basis, though with a new concern in the market for quality standards and the adequacy of credit analysis of the rating agencies and of issuing dealers.

Borrowing through commercial paper is an old practice dating back more than a century. Chart 14–1 traces the fluctuation in total volume of commercial paper outstanding in recent decades. The decline in the use of commercial paper during the 1930's will be noted, as well as the post–World War II increase, attributable largely to finance companies.

The finance companies have had a voracious and continuous need for

---

[1] *Economic Review,* Federal Reserve Bank of Cleveland, May, 1970, pp. 22–23.

Chart 14–1

Commercial Paper Outstanding at Year-End, 1918–70
(in millions of dollars)

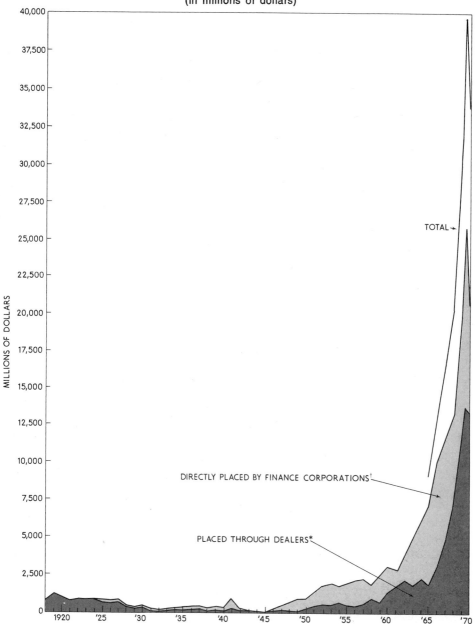

* As reported by dealers; includes finance company paper as well as other commercial paper sold in the open market and in 1969–70 paper of bank holding companies.

† As reported by finance companies that place their paper directly with investors. Also includes paper of bank holding companies in 1969 and 1970.

SOURCE: *Federal Reserve Bulletin.*

funds, and the relatively low cost of money in the commercial market has had great appeal to them as financial intermediaries living on the difference between the cost of money to them and what they can get for the money.

The great expansion in the late 1960's, and particularly in 1969, stemmed largely from heavy corporate demands for credit and restrictions on the bank's ability to compete ratewise for short-term funds through negotiable CD's. In effect, the growth of the commercial paper market represented a short circuiting of the banks' gathering of yield-sensitive short-term investment funds and short-term lending functions.

By mid-1970 some 653 companies carried NCO commercial paper ratings, roughly twice the number rated at year-end 1968. All but 34 of the companies were rated "prime." Total commercial paper peaked at $39.7 billion in May, 1970. This sum ironically included $7.5 billion *borrowed* by bank holding companies for their subsidiary banks. The lifting of some ceilings on CD's in mid-1970 and the subsequent decline of interest rates below these ceilings put the large banks back into more direct and complete competition with the commercial paper market. To what extent the banks will recapture business lost to the commercial paper market remains to be seen. Many new issuing companies, such as public utilities, got a good introduction to the advantages and disadvantages of commercial paper borrowing. A big advantage of borrowing through commercial paper is the relatively low interest cost at which this borrowing can be accomplished. The full costs savings come in part from the fact that interest rates at which commercial paper has been sold have generally been below the banks' prime lending rates. Chart 14–2 shows the relationship between important money market rates in recent years. Complicating cost comparisons have been the banks' requirements of compensating deposit balances to support credit lines (often 10% of the line) and actual borrowing (often 20% of outstandings). On the other hand, the issuers of commercial paper commonly have found it necessary to support the standing of their paper with backup bank credit lines that required deposit support. Moreover, there are some costs of issue—a dealers' commission of 0.125% to 0.25% on an annual basis for paper sold through dealers and the costs of a sales force for those large issuers, chiefly finance companies, that have marketed their paper directly to investors.

A potentially negative aspect of financing through commercial paper stems from its impersonal, arm's-length nature. Sensitized to loss possibilities by the Penn Central affair, the market is unlikely to be indulgent to issuers who encounter difficulties. Hence, all but the least vulnerable issuers must have some concern about how they could cope with maturing notes under conditions that made the sale of new paper difficult.[2]

---

[2] On this point the head of a note issuing finance company commented at the October, 1970, convention of commercial finance companies: "Apart from the comfort the commercial paper purchaser has in knowing that outstanding commercial paper is substan-

Chart 14–2

Selected Short-Term Money Rates, Monthly, 1951–70

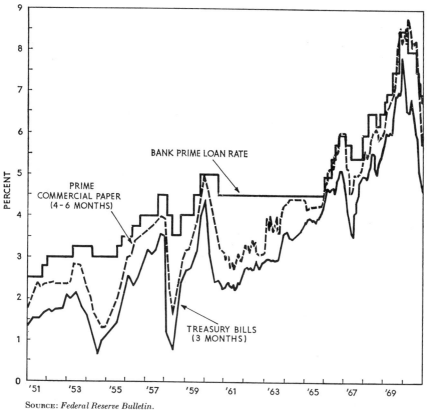

SOURCE: *Federal Reserve Bulletin.*

Notes sold in the commercial paper market do not provide for interest as such. Instead, an effective interest rate is established by sale of the notes at a discount from face value. Thus, a 6-month note for $100,000 sold by a *prime name* in April, 1970, at the then prevailing market rate of 8.00% per annum would net the borrower $95,875, which is the amount left after deduction of interest discount of $4,000 and the dealers' commission of 0.125%, $125.

Finance Companies

The label *finance company* is used loosely in business circles. In the absence of a more crisply definitive term, we use the term *finance companies* to refer to the several thousand firms that are in the business of lend-

tially covered by unused bank lines, one thing must be kept in mind; no matter how fickle we may consider the banking industry to be, as a group they offer much greater loyalty than the note buyers in the commercial paper market. Banking relationships are extremely important in spite of their cost, and they become even more important at times when the commercial paper market is difficult."

ing money, yet cannot be classified as banks, insurance companies, or other forms of traditional financial institutions. This rather broad definition includes many companies which specialize in one or more of several widely different types of lending. However, a few of the largest finance companies, such as the Commercial Credit Company and C.I.T. Financial Corporation (C.I.T.), directly, or through subsidiaries, offer a wide range of lending services. Finance companies, regardless of their special lines of business, raise their funds in much the same general fashion. Almost all are corporations with a significant ownership equity, often in the form of both common and preferred stock. On the basis of the equity investment and profitable records, finance companies have been able to borrow relatively large amounts through short-term bank loans and through sale of commercial paper and a variety of long-term debt instruments. For example, the consolidated balance sheet of C.I.T. on December 31, 1969, showed ownership funds of approximately $532 million compared with total debts of $2,964 million. By borrowing at lower rates than they charge on their loans, the finance companies hope to cover their expenses and enhance the return on their stockholders' investment.

Most of the finance companies specialize in direct lending to individuals and are called *personal finance* or *consumer finance companies*. Household Finance Corporation is the largest company of this type. On June 30, 1970, these firms had outstanding instalment loans of $9.7 billion.[3] Another group of firms are known as *sales finance companies*. These firms specialize in the purchase from retailers of the instalment receivables arising out of retail sales of automobiles, household appliances, industrial equipment, farm equipment, mobile homes, boats, and other durable goods sold on the instalment payment plan. The total instalment credit held by sales finance companies at the end of 1970 was estimated at $16.8 billion.[4] Given the fact of widespread instalment selling, the sales finance companies in effect supply the funds that firms selling on instalment credit would have to acquire elsewhere if they were to carry the investment in receivables themselves. In addition, these firms do a large volume of wholesale financing; that is, they loan to distributors and retailers of the above items to finance their inventory of unsold merchandise. The inventory serves as security for these loans, which typically are on a continuing basis.

Still another group of firms, variously termed *business finance companies* or *commercial finance companies*, lend directly to a wide variety of businesses, mainly small and medium size. The bulk of their lending is against the security of assigned accounts receivable, but they also do a significant amount of lending on inventory and equipment. Under special circumstances, these firms also extend unsecured loans to valued clients, but the volume of their unsecured lending is small. Rates charged are

---

[3] *Federal Reserve Bulletin*, January, 1971, p. 55.
[4] *Ibid.*

relatively high compared to bank rates. Thus, an executive of a leading finance company put their return on a typical receivables financing in early 1971 at about 14%. Most of their business customers are ones that could not qualify for equivalent bank credit; the borrowing relationship typically is a continuing one over a period of years, ending when the position of the borrower has sufficiently improved so that it can shift to lower-cost sources.

Industry sources estimated the combined volume of commercial finance and factoring in 1970 at $30 billion, up from $2.67 billion in 1945. Some $20 billion of this was in commercial financing, $10 billion, factoring.[5] In view of the turnover of receivables and other assets against which the total advances were made, the credit extended at any one time was only a fraction, some 10%–15% of the $30 billion annual total. Nevertheless, the volume of such credit is significant and has grown steadily through boom and recession years alike.

A limited number of finance companies specialize in providing a distinctive financing service known as *factoring*. Factoring is essentially the purchase of accounts receivable. It has become sufficiently important to warrant separate discussion later in this chapter.

As we have suggested, the lines between the various types of finance companies often are blurred. A breakdown of the receivables acquired during 1969 and those outstanding on December 31, 1969, in the course of the finance company operations of Commercial Credit Company and its subsidiaries indicates the varied kinds of financing supplied by this leading diversified firm:

Receivables Acquired during 1969
(in millions)

Motor retail	$ 574.2
Mobile homes retail	360.2
Farm equipment and other retail	354.3
Personal loans	630.3
Motor, mobile homes, and other wholesale	1,273.3
Business loans and factoring	2,339.0
Leasing and lease financing	424.6
	$5,955.9

Receivables Outstanding on December 31, 1969
(in millions)

Motor retail	$ 678.6
Mobile homes retail	623.1
Farm equipment and other retail	492.5
Personal loans	552.3
Motor, mobile homes, and other wholesale	327.4
Business loans and factoring	371.9
Leasing and lease financing	636.5
Other accounts and notes	39.8
	$3,722.1

SOURCE: *Commercial Credit Annual Report for 1969.*

---

[5] National Commercial Finance Conference, Inc., *Annual Convention of the Commercial Finance Industry, 1970* (New York, the Conference), p. 34.

The diversified lending operations of companies like Commercial Credit Company suggest a characteristic important to many business borrowers. Generally, the better finance companies have won a reputation as venturesome and imaginative lenders. Their willingness to consider lending to companies in difficult situations, and their skill and resourcefulness in setting up lending arrangements that meet the pressing needs of borrowers yet hold the lender's risks to tolerable proportions, have made them an invaluable source of credit for many companies and have won them an important role in the economy.

The Use of Factoring

As an alternative method of converting accounts receivable into cash, many firms can look to factoring, a service offered by factoring concerns and a very limited number of commercial banks.[6]

For many decades, factoring has been very important in the textile industry, and this industry is still the source of a large percentage of total factoring business. In recent decades its use has spread to many other industries. Factoring perhaps can best be understood if major distinctive aspects of a factoring arrangement are compared with those of a loan secured by assignment of accounts receivable. As we shall see in Chapter 15, under the typical accounts receivable loan arrangement the borrower still holds title to his accounts receivable,[7] and the lender expects him to absorb losses if particular accounts are not paid. The firms owing the accounts normally are *not* notified that their account is pledged and continue to send their payments to the borrower. In contrast, the typical factoring arrangement has the following characteristics:

1. The factor *purchases* accounts acceptable to him without recourse. That is, if the accounts are not paid, the loss is the factor's. The client no longer carries factored accounts receivable on his balance sheet, in effect having converted them into cash.[8]

2. Firms owing the accounts receivable to client firms are notified that

---

[6] Among the larger firms active in factoring are two subsidiaries of C.I.T. Financial Corporation, Meinhard-Commercial Corporation and William Iselin & Company, Inc.; a subsidiary of Commercial Credit Company, Textile Banking Company, Inc.; W. E. Heller and Company; James Talcott, Inc., and John P. Maguire and Company, Inc.

The First National Bank of Boston, The Trust Company of Georgia, and the Bank of America N.T. and S.A. have for some years operated factoring services on an important scale. In recent years a number of major banks, including First National City Bank of New York, Citizens and Southern National Bank, and United California Bank, entered the field by purchasing factoring firms.

[7] The borrower pledging accounts receivable shows the pledged receivables on his balance sheet. Good accounting practice requires note, however, of the fact that they are pledged as security.

[8] Where the factor advances less than 100% of the receivables, the borrower carries his equity in the receivable among his assets. Thus, if $500,000 of accounts are factored but only 90% is advanced, the client would show accounts receivable of $50,000 on his balance sheet.

the account has been sold to the factor and are asked to remit directly to the factor.

3. As implied above, the factor seldom agrees to buy all of the accounts receivable of a client firm; instead, he retains the right to screen the accounts and select those acceptable to him. The client firm can continue to sell to customers whose accounts are unacceptable to the factor, but it must carry them itself and assume all risks on them.

4. Under the typical factoring arrangement the client maintains a running account with the factor. As receivables are sold to the factor, the proceeds are put at the client's disposal in this account. Often, clients are given the privilege of overdrawing their account with the factor, or, in effect, of borrowing on an unsecured basis, in addition to drawing against the proceeds of the factored accounts. Also, interest is normally credited by the factor on funds left with him.

Usually, the factor's charges are computed and assigned to the client's account once a month. The computation of the factor's net charges, involving a variety of charges and credits, is a somewhat complex one. This complexity, together with the fact that the factor provides certain distinctive services, such as credit investigation, collection, and the absorption of bad-debt losses, makes difficult a clear-cut comparison of the costs of factoring with the costs of alternative methods of raising funds. However, factoring is widely regarded as a relatively high-cost method of financing. Outside the textile industry, factoring has been used most widely by firms with annual sales in the $500,000 to $10 million range.

Private Lenders

In past decades a number of private individuals who had accumulated considerable wealth, particularly in the smaller cities and towns of the nation, made a practice of lending money. While most of their loans took the form of long-term notes, they did some short-term lending to businesses, particularly smaller local concerns. While no statistical information is available on the loans of individuals to businesses, there is strong reason to believe that the amount of such lending currently is small.

In the larger cities there are still individuals who make business loans, usually to firms that cannot find enough credit elsewhere. Rates charged are very high, often amounting to annual rates of 24% or more on the funds supplied. The little information that is available about such lenders suggests that they are truly a "source of last resort" and that they should be dealt with most cautiously—preferably not at all.

Customer Advances and Prepayments

Some companies are able to get substantial aid from customers in the form of advances against orders for future production and delivery, or by special arrangements under which partial payments are received prior to completion of an order or contract. Such financial aid from customers is most important to producers of large, specialized equipment, where the time and expense involved in production are great. For example, United Aircraft Corporation, whose major product is jet engines, reported customer advances on sales contracts of $110 million on December 31, 1969.

Most contract builders also depend heavily on customer advances and/or contractual agreements under which they are authorized to bill customers as certain costs are incurred in connection with the partially completed contract. For example, Combustion Engineering, Inc., designs, manufactures, and installs complete steam power plant and other such installations. At the end of 1969 Combustion Engineering showed on its balance sheet advance payments from customers of $101.4 million or 18% of total assets of $562.4 million. In addition, contract terms which permitted billing as progress was made on incomplete contracts helped very materially to reduce the financial needs from what they would have been if Combustion Engineering had not been able to collect from customers in advance of completion of the contracts.

Special Credit from Suppliers

In our earlier discussion of trade credit from suppliers as a spontaneous source, we did not discuss the possibilities of obtaining through negotiation special additional credit from suppliers. Under certain circumstances, sellers are willing to grant somewhat longer terms than those made available in routine to all their credit customers. In a number of instances, buying firms have been able to negotiate with the seller special terms for the financing of an especially large or otherwise unique purchase order. Illustrative of such possibilities was the reported willingness of the Hammond Organ Company in 1960 to offer to new distributors of Hammond's products term credits as large as twice the distributor's equity investment. According to the vice president of finance of Hammond: "We will offer loans up to 200%, to be retired in three years, at an attractive interest rate. This capital financing program will help us put into business those who have expressed interest in owning a studio but who have not had the necessary capital."[9]

Not infrequently, hard-pressed firms are able to arrange with important suppliers to put outstanding overdue open-account payables on a note basis with maturities deferred for a period of months or years. In such cases it is usually expected that new purchases will be on open account and regular terms and will be paid promptly when due; it is the prospect of further business and an improved relationship that encourages suppliers to accept deferred payment arrangements on old payables. Needless to say, suppliers enter into such deals with reluctance.

---

[9] *The Wall Street Journal*, October 31, 1960.

Another form of special credit is the use of special credit terms designed to encourage inventory stocking by distributors or retailers well ahead of their normal selling season. In such cases the supplier offers "seasonal datings," that is, special credit terms which require payment only after the retail selling season is well advanced. Special credit terms also are often made available in the case of promotional stocks.

A number of firms have formed finance company affiliates to help dealers finance inventories of their products as well as to take over retail instalment sales contracts. Some firms are willing to support bank borrowing by customers with credit guaranties or agreements to buy back unsold inventories of their products. Suppliers also may provide financial aid to their customers to permit them to acquire specialized equipment necessary to handle their products. A number of dairy products producers help customers acquire refrigeration equipment. Grain companies may finance customers' purchases of bulk feed storage facilities. Oil companies may help finance the construction of filling stations.

Speaking generally, suppliers are most likely to consider granting special credit terms when all or most of the following circumstances exist: The customer is one who can be expected to buy important quantities of goods in the future if the special terms are granted; the customer can get equally satisfactory products from other suppliers; the supplier itself is well financed; the supplier expects to operate at a rate short of full capacity, and marginal production costs are low; and there is evidence that the need for special credit will not last indefinitely. If the supplier is making a large profit margin on marginal increments of sales, the chances of his agreeing to a special credit deal are enhanced greatly.

Reliance on suppliers for unusual credit arrangements can have weighty disadvantages, including the loss of bargaining power on price, delivery, and other terms. However, firms hard pressed for funds should not overlook the possibility of negotiating special credit terms for new purchases, extended payment terms on existing payables, or other forms of assistance from major suppliers.

Credit Instruments Used Predominantly in Foreign Trade: The Banker's Acceptance

Certain credit instruments, of which the *banker's acceptance* is the most important, are used primarily in connection with the financing of imports from and exports to foreign countries. The financing of foreign trade involves many distinctive instruments and practices, detailed description of which is best left to specialized books on the subject. We shall briefly discuss here the banker's acceptance and its use, both because of its importance in foreign trade and as an example of the specialized instruments of credit that have been developed to meet special needs.

The banker's acceptance begins as a *draft* or demand for payment, drawn on a bank, asking the bank to pay a stated amount to a stated firm or its assignees at a definite date. When the bank on which it is drawn agrees to make the payment by writing "Accepted" on the draft (along with the signature of an authorized official of the bank), it becomes a banker's acceptance—or an obligation of the accepting bank. Of course, the bank will only accept drafts in behalf of customers who have made the necessary previous arrangements with the bank and convinced it that they in turn will repay the bank upon maturity of the acceptance. The accepting bank charges a commission of $\frac{1}{2}\%$–$2\frac{1}{2}\%$ depending on the credit quality of the bank's customer.

An illustration may help to explain how the banker's acceptance is used as a source of credit by business firms. Let us assume that a New York manufacturer of topcoats desires to import a $20,000 shipment of Harris tweed from a manufacturer in Scotland. The Scottish manufacturer is anxious to make the sale and will be willing to defray the costs of extending the credit the American importer wants on the deal—say, 90 days from shipment.

The New York garmentmaker—who, we shall assume, has a good credit standing with his New York bank—arranges to have his bank open a *letter of credit* in favor of the Scottish tweed manufacturer. This document states that the New York bank will honor—or accept—drafts drawn on the New York firm, provided they are drawn in accordance with detailed terms stated in the letter of credit. When shipment is made, the Scottish firm prepares a 90-day draft on the New York firm in accordance with the letter of credit and presents it to its Scottish bank. That bank will advance the funds—actually, the pound equivalent of $20,000 less interest and fees—to the Scottish company and forward the draft along with shipping papers, the ocean bill of lading, etc., to its New York correspondent bank, which presents it to the New York manufacturer's bank for acceptance. If all papers are found to be in order, the New York manufacturer's bank accepts the draft, and it becomes a *banker's acceptance*.

Since there is an open market in bankers' acceptances based on their very strong credit standing as a result of the bank's acceptance, the Scottish bank could readily arrange its sale and thus recoup the dollar equivalent of the funds it had advanced. The American manufacturer gets the credit he wants, the risks to all parties except the accepting bank are minimal, and the sales transaction is completed. The credit transaction is completed when in 90 days the acceptance is presented to the New York bank and paid by it; and the bank, in turn, looks for repayment to the New York manufacturer.

Of course, the accepting bank depends heavily on the credit of its customer—the New York importing manufacturer. It may release the goods to him upon arrival only under a security arrangement, or it may satisfy itself that it can safely accept the draft without requiring security when the goods are released to the manufacturer.

Since the Scottish firm, or its bank, usually is in a poor position to assess the creditworthiness of the American customer, the use of the letter of credit and the insertion of the American bank's credit into the picture through its acceptance is an important, and often vital, part of the trade arrangement.

Although bankers' acceptances are used predominantly to finance the movement of goods in international trade, they are also used to a modest extent for domestic transactions where goods are used as security. In one field, the domestic storage and sale of raw cotton by cotton dealers, bankers' acceptances are a major method of financing. At the end of November, 1970, bankers' acceptances outstanding were estimated at $6,267 million. Bankers' acceptances, like commercial paper, are bought and sold on a discount basis. Discount rates during December, 1970, averaged 5.25%, a rate below that of prime commercial paper, and only modestly above the rate of U.S. government 90-day bills.[10] The low rate reflects the high credit standing of bankers' acceptances as obligations of the banks.[11]

State, Regional, or Local Development Credit Corporations

In a number of states and localities, development credit corporations have been established to support and develop economic activity and employment in their areas by extending financial or other support to firms that cannot secure needed funds from conventional lenders. Most of the development credit corporations operate with local government encouragement; some operate with public funds, but most are privately financed. Although they make short-term loans, their loans are more commonly of intermediate term and call for instalment repayment. One of the first of these, the Massachusetts Business Development Corporation, had in 16 years through 1969 made loans of more than $45 million.

The total financing provided by the local development corporations represents only a small fraction of the credit extended by banks or trade creditors. But their existence does add a possible alternative to firms having difficulty meeting their needs elsewhere.

U.S. Governmental Sources of Short-Term Funds

In recent decades the United States Congress has enacted a number of laws providing for federal government financial assistance to business enterprise. Most of these programs have been directed at meeting financial needs which have been intermediate or long term rather than short term as we have defined it. In view of the great variety in the provisions for

---

[10] *Federal Reserve Bulletin,* January, 1971.

[11] For a more complete description of the use of acceptances and the market for them, see Federal Reserve Bank of Cleveland, *Monthly Business Review,* July, 1970.

governmental financial assistance, however, a classification of the purposes of federal financial assistance to private concerns may be helpful. The legislation providing for governmental financial assistance seems to fall into four rough categories.

1. Broad-scale government loans to business under depression conditions, in which the normal sources of financial assistance to business are inadequate for business needs, or where the economic welfare of the country suggests the wisdom of lending standards more lenient than those normally considered appropriate by lenders for profit.
2. Legislation under which governmental agencies seek to fill gaps in the financial structure of the country believed to exist under normal economic conditions.
3. Aids to suppliers to the government of military items.
4. Special aids to particularly deserving groups such as military personnel returning to civilian life and the victims of floods, tornadoes, or other disasters.

Broad-Scale Government Financing to Business under Depression Circumstances

During the depression of the 1930's, several governmental agencies were established to loan public funds to business firms in need of aid because of depressed conditions. The Reconstruction Finance Corporation was the most important agency set up for this purpose, and it granted loans on a massive scale to a wide variety of businesses, both large and small. Most of the RFC loans called for periodic repayment over a period of years. During World War II, this agency also provided much aid to industries vital to the war effort. Finally, in 1953, after having loaned more than \$12 billion, the RFC was phased out. In the event of another depression, the federal government probably would again establish credit facilities of the RFC type.

Government Efforts to Fill Gaps in the Availability of Credit

Even under prosperous conditions, Congress has concluded that private financing agencies have not met fully the needs of all segments of socially desirable business. Most important of the gaps have been in the availability of intermediate loan capital for smaller businesses, in the loan capital available to farmers, in credit on export sales, and mortgage funds for housing. Various agencies have been set up to assist small businesses to meet their capital needs. The most recent of these, the Small Business Administration, in 1953 was given the authority both to make direct loans and to guarantee portions of loans to small business by banks and other private lenders. The Small Business Administration has described the business loan program in these words:

Section 207(a) of the Act gives the Small Business Administration authority *to make loans to small business enterprises when credit is not otherwise available on reasonable terms.* The loans are intended to fill a gap in the financing provided small firms by private financial institutions and are designed to stimulate and preserve the initiative, independence and enterprise of small businesses. To the greatest extent possible, the Small Business Administration is striving to provide this credit in cooperation with private lending institutions. Its success in this is evidenced by the fact that about two-thirds of all loans approved are in participation with banks and other financial institutions.

In order to expand financial assistance to small business concerns and to promote a balanced national economy, the Bank–Small Business Administration participation loan plan offers the greatest possible benefit to the participating institution consistent with the intent of the Small Business Act. For example, the plan enables a bank to broaden its lending activities, while maintaining desired liquidity of assets. The bank is assured a fair return on money loaned and is able to give better service to its depositors.

In the administration of its lending program under Section 207(a) of the Small Business Act, the Small Business Administration is governed by the policies established by the Agency's Loan Policy Board and the requirement of the Act that *"loans be of such sound value or so secured as reasonably to assure repayment."*[12] The Agency applies the most liberal interpretation of these policies and requirements possible, consistent with sound credit principles, but at the same time is fully aware of its responsibility to protect Government funds. Therefore, each loan application is thoroughly analyzed and a loan is never approved or declined without full consideration of all factors concerned. The Agency's lending program is under continual study, and the area in which credit can be provided safely is being constantly reviewed.

In the decade of the sixties, SBA lending activity grew to an annual rate of $800 million, four times the annual rate of 10 years earlier. Loans are granted under several programs, the largest of which, "Business Loans," involved loans of slightly over $500 million in both 1968 and 1969. Average loan size approximated $33,000 in 1969; few exceeded $500,000. Banks provided 60% of 1969 loan funds. The maximum rate the SBA can charge on business loans is $5\frac{1}{2}\%$.

Losses, actual and projected, on SBA business loans through June 30, 1969, amounted to $106 million or 3.5% of the $3 billion actually disbursed by the SBA to that date.

Under Section 207(b), as amended, of the Small Business Act of 1953, the SBA is also authorized to make loans to assist in the rehabilitation of homes and businesses which have been damaged by floods, storms, or other natural disasters. In addition, the SBA is empowered to give loan assistance to businesses suffering economic loss as a result of drought conditions where there is any reasonable chance of rehabilitation. In the words of the SBA: "Loans can be made only to the extent of actual losses

---

[12] Italics supplied.

(apart from those of drought) not covered by insurance, and, as in the case of regular business loans, cannot be approved if the financing is otherwise available on reasonable terms."

Since the disaster loans are intended as a rehabilitation measure, much more liberal credit standards are applied to them than would be prudent for the Agency's business loans. Interest rates, too, are lower (3%).

The most costly disaster in SBA's history occurred when Hurricane Camille struck the Gulf Coast area on August 17, 1969. In the following 4 months 7,612 disaster loans totaling $85 million were approved.

As might be expected, SBA estimates of ultimate loss on disaster loans were higher, at 3.86% of disbursements, than on business loans.

The SBA also has important administrative responsibilities under the Small Business Investment Act. This act provided for certain government tax and financial aids to privately owned investing firms organized under the regulations established for Small Business Investment Companies. By 1970 some 450 "SBIC's" with combined assets of about $600 million were in operation.[13] These firms make loan or equity investments in small businesses. Usually, the loans are for a period of years. By mid-1970, SBIC's had invested more than $1.8 billion in more than 37,200 small companies. In a later chapter we shall discuss further the work of the SBIC's in supplying funds to small business.

Governmental financial aid to farmers has taken a variety of forms. Suffice it for our purpose here to recognize that sizable governmental programs exist to help the farmers finance both long-term and short-term needs.

One student of the subject commented that government programs of loans to private business, such as those of the RFC and the SBA, shared the following characteristics:

1. Avoidance of competition with private lenders and the related emphasis on participation arrangements with private lenders.
2. Emphasis on secured loans.
3. Elaborate procedure of loan processing involving counseling on business management matters.
4. Large proportion of loan applications denied.
5. Relative inflexibility of interest rates over time and absence of differentials for varying size, risk, and maturity of loans.
6. Intermediate-term financing for working capital purposes.
7. Large proportion of loan approvals for manufacturing enterprises.
8. Subsidy aspects of programs.[14]

Especially important among the government-sponsored organizations active in the support of export sales by U.S. firms has been the Export-

---

[13] Small Business Administration, *Annual Report to the President and Congress for 1969* (Washington, D.C.: U.S. Government Printing Office, 1969).

[14] Carl T. Arlt, *Financing Small Business* (Washington, D.C.: Board of Governors, Federal Reserve System, 1958), chap. xii, "Government Loan Programs for Small Business."

Import Bank of the United States, a government-owned corporation. The Eximbank makes direct loans to foreign governments and private concerns which permit them to purchase capital goods and other products from U.S. firms. In addition, the Eximbank has participated with American exporters and U.S. commercial banks in extending short- and intermediate-term credit to foreign buyers on specific export transactions, such as the sale of textile machinery to a Colombian textile manufacturer. Since July 1, 1963, the Eximbank has had an active program of guaranteeing medium-term and long-term credits to foreigners by U.S. exporters of capital goods. This has facilitated the efforts of the U.S. vendor firms to have banks take over these credits without recourse to the exporter if the foreign customer failed to complete his payments. The Eximbank has also had an important role in the development of programs of insurance against certain of the risks in extending routine export credit.[15]

The scale of Eximbank lending, guaranty, and insurance activity has been substantial. In the year ended June 30, 1970, Eximbank authorized a total of $3,968 million in loans, guaranties, and insurance. Total loans authorized over its life through June 30, 1970, amounted to $24 billion; on June 30, 1970, outstanding loans were approximately $5.7 billion.[16]

Financial Aids to Military Suppliers

Considerations of national defense make it important that vital defense suppliers not be hampered by financial limitations. A variety of forms of aid to military suppliers have been developed including the following:

1. Government construction and equipping of plants with government money.
2. Authorization of rapid amortization of defense-oriented new equipment and facilities owned and operated by private concerns.
3. Government guaranties of commercial bank loans to military contractors.
4. Progress payments.
5. Advance payments.

The first four of these were used widely in World War II and during the Korean conflict. By the 1970's, only progress payments remained a highly important source of government funds for its suppliers. Military contracts may authorize predelivery payments to the contractor, as work proceeds, on the basis of costs incurred or upon accomplishment of stages of completion of the project. It is common practice for contracting agencies to provide for progress payments on sizable contracts. As of Septem-

---

[15] For an extended exposition of the export financing assistance programs of the Eximbank, see Export-Import Bank of the United States, *U.S. Export Financial Programs*, (3d ed.; December, 1970).

[16] Export-Import Bank of the United States, *Annual Report—FY 1970* (Washington, D.C.: U.S. Government Printing Office, 1970).

ber 30, 1970, the Defense Department had progress payments of $9.8 billion outstanding. After March 1, 1968, "customary" progress payments on new contracts based on costs were 80% of the contractor's total cost outlays, or in some cases 100% of his direct labor and materials costs. Provision was also made for the approval, under exceptional circumstances, of "unusual" progress payments at greater percentages of the contractor's incurred costs.

Advance payments differ from progress payments in that payments may be made in anticipation of performance under the contract, without regard to costs incurred or the stage of project completion. Advance payments are made only if no other method of financing will meet the contractor's needs. Such payments are most widely used to finance contracts with nonprofit institutions. In the third quarter of 1970, new contracts with nonprofit institutions were at an annual rate of $50 million.

Programs of Aid to Especially Deserving Groups

An example of programs of this sort is the provision by legislation for governmental guaranties of certain loans by banks or other private agencies to ex-servicemen. Greatest use of these loan guaranties by veterans has been for the purchase of homes; through November, 1970, almost 8 million home loans of $79 billion had been granted under this program. For veterans serving before February, 1955, guaranties of up to 50% and a dollar amount of $2,000 could be obtained for business ventures that had good promise of success. Some 254,000 such loans, totaling $652 million, were made. Defaults under this latter program proved substantial (on 18% of the loans through 1963) and claims for Veterans Administration reimbursement were filed on about 7%.

chapter 15

The Effective Use of Security in Business Borrowing

A vital feature of much business borrowing is the granting to lenders of a security interest in particular assets of the borrower. A large percentage of the commercial bank credit, and virtually all of the credit granted business by commercial finance companies and governmental agencies, is predicated on the granting of security.

The importance of security in bank borrowing is documented by comprehensive studies of business loans by member banks of the Federal Reserve System. Key findings relative to the use of security are summarized in Tables 15–1 and 15–2 (page 277). Although the most recent Federal Reserve studies took place in 1957 and 1955, there is no evidence of great change in the use of security in bank borrowing since the dates of the studies.

As Table 15–1 brings out, 66.8% or 856,000 of the 1,281,000 business loans outstanding at these banks were supported by collateral. Comparison with results of earlier studies in 1946 and 1955 indicated that the use of security in commercial bank lending to business had increased moderately in the 1946–57 period.

The use of security is particularly important in the bank borrowing of small and medium-sized firms. This conclusion is supported by the Federal Reserve study, which disclosed that secured loans, while representing 66.8% of the total *number* of business loans, accounted for $20,426 million, or 50.3% of the total *amount* of bank credit to business.[1] The lower dollar amount percentage reflects the fact that most large loans are

---

[1] *Federal Reserve Bulletin*, April, 1958.

Table 15–1

Relation of Secured Loans to Total Business Loans of Member Banks, 1957,
within Size-of-Borrower Groups

Size of Borrower by Assets (in $ 000)	Loans by Amount ($ in Millions)			Loans by Number (in Thousands)		
	Total Loans	Secured Loans	Secured as % of Total	Total Loans	Secured Loans	Secured as % of Total
All*.................	$40,618	$20,426	50.3	1,281	856	66.8
Less than 50..........	1,456	1,141	78.4	505	344	68.2
50–250..............	5,256	4,023	76.5	494	325	65.7
250–1,000...........	6,302	4,543	72.1	158	104	65.9
1,000–5,000.........	6,775	4,056	59.9	48	29	60.7
5,000–25,000........	5,912	2,661	45.0	13	6	48.5
25,000–100,000......	4,893	1,381	28.2	5	2	31.7
100,000 or more......	8,815	1,546	17.5	6	2	34.7

* Includes a small number of loans to companies whose size was not ascertained.
Source: *Federal Reserve Bulletin*, April, 1958, p. 403.

made on an unsecured basis. As might be expected in view of the general tendency for the financial strength of business firms to increase with asset size, the study showed that the use of security varied inversely with the size of the borrowing firm. Thus, 76.5% of the bank credit extended firms with total assets of between $50,000 and $250,000 was on a secured basis, while only 17.5% of the credit extended firms with assets above $100 million was secured.[2]

As we have seen, commercial finance companies are important lenders to business. A very high percentage of their loans to business is extended against security. Since the finance companies generally have been willing to loan to companies inherently more risky than commercial banks have cared to accommodate, they have been especially vigorous and imaginative in developing ways of taking security as a means of curbing their risks in lending.

The lending to business by governmental and semigovernmental agencies has been predominantly on a secured basis. A major proportion of the Reconstruction Finance Corporation loans were made against specific security. The loans currently made by the Small Business Administration, and loans supported by governmental guaranties to aid in the financing of military contracts typically are predicated on the grant of a security interest to the lender.

Why Borrowers Offer Security to Lenders

The paramount reason why most borrowers offer lenders a security interest in their assets is simply to enhance their borrowing power. Many

[2] *Ibid.*

American concerns, particularly very large ones, enjoy such excellent profit prospects and strong financial positions that they do not need to offer security—they can get sufficient credit on suitable terms on an un-secured basis. But a great many more enterprises are able to boost their attractiveness to lenders materially by skillful concession of security inter-ests in their assets.

To many firms with uncertain prospects or limited ownership funds, little or no credit, other than that from the spontaneous sources described in Chapter 11, is available on an unsecured basis. Only by offering se-curity attractive to lenders are they able to get loans at all. In other words, to these firms, use of security in borrowing is not really a matter of choice but the *sine qua non* of any debt financing. Still other, less weak, concerns could arrange some bank credit on an unsecured basis but can get more by offering security.

In the case of other borrowers, offering security may be desirable primarily as a means of obtaining more favorable credit terms—lower interest rates, longer maturity schedules, or less restrictive covenants—than could be obtained through unsecured borrowing. For example, many railroads use locomotives or other rolling stock as security under equip-ment trust certificates, a borrowing device referred to later in this chapter. The repayment record of equipment trust certificates over past decades has been so excellent that it is usually possible for even the strongest railroads to borrow through equipment trust certificates at lower net interest rates than could be obtained through unsecured borrowing for comparable periods.

Why Security Is Valuable to the Lender

Why do lenders so frequently prefer a *secured position* to the status of an unsecured creditor? As suggested earlier, lenders take collateral pri-marily as a means of reducing the risk of loss through nonrepayment of their loans. The risks of loss may be reduced by a secured position in several ways:

1. Under many security arrangements, close contact with the borrower is required in order to maintain an effective secured position. As a by-product of the security arrangement, the lender often gains a more complete and up-to-date acquaintance with the borrower's affairs than he would have obtained as an unsecured creditor.

2. Under many security arrangements the lender obtains a close and continuing control over assets vital to the borrower's business. This control helps to prevent the sale or diversion of assets that the lender is looking to as an ultimate source of repayment of his loan. Some lenders would be willing to accept an unsecured status *provided* no other creditor could obtain a prior claim. By taking key assets as security, the lender assures himself that these assets cannot be pledged to another creditor

who would thereby gain priority over unsecured lenders. If the lender has full confidence in the borrower, he may seek to gain this same objective through an agreement that the borrower will not pledge assets to other lenders. Such compacts, known as *negative pledge* agreements, are used with some frequency.

3. Finally, and most basically, if the borrower encounters serious financial difficulties and cannot meet his obligations, the secured lender expects to enjoy a prior claim to the security and to the net proceeds from its disposition. Under certain circumstances, if the borrower cannot meet his commitments to the secured lender, the lender can seize and sell his security to satisfy his debt without ever becoming a party to developing bankruptcy proceedings. Alternatively, if all of the distressed borrower's assets are placed under the supervision of a bankruptcy court for distribution to creditors or for reorganization of the business, the secured lender expects to be able to establish his prior claim over unsecured creditors to the proceeds of his security.

Taking over security does not necessarily mean the full satisfaction of the debt obligation. In the event that sale of the security does not net enough money to pay off the debt in full, the secured lender usually can obtain a *deficiency judgment* for the unsatisfied portion of the debt. However, for this portion of his debt, the lender ranks as an unsecured or general creditor of the firm and shares pro rata with other unsecured creditors in any proceeds available for them.

Most sizable firms that enter bankruptcy do not undergo complete liquidation of their assets. Very often, the total value of the firm as a reorganized, going concern is judged to be greater than the probable net proceeds from liquidation and dispersal of its assets. Consequently, the firm is reorganized and continues in business. The treatment accorded secured creditors in reorganization is influenced strongly by the value of the secured assets under the alternatives of liquidation or reorganization. Secured creditors with claims on assets vital to the operation of reorganized firms frequently have been paid in full while unsecured creditors suffered heavily. Consequently, the priority ranking of creditors strongly influences their vulnerability to loss in reorganization, as well as in bankruptcy leading to complete liquidation. At worst, secured creditors of bankrupt concerns generally fare substantially less badly than unsecured creditors.

It should be emphasized that the legal rights to a security interest in particular assets can be no more valuable than the assets themselves. If the assets prove of limited value in sale or use, the priority that attaches to the proceeds of this security likewise will be of limited value.

What Assets Make Good Security

Not many decades ago, only *real property*—land and buildings—and marketable securities found widespread use as security for loans. In recent decades the situation has changed markedly. Today, every major type of business asset is used as security for loans in significant volume. Accounts receivable, inventory, equipment, and even claims not yet appearing as assets on the balance sheets of borrowers (such as anticipated rental receipts for property rented under long-term leases) now serve as collateral on an important scale.

Back of the broadening security base for business borrowing have been several developments. Important among these have been major improvements in the legislation covering the use of business assets, such as inventory and receivables, as security. Further, lenders have much improved their skills and techniques in taking and administering a secured position. Vitally important, too, has been the increasing conviction on the part of lenders broadly that such assets as accounts receivable, properly handled, can constitute good security against loss to the lenders.

Of course, this does not mean that in a specific situation a potential lender will conclude that all or any of the firm's assets represent good collateral. Rather, it means that lenders increasingly are willing to take a searching look at almost any asset for its possible value as security. If lenders are to regard a particular asset as attractive security, it must meet four basic tests:

1. The lender must be able, under applicable laws (usually state legislation) to obtain a legal security interest in the asset that clearly is valid and sustainable against challenge in the courts.
2. The lender must be able to achieve a reasonable degree of protection against loss through fraud. This requirement is especially critical in respect to these assets which the lender for practical reasons cannot take into direct and continuous possession.
3. The mechanics of the security device and of supervision of the security interest must be such that they can continue in force without undue expense and trouble to either borrower or lender.
4. The asset must be one that can reasonably be expected to continue to have value over the projected life of the loan. This value must be recognizable and realizable; that is, the lender must be able to forecast with some confidence that even under adverse conditions, he will be able to convert the asset into enough cash to cover his advance.

Establishing a Legally Valid Security Interest

Although certain provisions of federal bankruptcy law may be applicable, the legislation governing the taking of a security interest and the rights and obligations of secured lenders is primarily that of the 50 states. Until recently the state legislation dealing with the granting of security interests was characterized by diversity, complexity, and more than a little obscurity. This was particularly true of the law and practice related to the use of *personal property*—assets other than real estate—as security.

It is pleasing to acknowledge the great progress achieved in recent years toward relative uniformity in state legislation related to many aspects of commercial transactions, including the granting of security. This progress has taken the form of adoption by the states of model legislation called the Uniform Commercial Code. Since the Code went into effect in Pennsylvania in 1954, it has been adopted with limited changes by virtually all the states.

A great deal of effort by outstanding members of the bar and other interested parties went into the drafting of the provisions of the Uniform Commercial Code. Section 9 of the Code was devoted to security interests; its provisions sought to clarify both basic concepts and legal mechanics of granting a security interest. For example, the pre-Code requirements of the various states were particularly diverse regarding the methods by which other interested parties could inform themselves of the fact that particular creditors were being extended a security interest in accounts receivable. Clearly, in fairness, trade creditors and other interested parties were entitled to a warning that a security interest had been granted and that the debtor did not hold the accounts receivable free and clear. While agreeing generally to the need for a warning mechanism, the states disagreed as to what form it should take.

The objectives of notification are served under the Uniform Commercial Code by requirement of *notice filing* at a designated public office, often that of the secretary of state at the state capitol, to put other creditors on notice that the debtor has given, or may in the future give, to one or more specified creditors, an interest in the accounts receivable (or other assets if they are covered). Notice can take the form of filing the signed security agreement between borrower and lender or, alternatively, by the filing of a financing statement which either may relate to a particular transaction or may give generalized warning of present and future transactions in receivables or other types of assets.

Although widespread adoption of the Uniform Commercial Code has reduced much of the pre-Code ambiguities and uncertainty related to taking a security interest, a cautionary generalization still has broad validity: *Lenders must exercise great care in taking a security interest and in maintaining it.* If the borrower gets into financial difficulties and bankruptcy ensues, typically, unsecured creditors also will be in the picture. It will be to the unsecured creditors' advantage to have as much as possible of the proceeds of the bankrupt's assets put in the pool for division among unsecured creditors. Consequently, counsel for unsecured creditors can be expected to exploit any opportunity to challenge the claims of secured creditors to a priority security interest in the more valuable assets. If counsel for unsecured creditors can find significant flaws in the prior claims, they may well succeed in having the court deny the validity of the security interest, so that the secured lender finds himself unwittingly and unwillingly a general creditor. In effect, lenders against security still must walk a legal tightrope in order to ensure that their claim to a security interest can stand up under challenge in the event the claim needs to be asserted.

BORROWING AGAINST RECEIVABLES

Discounting Notes Receivable

In an earlier chapter we noted that it was once common practice for manufacturing and wholesale firms to sell to retailers on credit terms of several months. The credit instrument in such sales was the unsecured promissory note of the customer. Commonly, the seller *discounted* or borrowed against these notes at his bank. The bank held such notes in its possession and presented them, through correspondent banks, for collection at maturity. Since the discounting bank required endorsement of the notes by the seller, they were known as *two-name paper;* and if either buyer or seller had a good credit standing, the notes represented good support for the bank's advance. No priority of claim over unsecured creditors of either firm was involved, however.

In recent decades the volume of business borrowing through discounting of notes receivable has shrunk.[3] The decline in such financing has resulted not from bankers' unwillingness to discount notes of responsible concerns but from changing business practice in terms of sale. As we noted earlier, most businesses now sell on short terms and on open account. Consequently, even though those firms still selling on notes from creditworthy customers have little trouble converting such notes into cash, the overall volume of such transactions in domestic trade now is small.

While the use of notes receivable in routine trade credit has declined, there has been a sharp increase in the sale of machinery and equipment and consumer durable goods on terms which call for monthly instalment payments over a period of several years. Typically, the manufacturer or retailer granting such credit retains legal title to, or a security interest in, the equipment, and the debt is evidenced by notes or sales contracts which are assignable to lenders. The discounting of notes secured by equipment will be discussed later in this chapter under "Borrowing against Equipment."

Borrowing against Accounts Receivable as Collateral

Since most business concerns sell on credit and on open account, the typical firm has a large investment in accounts receivable. The attitude of banks and other commercial lenders toward accounts receivable as security has changed substantially in the last 25 years. In earlier periods,

---

[3] In Western European countries and many others around the world, the sale of goods on bills of exchange and their discounting still is commonplace.

many lenders, particularly commercial banks, hesitated to enter into loan agreements with accounts receivable as security. Generally, they took accounts receivable as security only as a means toward the "working-out" of loans which had "gone sour." As a consequence, the use by a business of its accounts receivable as security for loans was widely regarded as evidence of serious financial weakness on the part of that firm.

Despite this early stigma and the problems involved in lending against accounts receivable, this form of lending has become important in recent decades. Basic to the growth is the solid fact that accounts receivable represent the closest asset to cash timewise and the asset of soundest value of many would-be borrowers. For example, many small, financially weak shoe manufacturers sell on short terms to large retail chain stores or department stores whose credit is excellent. Too, much progress has been made in the development of procedures for efficient and low-cost handling of the extensive paper work necessarily involved in lending against accounts receivable. Aware of fraud hazards in this sort of lending, lenders have had considerable success also in developing policing techniques which reduce the opportunities and temptations for fraud. These include periodic inspection of the borrower's receivables records, selective verification, often through a public accounting firm, of the receivables through confirmation by the customers of the amounts they owe the borrowers, and especial effort to see that the accounting procedures for crediting returned merchandise are adequate and are followed carefully.

Other important measures of curbing the risk in loaning against accounts receivable have come into widespread use. Perhaps most important among these are the following:

1. Lenders reserve the right to select the accounts that will be acceptable to them as security. Effort is made to screen out and exclude from the security base overdue accounts and current accounts from concerns financially weak or with a poor reputation for payment.
2. Accounts typically are accepted *with recourse*. That is, the borrower agrees to replace those accounts that are not paid reasonably promptly with acceptable accounts not overdue, or to reduce the loan accordingly.
3. Perhaps most important is the usual practice of loaning only a percentage of the full face amount of the accounts pledged. For example, if the lender advances only 75% of the face value of the accounts pledged, the 25% margin is available to cover prompt payment discounts, goods returned by the customer for credit, and demands for allowances for faulty merchandise or damaged goods, and accounts that prove uncollectible. If these are expected to be high, a wider margin of safety is sought through establishment of a lower percentage of loan to accounts pledged.
4. Typically, a maximum limit also is established on the total amount

that will be loaned, regardless of the total value of the security. This ceiling recognizes that the general credit of the borrower is also back of the loan and that this added protection is diluted when the receivables loan becomes very large relative to the total resources of the borrower.

Now, let us get some idea of the mechanics of receivables borrowing by reviewing typical terms of loan agreements drawn up to cover bank loans against receivables. Points covered in the loan agreement or other papers establishing the loan arrangements commonly include the following:

1. The term of life of the lending arrangements. Although provision often is made that the loan secured by receivables is payable on demand of the lender, there is usually an understanding that the loan will continue for a considerable or indefinite period. Many receivables loans continue for years, terminating only when the company no longer needs to borrow or has prospered to a point where it can get satisfactory credit on an unsecured basis.

2. Agreement that the bank may screen the accounts to determine which represent acceptable security, and an outline of the procedures by which accepted accounts that become overdue are replaced or the loan base is reduced.

3. The percentage that the bank will loan against the face amount of receivables.

4. The maximum dollar amount of the loan against receivables.

5. The evidence that the borrower must submit in support of the validity of the accounts. In some cases, only a simple listing of the customers and the amounts owing from each is required. In other cases the borrower may be required to submit such evidence as original invoices, or signed receipts from shipping companies, for the goods giving rise to the account receivable.

6. Authorization to the lender to inspect the borrower's books upon demand or to undertake other methods of checking up on the validity of the receivables given as collateral.

7. The frequency with which the borrower can bring in new accounts to add to the security base and thus permit greater borrowing, as well as the interval within which he must bring in the money collected from pledged accounts to pay down the loan. In some cases, collections and new accounts added are brought in daily, and a new calculation is made of security base and loan balance. Since most firms make new credit sales and collections each day, both the gross value of the accounts given as security and the loan amount totals are shifting ones. Specific receivables pledged change, and the totals pledged and borrowed rise and fall; but normally, some accounts remain outstanding, and so does the loan against the receivables.

What Lenders Make Accounts Receivable Loans?

Commercial banks, commercial credit companies, and factoring concerns are the principal financial concerns that lend against accounts receivable on a major scale. In commercial banking circles it is now widely recognized that accounts receivable can represent satisfactory security, and most large banks now stand ready to make such loans as part of a well-rounded lending service to business. Since such lending often implies relatively steady lending, requires more paper work and generally more trouble to service than most loans, and necessitates some specialized knowledge and procedures, many smaller banks have shown little interest in making such loans.

As indicated earlier, commercial credit companies pioneered in accounts receivable lending, and such lending still accounts for a substantial portion of their total lending volume. While factoring concerns, as explained earlier, finance receivables primarily on a purchase basis, they also do a certain amount of lending against pledge of receivables.

Costs of Borrowing against Accounts Receivable

Since companies borrowing against receivables tend to be of less than average financial strength, and since the continuing borrowing arrangement involves relatively high expense and trouble to the lender, the costs of such borrowing tend to be higher than on unsecured loans to stronger companies. When the interest rate charged by banks to prime credits on an unsecured basis is around 6%, the interest rate on accounts receivable loans will likely be 8% to 9%; and additional charges for servicing the account, amounting to an annual cost of 1% or 2%, are common. Total charges by nonbank lenders commonly amount to an annual rate of 12% to 16% of the credit supplied, and often may be higher.

BORROWING AGAINST INVENTORY

As we have seen, most business firms have a substantial portion of their resources invested in inventory. And many in need of credit have inventory with characteristics that make it good collateral for borrowing. Of the 799,100 secured bank loans covered in a 1955 Federal Reserve study summarized in Table 15–2, some 47,400 loans representing 9.2% of the total amount and 5.9% of the number were secured by inventory.

What Inventory Makes Good Collateral?

An outstanding characteristic of the investment in inventory of a great many firms is its heterogeneity. The typical manufacturer, for example, has on hand raw materials, work in process, finished goods, and supplies; and each of these categories consists of a variety of items of different

Table 15–2

Business Loans at Member Banks of Federal Reserve System, October 5, 1955
(estimates of outstanding loans)

	Amount of Loans (In Millions)	Number of Loans (In Thousands)	Percentage Distribution	
			Amount	Number
Unsecured...................	$15,105	386.1	49.0	32.6
Secured....................	15,700	799.1	51.0	67.4
Total, all loans.............	$30,805	1,185.2	100.0	100.0
Secured Loans (by type of security):				
Endorsed, comaker, or				
guaranteed.................	$ 2,755	185.9	17.5	23.3
Receivables and other claims......	2,813	52.9	17.9	6.6
Inventories..................	1,448	47.4	9.2	5.9
Equipment...................	2,194	218.5	14.0	27.3
Plant and other real estate........	3,592	164.4	22.9	20.6
U.S. government securities........	182	8.5	1.2	1.1
Other bonds.................	165	2.6	1.0	0.3
Stocks......................	1,002	39.1	6.4	4.9
Life insurance and savings				
accounts...................	447	53.8	2.8	6.7
Other security................	1,102	26.1	7.1	3.3
Total, secured loans..........	$15,700	799.1	100.0	100.0

Source: "Security Pledged on Business Loans at Member Banks," *Federal Reserve Bulletin*, September, 1959.

sizes, shapes, and grades. In considering the possibilities of bolstering a credit application by giving the lenders a security interest in particular inventory, it can be helpful to appraise the inventory in terms of the qualities that lenders look for in deciding whether a particular commodity will be good security.

The physical characteristics of the goods are of basic importance. Clearly, lenders prefer products that are not vulnerable to physical deterioration during the terms of the credit. Wheat of low moisture content, properly stored, resists deterioration for long periods, for example, in contrast to fresh peaches, which may go soft, even under refrigeration, in a matter of hours. While conditions of storage can affect perishability risks, it is possible to generalize that lenders are little interested in taking as security those commodities subject to substantial risks of physical deterioration.

Relatively homogeneous products generally are preferred to commodities whose grade or quality is diverse or hard to measure. For example, lumber of a single type, grade, size, and shape would be easier to appraise and keep tallied than lumber of diverse kinds, grades, and shapes.[4]

[4] At a 1964 convention of the commercial finance industry, a participant on an industry panel was asked, "Do you find, in the event of liquidation, that the inventory mix is

Although bulk is not necessarily undesirable, commodities of high value relative to bulk generally are preferred.

It is perhaps more important that the commodity be one that reasonably can be expected to continue to have resale value. No lender wants to take over inventory and have to dispose of it. But he wants to be confident that if he must, he can find a ready buyer at a good price. What factors help build such confidence? First is a record of price stability in the past. Some products, such as wool, have records of rapid and wide price fluctuations in contrast to the relative price stability of such items as sheet steel.

Second, the existence of a broad, local market for the commodity heightens the possibility that buyers can be found at a relatively small reduction in price. Such a broad market is more likely to exist if the commodity is a relatively standard one. High-style items with a narrow local market, such as women's high-style dresses in a small midwestern town, could be compared with uncut yard goods of a popular grade and color suitable for men's suits, located in New York City, center of the garment industry. Usually, raw materials have a broader market than semiprocessed or finished goods where the process of manufacture has created distinctive features. Most lenders are very reluctant to lend much on in-process inventories.

Third, the existence of frequent selling transactions in an organized market with published price quotations helps the lender to follow trends in value of the product with minimum effort.

Fourth, as is true of any asset considered as security, the commodity must be such that the borrower can give the lender a clear-cut security interest without undue inconvenience or disruption of his business operation and associated expense. For many would-be borrowers against inventory, this is a major problem area. Consider the highly diverse circumstances under which inventories are held—pulpwood at the paper mill awaiting processing, cattle in the farmer's feed lot for fattening, refrigerators on the floor of the appliance retailer, oil reserves still underground, the food processor's stocks of frozen foods located in cold-storage warehouses in a number of cities. These few items suggest the need for a variety of legal procedures and for imagination on the part of lenders if they are to obtain a valid security interest and keep track effectively of their collateral. And indeed, much progress has been made in the

---

different from the going concern's mix?" The answer of the experienced lender was, "I think we will always find that. . . . When you liquidate an inventory, you are always going to find that the less desirable items are on hand. I recall one recently where we thought we had a pretty good mix on a lumber inventory, but when it went into bankruptcy all we had—or at least eighty per cent of it—were moldings, which were very hard to sell. This poor mix occurs even with the finished goods; hence, the only product you can be sure of is probably raw steel." (*Proceedings of the Twentieth Anniversary Convention of the Commercial Finance Industry* [New York: National Commercial Finance Conference, Inc., 1964], p. 85.)

development of legal and operational procedures that can offer adequate protection to the lender while minimizing the inconvenience and expense to the borrower.

Several different methods of giving lenders a security interest in inventory are in widespread use. The basic features of the more important types of arrangements will be described briefly.

1. BORROWING AGAINST INVENTORY COVERED BY WAREHOUSE RECEIPTS. Under this well-established method, physical custody of the goods is placed in the hands of a warehousing company which, at the direction of the borrower, issues a *warehouse receipt* made out in favor of the lender. As custodian of the goods, the warehousing firm releases them only upon the instructions of the lender. Properly handled, the warehousing arrangement gives the lender firm control over the collateral. Much of the moral risk inherent in other kinds of inventory financing, where physical control of the goods is left with the borrower, is avoided. The legislation of the various states relating to the pledge of commodities under warehouse receipts is relatively uniform and well tested, so that the legal uncertainties that relate to many aspects of secured lending are relatively small in the case of lending against warehouse receipts.

Warehousing arrangements are of two major types—*public* and *field*. In the case of public warehouses the goods are brought to the warehouses for storage—for example, wheat moved into the public grain warehouses that dot the skylines of farm belt towns and cities. Lenders have long looked with favor on the public warehouse receipt security arrangement, and it has worked well from the borrower's viewpoint in the case of commodities that can be left undisturbed in the warehouse for long periods of time—such as whiskey being aged or wheat stored after harvest awaiting processing into flour.

Yet, many firms have their own storage facilities convenient to their manufacturing facilities or markets and want to avoid the trouble and expense of moving inventory to and from the warehouseman's facilities. Further, they wish to add to and draw from warehoused stocks frequently or continuously. To meet such needs, several warehousing firms[5] offer a *field warehousing* service. Under a field warehouse arrangement the warehousing firm leases storage facilities of the borrower and posts signs to signify that goods stored therein are in its exclusive custody, to be used as security. Commodities are put in the custody of the warehousing firm,[6] which issues warehouse receipts covering these segregated goods in the name of the lender. We should make clear that the warehousing firm performs only a warehousing function, making it possible for banks or other lending organizations to advance loans against the security of the

---

[5] The leading field warehousing firm is Lawrence Warehouse Company.

[6] Care must be taken that the borrower in fact has no control over the goods. To be legally valid, the warehousing arrangement must put "continuous, exclusive, and notorious possession" in the hands of the warehousing firm.

goods covered by the warehouse receipt. Under the typical field warehouse receipt loan, the lender advances a percentage of the value of the commodities covered by the warehouse receipt. When the borrowing firm wants to withdraw goods for processing or sale, it arranges with the lender to pay down that portion of the loan advanced against the particular goods involved, and the lender authorizes the warehouseman to release the goods to the borrower by surrendering the warehouse receipts.

The field warehousing arrangement is a highly ingenious method of facilitating the extension of credit and has come into widespread use in recent decades. One of the first industries to make heavy use of field warehousing was the California food-canning industry. The typical canner's manufacturing operation was highly seasonal, but sales were spread through the year. Customarily, the canner had a large investment in finished goods at the end of the canning season. The field warehousing arrangement permitted the canners to get substantial bank credit against the collateral of the canned goods and yet fill shipment orders through the year with minimum inconvenience and expense.

Over the years, field warehousing has been used for a wide variety of commodities, including such items as coal in hopper cars on a railroad siding (locked switches into the main railroad line were in the control of the field warehouseman), logs in a mill pond, and watch movements stored in a large file cabinet.

The foregoing paragraphs dealing with borrowing against inventory covered by warehouse receipts have been carried forward exactly as they appeared in an earlier edition of this book (except for footnote 5, which has been revised to reflect the demise through bankruptcy of American Express Field Warehousing Corporation). Note the implicit confidence in the integrity and competence of the field warehousing companies. Our confidence reflected the general attitude of banks and other lenders toward the field warehouse receipts of well-known warehousing companies. It is also interesting to note that a basic commodity such as soybean oil, used in a variety of important products, and for which there is an active market, has the characteristics that make for valuable collateral—as we had listed them.

These basic considerations—widespread confidence in field warehouse companies and the validity of their receipts and confidence in the security value of basic commodities like soybean oil—help to explain how 51 companies and banks lost many millions of dollars in credit extended against field warehouse receipts for soybean and other vegetable oils that proved nonexistent. The total inventory shortage discovered in the wake of the failure of the presumed owner, Allied Crude Vegetable Oil Refining Corporation, in late 1963, was reported to be 1,854 million pounds of oil with a stated value of $175 million.[7] Incorrect or fraudulent warehouse

---

[7] The figures quoted here are from Norman C. Miller's *The Great Salad Oil Swindle* (New York: Coward McCann, Inc., 1965).

receipts had served as the basis for what appears to have been well over $100 million of credit. The proceeds of insurance and payments from the parent company of one of the warehousing firms, American Express Company, significantly cut the gross losses but net losses were huge. Altogether the "Great Salad Oil Swindle" stands as one of the worst of all times and one especially striking because of the nature of the major victims, sophisticated and prominent business, financial, and commercial banking firms.

2. BORROWING AGAINST INVENTORY COVERED BY TRUST RECEIPTS. A long-established method of borrowing against inventory that has continued under the Uniform Commercial Code involves the use of trust receipts. Lending arrangements under trust receipts typically involve three parties: for example, the manufacturer of automobiles, the automobile dealer, and the commercial bank lending to the dealer. If a shipment of cars to the dealer is to serve as security, the manufacturer transfers title to the cars and receives payment for them from the lending bank. The lending bank, in turn, delivers custody of the cars to the borrowing dealer under a *trust receipt agreement*, which specifies what the borrower may do with the cars. In the case of finished goods held for resale, such as the automobiles on the premises of the dealer, the agreement will provide that the goods may be sold but that the borrower will use the proceeds from sale promptly to pay off the loan.

The goods in trust should be specifically identified in the trust receipt, and the lender must devote reasonable care to policing the agreement to insure that the borrower carries out his responsibilities under the trust agreement. The fact that the borrower can put the material into process or sell it, as the trust agreement specifies, *before* he makes settlement with the lender can be a major convenience to the borrower, but it also involves risk to the lender. Accordingly, the moral standing and reputation for integrity of the borrower are particularly important to the lender considering a trust receipt financing arrangement—more so than in the case of warehouse receipt financing.

The trust receipt device has been heavily used by distributors and retailers of new automobiles and of major equipment and appliance items, who borrow to finance their working inventories of these items. Since the trust receipts must specifically identify the security, new trust receipts must be prepared as the borrower adds and disposes of particular items of inventory. The problem of specific identification and the burden of paper work in trust receipt financing makes the trust receipt an awkward or unsuitable device for securing highly diverse, fast-moving, or hard-to-identify inventory such as work in process.

3. BORROWING AGAINST INVENTORY COVERED BY A FLOATING LIEN UNDER THE UNIFORM COMMERCIAL CODE. The Uniform Commercial Code provides that lenders may be given a very broad security interest in inventories of the borrower. The security interest can extend to all the

stocks of the borrower, raw materials, in-process, or finished goods. Specific identification is not required; indeed, the lien can extend to inventory yet to be acquired. The security interest can extend over long periods of time, during which the actual stocks held by the borrower may turn over several times and the dollar value can rise and fall substantially. Moreover, the security interest can extend to receivables and the proceeds of collection of the receivables, so that the lender can have both inventory en masse and receivables as security.

As in the case of the trust receipt arrangement, the floating lien leaves practical control over the inventory with the borrower and calls also for a strong sense of moral responsibility, as well as accounting care, on the part of the borrower. Too, much of the inventory, particularly if work in process is a large percentage of the total, may have a low value upon forced sale. Consequently, lenders under the floating lien arrangement usually are willing to loan only a modest percentage of the book value of inventory covered. In one case known to the authors, where a factor was lending to a manufacturer of venetian window blinds, the factor determined that he could safely advance only 20% of the cost of the inventory. Since the floating lien arrangement is adaptable to heterogeneous, fast-moving inventory, it is expected to find growing usage by banks, business finance companies, and factoring concerns.

4. INVENTORY PLEDGES UNDER CHATTEL MORTGAGE, AN INSTRUMENT WHICH CONVEYS TO THE LENDER A SECURITY INTEREST IN SPECIFICALLY IDENTIFIED GOODS. The chattel mortgage is an old, well-established, and widely used legal device. Farmers holding cattle in feed lots for fattening over a period of months have made particularly heavy use of the chattel mortgage in posting such livestock as security for bank loans. As we shall see, however, the chattel mortgage instrument is more widely used for items of machinery and equipment than for inventory.

BORROWING AGAINST FIXED ASSETS

Borrowing against Equipment

The continuing long-term trend toward mechanization in manufacturing, farming, service, and even retailing (use of vending machines, etc.) has been accompanied by increasing investment in equipment by firms in these fields and by the growing use of equipment as security for loans.

Much of the credit to businesses secured by equipment is extended initially by manufacturers or sales concerns supplying new machines. Many vendors of important items of new equipment accept from purchasers who make a significant down payment (often 20% to 33%) notes calling for payment of the remainder of the purchase price plus interest and other charges over a period of months, in some cases as many as 60. Generally, the seller requires a down payment and monthly payments sufficiently large so that the outstanding debt over the life of the credit remains less than the estimated net resale value of the equipment if repossession becomes necessary. The seller takes a security interest in the equipment, a common instrument being a *conditional sale contract,* under which the seller retains legal title until the buyer has met all terms of the sale agreement. Under the terms of the conditional sales contract, the seller has the right to repossess the equipment if the contract terms of payment are not met. Alternatively, chattel mortgages are taken on the equipment, but their use is less frequent.

Many vendors who offer instalment payment terms to purchasers of their equipment cannot, or prefer not to, maintain a large investment in such instalment receivables. Most finance companies, and in recent years a number of commercial banks, have been willing to extend credit based upon such instalment notes secured by an assignment of the vendor's security interest (the conditional sales contract or chattel mortgage) in the equipment. Usually, financing of the instalment notes receivable is with recourse to the vendor, so that the financing agency has the obligation of the buyer of the equipment, the assigned security interest in the equipment, and the right of recourse to the vendor to support the obligation. In addition, a portion of the payment to the seller is often withheld by the financing agency as a "dealer's reserve" until the note is paid.

A number of manufacturers and a few large retailers of equipment and consumer durables have set up wholly owned subsidiaries to take over the parent firm's investment in extended receivables. Typically, these "captive finance companies" borrow heavily from banks and through bond issues; frequently, their debts are supported by parent company guaranties.

Concerns purchasing new equipment may find it cheaper or otherwise preferable to borrow directly from banks or finance companies in order to pay the vendor the full purchase price in cash. Such a direct lender often takes a chattel mortgage on the equipment to secure his advance, normally an amount significantly less than the purchase price. Repayment of the notes is scheduled on an instalment basis, again at a rate calculated to keep the loan balance below resale value upon repossession.

Instalment financing is used for a great variety of equipment—from barber chairs to giant diesel earthmovers—and by a wide variety of businesses. Large corporations of strong credit standing are less likely to use the device, but many strong railroads are outstanding exceptions to this generalization. For a long time, major railroads have been buying locomotives and other rolling stock through use of *equipment trust certificates,* which can in many ways be regarded as a specialized form of instalment equipment financing. Insurance companies have been major buyers of equipment trust certificates.

Speaking broadly, credit against equipment is restricted mainly to new or highly serviceable used machinery. The rapid obsolescence of many types of equipment reduces the resale value of much used, though serviceable, equipment to near scrap values. Consequently, a would-be borrower will find it much easier to get substantial credit on new than on old equipment, even though the used equipment is physically sound and is carried on the owner's books at substantial value.[8]

Costs of credit against equipment vary widely. Equipment trust certificates of strong railroads have long carried low interest rates, while financially weak concerns buying equipment subject to rapid depreciation in value may well pay fees amounting to an annual interest rate on the balance owed of from 12% to 24%.

More than 27% of the secured commercial bank loans covered in the 1955 Federal Reserve analysis were secured by equipment. Since the equipment loans were typically for small amounts, they were about 14% of the total dollar amount of secured loans.

Borrowing against Plant or Other Real Estate

Businessmen are inclined to regard their investment in brick and mortar—in plant and built-in or fixed equipment—as excellent potential security under mortgage arrangements.[9] Particularly is this impression

---

[8] An experienced officer of a commercial finance firm that loaned extensively against equipment commented as follows on the assessment of the security value of equipment, "Basically, the equipment should affirmatively answer the question, 'Will a forced sale of the equipment securing our loan recover the unpaid balance due us?' The answer, of course, is not so simple, nor is it so elusive. Over and above a *knockdown* appraisal from a competent and recognized appraiser in his specialized field, in whom you have complete confidence, consideration of the following criteria will suggest a solution:

a) Is the equipment specialized or intended for a unique application?
b) Is it to be used in a volatile industry where obsolescence is a good possibility in the very near future?
c) Is it to be used in a limited industry, therefore having a very restricted resale market?
d) Is its geographical location to be in a remote area, far removed from an industrial center containing similar industry?
e) What is its normal depreciable life?
f) Is the industry itself in which it is being employed growing, dying or stable?
g) Does the equipment schedule contain a large number of the same machine which, if offered for sale at the same time, would depress the price of all?
h) Is the machinery or equipment so affixed to or located in the building that the cost of its removal would be prohibitive?
i) Is the loan based on one large, single piece of equipment?
j) What effect is inflation likely to have on resale value? What is the current replacement price?
k) What is the current availability of the equipment vis-à-vis current and anticipated demand?" (*Proceedings of Twentysixth Convention of the Commercial Finance Industry* [New York: National Commercial Finance Conference, Inc. 1970].)

[9] The mortgage device of granting to lenders a security interest in real estate is a very old one. Since ownership of residential property is so commonly financed by borrowing, with the home used as security under a mortgage (or a similar form, used in several states, called a deed of trust), mortgage law has become detailed and complicated in all of the states. Generally, commercial or industrial real estate is mortgaged under the basic mortgage laws applying to residential property.

likely to be strong if the plant facilities are handsome, costly, and built to last for a long time. Yet, our earlier observation that few lenders are willing to make a loan against security if they really expect to have to take over and liquidate the security in order to settle the loan is particularly valid in the case of loans against plant as security.

Industrial plants have, in the view of many lenders, particular weaknesses as loan collateral. A first weakness is that firms wanting to borrow against fixed assets often want the money to finance added investment in fixed assets. Since recovery of this investment by the borrower through depreciation or added profits normally takes many years, his investment is relatively illiquid. Further, action to seize and sell, or *foreclose*, a company's productive establishment is indeed a drastic step, often fatal to the company, and hence one taken by lenders with real reluctance. Third, the process of foreclosure is, in many states, a time-consuming one, with the debtor retaining rights to reclaim his property over a considerable time. Fourth, and most basic, is the high degree of uncertainty regarding resale value upon foreclosure. If the difficulties of the borrower that lead to default and foreclosure are the result of generally depressed conditions in his industry, as frequently is the case, the number of firms interested in buying the foreclosed plant may be limited indeed. Prosperous and expanding companies which might be buyers often prefer to build a new plant designed and located to meet their particular requirements. In such circumstances the added expense of building to their own needs may result in lower operating costs and in long-run economy, so that they are not interested in the older, foreclosed plant at any price.

Furthermore, relatively few plants are truly general-purpose facilities. Most contain much built-in equipment or special features for a particular productive activity that limit the potential market for the property. Highly specialized plants such as foundries have attraction and value only to other foundry companies, and they may well share the slack business or other unfavorable developments that led to the trouble of the borrower.

This is not to say that industrial facilities have no value as collateral. There is widespread mortgaging of plants as security—almost 21% by number and 23% by volume of secured loans in 1955 were secured by plant and other real estate. But much of their use as security is not due to the attractiveness of plants as collateral. Lenders often take the security as a means of added control over a borrower for a loan they are making essentially on an unsecured basis. That is, many loans that are nominally against plant security are in fact regarded by the lender as primarily unsecured, with some possibility of added security in the plant because of its value to the borrower. If the property is essential to the borrower, or to a reorganized company in the event of bankruptcy, the lender may get better treatment at the hands of the court owing to his claim against the vital, if nonresalable, plant.

BORROWING AGAINST SECURITIES AND LIFE INSURANCE

For various reasons, concerns owning government bonds or other securities may prefer to raise needed funds by borrowing against the securities rather than by selling them. The mechanics of pledging securities are relatively simple and easily accomplished. Although the borrower retains ownership of the securities, he assigns an interest in them to the lender, who holds physical possession as security for the loan. The note or other debt instrument specifies the terms upon which the lender can dispose of the securities and apply the proceeds toward the debt.

If the securities are marketable government bonds or corporate securities traded actively on national security exchanges, the borrower seldom will have difficulty finding lenders willing to loan a high percentage of the market value of the securities.[10] If the securities are those of little-known subsidiaries or other companies whose securities have limited markets, prospective lenders can be expected to consider carefully the factors that will probably affect the future value and marketability of the securities and to loan only a portion of their appraisal of the value of the securities. In 1955, 6.3% of the total number of secured member bank business loans and 8.6% of the total amount were against pledged securities.

Many firms carry life insurance policies on key personnel of types that in time accumulate considerable cash surrender value. The rights to matured or cash surrender value can be assigned to bank or other lenders as security for loans. Much of the lending against securities or cash surrender values of life insurance policies is by commercial banks, ordinarily at near prime interest rates.

USE OF COMAKER, ENDORSEMENT, OR GUARANTY OF LOANS

Over 23% of the secured member bank loans to business in 1955 were secured in the sense that other concerns or individuals accepted direct or contingent obligations for the loans. An ordinary note can be signed by several parties, each party becoming a *comaker* of the note, and all parties jointly and severally assuming the obligations of the promise to pay. As another technique of security, a lender may ask for an *endorsement* of a borrower's note by a third party. The third party, by signing a note on the reverse side, grants to the lender full recourse to his resources (unless otherwise stated) in case the borrower fails to honor the debt. In a third and more flexible arrangement, a third party signs a guaranty agreement covering all debts of the borrower to the lender and

---

[10] Full freedom to use listed stocks as security for loans may be subject to the restrictive provisions of Regulation U of the Board of Governors of the Federal Reserve System. These restrictions are designed to curb speculative buying of stocks "on margin."

thereby obviates the necessity for each note or other debt instrument being individually endorsed. Guaranty agreements are particularly common in the case of closely held corporations whose owners have substantial personal resources and are willing to put these resources behind the firm's borrowing. Also, it is common for parent companies to guarantee loans to their subsidiaries.

Obviously, the value to lenders of any of these arrangements varies with the financial resources of the comaker, endorser, or guarantor. It is interesting to note that lenders, by obtaining endorsement or guaranty of corporate debts by share owners, in effect break through the limited liability feature of the incorporated business.

We should make it clear that the comaker, endorsement, or guaranteed loans are not secured loans in the sense that the lender gets any priority over the other general creditors of either the comaker or endorser of the note. The use of the comaker simply gives the lender a general claim on two persons or firms, rather than one.

SUBORDINATION OF CERTAIN DEBT CLAIMS TO OTHER OBLIGATIONS

In recent years the practice of subordination by a creditor or group of creditors of certain of their rights as creditors to another creditor or class of creditor has become sufficiently important to deserve attention here. Subordination is accomplished through contract between the interested parties and as such can take whatever form the interested parties can agree upon.

One of the most common uses of subordination is by stockholders of closely held corporations who are also creditors of their corporations. Tax considerations have been especially important in recent years in stimulating stockholders to make part of their investment in their company in the form of loans to the company. In negotiating bank credit, agreement by the stockholder-creditors to subordinate their own loans to those of the bank may materially improve the chances of getting bank loans. In such cases the subordination is usually stated both in terms of maturity (for example, agreement that no debt to stockholders will be repaid so long as the bank loan is unpaid) and in terms of bankruptcy leading to reorganization or liquidation. The subordination agreement often is drawn to provide that in the event of bankruptcy the favored creditor—in this case, the bank—is entitled to stand in the place of the subordinated creditors when assets are distributed and thus be entitled to payment in full before the subordinated creditors are entitled to anything.

Often it is said that such subordination agreements, from the viewpoint of the favored creditor, make the subordinated debt money the equivalent of equity funds as a protective cushion in the event of bankruptcy. Actually, from the viewpoint of the favored creditor, debt subordinated to his debts may be better than equity because the favored creditor acquires, for his exclusive benefit, the subordinated creditor's rights as a *creditor* of the company.[11]

Consider the following simplified examples:

Balance Sheets, in Summary, before Bankruptcy

Company A		*Company B*	
Total assets.................	$500,000	Total assets.................	$500,000
Bank loan..................	$100,000	Bank loan..................	$100,000
Due trade and other		Due trade and other	
creditors.................	200,000	creditors.................	200,000
Loan from stockholders,		Common stock and surplus....	200,000
subordinated to bank.......	100,000		
Common stock and surplus....	100,000		
Total liabilities.............	$500,000	Total liabilities.............	$500,000

Note that the only difference between the two balance sheets is that $100,000 of the owners' investment in company A is in the form of debt which has been subordinated to the loan to the company from the bank. Now, assume that each company found it impossible to meet maturing obligations and was forced into bankruptcy leading to liquidation. Assume that in each company, enough cash was available to pay the expenses of bankruptcy and to pay certain preferred creditors in full, leaving thereafter $220,000 in cash for all other creditors.

In company A, a 55% distribution to creditors ($220,000 divided by 400,000) is sufficient to pay the bank in full, since it is entitled to $55,000 on its debt directly and, under the subordination agreement, is entitled to enough (in this case, $45,000) of the subordinating creditor's share to permit repayment of the $100,000 due the bank in full.

In company B, however, a similar net amount for distribution to all creditors, $220,000, would permit a 73.3% payout to each creditor ($220,000/$300,000). In this instance the bank is able to collect only $73,333 on its $100,000 credit. Trade and other creditors fare better than in company A, getting paid $146,666 in comparison with $110,000 in company A. The owners get nothing in either case.

In the discussion and examples above, we have considered only one of the important types of subordination agreements. Other circumstances in which subordinations are used include subordination by an entire class of creditors, such as trade creditors, as a means of encouraging new credit to keep a valued customer in business. Further, in nondistress circumstances, many concerns, particularly finance companies, have succeeded in selling to the public subordinated debentures which by their terms subordinate certain rights of the holders of these securities to those of other creditors.

---

[11] A disadvantage is that the holder of the subordinated debt may have greater power than the holder of an equity of the same amount to initiate bankruptcy proceedings at a time when the favored creditor would prefer to avoid such proceedings.

Some Cautions Regarding the Giving of Security

Earlier in this chapter, advantages that borrowers might obtain from effective use of their assets as security for loans—greater credit, lower interest rates than on unsecured borrowing, etc.—were discussed. It is appropriate at this point to consider the serious disadvantages that can result from injudicious giving of security.

First, the increased availability of credit by giving security may encourage excessively heavy use of debt. Any borrowing involves risk to the borrower—financial risk added to the normal risks of doing business. The increased risks of debt should be appreciated and accepted only after careful and full consideration.

Second, for many firms, there is great advantage (not to say comfort) in retaining reserves of borrowing power for use in financial extremity or to finance particularly desirable investment opportunities that may develop. Obviously, security, once committed, no longer is available as the basis for further credit; and the firm that ties up all of its attractive security is in the same exposed position as the general who has committed all his reserves to battle. When secured borrowing is undertaken, the borrower should appreciate that if he concedes more security than really is required and further credit subsequently is needed, it may be hard indeed to get the old lender to release security or to dilute his own cushion by lending more against the same security.

Third, most firms depend heavily on continued trade credit from suppliers, extended on an unsecured basis. As the firm commits more and more of its best assets as security for loans, the trade creditors increasingly depend on the shrinking and poorer assets left unpledged. While it is difficult to determine in advance the exact extent to which pledging of assets can be carried without jeopardizing the continued availability of trade credit, excessive pledging of assets *can* result in impairment or loss of credit from alert suppliers and other unsecured creditors.

PART VI

THE SOURCE OF LONG-TERM CORPORATE CAPITAL

chapter 16

External Sources of
Long-Term Capital

In this chapter we shall consider first the extent to which American corporations raise funds through the sale of new securities. Then we shall focus our attention on the markets for corporate securities. It is axiomatic in marketing that selling programs should be built on a foundation of knowledge about the potential customers. We shall present basic information about the major buyers of corporate securities, indicating the types of securities they buy and their relative importance in absorbing new issues of securities. In the following chapter we shall discuss the major means by which corporate sellers of securities can tap these markets—the principal methods of distributing new issues and the major institutions, particularly the investment banking industry, which exist to facilitate distribution of new issues. Finally, we shall review the markets for outstanding securities and how they relate to the sale of new securities.

The Use of Long-Term External Capital in Perspective

To what extent have American corporations turned to the long-term capital markets for funds to meet their expanding total need for funds? And how does the total amount provided by the sale of long-term debt and by issues of preferred stock and common stock compare with the amounts provided by internal sources, bank borrowing, expanded trade credit, and other sources of financing? Helpful in answering these questions and thus in putting the use of external long-term sources into proper perspective are the data on corporate sources and uses of funds during the post–World War II years presented in Table 16–1. Strikingly apparent from the table is the continuing importance of the internal or operational sources—

Table 16-1

Sources and Uses of Funds, U.S. Corporations (Excluding Financial Corporations and Farms)
(dollar figures in billions)

	Annual Average			Yearly Figures					Percentage of 1969 Total
	1946–49	1950–59	1960–64	1965	1966	1967	1968	1969	
USES									
Increases in:									
Cash and marketable securities	$ 0.2	$ 1.9	$ 2.0	$ 1.7	$ 1.9	$ 0.6	$ 10.1	$ 2.3	2.0%
Inventories	4.8	3.9	4.0	9.6	16.2	7.5	9.7	12.6	10.8
Receivables	3.5	6.7	8.6	16.3	12.5	9.7	16.5	18.6	15.9
Gross fixed assets	15.8	26.5	39.6	54.8	62.7	66.0	70.3	79.8	68.4
Other assets	0.8	1.4	2.7	5.1	1.0	3.2	0.1	3.4	2.9
Total uses	$25.1	$40.4	$57.1	$87.5	$ 94.3	$87.0	$106.7	$116.7	100.0%
SOURCES									
Increases in:									
Trade payables	$ 1.6	$ 3.9	$ 3.9	$ 9.1	$ 7.3	$ 2.6	$ 5.7	$ 10.9	8.8%
Accrued income taxes	(0.3)	0.6	0.4	2.2	0.2	(4.1)	3.7	0.8	0.6
Bank loans	1.2	2.2	2.6	10.6	8.4	6.4	9.6	10.9	8.8
Mortgages	1.3	1.6	3.9	3.9	4.2	4.5	5.8	4.3	3.5
Other loans	(0.5)	....	0.7	0.6	1.4	1.4	3.6	6.2	5.0
Other liabilities	1.7	2.3	3.6	4.6	6.5	5.2	6.9	6.5	5.2
Retained earnings	11.2	11.3	12.9	23.1	24.7	21.2	22.0	19.9	16.1
Capital consumption allowances	6.2	15.7	28.5	35.2	38.2	41.2	44.3	48.0	38.7
Net new security issues:									
Bonds	2.8	3.8	4.1	5.4	10.2	14.7	12.9	12.1	9.8
Stocks	1.2	2.0	1.2	....	1.2	2.3	(0.8)	4.3	3.5
Total sources	$26.4	$43.4	$61.8	$94.7	$102.3	$95.4	$113.7	$123.9	100.00%
Discrepancy	($1.3)	($3.0)	($4.7)	($7.3)	($8.0)	($8.4)	($7.0)	($7.2)	

SOURCES: *Survey of Current Business*, November, 1969, p. 14, and "Sector Statements of Savings and Investment," *Federal Reserve Bulletin*, August, 1970, Table A 71.4.

retained earnings and capital consumption allowances, a comprehensive term that includes both depreciation and depletion. These internal sources accounted for 54.8% of the total in 1969. Also notable is the continued growth, both relatively and in absolute terms, of the funds inflow related to capital consumption allowances. Even though overshadowed by the internal sources, corporations did draw $62.3 billion from the capital markets through the sale of bonds and stocks during the 5 years, 1965–69, and an additional $22.7 billion through mortgage financing during the same period. In 1969, $20.7 billion or 16.7% of the total net sources of funds was raised through mortgage, bond, and stock financing. Clearly, for American business broadly, the availability of longer-term debt and equity on tolerable terms has helped to make possible the great expansion of the U.S. economy in recent years.

The Volume of Funds Raised through Sale of New Securities

Data on new issues of corporate securities in 1934, 1940, 1950, and 1955 through 1969 are presented in Table 16–2. Retirements of outstanding securities are also shown. There is much of significance to the student of finance in these data. Especially notable is the upswing in net new issues over the period from the earlier years when corporations were supplying rather than drawing long-term funds from the capital markets. In the earlier years much of the sale of bonds was for the purpose of refunding old issues at the very low interest rates which prevailed in the late 1930's and 1940's. Total new issues reached $28.8 billion in 1969.

As can also be seen from Table 16–2, corporations have made particularly heavy use of debt securities in tapping the capital markets. While the data do not separate common and preferred stocks, other sources indicate that common stocks accounted for the bulk—and in recent years the predominant portion—of the proceeds from stock sales; in 1969 common stocks represented 91.9% of the total, preferred stocks the remaining 8.1%.[1]

While the data in Tables 16–1 and 16–2 give an idea of the role of sale of securities in the financing of corporations generally, it should be recognized that these are aggregate figures for corporations as a whole. As such, the aggregate figures conceal such important differences as those between various industries, between groups of companies by size, and between individual concerns. For example, the electric utility industry has made particularly heavy use of the sale of new securities in financing its expansion. In recent decades the electric utilities as a group have paid out a relatively high percentage of their earnings in dividends; hence, retained earnings have been of less importance than in the case of manufacturing companies, which have made less heavy use of the capital markets through sale of stocks or bonds.

---

[1] Securities and Exchange Commission, *Statistical Bulletin*, March, 1970, p. 16.

Table 16-2

Net Changes in Outstanding Corporate Securities

(in millions of dollars)

Year	Bonds and Notes			Common and Preferred Stocks*			Total		
	New Issues	Retirements	Net New Issues	New Issues	Retirements	Net New Issues	New Issues	Retirements	Net New Issues
1934	391	635	— 244	154	78	76	545	713	— 168
1940	2,477	2,814	— 337	324	260	64	2,801	3,074	— 273
1945	4,924	5,996	—1,072	1,533	910	623	6,457	6,906	449
1950	4,806	2,802	2,004	2,418	698	1,720	7,224	3,501	3,724
1955	7,571	3,383	4,188	4,903	2,216	2,687	12,474	5,599	6,875
1956	7,934	3,203	4,731	5,267	1,836	3,432	13,201	5,038	8,162
1957	9,638	2,584	7,053	3,321	618	2,703	12,959	3,202	9,756
1958	9,673	3,817	5,856	3,070	964	2,106	12,743	4,781	7,962
1959	7,122	3,049	4,073	3,378	1,002	2,376	10,500	4,051	6,449
1960	8,072	3,078	4,994	2,725	1,029	1,696	10,797	4,107	6,690
1961	9,194	4,024	5,170	4,454	1,804	2,650	13,648	5,828	7,820
1962	8,613	3,749	4,864	2,255	1,567	688	10,868	5,316	5,552
1963	10,556	4,979	5,577	1,948	2,197	— 249	12,504	7,176	5,328
1964	10,715	4,077	6,637	3,748	2,317	1,431	14,463	6,394	8,068
1965	12,747	4,649	8,098	3,205	3,242	— 37	15,952	7,891	8,061
1966	15,629	4,542	11,088	4,169	3,000	1,169	19,799	7,541	12,258
1967	21,299	5,340	15,960	4,664	2,397	2,267	25,964	7,735	18,229
1968	19,381	5,418	13,962	6,057	6,959	— 900	25,439	12,377	13,062
1969	19,523	5,767	13,755	9,318	5,046	4,272	28,841	10,813	18,027

* Through 1956 the data on stocks include investment companies. After 1956, investment companies are excluded.
Source: *Federal Reserve Bulletins.*

For reasons discussed in more detail later, the typical small corporation finds the problems in effective sale of securities much more formidable than does its large counterpart. Consequently, smaller concerns have relied more on internal and short-term sources than have large corporations. Indeed, the hundred largest corporations account for a very substantial portion of the sale of new securities each year. A.T.&T. and its operating subsidiaries of the Bell System raised some $2.46 billion in new capital, mostly through bond issues, in a single year, 1969, and in May of 1970, A.T.&T. raised over $1.5 billion through a single offering to shareholders of debentures and warrants.

A few companies have been able to grow to great size without recourse to the sale of securities to the public. The Ford Motor Company, which from its inception through 1955 drew no funds from the capital markets through stock or bond issues, and yet amassed total assets of almost $2.6 billion, is a striking example of a large enterprise that long relied entirely on internal and short-term sources of funds for expansion (though even Ford found it necessary to finance part of the major expansion program in 1956 and 1957 through a large private placement of debt securities).

The External Sources of Funds for Purchase of Corporate Securities

This chapter has been headed "External Sources of Long-Term Capital." It should be emphasized that there is no single homogeneous market for new issues of corporate securities. Instead, it is more useful to think of the buyers of corporate securities as being grouped in a number of more or less tightly compartmented segments with differing investment objectives and operating under distinctive investment policies and practices. For some of the segments or individual markets, available information permits fairly precise, summary description; in other segments, few data are available, and our comments must be more general and tentative.

The savings of individuals are the most basic source of funds for investment in corporate securities. If individuals in the United States spent all their income for current consumption, few corporate securities could be sold. Indeed, in many of the less developed countries, the inability or unwillingness of the people to forgo current consumption makes it extremely difficult for private industry to accumulate the long-term capital necessary for large-scale and expensive industrial development. In other less developed countries, such as India, the problem of raising funds for private industrial development is further accentuated by a long-standing preference on the part of many of those who have been able to save and accumulate capital for investment in gold, precious jewels, real estate, or other material wealth rather than in intangibles such as stocks and bonds of corporations.

In the United States the people have turned over much of their savings to financial institutions, which have invested the funds entrusted to them.

Thus, such financial institutions as insurance companies, mutual funds, savings banks, etc., have been the actual buyers of many of the new securities issued by corporations. Since the financial institutions, other than commercial banks, do not create funds, they must be thought of rather as conduits or intermediaries in the flow of savings from the people into effective investment.

Although a large and generally increasing share of the financial savings of the people reaches the capital markets *through* financial institutions, many individuals, particularly the more affluent, buy corporate securities for their own account.

Competing Demands for Savings

Corporations must compete for bank credit or investment savings with several other avid sectors of demand for funds. As Table 16–3 brings out,

Table 16–3
Funds Raised by Major Sectors of the Economy
(in billions of dollars)

	1965	1966	1967	1968	1969
U.S. government and government-sponsored agencies	$ 3.8	$ 8.7	$12.6	$16.8	$ 5.5
State and local governments	7.6	6.4	7.9	10.2	8.9
Households (chiefly through home mortgage and consumer credit)	28.8	23.2	19.7	31.8	31.6
Nonfinancial business	29.6	33.8	37.9	39.1	47.8

Source: "Flow of Funds Accounts," *Federal Reserve Bulletin*, August, 1970, Table A 71.1.

the U.S. government and government-sponsored agencies like the Federal Home Loan banks, have placed fluctuating, but at times highly material, demands on the capital markets.

The demand for mortgage loans to finance individuals' purchases of homes has been a particularly strong and significant one. The total of outstanding mortgage debt secured by one- to four-family homes has grown from $18.6 billion on December 31, 1945 to $271.7 billion on June 30, 1970. Mortgages outstanding on all properties grew from $35.5 billion to $435.6 billion in the same postwar years. The increasing demand by consumers for credit to purchase automobiles, other durable goods, or to support current expenditures has resulted in a growth in consumer credit outstanding from $5.7 billion at year-end 1945 to $122.5 billion on June 30, 1970. Of the increase, $66.4 billion came during the 1960's. Some 80.7% of this debt called for repayment in instalments.

During many of the years since 1945, the operations of the federal government have been at cash deficits necessitating public sale of bonds.

In addition, "government-sponsored agencies" such as the Federal Home Loan banks, have issued bonds to finance their operations—in the case of the FHLB's, to gather funds to advance to savings and loan associations for further investment in mortgages. The total governmental "demands on the markets" have shifted widely from year to year; in some years cash surpluses have permitted the government to supply funds to the market through net debt retirements.

State and local governments have also stepped up their borrowing through bond sales. Capital outlays for such facilities as new public schools and highways are typically financed by bond issues, and the heavy activity in these two fields has been the source of much demand for long-term capital by states, cities, toll road authorities, and other public agencies. Interest income on the bonds sold by the state and local governmental units, unlike the interest on U.S. government bonds issued since 1941, is essentially exempt from federal income taxation; and this feature of *municipal securities*—the term applied to securities issued by states and any other governmental unit, other than the federal government—makes them particularly attractive to some investors.

The main point we want to support through this brief review of the major sources of demands for capital funds is that corporations experience vigorous competition from other major capital-hungry sectors for the available funds. When demand is great and supply is not unlimited, corporations must be prepared to sweeten the terms of the securities they offer and/or scrutinize more rigorously the projects and plans that call for additional capital so as to lessen the need to go to the market under unattractive capital market conditions.

The Institutional Market for Corporate Securities

As we noted earlier, much of the financial savings of the people flows into institutions which have the task of putting it to work. Most major financial institutions fall into two main groups—the deposit type, such as commercial banks, savings banks, and savings and loan associations; and the contractual type, such as life insurance companies, corporate pension funds, and governmental unit pension funds. Another important institutional intermediary, the investment company or mutual fund, does not fall readily into either category. Estimates placed total personal financial savings during the 1950's at $220 billion. Of this total, some 40% was estimated to have flowed into deposit-type institutions, 40% into the contractual type, and the remaining 20% to have been invested directly in securities or through investment companies or personal trust funds.[2]

Data for more recent years regarding the amount and composition of

[2] Jules I. Bogen, "Trends in the Institutionalization of Savings and in Thrift Institution Policies," *Proceedings of 1960 Conference on Savings and Residential Financing* (Chicago: U.S. Savings and Loan League, 1960).

individual financial savings are shown in Table 16–4. Note that the amount of savings had grown greatly—$241.5 in 4 years of the late 1960's versus the estimate of $220 billion for the 10 years of the 1950's. Particularly evident was the surge in direct investment in bonds in 1969 at the expense of savings deposits as the interest rate savings institutions could pay was restricted, while interest rates on new bond issues moved up to the highest levels of the 20th century. Also striking is the heavy net sale or disinvestment in corporate stocks ($35.3 billion over the 4 years) offset somewhat by a $15.8 billion purchase of investment company (mutual fund) shares, most of which was invested by the mutual funds in corporate stocks.

Highly noteworthy was the continued flow of individuals' savings into life insurance and pension fund intermediaries.

Fortunately, rather reliable data are available as to how the more important institutional intermediaries invest the funds entrusted to them, so that we can assess the past, current, and probable future importance of the various institutions as buyers of corporate securities.

Institutional investors currently or potentially important as buyers of corporate securities include the following:

1. Life insurance companies.
2. Property-liability insurance companies.
3. Private noninsured pension funds.
4. State and local government pension funds.
5. Investment companies.
6. Commercial banks—as investors of deposit funds and as trustees for private trust funds.
7. Mutual savings banks.
8. Savings and loan associations.
9. Religious, educational, and charitable funds.

The Life Insurance Companies as Buyers of Corporate Securities

The life insurance companies of the country represent a large and ever-growing segment of the institutional market for corporate securities. The total assets of the U.S. life insurance companies grew from $19 billion in 1930 to $197 billion on December 31, 1969. This great growth in assets was the result not only of the increase in outstanding policies as more life insurance was sold but, even more importantly, the accumulation of premiums paid in over a period of years before the maturing of the obligation of the insurance company to pay at the death of the insured (or maturing of annuities) on an ordinary life policy. The young man of 30, on an actuarial average, will pay into the insurance company annual premiums which the company can use over the years until his death calls for the policy to be paid. One insurance company executive has estimated

Table 16–4

The Financial Savings of U.S. Individuals, 1966–69
(dollar figures in billions)

	1966	1967	1968	1969	Total	Percentage of Total
Additional investment in:						
Deposits:						
Currency and demand deposits............	$ 3.1	$11.5	$ 6.9	$ 3.7	$ 25.2	10.4%
Savings accounts......................	19.1	32.5	27.7	10.8	90.1	37.3
Direct investment in securities:						
U.S. government and governmental agencies....	7.4	0.7	7.1	14.3	29.5	12.2
State and local government.............	2.1	(2.1)	(0.2)	4.4	4.2	1.7
Corporate and foreign bonds............	2.0	4.0	4.6	4.0	14.6	6.0
Corporate stocks.....................	(4.7)	(7.4)	(12.4)	(10.8)	(35.3)	(14.6)
Through nondeposit institutions:						
Private life insurance reserves...........	4.5	4.7	4.6	4.5	18.3	7.6
Private insured pension reserves..........	2.1	2.6	2.9	3.0	10.6	4.4
Private noninsured pension reserves.......	6.1	6.7	6.4	6.6	25.8	10.7
Government insurance and pension reserves....	5.3	6.0	5.6	7.8	24.7	10.2
Investment company shares.............	3.7	2.5	4.7	4.9	15.8	6.6
Miscellaneous financial assets...........	3.7	4.8	5.7	3.8	18.0	7.5
Total net financial savings in year......	$54.4	$66.5	$63.6	$57.0	$241.5	100.0%

Source: U.S. Securities & Exchange Commission, *Statistical Bulletin*, April, 1970, p. 30.

Table 16-5

Distribution of Assets of U.S. Life Insurance Companies
(dollar figures in millions)

	December 31, 1940		December 31, 1950		December 31, 1960		December 31, 1969	
	Amount	Percentage	Amount	Percentage	Amount	Percentage	Amount	Percentage
U.S. government bonds	$ 5,767	18.7%	$ 13,459	21.0	$ 6,427	5.4%	$ 4,124	2.1%
Foreign government bonds	288	1.0	1,060	1.7	437	0.3	647	0.3
State, provincial, and local bonds	2,392	7.8	1,547	2.4	4,576	3.8	5,463	2.8
Railroad bonds	2,830	9.2	3,187	5.0	3,668	3.1	3,608	1.8
Public utility bonds	4,273	13.9	10,587	16.5	16,719	14.0	17,963	9.1
Industrial and miscellaneous bonds	1,542	5.0	9,526	14.9	26,728	22.4	49,968	25.3
Stocks	605	2.0	2,103	3.3	4,981	4.2	13,707	7.0
Mortgages	5,972	19.4	16,102	25.1	41,771	34.9	72,027	36.5
Real estate	2,065	6.7	1,445	2.3	3,765	3.1	5,912	3.0
Policy loans	3,091	10.0	2,413	3.8	5,231	4.4	13,825	7.0
Miscellaneous assets*	1,977	6.3	2,591	4.0	5,273	4.4	9,964	5.1
Total assets	$30,802	100.0%	$64,020	100.0%	$119,576	100.0%	$197,208	100.0%

* Includes cash.
SOURCE: Institute of Life Insurance, *1970 Life Insurance Fact Book* (New York, 1970), p. 70.

that if no further policies were sold, the assets of his company would continue to increase for more than 12 years.

The continued growth, stability, and predictability of their funds have enabled the life insurance companies to invest a major portion of their huge assets, which represent largely reserves held against policy obligations to millions of policyholders, without primary emphasis on liquidity. Since only a small portion of these policies is expected to mature during any year or at any single time, the insurance companies hold only a small percentage of their assets in cash and feel free to invest the bulk of their funds in income-producing securities on a long-term basis.[3]

In their investment policies, however, the life insurance companies are subject to certain legal restrictions imposed by the states in which they operate. The restrictions are designed to insure protection of principal, and tend to limit investment primarily, although not exclusively, to low-risk debt instruments.

Table 16–5 presents a breakdown of the assets of U.S. life insurance companies as of December 31, 1940, 1950, 1960, and 1969. Especially noteworthy, along with the more than sixfold growth in assets during the 29 years, was the great increase in the life insurance companies' investment in industrial and miscellaneous bonds. Total corporate bondholdings amounted to $71.5 billion, or 36.2% of their total assets in 1969. In addition, some of the mortgage loans represented intermediate credit to business firms.

The life insurance companies also are seen to have a significant and growing investment in common stocks.

Perhaps even more revealing as to the continuing importance of life insurance companies as buyers of corporate securities are the data on their sources and uses of funds over several years, presented in Table 16–6. These show only the *net* new funds the insurance companies have to invest. Actually, their annual inflow of funds for investment is swelled as payments are received on outstanding mortgages and other debt securities, and as particular security holdings are sold, mature, or are called for redemption by the issuers.

In many recent years insurance companies along with some pension funds have been active buyers of debt issues offered them privately. Many such issues have been somewhat less than top quality and have offered relatively generous yields and/or equity "sweeteners." During the tight money years of 1969–70, insurance companies largely confined their bond purchases to publicly marketed issues.

During the late 1960's many insurance companies acquired or started

---

[3] During recent periods of tight money and high interest rates, many policyholders have availed themselves of their legal right to borrow accumulated values, usually at the prescribed rate of 5%. The demand for such *policy loans* has represented a major and largely unpredictable cash need in these periods.

Table 16–6

Sources and Uses of Funds, Life Insurance Companies, 1955, 1960, 1965–69
(in billions of dollars)

	1955	1960	1965	1966	1967	1968	1969
Sources of funds:							
Increase in admitted assets*....	5.7	6.0	8.9	8.9	9.5	9.9	10.2
Use of funds:							
Mortgages.................	3.5	2.6	4.9	4.6	2.9	2.5	2.3
Corporate bonds.............	1.6	1.4	2.4	2.2	3.7	3.7	2.4
Corporate stocks*............	0.1	0.4	0.7	0.3	1.0	1.4	1.5
All other assets..............	0.4	1.7	1.1	1.8	1.8	2.4	9.0
	5.7	6.0	8.9	8.9	9.5	9.9	10.2

* Net of appreciation or depreciation in market value.
Source: Bankers Trust Company, *The Investment Outlook for 1963; The Investment Outlook for 1970* (New York, 1970), Table 15.

mutual fund companies. One estimate put the total assets of mutual funds related to life insurance companies at $8 billion.[4]

Property-Liability Insurance Companies

Property-liability insurance companies (also referred to as fire and casualty companies) are also important investors in corporate securities. Total assets of these companies amounted to $46.6 billion at the end of 1967, up sharply from $5.1 billion in 1940 and $7.9 billion in 1945. In general, these companies are subject to much less rigid legal restrictions in their investment policies than the life insurance companies, and they have invested relatively heavily in common stocks. A breakdown shows holdings of corporate bonds of $3.85 billion, or 8.4% of total assets; corporate preferred stocks of $1.28 billion, or 2.8%; and common stocks of $14.75 billion, or 32.1%. Holdings of government bonds were also large.[5]

In recent years these companies have been significant buyers of corporate bonds and stocks and of tax-exempt bonds as well, taking up more than $1 billion annually of each of these three types of investments.

Private Pension Funds

Private pension funds, which accumulate funds paid in by employers and to a lesser extent by employees, are largely a post–World War II development. The assets being accumulated against present and future

---

[4] Weisenberger Services, Inc., *Investment Companies 1970: Mutual Funds and Other Types* (30th ed.; New York, 1970).

[5] *Best's Fire and Casualty Aggregates and Averages 1969* (New York: Alfred M. Best Co., Inc., 1969).

obligations to pay pensions to retired employees have grown from a modest figure in 1947 to an estimated $126.2 billion in 1969. A significant portion of these funds, $39.0 billion at the end of 1969, was held by life insurance companies under "insured plans" and largely was commingled for investment purposes with their other assets. A larger amount, $87.2 billion at year-end 1969, was held and administered by trustees, frequently banks, appointed for the purpose.[6] Strictly speaking, it may be inaccurate to classify funds so managed as "institutional"; but to the extent that the pension funds are run by full-time investment managers on a continuing professional basis, in operation they are handled much like institutional funds, and so we discuss them under the institutional heading.

Most pension fund managers believe that they can, like life insurance companies, invest appropriately in long-term corporate securities. The investment income of pension trusts is free of federal income tax. Table 16–7 shows the distribution of assets of noninsured pension funds on

Table 16–7

Distribution of Assets of Private Noninsured Pension Funds,*
December 31, 1969
(dollar figures in billions)

	Book Value	Percentage of Total
Cash and deposits..............	$ 1.59	1.8%
U.S. government issues...........	2.59	3.0
Corporate bonds................	26.64	30.5
Preferred stock.................	1.74	2.0
Common stock..................	45.96	52.7
Mortgages.....................	4.01	4.6
Other assets...................	4.74	5.4
Total assets..............	$87.24	100.0%

* Includes funds of corporations, nonprofit organizations, and multiemployer and union plans.
Source: U.S. Securities and Exchange Commission, *Statistical Bulletin*, September, 1970, p. 26.

December 31, 1969. Note the heavy emphasis on corporate securities, including common stocks.

The chief significance of the pension funds as investors in corporate securities lies not so much in the size of their present holdings as in their impressive growth in recent years and the currently large additions to their holdings through new purchases each year. The noninsured pension funds alone between 1960 and 1969 added more than $10.9 billion to their holdings of corporate bonds and almost $36.2 billion to their investments in corporate stocks. In 1969 alone, these funds increased their corporate

---

[6] Securities and Exchange Commission, *Statistical Bulletin*, May, 1970, p. 24. This amount includes funds of nonprofit organizations and multiemployer plans.

bond portfolio by $0.5 billion and their common stocks by $5.7 billion.[7]

Most private pension funds were established as a result of collective bargaining with labor unions, and pressures from unions should tend toward increasing the long-term importance of the pension funds. For this and other impressive reasons, we anticipate that the pension funds will continue to grow robustly and that they will represent a continuing, important source of funds for investment in corporate securities. If the trends of recent years continue, these funds will be especially important buyers of common stocks.

Public Pension Funds

Like the private pension funds, the retirement funds of state and local governments are accumulated in order to meet obligations to pay pensions. The total amount of such funds at the end of 1969 was estimated at $52.0 billion.[8] In 1969 payments into such funds and investment income were estimated to total $9.4 billion, while benefit payments amounted to only $3.3 billion.[9] Until relatively recent years, their assets were invested predominantly in U.S. government and state and municipal bonds. More recently, the investment managers of many funds have taken advantage of eased restrictions on their investing policies to seek the higher investment returns available from corporate bond issues. In 1969 these funds added $3.8 billion of corporate bonds and notes to their portfolios.[10] There is every reason to expect that these funds will continue to be an important and growing source of demand for corporate debt issues.

Some funds have begun to buy common stocks. It was estimated that they added $1.7 billion of common stocks to their investment funds in 1969.[11]

Social security and retirement funds administered by the U.S. government can be acknowledged as representing a huge and growing accumulation of savings. These funds are invested exclusively in U.S. government securities. As of July 31, 1970, these funds, along with other U.S. government agencies and trust funds, held $94.8 billion of U.S. government securities.[12] This compares with a total figure for such holdings of $27 billion at the end of 1945. Since they have absorbed U.S. government bonds that otherwise might well have been sold in competition with corporate securities, these funds have had a significant, though *indirect*, effect on the markets for corporate securities.

---

[7] *Ibid.*, p. 23.

[8] *Ibid.*, p. 24.

[9] Bankers Trust Company, *The Investment Outlook for 1970* (New York, 1970) Table 17.

[10] *Ibid.*

[11] *Ibid.*

[12] *Federal Reserve Bulletin*, September, 1970, p. A42.

Investment Companies

On June 30, 1969, 1,049 companies engaged primarily in the business of investing in securities that were registered with the Securities and Exchange Commission as *investment companies.*[13] In the broadest terms these companies gathered the funds of investors, typically in small increments, for investment in the securities of other firms. The most important type of investment company was the open-end mutual fund; 679 funds had a total market value on June 30, 1969, of $54.5 billion. Many new mutual funds were formed in the late 1960's, 200 during the fiscal year ended on June 30, 1967. The assets of the open-end mutual funds have grown with market appreciation over the years and as the result of vigorous sales efforts. In effect, these funds offer small, as well as large, investors an opportunity to participate in a professionally managed and diversified portfolio of securities. Many investors in mutual funds do not have important other holdings of securities.

Chart 16–1 shows the growth in total market value of investment companies. Table 16–8 shows the great growth of open-end mutual funds during the 1960's and the way these companies have invested their assets. In contrast to the policies of other institutional intermediaries, the mutual funds consistently have invested predominantly in common stocks. For the most part, these funds invested in the stocks of the established and larger "blue-chip" companies. During the 1960's many fund managers adopted more aggressive and speculative investment policies in a search for superior performance. Many were highly successful for a time, but those which had invested heavily in smaller, less substantial or marginal firms, saw their values melt down severely in the bear markets of 1969–70.

Despite the setback in the bear market and despite the prospect of regulatory curbs of some aggressive selling and management practices of the funds, we anticipate that the funds will be able to make the adaptations necessary for them to resume their growth and to continue as a major buyer of corporate equities.

---

[13] Investment companies are of several types, two of which, the *open-end* and the *closed-end* types, are of special importance. The open-end companies, of which Investors Mutual, Inc., with assets of $2,681 million on December 31, 1969, is the largest, have no fixed number of shares of common stock. Instead, they offer new common shares for sale continuously. The price of the shares is established by the current per share value of the company's assets plus a "loading" to cover sales commissions and other expenses of selling the new shares. The open-end companies typically contract to repurchase their shares at the per share asset value of the investment company on the date they are presented for redemption. In recent decades the sales of new shares of the open-end companies have far exceeded the redemptions, so that the assets available for investment have grown for this reason, as well as because of market appreciation of holdings over the years. The bear market of 1969–70 cut substantially into total market values and into net sales.

The closed-end trusts operate with a fixed number of shares. These shares are traded on the stock exchanges or over-the-counter and may sell at wide discounts or premiums over their asset values. Tri-Continental Corporation, which had total investment assets of $639.1 million on December 31, 1970, is an example of a closed-end investment company.

Chart 16–1

Estimated Aggregate Market Value of Investment Company Assets as of June 30*
(in millions)

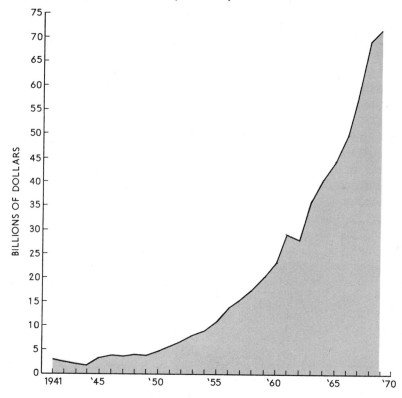

* The increase in aggregate assets reflects the sale of new securities as well as capital appreciation.
SOURCE OF DATA: U.S. Securities and Exchange Commission, *35th Annual Report, 1969* (Washington, D.C., 1970), p. 126.

Table 16–8

Distribution of Mutual Fund Assets at End of Years, 1960–69
(dollar figures in millions)

	Total Net Assets	Net Cash and Equivalent		Corporate Bonds		Preferred Stocks		Common Stocks	
1960.....	$17,026	$ 973	5.7%	$1,247	7.3%	$ 707	4.2%	$14,099	82.8%
1961.....	22,792	980	4.3	1,587	6.9	775	3.4	19,477	85.4
1962.....	21,271	1,315	6.2	1,617	7.6	738	3.5	17,601	82.7
1963.....	25,214	1,341	5.3	1,788	7.1	729	2.9	21,356	84.7
1964.....	29,116	1,329	4.6	2,149	7.4	687	2.4	24,951	85.6
1965.....	35,220	1,803	5.1	2,554	7.3	595	1.7	30,268	85.9
1966.....	34,829	2,971	8.5	2,915	8.4	505	1.4	28,438	81.7
1967.....	44,701	2,566	5.7	2,959	6.6	755	1.7	38,421	86.0
1968.....	52,677	3,187	6.0	3,408	6.5	1,675	3.2	44,407	84.3
1969.....	48,291	3,846	8.0	3,586	7.4	1,190	2.5	39,669	82.1

SOURCE: Investment Company Institute, *1970 Mutual Fund Fact Book* (Washington, D.C., 1970), pp. 79, 80.

The Commercial Banks

The commercial banks long have been major investors in the debt securities of the U.S. government and its agencies and in the tax-exempt bonds and notes of state and local governments. On June 30, 1970, commercial banks held $62.1 billion of U.S. Treasury and agency securities and $63.2 billion of the obligations of state and local governments. Banks have legal sanction to invest in corporate bonds but in recent decades have so invested only to a minor degree. Speaking generally, banks are not permitted to invest bank funds in common stocks.

Earlier we noted that banks acting as trustees administer a very substantial portion of noninsured corporate pension funds. Further, the banks administer a huge volume of assets held in personal trusts and advisory accounts. The assets at market value held in personal trusts administered by commercial banks have grown sharply in recent years—from $49.7 billion at year-end 1958 to an estimated $126.2 billion at year-end 1967. Available data on the distribution of the assets of these funds at an earlier date is shown in Table 16–9.

Table 16–9

Asset Holdings in Personal Trust Accounts Administered by Commercial Banks

Type of Asset	December 31 1963	
Common stock	$54,017.1	65.7%
State and municipal securities	11,644.0	14.1
Participation in common trust funds	4,749.3	5.8
Corporate bonds and debentures	3,032.5	3.7
U.S. government securities	2,772.7	3.4
Preferred stock	1,315.6	1.6
Mortgages	941.7	1.1
Cash	552.0	0.7
All other assets	3,215.9	3.9
Total	$82,240.8	100.0%

SOURCE: Gordon A. McLean, "Report of National Survey of Personal Trust Accounts," *The Trust Bulletin*, published by the Trust Division of the American Bankers Association, Vol. 44, No. 4 (December, 1964), p. 9.

The very large investment of personal trust funds in common stocks is strikingly apparent in Table 16–9. Banks buying for various trust accounts represent the largest institutional investment source of demand for common stocks, outstripping even the investment companies.

Also especially noteworthy from Table 16–9 is the heavy use made of the tax-exempt bonds of states and municipalities. This reflects the fact that the income beneficiaries of trusts commonly are in high income tax brackets and they can net more income after taxes from the tax-exempt interest available from municipal bonds than on the higher yielding but taxable return available from governments and corporates. In other words, investors in a high tax bracket normally find tax-exempt bonds more attractive investments than U.S. government or corporate bonds.

The banks have had some success in devising trust arrangements especially for persons with a small or moderate amount of capital for management. If continued progress along these lines can be made, the growth of bank-administered trust funds will be very much greater than if the banks are forced, for cost and other reasons, to restrict their interest to trust accounts of $200,000 or more.

Mutual Savings Banks

The mutual savings banks, largely concentrated in New England, New York, and Pennsylvania, had assets amounting to nearly $76.3 billion on June 30, 1970. The mutual savings banks have invested primarily in home mortgage loans and in U.S. government bonds. Although subject to close legal restriction in their investment in corporate securities, a breakdown of their assets at the end of 1969 showed holdings of $5.9 billion in corporate bonds and $2.2 billion in corporate stocks.[14] Should the recently abundant opportunities for investment in home mortgages decline importantly, the savings banks may well prove a more important market for corporate securities, mainly high-quality bonds of intermediate and long maturities.

Savings and Loan Associations

In recent years savings and loan associations have been particularly effective in competing for individuals' savings. Their total assets on June 30, 1970, amounted to $174.6 billion.[15] Regarded by many savers as the approximate equivalent of savings banks, the savings and loan associations have invested predominantly in home mortgages and to a much lesser extent in government bonds. To date, their investment in corporate securities has been negligible, but they represent a possible source of demand for corporate securities should the supply of mortgage investments available to them shrink greatly and legal restrictions on bond investment be eased.

Religious, Educational, and Charitable Funds

The assets of the various nonprofit institutions of the country are largely invested in corporate securities. They are relatively free of income

---

[14] Federal Deposit Insurance Corporation, *Annual Report, 1969* (Washington, D.C., 1970).

[15] *Federal Reserve Bulletin*, May, 1970, p. A38.

taxation and of legal restrictions on their investment policies, and their security holdings include substantial amounts of common and preferred stocks as well as bonds. An analysis of the investment portfolios of 71 college and university endowment funds on June 30, 1969, showed 20.9% of the total market value of the endowment funds invested in bonds, 0.6% in preferred stocks, 4.8% in convertible securities, and 60.3% in common stocks. The total market value of the 71 endowment funds was $7.64 billion.[16]

The assets of other nonprofit organizations total several billion dollars and also include a substantial amount of corporate equities.

The inflow of funds to the nonprofit funds is relatively slow, so that they are net buyers of corporate securities only in moderate amounts.

Summary of the Institutional Market for Corporate Securities

Before turning to a review of the noninstitutional, or individual, investor segments of the market, we can appropriately summarize some key points about the institutional markets for corporate securities. We have reviewed briefly the investment practices of the institutions with important amounts of funds to invest in corporate securities along with other segments—pension funds and institutionally administered personal trust funds—of the market that are professionally managed. We have seen that institutions, broadly considered, have very important holdings of corporate bonds. Further, the institutions are continuing to buy a dominant portion of new issues of corporate debt securities, and there is evidence to support the view that they will continue to be the principal purchasers of new issues in the future.

We have noted very wide differences among the major types of financial institutions in investing in common stocks. At one end of the spectrum are mutual funds which invest primarily in common stocks. At the other extreme, deposit-type institutions have invested very little in equities.

By the end of 1969 institutions held nearly $152 billion of stocks listed on the New York Stock Exchange. Their holdings represented 24.1% of the total market value of NYSE-listed stocks at that date.[17]

In recent years institutions, especially private pension funds, have been heavy net buyers of common stocks. Reflecting the increased importance of institutions in the market for equities, and the high trading activity of mutual funds, the percentage of total dollar value of trading on the New York Stock Exchange done by or through institutions grew from 39.3% in 1960 to 60.3% in 1969.[18]

---

[16] Boston Fund, Inc., *The 1969 Study of College and University Endowment Funds* (Boston, 1970, p. 4).

[17] New York Stock Exchange, *Fact Book 1970* (New York, 1970). This tally of institutional holdings largely excluded bank-administered trust funds.

[18] *Ibid.*

The Noninstitutional Market for Corporate Securities

Now let us turn to the noninstitutional or "individual investor" segment of the market for corporate securities. While fully reliable and detailed information on this important part of the market does not exist, the available evidence does permit some useful general observations about how individuals have invested their savings.

First, over the years individuals have been important but secondary buyers of corporate bonds. Since institutions have come into importance as buyers of corporate equities only in recent decades, individuals necessarily have been the dominant holders of corporate stocks over the years. By the end of 1961, one major study estimated institutions held 81.4% of the $107 billion of corporate notes and bonds then outstanding but only 22.1% of the $546.2 total value of stocks outstanding. Despite interesting trends of more recent years noted shortly, we can generalize that individuals have left bond investment largely to the financial intermediaries while still holding the major share of corporate stocks.

Now let us look more closely at data on how individuals have been investing their savings in recent years. First, as Table 16–4 shows, individuals have directed a large part of their total financial savings in recent years—47.7% in the years 1966–69—into deposit institutions. During this same period some 32.9% of the savings was in the form of pension fund or insurance reserves.

While the predominant amount of their savings went to institutional intermediaries, individuals did add to their direct investments in government and corporate bonds during these years, particularly in 1969 when new issues of U.S. and corporate bonds offered the highest interest yields in recent decades, while interest paid by deposit institutions was subject to regulatory ceilings.

The data show a major disinvestment (more selling than buying) in corporate stocks by individuals broadly during these years of generally strong stock markets. This net selling of $35.3 billion of direct stock holdings during the 4 years was partially offset by the net purchase of $15.8 billion of investment company shares. As we have seen, individuals still hold directly the lion's share of outstanding stocks. But in recent periods institutions have become major net buyers of stocks from individuals. Students of the stock markets understandably have devoted much attention to the consequences of the growing importance of institutions in the market for equities and the extent to which this trend will continue in future years.

What is known about that portion of the American public that has invested in corporate securities?

One inescapable characteristic of the individual investor segment is its heterogeneous nature. The investment objectives of the various individual holders of corporate securities, for example, are widely varied, running all the way from the needs of the almost impecunious widow, who desires most the protection of her small principal but who also needs income, to that of the speculator, who is willing to risk his money on the most hazardous issue in hope of large return through capital gains.

The degree of investment sophistication and skill is also extremely varied. The Kansas farmer with a large supply of extra cash from the last wheat crop obviously is a prospective investor quite different from the seasoned speculator who has survived many years on Wall Street. The diverse character of the individual market in this respect contrasts with the institutional market, in which it is presumed that most important firms have the resources and personnel for careful, informed investment management.

On the basis of a "Census of Shareownership" in early 1965, the New York Stock Exchange concluded that some 20.1 million individuals or one in six adults owned shares in publicly held corporations.[19] More than 13% of the total residents in New England and the Middle Atlantic states owned shares but only 5.8% in the South Central region. By 1969 the NYSE estimated the number of shareholders had grown to 26.4 million.

While the growth in total number of shareholders sounds impressive, this statistic may give a misleading impression of breadth of direct stock ownership. First, the total includes many millions who have very small holdings.

Second, there is abundant evidence that a high percentage of the total stockholdings of individuals are held by a relatively small number of high-income investors. Table 16–10 presents data on dividend and interest income received by taxpayers in various income groups. Note, for example, that taxpaying units with more than $20,000 income accounted for only 17.5% of total adjusted gross income but for 66.9% of dividend income. Interest income was much more evenly distributed, with taxpayers over $20,000 receiving only 27.1% of interest income. This lower figure reflects the great importance of interest paid on savings deposits and savings bonds to persons with moderate incomes.

Perhaps significant was the correlation of shareownership with educational achievement, revealed in the NYSE study. Of the total population of college graduates, 59.1% were shareholders, while only 5.6% of the adults who had not finished high school owned shares.

As might be expected, shareownership was most common among individuals in the 45-to-54-year age group. Of the population in this age group, 21.8% owned stock.

Interestingly enough, and for whatever significance it has, women shareholders outnumbered the men, 51% of the adult shareholders being women, mostly housewives.

---

[19] *Shareownership U.S.A.: 1965 Census of Shareowners* (New York: New York Stock Exchange, 1965).

Table 16-10

Dividends and Interest Received by Individuals in Various Income Groups, as Reported in Income Tax Returns for 1967
(dollar figures in millions)

Adjusted Gross Income Group	Adjusted Gross Income	Percentage of Total	Cumulative Percentage	Dividend Income (after Exclusions)*	Percentage of Total	Cumulative Percentage	Interest Received	Percentage of Total	Cumulative Percentage
Under $5,000........	$ 58,491	12.0%	12.0%	$ 596	4.4%	4.4%	$ 2,155	16.6%	16.6%
$5,000–$10,000......	172,615	35.4	47.4	1,491	11.0	15.4	3,521	27.0	43.6
$10,000–$15,000.....	124,171	25.5	72.9	1,304	9.7	25.1	2,479	19.0	62.6
$15,000–$20,000.....	46,762	9.6	82.5	1,077	8.0	33.1	1,334	10.3	72.9
$20,000–$50,000.....	54,914	11.3	93.8	3,521	26.1	59.2	2,275	17.5	90.4
$50,000–$100,000.....	17,162	3.5	97.3	2,198	16.3	75.5	738	5.7	96.1
$100,000–$200,000.....	6,737	1.4	98.7	1,435	10.6	86.1	290	2.2	98.3
$200,000–$500,000.....	3,619	0.7	99.4	1,026	7.6	93.7	140	1.1	99.4
$500,000–$1,000,000..	1,383	0.3	99.7	385	2.9	96.6	43	0.3	99.7
$1,000,000 or more....	1,590	0.3	100.0	463	3.4	100.0	41	0.3	100.0
Total.........	$487,445	100.0%		$13,497	100.0%		$13,016	100.0%	

* Taxable and nontaxable returns.
SOURCE: U.S. Internal Revenue Service, *Statistics of Income, 1967: Individual Income Tax Returns* (Washington, D.C.: U.S. Government Printing Office, 1969), Table 4.

chapter 17

Tapping the Sources of Long-Term Capital

Earlier, we pictured the relative importance to American corporations in recent years of capital raised through the sale of new issues of securities, and we sketched in broad-brush terms the nature of the ultimate market for these securities. In this chapter we shall discuss the major means by which corporations issuing new securities reach buyers for their securities and thus avail themselves of long-term capital. Although numerous methods of distribution of corporate securities have been developed, our discussion will center on the few basic methods that are of particular importance.

Relation of the Markets for Outstanding Securities to the Distribution of New Issues

It is important at this point that the reader carefully distinguishes between the sale by corporations of newly issued securities, or *primary* distribution, and the trading of *outstanding*, or "old" issues in the *secondary* markets like the New York Stock Exchange. Our major focus in this chapter is on primary distribution of securities, but later in this chapter we shall look briefly at the secondary markets and their somewhat distinctive activities, institutions, and mechanisms.

The existence and operations of the secondary markets are important to, though distinct from, the primary distribution of securities. Each new issue of securities competes, directly or indirectly, with outstanding securities for the ultimate investor's favor and dollars. The terms and price of new offerings must be made temptingly attractive in comparison with those of outstanding securities which can be bought in the secondary markets. Also, the attractiveness of a newly issued security to potential investors is enhanced by the prospect that a good secondary market for the securities will develop.

Major Types of New Offerings

Most new securities for cash sale are sold through one of three basic methods of distribution:

1. *A public offering involving the issue of subscription rights to existing shareholders.* The rights to subscribe to the new offering, typically at a price well below the market for outstanding shares, are extended pro rata to existing shareholders. The subscription rights typically are transferable, so that a shareholder who does not want more shares can sell his rights to someone who does want to subscribe.

2. *A public offering without rights,* in which the new issue is offered for sale to the public.

3. *Private placements,* which represent the offering of an entire issue to a single or limited number of investors who buy as ultimate investors rather than for early resale. This method is used primarily for new issues of debt securities.

Corporations have employed the public offering method predominantly in marketing new issues of equity securities but have made heavy use of private placement in selling debt issues. Chart 17–1 shows the amount of corporate debt issues sold in recent years and the portions placed privately. As can be seen from the chart, corporations have utilized both public issues and private placement in selling debt issues. As recently as 1965, well over half of the total amount was placed privately. As the total supply of debt issues grew faster than the institutional appetite for new issues, issuing corporations turned increasingly to public offerings aimed at the noninstitutional market as well. In the preceding chapter we saw that individuals were significant buyers of government and corporate bonds in the late 1960's.

Industrial concerns have made very much heavier use of private placement than utilities or other issuers. The growth of private placement in the 1950's and early 1960's was facilitated by the continued growth and importance of institutions—notably life insurance companies and state and local pension funds—as buyers of corporate debt securities. The larger of these institutions represent an identifiable and concentrated market. At times their investment managers have been eager to garner the higher yields of privately purchased bonds over those available in public issues.

During the later 1960's, the institutional markets for bonds failed to expand and in addition some institutions shifted to predominant purchase of public issues. This in part stemmed from renewed concern about their own institutional needs for liquidity and for an increased appreciation in these circumstances, for the flexibility in portfolio policy afforded

Chart 17–1

Total New Issues of Corporate Bonds, Gross Proceeds
(in billions)

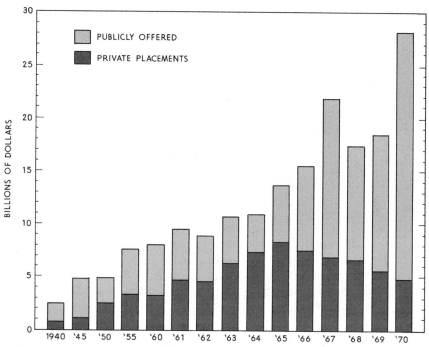

SOURCE OF DATA: *Federal Reserve Bulletins.*

by the very much greater marketability of many of the publicly issued bonds. Further, the high yields available on public issues of good quality during this period diluted some of the added-yield appeal of private placements.

Why have corporations been willing to offer higher yields to private buyers than they would have to offer if bonds were sold publicly?[1] Several advantages of private sale appear of importance to corporate issuers. First, the registration and disclosure procedures of the Securities and Exchange Commission, which are a necessary part of public offerings, are not required if the securities are sold privately. Avoiding these procedures may save time, trouble, and some expense. Second, the issuer may be able to arrange more satisfactory covenants in direct negotiation with the informed and sophisticated institutional buyers than would be the

---

[1] The public offering also may afford the issuing corporation opportunities over the life of the issue to buy up and retire bonds at favorable prices. Depressed market prices are likely if the level of interest rates rises above the interest rate of the bond. In the case of bonds placed privately, there is no market for the securities, and so parallel opportunities do not exist.

case in a public offering. Third, the mechanics of making agreed changes in the terms of private placements are not difficult; in contrast it may be extremely difficult to garner the necessary consents of scattered public bondholders to even minor changes. Fourth, the costs of issue are usually significantly smaller under private placement, since the costs of distribution involved in issues to the public are largely avoided. While the costs of public bond issues are less than those of public common stock offerings, they can be material. We shall speak later in more detail regarding costs. Fifth, under private placement there is somewhat more flexibility in arranging for instalment or deferred takedowns or for other special needs. For example, in December, 1965, Southland Paper Mills, Inc., with the agency help of Lehman Brothers, arranged the sale to institutional investors of $35 million of $5\frac{1}{4}\%$ notes due in 1986. Of the total, $15 million was to be taken down in the third quarter of 1966 and another $15 million in the first half of 1967. In addition, Southland had the option of borrowing an additional $5 million from the institutional buyers of the other notes.[2]

Private placement of equity issues has increased in recent years, with the total reaching a record $825 million in 1969.[3] Some of these were unregistered or "investment letter stock" in which buyers attested that they were buying for purposes of investment rather than resale. Many buyers of such stock had to sit immobile with these investments as their market values moved up smartly, then melted away in the bear market of 1969–70. It is by no means clear that private placement of equities will continue to grow.

The Role of Investment Bankers in Distribution of New Issues

The issuing corporation usually is free to undertake without outside help all aspects of the job of designing a new security issue and selling it to investors; in most cases, however, it has enlisted the help of investment bankers who are specialists in the marketing of new security issues. Basically, investment banking firms perform a distributive function, acting as middlemen between issuing corporations and the ultimate buyers of new securities. In recent years investment banking firms have been willing to make their services available on a variety of different arrangements, although several are of particular importance.

In outline form the major arrangements under which investment bankers assist in the distributive functions are:

1. Underwritten issues:
    a) Fully underwritten public issues.
        (1) Negotiated underwritings.

---

[2] *Investment Dealers' Digest*, December 20, 1965, p. 14.

[3] *Investment Dealers' Digest, Corporate Financing Directory*, Sec. II, September 22, 1970, p. 23.

Table 17–1

Number of New Security Issues by Type of Transaction, 1935–49

	Bonds*		Preferred		Common		All Securities	
	Num-ber of Issues	% of Total Number	Num-ber of Issues	% of Total Number	Num-ber of Issues	% of Total Number	Num-ber of Issues	% of Total Number
Total......	3,215	100%	973	100%	718	100%	4,906	100%
Underwritten ne-gotiated........	856	26.6%	706	72.6%	438	61.0%	2,000	40.8%
Underwritten pub-lic sealed bidding	502	15.6	89	9.1	32	4.5	623	12.7
Total under-written...	1,358	42.2%	795	81.7%	470	65.5%	2,623	53.5%
Nonunderwritten agency........	32	1.0%	47	4.8%	62	8.6%	141	2.9%
Nonunderwritten, no investment banker........	42	1.3	45	4.6	162	22.6	249	5.1
Total nonun-derwritten	74	2.3%	92	9.5%	224	31.2%	390	7.9%
Private placement agency........	818	25.4%	52	5.3%	6	0.8%	876	17.9%
Private placement, no investment banker........	965	30.0	34	3.5	18	2.5	1,017	20.7
Total private placements	1,783	55.5%	86	8.8%	24	3.3%	1,893	38.6%

* Including bonds, debentures, notes, etc.

Source: *United States of America* v. *Henry S. Morgan, Harold Stanley, et al., Doing Business as Morgan Stanley & Co., et al.,* U.S. District Court for Southern New York, Civil No. 43–757, Defendants' Preliminary Memorandum for the Court, p. 24.

(2) Underwritings won under competitive biddings.
    b) Standby underwriting of issues offered with subscription rights.
2. Issues in which investment bankers work on an agency basis:
    a) Nonunderwritten agency basis on sales to the public.
    b) Agency basis in private placements.

Particularly complete and reliable data concerning the relative impor-tance of the various major arrangements are available for the years 1935–49, and these are summarized in Table 17–1. It will be noted that more than half of the issues in these years were on an underwritten basis.

While equally complete and parallel data are not available for the years since 1949, the basic pattern of investment banking activity has not changed greatly from that reflected in Table 17–1.

Underwritten Public Issues—Negotiated Deals

In underwritten issues, one or a group of investment banking firms working together on an issue assure the issuing firm a definite sum of money for the issue at a definite time. The underwriting investment banking firms are willing to back their judgment as to the marketability of the issue at the proposed public offering price by agreeing to purchase the entire issue at a firm, agreed price, assuming the risks that they will be unable to resell the issue to the public. In other words, they assure, or *underwrite*, the success of the issue, and add the function of risk taking to their selling function.

At this point, it is well to distinguish between underwritten issues in which the arrangements between issuer and investment bankers as to price and other key factors are arrived at by *negotiation* between the parties and those other underwritten issues in which the terms of the new security issue are drawn up by the issuer and the issue is placed with underwriting investment bankers on the basis of *public sealed bids*. Under the public sealed bid arrangements, commonly known as *competitive bid* deals, the issue is, in effect, put up for sale to the highest responsible bidder. Use of competitive bidding is confined almost exclusively to security issues of regulated industries or governmental units.

Investment banking sources reported that 172 issues of bonds, totaling $7.5 billion, were sold through negotiated underwritings in the first 6 months of 1970. In the same period, 81 underwritten bond issues, totaling $2.6 billion, were sold at competitive bid. The totals for bonds, preferred stocks, and common stocks were 653 issues, $10.5 billion, negotiated; and 95 issues, $2.9 billion, at competitive bid.[4]

The negotiated arrangement is the traditional form of underwriting and is favored by investment bankers generally. In a negotiated under-written public offering, the services of the investment bankers may be utilized, to the extent the issuer wishes, in every stage of the process from the design of the security through its actual distribution to the public. An investment banking firm, which will act as manager of the syndicate of banking firms it selects to assist in the underwriting and sales operation, will be chosen at a very early stage. Morgan Stanley & Company, for example, from 1935 through 1967 served as manager or comanager in public offerings totaling nearly $30 billion. The firm selected as manager or comanager undertakes a searching and detailed investigation and analysis of the affairs of the issuer, with especial emphasis on its current and future financing needs. Working with company officers, the managing firm attempts to work out details on an issue which effectively reconcile the objectives of the issuer and the requirements of investors under the anticipated market conditions upon offering of the security. Typically, the investment bankers assist corporate management in reaching decisions as to the type or types of securities to be offered, their provisions, and the timing of the offering. The banker and his counsel also help in the drafting of the registration statement and prospectus usually required by the

---

[4] *Ibid.*, p. 20.

Securities and Exchange Commission, and in the filing of other documents necessary to qualify the issue legally for sale. Since most companies undertake public issues only infrequently, the market *expertise* of the investment bankers can be highly valuable to the issuer.

About the time the prospective new security takes tentative form, the investment banker undertakes to line up other investment banking firms to join in a group of firms or *syndicate* to share the risks of underwriting and the job of selling. In a large issue the syndicate will usually include many firms. The size of the syndicate formed and the number of selling dealers enlisted tend to increase with the size of the issue. In the huge offering of Ford Motor Company common stock owned by The Ford Foundation—10.2 million shares sold to the public at $64.50 for a total of $657.9 million—in January, 1956, seven firms served as comanagers of the underwriting syndicate, which was composed of 722 firms. In addition, the syndicate employed the services of 1,000 security dealers in selling the issue. The issue was quickly oversubscribed.

Firms joining the syndicate as underwriters also act as selling firms; in large deals, additional firms commonly are brought in only as selling dealers, as was the case in the Ford issue. Because the security issues often are large in relation to the capital resources of individual investment banking firms and because it is helpful in tapping as wide a market as possible to have a number of firms with customers throughout the country, syndicate arrangements under which various firms band together on a single issue have become typical for all but the smallest issues. The composition of the syndicates and the percentage participation of each firm differ from one issue to another, but certain firms tend to work together on many issues.

Tentative understandings as to probable price both to the company and to the public (thus approximating the anticipated *banker's spread*, or gross margin of profit, on the deal) may be reached early in the discussions. Shortly before the registration statement becomes effective and the issue legally can be sold, definite prices and terms of the issue are established in final negotiation between bankers and issuer.

To be fully satisfactory to all concerned, such a pattern of operation requires a high degree of mutual confidence and trust on the part of all parties. One of the prime assets of a successful investment banking firm is its reputation for fair and effective operation over the years, and such reputations are jealously guarded. This feature also helps to explain why many issuing firms have developed close relationships with particular investment banking houses and continue to do business with them in successive issues over long periods of years.

The investment bankers make strenuous efforts to sell new issues quickly—both to achieve rapid turnover of their capital and to minimize the risk that a downturn in the market will leave the securities "on the bankers' shelves" at what become unattractively high prices. Despite the bankers' best efforts at close pricing, relatively minor downturns in the market may leave an issue unsold at the issue price, necessitating either sale at reduced prices or holding for an upturn in prices, which may not materialize and in any case ties up the investment bankers' capital. The spread between the price that the bankers pay the issuers and the resale price to the public is usually so small that even a small break from planned prices may result in losses to the bankers.

It is common practice for the syndicate manager to retain a portion of the securities for sale to institutional buyers for the "pot," that is, the account of the whole underwriting syndicate. This is in addition to the managing firm's own selling commitment.

In compliance with regulations that control the practice, the manager for the syndicate generally is authorized to—and when the occasion requires, does—undertake buying and selling in the market designed to *stabilize* the market price of the security during the period in which the new securities are being sold by the syndicate. Profits and losses stemming from the stabilizing operations are for the account of the whole syndicate.

Important prospective buyers are supplied with copies of the prospectus describing the issue, complete except for final price and a few other terms, for their study well before the offering date. Many make their decision to buy, contingent on the final price, before the actual offering. Consequently, if the issue is to be a successful one, it usually "goes out the window," that is, it is entirely sold out, in a matter of hours or a few days after the initial offering—and the syndicate is quickly terminated. When sales are slow, the syndicate typically continues in operation for a longer time with sales only at the agreed, announced price. If the offering is not sold out in a few weeks, by agreement the syndicate usually breaks up, stabilization activities are abandoned, and each investment banking underwriter is free to hold or dispose of his inventory of securities as he sees fit.

The foregoing description imputes a rather passive role in the marketing effort to the selling company. In actual fact, officers of the selling firm may be drafted to help explain the company and its future to potential buying interests around the country. For example, when the securities of a number of new Real Estate Investment Trusts (REIT's) were brought to market in the bearish atmosphere of 1970, it was common for corporate officials to join representatives of the underwriters in a "dog and pony show" circuit or series of speaking and question and answer sessions before syndicate sales personnel and potential investors around the country.

An additional variable was important in the sale of securities by the REIT's and has been in a number of other negotiated underwritings. The amount of the issue as well as certain terms often was left somewhat open-ended until the underwriters could make a last-minute assessment of the capacity of the syndicate to sell and the market to absorb the new securities. Reportedly particular REIT issues in 1970 were adjusted upward or downward by 10%, 25%, or even 40% and some planned issues were repeatedly postponed or never materialized. In other words, a high element of "feel your way" or "cut and try" may be involved in some "firm underwritings."

In Exhibit 17–1 we have reproduced a proposed time schedule and assignments sheet submitted by an underwriting firm, Lehman Brothers, Inc., to a real estate investment trust considering a large issue of senior notes early in 1971. As the schedule indicates, some 53 days were allotted for the process from first meeting until the issuer received payment from the underwriters at "closing." Although a number of the detailed items are not self-explanatory or explained, we have included the exhibit to give the reader an idea of the mass of time-consuming procedural and legal activities incident to an underwritten negotiated public offering.

Underwritten Issues under Competitive Bidding

Security issues under public sealed bidding generally follow this basic pattern: The issuing firm offers an entire issue, generally of bonds or preferred stock, for outright purchase by the bidder offering the highest price—in terms of the lowest cost of money to the issuer. Bidding typically is by investment banking syndicates formed for the purpose of bidding on the specific issue. Unlike the pattern in negotiated underwritings, the investment bankers come into the picture at a late stage in the financing process. The investment bankers who bid on the issue do not act as consultants to the company in designing the issue—in fact, they are forbidden by administrative regulation to do so. The issuer and its counsel, or other expert advice, design the issue entirely by themselves and solicit by advertisement sealed bids for the definitively designed issue (see Exhibit 17–2).

The process of bidding and sale under competitive bidding has been described in the following terms:

Normally, numbers of bankers associate together to form accounts to bid for a specific issue. The reason for such association is the same as in the case of a negotiated transaction—to spread the risk and to accomplish distribution of the securities. After analyzing the registration statement, prospectus and other general data available as to the issuer and the issue to be offered, and after meeting with the issuer at a prebidding information session, the bankers comprised within each account meet together just before the bidding date to determine a bid. In the light of their estimates of the highest price at which the securities can be sold to the public based on then current market conditions, prices of comparable securities, and other relevant factors, each account determines the bid it will make for the entire issue. It frequently occurs that underwriters withdraw from the [syndicate] account because their views of the proper bid are lower than the bid price set

Exhibit 17–1

Proposed Time Schedule and Assignment Sheet

Summary Time Schedule

First day: General Meeting to discuss terms, time schedule and assignments.

Eighth day: Circulate first proofs of Registration Statement, Underwriting Agreements, and Indenture.

Sixteenth day: Registration Statement filed.

Forty-fifth day: Determine interest rate and price.

Forty-sixth day: Sign Underwriting Agreement, Registration Statement effective. Public Offering.

Fifty-third day: Closing.

Code for Assignments

T = Real Estate Investment Trust Issuing the Senior Notes.

R = Managing Underwriters.

M = Counsel for Issuing Company (the REIT).

UC = Counsel for the Underwriters.

Aud = Auditors for Company.

I = The Indenture Trustee.

Day and Activity	*Assigned to*
1 General Meeting to discuss terms, time schedule, and assignments...	T, R, M, UC Aud
2 Commence preparation of the following:	
a) Indenture...	UC
b) Registration Statement:	
(*i*) Facing page, Underwriting, Description of Notes.......	R, UC
(*ii*) Financial statements.............................	Aud
(*iii*) Remainder including exhibits........................	T, M
c) Trustees' questionnaires................................	M
d) Powers of attorney for Registration Statement and amendments..	M
e) Underwriters' questionnaires............................	R, UC
f) Underwriting Agreements and Powers of attorney for Underwriters..	R, UC
g) Blue-Sky and Legality Surveys...........................	UC
h) Trustees' resolutions...................................	M, UC
3 Advise banknote company of proposed schedule................	T, M
8 Circulate first proofs of Registration Statement, Underwriting Agreements and Indenture.	
9 First meeting to discuss Registration Statement, Underwriting Agreements and Indenture................................	T, M, R, UC Aud
11 Give Note language to banknote company.....................	T
Give Indenture proof to Trustee. Request Trustee to prepare Form T-1 and give comments on Indenture...................	T, UC
12 Obtain Powers of attorney and questionnaires from Trustees......	T
Circulate proof of Registration Statement to Trustees...........	T
Advise New York Stock Exchange of proposed financing........	T
Second Meeting to discuss Registration Statement, Underwriting Agreement, and Indenture.	

Exhibit 17–1 (Continued)

14   Determine requirements for preliminary material and give printer instructions.. T, R

15   Prepare transmittal letters to Underwriters and dealers to accompany preliminary material; give mailing instructions to printer...................................... R

Meeting of Trustees to approve financing program, including resolutions relating to:.................................... T, M

    a)   Authorizing issue, sale, and delivery of Notes.

    b)   Approving Indenture and Form of Note and authorizing execution thereof.

    c)   Approving form of Underwriting Agreements and authorizing execution thereof.

    d)   Appointing Trustee under Indenture.

    e)   Executing of Registration Statement and amendments.

    f)   Blue-Sky matters.

    g)   Listing of Notes on New York Stock Exchange.

Execute Registration Statement.............................. T

16   Registration Statement filed with SEC in Washington.*......... T, M

Brief press announcement of filing released.................... T, R

File Listing Application with New York Stock Exchange........ T, M

Proceed with Blue-Sky registration, where necessary............ UC

Mail to Underwriters Registration Statement, preliminary prospectus, Blue-Sky and Legality Surveys, questionnaires, preliminary Indenture and Underwriting Agreements and Powers of Attorney...................................... R

38   Obtain Notice of cursory treatment from SEC (or timing of comments, if any)... T

—   "Due Diligence" Meeting.................................. T, R, M, UC Aud

43   Receive questionnaires and powers from Underwriters........... R

Furnish SEC with Trustees' and Underwriters' request for acceleration and Rule 460 Preliminary Prospectus distribution information.. R

44   Notes approved for listing on New York Stock Exchange on notice of issuance and subject to adequacy of distribution and Exchange so advises SEC, if necessary.

45   Informal agreement reached between Trust and managing underwriters as to terms of Notes (i.e. interest rate, offering price, etc.) (3:30 P.M.)... T, R

Meeting of Trustees to adopt resolutions relating to terms (i.e. interest rate, offering price, etc.).............................. T

Give printer labels and mailing instructions for final prospectus.... R

46   Sign Agreements Among Underwriters in New York (9:00 A.M.)..... R

Sign Underwriting Agreement (9:15 A.M.)...................... T, R

Representative in Washington files pricing amendment with SEC at 9:05 A.M... T

Registration Statement effective with SEC (10:00 A.M., New York Time).

Complete Blue-Sky registration.............................. UC

Release wires to Underwriters and Dealers.................... R

Public Offering... R

Exhibit 17–1 (Continued)

	Release advertising...	R
	Release price information to press...........................	T, R
47	Mail to SEC 25 copies of Final Prospectus under Rule 424 (b).....	T
	Underwriters' advertising appears...........................	R
	Furnish Trust and Indenture Trustee with names and denominations for Notes..	R
52	Preliminary closing conference (2:00 P.M.).....................	M, UC
53	Closing (10:00 A.M.)..	T, R, M, UC
—†	Advise New York Stock Exchange of distribution of Notes and termination of Syndicate...................................	R
	Registration of Notes under Securities Exchange Act of 1934 effective.	

* Should either the SEC elect not to give the Registration Statement accelerated or cursory review or the State Securities Commissions proceed slowly, the time period will be lengthened by as much as two weeks. Accordingly, this date and subsequent dates should be regarded as tentative and subject to change. Since the Mortgage and Realty Trust offered securities as recently as June 4, 1970, the likelihood of prompt action on the part of the SEC and State Securities Commissions is enhanced. In addition, since the Shares of Beneficial Interest are listed on the New York Stock Exchange the number of states in which the Notes will have to be qualified is substantially reduced.

† Subsequent to closing date.

by the other members of the account, or for other reasons. If the number of such "dropouts" is large, it may be impossible for that account to submit a bid at all, in which case it disbands without further action unless other bankers will come in.

Each bid submitted indicates that the members of the account, as then constituted, offer to purchase the entire issue on a several basis[5] at the bid price.

The underwriters in the winning account then determine by themselves, and without reference to the issuer, the public offering price, the method of sale, and any concessions or reallowances, subject, where and to the extent required, to the approval of the proper regulatory authority. The difference between the public offering price and the bid price establishes the level of anticipated gross compensation for the underwriters of the issue.

The offering to the public in public sealed bidding issues usually differs from that of a negotiated underwritten public offering in the extent of distribution. Since the winning account knows that it has been successful only a very short time in advance of the public offering and has had no assurance that it would win the issue, there has been little time and no assurance of reimbursement for the advance work of educating dealers or investors in the special characteristics of the prospective issue. As a result, and in view of the fact that such issues are generally of the higher grades permissible or suitable for institutional investment, the underwriters frequently sell much of the issue in large blocks to institutions. The underwriters have no undertaking to the issuer to try to place the securities with any particular class or classes of investors or in a particular or widespread geographical area, and the cost of organizing selling efforts through dealers

---

[5] Purchase by the underwriters on a "several basis" means that each member of the syndicate is legally obligated to the issuer to take only that portion of the issue subscribed to by it. [Authors' note.]

Exhibit 17–2

Illustration of Invitation for Bids for a New Issue of Bonds

UNION ELECTRIC COMPANY

Public Invitation for Bids for the Purchase of $50,000,000 Principal Amount of First Mortgage Bonds,   % Series due 2001

Union Electric Company (the "Company"), a Missouri corporation, hereby invites bids for the purchase from it of $50,000,000 principal amount of its First Mortgage Bonds,   % Series due 2001 (the "Bonds"). Such bids will be received by the Company at the office of Bankers Trust Company, One Battery Park Plaza (State and Pearl Streets), New York, N. Y., Sixteenth Floor, Room A, up to 11 A. M., New York Time, on January 6, 1971, or on such later date as may be fixed by the Company as provided in the Statement referred to below. Copies of a Prospectus relating to the Bonds, dated December 29, 1970, of a Statement of Terms and Conditions Relating to Bids for the purchase of the Bonds, dated December 29, 1970, and of other relevant documents referred to in said Statement may be examined, and copies of certain of such documents may be obtained at the above address and at the office of the Company, One Memorial Drive, St. Louis, Missouri 63166. Bids will be considered only from bidders who have received copies of such Prospectus and only if made in accordance with and subject to the terms and conditions set forth in said Statement, including the filing of questionnaires on or before the time specified in such Statement.

Officers and representatives of the Company, counsel who will act for the successful bidders, and representatives of the auditors for the Company will be available at the office of Bankers Trust Company, One Battery Park Plaza (State and Pearl Streets), New York, N. Y., Sixteenth Floor, Room A/B, on January 5, 1971 at 10 A. M., New York Time, to meet with prospective bidders for the purpose of reviewing with them the information with respect to the Company contained in the Registration Statement and Prospectus. All prospective bidders are invited to be present at such meeting.

UNION ELECTRIC COMPANY

Dated: December 29, 1970   By Charles J. Dougherty, *President*.

---

may not be warranted by the spread which may exist for the particular issue, so that wide distribution is often not achieved.

If the issue is successful the compensation received may (although not always, even in a successful issue) cover the function of carrying the risk of the issue, the distribution function and the services of the manager in managing the distribution. Since no services have been performed in the design of the issue, and in view of the nature of the distribution, the services of the manager are much less than in a negotiated issue and the compensation, if any, is substantially less.[6]

---

[6] This description is taken from the Defendants' Preliminary Memorandum for the Court in the case of *United States of America* v. *Henry S. Morgan, Harold Stanley, et al., Doing Business as Morgan Stanley & Co., et al.*, U.S. District Court for Southern New York, Civil No. 43–757, pp. 89–90.

Use of competitive bidding has been restricted largely to firms in the public utility and railroad industries, which are required to use it by administrative agencies—chiefly the Securities and Exchange Commission, the Interstate Commerce Commission, the Federal Power Commission, and various state agencies regulating public utilities.[7] Use of competitive bidding received a great boost in April, 1941, when the SEC issued Rule 50, which required its use, subject to certain exceptions, for issues by public utility holding companies under its jurisdiction under the so-called "Death Sentence Act"—the Public Utility Holding Company Act of 1935. In announcing the rule, the SEC argued:

After weighing the evidence and considering all aspects of the problem, the Commission concluded that there was no way short of competitive bidding that would afford it satisfactory means of determining the reasonableness of spreads [investment bankers' gross margins] or the fairness of prices [of new issues bought by investment bankers], assure disinterested advice in financial matters to the companies concerned, and effectively control their dealings with affiliates.[8]

Whatever the merits of competitive bidding from the issuer's viewpoint, the investment bankers generally have taken a dim view of its merits relative to those of negotiated bidding. And it is significant that competitive bidding has been little used by issuers who are not under pressure from regulatory agencies to use it. Indeed, the record in recent years shows that public utilities that have come out, through reorganization, from under SEC jurisdiction as holding company units or subsidiaries and that had had experience with competitive bidding, have generally chosen not to use it when they subsequently have had free legal choice in the matter.

During the period from May 7, 1941, the effective date of Rule 50, to June 30, 1969, a total of 1,053 issues of securities with an aggregate value of $16,908 million has been sold at competitive bidding under the rule.[9]

Investment Bankers' Activities in Nonunderwritten Public Issues

In some public issues the issuing company is willing to stand the risk of an unsuccessful offering but desires to use the services of investment bankers on an *agency* basis. Under such arrangements the investment banking firm, for a fee, typically assists the issuer in surveying and gauging the market for the issue, in the design of the security, in setting fees the issuer will pay for distribution services, and in organizing dealers to distribute

---

[7] Most new bond issues by state and local governmental units are sold to investment bankers through competitive bidding.

[8] Securities and Exchange Commission, *Seventh Annual Report, 1941* (Washington, D.C., 1942), p. 101.

[9] Securities and Exchange Commission, *Thirty-Fifth Annual Report, 1969* (Washington, D.C., 1969), p. 155.

the securities for the account of the issuer. Under the usual agency arrangement the dealers receive a commission based on the amount they are able to sell. The bankers may also assume greater responsibility by agreeing with the issuer that they will use their *best efforts* to sell the entire issue and will receive commissions for the sales made as a result of their efforts.

Sale of New Issues to Existing Security Holders

The existing security holders represent a significant and identifiable potential market for further issues of securities; and a substantial percentage of new issues of common stock, and of bonds and preferred stocks convertible into common stock, is offered first to existing common stockholders. Some corporations have free choice in deciding whether or not to offer new common shares first to present stockholders, but in many companies the present common shareholders possess a legal right to receive *privileged subscriptions* to new issues of common stock. The legal right to privileged subscriptions is termed a *preemptive right*. Where it exists, corporations have no choice but to offer new issues of securities for cash pro rata to the security holders having the preemptive right. We shall discuss this further in Chapter 24.

A corporation that has decided to offer a new issue of stock to its stockholders usually distributes to them purchase warrants known as *rights*. The rights state the privilege of the holder to subscribe at a specified subscription price to a stated number of the new shares. Usually, such stock purchase rights must be exercised within a limited period of time, seldom more than 30 days. Such shares as remain unsubscribed on the date the rights expire may then be offered to the public at the same or at a higher price.

In most instances the rights are freely transferable, so that a stockholder who does not care to exercise his rights can sell them to someone who does want to use them to buy the stock at the subscription price. When the issue of rights relates to an actively traded stock, active trading in the rights usually develops and continues until the date the rights expire. In trading, the price of a right is the price of the subscription privilege derived from ownership of one old share.

Illustrative of the process of selling new shares through a rights offering was the offering by the Chrysler Corporation in April, 1965, of 5,611,360 new common shares to existing shareholders on the basis of one new share for each seven held of record on April 23. At the close of the market on April 23, the Chrysler stock sold at 54⅞. Subscription rights were issued to common stockholders entitling them to buy new shares for $48 plus seven rights per share. The rights were transferable, and active trading in the rights on the New York Stock Exchange continued until the announced terminal date of May 12, 1965.

During the April 23–May 12 subscription period when the rights were effective, anyone wanting to invest in Chrysler could have bought the common shares directly in the market; alternatively, he could have purchased the necessary rights (seven per share) and subscribed to the new stock at $48 a share. During the offering period the new issue would be attractive at $48 and the rights would have much value only if the current market price stayed above $48. A decline below $48 for a protracted time during the offering period would have jeopardized sale of the new issue. The setting of the subscription price, therefore, in such offerings to stockholders involves prediction of likely market prices for the security during the life of the rights. Some companies attempt to set the subscription price close to the market; others price the new issue well below the market in order to provide maximum inducement for use of the rights and successful sale of the issue. In the Chrysler case the market sagged somewhat during the offering to a low of 51⅞ for the stock and ½ for the rights on May 11. As might be expected from the fact that the market price stayed well above the $48 subscription price, the issue was more than 98% taken up, leaving only 97,562 shares unsubscribed.

In offering securities to existing shareholders, the issuing companies frequently elect to dispense with the services of investment bankers and absorb any risks that market declines will cause the offering to fail.[10] For example, A.T.&T. and its subsidiaries commonly set low prices on new issues of common shares offered with rights and do not arrange for underwriting. In other cases, such as the Chrysler offering, the issuer employs investment bankers on a *standby underwriting* basis. In the Chrysler instance, a syndicate of 310 investment bankers headed by the First Boston Corporation agreed to buy all unsubscribed shares at the subscription price. The underwriting fees were reported to be $1.10 a share.

Relatively seldom are nonconvertible bonds and preferred stocks offered through rights to existing shareholders of sizable concerns. As indicated above, this method is quite important in the sale of common shares or securities convertible into common stock.

The Investment Banker as Agent in Private Placements

As private placement grew, investment bankers demonstrated increasing interest in working with corporate clients on an agency basis in placing new issues. Some corporate financial officers prefer to deal directly with institutional buyers without use of investment bankers, particularly in cases where they are going back to institutions with whom they have had long-standing relationships. A great many issuing firms do enlist the assistance of investment bankers in planning the offering, in

---

[10] A study covering 177 offerings of common stock through rights in 1963–65 reported that 91 issues accounting for 30% of the $3 billion total involved investment banker participation on a standby basis (Securities and Exchange Commission, *Cost of Flotation of Registered Equity Issues, 1963–1965* [Washington, D.C., 1970]).

finding likely buyers, and in taking over, or helping in, the negotiation of the final terms of an issue.

Investment bankers argue, with great justification in many cases, that they are in a position to more than earn their fee. First, they point out that they are in virtually continuous contact with the state of the market and with prospective buyers. Thus, they can closely gauge market conditions and the terms the company should get. Moreover, they can get to know well the various preferences, prejudices, and money positions of the different institutions and hence are in a good position to find buyers for the issue. As one young banker put it, "I know key investment officers in seventy-five or a hundred top insurance companies and pension funds. I am learning a great deal about what each of these fellows does and doesn't want and what kind of a reaction I can get from them on a given deal." In contrast to the investment banker's continuing, intimate contact with the market, the corporate financial officer may have a major financing only every few years and have been only in loose contact with the market in the interim between issues.

Second, the investment bankers bring a degree of objectivity to each transaction and can help the issuer define the limits within which bargaining is possible and recognize when he has got the best price and terms he is likely to get. Sometimes the banker can suggest changes in the policies or practices of the issuing firm that make its securities more attractive.

Third, they argue that the usual fees for direct placement work are not large except in unusually difficult or time-consuming issues. Fees of one half of 1% of the amount involved are common and seldom exceed 1% for sizable issues (see also Table 17–5). Hence, it is not hard, they say, for them to get the company a deal enough better than it could have gotten alone to cover the fee.

In any case, work as agents in private placements has become a major activity for many investment bankers.

Direct Sale of Common Stock to Employees, Suppliers, or Other Special Groups

Although the total amount of new issues sold to employees and other special groups is not such as to make it a major means of raising capital, it does deserve brief mention. Many companies make stock available to key employees on an option basis, and some have special plans on a continuing basis to permit employees to buy new shares. Usually, the motives of the issuer in such security issues are not primarily financial— that is, not primarily to raise capital—but rather to provide additional incentive compensation or to encourage or cement employee loyalties to the company. In a few instances, however, amounts of capital raised thereby have been quite consequential—as in the case of A.T.&T., where 71,288,000 shares had been purchased by employees when the Employees' Stock Plan terminated in 1968 after 10 years.

During the 1920's a number of companies, especially public utilities, made strenuous efforts to sell securities to employees and to customers, largely with the aim of increasing the goodwill of these groups toward the companies. Many found, however, that subsequent declines in the market values of the securities sold these groups resulted in ill will rather than good feeling toward the company. Another objection to this practice is that employees are, in effect, being asked to compound their risks when they are asked to invest their savings in the same enterprise on which they are dependent for a livelihood.

Costs of Sale of New Security Issues

So far we have referred to the costs of direct placement and of underwriting in specific cases. Fortunately, considerable data are available which permit a useful general view of the costs to issuers connected with the public sale of new issues.

Underwriting compensation or *underwriting spread* is the term applied to the compensation of investment bankers and security dealers for their participation in public issues. This spread is measured by the difference between the price the bankers pay the issuing firm and the price at which they sell to the public. It is a gross figure and must cover a variety of expenses.

In Table 17–2 we present data regarding underwriting spreads on underwritten issues registered with the SEC in 1951–53–55, 1963, and for equity issues in 1963–65.

One of the striking features to be noted from the data is the relatively low spreads on debt securities sold to the public in comparison with those of common stock. In all size groups, bonds were sold at lower spreads than were common stocks. Preferred stock spreads fell between those of bonds and common, tending to be closer to the costs of bonds than of common stock.

Why are the spreads in sale of common stock so much higher than those for bonds? A basic reason is the difference in the nature of the markets. As indicated in the preceding chapter, a large percentage of the new bond issues is sold to the relatively concentrated, easily reached institutional market. In the case of common stock a much higher percentage must be placed with the diffuse individual buyer market. Hence, typically, it is much easier and cheaper for investment bankers to sell bonds than common stocks.

Generally, more selling effort is required for common stocks than for bonds, where institutional buyers pretty much decide for themselves whether or not to purchase. Except in the case of "hot" issues, the investment bankers have to sell new issues of common stock aggressively. Further, their selling largely takes the form of recommending the issue to their customers as a "good buy." For their efforts and for "putting on

Table 17-2

Weighted Average Underwriting Spreads, as a Percentage of Gross Proceeds, on Underwritten Securities Registered with the Securities and Exchange Commission, 1951–53–55 and 1963–65*

Issues by Type (Numbers of Issues in Parentheses)

Size of Issue (Millions of Dollars)	Debt Issues		Preferred Stock Issues†		Common Stock Issues	
	1951–53–55	1963	1951–53–55	1963	1951–53–55	1963–65
Under 0.5	7.53 (5)	4.73 (2)			20.99 (13)	10.0 (24)
0.5–0.999	5.80 (15)	7.89 (7)			17.12 (43)	9.4 (45)
1–1.999	2.37 (29)	3.87 (9)			11.27 (60)	8.7 (93)
2–4.999	1.01 (44)	1.61 (17)	2.93 (21)		8.47 (62)	7.3 (119)
5–9.999	0.88 (72)	0.89 (24)	2.40 (19)	1.24 (4)	5.31 (24)	6.0 (57)
10–19.999	0.85 (79)	0.80 (41)		1.36 (6)	4.20 (17)	5.0 (30)
20–49.999	0.88 (21)	0.79 (24)			4.98 (11)	4.9 (11)
50 and over					...... (....)	......
Total (dollar amount in millions)	$5,900 (265)	$3,907 (124)	$850 (120)	$133 (15)	$1,000 (230)	......
Weighted average spread	0.92	0.87	2.98	1.52	6.54	......

* Data for 1963 include only new issues of domestic corporate securities not offered via rights. Not included are issues in intrastate sales, Registration A exemptions, exempted industries, and issues registered with the Interstate Commerce Commission. Data for earlier years are from the Securities and Exchange Commission, *Cost of Flotation of Corporate Securities, 1951–1955* (Washington, D.C.: U.S. Government Printing Office, June, 1957).

† The number of issues in other categories was too small for useful comparisons.

SOURCE: Investment Bankers Association of America, *Statistical Bulletin*, June, 1964, and Securities and Exchange Commission, *Cost of Flotation of Registered Equity Issues, 1963–1965* (Washington, D.C., 1970).

Table 17-3

Costs of Sale as Percentage of Proceeds*

(securities offered general public in selected years: 1951, 1953, 1955)

Size of Issues (In Millions of Dollars)	Bonds, Notes, and Debentures			Preferred Stock			Common Stock		
	Compensation	Other Expenses	Total Costs	Compensation	Other Expenses	Total Costs	Compensation	Other Expenses	Total Costs
Under 0.5	...	...	...	...	...	...	20.99%	6.16%	27.15%
0.5–0.9	7.53%	3.96%	11.49%	8.67%	3.96%	12.63%	17.12	4.64	21.76
1.0–1.9	5.80	2.37	8.17	5.98	2.09	8.07	11.27	2.31	13.58
2.0–4.9	2.37	1.41	3.78	3.83	1.05	4.88	8.47	1.50	9.97
5.0–9.9	1.01	0.82	1.83	2.93	0.79	3.72	5.31	0.86	6.17
10.0–19.9	0.88	0.64	1.52	2.40	0.52	2.92	4.20	0.46	4.66
20.0–49.9	0.85	0.48	1.33	2.34	0.35	3.20	4.98	0.38	5.37
50.0 and over	0.88	0.32	1.19	2.12	0.38	2.51	...	...	...

* Data on compensation do not include the ultimate burden involved in the granting to underwriters of additional but contingent compensation in the form of options or warrants to purchase common stock at what may prove to be bargain prices. Options are particularly common in the case of small issues of common stock.

† Only securities registered with the Securities and Exchange Commission are included. Bank stocks and railroad equipment trust certificates are the major types of public sales excluded.

Source: Securities and Exchange Commission, *Cost of Flotation of Corporate Securities, 1951–1955* (Washington, D.C.: U.S. Government Printing Office, June, 1957).

the line" their own reputations as shrewd analysts of value, they expect more compensation.

Reliable evidence not cited here shows that common stock issues undertaken by investment bankers on a best efforts basis carried higher spreads than did fully underwritten issues. This seemingly reverse phenomenon is explained by the fact that the best efforts arrangements commonly were for issues of new or little-known firms, firms with poor records or with other features that would discourage underwriters from a firm commitment. Presumably, the higher fee reflects the greater sales effort anticipated by the bankers under such circumstances.

It will be noted also from Table 17–3 that the percentages of costs of sale of securities are very much higher for small issues than for large. The costs of selling small issues of common stock are particularly high in comparison with those of large issues. There are several reasons for the higher costs of smaller issues. First, many of the costs of investment bankers in investigating an issue, in preparing an issue for sale, and in selling it are relatively fixed. Since the absolute amount of the costs does not increase proportionately as the amount of the issue is increased, the costs in percentage terms of the smaller issues are much greater. In addition, the larger issues tend to be of firms that are well known to investors and hence require less selling effort. Institutional buyers are more likely to represent an important potential market, easily reached, in the case of issues of strong, large companies. The investment quality of the security generally *tends* to be higher with size of the issuer. Small issues of companies with uncertain futures tend to involve considerable price risk to investment banker-buyers. Again, when an investment banker with a fine reputation takes on the job of selling the securities of a small, little-known firm, the banking firm is selling its reputation as much as, or more than, that of the issuing firm—so the banker expects a compensating margin for his contribution and risks.

Issuing concerns also encounter significant other expenses in addition to the compensation of the underwriters. These include legal and accounting fees, printing costs, certain federal and state taxes and fees and, in the case of bond issues, trustees' fees. The SEC has estimated the expenses of public issue, other than compensation, for an "average debt issue" of $15.5 million at about $110,000, broken down as follows:[11]

Legal fees	$16,700
Printing and engraving of the bonds, prospectus, etc.	30,500
Accounting fees	5,300
Engineering fees, etc.	9,100
Federal and state stamp taxes and fees	21,400
Trustees' fees	16,300
SEC fees	1,600
Miscellaneous costs	9,900

[11] Securities and Exchange Commission, *Cost of Flotation of Corporate Securities, 1951–1955* (Washington, D.C., 1957), p. 11.

Table 17–3 shows the total costs of sale of new issues publicly offered in selected years. The "total costs" do not include warrants and other indirect compensation given investment bankers in some common issues. As can be readily noted, "other expenses" are a much higher percentage of small issues than of large and are significant in all size categories.

As will be seen from Table 17–4, the costs of issuing common stock

Table 17–4

Costs of Sale as Percentage of Proceeds
(registered underwritten common stock offerings through
rights to existing stockholders, 1963–65)

Size of Issue (In Millions) of Dollars	Underwriters' Compensation as a Percentage of Proceeds	Other Expenses as a Percentage of Proceeds	Total Costs
Under 0.3	1.7%	5.1%	6.8%
0.3–0.5	8.3	4.0	12.3
0.5–1.0	3.6	4.0	7.6
1.0–2.0	5.4	3.0	8.4
2.0–5.0	2.9	2.1	5.0
5.0–10.0	3.6	1.3	4.9
10.0–20.0	1.2	1.0	2.2
20.0–50.0	2.0	0.8	2.8
50.0–100.0	1.4	0.4	1.8
100.0–500.0	1.9	0.3	2.2

Source: Securities and Exchange Commission, *Cost of Flotation of Registered Equity Issues, 1963–1965* (Washington, D.C., 1970), Table 9, p. 26, and Table B–9, p. 57.

through first offer to existing shareholders typically are smaller than those of selling common stock to the general public. The chief saving is in the compensation paid investment bankers. As we have seen, in some offerings to stockholders, standby underwriting is avoided altogether. Where used, standby underwriting fees and other investment banking charges typically are smaller than in the case of underwritten issues sold to the general public.

The costs of placing securities privately include certain accounting, legal, and other expense in addition to the fee paid investment banks when they are used as agents. Cost data covering a large number of private placements during 1951, 1953, and 1955 are shown in Table 17–5.

We should caution the reader that the costs of sale, as we have discussed them here, include only the costs of getting the new issue out and sold. They do not include the continuing costs associated with the issue once it is outstanding. Thus, the concern that must pay a higher interest rate on bonds sold privately than it would have had to pay on bonds sold to the public may well use up in higher interest costs over a period of years any savings in issue costs achieved through private placement.

Table 17-5

Costs of Sale as Percentage of Proceeds*
(securities placed privately in selected years: 1951, 1953, 1955)

Size of Issue (In Millions of Dollars)	Bonds, Notes, and Debentures†	Preferred and Common Stock†
Under 0.3	1.49%	1.25%
0.3–0.4	1.06	0.13
0.5–0.9	0.83	0.53
1.0–1.9	0.59	0.61
2.0–4.9	0.43	0.50
5.0–9.9	0.34	0.38
10.0–19.9	0.32	0.14
20.0 and over	0.22	. . .

* Median percentages in each size category.
† Data are drawn from 1,846 issues of bonds, notes, and debentures and from 108 issues of preferred and common stock.
SOURCE: Securities and Exchange Commission, *Cost of Flotation of Corporate Securities, 1951–1955* (Washington, D.C., 1957), p. 66.

The Secondary Markets for Corporate Securities

As we indicated earlier, the existence of good markets where investors can buy or sell outstanding securities has an *important, though indirect,* effect on the ability of corporations to raise new capital through the sale of securities. In this section we shall briefly review the secondary markets for corporate securities.

THE ORGANIZED SECURITY EXCHANGES. Much of the secondary trading in corporate securities takes place on organized security exchanges such as the New York Stock Exchange (NYSE). The exchanges essentially provide central marketplaces where individual and firm members execute buying and selling orders for securities admitted for trading. Member brokers act primarily as agents of customers wishing to trade particular securities, executing buying or selling orders in their behalf. In return for executing the orders and related services, the broker charges a commission, the amount of which is determined by reference to a standard schedule of fees established by the exchange.

Trading on the organized exchanges is conducted on what can be termed a "two-way auction" basis. Members with buy orders compete with each other to purchase the shares at the lowest possible prices. At the same time, sellers compete to get the highest possible price. A transaction is made when the highest bidder and the lowest offerer get together. The prices at which sales are made are recorded and immediately publicized. Consequently, the prices for exchange transactions reported in the newspaper represent actual transactions, and the person for whom orders to buy or sell are executed can assure himself that the prices reported to him by his broker represent reasonable prices, given the state of the market at the time of the transaction.

Obviously, the exchange and its member brokers do not create the prices at which securities are traded; instead, the prices arrived at by buyer and seller are the reflection of relative supply and demand for the security at the time it is traded.

Issuing firms must take the initiative in getting their securities listed for trading on the exchanges. To qualify its securities for listing, the corporation must meet certain requirements of the exchange and of the SEC. The NYSE requires that the concern be a going business with substantial assets and earning power. The company's stock should have sufficiently wide distribution and potential activity that a reasonable auction market may be expected to develop.[12] In addition, the company must conform to various SEC or stock exchange rules requiring independent outside audit, publication of financial statements, and the like. The other exchanges also have rules relative to the listing of stocks for trading but, in addition, permit trading in stocks not fully listed under certain conditions, which include the permission of the SEC. There has been a marked tendency over the years toward stricter requirements for listing.

At year-end 1969, 1,250 U.S. and 28 foreign corporations had common shares listed on the NYSE. These 14.6 billion shares had a total market value of $606.8 billion. In addition, 499 preferred stock and 1,574 bond issues were listed.[13]

Virtually all the trading on exchanges was done on 11 stock exchanges registered with the SEC and subject to its regulations. Table 17–6 shows the volume of trading on each of these exchanges in 1969. The dominant position of the NYSE, where 73.9% of the trading in stocks on exchanges took place is apparent. Since the American and National exchanges are also located in the Wall Street area, the importance of New York City as a trading center for stocks also is noteworthy.

What is the extent of market turnover for all stocks listed on the NYSE? The total market value of all equity shares listed on the NYSE

---

[12] With respect to the specific requirements of the NYSE for initial listing of securities, the exchange commented as follows:

Initial Listing: While each case is decided on its own merits, the Exchange generally requires the following as a minimum.

1. Demonstrated earning power under competitive conditions of $2.5 million before Federal income taxes for the most recent year and $2 million pre-tax for each of the preceding two years.
2. Net tangible assets of $14 million, but greater emphasis will be placed on the aggregate market value of the common stock.
3. A total of $14 million in market value of publicly held common stock.
4. A total of 800,000 common shares publicly held out of 1,000,000 shares outstanding.
5. Round-lot shareholders numbering 1,800 out of a total of 2,000 shareholders.

(Quoted from New York Stock Exchange, *1970 Fact Book* [New York, 1970], p. 26.)

[13] New York Stock Exchange, *1970 Fact Book* (New York, 1970), pp. 28, 78, 79.

Table 17–6

Sales of Stocks on Registered Exchanges during 1969
(dollar figures in millions)

	Sales at Market Value	Percentage of Total
New York............................	$129,603	73.9%
American............................	30,074	17.2
Midwest............................	5,988	3.4
Pacific Coast........................	5,422	3.1
Philadelphia-Baltimore-Washington.....	2,528	1.5
Boston.............................	1,191	0.7
Detroit............................	217	0.1
National...........................	180	0.1
Pittsburgh*.........................	47	. . .
Cincinnati..........................	19	. . .
Salt Lake...........................	18	. . .
Spokane............................	11	. . .
	$175,298	100.0%

* The Pittsburgh Stock Exchange was merged into the Philadelphia-Baltimore-Washington Stock Exchange as of the end of 1969.
Sources: Securities and Exchange Commission, *Statistical Bulletin*, March, 1970, p. 11, and *Thirty-Fifth Annual Report, 1969* (Washington, D.C., 1970), p. 69.

was $692.3 billion on December 31, 1968, and $629.5 billion on December 31, 1969.[14] The market value of shares traded in 1969 was $129.6 billion, or 19.6% of the average market value of the listed shares. Total value of all bonds listed for trading on the NYSE at the end of 1969 was $100.6 billion;[15] but trading in bonds on the NYSE was very light—only $3.6 billion in 1969—most of the trading in bonds being done in the over-the-counter market, to be discussed later. In other words, the NYSE is a very important market for stocks and relatively unimportant for bonds.

The Over-the-Counter Markets

Like the organized exchanges, the over-the-counter markets (OTC) perform the basic economic function of promoting liquidity—or more accurately, transferability—for investors in securities. In contrast to the exchanges, the OTC does *not* represent auction markets where buying bids and selling offers of many customers are brought together. Instead, prices are arrived at by negotiation between dealers and between dealers and investors. In this trading, the dealers usually act as principals for their own accounts rather than as broker-agents for customers. Publicity of prices is limited to the furnishing of bid and asked quotations rather than the public reporting of actual sales prices. Many OTC dealers specialize in

[14] *Ibid.*, p. 70.

[15] *Ibid.*, p. 25.

a limited number of selected issues and "make a market" for these securities by carrying an inventory of the securities and standing ready to buy or sell the securities to customers or other dealers.

As suggested above, the size of markups (or markdowns) in principal transactions and commissions in agency transactions is not governed by a fixed schedule in the OTC markets. Principal markups usually are higher than agency commissions.

The OTC markets are very heterogeneous in character and in technical quality. An SEC report commented,

. . . the securities and markets constituting the broad over-the-counter category range from well-known, established companies with a substantial number of dealers making a close and competitive market at one extreme, to obscure, recent issues with a single dealer dominating the market, quoting widely spread bid and asked prices, and combining wholesale and retail trading at the other extreme, and with many variations and gradations between the two extremes.[16]

What securities are traded over-the-counter? The answer is a bit involved. A very important segment of the market is composed of U.S. Treasury and federal agencies issues. Although some U.S. bond issues are listed on the NYSE, an overwhelming percentage of total trading in governments is carried on in the over-the-counter markets, with 20 dealer firms handling the bulk of the volume. Trading in U.S. securities has often been very heavy. Traded over-the-counter exclusively are the bonds of some 150,000 state, municipality, school district, and other local governmental units, known as *municipals*. A number of dealer firms specialize in municipals, a few firms dealing exclusively in them. It is interesting to note that commercial banks have authority to act as dealers in government bonds and in certain classes of municipal bonds, and a few large commercial banks are among the leading dealer firms in this activity. Trading in corporate bonds is also accomplished mainly in the OTC markets, although many are listed on the NYSE.

The common stocks of many commercial banks and insurance companies are traded in the OTC market. The industrial and utility issues traded over-the-counter are typically those of small or medium-sized companies whose securities are narrowly distributed and whose trading is relatively inactive. Since the securities of a large number of the corporations in the country are so characterized, the total number of issues of corporate stocks traded in the OTC market in the course of a year is large. The National Quotation Bureau, a private concern circulating quotations for OTC stocks, reported about 26,000 security issues in its October, 1965, volume, which is a cumulative record covering a period of years. The daily quotation sheets, or *Pink Sheets*, of the Bureau carry more than

---

[16] Securities and Exchange Commission, *Report of Special Study of Securities Markets* (Washington, D.C.: U.S. Government Printing Office, 1963), Part 5, p. 123.

10,000 separate issues of stocks and bonds, many of which are listed on a U.S. or Canadian stock exchange. That many of these are small or closely held is suggested by SEC estimates for 1963 that there were about 4,400 stocks of U.S. corporations, exclusive of investment companies, with 300 or more stockholders each, whose stocks were quoted only over-the-counter. These stocks were estimated to have a total market value in 1963 of about $98.8 billion.[17]

In addition to the trading in corporate stocks not admitted for trading on organized exchanges, there is considerable trading over-the-counter in stocks that are also traded on the exchanges. Many large blocks of listed stocks are traded in negotiated deals off the exchanges, despite progress by the exchanges in developing specific techniques for handling effectively large-block transactions on the exchanges.[18]

In early 1971 an automated Quotation system to carry quotations on OTC stocks to the nearly 4,000 broker-dealers of the National Association of Security Dealers was put into service. The automated system started with 2,150 securities; it has a capacity to handle some 20,000. Improved technology of this sort has been seen as a long-term threat to the physically centralized trading on the exchanges.

A Look at the Firms Doing Business in the Primary and Secondary Security Markets

The piecemeal references to financial houses in this chapter, variously speaking of "investment bankers," "brokers," "broker-dealers," "traders," etc., has probably been confusing to the reader. At this point, clarity may be served by a recapitulation of the major functions served by financial houses and a brief elaboration of their patterns of operation.

We have at various points identified several major functions performed by financial firms:

1. Participation as underwriters of new issues and related activity in selling new issues.
2. Selling of new issues without underwriting participation.
3. Brokerage activity as agents, for a commission, in the buying and selling of outstanding securities.
4. Trading as principals in the buying, holding for trading, and selling of securities in the over-the-counter market.

Not noted earlier are additional roles assumed by many firms. For example, some firms invest in securities for continued holding as investors

---

[17] Securities and Exchange Commission, *Thirtieth Annual Report, 1964* (Washington, D.C., 1965), p. 55.

[18] For example, on February 9, 1971, a single block of 3,248,000 common shares of Allis-Chalmers Manufacturing Company was sold on the NYSE for $58.5 million. This was the Big Board's largest single trade measured in number of shares.

rather than for early resale. Related but distinct are the activities of some firms in trading for their own account for short-run gains. This may take the form, for example, of *arbitraging*—taking advantage of aberrations of the market which present opportunities for profitable two-way simultaneous transactions in equivalents, in which one security is bought and its equivalent sold at about the same time, as in the case of stock purchase rights and the security they can be used to buy.

Some large firms, such as Merrill Lynch, Pierce, Fenner & Smith, Inc., or Loeb, Rhoades & Co., although best known as brokers, actually are engaged in all the major types of activity summarized above. Other firms specialize, a few exclusively, in performing one of the above functions. Thus, Morgan Stanley & Co. specializes in underwriting and, indeed, in the management of underwriting syndicates; while Aubrey G. Lanston & Co., Inc., operates as a dealer in U.S. government and federal agency bonds in the over-the-counter market.

Some 700 securities firms—out of several thousand registered securities dealers—are members of the Investment Bankers Association of America and presumably do a significant amount of investment banking. While they may refer to themselves as investment bankers (this activity appears to carry more prestige than does brokerage or trading), most of these firms derive the bulk of their revenues from the brokerage and other functions described earlier.

Secondary Offerings through Investment Bankers

Throughout this chapter we have tried to emphasize the distinctions between the primary and secondary markets. In so doing, we have implied that investment bankers are involved only in primary distributions. Perhaps without confusing the reader, we now can acknowledge the developing importance of a kind of security sale that technically is a secondary distribution but is commonly handled by investment bankers much as they handle primary issues. We refer to the sale of large blocks of stock by their owners through investment bankers. For example, a syndicate of investment bankers headed by the First Boston Corporation underwrote the sale in June, 1970, of 525,000 shares of Eastern Gas and Fuel Associates. This issue was registered with the SEC and a prospectus was issued, but the shares were sold, not by the company, but by several stockholders.

In many cases in recent years, company and leading shareholders have joined in a public offering of shares. Investment banking sources reported $2,188 million SEC-registered secondary offerings (572 issues) and $335 million nonregistered secondaries (71 issues) in 1969.[19]

---

[19] *Investment Dealers' Digest, Corporate Financing Directory,* March 3, 1970, Sec. II, p. 19.

PART VII

THE LONG-TERM
CAPITAL STRUCTURE

chapter 18

The Basic Security Types

Having now considered the nature of the market for external capital, we are in a position to turn our attention to the basic contractual arrangements by means of which these external funds are obtained from time to time. Because it is one of the most critical aspects of financial policy, the question of the optimum mix of securities and internal funds will occupy our attention over the next four chapters. As we shall see, the choice of dividend policy is not separate from this decision, since it must be considered along with new equity issues in the balance of debt and equity funds. However, we shall approach the problem as the corporate management normally does; namely, on the expectation that predicted needs will at times exceed internal funds flows (under the existing dividend policy), and therefore a new security issue must be brought into the financial plan. This chapter is designed to provide the background of information about these securities which will enable us to carry forward the analysis upon which a decision will be based.

Earlier in this book it was pointed out that corporate securities fall into two main classes: contracts of debt and participations in ownership. Three main types were named: bonds or notes in the first class and preferred stock and common stock in the second. The reader may already be aware that there are in common use a great many different kinds of debt contracts as well as a variety of preferred and common stock forms. To the beginner in finance, it would be a very difficult assignment to get this confusing array of securities clearly fixed in mind.

Fortunately, this is not at all necessary or desirable, for, as will be brought out in this chapter, the first step is to gain a clear understanding of the fundamental characteristics of the three basic security forms—the bond, the preferred stock, and the common stock. It is these characteristics which are of primary importance in decisions relating to long-term finance. Later, when the basic analysis has been well established, we shall introduce the subject of the bargaining process between issuer and investor and the many special kinds of bonds and stock that have been produced in an effort to meet special needs and circumstances. It will be seen that the concepts and analytical approaches developed in this chapter and the two which follow will be directly applicable to the many different forms of long-term debt and equity contracts in our illustrative examples and cases.

THE BOND

The Basic Promises

The responsibility of a company to those who have supplied funds through the purchase of its bonds is essentially the very simple obligation of anyone who has borrowed money, namely, to repay the sum at the promised time and to compensate the lender for the use of his money by the payment of an interest charge while the debt is outstanding. A formal statement of this obligation is found on the face of the *bond certificate* held by each individual or institution participating in the loan. The precise details of the legal contract between the issuing company and the bondholders are to be found in a document known as the *bond indenture*. A copy of this document is held and enforced by a *trustee under the indenture*, who represents the bondholders as a group.

The following is a portion of the wording of a certificate of a recent issue:

Westinghouse Electric Corporation, a Pennsylvania corporation (hereinafter called the Corporation) for value received, hereby promises to pay to [name of owner][1], or registered assigns, [one thousand dollars][2], on September 1, 1995, and to pay interest on said sum at the rate of 8⅝% per annum, semi-annually on September 1 and March 1 in each year until payment of said principal sum shall have been made or duly provided. . . .

. . . .

This Debenture is one of a duly authorized issue of debentures of the Corporation, limited to the aggregate principal amount of $200,000,000 designated as its 8⅝% Debentures, due September 1, 1995. . . .

On August 27, 1970, Westinghouse sold $200 million face value of bonds in an issue known as 8⅝% debentures, due September 1, 1995. It was estimated that $197,525,000 was realized by Westinghouse from

---

[1] It will be seen that this certificate has registered the name of the owner. Although in the past most bonds were issued payable to bearer and many such bonds remain outstanding, the current practice is to register the owner's name and address as is done with stock issues.

[2] Bonds are seldom issued for less than $1,000. The $1,000 face value bond is the unit usually referred to when one speaks of "a bond."

this sale (Prospectus of issue, page 1). In exchange for the use of these funds for a period of 25 years, the company contracted as follows:

The Corporation will duly and punctually pay the principal of and premium, if any, of each of the Debentures, and the interest which shall have accrued thereon, at the dates and place and in the manner described in the Debentures, according to the true intent and meaning thereof. . . .[3]

There are no qualifications to this time series of payments. The certificate does *not* say "if earned" or "if the financial condition of the company permits"—but simply, "hereby promises to pay." To fail to do so at any point constitutes a breach of a legal contract, which act (under almost all bond contracts) entitles the bondholders to declare the entire sum due and payable and to take court action to recover the loan. This process is known as *acceleration of maturity*.[4] It is clear that if the business is to continue without a financial crisis, there is no alternative to a literal adherence to its promises. Herein lies the hazard of debt financing to the issuer and the advantage of bond ownership to the investor. A bond will not be well regarded unless both sides see a considerable margin of safety to assure the performance of the promises in the bond contract even if events turn out badly.

The debtor must meet each promise to pay at the time it becomes due, and the payments must be in cash. The margin of safety, therefore, must be seen in the company's ability to generate the needed funds. As has been made clear often in this book, corporate gross revenues fluctuate from year to year, and funds availability is conditioned by this fact and by the need to fund expansion programs as well. The range of possible fluctuation varies, of course, from one industry and one company to another. Later in this chapter we shall present several ratios that help to determine whether the needed margin exists.

Sinking Funds

Although the whole principal of an issue must be paid at maturity, this Westinghouse issue is an example of the frequent practice to have debt contracts provide for partial repayment of the debt at intervals, usually yearly. Such requirements are generally referred to as *sinking funds*. In the case of the Westinghouse issue, the bond indenture requires that in addition to interest payments the corporation must make sinking fund payments of $10 million to the trustee on September 1 of each year, beginning in 1976. The payments may be made in the face value of bonds that Westinghouse has purchased in the market, or in cash. In the latter case, the trustee will call bonds by lot and pay them. The corporate lia-

---

[3] Indenture, p. 22.

[4] Debtors are not permitted to default willfully in order to pay off burdensome debt.

bility will thus sink so that the final payment in 1995 is $10 million instead of the entire $200 million.

Sinking fund payments do not always provide for complete retirement of the debt by maturity; often, there is a substantial final payment on the maturity date, commonly known as a *balloon maturity*. However, to the extent that the sinking fund provision requires a portion of the debt to be repaid prior to the official maturity date, these funds must be provided by the debtor at the times specified.[5]

It is to be noted that these repayments of the principal are just as mandatory as the payments of interest, and any failure to pay on the dates specified will accelerate the maturity of the whole issue. It is obvious that management must consider the sinking fund, as well as the annual interest payments, when deciding whether or not to issue bonds.

The Flow of Funds Related to the Bond

As has just been said, a bond is an instrument that commits the corporation to certain outflows of funds at specified times. The combined amounts of interest, sinking fund, and final maturity payments are referred to as the *burden, service,* or *cash drain* of the bonded debt. In addition to the obligation to meet the burden annually, there is also the obligation to repay at maturity that portion of the original issue which has not been redeemed by the application of the sinking fund. This would not present a problem in the Westinghouse case. Many bond issues, however, either have no sinking fund provision or provide for only a partial retirement by this means. As a result, the sum outstanding and due for repayment at the maturity date is of an entirely different order of magnitude from that required for annual servicing of the debt. For example, the recently issued $350 million, 32-year, 8.70% debenture of American Telephone and Telegraph Company, due in 2002, has no sinking fund at all.

The fulfillment of this obligation might well appear to present an impossible strain on the earnings and cash position of the company in the year 2002. A management may, however, have no intention of terminating its borrowings at that point. Under a *policy of perpetual debt* it expects to find the solution in a new issue of bonds, the proceeds of which will be used, in whole or in part, to repay the holders of the old bonds. This process, known as *refunding*, will be discussed in more detail in Chapter 25. It can, nevertheless, be noted that one of the major immediate causes of business failures is the inability to pay maturing obligations. Usually, there are other underlying causes, but a large maturity is often the event that makes continuation impossible.

---

[5] In some issues a corporation has the option to use funds to retire some of the debt or to buy new assets of specified types. It is argued that the new investment substitutes for debt reduction by adding to the value and earning power supporting the debt.

The Tax Implications of Debt Service

In observing the role played by debt and other basic security types in the long-term financing of individual companies, it is necessary to develop one or more simple measures of significance so that objective comparisons can be made among companies and over time. Before we turn to a description of these measures, however, it will be helpful to identify one of the important elements of such comparisons, namely, the effect of the associated payments on the company's corporate income tax position.

With regard to debt, it is particularly important to have a clear understanding of the differences between interest and sinking fund payments in this respect. In the United States, income taxes are levied on *net income,* that is, on the sum remaining from gross income after the deduction of all costs. Among the expenditures accepted as "costs" for tax purposes, and thus deductible in computing the income upon which the tax is based, is interest on debt.

In order to bring out the significance of this factor, we have taken figures from the 1969 annual report of Westinghouse Electric Corporation. This company experienced an income tax charge of 49.1% in the year, and that rate is used in our examples to be consistent with the published report.

		(In Millions)
Sales and other income....................		$3,563
Cost of sales...........................	$2,679	
Distribution and other expenses..........	489	
		$3,168
Funds provided by operations.............		$ 395
Depreciation............................		70
Earnings before interest and tax..........		$ 325
Interest paid........................		31*
Taxable earnings........................		$ 294
Income tax (49.1%)...................		144
Net income............................		$ 150

* This includes amounts paid during the year to support short-term loans. The annual report does not permit a separation to be made between the costs of long- and short-term debt, but it is sure that most of the interest expense referred to long-term obligations.

Now let us suppose that instead of financing by using borrowed funds, the company had a larger stock issue outstanding. There would then be no interest expense, and the lower portion of the income statement would have appeared as follows:

Earnings before interest and tax..........	$325
Income tax...........................	160
Net income...........................	$165

The tax liability in this case is $15 million larger because the interest of $31 million could not be used as a deduction before the calculation of the tax, and $31 million multiplied by the tax rate, 49.1%, is $15 million. We call the amount of income tax saved by taking an allowable expense the *tax shield* and contrast it with *tax exposure*, which is the amount of income tax related to an element of income.

It is a common observation that corporate borrowing is cheaper than appears at first glance, because of the tax shield that is developed. Thus, it can be said that the $8\frac{5}{8}\%$ cost of the recent Westinghouse issue should be regarded as $4\frac{5}{16}\%$ (assuming a 50% tax rate). Certainly this observation is true if one remembers the limitation that a taxpayer must have income (and therefore tax exposure) before he can use a tax shield.

It must be emphasized that the privilege of deducting debt costs for purposes of income tax computation does not extend to sinking fund payments. Although such payments involve a cash drain similar to the payment of interest, the sinking fund payment is in fact a repayment of part of the liability, which is the principal of the bonds, and cannot be counted as a cost any more than the original proceeds of the loan received by the company would be counted as income. A sinking fund should therefore be regarded as a contractual commitment defining how earnings, or a part of earnings, shall be used. That is to say, they must be retained in the business to permit the repayment of a portion of the debt. Interest, on the other hand, is an expenditure necessary to have the use of the funds, just as wages are an expenditure necessary to obtain the services of employees.

The latter line of reasoning does not apply to dividends on stock. In contrast to the treatment of bond interest as a cost, dividends are considered as a distribution of the net income of the business to the owners and, as such, cannot be deducted when computing the corporate income tax. This rule applies to dividends on preferred stock as well as to dividends on common stock.

The Burden of Debt: Measures of Significance

The owners of a company which issues bonds or other debt contracts are adding to the danger that the company may find itself *insolvent*, that is, unable to pay its obligations at the times specified. As we have pointed out, the problem is one of matching inflows and outflows. Analysts have developed a number of ratios to give indications of the risk that exists in a particular case, and we shall introduce them here. First, however, the relevant flows must be determined.

The reader has already been told the elements of the cash flow that represent the burden of the debt. These are:

1. The interest.
2. The sinking fund.
3. The final payment at maturity.
4. The tax related to the above items.

A table describing the burden of debt for a certain time period can be prepared in the form shown in Table 18–1. We have chosen information for the year 1969 from the annual report of the Westinghouse Electric Corporation, and entered the numbers that are taken directly from that report in boldface type.[6] The reader should note carefully that some of the initial information appears in the column headed "Amount before Tax" and some in the column for "Amount after Tax." Great care must be taken to assign the initial information to its proper class, for any combination of before-tax with after-tax figures is as meaningless as the familiar example of adding oranges and apples.

Table 18–1

The Burden of Debt
(dollar figures in millions)

	100.0% Amount before Tax	49.1% Tax Exposure (e) or Tax Shield (s)	50.9% Amount after Tax
Funds requirement			
A.　Interest...................	$ 30.6	$ 15.0 s	$ 15.6
B.　Sinking fund...............	43.8	21.5 e	22.3
C.　　　Total contractual burden.....	$ 74.4		$ 37.9
Funds availability			
D.　Funds provided by operations.....	$394.6	$193.7 e	$200.9
E.　Depreciation...............	69.6	34.2 s	35.4
F.　Earnings before interest.........	$325.0	$159.5 e	$165.5

The next step is to complete the table. The formula for converting before-tax to after-tax amounts, or vice versa, where r is the applicable tax rate, as a decimal, is (Before $) $(1 - r)$ = (After $). The percentage figures at the top of the table show the mathematical relationship in numerical form.

The table has two sections. In the upper section are collected the numbers for the elements of the debt burden. In this section the first line (A) tells us that the expenditure of $30.6 million for interest can be regarded as reduced to $15.6 million because of the tax shield that interest, as a recognized expense, develops. The second line (B) tells us that the payment of $22.3 million requires the company to earn $43.8 million in order to cover the tax exposure that intervenes before a payment can be made out of after-tax earnings. The total of the two items (C) pictures for the year 1969 the financial burden obligatory under debt contracts. We refer to this as the *contractual burden*.

In the lower section of Table 18–1 are collected numbers that picture

---

[6] The amount for sinking fund was approximated, and the total of interest was assumed to apply to long-term debt.

inflows in various ways. As before, the information from the Westinghouse annual report is printed in boldface type. The first line (D) titled "Funds provided by operations" is, in the first column, the net of all operating income and expenses that provided or required funds during the year. The tax exposure is the tax liability that the company would have paid if depreciation were not deductible as expense, and the final figure is the after-tax position. The line for depreciation (E) shows, in the first column, the amount of the expense that the company reported. This expense provided a tax shield of $34.2 million leaving $35.4 million of depreciation expense not offset by any tax shield. Thus, the third line of this section (F) presents in the first column the familiar E.B.I.T. number, next the net tax exposure before considering financial costs, and

Table 18–2

Ratios of Burden Coverage
(dollar figures in millions)

		Before-Tax Basis	After-Tax Basis
Times interest earned	$\dfrac{F}{A}$	$\dfrac{325.0}{30.6} = 10.6$	$\dfrac{165.5}{15.6} = 10.6$
Times burden earned	$\dfrac{F}{C}$	$\dfrac{325.0}{74.4} = 4.4$	$\dfrac{165.5}{37.9} = 4.4$
Times burden covered by operating funds	$\dfrac{D}{C}$	$\dfrac{394.6}{74.4} = 5.3$	$\dfrac{200.9}{37.9} = 5.3$

NOTE: Letters "F," "A," etc., refer to items in Table 18–1.

finally the available earnings after taxes but before financial costs. We are now prepared to make some comparisons.

As we have pointed out, the amount of burden cannot be judged to be large or small except as it is compared with the inflows available to meet it. Ratios are a useful way to make such comparisons. We now have figures for inflow and ouflow that are consistently measured, and we can use either the before-tax or the after-tax column to calculate the ratios that appear in Table 18–2.

The ratio of *times interest earned* is one that has been most frequently used by analysts in the measurement of the safety of bond issues. It is presented by every standard financial manual; and it is embedded in the laws of some states which regulate the investment practices of certain types of investors, such as trustees, insurance companies, and savings banks. Despite this use, it is now becoming clear that more comprehensive analytical tests are required to avoid comparing only income and cost figures. The question of solvency requires looking into funds flows of all kinds.

The first addition is the ratio that compares the total burden to the earnings. By using this ratio, we examine the power of the company to meet both interest and debt retirement out of earnings without resorting to outside sources of funds.

Going further, we may compare the burden to the funds provided by operations. No firm can, over the long run, avoid the need to make expenditures to replace depreciating equipment, but it may well postpone them, so the third ratio shown in the table indicates the margin by which the company's operating funds flows exceed the contractual burden.

Each of the ratios, in the case of Westinghouse in 1969, is well over the minimum needed to preserve solvency. Such results support the inference that a depression year when operating funds are low will not bring a challenge to the company's ability to pay.

We shall have more to say later on about these ratios and the others we shall encounter in this chapter. The reader should be sure that he understands what they are, how they are computed, and what lies behind them. May we emphasize that no method which gives unequal ratios from before-tax and after-tax figures is properly designed. It is also to be remembered that before-tax and after-tax figures cannot be combined. A very common error, for example, is to add interest and sinking fund without taking account of the tax-related items. Thus, it would be a mistake to calculate the burden of the Westinghouse debt as being the sum of the interest charges of $30.6 million and sinking fund payments of $22.3 million, since one is in before-tax dollars and the other is in after-tax dollars.

There are reasons which lead us to recommend that the reader make it a practice, where possible, to use the before-tax basis for these ratio comparisons: (1) In comparisons of different companies, there can be significant differences in the tax levy which are not apparent in the information available. (2) For the same company over a period of time, there will surely have been significant changes in the basis and rate of tax from one year to another, which will affect the results and again may not be apparent in the data used. (3) Finally, if the company should sustain a loss in any year, the full interest payment must still be met. (Of course, to the extent that the bond interest increases the deficit for the year, a tax credit may be taken against earnings of other years.) For these reasons, our comparisons will be made primarily in terms of burden before taxes, earnings before interest and taxes, and depreciation charged.

Debt Ratios from the Balance Sheet

The ratios just described compare the sizes of outflows and inflows of funds. It is also possible to indicate the burden of indebtedness by reviewing ratios taken from the balance sheet. The comparison to be made is between the amount of funds raised by the use of debt contracts and the amount of the stockholders' investment in the corporation.

For a numerical example we take the balance sheet of the Westinghouse Electric Corporation at the end of 1969 and select the numbers shown in Table 18–3. The relationship of debt to equity can then be shown either by calculating *capitalization ratios,* usually expressed in percentage terms, or by comparing the size of the equity to the size of the debt.

The *debt ratio* (debt as a percentage of total capitalization) of Westinghouse is 22%. The smallness of this figure suggests that the burdens of the debt will be small relative to operating inflows. But, since interest rates are sometimes high or low (Westinghouse borrowed at $8\frac{5}{8}\%$ in 1970 but at $2\frac{5}{8}\%$ not many years before) and sinking funds are fast or

Table 18–3

Debt and Equity Ratios from the Balance Sheet
At December 31, 1969

	Amount in Billions of Dollars		Capitalization Ratio	Ratio of Equity to Debt
Long-term debt..........		$ 393.3	22%	
Stockholders' Equity				3.5
Preferred stock...........	30.5			
Common stock*...........	1,358.8	1,389.3	78%	
Total		$1,782.6	100%	

* Surplus plus retained earnings.

slow in debt retirement, any ratios derived from the balance sheet are far less helpful than those in Table 18–2, which compare funds flows.

THE COMMON STOCK

In contrast to the bondholders, the common shareholder has no promise from the company to which he may turn for an assurance of income or the return of his investment. The absence of any specific financial commitment on the part of the corporation to the shareholder is reflected in the wording of the stock certificate, an example of which appears below:

> This is to certify that _____ is the owner of _____ fully paid and nonassessable shares of the par value of $20 each of the common stock of the A.B.C. Company, Inc. . . . A statement of the designations, preferences, privileges and voting powers, and the restrictions and qualifications thereof, of the Preferred Stock . . . and of the Common Stock . . . is printed on the reverse side hereof, and this certificate . . . shall be subject to all the provisions of the Certificate of Incorporation . . . to all of which the holder by acceptance hereof assents.
> Dated _____ Signed _____

The basic purpose of the certificate is simply to indicate that the person named is a shareholder of the company and to indicate the extent of his participation as measured by the number of shares owned. No payment in the form of dividends is promised or implied. No repayment of the original principal is anticipated, since the money supplied by the common shareholder is considered to be an investment for the life of the business. The principal assurance given the holders of the common stock is the basic right of ownership—the right to decide matters of corporate policy either directly, by vote at regular or special meetings of the shareholders, or by delegating their powers of control to a board of directors of their own choosing.

Thus, the corporation has no specific financial commitments to its shareholders of a nature that would make the distribution of cash at any point of time mandatory. Of course, profits which are not paid out in cash dividends remain in the business; and if wisely used, they will add to the value of the common shareholders' residual claim on the assets and earning power of the business. Even so, it must be recognized that the realizable value to the shareholder of reinvested earnings depends on the extent to which they are reflected in a higher market price for the stock.

It is this absence of specific financial obligations that makes common stock so attractive and necessary as a basis of long-term finance in the business corporation, characterized as it is by fluctuating earnings in greater or lesser degree. Dividend payments can be adjusted year by year to the financial circumstances of the moment. This is not to imply that the management is free from pressures of a nonlegal sort for payment of dividends. It is apparent that a board of directors elected by the common shareholders will probably be sensitive to the wishes of those shareholders. Even when the directors are representative of the shareholders in name only, significant pressures are likely to exist. The most important of these relates to future financing. Companies which face a long-range program of growth, or even just the possibility of such growth, must keep in mind the fact that at some time in the future they may have to supplement existing equity capital with a new issue of stock. In order that the new stock be readily marketable, the outstanding stock must have an attractive record of stability and strength. A pattern of stability and growth in dividend payments is often the foundation for stability and growth in the market price of the stock. Obviously, then, the necessity for a sale of stock at a favorable price in the future can be a very practical and powerful incentive to pay dividends in the present.

However, the essential feature of stock remains, namely, that management can, if necessary, disregard these urgings and reduce or suspend dividend payments without breaking a legal contract or interfering in any way with the continuity of the business. This gives management a flexibility which it does not possess with fixed charge debt obligations.

In view of the absence of assured income in the case of common stock, it may seem surprising that many investors prefer to invest in stocks rather than in bonds. The reason is, of course, that the residual claim of the shareholders has its advantages as well as its disadvantages. The holder of a bond of Westinghouse, cited earlier, will never under any financial circumstances receive for each bond more than $86.25 per annum interest income or more than $1,000 at maturity. There is a limit to his gains which goes along with protection against loss. The shareholder, on the other hand, has no limit placed on possible participation in earnings. If the business prospers, it is quite likely that he will receive dividends which pay him a rate of return substantially above that paid to the bondholder; and if he liquidates his investment, he may also realize a capital gain over and above his original investment. Counterbalancing the uncertainty associated with a return which is dependent on earnings and the policy decisions of the directors is the prospect of greater rewards than can be obtained when the return is guaranteed.

The advantages of owning common stock seem all the greater in periods of general inflation, when the fixed income of bondholders becomes less and less attractive from the point of view of purchasing power. Many companies enjoy not only increasing profits in such periods but also increasing monetary values of their fixed assets, so that their common stocks are considered especially attractive investments. It is anticipated that the price will rise and the holder may obtain profits through sale.

The Flow of Funds Related to Common Stock and Its Measurement

In the case of bonds, we identified certain outflows of funds as committed because the corporation had entered into the bond contract. Al-

	(*In Millions*)
Earnings before interest and tax.............	$325
Interest paid...........................	31
Taxable earnings.........................	$294
Income tax (49.1%)......................	144
Net income..............................	$150
Preferred dividend requirement............	1
Income available for common stock..........	$149
Net earnings per common share.............	$ 3.76
Dividend per common share................	$ 1.80
(39,628 thousand shares)	

though no such enforceable commitments are made to the common stockholder, two kinds of funds flows must be identified with this type of security. The first of these is an actual outflow of funds to the shareholder, in the form of such cash dividends as may be paid. The amount of the dividend is, therefore, an important number. It is usually computed and expressed as the *dividend per share*. This flow is, as we have said, on an after-tax basis because the law does not regard it as a cost.

The special nature of the common stock interest brings another flow into consideration. Since the common shareholder has the residual equity, he is entitled to consider as his all the earnings after prior charges, whether or not they are to be distributed as dividends. Funds earned but not paid out serve to add to the value of the stockholder's interest. A measure of equal importance to *dividend per share* is, therefore, *earnings per share*.

These two measures can be illustrated by referring to the Westinghouse financial statements on page 349, and adding other data from the annual report.

Note that the figures of $3.76 and $1.80 per share are on an after-tax basis but that they may also be considered on a before-tax basis. Thus, in this case, it takes $292 million of before-tax earnings to produce the $149 million of earnings after taxes to which the common shareholders have claim. On a similar basis, it takes $140 million of before-tax earnings to enable the company to pay $1.80 per share in dividends.

A measure of the same nature as the ratio of earnings coverage for bonds is computed for common stock and known as *dividend cover*, in this case:

$$\text{Earnings per Share} \div \text{Dividend per Share} = \text{Cover}$$
$$3.76 \div 1.80 = 2.1 \text{ times}$$

It is more common to see and hear about this ratio in its inverse form, when it is known as the *payout ratio*, and expressed as a percentage.

$$1.80 \div 3.76 = 48\%$$

Either of these ratios gives the shareholder some idea of the degree of risk that his dividend may be reduced if earnings fall.

It is a common practice of investors to relate earnings per share and dividends per share to the market price of the stock. Thus, *dividend yield* is the dividend expressed as a percentage of the market price at whatever point of time is significant in the analysis. The average market price for Westinghouse common stock during 1970 was $61.50. Thus, the yield based on this price would be:

$$\text{Dividend per Share} \div \text{Price per Share} = \text{Dividend Yield}$$
$$1.80 \div 61.50 = 2.9\%$$

The relationship between earnings per share and market price is most commonly expressed in terms of the *price-earnings ratio*, which in the Westinghouse example would be:

$$\text{Price per Share} \div \text{Earnings per Share} = \text{Times}$$
$$61.50 \div 3.76 = 16 \text{ times}$$

Thus the stock is said to be selling at 16 times earnings. This also can be expressed in inverse form as an *earnings yield* similar to the dividend yield, as follows:

$$\text{Earnings per Share} \div \text{Price per Share} = \text{Earnings Yield}$$
$$3.76 \div 61.50 = 6.1\%$$

The ratio of dividend cover may also be reached as follows:

$$\text{Earnings Yield} \div \text{Dividend Yield} = \text{Cover}$$
$$6.1 \div 2.9 = 2.1 \text{ times}$$

Summary: Common Stock

In summary of this section on common stock, we can say that the holder of this stock has no enforceable promises relating to monetary payments. He shares in the residual values of the company, and benefits or loses as the company prospers or declines. The value of the stock depends not on promises to pay but on the ability of the company to grow in value, and thus reinvested earnings will influence the price of the stock. Dividends depend upon management decisions, but there are several reasons why management will consider paying dividends when earnings exist. Useful measures of the position of a common stock include earnings per share, dividends per share, the payout ratio, and ratios of earnings or dividends to price.

THE PREFERRED STOCK

The preferred stock represents a type of corporate financing which is somewhat paradoxical as between its nominal characteristics and its practical application. On the surface, it appears to provide the corporation with a security coupling the limited obligation of the bond with the flexibility of the common stock—a combination that would be unusually attractive to the issuer. Unfortunately, general experience does not bear out such expectations.

From the purely legal point of view the preferred stock is a type of ownership and thus takes a classification similar to that of the common stock. Accounting practice recognizes this by placing preferred stock along with common stock in the net worth section of the balance sheet, and tax laws interpret preferred dividends as a distribution of net profits to the owners rather than a cost of the business, as in the case of bond interest.

Most analysts include the amount of the preferred stock as equity in computing capitalization ratios, as shown on page 354. The preferred stock certificate is much the same as that for the common stock, stating that the named individual is the owner of a number of shares of preferred stock with such "designations, preferences, privileges, and voting powers, and the restrictions and qualifications thereof," as are shown on the face and reverse side of the certificate. Unlike the bond, the preferred stock does not contain any promise of repayment of the original investment; and as far as the shareholders are concerned, this must be considered as a permanent investment for the life of the company. Further, there is no legal obligation to pay a fixed rate of return on the investment.

The special character of the preferred stock lies in its relationship to the common stock. When a preferred stock is used as a part of the corporate capital structure, the rights and responsibilities of the owners as the residual claimants to the asset values and earning power of the business no longer apply equally to all shareholders. Two types of owners emerge, representing a voluntary subdivision of the overall ownership privileges. Specifically, the common shareholders agree that the preferred shareholder shall have "preference" or first claim in the event that the directors are able and willing to pay a dividend. In the case of what is termed a nonparticipating or *straight preferred stock,* which is the most frequent type, the extent of this priority is a fixed percentage of the par value of the stock or a fixed number of dollars per share in the case of stock without a nominal or par value.

For example, the Westinghouse Electric Corporation had outstanding in 1969 a cumulative 3.80% preferred stock, par value $100. According to the terms of the contract of issue, each preferred share was entitled to $3.80 per share before the common shareholders would be allowed to receive a cash dividend. The issue was *cumulative,* which is true of most preferred issues, and which means that before any common dividends can be paid, not only must the current preferred dividend have been paid but also the preferred dividends of previous years that have remained unpaid.

A measure of interest to preferred stock is the yield, obtained by the following calculation (using the 1970 average price of the preferred stock):

$$\text{Dividend per Share} \div \text{Price per Share} = \text{Yield}$$
$$3.80 \div 55 = 6.9\%$$

The reader should note that the liquidation value of $100 given each preferred share has no noticeable influence on the price, which reflects the current level of interest rates.

It must be emphasized that the prior claim of the preferred stock does not guarantee a fixed and regular rate of return similar to that on a bond —it merely establishes an order of priority in which the board of directors will pay dividends *if* it decides to do so. At the same time, it establishes a definite upper limit to the preferred shareholders' claim on earnings. Whatever the profitability of Westinghouse, the preferred shareholders of this issue will never receive more than the $3.80 per share per annum dividend.

In most cases the prior position of preferred stock also extends to the disposition of assets in the event of liquidation of the business. Again, the priority is only with reference to the common stock and does not affect the senior position of creditors in any way. It has meaning and value only if asset values remain after creditors have been fully satisfied—a condition which is by no means certain in the event of liquidation following bankruptcy. In the preferred issue cited above, the shareholders are entitled to receive $100 per share plus accrued dividends, in the event of involuntary liquidation, before the common shareholders participate in the remaining assets.

So far, we have considered the preferred stock in terms of the formal rights and responsibilities inherent in this type of security. The impression created is that of a limited commitment on dividends coupled with considerable freedom in the timing of such payments. In reality, experience with preferred stocks indicates that the flexibility in dividend payments is more apparent than real. The management of a business which is experiencing normal profitability and growth desires to pay a regular dividend on both common and preferred stock because of a sense of responsibility to the corporate owners and/or because of the necessity of having to solicit further equity capital in the future. The pressure for a regular common dividend in many cases assures the holder of a preferred stock that his regular dividend will not be interrupted, even in years when profits are insufficient to give common shareholders a comparable return, for it is very damaging to the reputation of a common stock (and therefore its price) if preferred dividend arrearages stand before it. The fact that most preferred issues are substantially smaller in total amount than the related common issue means that the cash drain of a preferred dividend is often less significant than the preservation of the status of the common stock.

The result is that management comes to view the preferred issue much as it would a bond, establishing the policy that the full preferred dividend must be paid as a matter of course. The option of passing the dividend still exists, but it is seen as a step to be taken only in case of unusual financial difficulty.[7] Under such a circumstance, the obvious question presents itself: Why, then, use preferred stock as a means of raising permanent capital? Why not use bonds instead? The primary advantage of the preferred stock becomes identical with that of a bond, namely, the opportunity to raise funds at a fixed return which is less than that realized when the funds are invested. On the other hand, the dividend rate on preferred stock is typically above the interest rate on a comparable bond and has the additional disadvantage of not developing a tax shield. Of course, the bond is more likely to have a sinking fund, so that the *burden* of bond and preferred stock may not be greatly different.

The differential in cost between a preferred stock and an alternative debt issue may be considered a premium paid for the option of postponing the fixed payments. If management is reluctant to exercise this option, it is likely that the premium will be considered excessive. However, the closer a company gets to its recognized debt limits, the more

---

[7] The experience of the 1930's is evidence of the fact that such periods do occur; and it must be recognized that in such conditions of severe economic recession, large numbers of preferred issues will stand in arrears.

management is likely to appreciate the option to defer the dividend on a preferred stock issue and to be willing to pay a premium for this potential defense against a tight cash position.

The Flow of Funds Related to Preferred Stock

The fact that most managements have established the policy to pay the full preferred dividend as a matter of course leads us to recommend that, for internal planning purposes, the preferred dividend requirement (and preferred sinking funds, if any) be listed as fixed charges. The recommended management approach is seen in the following calculations. In the Westinghouse example the total annual preferred dividend payment in 1969 was $1,190,525. Like common dividends, preferred dividends are treated for tax purposes as a distribution of profits and not as a cost. Consequently, the sum of $1,190,525 which is a payment after taxes, must also be considered in terms of the before-tax income necessary to cover this payment. Using the 49.1% federal corporate income tax experience of Westinghouse, the figure would work out approximately as follows:

Preferred dividends..........................	$1,190,525
Tax exposure................................	1,148,424
Required before-tax income.................	$2,338,949

As a measure of the degree of assurance that the investor may place in the continuity of this dividend, we may use the same criterion suggested for bonds, namely, coverage. In discussing the ratios of times interest earned and times burden covered in connection with bonds, it was suggested that whatever particular issue happens to be under consideration, the calculation should include in the denominator the interest and sinking fund charges on all fixed debt.

Likewise, in considering preferred stock, our calculations should include the total burden of all securities that are equal or senior to the issue in question, because all must be paid if this class is to be. Thus, the ratio of times burden covered for preferred stock should have in the denominator the total of the following, where they apply:

1. Total bond interest.
2. Total sinking funds on bonds plus tax related.
3. Total preferred dividends plus tax related.
4. Total sinking funds on preferred stock (if any) plus tax related.

The Westinghouse Electric Corporation had a number of debt contracts in force in 1969, and one issue of preferred stock was outstanding. The pertinent information to allow a test of the company's ability to maintain dividend payments can be tabulated as in Table 18–4. Some of the data found there is a repetition of Table 18–1. The ratios in Table 18–5 are the same as shown in Table 18–2 except that the amounts of contractual

Table 18–4

The Burden of Debt and Preferred Stock
(dollar figures in millions)

		100.0% Amount before Tax	49.1% Tax Exposure (e) or Tax Shield (s)	50.9% Amount after Tax
Funds requirement				
A.	Interest......................	$ 30.6	$ 15.0 s	$ 15.6
B.	Sinking fund..................	43.8	21.5 e	**22.3**
C.	Total contractual burden...	74.4	36.5	$ 37.9
G.	Preferred dividends.............	2.3	1.1 e	**1.2**
H.	Total prior payments......	$ 76.7	$ 37.6	$ 39.1
J.	Common dividends.............	137.1	67.3 e	**69.8**
K.	Total funds requirement....	$213.8	$104.8	$108.9
Funds availability				
D.	Funds provided by operations.....	**$394.6**	$193.7 e	$200.9
E.	Depreciation...................	**69.6**	34.2 s	35.4
F.	Earnings before interest.........	$325.0	$159.5 e	**$165.5**

Table 18–5

Ratios of Burden Coverage—Debt and Preferred Stock
(dollar figures in millions)

		Before-Tax Basis	After-Tax Basis
Times interest and preferred dividend earned	$\dfrac{F}{A + G}$	$\dfrac{325.0}{32.9} = 9.9$	$\dfrac{165.5}{16.8} = 9.9$
Times debt and preferred burden earned	$\dfrac{F}{H}$	$\dfrac{325.0}{76.7} = 4.2$	$\dfrac{165.5}{39.1} = 4.2$
Times debt and preferred burden covered by operating funds	$\dfrac{D}{H}$	$\dfrac{394.6}{76.7} = 5.1$	$\dfrac{200.9}{39.1} = 5.1$
Times interest and all dividends earned	$\dfrac{F}{A + G + J}$	$\dfrac{325.0}{172.4} = 1.9$	$\dfrac{165.5}{87.8} = 1.9$
Times all burden earned	$\dfrac{F}{K}$	$\dfrac{325.0}{213.8} = 1.5$	$\dfrac{165.5}{108.9} = 1.5$
Times all burden covered by operating funds	$\dfrac{D}{K}$	$\dfrac{394.6}{213.8} = 1.8$	$\dfrac{200.9}{108.9} = 1.8$

burden that were used before have been replaced. First there are ratios to test the margins that cover the total burden prior to common dividends; then there are ratios to show the cover of all financial charges.

Summary: The Preferred Stock

To summarize what has been said about preferred stock, it is a security that offers no contractual guaranty of dividends, although it does define the amounts that may be received and usually provides for the accumulation of dividends that are not paid. In fact, most preferred stocks are issued with the intent of management to pay the dividends on time; and therefore, for analytical purposes, they should be treated as a kind of debt, although they are not legally so considered. Preferred dividends cannot be considered as costs, and the income tax related to the dividend is part of the burden of the issue. If there is a sinking fund, it is part of the burden, too.

GENERAL SUMMARY

As mentioned at the beginning of this chapter, we have confined our attention to the basic security types—bonds, straight preferred stock, and common stock. This has enabled us to examine the fundamental characteristics of these securities free of the distractions which would result if the discussion were extended to include the many modified forms of bonds and stocks. Later, in Chapters 23 and 24, it will be seen that these modified security forms evolve in the bargaining process between issuer and investor as variations in, or modifications of, the normal distribution of risk, income, and/or control found in the basic types.

We have in this chapter illustrated certain quantitative measures which we have found most useful in appraising the financial significance and effects of these basic security types. In particular, we have emphasized the ratios of times interest earned and times burden covered for senior securities and the measures of earnings per share, payout, price-earnings ratio, and dividend and earnings yields for common stock. Throughout, a careful distinction has been drawn between before-tax and after-tax comparisons. Whether or not the reader accepts our preference for before-tax comparisons, it is essential that the calculations be consistently on one basis or the other and that the analyst be ready to use either. Finally, the examples in this chapter have been confined to data available to both the external and the internal analyst. In the chapters which follow, we will develop ideas for a more detailed analysis by the internal financial staff, which is made possible by access to privileged financial information.

chapter 19

The Use of Securities to Allocate Income, Risk, and Control

In Chapter 18 we described important characteristics of the basic security types taken separately. We shall now begin to consider how these securities relate to one another when they are used in combination in the financing of a single corporation. It is in the power of management to decide from time to time what type or types of security shall be used. It might be desirable to use debt, preferred stock, new common stock, or retained earnings—most often, in fact, some combination of these. It is therefore one of the tasks of financial management to decide on the "mix" of securities most suitable to the policies of the company.

As we begin to explore the determinants of the management decision about the most desirable capital structure, we shall find that the types of securities available permit the allocation of certain attributes of business activity to security holders in varying proportions. There are three categories to consider when we talk of the allocation of the attributes of the business. The first we shall discuss is *income*. Seen from the investor's point of view, this category has to do with the size of his income. To the issuing corporation, the same category appears as a cost.

The second category of business attributes is that of *risk*. Seen from the investor's point of view, the risk is that of loss of expected income or market value of the security he holds. Seen from the point of view of the issuing corporation, the risk is that it may not be able to meet the obligations it has undertaken.

The third category of attributes that may be assigned in different ways is that of *control*. Control, in the first instance, has to do with the power to elect the firm's directors, but it is also important to remember that many security contracts contain provisions that guide or limit what management may do, and thus act to control its decisions, also.

In this chapter we shall see how these elements have been subdivided in a specific corporation, as an illustration. It is the Westinghouse Electric Corporation, with which we already have some familiarity. It serves the purpose well, for it has a relatively uncomplicated capital structure made up of long-term debt, preferred stock, and common stock.

A Company's Capitalization

The balance sheet of this company appears with some condensation in Table 19–1. At the moment our interest lies in the outstanding obliga-

Table 19–1

WESTINGHOUSE ELECTRIC CORPORATION
Condensed Consolidated Balance Sheet as of December 31, 1969
(in millions)

ASSETS

Current assets.............................	$1,404.5	
Investments in securities of other companies...	179.7	
Plant and equipment.......................	751.3	
Other assets..............................	142.0	
Total assets........................		$2,477.6

EQUITIES

Current liabilities.........................	$ 695.0	
Long-term debt...........................	393.3	
Total liabilities.....................		$1,088.3
Preferred stock...........................	$ 30.5	
Common stock actually outstanding }	501.1	
Capital surplus }		
Retained earnings.........................	857.7	
Total stockholders' equity............		$1,389.3
Total equities.....................		$2,477.6

tions that the company has incurred in order to have the assets with which it does business. More particularly, we are interested in the pattern of the long-term obligations, and so we shall mention the current liabilities only enough to recognize their existence. We have given them adequate attention elsewhere in this book.

The term *capitalization*, or *invested capital*, is used to refer to the total of the long-term liabilities together with all the kinds of stockholders' equity. Taking this total as 100% we can calculate the capitalization ratios of Westinghouse as follows:

Long-term debt......................	$ 393.3	22%
Preferred stock.....................	30.5	2
Common stock accounts..............	1,358.8	76
Total......................	$1,782.6	100%

The obligations totaling $393.3 million are found in several instruments, representing the results of bargains made at various times between Westinghouse and the lenders. They reflect the market conditions at the time the debt was issued as well as the relative powers of the parties to the bargain.

The funds provided by direct shareholder investment came in part from a preferred stock issue as well as from the sale of common stock. The preferred shareholders of Westinghouse have made their funds available to the management on the promise of limited dividends of $3.80 on a share with a par value of $100.

The debt ratio of Westinghouse, as it is commonly expressed, is 22%. For internal planning purposes we would regard as more useful the ratio of 24%, including the preferred stock. But perhaps the most useful way of making a brief statement about Westinghouse's sources of long-term financing is to say that the common equity is 76% of the capitalization. This statement avoids the argument of whether preferred stock is to be regarded as debt or equity. If we could influence the language of the trade, this is one of the places we would do so.

The rest of the equity capital came through the sale of common stock or the reinvestment of earnings. The stock, 39,485,635 shares actually outstanding, on December 31, 1969, has altered over time in both form and amount as new shares have been issued and changes in the capital structure have occurred. The shareholders, both preferred and common, invested without promised maturity and hence for an unlimited period so far as they were concerned. These issues make up an investment base which can be as permanent as the business itself. The amounts received from stock sale total $501.1 million.

The remaining item is the total of *retained earnings*. The figure of $857.7 million is the sum total of those profits which have been realized over the years since incorporation (net of any losses) and which have been reinvested in the business rather than distributed in the form of dividends. These earnings stand to the credit of the common shareholders, and the common shareholders' equity therefore includes them. Unlike the investment in stock, the earned surplus is an amount that the board of directors is legally entitled to distribute completely to the shareholders at any time. In practice, however, a complete distribution is unlikely to take place, since most, if not all, of the funds provided by profits have long since become a permanent part of the asset structure upon which the present earning capacity is based. The reader is reminded that surplus represents a surplus of historical values, not of liquid assets, as some ill-informed people believe.

With these details of capitalization before us, we now turn to the ways in which the characteristics of the company have been allocated to the three types of securities that have been used.

The Allocation of Income

The allocation of the income generated by a firm's activities is the first of the three categories we shall consider. We shall proceed from an example to a more general discussion and then to the presentation of techniques for studying the effect of alternative financial plans upon the income that may come through to the common stockholders.

The Westinghouse Electric Corporation reported for 1969 the amount of $325.0 million as earnings before interest and taxes. This sum can be related to the invested capital of the company, $1,782.6 million as shown on the December 31 balance sheet, to show a return of 18.2%. At the same time as the corporation had this rate of return, it paid $30.6 million in interest to satisfy long-term debt of $393.3 million, an average rate of 7.8%.[1] The preferred stock was issued in a period when rates were low, and carried a dividend of $3.80 per share. Expressed on a before-tax basis, this payment required 7.6% on the par value of the issue.

Clearly, the holders of the senior securities of this company were satisfied with relatively low returns on their investment. They chose to receive fixed incomes and to enjoy stable market values rather than to participate in all the risks of the business.

The safety granted to these holders of senior securities was obtained by increasing the risk of the investment of the common equity shareholders, who promised fixed returns and granted priorities in liquidation to the holders of the bonds and preferred stock. By this acceptance of greater risk, the common equity created for itself the expectation of greater return on the investment of the common stock. This process has long been known as *trading on the equity*, a term which indicates that a bargain has been made between the classes of securities, as is indeed the case. It is the equity that is traded on because the common stock equity position is affected by the privileges granted to owners of senior securities. The process is also referred to as *leverage*.

Trading on the Equity

A diagram will serve to indicate the nature of the bargain so far as the allocation of income is concerned. Chart 19–1 has been drawn with a horizontal axis representing the $1,782.6 million invested capital of Westinghouse. The line has been subdivided into the amounts provided by the various classes of securities, as tabulated in Table 19–1. The vertical axis represents rates of cost or return, so that the area of the rectangle ABCD is the product of the rate of return on capital, 18.2%, and of capital itself, or the $325 million earnings before interest and taxes.

---

[1] The amount of the interest on long-term debt is overstated, as explained in a footnote on page 349.

On the base representing the capital contributed by each of the senior securities, rectangular areas are shown which represent the amounts of cost required to support these securities. These claims must be met before the common equity can receive anything, thus adding some risk to the equity position. On the other hand, the amount of the senior claims is

Chart 19–1

Effects of Trading on the Equity in Westinghouse Electric Corporation
(1969 operations)

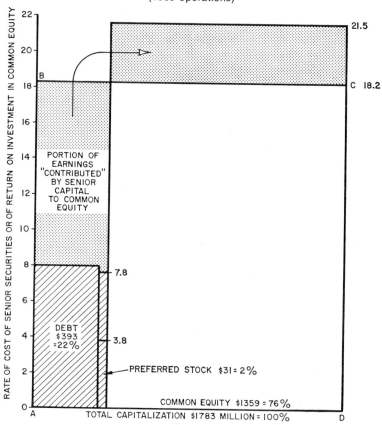

fixed, and any earnings above these fixed amounts benefit the common shareholders. We have shown this in our diagram by transferring the irregular area above the fixed charges to an equal area based on the amount of the common equity. It will be seen that the effective return on the amount of common equity capital has been increased by trading on the equity from 18.2% to 21.5%. These rates are, as will be recalled, on a before-tax basis.

By comparing these two percentages we have a precise measure of how the use of debt and preferred stock has worked to the benefit of the equity holders of Westinghouse in the year 1969. It has worked to their advantage for several reasons, two of which will be mentioned here. The first is the fact that the buyers of the debt and preferred stock have, by contributing their funds, made it possible for the common stockholders to manage a total of assets which is larger in amount than what they invested themselves.

The second advantage is found in the fact that the lenders have asked for a lower rate of return than the one that Westinghouse management was able to obtain in 1969. The benefit went over to the side of the common equity, as the diagram shows.

Trading on the equity is defined as: the use of fixed charge securities in the capitalization of a company. It gives to the owners of the common equity a rate of return which is different, when referred to their share of the invested funds, from the rate of return on the entire capitalization.

Let us assume for the moment, in order to emphasize the point, that the senior money is cost free. There is no interest or preferred dividend to pay. In such a case, the benefit conferred by the lender is one that multiplies the rate of return on all the capital (Rc) by the ratio of the total invested capital (c) to the equity portion (s). The elements of this ratio can be expressed in either dollar terms or capitalization ratios.

$$Rc\left(\frac{c}{s}\right) = Re$$

where Re is the rate of return on the common equity. For Westinghouse[2] in 1969:

$$18.2\left(\frac{1783}{1359}\right) = 18.2\left(\frac{100}{76}\right) = 23.9\% \ .$$

This delightful result is not always obtained, because the corporation must pay for the use of the borrowed money, thus reducing the amount of earnings going into the calculation of the rate of return. The factor for reduction that must enter the formula takes into account the earnings before interest and taxes (Y) and the fixed charges (F). Care must be taken, as always, to state these numbers in consistent terms, either before or after tax. It is easier to use dollar numbers in this case.

So the whole formula becomes:

$$Rc\left(\frac{c}{s}\right)\left(\frac{Y-F}{Y}\right) = Re$$

or, for Westinghouse,[3]

$$23.9\left[\frac{325 - (31 + 2)}{325}\right] = 21.5\% \ .$$

---

[2] Figures taken from page 354.

[3] Figures taken from Table 18–4.

This has been shown already in Chart 18–1. By the use of this formula, it is possible to determine precisely what advantage has been created in the income position of the common equity by the acceptance of the risks implicit in the promises to pay the charges for senior securities.[4]

The demonstration we have just made refers to a certain level of earnings, which obviously for any real company is not going to remain constant. Let us see what happens to the rates of return on invested capital and on the equity portion when a change in the E.B.I.T. takes place without any change in the funds made available. Here we have a real instance of the case we assumed earlier, for the increase of earnings is obtained without added cost, and leverage has its maximum effect.

For purposes of illustration, we have assumed a corporation in which the common equity makes up 50% of the capitalization, the debt portion cost 9% to support, and the normal, or average, earnings base is 10% on the invested capital.

At this level, if all the capital were supplied by one class of common stock, the return would be unlevered, at 10% per dollar invested. But under the conditions just assumed, the levered rate would be 11% per dollar on the smaller amount of common equity.[5]

$$10(2)\left(\frac{10 - 4.5}{10}\right) = 11\%.$$

Now let us abandon the assumption that the 10% normal rate will be experienced steadily. Let us look first at a period in which the company is enjoying a prosperous phase and is able to earn at a higher rate on its invested capital. As the unlevered rate rises, the levered rate moves ahead also, and at a faster rate. This relationship is shown in Chart 19–2. We have used a ratio scale to show the relationships more clearly.

Certain characteristics of the levered-unlevered comparison need emphasis. When the rate of return on total capital is equal to the cost of borrowing, 9%, the levered rate is the same, and the only advantage of using borrowed funds is that the equity owner can manage a larger investment than he could provide with his own funds.

When the rate of return on total capital is less than the cost of capital, as may happen in recession or because of poor forecasting, then the levered rate falls below the unlevered rate and reaches the area of loss sooner. It is easy to find examples of this side of leverage in 1970 as these words are being written. But in 1968 and other boom years, there were many who did not look at the down side as they made their plans.

A third and most important advantage in the process of trading on the

---

[4] For further discussion, see Pearson Hunt, "A Proposal for Precise Definitions of 'Trading on the Equity' and 'Leverage,'" *Journal of Finance*, September, 1961, pp. 377–86.

[5] The value of 4.5 used in this calculation results from the application of the 9% cost of borrowing to 50% of the capital.

equity, demonstrated by Chart 19–2, is that companies forecasting a certain rate of growth in earning power can transmute that growth rate to a higher rate of growth as well as a higher rate of return for their common shareholders by the use of fixed-charge senior securities. Thus, leverage under favorable circumstances not only raises the average rate of return on the common equity but raises the rate of growth where growth is experienced. In some actual cases the results have been dramatic—both

Chart 19–2

Effect of Leverage on Rate of Return per Dollar of Equity Investment

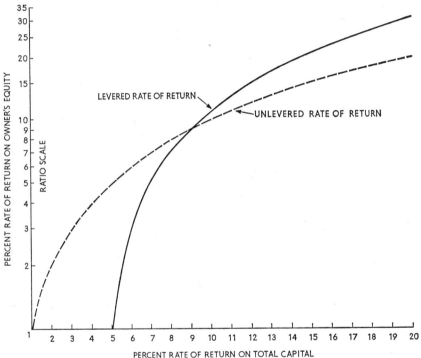

on the up side and on the down side—and they have been reflected in the market prices of stock, also.

As an illustration of how the effects of leverage upon the earning power of common stock might be presented graphically in a situation where alternative means of financing are being considered, let us take a company that needed to raise $10 million. It had no long-term debt at the time, but was considering the alternative of raising the money by the sale of bonds on a 7.5% basis or through the sale of 400,000 shares of common stock at the price of $25 per share. There were 1 million shares of stock outstanding at the time.

Studying recent experience, the company concluded that its E.B.I.T. might range from $5 million to $12 million per year. The higher figure included the increase of earnings due to the new investment.

Many people use the amount of earnings per share as the primary index of the value in an investment in common stock. Following this assumption, Table 19–2 can be made, showing for two levels of earning power the resulting earnings per share.[6] The table clearly shows that the effects of dilution (that are the result of issuing new shares) more than offset the costs of borrowing in the range of E.B.I.T. that the company has specified.

Chart 19–3 has been made to show the results graphically over an entire range of possible levels of E.B.I.T. When this chart was introduced,

Table 19–2

Calculation of Earnings per Share from E.B.I.T. for Alternate Financing Proposals (in thousands of dollars)

	Bonds	Stock	Bonds	Stock
E.B.I.T.	5,000	5,000	12,000	12,000
Interest	(750)	. . .	(750)	. . .
Taxable earnings	4,250	5,000	11,250	12,000
Tax @ 50%	(2,125)	(2,500)	(5,625)	(6,000)
Earned for common	2,125	2,500	5,625	6,000
Earned per share				
÷1,000	2.13		5.63	
÷1,400		1.79		4.28

we called it a *Range-of-Earnings Chart,* but it has become known as the "E.B.I.T. Chart" to most of its users.

Before we leave the chart, however, we can emphasize certain points. We saw in the previous chart, 19–2, that leverage produces a lower rate of return on the equity when the cost of borrowing exceeds the rate of return on the invested capital. This same condition is seen in Chart 19–3, to the left of the crossing of the lines which occurs when the E.B.I.T. is $2.625 million. This time the measurement is the quantity of earnings per share, but the point is the same.

It may also be noted that the earnings per share related to the issue of bonds becomes zero at an E.B.I.T. of $750 thousand—which is due to the cost of the borrowing that has become a financial charge that is prior to the claim of the equity on earnings.

From this chart, we can see that earnings per share will be higher if bonds are issued at all values of E.B.I.T. within the range set by the company's management. If we follow the assumption that the value of the shares responds to the amount of earnings per share, then the use of

---

[6] Any two levels can be used, but it is best to choose levels of E.B.I.T. not far from the range that the planners consider possible.

Chart 19–3

Effect of Leverage on Earnings per Common Share

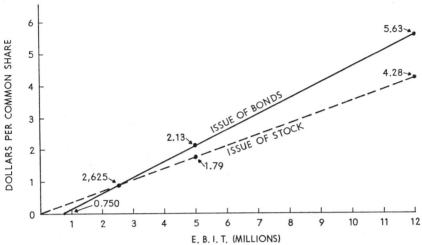

bonds is clearly the better alternative from the value point of view. This is the assumption that lies behind the policies of firms that regularly use borrowed funds to supplement the amounts contributed by their common shareholders. But there are other considerations, notably the effect upon the common stockholders' values of the risks created by the insertion of the contract terms that provide leverage. We must, therefore turn to the subject of risk.

The Distribution of Risk—Priorities

When seen from the point of view of the holders of the common stock, the use of senior securities that we have presented is usually regarded in a favorable light. If this be so, why do corporations not adopt the policy of borrowing all that anyone can lend? There are two important reasons for reluctance, although the second is only a reflection of the first.

Under a private enterprise system the prospects for individual gain are inevitably associated with the possibility of loss, and this hazard rests most heavily on those who have supplied the capital. The hazard shows itself both in the uncertainty of the income to be received and of the recovery of the original principal invested. We turn to these uncertainties under the heading of "risk."

If a firm continues to spend more money than it takes in, the time will come when it is unable to meet its current obligations. When there is no longer enough to go around and some legal claims against the business remain unsatisfied, the company is said to be *insolvent* or *bankrupt*. If this occurs, certain legal procedures are instituted to assure a fair and orderly distribution of the remaining assets (in liquidation) or revision of claims (in reorganization), following a pattern of priorities established by the terms previously negotiated for the outstanding obligations of the company (see Chapter 29).

Among the debts, certain claims have top priority over all others. These are established by law and include tax liabilities and the legal expenses that will arise if the firm enters bankruptcy. All other debts have equal priority unless some specific collateral has been provided. Let us assume that the values of the assets of a bankrupt company amount to 90% of the debts remaining after paying the special types mentioned above. Then all debts in this general category should receive 90% of their amount, regardless of their form. The open account payable to a supplier ranks equally with the formal bond.

As we saw in Chapter 15, persons negotiating debt contracts can improve their position against the prospect of bankruptcy by arranging to have a secured position. In the field of long-term debt, a real estate mortgage is a common type of such a pledge, though many other forms exist, as will appear in a later chapter. We have already discussed the limits to the significance of collateral—the claim has priority only as to the value of the specified assets; and if the asset has ceased to produce a return on investment, that value may be seriously in question. Nevertheless, properly selected collateral can add substantially to the relative position of a debt claim in a bankruptcy.

The existence of such priorities as those just mentioned further strengthens the position of a creditor as contrasted with any holder of any equity security and further contributes to a creditor's willingness to lend funds and to take a fixed rate of return in the form of interest instead of requiring a proportionate share in the profits. The relatively low cost of raising money by the use of debt comes from the more certain position of the investor derived from his creditor position, supplemented in some instances by collateral.

It may be emphasized at this point that the position of creditor is a negotiated one, the result of a bargain between the firm obtaining funds and the person or institution supplying them. The division of risk, therefore, is voluntary on both sides and must be consistent with the established policies of management. The management of a firm has a large amount of choice as to whether or not to permit debt and to give priorities, the alternatives being to raise funds by the issuance of equity securities or to operate a smaller business.

The preferred stock contract is like a debt contract in that it confers a priority on its owner, but this is only superior to the common equity. All debts must be fully settled before any claim arising from a preferred stock can be met. In the previous chapter we suggested that management should, for planning purposes, view preferred stock as if its claims were debt claims. While this is the appropriate posture for management, the preferred holder should always be aware that he does not have the protection against the ultimate risk of bankruptcy that any holder of a debt has. The intermediate position of preferred stock as to risk is normally reflected in a dividend rate somewhat higher than the interest rate on a bond of the same company issued at the same time.

Although financial failure occurs in only a minority of instances, and hence may seem unimportant, a priority position also influences the market value given to the securities of going concerns. Since the future is never wholly certain, the bonds of strong firms enjoy better markets than those of weak ones, and the bonds of any firm can be expected to exhibit more stable prices than the equity issues of the same firm, both in periods of poor economic results and in days of prosperity.

THE INVESTOR'S RISK. It is, therefore, within the power of a firm to increase the stability of the market price of some of the securities it issues, but only within the limits of the firm's capacity to stabilize, given its inherent cash flow characteristics, and only by creating a greater risk for the junior issues of the company.

Little needs to be added about the position of common stock with reference to the allocation of risk, because the matter is implicit in the preceding paragraphs. Management can weaken the position of common stock with reference to claims on assets for advantages which will appear below but cannot strengthen it, since the common stockholder is last in line and there is no one to whom he may turn for greater assurance of income or principal.

While the market price of a security is the result of many forces, it reflects in its stability or instability the degree of confidence that investors have in the security. In illustration of the effect of the uneven distribution of risk on the market prices of bonds, preferred stock, and common stock, we have chosen the 1957 record of three issues of the Erie Railroad and plotted them in Chart 19–4. The first is one of the bond issues under the consolidated mortgage. Not only is it a debt instrument, containing firm promises to pay interest and principal, but it is secured by the existence of a mortgage of property whose value is directly tied to these bonds, whatever happens to the Erie Railroad corporation.

Erie's preferred stock comes below a number of issues of bonds, so far as priority of claim for dividends is concerned. It would receive nothing in liquidation until every debt of any nature had been settled in full. Thus, it is not surprising to find that its price was more responsive to the developing pessimism in 1957.

Erie's common stock, which bore not only the risks of the railroad business but also those created by the promises made to bond and preferred issues (those *senior* to it), was considered much more risky, as Chart 19–4 shows.

For the same basic reasons, if the outlook in 1957 had been for growing railroad prosperity, one could expect the common stock to rise as

Chart 19–4

Changes in Market Price of Three Securities, Weekly, 1957
Prices of Week Ended January 4, 1957 = 100*

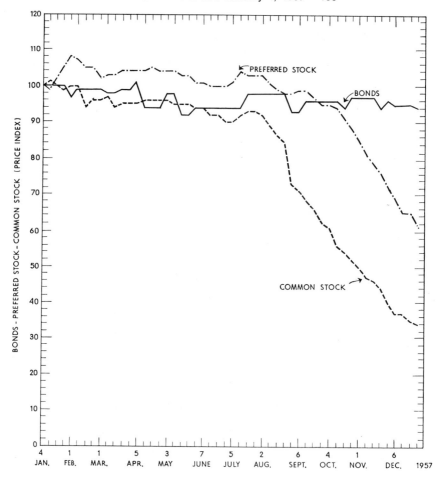

* Prices for week ended January 4, 1957, were as follows: bonds, 92; preferred, 72½; common, 20.
SOURCE: *Commercial and Financial Chronicle*, issues for 1957.

steeply as it fell. The preferred and bond issues would respond in a less pronounced upward movement.

THE BORROWER'S RISK.   From the point of view of management in a going business, what happens in the event of failure is secondary to the question of what needs to be done to avoid failure. The practical concern of management at the time of signing a debt contract, as far as risk is concerned, is the extent to which the increase in the total of fixed cash payments resulting from the new interest and sinking fund commitments makes the task of avoiding failure (cash insolvency) more difficult. A rational appraisal of the risk element would relate expectations on the magnitude and timing of cash inflows to cash outflows, particularly to mandatory cash outflows, in an effort to anticipate the chances of being "out of cash" at some time in the future and to determine how these chances are affected by the fixed cash commitments that constitute the burden of financing.

To accomplish this essential study, it is necessary to consider the type of detailed information that is presented in Table 18–4 (page 362)— although only one set of consistent figures, either before or after tax, is necessary. Such information must be estimated for future periods as well in order to enter into company plans as the mix of policies is determined. Thus, for example, the terms of the Westinghouse issue in 1970 must have been translated into annual burden figures and "spread" in a planner's work sheet for study with all related matters before they were accepted by management. The details of making such a work sheet will be formed in Chapter 20. It permits studying financial proposals from the risk point of view to supplement the range of earnings studies described above.

Since the terms of debt on preferred stocks are negotiated and are open to a considerable range of variation, it can be seen that the degree of risk presented by an issue of any given amount can be altered somewhat by management if it chooses to give priority to this in its negotiations with the creditor before the signing of the contract. Thus, for example, reducing the life of the Westinghouse loan by 10 years could substantially increase the annual cash drain required to retire the debt by the maturity date. Naturally, the opportunity to modify the risk in this manner will depend heavily on the bargaining position of the borrower and the risk standards of the lender, as well as consideration of cost.

Effects on the Cost of Capital

In considering the effect of variations in debt proportions on the cost of capital to the corporation concerned, it is necessary to take account of some differences which appear to exist between rational expectation and observed behavior. To begin with, it is generally agreed that as the proportion of debt increases, and the capacity of a business to service that debt without default decreases (all other things remaining equal), the debt becomes a more risky investment in the mind of the lender, and he will expect a higher interest rate to compensate for the increased risk. If the debt is sold publicly and the increase in the debt is large enough, this change will be apparent in a lower rating for the bonds, and there will be the dual effect of rising interest costs on new issues and a narrowing of the market interest in the issue. The latter will be particularly apparent when the rating slips below the "A" rating required for certain institutional investments.

Increased proportions of debt may also be expected to have an effect on the cost of the underlying security issues, particularly the common equity. As we have just illustrated, the volatility, and therefore the riskiness, of the common stock is increased, and reason would lead us to expect an adverse effect on the market price of the common stock, a decline in the price-earnings ratio, and a consequent rise in the earnings yield on this stock. And so it would appear that any change in the debt ratio will, in theory at least, be reflected in the cost of each of the elements of the capitalization.[7]

The net effect of these changes and the ultimate implications for the market value of the common stock of leveraged companies is currently a matter of hot debate in the academic literature and, on a much reduced scale, in the business community. In particular, the famous Modigliani-Miller thesis that the total market value of all the securities in the capitalization of a company will not change despite the particular debt-equity mix has challenged a very common assumption in business that borrowing lowers the overall cost of capital.[8] Their argument, in simple terms, is that the advantage in improved earnings on the common stock derived by using higher proportions of low-cost debt is exactly offset by the deterioration in the price-earnings ratio due to the increased risk.

Experience strongly supports the view that there are in practice certain debt levels which are regarded by investors as "reasonable" for certain industrial or commercial categories. It follows from this that the adverse market reaction to higher levels of debt is largely reserved for those companies which are clearly out of line with what is regarded as reasonable or normal. This is consistent with the generally observed phenomenon that market behavior in practice is less continuous than market behavior in theory. It is also relevant that whatever the theoretical or logical facts, if a large segment of the business community *believes* debt is a means of reducing the overall cost of capital, this is a factor to be taken into account. Nor is this necessarily "irrational" behavior, since in practice the decision makers may be concerned about aspects of the decision which lie beyond the maximization of the market value of common stock at a point in time. Not the least of these is that borrowing increases the size of the investment being managed by the equity.

We therefore conclude that the debt-equity mix is not a matter of indifference so far as management and the stockholder are concerned and that there are opportunities for lowering the overall cost of capital which should be explored—even though there are theoretical and practical limits on the extent of the expected benefits.

---

[7] For further discussion, see Eli Schwartz, "Theory of the Capital Structure of the Firm," *Journal of Finance*, March, 1959, pp. 18–39.

[8] See Franco Modigliani and M. H. Miller, "The Cost of Capital, Corporation Finance, and the Theory of Investment," *American Economic Review*, June, 1958, pp. 261–97.

A final note concerns the reference above to debt level norms. It is generally recognized that there are different norms for such industry categories as public utilities, retail food chains, finance companies, oil and gas companies, and so on. There is some tendency to lump manufacturing companies together in this respect, where there is a debt standard commonly applied of 33⅓% of capitalization. However, such generalizations must not be taken too literally, and practice clearly shows a wide range of behavior. The following debt-equity ratios, by industry aggregates for the end of the third quarter of 1970,[9] may be of some interest:

All manufacturing corporations, except newspapers................ 30.6%
Manufacturers of motor vehicles and equipment.................... 17.3
Manufacturers of lumber and wood products, except furniture........ 39.7
Manufacturers of textile-mill products........................... 32.4
Manufacturers of apparel and other finished products.............. 39.8
Manufacturers in petroleum refining and related industries............ 21.9

The Location of Control

The control of a corporation can be considered as being in the hands of those who have the voting power to elect the board of directors of the corporation. Such power is obviously centralized when a person or group holds a majority of the voting stock. On the other hand, many corporations, even among those of small size, have issued some voting shares to holders who are not part of the management group, so that a threat to control may develop if new issues of voting shares are created or, perhaps, if a preferred stock dividend is passed.

In many cases, therefore, the location and distribution of voting power is an important part of the planning of security issues. There must always be a voting stock outstanding.[10] Sometimes, however, the common stock is "classified," with one class having all the rights of such stock and the other class having all of them except voting power. Many investors are not interested in participating in management, even to the minute degree of making use of a proxy; so there is a market for nonvoting common shares. In 1926, however, the New York Stock Exchange adopted a rule against accepting any future nonvoting common stocks; and although

---

[9] Based on data in U.S. Federal Trade Commission and Securities and Exchange Commission, *Quarterly Financial Report for Manufacturing Corporations, Third Quarter, 1970* (Washington, D.C.: U.S. Government Printing Office, 1970).

[10] For many years (1890–1954), the Great Northern Railway Company had only one class of stock outstanding, designated as a $6 noncumulative no-par preferred stock. Each share had one vote. In 1954 the stock was split two for one and reclassified as a common stock. There is also the unique case in Virginia where a corporation acquired all its voting stock from a bank which had taken it over as collateral from the owner, who had defaulted on a loan. Although sympathizing with the management for its efforts to "bail out" the former owner, the probate court ordered the transaction rescinded. It is beyond the powers of a company to extinguish all its voting stock.

other exchanges have not been as rigid in this respect, nonvoting common has become a device that is very seldom adopted.

There are also instances where voting power is not proportionate to the number of shares held. Most cooperative corporations allow but one vote to each stockholder, for example. A "reform" of corporate voting power, which has strong proponents and opponents, is the scheme of *cumulative voting*, where all the nominees for office are voted for at once, and a shareholder is allowed the number of votes resulting from his number of shares multiplied by the number of persons to be elected to the board. The reader will see that this system allows minorities to elect members to the board roughly in proportion to their relative shareholding. The argument rages as to whether such minority representation assists or hinders the proper working of a board of directors. The right to vote cumulatively is available on a mandatory or optional basis in all states except Iowa, Massachusetts, New Hampshire, and Wisconsin.[11] All national banks also have cumulative voting.

In recent years preferred stocks have not received general voting power, although there are still outstanding many older issues with full voting privileges. Instead, it has become customary to confer voting power on the preferred in the event that its dividends or sinking funds fall into arrears for longer than a specified period. Provisions range from the transfer of all voting power from the common to the preferred, a most rare case, to the power to elect a minority of the board of directors to represent the interests of the preferred stock. Such a power in the case of nonpayment of the preferred dividend is very different from the acceleration of maturity which occurs upon the default of a bond, and it has led one of the authors to say that a preferred stockholder has a pillow while a bondholder has a club with which to threaten management.

Before one can take into account the question of the location of voting power, one must have a thorough understanding of the way in which the holders of voting power can be expected to use it. Many corporations have well-established managements whose direct supporters have very few votes. Yet, their nominees are regularly elected to the board of directors through the operation of the proxy system. A successful proxy fight could unseat the existing management; but if the nonmanagement shareholders are widely scattered, and if there are no large blocks held by persons ready to take leadership, the proxy system can be relied on to provide the necessary support for management.

There is risk in minority control, however, and many managements holding majorities find it almost impossible to consent to any plan which endangers the "absolute" control which they have. (It is not in fact "absolute," for minority interests must always be considered fairly when

---

[11] For details of the procedures necessary, see the latest Commerce Clearing House, Inc., *Corporation Law Guide* (Chicago).

policies are made.) In our view, small and growing corporations have too often chosen to borrow rather than to sell voting shares because of excessive fear of the risks to management of a public holding of voting control. But the actual appraisal of the risks is too complicated for a general statement. The matter must be studied on a case-by-case basis.

Bondholders, like other creditors, do not have a vote; and as long as the corporation lives up to the terms of the debt contract, they can take no action. The actual situation, however, is less permissive than it seems to be at first glance, for both bond indentures and preferred stock contracts usually contain clauses known as protective provisions specifying what the corporation will do (*affirmative covenants*) or will not do (*negative covenants*) during the time the particular security is outstanding. To cite a few examples: corporations may promise not to pay dividends, even on preferred stock, unless earned; they may promise to set aside certain funds for the replacement of assets; and so on. The existence of such clauses leads us to suggest supplementing the definition of control, given a few pages ago, so that it reads: ". . . We may say for practical purposes that control lies in the hands of the individual or group who has the actual power to select the board of directors (or its majority). In most corporations a measure of control is exercised by the promises that have been made in contracts in force at any moment."

We now return to the instance of Westinghouse to cite some examples of major ways in which the control of its policies has been determined by the terms of senior security issues.

1. *Debentures.* Neither company nor any subsidiary will mortgage or pledge any property or assets unless the debentures are equally and ratably secured, except for purchase money mortgages or existing liens on after-acquired property and the pledge of certain assets in connection with current operations.

Company will not create, assume, or guarantee any funded debt (except extensions, renewals, or refundings of funded debt, currently outstanding or retired within six months preceding) unless thereafter consolidated current assets at least equal consolidated total liabilities.

Company may not enter into sale and leaseback arrangements unless it or any manufacturing subsidiary could incur funded debt secured by a mortgage on the property without equally securing the debentures or if the company applies an amount equal to the fair value of the property so leased to the retirement of any debt that matures more than one year after the signing of the lease.

Company will not declare or pay any dividends (except stock dividends) or make any distribution on common unless thereafter consolidated current assets at least equal consolidated total liabilities.

2. *3.80% cumulative preferred; par $100.* Has no voting power unless four quarterly dividends are in arrears when preferred, voting separately as a class, is entitled to elect two directors.

Affirmative vote of $66\frac{2}{3}\%$ of preferred necessary to (1) increase authorized preferred or create any stock prior or equal thereto; (2) change the rights of the preferred prejudicial to the holders thereof; (3) sell or transfer substantially all assets or merge or consolidate (except with a subsidiary) ; or (4) create, assume, or guarantee any funded debt or permit any consolidated subsidiary so to do, except for extensions, renewals, and refundings of funded debt or refundings of funded debt retired within six months preceding, unless consolidated tangible assets less consolidated total liabilities (except consolidated funded debt) plus proceeds of proposed issue not applied to acquisition or retirement of consolidated debt or preferred or stock prior or equal thereto, are at least twice par of all consolidated funded debt and liquidation value of all preferred.

Company will not pay any dividend (except in common stock) or make any distribution on or purchase any common if thereafter (1) consolidated net assets applicable to common would be less than four times the liquidation value of all preferred; or (2) consolidated current assets would be less than consolidated total liabilities (as defined).[12]

These are samples of the many types of *protective covenants* found in security issues. It is one of the places where the limit of possibility is set only by the ingenuity of the draftsman. The actual terms of issues are reached by bargaining between the issuing corporation and some agency representing the investors' interests. We shall deal further with this subject in the chapters on the bargain for funds. Suffice it to say here by way of summary that questions of control enter into the selection of corporate securities not only with reference to the powers granted to vote at annual meetings but also in terms of the detailed contractual provisions that may be agreed upon for specific issues.

Dilution and Control

Neither a new bond nor a nonvoting preferred stock would alter the control of the business as exercised through shareholder meetings and the board of directors. The issue of common stock, however, does involve the problem of control directly, since each new share adds one new vote. To the extent that the stock is sold to new shareholders, there is a dilution of the control of the existing shareholders, the magnitude of which will be measured by the amount of new stock in comparison with the amount of stock presently outstanding.

A convenient measure of dilution may be made as follows: Divide the old number of shares by the total of old and new to be outstanding under the proposed plan. In the case of an electric utility, the raising of $8.0 million required increasing the outstanding 2,555,000 shares by 174,000 new shares.

$$\frac{2,555}{2,729} = 94\%$$

---

[12] Abridged from *Moody's Industrial Manual, 1970*, pp. 2664–69.

Table 19-3

Summary Grid of Characteristics of Security Types Illustrated by Data on
Westinghouse Electric Corporation, December 31, 1969

Basic Security Types	Income	Risk	Control
Debentures	Fixed payments ranging from 2⅝% to 6¼% on outstanding debentures through April, 1992. Twenty-two percent of capitalization of consolidated companies.	Contractual obligation to pay interest and repay principal on specified dates. Total outstanding debt as of December 31, 1969, $393 million includes $11 million deferred taxes.	No voice in management other than through terms of loan.
Preferred stock	Prior claim to earnings of $3.80 per share before payment of dividends on common. Dividends cumulative. Two percent of capitalization.	Board has power to suspend dividends or sinking fund without penalty other than (1) suspension of common dividends and (2) election of two directors by preferred shareholders. Cumulative sinking fund to retire annually two percent of all preferred theretofore issued.	No voting power unless four quarterly dividends are in arrears, when preferred as a class may elect two directors to a 16-man board. Terms of issue control some policies.
Common stock	Entitled to all earnings remaining after all prior claims deducted. In 1969 this amounted to $3.76 per share, of which $1.80 was paid out in dividends. Ratio of trading on the equity 1.3 (based on 1969 charges and earnings).	Basic risks of the business rest on the common shareholder, who has no legal claim except to the ownership of whatever remains after all other claimants have been satisfied. Debt and equity proportions at the end of 1969 were 22% debt, 2% preferred, and 76% common equity.	Common shareholders elect the board of directors on the basis of one vote per share. Cumulative voting permitted in such elections.

The figure of 94% is the proportion of voting power that would remain for the old holders after the dilution. It is a factor that can be used by any holder to determine his future position. Thus, if a group held 51% of the voting stock before the dilution, it would have (0.51) (0.94) = 48% afterwards.

The analysis of alternatives so far as the issue of control is concerned is so simple and direct that it hardly warrants description. It is for this reason that the theoretical discussions of capital structure virtually ignore control, and focus on the more analytically complex issues of income and risk. It is not to be inferred, however, that control is, therefore, unimportant in the actual choice between voting and nonvoting securities. On the contrary, control often is the dominant consideration. Even in companies with widely dispersed stockholder groups, management is always sensitive to the effect of new common stock issues on actual or potential locations of voting power.

Summary Grid

The contrasting characteristics of bonds, preferred stock, and common stock with respect to the distribution of income, risk, and control may be summarized in the form of an analytical "grid." We recommend that students use such a grid in getting an overall appraisal of the balance of security types in the capital structure of a corporation. After a time the scheme of classification will become habitual and need no longer be done on paper, unless the structure is very complex. The grid in Table 19–3 is illustrated with reference to the capitalization of Westinghouse as of December 31, 1969.

chapter 20

Deciding on the Mix of
Security Issues

In the two preceding chapters, we have focused attention on the basic contracts by means of which a corporation acquires the use of external funds on a long-term basis. The reader is now familiar not only with the nature of these contracts—the common stock, the preferred stock, and the bond—but also with the effect each has on the incidence of the fundamental elements of investment—income, risk, and control.

The reader has also seen, in Chapter 19, certain devices, notably the range of earnings chart, that assist the management of an individual corporation facing a need for external funds at a point in time. Later in this chapter we shall refer to these methods, adding others which are necessary to assist management in the difficult task of deciding upon the proportion of each type of security to best assure the results it desires. As we proceed, however it will become clear to the reader—if it is not clear already—that a decision on the "right" balance of security types can be made only within the boundaries of the individual corporation at a specific stage in its history, in full knowledge of, a) its special circumstances, b) the attitudes and objectives of its owners and management, and c) the current condition of the capital markets.

The extent to which the choice of security types occupies the time and attention of the financial officer and the board of directors varies greatly from one company to another and within a single company from period to period over its life-span. Obviously, the problem is presented when the company is first organized, though the choice may be simplified by the fact that one or more of the security types may not be available to a new, untried company. Subsequently, the frequency with which this type of decision has to be made depends on the rate of growth of the business, the capital requirements to support the growth, and the extent to which the needed funds can be generated and retained internally. In many businesses, new securities have been floated no more than three or four times over a 20-year period. In contrast, there are some companies which are issuing new securities frequently.

Even where the question of the balance among security types is presented infrequently, however, it is of critical importance, with long-term financial implications. Usually, the need for additional external funds can be anticipated well in advance, so that there is time for a careful weighing of all relevant considerations. Further, it should be pointed out that, although by far the largest proportion of funds for new business investment comes from internal sources, the choice between internal and external sources is an ever-present aspect of long-term financial planning. Every management has some control over the corporate rate of growth and the rate of earnings retention and, therefore, over the extent to which the need for external funds presents itself. Those managements which consciously work to avoid the need for selling securities are probably restricting growth by denying their company funds that could be provided by the sale of stock or bonds. Their choice is rational only if it includes a careful analysis of the effects of new external sources of funds.

Some Basic Premises

Before we introduce analytical procedures for handling the necessary quantities, we shall establish some basic premises. First, we believe that it is the task of financial managers to assist in the creation of value while at the same time preserving the solvency of the firm. But "value" and even "solvency" are indefinite terms unless we establish a point of view from which they are to be considered. In studying what has occurred in actual cases, one can recognize several distinctly different viewpoints—such as those of the creditors, the management, "the company," the existing shareholders, and the prospective shareholders. It is clear that the relative advantages and disadvantages of securities in the corporate capital structure will appear very differently to individuals with different relationships to the corporation. What is considered "best" by the bondholders may be viewed as less than best from some other point of view. Thus, for example, the sale of a new block of common stock would be welcomed by bondholders, since they would have prior claim to the earning power and residual values of the funds so acquired. In other words, the solvency of the firm would be assured more than before. The existing common shareholders, on the other hand, could be strongly opposed, particularly if the stock was sold below market price, because the new shares would dilute their participation in future earnings. For management to reach a meaningful decision in a given situation, a point of view must be adopted and adhered to consistently.

In the analysis that follows, we adopt the viewpoint of the holder of common stock. It is his interests which are most clearly and intimately connected with the long-term prospects and objectives of the business. It is he who accepts (knowingly or not) the basic risks of ownership and it is his resources that are committed for the protection of others, including senior security holders. In contrast to this, the interests of the bondholder and the preferred shareholder are negotiated and limited by contract. It is the common stockholders, acting as a group, who have the power to elect the board of directors, thus making the board—legally, at least—accountable to them. We therefore assume that the basic objectives of management will be identical with the objectives of the common shareholder and that management in its decisions will reflect this identity of interest.[1]

Of course, this is not to say that in practice management will always take this point of view, or that it should be interpreted so narrowly as to exclude from consideration the valid interests of others toward whom the company has important responsibilities—creditors, employees, customers, the general public. It is, however, an appropriate starting point for the consideration of a number of issues, including the one posed in this chapter. It should be emphasized that if a new stock issue is in prospect, we narrow the point of view still further by identifying the company's interests with those of the *existing* common shareholders as opposed to the *new* common shareholders where a possible conflict of interest may develop (as, for example, in the pricing of the new issue).

It will be apparent that the choice of securities is a problem which cannot be solved in general terms or by any simple formula. There are pros and cons for each alternative, and the final choice must be left to individual judgment in each particular case. At the same time, however, if the analysis of these considerations is carried out in a thorough and objective manner, the resulting capital structure should, within limits, fit into a general pattern suited to the character of the industry in which the business operates.

The Method of Analysis

A basic assumption concerning the value of the interest of common stockholders is that it responds to the level of earnings that are made available to that interest—operating profits after deduction of the costs of senior securities. The degree to which value varies in proportion to earnings is, as we discussed in Chapter 19, much conditioned by the factor of risk. Nevertheless, we can say that some degree of leverage is likely to create value in almost all firms, if (a very important "if") solvency can be assured. We turn, therefore, to a newly developed procedure for

---

[1] For a discussion of some points of difference, see Gordon Donaldson, "Financial Goals: Management vs. Stockholders," *Harvard Business Review*, Vol. 41, No. 3 (May–June, 1963), pp. 116–29.

studying the effect on a company's solvency of such alternative financial programs as the managers of a firm may wish to analyze.

The problem is necessarily complex, for not only are several factors to be considered but they are interrelated so that a proposed change in one of them will change the desirability of a planned level of another. For example, a proposal to increase the level of a cash dividend will reduce the amount of funds available to support business expansion *unless* new money is raised by a security issue. Three variables are interrelated in this example. There are sometimes more.

Our readers who are acquainted with computers and the techniques of managerial economics will recognize that such a situation responds well to computerized simulations and, in some cases, to the mathematics of programming as well. We shall not ask our readers to turn at once to a computer, but we do present a format for analysis that adapts itself to computerization more easily than do older procedures.

The method we propose calls for the same kinds of quantities as appear in the traditional financial statements, but in a substantially altered arrangement. We emphasize that it is not necessary to construct the forecast balance sheet or income statement for each of the planning periods, for the two work sheets we propose give all the numbers necessary for the guidance of financial policy.

Since the procedure is best explained by the use of an example, we have chosen the planning problem of an electric utility company. The nature of its business permits forecasts of earnings within acceptable levels of uncertainty for periods as long as 5 years. In 1969 the estimates for the ensuing 5 years reflected an increasing rate of growth of revenues, which could not be realized without large additions to capacity.

Forecasting Operating Funds Flow

Two tables are to be prepared. Table 20–1 is to be begun first, as figures derived in it (line 6) are needed to begin the second table.

The estimates of E.B.I.T. provided by the company appear in the first line of Table 20–1. It is the first of several lines under the general heading of Operations. But if estimates are provided in items of E.B.I.T., one must immediately eliminate the effect of taking as expense certain allocations of cost that will not require funds. Depreciation (2) is the chief but by no means the only, one of these, and it is added to E.B.I.T. in order to give us the number which is basic to all our work, the Funds provided by operations, on a before-tax basis (3). We can refer to it as FPO (BT). In fact, since the previous two numbers were entered only to help us arrive at the estimate of FPO, they can well be omitted if permitted by the forecasting procedures used in estimating the results of operations. Another correction may be necessary. For our purposes the FPO must result only from the operating revenues and expenses that may be derived from the use of the company's resources, however they may have been obtained. It is important to recognize that there is a basic flow developed through the use of resources, and this information should not be polluted by burying financial costs into the total operating costs to produce an estimate of operating results. They must appear separately, later in the table.

Whenever, as is the case here, the FPO (BT) is a positive number, there is a concurrent amount of tax exposure to be related to the operating inflow. This has been computed and entered at the rate of 48% (4). The reader will note that this set of numbers is entered in parentheses. We have chosen to enter in this way all numbers that tend to reduce the cash position of the company.

The numbers in the next line (5) must be selected with care. It is a frequent practice for companies to use one scheme of depreciation when estimating the earnings that will be reported to their shareholders and another scheme of depreciation in their tax returns. The analyst must obtain, before he enters the numbers in line 5, an estimate of the depreciation expense that will be used for tax purposes. In the case of the company we are using as our example, the figures in line 2 were taken from internal planning documents and did represent the depreciation as it would appear in the tax return. The quantities of tax depreciation are then multiplied by the tax rate. The products, being the tax shield created from the expense, supply the numbers for line 5, captioned Tax shield, depreciation. The importance of the use of tax depreciation at this point is that the only effect of depreciation upon the operating funds position of the company is from its effect in reducing the tax exposure. The tax shield we have computed is this effect.[2]

The sum of lines 3, 4, and 5 is found in line 6, and is the amount of the Funds provided by operations, after tax. It may be referred to as FPO (AT). This number, most important as a basis for financial planning, is seldom seen in company reports. It represents the funds contribution of the internal sources of the firm to its needs for expansion and the support of its financial contracts.

Forecasting Earnings

Table 20–2 may be made concurrently with Table 20–1, or at a later time. Its purpose is to show the effect of the policies being investigated on the profits that will be reported, and thus to bring consideration of values, as measured by anticipated earnings, into the study.

At this point, we ask the reader to note that the earnings table begins with the numbers of Funds provided by operations after tax, line 6 of

---

[2] The algebraic sum of lines 4 and 5 will not equal the reported tax accrual in the income statement of any firm that has tax-deductible financial costs. These costs develop additional shields, as in line 11 of our example.

Table 20–1

Emphasizing Solvency

(dollar figures in millions)

		1970	1971	1972	1973	1974
	OPERATIONS					
1	Earnings before interest and taxes	$ 14.1	$ 15.4	$ 15.2	$ 15.8	$ 18.5
2	Depreciation eliminated	4.7	5.0	4.8	5.2	5.5
3	Funds provided by operations, before taxes	$ 18.8	$ 19.4	$ 20.0	$ 21.0	$ 24.0
4	Tax exposure (48%)	(9.0)	(9.3)	(9.6)	(10.1)	(11.5)
5	Tax shield, depreciation	2.3	2.4	2.3	2.5	2.6
6	Funds provided by operations, after tax	$ 12.1	$ 12.5	$ 12.7	$ 13.4	$ 15.1
	INVESTMENT					
7	Additions to property	(15.6)	(15.4)	(15.7)	(18.5)	(20.0)
8	Increases in noncash working capital	(0.5)	(0.5)	(0.7)	(0.9)	(1.0)
9	*Funds profile*	$ (4.0)	$ (3.4)	$ (3.7)	$ (6.0)	$ (5.9)
	FINANCING PAST COMMITMENTS					
	Costs–Dividends					
10	Interest expense	$ (2.9)	$ (2.1)	$ (2.3)	$ (2.3)	$ (2.3)
11	Tax shield, financing	1.4	1.0	1.1	1.1	1.1
12	Preferred dividend	(1.3)	(1.5)	(1.8)	(1.8)	(1.8)
13	Common dividend	(3.1)	(3.3)	(3.6)	(3.8)	(4.0)
	Repayment					
14	Maturing debt	(6.7)	(9.4)	(1.4)	(1.4)	(7.0)
15	*Financial specification*	$(16.6)	$(18.7)	$(11.7)	$(14.2)	$(19.9)
	PROPOSED FINANCING					
16	Reserves used	1.5	0.7			
17	Sale of bonds: Proceeds	10.0	10.0			
18	Burden: Interest	(0.4)	(1.1)	(1.1)	(1.1)	(1.1)
19	Tax shield	0.2	0.5	0.5	0.5	0.5
20	Sale of preferred stock—proceeds and burden		6.0	(0.5)	(0.5)	(0.5)
21	Sale of common stock	8.0	....			
22	*Change in cash*	$ 2.7	$ (2.6)	—	—	—
23	Balance, beginning of period	5.2	7.9	—	—	—
24	Minimum cash balance	(5.2)	(5.2)	—	—	—
25	*Cumulative free cash*	$ 2.7	$ 0.1	—	—	—

Table 20–2

Emphasizing Earnings
(dollar figures in millions)

		1970	1971	1972	1973	1974	1975
	OPERATIONS						
1	FPO (AT)............	$12.1	$12.5	$12.7	$13.4	$15.1	
2	Depreciation as reported to stockholders.....	(4.3)	(4.2)	(3.6)	(3.5)	(3.4)	
3	Deferred taxes........	(0.2)	(0.4)	(0.6)	(0.9)	(0.6)	
4	Earnings before financial charges and related taxes.....	$ 7.6	$ 7.9	$ 8.5	$ 9.0	$11.1	
5	Interest expense*.....	(3.3)	(3.2)				
6	Tax shield, financing*...	1.6	1.5				
7	*Net earnings*.......	$ 5.9	$ 6.2				
8	Preferred dividend requirement*.......	(1.3)	(1.5)				
9	*Earnings available for common stock*......	$ 4.6	$ 4.7				
10	Common dividend*.....	(3.1)	(3.3)				
11	Retained earnings......	$ 1.5	$ 1.4				
12	Earned per share (800,000 shares outstanding)......	$ 1.88	$ 1.75				

* Existing and proposed commitments.

Table 20–1. The next line allows the deduction of the depreciation expense. But this time we must enter the amounts as they will be reported to shareholders, and not the tax deductions that supplied the shields we entered in line 5 of Table 20–1 because the shareholders will see the earnings figure so derived, and not the earnings reported for tax purposes. The figures in Table 20–2 represent the straight-line depreciation that will be used in financial reports. The values in line 3 represent the recognition of tax deferral, as recommended in a recent opinion of the Accounting Principles Board.[3] The amounts are obtained by taking the difference between the tax depreciation and the reported depreciation and multiplying by the tax rate.

The combination of the first three lines of Table 20–2 gives us the published net earnings after taxes but before financial costs and their tax effects. The amounts show what the reported net earnings would be if the company were entirely financed by the common equity.

Forecasting the Capital Budget

The accountant enters depreciation as an expense because it is necessary to record the expiration of values in assets that have been carried over from past periods. By contrast, in studying solvency, the financial manager is interested not in the expiration of past costs but only in the amounts of funds that will be needed for assets to be acquired. In the case of our utility company, the sums are substantial. Estimates taken from engineering studies furnished the figures in line 7 of Table 20–1, while the controller's office gave the corollary estimates in line 8. This firm has not forgotten that expansion calls for working capital, too.[4]

The contrast between the entry of an expense in Table 20–2 and a budget in Table 20–1 should not be allowed to obscure the fact that the concepts involved are analogous. The difference is in the timing of the recognition in periodic figures. In the table emphasizing solvency, we enter forecasted uses of funds for capital assets. In the table emphasizing earnings, we enter the amortization of past investments in capital assets.

The Funds Profile

Line 9, the last line in Table 20–1 that will ignore financing, is called the *Funds profile* because if one charted the amounts on this line from year to year one could see the changing situation that financial planners must meet. More precisely, one situation occurs when the Funds profile is positive. Then the amount shows the funds that are provided by the business to meet the financial obligations that have been entered into by

---

[3] AICPA, "Accounting for Income Taxes," *APB Opinion No. 11* (New York, 1970).

[4] The analyst must be careful to pick up all expenditures for fixed assets, for instance, purchase of securities for investment purposes, etc., etc.

the management. If it is negative, we see the specification of how much must be provided by the financial officers to supply the needs of the firm.

The Funds profile is determined by the basic economic cycles of investment and operations that characterize the segment(s) of the economy in which the firm operates. After some experience with the profiles of various industries and after learning a few details about a particular company, one can rather easily predict whether the company's Funds profile will be running ahead of forecast earnings, or below.

In the utility company of our example, which is in a phase of growth in sales, and in a capital-intensive industry requiring large investments to support new revenues, the Funds profile, with its negative quantities, makes a striking contrast with the earnings estimates of line 4 of Table 20–2. Although in this case the Funds profile results of each year are negative, the plans of other companies will often show positive numbers at this level of the study. Such is likely to be the case, for example, in a company enjoying good profit margins with little or no need to expand. The specification derived from such a profile is that the planners have internal sources of funds to rely on. But for the company in our example, we are told that previously accumulated liquid balances or other reserves must be drawn down or that more financing must be planned to supply the need in the years shown.

Flows Related to Existing Financing

Any going concern is almost certain to have contractual and policy burdens (see page 351 for definition) in existence as a planning period begins. Lines 10, 11, 12, and 13 of Table 20–1 list these, so far as annual interest expenses or dividends are concerned. Line 14 lists the cash flow consequences of sinking funds and maturities, and line 15 shows the combined effect of existing commitments of a financial nature and the needs to support operations shown as the Funds profile in line 9. We caption this line *Financial specification*.

Meeting the Financial Specification

In the company used in our example, it was felt that there were $1.5 million in cash items that could be devoted to meet the financial specification in 1970 and that the sale of vacation properties near an expanded hydro development would bring in $0.7 million in 1971. These small contributions, however, did not meet the need.

At the time our interview took place, plans for ways to meet the financial specification were well settled for the years 1970 and 1971. These included the issue of $10.0 million in bonds in each of the two years, without sinking funds and with an interest cost of 7.75%, and in 1970 the raising of $8.0 million through capital stock without increasing the amount of the cash dividend budgeted (already set to increase at 5% per year). Toward the end of 1971, a new issue of $6.0 million of 8% preferred stock would be issued. The quantities of these forecasts have been entered in lines 17 through 21 of Table 20–1. Line 22, which combines lines 15 through 21, gives the net result of all the forecasts in terms of the change in cash to be expected in each year.

We proceed to the final section of the work sheet, entering in line 23 of 1970 the amount of the cash balance that the company had on hand at the beginning of 1970. In line 24 we offset this number by the working balance that the management feels must be held as a minimum. The resulting figure, appearing in line 25 for 1970, is then accumulated with the amounts for subsequent years taken from line 22. We call this line the *Cumulative free cash.*

The behavior of the figures on this line may be used as a guide to the suitability of all the plans whose quantities were entered above.

When the predicted balance is stable and not excessively large, we have an indication that the policies being analyzed are acceptable. If they go into negative numbers, and especially if they grow larger in the negative direction as time goes on, the proposed policies will not work.

If they grow ever more strongly positive over time, we have an indication that the firm will accumulate *excess* resources. Plans should be made to use the resources or to distribute them.

If the predicted cash balance fluctuates cyclically around a satisfactory average, there is opportunity to save financial costs by arranging loans with scheduled repayments which fit the cycle.

There may, of course, be several combinations of operations, investment, and financing that lead to stability in the company's liquid position. In the company used as our example, the plans described for 1970 and 1971 do meet the test of a relatively stable, not excessive amount of free cash. We can conclude that the proposed program meets the test of solvency, and can turn again to the question of whether it is a combination that creates value for the shareholders.

To help with this problem, Table 20–2 has been completed for the years 1970 and 1971. Lines 5 and 6 reflect the new fixed charges as well as the continuing ones. The last 3 years have been left uncompleted, because the numbers cannot be supplied until Table 20–1 has been worked on.

We now suggest to our readers that they experiment with possible plans for the public utility used in our example for the last 3 years of the planning period, and complete the tables for each alternative plan. A chart of the kind shown in Chapter 19 (19–3) may also be helpful.

The following assumptions may be used.

1. Maturing debt may be replaced by new issues. The interest rate expected is 7.75%. Long-term debt was $40 million at end of 1971.

2. New debt can be created as earnings are retained, but the amount borrowed may not be above 2.0 times the amount of the retention.
3. In addition, preferred stock can be created to 0.3 times the retained earnings, but it must offer the investor 1% more than a bond offers. Preferred stock was $13.5 million at the end of 1971.
4. Common stock can be sold with a price now estimated at 12 times earnings. Common stock was $40 million at the end of 1971.
5. Some members of management feel that the policy of steady increase in the cash dividend can be changed to more infrequent increases without damaging the value of the stock in the market. They believe that the value of the stock is primarily influenced by earnings per share.

The Analysis of Risk in the Individual Company

Now that we have made our readers acquainted with two related work sheet formats, we think they are better prepared to take up once again the subject of permissible levels of senior securities in a firm's financial planning.

In Chapter 18 we showed how one can compute ratios óf burden coverage and capitalization ratios. We said that the financial world uses certain standards or rules of thumb to appraise the ability of a firm to carry indebtedness, and we suggested that better ways could be found. We think the use of the work sheet format exemplified by Table 20–1 is a better way.

The traditional approach to risk by the criterion of burden coverage takes earnings as defined by accounting practice as the index of ability to pay debt servicing charges. In fact, of course, debts are serviced by cash payments, and it is cash flow and cash reserves that determine whether a problem of servicing exists. We know that it is the variations in cash outflow unmatched by compensating changes in inflow that create problems for management. The more management adds to the fixed element of outflows, including large capital expenditures and cash dividends, the greater the threat from unexpected and prolonged declines in inflow. Thus, a serious approach to analysis of the risks of indebtedness must be expanded to include consideration of *all* those factors that significantly influence the behavior of cash inflows and cash outflows over extended periods of time. This information is accessible to the internal analyst, and it should be used as a means of coming to an independent judgment on capital structure policy.

Tables 20–1 and 20–2 can serve as models for the necessary analysis. They can be refined by adding greater detail as necessary and programmed for a computer.[5] In any case, crude or refined, the study of the

---

[5] See, for example, the exhibits in the case of the Inconco Corporation, p. 627.

corporate system of cash flows must have as one of its parts the simulation of a range of adverse conditions so that the effect on net cash flows and cash reserve position can be measured. In the more refined models a considerable array of results can be developed over a wide range of recession conditions and can be used to develop a measure of the probability of cash insolvency or inadequacy for any combination of debt, equity, growth, and dividends. The analysis will also show how this probability of insolvency is increased for any given change in policy.

We suggest that the reader add 1975 to his work on the utility company, and examine the consequences of a 15% decline in the before-tax FPO in that year. Can solvency be preserved? What policies are indicated by such a recession year?

Although many managements rely on estimates using single "most probable" figures, we feel that they could strengthen their decision making by using estimates covering the range of uncertainties—estimates developed from the specific circumstances of their own company and industry and reflecting their own financial priorities. But it must be recognized that an improved measure of risk magnitude does not provide the final answer. There is also the subjective dimension of the financial mix decision—willingness to bear risk. Here is renewed evidence that generalized rules must always be viewed with suspicion and not used as the primary basis for the policy related to financing. It is a choice to be reserved solely for those who bear the risk—the common shareholders—or their duly elected representatives—the board of directors and the top management they appoint.[6] They alone can say whether any given level of risk of insolvency is acceptable to them.

The Question of Marketability

However much care and detail may have been put into the number work described above, the analysis will inevitably be only a contribution to the final decision. It must be remembered that the wishes of the prospective security holder are just as important as the wishes of the managers of the issuer in bringing the two together successfully. So far, we have shown how the managers may decide about how far to use debt in their endeavor to add value to the stock through the use of leverage. They can obtain an estimate of the firm's *debt capacity*.

Given both the willingness of the market to lend and the willingness of the management to borrow—one of the two limits will be the controlling one—then the question is one of how much of this debt capacity to use at a point in time. Here again, judgment must be exercised, for the problem is then one of sensing the reaction of the stock market to de-

---

[6] The fact that many managements are not made up of persons with important shareholdings raises many difficult problems. Should managers apply their own risk preferences or attempt to learn and apply the preferences of stockholders?

termine whether as the use of debt approaches the prescribed limit, the price-earnings ratio for the common stock will be substantially affected by the risk consideration. Here customary debt levels are important—what the industry does; but the market also considers the quality of management and other factors in the nature of its response, and the outcome is very difficult to predict in general terms.

Finally, we reach the point where we are working with a debt limit that is acceptable to both the market and the company and that promises desirable gains in the value of the common equity. Then the decision becomes whether to use debt rather than equity at this particular time for this particular financing.

The securities market is at best highly complex and constantly changing. The services of men experienced in the ways of the market and in constant touch with it are required to approach a statement of the possibilities at a given point of time; and even then the statement will be tentative. The acceptable type, amount, and terms of security to be offered will vary from time to time. This is not to suggest that our utility company, which is regarded as strong and well managed, cannot market all three types of securities indicated between 1970 and 1975 but simply to indicate that the market must not be taken for granted. In a given situation, the factors considered of primary importance to the company and the common shareholders may be overshadowed by the consideration of what is acceptable to the prospective security holder.

Timing the New Security Issue

Related to the question, "Can the issue be sold?" is the question, "Is this the best time to sell it?" In prosperous times the large and successful business can usually sell an issue, provided it is willing to meet the investors' terms. However, we know that the securities market is dynamic, so that within brief periods of time the investors' terms on any or all types of securities may have changed so significantly that an issue no longer seems desirable.

How this affects our decision depends entirely on our expectations as to the future trends in the securities market. If a consideration of income, risk, and control in this case pointed to the choice of common stock, for example, as the desirable medium for financing current needs, management might still pause in its decision if it felt that by waiting for, say, a year, the stock could be sold substantially above its current price. Since usually one can assume that a company could sell any of the three security types, an expectation of rising common stock prices could lead to a decision to finance through debt on a temporary basis until a more advantageous price for the common stock could be obtained. Far-thinking management recognizes that financing in the long run will be through a combination of debt and equity sources, and its ideal is to time its approaches to the market so as to minimize both the cost of senior securities and the dilution resulting from new common stock issues.

There are, of course, certain obvious limitations to the achievement of this ideal. The most basic is the dynamic nature of the market and our very limited capacity to anticipate market behavior. Obviously, there are considerable risks in waiting a year for this hoped-for rise in the market price of common stock. The company's expectation could be entirely wrong, and it might ultimately be forced to sell the common stock below its current price. This brings up a second limitation, namely, that the issuing company cannot postpone equity financing indefinitely, since it cannot continue to create burden without the margin of safety that equity affords through the earnings on the equity itself. The opportunities for taking advantage of market trends have certain time limits placed upon them by these circumstances.

Historical Behavior of Costs of Capital

An alert financial manager will recognize that the costs of various types of securities are constantly changing. This fact can be observed not only from the terms that his company obtained whenever it did issue new contracts but also and more continuously from the behavior of the issues of his company and similar issues in the market. As was pointed out earlier, the historical costs of a particular issue are not so important to the management as the likely costs of the next issue; and costs in the near future may be inferred, as a first approximation, from the present level and historic behavior of the market. For this reason, we present in Chart 20–1 certain measures of cost since 1950.

The data for the chart were taken from the tabulations which show the "yield" of various issues to a buyer. In order to make these statistics useful from the point of view of a corporation considering an issue, the yield rate on debt instruments was reduced to an after-tax figure, using rates appropriate for each year. The costs of stocks and bonds were thus made comparable for our purposes, and no longer useful to potential buyers.[7]

With this presentation, we see that the ordering of costs is what our theoretical descriptions would suggest; short-term debt is normally the cheapest and bonds come next. Costs do not change greatly in these categories. The fact that the dividend yield on common stock has descended recently below that of preferred stock and debt instruments is worthy of note. It confirms our argument that the buyer of common stocks is finding value in something in addition to his dividend.

The major change to be noted is the movement downward of the

---

[7] Actually, since these data were taken from seasoned issues, they slightly understate the cost of new issues, which often are offered at favorable prices and always bear registration and other costs.

Chart 20–1

Indicators of Costs of Corporate Issues, 1946–65
(after tax on debt instruments)

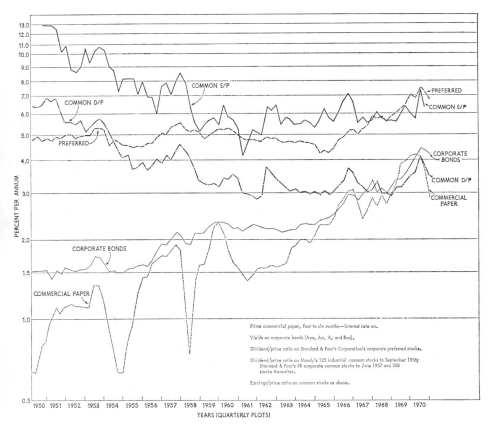

SOURCES OF DATA USED: Office of Business Economics, Department of Commerce, *Statistical Supplements to Survey of Current Business* for stock data to December, 1951; *Federal Reserve Bulletins*, for all other data.

common stock earnings-price ratio, and its relatively stable relationship to the dividend yield on common stock since 1958. Certainly there is evidence that the attitude of buyers toward common stocks has changed greatly. The "rule of thumb" that common stock can be sold only in a few months of the business cycle can certainly be challenged from the facts shown in the chart.

As we are writing this chapter, in March, 1971, we are seeing the end of a period in which the "spread" between the yield to buyers of common stock and the yield to buyers of bonds is very close. But, viewed from the issuer's position, borrowing is still notably less costly than stock financing, because of the tax deductibility of interest.

The Need for Flexibility

Although the matter of flexibility is involved in some of the considerations already discussed, it requires special emphasis. By flexibility, we mean the capacity of the business and its management to adjust to expected and unexpected changes in circumstances. Another way of expressing the idea would be to say that management desires a capital structure which gives it maximum freedom to maneuver at all times. Flexibility is a consideration each time management changes its capital structure by a new issue of securities.

Of course, a goal of "maximum freedom to maneuver at all times" is an ideal never attained, short of holding all resources in cash and never taking any action or position. Every act to commit resources to specialized use means a denial of these resources to other uses and therefore a reduction in maneuverability. And as management presses for maximum return on capital through full utilization of resources, it is reducing its capacity to shift quickly if its judgments prove to be less than optimum. This is the essence of business risk, and it is part of the game of business that the use of funds for one purpose today is a restriction on their use for another purpose tomorrow—a use that may turn out to be more profitable or even vital to survival.

Financial flexibility or mobility is a much broader issue than the question of capital structure. As suggested above, it pervades the whole spectrum of uses and sources of funds. In its most obvious form it is concerned with liquid balances—cash and marketable securities. However, of greater importance in most companies than the "stocks" of liquid funds are the flows of these funds—the rate of conversion into and out of specialized use and the variability over time. In addition to those assets that are quickly convertible into cash as a matter of business routine, there are assets that are potentially convertible into cash, and these also are part of the picture of mobility. Finally, there are the various short-term and long-term sources of funds and their potential role in providing new capital when an unexpected need arises. An adequate strategy for financial flexibility must bring all of these into balanced consideration.[8]

In this chapter we are concerned only with the question of how flexibility influences or should influence the capital structure decision—the use or conservation of sources of funds tapped through the basic security contracts. It will be recalled that our analysis does deal with the question of the unexpected need for funds, and the analysis of cash flows as presented in Table 20–1 and the text describing it was an effort to explore the range of possible future circumstances and determine the magnitude of the chance of a cash deficiency. Since this dealt with all elements of cash flow and was used to observe the impact of various debt levels on

---

[8] See Gordon Donaldson, *Strategy for Financial Mobility* (Boston: Division of Research, Harvard Business School, 1969).

the cash position, it can be argued that we have already included the consideration of flexibility in our analysis. In other words, one can explore the unexpected, assess the probability of being unable to meet cash needs, and decide if he is willing to live with whatever probability is associated with the approved debt limits. Implicit is the acceptance of some degree of inflexibility, and the choice of degree is up to management.

Most financial officers prefer to hold some of their debt capacity in reserve. Along with excess cash this forms the first line of defense in their strategy of flexibility. These are the funds they can lay their hands on confidently and quickly when the unexpected need suddenly presents itself. The questions arise: Is this widespread practice of hoarding debt capacity rational, particularly if we can assume that a comprehensive risk analysis has been made and debt limits have been based on a recognition of apparent risk magnitudes? If management knows its limit of debt and debt is in fact the low-cost source, why not push to the limit and stay there?

Without an attempt at an exhaustive answer to this important set of questions, some points should be made. One is that there is a potential element of inconsistency in asserting on the one hand that we are willing to live with a given level of risk and on the other that we need to keep some idle resources to protect ourselves if that risk materializes. We can be guilty of creating the appearance of risk bearing while at the same time carrying an "insurance policy" to cover it.

At the same time, from a practical viewpoint one can see rather persuasive arguments for not being fully "borrowed up" at all times. An obvious one is that in practice financial analysis, including the analysis of debt capacity, is a crude and imperfect art, and even the analysis we propose must not be considered an exact science. Experience teaches that one's best judgment can be wrong. Beyond this, however, is a concern which is perhaps the essence of the practitioner's view of flexibility. It is that the stream of investment needs or opportunities includes some which prove to be critical in the growth and development of a company, and the timing of these is often beyond management's ability to predict. In the face of this, there is a natural reluctance to fully commit the company's most reliable and readily available external source, debt, on investments which, even though profitable, are not critical to the company's future. The critical need or opportunity may be just around the corner, and that may be the very time when other means of financing, such as the common equity market, may be very unattractive and uncertain alternatives.

Hence comes the common practice of a dual debt limit: the one reflecting the amount of debt available at an acceptable level of risk and the other the amount of debt the company is willing to commit to "normal" investment opportunities.

chapter 21

Reinvestment of Earnings
and Dividend Policy

The preceding three chapters have examined the various sources of external long-term funds and have explored their costs and other characteristics. Methods of analysis by which the choice among these alternative sources is made have also been demonstrated. Little has been said, however, about the most important source of all: the funds generated by the company's own operations. In recent years approximately two thirds of all the funds used by business corporations have come from internal sources—which are divided between depreciation and retained earnings.

In terms of dollar volume the amount assigned to depreciation exceeds that of retained earnings. The choice of a depreciation method is an important decision. Once a depreciation method has been selected, however, the process is essentially automatic.

Retained earnings are a very different matter. Management—or more specifically, the directors—must decide how to allocate the company's after-tax earnings between retention in the business and distribution to the stockholders as cash dividends. This decision is of prime importance and great complexity. The importance of retained earnings as a source of funds to finance the company's continued growth must be set against the importance of dividends to the company's owners and their effect upon the value of the company's stock. Much of the complexity of the decision will become clear in the course of this chapter.

The Nature and Form of the Dividend

A dividend payment is a distribution to the shareholders of something that belongs to the company. In this chapter we shall be concerned primarily with *cash* dividends. Dividends may, however, be paid by distributing other assets: the stock of another company, or even the company's own products. In the accounting sense, the counterpart of the distribution of the asset is the reduction of the net worth of the business.

Distribution of the company's own stock as a dividend is increasingly used; but payment of stock dividends does not in itself reduce the net worth of the company. Stock dividends are discussed elsewhere in this book (page 481). We are here concerned with true dividends: the reduction of the company's net worth by the distribution of a valuable asset to the stockholders.

In the United States the power to declare dividends rests in the discretion of the directors of the corporation. (In some foreign countries the shareholders themselves have the right to vote upon dividend policy.) There is never—and legally cannot be—any contractual obligation to pay dividends. This applies equally to common and preferred stock and is one of the basic distinctions between equity and debt. There are, however, well-established legal rules which define the circumstances in which dividends cannot be paid. These rules differ from state to state, but the basic principle is the same—that dividends may be paid only out of realized earnings so as not to impair the company's original paid-in. capital. In other words, dividends are paid out of the "unreserved and unrestricted earned surplus of the corporation."[1]

According to U.S. law, then, a company may pay out cash dividends greater than its current earnings, so long as there is an amount of earned surplus large enough to absorb the payment. (It is interesting to note that in some other countries companies are not permitted to draw upon past earnings in this way.) Such a policy would make little sense on a continuing basis. As a temporary measure, however, it may make very good sense indeed. A company that experiences a reduction in current earnings but can confidently forecast that the setback is only temporary may be very wise to maintain dividends at their previous level, rather than reduce them and thereby adversely affect its stock price and its reputation with the investment community. Paying dividends in excess of earnings might also be a justifiable policy for a company which has reached a stage of corporate maturity, has few attractive investment opportunities open to it, and finds itself with a large positive funds profile.

Restrictions on the payment of dividends also arise out of the process of bargaining for external funds. These restrictions take the form of *protective provisions* in loan agreements and senior securities, which have been referred to previously. The type of contractual limitation which restricts the freedom of the company to declare dividends is usually expressed in terms of the necessity to maintain a certain financial position

---

[1] Model Business Corporation Act (revised 1959) prepared by the Committee on Corporate Laws of the American Bar Association.

or a certain level of earnings. For example: "Company may not pay cash dividends on common or acquired stock in excess of consolidated net income after December 28, 1957, plus $2,500,000 [of retained earnings] and provided consolidated net working capital is not less than $10,000,000. At December 26, 1959, $4,073,247 of retained earnings were not so restricted."[2]

The payment of dividends on the common stock is often further restricted by provisions in the preferred stock contract. The most common is the provision that identifies the preferred as a cumulative one by stipulating that unpaid preferred dividends shall be accumulated and that no common dividend can be distributed unless and until both current and accumulated preferred dividends are paid. Such a provision might typically read: "If in any quarterly dividend period dividends at the rate of $6 per annum per share shall not have been paid upon, or declared and set apart for, the $6 preference stock, the deficiency shall be fully paid or declared and set apart for payment before any dividends shall be paid upon, or declared and set apart for, common stock of the company."

Taxation and Dividend Policy

Before we leave the topic of the legal rules imposed by statute and contract which limit freedom in the area of dividend policy, we should make brief reference to the laws of taxation, for there one can find examples of provisions which give strong incentive either to pay dividends or not to pay them, depending upon the law and the particular circumstances of a company. For example, frequent reference is made in financial journals to the paradoxical situation of the stockholder who does not want to receive dividends because he must pay a higher rate of personal income tax upon the dividends that he might receive than on the capital gains he may realize by selling the stock later on. Publicly owned corporations with scattered shareholders may not have to worry about stockholders of this kind, but closely held companies do sometimes give consideration to this factor in determining the amount of cash dividends to be distributed. In view of this fact, there exist Sections 531–37 of the United States Revenue Code. This provision of the Code may be used to penalize those corporations which unnecessarily retain earnings for the purpose of benefiting the personal income tax position of their shareholders. There exists a considerable body of specialized knowledge about how this provision must be regarded, but it will not be discussed here because of the narrow range of companies to which in fact it might be applied.

---

[2] Term Loan of General Baking Company, as stated in *Moody's Industrial Manual, 1960*, p. 1136.

Voting and Distributing the Dividend

Most U.S. corporations distribute dividends on a quarterly basis. Again, foreign practice is different, particularly in those countries in which dividends may not legally exceed current earnings and in which the dividend is paid at the end of the year when earnings are known. A few U.S. corporations pay only once a year, and an even smaller number pay a monthly dividend. The quarterly distribution may be considered standard practice, however.

When dividends are being paid on a regular basis, a certain meeting of the board comes to be recognized as the *dividend meeting*. At this meeting the directors decide the amount of the dividend and the form it will take: the date of payment and the *record date*. At the conclusion of the meeting a formal notice is often released to the financial press. Such a notice typically states that "The board of directors has this day declared a quarterly dividend of 25¢ per share on the capital stock of this corporation, payable September 15, 1971, to shareholders of record August 30, 1971." In other words, in order to have dividend checks available for all shareholders by September 15 the company has established a cutoff date of August 30: any investor who purchases the company's stock after August 30 will not receive a dividend check from the company. In the case of securities that are traded on registered stock exchanges, an *ex-dividend date* is established by the rules of the exchange. This date is based upon the record date minus a few days to provide for the mechanics of the delivery and transfer of securities. On and after this ex-dividend date the stock is sold without any claim to the dividend—which goes to the former owner—and, at least in theory, the market price of the share falls on the ex-dividend date by the amount of the dividend.

The Concept of a Dividend Policy

By a dividend policy we mean some kind of consistent approach to the distribution versus retention decision, rather than making the decision on a purely *ad hoc* basis from period to period. We should take note of the fact that some companies pay no cash dividends. This may simply arise from an inability to generate earnings, in which case the term "policy" is hardly applicable. There are, however, some situations in which earnings are being retained in full to finance further growth: this, as we shall demonstrate later in this chapter, may be a viable and indeed an optimal policy at some stage in the company's development. Few companies, however, state that nonpayment of dividends is their *long-term* policy. In general, therefore, the problem is not whether to pay a dividend but when and how much to pay.

The fact that a company makes a practice of paying cash dividends does not of itself constitute a dividend policy. Some companies act as if each dividend decision were completely independent of all previous decisions. In most cases, however, there is an element of continuity, and the current dividend decision is strongly related to previous dividend payments. This fact is recognized in the term *regular dividend*. In the usage of the securities market the regular dividend is that portion of a cash dividend which is expected to continue from year to year. Any extra payment which is not expected to be repeated in subsequent dividend periods is called a *special* or *extra dividend*. If, however, the additional earnings out of which the extra dividend has been paid prove to be permanent, the "extra" component is likely to be incorporated into an increased regular dividend. There is, in fact, a tendency for the market to expect any "extra" that has been paid for two or three consecutive periods to be repeated in all subsequent periods, and failure to do so may adversely affect the price of the company's common shares.

Determining Dividend Policy

We have shown that the decisions whether or not to pay a cash dividend—and if so, how much—are matters for the board's discretion. Are these important decisions? To answer this question, we must return to our basic objective of all financial management, the maximization of shareholder wealth.

The wealth that a shareholder attains through his ownership of common stock has two components: any cash dividends he receives and the capital gain he realizes when the stock is eventually sold. At first sight it would seem obvious, then, that the company's dividend policy is a direct determinant of stockholder wealth and a very important decision indeed. But this is an oversimplification. We have already pointed out that the common stockholders are the *owners* of the company. If a dollar is retained in the company for investment in assets instead of being paid out as a cash dividend, the common stockholders still own that dollar. The essential difference is that they cannot spend the dollar on current consumption needs. But if they still own the dollar, has the decision not to make a cash dividend distribution really had any effect on their wealth? Certainly the company's book value is increased by the dollar of retained earnings. But book values cannot be translated into capital gains automatically. The stockholder's potential capital gains depend not on the size of the company's asset base but on the market valuation of the company. The fact that a dollar has been retained in the company does not directly benefit the common stockholder, because neither now nor in the future will that dollar be available to him to spend. The question is, rather, whether the use of the dollar that has been retained will increase the company's market value—and therefore his own potential capital gain—enough to offset the loss of a dollar of current income. If in the shareholder's judgment the change in the company's market value will exactly offset the reduction in the stockholder's current cash income because earnings have been retained, the equity owners will be quite indifferent to the size of the cash dividend, and the distribution versus retention decision will be trivial. If not, the company's dividend policy will be an important factor in the determination of stockholder wealth.

We must now introduce a further complication. Any funds that are retained rather than paid out as cash dividends will presumably be used for productive purposes such as investment in new machinery. If the funds were distributed as dividends, it would presumably have been necessary to use debt funds to finance the new equipment or to sell additional equity. But there are situations in which the company can neither increase its debt any further without exceeding its debt capacity nor sell more stock. In such cases the distribution versus retention policy takes on an added importance, because the use of funds to pay cash dividends would inhibit the rate of growth of the company's earnings. We shall return to this situation later in the chapter. For the moment, however, we shall assume the simpler case that the distribution versus retention decision does not affect the company's future growth. Given this assumption, does dividend policy have any effect upon stockholder wealth? There has been considerable controversy on this point, and we shall briefly review the arguments advanced before we indicate our own position.

The hypothesis that stockholder wealth is essentially independent of dividend policy has been most ably advanced by Professors Franco Modigliani and Merton H. Miller,[3] and we shall follow a well-established precedent by referring to this school of thought as "M.M." The basic M.M. hypothesis is that, given a specific capital investment program, the firm's dividend policy is not important (remember that we are assuming for the moment that dividend policy does not affect the size of the capital investment program). M.M. presents a theoretical model, which is based upon a number of assumptions: (1) that all investors have access to all information, (2) that they behave rationally on the basis of that information, (3) that there are no transaction costs involved in buying or selling stock, and (4) that there is no difference between the tax rates on cash dividends and those on capital gains. Initially, they also assume certainty—that is, that investors know what the future earnings of every company are going to be. They show that under these circumstances dividend policy would indeed be unimportant. If the company decided to distribute some amount as a cash dividend and to replace by external financing the funds that would otherwise have been retained, then the

---

[3] Merton H. Miller and Franco Modigliani, "Dividend Policy, Growth, and the Valuation of Shares," *Journal of Business*, Vol. 34 (October, 1961), pp. 411–33.

external financing will depress the value of the preexisting common stock by exactly the amount of the dividend. The logic of M.M.'s arguments—given their assumptions—is impeccable.

Critics of the M.M. hypothesis have sought to show that differential tax treatment is *not* the only factor linking dividend policy and shareholder wealth. The major issue here is the effect of uncertainty. It has been argued, primarily by Professors Myron J. Gordon[4] and James E. Walter,[5] that as soon as it is accepted that investors do *not* know what the future earnings and dividends of corporations will be, they will demonstrate their inherent risk aversion by valuing a dollar of dividend paid now higher than a future payment that has a nominal "present value" of one dollar. Also, conditions of uncertainty will make them unwilling to supply their current consumption needs by borrowing as they await cash. In short, on the principle that "a bird in the hand is worth two in the bush," stockholders will consider present dividends less risky—and therefore more valuable—than dividends to be received at some time in the future.

We suggest that in practice there is no doubt that dividend policy *does* affect stockholder wealth. None of the M.M. assumptions apply in real life. There are important differences between the tax rates applied to cash dividend income and the tax treatment of capital gains. Most investors *are* risk-averse, and must always operate on the basis of limited information. The cost of obtaining *better information and the transaction costs* on the purchase and sale of stock *are* significant, especially for the small investor. Therefore, the M.M. hypothesis, interesting though it is, has no practical application, and stockholders do consider the corporation's dividend policy to be an important determinant of their wealth—or, more precisely, the utility they derive from it. Dividend policy is a most important management decision, and we cannot avoid discussing it in greater detail.

Dividend Policy under Capital Adequacy

We shall continue to assume, for the moment, that the corporation has ready access to additional external capital and the decision to pay a cash dividend does not make it necessary to forgo a profitable capital investment. In other words, the company's rate of growth in earnings is independent of dividend policy.

Under these circumstances the optimum dividend policy becomes a matter of selecting the balance between distribution and retention that maximizes the current share price. To be able to make this decision we

---

[4] Myron J. Gordon, *The Investment, Financing, and Valuation of the Corporation* (Homewood, Ill.: Richard D. Irwin, Inc., 1962).

[5] James E. Walter, "Dividend Policy: Its Influence on the Value of the Enterprise," *Journal of Finance*, Vol. 18 (May, 1963), pp. 280–91.

need a "market model" to relate the market value of the firm to earnings and dividends. Building such models has been another favorite occupation of finance writers in recent years. The results range from simplistic rules of thumb to highly complex formulations.

One of the most basic and best known valuation models was suggested by Professors Myron J. Gordon and Eli Shapiro.[6] Their article focused upon the rate of return at which a company's stock may be expected to sell—on the basis that the wealth of the stockholders will be maximized by equating the marginal rate of return on investment with this rate. They concluded that this rate of profit would be equal to the current dividend yield (current dividend divided by current price) plus a growth factor to represent the anticipated rate of growth of the company and its dividends:

$$K = \frac{\text{DIV}}{\text{PRICE}} + g \, .$$

Many more sophisticated models have since been developed, and we have discussed them in Chapter 10.

Most recent attempts to produce stock valuation models are based on the assumption that the value of a common share is equal to the present value of the certainty equivalents of the expected stream of future dividends on that share. We believe that this view is theoretically correct, taking into account as it does the time value of money, the pattern of future dividend payments, and investor risk aversion. Unfortunately, such models are not very useful as guides to dividend policy. Professors Alexander A. Robichek and Stewart C. Myers present one of the best explanations of such a model, but having done so they caution, "We do not expect the financial manager to be able to *compute* the optimal financing decision, at least in the foreseeable future . . . the problem in computation lies not in the implausibility of [the model] but in separating the effects of the independent variables."[7]

If there is as yet no fully satisfactory stock valuation model, how can the practicing financial executive decide what the company's dividend policy should be? We can give no ready-made answer to fit all circumstances, but there are some important generalizations to be made. Since dividends constitute taxable income for the shareholder, there is reason to consider retention favorably, but this must depend upon the preferences of the stockholders insofar as management is able to determine what these preferences are. Some companies have a high proportion of stockholders who rely on cash dividends to supply their consumption needs and have a very great preference for current over future dividends. A change to a high-retention/low-payout policy will clearly displease these

---

[6] Myron J. Gordon and Eli Shapiro, "Capital Equipment Analysis: The Required Rate of Profit," *Management Science*, Vol. 3 (October, 1956), pp. 102–10.

[7] Alexander A. Robichek and Stewart C. Myers, *Optimal Financing Decisions* (Englewood Cliffs, N.J.: Prentice-Hall, Inc., 1965), p. 108.

stockholders, and in the short run at least may lead to heavy selling and a decline in the price of the stock. Companies sometimes pay cash dividends and at the same time raise additional investment funds from the existing stockholders through preemptive issues of new common stock. This is a very questionable policy. The company would be better advised to retain the funds and thereby let the stockholders avoid the payment of income taxes on funds that are going to be reinvested in the company rather than used for current consumption.

Finally, it is clearly a highly suspect policy to pay out a cash dividend if the use of funds in this way makes it necessary to forgo potentially profitable investments and thus restricts growth. This brings us to the next subject.

Dividend Policy under Cash Inadequacy

We now relax the assumption that the corporation has free access to new external capital funds and that the dividend versus retention decision does not affect the scale of the capital investment program. There are many firms that cannot readily obtain additional funds. Earlier chapters of this book have pointed out that a company's debt capacity is not unlimited. A level of debt may be reached at which the debt burden is as much as can be safely carried, and the prudent executive will not add more burden to endanger the company's solvency. Even if the executives have not performed a debt capacity analysis of the kind we advocate, there comes a point beyond which lenders decline to provide further debt funds or charge a prohibitively high rate of interest for doing so. The sale of additional common stock is a possible alternative, but if the stock is selling at an unusually low price-earnings ratio, this route may be very unattractive. Considerations of control may also preclude the sale of additional common stock. In such a combination of circumstances there is an effective funds constraint, and any payment of cash dividends reduces the funds available for capital investment.

Another, less obvious situation exists when the management of the company imposes an artificial capital budget constraint. Many writers have pointed out that the interests of professional managers often differ from those of the company's owners. These professional managers are risk-averse and may value the safety of the company—and their own jobs—more than the maximization of stockholder wealth. This sometimes leads to a reluctance to use long-term debt funds and to a policy of financing all investments out of retained earnings, even though the company has not approached the limit of its safe debt capacity. If the common shareholders become aware that their management is adopting such a policy, the remedy is in their own hands.

Where the capital budget constraint is real rather than "administrative," however, the company's dividend policy becomes a major determinant of its possible rate of growth. Assuming that profitable capital investment opportunities are available in excess of the funds available from internal operations—that is, that inclusion of these projects produces a negative funds profile—then every dollar paid out as a cash dividend reduces the funds available for capital budget projects by *more than one dollar*. If, for example, the company has set itself a limiting debt-to-equity ratio of 40% and has reached that limit, then the switching of one dollar from dividend distribution to retention and reinvestment increases equity by one dollar and makes it possible to borrow 40 cents to restore the debt-to-equity ratio: capital budget funds have been increased by $1.40. In practice we do not advocate the use of such an arbitrary debt limit. A thorough "debt capacity" analysis should be performed. But the principle remains the same: adding to the equity base makes it possible to increase the debt burden without increasing the risk of insolvency beyond acceptable limits.

The dramatic effect that a reduction in cash dividend distribution may have on a company's growth in such circumstances is best shown through an example.

One of the cases in this book, Nautilus, Inc. (page 793), describes a situation in which management must face up to the problems we have just described. Nautilus, a company with very considerable growth potential, will not be able to realize this potential unless its capital budget constraints can be relaxed. These constraints arise out of the preferences and prejudices of various interest groups. The company's founders have recently agreed to an issue of common stock that will produce a one-third dilution in their control of the company and are very unlikely to accept any further equity financing for some time. The company's commercial bank urges that debt should be limited to one third of total capitalization. The investment bankers who are underwriting the current equity issue insist that the company should undertake to start laying out 50% of its net after-tax earnings as cash dividends after a few years. The combination of these factors means that funds available for capital investment and for additions to working capital will be limited to one half of net after-tax earnings plus the additional debt that can be matched with these retained funds without infringing the 33% debt constraint. This means that each $2 of earnings will generate only $1.50 of capital investment funds: the $1 retained from earnings plus 50¢ of additional debt to maintain the maximum permissible debt-equity ratio.

The various exhibits to the case show how these constraining factors can be expected to inhibit the company's growth. Given free access to additional long-term funds, the company's potential growth would be limited only by demand, and in the 10-year planning period used in the case, its total revenues could reach $55 million, with after-tax earnings of $4.4 million (Exhibit 3). Given the limits on external financing, however, the adoption of a 50% dividend distribution halfway through the planning period would limit end-of-period sales to $42 million and after-tax earnings to $3.2 million (Exhibit 6). Having said this, we have by no means "solved" the case. It remains to be decided what changes, if any, the company should make in its policies, and we have not discussed one of the major issues relative to this decision. It is conceivable that the 50% distribution policy, though it clearly does not maximize the company's growth, does maximize the shareholders' wealth. The important thing is that the decision maker must be aware of the effect of the distribution policy upon growth rate as one of the major inputs to his decision problem.

A somewhat similar situation can be found in the SCM company case (page 807). The primary topic of this case is a choice between stock dividends and cash dividends, and their respective contributions to stockholder wealth. The reader will find it interesting, however, to determine for himself how a more generous cash dividend distribution might affect the company's growth. The approach used in Nautilus can readily be adapted to this case.

We have now demonstrated that in certain circumstances a policy of generous cash dividend distribution—or indeed any cash dividend distribution—may constrain the company's growth. The key issue is whether or not such a constraint will also reduce stockholder wealth. Once again, we can give no universal, ready-made decision rule. We need a stock valuation model which tells us what weights or preferences investors will apply to expected rates of growth in sales and earnings versus dividend payments. No fully operational model exists. An approach developed by Professor James E. Walter[8] is of considerable interest, however. Walter suggests that the key factor should be a comparison between the internal rate of return available on investment projects and the "market rate" demanded by investors: if the internal rate is greater than the market rate, the stock price will be maximized by retentions and will vary inversely with dividend payout. We do not believe that Walter provides convincing proof of his model, or that the relationship is quite as simple as this—or that a "market rate" is easily determinable. Nevertheless, his approach has intuitive appeal, and the direction of the relationship is undoubtedly correct. In other words, a company such as Nautilus, faced with highly attractive investment opportunities and limited investment funds, will maximize the wealth of its stockholders by paying no cash dividends during this growth phase of its corporate history.

We must emphasize at this point an observation that was made earlier in this chapter. The "double taxation" on funds distributed as cash dividends makes it undesirable for a company to distribute its earnings while at the same time selling additional common stock to raise funds.

---

[8] James E. Walter, "Dividend Policies and Common Stock Prices," *Journal of Finance*, Vol. 11 (March, 1956), pp. 29–41.

In a company experiencing financing constraints of the kind described above and working under capital rationing, such a policy is even more difficult to justify. The Nautilus case is again relevant. The company is clearly undercapitalized in relation to its growth opportunities and needs to increase its equity base—a fact which the treasurer clearly recognizes. The impairment of the equity by a generous cash dividend distribution simply exacerbates the problem.

The Dividend as Information

Up to this point we have been concerned with the absolute level of dividends and their effects upon growth, share prices, and stockholder wealth. We now add one further complication. When a company makes a change in its dividend policy, the change alone may significantly affect share prices, irrespective of the absolute level of the dividend. This phenomenon exists because dividend policy is a form of communication between the company's management and its stockholders.

The real world is characterized by uncertainty. Investors do not know what the future earnings or dividends of companies are going to be. The information available to them is limited. The best source of such information is corporate management. Management's predictions may be transmitted to investors either indirectly (through security analysts) or directly (in the annual report and other media). But investors are eager for more information, and management's actions are interpreted as signals of management's beliefs about the company's future. Thus, an increase in the dividend payout is likely to be seen as a signal that management believes the company to be entering a period of ample cash flow. A reduction in the dividend, on the other hand, is seen as a signal that things are going wrong—probably much more so than the company is admitting in its published statements.

The information content in the dividend policy produces something of a paradox for the growing company operating under a capital budget constraint. The appearance of unusually attractive investment opportunities that cannot be financed out of external sources probably means that the cash dividend should be reduced or eliminated, and such a policy change would in fact be a sign of strength. But it is likely to be interpreted by stockholders and the investment community in general as a sign of weakness unless the company has undertaken a very careful public relations campaign. The moral is, rather obviously, that management should be reluctant to establish the dividend distribution at any level if there is any possibility that it cannot be maintained at that level indefinitely. We suggest that a company's true income—using "income" to mean funds available for financial expenditures such as the burden of debt and cash dividends, rather than the figure calculated by accountants—is simply whatever is left over *after paying the price of staying in the business.*

In high-growth, high-technology industries this price may be high—certainly much higher than simple provision for replacement of existing equipment—but unless this price is paid, there can be no certainty that payment of dividends in the current period is not damaging the company's ability to maintain that level of dividend in the future. The need for some way of determining a figure for true income—the discretionary funds, if any, left over after capital investment and working capital needs have been met—is, of course, precisely why we developed the concept of the "funds profile" introduced in Chapter 20.

Dividends in Practice

Dividend policy is, as we have shown, both an important decision and an extremely difficult one. No basis for computing an optimum policy that will maximize long-run stockholder wealth is yet available, and the distribution decision must still be largely intuitive. It is hardly surprising, then, that wide variations exist in practice, from the high but arbitrary cash payout to the opposite extreme in which the dividend is regarded as a pure residual after all investment needs have been met.

There is growing evidence, however, that many companies do make use of a policy that broadly agrees with the recommendations made above. Downward dividend fluctuations are avoided where possible because of the negative information content that such fluctuations carry. Companies tend to use caution in raising the level of dividends, making increases only when there is reasonable certainty that the new level can be maintained. Professor John Lintner published an important paper in 1956,[9] in which he concluded that when companies experience increased earnings, they tend to increase dividends only after a time lag, and not by the full extent of the earnings increase. Conversely, companies are unwilling to reduce dividends even when earnings decline.

There is some evidence that the stock market's expectations—that is, the way Wall Street believes that companies *should* behave—closely resemble the Lintner model. Companies that enjoy increasing earnings are expected to pass some part of this increase on to the stockholders in the form of increased dividends. It is recognized, though, that the prudent company will want to wait and make sure that the higher level of earnings will be maintained, and a time lag between earnings increase and dividend change is not penalized.

A most interesting recent study by John A. Brittain[10] sought to determine the basis upon which companies make their dividend decisions by testing various decision models against empirical data. The model

---

[9] John Lintner, "Distribution of Incomes of Corporations among Dividends, Retained Earnings and Taxes," *American Economic Review*, Vol. 46 (May, 1956), pp. 97–113.

[10] John A. Brittain, *Corporate Dividend Policy* (Washington, D.C.: Brookings Institution, 1966).

giving the best fit was a modification of Lintner's, substituting cash flows for corporate earnings. In other words, companies appear to increase dividends some time after an improvement in their internal cash generation becomes apparent, and the payout is raised only to a level that management believes can safely be maintained. The reader may like to explore for himself the implications of a further modification of this model, substituting the funds profile for corporate cash generation.

PART VIII

THE BARGAIN FOR FUNDS

GENERAL INTRODUCTION TO PART VIII

Each corporate security issue is made up of a number of rights and duties running between *the issuer*, the corporation that offered the security, and the person who owns the security. Some of these are established by law and apply to all securities of a certain type. For example, interest on bonds may be deducted by the issuer among the tax-deductible expenses, while the dividends on preferred stock may not. Or, common stockholders may hold corporate directors responsible to make decisions in their interest, while bondholders can ask for no more than strict accordance with their contract.

The greater part of the conditions of a security issue, despite the increasing complexity and volume of legislation in this area, is set by the terms of its particular contract, which is drafted while negotiations progress. It is, therefore, correct to say that the specific terms under which a group of investors makes funds available to a business are the result of a bargaining process between the investors and the management of the corporation. As in any bargain, the final terms represent a workable compromise which embodies the essential objectives of both parties. For example, it is obvious that any investor will want to have the highest possible return on his investment and at the same time have the maximum assurance that his income will be received and his principal protected. The issuing company, however, will wish, from the point of view of its common shareholders, to minimize the costs associated with the financing and to preserve maximum flexibility in the payments and terms to which it becomes committed. The terms of the actual security issue must somehow reconcile these conflicting objectives.

Despite the fact that all categories of investors are anxious to achieve a "maximum" return on their investment, an agreement is possible because different kinds of investors want their position guaranteed by safeguards of varying strength. An investor who is concerned about steady, moderate income and the safety of his capital, for example, might easily furnish funds with adequate safeguards to a risk taker who is willing to run a substantial chance of losing all his capital if he can double his money in a short time. The first man might accept relatively low rewards if the venture was a success in return for the safety given by first claim on certain valuable assets if it failed. The risk-taking investor would gain the majority of the fruits of success but, in return for assistance in financing this opportunity, would stand to lose much more heavily in the event of a failure. Needless to say, each category of investor is anxious to secure his objectives as much as possible by placing limitations on the positions of the other classes of investors. Over the years a large variety of investment forms and terms have been developed to define these relationships, and it is in the negotiation of the specific terms that the bargaining takes place.

In a sense the bargaining process does not stop when the terms are set and the issue sold but can continue on in the form of negotiations for modification of the terms of the agreement to meet changing operating conditions and financial needs. With respect to this process, there is a major difference between a private sale to a few institutional investors (or a term loan from a bank or a lease) and a public issue of bonds. The direct relationship between the company and its security holders implicit in the private placement affords greater opportunities for the borrower to renegotiate any terms that have been found unduly burdensome. The investment officers of the institution, which perhaps may be eager for future business from the company, can examine the situation and relatively quickly determine what modifications are reasonable. The two parties can thus understand each other's positions quickly and reach a decision on the action required.

In a public issue, on the other hand, a change in the provisions may require soliciting the vote of hundreds or thousands of individual security holders. With unregistered securities the task of merely identifying the owners can be staggering, requiring a major expenditure of corporate managerial resources. The investment banker can help in the process of solicitation, but unlike his role of "representing the investor" in the initial negotiations, he himself cannot commit the investors to a position. Because changes in the terms of a public issue are so difficult, corporations issuing such securities are wise to seek the maximum flexibility in the construction of the agreement which the investment banker believes investors will accept.

It should not be inferred from the concept of security planning as a negotiated procedure that each and every term of the issue is carefully weighed and debated before it is included. In fact, manuals exist in which many standard clauses are to be found. We start with the three basic and considerably standardized security forms of bonds, preferred stock, and common stock, the primary features of which have been well established in company law, corporate charters, and investors' standards. The precedent of accepted corporate practice in a given industry has a great deal to do with the form which new issues take. There are also the regulations of government agencies such as the Securities and Exchange Commission, which have an influence on the terms that shall be included or excluded, as well as the regulations of the organized exchanges. The general economic and business conditions at the time of issue have a bearing. All these things tend to narrow the range of security features which may be negotiated before the precise form of the security is finally decided.

It is important to recognize that when company officials make some concession in price, income, or other terms to a group of security holders in order to have a successful offering, what they concede is a portion of what would otherwise belong to other security holders. It is a process of allocating the benefits that exist, not of creating values out of nothing. The tangible gain to the company resulting from a security sale on unusually favorable terms is a gain to the other security holders. A sale of bonds at a relatively higher interest rate means lower net earnings per share of common stock. A preferred stock which has the cumulative feature means a greater hazard to common dividends than would be the case if it was noncumulative. A further common issue offered to new stockholders and priced at an unusual discount from market price in order to assure ready sale means added dilution of the investment of existing common shareholders. Thus, the ultimate bargain is not between the new security holders and management as such but rather between one class of security holders and another. In this connection, we remind the reader that we have consistently emphasized the essential responsibility of management to act as the representative of the common shareholder. Despite the inability to create something out of nothing, one can bring a greater part of the benefits to each equity dollar received, and this often increases the value of the equity holding.

We are now ready to extend our consideration of long-term finance to take account of the influence which variations in the circumstances and objectives of both issuers and investors have on the terms of the investment contract. Over a period of many years the basic security types have been subject to a considerable variety of modifications in an effort to have them meet more precisely the special needs of particular investors and business corporations. A complete catalog of kinds of securities would be almost endless and never quite up to date, for the possibilities of special arrangements are limited only by the imagination of the draftsman.

Our purpose is to show, by reference to the more commonly used variations, how these features come into being in the bargaining process between issuer and investor. A review of these features should stimulate the reader to invent new terms when necessary to suit the conditions of particular problems that he one day comes to face.

We shall first introduce the form of financing known as the lease, so far not described in this book. It often serves as a special form of debt. In Chapters 23 and 24 we shall return to the variations in the details of bonds, preferred stock, and common stock as they may be negotiated at the time of issue. In Chapter 25 we shall describe how changes may be made in issues after they have become outstanding. Finally, in Chapter 26, we shall take up the influence on corporate financial practices of the federal regulatory agency known as the Securities and Exchange Commission, and other agencies.

chapter 22

Leasing as an Alternative
to Ownership

The common purpose of the various types of security contracts is to raise funds which are used to acquire the assets used by a firm. But since the use of assets for a desired period of time can often be made fully available through rental rather than ownership, financial managers often have the option to arrange contracts of rental rather than being limited to ways to finance ownership. We shall deal with the advantages and disadvantages of this alternative in this chapter.

Long-term rental arrangements are usually called leases. From the points of view of finance and accounting, the unique feature of a leasing contract is that although the lessee is entitled to the use of the asset, legal title is retained by the lessor, who continues to own it. Thus arises the term *off-the-balance-sheet financing,* for under present accounting conventions the user of the property cannot show it among his assets, and the periodic obligations to pay rent are not shown as liabilities until they become due. At the same time, of course, the value of the property appears on the balance sheet of the lessor, who is the holder of the legal title.

There are many types of rental arrangements which are of short duration, or cancelable, or otherwise not important as alternatives to long-term ownership. A *financial lease,* with which we are now concerned, has two distinguishing characteristics. The first is the fixed nature of the obligation. Whenever a lease is noncancelable and runs over a long period of time, it produces a financial burden on the lessee similar to that of a debt. Second, under a financial lease a lessee promises payments which, in total, exceed the purchase price of the assets that are leased. Usually also, though not necessarily, a financial lease is a "net" lease. That is, the tenant agrees to pay property taxes, maintain the property, etc., as if he were the owner. Thus, a financial lease can be described as "a practicable alternative to ownership of the asset by the company, with the decision between owning and leasing turning on financial rather than operating consideration."[1]

Thus, once more, we see that the scope of finance is broader than the confines of a balance sheet. Management must provide the firm with the use of properties needed for its activities, either by ownership or by rental. We are familiar with the idea that assets are acquired by the creation of securities which appear as liabilities. The promises made under lease contracts are just as binding as those under security contracts, although no asset or liability appears. In fact, we regard payments under long-term lease arrangements to be part of the burden of financing and in the same category as the servicing of a bond issue. In doing so, we are continuing our assumption that obligations should be compared as they are seen by solvent, going concerns as they plan their financial commitments.

Nevertheless, the reader should know that the ultimate consequences of default under a lease are different from those if bonded debt exists. In case of breach of contract (known in the financial world as *default*), the lessor may repossess his property,[2] but in bankruptcy his claim for damages may not exceed 1 year's future rent if a liquidation results from the failure, or 3 years' rent if the company undergoes reorganization, no matter how long the lease had to run. The holder of a bond, on the other hand, is a creditor for the entire principal of his claim against a defaulting debtor. But even if the bond is secured by a mortgage, the property cannot be taken away without a court order, which is seldom forthcoming unless a complete liquidation has been decided upon. He is "locked in" to the situation, although the value of the mortgaged property is recognized as assigned to him.

Examples of Leasing Arrangements

The parties to contractual relationships that are found in a financial lease can be diagrammed as in Chart 22–1. In studying this chart, the reader should remember that the functions of selling, titleholding, and investing may be performed by one company, two companies, or three.

For example, we refer to the financing arranged by American Airlines, Inc., to provide the engines for its jet fleet. The producers, to use the term in the chart, were the manufacturers of the engines. Each of these producers established a leasing subsidiary to act as titleholder of the engines. The engines were purchased by these subsidiaries, using funds provided by investors, and leased to the airline on terms that amortized

---

[1] D. R. Gant, "Illusion in Lease Financing," *Harvard Business Review*, March–April, 1959, p. 122.

[2] If the tenant, although in default on other obligations and bankrupt, continues rental payments, the landlord may not repossess the property.

the purchase price and provided interest at about 4⅛% per year. The transaction "saved" the airline a capital investment estimated at $67 million at a time when public placement of stock would have been possible only at depressed prices, and when the company, because of existing loans, would probably have had to use subordinated debt if it had attempted to borrow in the investment market. Other airlines have followed this initiative.

A variant on the use of a private company as titleholder is found when a corporation leases a property from a municipality, which borrows the funds needed to build the plant by issuing revenue bonds, whose interest is tax-exempt. The tax exemption feature usually permits the setting of much lower rental charges than would otherwise be possible, and these low charges have been used as inducements to industry to locate in a certain place.

Chart 22–1

Relationships in a Typical Financial Lease

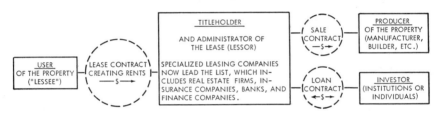

No doubt this arrangement was developed from the model provided for many years by the "equipment trust," widely used to supply rolling stock to railroads. It is one of the earliest examples of a specialized financial lease. Today, the varieties of leasing arrangements are almost endless, with new variations being heard of frequently, as the use of this extremely flexible form of financing is extended. It is in the extension of its use that one sees the change. One can now find leasing arrangements offered for such items as office equipment, large and small computers, all kinds of production tooling, engines for aircraft, the aircraft themselves, entire corporations, general-purpose buildings, buildings built to the tenant's specification, and many fleets of cars and trucks. In fact, leasing companies are ready to offer terms for consideration almost any time a firm is studying how to finance the acquisition of a specific property.

A great advantage of the leasing arrangement is that it is available to finance amounts too small to be of interest to major institutional lenders or the public market. It is an important device in the expansion period of a small business and a very convenient one for larger companies when their needs are small and a specific asset is to be purchased.

Immensely popular in the 1930's and 1940's, and still a device in use, is the *sale-and-leaseback* arrangement. This is a device which exists if company A, already the owner of a property, sells it to B and immediately leases it for continued use. The new lessee, A, then has in his possession the use of the property as well as the cash received from the sale. For a time this seemed like magic to many people in the financial world, but it is now recognized that the device has the same essential feature as any lease: namely, the granting of the use of a property in return for a series of rental payments. It is dramatic to see an existing property exchanged for cash while the property continues to be used as before, but the financial effects are the same as they would be if the property were newly acquired.

The Avoidance of Investment

By surrendering the benefits of holding title to a property, a lessee may avoid the need to buy it. In order to be concrete, we shall use the actual problem of a chain of variety stores which projected a new branch to cost $225,000, a sum made up of land, $25,000; building, $150,000; and certain basic equipment, $50,000. The financial officers of the chain store company found a group of investors who operated in the area of the proposed store. This group offered to build the store to the tenant's specifications and to lease it for 25 years, with annual rentals as follows: first 10 years, $22,035; next 15 years, $11,583. If this lease were accepted, the variety chain would not have immediately to pay out $225,000 to establish the new outlet.

But the belief that the company in this example has "released" $225,000 for other business purposes by using a lease is quite superficial. Such an idea contains the implicit assumptions both that the funds in question exist in the business already and that we can ignore the way in which they were obtained. We cannot. The lease should be regarded as a case of a loan of 100% of the needed funds—$225,000. The outflows to meet the obligations of the lease are fixed and represent the burdens of financing just as much as the promises which accompany borrowing. Surely, the acceptance of the proposed lease will consume a portion of the company's total capacity to arrange debt financing. In purely logical terms the debt capacity that is consumed must be equal to that of borrowing to raise the same amount of funds. If the advantages of the lease are to be tested against alternatives, the comparison should be made between the obligations of the lease and those of a debt contract that might actually be arranged. The latter financing would create a balance sheet asset of $225,000, balanced by a debt of the same amount.

Further on in this chapter we shall describe an analysis to determine whether it is better to borrow or to lease the property. Here, it is sufficient to point out that a lease uses up credit. One might expect that it would use up as much of the company's borrowing capacity as a loan of equivalent terms. Altogether too many leases have been signed without recognition of this matter, as evidenced from time to time by the bankruptcy of a firm with small debts but heavy rental obligations.

The frequent appearance of a prohibition or limitation of the extent of leasing as well as of further borrowing among the protective provisions of loan contracts is additional evidence that the financial world is recognizing the essential similarity of lease obligations to those incurred by long-term borrowing. Thus, in the case of the variety chain, the firm will obtain $225,000 in funds (in the form of the desired store) in return for fixed contractual obligations to pay rent, as stated above.

Effect on Borrowing Capacity

Two factors exist, however, which sometimes permit a company to raise more funds by leases than by debt. One of these factors is that the title to leased property remains in the control of the lessor. It cannot be touched by the creditors of the lessee. If, instead, the property in question had been bought and financed by a mortgage and there were a default, the investor would have to await foreclosure, which is at best a slow and expensive process. In fact, if the property can be expected always to have a value to others, a lease may be the only way a financially embarrassed corporation can obtain the use of new equipment. For example, Northeast Airlines, Inc., financially weak at the time, obtained the use of new jet-powered equipment through a leasing arrangement, and many a weak manufacturer has leased new tools when its general credit was exhausted. In order to obtain such a result, however, the criterion that the property is sure to be valuable to others must be met without any possibility of doubt. The more the leased property becomes special purpose, the more the general credit of the company limits its power either to lease or to borrow.

A second factor that may sometimes permit a company to raise more funds by lease than by debt is that the burdens the lease creates are not evidenced by liabilities on the balance sheet. The result may be that certain grantors of credit will not take the leasehold obligations fully into account and thus will be more liberal than if an equivalent debt were to appear. There is evidence that this situation does exist, despite the efforts of accountants, the Securities and Exchange Commission, and others to provide full disclosure.[3] At the present time, however, this condition has dwindled in importance. What is more important to say in this book is

---

[3] The Accounting Principles Board of the American Institute of Certified Public Accountants, in *Opinions of the Accounting Principles Board*, No. 5 (September, 1964), recommends that "financial statements should disclose sufficient information regarding material, noncancellable leases . . . to enable the reader to assess the effect of lease commitments upon the financial position and results of operations, both present and prospective, of the lessee." This information is to be given in the statements themselves, or in accompanying notes.

that no financial manager who contemplates a lease obligation should allow himself to be deceived. Contractual rental obligations from his point of view are charges as fixed as the elements of the burden of bonds.

The Question of Terminal Values

The lease is a device which separates the possibility to use the property from its ownership for the period of the lease. At the expiration of the lease, the property is returned to the lessor together with all permanent improvements installed by the lessee. Thus, the managers of the variety chain must recognize that the lease gives them less than full ownership would. An argument favoring ownership over leasing that is frequently heard is, therefore, that the values that will exist at the terminal date of a lease are too great to give up. Certain types of property may enjoy a high sale value at the time the lease expires, and it may be desirable to hold title for the purpose of gaining from this residual value. The argument is especially attractive for well-situated real estate, since it is well known that substantial profits are often made in this way. While conceding the attractiveness of this line of thinking, we urge the reader to note carefully the fact that money which may be received in the distant future has far less value in the present than its future amount makes it seem to have. It is often far better to conserve funds for immediate purposes, as the earnings thus obtained will be more than the expected long-run windfall. We shall test this point as we develop the example of the variety chain.

It is also to be noted that the terms of many leasing contracts are now being written with an allowance for a terminal value which alters the required lease payments in favor of the lessee, implicitly or explicitly. It is our conclusion that careful negotiation of the terms of a lease can overcome the disadvantage of loss of title, unless major capital gains are very certain. We shall discuss this matter further, later on in this chapter.

Tax Advantage in Leasing

While the owner of property must suffer taxes on the income it produces, he has depreciation expense to create tax shields. This is the situation of lessors, like all other owners. The person using property belonging to another must also suffer taxes on the income it produces, but tax shields are created by the rental payments he must make. Out of these facts arise the possibility that the tax shields available from leasing as an alternative to ownership may be more desirable. There is little doubt that the lease came into popularity in the 1930's largely because it would permit a far more favorable schedule of tax shields than was available to owners under the then existing laws and regulations.

For example, when straight-line depreciation was substantially the only method owners could use for tax purposes, and a commercial building was often required to be depreciated over 67 years, the maximum tax shield in any year, per thousand dollars of such an investment, was ($1,000 ÷ 67) (0.48) = $7.17, given a tax rate of 48%. With such constraints on ownership, it was easy to set up a lease obligation under which the rental payments produced larger tax shields in the early years of the life of the property. For example, a 25-year lease with equal payments of the capital value would create a tax shield on $1,000 invested in a building of $19.20 instead of $7.17, but, of course, only for the 25-year period of the lease.

Today, when the term of depreciable life has been shortened by the new "guidelines" and one may select a scheme of depreciation with heavy charges in early years, it is much less likely that a lease will offer tax-shield advantages that preempt any consideration of other advantages and disadvantages of leasing. Advantage may remain in favor of the lease when the property contains a good proportion of land, which is not depreciable, or when some asset must be depreciated more slowly than over the period of the lease, or when the lease, as in the case of the variety chain, has heavy rental payments in the early years. But even these advantages are small, if any terminal values for the land or slowly depreciating property have been allowed for in the terms of the lease.

Substantial tax advantages still exist for certain types of lessors, but this side of the matter will not be explored here.

The Cost of the Arrangement

It is as necessary to have some idea of the cost of raising funds by leasing as it is to have a figure for the cost of borrowing. In the first place, it is an important part of the average cost of capital (page 192) which is too often forgotten. Sometimes, the cost is explicitly stated. If not, it is useful to know that studies show that the interest cost of funds provided by lease runs from a minimum of the same rate to 2% higher than could be negotiated on a loan of equivalent amount and terms. The discrepancy varies according to several factors, including the general credit standing of the lessee and the ease with which the leased property could be transferred to other use following a default.

The implicit cost of a lease may be computed, as in the case of a bond, by tabulating the outflows it requires, considering the initial value provided and the terminal value to be expected, and working out the internal rate of return (page 168). But this is sometimes easy to say and hard to do, because some of the required quantities may be difficult to obtain. The schedule of rents is not always absolutely fixed, it is often not possible to know the terminal value that should be used for the value of the remaining property, and it may even be difficult to learn the price at which the property could be acquired for cash—a number which to most analysts represents the value provided by the lease financing.

The variety store in our example knows the cash price of the property it may lease; it is $225,000. To avoid paying out this sum, the firm accepts the schedule to pay $22,035 annually at the end of each of the first 10 years, and $11,583 at the ends of years 11 through 25. The "internal rate of return" worked out from these figures is 6% before taxes, which reduces to 3.12% after a 48% tax shield is taken into account. The calculation ignores the question of terminal values, which will be dealt with below.

Years	Amount	6% Factor	Present Value
1–10.................	$22,035	7.3601	$162,180
11–25.................	11,583	5.4233	62,818
			$224,998

Ownership versus Leasing, an Example

If the reader has accepted our position that a lease, because of its fixed obligations, must be regarded as a form of borrowing by a potential lessee, its desirability can only be tested against the alternative of borrowing an equivalent amount of funds. In practice one compares with alternatives that are possible. They may call for payments on slightly different terms. Here, in order to focus only on the two distinguishing features of leases, we assume the alternative of a debenture debt for the whole $225,000 with the same repayment terms and interest rate as the lease. This gives us the opportunity to compare ownership with leasing in an instance where the differences are confined to the tax treatment which is afforded the lease payments, as contrasted with the depreciation which is granted with ownership, and to the ownership of the terminal value. We shall deal with these in the order named.

The schedule of after-tax cash flows demanded by the lease is easily derived, for if the lease is used, all of the annual rent is a tax-deductible expense. In each of the first 10 years, the payment of $22,035 results in a tax shield of $10,577 (at 48% rate), so that the net cash flow is $11,458. In the ensuing period, the annual rent is $11,583, and the net cash flow is $6,023. These net cash outflows called for by the lease are pictured cumulatively, in Chart 22–2. The total of the yearly after-tax figures over the 25-year period is $204,925.

To make a schedule of the after-tax cash flows for the borrowing is more difficult, because not all the annual payment is to be treated as expense for tax purposes. Instead, a tax shield must be computed from the total of the interest paid on the loan plus the allowable depreciation expense. This total is then deducted from the before-tax payment to produce the after-tax cash outflow to be compared with the lease. The authors have done this work for each of the 25 years, and the cumulative figures appear

Chart 22–2

Accumulated After-Tax Cash Outflows in Bond versus Lease
Methods of Financing an Investment of $225,000

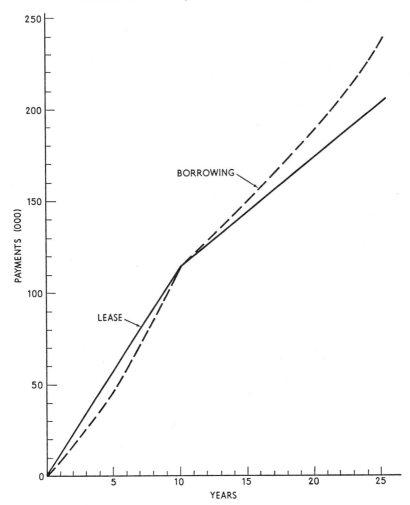

in Chart 22–2. We shall give the details from our table only for the first 2 years, to show the way the numbers change.

The assumed loan, following the payment pattern established by the lease, contains two parts. One part is a fixed loan for the first 10 years of $112,500. It is amortized in years 11–25 by the annual payment of $11,583. In each of the first 10 years, it requires interest expense at 6% of $6,750.

The second part of the loan is also $112,500, to be amortized in the first 10 years.

The first annual payment of $22,035 may be subdivided as follows:

$ 6,750—Interest on the first (constant) part of the loan.
 6,750—Interest on the second part of the loan.
$13,500—Total interest expense.
 8,535—The balance, used to reduce the principal of the second part
         of the loan.

The second annual payment, reflecting the reduction of the second part of the loan by $8,535 from $112,500 to $103,965, may be subdivided as follows:

$ 6,750—Interest on the constant part of the loan.
 6,238—Interest on the reducing part of the loan.
$12,988—Total interest expense.
 9,047—The balance, used to reduce the principal.
$22,035

Following this procedure, the interest expense for each of the 25 years may be computed.

	Year	
	1	2
Interest.	$13,500	$12,988
Depreciation.	17,500	15,125
Total expense.	$31,000	$28,113
Tax shield, 48%.	$14,880	$13,494
Before-tax payment.	22,035	22,035
After-tax payment.	$ 7,155	$ 8,541

Having obtained the interest expense, we must also know the depreciation expense in order to have the total expenses from which we may compute the tax shield, year by year. In the case of ownership of the $225,000 investment, the $25,000 cost of land may not be depreciated. The new "guidelines" permit a 10-year schedule for the equipment and 40 years for the building. The greatest tax advantage lies in using one of the accelerated methods now available, and we have chosen to use the "double-declining-balance-shifting-to-straight-line" scheme. On this basis, the depreciation for the first year is $10,000 and $8,000 for the second year on the equipment costing $50,000. It is $7,500 for the first year and $7,125 for the second year for the $150,000 building.

The tax-deductible expenses for the first 2 years appear in the accompanying table, together with a computation of the tax shield. We are now able to calculate the net after-tax cash outflow related to the loan.

Having completed work of this kind for each of the 25 years, we find the total of the outflows to be $236,282, which is $31,357 larger than the total of after-tax outflows demanded by the lease. It is interesting to ask ourselves why this difference exists. It must be due to the difference in tax shields, because other possible variables, such as the rate of interest and the schedule of payments, were assumed to be the same. The lease permits the tenant to take as expense all of the $225,000 invested in the property. But in the case of ownership, only the equipment is fully depreciated. Therefore, only the first 25 years of the 40-year schedule for the building has been used, totaling $109,672. And the land is not depreciated at all. These figures show that in 25 years ownership will develop a tax shield of ($159,672) (0.48) = $76,643, or $31,357 less than the tax shield the lease provides, ($225,000) (0.48) = $108,000.

Chart 22–2 shows that the lease payments are more demanding than the bond payments during the first 10 years but that the opposite is true during the second period, after the rental rate falls. Since the eye is not able to perform "time adjustment" calculations, it is necessary to find a present value for each of the two schedules in order to have commensurate figures for our use. We have done this work at the rate of 3.12%, which is the after-tax cost of a loan at the before-tax rate of 6%. This is taken as the opportunity cost of credit for the case at hand. The total of the present values of the annual outflows under the lease is $149,421, and under the borrowing, it is $164,784. From this we learn that the initial advantage of the borrowing is more than overcome by the later advantage of the lease.

But we cannot leave the matter at this point. The question of terminal value still faces us. By accepting the lease arrangement, the management of the variety chain would be giving up whatever the terminal values may be, and we need to know whether these values are less than or greater than the difference that, so far, favors the lease. The difference in the present values is $15,363, but this is a number evaluated at the outset of the financing. It tells us that the lease form of providing its needs will leave the firm with funds for other uses that are the equivalent of the immediate investment of $15,363. We have gone to the statements of the variety chain in question and found that it can be expected to earn 9% after taxes. By compounding at this rate, we find that $132,476 is the equivalent sum, the present value of $15,363, at the end of the 25th year.

Although there are reasons behind the ruling of the tax authorities that land does not depreciate, and also reasons why store buildings are depreciated over 40 years, it would be hard to predict that these assets, with a book value of $65,000, will have a realizable value over twice as much at the end of the 25th year. We would feel safe in advising the managers of the variety chain to take the lease arrangement.

Nevertheless, we must remind the reader that the question of terminal values is always present. Where the tax advantages of a lease are not as great as in our example, some bargaining over the matter can be expected, resulting in terms of a lease more favorable to the lessee. It is more and more being recognized that the $225,000 in funds provided by the lease is only for the use of the property and that a lessee who gives up ownership is in reality adding the forgone terminal value to the more easily seen costs of his lease.

Lease Obligations, Burden Coverage, and Debt Ratios

In Chapter 18, at page 348, we defined the burden of a debt and we suggested certain ratios that are useful to relate the burden to the earnings or cash inflows of the borrower, and to measure the degree of trading on the equity. For analyzing a company with large lease obligations, we recommend including these lease payments as part of the financial burden and relating the burden thus found to earnings before interest, lease payments, and taxes (E.B.I.L.T.) instead of earnings before interest and taxes (E.B.I.T.). The necessary amounts can be determined from most published statements, and will, of course, be available to the management of a specific company.

Suppose, for example, we are to analyze the debt position of a company that reports an invested capital of $65,000, made up as follows:

Long-term debt...............	$15,000
Capital stock and surplus.......	50,000
	$65,000

The income statement shows:

E.B.I.T.....................	$14,000
Interest expense..............	750
Taxable income.........	$13,250

We also learn from footnotes to the company's statements that there are long-term lease payments of $3,000 a year and that assets with a cost of $50,000 were provided under the lease. The figures above can be adjusted as follows:

Long-term debt and leasehold value.....	$ 65,000
Capital stock and surplus...........	50,000
	$115,000

E.B.I.L.T............................	$ 17,000
Burden of debt and leases............	3,750
Taxable income...............	$ 13,250

We then find:

Burden coverage:

$$\text{Unadjusted} \ldots \ldots \ldots \ldots \frac{14,000}{750} = 18.7$$

$$\text{Adjusted} \ldots \ldots \ldots \ldots \frac{17,000}{3,750} = 4.5$$

Equity ratio:

$$\text{Unadjusted} \ldots \ldots \ldots \ldots \frac{50,000}{65,000} = 77\%$$

$$\text{Adjusted} \ldots \ldots \ldots \ldots \frac{50,000}{115,000} = 43\%$$

Ratio of trading on the equity:

$$\text{Unadjusted}\ldots\ldots\ldots \left(\frac{1}{0.77}\right)\left(\frac{17.7}{18.7}\right) = 1.2$$

$$\text{Adjusted}\ldots\ldots\ldots\ldots \left(\frac{1}{0.43}\right)\left(\frac{3.5}{4.5}\right) = 1.8$$

If one is inside a firm, the alternate purchase price of leased property is usually available for such a purpose as that just mentioned. Analysts "on the outside looking in" may be forced to capitalize annual lease payments at some rate in order to get a figure to use. Controversy rages over the rate to be used, but the present authors feel that the yield on debenture debt in the industry is a rate that will serve for most cases. It should, however, be applied to the payment schedule over the time of the lease, through the use of present-value factors.

Summary

We can summarize the place of the financial lease in the area of bargaining for funds by saying that its obligations are to be regarded as a form of debt, treated in financial analysis in the same way as the burden of a bond issue. Leases are used for both small and large transactions, and their variety is great. The tax treatment accorded to lease payments may make them less burdensome than an equivalent borrowing, although this is not always the case. Leases often assist in financing small or financially weak companies. They are often used by large companies to finance specific projects where the property is available on favorable terms, or when for some reason the time is not deemed propitious for the issue of new securities.

Perhaps this is the place to point out that the special advantages of leases in the tax field have led to very careful scrutiny of the real situation that lies behind the formal lease. Expert legal counsel is required for the complex task of drafting lease arrangements that will stand up against possible legal attacks either from creditors of the lessee (who would like to have the value of the property declared an asset of the lessee) or from the tax authorities (who would prefer to have the lease payments taken as instalments for an ultimate purchase). It is no game for the superficial or the unwary. In fact, we have been told by one expert that the variety chain lease that we have used as our example might not be recognized as a lease for tax purposes! Wherever this occurs, the question of ownership versus leasing becomes one of finding convenient sources of funds, rather than one of cost advantage, for the tax shield pattern will be unchanged.

chapter 23

Modifications of the Distribution of Risk

We ended Chapter 19 by showing how a grid, or cross-classification, could be made, showing for each security type how it affected the allocation of risk, the distribution of income, and the location of control. We now turn to exploring the relationship between the terms of security issues which may result from the bargaining process and these three categories. As with most classifications, the approach has its limitations. The security known as a subordinated income bond represents a modification of risk as well as income and could fit with equal justification under either category. This is not a serious problem, however, provided the classification is recognized as secondary to the objective of a clear understanding of the security in question.

By the term *risk* we refer to uncertainty both with respect to the receipt of income and to the return of the principal invested. It would be impossible to guarantee absolutely either of them, but much can be done to bring assurance through contractual provisions. In this chapter we shall deal with attempts to assure the ultimate repayment of the principal value of a particular issue despite the possibility that the issuer might at some future time be unable to meet all its obligations.

Types of Protection

The terms of a security may provide the security holder with any or all of three major types of protection. First, the company may agree to a variety of *controls over the creation of additional obligations*. These will limit the amount and/or the form of other securities which the firm may issue. Second, the provisions may grant the security holder some *control over funds flows* within the company and between the company and its external suppliers of funds. Such controls may prevent actions that otherwise might bring insolvency. The final type of protection, one which most security purchasers hope they never have cause to use, provides *protection in case of default* by creating for one class of security some priorities of claim over specific assets. These terms can provide additional bargaining strength in the event of failure. We shall discuss each of these methods of allocating risk, bearing in mind that specific provisions often can be placed in more than one category. Before turning to these details, however, it is necessary to look more specifically at the nature of default.

The Nature of Default

A company is surely in *default* when it is unable to make payment on contractual obligations. These obligations may range from accounts payable to long-term bonds. In the case of bonds, default will normally occur when the company is unable to meet either interest or principal payments. At the time of default (or after a grace period of a few weeks), the creditors may begin to take formal action to secure the funds due them, and the company must pay or be declared bankrupt (Chapter 29).

Some security holders, of course, are not guaranteed fixed payments by their relationship with the company. When payments are suspended upon a preferred stock, the stock is said to be in *arrears*, but the actions the owners of the stock can take do not include the right to sue for their dividends. Their contract may provide for some change in their relationship with the company, such as giving them the right to elect directors. But it will not allow them to bring bankruptcy. Common shareholders are even more restricted in the actions they can take when payments to them are terminated. Usually, their rights do not change.

Once a business has been forced into formal bankruptcy, its relations with creditors, suppliers, and customers become complicated. Legal expenses rise. The company's ability to act rapidly is reduced, and it may ultimately be forced to discontinue its business and liquidate. Consequently, security holders who are concerned about the protection and return of their capital often wish to have a voice in the company's operations in advance of a liquidity crisis.

Technical Default

Bondholders' contracts with a corporation do not permit them to vote on corporate actions. Therefore, whatever controls they require must be written into the agreement at the time it is drawn up. *Acceleration of principal* is a device used frequently to protect the senior security owners. The bond covenant will provide that if the company takes certain actions or if certain events should occur, a *technical default* will have taken place and the principal of the security will become due immediately (or within 30 to 90 days). Few firms would be able to meet such accelerated maturities, and therefore, unless revisions could be negotiated with the bondholders, default of payment on the principal of the bond would occur.

The purpose of these terms, however, is not to force the company into bankruptcy but to put the lender in a position to insist on measures he thinks will help the situation *before the financial position of the company has become desperate.* The terms are thus written with an expectation that they will become effective while a margin of safety still exists. At this point, the senior creditors may still have time to improve their position by negotiation. Management and the more junior creditors will probably still be willing to work toward a negotiated agreement. At the time of technical default they should have something promising to negotiate toward rather than accepting immediate bankruptcy.

The terms which define technical default are subject to infinite variation. We shall discuss three major categories:

1. Change in the nature of the business.
2. Diversion of assets.
3. Degeneration of corporate financial position.

1. CHANGE IN THE NATURE OF THE BUSINESS.   The first set of provisions represents assurance against changes that could substantially alter the nature of the borrower's business and hence the position of the senior securities. These terms might include prohibitions during the life of the security of the following:

1. Sale of the assets of the company other than in the normal course of business—for example, sale of an obsolete machine would be permitted; sale of a plant would not.
2. Merger of the company with other companies.
3. Major changes in the management of the company except by normal processes such as retirement.

If any of these actions in a particular case were found to be consistent with sound operation of the firm, the debtholders would undoubtedly agree to modify the prohibitions or to grant waivers for specific actions. But they, by providing the limitation, give themselves the right to review the scheme.

2. DIVERSION OF ASSETS.   The second group of restrictions guards against undesirable diversion of the assets of the firm. One of the most common and direct of such clauses is explicit limitation of the salaries or other benefits paid top management. Such a limitation is particularly common in the case of small, closely held companies where major stockholders are also employees and could, in the absence of restrictions, siphon

off funds required for the protection of the senior creditors through excessively large salary withdrawals.

Potentially more important in the case of larger companies is the restriction of dividend payments, particularly to common stockholders. The restriction of dividends takes various forms and degrees of severity, depending largely on the strength and bargaining power of the borrower. Even for the strongest borrowers, lenders frequently insist that future dividends be paid only out of future earnings, so that the surplus cushion at the time the loan is granted is not reduced. In other instances, dividends may be prohibited entirely until repayment of a debt has been completed or has reached a lower level. Dividends may also be restricted to a certain proportion of each year's income.

It pays to be familiar with the exact phrasing that is sometimes used in such restrictions. A fairly typical one is this clause in a U.S. Plywood–Champion Papers, Inc., offering:

> The company covenants that it will not declare or pay any dividends, other than dividends payable in stock of the company, or acquire any of its stock or make any other distribution to its stockholders, except in its stock, or permit any restricted subsidiary to purchase such stock if after giving effect thereto, the aggregate amount of such dividends declared or paid, and the aggregate amount of payments made in connection with all such purchases, subsequent to December 31, 1970, exceeds (a) $50,000,000 plus ($b$) net income earned subsequent to December 31, 1970, plus (c) the amount, if any, by which the aggregate net proceeds received by the company from the issue or sale subsequent to December 31, 1970 of stock of the company, options to purchase stock of the company and indebtedness of the company which has been converted into or exchanged for stock of the company subsequent to December 31, 1970 exceeds the aggregate amount expended since that date to acquire stock of the company.

The effect of the clause quoted is to freeze surplus at the time of issue. Nevertheless, the situation in which the issuing company would find such a clause seriously restrictive is likely to be unusual. For this reason, and also because this feature has become so common since the 1930's, it is not often a major bargaining consideration. Where it is likely to be a problem, as in the instance when a smaller, family-owned company is bargaining with a financial institution, it may well be worth substantially more attention than is usually the case.

3. FINANCIAL DEGENERATION. The last group of provisions seeks to encourage management to prevent certain events and actions which would be harmful to the lenders. Many of these terms are written to ensure that the corporation maintains a strong current position. The long-term profits looked to for loan repayment may be jeopardized if the borrowing firm does not maintain sufficient working capital and credit standing to permit normal conduct of its business. Furthermore, in the

event of serious trouble, when the lender may be forced to look for repayment from liquidation of the borrower's assets, the lender would like to have the prospect of substantial payout from current assets. These are typically the most liquid and often the highest-yielding assets in bankruptcy, and heavy current borrowings would dilute the lender's prospects of repayment from their liquidation.

With these points in mind, many lenders rely on a requirement that the current ratio of the borrower be maintained above a minimum figure, such as 2 to 1, counting on this requirement for protection against excessive reduction of working capital. A minimum "net quick" ratio is also frequently included. These restrictions may be stated alternatively (or concurrently) in absolute dollar amounts or in terms of some multiple of the long-term debt outstanding. Usually, the lender's desires in this area can be expressed in a clause which expresses what a prudent borrower would plan to do anyway.

Definitions of the sort described can be quite effective in maintaining control over short-term borrowing. At the same time, a frequent source of strain on working capital is the investment of funds in fixed assets. Undue diversion of cash into plant, equipment, or long-term investments may hamper normal operations and jeopardize repayment of the senior securities. Consequently, holders of long-term debt may also require restrictions on the amount of fixed assets acquired each year. For example, the corporation may be limited to investing the amount supplied by annual depreciation charges. Such limitations are often the subject of vigorous bargaining and, over the full life of the loan, are among the provisions most frequently modified by mutual agreement.

Senior lenders may also wish the protection of a clause providing that a default on any of the company's obligations, including rental of leased property, will accelerate the maturity of the issue.

Because provisions of the type mentioned are intended as guides and to give the company's debtholders an opportunity to strengthen their position early in case of difficulty, the provisions may be modified by joint consent when sound business reasons exist for changes. A company with good reason to sell its assets or to merge would undoubtedly get permission to do so, although in return the lender might well wish to have his protection increased. If a major asset were sold, for example, permission for the sale might require the company to use part of the proceeds to repay a portion of the loan. If a company wished to invest more heavily in fixed assets because sales and profits were rising rapidly, the lenders might agree on the condition that the term of the debt be reduced or the interest rate be increased, or the dividend restriction be tightened.

In a prospectus covering a secondary offering of common stock in Braniff Airways, Inc., by Ling-Temco-Vought, Inc., prospective investors were informed that on December 31, 1970, Braniff had a long-term debt-to-equity ratio of 254%. They also were informed that Braniff was then negotiating with banks and insurance companies regarding some lengthening of the maturities and other terms, principally the interest cost, of the various notes in question. Part of the debt was represented by $36 million in revolving credit notes held by 10 banks and due June 30, 1972. Braniff was negotiating an extension of the maturity—not a change in interest rate arrangements—so that they would become payable in three equal instalments starting December 31, 1972.

Then, there was this comment, which clearly brings home the lesson about risk modification. The prospectus said:

> In this connection, the company would be subject to certain additional covenants—the details of which are still subject to negotiation—including additional limitations on indebtedness restricting the company's total long-term and short-term indebtedness to approximately $215,000,000 until June 30, 1972, provisions of certain rights of disapproval on the part of the lenders with respect to the company's commitments for airframes, and the imposition of certain additional restrictions on the payment of dividends other than stock dividends.

By way of information, at the time Braniff's long-term indebtedness totaled about $205 million, which obviously left little margin for error.

Sinking Funds

It is undoubtedly obvious that many of the provisions defining the conditions of technical default also exert control on the flow of funds. Those terms apply generally to internal operations of the company or protect one set of security holders from actions harmful to them but favoring another set. The terms discussed in this section relate more directly to regulating the flow of funds between the firm and a specific set of its creditors.

It is characteristic of uncertain conditions that the longer the period of his contract, the greater the risk to the bondholder. The longer he has to wait for the repayment of principal, the more difficult it becomes to forecast with accuracy ability to pay, and the less meaningful is the record of the immediate past upon which confidence is usually based. It follows from this that the risk to the bondholder may be modified by varying the timing and method of repayment of the debt. It also follows as a consequence that a significant lengthening of the maturity date of an issue will probably require a somewhat higher yield to the bondholder or some other concession in order to induce him to accept the increased risk.

Bondholders may attempt to reduce their risk by requiring periodic repayment of principal over the life of a loan, an arrangement which reduces the principal exposed to default. A number of these provisions will be discussed below. It is worthwhile mentioning, however, that bondholders' desires for income may occasionally conflict with their concern for orderly retirement of their principal. When interest rates are high, lenders may want lower annual payments so that they may earn high interest rates on their funds for a longer time. In particular, investors may insist on terms preventing the company from retiring the debt when the company's purpose is to refinance the loan at a lower rate. Because debt issues which cannot be retired may put the firm in a relatively inflexible financial position, management must be careful to insure that covenants designed to protect the lender's interest rate do not interfere with arranging a sound financial structure.

The basic bond is repayable in a lump sum at a single known future date, which may be 15 or 20 years from date of issue. A very common modification of the lump-sum repayment of a bond issue is found in the *sinking fund bond*. Previous chapters have made the reader aware that some bonds require the issuing company to set aside a sum of money each year for the repurchase and retirement of some of the outstanding bonds instead of leaving repayment to the uncertain financial capacity in the year of maturity. In the past, most bonds were written to remain outstanding until maturity, and the sinking fund was accumulated elsewhere. This practice still continues in many countries, but it is open to the consequences of mismanagement of the accumulating fund. Experience in the United States has counseled the present practice of retiring some of the debt itself with each sinking fund payment.

A typical covenant regarding sinking funds is found in the F. W. Woolworth Company debentures of 1996, (issued in 1971) which states:

The debentures will also be subject to redemption on at least 30 days' notice by mail through the operation of a sinking fund on April 1, 1977, and on each April 1 thereafter to and including April 1, 1995, at 100% of their principal amount together with accrued interest to the date fixed for redemption. The sinking fund will provide for the redemption of $6,250,000 principal amount of debentures on each date.

There are variations on the theme, such as sinking fund payments which are contingent upon earnings of the enterprise. Under such circumstances, there will be a minimum sinking fund requirement, and an additional one dependent on the level of profitability. For example, Erie Forge & Steel Corporation first 5¾'s of 1977 has a *contingent sinking fund* provision which requires the company to make sinking fund payments equivalent to 40% of earnings in excess of $550,000. These payments would usually be credited against the most distant maturities, so that the company's more immediate obligations are not reduced by the contingent payments.

There usually are also provisions that allow a company to contribute to the sinking funds, in place of cash, debentures purchased on the open market. This way, particularly during periods of low market prices, bonds may be bought below par, enabling the company to (1) buy its bonds back cheaper and (2) through some accounting legerdemain realize a profit in its income statement from the transaction.

The decrease in risk to the bondholder resulting from a sinking fund is a significant bargaining point when setting up the terms of a bond issue and one which should give the issuer a more favorable bargaining position in other respects. The disadvantage of such a feature to the common stockholders stems from the fact that the retention of earnings to meet the sinking fund requirements means, in effect, a gradual substitution of high-cost equity capital for low-cost debt. Alternatively, the earnings could have been applied to new investments within the company or withdrawn and invested elsewhere. However, the practical significance for the stockholder may be small if the company is maintaining a continuous debt position through new bond issues which overlap the old.

Variations on the sinking fund principle occasionally require separate establishment of additional special accounts such as a *maintenance and replacement fund*. Cash, in an amount determined by the bonds outstanding, total capital investment, or some other figure, is deposited with a trustee. The trustee may release the money back to the company to spend on certain specified types of assets, which then become security for the bonds already outstanding. In the event that the fund is not exhausted by these withdrawals, the money is applied to the repurchase of debt. These techniques give the lenders additional control over company expenditures without necessarily removing the money from the company. At the same time, the provisions can be made quite flexible from the company's standpoint. We think this is a very desirable arrangement.

Another type of bond which has an effect somewhat similar to a sinking fund requirement is the serial bond, where specific groups of bonds, all of which are covered by the same indenture, are repayable at predetermined dates. The significant difference between this bond and the sinking fund bond is that the bondholder knows in advance the exact life of his particular bond and can take this into account in the price he pays for it. The serial feature is not nearly so common as the sinking fund provision, but it continues to fill a need in certain situations and is frequently used in municipal finance. An example of a public utility issue is Indiana and Michigan Electric Company's 3.25% serial notes, due in 1957–67 (issued on January 1, 1952). These notes were floated "for construction" and were sold to yield 2.75% for the nearest maturity to 3.2% for the farthest maturity. The various series were due as follows: $250,000, 1956–60; $500,000, 1961–62; $750,000, 1963–67.

Preferred Stock

Because preferred shareholders, like bondholders, desire greater certainty, the sinking fund provision has, with increasing frequency, been written into the terms of preferred issues. As mentioned previously in connection with bonds, the sinking fund presents a possible disadvantage from the common shareholder's point of view. Nevertheless, investors—especially the casualty insurance companies which are major buyers of preferred stock—have demanded it. The reason lies in part in the unhappy experience of arrears on many oversized preferred issues in the 1930's. It is also recognized that the market price of the stock benefits from some compulsory buying on the part of the issuing company.

The payment may be required as a flat sum annually or may be tied to earnings on a percentage basis, thus automatically relieving the company of payments in years of losses. The following is the sinking fund provision of the St. Regis Paper Company 4.4% cumulative first preferred, series A, par $100:

Sinking Fund—Annually, and cumulative to extent of net income (after deduction of dividends on preferred and prior or equal stock, and sinking fund for any funded debt not to exceed the lesser of 3% of such debt or $1,200,000) for succeeding years, sufficient to retire by purchase or redemption at $100 per share and dividends, for (*a*) first 2 years, 2½%, (*b*) next 20 years, 4%, and (*c*) succeeding 3 years, 5%, of greatest number of shares of preferred at any time outstanding.

It should be noted again that if the provision is in the form of a flat sum, failure to pay will not precipitate bankruptcy but may affect the relative voting position of the preferred and common shareholders. This is distinctly different from the effect of default of the sinking fund provision on a bond. The terms of the American Cement Corporation class A cumulative preferred stock 6.25% series sinking fund provision illustrate the relatively weak position the preferred shareholder holds in contrast to a typical bondholder:

The Company will have no obligation or liability with respect to the sinking fund or the redemption of shares of the 6.25% Series. Holders of shares of the 6.25% Series will have no remedy whatsoever in the event of the Company's failure to make sinking fund payments or to redeem shares of said series, their rights being limited solely to the restriction on declaration and/ or payment of Common Stock dividends, the restrictions on the purchase of Common Stock and the majority voting requirements set forth above.

Truly, the preferred shareholder has a pillow and not a club with which to influence management!

As in the case of bonds, the risk to management and to the common shareholder which preferred stock presents in the form of a rigid prior claim to earnings may be reduced by making the preferred callable or redeemable. This is essential in the issue where a sinking fund is required and is desirable in any case to give the company needed flexibility. The possible effect of this provision on market price of the preferred is the opposite of that of the sinking fund. The general effect of purchases for the sinking fund is to support the market price. The effect of a call feature, where the possibility of call appears a reality, is to hold the market price down to the call price when the general condition of the market might push it higher. An investor is seldom willing to pay more than the call price, even were yield attractive at the higher price, if the company might pick his number for redemption.

Control over Other Obligations

DEBT ISSUES.   Since the terms of a security issue establish the rights and responsibilities of the parties to the agreement, the owners of a security will want to prevent the company from modifying those terms by the act of issuing other securities whose rights jeopardize previous agreements. For this reason, holders of senior securities will usually insist on terms which limit the ability of the company to issue additional obligations.

Two types of clauses are quite effective in this respect, so we shall mention them briefly at this point. Their primary characteristics, however, dictate deferring a full discussion until the section on protection in the event of default. The first provision is that of taking a *pledge of specific assets* as security for a loan. This agreement limits the firm's ability to secure additional debt by making some assets unavailable as prime security for additional debt issues. To the extent that the limitation is successful, it acts to hold down the overall proportion of debt in the capital structure, thereby improving the earnings coverage of the outstanding bonds beyond what it would be otherwise. This reduces the risks assumed by the existing bondholders. From the company's viewpoint the acceptance of such limitations may be a means of gaining advantages in other ways, such as a lower interest rate and/or a better selling price for the bonds.

A second form of protective provision is found in some debt contracts which provide that property acquired after the securities are issued will also become part of the collateral against which the lenders may take a claim in the event of default. This provision, known as the *after-acquired property clause* not only provides protection for the lender against additional issues of debt but increases the strength of his position by adding to the property against which his claims are secured.

Another way of preventing claims from rising to dangerous levels is to forbid further borrowing. Clauses of this type are known as *negative pledge clauses*. The prohibition against additional debt may be as direct, specific, and complete as the company is willing to accept. Additional pledges of assets can be prohibited. The company can be prevented from entering into sale-and-leaseback agreements. It is even possible to forbid additional borrowing of any type.

In cases where all parties agree that the company has capacity and needs for further borrowing (or is likely to have in the future), the terms

444 Basic Business Finance

of the debt agreement can be made more flexible. Then the agreement can define the circumstances in which more debt might be raised rather than strictly prohibiting all additional loans. Then, if the company continues to prosper and remains strong, more money can be raised without having to renegotiate the outstanding debt agreements. For example, the terms of a loan might permit the company to borrow on a short-term basis, either a specified amount or as much as needed, provided certain working-capital ratios are not violated. If longer-term funds are a possible requirement, the agreement might permit the company to pledge certain assets or to issue subordinated loans up to a specified amount. A frequently found limit to the debt of industrial companies is one third of the total capitalization (see table, page 379). Subordinated debt could, for instance, be limited to the smaller of 200% of senior, secured debt or 300% of tangible net worth. Terms of this kind can also be used to control the nature and amount of borrowing by subsidiaries. The lenders and the corporation could negotiate any of a wide variety of specific terms that would permit additional borrowing while controlling its amount and form.

It is often the case that a *debenture,* an unsecured form of bond, is the only bond issue of a particular company. In order to protect against the hazard of a subsequent bond issue secured by a lien on assets, which would then take precedence over the debenture as to these assets, the terms of the debenture normally prohibit a future pledge of assets or outline the conditions under which such a pledge would be acceptable. For example, the Allied Chemical debenture $3\frac{1}{2}$'s, due in 1978, are covered by the following provisions, known as the *equal and ratable security clause:*

Company and any subsidiary will not mortgage property unless debentures are equally and ratably secured therewith, except for (1) purchase money or existing mortgages up to $66\frac{2}{3}\%$ of lower of cost or fair value of property, as provided and (2) other permitted liens. If on any consolidation or sale of substantially all properties, any property would become subject to a mortgage, debentures will be secured by direct prior lien thereon except for any existing lien.

OWNERSHIP CONTROL OVER NEW OBLIGATIONS. Preferred and common shareholders, having been willing to accept greater risk in hopes of greater income, receive less specific control over the additional obligations their company can issue. Within the ownership position itself, of course, the major redistribution of risk occurs when a preferred stock is created. Unless the preferred is issued as part of a corporation's initial capitalization, most states require a two-thirds vote by the common stockholders to amend the company's charter to create a new preferred stock. The common shareholders are protected in this way against dilution of their ownership without the consent of a large majority.

1. PREFERRED STOCK. One of the potential hazards associated with preferred stock is the creation of additional securities at a later date

which have an equal or senior position in the capital structure. Protection against this hazard in preferreds is a relatively new idea, but many issues currently outstanding contain restrictive provisions in this regard. These vary in the degree of limitation placed on management. They may apply only to new stock issues, or they may apply to new debt as well. The following example of the Kendall Company $4.50 cumulative preferred A illustrates the latter type:

Consent of two-thirds of preferred necessary to (1) issue or assume any funded debt . . . if thereafter consolidated funded debt plus involuntary liquidating value of outstanding preferred of subsidiaries and of preferred and of any stock having priority or on a parity with preferred exceeds 75% of excess of consolidated tangible assets over consolidated current liabilities, (2) create or issue any stock having priority over preferred (3) alter or amend provisions of preferred.

Consent of a majority of preferred necessary to create or issue additional preferred or any stock on a parity therewith. . . .

2. COMMON STOCK.   To the extent that the risks borne by senior security holders are lessened by the specific terms attached to their securities, the risks associated with the junior securities are likely to be increased, since the modification does not normally remove the risk but merely shifts it. Because the common stock stands last in line, there is no opportunity for a favorable shifting of the basic risks by qualifications in the terms of the issue.

There is, however, one respect in which the risk may be reduced, and that is with regard to the dilution of equity values through additional issues of the same class of stock. The feature aimed at safeguarding the interests of existing stockholders is the *preemptive right*. This is the right to buy any additional issues of common stock on a pro rata basis, before it is offered to new stockholders, on terms which are at least as favorable as those offered to the new shareholders. If dilution is involved in the offering price, the old shareholder can protect his position by buying a block of the new stock in proportion to his present holdings. This right may be required by state law, or it may be left to the bargaining process between the company and the shareholders. For common stock which does not have the preemptive right, new issues of common may or may not be first offered to existing shareholders before being offered to the public at large, depending on the decision of management. If the new common is priced substantially under the market, then it may result in lowered market value and earnings per share on the outstanding stock. We shall give further attention to various aspects of rights offerings of common stock in the following chapter.

The Call Provision

In contrast to the serial and sinking fund bonds, which work to reduce the risk to the bondholder, the *call provision* provides a means by which the terms of a particular debt can be canceled. The call feature gives the company the option of repaying all or some portion of the debt prior to maturity, as in the following example of Texas Company debenture 3⅝'s, issued in May, 1958, and due in May, 1983:

Callable—As a whole or in part at any time on 30 days' notice to May 1 incl. as follows:

1961	104½	1964	104
1967	103½	1970	103
1972	102½	1974	102
1976	101½	1978	101
1980	100½	1981	100¼
1983	100		

Optional redemption is also permitted up to $5,000,000 of debentures during each 12 months' period ending May 1, beginning with period ending May 1, 1969, at 100 and interest.

The call feature gives the company the very real advantage of greater flexibility in its capital structure so that it can time repayment to suit its needs and objectives as they develop. It also enables the company to take advantage of lower market interest rates, should they occur prior to maturity, by calling in the old bonds and replacing them with new bonds at the lower rate. In this respect the company's gain is the bondholder's loss; thus, the question of having a call feature may be a hotly debated issue. The small call premium may be quite inadequate to compensate the bondholder for having to reinvest his funds for the balance of the period at a lower rate of return. It is apparent that the call feature is one which may affect the distribution of income as well as risk.

The call provision is a good example of an indenture clause which is subject to change over time as the condition of the money market and the bargaining position of the borrower and lender change. In the period of declining interest rates which prevailed for many years, an unrestricted call provision was considered highly desirable by the borrower and was almost invariably included in the indenture as long as a strong demand for bonds by investors persisted. However, whenever their bargaining position permits, and this is likely to be strong when interest rates are high, lenders are inclined to demand that limitations be placed on calls so as to slow down their turnover of investments and to preserve higher yields for a longer period of time. This is certainly the case as this book goes to press.

Having observed many occasions where the absence of the call feature has forced firms to continue obligations that there is every reason for them to avoid, the authors urge all who bargain for funds not to give up the call feature entirely. One may agree on noncallability for a few years, or accept a high premium cost if call is decided upon, but to approve a completely noncallable arrangement is a sign of lack of foresight. The only exception, in our view, for which argument can be made may exist in term loan agreements of short duration where there is no reason to foresee either having excess funds on hand or being embarrassed by one of the contract clauses.

Protection after Default: Priority

If a company does encounter severe and prolonged difficulty, advance efforts to protect the position of the security holders may fail. It is possible that the company would then go into bankruptcy proceedings and be liquidated. Even if this event is avoided, the company's creditors may have to agree on a settlement in order to keep the firm operating. In either case the holders of the firm's securities will find themselves in quite different positions according to how they secured their advances against the assets of the company. For example, a lender whose loan is secured by the primary productive assets of the company not only has his principal protected by first claim on the proceeds of those assets in the event of liquidation but he is also in a very strong bargaining position during the settlement negotiation.

Thus, the effect of a pledge is to give a certain priority to one group of creditors over the claims of others. The obvious reason for a pledge of, or a lien against, *specific* assets is to decrease the risk to the bondholder, which may mean that the issue is salable at a somewhat lower interest rate as a result. On the other hand, the primary protection for any bond lies in the earning capacity of the issuing company, so that the debenture of one company may involve less risk to the investor than the secured bond of another.

Pledges do not come into action until after default, which is avoided through favorable operations and not through the pledge. The pledge merely confers on the privileged creditor a priority of claims on the value of the assets pledged to him. There is no way in the United States to create a general priority over other creditors. The pledge is of a specific asset.

THE MORTGAGE. Almost any corporate asset may be pledged, but the laws are intricate, and so the forms of contract differ according to the type of property. The most common form of secured bond is that secured by a mortgage on all or some of the fixed assets of the business—in the form of real estate; land and buildings. This type of issue is known as a mortgage bond and is frequently found in industries which combine relatively stable earnings with a high proportion of the total investment in fixed assets, such as public utilities and railroads or companies owning income-producing real estate. The mortgage will contain a detailed description of the property pledged, so that it can be accurately identified in event of default. An abbreviated statement of such security is seen in the following example of Inland Steel Company first 4½'s, Series L, issued in February, 1959, and due in February, 1989:

Secured equally and ratably with other series by first mortgage on (1) Indiana Harbor and Chicago Heights plants, (2) certain iron ore properties in Iron and Marquette Counties, Mich., and St. Louis and Crow Wing Counties, Minn., (3) coal properties of company, subject to certain exceptions, and (4) approximately 800 acres of vacant land in Porter County, Ind.

It is a recognized fact that in the event of liquidation, business assets generally undergo shrinkage in value. This is particularly true of specialized fixed assets, where the cash realized in sale is likely to be considerably below the book value. In view of this, it is a general rule that the value of fixed assets pledged as security for a bond issue will be substantially larger than the amount of the debt. The usual upper limit for mortgage loans is two thirds of the cost of the pledged assets; and in some cases, it may be as low as one half.[1] Obviously, this is one of the ways in which the creditor seeks to limit the risks involved in investment.

There are occasions when a bond issue is secured by a *second mortgage* on assets which have already been pledged on a previous issue. As the term implies, the holders of such securities take a secondary position to the holders of the first-mortgage bonds in the event of foreclosure and sale of the particular assets. On the other hand, they rank before other creditors as regards these assets. It will be apparent that a second mortgage has an appeal to the potential bondholder only when the value of the pledged assets is substantially in excess of that necessary to provide protection under a first mortgage.

Some security provisions include property "hereafter acquired" as well as property in existence at the time of the mortgage. This is known as an *after-acquired property clause* and is found in many such mortgages as a feature to increase further the confidence of the investor by adding new assets to the pledge. More significantly, the effect of the clause would be to exclude additional first-mortgage debt, which would otherwise increase the fixed charges against earnings and thereby the risk to existing bondholders. The mortgage may also include a statement of certain exceptions to this clause in the case of property which bears a prior lien at the time of acquisition.

As an instance of the type of bargaining which is appropriate when a bond contract is being designed, let us look at the consequences to a debtor of accepting the after-acquired clause. It prevents borrowing on mortgage when new property is acquired. Therefore, if this clause is requested, an alert management will suggest that the terms should also include some degree of permission to increase the amount of the borrowing under the existing mortgage to finance additional assets. This is usually

---

[1] Some investors, such as insurance companies, often have maximum loan ratios set by law. At the same time, however, the value against which the loan is made is frequently subject to negotiation. If the value is not determined by the cost of the building but by appraised valuation, it is possible for several appraisers to place quite different values on the property and the lender may choose the one he wishes to use.

arranged by some type of an *open-end clause* which permits additional issues of bonds under the same mortgage provided certain conditions are met. An example of this is the Michigan Consolidated Gas Company first-mortgage 3½'s, series due in 1969. These bonds have an open indenture with the following provision regarding further issues:

Additional bonds may be issued (unlimited except as provided by law) equal to (1) 60% of lower of cost or fair value of net property additions after December 31, 1943, not theretofore bonded . . . (2) bonds issued hereunder and prior lien bonds returned but not theretofore bonded; (3) cash deposited with trustee for such purpose, but only if net earnings available for interest and depreciation for 12 out of 15 months next preceding are at least 2½ times annual interest on bonds to be outstanding and on all prior lien bonds outstanding; except that, in general, no earnings test is required to issue bonds (a) for refunding bonds issued by company or prior lien bonds, or (b) to reimburse company for monies expended or repay loans incurred for such refunding.

Even an open-end mortgage bond issue usually contains provisions designed to preserve a certain minimum protection of asset values and earning power for the bondholder. At the same time, the clause gives the issuer a degree of flexibility in the further use of debt. The specific terms of this provision are of obvious importance to both parties and would be a subject for negotiation in discussions preliminary to the sale of the issue.

OTHER FORMS OF PLEDGE. A second type of property which may become security for long-term debt is movable physical assets such as equipment, commonly referred to as chattels. The mortgages which cover such assets are broadly classified as *chattel mortgages*. This form is widely used in the transportation industry. An example of a straight chattel mortgage is Trans World Airlines, Inc., equipment mortgage sinking fund 3¾'s issued in 1954, due in 1969, and secured by a general mortgage on aircraft and engines owned as of December 31, 1957, with the exception of certain specific aircraft and engines pledged under a bank loan or purchased under a conditional sale contract. TWA has continued to use this device up to the present time.

A third type of property frequently pledged by certain types of businesses is investments in stocks and bonds or other instruments such as notes receivable. A bond secured by a pledge of such securities is known as a *collateral trust bond*. This type of collateral may be more or less effective as protection against the risk of default, depending on the character of the pledged securities and the strength and stability of the market for them. Such bonds would not normally be used by industrial companies, since few of them carry a sufficient investment in marketable securities to support a bond issue. On the other hand, they are a natural form of bond issue for finance companies, which have large portfolios of notes receivables from those to whom they have made advances.

THE FLOATING CHARGE. In countries which have modeled their laws on the British statutes, the *floating charge* appears. This is just the opposite of subordination, since it is an arrangement by which groups of assets are pledged by categories to a certain creditor. They are not pledged specifically with detailed descriptions, as in the United States, but by kind. Thus, a certain secured issue may have a floating charge on all the real estate and/or other categories as each may exist at the time of default. The floating charge "fixes" at that time, so that to speak of "fixed charges" in London is to raise images in the hearers' minds quite different from those that would result from the use of the term in New York.

In our view there is a great deal to be said for this device, which permits the bargainers to confer priorities of claim without reference to particular assets. Those who are interested in the improvement of commercial law in the United States would do well to study it. We mention it here as an example of the fact that not all the best practices in finance are to be found in the United States.

UNSECURED DEBT, SUBORDINATION. As we progress down the list of priorities, we must not forget the many kinds of unsecured debt, from the formally engraved debenture bond to the verbal contract that created a purchase on credit. The features mentioned so far have been designed to reduce the risk to the investor. On occasion a feature is introduced which acts to increase the risk to the investor. Such is the case of the *subordinated debenture.* As we indicated in Chapter 15, a subordinated debt is one which would in the ordinary course of events be equal to or have priority over other debt but which for some reason has been placed in a secondary position to such debt. An example of the subordinated debenture is W. R. Grace and Company convertible subordinate debenture 3½'s, due in 1975, which were sold in 1955 for additions to plant, facilities, and working capital, and were "subordinated to all senior debt, including bank borrowings, current loans, etc." Such subordination is necessary for new debt when existing debt contracts prohibit additional debt having equivalent or senior claim on assets and earnings. In order to make such bonds acceptable to the prospective holders, a higher interest rate may be necessary.

Convertible bonds often are subordinated—testimony that they are thought of as a kind of equity investment.

The convertibles of Uniroyal, Inc. provide that the payment of the principal, sinking fund requirements and interest on the debentures is subordinated in right of payment, to the prior payment in full of all superior indebtedness of the company whether outstanding on the date of the indenture or thereafter incurred. There are no restrictions in the indenture upon creation of superior indebtedness or any other indebtedness.

PREFERRED STOCK. Preferred shareholders usually, but not necessarily, receive a preferred position ahead of common shareholders but after all forms of debt in the event of liquidation of assets. The terms may be stated, for example, as a certain dollar amount to which will be added any accrued dividends. At times the amount assigned to the preferred shareholders will be larger if the liquidation is voluntary than if it is involuntary. On the other hand, the preferred shares are not secured against any particular assets, which makes their claim relatively weak. Countless cases suggest that preferred shareholders may receive the least satisfactory treatment of any security holders in a liquidating company as compared with the agreed terms of their security.

The common shareholders are in the position of having to take what is left in event of a liquidation. They have invested in the company with the objective of increasing their wealth by receiving the major portion of the benefits of success and at the risk of losing their investment in the event of failure. It is appropriate for their claims to be for leavings, be they large or nonexistent. In bankruptcy or reorganization, their interest may have no value at all.

chapter **24**

Modifications of the Distribution of Income and Control

We may regard the funds flow derived from operations (FPO) as the contribution made by efficient use of the assets at the disposal of the firm and therefore as the source of the values of these assets as they are used in the going concern. When the managers of a firm cause it to issue securities with special claims to funds, they are allocating the flows and thus allocating value among the securities the firm issues. If this is wisely done, the result will be increased return on each dollar invested by the common shareholder without a corresponding increase in risk. The process will, therefore, provide greater value for the common shareholder. This result is in accord with the obligation of management to the owners of the common equity: to arrange the terms of security contracts with the goal of maximizing the value received by the holders of the common stock, as that holding exists at the time a choice of financing is under consideration.

Commitments to Fixed Payments

The complement of a desire for greater security of principal is a willingness to accept less income. Security holders who are averse to risk are also interested in insuring the safety of that income, however small. This can be accomplished by the establishment of fixed payments with priority over disbursements to other security holders. The fixed obligations of interest owed bondholders, lessors, and the like fall at one end of the spectrum with the dividends paid common shareholders, which are declared at the discretion of the directors, at the other. Dividends on preferred shares are also paid at the discretion of the directors. Never-

452

theless, because preferred dividends are often cumulative and failure to make payments can frequently have unattractive repercussions upon the common shareholders' position, management usually considers preferred dividends as fixed requirements.

Given that interest payment is to be granted priority, the problem of setting an interest rate on a specific issue is an extremely important one. In fact, in the bargain between the corporate borrower and the bondholder, there is no issue more vital to both than the interest rate which will be necessary to market the issue completely and quickly. In a private placement this can be settled by direct negotiation, whereas in a public offering the issuer and his investment banker must estimate in advance of the offering what will be the minimum yield acceptable to the bondholder. In either case, however, once the coupon rate is accepted by both parties, the specific terms of payment follow a standard pattern—typically, a regular semiannual payment of fixed amount of money. The only way to make a change after the issue is to call the issue and replace it, unless the issue is closely enough held to permit a negotiated adjustment. Replacing or amending an issue is an expensive operation, infrequently used.

The primary determinant of the interest rate (or preferred dividends) which a firm must concede to its lenders (or preferred shareholders) is the general level prevailing at the time of issue for companies whose risks are adjudged to be approximately the same as those of the issuing corporation. Small changes in the rate can sometimes be arranged if concessions are made elsewhere in the contract. Generally speaking, lower rates can be obtained by including clauses which reduce risk (such as the variety of pledges, covenants, and maturity arrangements described in Chapter 23). On the other hand, the preservation of some freedom (permission to borrow further, smaller sinking fund) can often be arranged by concession on the rate. One large corporation, for example, was told that its insistence on a call feature in its issues was costing it an additional $3/8\%$ to $1/2\%$ on the rate. Yet it wisely (in our view) did insist on the flexibility that the call provision provides.

Convertibility

It is often desirable to provide part of the income to senior holders on a contingent basis. For example, it may be possible to raise funds less expensively (from the existing common shareholders' point of view) by offering a security containing some elements of both a bond and a stock rather than selling securities which are pure examples of either type. Alternatively, it may be necessary to concede additional, contingent income in return for terms of the contract which management believes to be essential. In some instances lenders may refuse to make a risky loan unless they are provided with a share in the anticipated profits. Traditional or legal restraints may also prevent them from requiring fixed interest compensation adequate to allow for the risks they accept. A wide variety of instruments have been developed to meet the demand for protected securities with contingent compensation.

A significant modification of the normal fixed income position of the bondholder and preferred shareholder is to be found in the convertible issue. The convertible bond gives the bondholder the option of retaining his normal contractual claim or exchanging his security for another security, usually common stock, on a ratio fixed at the time of issue of the bonds. The terms may be illustrated by Continental Baking Company convertible subordinated debenture 3⅝'s, issued on March 1, 1955, and due in 1980. The provision for conversion into common stock was stated as follows: "The basic conversion price shall be $34.50 per share of Common Stock to and including February 28, 1958, $37 thereafter to and including February 28, 1961, and $39 thereafter to and including February 28, 1965." Cash was to be paid in lieu of fractional shares, and there was to be no adjustment for interest or dividends. The conversion privilege was protected against dilution. As a result, when a stock dividend was paid on the common stock in September, 1955, the conversion prices were changed to $32.50 to February, 1958; $34.85 to February, 1961; and $36.73 to February, 1965.

It will be apparent that this privilege has no realizable value to the bondholder unless and until the earnings and/or dividend performance of the common justifies a market price of the stock in excess of the conversion prices quoted. At that time the bondholder is able to acquire common stock at a bargain price and either take an immediate capital gain by selling the common or hold it for income and further appreciation. Thus, the bondholder has the option of retaining his contractual but limited claim on earnings or of taking advantage of the more favorable income position of the stockholder if and when this becomes a reality. It would appear that if there is any real prospect of conversion under favorable terms, the holder of the convertible bond has "the best of all possible worlds"—the protection of a bond plus the speculative opportunities of a stock. In this respect the bondholder's gain is the common shareholder's loss. When conversion takes place, high-cost equity capital is substituted for low-cost debt, and the common shareholder's equity is diluted by the addition of stock "sold" at a (conversion) price below market.

There are two principal reasons why companies are willing to consider a convertible bond. One is that circumstances may make it difficult to market a particular bond (for example, a subordinated debenture) at a reasonable coupon rate, and the speculative feature is added to put the issue across. Thus, the conversion feature is often a sign of weakness, and convertible bonds often are found to have relatively low ratings. A survey by the New York Stock Exchange firm of Salomon Bros. in 1970 showed that of the $12.4 billion of convertible bond issues listed in Moody's

Manual, "only $1.4 billion or 12% is rated A or above, $1.7 billion or 14% is rated Baa, and the balance, $9.3 billion or 74% is rated Ba and lower."

The other and perhaps more justifiable reason for a convertible issue is found in the case of a company which prefers to finance by stock rather than bonds but finds the current stock market unfavorable. Being unwilling to sell stock at the price dictated by the existing market and at the same time able to sell a bond which is convertible into stock at a higher price, the company sells the convertible bond in the expectation that it will be fully converted in the near future. If conversion takes place, the company has, in a sense, sold common at the higher price in an indirect manner.

To illustrate, the range of Continental Baking common in the year preceding the debenture issue of March 1, 1955 was 20¾–33, with the high prices being recorded in March. At the time the decision to float this issue was made, it was highly uncertain whether a common issue could be sold at or near $34.50. On the other hand, it was quite within the realm of possibility that even within the year the market price of the common could rise above this figure and thus make conversion attractive to the bondholders.

In practice, it is possible for the bondholder to realize his capital gain without actual conversion. The reason for this is that once the market price of common stock rises above the conversion price, the market price of the bond tends to rise along with it. The bond is no longer valued as a bond but rather on the basis of its conversion value. As a consequence, the bondholder can take his capital gain simply by selling the bond. This market result tends to prevent the issuing company from realizing its objective of replacing debt with common equity capital. In order to assure that this objective will be realized, convertible bonds must be made callable.

For example, the Continental Baking convertible debentures were callable at 105 to February 28, 1958, and thereafter at 104¾ to February 28, 1961. If the hoped-for rise in the price of the common stock occurred (above $32.50 after September, 1955) and the price of the debentures began its corresponding rise but no conversion actually took place, the company could precipitate conversion at any time that the debentures rose above 105 by issuing a call for redemption. The bondholders would then convert to avoid being paid off at the lower call price.

At the beginning of 1958, about $3.8 million of the $13 million issue of Continental Baking debentures already had been converted. The common stock price began a steady rise from 27¾ early in 1958, and the debentures were called for redemption on October 1, 1958, at 104¾. At the time of call the common price was 41½. Almost $9.2 million debentures were converted during 1958, and only $36,000 were redeemed.

The critical decision in establishing the terms of a convertible issue is setting the conversion ratio or conversion price. Normally, this price is above the current market price of common, although there have been issues where the convertible bond had a guaranteed value in conversion. A convertible issue of the Continental Investment Corporation guaranteed a future discount on the market price of the stock. The 20-year convertibles carried a 9% coupon, and were noncallable and nonconvertible for three years from date of issue. Then, however, they were convertible into stock at a price 18% below the average price for a five-day period immediately preceding the end of the three-year period. It is in the interests of the existing common shareholders to set the price as high as possible; but on the other hand, it must not be so high as to make conversion very remote and therefore valueless in the mind of the prospective bondholder. The setting of the conversion price on the Continental Investment issue is an example of an attempt to guarantee both objectives.

It should be noted that the terms of convertible issues almost always include protection against dilution. This term means that the basis of conversion will be adjusted in the event of a subsequent stock split or stock dividend so as to preserve the original advantage. Thus, if the common stock is split 2 for 1, the conversion price offered to the bondholder will be cut in half.

Just how imaginative things can get for issuers of convertible financing was underscored by one issue floated by Pennzoil United, when it sought funds for an offshore Louisiana lease sale. It put together a new subsidiary known as Pennzoil Offshore Gas Operators (POGO), in which it sold debentures and stock to the public. The convertible part of the package had only a nominal 1% yield for the first five years, after which the interest jumped to 6%. The bonds were convertible at $6 per share into the POGO common. However, there was always a chance the new venture might come a cropper. And so Pennzoil agreed that if POGO defaulted on either interest or principal it would convert the bonds into its own common, or at Pennzoil's option, pay off the debentures in cash at par plus accrued interest. Thus, Pennzoil was able to obtain its necessary financing—the deal brought it $121.6 million—and because Pennzoil commanded 80% of voting power in POGO it was able to consolidate for tax purposes POGO's losses or profits as well as charge off intangible drilling costs.

Elaborate schemes of this nature sometimes fit special conditions. A general rule is to avoid them because they confuse the analyst and lead him not to recommend them.

A *convertible preferred* stock is also placed on the market. Since the characteristics of this security are very similar to those of the convertible bond as far as this feature is concerned, it will be discussed very briefly. Like the bond, it gives the senior security holder an opportunity to profit from his investment in the business beyond the fixed limits of his security type. To the extent that he does, it is at the expense of the common shareholder. If the security is issued as an intermediate stage in a plan for ultimate common stock financing, it will be necessary to include the call feature in order to be able to force conversion when the time becomes appropriate.

Typical of the terms of such an issue is Abbott Laboratories 4% convertible preferred, par $100:

Convertible into common at any time to Dec. 31, 1961 incl., on basis of 1.7 common shares for each preferred share, with no adjustment for dividends and with scrip for fractional shares. Conversion rights subject to adjustment in certain events. Right to convert preferred called for redemption prior to Jan. 1, 1962 will terminate not earlier than seventh day prior to redemption.

Callable as a whole or in part on not less than 30 days' mailed notice at any time at $105 per share and dividends.

It is interesting to note that the 1960 price range for Abbott Laboratories common stock was 69½–50 and for the convertible preferred, 114½–98¼. At the high for the common of 69½ the gain from conversion would have been $18 over the par value of the preferred and $13 over the call price.

Convertible preferred stock has been used in recent years as a vehicle for effecting mergers. One advantage is that an exchange of common stock for a preferred stock is not considered a taxable transaction at the time of the exchange. The exchange of stock for a bond is taxable. More important, however, a convertible preferred provides a chance to negotiate a mutually satisfactory merger in conditions where the earnings per share, dividends, and market price of the two companies are not in the same relationships. For example, on June 1, 1965, *The Wall Street Journal* reported a proposal for merging Beneficial Finance Co. and Spiegel, Inc., a Chicago mail-order house. In exchange for each share of his company's common stock a Spiegel shareholder would receive ⅓ share of Beneficial common stock and ½ share of a new Beneficial $50 par cumulative convertible preferred stock with a $2.15 dividend. Each full share of the new preferred could be converted into 0.7 share of Beneficial common stock at any time during a 12-year period. Beneficial could not call the stock for 5 years. Thereafter, Beneficial could call the stock at prices which gradually declined to $52.50 a share.

At the time of the announcement, earnings, dividends, and price of the common stocks of the two companies were as follows:

	Market Price May 28, 1965	1965 Indicated Dividend	1964 Earnings per Share
Spiegel, Inc.	$36.625	$1.50	$2.61
Beneficial Finance Co.	60.125	1.40	2.92

The terms of the merger gave Spiegel shareholders an increased dividend rate of $1.54 if they did not convert their preferred stock. To have provided them a similar income from Beneficial common stock would have required more than one share of Beneficial for each share of Spiegel and would have entailed dilution of Beneficial's earnings per share. Under the terms suggested, Spiegel shareholders (assuming immediate conversion) would in fact have their per share earnings diluted but would receive stock with a market price of about $45 to compensate them for the earnings drop assuming that the new preferred would sell at its par value. Although neither set of shareholders received all the benefits, as befits a satisfactory negotiation, they each improved their position in some respect to compensate for their concessions in others. The flexibility of the convertible preferred was apparently an extremely important factor in permitting a satisfactory distribution of the benefits of the merger.

Warrants, Units

Occasionally, the opportunity for capital gains is offered a senior security holder in a manner that does not require him to give up his preferred position. This is accomplished by attaching to the senior security stock purchase warrants, which entitle the holder to acquire common stock at a fixed price, intended to be favorable. If and when the warrants are exercised, the senior security remains outstanding—in contrast to the convertible security. Once again, to the extent that the senior security holder gains, the common stockholder loses.

For example, March 23, 1971, Amerada Hess Corporation sold 6¾% subordinated debentures, with warrants so that each $1,000 bond received warrants to buy six shares of the common stock of Louisiana Land & Exploration Co., owned by Amerada Hess.

The warrants could be exercised at the price of $81 on and after June 15, 1971. As we went to press, the stock was quoted at $88. Thus the warrant holder could look forward to a gain, because the corporation had committed itself to give him stock at a price that was expected to be below what the corporation could otherwise have obtained by a direct sale—the corollary being that the existing stockholders of Amerada Hess were paying a price to obtain success in the distribution of the debentures.

Another technique for providing a security purchaser with a mix of protection and income is to offer a *unit* composed of two or more securities. These may be any combination of debt, preferred stock, and common stock of several classes. In some respects a unit issue of securities gives the purchaser a preconverted issue for which there is no clearly separable cost or a warrant which requires no additional payment to be exercised. For example, in 1960 the Mid-America Pipeline Company offered to the public $20.5 million of 6½% subordinated debentures in units of a $50 debenture and 3½ shares of common stock for a total price of $73.50 a unit.

Contingent Payments

Another form of senior issue with a contingency clause is a security whose provisions relate payments to the security holder with the income of the company. The *income bond* is one example. Briefly stated, an income bond is one in which the interest payment is made contingent on earnings. The payments may be cumulative or noncumulative. It differs from a preferred stock in the respect that the payment is mandatory if earned, whereas the preferred dividend is still at the discretion of the board of directors.

There has been a growing interest in income bonds by solvent and profitable businesses. The primary reason is that under current conditions of heavy corporate income taxation, the security offers the elements of flexibility found in a preferred stock, combined with the tax advantage of interest payments deductible as a cost. The result has been that the income bond has taken on a new respectability. This is another example of how attitudes toward security forms are modified as circumstances change.

The following terms of the Security Banknote Company convertible subordinated income debenture 5's, dated June 1, 1956, and due in 1976, illustrate the principal features of this type of security:

Interest payable . . . at 5% per annum, to extent earned; noncumulative.

Sinking Fund—Annually, April 30, 1957–75, cash (or debentures) equal to 10% of consolidated net earnings, for redemption of debentures at 100.

Security—Not secured; subordinated to prior payment of senior indebtedness, including bank borrowings.

Dividend Restrictions—Company may not pay cash dividends on common while interest, principal or sinking fund installment is in default.

Issued—Series A . . . in exchange for preferred at rate of $20 of debentures for each preferred share; series B issued in payment for preferred dividends in arrears.

Note that in this particular case the bond issue is further weakened by subordination.

In recent years the Interstate Commerce Commission has authorized a number of railroads to issue income debentures for the purpose of retiring preferred or class A common stock. The Commission commented on these developments as follows, in 1957:

There was a continuance of the trend which began several years ago for railroads to substitute interest-bearing obligations for preferred stock, with payment of interest generally contingent upon earnings, in order to reduce Federal income taxes. Interest on debentures is deductible whereas dividends on preferred stock are not.

A preferred stock offering a shareholder an opportunity to participate in income beyond the stated dividend is known as a *participating preferred*. Unlike the income bond, which places a ceiling on the income the bondholder can expect, the maximum income of the participating preferred shareholder is often unrestricted. The terms of the Virginia-Carolina Chemical Corporation 6% cumulative participating preferred illustrate this form:

Dividend Rights—has preference over common as to cumulative dividends of 6% annually. . . . After common has received $3 per share in any fiscal year entitled to participate share for share with the common in any additional dividends in such fiscal year.

It is obvious that such a feature can result in a major income concession to the preferred shareholder at the expense of the common shareholder; and for this reason, it is not found very frequently in preferred stock issues. Its presence indicates that at the time of issue the company and/or the common shareholder were in an unusually weak bargaining position.

The Cumulative Preferred Dividend

Almost all the preferred stocks now issued contain the cumulative feature. While it must be recognized that any dividend must be declared by the directors of the corporation before it becomes an enforceable financial obligation, it is possible to arrange by contract that if a dividend on preferred stock is not declared, no dividend on the junior stocks of the company will be paid until all *dividends in arrears* have been made up. This is the *cumulative feature*. In addition, in situations where dividends are not declared on a preferred stock, the preferred stockholder is usually put in a position where his representatives have more direct control over the use of funds than the provisions of the security would allow in normal circumstances. The degree of influence may vary from the right to elect only one or two members of the board of directors to the right to elect all the directors until such time as the arrears have been completely eliminated. On the other·hand, the terms of this power can define it very narrowly. A case is known where, despite the accumulation of substantial dividends in arrears on a preferred, the common shareholders have remained in control by virtue of paying every fourth preferred dividend. The terms of the preferred issue provided for preferred voting power only in the event four *consecutive* dividends had been passed.

Classified Common Stock

Generally the common shareholders exercise their control over the funds of the company, on which they have the last call, through their ability to elect the directors. In a few companies, however, two classes of common stock have been created where the burden of risk is divided unequally. Such stock, referred to as classified common, may differ only in respect to voting privileges and may be equal in all other respects. On the other hand, one class may be set up with a prior claim to dividends, in which case it becomes in essence a type of preferred stock, even though not so named. Such a provision obviously effects an uneven distribution of risk among the common shareholders. An example of this is Crown Cork International Corporation's $1 cumulative participating class A stock: "Has preference as to cumulative dividends of $1 per share and participates in any further distribution equally, share for share, with class B stock after latter has received noncumulative dividends of $1 per share in any year."

Another interesting example of classified common stock is the A and B common issues of the Citizens Utilities Company. Both A and B stock carry one vote per share. However, the dividends on class A stock are paid only in stock, whereas the dividends on B stock are paid in cash. Class A stock is convertible into B at the holder's option, share for share, except at the time of cash dividend payments. The two classes were issued as a part of a stock reclassification plan.

Dilution and the Position of Common Stock

Aside from the very important ways in which the income and control position of the common equity can be affected by the terms of securities senior to it, the value of an existing stockholder's interest is challenged every time new shares are to be issued. If an expanding corporation proposes to issue new shares, it inevitably creates a situation where those who formerly held all the equity must either invest additional funds to maintain their position, or concede a portion of the equity to others. Under such circumstances even actions that promise to increase the value of the equity may sometimes reduce the portion of it that represents the present investment of the present ownership group. In this, we are only saying again what was said in the discussion of the cost of equity capital.

Let us look at the situation this time in terms of numbers of shares, recognizing that any increase in the number of shares is a value-reducing event from the viewpoint of the existing ownership. Only when positive factors exist to offset the effect of increasing the "number of mouths to feed" should the new issue be considered.

First, we see a negative force, termed *immediate dilution*, which can be defined as the relative loss or weakening of the equity position caused by the issuance of new shares. The degree of this dilution can be measured precisely by the fraction

$$\frac{N}{N + \Delta N}$$

where:

N = Existing number of shares.
ΔN = Proposed added number of shares.

This tells us the proportion of the total shares that the former owners of the equity will hold after the new shares are issued (unless they commit additional resources to the corporation).

The same fraction, therefore, indicates the percentage of control, through voting power in stockholder meetings, which will remain with the group that had a certain fraction of these votes. For instance, suppose a management group controls a corporation by holding 60% of the 100,000 shares of common stock. If the corporation issues 20,000 more shares to new investors, the 60% interest becomes:

$$0.60 \left(\frac{100,000}{120,000} \right) = 0.50 \ .$$

This is barely enough to retain unquestionable control, and the controlling group may not wish to consent to any larger issue, no matter what the attractiveness of the opportunity in terms of its contribution to value.

Putting questions of control aside, despite their importance, and dealing solely with value, the existing shareholders will not find their value position protected unless some value-creating event results from the issue of the new shares which at least offsets the effects of the initial dilution. This occurs when the proportionate increase in the number of shares is at least the same as the proportionate increase in the value to be expected. To use the numbers just assumed, there must be a 20% increase in the total value of the equity if 20,000 shares are to be added to a 100,000 share base. This condition is theoretically necessary even if rights are issued to the existing shareholders. Since this important point is overlooked by many experts, we shall discuss it at length.

Privileged Subscriptions: Rights

The existing security holders represent a significant and identifiable potential market for further issues of securities; and a substantial percentage of new issues of common stock, and of bonds and preferred stocks convertible into common stock, is offered first to existing common stockholders. Some corporations have free choice in deciding whether or not to offer new common shares first to present stockholders, but in many companies the present common shareholders possess a legal right to receive *privileged subscriptions* to new issues of common stock. The legal right to privileged subscriptions is termed a *preemptive right*. Where it exists, corporations have no choice but to offer new issues of securities for cash pro rata to the security holders having the preemptive right.

What determines whether a particular security issue has this preemptive right? In most cases the status of the preemptive right is governed by specific provisions on the subject in the charter or bylaws of the corporation. If the status of the right is not clearly established in this way, the laws on the subject of the state of incorporation must be studied. In the absence of both charter and statutory definition of the preemptive right, reference must be made to the common law.

Whether conferred by law, corporate charter, or as a privilege extended at the discretion of management, the right to subscribe to new securities has important implications for income and potential capital gains. In many instances the right to subscribe to a given number of new securities is made at a price below the normal market price, and this means that those who hold the rights have a measurable advantage over those who do not.

It will be the primary purpose of this section to describe the effect of rights on the market price of the outstanding stock. The privilege of subscribing to new securities on favorable terms may be offered to any class of security for the purchase of the same or another class of security. The most common example, however, is a right extended to common shareholders for the purchase of additional shares of the same stock. We deal with this situation here.

We shall use as an example the National Aviation Corporation, which in 1956 offered its stockholders the privilege of subscribing to one new share for each four old shares held. In this case, one right was the privilege to subscribe to one-quarter share. In practice, while this right could be sold independently, it could only be exercised in conjunction with three other rights, to permit subscription to one share of the new issue.

If the stock is traded on an exchange, the exchange typically designates a date after which the stock will be traded free of the rights, or *ex rights*. Until that date, trading is on a *cum-rights* basis (also termed *rights on* and *with rights*). When stock is sold cum rights, the seller of the stock agrees that the buyer is to receive, in addition to the shares of stock, any rights that have been or are being issued on that stock.

Referring again to the National Aviation Corporation illustration, stock rights to expire on May 22, 1956, were mailed to stockholders of record as of May 8, 1956. The stock was traded on the New York Stock Exchange cum rights through May 9, and thereafter on an ex-rights basis. During the ex-rights period the stock and the rights were traded separately with independent quotations.

But before we look at the period when the rights are traded, let us look at the likely behavior of the market price cum rights, after the announcement of the plan to undertake rights financing and before the ex-rights date. Suppose it were generally believed that the new money was to be used on projects which would not contribute proportionately to future earnings. We have shown that, under such conditions, the average value of all the shares will fall. In a perfect market this fall will take place in anticipation of the ex-rights date. Nothing in the rights procedure can overcome such a loss. *Thus, an implicit assumption of thinking about rights must be that the proposed expansion meets the criterion already stated.* If so, the price, cum rights, will hold steady. Specifically, we assume that the proposed use of funds by National Aviation was justified.

During that time that rights are effective, the ex-rights period, any person planning to invest in the stock of the company has alternative ways to acquire it. He may buy a share on the market at the current market price, or he may buy the proper number of rights and then subscribe at the subscription price. In the latter case his total cost is the price of the rights plus the subscription price.[1] It is clear that investors will not be attracted to the new issue unless the subscription price is less than the going market price of the outstanding stock. Consequently, the setting of the subscription price contains the problem of predicting likely market prices for the security during the life of the rights. Some companies attempt to set the subscription price close to the market in order to minimize dilution. Others price the new issue well below the market in order to provide maximum inducement for use of the rights and to protect against the possibility that downward pressure on market price during the offering period will render the rights valueless.

In practice, the question of dilution of market values arises in every case, because the subscription price for the new stock is at least somewhat lower than the recent market price for the existing issue. In fact, it will appear from the following discussion that the market value of a right represents the amount of the dilution of the previous market values which is implicit in the new offering at favorable subscription prices.

EFFECT ON MARKET VALUE OF ISSUE OF STOCK AT LESS THAN OLD MARKET PRICE. Perhaps the effect on market value can be pictured best by first examining the theoretical effect on market value of a *stock split;* for in a stock split the number of shares of stock is increased, but the net worth of the company does not change. From the standpoint of the stockholder, his total values remain the same; and in theory, he has gained or lost nothing as a result of the split.

For example, a 4-for-1 stock split is announced for a stock selling at 120. Since the corporation will acquire no new money as a result of the split, its stock will have gained or lost nothing in value. A total value of 120 is now represented by four shares. Hence, the new stock would be expected to sell at

$$\frac{120}{4} = 30 .$$

(Further reference to the stock split will be found in Chapter 26 on refunding and recapitalization.)

Now, let us return to the National Aviation illustration of the sale of new stock. Although the old stock was selling at about $41\frac{1}{4}$ cum rights, stockholders received rights to purchase at 30 one new share for each

---

[1] We ignore brokerage.

four shares held. What dilution of market value of the old shares results from the issue at 30? In answering, let us consider a stockholder who owns four old shares. Before the stock went ex rights, his four shares represented a value of \$165 (41¼ times 4). In exercising his rights to purchase one new share, he added an investment of \$30 in cash, making a total investment of \$195 now represented by five shares. One new share, then, could be expected to have a value of

$$\frac{\$195}{5} = \$39 .$$

Actually, the first sale on the first day of trading ex rights was 39⅛, and the market closed at 39.

A formula incorporating this reasoning is widely used as a rough measure of the theoretical effect of issuance of stock at less than the market on the ex-rights market price of the stock. In the formula the following notations are used:

M = Market value of one share cum rights .
N = Number of old shares that entitle the holder to purchase one new
        share .
P = Theoretical market value of one share ex rights .
S = Subscription price .

Using the above notations, the formula is:

$$P = \frac{MN + S}{N + 1} \text{ (Theoretical Market Price after Exercise of Rights) .}$$

Substituting the facts from the National Aviation illustration:

$$P = \frac{(41\frac{1}{4} \times 4) + 30}{4 + 1} = \frac{195}{5} = 39 .$$

VALUATION OF STOCK RIGHTS. If the stockholder does not care to exercise his right to purchase, at what price will he be able to sell the right in the market? Once the stock is selling ex rights, the calculation of the value of one right is relatively simple. The value of one right is the difference between the ex-rights market price of one share and the subscription price, divided by the number of rights necessary to purchase one share. In the National Aviation case the first market price on the first day of trading ex rights was 39⅛. With four rights an investor could buy one share at an effective discount of 9⅛, since the subscription price was 30. Hence, one right had a worth of about 2¼.

Expressed in a formula, this relation is:

$$\frac{P - S}{N} \text{ (Theoretical Market Value of One Right, Ex Rights)}$$

$$= \frac{39\frac{1}{8} - 30}{4} = 2\frac{1}{4} .$$

Before the ex-rights date, when the stock is still selling cum rights, the value of one right can be predicted by use of the following formula:

$$\frac{M - S}{N + 1} \text{ (Theoretical Value of One Right, Cum Rights)}.$$

Using the National Aviation illustration again, with the cum-rights market price of 41¼:

$$\text{(Theoretical Value of One Right)} = \frac{41\frac{1}{4} - 30}{4 + 1} = \frac{11\frac{1}{4}}{5} = 2\frac{1}{4}.$$

It will now be apparent that the value of one right, in theory, will equal the anticipated dilution of market value of one old share. Hence, if brokerage fees and income tax questions involved in sale of the rights are ignored, the stockholder who sells his rights theoretically receives enough cash from the sale so as to sustain no net loss or gain in total market value of his holdings. From this point of view, a privileged subscription, if exercised or sold, prevents dilution of the market value of the total interests of the existing shareholders.

As a matter of interest, the following is the actual record of National Aviation Corporation common stock during the period (taken from *The Wall Street Journal*):

| | Price of Common* | | Price of |
Date	Cum Rights	Ex Rights	Right
May 7, 1956	41⅜	. . .	. . .
May 8, 1956	41½	. . .	. . .
May 9, 1956	41¼	. . .	. . .
May 10, 1956	. . .	39	2⅛
May 11, 1956	. . .	38⅜	2¼
May 14, 1956	. . .	38⅜	2⅛
May 15, 1956	. . .	38¼	2
May 16, 1956	. . .	38⅜	2
May 17, 1956	. . .	38⅜	2⅛
May 18, 1956	. . .	38½	2⅛
May 21, 1956	. . .	38	2¼
May 22, 1956	. . .	38½	2⅛

* Closing prices only.

The discussion above was based on an issue of common stock. In valuing rights to subscribe to issues of straight preferred stock or bonds (an event much less frequent than in the case of common stock), the ex-rights formula given above, $(P - S) \div N$, may be used in all instances, since dilution is not involved. If a valuation of the rights to buy preferred stock or bonds in advance of the establishment of a market price for the issue is desired, a probable market price, P in the formula, must be assumed.

Rights offerings are generally made with the presumption that a large proportion of the new shares will be subscribed for: 90% subscription is regarded by many financial analysts as the lower limit of a "successful" rights sale. Under such circumstances, the issuing company can either withhold the few unsubscribed shares from the market or sell them to the general public. In order to increase the chances that a large part of the issue will be taken up by stockholders, a number of companies offer *oversubscription* privileges, sometimes known as *the second bite*. Under this arrangement, stockholders are allowed not only to subscribe to the new issue on a pro rata basis but also to oversubscribe any shares not bought on the initial subscription.

The use of rights in connection with new issues gives an existing shareholder two types of protection. He may preserve his proportionate control, but only by buying the shares offered to him. He may overcome the effect of the discount that is used to assist in the sale of the new shares, either by subscribing to the new shares or by selling rights. But there is *no way for him to overcome the loss created by expansions which do not create new value in proportion to the increase in the number of shares.*

Before leaving the subject of rights, we call the reader's attention to the widespread use of executive stock options which grant executives, and sometimes other employees, the right to purchase a specified number of the company's common shares at a fixed price within a certain time period. This practice must be considered not as an aspect of the bargain for funds but rather as an aspect of the bargain for executives. Nevertheless, from a strictly financial viewpoint the effect on the common shareholders is the same as if the right to buy common stock had been extended to another group of security holders.

Of course, the attractiveness of such plans depends on a rising market price, and it is not surprising that some of the enthusiasm wears off in periods of recession. This was evident in the period of declining profits and uncertain market prices of stock in recent months.

Stock Purchase Warrants

Earlier in the chapter we mentioned the function of *stock purchase warrants* as a device for providing potential capital gains to holders of senior securities. Warrants, which threaten the common shareholder with the same sort of dilution that any type of new issue does, need not be issued only to purchasers of bonds. They can serve other purposes, but of course should be used only after careful exploration has indicated they provide the best way for protecting the common shareholder's position. For example, warrants are sometimes issued to individuals in return for their services to the company. Lawyers, underwriters, and promoters may be granted warrants as part of the remuneration for their efforts to found a company or to secure new capital for it. Executive stock options are a form of warrant. In one instance, a corporation has sold warrants directly to the public. In 1964 Mid-America Pipeline Company offered warrants at 9 cents each to its common shareholders on the basis of one warrant for each six common shares held. Each warrant entitled the holder to purchase a share of Mid-America common stock at $9 through March 31, 1972.

More frequently, warrants are used as an added inducement to complete a financing. When American Telephone and Telegraph in 1970 decided to raise $1.57 billion via the debt route from stockholders, it also used warrants that were exercisable at $52. The stock at the time was around the mid-$40 range. Thus the buyers of the bonds had a position in the equity values of the company.

Typically, a warrant will be combined with either preferred, common stock or a debenture in a *unit*. Tampa Electric, for example, came to market with a 150,000-share straight preferred issue, and accompanying each share of preferred was a warrant exercisable into two shares of common at $23 for a five-year period. The utility's stock then was selling around $20. Thus, while the warrants if fully exercised would present the company with a 2.8% dilution, Tampa Electric didn't fret since its planners foresaw some equity financing about six years out. The risk was that if the stock appreciated greatly over that time, the company had obviously committed its stock via the warrants too cheaply. The issue of preferred, however, because of the warrant sweetener, carried an 8% yield, whereas a straight debt preferred might have gone for 9.5%. In terms of annual dividend payments, that worked out to a savings of $225,000.

Similar savings have been used by others, and not always with warrants on their own stock. Cities Service, for example, was under court orders to divest itself of its holdings in Atlantic Richfield. So, when it sought to raise $100 million in debt it attached warrants to purchase 500,000 shares of its Atlantic Richfield holdings. At the time, Cities Service figured the warrant feature saved it almost a point in interest charges. Moreover, the warrants were exercisable at $110, and when Atlantic Richfield stock declined to near $50 the possibility was raised that the warrants never would be exercised, so that Cities Service would then be free to otherwise dispose of the committed shares.

Modification of the Distribution of Control

In Chapter 19 the normal distribution of control among the basic security types was discussed. It was brought out that normally, voting power rests in the hands of the common shareholders alone, although certain contingent voting privileges may be reserved for the preferred shareholders in event of suspension of dividend payments.

In a few cases the preferred stock does have a share of the voting power at regular shareholders' meetings. The extent varies from one issue to another. The holders of Sperry Rand Corporation $4.50 cumulative preferred have full voting rights of one vote per share along with the common. The holders of Mead Johnson & Company 4% cumulative preferred are entitled to one vote per share, to use these votes cumulatively in voting for directors, and on some issues, to vote as a group. Under certain circumstances, the voting power of the preferred shareholders could be a major consideration in the minds of the common shareholders and hence an important issue in setting the terms of the preferred.

It has been mentioned previously that some companies have subdivided their common stock into two classes. Usually, the primary purpose of this is to reserve the voting power for one class and use the other class as a means of raising capital from the investing public. Obviously, such nonvoting stock can be sold only to shareholders who are first and foremost investors and therefore attach only secondary importance to the voting privilege. It is a significant fact that nonvoting common stock is not accepted for listing by the New York Stock Exchange.

Although bondholders and most preferred stockholders do not have a direct voice in management, they nevertheless influence the actions of management by means of positive or negative covenants in the bond indenture or in charter provisions relating to preferred stock (described in the previous chapter). Further, if the issue is in default and/or the company in bankruptcy, these investors or their representatives will have a strong influence on management decisions, and this influence may be perpetuated in a reorganization under which old securities are exchanged for new securities with voting power. The full implications of reorganization will be taken up in a later chapter.

Summary

In this and the preceding chapter we have developed the idea of the security form as a product of the bargaining process between the corporate user of funds and those individuals and institutions which supply the funds. It has been seen how certain security features are to the advantage of the issuing company and its common shareholders and that other features are to the advantage of the senior security holder. The resultant security is basically a compromise of objectives which is acceptable to both parties to the contract. We have stressed that the fundamental give-and-take of this process is not really between management as such and a group of security holders but rather between one group of security holders and another—between the common shareholders, on the one hand, and the senior security holders, on the other.

Because of the wide variation of circumstances and objectives, it is not surprising that this bargaining process has produced a complex of special security types. We have reviewed the major variations in general use; but as we stated at the beginning, this is by no means a catalog of all possible types. The reader is referred to the appendix of the first edition of Graham and Dodd's *Security Analysis* for a list of illustrations of unusual variations of the common security forms.[2] This list includes such securities as bonds payable at the option of the bondholder, noninterest-bearing bonds, preferred issues with little or no claim as to assets, preferred stock with a mortgage lien, and common stock with a claim to income senior to another issue. The perusal of such a list brings home the importance of judging a security not by the name which the company has applied to it but rather by the specific terms which determine its true nature.

[2] Benjamin Graham, and David L. Dodd, *Security Analysis* (1st ed.; New York: McGraw-Hill Book Co., 1934), Appendix, Note 3, pp. 618–35.

chapter 25

Refinancing

Definitions

In considering the management of long-term finance, it is natural that our attention should have been concentrated on the issuance of securities for the purpose of acquiring new capital. This is a primary concern of both new and growing businesses. In prosperous times the purpose of raising new money is the dominant one in corporate security offerings.

There are, however, other reasons why corporations issue securities. For the more mature business, there is likely to come a time when new securities will be issued not to add to the funds invested but rather to replace some portion of the existing investment. When a new issue of securities is sold to a new group of security holders and the proceeds are applied to the retirement of an existing issue of securities, the company is said to be engaged in *refinancing*. The most common form of refinancing is the sale of a new bond issue to replace an existing bond issue, and this is known as *refunding* the debt. The similar process of retiring a preferred stock with the proceeds of a borrowing is known as *funding*. There are also those situations where a group of existing security holders accepts a new issue in voluntary exchange for the issue it now holds. This process of modifying the capital structure is referred to as *recapitalization*.

In our discussion in this chapter, these distinctions will be preserved, although in practice, new financing, refinancing, refunding, and recapitalization may be linked together in some degree in one operation. For example, a new issue of securities may be in part new money and in part refinancing. Similarly, the refunding of a bond at maturity may be accomplished in large measure by the existing bondholders taking new bonds in exchange for the old, thus coming under the definition of recapitalization. However, the problems associated with each of these types of capital structure changes are sufficiently different to warrant separate treatment.

471

Refunding Bonds at Maturity

The reader is now well aware that a corporate bond involves the contractual obligation to repay the face value of the bond in cash at a fixed maturity date. The setting of the life period of a bond is determined more by market conditions at the time of issue than by the issuer's long-range plans. At the time of issue the conditions and needs many years hence cannot be foreseen with any degree of accuracy. Thus, it will normally be mere coincidence if the maturity date coincides with a time when disinvestment or a change in the debt-equity balance of the issuer is desired. On the contrary, it will frequently be true that a business finds it continues to need the funds supplied by the bondholders and is confident that the existing debt-equity balance is one that can and should be preserved.

Under these circumstances, the company will desire to refund the old issue. The normal procedure is to create a new issue of bonds approximately equal in amount to the maturing issue. It may be sold generally or offered to the present bondholders in exchange for the maturing bonds. The existing bondholders are, of course, entitled to receive cash and will be paid in cash if they so desire. On the other hand, it is likely that if they have been satisfied with the bonds of this company up to the present, they too will be interested in continuing the investment. Provided the new bonds are offered on terms which are attractive to the investors, a large percentage of them are likely to take advantage of the exchange. The balance can then be paid off in cash provided by the sale of the unexchanged refunding bonds.

It is almost certain that the refunding bonds will not contain precisely the same terms as the bonds they are replacing. Both the company and the investment market will have changed significantly between time of issue and time of maturity. Whether the net result will run toward more favorable terms for the issuer or for the bondholder depends on the individual circumstances. Normally, it is to be expected that the financial condition of a successful and profitable business would improve over a period of 15 or 20 years to the point where the company's bargaining position in the market would be reflected in an upgrading of its bonds. Thus, it might be expected that the new bonds could be offered at a lower interest rate or with other terms more favorable to the issuer. On the other hand, the company must reckon with the general market trends and with the general demand for and supply of investable funds at the time of maturity. It may well be that a weakness in the market at that time could more than offset any improvement in the company's financial position and risk status.

It would appear that the occurrence of a maturity is an event which involves considerable uncertainty for the issuing company and, at the same time, one in which the outcome is largely outside the discretion of management. It is quite conceivable that a large bond issue could come due in a soft bond market, which would make it difficult to refund except, perhaps, on unfortunate terms. It would also appear that there is little management could do about this, in view of the fact that it cannot influence the timing of refunding or the market conditions.

In practice, both the hazard and the limitation of management discretion may be considerably reduced. In various ways the amount of the debt may be substantially diminished by the time of ultimate maturity. As previously mentioned, many bond issues today carry sinking fund provisions which make retirement of a substantial portion of the debt prior to maturity mandatory. Companies with large amounts of debt are well advised to use several issues to spread their maturities. Further, there is nothing to prevent a company from acquiring its own bonds on the open market at any time before maturity, with or without a sinking fund provision, thus reducing the outstanding obligation.

Refunding after Call

We have noted that a call, or redemption, privilege is one that is included in the terms of most of the corporate bonds and preferred stocks issued in the United States. The existence of this feature enables management to choose its own time to retire an issue and thus to take advantage of favorable conditions to revise its bargains with investors by replacing the called security by a refunding issue. The call feature adds great flexibility to managerial discretion, since a bond may be retired before maturity, and a preferred stock, which has no maturity, may also be retired. Thus, a management may consider a refunding at any time it feels that the terms of financing can be significantly improved.

Although it is sometimes decided to retire an issue to stop the effect of some burdensome protective provision, the most significant incentive to refunding is to gain a lower cost of funds for the issuer. Apart from changes within the firm which might change favorably the quality rating of its bonds and preferred stocks, shifts in the structure of interest rates sometimes make refunding very attractive. In the late 1940's there was such a period, but there has been little opportunity since so far as bonds are concerned.

During the summer of 1965 the officers of the General Telephone Company of California, who were considering the issue of bonds for a number of purposes, decided to raise $16.5 million more by borrowing in order to call and retire the 750,000 shares of outstanding $5\frac{1}{2}\%$ cumulative preferred stock. The redemption price was, at the time, $22 on shares with $20 par value. This call was made, effective August 31, and the stock was retired.

It happened that, after the call had been announced (and therefore could not be rescinded), conditions in the bond market seemed unfavorable, and the company chose to borrow temporarily from banks. On

December 8, the funding was accomplished by the successful issue of $40.0 million of 5% first-mortgage bonds due December 1, 1995. The prospectus accompanying the issue stated that $16.5 million of the proceeds was to be used to repay the bank loans referred to above. The delay described above serves as an example of the problems of timing that are sometimes encountered when one attempts to raise funds.[1]

The interest cost of the new issue, calculated from the price paid by the banking syndicate to the telephone company, is 5.02%. The cost of the retired preferred, based on the redemption price of $22, is 5%. But bond interest is tax deductible while preferred dividends are not. With taxes at 48% taken into account, we have the following comparison, which shows a significant saving.

	Before Tax	After Tax
Preferred, 5½% @ 22	9.62%	5.00%
Bonds, 5's @ 99.7097	5.02	2.61

The comparison can also be made in terms of outflow of funds. The 750,000 shares of preferred stock required the payment of dividends amounting to $825,000. To raise $16.5 million by bonds priced at 99.7097 requires a par value of $16,548,039, on which 5% interest is $827,402. With a 48% tax rate, the tax shield on this interest is $827,402 × 0.48 = $397,153. So the after-tax cost of the bond interest is $827,401 − $397,153 = $430,248. The comparison with the burden of the preferred is much in favor of the bond.

In the language of capital budgeting, the "net funds inflow" of this refunding is the after-tax cost of the preferred less the after-tax cost of the bonds, $394,752 per year. We may ignore the funds flows related to the sinking fund on the new bonds, because for purposes of comparison with a preferred that had no sinking fund, we should assume that any bonds retired would be replaced by new borrowing at the same rate.

One is tempted to calculate a rate of return on the investment, because apparently there has been an investment of the call premium that the preferred stock required, $1.5 million. But such a calculation is misleading. The fact is that the telephone company has increased its debt capacity by the funding, despite the apparent increase in its obligations. It has the same assets as before, and it has less to pay for the financing that provides them. Our thesis is that what we have named "burden" is the significant measure of the obligation of a bond or preferred stock, not the book values on the balance sheet. The burden has been reduced and that is the important fact. The total sum paid out over the life of the bonds and at

---

[1] The fact that the stock was sold in 1957 at a cost of 5.77% is of no significance now.

their maturity is less than would have been required by preferred stock over the same period plus a call of the preferred in the year 1995. In detail, the comparison appears in Table 25–1, which shows the actual dollar amounts and their time-adjusted equivalents at 2.61%, the after-tax cost of the borrowing. What these figures tell us is that the company can carry the obligation for 30 years and then retire it with a present commitment which is $8.2 million less if the bonds are used.

We may emphasize the point of recent paragraphs by saying that a successful refunding operation should never be regarded as competing with a project to acquire new assets. The success of the refunding makes it easier to finance the desired assets, because the total financial burden of

Table 25–1

Comparison of Funds Flows, 1965–66
(5½ % preferred vs. 5.02% bonds)

Time	Event	Preferred	Preferred Present Value @ 2.61%	Bonds	Bond Present Value @ 2.61%
1–30	Annual dividend on preferred	$ 825,000	$17,091,750	. . .	. . .
1–30	Annual interest on bonds	. . .	. . .	$ 430,249	$ 8,876,037
30	Call preferred in 1995	16,500,000	7,623,000	. . .	. . .
30	Maturity of bonds	. . .	. . .	16,548,039	7,645,194
			$24,714,750		$16,521,231

the company is made lower. Any call premium (and other expenses of the refunding operation) is not to be regarded as an investment at the time, but rather an increase in the ultimate repayment at maturity.

Recapitalization

The term *recapitalization* normally refers to the voluntary exchange of one security for another. While the term is broad enough to cover a variety of different exchange combinations, certain forms of recapitalization have been more common than others, and these will be given special attention in this section. The use of the adjective *voluntary* is designed to exclude from the discussion those exchanges which take place under conditions of bankruptcy and receivership where the choice on the part of the existing security holders can hardly be described as free. Such exchanges of securities will be discussed in Chapter 29, which deals with this subject. Also excluded here are those exchanges of the securities of one company for another which are covered in the chapter on mergers and acquisitions, Chapter 28.

The terms of a legal contract are binding during its life, unless a specific procedure for change has been agreed upon and made a part of the contract. Therefore, for a corporate issuer to attempt to modify the terms of an issue or to make a substitution of a new security without the consent of the holder would not only be without legal foundation but would also justify a legal action for enforcement of the original contract and recovery of damages, if any. But in practice the need for change has been foreseen. For example, most of the existing preferred stock contracts provide for change, if approved by a large majority (frequently two thirds) of the shares. Modern bond indentures also make provision for change, if approved by a similarly large majority in amount of the issue. Such privileges are, however, almost never extended to the basic conditions of the issue, such as the rate of interest, the maturity date, the priority of claim over other creditors, the call premium, etc. Nevertheless, especially since many new bond issues are issued in registered form so that the issuer knows who the holders are, and can reach them, it can no longer be said absolutely that the terms of senior securities are unalterable without unanimous consent.

Since common stock is the voting stock, it is normally considered that the power to elect the board of directors is sufficient protection of the best interest of this stockholder group. The one specific right which may be attached is the preemptive right, which is intended to protect the individual shareholder against dilution of the voting privilege and of the value of his investment (see page 445).

The need to obtain the necessary consent in recapitalization presents a phase of the problem which was absent in the cases of refinancing previously discussed. Through maturity or by exercising the call provision, the company legally discharged its obligation to the old security holders and replaced them with a new group of security holders who were prepared to accept the terms of the new issue. In such cases there was no need to consult the holders of the redeemed securities. In other cases where the privilege to change with the consent of a specified majority has not been provided, there is a question of what becomes of the stockholder who refuses to go along with the proposal. As a general rule, those who do not consent remain with their previous holding. Many corporate balance sheets show small amounts of such issues. But the corporation law of many states now provides the alternative that such dissenting stockholders must be paid off in cash at a price to be set by independent appraisal or arbitration. Since there is no quick answer to the problem of valuation, the value which will finally be set as a basis for compensation is difficult to estimate in advance.

In order to keep recapitalization in perspective, it should be borne in mind that the typical industrial corporation has a relatively simple capital structure made up of some combination of bonds, preferred stocks, and common stocks, and that if this structure is changed at all by recapitalization during the life of the corporation, it is only at infrequent intervals and under unusual circumstances.

In August, 1965, the United States Steel Corporation announced that a special meeting of shareholders would be held November 24 to obtain approval, among other proposals, of a plan to create a new issue of subordinated debentures to be offered to the holders of the existing 7% preferred stock. Concerning the details of the new issue, the chairman of the board of the corporation said only that they would be priced "somewhat in excess" of the current market value of the preferred stock (about $152 per share).

The 7% preferred stock of the United States Steel Corporation was one of the last of a group of "noncallable" preferred stocks that had been created by corporations in the early years of this century when the noncallable feature had been considered necessary to attract investors. In view of this protection against call, the high 7% rate, and the financial standing of the issuer, the stock sold well over par, and the yield followed that of the less highly rated industrial bonds. At 150, for example, the yield was $4\frac{2}{3}\%$.

Over the years, often attracted by the fact that preferred dividends are not allowed as expenses for tax purposes, most of the noncallable preferreds had been retired, or reduced to small amounts, by exchange offers and other devices. Now the United States Steel Corporation made its move by requesting the shareholders to approve a recapitalization.

On September 29 the exact terms of the exchange were made public. Each $100 par value share of the 7% preferred could be exchanged for $175 par value of $4\frac{5}{8}\%$ subordinated debentures of 1966, with no call permitted for 10 years and then callable at a small premium. The preferred holder might well expect that the market price of his holding of the new bonds would be greater than recent levels of the preferred, and his new income would rise to $8.09\frac{3}{8}$ per year. It was, however, expected that the transaction would be taxable as a capital gain, measured between the market price of the new bonds and each preferred shareholder's cost.

The United States Steel Corporation received a large favorable vote at its meeting in November, and it proceeded to make the exchange offer as described. "When issued" trading opened in the new bonds as soon as the vote was taken. Thus, the preferred holders were given more definite information about the terms. The opening quotations of the bonds were $95\frac{1}{2}$, and the preferred stock, of course, traded at $167\frac{1}{8}$. Only one stockholder gave notice of dissent to this refinancing and he did not pursue his claim.

It is perhaps worth noting that while most of the opinions the authors heard "on the Street" were to the effect that the move was a constructive one for the corporation because it would create new tax shields, there were a few "old-timers" who grumbled because the debt ratio of the United States Steel Corporation was almost doubled, and the fixed charge coverage fell from about 7 times to about 4 times. There was also a substantial reduction in the corporate surplus, due to the creation of $175 in debt for each $100 of stock.

We present here the history of a recapitalization within Litton Industries, Inc. as a further example of refinancing.

On January 30, 1964, Litton Industries, Inc., offered to its common shareholders a share-for-share exchange of the common stock into a new $3 dividend cumulative preference stock (par $5 per share, involuntary redemption price after 1972, $100). The preferred stock was convertible at the option of the holder into one share of common stock, and this privilege was protected against dilution. Only 428,141 preferred shares of a larger authorization were offered for exchange. Convertible preferred stocks were coming into fashion as a means of accomplishing acquisitions (page 445). In such negotiations it is desirable to know the likely market value of what is being offered, so it is not surprising that Litton stated as its purpose for offering the new shares in exchange for common: "to create an ascertainable market value for the preferred and a ready market therefor."[2] It is also not surprising, in view of the intended use of the unissued portion of the preferred stock, that it was provided that shares reacquired in any manner, including those surrendered for conversion, might be reissued.

The offer was a great success, as about 7.6 million common shares out of 10.7 million were tendered for the exchange. The actual issue was distributed in proportion to all those tendering, each holder receiving about 4% of the number of shares he requested.

During the year 1964, among other acquisitions, Litton Industries acquired the Fitchburg Paper Company by issuing Litton common and preferred stock, and the Royal McBee Corporation by issuing Litton preferred in return for Royal McBee common stock. Negotiations to acquire the Streater Corporation in return for cash and Litton preferred were reported.[3] So the new preferred was quickly proved to be very useful.

RECAPITALIZATION AND THE BARGAIN FOR FUNDS. We have now seen that there are a number of ways in which a business corporation may modify its capital structure from time to time. The usual methods by which this comes about and the immediate and potential benefits have been illustrated. It is clear that the basic objective of refinancing and recapitalization is to improve the position of the company and (usually) its common shareholders through a modification of the terms of the existing security forms.

Properly considered, these activities on the part of the issuing company are a continuation and extension of the bargaining process we discussed in the preceding two chapters. Such changes usually would not

---

[2] *New York Stock Exchange Listing Statement*, No. A 21504 (January 14, 1964).

[3] *The Wall Street Journal*, April 3, June 12, September 9, 1964.

be initiated by the company unless an advantage, through a change in the market and/or the bargaining strength of the company, was anticipated. On the other hand, it must also be true that if there is to be a change at all, it must be generally acceptable to the other security holders and realistic in terms of existing market conditions.

Stock Splits

A *stock split* is a type of recapitalization designed to increase the number of shares outstanding. There is also a *reverse split*, in which the number of shares outstanding is reduced. In a stock split the shareholders receive more shares of the same class of stock (for example, 1½ to 1, or 2 to 1) for each old share previously held. Thus, the number of certificates of ownership outstanding is increased by a multiple without any change taking place in the total value of the investor's holding. It will be apparent, however, that the one thing that is affected is the value of one share. Since no new funds have been added and nothing has happened to the basic determinants of the value of the business as a result of this exchange of paper, reason would suggest that the value of one share after a stock split will be that fraction of the value before the split which is the inverse of the increase in the number of shares. If it is a 3-for-1 split, for example, three new shares for one old, then the value of each of the new shares would be one third the value of one of the old shares, so that the total valuation "per stockholder" of the stock after the split is exactly equal to the total valuation before the split. It should be noted that when a company splits its stock, it is usual to make a parallel downward adjustment in the per share dividend, so that the total payment is the same as before.

The reason usually advanced for a stock split (or stock "split-up") is that of providing a broader and more stable market for the stock. It is argued that a larger volume of lower-priced securities should make for a more continuous market and therefore one which is less subject to erratic fluctuations. Officials of the New York Stock Exchange have estimated that the most satisfactory price to induce active trading is between $18 and $25 per share.[4]

The pressure for a stock split is usually found in a company which has demonstrated consistent profitability over a number of years. As a result of this, the market price of the stock has appreciated considerably. There may be a feeling that the price of the stock has moved out of the price range of many investors and that this is detrimental to the future growth of the stock. In fact, it is often seen that the number of shareholders increases after a split.

Although it is not always explicitly stated, there is often the additional hope that the market reaction to the split will be irrational to the extent of

---

[4] New York Stock Exchange, *Company Manual*, § A 15.

giving the three new shares a combined market value in excess of one old share. As a result, some capital appreciation will have been realized by the holders of the old shares. The one valid reason for expecting such a result is that the old stock has been somewhat undervalued in a market which is "narrower" because of its relatively high price. This line of reasoning would argue that the split restores the stock to the full impact of market demand and thus to "proper" valuation.

Whether or not stock splits actually increase the overall market valuation is a hotly debated issue. This would seem to be a debate easily resolved by reference to the facts of market price. However, the problem is one of isolating the effects of the split from the many factors which can have a cause-and-effect relationship with market price. Those who see a capital gain advantage can point to cases where a higher overall valuation obtained after the split; but to prove the precise cause is difficult, if not impossible. Those who oppose the stock split claim that if there is any benefit at all, it is only a temporary one resulting from speculative activity.

The problem may be illustrated by the case of the American Telephone and Telegraph Company. Between 1936 and 1959 the common stock of A.T.&T. did not sell below $100, and there was a steady upward trend, which brought the price to the 224–65 range in early 1959. For many years there had been strong pressure on management to split the stock, pressure which management resisted. This activity culminated in a vote on the issue in 1957, at which time the split was rejected by a substantial majority. At the annual meeting of the previous year, 1956, the president of the company commented on the stock split proposal, in part, as follows:

When there is an announcement of a stock split, the price of stock goes up, there isn't any question about that at all. You will get a flurry in the stock market and a rise in the price of the stock. But if there is no substantial dividend increase . . . at the time of the stock split, or shortly thereafter, that stock goes down in the market. And in almost every case it goes down below where it was before. . . . So I think if the telephone company were to split without a dividend increase, you would see our price go up on the market temporarily. That would benefit some people who bought our stock on a short-term basis. It would not benefit you people that want to keep your stock on a permanent investment.[5]

In 1959, however, the management split the stock 3 for 1, and at the same time increased the cash dividend. The following explanation of the change was given by the president at the annual meeting in 1959:

Conditions have changed from two years ago. The Company has consistently opposed a stock split with no dividend increase, and at the time referred to [1956] an increase could not be justified. Recently our growth in share owners has slowed down—it is important to encourage more people to

---

[5] American Telephone and Telegraph Company, *Report of the Annual Meeting of Share Owners, April 18, 1956,* pp. 7–8.

invest in the business—an increased dividend is needed to maintain investors' confidence—and the Company's improved financial situation permits us to pay it. . . .[6]

Previous to the 1959 split, the dividend had been $9 per share, unchanged since 1922. The dividend rate at the time of the split was established at $3.30 per share. It was made $3.50 in 1962. In that year the stock was again split, 2 for 1, and the dividend rate of $2 per share was established. It had reached $2.60 in 1970. The reader is asked to calculate what is a proper adjustment to make to compare the present rate of $2.60 per share with the old $9 rate.

Stock Dividends

An alternative to the stock split as a means of increasing the number of shares outstanding is the stock dividend. For example, the number of shares in a company could be doubled without an increase in the funds invested in one of two ways: (1) by splitting the company's capital stock so as to have twice as many shares representing the same total nominal or par value as shown on the balance sheet; or (2) by declaring a 100% dividend in stock, issuing each shareholder one new share for each share now held and transferring from the Earned Surplus account to the Capital Stock account an amount representing the value of the newly created shares.

The difference in accounting procedure may be illustrated. Suppose a company to have the following net worth:

```
Capital stock:
    Common, $10 par, 100,000 shares...........   $1,000,000
    Earned surplus............................    3,000,000
                                                 $4,000,000
```

After a 2-for-1 split, this would appear as follows:

```
Capital stock:
    Common $5 par, 200,000 shares.............   $1,000,000
    Earned surplus............................    3,000,000
                                                 $4,000,000
```

After a 100% stock dividend the net worth would show as follows (using par value as a basis for the transfer).[7]

```
Capital stock:
    Common $10 par, 200,000 shares............   $2,000,000
    Earned surplus............................    2,000,000
                                                 $4,000,000
```

---

[6] American Telephone and Telegraph Company, *Report of the Annual Meeting of Share Owners, April 15, 1959*, p. 12.

[7] The New York Stock Exchange requires that the transfer be at "fair value" instead of par value. NYSE, *Company Manual* § A 13. Such a transfer is also the recommendation of the Accounting Practices Board. American Institute of Certified Public Accountants, *Accounting Research and Technology Bulletins* (Final Edition, 1961), p. 51.

While the accounting procedure is different and the balance sheet will appear differently in each case, the net effect is the same as in a stock split, namely, to double the number of shares by a paper transaction with no increase in funds invested or in earning capacity as a result of these changes. Thus, a stock dividend can be a means of bringing about this type of recapitalization, provided, of course, that the authorized capital stock permits and earned surplus is large enough to cover the transfer.

Since it has been argued in terms of logic that a stock split should bring a reduction in per share market value which is exactly the inverse of the increase in the number of shares, so it would appear to follow that a stock dividend will bring a similar lowering of market price. If all that has happened as a result of the dividend is that the shareholders hold twice as many certificates as before, each certificate should be worth one half of what it was worth before the dividend with no net increase in the total market valuation of the company. An important distinction must be made, however, between the large-scale stock dividend, illustrated above, which is basically a stock split in a different form, and the small-scale stock dividend which is in the range of 1%, 2%, or 5% of the outstanding stock.

Stock dividends on a modest scale have become quite popular with management in recent years. In some companies such dividends have been issued as a supplement to cash dividends on a regular basis over a period of several years. The argument usually advanced for such stock dividends is that in this way, management is recognizing the shareholders' additional contributions through retained earnings in a tangible form which can be either retained or sold, as the individual shareholder chooses. The inference is that the declaration of the stock dividend has, in and of itself, added something to the value of the shareholder's existing investment. Thus, if he sells the stock received as a dividend, the remaining investment will be as valuable as it was before the stock dividend.

The facts of the situation run contrary to this argument. If any value has been added, it is the result of the earnings which have been realized and retained, and this will be reflected on the balance sheet and in the market price of the existing shares without any assistance from the formalities of a stock dividend. Rationally, the effect of a small stock dividend should be the same as that of a large one—simply to spread existing values over a large number of shares, thus leaving each shareholder exactly as he was before, with the exception that he has certificates for more shares of stock. If he sells the shares received as a "dividend," he is in fact liquidating a portion of his investment. This is not "income" but rather a conversion of principal into cash.[8]

Having recognized this basic point, we can now proceed to note how a

---

[8] The available evidence indicates that few shareholders do sell the dividend shares they receive.

stock dividend may have some real meaning and value to the shareholder. It will be recalled in the reference to A.T.&T. that the president qualified his criticism of a proposed stock split in saying "if there is no substantial [cash] dividend increase." In the case of a stock split or large stock dividend, it would be an unusual company which could maintain the per share cash dividend paid before the split or stock dividend. However, in the case of a small stock dividend of, say, 2% or 5% of the outstanding issue, it is quite possible that the company could maintain the existing per share cash dividend, thus increasing the dollar dividend payout in the period following the stock dividend payment.

Thus, if a person held 100 shares and was receiving a $2 per share cash dividend, a 5% stock dividend would give him 105 shares and a total cash dividend in the following year of $210 rather than $200. A number of companies which have a stable cash dividend policy declare periodic small-scale stock dividends with this in mind. The stock dividend becomes, in effect, a promise of increased cash dividends in succeeding years. Of course, the same result could be obtained by raising the cash dividend on the old number of shares.

In view of our suggestion in Chapter 21 that dividends may play an important part in a shareholder's appraisal of the value of his shares, the small periodic stock dividend may have real future value in the eyes of the shareholder; and this, coupled with the conflicting evidence regarding the reaction of the market price, gives the stock dividend considerable appeal among shareholders. In addition, for management, there is a possible advantage in a lower market price and a wider and more stable market for the stock. Again, however, we must say that statistical studies have not succeeded in isolating the effect of the policy.

Conversion as a Means of Recapitalization

Significant changes in the capital structure can be effected by the exercise of the conversion privilege attached to bonds or preferred stock. However, unlike the forms of recapitalization already mentioned, conversion is not initiated by management at a time of its own choosing but rather is negotiated when the security is first issued and is at the discretion of the security holder, if and when he finds reason to do it. Conversion involves a voluntary exchange of securities and brings about the replacement of one type of security by another of distinctly different form. The factors involved in conversion have already been discussed in Chapter 24.

While it is true that management cannot "make" a favorable market price or decide for the shareholder whether he wants to be in a preferred position or a common equity position, it can nevertheless have a great deal to do with the timing of conversion. By having a call provision in the terms of the convertible security, management is in a position to precipitate a mass conversion at an early date, by calling the security at a time when the market price is above the call price. Of course, a company's managers cannot guarantee a rising market price of the common stock. Nevertheless, many issues of convertible securities are sold by companies which have a definite plan for forcing conversion at the earliest favorable opportunity.

The Repurchase of Outstanding Common Shares

In this final section of the chapter on refinancing we shall turn to a process that does alter the proportions of an existing capital structure, but by reducing the amount of the outstanding equity interest instead of by rearranging security contracts.

The corporation laws in the United States permit corporations to buy their own outstanding shares, and the rules of the national stock exchanges and of the Securities and Exchange Commission only require that corporations make public the number of shares they have purchased after the purchase has taken place. Many firms have availed themselves of this privilege, though most of them have advised their shareholders of their intention in advance of the purchasing.

The privilege to repurchase shares has long been used to buy small amounts of outstanding shares, for example, to supply shares for stock options being exercised or, in the case of a closely held company, to assist a stockholder who desires to liquidate his interest.[9] In recent years, however, the amount of repurchasing by major corporations has made this activity one of great importance.[10] Such companies as General Motors, General Electric, and the Standard Oil Company (New Jersey) have themselves accounted for over 14% of the annual volume of trading in their securities, and over 125 of the companies listed on the New York Stock Exchange have purchased over 5% of their volume. It was estimated in 1965 that, since 1962, the money spent for such purchases (over a billion dollars a year) exceeded the net amount of cash funds raised by new common stock issues to the public. Here is a phenomenon worthy of far more attention than it has yet received in the legislative and academic worlds.

Most of the countries around the world have prohibited the retirement of corporate capital without a finding by some tribunal that the proposed retirement does not (1) damage creditors by unduly reducing the equity base, (2) represent an attempt to avoid the taxation that would fall on a dividend distribution, and (3) represent an attempt by "inside" interests

---

[9] In one of the developing countries, Ghana, the new corporate law specifically provides power to purchase shares in order to encourage the spread of stock ownership that would otherwise be limited by the fear of being unable to liquidate the holding.

[10] The information in this section is drawn from an unpublished thesis of Leo A. Guthart, and his article "More Companies Are Buying Back Their Stock," *Harvard Business Review*, Vol. 43, No. 2 (March–April, 1965), pp. 40–53, 172.

to buy out other shareholders who are not fully informed of the firm's prospects. These are the three principal dangers that must be avoided in the United States by other means than a governmental review, if the practice is to be endorsed. To quote Guthart:

At the present time, the SEC has no specific requirements concerning share repurchases, and the body of corporate law concerning this particular activity is not clear regarding the potential conflict of interest that may exist. Conclusive definitions of responsibility in this area are urgently needed.[11]

In this brief presentation we shall concentrate on the questions that arise from the point of view of the company's shareholders. What does repurchase mean to the "typical" shareholder who must rely only on the information that will be made public? Our first point here is the assumption that the repurchases are decided upon by the managers because they believe that the repurchasing will benefit the firm. If so, it seems reasonable to suggest that the persons who decide for the action expect that the value of the shares which will remain outstanding will increase, relative to the value at which the purchase shares are obtained. Whether the expectation will prove correct, of course, is a very important question as to which a shareholder might well reach an opposite conclusion. But the shareholder who does not know of the proposed action has no chance to make his decision.

Such reasoning has led the great majority of persons who have considered the matter to recommend that all shareholders be put on notice of the company's intentions before purchases begin. The argument that if the corporation buys through a broker it can only obtain shares from someone who has decided to sell anyway and who therefore is not damaged, does not hold water, because the fact is that the company is reducing its outstanding shares to increase the value of each remaining share. It is thus a very "material fact" (using the words of the Securities Act) and it must be disclosed.

The principal reasons given by corporations for the retirement of their shares are as follows:

1. To use liquid funds that have accumulated beyond the level necessary for the conduct and expansion of the business.
2. To have treasury stock which can be used instead of the new shares otherwise necessary when shares are needed:
   a) For acquisitions.
   b) For satisfying stock options as exercised.
   c) For meeting the conversion of convertible issues.
   d) For regular or occasional stock dividends.
   e) For meeting obligations under employee stock purchase plans.
3. To improve the record of earnings per share.

---

[11] *Ibid.*, p. 53.

The diversity of these reasons, in Guthart's words, leads "unmistakably to the conclusion that no comprehensive theoretical solution exists to the problem of when, and at what price, a corporation should buy back its own shares. Furthermore, no attempt has been made to solve the problem of how to allocate funds among share repurchase, dividends, and new investments in plant."[12]

Two methods of accomplishing stock repurchase are prevalent. We shall do no more than name them here, because they are well described in the case of the Extone Chemical company, at page 857. One method, which assures that every shareholder has a notice of the program sent to his address, is the invitation to shareholders to *tender* their shares. In this method the prospective buyer announces its intention of making purchases under specified terms and invites owners to indicate their acceptance, that is, to tender their securities. The terms offered may be fixed in price and quantity, as in the example at page 869. Or, they may be dependent on the demand which develops, as in the procedure announced by the Universal Leaf Tobacco Company. This is very similar to a procedure that has been used to offer new issues of securities in England.

Universal Leaf is letting shareholders name their own price for the shares and is reserving the right to reject all offers that exceed a maximum price— a price which hasn't yet been set by company officials.

The Company will pay stockholders of all shares accepted the same maximum price per share, with stockholders tendering their shares at the lowest price to be the first in line, according to Gordon L. Crenshaw, president.

Thus, a stockholder who offers to sell his preferred stock at $100 a share may be first to get paid $250 a share if the company decides to pay $250. He also may get paid $150 a share, if officers set the price at that level. Another shareholder asking $250 for each of his shares may get turned down if the company sets the price at $225 a share.

"We are going to set one price at which we're willing to pay and everybody who tenders their stock at that price or under will get paid the same price, with the lowest prices offered us getting first considerations," said Mr. Crenshaw.[13]

The second method of acquiring shares is simply to buy them through brokers in the ordinary way. Some firms issue elaborate instructions to minimize the effect of this special source of demand on the price (no one is so naïve as to think that there is no effect). Others are less careful. With reference to the possibility that the corporation might, with "inside" knowledge, take advantage of the outside shareholders, some firms cease buying when such information comes to light until it has been made public. Other firms, again, are not so meticulous. Surely Guthart is right in his conclusion that, "Conclusive definitions of responsibility in this area are urgently needed."

---

[12] *Ibid.*, p. 172.

[13] *The Wall Street Journal*, December 7, 1965.

In this connection, we might quote one of the authors of this book, although others would not go so far:

I must admit that I share some of the questionings [which others have expressed] about the current wave of stock repurchasing. I know that I would favor any kind of regulation that would make it certain that companies would inform their shareholders of their intentions before they start purchasing, and I would even consider the possibility of limiting the methods of acquiring the shares to such procedures as an invitation to tender, or even of making a distribution of surplus funds equally to all shares in lieu of purchasing shares at all. . . .

. . . . Concentrating the number of shares does of course distort the record of earnings per share. In fact, some companies seem to be expecting that the increase in earnings per share will be received with the same enthusiasm as if it represented growth. On the whole, I think they have been disappointed— since investors are not quite as gullible as one sometimes assumes. . . .

In fact, I am critical of those companies which for too long hold large amounts of liquid funds invested at low returns. . . . Many of the companies which are now embarrassed with excess funds might avoid the embarrassment if they reconsider their dividend policy!

Like almost everything else in finance, the fine points of a decision seem to rest on the facts of a particular case. We have collected instances where it seems obvious that the accumulation of funds was due to a stingy dividend policy, and, on the other hand, we have cases where some sort of a nonrecurrent capital disinvestment has created funds that can quite properly be returned through repurchase. With sufficient notice, on such facts as the latter, I cannot criticize the action.[14]

---

[14] Pearson Hunt, letter to the editor, *Harvard Business Review*, Vol. 43, No. 4 (July–August, 1965), pp. 36–37.

chapter 26

The Nature and Effects of Government Regulation on Long-Term Finance[*]

The federal and state governments have both come to exert a very considerable and increasing influence on the subject of long-term corporate finance. Because the corporation as a creature of the state derives its characteristics from a charter issued pursuant to a state corporation law, this influence has always existed to some degree. However, the impact of government regulation on corporate finance through the state incorporation laws has become increasingly less important as such corporation laws have been liberalized. The intervention of the state and federal governments in the capital markets has been more important.

Except for the railroads, the extensive federal regulation of the security markets, together with the resulting impact on corporate finance, had its origins in the 1929 stock market crash and the severe depression that followed. Nowhere was the widespread collapse of confidence more apparent than in the financial sector of the economy. As a result, direct governmental response in the form of vigorous legislation came early during the New Deal. A review of the pervasive nature of this response—which forms the backbone of the institutional environment in which corporate financing must today exist—discloses the major objectives of this legislative program.

The radical overhauling of certain key financial institutions must be mentioned first. In particular, the separation of commercial banking from investment banking functions pursuant to the Glass-Stegall Act of 1933 and the regulation of security exchanges and trading in securities pursuant

* The authors wish to thank Peter J. Barack, J. D., Assistant Professor at the Graduate School of Business Administration, Harvard University, who revised this chapter.

to the federal security laws were designed to eliminate weaknesses which had contributed to the financial collapse and to the general decline in economic activity and employment. Furthermore, a new and continuing governmental overview of the major institutional components of the financial sector began with the birth of one major administrative agency, the Securities and Exchange Commission, and the strengthening of others. Second, the legislative program was designed to protect the investor, particularly the small-scale, unsophisticated investor, from unnecessary losses in stock and security holdings and bank deposits. With the restoration of investor confidence in the capital markets, the hope was that savings would again flow into productive activity and so revive the vital allocational function of this market. Finally, there was the objective of protecting the public as consumers in certain key industries, such as the public utility industry, from a decrease in efficiency and an increase in costs resulting from weaknesses in or abuses of corporate financial policy.

If an estimated 10.0 million stockholders[1] realized losses in the 1929–32 debacle, any similar event in the 1970's would affect a much larger number and proportion of the population of the United States. The Census of Shareholders of the New York Stock Exchange has, for example, estimated a jump in the number of stockholders from 8.6 to 30.8 million over the period from 1956 to 1970.[2] Moreover, millions of additional Americans indirectly hold corporate stock and securities through their interests in the institutional investors—the mutual funds, insurance companies, and corporate and union pension plans.[3] This overwhelming growth has greatly increased the importance of securities regulation in our economy.

FEDERAL REGULATION OF NEW ISSUES

The Securities and Exchange Commission, created in 1934, is the principal federal agency charged with administering the six federal securities laws.[4] This series of acts and the subsequent amendments to them give the Commission broad authority to regulate most aspects of the American capital markets. The first two in this series, the Securities Act of 1933 and the Securities Exchange Act of 1934, deal primarily with regulating the initial distribution of and post-distribution trading in se-

---

[1] Edwin B. Cox, *Trends in the Distribution of Stock Ownership* (Philadelphia: University of Pennsylvania Press, 1963), p. 33.

[2] New York Stock Exchange, *Census of Shareholders*, 1965 and 1970.

[3] At the beginning of 1969, over 23 million persons were covered by private non-insured pension plans (Institute of Life Insurance, *1970 Life Insurance Fact Book* [New York, 1970], p. 35). At the end of 1969, there were also over 9 million personal, mutual fund shareholder accounts (Investment Company Institute, *1970 Mutual Fund Fact Book* [Washington, D.C., 1970], p. 16) ; and over 130 million individual policyholders had legal reserve life insurance (Institute of Life Insurance, *ibid.* at p. 19).

[4] The Securities Act of 1933, the Securities Exchange Act of 1934, the Public Utility Holding Company Act of 1935, the Trust Indenture Act of 1939, the Investment Company Act of 1940, and the Investment Advisers Act of 1940.

curities. Because primary reliance is placed by these acts on the ability of the investor to make a wise decision following a full presentation of the facts, they are often referred to as the "full-disclosure laws." While having the power to force full and fair disclosure, "the Commission has no authority to pass on the merits of the securities to be offered or the fairness of the terms of distribution."[5]

The Securities Act of 1933 requires registration with the SEC of most securities that are to be offered for sale to the public through the mails or any other "instrumentality of interstate commerce." Although this jurisdictional base is hard to avoid, the act does exempt certain securities and certain transactions. The securities of several types of corporations, including banking institutions supervised by state officials and common carriers regulated by the Interstate Commerce Commission, are exempt. Those securities which are a part of an issue that is offered and sold wholly within one state by a corporation incorporated and doing business in that state are also exempt. In addition, the issuance of securities by a corporation not involving any public offering is exempt. Such a "private placement" might include, for example, the offer by a corporation of its long-term debt securities to a handful of insurance companies—for long-term investment rather than trading purposes—and the sale of such securities to an even smaller number of insurance companies. These private placements yield economies of time and cost, and supply a considerable proportion of new financing. For example, in 1969 they made up 27.2% of new corporate securities offered for cash.[6] Finally, where the aggregate amount of securities in an issue totals less than $500,000, the issuer need only file with the SEC a more limited amount of information.

Pursuant to the disclosure philosophy of the 1933 act, *issuers* that propose to sell or offer for sale securities not exempted under the act must file a *registration statement* containing detailed information. Such an "issuer" is defined, in effect, to include not only the corporation whose securities are being offered but also any person in control of or controlled by the corporation. As such, not only the *initial distribution* of such securities by the corporation but also certain *secondary distributions* of these securities by controlling persons must be registered. The registration statement, in addition to describing the company, stating the purposes for which funds are to be raised, and presenting audited financial statements, must disclose "such matters as the names of persons who participate in the management or control of the issuer's business; the security holdings and remunerations of such persons; . . . underwriters' commissions; payments to promoters made within 2 years or intended to be made; the interest of directors, officers, and principal stockholders in

---

[5] Securities and Exchange Commission, *Thirty-Fifth Annual Report, 1969* (Washington, D.C., 1970), p. 26 [hereinafter cited as SEC 1969 Annual Report]. This federal regulatory philosophy is in contrast to the approach to securities regulation taken by many of the states.

. [6] New York Stock Exchange, *1970 Fact Book*, pp. 66–67.

material transactions with the issuer; . . . [etc.]"[7] As soon as it is filed, the registration statement is open to public inspection. Accompanying the registration statement is a copy of the *prospectus,* a document containing most of the information in the registration statement. The prospectus must be sent to prospective and actual buyers of the proposed issue as well as to any other person requesting it.

Upon receiving the registration statement and the prospectus, the Commission will review both documents to determine whether all *material facts* have been disclosed. While the responsibility of the Commission does not extend to a consideration of investment quality and security risk, the SEC will require the prominent presentation of certain types of material facts:

Where appropriate to a clear understanding by investors there should be set forth immediately following the cover page of the prospectus under an appropriate caption a carefully organized series of short, concise, paragraphs, . . . summarizing the principal factors which make the offering one of high risk or speculative. These factors may be due to such matters as an absence of an operating history of the registrant, an absence of profitable operations in recent periods, an erratic financial history, . . .[8]

Although a registration statement will automatically become effective 20 days after filing, the Commission will require the filing of delaying amendments until it is satisfied the full-disclosure standard has been met. During this waiting period between time of filing and the effective date, the SEC reviews and analyzes the registration statement and prospectus, prepares and delivers a letter of comment, and receives from the registrant substantive amendments and additions. When satisfied, the SEC will accelerate the effective date to just after the filing of the last amendment. In practice, because of the volatility of the capital markets, this is almost always the price amendment setting the price at which the issue is to come onto the market.

In fiscal year 1969, the median lapse of time between the date of filing a registration statement and the effective date was estimated at 65 calendar days.[9] During this waiting period, the issuer, underwriters, and brokers may only make *offers* to sell the security in registration. Once the registration statement becomes effective, the securities may be actually offered and *sold* to the public, provided that each investor receives a copy of the prospectus before or at the time he receives the securities.

Whenever it becomes apparent, either during the waiting period or after the effective date, that the registration material is misleading, the SEC may issue a *stop order* suspending the effectiveness of the registration statement. The Commission is also empowered to request a *court injunction* whenever it appears that a person is engaged in or is about to

---

[7] SEC 1969 Annual Report, p. 27.

[8] SEC Securities Act Release No. 33–4936 (December 9, 1968).

[9] SEC 1969 Annual Report, p. 32.

engage in activity that is or will be in violation of the act. Moreover, any person who wilfully violates any section, rule, or regulation of the 1933 act will be liable for criminal penalties.

Because there have been few criminal prosecutions, the possible civil liabilities under the act are of more general importance. First, any person who offers or sells a security in violation of the registration and prospectus provisions will be liable to the purchaser for damages or rescission. Second, any person who offers or sells *any* security, whether or not registered or exempt from registration, by means of a material misrepresentation will also be liable to the purchaser for damages and rescission. Third, the 1933 act also includes a general antifraud provision declaring it unlawful for any person to employ any fraudulent device or misrepresentative statement in the offer or sale of any security. Finally, to ensure compliance with the full-disclosure standard, the 1933 act holds the following parties liable to the purchaser for any misstatement or misleading omission of material fact in the registration statement and prospectus: the issuing corporation, its directors, any experts named as responsible for a portion of the registration statement, the underwriters, and all signers of the registration statement, among whom must be the company's chief executive, financial, and accounting officers. To escape liability, such a party, other than the issuer, must show that the allegedly misleading statement was only made after a reasonable investigation with due diligence on his part.[10]

Through the forceful application of this full-disclosure philosophy by the Commission, the Securities Act of 1933 has been effective in protecting the purchaser of securities during the initial distribution process. As such, significant benefits have also accrued to the corporate issuers. Honest corporate reporting under the auspices of the Securities and Exchange Commission cannot help but build public confidence in the securities markets. With the reduction in possibility of misrepresentation or fraud, the demand side will accordingly be strengthened. These market benefits most likely outweigh the costs of such government intervention. These costs include not only the time and expense of the formal registration procedure but also a concomitant increase in rigidity in the distribution process. In a highly volatile securities market, maximum flexibility is required in order to ensure a successful sale, in terms of both volume and price.

FEDERAL REGULATION OF SECURITIES TRADING

As a complement to the Securities Act of 1933, the Securities Exchange Act of 1934 is designed to ensure a fair and honest securities market

---

[10] As a general rule, a reasonable investigation in most circumstances cannot stop with the questioning of company officials but must include independent verification of their answers (*Escott* v. *BarChris Construction Corp.*, 283 F. Supp. 643 [S.D.N.Y. 1968]).

through the regulation of post-distribution trading in securities. As such, the 1934 act is a comprehensive piece of legislation with an impact in four basic areas: the disclosure of information on most widely held securities, the regulation of the securities markets, including the exchanges and brokers-dealers, the prevention of fraud and manipulation, and the regulation of credit extended on security purchases in the markets.

Full Disclosure

Those companies whose securities are listed and traded on a national securities exchange or which have total assets in excess of $1 million and a class of equity securities held by over 500 persons must register such securities with the SEC. The registration statement required must contain much the same information as is required for new issues under the 1933 act. However, this information must be kept current through the filing of annual (the so-called "10–K" report) and other reports "as the Commission may prescribe as necessary or appropriate for the proper protection of investors and to insure fair dealing in the security."

PROXY SOLICITATIONS. The Securities Exchange Act of 1934 has also emphasized the technique of full disclosure in its regulation of the proxy solicitation process. The ultimate objective of this regulation is to secure the full and informed exercise of the corporate franchise. Insofar as the large, widely held corporation draws its equity financing from a large number of shareholders while being managed by a small group of executives, the modern corporation has divorced its ownership interests from their effective ability to control. Although the shareholder-owners retain ultimate control in their power to elect directors and approve certain fundamental corporate policy decisions, their sheer numbers, inability to attend many of the shareholders' meetings, and lack of cohesiveness oftentimes contribute to a generally passive investment—rather than ownership—status. Frequently, if a stockholder's vote is to be counted at all, the stockholder who is unable to attend a shareholders' meeting must designate someone who will attend and vote as his proxy. Indeed, it has now become a common practice for the existing directors regularly to solicit the proxies of shareholders. While thus a device for maintaining ownership status, the proxy solicitation process has all too often proved ineffective, as stockholders frequently are ill-informed on management matters, sign their proxies only as a matter of course, or ignore entirely their right to vote. As a result, existing management can often perpetuate itself indefinitely without ever rendering full account to the shareholder-owners.

To prevent or remedy the most egregious abuses of this process, the SEC regulates the solicitation of proxies from the holders of all securities registered under the 1934 act. Although the proxy rules even prescribe the appropriate proxy form, the thrust of this regulation has been to provide full disclosure to the stockholder. Accordingly, no solicitation of a proxy may be made unless each person solicited is furnished with a written proxy statement previously filed with the SEC. In addition to stating on whose behalf the proxy is being solicited and identifying each matter to be acted upon at the meeting, the proxy statement must contain much the same information as is required under the 1933 act registration statement. Violations of the proxy rules, including the presence of material misrepresentations in the proxy statement, may be remedied through suit by aggrieved stockholders for damages or other relief, including the possible abrogation of matters approved at the shareholders' meeting pursuant to the misleading statement.[11] For example, such other relief, as the circumstances require, could include not only the declaration as void of the election of directors but also the rescission of a consummated corporate merger.

The SEC proxy rules also attempt to equalize so far as is practicable the rights of management and of opposition security holders. Whenever the management of a company intends to make a solicitation subject to the proxy rules, it must also, at the request of a security holder desiring to communicate with other security holders for a proper purpose, either furnish him with a list of all security holders or mail his proxy material for him. Moreover, a security holder may require management to include in its own proxy statement any legitimate proposal of the security holder and, if the management opposes such a proposal, a 100-word statement in its support.[12] For example, in 1970 the General Motors Company was required by the SEC to include with its proxy materials two proposals along with supporting statements—one suggesting an increase in the board of directors and the other establishing a special shareholders' study committee—as put forth by the Project on Corporate Responsibility.

The proxy rules thus greatly shape one of the more spectacular phenomena of modern corporate life—the proxy fight. Although such fights are relatively rare,[13] to the extent that the rules equalize the solicitation rights of stockholders and alert the shareholders to their potential ability to control top management, the possibility that existing management may be challenged from without grows in significance. In the event of a contested corporate election, special rules apply which require the participants to file with the SEC additional information, including a statement as to any material proposed transaction involving the issuer. When a rival individual or group seeks to replace the established board of direc-

---

[11] See *J. I. Case Co.* v. *Borak*, 377 U.S. 426 (1964).

[12] During the 1969 fiscal year, 173 proposals submitted by 27 stockholders were included in the proxy statements of 118 companies; and 48 proposals submitted by 21 stockholders were omitted from the proxy statements of 19 companies. In total, 5,316 proxy statements in definitive form were filed by management and 32 by nonmanagement groups or individual stockholders (SEC 1969 Annual Report, pp. 46–47).

[13] Twenty-five in fiscal 1969 came under SEC jurisdiction (*ibid.*, p. 48).

tors, both groups will actively solicit the proxies of the large numbers of independent shareholders. Depending on a whole host of factors—including the persuasiveness of the rival parties, the size of the independent vote, and the form of voting, whether cumulative or otherwise, used by the corporation—the outsiders may fail completely, elect a minority of directors, or sweep the "old guard" out of office.

On balance, while the whole framework of the proxy solicitation rules may have little direct impact on the corporate decision-making process, they most likely have a healthy indirect impact on corporate management. The disclosure rules together with the stockholder right to submit proposals help to keep corporate management alert and responsive to the interests of shareholders. Moreover, the proxy approach to corporate democracy provides an opportunity to shareholders to become conscious of their responsibilities as the source of ultimate authority in the corporation. In the end, the symbolic significance of the proxy process should not be underestimated "in an area in which no alternative philosophy has yet been developed for the classic theory of managerial responsibility to the owners of the business."[14]

TAKEOVER BIDS. While proxy fights have been the traditional arena for contests over corporate control, the 1960's witnessed the increasing use of an equally spectacular weapon in the corporate arsenal, the takeover bid. Here, the bidding corporation or group makes a tender offer[15] in cash or securities to the stockholders of the target corporation for a controlling interest in the target. To many acquisition-minded companies, the takeover bid may appear relatively more advantageous than the prospect of a proxy fight. In the long run a tender offer might be less costly than a proxy battle. Stock acquired in the target company by the acquiring company could, if a controlling interest were not tendered, always be held as an investment or sold—and, frequently, at a profit. The quest for corporate control via a takeover bid will, moreover, probably be settled, one way or the other, in a shorter period of time than through a proxy fight. (And, prior to 1968, unless the tender offer were in securities registered under the 1933 act, surprise was even possible insofar as takeover bids were subject to little regulation.) In response, however, to the rash of takeover bids in the middle 1960's and with the intent both to close gaps in the full disclosure provisions of the 1934 act and to put cash tender offers on the same footing as proxy contests for control, Congress enacted the Williams bill in 1968.

These amendments to the Securities Exchange Act of 1934 provide first for full disclosure by the bidding company. Any person who acquires or makes a tender offer to acquire more than 5% of any class of equity

---

[14] Louis Loss, *Securities Regulation* (2d rev. ed.; Boston: Little Brown & Co., 1961), p. 911.

[15] A tender offer can also be made to the stockholders by the issuing corporation itself pursuant to a stock repurchase program. See Extone Chemicals, Inc., p. 857.

securities registered under the 1934 act must file a statement with the SEC in addition to sending a copy to the issuing corporation and to each stock exchange on which the security is traded. Such a statement must disclose such facts as the source and amount of funds used in making the stock purchases, the purposes underlying such purchases—whether or not to acquire control of the issuer—and whatever plans or proposals are contemplated—whether "to liquidate the issuer, to sell its assets or to merge it . . . , or to make any other major change in its business or corporate structure." Moreover, to equalize the position of the competing groups, the target company itself may not reacquire its own securities unless it too files a statement with the SEC and complies with the rules of the Commission. Finally, any solicitation of or recommendation to a security holder of the target company must comply with the rules of the Commission.

The 1968 Williams bill amendments also substantively regulate the tender offer procedure. First, any acceptance of an offer by a shareholder of the target company may be revoked both within the first 7-day period after the offer was first made and any time after 60 days from when the offer was made. Second, if there is an overacceptance of a tender offer on the part of shareholders in the target company within the first 10-day period after the offer was made, the securities tendered by each shareholder must be taken up on a pro rata basis by the acquiring company. Finally, if the offer price is increased before the expiration of the offer period, the higher price must be paid for all securities taken up, whether they were tendered before or after the step-up in the offer price. Because these amendments to the 1934 act are so new, whether they unduly favor management or the bidding company is as yet uncertain. However, one perverse result has been suggested. Insofar as the disclosure provisions may segregate the corporate "raiders" from the more reputable corporate bidders, security holders in the target company may not tender their shares or, alternatively, may demand a higher offer price—and thereby make a takeover more difficult—when the bidder is a more reputable company.[16]

Regulation of the Securities Markets

The Securities Exchange Act of 1934 has played a vital role in the restructuring of the American capital markets through its regulation of the exchanges and of broker-dealers. All national security exchanges must be registered with (or exempted by) the SEC. Although 13 exchanges were so registered (and 3 exempted) in 1970, the New York and American Stock Exchanges in New York accounted for 91.3% of all trading

---

[16] Loss, *op. cit.*, Supp. to 2d ed. (Boston, Little Brown & Co., 1969), p. 3665.

in stocks on the registered exchanges in 1969.[17] Because it would be unrealistic for the Commission to undertake detailed regulation of the entire trading process, the statutory scheme is essentially one of self-regulation. To register, an exchange must file the appropriate documents, promulgate rules which are "just and adequate to insure fair dealing and to protect investors," and make provision for disciplining exchange members for conduct inconsistent with "just and equitable principles of trade."

While the exchanges are thus self-regulated, the SEC does play a strong supervisory role, one major aspect of which is "the continuous review . . . of the existing rules, regulations, procedures, forms, and practices of all exchanges."[18] Moreover, while limited, the Commission does have authority to order compulsory rule changes in certain areas, including "the fixing of reasonable rates of commission, interest, listing, and other charges." And, in addition, the SEC has authority both to suspend or expel a member from a national securities exchange for violations of the act or the Commission rules and to suspend from trading any security listed on such an exchange. While such authority is potentially Draconic, the mere threat of such action must be a powerful weapon against dishonesty on the national securities exchanges.

RECENT INSTITUTIONAL PROBLEMS. Recent years have witnessed the surfacing of a number of problems within the institutional framework of the exchanges. Over the years from 1965 to 1969, exchange members were increasingly unable to handle the back-office paper work required by the rising trading volume on the exchanges;[19] as a result, they experienced a serious increase in "security delivery failures," as securities sold by one person were not delivered to the purchaser in the time allowed for the transaction to settle. With the cooperation of the Commission, the security exchanges, and the National Association of Securities Dealers, studies have been commenced looking toward the automation of trading and trading information systems. Of even greater concern has been the occasional inability of member firms to meet the net capital rule of the New York Stock Exchange[20] and the failure and liquidation of some of these firms with the bear market of 1970. Unfortunately, the New York Stock Exchange Trust Fund designed for these contingencies was not large enough to cover the liabilities of these bankrupt firms to investors who had left cash and securities on account with them. As a result, the

---

[17] SEC 1969 Annual Report, pp. 68–69; Securities and Exchange Commission, *Statistical Bulletin*, March, 1970, p. 11.

[18] SEC 1969 Annual Report, p. 69.

[19] *Ibid.*, p. 1.

[20] New York Stock Exchange Rule 325. All member firms must maintain a 20 to 1 ratio of aggregate indebtedness to net capital. See Rule 15c 3–1, Securities Exchange Act of 1934, which imposes a similar rule on over-the-counter brokers and dealers registered with the SEC.

Securities Investor Protection Corporation Act was enacted in late 1970. As an organization analogous to the Federal Deposit Insurance Corporation, the SIPC is designed to increase investor protection by establishing a fund to cover the customer liabilities of liquidated broker-dealers.

As a response to the need of NYSE member firms for more permanent capital and in realization that more and more large blocks of NYSE listed securities are being traded off the floor, on regional exchanges, and on the "third market," the SEC and the NYSE have finally begun to grapple with two fundamental issues, the structure and level of commission rates and public ownership of securities of exchange members. Commission rates for trading in listed securities on the exchanges have for a long time been characterized by a fixed schedule of minimum rates with few volume discounts. Now under intensive review, the structure of future rates may include maximum rates for small-volume trades and higher discounts for large-volume trades, if not completely negotiated rates in disregard of any schedule. The constitution and rules of the New York Stock Exchange have until recently been clearly incompatible with the public (as distinguished from the private, closely held) ownership of member firms. Many member firms have, however, indicated that the raising of capital funds through the public distribution of their own securities will be required to meet the growing problems in their industry. The Board of Governors thus endorsed in 1969 the concept of public ownership. And, by late spring 1971, several NYSE member firms had already made an initial public distribution of their securities. Now, the appropriate safeguard provisions have to be agreed upon: those dealing with member firms that are subsidiaries of nonbroker-dealer companies and those dealing with the amount of commission business a member firm may do for any institutional investor that has effective control over it.

The present problems engulfing the securities industry evidence the growing divergence of industry developments over the past 25 years from the institutional and statutory framework devised in 1934 in response to the then prevailing economic conditions. Whether these problems may be resolved without any major alteration in that framework remains to be seen.

REGULATION OF THE OVER-THE-COUNTER DEALERS. In an attempt to place the over-the-counter market on a par with the exchange markets, the Securities Exchange Act of 1934 provides for the registration of all brokers and dealers who deal on the OTC market. Essentially, registration entails filing an application and annual reports which meet the full-disclosure standards. To enforce these standards the SEC may censure or suspend any broker or dealer who makes any misleading statements to the Commission, employs a manipulative or fraudulent device in an OTC transaction, or otherwise violates the federal securities laws. In addition, the SEC has applied a minimum net capital rule to all such registered broker-dealers.

Just as the national securities exchanges are self-regulating, the 1938

Maloney Act amendments to the Securities Exchange Act of 1934 provide for self-regulation of all broker-dealers. Brokers and dealers may voluntarily form for this purpose a national securities association. The only such association to register with the SEC is the National Association of Securities Dealers, Inc. The NASD has the general responsibility of supervising its membership and promulgating rules "designed to prevent fraudulent and manipulative acts and practices, to promote just and equitable principles of trade, to provide safeguards against unreasonable profits. . . , and, in general, . . . to remove impediments to and perfect the mechanism of a free and open market." In addition, all members, and associates of members, of the NASD must meet certain qualifications as to training, experience, and otherwise. As with the national securities exchanges, the SEC exercises a broad supervisory role over the NASD and all registered brokers and dealers.

Prevention of Fraud and Manipulation

The third basic area with which the Securities Exchange Act of 1934 is concerned is the prevention of fraud and manipulation in securities trading itself. In an attempt to provide investors with a free and honest securities market, the 1934 act generally prohibits all manipulations of security prices. Regulation of certain specific activities, such as short selling or stabilization in the after-market in aid of security distributions, is provided for.

Of widespread recent interest has been the judicial interpretation of Rule 10b–5—a rule prohibiting the employment of manipulative or deceptive devices in the purchase or sale of any security. This rule not only prohibits any material misrepresentation but also imposes an affirmative duty to disclose material facts on a corporate insider before he may enter into a securities transaction. Thus, in the celebrated case of *SEC v. Texas Gulf Sulphur Co.*,[21] corporate employees who purchased stock in their company after being informed of a potentially very wealthy ore strike, but before this information had become public, were found to have acted illegally. As Judge Waterman stated:

Anyone in possession of material inside information must either disclose it to the investing public, or, if he is disabled from disclosing it in order to protect a corporate confidence, or he chooses not to do so, must abstain from trading in or recommending the securities concerned while such inside information remains undisclosed.[22]

Hence, insofar as an insider may be defined to include anyone in possession of material inside information, even "tippees" of such information

---

[21] 401 F. 2d. 833 (2nd Cir. 1968), cert. den. sub. nom. *Kline* v. *SEC*, 394 U.S. 976 (1969).

[22] *Id.* at 848.

not associated with the corporation in whose stock they deal must be careful that they do not violate Rule 10b–5.

The Securities Exchange Act also provides a more direct restraint on the possible abuse of a position of influence for personal gain by corporate officers, directors, and major shareholders. Officers and directors of issuers of registered securities and owners of more than 10% of such securities must report to the Commission both their holdings of such securities and any subsequent changes in these holdings. This information is made available to the public. Moreover, "for the purpose of preventing the unfair use of [inside] information," any profits realized by such an "insider" from the purchase and sale of equity securities of the issuer within a 6-month period may be recovered by the issuing company.

Credit Regulation

To limit the amount of credit "directed by speculation into the stock market and out of more desirable uses of commerce and industry," to provide an instrument of monetary policy, and to protect the margin purchaser, the 1934 act authorizes the Board of Governors of the Federal Reserve System to limit the amount of credit extended for the purchase or carrying of securities by broker-dealers, banks, and other lenders. At the end of 1970 the maximum loan value on purchases of listed equity securities was restricted to 35%, of listed convertible securities to 50%, and of short sales to 35%.[23] Insofar as these margin rules limit the possible leverage of a private investor, they also limit the possibility of loss stemming from forced sales following additional margin calls.

STATE REGULATION OF SECURITIES AND SECURITY TRADING

The so-called state blue-sky laws[24] regulate securities and security trading in the states. Although the beginnings of securities regulation by the states date from the mid-19th century, the blue-sky movement experienced its greatest growth over the period from 1910 to 1933. Although the immediate thrust for federal regulation in this area came from the market collapse of the 1930's, state securities regulation had, in any event, up to that time generally proved insufficient. Not only was the statutory coverage of the state blue-sky laws uneven, but also state efforts at enforcement were never uniformly effective. However, of greater significance was the basic inadequacy of state legislation in an interstate economy. State laws regulating intrastate transactions could hardly resolve what was essentially an interstate—if not an international—problem. As a result, with

---

[23] 12 Code of Federal Regulations § 220.8 (1970).

[24] "The name that is given to [such a] law indicates the evil at which it is aimed; that is . . . 'speculative schemes which have no more basis than so many feet of "blue sky"'." (*Hall* v. *Geiger-Jones Co.*, 242 U.S. 539, 550 [1916]).

the enactment of the federal securities laws, federal regulation has assumed the dominant role in this area.

The state blue-sky laws do, nevertheless, still regulate securities transactions within each state. Such laws may be general antifraud statutes or they may provide for the registration of brokers and dealers or for the registration of most securities sold in the state. In contrast to the dominant disclosure philosophy of the federal laws, the objective of many blue-sky laws is "to give the investor a 'run for his money' by excluding from the state those securities which do not satisfy the statutory standards."[25] For these states which do go beyond the full-disclosure standard, the state administrator may review such issues as the reasonability of all selling commissions and of all participations, options, and profits accruing to the promoters and corporate insiders as well as the general investment risk associated with the security. The blue-sky laws of some states, including especially California and Kansas, leave the state administrator with a wide degree of discretion. Undoubtedly, some able administrators have under these substantive standards stopped some fraudulent securities transactions long before their true nature would have been revealed under the federal disclosure laws. On the other hand, regulation under these standards has also interfered with the allocational function of the capital market mechanism. In particular, such state government intervention may have its greatest impact on newer and presumably more risky business ventures. Small companies unable to obtain debt financing may find registration especially difficult in states where the regulatory standard is so broad that wide discretion is left to the state administrator. A final balance of advantage versus disadvantage is hard to draw.

THE FUTURE REGULATORY PATTERN: SEC STUDIES AND INVESTIGATIONS

The capital markets in the United States are constantly in a process of change. Although surely with a pronounced lag, the federal securities laws do evolve to meet these changes so as to insure that they are not inconsistent with the public interest and the protection of investors. New laws and major amendments to old laws have in the past frequently followed exhaustive SEC studies of new problems or the "loopholes" in old ones. Thus, the Investment Company Act was enacted after a 4-year SEC study of the mutual fund industry ordered by Congress in the 1935 Holding Company Act. Such comprehensive amendments to the securities laws as the Securities Acts Amendments of 1964 and the Investment Company Amendments Act of 1970 followed respectively the 1963 Special Study of the Securities Markets and the 1962 study by the Wharton School of Finance and Commerce (commissioned by the SEC) of mutual

---

[25] Loss, *op. cit.* (2d ed.; Boston, 1961), p. 34.

investment companies.[26] Of possibly equal productivity in the future are two major SEC studies, the 1969 "Wheat Report" on disclosure policy and the Congressionally initiated 1970 Institutional Investor Study.

The Wheat Report, entitled *Disclosure to Investors—A Reappraisal of Federal Administrative Policies Under the '33 and '34 Acts,* is an intensive examination of the disclosure philosophy underlying the securities laws. Disclosure is deemed central to national policy in the federal securities laws for two major reasons: (1) disclosure enables investors to arrive at their own informed decisions; and (2) disclosure tends to deter questionable practices and to elevate standards of business conduct. In particular, the Wheat Report is an attempt to make disclosure more effective by suggesting ways to enhance the degree of coordination between that disclosure required under the Securities Act of 1933 and that under the Securities Exchange Act of 1934, to make prospectuses less complex and more readable, and to provide more consistent treatment of secondary distributions of securities by controlling persons of the issuer.

Pursuant to congressional authorization, the SEC was in 1968 directed to make a study of

. . . the purchase, sale, and holding of securities by institutional investors of all types including, but not limited to, banks, insurance companies, mutual funds, employee pension and welfare funds, and foundation and college endowments, in order to determine the effect of such purchases, sales, and holdings upon (A) the maintenance of fair and orderly securities markets, (B) the stability of such markets, both in general and for individual securities, (C) the interests of the issuers of such securities, and (D) the interests of the public, in order that the Congress may determine what measures, if any, may be necessary and appropriate in the public interest and for the protection of investors.[27]

Appearing in March, 1971, the Institutional Investor Study may well have a wide ranging impact on the statutory framework in which these institutions must exist. In particular, the institutional investors may in the future be required to meet full-disclosure standards in their investment policies as well as possible substantive restrictions on such policies, including, for example, possible maximum limits on the amount invested in any one security or even maximum limits on turnover levels.

FEDERAL REGULATION OF CORPORATE FINANCIAL POLICY

Federal regulation of securities trading and the capital markets has been directed towards the development of a free and fair securities market in which the basic rights of an investor are assured and his decisions

---

[26] Irwin Friend *et al., A Study of Mutual Funds Prepared for the Securities and Exchange Commission* (Report of the Committee on Interstate and Foreign Commerce, H. R. Rep. No. 2274, 87th Cong., 2d sess. [Washington, D.C.: U.S. Government Printing Office, 1962]).

[27] Securities Exchange Act of 1934 § 19(e)(1), (1964).

informed. The primary instrument relied on to reach this objective has been the requirement of full and honest disclosure. On balance, such regulation may be said to have reached this goal and, in doing so, to have facilitated the task of raising long-term funds for legitimate business ventures. Of course, any such comprehensive government intervention into the free market mechanism must result in some misallocations, and, to the extent that they are not justified by market imperfections or economic externalities, they must be viewed as the cost to such regulatory benefits. However, in the main, government regulation of securities markets must not be considered as a serious encroachment on the freedom of action of corporations in their financial activities and decision making. Nonetheless, there is one industry in which government regulation does invade the once inviolate, private area of corporate financial policy. While the authority of the SEC to intervene directly in such financial decision making is limited to the electric and gas utility industry, this intervention does have considerably broader implications. To the extent that the Commission's financial standards are formally adopted and become known and accepted by the investing public, they are bound to have an influence on investment standards in other industries.

After a bitter struggle the Public Utility Holding Company Act was enacted in 1935 to put an end to certain freewheeling corporate practices which had been widely followed in the electric utility industry during the preceding decade. Through the creation of nonoperating holding companies—for the sole purpose of controlling ownership in subsidiary operating companies—vast electric utility pyramids were constructed, resulting in the concentration of control of the industry in the hands of relatively few men. By retaining voting control of the common stock of a utility while issuing large quantities of nonvoting senior securities to apparently indifferent investors, holding companies would gain control of a utility with a disproportionately small investment. With the funds so produced and the assets so controlled, the utility in question could be used as a base for the acquisition of voting control in other utilities; and they, in turn, would become the means of bringing more operating companies and other holding company systems within the orbit of the parent holding company. Theoretically, such pyramiding of control was without limit.

This increasing concentration in the public utility industry together with the economic abuses it engendered was to eventually require the regulatory response of the federal government. First, the concentration of control at the top of the pyramid in private hands in such a vital industry affected with the public interest was, if not responsibly exercised, a potential challenge to that public interest. Second, while regional integration for such an industry that is to some extent a natural monopoly did make economic sense, many of the public utility holding companies linked together noncontiguous operating subsidiaries (and even diverse subsidiaries outside of the industry) to the detriment of the consuming public where no conceivable economic advantage could be gained. Finally, with the pyramiding of control more important than increasing operating efficiency, financial excesses developed: corporate funds were drained off to acquire control of other companies; and the top-heavy, highly leveraged capital structures of the holding company systems overly burdened earnings and threatened solvency.

The eventual government response was the Public Utility Holding Company Act of 1935. All holding companies, defined as any company which owned 10% or more of the outstanding voting securities of a public utility company or of another holding company, were first required to register with the SEC. Then, in order to reverse the trend towards uneconomic concentration, the SEC was empowered under the so-called "death sentence" provisions to restrict each holding company to a single economically and geographically integrated gas or electric utility system together with such other businesses that were reasonably incidental or economically necessary to the operation of the integrated system. As a result, from a total of 216 registered holding companies in 1955, there remained in existence in 1969 17 active registered holding company systems representing some 174 system companies.[28]

The continuing task of geographical and functional integration has been paralleled by continuing efforts to simplify the intercorporate relationships and capital structures of the remaining public utility holding companies and their operating subsidiaries. Indeed, all new security issues of such public utility systems must be found by the Commission to meet certain statutory standards. Thus, through a gradual process of retirement and consolidation of issues, the SEC has hoped to replace the confusing maze of senior securities characteristic of these systems in the 1920's with a clear-cut bond, preferred stock, common stock capital structure. The jurisdiction of the Commission here extends far beyond disclosure "to the type, amount, price and other terms of the securities which [the] company proposes to issue for the purpose of financing the business in which it is lawfully engaged."[29] Consequently, a more detailed look at the standards which the SEC has applied to such financial

---

[28] SEC 1969 Annual Report, pp. 145–46. While the number of holding companies has thus sharply declined, "far from proving to be [a] . . . death sentence . . . , the . . . program has given a new lease on life to private power under public control. . . . [And] now that the integration and simplification process has been substantially completed, there are indications of a trend towards the creation of new holding company systems that will reflect technological developments over the past few decades, toward the end of achieving economies for the consumer consistently with the statutory standards" (Loss, *op. cit.* [2d. ed.; Boston, 1961, and supp. ed., 1969] pp. 141, 2276).

[29] *Alabama Power Co.*, Holding Co. Act Rel. 15,252 (1965) 3–4, aff'd sub. nom. *Alabama Electric Cooperative, Inc.* v. *SEC*, 353 F. 2d 905 (D.C. Cir.), cert. den., 383 U.S. 968 (1965). "Obviously, Congress intended not that the Commission should be a mere slot-machine, automatically emitting approvals once an application had been filed, but rather that it should examine applications in the light of existing facts in order to see to it that management complied with the standards fixed by the Act" (*Consumers Power Co.*, 6 SEC 444, 459 [1939]).

decision making will be of real significance beyond this one industry insofar as it is an example of what government regulation can mean in the area of corporate finance. Because of the great influence of the SEC in the securities markets, the standards it applies and the reasoning behind them may have an indirect but significant impact on corporate practices generally.

Debt-Equity Balance

In setting standards of sound financial practice for the public utility industry, the SEC has had as one of its major objectives the reduction of the excessive amounts of debt and other senior securities and the increase of common stock equity. This concern derives from the overly top-heavy capital structure of many of the holding company systems in the past. After the example of the 1930's, when many public utilities experienced a significant shrinkage in earnings and when some were forced, because of excessive debt, to default on interest and dividend payments, it has become clear that considerations of safety dictate some limit to the proportion of securities bearing a fixed commitment to the investor. Furthermore, such a limit should provide for some reserve of borrowing power in anticipation of future financing and the need for flexibility in the timing of new issues. As the SEC itself has stated: "By insisting that parent holding companies undertake common stock financing periodically to match increases in system debt financing, the Commission seeks to prevent a return of the high-leveraged, unwieldy structures which led to the legislation it now administers."[30] Common stock equity was also to be increased "by requiring the conversion of open accounts, bonds or preferred stock held by the parent company into common stock of its subsidiary . . . ; by the parent's increasing its equity in its subsidiaries either through outright cash contributions or through the purchase of additional common; and by imposing restrictions on the payment of common stock dividends."[31]

In interpreting the statutory standard that newly issued securities be "reasonably adapted to the security structure of the . . . [company] and other companies in the same holding company system," the SEC has most often examined a company's capitalization ratios: "Although the Commission has not attempted to prescribe optimum or ideal capitalization ratios, nor assumed that the 60–10–30 policy [with respect to debt, preferred, and common] . . . sets a fixed or permanent standard to be applied in all systems, these ratios have been generally regarded as embodying the present working policy of the Commission."[32] That this

---

[30] Securities and Exchange Commission, *Sixteenth Annual Report, 1950* (Washington, D.C., 1951), p. 104.

[31] Loss, *op. cit.* (2d ed.; Boston, 1961), p. 382.

[32] Securities and Exchange Commission, *Twenty-Second Annual Report, 1956* (Washington, D.C., 1957), p. 159.

policy is flexibly applied may be seen in the case of *Kentucky Power Company*.[33] There, because the subsidiary company and other system companies had substantial amounts of accumulated credits in restricted surplus accounts resulting from accelerated amortization and liberalized depreciation, the SEC approved of a new financing where (1) common stock equity would not fall below 30%, (2) mortgage debt would not exceed 60%, and (3) long-term debt would not exceed 65% of total capitalization, excluding the accumulated balance sheet credit.

Standards directed towards the establishment of more balanced capital structures in public utility holding company systems have also been expressed in terms of earnings coverage—the extent to which earnings available for the payment of fixed charges exceed these fixed charges. Indeed, the Public Utility Holding Company Act provides that the SEC may not approve of a company's new financing if "the security is not reasonably adapted to the earning power of the company." In construing this statutory standard, the SEC in an early case, *New England Gas and Electric Association*,[34] approved of a bond financing where the indenture required a 1% sinking fund, a ceiling limit of 60% of debt to consolidated capitalization of New England and its subsidiaries, and, as a condition to the issuance of any additional debt, an earnings coverage of at least 2½ times the annual interest charge to be outstanding. More recently, the SEC set forth a more liberal standard in a 1956 statement of policy.[35] Unless the purpose is to refund an outstanding series of bonds issued under an indenture with a higher interest rate than the contemplated additional bonds or with a maturity date less than 2 years away, net earnings must cover by at least *2 times* the annual interest payments on all bonds and prior lien obligations, including the contemplated additional bonds.

The SEC is empowered under the Holding Company Act to review the financial provisions of those indentures governing the proposed bond issues of registered public utility systems. This is in contrast to the standards expressed in the Trust Indenture Act of 1939 (to which utility systems are also subject), which focus not on the strictly "business" features of an indenture but on those provisions relating to the protection and enforcement of the rights of the investors. After an initial period of *ad hoc* case-by-case review and "as modified in the light of experience . . . and in the further light of comments received,"[36] the Commission promulgated its policy with respect to first-mortgage bonds in a 1956 release. While traditionally the typical utility indenture had been "open-ended," and "in the days before the Holding Company Act the principal

---

[33] 41 SEC 29 (1961).

[34] 23 SEC 433 (1946).

[35] *Statement of Policy Regarding First Mortgage Bonds Subject to the Public Utility Holding Company Act of 1935*, Holding Comp. Act Release No. 35–13105 ¶(a) (1956).

[36] Securities and Exchange Commission, *Twenty-Third Annual Report, 1957* (Washington, D.C., 1958), p. 141.

amount of additional bonds issuable used to be 70 to 80 percent of the 'fair value' of any additional property acquired by the obligor,"[37] the Statement of Policy is more stringent. The trust indenture must provide that additional bonds may be issued only if limited to 60% of the bondable value of net property additions. Insofar as the asset structure of operating utility companies primarily consists of fixed assets, this standard bears a close resemblance to the capitalization ratios cited above.

The Statement of Policy by the SEC also evidences a concern that the value of a mortgage bond should not be eroded to the detriment of new and existing investors by the ill effects of inadequate depreciation. To prevent such an erosion of the pledged properties and to preserve operating efficiency, the Commission has insisted that all mortgage indentures either require the company to use new capital funds in constructing property additions or provide for an equivalent deposit of cash or bonds with the indenture trustee. As, in effect, a minimum depreciation requirement these deposits or additions must on a cumulative basis provide for the replacement of the book cost of the depreciable mortgaged property of the obligor over its estimated useful life.

The Statement of Policy regarding first-mortgage bond indenture provisions further establishes standards for the gradual reduction of outstanding debt of system companies. The indenture must obligate the issuing company to deposit annually in a sinking and improvement fund with the indenture trustee an amount equal to at least 1% of the aggregate principal amount of bonds outstanding under the indenture. Alternatively, in lieu of cash the issuing company may apply against the sinking fund requirement an amount equal to the principal amount of retired bonds or 60% of the bondable value of net property additions. As the Commission has stated: "The primary function of a sinking fund is to improve the ratio between debt and net property."[38]

To ensure further the maintenance of adequate equity capital and as an additional means of protecting senior security holders, the Statement of Policy also places a limitation on dividends. In effect, the trust indenture for any bond financing must limit common stock dividends and common stock repurchases to (i) earned surplus accumulated after the date of issuance of such bonds, plus (ii) an amount approximately equal to current annual dividend payments on the preferred and common stock then outstanding (or currently proposed to be issued), plus (iii) any additional payments which the issuer has demonstrated "would not materially and adversely affect existing capitalization ratios or otherwise be inconsistent with the protection of the holders of the securities of the . . . [issuer] in the light of the ratio of mortgage debt to net fixed property."[39]

---

[37] Loss, *op. cit.* (2d. ed.; Boston, 1961), p. 385 n. 47.

[38] Securities and Exchange Commission, *Thirteenth Annual Report, 1947* (Washington, D.C., 1948), p. 89.

[39] Holding Company Act Release No. 35–13105 ¶(h) (1956).

Finally, the Statement of Policy makes provision for the refunding of bond issues. Essentially, this concern over redemption policies reflects the need of public utility systems for financial flexibility. "Public utilities, unlike most other industries, are usually faced with the problem of expanding plant facilities in periods of depression as well as prosperity. A high degree of financial flexibility is therefore essential in order to insure maintenance of adequate service to consumers."[40] More directly, since one of the statutory objectives of the act is to ensure "economies in the raising of capital," the bond indenture was required to provide "for redemption at any time upon reasonable notice and with reasonable redemption premiums, if any," in order to take advantage of any significant decrease in money rates. However, this policy has been under continuous review and, in fiscal 1965, 1966, and 1968, SEC statistics indicated that, from a financial marketing standpoint, the nonrefundable issues were more successful than the refundable. As a result, in May, 1969, the Commission revised its policy by permitting holding companies subject to the act to include in their indentures governing new issues of long-term debt securities a provision prohibiting, for a period of not more than 5 years, the refunding of such securities by the issuance of other debt securities at lower interest costs.[41]

The Securities and Exchange Commission has, through the standards discussed above, attempted to force the public utility industry to accept a set of objective yardsticks by which to measure the limits of a sound and flexible capital structure debt-equity balance. At the same time as the public utility companies are required to observe these standards, investors are bound to become accustomed to examining similar yardsticks in their evaluation of the debt instruments of companies in other industries.

Cost of Financing

One of the primary objectives of the Public Utility Holding Company Act has been, as mentioned above, the achievement of "economies in the raising of capital." To secure such economies and to meet the Congressional concern that public utility companies had, prior to the Act, entered into high-cost financial "transactions in which evils [had] result[ed] from an absence of arm's-length bargaining or from restraint of free and independent competition," the Commission promulgated in 1941 its highly controversial rule requiring *competitive bidding*. Under this form of financing, the prospective issuer will ask for bids on the underwriting and select the lowest cost bidder rather than negotiate the underwriting fee with the proposed investment banker. Prior to this time, competitive bidding had seldom been the accepted financing procedure

---

[40] Securities and Exchange Commission, *Seventeenth Annual Report, 1951* (Washington, D.C., 1952), p. 105.

[41] Holding Company Act Release No. 35–16369 (May 8, 1969).

except for municipalities and public instrumentalities. Instead, the issuing corporation would select a banking house early in its planning process. The advantages of specialized advice obtained in this way are to be compared with the disadvantages of being committed to the services of a certain banking house before the price for these services has been fixed.

Rule 50 of the Holding Company Act now requires competitive bidding by investment bankers seeking to underwrite new issues of registered public utility companies and their operating subsidiaries. While exemptions are provided for some issues—including preemptive rights offerings, certain private placements, certain sales to other public utility companies, sales under $1 million, and by special order of the SEC—over the period from the effective date of the rule to June 30, 1969, 1,053 issues aggregating $16.908 billion had been sold at competitive bidding; and only 239 issues aggregating $2.668 billion had been sold pursuant to exemption orders.[42] The requirement of competitive bidding has undoubtedly resulted in a significant decrease in costs and increase in net proceeds to the public utility issuer relative to that possible through private negotiation.[43] For example, the SEC has concluded after a study of the costs of underwriting preferred stock issues: "issues acquired by underwriters through competitive bidding tend to have smaller underwriting spreads than do negotiated offerings."[44]

The objective of greater economies in financing has also led the Commission to encourage the use of preemptive rights and rights offerings in additional sales of common stock. A new issue which is taken up largely, if not entirely, by the existing shareholders minimizes or, if the rights offering is not underwritten, eliminates the services and costs of the "middleman," the investment banker. As the SEC has stated:

It is, and has long been, our opinion that when holding companies and public utility companies subject to our jurisdiction sell additional shares of common stock, their own interests, as well as the interests of their common shareholders are, absent special circumstances, best served by allowing common shareholders the right to purchase their proportionate shares of the new issue.[45]

However, because of the Commission concern that there be leeway for "situations in which the length of time necessarily required for preemptive rights offering to stockholders . . . involve[s] a serious risk of an unsuccessful offering, at a time when funds are urgently needed,"[46] the SEC has not, since 1953, strictly required a rights offering when the issuer can show the advantages of an underwriting by competitive bidding.

---

[42] SEC 1969 Annual Report, p. 155.

[43] Securities and Exchange Commission, *Cost of Flotation of Registered Equity Issues 1963–65* (Washington, D.C., 1970), p. 49.

[44] *Ibid.*, p. 29.

[45] Public Utility Holding Company Act Release No. 9730 (1950).

[46] *Columbia Gas System, Inc.*, 31 SEC 202, 204 (1950).

Notwithstanding this policy, at least over the period 1963–65 the bulk in dollar value of the common stock financing of public utility companies has been through rights offerings.[47]

Preferred Stock

A principal financial concern of the Commission under the Public Utility Holding Company Act has been the establishment of balanced capital structures. Prior to the act the highly leveraged electric utility pyramids were constructed with the use of excessive amounts of nonvoting senior securities, including both debt and preferred stock. The effort of the Commission to reduce the excessive amounts of debt in public utility systems has been paralleled by an effort to control the use of preferred stock in such systems. This is consistent with the statutory standards in the act opposing the issuance of preferred stock except under limited conditions. For example, the Commission has permitted the issuance of preferred stock primarily in the case of operating public utility companies. Moreover, because the financial characteristics of preferred stock make it a senior security, the SEC has required in its "Statement of Policy Regarding Preferred Stock Subject to the Public Utility Holding Company Act of 1935"[48] that the corporate charter of any issuer of preferred meet certain standards in the interests of financial safety and flexibility.

This Statement of Policy contains provisions designed to protect the holders of such preferred stock and other provisions designed to maintain a balanced capital structure. Among the latter is a provision prohibiting the issuance of additional securities representing unsecured debt when all such unsecured debt outstanding (including that proposed to be issued) exceeds "20% of the aggregate of all existing secured debt of the Corporation and the capital stock, premiums thereon, and surplus of the Corporation, as stated on its books."

The Statement also includes a provision limiting the payment of dividends on or the repurchase of stock ranking junior to the preferred when the junior stock equity falls below a certain percentage of total capitalization of the issuer. In effect, this helps to insure the maintenance of a minimum cushion of common equity in the capital structure. As one public utility company has put it: "[Such] a 'cushion' . . . will enable the company to absorb variations in income to meet the interest and amortization claims of its preferred stock. . . . This 'cushion' preserves the company's ability to issue senior securities even when economic conditions are unfavorable for the issuance of common stock . . ."[49] Finally, the Statement of

---

[47] Securities and Exchange Commission, *Cost of Flotation of Registered Equity Issues 1963–1965* (Washington, D.C., 1970), pp. 24, 43.

[48] Holding Company Act Release No. 35–13106 (February 16, 1956).

[49] *Pennsylvania Electric Company,* 40 SEC 711, 715 (1961). The quotation continues: "But that once common stock equity adequately meets this requirement further increases therein result in higher revenue requirements which are contrary to the interests of investors and consumers" (*ibid.*).

Policy provides that such stock may be called for redemption by the company at any time upon reasonable terms. However, as with the refunding of bond issues, the SEC has recently revised its redemption policy to allow a prohibition against the redemption of such preferred stock for a period of not more than five years.[50]

Although there has thus been a concern over excessive amounts of preferred stock in a public utility company's capital structure, the position of the Commission towards preferred stock has at times been somewhat ambiguous. As pointed out in Chapter 13, preferred stock does present a special problem because of its somewhat paradoxical position halfway between a fixed charge security and a true equity security. This makes a satisfactory classification of the security difficult. While, for some purposes, preferred should be treated as a senior security with a fixed claim on earnings and a resulting mandatory drain on cash, for other purposes it should be treated as a part of equity capital. For example, because interest is a deductible expense while dividends are not, for several years there has been a trend towards a decrease in the dollar amount and relative proportion of preferred stock financing of public utility companies. Thus, while approving a bond financing of a company that also announced its intention to abandon any further issuance of preferred and to give early consideration to the feasibility of retiring its outstanding preferred stock, the Commission stated:

We recognize of course that the cost of capital and related income taxes to a company issuing debt is generally less than that of issuing preferred stock. Nevertheless, the deductibility for tax purposes of interest on debt capital should not be employed as a basis for permitting an excessive debt ratio, for . . . the stock equity of a company should be sufficient to enable it to withstand economic adversity.[51]

While the authors fully concur with the intent of the last sentence of this quotation, we feel that debt ratios are an insufficient guide to conclusions about policy. The study of funds flows will bring the matter into far sharper focus. (Chapter 20.)

Shareholders and Voting Control

Insofar as the public utility companies constitute an industry which is affected with the national public interest, the regulation of the industry by the Securities and Exchange Commission is directed toward protecting that public interest, the interests of consumers of electric energy, and the interests of investors in the securities of holding companies and their subsidiary companies and affiliates. Among the latter group are the preferred and common stockholders of the public utility companies. Be-

---

[50] Holding Company Act Release No. 35–16758 (June 22, 1970).

[51] *Pennsylvania Electric Company*, 40 SEC 711, 715 (1961).

cause, prior to the act, the highly leveraged corporate structures allowed control to be exercised through "disproportionately small investments," the Congress authorized the SEC to take such acts as to ensure that "the corporate structure . . . does not unduly or unnecessarily complicate the structure, or unfairly or unequitably distribute voting power among security holders, of such holding company system." In meeting this standard, the SEC has in a sense been attempting to protect the stockholder-owners of such companies from their own shortsightedness and neglect.

The SEC Statement of Policy Regarding Preferred Stock contains several provisions designed to protect the ownership position of preferred stockholders under this standard. First, the dividends on any such preferred stock must be cumulative. Second, and perhaps more extreme, is a provision providing for the shifting of corporate control under certain conditions:

If and when dividends on any series of preferred stock shall be in arrears in an amount equal to four full quarterly-yearly payments or more per share, the holders of all series of the preferred stock voting together as a class shall be entitled to elect the smallest number of directors necessary to constitute a majority of the full board of directors until such time as all dividend arrears on the preferred stock shall have been paid or declared and set apart for payment.[52]

Finally, the Statement of Policy provides that approval by at least a majority vote of the preferred stockholders is required for any merger or consolidation of the issuer and for the issuance of additional shares of the preferred stock; and that approval by two-thirds vote of the preferred stockholders is required for any alteration of the rights, preferences, or powers of such stock and for the authorization and issuance of any class of prior preferred stock.

Financial Planning

One natural and beneficial by-product of the careful reordering of public utility capital structures by the Commission has been an emphasis on careful planning for future needs. Where necessary, the SEC has insisted on a forecast of future capital expenditures and a plan for financing these expenditures which preserves the desired debt-equity balance. Because of the long-term growth characteristics of the utility industry and of the uncertainties of the capital market over the long run, the Commission has stressed the need for an adequate common equity cushion. Such a desirable margin of borrowing power is thus a necessary prerequisite to financial planning and to the appropriate timing of new issues in the public utility as well as in other similar industries.

---

[52] Holding Company Act Release No. 35–13106 ¶ (a) (February 16, 1956).

SUMMARY

It has been the intent of this chapter to review the various ways in which the federal and state governments impact upon the financial decision-making process of private business concerns. Whether this government impact consists of setting the institutional stage on which private financial decisions are made or consists of a more direct intervention into the decision-making process, the fact remains that most such financial decision making must take into account the government regulation in the area. Although the traditional federal government approach towards such regulation has been that of disclosure, it is now apparent that in many areas Congress, the courts, and the SEC have turned towards a more substantive, regulatory approach. To the extent that this does indeed become an established trend, the possibility of unnecessary misallocations from the market solution will also exist. The clear presence of market imperfections or economic externalities that can not be remedied by a disclosure solution should first be established before the regulatory approach becomes substantively oriented. In one situation, the public utility holding company industry, this was clearly the case, and the result was the Public Utility Holding Company Act of 1935. Parts of this chapter have thus focused here more intensively in order to illustrate what substantive government intervention can mean in the area of decision making in long-term finance.

PART IX

FINANCING GROWTH
AND DEVELOPMENT

chapter 27

Financing the New
Small-Scale Enterprise

In financing the new small-scale business enterprise, certain variations in the financial problems and practices occur which are peculiar to a business at this stage of its development. This chapter is designed to bring out the nature and significance of the more important of these variations. A primary objective will be to draw a distinction between the problem of smallness in business and the often related but different problems of newness, inexperience, and incompetence.

In view of the large numbers of new businesses that are being formed every year, it is obvious that each year a substantial percentage of the business owner-manager population is going to be preoccupied with the special problems of a business in formation. When these figures are considered in relation to those on business termination, it is also apparent that a great many businessmen cope with these problems unsuccessfully. A study made annually by Dun & Bradstreet of failures among the large number of businesses which come under their survey of credit information shows remarkable consistency in the age distribution of the failures. Of the total number of failures listed in 1969, 53.2% had been in business for 5 years or less and another 24.4% had been in existence for 6 to 10 years.[1] An earlier study of business turnover suggested that about half of the businesses formed are sold or liquidated within 2 years and that only one in five survive for 10 years.[2]

Statistics such as these, which have been available and widely circulated for many years, are not likely to encourage an attitude of optimism toward new businesses on the part of those who are asked to supply

---

[1] Dun & Bradstreet, Inc., *The Failure Record Through 1969* (New York, 1970) p. 10.

[2] "Age and Life Expectancy of Business Firms," *Survey of Current Business*, December, 1955, pp. 15–19.

capital to such businesses. Of course, aggregate statistics cannot provide a satisfactory basis for judgment in the individual case. Unfortunately, however, a new business is by definition a business without a record of performance by which potential can be measured; consequently, there is little if any basis for differentiating it from what is assumed to be typical. A new and small business must have some unusual appeal before it can be considered an exception from the general expectation of great risk and probable failure, an expectation which continues to be supported by experience even in times of high-level prosperity.

Newness as a Financial Problem

A new business which is well conceived and well planned possesses certain inherent competitive advantages. At the same time, the fact of its newness may have significant financial disadvantages. One of these comes in financial planning. The starting point of any program for the financing of a business is a careful estimate of requirements. The usual starting point in business forecasts is the record of the immediate past, modified for foreseeable variations during the forecast period. Without the advantage of a period of actual performance upon which to base assumptions, it is exceedingly difficult to anticipate such vital information as the amount and timing of customers' orders, credit experience with customers, and profit margins with the degree of accuracy necessary to make the forecast useful. The possibility of substantial errors of forecast is great. Unfortunately, the spirit of optimism which is a necessary accompaniment of new ventures in business tends to produce underestimates rather than overestimates of the needed funds.

To the inherent difficulty of forecasting the need for funds may be added another problem. New businesses frequently involve new and inexperienced management. Since the idea which sparks the drive for independence in business normally grows out of experience in areas other than finance, the basic problem of forecasting the need for funds is often complicated by a lack of understanding of the means by which business transactions are translated into financial terms. Errors in projecting needs which result from inexperience are particularly common in the calculation of absorption of funds into working capital as production and sales develop.

Incompetence in the financial area may not be disastrous. The effects of ignorance depend on the nature and magnitude of the errors, the circumstances which may either magnify or cushion the effects, and the rapidity with which management can recognize and correct its mistakes. On the other hand, managerial incompetence is considered to be the primary cause of failure among new and small businesses. It is difficult in practice to separate incompetence in the financial area from incompetence in other areas of managerial responsibility, since most important decisions have their financial implications. Thus, "receivables difficulties" may have resulted from overenthusiastic selling, inadequate credit control, or an inability to anticipate the working capital requirement of credit to customers. There is no doubt, however, that the typical manager of a new business is much better prepared for his responsibilities in the areas of production or sales than he is in finance.

The disadvantage of newness is also to be found in relations with suppliers of capital. For those suppliers who are motivated by purely business considerations (as distinct from friends and relatives who play an important part in financing many new ventures), the principal guide to future performance is again the record of the immediate past. In the absence of operating statements, balance sheets, and credit and other records which lend some degree of objectivity to a judgment of future prospects, the prospective creditor or shareholder lacks a firm basis for the assumption of the very considerable risks involved. The inevitable result is that many sources, particularly institutional sources, refuse to assume these risks or insist on protective provisions such that the extent of their participation is seriously limited. Thus, a bank may be prepared to make a limited short-term loan, provided it is well protected by high-grade collateral with a value substantially in excess of the amount of the loan. A loan which is only a fraction of the value of inventory or accounts receivable will not solve the working capital problem of a new and growing business.

One business source of capital which frequently departs from the attitude suggested above is trade credit from suppliers. Primarily because suppliers wish to develop new customers, they often show a very tolerant attitude toward the new business, provided the management gives evidence of good faith in its dealings. In this regard, openness about financial difficulties in discussions with suppliers usually yields better results than secretiveness. It is because of this policy on the part of suppliers that trade credit ranks as one of the major sources of short-term funds in new and small businesses. It is unfortunately true that many new businesses under financial pressure will abuse trade credit, going on the assumption that the supplier will not get tough because he is anxious for business and will wait for his money (and even ship more inventory on credit) when a bank or finance company would not.

A partial substitute for lack of a performance record in the new business is to have management which has had a record of satisfactory performance in other business situations. If such is the case, the persons in question know and are known by suppliers of debt and equity capital and may be able to overcome their suppliers' natural reluctance by the confidence they personally inspire. Confidence inspired by individuals must, of course, be supported by early indications of strength in the new venture.

As a result of one or more of these disadvantages of newness, the founder of the new business may well find himself in an unusually weak bargaining position until such time as he is able to give clear proof of profit potential. If the founder needs further capital in the intervening period (which may last several years) and is not able to supply it himself or obtain it through normal channels such as trade credit, he may not be able to obtain the extra funds except on unfavorable terms. On the one hand, he himself is committed to the business and cannot withdraw at this stage without the chance of serious loss. On the other, there is little by which independent investors can be attracted to the business except the enthusiasm of those who need the money. The prospective creditor or shareholder is in a position to drive a hard bargain.

The Related Problem of Smallness

In the large majority of cases the new business is also a small business —small in the sense that the entire responsibility of management rests on one or two men. How far this statement is true can be seen from Table 27–1, which shows the results of a study of the business population classi-

Table 27–1

Percentage Distribution by Employment Size of Company of Total Business Population and of Sales and Receipts, 1958 and 1963

	1958		1963	
Employment Size of Company	Percentage of Total Business Population*	Percentage of Sales and Receipts†	Percentage of Total Business Population*	Percentage of Sales and Receipts†
No employees	39.9%	2.7%	38.0%	2.0%
1 to 19 employees	54.8	28.2	56.5	26.1
0 to 19 employees Subtotal	94.7%	30.9%	94.5%	28.1%
20 to 99 employees	4.5	17.9	4.6	17.9
0 to 99 employees Subtotal	99.2%	48.8%	99.1%	46.0%
100 to 249 employees	0.5	7.5	0.5	7.2
0 to 249 employees Subtotal	99.7%	56.3%	99.6%	53.2%
250 to 499 employees	0.2	4.7	0.1	4.4
0 to 499 employees Subtotal	99.9%	61.0%	99.7%	57.6%
500 employees and over	0.1	39.0	0.3	42.4
	100.0%	100.0%	100.0%	100.0%

* The number of companies in the total business population of all economic census industries was 3,229,000 in 1958 and 3,293,000 in 1963. The economic censuses include mining, manufacturing, wholesale trade, retail trade, and selected service industries, which represent approximately two thirds of all national income produced in the private sectors of the U.S. economy. However, they account for only about one third of the total corporation assets reported to the Internal Revenue Service in 1963.

† Sales and receipts of all census industries were $742,243 million in 1958 and $935,506 million in 1963.

Source: U.S. Congress, Senate, Select Committee on Small Business, *Nineteenth Annual Report* (1969), (Washington, D.C.: U.S. Government Printing Office, 1969), p. 75.

fied by number of employees and related percentages of sales and receipts. It shows that businesses with fewer than 20 employees account for 95% of the total business population. It also shows that these companies account for only 29% of total sales and receipts. Thus, small companies clearly dominate in terms of numbers, but large companies dominate in terms of volume of business. In view of their numerical importance, consideration of the problems peculiar to the new business must be supplemented by a consideration of those associated with smallness of scale of operations.

One of these problems is the highly personal character of businesses of the size indicated above. The business typically stands or falls on the experience, intelligence, and initiative of one man. This can be a very real asset, and it is this which makes the small business so well suited to certain types of business activity. It can also give rise to difficulties. A business at this stage is merely an extension of an individual's personal activities, and its business decisions—particularly financial decisions—may be strongly influenced by purely personal considerations. So, for example, the absence of debt in the capital structure may result from a deeply rooted personal feeling against borrowing in general, although the circumstances of the business may indicate that a limited use might be highly desirable and financially sound. In the larger business with a management group and possibly with a separation of ownership and management, personal considerations are more likely to be subordinated to the common goals of the business.

The attitude of suppliers of capital may be influenced adversely by the fact of one-man management. The possibility of death or withdrawal of this individual presents a significant risk. Here, insurance can be of some help, but continuity of the business as a profitable unit independent of particular persons is much to be desired in financial contracts. The corporate form provides the legal fiction of continuity of life, but it becomes a reality only through the development of a competent and reliable management group capable of reproducing itself.

Another aspect of one-man management is the pressure of time, which frequently bears down on one individual who is attempting to discharge all the demands made on him as owner-manager in addition to the many operating tasks which others in the business are not capable of doing. The inevitable result is to give low priority to those things which appear to him to be less important at the moment, less interesting, or by nature more postponable. Financial matters often fall into this category. Insufficient time is given to keeping informed on the financial implications of action, to careful projection of needs, and to the cultivation of sources of capital so important in the rather informal capital market in which the small business often operates.

This raises another aspect of the small-scale business—the peculiarities of its market for funds. Since the depression of the 1930's, the organized capital market has been under attack for being insensitive to the needs of small business. There are good and obvious reasons why financial institutions are likely to be less interested in the small business than in the large business. Banks and insurance companies have a primary responsibility to depositors and policyholders to maintain high standards of safety in their investments. The record of solvency in small business has not been encouraging; and while this does not mean that large-scale business is necessarily a safer investment, these investors tend to be wary of heavy involvement in new and small-scale businesses. Further, there is the obvious point that the return to be derived from the small account is less interesting than that from the large account, particularly in view of the relatively fixed costs of servicing the account. It is for this reason that the machinery which has been developed in the capital market for such tasks as the marketing of securities is primarily designed for the larger sums required of large-scale enterprise.

This does not mean that a small business cannot satisfy its need for funds in the normal capital market. Many mature and profitable small businesses are more than adequately supplied in this way. What is does mean is that the small-scale businessman may have to spend considerable time and effort cultivating this market before the desired results are obtained.

New businesses are typically small for two reasons: The scale may be that which is best suited to the particular activity, or the resources of the founders are such that a larger and more efficient scale is not possible at the outset. Through either ignorance, impatience, or sheer venturesomeness, many businesses are started on a scale far below that which the industry and the market require as a prerequisite for permanence, stability, and profitability. For such a business, rapid growth is vital to survival. There is a great sense of urgency to obtain the break-even point of profitability in the shortest possible time; and if the business has promise, there may be the opportunity to grow as rapidly as financial, physical, and human capacities permit. It is not unusual to find a business in its early years doubling or tripling sales volume from one year to the next. Such a rate of growth gives the business an almost insatiable appetite for new capital. Until it reaches and passes the break-even point, however, the business has little appeal to outside investors and little, if any, throwoff of funds from internal sources. Operations in this early period may constitute a drain on funds because of a net excess of costs over revenues. A business in these circumstances has little staying power, and the slightest reverse creates a major financial crisis.

The Sources of Funds for New Enterprise

In many respects, the financing of a new small-scale business is no different from that of business in general. By calling attention to certain peculiarities which have widespread occurrence among such businesses, there is a danger of leaving the impression that they exist in a financial world of their own. On the other hand, it is important to be alerted to the fact that certain variations in the normal pattern of business finance can be traced to the age and size of the business unit.

Table 27–2 gives some indication of the differences in sources of funds between small-scale and large-scale business. It shows a percentage breakdown of composite balance sheet data on manufacturing companies with

Table 27–2

Balance Sheet Percentages for Manufacturing Corporations with Assets under $1 Million and Assets of $1,000 Million and Over, End of Third Quarter, 1970

	Under $1 Million	$1,000 Million and Over
Cash and U.S. governments	10.4%	3.5%
Receivables	28.4	14.3
Inventories	21.2	19.5
Other current assets	4.1	3.6
Total current assets	64.1%	41.0%
Property, plant, and equipment	62.6	88.4
Deduct: reserve for depreciation and depletion	32.4	41.9
Net property, plant, and equipment	30.2%	46.5%
Other noncurrent assets	5.7	12.5
Total assets	100.0%	100.0%
Short-term loans from banks	5.9%	3.4%
Advances and prepayments by U.S. government	0.1	1.6
Trade accounts and notes payable	17.9	6.6
Federal income tax accrued	2.1	1.8
Instalments due in one year or less: Bank loans	1.4	0.4
Other long-term debt	1.6	0.8
Other current liabilities	5.9	8.1
Total current liabilities	34.8%	22.7%
Long-term debt due in more than one year: Loans from banks	4.6	2.9
Other long-term debt	11.0	14.3
Other noncurrent liabilities	0.8	5.0
Total liabilities	51.2%	44.9%
Reserves not reflected elsewhere	—	—
Capital stock, capital surplus, and minority interest	19.1	18.3
Earned surplus and surplus reserves	29.8	36.8
Total stockholders' equity	48.8%	55.1%
Total liabilities and stockholders' equity	100.0%	100.0%

SOURCE: Federal Trade Commission and Securities and Exchange Commission, *Quarterly Financial Report for Manufacturing Corporations, Third Quarter, 1970*, pp. 29 and 33.

assets under $1 million versus companies with assets of $1,000 million and over. The most notable statistic is the much heavier reliance on trade credit in the smaller business—17.9% versus 6.6% of total liabilities plus equity.

There are obvious reasons why trade credit plays such an important role. The supplier of trade credit is in business to sell a product at a profit. Competition for sales volume forces him to reach out for new, small, and often financially weak customers by offering delayed payment. When such customers abuse normal credit terms such as net 30 days by holding back payment for 45 or 60 days, the supplier hesitates to act harshly in order to collect payment, for it may mean loss of a promising customer. If there is no discount for prompt payment or if the discount date is passed, it is in the interest of the customer to delay payment as long as possible, since this minimizes the overall cost of capital. Small businesses that are hard pressed for funds often become very skillful in juggling payables so as to gain the maximum credit without losing their sources of supply.

A second characteristic of the small business seen in Table 27–2 is the relatively heavy reliance on banks among institutional sources of debt capital—11.9% versus 6.7%. Unlike an insurance company, a commercial bank is not just supplying capital for an interest income. It has an interest in developing new businesses in the community as depositors, as users of bank services, and as a means of increasing employment. If the bank can establish a sound relationship, person to person, early in the life of a business, that relationship is likely to be lasting. The statistics of Table 27–2 show that bank funds supplied were both seasonal loans and term loans.

A development in recent years that may hold considerable significance for new and small-scale businesses is the interest shown by insurance companies and some other lenders in an equity type of participation as a part of a loan agreement. The option to purchase a block of common stock at a favorable price is regarded as an inducement to make a loan that would otherwise be considered unattractive at fixed interest rates within the customary range. This suggests a possible formula whereby some conservative financial institutions which are not now considered as a primary source of capital for small business may be induced to divert some funds into this market. So far, however, loans of this type form a modest part of the portfolios of the lending institutions making use of them.

The primary source of equity capital in the new small-scale business is the personal savings of the founder and the earnings of the business. The savings of the founder are often supplemented by those of relatives and friends. The extent to which such resources can be the sole external equity base depends entirely on the rapidity with which the business becomes profitable, the degree of profitability, and the rate of profit relative to the rate of growth of the business. Unfortunately, it is often true that the earnings of a business in the early years, when need is greatest, are small or nonexistent. Among other causes, this may result from a volume of sales below the break-even point for the industry or because of the inevitable time lag in reaching maximum efficiency. This situation will be particularly serious if it has not been anticipated or if the reverse has been expected and plans made accordingly. All too frequently, the optimism of the founders leads to the hope of large profits immediately, profits which are counted on to contribute essential capital for stabilization and growth.

Personal sources of equity capital may be supplemented by recourse to the informal equity market in the community in which the business is located. Certain well-to-do individuals, such as doctors or lawyers, become known as potential investors in attractive equity situations. In larger centers such capital may be directed through the more formal and systematic channel of a venture capital company. The primary concern of the founder seeking such equity capital is the distinct possibility that his control may be diluted or destroyed if such sources are invited to participate.

For some new businesses a public offering of equity securities is a possibility if the business and its management have an investor appeal and if the size warrants it. However, studies made over the years have clearly demonstrated that the costs of floating a public issue are to a considerable extent fixed, and this makes a small issue expensive, perhaps prohibitively so.

The Securities and Exchange Commission has made several studies of the cost of flotation of securities, the latest for the years 1963–65. Although such costs have declined for all sizes of issues, they still remain high for small issues. In 1963–65, for primary common stock issues offered through security dealers, the total costs as a percentage of proceeds for issues under $500,000 were 18.5%, to be compared with 9.1% for issues between $2 million and $5 million. Compensation as a percentage of proceeds was 11.3% for issues under $500,000 and 7.4% for issues between $2 million and $5 million; other expenses were 7.3% and 1.7% respectively.[3]

Public offerings under Regulation A of the Securities and Exchange Commission, that is, offerings not in excess of $300,000 including underwriting commissions, increased from 383 in 1967 to 1,043 in 1969. Most of these offerings in 1969 were in the $200,000–$300,000 group.[4] Testimony before the Senate Committee on Small Business in 1967 was that the SEC had found no evidence that small businesses had had difficulty in finding investment bankers or broker-dealers to distribute their securities when the securities were truly marketable.[5]

A perennial issue for political investigation and debate has been the

---

[3] U.S. Securities and Exchange Commission, *Cost of Flotation of Registered Equity Issues, 1963–1965* (Washington, D.C., 1970).

[4] SEC 1969 Annual Report (Washington, D.C., 1970), p. 38.

[5] U.S. Congress, Senate, Select Committee on Small Business, *Status and Future of Small Business* (Washington, D.C.: Government Printing Office, 1967), p. 368.

question of whether small business has been stifled for a lack of equity or debt capital and in particular, whether the organized capital markets favor the larger, more mature business. We have already reviewed some of the reasons why the new, untried business and management may have trouble interesting risk-sensitive sources of debt and equity capital. Undoubtedly a gap between perceived needs and available sources often exists. This is particularly likely to be true for medium-term debt capital and equity capital with no strings attached.

Evidence for this is seen in two surveys conducted by the Federal Reserve in 1959 and 1960, one covering about 3,000 manufacturers and the other about 8,500 unincorporated retailers. Both confirmed the widely accepted view that the small-business financing gap was for more or less permanent funds, that is, intermediate and long-term credit and equity capital. Both indicated that small concerns were much more successful in meeting their needs for short-term credit than in obtaining longer-term credit or equity capital. In manufacturing, for example, about three fourths of the small companies reporting a need for short-term credit were able to obtain such funds in amounts and on terms that they regarded as satisfactory. But only one third of the small companies needing long-term credit, and only one tenth of those needing equity capital, obtained it on a satisfactory basis.[6]

A point which has been observed to be significant to many new and small businesses is the time and effort required in the cultivation of capital sources. When a business must supplement regular sources such as trade credit and bank loans by recourse to the secondary capital market of relatives, friends, business acquaintances, customers, finance companies, and the like, there are very few reliable guides. Each source must be explored carefully and exhaustively to pin down the precise terms upon which the money will be made available. Even when terms are established, the reliability of the lender may be in doubt, especially if the agreement extends over a considerable period of time. In such situations the negotiations for capital can consume a great deal of time and effort, and the task cannot be delegated by the owner-manager.

Special Assistance to Small Businesses

The widespread acceptance of the idea that small business is confronted with unusual problems peculiar to it has resulted in efforts on the part of government and private agencies to diminish or eliminate these problems. For many years, government has assumed the role of custodian of the competitive system, and one of the key elements in such a system is a business climate favorable to the formation of new competitive units where the need exists. It is natural, therefore, that the government would

---

[6] Testimony of William McChesney Martin, Jr., in Senate, Select Committee on Small Business, *Status and Future of Small Business*, p. 617.

take it upon itself to keep the opportunities for new and small business alive.

All levels of government have hastened to pay at least lip service to the needs of small business, but the most noteworthy service has been offered by the federal government. Congress created the Small Business Administration in 1953 and small-business investment companies by the Small Business Investment Act in 1958 to meet the gap in financing. Later legislation has liberalized the requirements. The work of the SBA has significant financial implications for the small business that seeks and qualifies for its assistance.

One of the responsibilities of the SBA has been to assist small businesses to get their share of government contracts, both directly and as subcontractors. This it does by acting as a source of information for government purchasing agencies as well as potential suppliers, by certifying businesses as being financially and technically competent to undertake government contracts, by helping to form production pools, and by setting aside certain government purchases for competitive bidding by small firms. In 1969 the SBA took about 50 government contracts directly and awarded them to minority manufacturers. It also worked with franchisers to assist minority businessmen in establishing franchised businesses.[7]

The SBA is also authorized to assist in the financing of small business either by making direct loans or by participating with banks or other private credit institutions. The loan may be used to finance plant and equipment or for working capital. There are a number of restrictions as to the circumstances under which a loan will be made, one of which is that all other reasonable sources, internal and external, must first be exhausted. The SBA is a lender of last resort—a possible alternative to the high-cost secondary money markets so frequently used by small businesses.

The principal types of loans made by the SBA in 1970 were these:[8]

1. *Regular business loans,* authorized under Section 7 (a) of the Small Business Act, and subdivided into direct, immediate participation, and guaranteed loans. These were loans with a maturity limit of 10 years (15 years for construction of facilities) and a total limit of $350,000. SBA regulations as of 1970 established limits of $100,000 for direct loans; $150,000 as SBA's share of immediate participation loans, with a usual limit on SBA participation of 75%; and $350,000 for SBA's share of guaranteed loans, with a 90% maximum. Interest rates were 5½% on

---

[7] Small Business Administration, *1969 Annual Report* (Washington, D.C., 1970), p. vii.

[8] See U.S. Congress, Senate, Select Committee on Small Business, *Review of Small Business Administration's Programs and Policies—1969* (Washington, D.C.: U.S. Government Printing Office, 1969), pp. 21–25; and U.S. Congress, House, Select Committee on Small Business, *Organization and Operation of the Small Business Administration (1969–70)* (Washington, D.C.: U.S. Government Printing Office, 1970), pp. 3–4.

direct loans and the SBA share of immediate participation loans, 8% on the bank share of immediate participation loans; and generally two points above the prime rate on guaranteed loans.

From the inception of the SBA through April, 1969, it furnished more than 93,000 loans to small firms, totaling about $4.3 billion. This type of loan has been the principal activity of the agency.

2. *Economic opportunity loans*, limited to $25,000 and a 15-year term in 1970. In order to be eligible to apply for an EOL loan, the applicant must be a low-income individual or a person who due to social or economic disadvantage has been denied the opportunity to acquire adequate business financing through normal lending channels on reasonable terms. This expanded the SBA service beyond the entire small-business community to emphasize the assistance to the deprived sector of this community. From the beginning of the program in 1964 through April, 1969, the SBA approved 11,245 loans for $125 million. Both immediate participation and guaranteed loans were included.

3. *Development company loans.* Under Sections 501 and 502 of the Small Business Investment Act, the SBA may lend to both state and local development companies, which in turn assist small businesses in their areas. Through April, 1969, the SBA approved 2,184 loans totaling $311 million to local development companies to finance projects costing $446 million and 24 loans totaling $15 million to state companies.

4. *Displaced business loans*, with no dollar limitation but a 90% limit on the SBA share of immediate participation and guaranteed loans. From the inception of this program in 1961 through April, 1969, the agency approved 1,679 loans with a total of $150 million. The purpose of these loans was to aid businessmen displaced or suffering injury from federally aided construction projects.

5. *Disaster loans*, made to both businesses and home owners suffering from natural disasters. From its inception the agency has approved 75,661 loans with a total of $667 million.

6. *A lease guarantee program,* begun in 1967 and expanded in 1968. The purpose of this program was to provide small businessmen with rental space in desirable locations that they would otherwise be unable to obtain. This was intended to be a self-sustaining program, with premiums paid. Although the SBA has made direct guarantees, it has also interested private insurance companies in insuring lease payments. By the end of fiscal 1969 the SBA had approved 207 applications for lease guarantee, 81 of them in participation with private insurance companies. The total amount of rent to be guaranteed was $101.7 million. Total premiums were $2.5 million, with SBA's share $1.7 million.

7. *The Small Business Investment Company program.* Recent actual and estimated loan levels in most of these categories are shown in Table 27–3. The data bring out several significant developments. Funds availa-

Table 27-3

Loan Levels of the Small Business Administration, 1968–70
(in millions)

	Fiscal Year 1968, Actual		Fiscal Year 1969, Actual		Fiscal Year 1970 Estimate	
	Gross	SBA	Gross	SBA	Gross	SBA
7(a) business loans						
Direct........................	$ 54.3	$ 54.3	$ 15.1	$ 15.1	$ 18.0	$ 18.0
Immediate participation........	205.0	144.1	149.9	100.5	154.0	98.0
Guaranteed..................	236.3	186.3	378.7	308.8	469.5	389.0
Total....................	$495.6	$384.7	$543.7	$424.4	$641.5	$505.0
Economic opportunity loans						
Direct and immediate						
participation..............	$ 26.8	$ 26.4	$ 29.4	$ 28.6	$ 32.0	$ 32.0
Guaranteed.................	4.4	4.0	21.9	20.1	48.9	44.3
Total....................	$ 31.2	$ 30.4	$ 51.3	$ 48.7	$ 80.9	$ 76.3
Displaced business loans						
Direct and immediate						
participation..............	$ 44.2	$ 41.8	$ 32.0	$ 29.6	$ 35.0	$ 33.0
Guaranteed.................	1.0	0.7	0.6	0.6	15.0	12.0
Total....................	$ 45.2	$ 42.5	$ 32.6	$ 30.2	$ 50.0	$ 45.0
Development company loans						
Direct and immediate						
participation..............	$ 47.7	$ 44.8	$ 52.6	$ 50.5	$ 54.0	$ 51.0
Guaranteed.................	4.9	4.3	12.8	11.4	39.0	35.0
Total....................	$ 52.6	$ 49.1	$ 65.4	$ 61.9	$ 93.0	$ 86.0
Investment company						
Assistance...................						
Direct......................	$ 24.6	$ 24.6	$ 9.0	$ 9.0	$ 15.0	$ 15.0
Guaranteed.................	—	—	0.8	0.8	40.0	40.0
Total....................	$ 24.6	$ 24.6	$ 9.8	$ 9.8	$ 55.0	$ 55.0
Total direct and IP.......	$402.6	$336.0	$288.0	$233.3	$308.0	$247.0
Total guaranteed........	246.6	195.3	414.8	341.7	612.4	520.3
Total.................	$649.2	$531.3	$702.8	$575.0	$920.4	$767.3

Source: U.S. Congress, Senate, Select Committee on Small Business, *Review of Small Business Administration's Programs and Policies—1969* (Washington, D.C.: U.S. Government Printing Office, 1969), pp. 32 and 518.

ble to the SBA for the business loan and SBIC programs have been drastically cut. In 1969 the SBA Administrator commented as follows on the effect of the Revenue and Expenditure Control Act of 1968:

The application of this outlay limitation forced us to reduce the level of our direct and immediate participation loan programs by $173 million from a planned level of $407 million to a revised level of $236 million. In order to achieve these reductions, it was necessary to practically discontinue the direct business loan program in the latter part of the fiscal year and after an initial outlay of $8.7 million direct funds in the SBIC program, we had to completely discontinue direct lending in that program early in the fiscal year.

The outlook for the fiscal year 1970 on the direct and immediate participation loan programs, specifically the 7 (a) business loan and SBIC programs are equally bleak.[9]

Because of the limitations on SBA funds, efforts to increase participation by banks and other private sources of funds, such as pension funds, have gained further importance. From 1961 through 1966, banks participated in 27,379 loans in a total of 48,981 loans. In dollar amount their participation was about 19%.[10] In fiscal 1969, banks provided $471 million in participation and loan guarantee plans, at the rate of about 81% of the dollars made available through business loans and 41% of the dollars in economic opportunity loans.[11]

Also to be noted is that the cut in the SBA share of business loans has been more severe than the cuts in other programs. Recent emphasis has been on help to deprived areas and minority entrepreneurship.

From the beginning of the program through June 30, 1969, the SBA had charged off $56.6 million of principal on 4,465 regular business loans and estimated that there would be additional losses of $35.5 million on other loans for a combined total of actual and estimated principal loss of $92.1 million, equivalent to 3.09% of disbursements. Furthermore, since the loans disbursed in the last two or three years had not matured to the point of reliable estimates, experience suggested that there would be a total loss of 3.82% of disbursements. This would mean an ultimate loss of $106 million on the SBA share of $3 billion disbursements through June 30, 1969.

Actual and estimated losses of $15.6 million on economic opportunity loans would amount to 14.6% of $106.8 million disbursements. On displaced business loans, actual and estimated losses would be 0.49% of $113.8 million disbursements; on disaster loans, 3.86% of disbursements; on development company loans, 2.04% of SBA disbursements. On loans to investment companies, the SBA had charged off $3.4 million and set up reserves for loss of $35.8 million.[12]

In 1958 the Small Business Investment Act made the SBA the channel through which a new form of federal assistance became available to small businesses. This act provided for the licensing and incorporation of investment companies to supply equity as well as debt capital to small business. Minimum initial capital required for such an investment was $300,000, half of which might be provided by the federal government through a long-term loan and at least half by private investors through

[9] Senate, Select Committee on Small Business, *Review of . . . Programs*, p. 5.

[10] From table presented by First Deputy Comptroller of the Currency at a hearing on the future of small business (Senate, Select Committee on Small Business, *Status and Future of Small Business*, p. 648).

[11] Small Business Administration, *1969 Annual Report*, p. 11.

[12] Small Business Administration, *1969 Annual Report*, p. 35.

the purchase of stock. The intent of the act was to encourage private investment in small business and to recognize the critical need for equity funds as well as debt capital.

The response to the Small Business Investment Company (SBIC) concept was substantial. By the end of 1964 there were 700 such companies in operation with an investment of $500 million in 10,000 small businesses. Their performance, however, was less impressive than some of the founders had been led to expect. A problem in identifying investment opportunities having the appropriate risk and profit characteristics led to delays in reaching full employment of resources and profitability in the SBIC's. Inevitably there was some mismatching of investors, SBIC management, and small business investment opportunities.

In 1964 the federal government moved to relieve some of the problems which had emerged. The changes which were instituted included a higher initial investment hurdle for new SBIC's (now $300,000 of private capital), increased opportunity for investment by the government itself through the SBA in the form of direct loans to SBIC's (maximum raised from $400,000 to $700,000) and guarantees, and more freedom for the SBIC's in the risk and profit characteristics of their investments. In general, the problems of the SBIC's for which these moves were designed as a partial solution merely reflect the basic difficulties of equity investment in the new and small business, to which we have already referred.

The SBIC program completed 10 years of operation in 1969. During that period the SBA approved $387 million to finance their activities and SBIC's had provided some $1.4 billion to finance small business concerns. There had been a decline in the total number of SBIC's, however. In contrast to the 700 SBIC's in 1964, there were 498 in 1968 and 479 outstanding licensees in June, 1969. Of these, 128 were in some stage of dissolution. The SBA expected the shrinkage to stop at about 350 effective companies, to leave a stable number of quality companies in the program.[13]

There were several reasons for the decline. Some SBIC's lost money, others found the business too difficult. This was particularly true of the small companies started with the original minimum private capital of $150,000. Mergers and consolidations resulted in stronger companies, although they reduced the total number. Some companies were eliminated through regulatory and legal action by the SBA against inactive companies and companies in violation of the regulations. The Small Business Investment Act Amendments of 1966 had given the SBA additional means of proceeding against SBIC's and their principals who violated the act, and during the next years the SBA continued its effort to elimi-

---

[13] Senate, Select Committee on Small Business, *Review of . . . Programs*, p. 24.

nate undesirable companies while protecting the small businesses in the portfolios.[14]

The curtailment of funds to the SBA in 1968 and 1969, together with rising interest rates, made it difficult for SBIC's to get the necessary funds for investing in additional small businesses. The executive director of the National Association of Small Business Investment Companies testified in June 1969 concerning the financial crisis as follows:

. . . for fiscal 1968, Congress appropriated $55 million for SBA to use in making loans to SBIC's. Of this amount, the Bureau of the Budget released only $15 million to SBA, so the agency went into fiscal 1969 with $8.7 million in approved loans which it could not disburse. For fiscal 1969, Congress appropriated $30 million for SBA loans to SBIC's, but the Budget Bureau released only $8.8 million to fund the approved loans pending at the beginning of the year. Therefore, SBA has not been able to make a single dollar available for SBIC's since the first of July 1968.

SBA was authorized, however, to utilize a guarantee program under which SBIC's would be able to try to get loans from private lenders and those loans would be backed by a 100-percent default guarantee.

. . . our separate and joint efforts have not borne significant fruit. The ever-increasing interest rate has frustrated us on several occasions. . . .[15]

The Senate Select Committee on Small Business summed up the problem as follows:

The 1967 amendments to the Small Business Investment Act increased SBIC leverage from $4.7 million to $7.5 million and, under certain conditions, to a maximum of $10 million per company. This, coupled with rising interest rates and a tighter money market, placed a great demand on SBA for Government funds. The problem has been compounded by a curtailment of Government expenditures in fiscal year 1969, resulting in a reduction, from $30 million to $8.7 million, of funds allocated to the SBIC program. This permitted SBA to honor only those applications filed by June 30, 1968. SBA has not approved or disbursed any funds on applications received from SBIC's since July 1, 1968. As of this date the agency has in excess of $20 million of applications awaiting a source of funds.[16]

In November, 1969, the Small Business Administration undertook to organize Minority Enterprise Small Business Investment Companies (MESBIC's) to create venture capital for small business concerns in which at least 50% of the ownership represented disadvantaged persons. They are to offer venture capital and long-term loans, plus competent management and marketing assistance. At the end of June, 1969, three MESBIC's were in operation and 15 more were expected to be licensed soon.[17]

---

[14] Small Business Administration, *Annual Reports.*

[15] Senate, Select Committee on Small Business, *Review of . . . Programs,* pp. 274–75.

[16] Senate, Select Committee on Small Business, *Nineteenth Annual Report,* p. 6.

[17] Small Business Administration, *1969 Annual Report,* p. 17.

Another and quite different means by which governments have sought to assist small-scale business is through relief from taxation. The primary tax on business income is the corporate income tax. Since many small and new businesses are not incorporated, they escape this tax. Whether or not this is an advantage depends on circumstances. The owner escapes the business income tax but must pay the personal income tax on all business income, whether withdrawn or not. The problem comes down to a comparison of corporate and personal income tax rates for the sums involved.

Within the federal corporate income tax, there is presently a degree of relief for the small business in the breakdown between the so-called normal tax and the surtax, which applies only to income in excess of $25,000. Under the tax reduction introduced in 1964, the normal tax rate to be applied in 1965 and later years is 22% and the surtax is 26%. This compares with the previous rates of 30% and 22%. For the very small corporation the advantage of this provision can be significant. It is interesting that, to date, tax concessions of this type have been solely in terms of size of a business (measured by taxable income) rather than some combination of size and age of the business. There is reason to believe that if tax relief is justified in the broad economic sense, it would be for the new business rather than the small business as such. Greater competitive stimulus might well result from substantial but temporary relief for the new business rather than permanent shelter for the small business.

While generally less ambitious in scope, programs have been established by state and local governments in aid of the small-scale business. Such programs generally have the twofold objective of helping existing businesses to become more efficient and profitable and of attracting new business ventures, large and small, to a particular area. For many years, New York State has been one of the leaders in encouraging better-informed and better-qualified small business management. Through various publications the State Department of Commerce gives general advice on starting and operating small business, specific counsel and information on the operation of many different types of small businesses, such as restaurants and electrical appliance stores, a variety of pertinent business statistics for the state as a whole and by districts, and other information which is not readily available to the small-scale operator. In addition, personal counsel is available through regional offices of the Department and by the operation of regional workshops and forums.

As a general rule, state and local governments refrain from becoming involved in financial assistance to small business. They have, however, lent encouragement to the establishment of an institution of some real significance in this respect—the business development corporation. These corporations have as their primary objective the encouragement of industrial growth in an area, working on the assumption that one of the chief obstacles, particularly for smaller businesses, is a lack of medium- and long-term debt capital. An example of this type of institution is the

Massachusetts Business Development Corporation. Its capital is derived from loans from banks with which it is associated and from the sale of stock. The loans made by this corporation are primarily of a medium- and long-term character. For the most part, they have been secured by one or more of the following types of collateral: first or second real estate or chattel mortgages, liens on accounts receivable and inventories, and assignments of life insurance policies and leases.

In summary, it may be said that at the present time the presence of various governmental and private agencies in the small business capital market has not made a radical change in the general financial position of the new and small business. However, for particular businesses, they have often meant the difference between continued operation and liquidation. Further, they appear to have become a permanent part of the financial scene.

The Conservation of Scarce Funds

Because the typical new and growing enterprise is faced with a persistent shortage of funds, which places serious restrictions on management's freedom of action, it is necessary not only to explore all possible sources of capital but also to consider ways and means of making available funds go as far as possible. In every business, there are certain physical facilities, stock-in-trade, and personal and other services which must be provided in order to operate at all. On the other hand, these requirements normally have some element of flexibility, and there may be two or even several ways of providing some requirement which have significantly different financial implications. Hard-pressed small business managers must of necessity use as much persistence and originality in managing the productivity of each dollar raised as they do in raising it.

Without attempting to provide a complete catalog of the ways in which the business investment dollar may be made to go farther, the job of conservation can be illustrated by reference to several approaches which are in common use by small business managers. The investment in the physical facilities necessary for a given scale of operations may be minimized as follows:

1. Rent factory or store space, and rent equipment rather than purchase. Store or office space is usually easier to find on a rental basis than is factory space, because the former is a more standardized commodity. The opportunity for rental of machinery and equipment depends a great deal on the industry, since practices differ.
2. Purchase secondhand rather than new machinery and equipment. The availability of good secondhand equipment varies with the degree of standardization of the equipment to be used and the size and character of the industrial area in which the new business is to be located. For example, it is quite feasible to pick up suitable secondhand equip-

ment for a garment factory in the New York City area, where the industry is well established.

3. Purchase an existing business in financial difficulties. The opportunity to begin business in this way depends a great deal on the patience and flexibility of the individuals involved and the timing of the misfortunes of others. The individual who cannot or will not delay his start and who is strongly wedded by experience or prejudice to one line of activity is unlikely to find a favorable opportunity just when he wants it.

4. Build rather than buy ready-made. Many small business owners have saved scarce dollars by undertaking to construct their own physical facilities and, at least to some extent, make their own equipment. The possibilities here obviously depend on the capacities of the people involved and the nature of their business.

5. Assemble rather than manufacture. It is very common to find new businesses in the manufacturing area doing what is essentially an assembly operation. This helps to minimize the initial investment in plant and equipment. As they prosper and grow, they tend to take on more and more of the manufacturing, with the timing largely influenced by the growth of their financial resources.

6. Substitute labor for equipment. The initial financial burden in a new business may be minimized by purchasing only that equipment which is absolutely necessary and using labor wherever possible. Labor-saving equipment may then be added at a later date as funds permit.

In other ways the basic investment in working capital may be reduced by:

1. Keeping inventory down to what is absolutely necessary for continuous operation—and running some risk of inability to meet customer orders or of work stoppages.

2. Handling product lines which are available on favorable credit terms and avoiding lines which are not.

3. Restricting sale to those customers who are prepared to pay cash on delivery or within a brief credit period.

4. Scheduling production so as to produce salable products in the shortest possible time. The objective here is to produce an account receivable in the shortest possible time. Efficient production scheduling is not necessarily based on individual customers' orders, but it may be forced into this pattern if the need for release of cash is great.

5. Operating in whole or in part as a subcontractor to a larger business which may be willing to ease the financial burden by such means as supplying the raw materials for the operation out of its own inventory.

These devices are examples of what may be termed legitimate efforts to pare down the financial requirements of the business. It must be added that under extreme financial pressure, businesses sometimes resort to tactics which have a similar end result but which hardly qualify as sound financial practice. One of these is to abuse trade credit by allowing obligations to remain outstanding well beyond the limits set by the supplier. This practice is based on the assumption that because the supplier wants the business, he will not react by cutting off the supply and enforcing payment. A little experimentation along these lines shows up the soft spots. Another practice is to rely on the "float" of issued but uncashed checks to extend the usefulness of the bank account. Checks may be issued without being covered at the moment by cash in the bank in the hope that they will not be cashed immediately and that, by the time they are, deposits will have covered the amount. It is hardly necessary to say that this kind of "shoestring" financing is at best a questionable device for getting over the occasional tight spot and cannot be a part of a sound long-run financial policy.

In a review of the various ways of effecting some reduction in the need for funds during the initial stages of business life, it becomes apparent that the ultimate financial implications are not always the same. Four distinctly different effects can be observed:

1. A genuine reduction in the capital required to conduct the business—as illustrated by the purchase of assets at distress prices or the sale of products for cash rather than on extended credit terms.
2. Illusory economies of capital which simply defer the outlay—as illustrated by the purchase of secondhand plant or equipment which requires drastic overhaul or replacement in the near future.
3. The exchange of one financial problem for another—principally the exchange of a large initial outlay for a series of smaller payments over a period of time. This is illustrated by the "rent versus buy" alternative and the substitution of labor for machinery.
4. A reduction in the initial capital required in exchange for some loss of efficiency and profitability. This is seen in the subcontracting of aspects of a manufacturing process, in small and frequent purchases of raw materials, and in the scheduling of production in terms of orders rather than economical runs (when these conflict).

In taking a course of action that postpones an expenditure or changes its form from a lump sum to a series of smaller payments, the manager is primarily motivated by a desire to buy time. Such a step may be based on a careful projection of the future financial position of the business or may merely reflect an impatience to get under way and a blind optimism that things will work out somehow if only a start is made. If, as often happens, the shortage of funds is solved by "economies" which reduce efficiency, increase costs, and lower profit margins, the business manager may merely be postponing the evil day. The immediate financial relief is bought at the cost of lower profits in the future—profits which are a vital source of funds for consolidation and expansion. The hazards of such an approach to a shortage of capital are heightened by the fact that many men new to the role of the independent business operator may be ignorant of the effect on profit or, if aware of this possibility, are unable to assess its magnitude and tend to ignore it.

Summary and Conclusion

In this chapter we have outlined some of the financial problems and practices commonly associated with the new and small-scale business. It would be unfortunate if, in doing so, we overstated the differences between small-scale and large-scale business. In fact, businesses on both sides of this rather arbitrary classification are faced with the same basic financial problems involved in planning, raising, managing, and conserving the capital necessary to carry on their activities. In general, the approach to and analysis of the problems we have described throughout this book can be applied with equal advantage to both small-scale and large-scale business. Thus, for example, the usefulness of a detailed cash budget has nothing to do with the size of the operation.

It is true, of course, that much of our discussion, particularly as it relates to long-term finance, has been in terms which are more familiar to the large business. Even here, however, the careful reader will observe that, for example, the public stock offerings and privately placed bond issues of the multimillion-dollar corporation have their modest counterpart in the equity and debt arrangements of the one-man business and present the same basic questions as to the proper apportionment of risk, income, and control. Similar parallels could be drawn in regard to such problems as capital budgeting, the bargain for funds, and income administration. It was the major purpose of this chapter to assist the reader in making the necessary modifications of his analysis when dealing with a new or small-scale business problem.

chapter **28**

Growth through Merger or Acquisition: Financial Aspects

Internal versus External Growth

In corporate finance it is customary to think of investment as investment in real assets of the kind recorded on the balance sheet—inventory, plant, equipment, and so on. In considering investment growth it is customary, as we did in the chapters on capital budgeting, to think of internal expansion through a series of expenditures in which existing operations are extended to provide new capacity and new products and to serve new markets. This all takes place within the same corporate entity, through the same organization, and under the same management. It is part of the process of economic and financial evolution of the business firm. Internal investment normally follows a relatively gradual and predictable course as the business seeks out the natural growth available to it in areas in which it has an established position.

In recent years substantial publicity has been given to an alternative approach to growth, namely, growth through acquisition of, or merger with, the existing business activities of another firm. For a variety of reasons this form of corporate expansion has been more visible, more dramatic and more stimulating to investors, analysts, and students of finance than has been true of year-to-year internal growth. Very recently, events have conspired to destroy some of the glamour attached to acquisitions and the whole conglomerate phenomenon, and some important financial as well as general management lessons can be learned from this experience. We will discuss this later in the chapter. First, we need some background on terminology and on historical perspective.

Definition of Terms

The term *merger* implies a combination of two or more formerly independent business units into one organization with a common management and ownership. In business practice the term is loosely used to cover a variety of legal and financial devices by which this union of ownership and management is achieved. Other terms—*consolidation, amalgamation, acquisition*—are used in a similar context, and the lines of distinction are often unclear. Since an event of this sort has major legal implications, it might be helpful to begin with the legal concept. The statement that follows covers the basic legal framework. It is not intended to cover all the variations that have come into existence, the use of which has been strongly influenced by tax considerations.

Formal statutory provision for corporate mergers is to be found in the corporation laws of the various states. To choose a prominent example, the corporation law of the state of New York makes specific provision for both mergers and consolidations. According to this law, a *merger* takes place when two or more domestic corporations merge into a single corporation which is one of the constituent corporations. A *consolidation*, on the other hand, takes place when two or more corporations consolidate into a new corporation to be formed pursuant to the consolidation. In both mergers and consolidations the plan usually must be authorized by vote of holders of two thirds of all outstanding shares, by class and in total, entitled to vote thereon. However, a parent company owning 95% of the stock of a subsidiary may merge with the subsidiary without a shareholder vote. In a merger the certificate of incorporation of the surviving corporation, as amended by the merger plan, becomes the certificate of incorporation of the merged company. In a consolidation a new certificate of incorporation must be drawn up for the consolidated corporation. Both surviving and consolidated corporations possess all the rights, property, and the like of the constituent corporations, and assume all their liabilities. In both cases, provision is made for the appropriate treatment of those shareholders who formally protest the decision within the stated time limit.[1] Dissenting shareholders typically receive cash compensation on the basis of an appraised value for their shares.

In contrast with the rather narrow and precise legal definition, we have the relatively loose and all-inclusive concept of a merger as used by the Federal Trade Commission. With an obvious interest in the monopolistic implications of mergers, the FTC is concerned with any act which causes the disappearance of a formerly independent business. It prefers to use the term *acquisition*, which includes "all business and corporate organizational and operational devices and arrangements by which the owner-

---

[1] See *The Corporation Manual* (1970 ed.; New York: U.S. Corporation Co., 1970), Vol. II, New York, pp. 54–59.

ship and the management of independently operated properties and
businesses are brought under the control of a single management."[2] Accordingly, this term includes mergers which are defined as acquisitions
of large companies, as contrasted with those where the acquired company
is small compared to the acquiring company. In this sense, mergers are
numerically less important than acquisitions.

Within the framework of this book, we are primarily concerned with
the financial implications of mergers. Thus, definitions which are useful
for legal or regulatory purposes are not completely satisfactory for our
purposes. A statutory merger of company A with company B, where A
already owns 100% of the stock of B, is largely a legal formality with no
major financial implications at this time. Similarly, there could be acquisitions which appear highly significant to the FTC, in terms of potential
control of output or markets, which do not give rise to major financial
problems for the businesses concerned. It will therefore suit us best to
use an all-inclusive definition of a merger and ignore those forms which
are of a nonfinancial character. Such a broad definition was suggested
at the outset: the concept of a merger as a union of two or more independent business units into one organization with a common ownership
and management.

The Merger Movement

What is termed *the merger movement* refers to the periodic rise and
fall in the number of mergers taking place, roughly corresponding to
cyclical swings of prosperity and depression. The Federal Trade Commission has brought up to date a statistical study of mergers begun by the
Temporary National Economic Committee. A graph showing the number
of mergers taking place in the years from 1920 through 1969 is reproduced in Chart 28–1. As indicated by the FTC, certain limitations of
the study make the absolute figures unduly conservative, but the relative
changes in merger activity are unmistakable. As can be seen, the first
wave of merger activity shown in these data came after World War I and
subsided in the period of economic uncertainty during the early 1920's,
to be followed by another and greater wave during the period of prosperity that terminated in the economic and stock market collapse of
1929. A third modest upsurge came toward the end of World War II
and terminated in 1948. The last and most dramatic wave of mergers
and acquisitions started in 1950 and continued until 1968, reaching the
all-time peak of 2,400 in manufacturing and mining in that year. The
break in the stock market and the associated deterioration in the economy
once again resulted in a decline of this activity in 1969 and 1970.

These fluctuations in mergers and acquisitions naturally raise questions

---

[2] Federal Trade Commission, *Report on Corporate Mergers and Acquisitions* (Washington, D.C.: U.S. Government Printing Office, May, 1955), p. 8.

Chart 28–1

Mergers and Acquisitions in Manufacturing and Mining

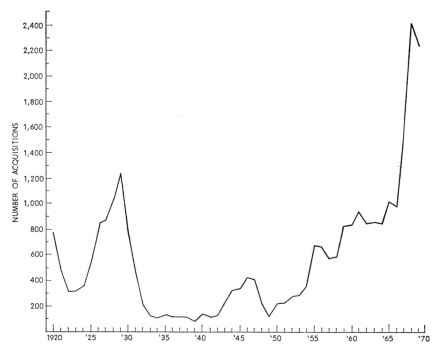

SOURCES: Data for 1920–39 from U.S. Temporary National Economic Committee, *Investigation of Concentration of Economic Power* (Monograph No. 27, "The Structure of Industry" [Washington, D.C.: U.S. Government Printing Office, 1941]), p. 233. Data for 1940–69 from U.S. Federal Trade Commission, *Current Trends in Merger Activity, 1969* (Washington, D.C., 1970), p. 9.

as to the fundamental cause or causes. In a broad sense it is apparent that the cyclical changes in merger activity roughly parallel fluctuations in general business activity, and this is to be expected when mergers and acquisitions are viewed as one dimension of corporate growth. However, questions persist around the specific reasons why individual businesses are motivated to give up their individual identity and pool their opportunities and their risk with another business, particularly when independence of control and of opportunity is such a powerful motivating factor in the formation of business enterprise. A number of factors are involved.

First among these are the management and corporate objectives of the acquiring or "surviving" business. So long as these objectives can be satisfied within traditional product lines and market areas and are within the share of market potential of the company attainable through internal growth there will be little incentive to initiate a merger or acquisition. On the other hand, it may be determined that despite the best efforts of the existing organization a strong, sustainable, and profitable competitive position cannot be produced without a significant change in share of market. Managerial talent, productive capacity, and technology may be involved along with sales volume. The action may be either defensive or aggressive. Obviously, some real or arbitrary time dimension is also involved. Whether founded on real or contrived competitive considerations, the only way to close the gap between expectations and realization quickly is by merger or acquisition. For this event to occur there must be other businesses in the same industry which feel similar or related competitive pressures and out of different circumstances and motives are willing to be acquired.

Management and corporate objectives may also move in quite a different direction, that of diversification. The desire to diversify may arise out of the realization that the underlying industry is maturing and demand is flattening out or that the business has reached the limits of its growth in share of market or that the business is inherently cyclical and greater stability in year-to-year volume and profit is desirable. For whatever reason, when industry and product diversification is desired, acquisition and merger is often the only realistic approach. The substantial differences which exist among industries and product lines with respect to managerial know-how, product and production technology, and marketing expertise are major barriers to internal development. The only way is to go out and buy these in a ready-made package as they exist in another organization. Of course, there are major risks, for it is hard to appraise beforehand the real potential of the packages offered on the acquisition market at the time diversification is sought. Some businesses have approached this task of evaluation with great skill, and others have proceeded almost blind.

A third aspect of corporate objectives which may lead to acquisition as a means of growth is related to what are or appear to be arbitrary growth rate objectives. Often these objectives, which are typically stated in terms of growth in sales volume and profits, are financially inspired— meaning that they are considered necessary to produce some real momentum in the growth of equity values. At other times they appear to be more management oriented in that they are considered essential to management motivation and development. In any case an aggressive growth rate objective beyond the historical rate of internal growth may be suddenly imposed on an organization by revitalized management, and once again the attractiveness of the quick acquisition route as opposed to the slow and difficult internal growth route is apparent.

It is difficult in practice to identify the cause and effect relationships in specific mergers—whether competitive necessity, diversification, or the creation of equity values has dominated the decision. Undoubtedly these considerations are used from time to time as an after-the-fact rationalization of the personal drive of a chief executive seeking to prove his leadership capabilities. In most cases there is probably a combination of economic and personal forces at work, as is true of any management decision. On the side of the acquired company, personal considerations may also be a factor, such as when a family business faces problems of management succession.

Any reference to considerations involved in acquisitions must include accounting and tax aspects. It is clear that an important element of incentive in the past decade has been the possibilities of increasing earnings per share by taking advantage of the accounting and tax treatment when two companies are joined together. Later sections will deal at some length with these considerations from the acquiring company's viewpoint. From the acquired company's viewpoint there are two primary advantages. One is that if the acquired company has been experiencing losses, these may become salable to the acquiring company, which may use them as an offset to the merged company's profits. The other major advantage lies in the fact that an exchange of equity for equity may not be treated as a sale for tax purposes, and the capital gains tax which might be involved in a cash sale is avoided, or rather postponed until the stock of the acquiring company received in the tax-free exchange is sold.

The Procedure of Mergers

We have already mentioned the formal procedures which have been prescribed by state law for the effecting of corporate mergers and consolidations. Such *statutory mergers,* as they are called, represent one of the ways in which businesses are brought together under common management and ownership. The steps taken under corporation law for the dissolution of the merged company may in fact be merely giving formal recognition to a union which has been in effect for some years. It is the purpose of this section to describe how mergers commonly come about.

Mergers may be initiated by either of the parties to the merger or by an outside organization such as an investment banking firm which sees in it some direct or indirect advantage to itself. Negotiations may be conducted between or among the top managements concerned or directly with the owners. At times, top management may be deliberately bypassed where it is expected to be antagonistic to the change. The most frequently used procedure for bringing ownership and management together is for one company to acquire ownership of all or a substantial portion of the voting stock of the other. In the initial stages, therefore, the company to be merged is likely to retain its identity, and the two companies are in a parent-subsidiary relationship. This relationship may continue for a very brief period or sometimes for years before actual merger takes place. If the acquiring company does not gain 100% ownership in the original transaction, it may find it necessary or desirable to add to its ownership before initiating merger proceedings. Even if it has the majority necessary to vote approval of the merger by the company to be merged, it may wish to reduce further the minority interest, which will have to be reimbursed in cash at an arbitrated price. In the meantime, the fraction of the stock originally acquired may be quite sufficient to operate the two companies as if they were parts of a single organization.

The voting stock of the company to be merged may be acquired in several ways. It may be obtained in a private negotiation between the acquiring company and a single owner or small group of owners. In the case of a publicly owned company, the stock may be purchased gradually on the open market at the market price in effect at the time. It may be purchased by a public offer to buy all or a stated number of shares of the company at a price which is usually above the market price. This offer may be made with or without the knowledge and blessing of the management of the company to be merged. As an alternative to the payment of cash for the stock, the acquiring company may offer its own stock in exchange at a ratio which is expected to be attractive. In this way the shareholders of the merged company become shareholders of the surviving corporation. Apart from the possible advantages of the exchange itself, there may be considerable attraction in becoming a part of a larger and more diversified organization.

The other alternative to the acquisition of the stock of a going concern is to purchase its assets. This might appear to be a more direct and therefore more satisfactory procedure for the acquiring company, since the ultimate purpose in acquiring stock is to have the use of these assets. Instead of the shareholders receiving the payment directly, the acquired corporation receives it and ultimately disburses it to the stockholders as a liquidating dividend when they dissolve the company. The acquiring company is thus relieved of the formal merger proceedings and the problems of minority interests. However, in practice, the purchase-of-stock route often proves to be the quicker and more effective procedure, as evidenced by its use in a majority of cases. Where there is an established market price for the stock, the key problem of valuation is greatly simplified. Further, the purchase of stock is a way of bypassing antagonistic management, and it may be done with a minimum of publicity through the impersonal medium of the stock market.

When a company is acquired through the purchase of stock, the acquiring company indirectly takes on responsibility for its liabilities as well as its assets, since it has assumed the responsibilities of ownership. When a direct purchase of assets is made, there is no necessity for the acquiring company to assume the liabilities as well, although this may be a part of the deal, especially where the merged company is in a weakened financial condition. Otherwise, the company concerned is simply converting earning assets into cash, and it retains responsibility for discharging its own obligations before it is dissolved and any cash is disbursed to its shareholders.

Some Accounting Aspects of Business Combinations

In recent years a number of aspects of accounting practice as it relates to business combination have come in for close examination and criticism. A substantial area of discretion within "generally accepted accounting principles" has existed, and this has had important implications for the reporting of value and earnings per share following the event of acquisition or merger. It has been alleged that this area of discretion has been abused with the intent of inflating records of performance and misleading the investing public. Among others, the Securities and Exchange Commission and the Accounting Principles Board of the American Institute of Certified Public Accountants have been drawn into the debate. Some of the issues are worthy of comment in this chapter.

The most fundamental issue which has been subject to vigorous pressure from conflicting viewpoints concerns the manner in which the combined assets and liabilities are joined together as the basis for future reporting. The traditional method of accounting, referred to as the *purchase method*, views a business combination as one company acquiring another just as if the acquired company was a bundle of assorted assets— land, buildings, machinery and so on. As in any purchase, the value to be recorded on the acquiring company's books is the value of the acquired's assets arrived at for purposes of the exchange and not the historical cost on the books of the acquired company. This is particularly significant because periods of high merger activity coincide with buoyant economic conditions and rising values, so that the purchase price of an acquired company is often substantially above the book values of its assets. If the premium paid above book value is then placed on the books of the acquiring company, it increases the costs being charged to future income and results in a lower reported income than would be true if book values alone were used.

The alternative method of accounting for a business combination is called the *pooling-of-interests* method. This method, which relates most directly to the situation where an acquisition or merger takes place through an exchange of common stock, rather than for cash, views the transaction not as a purchase of assets but as a mutually advantageous combination of two formerly independent ownership groups, which does not change the underlying asset values of the corporate entities involved. Thus, in a combination effected through the pooling-of-interests method, the two balance sheets are "pooled" at existing book values regardless of the premium implicit in the rates at which the stock is exchanged. The obvious advantage of this method is that asset values subject to write-off against income are minimized, and future earnings performance is thereby improved.

The issues involved here are far more complex than this brief statement indicates.[3] In the main, the support of the pooling-of-interests concept comes from acquisition-minded businessmen who seek to place growth through acquisition in the most favorable light consistent with accepted accounting principles. Some would argue that to enforce the purchase method on all acquisitions would be to eliminate much of the advantage of and incentive for growth through acquisition. Opposition to the pooling-of-interest method and support for the purchase method comes primarily from two sources—those professional accountants who favor the purchase method on principle and those accountants and businessmen who favor conservative reporting of income. It is interesting to note that some businesses in the past have not felt bound by the concept of consistency and not only have varied the method from one acquisition to another but have even combined them on the same acquisition. With improvement in earnings performance as the primary consideration, the purchase method helps when a company is acquired below book value and pooling of interests helps when the cost of acquisition is above book.

The handling of other aspects of financial reporting is also at issue in business combinations. The event of combination inevitably calls for action to make the two accounting systems compatible and is an opportunity to liberalize the accounting system of the acquired company if the new management is so inclined. Modifications of inventory valuation, depreciation policy, and other elements of value and therefore of cost can result in significant improvements in earnings per share.

The heated debate of recent years surrounding accounting for business combinations, particularly in the case of businesses which have become habitual acquirers of other businesses, has raised the clear suggestion of manipulation of financial information to the detriment of existing and potential investors, private and public regulatory agencies, and the public in general. The evidence strongly suggests some of this has gone on. On the other hand, some real issues of accounting principle have been raised where legitimate differences of opinion and judgment exist. It is precisely because there is room for legitimate debate that the opportunity for abuse has existed. The opinion handed down by the Accounting Principles Board cited in footnote 3 clearly indicates that the debate is not at an end.

The Conglomerate Phenomenon

Perhaps the most spectacular financial phenomenon to come on the business scene in the 1950's and 1960's has been the so-called conglom-

---

[3] See American Institute of Certified Public Accountants, *Opinions of the Accounting Principles Board,* No. 16, "Business Combinations" (New York, 1970).

erate corporation. This is a business corporation where the theorists' normative model of maximization of equity values becomes the dominant element in corporate strategy to the point where external growth through acquisition, as the vehicle whereby the rate of growth is accelerated, is largely or entirely indifferent to the nature of the business acquired. The word *conglomerate* suggests a combination of unlike bodies. Since these corporations have had an unusual glamour in the minds of investors and students of business, as well as substantial economic significance, it is worth examining the financial strategy involved. There are several parts to the strategy.

The most essential element of this strategy is that the basis upon which another company is acquired must produce an increase in earnings per share as a result of the merging of the two income statements. This happens as follows. Assume company A, the acquiring company, has 2 million common shares outstanding, current E.P.S. of $3.50, and a market price of $70 (a price-earnings multiple of 20). Assume company B, the one to be acquired, has 1 million common shares outstanding, E.P.S. of $4, and a market price of $60 (a price-earnings multiple of 15). Suppose that A and B agree to combine by an exchange of common stock in proportion to their current market values, or 100 shares of B is exchanged for 86 shares of A. The former shareholders of B thus receive in total 860,000 new common shares of A. The outstanding issue of the surviving company A is now 2,860,000 shares, having combined earnings of $11 million or $3.84 per share, 34 cents higher than before.

The acquisition has thus produced an instantaneous increase in E.P.S. which, assuming the same price-earnings ratio for A as before, will result in a higher market value for the stock of A. Will it remain the same? A rational mind would want to examine what the acquisition of B did to the variability and trend of A's earnings. But if A's management has the true conglomerate philosophy, it will not wait for the evidence on earnings to unfold but will soon have another acquisition on the books with another instant improvement in E.P.S. A succession of acquisitions where a company with a higher price-earnings ratio acquires other companies with lower price-earnings ratios can create a momentum of increases in earnings per share which the market begins to build into expectations and which becomes reflected in a rising price-earnings ratio. The higher the ratio, the higher the bargaining power and gains to the acquirer.

This strategy works well so long as the stock market is buoyant and acquisitions continue. But when the acquisitions stop the artificial growth resulting from a series of one-shot gains is withdrawn, leaving internal growth as the only support for E.P.S. If the conglomerate has not exercised good judgment to assure that its acquisitions are basically profitable or is unable to manage them effectively, the subsequent trend in earnings may be in sharp contrast to the period of acquisitions, with disastrous consequences for the price-earnings ratio and market value. When this situation happened to coincide with a general economic slowdown and a break in the stock market, as in the early 1970's, disillusionment with the so-called conglomerate strategy was almost universal.

Some of the companies which employed this strategy for purposes of creating high price-earnings multiples used other means to add to the short-term momentum of earnings per share. By acquiring debt-free companies and putting their debt capacity immediately to work, by taking quick action to terminate parts of the operation which were a drain on earnings, and by using convertibles as means of postponing the dilution of the eventual increase in common shares outstanding, the short-term impact on earnings performance could be magnified. When coupled with "liberal" accounting practices, the results were even more spectacular. Taken separately and in the right context, these actions could be quite legitimate, but they had the common characteristic of being one-time gains which could be repeated only by continuing the acquisition sequence.

It is unfair to tar all multiproduct companies that have come into existence through the acquisition process with the brush of cynical financial policy and inflated equity values. For some at least, diversification into unrelated industries was a legitimate strategy for extending the span of competent management and for minimizing risk. Its legitimacy could be and was strengthened by the use of conservative or at least consistent financial reporting practices. Where abuses arose, the investment community was not entirely blameless in its uncritical acceptance of the earnings record.

Undoubtedly, stricter guidelines for reporting required by the SEC, clearer directives from the accounting profession, and a more alert investment community will work against an early repetition of what happened in the 1960's. However, the underlying problem of identifying and interpreting trends in earnings per share and their relation to market value remains.

Valuation

The issue of valuation is one which pervades the whole of financial management. From the stockholder viewpoint the end product of successful financial management is the creation of value and its growth over time. The ultimate measure is the change in the market price of the ownership certificate as compared with other similar equity investments. This is now a familiar concept to the reader, and we have raised the issue many times and in a variety of contexts. However, we have deferred a summary of concepts of valuation until this chapter for two reasons: one is that it is a central issue of the financial aspect of mergers and acquisitions; and the other is that it is a very appropriate core around which to summarize the many dimensions of financial management discussed throughout this book.

It should be stated at the outset that a review of the literature of finance as it refers to the question of valuation leaves one with a feeling of disappointment at the apparent lack of objective and definitive treatment of the subject. Further, it is unlikely that this chapter will do much to change that impression. The subject remains as one of the great challenges to financial practitioners and theorists. The reasons are not hard to find. Economic value is something which has little if any meaning in the abstract. The concept of value has practical meaning only when the parties concerned have been identified and the circumstances of the need for valuation spelled out. There is a great deal of truth in the statement that "value is what people agree it is," and this opens up the whole elusive dimension of opinion and judgment and bargaining position.

Thus, one may easily conclude that value cannot be generalized and that it is objective only in the historical sense of what was agreed upon by particular individuals at a point in time. Nevertheless, even where value is being set by the give and take of direct negotiation between two parties, there is usually an attempt to appeal to the impersonal arbiter of objective criteria. Each party will seek to support his position by such evidence as appears at least to remove the elements of opinion and bias and substitute therefor fact. As we shall see, however, when we review the commonly accepted bases of valuation, it is impossible to escape from a degree of subjectivity, since value relates to an individual (or group) and his (their) participation in unknown future events.

When two or more independently owned businesses are merged, a problem of valuation is inevitably involved. If it is done by the purchase of stock or of assets, the cash equivalent must be established. If the merger is accomplished by an exchange of stock, then the relative value of each component part must be determined in order to find the share which each of the formerly independent stockholder groups will have in the surviving corporation. It will be apparent that this valuation will be the key issue in negotiations between or among the parties to the merger. It is appropriate, therefore, that we take up the problem of the valuation of a going business concern in some detail at this point.

While valuation is of special significance in business mergers, this is not by any means the only situation in which this problem arises. The question of the value to be placed on a going business, either as a whole or on a fraction thereof (a share or block of shares), also comes up in the pricing of new issues of securities; in the purchase, sale, taxation, or pledge of existing securities; in recapitalization; and in reorganization and liquidation. Because of this, the following discussion of valuation should be read not only in relation to the question of mergers but also in terms of its wider application to these other situations.

Kinds of Value

The term *value* is used in economic, business, and legal phraseology with a wide variety of meanings. Some of the many kinds of value confronting the student of finance are *assessed value* for purposes of property taxation; *condemnation value* awarded as payment in takings by right of eminent domain; *book value*, as derived from accounting statements; *reproduction value* of existing fixed tangible business assets; *going-concern value* of assets of at least potentially profitable business enterprises; *liquidating value* of assets on dissolution of a business; *collateral value*, representing the amount that may be borrowed on the pledge of an asset; *fair value*, used as a base for public regulation of utility rates; *sale value*, representing the anticipated realization upon sale under various conditions; *market value*, usually determined from actual prices, or bids and offerings in some sort of "market" (which implies the existence of potential buyers and sellers), though it may be imputed by estimate; and *fair market value* that adds to the concept of market value the assumption of the existence of a large number of buyers and sellers and sometimes the assumption that those buyers and sellers are well informed and entirely rational in their evaluations. The value derived under this last assumption is also called *intrinsic value* or *investment value*, distinguishing it from market price.

Despite the variety of the concepts of value indicated above, most of the methods of security valuation fall into three main categories: those based on the capitalization-of-earnings concept, those that emphasize asset values, and those that stress actual or imputed market prices. The outlines of each major approach will be drawn in succeeding pages. For purposes of simplicity, each approach will be discussed in terms of the valuation of a single share of stock. It will be apparent that whether we are placing a value on the business as a whole or on a fractional interest in the business, the concepts will be the same, and there will be a direct relationship between the two.

The reader will soon become aware of the fact that there is no single, always reliable method of determining *the* value of a business or its securities that can be applied to all situations. Often, several methods of getting at an answer, or various combinations of methods, will be useful in a particular situation. As we said earlier, valuations are undertaken for a definite purpose and from a definite point of view, and the choice of approach and the final appraisal will inevitably reflect that purpose and point of view. For example, a businessman who is considering the purchase of the majority stock of a street railway company with intentions of liquidating the company for the scrap value of its property would obviously approach the problem of placing a dollar value on the stock differently from an investor who plans to acquire the stock for the income it may produce from continued operation.

The Capitalized Earnings Approach

The capitalized earnings approach to the evaluation of common stocks rests on the philosophy that the current value of property depends on the income it can be made to produce over the years. Hence, it is argued, ownership shares in the assets of a business concern are properly valued on the basis of the earning power of the business. It is the earning power that will provide income to the shareholder, and it is income that he values rather than the physical assets themselves. The basic validity of the concept that value rests on earning power, or potential earning power, is seldom challenged. It is in the application of the concept to actual situations that major questions arise.

In other chapters of this book, particularly the chapters which deal with capital budgeting, the reader is introduced to the idea and method of establishing a present value for a stream of earnings (or savings) extending into the future. In those chapters, however, we were primarily concerned with the internal investment opportunities commonly available to a going concern in a period of growth. The required investment was generally taken as given, and the question was one of determining the time-adjusted rate of return to be realized from the expected earnings or savings. This was then compared to a standard set by the company's cost of capital or some other criterion.

The problem we now take up is largely an extension of this line of reasoning, although the form of the question has changed. Attention shifts from the determination of an expected rate of return on a given investment of capital to the determination of what this investment of capital should be. From the point of view of the one acquiring the investment, the question is: What is the maximum amount I am willing to pay for this stream of earnings? From the point of view of the one selling the investment, the question is: What is the maximum amount I can reasonably expect to get for this stream of earnings? Unlike the capital budgeting problems, the problem we are now considering involves an investment which is an entire business entity (or group of entities); consequently, the "earnings" in this case are the total net profits of the business (after taxes).

There are two basic problems involved in arriving at an earnings valuation of a business. One of these is the determination of the annual earnings (or earnings per share) which the business can be expected to produce in the future. The other basic problem is the determination of the rate of capitalization to be applied to these earnings. We shall discuss these in order.

ESTIMATE OF EARNINGS. Before considering the problem of estimating earnings, we should note another difference between our analysis here and our capital budgeting problems. There, specific investment opportunities are considered to have an income stream of limited duration.

A business entity, on the other hand, must, in the absence of evidence to the contrary, be considered as having an unlimited future; therefore, its income stream must be treated as if it will continue to infinity. Thus, it is natural that we think of earnings figures in terms of earnings per unit of time—the amount per year.

In assessing future earning power, the starting point is obviously the record of the past, and the first step is to get this record straight—or as straight as is possible and useful. The obstacles to reliable data we have discussed many times before, particularly in the chapter on interpreting financial statements. They derive from the fact that the person making the valuation may not have access to all the data he would like and even when he has, he is somewhat at the mercy of the whims of accounting practices. The inevitable adjustments will be a part of converting earnings data to a basis appropriate for the comparisons that are to be made. Where companies are being merged, it is essential that comparability of treatment of cost and revenue terms be established. Obviously, a great deal rests on the good faith of the parties concerned, since there is both an opportunity to conceal or distort the data and the temptation to do so.

Given a reasonable approximation of recent earnings performance, there is then the perplexing problem of how to allow for apparent trends. If the earnings are reasonably stable or fluctuating around a more or less horizontal trend line, the meaning of an annual earnings rate is fairly clear. If, on the other hand, there is an apparent trend upward or downward, an allowance must be made, and although the direction of the allowance is clear, the magnitude is not. The problem is one of identifying the extent to which a rate of increase in the earnings level is inherent in the particular business entity being acquired (and therefore an asset commanding a price) or simply a function of the general industry environment or of the efforts of the new ownership and management. It is obvious that a company will not pay for results it will produce itself. On the other hand, the prospect of rising earnings resulting from a unique product, market position, or management team is a salable asset and one which will strongly influence negotiated value.

As a practical matter, what the latter case suggests is an estimate of future earnings over an arbitrary time horizon as supported by the apparent trend in the past and present expectations. The horizon would presumably be a period short enough to justify a reasonable degree of confidence in the expected earnings, and the resultant estimate of earnings would be an upper limit for bargaining purposes. In practice, there is a strong correlation between eagerness to acquire certain earning properties and the willingness to pay for tomorrow's earnings rather than today's or yesterday's.

Let us assume that the analyst, as a result of a reasonably complete consideration of the various factors affecting the profitability of company X, forecasts annual earnings of $3 a share. How much is the probable earnings stream of $3 per share worth? What value should be placed on a share of this stock?

RATE OF CAPITALIZATION.   Once we have an annual earnings rate for the company as a whole or per share—or possibly a range of earnings rates—the next step is to apply *a capitalization rate* to arrive at the prospective investment value. This is the sum which, if invested at the assumed capitalization rate, will yield the expected annual earnings in perpetuity. This assumes, of course, that the earnings rate has been calculated net of whatever capital expenditures are necessary to assure their perpetuity. Thus, if the capitalization rate is taken as 10%, the $3 of earnings per share are worth $30 and presumably this is what someone who accepted these data would describe as the "value" of the share.

However, all this is deceptively simple; and in fact, the determination of the appropriate rate of return is the most difficult and subjective aspect of the problem. In general, the selection of a rate of capitalization is determined by the relative certainty of the estimated earnings actually being realized. The more certain the prospective buyer is that the earnings will materialize, the more he will pay for the claim to the earnings. On the other hand, where uncertainty is great—or in other words, where the risk is believed high—the buyer will insist on a high rate of return. For example, in the case of a small concern producing a highly competitive item of uncertain demand, the buyer of stock may insist on a price which will yield a return of 25% on his investment. That is, he would capitalize estimated earnings of $5 a share at 25% and reach a valuation of $20 for one share of the stock. Another commonly used way of expressing this is to say that the risk justifies a value of "four times earnings." If, however, the business in question were a very stable one with every prospect of steady earnings at the $5 level, the buyer might well be willing to accept a capitalization rate as low as 5%, in which case he would value one share of stock at $100, or "20 times earnings."

In the example of the high-risk situation above, the analyst might prefer to adjust for the risk by writing down the estimate of earnings to, say, $2.50. To the extent that he has thus made allowance for the risk factor through a conservative estimate of earnings, a duplicate allowance for the uncertainty would not be made through the capitalization rate. In other words, if the earnings estimate were written down from $5 to $2.50 to allow for the risk, then a capitalization rate of 12½% rather than 25% would be in order. This, however, seems to us to be an undesirable way to approach the problem. It makes for a "cleaner" analysis to separate so far as possible the measurement of earnings magnitudes from the assessment of the variability or certainty of those magnitudes as expressed in the multiplier or capitalization rate. In any case care must be exercised not to double-count the risk allowance as may well happen, particularly when several people are involved in the evaluation process.

Since the factors that go to determine the risk in a particular situation are complex and the weighing of them is a matter of judgment, it is apparent that the selection of a capitalization rate appropriate to the risk is subjective. It is also clear that a small change in the rate of capitalization applied will make a substantial change in the final valuation figure. In practice, many analysts tend to classify industries by groups and to develop rules of thumb governing appropriate rates, however questionable on theoretical grounds. Thus, for many years, it was widely felt that the more stable industrials with good prospects were "worth" about 10 times conservatively estimated earnings.

Before concluding this section on the capitalized earnings approach to value, we remind the reader of the growing body of theoretical literature concerning the determinants of value in the securities market and in particular of the continuing debate regarding the relative impact of earnings and dividends on market price (see Chapter 10). Since our discussion here has been in the context of value for corporate acquisitions, the focus has been on earnings alone. When one company buys another, it buys sales and earnings. Dividend payments, to the extent that they enter the picture at all, are more likely to detract from rather than add to value, since they represent a cash drain which must be assumed. However, it is recognized that the dividend aspect is of very real and positive significance to the individual investor in securities. This merely emphasizes once again how the concept of value changes as the beneficiary and circumstances change.

Asset Approaches to Valuation

Several methods of valuation can be termed *asset approaches*, since they center attention more on the assets to which the shares of stock have claim than on income data. Among the more significant of these concepts of value are book value, reproduction value, and liquidation value.

As the terminology suggests, *book value* is derived from the asset values shown on the company's own books and presented in its most recent balance sheet. The excess of assets over debts represents the accounting net worth of the business and hence the book value of the stockholder's investment. Where preferred stock is outstanding, a value for the preferred shares must, of course, be deducted to determine the net worth applicable to common. The net worth available to common stock divided by the number of common shares outstanding yields book value per share.

Many refinements on this direct method of computing book value are in use. Some analysts prefer to exclude from net worth some or all of such intangible assets as good will, patents, bond discount, organization expense, and deferred charges. Others analyze reserve accounts and add to net worth those reserves which are felt to be essentially segregations of surplus. A few inject a measure of the capitalized earnings approach by allowing good will (or even adding it when none is shown on the books) if the earnings have been large enough to support a contention that the concern has a "going-concern" value in excess of the stated value of the tangible assets.

Despite the variance in method of computation, book values are relatively easily and simply determined. To the unsophisticated, they are exact and clear-cut and, until relatively recent times, were widely accepted as standards of security value.

The student of accounting, however, will immediately recognize the fact that the figures for book value for a particular company will be influenced by the accounting policies of that company. The variations between companies in accounting for current assets are relatively small, with the possible exception of inventories. The lack of standardization of accounting practice is particularly significant in the valuation of fixed assets and in the treatment of intangibles such as patents and good will. Hence, a firm with a rigorous depreciation policy would show lower net fixed assets and thus lower book values than would a similar firm that had charged less depreciation. When book values are used in comparing the value of the security of one company against that of another, the analyst must attempt the often difficult task of reconstructing reported figures so as to get them on a comparable basis.

Even if a company follows "conventional accounting practice" in all respects, it will arrive at its balance sheet values by reference to conventions rather than sheer logics of value. Hence, inventories are generally carried at cost or market, whichever is lower. More important, fixed assets are typically carried at historical cost less depreciation rather than at current values.

An even more important weakness than the influence of vagaries of accounting convention and practice is the failure of the book value approach to give consideration to the earning power of the assets as the real test of their worth. For example, IBM reported earnings per share of common stock of $8.21 for the year 1969. Yet, the net tangible assets in 1969 amounted to $46.40 per share.[4] Clearly, the book figures were not a reasonable indication of the worth of IBM stock. On the other hand, there are companies—for example, certain railroads—where book values substantially overstate the worth of the company if earnings are taken as the standard.

Book values are most useful in appraising companies whose assets are largely liquid and subject to fairly accurate accounting valuation (i.e., banks, investment trusts, and insurance companies); but even in these instances, book values used alone are seldom reliable standards of value.

Reproduction value, or the cost of reproducing the assets of a concern at current prices, is of significance mainly in the case of public utilities,

---

[4] *Moody's Industrial Manual, 1970,* p. 2332.

where it sometimes becomes a factor in the determination of rate schedules by governmental regulatory bodies. As a single standard of value, it is seldom used. A major objection lies in the inescapable fact that the typical business is much more than the sum of its physical assets. While costs of replacing physical properties can be calculated with some exactness by painstaking appraisal, the cost of duplicating the business organization, its experience, know-how, and reputation, apart from the physical assets, is most difficult of determination.

When physical assets are the principal things of value to a concern, however, and when they can be readily reproduced, the cost of reproducing the assets will tend to serve as a ceiling on valuations reached by other methods. For example, in the case of a concern the principal asset of which is a residential apartment house, few buyers would pay more for the shares of the apartment house concern than the cost of erecting and getting into operation a similar apartment house, regardless of the earnings of the present concern.

On the other hand, *liquidation values* tend to put a floor under valuations reached from other approaches, since there are many firms which will purchase concerns when valuations placed on the business become so low as to create an opportunity for worthwhile profits through their liquidation. During depression periods, when earnings are low or nonexistent for a number of firms, liquidation values may become widely significant.

It might be noted at this point that even in the liquidation approach the valuation of the assets is based indirectly on their potential earning capacity. Unless they are to be sold for scrap value, the assets will ultimately find a market in someone who feels that he can use the assets effectively—that is, make them earn him a profit.

In certain cases in which the business as a whole is being valued, a combined capitalized earnings and asset approach may be appropriate. The appraiser may find, after valuing the shares on the basis of the earning power of the business, that the concern owns certain assets which may be sold or distributed to security holders without impairing the earning capacity of the company. Unneeded cash, government securities, or unused plant may fall in this category. These "extra" assets may properly be valued without reference to the earning power of the business and their net realization value added to the capitalized earnings value in the final determination of the worth of the stock. This is known as the *redundant asset* method.

Conversely, when additional investment by the purchasers is needed in order to realize the estimated earning power, the additional investment required may appropriately be subtracted from the value arrived at by capitalized future earnings based on the assumption that the additional investment will be made.

Asset approaches to valuation, particularly book value, have come under severe criticism as unrealistic measures of value except for the rather limited purposes of law and accounting. At the same time they persist as important guides to the determination or negotiation of value in practice. One reason is that book value is a matter of record—a number independently derived and precisely stated. In an uncertain world precise and apparently unbiased numbers are highly prized—however invalid they may be.

Another and perhaps more important reason for the appeal of book value is that it represents the commitment once made, and particularly in deteriorating situations investors are naturally inclined to cling to the notion that if they can recover what they originally invested they will be satisfied. Anything less represents "loss"—loss of money and, perhaps equally important, loss of face as a measure of bad judgment or bad management. These are some of the human factors which in practice have a strong influence on the positions taken by parties negotiating a value. They tend to lie in the gray area between what is rational and what is a rationalization.

Market Value Approach

Another major approach to value looks to the prices set for the security in actual transactions between buyer and seller—to "the bloodless verdict of the marketplace." Proponents of this approach argue that actual market prices are set by buyers and sellers acting in basic self-interest. Thus, they are appraisals of supposed experts who are willing to support their opinions with cash. Therefore, it is maintained that the prices at which sales take place are practical expressions of value which are definitely to be preferred to theoretical views of value.

Supporters of market price as a standard argue that the market price at any particular time reflects the value of the security sold in relation to all other securities or opportunities for investment and that all values are basically relative. Hence, the price of a security in a free market serves as an effective common denominator of all the current ideas of the worth of a security as compared to other investment opportunities. Also, market price is a definite measure that can readily be applied to a particular situation. The subjectivity of other approaches is avoided in favor of a known yardstick of value.

Whatever truth is embodied in these arguments, there are many problems in applying market price as a standard of value. In the first place, recent market prices are available for the common stocks of only the larger companies. In the period July, 1967–June, 1968, there were almost 1,535,000 corporate income tax returns filed for active corporations in the United States.[5] Yet, even in 1969, only 2,880 issuing com-

---

[5] Internal Revenue Service, U.S. Treasury Department, *Preliminary Reports, Statistics of Income—1967, Corporate Income Tax Returns* (Washington, D.C., 1970), p. 1.

panies had securities listed on securities exchanges in the United States.[6]
Further, "listing" does not in itself create an active group of buyers and
sellers, and many listed stocks are traded on a very desultory and infrequent basis.

Where there are few prospective buyers and sellers for a security, a
"thin market" is said to exist. Markets are particularly thin for many
securities traded in the over-the-counter market, where one will often find
such wide spreads between bid and asked prices as "16 bid, 19 asked."
The release of a relatively small number of shares on such a thin market
may be enough to depress market prices substantially. Further, the
market price for a particular stock on a given date may be influenced by
artificial means. Stabilization, or price-support activity, is legal in a
number of instances and is typical during the period in which a new issue
is being marketed by the underwriters.

Another question often arises in the valuation of large blocks of
securities. Recorded sales prices for the date in question may be based on
the sale of one or two hundred shares. Is it fair and appropriate to apply
the price set on a small scale to a large block of shares?

A more basic objection frequently raised is the contention that the
market itself tends to exaggerate major upward and downward movements in stock prices. For example, it is argued that speculative influences pushed common stock prices for certain widely traded stocks
in the historic boom of 1929 far beyond "reasonable" levels. Conversely,
it is claimed that prices in 1932 were so depressed by purely psychological factors and by technical pressures for liquidity as to be manifestly
poor standards of long-run value. Other, though perhaps less dramatic,
examples could be cited from more recent experience of market and
individual company price fluctuations.

Partially in answer to some of the objections above noted, the theory
of *fair market value* or *intrinsic value* has been developed. Under this
approach, fair market value is the value at which a sale would take place
if there were willing buyers and willing sellers actually in the market,
each equipped with full information on the security and prepared to act
in an entirely rational manner. This concept does meet most of the
objections stated; yet, per se, it raises a need for other standards of
valuation than market quotations and suggests recourse to something like
capitalized earnings as a more valid appraisal of "intrinsic worth."

At any rate, largely because of their ease of application, market prices
are widely used by the courts and by tax authorities, although not to the
exclusion of other standards where they are deemed appropriate. Regardless of theoretical weaknesses of market price as a measure of intrinsic
value, where a market price exists for even one share of stock, it will

---

[6] Securities and Exchange Commission, *Thirty-Fifth Annual Report, 1969* (Washington, D.C., 1970), p. 72.

inevitably affect the appraisal of a prospective buyer or seller, however large the potential transaction. The seller will, in ordinary human nature, hesitate to take a price much less than the price label established in the market, and the buyer will resist evaluations substantially higher than the market quotations.

Valuation in Practice

These three approaches to valuation represent attempts to remove the problem from the realm of personal opinion and to place it on an objective basis. In this respect they are only partially successful; and in each, some element of individual judgment remains. It must be remembered, also, that in mergers and in most other valuation situations, the final determination of value is a part of a bargaining process and that a compromise value is therefore likely to result. In such cases it would be largely a matter of coincidence if the agreed-on value corresponded exactly to that indicated by any of the objective approaches. This does not mean that they are therefore of no value in practical situations, for they will normally play a significant role in setting rational limits within which the negotiated value will fall. It is not surprising to find that each party to the negotiation will champion the method of valuation most favorable to its interests.

A study of the bases of valuation used in corporate mergers during the years 1953–54 indicated that present and future earnings were of "overwhelming importance."[7] At the same time, it indicated that book values were comparatively unimportant, except in cases where liquidation was a definite possibility. These conclusions are helpful in suggesting the nature of recent precedent in the "court" of corporate practice. In addition, they lend support to the observation that a negotiated price does not necessarily imply one based on nonrational considerations. It must not be interpreted, however, to mean that capitalized earnings value will, or even should, govern every valuation decision. Each case must be considered on its own merits. Without a careful analysis of the particular circumstances, there is no way of distinguishing the exception from the rule.

---

[7] C. C. Bosland, "Stock Valuation in Recent Mergers," *Trusts and Estates*, June, July, and August, 1955.

PART **X**

BUSINESS FAILURE

chapter 29

Liquidation or Reorganization[*]

Definitions

The decision to terminate a business venture may be reached for a variety of reasons. Terminations are, in general, customarily associated with *failure*—with *insolvency* and *bankruptcy*. Insolvency and bankruptcy will, consequently, be the primary concern of this chapter. However, it is necessary to keep in mind that many businesses are terminated while they are still quite solvent and even profitable. Disregarding personal reasons, which are of considerable importance as a cause of termination in closely held businesses, the circumstances surrounding the decision may vary widely. In the financial sense a specific business is an investment opportunity whose value is to be considered in relation to other alternatives. It may cease to be the most attractive alternative long before profits turn into losses. In a sense, it may be said to have failed if and when this fact becomes apparent. In everyday business usage, however, we apply the term *failure* only to those cases of termination where it is financially impossible to continue normal business activities. Dun & Bradstreet, Inc., the primary source of statistics on business failures, uses the term to mean "a concern that is involved in a court proceeding or a voluntary action that is likely to end in loss to creditors."[1] It is in this sense that we shall be using the term in this chapter.

Before proceeding, the meaning of two other terms used in conjunction with failure—*insolvency* and *bankruptcy*—should be explained. A firm is

---

* The authors wish to thank Peter J. Barack, J.D., Assistant Professor at the Graduate School of Business Administration, Harvard University, who revised this chapter.

[1] U.S. Department of Commerce, Office of Business Economics, *1969 Business Statistics: 17th Biennial Edition: A Supplement to the Survey of Current Business*, p. 38.

insolvent when either of two conditions exist: (1) the firm is unable to pay its maturing obligations; or (2) the total liabilities of the firm are in excess of the fair and realizable value of its assets. Although the former condition should in any particular situation be readily apparent, the latter may require proof of the values involved. This is because book values are often inadequate indicators of the realizable values of the assets in a company. It is important to recognize, however, that a firm is not legally *bankrupt* unless it has been adjudged to be so by a federal court upon application of the tests listed in the Federal Bankruptcy Act. These tests, listed as *acts of bankruptcy,* will be applied, on the one hand, when creditors petition a federal court to find their debtor bankrupt. Among such acts of bankruptcy are included the transfer of property by the debtor with intent to defraud his creditors, the preferential transfer of property by the debtor to the benefit of certain creditors prior to the anticipated filing of a bankruptcy petition, and the suffering by the debtor while insolvent of the appointment of a receiver to take charge of his property.

A debtor may petition the court himself, admitting his inability to pay his debts and his willingness to be adjudged a bankrupt. If so, the action is termed a *voluntary* bankruptcy. If, however, the creditors must petition the court and prove the existence of an act of bankruptcy, the proceeding is termed *involuntary.* In fact, the great majority of bankruptcy proceedings are voluntary.

Although many persons use the term bankrupt generally in reference to any firm which has "failed," it should be remembered that bankruptcy is a legal "word of art." Of wider expanse is Dun & Bradstreet's use of the term *failure* to include:

All industrial and commercial enterprises that are petitioned into the Federal Bankruptcy Courts. . . . Also included . . . are: Concerns which are forced out of business through such actions in the State courts as foreclosure, execution, and attachments with insufficient assets to cover all claims; concerns involved in court actions such as receivership, reorganization, or arrangement; voluntary discontinuances with known loss to creditors; and voluntary compromises with creditors out of court.[2]

Statistics of Business Failure

Although businesses are terminated for many reasons, those terminations coming under the Dun & Bradstreet definition of failure have in recent years represented a relatively insignificant proportion of the total business population. For example, Table 29–1 indicates an approximate failure rate of 0.44% of the total business population in 1970. Moreover, even in the depths of the great depression, total failures reached only

---

[2] Dun & Bradstreet, Inc., *The Failure Record through 1969* (New York, 1970), p. 1.

Table 29–1

Total Industrial and Commercial Failures in the United
States, 1955–70
(failure rate per 10,000 concerns)

1955	41.6	1963	56.3
1956	48.0	1964	53.2
1957	51.7	1965	53.3
1958	55.9	1966	51.6
1959	51.8	1967	49.0
1960	57.0	1968	38.6
1961	64.4	1969	37.3
1962	60.8	1970	43.8

SOURCE: *Economic Report of the President, 1971* (Washington, D.C.:
U.S. Government Printing Office, 1971), p. 290.

32,000 in 1932, as compared with 10,748 in 1970.[3] On a percentage
basis the average annual failure rate over the period 1900–1960 has been
estimated at 0.7% of the total population.[4]

However, it should not be forgotten that "business failures, although
the most drastic evidence of turnover in the economy, represent just a
fraction of the annual change in business population. Each year in recent
years over 400,000 firms were started annually, between 350,000 to
400,000 discontinued, and ownership or control was transferred in a
slightly larger number."[5]

Thus, while failure narrowly defined is a problem experienced by only
a small minority of business owners, in a broader sense the liquidation or

[3] *Ibid.; Dun's,* February 1971, p. 91; Paralleling the general business downturn of
1970 has been an increase in the number of business failures. This can be seen in the
following monthly figures for 1970 for failures and for seasonally adjusted annual failures
per 10,000 enterprises listed in the Dun & Bradstreet *Reference Book.*

	Seasonally Adjusted	Number of Failures
January	33.7	734
February	39.4	817
March	40.1	921
April	43.7	992
May	42.1	891
June	43.4	912
July	46.8	917
August	47.4	910
September	50.0	906
October	45.9	941
November	50.8	939
December	44.5	869

SOURCE: *Dun's,* January, 1970–January, 1971.

[4] Small Business Administration, *Fourteenth Semiannual Report, for the Six Months
Ending June 30, 1960* (Washington, D.C., 1960), p. 12.

[5] Dun & Bradstreet, Inc., *The Failure Record through 1969* (New York, 1970), p. 1.

sale of a business under unfavorable circumstances is not an uncommon occurrence. Furthermore, the above statistics of *actual* failures and terminations understate the number of times the prospect of liquidation has entered the minds of management as a very real alternative, perhaps under distressing circumstances which later proved to be temporary.

The Causes of Business Failure

There is some question as to how much can be usefully said about the causes of failure in business. Dun & Bradstreet prepares the best-known continuing study of causes of business failure. Table 29–2 presents the breakdown of apparent causes for 1969.

Dun & Bradstreet's *The Failure Record through 1969* goes on to comment:

Managerial inexperience and ineptitude account for almost 90% of business failures, a percentage that varies but slightly over the years. However, the economic climate [also affects] . . . the problems management must face. For example, [uncollected] receivables were more serious in 1969 than a year earlier in every category except retailing. Although the proportion of failures triggered by out-of-control expenses dropped a little from 1968's record high, the total was still two and a half times as large as ten years [earlier]. Inadequate sales [as a cause of failure] claimed a new low in 1969, with one glaring exception—the depressed construction industry where 30% of recorded failures were traceable to the current slump in home building.[6]

To try to establish a single dominant cause of failure in each case, as is attempted in the Dun & Bradstreet studies, would in one respect be a mistake. Invariably, there are several factors to any case of failure, with each reinforcing the others. This is especially apparent in the so-called "financial" causes of failure. An examination of unsuccessful businesses will demonstrate such financial weaknesses as insufficient working capital, overextension of credit, overinvestment in inventory, excessive debt, and excessive withdrawals of profits. Yet, each of these weaknesses may be

---

[6] *Ibid.*, p. 2. O. D. Dickerson and Michael Kawaja summarize in "The Failure Rates of Business," in Irving Pfeffer (ed.), *The Financing of Small Business* (New York: Macmillan Co., 1967), the findings of three state studies made within Rhode Island, Michigan, and Illinois on causes of failure. They consider these findings to be more specific than the Dun & Bradstreet classifications. The most important conclusions are: (1) owners with fewer years of schooling had a higher rate of discontinuance; (2) there was little relationship between previous experience in the same line of business and discontinuance; (3) individuals who had owned a business before had a much lower rate of failure than those who had never before been in business—in other words, entrepreneurial experience was more important to success than experience in the same occupation; (4) management teams of two, three, or four persons were much more successful than single managers; and (5) in general, the larger the amount of capital invested initially and the higher the proportion of equity, the lower the failure rate was.

Table 29–2

Why Businesses Fail—Year Ended December 31, 1969

Apparent Causes	Manufacturers	Wholesalers	Retailers	Construction	Commercial Service	All
Neglect	2.0%	3.3%	2.8%	3.2%	2.9%	2.8%
Fraud	1.1	2.0	1.1	0.9	0.9	1.2
Inexperience and incompetence						
Inadequate sales	43.9	43.4	39.7	30.8	38.3	39.0
Heavy operating expenses	14.7	9.0	8.4	14.1	13.7	11.2
Receivables difficulties	15.5	14.8	3.4	17.9	6.0	9.3
Inventory difficulties	3.3	6.3	6.5	0.6	0.9	4.2
Excessive fixed assets	6.7	1.5	2.7	3.5	4.4	3.6
Poor location	0.3	0.7	5.0	0.2	1.7	2.6
Competitive weakness	18.3	20.4	22.1	25.3	17.0	21.2
Other	1.7	1.4	1.4	1.8	0.8	1.4
Disaster	1.7	2.3	1.8	0.3	0.5	1.4
Reason unknown	3.4	4.3	7.2	6.9	14.1	7.1
Total number of failures	1,493	842	4,070	1,590	1,159	9,154

Source: Dun & Bradstreet, Inc., *The Failure Record through 1969* (New York, 1970), pp. 11–12. Classification based on opinion of informed creditors and information in credit reports. Because some failures are attributed to a combination of apparent causes, percentages do not add up to 100%.

traced back to some other underlying cause: for example, insufficient working capital to lack of intelligent planning; overextension of credit to a tough competitive situation; or overinvestment in inventory to a misjudgment of future trends in demand. Such weaknesses may also be interrelated: for example, there is probably a positive relationship between excessive debt, excessive withdrawals of profits, and insufficient capital.

The intention here is not to suggest, however, that it is either impossible or undesirable to search for causes of failure—even though to the parties involved in liquidation this research may appear purely academic. In a broad sense, such research is desirable in order that there be a useful transfer of experience regarding avoidable hazards. In the specific case, it may also be of vital importance. When a business is to be reorganized rather than liquidated, it is obvious that the new company must know— and, as far as possible, correct—the mistakes of the past in order to have any prospect of survival in the future. For these purposes, it is important to know all the important contributing factors of a business failure.

Insolvency without Bankruptcy

Only rarely has a healthy business become bankrupt overnight. More frequently, insolvency (and the resulting arrangement, reorganization, or liquidation) is the endpoint of a long struggle to preserve profitability and solvency. During this period, in the hope of reaching a financial turning point, such a declining business will have gradually exhausted the various means available of preserving solvency.

When a business is unable to show a profit and is experiencing a gradual depletion of its resources, one of a number of courses of action may be chosen in order to enable it to stay in operation. Setting aside for the moment the alternative of direct negotiations with the creditors of such a business, the more common courses of action for this purpose may include:

1. Converting nonessential assets into cash. What is considered "essential" will of course depend on the severity of the situation. For example, such assets may include,
    a)   Idle plant and equipment, or
    b)   Inventory above the bare minimum;
2. Cutting back or deferring all payments that are not absolutely required by contract. For example,
    a)   Accounts payable may be deferred, and
    b)   Preferred and common dividends may be cut;
3. Replacing debt of imminent maturity with debt of more distant maturity. This oftentimes requires recourse to higher cost loans; and
4. Obtaining new capital from those who have a reason for preserving

the company's existence—including, for example, officers, share-holders, suppliers, and customers.

For some declining companies, any or all of these steps or others may help to maintain the company long enough so as to enable it to reverse the trend towards insolvency and to reestablish itself on a sound financial footing. For others, such steps may only prove to be temporary expedients which merely postpone the more drastic steps of bankruptcy and liquidation.

If and when a business finds it impossible to continue to meet its obligations on time, even after full recourse to the types of emergency action suggested above, the only real remaining hope for preserving the business lies with reaching some type of *arrangement* with the firm's creditors, whether under the jurisdiction of or outside the bankruptcy courts. To avoid the costs of judicial proceedings, a business may make a direct appeal to its creditors in the expectation of some concessions from the rigid terms of its contractual obligations. The creditors of the debtor firm may well have many valid reasons in their own self-interest, apart from humanitarian considerations, for accepting less than that to which they are legally entitled. Trade creditors, especially, are apt to be lenient because of the expectation that future sales to the debtor will produce enough profits to justify any immediate sacrifice that an arrangement may call for. Bankers, on the other hand, operate on smaller "margins" and may be less amenable to this type of an adjustment. However, the more drastic alternatives to any such arrangement may well prove less satisfactory to the creditors. Not only are formal bankruptcy proceedings costly and time-consuming but also there is a strong likelihood that they will not produce full satisfaction of the creditors' claims. In fact, liquidation under court supervision most frequently involves a loss to at least some creditors. In addition, both creditors and debtors alike would rather avoid, if at all possible, the unpleasant publicity associated with bankruptcy proceedings. Thus, if the creditors trust the debtor's integrity and have any reason to share his hope for an improvement in his circumstances, they usually are willing to make an arrangement with the debtor and may in so doing be better off in the long run.

The type of arrangement agreed upon may take many forms. Moreover, the prospects for a permanent, or even a temporary, solution to the declining fortune of a business by this means depend upon all of the circumstances of the case. If the debtor firm continues to hope for a change in fortune, the arrangement may consist of an *extension* on any or all of the firm's obligations. Extensions usually involve a scheduled plan of repayment as well as a postponement of the immediate maturity date. Alternatively, with less appeal to the creditors, the arrangement may take the form of a common law *composition*. The composition is a legal agreement in which the creditors agree to accept from the debtor a stated percentage (less than 100%) of their claims in full satisfaction and discharge of what the debtor owes. Subsequent to a composition, the debtor is free to pursue his normal business activities. Such an arrangement may appeal to those creditors, particularly suppliers, who have an interest in preserving the business of the debtor and who see no hope in receiving full satisfaction for their claims. Aside from extension or composition, satisfaction in full of certain creditors' claims may be a part of any agreement that is worked out. For example, full payment of employee and small commercial claims can be considered a standard provision. The larger creditors usually approve of such a step in order to reduce the number of persons who will be party to the negotiations.

Any such arrangement consummated outside of the bankruptcy courts is particularly well adapted to disposing of the affairs of small debtors who scarcely warrant the safeguards and the expense of judicial proceedings. These arrangements may be carried out in an informal manner where the creditors are few in number or can be readily brought together for united action. The details of an arrangement may be worked out through direct negotiations between the debtor and the creditors or with a creditors committee, the services of a trustee, or an outside agency such as a credit bureau. Moreover, any such arrangement must be purely voluntary on the part of the creditors. Once accepted, the arrangement is final for those creditors who willingly participate; there is no need for court proceedings to make the agreement binding on these creditors. However, nonparticipating creditors will not be bound without their acquiescence in the proposed modification of the debt. In fact, any creditor who refuses to acquiesce with the arrangement must be satisfied according to the terms of his original contract. Otherwise, the debtor carries the risk of such nonparticipating creditors filing a petition for bankruptcy proceedings, for certain types of arrangements may constitute an act of bankruptcy.

In cases involving insolvency without bankruptcy, the role of the *creditors committee* often becomes important. The creditors of a declining business may at times be willing to work out an arrangement that will preserve the business of the debtor on the condition that a creditors committee is allowed to play an active, if not dominant, role in management during the period of rehabilitation. This desire for a part in management may reflect the creditors' lack of confidence in either the existing management's ability or willingness to fulfill its contractual obligations. Any arrangement of this sort must, of course, have the consent of the existing owners. However, in view of the possibly more drastic alternatives facing the debtor, the creditors' desire for an active creditors committee may well be recognized. Once the claims of the creditors have been fully satisfied according to the terms of the arrangement, they will withdraw, allowing full control to return to those who own the company.

A failing business that becomes insolvent may thus in these various ways avoid bankruptcy and liquidation. Although such informal procedures are less costly than court-supervised proceedings, they cannot be utilized without the consent, if not the active support, of the creditors. Generally speaking, however, creditors dislike liquidation as a means of realizing their claims and will give serious consideration to any alternative which offers a real hope of the ultimate return of their investment.

Bankruptcy without Liquidation: Chapters X and XI

Congress has provided in Chapters X and XI of the Bankruptcy Act two important procedures for reestablishing an insolvent business on a sound financial basis as an alternative to liquidation through ordinary bankruptcy. Chapter X of the Bankruptcy Act provides for the rehabilitation of an insolvent business through the route of corporate reorganization, frequently involving the adjustment of not only the secured and unsecured claims of creditors but also the equity interests of preferred and common shareholders. The procedures established for any Chapter X reorganization, moreover, provide elaborate and expensive safeguards for the protection of creditors, shareholders, and the public interest against potential abuse. On the other hand, Chapter XI of the Bankruptcy Act provides an alternate method for court supervision of arrangements between a debtor corporation or individual and its creditors for adjusting the unsecured obligations of the debtor. With an emphasis on economy and speed, few of the safeguards present under Chapter X reorganizations are found in Chapter XI arrangements.

Although to some extent a business corporation in financial difficulty is free to choose between Chapters X or XI of the Bankruptcy Act, the two chapters are clearly distinct and, when one is more appropriate than the other, the more appropriate proceeding will be required. Thus, for example, a petition filed under Chapter XI may be dismissed unless amended to comply with Chapter X upon the application of the SEC, or some other interested party, and the finding that the proceeding should have been brought under Chapter X. However, sometimes it is unclear as to which proceeding is the more appropriate.[7] On the one hand, the Supreme Court has stated that neither the character of the debtor, whether closely held or publicly owned, nor the size of the debtor, nor the nature of its capital structure is the controlling consideration in the choice between Chapter X or Chapter XI.

---

[7] As to the difficulty of this problem, Judge Friendly has stated: "We know of no scale sufficiently sensitive to weigh the near certainty of achieving a Chapter XI arrangement that may not be altogether fair and equitable against the possible emergence of a better plan from a Chapter X proceeding during which the patient may die before an operating room is ready or for which the fees of the surgeon and others in attendance may exceed the patient's means" (*SEC* v. *Canandaigua Enterprises Corp.*, 339 F.2d 14, 19[2nd Cir. 1964]).

Rather . . . [the Court has] emphasized the need to determine on the facts of the case whether the formulation of a plan under the control of the debtor, as provided by Chapter XI, or the formulation of a plan under the auspices of disinterested trustees, as assured by Chapter X . . . , would better serve "the public and private interests concerned including those of the debtor." . . . The essential difference is not between the small company and the large company but between the needs to be served.[8]

In applying any such judicial "needs" test, however, the small, more closely held debtor attempting to adjust its trade debts is likely to find Chapter XI more appropriate than the elaborate Chapter X machinery.

As a general rule Chapter X is the appropriate proceeding for adjustment of publicly held debt. . . . Public investors . . . are generally widely scattered and are far less likely than trade creditors to be aware of the financial conditions and cause of the collapse of the debtor. They are less commonly organized in groups or committees capable of protecting their interests. They do not have the same interest as do trade creditors in continuing the business relations with the debtor. Where debt is publicly held, the SEC is likely . . . to have become familiar with the debtor's finances, indicating the desirability of its performing its full Chapter X functions. It seems clear that in enacting Chapter X Congress had the protection of public investors, and not trade creditors, primarily in mind.[9]

Because the Chapter XI procedure is more likely to be applicable to a greater number of declining businesses than the elaborate Chapter X procedure, it is not surprising that many more petitions are filed every year under Chapter XI than under Chapter X. In fiscal 1968, for example, some 953 cases were initiated under Chapter XI while only 128 cases were initiated under Chapter X.[10] And, during the same fiscal year, the SEC actively intervened in only two cases, asking the court to find that the debtor's petition should have been brought under the full safeguards of Chapter X rather than under Chapter XI.[11]

Chapter XI Arrangements

In order to initiate Chapter XI proceedings, a debtor must file in the bankruptcy courts a Chapter XI petition alleging insolvency and setting forth the provisions of the proposed arrangement with his creditors. Such an arrangement is frequently the result of extended negotiations between the debtor and his creditors. It may include an extension or a

---

[8] *General Stores Corp.* v. *Shlensky*, 350 U.S. 462, 465–66 (1956).

[9] *SEC* v. *American Trailer Rentals*, 379 U.S. 594, 613–14 (1965).

[10] U.S. Administrative Office of the United States Courts, *Tables of Bankruptcy Statistics with Reference to Bankruptcy Cases Commenced and Terminated in the United States District Courts during the Fiscal Year Ending June 30, 1968* (Washington, D.C., 1969), p. 7.

[11] Securities and Exchange Commission, *Thirty-fourth Annual Report, 1968* (Washington, D.C., 1969), pp. 160–61.

composition and is defined as "any plan of . . . [the] debtor for the settlement, satisfaction, or extension of the time of payment of his unsecured debts, upon any terms." Within 10 days after the petition is filed, the court will provide for a meeting of the creditors to consider the proposed arrangement. At the same time, because a primary purpose of Chapter XI is to save the business of the debtor, the court will usually authorize the continued operation of the business. Moreover, frequently the debtor will be left in possession of his business and property. Only if a trustee in bankruptcy has previously been appointed or if the court has, upon application of a party in interest, found it necessary to appoint a receiver will the debtor not be allowed to continue to operate his business. At the creditors meeting, the court or a referee appointed by the court will verify or disallow the claims of the creditors and determine whether or not the arrangement as proposed by the debtor has been accepted.

In any such proceeding the unanimous acceptance of the arrangement by all the creditors affected by it is desirable and will act as a confirmation "if the court is satisfied that the arrangement and its acceptance are in good faith." However, unlike common law compositions, Chapter XI also provides that a confirmation by a majority of creditors will be binding on the nonassenting creditors. Thus, when an application for confirmation has been filed by the debtor and written acceptances have been received from a majority of the creditors, the arrangement will be confirmed by the court if, in its judgment:

1. The provisions of Chapter XI have been complied with.
2. It is for the best interests of the creditors and is feasible.
3. The debtor has not been guilty of any acts which would be a bar to the discharge of a bankrupt.
4. The proposal and its acceptance are in good faith.

The "best interests of the creditors" is the guideline according to which a proposed arrangement may be forced onto a minority of creditors by the majority. One interpretation of this "best-interests" guideline would limit this power of the majority to those arrangements which provide for a settlement of not less than what the creditors would realize in a straight bankruptcy liquidation. However, a settlement for less than the prospective liquidation value may at times be in the best interests of the creditors. Because of the possibility of a large divergence between the ongoing concern value of the debtor business and its liquidation value, this might be the case where the creditors hope to reestablish profitable business relations with the debtor in the future, even though an immediate sacrifice is called for. Moreover, determining the prospective liquidation value often involves no more than speculation. On the other hand, the legitimate interests of those creditors who wish to discontinue business with the debtor should not be sacrificed for those creditors who do see a good chance for future profits. Accordingly, prospective liquidation value is an important but not a conclusive test of the best interests of the creditors under the proposed arrangement.

Furthermore, unlike Chapter X reorganizations, the remedy available to a debtor's unsecured creditors through a Chapter XI arrangement need not satisfy the absolute priority rule (which is discussed later). Indeed, even though the claims of the creditors are not fully satisfied, the statute expressly provides: "Confirmation of an arrangement shall not be refused solely because the interest of the debtor, or if the debtor is a corporation, the interests of its stockholders or members will be preserved under the arrangement."

Even if a proposed arrangement has been accepted by all or a majority of the creditors, and has been found to be in the best interests of the creditors, it will not be confirmed unless found by the court to be *feasible*. The feasibility of a proposed Chapter XI arrangement does not center on the broad question of probability of success of the financial rehabilitation of the debtor. Rather, in view of the more limited concern of Chapter XI with adjusting the interests of unsecured creditors, feasibility will be found to exist when adequate assurance is given that the debtor is able to meet the terms of the proposed arrangement.

Upon confirmation a Chapter XI arrangement becomes binding on the debtor, upon any person issuing securities or acquiring property under the arrangement, and upon all creditors of the debtor. Moreover, the confirmation of an arrangement will "discharge a debtor from all his unsecured debts and liabilities provided for by the arrangement, except as provided in the arrangement. . . ." If, however, there is a failure to obtain confirmation of the proposed arrangement, the debtor may find himself in regular bankruptcy proceedings.

Chapter X Reorganizations

Whereas Chapter XI is oriented toward saving the business of the debtor, the financial rehabilitation of an insolvent corporation through a Chapter X reorganization is practically designed to enhance the prospects for a full realization of the creditors' claims or, more frequently, for a better realization than is possible through immediate liquidation. As such, the Chapter X corporate reorganization plan may involve a readjusting of the capital structure of the debtor corporation, including both secured and unsecured creditors and preferred and common shareholders. Unlike the voluntary recapitalization of solvent companies discussed in an earlier chapter, a Chapter X corporate reorganization may involve not only a more radical readjustment of the financial structure of the debtor but also the involuntary and noncompensated loss of interest in the debtor on the part of its shareholders and possibly some of its creditors.

A Chapter X petition may be filed not only by the debtor corporation but also, unlike a Chapter XI petition, by three or more creditors whose claims against the debtor total over $5,000. Such a petition must state that the corporation is insolvent or unable to pay its debts as they mature, in addition to a statement of the assets, liabilities, capital stock, and financial condition of the debtor. Once filed, the petition will be approved by the court if it has been filed in good faith and satisfies the requirements of Chapter X. Of more importance is the fact that a Chapter X proceeding will take precedence over any other action. Thus, a Chapter X petition once approved will operate as a stay of any prior pending bankruptcy, mortgage foreclosure, equity receivership proceeding, or any other proceeding to enforce a lien against the debtor's property.

After approval of the petition the judge will, if the aggregate indebtedness of the debtor is over $250,000, appoint a trustee for the property of the debtor. If the aggregate indebtedness is less than $250,000, the judge may either appoint a trustee or continue the debtor in possession as an agent of the court. Any trustee who is appointed, however, must meet stringent standards of disinterest. For example, a trustee may not be a creditor or stockholder of the debtor, nor may he be (nor may he have been within the past 5 years) an underwriter for any of the debtor's outstanding securities, nor may he have for any reason any' interest materially adverse to the interests of any class of creditors or stockholders.

A trustee for a debtor corporation under Chapter X proceedings has a variety of functions. Upon authorization of the judge, the trustee will continue the operation of the debtor's business. As such, the trustee may disaffirm burdensome contracts entered into by the debtor. These might include, for example, contracts of employment, unexpired leases, and long-term contracts of sale or purchase at fixed prices. While the debtor is thus relieved of such burdensome obligations, any person injured by such a rejection is entitled to damages and becomes an unsecured creditor of the debtor. The trustee will also examine the record of the debtor for any evidence of fraud, misconduct, or mismanagement on the part of any former officer, director, or others. If any malfeasance is found, the trustee will initiate legal proceedings on behalf of the debtor against those who are legally liable.

The primary function of the trustee is, however, to "investigate the acts, conduct, property, liabilities, and financial condition of the debtor, the operation of its business and the desirability of the continuance thereof, and any other matter relevant to the proceeding or to the formulation of a plan." The trustee must thus account for the debts of the corporation and estimate the values of its assets available to meet them. The initiative to formulate a plan of reorganization is, in addition, also on the trustee, under the direction of the court. The focus of a Chapter X proceeding is on reorganization and not liquidation. Thus, where the debtor is financially beyond repair and the petition for reorganization promises nothing more than liquidation, it will be dismissed as not filed in good faith; the creditor's remedy in that situation remains in an ordinary bankruptcy proceeding. However, at times liquidation will be the result of a course of action under Chapter X. In "emergencies where there is imminent danger that the assets of the ailing business will be lost if prompt action is not taken,"[12] the judge is empowered, upon the approval of a petition and on cause shown, to authorize a trustee to sell any property of the debtor, even if liquidation is the result. At other times, where the prospect for reorganization has dimmed since the original filing of the Chapter X petition, the plan for reorganization submitted by the trustee may provide for the sale of all or any part of the debtor's property "at not less than a fair upset price." Thus, one court has concluded:

Reorganization proceedings are for the purpose of readjusting a business life so that it can continue, not for dividing up its effects after the enterprise has died. Nevertheless, it is provided in the statute and courts have recognized that a sale of the entire assets of a debtor in reorganization is a proper part of Chapter X proceedings when the sale is made pursuant to a plan. . . .[13]

Once a plan of reorganization has been submitted by the trustee to the court, the court will call a hearing on the plan for consideration of any objections or amendments as may be proposed by the debtor, its creditors, or stockholders. Often, extensive and time-consuming hearings and negotiations are necessary before the conflicting interests of the claimants can be reconciled into a plan that meets the required legal standards. Moreover, where the schedule of indebtedness of the debtor exceeds $3 million, the judge must also submit the plan to the Securities and Exchange Commission for its consideration and recommendations. Where the schedule of indebtedness is less, submission by the judge to the SEC is optional; in any event, the recommendations of the SEC are advisory only. After the hearing and the filing of any SEC report, the judge will approve the plan if it complies with the Chapter X requirements and is fair, equitable, and feasible. Only if the plan is approved will the court submit it to all the parties affected by it together with the court's opinion, the SEC advisory report, and any other information of interest.

Before confirmation, a Chapter X reorganization plan must be accepted by creditors holding two thirds in amount of the claims filed and allowed of each class. Those creditors who are not affected by the plan are, however, not entitled to vote. This group will include those creditors whose claims are of no value by reason of their subordinate position in the hierarchy of priorities and the shortfall of assets of the debtor under that required to meet the more senior claims. Only if the debtor has not been found to be insolvent must the plan be accepted by stockholders holding a majority of each class of stock. Those minority creditors or stockholders who are part of a class which has accepted the plan by the requisite vote are, moreover, bound by that vote.

---

[12] *In re Solar Manufacturing Corp.*, 176 F.2d 493, 494 (3rd Cir. 1949).
[13] *Ibid.*

After acceptance of the plan by all parties affected by it (excluding those dissenting parties for whom provision has been made for the protection of their claims), the court will order a hearing for consideration and confirmation of the plan. Finally, and of utmost importance, the court will confirm the plan if, in its opinion, the plan meets the statutory standards. First, the court must assure that the plan of reorganization is *fair and equitable*. The words making up this standard, "fair and equitable," are "legal words of art" having an exact meaning. This is the *absolute priority rule*,

. . . The fixed principle, firmly established by Supreme Court decisions, that full recognition must be accorded to claims in the order of their legal and contractual priority either in cash or in the equitable equivalent of new securities and that junior claimants may participate only to the extent that the debtor's properties have value after the satisfaction of prior claims or to the extent that they make a fresh contribution necessary to the reorganization of the debtor.[14]

Thus, to be fair and equitable, any plan must preclude participation by the stockholders in any of the assets of the debtor until the prior rights of both secured and unsecured creditors have been fully satisfied. To maintain the relative priority of those who have an interest in the debtor is not enough; the rights of absolute priority must be respected. This does not mean, however, that senior creditors must be paid in cash; nor does it mean that they cannot receive inferior grades of securities. For example, to the extent that they are given inferior securities, they must receive, in addition, compensation for the senior rights which they are to surrender. Such senior rights may include among others a higher interest rate, a shorter maturity, and a fixed rather than contingent return.

To be confirmed, the plan of reorganization must, second, be found by the court to meet the statutory standard of *feasibility*. If the plan is not broadly feasible, it will not be confirmed even if it has been unanimously accepted by all the parties affected by it. This standard of feasibility reflects the "overriding public interest that the rehabilitation of distressed companies be soundly executed"[15] and that there be no danger of repetition of the bankruptcy. As such, the standard of feasibility must be recognized as limiting the area within which a "fair" plan may be worked out.

The judicial and administrative gloss that has developed about the statutory standard of feasibility has an important bearing on corporate financial policy. Insofar as the quest for a feasible plan often revolves about establishing a workable capital structure and generally acceptable

---

[14] Securities and Exchange Commission, *Seventeenth Annual Report, 1951* (Washington, D.C., 1952), p. 130. See also *Northern Pacific Ry. Co.* v. *Boyd,* 228 U.S. 528 (1913) ; *Case* v. *Los Angeles Lumber Products Co.,* 308 U.S. 106 (1939).

[15] Walter J. Blum, "The Law and Language of Corporate Reorganization," *University of Chicago Law Review,* Vol. 17 (1950), pp. 565, 583.

financial relationships, the standards promulgated may be looked to by the whole financial community. In this regard, the Securities and Exchange Commission has set forth the factors it will consider when advising on a Chapter X reorganization:

. . . In order to assure a reorganization which will not result in the debtor's return to Chapter X because of financial difficulties, the Commission gives a great deal of attention to the various factors affecting feasibility. Generally speaking these factors involve the adequacy of working capital, the relationship of funded debt and the capital structure as a whole to property values, the type and characteristics of the securities to be issued, the adequacy of corporate earning power to meet interest and dividend requirements, the possible need for capital expenditures, and the effect of the new capitalization upon the company's prospective credit.[16]

The feasibility standard thus requires that the proposed capitalization bear a reasonable relationship to the value of the debtor's assets and its prospective earnings. To be avoided in any Chapter X reorganization plan is the creation of securities whose value is contingent upon better than average performance on the part of the reorganized company. The SEC has in particular attempted to prevent the issuance of securities that have highly speculative characteristics. For example, in one advisory report, the SEC stated: "Nor is it appropriate under the auspices of the Court to effect a public distribution of securities whose market prices may reflect in large measure uninformed or speculative appraisals of the conjectural possibilities to which . . . no credence can be given."[17]

Central to the evaluation of any reorganization plan under the above two standards is the valuation of the debtor. Valuation is first necessary to ensure that the absolute priority rule is met. To resolve which claims are of value, what forms any new securities should take, and what patterns of allocation of new securities should be adopted as between bondholders and stockholders requires the accurate valuation of the corporate enterprise. Valuation is also necessary to the establishment of a feasible reorganization plan. The integrity and adequacy of the new capital structure cannot be appraised without an accurate valuation of the old enterprise.

Although in earlier chapters (Chapter 28) the presence of a number of different approaches to the valuation of a business has been noted, the courts have suggested the use of earning capacity to value an ongoing commercial enterprise. As Mr. Justice Douglas has stated:

[An] effort . . . to value the whole enterprise by a capitalization of prospective earnings [is necessary]. . . . Findings as to the earning capacity of an

---

[16] Securities and Exchange Commission, *Eighteenth Annual Report, 1952* (Washington, D.C., 1953), p. 156.

[17] *In re Bevis Shell Homes, Inc.*, SEC Corporate Reorganization Release No. 213 (May 25, 1964).

enterprise are essential to a determination of the feasibility as well as the fairness of a plan of reorganization. Whether or not the earnings may reasonably be expected to meet the interest and dividend requirements of the new securities is a *sine qua non* to a determination of the integrity and practicability of the new capital structure. It is also essential for satisfaction of the absolute priority rule. . . . Unless meticulous regard for earning capacity be had, indefensible participation of junior securities in plans of reorganization may result.

As Mr. Justice Holmes said . . . "The commercial value of property consists in the expectation of income from it." . . . The criterion of earning capacity is the essential one if the enterprise is to be freed from the heavy hand of past errors, miscalculations or disaster, and if the allocation of securities among various claimants is to be fair and equitable. Since its application requires a prediction as to what will occur in the future, an estimate, as distinguished from mathematical certitude, is all that can be made. But that estimate must be based on an informed judgment which embraces all facts relevant to future earning capacity and hence to present worth, including, of course, the nature and condition of the properties, the past earnings record, and all circumstances which indicate whether or not that record is a reliable criterion of future performance. A sum of values based on physical factors and assigned to separate units of the property without regard to the earning capacity of the whole enterprise is plainly inadequate.[18]

Liquidation

At the beginning of this chapter it was emphasized that the termination of a business, either through sale as a business unit or through sale of its assets separately, need not be an event forced on the owners by insolvency. Liquidation may in many cases take place with no loss to the creditors or even to the owners. Ideally, the investment in a business which has become less attractive than other opportunities will be withdrawn long before profits turn into losses, not to mention insolvency.

In other cases, however, the decision to terminate and undergo liquidation follows a realization by the owners of the inability to continue the business in operation. As discussed earlier, many declining businesses may exhaust a number of different courses of action, all looking to the reversal of a trend toward insolvency. Many businesses will try to continue in operation until either they have succeeded in reversing this trend or they have literally run out of cash. Often, resort may be had to preserving the business through a Chapter XI arrangement or a Chapter X reorganization. Otherwise, with creditors pressing for payment and with no cash either to pay them or to finance further sales, there is no alternative but to liquidate. Unfortunately, however, it is hardly ever easy to find a market for either an unsuccessful business or its assets.

The required liquidation may take the form of either an informal

---

[18] *Consolidated Rock Products Co.* v. *DuBois*, 312 U.S. 510, 525–26 (1941).

settlement or a formal court bankruptcy. An informal liquidation will be preferred when the advantages of speed, efficiency, and economy are sought. Such a liquidation may be an informal settlement in which the assets are sold and the proceeds are distributed among the creditors; or it may be a more formal assignment of assets to a third party—a trustee—who liquidates the business and distributes the proceeds. Here, the assignee may be any person or organization willing to perform the function and acceptable to the creditors, for example, a lawyer or a credit bureau. For an informal liquidation to work, however, the debtor must be trusted by the creditors, and the creditors must be in general agreement among themselves. It should be noted that a general assignment by a debtor of all of his assets for the benefit of his creditors is an act of bankruptcy under the federal Bankruptcy Act. Thus, following such an assignment, any dissatisfied creditor may institute formal court bankruptcy proceedings.

Many personal and business failures eventually wind up under the jurisdiction of the federal bankruptcy courts. During the year ended June, 1968, a total of 197,811 bankruptcy cases, both personal and business, were commenced in the federal courts. Of this total, only 16,545 were business bankruptcies, and of these 94% were voluntary.[19] Moreover, because liquidation is the usual result of business failure and reorganization is the exception, most of these cases were straight bankruptcies destined for liquidation rather than Chapter X or Chapter XI proceedings.

It is to be emphasized, however, that formal court-supervised liquidations are expensive. The administrative expenses incurred often take a large bite out of the available assets. These expenses include those required for the referee and the trustee, two court-appointed officers who oversee the sorting out of claims, the search for all valuable assets, and the reduction of these assets to their greatest possible cash value. Both debtors and their creditors will, as a result, attempt to avoid the bankruptcy courts. To illustrate these expenses, Table 29–3 presents the aggregate percentage distribution of a bankrupt's assets, including those which go to other than the creditors of the business.

A court-supervised liquidation in bankruptcy follows a procedure that centers on the basic tasks required. These include the preservation of asset values pending liquidation, the conversion of these assets into cash as soon as possible, and the distribution, according to the priority schedule, of cash through liquidating dividends to those creditors whose claims have been established. The court is assisted in handling these tasks by the two court-appointed officers mentioned above. The *referee* is responsible for overseeing the administrative details of the liquidation, including the

---

[19] U.S. Administrative Office of the United States Courts, *Tables of Bankruptcy Statistics* (Washington, D.C., 1969), Table F3.

preparation of lists of assets and creditors, the declaration of dividends, and the preservation of all records. The *trustee* is responsible for the more substantive duties of collecting and reducing to money the property of the debtor, examining the creditors' proofs of claim and objecting to those deemed improper, and paying the liquidating dividends.

The creditors of a bankrupt do not share equally in any liquidation. Rather, the creditors fall into three broad categories in the priority hierarchy. First must be mentioned the priority debts, which are entitled to payment in full before any liquidating dividends out of the debtor's

Table 29–3

Bankruptcy Cases in the U.S. Courts, Fiscal Year 1968

Distribution of Total Realization in Asset Cases $92,029,764 = 100%		Distribution of Administrative Expenses $22,517,054 = 100%	
Paid priority creditors:			
Taxes	10.3%	Attorneys	39.1%
Wages	1.8	Trustees' and receivers' com-	
Other	1.2	missions	19.1
		Referees' salary and expense fund	10.2
Administrative expenses	24.5	Trustees', receivers', and all other	
		expenses	15.0
Paid secured creditors	33.1	Auctioneers' fees and expenses	6.3
Paid unsecured creditors	25.2	Rental expenses	5.0
Other payments	3.9	Miscellaneous	5.3

SOURCE: U.S. Administrative Office of the United States Courts, *Tables of Bankruptcy Statistics with Reference to Bankruptcy Cases Commenced and Terminated in the United States District Courts during the Fiscal Year Ending June 30, 1968* (Washington, D.C., 1969), p. 10 and Tables F5 and F7.

estate are distributed to the other creditors. In their order of priority, the principal priority claims are:

1. The costs and expenses of preserving the estate.
2. Wages earned within the prior three months, up to $600 per claimant.
3. Federal, state, and local taxes.
4. Debts given priority by federal law or rents for the prior 3 months entitled to priority under state law.

Second, secured creditors have, of course, a property interest in the secured assets and, as such, are entitled to repayment from this secured interest, which is not considered to be a part of the bankrupt estate. However, to the extent that the claims of the secured creditors are not satisfied from the specific assets which have been pledged, they become general creditors for the balance. Finally come the general unsecured creditors. They are usually represented in the bankruptcy hearing and in any negotiations with the court by a creditors committee. They are entitled to liquidating dividends of an equal percentage for all proved and allowed claims. Because all outstanding liens and titles must first be honored and the priority creditors paid before the assets of the debtor are so distributed, it is not surprising that the unsecured creditors often receive only a fraction of their legitimate claims.

The adjudication of an individual as bankrupt by the court operates as an application for the discharge of his debts. Within 6 months after its adjudication as bankrupt, a corporation may file an application for discharge. Provided that the bankrupt has neither been granted a previous discharge within a 6-year period nor has engaged in any fraudulent acts or any acts contrary to the Bankruptcy Act, the court will grant the discharge.

Failure as a Management Problem

At the beginning of the chapter a distinction was drawn between the concept of business termination as the withdrawal of an investment from a business which no longer meets the original expectations of its owners and the concept of business termination as a failure of a business with its attendant distress and loss to creditors and owners. Once a business reaches the point of insolvency and must be terminated as a failure in bankruptcy, effective control of the business and its remaining assets shifts from its owners to its creditors or the courts. When a business has reached this state, management, if it has any role at all, becomes more of a participant than a dominant force directing events.

The management of a declining business will, however, be able to retain the initiative if it is able to recognize the hard facts of an unfavorable business environment. Unfortunately, this is often difficult to do, both because of human nature and, perhaps, because of the intricacy of the situation. Nevertheless, there will be many cases where a more realistic look at these hard business facts will enable the owners to minimize their losses and shift what remains of their investment to a more promising opportunity. At stake is not only the possibility of full satisfaction of the obligations of their creditors but also the preservation of an intangible but invaluable asset, their good credit record.

CASES

The Case of the Unidentified Industries

Despite variations in operational and financial policies and practices and in operating results between firms in the same industry, the nature of the industry has an important impact on the general patterns of the need for funds (asset allocation), the methods of meeting these needs, and the financial results of most firms in the industry. Presented in Exhibit 1 are balance sheets, in percentage form, and selected ratios drawn from the balance sheets and operating statements of 12 firms in 12 different industries. Recognizing the fact of certain differences between firms in the same industry, each firm whose figures are summarized is broadly typical of those in its industry.

See if you can identify the industry represented. Then, be prepared as best you can to explain the distinctive asset structures and ratios of each industry.

1. Basic chemical company.
2. Electric and gas utility.
3. Supermarket chain.
4. Maker of name-brand, quality men's apparel.
5. Meat-packer.
6. Retail jewelry chain (which leased its store properties).
7. Coal-carrying railroad.
8. Automobile manufacturer.
9. Large department store (which owns most of its store properties).
10. Advertising agency.
11. A major airline.
12. Commercial bank (fitted into the most nearly comparable balance sheet and ratio categories of the nonfinancial companies).

Exhibit 1

The Case of the Unidentified Industries

	A	B	C	D
Balance sheet percentages				
Cash and marketable securities............	4.0	7.6	5.1	15.7
Receivables...........................	3.9	8.6	16.4	26.8
Inventories...........................	. . .	24.9	11.0	23.2
Other current assets.....................	0.9	3.5	. . .	1.2
Plant and equipment (net)...............	78.7	44.6	49.5	33.4
Other assets..........................	12.5*	10.8†	18.0‡	0.7
Total assets....................	100.0	100.0	100.0	100.0
Notes payable........................	. . .	. . .	12.8	. . .
Accounts payable......................	2.9	23.9	5.3	29.3
Accrued taxes.........................	2.6	3.6	1.9	1.4
Other current liabilities.................	0.6	4.9	5.7	. . .
Long-term debt.......................	35.2	3.4	30.4	1.7
Other liabilities.......................	3.8	6.4	. . .	1.6
Preferred stock.......................	. . .	. . .	. . .	. . .
Capital stock and capital surplus..........	16.7	6.8	27.8	9.4
Retained earnings and surplus reserves.....	38.2	50.0	16.1	56.6
Total liabilities and stockholder equity.......................	100.0	100.0	100.0	100.0
Selected Ratios				
Current assets/current liabilities...........	1.45	1.38	1.25	2.06
Cash, marketable securities, and receivables/ current liabilities.....................	0.96	0.50	1.20	1.32
Inventory turnover (X).................	. . .	6.4X	6X	23X
Receivables collection period (days).......	20	19	64	18
Total debt/total assets..................	0.412	0.356	0.565	0.339
Long-term debt/capitalization............	0.403	0.055	0.425	0.025
Net sales/total assets...................	0.32	1.61	0.69	5.40
Net profits/total assets..................	0.052	0.059	0.057	0.080
Net profits/total net worth..............	0.102	0.105	0.137	0.121
Net profits/net sales...................	0.167	0.037	0.083	0.015

E	F	G	H	I	J	K	L
4.1	0.5	8.5	4.3	3.2	5.4	17.0	38.6
21.5	3.8	13.7	5.4	27.6	13.0	72.1	59.2
61.0	2.2	22.7	39.3	49.2	. . .	. . .	. . .
0.2	2.6	1.6	2.4	1.6	2.5	0.8	. . .
10.9	90.0	45.4	44.1	17.1	73.9	7.4	1.1
2.3	0.9	8.1§	4.5	1.3	5.2	2.7	1.1
100.0	100.0	100.0	100.0	100.0	100.0	100.0	100.0
5.1	3.1	0.8	5.2	2.0	. . .	. . .	. . .
12.6	2.6	10.0	25.3	10.5	8.3	50.3	84.4
6.6	1.4	2.7	2.4	3.1	. . .	. . .	. . .
1.2	2.6	12.0	10.4	5.8	7.7	2.6	. . .
5.8	43.3	25.6	3.8	20.6	45.6	3.3	1.6
1.0	1.8	7.5	8.2	. . .	10.9	1.0	5.9
2.2	9.4	4.9	. . .	0.1	. . .	. . .	. . .
31.0	25.3	11.9	12.0	17.4	8.4	6.8	5.1
34.5	10.5	24.6	32.7	40.5	19.1	36.0	3.0
100.0	100.0	100.0	100.0	100.0	100.0	100.0	100.0
3.41	0.92	1.85	1.19	3.81	1.29	1.44	. . .
1.62	0.44	0.33	0.22	1.44	1.13	1.24	. . .
2.1X	. . .	8.8X	12.8X	3.1X	. . .	. . .	. . .
64	44	30	4	66	69	42	. . .
0.313	0.530	0.510	0.471	0.420	0.619	0.663	0.918
0.078	0.490	0.382	0.078	0.262	0.628	0.090	0.191
1.30	0.32	1.65	5.03	1.51	0.69	5.33	0.06
0.085	0.048	0.077	0.056	0.065	0.026	0.081	0.008
0.124	0.107	0.211	0.125	0.112	0.095	0.240	0.112
0.065	0.153	0.047	0.011	0.043	0.037	0.015	0.131

* Includes 10.1% of investments in affiliated companies.
† Includes 9.2% of investments in affiliated companies.
‡ Includes 14.4% of investments in affiliated companies.
§ Includes 5.9% of investments in affiliated companies.

Shin Mitsubishi Financial

"Chris, Joe Fowler of Winkle, Brown & Company called me yesterday afternoon. He wanted to sound us out on an issue of new securities of a Japanese firm, Shin Mitsubishi Heavy Industries, Ltd. Although he wasn't positive, he thinks the underwriters and the company will agree on some sort of a convertible security.

"When I told him I'd barely heard of Shin Mitsubishi and didn't know anything about Japanese business, he likened the company to our General Electric. He said it wasn't entirely comparable but was as similar to GE as to any other U.S. company.

"I told him I'd take a look at it so we could give him an indication of any interest on our part in securities they might have to sell. Could you look into this? From the point of view of relating Shin Mitsubishi to what we're familiar with, why don't you begin with a comparison of its financial statements with those of GE? From what I do know about Japanese business, I understand some of their firms have pretty wild balance sheets. I'd really like to see what you turn up. Maybe I can learn something!"

With these comments, Mr. Alexander Peters, senior vice president in charge of investments of the Sun Rise Mutual Life Insurance Company asked Mr. Christopher Corbett, an analyst in his department, to do some staff work for him.

Sun Rise Mutual Life had in its files annual reports of General Electric Company, and the investment banker had sent along financial data on Shin Mitsubishi. Mr. Corbett thought he would begin with these. Exhibit 1 includes excerpts from recent published materials describing Shin Mitsubishi. Exhibits 2 and 3 show financial statements of Shin Mitsubishi; Exhibits 4 and 5 depict financial statements of General Electric Company.

Exhibit 1

Excerpts from Materials Describing Shin Mitsubishi's Product Line

The activities taken over by Shin Mitsubishi from its predecessor in 1950 included shipbuilding and ship repair and the production of various kinds of industrial machinery, motor vehicles, steel structures, and rolling stock. Most of the company's products at that time were products which the predecessor company had manufactured in prewar years, but they also included a limited number of new products (such as motor scooters, three-wheel trucks, and beverage bottling machines) which had been introduced by the predecessor in its process of reconverting to civilian production after the war.

Since 1950 Shin Mitsubishi's manufacturing operations have undergone a continuing process of diversification. A large number of new products have been added to the company's product lines, with the result that the importance to the company's business of the operations in which its predecessor historically was engaged, such as shipbuilding and ship repair, has substantially decreased and the importance to its business of the manufacture and sale of new products has substantially increased. In 1953 the company commenced the manufacture of pulp and paper equipment. In 1955 it began the production of jeeps and reentered the field of aircraft manufacture. In 1959 it began to produce four-wheel trucks and small passenger cars. In 1960 it started to manufacture construction machinery. Over the years, it has undertaken to make various new kinds of industrial machinery. The company's diversified operations are summarized in the table following, which shows net sales by major product categories for each of the fiscal years ending March 31, 1958 to 1962.

In recent years Shin Mitsubishi has commenced development work and production of a series of new products, none of which has so far materially contributed to sales. Under a licensing agreement with Vendo Company of the United States, Shin Mitsubishi has commenced the manufacture of vending machines for, among other products, bottled beverages, hot and cold beverages, foods, ice cream, and cigarettes.

The company has been active in the atomic energy field and is a partner with 26 other Mitsubishi companies in the Mitsubishi Atomic Power Industries, Inc., which was established in 1958. The Mitsubishi Atomic Power Industries was the general contractor in the manufacture of two 10,000 KW thermal research reactors for which Shin Mitsubishi as subcontractor manufactured doors, piping, heavy water circulating pumps, and thermal shields. The Mitsubishi Atomic Power Industries is also active in design studies and investigation of power reactors both for power generation and for marine propulsion.

Shin Mitsubishi has undertaken development work for the Japan Defense Agency in the field of medium range air-to-air and surface-to-air missiles for military purposes and has, out of its own resources, undertaken development work of a weather rocket.

The company has recently commenced production of gas turbines, reversible pump turbines, plastic injection molding machines, plastic extruders, finishing machines, and offset presses and intends to commence the sale of compressors for home refrigerators in fiscal year 1963. In February, 1963, Shin Mitsubishi expects to commence the sale of four-wheel diesel engine tractors for agricultural use.

The company has developed and sold a few small hydrofoil boats and is presently developing a design for larger hydrofoil boats. Shin Mitsubishi is also active in the design of flight simulators for jet planes and high-speed wind tunnels and linear accelerators for research purposes.

Exhibit 1 (Continued)

Breakdown of Net Sales by Product, 1958–62

(dollar figures in thousands)

Year Ended March 31	1958		1959		1960		1961		1962		Fiscal Year 1962 Net Sales as a Percentage of Fiscal Year 1958 Sales
Industrial machinery	$ 21,239	11%	$ 13,884	7%	$ 25,260	11%	$ 44,940	16%	$ 50,970	17%	240%
Power generating equipment	16,657	9	25,777	14	53,073	23	50,517	18	19,965	7	120
Small engines and agricultural machinery	11,321	6	12,057	7	15,098	6	22,489	8	28,439	10	251
Other machinery	12,527	7	9,517	5	11,452	5	17,409	6	26,096	9	208
Total machinery	$ 61,744	33%	$ 61,235	33%	$104,883	45%	$135,355	48%	$125,470	43%	203
Motor vehicles	45,094	24	47,121	25	47,653	21	72,674	26	96,704	33	214
Shipbuilding and repair	54,531	29	46,943	25	47,274	20	30,404	11	35,330	12	65
Aircraft	10,986	6	23,955	13	21,316	9	26,354	9	15,771	6	144
Rolling stock	10,058	5	6,202	3	7,805	3	11,759	4	12,074	4	120
Steel structures	5,809	3	2,659	1	4,048	2	5,617	2	6,836	2	118
Total	$188,222	100%	$188,115	100%	$232,979	100%	$282,163	100%	$292,185	100%	155%

Exhibit 2—SHIN MITSUBISHI HEAVY INDUSTRIES, LTD.

Balance Sheet

(dollar figures in thousands)

ASSETS	*March 31, 1962*
Cash and marketable securities	$ 47,217
Notes and accounts receivable net of allowance for bad debts	130,725
Inventories, less advances received on contracts*	92,303
Other current assets	13,764
Total current assets	$284,009
Long-term notes and accounts receivable	$ 43,991
Sundry investments and advances	10,228
Property, plant, and equipment	
Land	5,828
Buildings	50,683
Machinery and equipment	102,628
Construction in progress	24,253
Less: Accumulated depreciation	(54,123)
Property, plant, and equipment, net	$129,269
Other assets	7,111
Total assets	$474,608

LIABILITIES	
Notes and accounts payable	$125,773
Bank loans†	101,811
Current portion of long-term debt	13,925
Other current liabilities	37,603
Total current liabilities	$279,112
Long-term debt‡	
Mortgage debentures	$ 21,748
Secured loans from banks and insurance companies	27,303
Unsecured loans	35,751
Less: Portion due within one year	(13,925)
Total long-term debt	$ 70,877
Other liabilities	25,191
Total liabilities	$375,180
Common stock	$ 55,556
Capital in excess of par value	1,282
Revaluation surplus§	9,878
Retained earnings	32,712
Total equity	$ 99,428
Total liabilities and shareholders' equity	$474,608

* Inventories, at the lower of cost or market, include a substantial amount of in-process machinery and equipment for which customers are not billed until delivery.

† Represented by unsecured short-term notes bearing interest principally at 7.3%, generally 90 days, maturing at various dates to June 30, 1962. The company has in the past experienced no difficulty in renewing such notes upon maturity, if it considered such renewals advisable. Substantially all of these notes are with banks which have written basic agreements with the company to the effect that with respect to all present or future loans with such banks the company shall provide collateral or guarantors therefor immediately upon the bank's request if such action is deemed necessary by the bank; the company has never received such a request from the banks.

‡ Long-term debt bears interest rates of 3.55%–9.85% and matures from 1962-96. Aggregate annual maturities of long-term debt during the 5 years ending March 31, 1967 are:

Year Ending March 31	Thousands of Dollars
1963	$13,925
1964	18,220
1965	15,779
1966	11,703
1967	7,645
	$67,272

§ Property, plant, and equipment is stated principally at cost. Under Japanese laws, companies have been permitted to recognize, to some extent, the loss in purchasing power of the yen by revaluing their property, plant, and equipment on the basis of coefficients established under such laws, the last of which was enacted in 1953. The company's property, plant, and equipment accounts were increased by ¥8,371 million ($23,253 thousand), principally prior to March 31, 1955, as a result of revaluation made under these laws; corresponding amounts were credited to a revaluation surplus account.

Exhibit 3

Income Statements of Shin Mitsubishi Heavy Industries, Ltd.
for Years Ended March 31, 1958–1962
(dollar figures in thousands)

	1958*	1959*	1960	1961	1962
Sales and other income					
Net sales.	$188,222	$188,115	$232,979	$282,163	$292,185
Other income, principally interest.	2,118	3,256	4,167	5,031	8,846
Total revenue.	$190,340	$191,371	$237,146	$287,194	$301,031
Expenses					
Cost of sales.	$147,622	$145,369	$179,582	$233,388	$233,491
Depreciation.	5,812	7,263	8,217	9,008	11,996
Selling, general and administrative.	9,576	10,925	12,697	16,759	21,426
Interest.	5,042	5,949	6,303	9,192	13,053
Other, including research.	2,646	3,191	3,961	5,468	7,589
Typhoon loss.	.....	.....	5,407	.....	.....
	$170,698	$172,697	$216,167	$273,815	$287,555
Income before income taxes.	$ 19,642	$ 18,674	$ 20,979	$ 13,379	$ 13,476
Income taxes					
Current.	$ 8,916	$ 7,459	$ 9,591	$ 7,176	$ 5,090
Estimated future.	1,333	1,131	217	(104)	1,497
	$ 10,249	$ 8,590	$ 9,808	$ 7,072	$ 6,587
Net income.	$ 9,393	$ 10,084	$ 11,171	$ 6,307	$ 6,889

*Unaudited.

Exhibit 4

GENERAL ELECTRIC COMPANY

Balance Sheet

(dollar figures in millions)

ASSETS	December 31, 1961
Cash and marketable securities	$ 305
Notes and accounts receivable net of allowance for bad debts	671
Inventories, less advances received on contracts	476
Total current assets	$1,452
Long-term notes and accounts receivable	130
Sundry investments and advances	272
Property, plant, and equipment, at cost	1,673
Less: Accumulated depreciation	(956)
Property, plant, and equipment, net	717
Other assets	132
Total assets	$2,704

LIABILITIES	
Notes and accounts payable	$ 210
Other current liabilities	572
Total current liabilities	$ 782
Long-term debt: 3½% debentures due May 1, 1976	229
Other liabilities	90
Total liabilities	$1,101
Common stock	447
Capital in excess of par value	152
Retained earnings	1,004
Total equity	$1,603
Total liabilities and equity	$2,704

Exhibit 5

Income Statements of General Electric Company

Years ended December 31, 1959–61

(dollar figures in millions)

	1959	1960	1961
Sales	$4,350	$4,198	$4,457
Operating costs			
Inventories at January 1	$ 610	$ 626	$ 655
Wages and salaries	1,696	1,755	1,798
Materials and supplies	1,997	1,970	2,063
Depreciation	120	116	118
Taxes except those on income	38	37	39
Less: Inventories at December 31	(626)	(655)	(648)
Total operating costs	$3,835	$3,849	$4,025
Operating earnings	$ 515	$ 349	$ 432
Nonoperating income	51	54	63
Interest expense	(11)	(10)	(9)
Earnings before income taxes	$ 555	$ 393	$ 486
Income taxes	275	193	244
Net earnings	$ 280	$ 200	$ 242

American Motors Financial

"These figures you've worked up look interesting. But now I'd like you to back away from the figures and list the main points your figures seem to bring out as to where American Motors seems to be going, how it's like GM and the rest of the industry, and how it's different.

"While I'm out in Chicago, I'll be talking to Shares, Unlimited, the big mutual fund, about American Motors and the rest of the industry; so be sure that you cover points a common stock investor would be interested in. And as I pointed out, for years we've been after American Motors for a deposit account and some of their loan business. So, of course, we want all the insight we can develop about them and their financing. Also, point up any questions I ought to ask the treasurer when I see him. I'd like to have what you can pull out of your figures before I shove off tomorrow afternoon."

With these words, Gordon Olds, vice president of Northeast National Bank, tossed a folder containing the materials in Exhibits 1 through 4 to his young assistant, Weldon Dunn, and turned to other preparations for his forthcoming trip to the Midwest.

Exhibit 1

AMERICAN MOTORS

Consolidated Balance Sheets, as of September 30, 1964 and 1965

ASSETS	1964	1965
Cash	$ 34,778,575	$ 29,381,662
Marketable securities	15,985,946	6,491,170
Accounts receivable, net	54,974,011	54,880,694
Accounts receivable from affiliated companies	10,362,279	14,557,573
Inventories—at lower of cost (first-in, first-out method) or market	136,757,141	151,239,450
Prepaid insurance, taxes, and other expenses	5,335,113	8,773,590
Total current assets	$258,193,065	$265,324,139
Investments	45,870,355	50,842,297
Property, plant, and equipment	$239,288,590	$251,561,645
Less: Accumulated depreciation	102,414,114	110,726,041
Net property, plant, and equipment	$136,874,476	$140,835,604
Total assets	$440,937,896	$457,002,040

LIABILITIES		
Notes payable	$ 2,706,824	$ 52,040,472
Accounts payable	94,307,070	85,034,154
Salaries, wages, and amounts withheld from employees	14,532,269	10,788,891
Accrued expenses, including excise and miscellaneous taxes	31,650,294	30,337,440
Taxes on income	9,594,459	2,796,547
Total current liabilities	$152,790,916	$180,997,504
Other liabilities	6,450,285	5,681,321
Minority interests	2,978,466	3,074,209
Total liabilities	$162,219,667	$189,753,034
Capital stock, par value $1.66⅔ a share	31,774,774	31,775,774
Additional paid-in capital	50,062,865	50,069,529
Earnings retained for use in business	196,880,590	185,403,703
Total equity	$278,718,229	$267,249,006
Total liabilities and equity	$440,937,896	$457,002,040

Exhibit 2

AMERICAN MOTORS

Consolidated Statement of Net Earnings

Year Ended September 30, 1965

Sales	$1,044,079,873
Less: Excise taxes	53,461,164
Net sales	$ 990,618,709
Equity in net earnings of unconsolidated subsidiaries	833,247
Interest and miscellaneous	6,108,181
Total revenue	$ 997,560,137
Cost of products sold	$ 835,033,863
Selling, advertising, and administrative expenses	102,225,244
Amortization of tools and dies	28,317,705
Depreciation and amortization of plant and equipment	15,292,980
Cost of pensions for employees	9,197,895
Minority interest in net earnings of Kelvinator of Canada Limited	136,878
Total expenses	$ 990,204,565
Earnings before taxes on income	$ 7,355,572
Taxes on income	2,150,000
Net earnings	$ 5,205,572

Exhibit 3

Sales and Profit Figures for Four Automobile Manufacturers
First, Second, and Third Quarters of 1965
(dollar figures in millions)

	General Motors	Ford	Chrysler	American Motors
Sales, 1965				
First Quarter..............	$ 5,558	$ 2,912	$1,266	$ 215
Second Quarter............	5,657	3,086	1,370	240
Third Quarter.............	3,743	2,308	1,046	228
Net profit (loss), 1965				
First Quarter..............	636	201	57	2
Second Quarter............	638	237	62	7
Third Quarter.............	264	102	18	(13)
Sales, 12 months to				
9/30/64..................	17,973	9,672	3,935	1,095
9/30/65..................	18,796	10,849	5,118	991
Net profit, 12 months to				
9/30/64..................	1,866	545	187	26
9/30/65..................	1,913	642	224	5

Exhibit 4

Comparative Financial Ratios of Four Automobile Manufacturers

	General Motors Corporation Years Ended December 31					Ford Motor Company Years Ended December 31				
	1960	1961	1962	1963	1964	1960	1961	1962	1963	1964
Total assets (in $ millions)	7,838	8,273	9,169	9,641	10,293	4,701	5,120	5,416	5,949	6,459
Net sales (in $ millions)	12,736	11,396	14,640	16,495	16,997	6,798	6,709	8,090	8,743	9,671
Current assets, year end/Current liabilities, year end	3.2x	3.1x	3.2x	3.3x	3.0x	1.7x	1.6x	1.7x	1.7x	1.6x
Cash, marketable securities and receivables/Current liabilities	1.8x	1.9x	1.9x	1.9x	1.5x	1.0x	0.9x	1.0x	1.0x	0.8x
Inventory, year end/Sales	14.2%	15.8%	13.7%	13.5%	15.8%	13.1%	14.7%	13.4%	13.7%	14.9%
Sales/Inventory, average of beginning and ending	7.1x	6.3x	7.7x	7.8x	6.9x	7.6x	7.1x	7.8x	7.7x	7.3x
Receivables, year end/Sales	4.8%	8.7%	7.3%	7.6%	8.2%	3.1%	8.7%	7.1%	7.5%	7.8%
Receivables, year end/Average day's sales	17.4 days	31.6 days	26.7 days	27.7 days	29.8 days	11.3 days	31.8 days	25.9 days	27.4 days	28.5 days
Sales/Net plant	4.2x	3.8x	4.6x	4.9x	4.4x	3.4x	3.2x	3.8x	3.8x	3.7x
Sales/Total assets, year end	1.6x	1.4x	1.6x	1.7x	1.7x	1.4x	1.3x	1.5x	1.5x	1.5x
Net profit before taxes/Net sales	16.0%	15.5%	20.0%	20.3%	19.3%	13.0%	12.3%	12.4%	11.7%	10.3%
Net income after taxes/Net sales	7.5%	7.8%	10.0%	9.7%	10.2%	6.8%	6.3%	6.1%	5.7%	5.3%
Net income after taxes/Total assets, year end	12.2%	10.8%	15.9%	16.5%	16.9%	9.8%	8.2%	9.0%	8.4%	7.9%
Net income after taxes/Owners' investment, year end	16.5%	14.8%	21.9%	22.4%	22.8%	14.8%	13.1%	14.0%	13.1%	12.5%
Total debts (excluding reserves)/Total assets	23.1%	24.5%	25.1%	23.8%	24.0%	32.0%	35.4%	33.1%	33.6%	34.2%
Long-term debt/Total capitalization	5.0%	5.7%	4.9%	3.5%	3.0%	7.7%	7.8%	6.2%	5.2%	5.3%
Total equity/Total debt (excluding reserves)	3.2x	3.0x	2.9x	3.1x	3.1x	2.1x	1.8x	1.9x	1.9x	1.9x

Exhibit 4 (Continued)

AMERICAN MOTORS FINANCIAL

	Chrysler Corporation Years Ended December 31					American Motors Corporation Years Ended September 30				
	1960	1961	1962	1963	1964	1961	1962	1963	1964	1965
Total assets (in $ millions)	1,369	1,400	1,525	2,125	2,421	333	375	440	441	457
Net sales (in $ millions)	3,007	2,127	2,378	3,505	4,287	876	1,056	1,132	1,095	991
Current assets, year end/Current liabilities, year end	2.2x	2.3x	2.3x	1.7x	1.4x	2.0x	2.0x	1.7x	1.7x	1.5x
Cash, marketable securities and receivables/Current liabilities	1.2x	1.5x	1.6x	1.2x	0.8x	1.1x	1.1x	0.9x	0.8x	0.6x
Inventory, year end/Sales	10.7%	13.5%	11.7%	11.0%	13.1%	10.7%	9.1%	11.2%	12.5%	15.2%
Sales/Inventory, average of beginning and ending	9.1x	7.0x	8.4x	10.6x	9.1x	8.4x	11.1x	10.2x	8.4x	6.9x
Receivables, year end/Sales	4.1%	5.7%	6.1%	5.5%	5.4%	4.6%	4.7%	4.7%	5.9%	7.0%
Receivables, year end/Average day's sales	15.1 days	21.0 days	22.5 days	20.1 days	19.9 days	16.7 days	17.2 days	17.1 days	21.7 days	25.6 days
Sales/Net plant	5.9x	4.8x	5.9x	6.3x	4.9x	10.2x	11.9x	10.7x	8.0x	7.0x
Sales/Total assets, year end	2.2x	1.5x	1.6x	1.6x	1.8x	2.6x	2.8x	2.6x	2.5x	2.2x
Net profit before taxes/Net sales	2.2%	1.0%	5.3%	9.2%	9.4%	5.8%	6.9%	6.6%	4.1%	0.8%
Net income after taxes/Net sales	1.1%	0.5%	2.8%	4.5%	5.1%	2.7%	3.2%	3.3%	2.4%	0.5%
Net income after taxes/Total assets, year end	2.4%	0.8%	4.3%	7.4%	9.0%	7.1%	9.1%	8.6%	6.0%	1.2%
Net income after taxes/Owners' investment, year end	4.6%	1.6%	8.5%	16.5%	18.6%	10.4%	13.7%	13.8%	9.4%	2.0%
Total debts (excluding reserves)/Total assets	45.4%	45.4%	44.8%	50.5%	47.3%	31.2%	32.0%	36.6%	34.7%	39.6%
Long-term debt/Total capitalization	26.2%	26.0%	23.6%	21.1%	17.3%	0	0	0	0	0
Total equity/Total debt (excluding reserves)	1.1x	1.1x	1.1x	0.9x	1.0x	2.2x	2.1x	1.7x	1.8x	1.5x

The O. M. Scott & Sons Company

Between 1955 and 1961 management of The O. M. Scott & Sons Company launched a number of new programs aimed at maintaining and increasing the company's past success and growth. Largely in response to these activities, Scott's field sales force grew from 6 to 150 men, several entirely new and expanded production facilities went on stream, and the number of products in the company's product line tripled. Sales increased from about $10 million to $43 million. In late 1961 company officials were preparing to review the results of all these changes to ascertain how, if at all, Scott's plans and financial policies should be changed.

The O. M. Scott & Sons Company commenced operations in 1868, when it began processing the country's first clean, weed-free grass seed. Scott's early business came from a small but rapidly growing local market in central Ohio. Later, however, the company went through several stages in its growth. At about the turn of the century the company turned from supplying its local market to selling grass and other farm seeds over a wider geographic area by mail. As its success with its mail-order business increased, the company began to advertise extensively and in 1927 added a free magazine called *Lawn Care*, which has been widely distributed ever since. In all of these early promotional activities, the company sought to sell the Scott name and products as well as the idea of improved care of lawns. In the 1920's a special lawn fertilizer developed for home use was added to the company's product line. During the 1930's the company began to distribute its products on a small scale through selected retail stores and garden centers. Sales and profits grew steadily throughout these years. Scott continued to grow along these same general lines until 1945, by which time sales reached $2.7 million and net profits after taxes were about $30,000.

Over the decade immediately following the war, pioneering research by Scott led to the development and introduction of a wide range of new chemical weed and garden pest controls and special-purpose lawn fertilizers. In addition, the company's grass seed lines were upgraded and supplemented. Largely in response to the success of this research, sales increased to $11.4 million and profits to over $210,000 in fiscal 1955.

By 1955, however, despite the company's impressive postwar record of growth in sales and profits, management was convinced that neither Scott nor its competitors had begun to develop and tap the potential inherent in the national lawn care market. In Scott's own case this failure to develop and tap the national market was attributed to the fact that Scott's customers could not buy its products easily where and when they expected to find them. The company's distribution system had not evolved adequately in response to developing market opportunities, and in many instances the company's dealers either were poorly stocked or were not the right kind of dealer for the company's products.

Thus began a new stage in Scott's development. Early in 1955 the company launched a program to build a national field sales organization with the objective of increasing the number, quality, and performance of its distributors so as to capitalize more fully on the success of its product research and development efforts. When this program started, the company had six field salesmen. By 1960 Scott had a field sales force of 150 men serving almost 10,000 retail dealers across the country. These dealers were mainly department stores and small hardware stores and garden supply centers. The company's salesmen spent most of their time training the dealers how to do a better selling job with Scott products and were paid a salary plus a bonus based on factory shipments to dealers.

Scott's product development program continued apace with the buildup in the direct selling force, so that by the end of the 1950's the company was engaged in the purchase, processing, and sale of grass seed, and the manufacture and sale of fertilizers, weed and pest control products, mechanical spreaders, and electric lawn mowers. In 1959 sales increased to $30.6 million and profits to $1.5 million. A large proportion of these sales comprised new products that had been developed and patented by the company within the past few years.

Reviewing the company's progress again in early 1959, management was still not satisfied that the company was marketing its products as effectively as possible. For one thing, it was estimated that an annual market potential of at least $100 million existed for Scott products. Another important consideration was that several nationally known chemical firms had either begun or were expected to begin competing against Scott in certain lines. These facts led management to conclude that the most effective way for Scott to preserve its preeminent market position would be to push for immediate further market penetration. If successful, such a strategy would enable Scott to eclipse competition as completely as possible before its competitors could establish a firm market position against the company. In this context an annual growth rate in sales and profits of up to 25% was thought to be a reasonable goal for the company over the next few years.

Apart from the need to continue strengthening the company's field sales force and dealer organization, management thought in early 1959 that the most important factor standing in the way of further rapid growth and market penetration was the inability of the typical Scott dealer to carry an adequate inventory of Scott products. Because of the highly seasonal character of sales at retail of the company's products, it was essential that dealers have enough inventory on hand to meet local sales peaks when they came. Experience showed that in many parts of the country a large percentage of dealer sales were made on a few weekends each season. Failure to supply this demand when it materialized most often resulted in a sale lost to a competitor, although sometimes a customer simply postponed buying anything. The problem of assuring adequate dealer inventories had become more of a problem in recent years. The effectiveness of Scott's product development program meant that the dealer was expected to carry many more products than in the past. In addition, Scott had shifted its marketing emphasis from selling individual products to one of selling complete lawn and garden programs. And in order to sell a full lawn maintenance program, it was necessary that the dealer carry the complete Scott line and have it on hand when needed by the consumer.

Because of their small size and often weak working capital position, most of Scott's dealers could not realistically be expected to increase their inventory investment in Scott products. This meant that any desired buildup in dealer inventory levels would have to be financed in some way by Scott itself. In the past the company had extended generous seasonal datings to its dealers, as was industry practice. As a normal pattern, winter and early spring shipments became due at the end of April or May, depending upon the geographical area. Shipments during the summer months were due in October or November. The purpose of these seasonal datings was to enable and encourage as many dealers as possible to be well stocked in advance of seasonal sales peaks. Anticipation at the rate of 0.6% a month was offered on payments made in advance of these seasonal dates, although few dealers availed themselves of this opportunity. With purchases made outside the two main selling seasons, dealers were expected to pay on the 10th of the second month following shipment.

The company's past experience with seasonal datings suggested certain changes in the event Scott proceeded to finance a higher level of dealer inventories. Because of the seasonal nature of the business and the fact that most dealers were thinly capitalized, payment was not often received by Scott until the merchandise involved was sold, irrespective of the terms of sale. This meant that many dealers were continually asking for credit extensions. Another problem inherent in the seasonal dating policy was that Scott retained little or no effective security interest in the goods involved. A final problem was that in the past Scott had followed a policy of not selling to dealers that could not be relied upon to maintain prices at reasonable levels. It was thought that widespread selling at discount prices would undermine the company and the market image it was trying to project. Thus, in any decision to expand dealer inventories, management hoped to contrive a procedure whereby Scott would retain the right to reclaim goods from third parties in the event any of its dealers began selling at wholesale to a discounter.

After considerable study it was decided to continue the traditional seasonal dating plan and to introduce a new trust receipt plan as well. This combination was thought to fulfill all of the requirements outlined in the previous paragraph. As the particular trust receipt plan adopted by Scott worked, a trust receipt dealer was required to sign a trust receipt that provided for (1) immediate transfer to the dealer of title to any Scott products shipped in response to a dealer order, (2) retention of a security interest by Scott in merchandise so shipped until sold by the dealer acting in his capacity as a retailer, and (3) segregation of a sufficient proportion of the funds received from such sales to provide for payment to Scott as billed. Among other things, these provisions made it possible for Scott to move in and reclaim any inventory held by third parties that had been sold by a trust receipt dealer acting illegally as a wholesaler. Exhibit 5 (page 612)[1] shows the trust receipt form used by Scott. In addition to obtaining the trust receipt from its dealers, the company also was required to file a statement of trust receipt financing with the secretary of state in each state where a trust receipt plan dealer was domiciled. Such a statement is shown in Exhibit 6. Dealers using the trust receipt plan were charged an extra 3% on the cost of purchases from Scott. They also had to place all purchase orders directly through Scott's field salesmen, inasmuch as these account executives were held responsible by the company for controlling dealer inventories in connection with the trust receipt plan.

This last-mentioned role of Scott's sales force was absolutely central to the proper functioning of the trust receipt plan. Apart from simply policing the level and character of dealer inventories, the account executives also periodically inventoried the trust receipt dealers so that Scott could bill the dealers for merchandise sold. During the two peak retail selling seasons, these physical inventories were taken once a month and even oftener in the case of large dealers. In the off seasons the inspections occurred much less frequently. In any event, the terms of payment associated with the trust receipt plan required that the dealer pay Scott within 10 days of receipt of an invoice from the company for goods sold since the last physical inventory date.

---

[1] In this and in most of the succeeding cases, the exhibits will be found at the end of the case.

After introduction of the two payment plans in 1960, about half of Scott's sales were by seasonal dating and half by trust receipt. The trust receipt dealers were for the most part local garden centers and hardware stores, whereas the seasonal dating dealers were the larger chain garden centers and department stores. The company's overall collection experience with both plans was that about 75% of receivables were collected in the month due, another 16% in the following month, an additional 6% in the next month after that, and the balance thereafter.

The rapid growth in outstanding receivables resulting from the trust receipt program was financed largely by a combination of subordinated notes, a revolving line of bank credit, and increased use of supplier credit arising out of special deferred payment terms extended by the company's chemical suppliers. The company also retained almost all of its earnings each year as had been its policy in the past.

At the end of fiscal 1961 Scott and its subsidiaries had $16.2 million of long-term debt outstanding, of which $12 million comprised renewable 5-year subordinated notes of the parent company held by four insurance companies and a trustee and $4.2 million was publicly held bonds owed by Scotts Chemical Plant, Inc., a wholly owned subsidiary. The key terms associated with the $12 million of subordinated notes are summarized in the footnotes to Exhibits 1 and 2. The governing loan indenture limited the unconsolidated parent company's maximum outstanding debt at any time to an amount not greater than three times what was termed the company's "equity working capital" as of the preceding March 31. What was meant by equity working capital and the calculation of maximum allowed debt are shown in Exhibit 7. The note indenture restricted outstanding subordinated notes to only 60% of maximum allowed debt as determined by the above equity working capital formula. The agreement also required that Scott be out of bank debt for 60 consecutive days each year and that the company earn before taxes $1\frac{1}{2}$ times its fixed financial charges, including interest on funded and unfunded debt, amortization of debt discount, and rentals on leased properties.

In addition to the long-term debt just described, Scott also had a $12.5 million line of credit at the end of fiscal 1961 with a group of seven commercial banks. The purpose of this line was to provide for seasonal funds needs, and in recent years the maximum line had been used at some point during each year. An informal understanding covering this seasonal financing arrangement required that Scott maintain average compensating balances with the banks involved of 15% of the line of credit.

As far as accounts payable were concerned, Scott had negotiated an arrangement with its principal chemical suppliers whereby the company settled with these suppliers just once or twice a year. It had been possible to negotiate these favorable terms because the suppliers were persuaded that it was in their best interests to help Scott develop and expand the home lawn market. Generally, no interest or other charges were levied on these amounts.

As fiscal 1961 drew to a close, management was generally pleased with what appeared to have been the results of the trust receipt program, although final figures for the year just ending were not yet available. Company sales had increased from $31 million in 1959 to over $43 million in 1961. At this level of operations the company's break-even point was estimated at between $27.5 million and $30 million.

By the end of 1961, when company officials were reviewing the results of fiscal 1961 and preparing plans for the 1962 selling season, the audited statements shown in Exhibits 1 and 2 were available, as well as the un-audited and unconsolidated quarterly statements in Exhibits 3 and 4. In addition, on the basis of a physical inventory taken by the company's sales force, combined standard and trust receipt plan dealer inventories were estimated to be at a level of about $28 million at the end of calendar 1961. This compared with roughly $17 million at the end of 1960. On the basis of these and other data Scott's sales department estimated that in terms of cost of sales, dealer sales in fiscal 1961 reached an all-time high of over $30 million. The recent record of earnings, dividends, and market price range is shown in Exhibit 8.

It was against this background that company officials began their review and evaluation of recent operations and current financial position. They were particularly anxious to formulate any indicated changes in company plans and financial policies before the new production and selling seasons were upon the company.

Exhibit 1

THE O. M. SCOTT & SONS COMPANY AND SUBSIDIARY COMPANIES

Consolidated Balance Sheets for the Years Ended September 30, 1957 to 1961

(dollar amounts in thousands)

	1957	1958	1959	1960 (a)	1961 (e)
Cash	$ 533.9	$ 1,232.0	$ 1,736.4	$ 2,328.7	$ 1,454.3
Accounts receivable	2,640.0	4,686.5	5,788.4	15,749.7	21,500.5 (f)
Inventories	2,340.3	3,379.8	6,993.2	3,914.3	5,590.5
Total current assets	$5,514.2	$ 9,298.3	$14,518.0	$21,992.7	$28,545.3
Land, buildings, equipment	$2,253.5	$ 2,439.5	$ 7,364.6	$ 8,003.4	$ 8,370.2
Less: Accumulated depreciation	544.0	650.0	1,211.3	1,687.1	2,247.1
Net fixed assets	$1,709.5	$ 1,789.5	$ 6,153.3	$ 6,316.3	$ 6,123.1
Investment in and advances to affiliates	1,165.6	28.9	232.3	462.0	133.6
Other assets	488.5	376.6	837.5	1,132.0	937.8
Total assets	$8,877.8	$11,493.3	$21,741.1	$29,903.0	$35,739.8
Accounts payable	$1,540.8	$ 2,134.6	$ 4,140.2	$ 2,791.0	$ 6,239.2
Notes payable—banks	300.0		1,000.0		
Accrued taxes, interest, and other expenses	674.3	1,437.7	1,900.7	1,941.2	1,207.7
Current sinking fund requirements	77.0	173.9	324.3	382.5	512.5
Total current liabilities	$2,592.1	$ 3,746.2	$ 7,365.2	$ 5,114.7	$ 7,959.4
Long-term debt:					
Of parent company (c) (h)	$2,186.7	$ 2,059.7	$ 1,777.2	$ 9,000.0	$12,000.0
Of subsidiary (c) (h)			5,162.6	4,649.5	4,170.4
Total liabilities (d)	$4,778.8	$ 5,805.9	$14,305.0	$18,764.2	$24,129.8
Preferred stock (i)	$1,757.2	$ 2,432.2	$ 2,392.5	$ 2,347.5	$ 2,254.3
Common stock and surplus	2,341.8	3,255.2	5,043.6	8,791.3 (b) (g)	9,355.7
Total liabilities and net worth	$8,877.8	$11,493.3	$21,741.1	$29,903.0	$35,739.8

See Notes to Financial Statements following Exhibit 2.

Exhibit 2

THE O. M. SCOTT & SONS COMPANY AND SUBSIDIARY COMPANIES

Consolidated Income Statements for the Years Ended September 30, 1957 to 1961

(dollar amounts in thousands)

	1957	1958	1959	1960 (a)	1961 (e)
Net sales (b) (g)	$18,675.9	$23,400.2	$30,563.7	$38,396.4	$43,140.1
Cost of sales and operating expenses					
Cost of products sold, including processing, warehousing, delivery and merchandising (including lease rentals of $872,577)	$15,500.9	$18,914.7	$24,119.5	$30,416.8 (d)	$34,331.7
General and administrative, research and development expenses	1,817.2	2,134.1	2,499.3	2,853.6	3,850.7
Depreciation and amortization	263.2	185.9	377.6	584.2	589.6
Interest charges	199.8	212.7	410.6	881.6	1,131.5
Total cost of sales	$17,781.1	$21,447.4	$27,407.0	$34,736.2	$39,903.5
Earnings before taxes on income	894.8	1,952.7	3,156.7	3,660.2	3,236.6
Federal and state taxes on income	443.5	1,051.6	1,671.2	1,875.2	1,665.9
Net income after taxes	$ 451.3	$ 901.1	$ 1,485.5	$ 1,785.0	$ 1,570.7

See Notes to Financial Statements, following.

Exhibits 1 & 2 (Continued)

Notes to Financial Statements

(a)   1960 Auditor's Statement

THE BOARD OF DIRECTORS
THE O. M. SCOTT & SONS COMPANY
MARYSVILLE, OHIO

We have examined the statement of consolidated financial position of The O. M. Scott & Sons Company and its subsidiaries as of September 30, 1960, the related consolidated statements of operations, capital surplus, and retained earnings for the fiscal year then ended, and accompanying notes to financial statements. Our examination was made in accordance with generally accepted auditing standards, and accordingly included such tests of the accounting records and such other auditing procedures as we considered necessary in the circumstances.

In our opinion, the accompanying statements, together with the explanatory notes, present fairly the consolidated financial position of The O. M. Scott & Sons Company and its subsidiaries at September 30, 1960, and the results of their operations for the year then ended, in conformity with generally accepted accounting principles, except as described in note *(b)*, applied on a basis consistent with that of the preceding year.

PEAT, MARWICK, MITCHELL & CO.

COLUMBUS, OHIO
November 23, 1960

(b)   Sales

For several years the company has followed a prebilling system to obtain more efficient and economical control of production through the medium of unappropriated inventory. Under this system, the invoicing of customers predates shipment. Consequently, both fiscal 1960 and 1959 sales stated in the operating statement include firm orders received, billed, and costed out in late September which were shipped early in the immediately following October. Prior to September 30, 1960, the amounts involved were not significant, but toward the end of that month shipment was delayed by the company to facilitate the taking of physical inventories at storage warehouses as of the month end. The result of the foregoing is to include an additional amount of approximately $343,000 in net earnings for the year 1960. In management's opinion, the earnings on these sales are properly earnings of the year 1960.

(c)   Long-Term Debt

All long-term obligations of the parent company at September 30, 1959, were retired prior to December 31, 1959.

In fiscal 1960 the parent company sold 5-year subordinated promissory notes, principally to certain insurance companies, at the principal amount of $9 million, maturing October 13, 1964. The notes bear interest to October 10, 1960, at $6\frac{1}{2}\%$ per annum and thereafter to maturity at *(a)* 6% per annum, or *(b)* the New York prime commercial rate plus $1\frac{1}{2}\%$, whichever is higher.

The loan agreement provides, among other things, that *(a)* payment of principal and interest on the notes is subordinated to repayment of bank loans due within one year, *(b)* new or additional notes may be sold on October 28 of each future year, and *(c)* any holder of the notes may, before October 15 of each year, require payment by October 10 of the immediately ensuing year of all or part of the notes held.*

All holders of the notes at September 30, 1960, surrendered the notes then held in exchange for new notes having exactly the same terms but maturing October 28, 1965, at an interest rate of 6% per annum to October 10, 1961. Interest after October 10, 1961, accrues at the rate determinable under the provisions of the loan agreement.

Long-term obligations of subsidiary outstanding on September 30, 1960:

---

* Such payments were to be made in four equal annual installments beginning on October 10 of the immediately ensuing year.

Exhibits 1 & 2 (Continued)

20-year 5¾% first-mortgage bonds due March 15, 1977..........	$1,026,000
18-year 6% secured sinking fund debentures due Feb. 1, 1977......	2,840,500
10-year 6% sinking fund notes due March 15, 1967..............	178,000
10-year 6% subordinated debentures due Dec. 15, 1967..........	950,000
	$4,994,500
Less: Current sinking fund provision........................	345,000
	$4,649,500

The above obligations of a subsidiary are secured by property mortgages, and/or assignment of lease rentals payable by the parent company.

(d) Long-Term Leases

The main production, warehousing, and office facilities used by the company are leased from affiliated interests not consolidated, namely, the company's Pension and Profit Sharing Trusts, and also from a consolidated subsidiary, Scotts Chemical Plant, Inc. These leases, all having over 10 years to run, required minimum annual rentals in fiscal 1960 of $872,577. This represented less than 17% of net taxable profit before deduction for rentals, depreciation, and expenses based on net profits. It is anticipated that, in fiscal 1961, the fixed rentals under these leases will approximate the same amount.

(e) 1961 Auditor's Statement

BOARD OF DIRECTORS
THE O. M. SCOTT & SONS COMPANY
MARYSVILLE, OHIO

We have examined the statement of consolidated financial position of The O. M. Scott & Sons Company and its subsidiaries as of September 30, 1961, and the related statements of consolidated operations, capital surplus, and retained earnings for the year then ended. Our examination was made in accordance with generally accepted auditing standards and accordingly included such tests of the accounting records and such other auditing procedures as we considered necessary in the circumstances.

In our opinion, the accompanying statements of financial position, operations, capital surplus, and retained earnings present fairly the consolidated financial position of The O. M. Scott & Sons Company and its subsidiaries at September 30, 1961, and the consolidated results of their operations for the year then ended, in conformity with generally accepted accounting principles which, except for the changes (in which we concur) referred to in Notes (f) and (g), have been applied on a basis consistent with that of the preceding year.

ERNST & ERNST

DAYTON, OHIO
January 6, 1962

(f) Accounts Receivable

Accounts receivable are stated net after reserve of $740,000 for dealer adjustments, allowances, and doubtful accounts.

In 1959 the company adopted a plan of deferred payments for certain retail dealers. Accounts receivable include $16,033,093 for shipments under this plan which are secured by trust receipts executed by the dealers. The trust receipt arrangements provide for (1) immediate transfer to the dealers of title to the merchandise shipped in response to the dealers' orders, (2) retention by the company of a security interest in the merchandise until sold by the dealers, and (3) payment by the dealers to the company as the merchandise is sold at retail. The dealers, whether trust receipt or other, do not have the right to return any part of merchandise ordered by them and delivered in salable condition, but they may tender merchandise in full or part payment of their accounts in the event of termination by the company of their dealerships. To provide for possible adjustments and allowances in the liquidation of dealer accounts receivable, the company has provided an increase in reserve by a charge to net earnings of the current year of $150,000 and a charge to retained earnings at October 1, 1960, of $530,000.

Exhibits 1 & 2 (Continued)

(g)   Sales

In the financial statements for the year ended September 30, 1960, attention was directed to the company's policy of including in the operating statement firm orders received, billed, and costed out in late September which were shipped early in the immediately following October. During 1961 this policy was discontinued. In order to reflect this change in policy, prebilled sales at September 30, 1960, together with related costs and expenses included in operations of the year then ended, have been carried forward and included in the operating statement for the year ended September 30, 1961, with a resulting charge to retained earnings at October 1, 1960, of $429,600. This change in accounting principle did not have a material effect on net earnings for the year ended September 30, 1961.

(h)   Long-Term Debt: Five-Year Subordinated Promissory Notes

The notes bear interest to October 10, 1961, at 6% per annum and thereafter to maturity at a rate which is the higher of (a) 6% per annum, or (b) the New York prime commercial rate plus 1½%. The loan agreement provides, among other things, that (a) payment of principal and interest on the notes is subordinated to repayment of bank loans due within one year, and (b) elections may be exercised annually by the holders to (1) exchange the notes currently held for new notes having a maturity extended by one year, (2) purchase additional notes if offered for sale by the company, or (3) require payment of all or part of the notes held, such payments to be made in four equal annual instalments beginning on October 10 of the immediately ensuing year.

All holders of the notes at September 30, 1961, except for $1 million, surrendered the notes then held in exchange for new notes having exactly the same terms but maturing October 28, 1966, at an interest rate of 6% per annum to October 10, 1962. Subsequent to September 30, 1961, arrangements have been made for the note for $1 million not exchanged to mature September 1, 1962, and to issue a note to another lender for $1 million maturing October 28, 1966.

Obligations of Subsidiaries:

5¾% first-mortgage bonds, due March 15, 1977	$ 964,000	
6% sinking fund notes, due March 15, 1967	147,500	
6% subordinated debentures, due December 15, 1967	819,000	
6% secured sinking fund debentures due February 1, 1977	2,620,500	
	$4,551,000	
Less: Classified as current liability	414,000	$4,137,000
Real estate mortgage notes ($252 payable monthly for interest at 6% per annum and amortization of principal)	$ 34,383	
Less: Classified as current liabilities	1,000	33,383
		$4,170,383

The above long-term obligations of subsidiaries are secured by mortgages on property, plant, and equipment, and/or assignment of lease rentals payable by the parent company.

(i)   Preferred Stock

There were 22,460 shares of $5 cumulative preferred stock.

Exhibit 3

THE O. M. SCOTT & SONS COMPANY

Unconsolidated Quarterly Balance Sheets of Parent Company
for Fiscal Year 1961*

(dollar amounts in thousands)

	12/31/60	3/31/61	6/30/61	9/30/61
Cash..............................	$ 1,810	$ 2,140	$ 1,760	$ 2,070
Accounts receivable				
Standard plan......................	$ 1,500	$ 6,540	$ 3,110	$ 4,400
Trust receipt plan.................	8,660	15,880	11,890	16,830
Total receivables...............	$10,160	$22,420	$15,000	$21,230
Inventories				
Finished goods.....................	$ 7,390	$ 5,850	$ 6,420	$ 4,040
Raw materials and supplies..........	2,380	2,520	1,890	1,460
Total inventories...............	$ 9,770	$ 8,370	$ 8,310	$ 5,500
Total current assets.............	$21,740	$32,930	$25,070	$28,800
Land, buildings, equipment.............	$ 2,130	$ 2,190	$ 2,270	$ 2,290
Less: Accumulated depreciation.......	800	830	870	910
Net fixed assets......................	$ 1,330	$ 1,360	$ 1,400	$ 1,380
Other assets..........................	$ 1,990	$ 1,730	$ 1,720	$ 1,240
Total assets....................	$25,060	$36,020	$28,190	$31,420
Accounts payable.....................	$ 1,390	$ 3,680	$ 3,150	$ 7,040
Notes payable—bank..................	6,250	12,000	5,750	—
Accrued taxes, interest, and other				
expenses..........................	(390)	950	110	1,170
Total current liabilities..........	$ 7,250	$16,630	$ 9,010	$ 8,210
Subordinated promissory notes..........	9,000	9,000	9,000	12,000
Total liabilities..................	$16,250	$25,630	$18,010	$20,210
Net worth				
Preferred stock......................	$ 2,380	$ 2,380	$ 2,350	$ 2,250
Common stock and surplus...........	6,430	8,010	7,830	8,960
Total liabilities and net worth.....	$25,060	$36,020	$28,190	$31,420

* Excluding items relating to certain nonoperating subsidiaries. Unaudited and unpublished. For these reasons, Exhibit 3 does not correspond exactly with Exhibit 1.

Exhibit 4

THE O. M. SCOTT & SONS COMPANY

Unconsolidated Quarterly Income Statements of Parent Company for the Year Ended September 30, 1961*

(dollar amounts in thousands)

	Quarter Ended 12/31/60	Quarter Ended 3/31/61	Quarter Ended 6/30/61	Quarter Ended 9/30/61	Year
Net sales	$ 1,300	$15,780	$9,570	$14,740	$41,390
Cost of sales and operating expenses					
Cost of products sold including processing, depreciation, warehousing, delivery and merchandising	$ 3,250	$11,730	$8,670	$10,790	$34,440
General and administrative, research and development expenses	660	800	940	1,000	3,400
Interest charges	150	240	260	200	850
Total cost of sales	$ 4,060	$12,770	$9,870	$11,990	$38,690
Earnings (losses) before taxes on income	$(2,760)	$ 3,010	$ (300)	$ 2,750	$ 2,700
Federal taxes on income	(1,440)	1,570	(160)	1,390	1,360
Net income (loss) after taxes	$(1,320)	$ 1,440	$ (140)	$ 1,360	$ 1,340

* Excluding items relating to the operations of certain nonoperating subsidiaries. Unaudited and unpublished.

Exhibit 5

Trust Receipt

The undersigned Dealer, as Trustee, and Entruster agree to engage in Trust Receipt financing of the acquisition by Trustee of seed, fertilizer, weed controls, pest controls, applicators, mowers and other lawn and garden products, all bearing the brands and trade marks of The O. M. Scott & Sons Company. Entruster will direct said company to deliver said products from time to time as ordered by Dealer.

> (a) Dealer agrees to hold said products in trust for the sole purpose of making sales to consumers, functioning as a retailer and not as a wholesaler.
>
> (b) Dealer agrees to hold a sufficient proportion of the funds received from such sales for payment to Entruster as billed.
>
> (c) Either party may terminate this Trust Receipt on notice. In such event Dealer will surrender to Entruster his complete stock of The O. M. Scott & Sons Company products, proceeds thereof to be credited to Dealer.

Official Business Name   Accepted at Marysville, Ohio
of Dealer as Trustee:

_____   _____, 19__

Street & No._____

City_____Zone____State_____   THE O. M. SCOTT & SONS COMPANY
                                                      (*Entruster*)
Authorized
Signature_____

Date_____Title_____   *President*

Exhibit 6

Statement of Trust Receipt Financing

The Entruster, The O. M. Scott & Sons Company, whose chief place of business is at Marysville, Ohio, and who has no place of business within this state, is or expects to be engaged in financing under trust receipt transactions, the acquisition by the Trustee whose name and chief place of business within this state is:

of seed, fertilizers, weed controls, pest controls, applicators, mowers and other lawn and garden products, all bearing the brands and trade marks of The O. M. Scott & Sons Company.

Entruster: THE O. M. SCOTT & SONS   Date_____, 19__
                COMPANY   For the Trustee   (Dealer)

By:_____   By:_____
          President

Exhibit 7

Example Showing Calculation of Equity Working Capital and Maximum Allowed Debt of Parent Company for the 12 Months Following March 31, 1961*

(dollar amounts in millions)

Calculation of equity working capital:

Current assets..		$32.9
Current liabilities......................................	$16.6	
Long-term debt...	9.0	
Total debt..	$25.6	25.6
Equity working capital.................................		$ 7.3

Calculation of maximum allowed parent company debt:

300% of equity working capital.........................	$21.9
Actual parent borrowings—March 31, 1961...............	21.0
Available debt capacity................................	$ .9

Calculation of maximum allowed subordinated debt of parent:

60% of maximum allowed total debt ($21.9 million × 60%)...	$13.1

* Calculations based on figures taken from Exhibit 3.

Exhibit 8

Record of Earnings, Dividends, and Market Price Range, 1958–61

Fiscal Year	Earnings per Share	Dividends per Share	Market Price Range*
1958...............$0.69	10% stk.	$6⅛–1½
1959............... 1.15	10% stk.	32⅞–6⅛
1960............... 1.21	10% stk.	51 –31⅞
1961............... 0.99	10¢ + 5% stk.	58¾–30

* Calendar year; bid prices. Closing prices September 29 and December 29, 1961 were $49 and $32¼ respectively. Stock first sold publicly in 1958 and has traded over the counter since then. The company had about 4,100 common shareholders in 1961.

Union Paint and Varnish Company

On April 14, 1952, in Los Angeles, Mr. Robert Maple and Mr. Harry Hill, the credit manager and the regional sales manager, respectively, of the Union Paint and Varnish Company, met with Mr. Sidney G. Snider, president of Suburban Auto Stores Corporation, to discuss possible credit arrangements for sales of Union products to Suburban. After extensive discussion concerning the current financial position and future prospects of Suburban, Mr. Snider asked if Mr. Maple would approve 3-year terms on an initial order, amounting to some $35,000, for a basic inventory of the complete line of Union products. If such an arrangement could be made, Mr. Snider also wanted to know upon what credit basis "fill-in" orders to replace goods sold could be placed.

Union Paint (see Exhibit 1 for 1951 financial statements) was operating near capacity in the spring of 1952, but with the anticipated return to a buyers' market, Union began to prepare for increasingly keen competition. Accordingly, Union was aggressively seeking new outlets through which to sell the company's expanding volume. In this connection, Mr. Hill had pointed out that Suburban, whose account he had sought for several years, had an excellent reputation for being an aggressive merchandising organization; he stressed to Mr. Maple the fact that Union's weakest market coverage was "right in its own backyard," Los Angeles.

For about a year the sales department had been pursuing a nationwide promotional and merchandising program addressed to consumers. In addition, missionary salesmen worked to develop new dealerships, which frequently were excellent market outlets but financially undercapitalized. Although typical terms to retail accounts were 1/10, n/60, terms up to 5 years had been granted to enable new accounts of this type to purchase permanent display and backup stock. Such arrangements were believed necessary to get adequate market coverage and to continue large volume operations.

Mr. Hill told Mr. Maple of the opportunity at Suburban on April 2,

1952. The previous day, Mr. Hill had visited the offices of Suburban and talked with Mr. Snider, its president. Mr. Snider had said that he desired a 3-year payment plan to enable him to acquire the initial stock. Mr. Hill had replied that he could make no commitment, but believed that an extended payment plan could be arranged to cover the initial stock of paints and varnishes.

After this meeting, Mr. Hill concluded that Suburban could now be sold, and thought that steps should be taken promptly to "sew up" the potential accounts, for he realized that Union's competitors might also recognize Suburban's readiness to drop its current line. He asked Mr. Maple to act as promptly as possible to determine the credit standing of Suburban. Mr. Maple ordered a credit agency report and called his company's bank of account, Golden Gate Trust Company, in San Francisco, requesting information regarding Suburban.

On April 7, Mr. Maple received the credit report (see Exhibit 2) and a telephone call from John Farmer, an officer of the bank, who reported that the company was indebted to three Los Angeles banks for a total of $345,000, each bank participating equally. These loans, he said, were unsecured but endorsed by Mr. Sidney Snider, president of Suburban. Mr. Farmer said that the loans, which had been made on a 90-day renewable basis, matured on March 31, 1952, but that a temporary extension on a demand basis had been granted to permit the corporation to raise approximately $150,000, the estimated amount which Suburban had lost through operations for the fiscal year ended January 31, 1952. Although no specific time limit had been set for raising the $150,000, it was generally understood that this was to be accomplished by the end of May, 1952. The banks were not willing to comment on how long they would continue "to go along with" Suburban. Such action appeared to depend upon the company's ability to raise funds from outside sources to replace the operating loss.

The total cash balance among the three banks was reported to be slightly more than $60,000 at the moment. A few trade creditors in 1952 indicated a slow manner of payment, which had not been experienced previously. All, however, considered Suburban a desirable account.

Suburban's inventory position in March was reported to be in excess of $1 million despite vigorous attempts to liquidate a surplus of television sets and major appliances in late 1951. The banks were reported to be dissatisfied with this inventory, having concluded that substantial investment rested in types of goods which were moving too slowly. Furthermore, Mr. Farmer stated that the banks were unhappy about a new store opened in November, 1951, when funds were known to be needed to bolster a weak working capital condition. Nevertheless, Mr. Farmer added that the three banks unanimously agreed that they held the Suburban management in high regard as an aggressive merchandising organization.

On Tuesday morning, April 8, Mr. Maple met with Mr. Hill and the

Union sales manager, Mr. Joseph Carton, to discuss Suburban as a potential account. Mr. Maple said that it appeared to him inadvisable to make a definite decision regarding a deferred payment plan with Suburban until its financial status, especially the relationships with the banks, could be clarified.

Mr. Carton reported that he had learned that Suburban was interested in changing its line of paints because it was dissatisfied with the selling arrangements made by its current supplier, another nationally known manufacturer. Suburban was required to purchase paint products on a consignment basis, a procedure that was both bothersome and embarrassing.

Mr. Carton was anxious to get a decision on this account because he estimated, based on Suburban's sales of paint products in past years, that Union's sales should run in excess of $150,000 annually. He reemphasized that all Suburban's sales would be in territory new to Union, since only a few small hardware stores were handling Union's line in Los Angeles.

Mr. Hill commented that, although Mr. Snider had not mentioned it, he had learned through others in the trade that two other national paint manufacturers were currently attempting to sell Suburban their complete line. He further noted that Dun & Bradstreet, Inc., had rated the firm AA1 on January 16. Mr. Maple replied that nevertheless the company was short of working capital, was at that time negotiating with its banks regarding future loans, and that the Dun & Bradstreet report did not reflect the as yet unpublished January 31, 1952, statement.

The credit department of Union Paint and Varnish Company had classified its accounts in three categories: (A) well-financed customers—virtually no risk of loss; (B) moderately financed customers—average risk of loss; and (C) financially weak customers—great risk of loss.

As of April 1, category C accounts totaled nearly $440,000 for accounts sold on regular terms. In addition, about $75,000 of $750,000 receivables on extended terms (averaging 3 years) were in category C. Since Mr. Maple believed that the proposed account would be in the C group, he pointed out to Messrs. Carton and Hill that a decline in general business activity might bring substantial bad-debt losses. The fact that Union's bad-debt losses had been less than one half of 1% of credit sales since 1945 did not measure possible losses in a depression.

Mr. Carton quickly countered that since about one fifth of the company's total expenses continued regardless of sales, he was obliged continually to get more volume in order to spread those fixed charges as thinly as possible. Thus, Union had to take certain calculated risks to break into the Southern California market, where there was potentially great volume. Finally, Mr. Carton said that even if the Suburban account resulted eventually in a loss, in the meantime enough volume could well have been accomplished to more than offset the loss.

On April 10, Mr. Hill, at the request of Mr. Maple, had visited two of Suburban's banks of account to get the most recent information on the company. Officers in both banks expressed considerable faith in the management of Suburban. They indicated that, although the company had suffered a loss of more than $100,000 as a result of a drop in television and major appliance sales, this was typical of the retail trade during 1951. Both officers told Mr. Hill that they were willing to continue accommodating Suburban at least until July of 1952, when they could review operating results for the first 6 months of the year.

On April 11, Mr. Hill, concerned about the possibility of losing a large potential customer, arranged for Mr. Maple to visit Mr. Snider on the 14th in Los Angeles. At this meeting, Mr. Snider showed Mr. Maple summary figures as of January 31, 1952, stating that he wished to keep the statement confidential until it was made public in about a week. These figures are shown below:

SUBURBAN AUTO STORES CORPORATION
Balance Sheet as of 1/31/52

Cash	$ 64,975	Due banks	$ 345,000
Accounts receivable	102,695	Accounts payable	347,645
Inventory	1,227,760	Reserve for taxes	32,555
Total current assets	$1,395,430	Other current liabilities	117,875
Equipment, fixtures	185,725	Total current liabilities	$ 843,075
		Reserve	64,170
Prepayments	23,000	Net worth	696,910
Total assets	$1,604,155		$1,604,155

Mr. Snider said that, although the television inventory had reached a high point during the last year of $500,000, the inventory position in April amounted to only $125,000. He also stated that the gross profit on television sales throughout the country dropped considerably between 1950 and 1951. For Suburban, this drop was from 22% to 16%, thus causing a $148,000 loss in spite of the fact that sales volume and gross profit on most other items sold by the company remained at very even levels. It was Mr. Snider's opinion that rapid progress could be made, since the newest store of the chain was just getting established.

Mr. Snider asked Mr. Maple whether 3-year terms might be given his company on an initial order of about $35,000. He said he understood that fill-in orders were usually offered on a 1/10, n/60 basis. It was his estimate that Suburban should be able to do an annual volume with Union of over $200,000 if such terms were offered.

Exhibit 1

UNION PAINT AND VARNISH COMPANY

Balance Sheet and Income Statement for Year Ending December 31, 1951

(dollar figures in thousands)

BALANCE SHEET

CURRENT ASSETS			CURRENT LIABILITIES		
Cash........................		$ 14,991	Accounts payable..............		$ 5,675
Accounts receivable* (net)......		22,317	Federal and state income taxes..		10,790
Inventories.................		35,777	Miscellaneous accruals........		1,516
Total.................		$ 73,085	Current portion term loan......		1,725
			Total.................		$ 19,706
Real estate, plant and equipment	61,188				
Less: Reserve for depreciation..	25,659		Term loan—banks†............		14,950
		$ 35,529	Common stock...............		29,587
Prepaid and deferred charges....		1,641	Surplus......................		46,012
Total assets............		$110,255	Total liabilities.........		$110,255

    * Bad-debt reserve, $601,831.

    † Term loan with five banks at 3%, payable at rate of $1,725,000 each January 15 to 1961, when final payment is $2,875,000.

INCOME STATEMENT

Net sales.....................................	$262,801
Cost of sales.................................	214,282
Gross profit..................................	$ 48,519
Selling, general and administrative expense.........	30,224*
Operating profit..............................	$ 18,295†
Provision for federal income taxes.................	8,314
Net profit....................................	$ 9,981

    * Includes $152,725 for bad debt expense.

    † Total costs were composed of approximately 20% fixed costs, with 80% variable with volume of production.

Exhibit 2

UNION PAINT AND VARNISH COMPANY

West Coast Credit Reports, Inc.

October 15, 1951

SUBURBAN AUTO STORES CORPORATION   Los Angeles, California
SIDNEY G. SNIDER—*President and Treasurer*
JACK BINSTEIN—*Exec. Vice President*
LAURA B. GOODE—*Secretary*

SUMMARY

CORPORATION FORMED 1932; HOLDS A PROMINENT POSITION LO-
CALLY IN RETAIL TRADE. OPERATIONS HAVE SHOWN A PROFITABLE
TREND IN RECENT YEARS ON AN EXPANDING VOLUME. FINANCIAL
STATEMENTS OF JANUARY 31, 1951, SHOWED TANGIBLE NET WORTH
$855,000 AND A GENERALLY SATISFACTORY FINANCIAL CONDITION.
SUBSTANTIAL UNSECURED BANK ACCOMMODATION AVAILABLE,
WITH ACTIVE USE MADE OF BORROWING FACILITIES. TRADE PAY-
MENTS SATISFACTORY.

PERSONNEL

Sidney G. Snider, born 1898, married; started business in this line in 1921 with his
older brother, Julius Snider, operation under the trade name of Julius Snider Company,
Inc. On May 4, 1932, a 50% settlement was made with creditors on an indebtedness of
$168,000. Julius Snider Company, Inc., continues active in the automobile supply line
with Julius Snider, President and Treasurer, and Sidney G. Snider as Executive Vice
President of this corporation.

Jack Binstein, born 1906, married; was elected Executive Vice President in June, 1949.
He was formerly employed as an accountant for the company.

Laura B. Goode was appointed Secretary of Suburban Auto Stores in 1947, having been
employed by Sidney Snider as his personal secretary since 1936.

HISTORY

INCORPORATED: Under California laws, October 10, 1932, as a new business.
Authorized Capital Stock: 250,000 shares of Common Stock.

General Background Information: From its inception, this organization grew rapidly,
opening new stores from time to time; and by the end of the fiscal year of 1941, the
chain operated a total of 32 stores. During the war years, 17 of these stores were closed
as the result of war shortages. In the postwar period, five of the original stores have
been enlarged and modernized and four stores added. Until 1941, the company was engaged exclusively in the retailing of automobile accessories and equipment. Since 1942,
new lines have been added from time to time, so that the automotive merchandise now
constitutes less than 50% of the total volume. Merchandise now carried includes radios,
television sets, major electrical appliances and minor appliances, work clothes and related apparel, hardware, housefurnishings, unpainted furniture, house paints, glass-
ware, automobile supplies, tires and accessories, batteries and supplies, toys, luggage
and sporting goods.

Locations: All the store locations are leased. Executive offices are maintained at South
Flower Street, Los Angeles, where the corporation leases approximately 50,000 square
feet of floor space.

Number of Employees: Total 335 employees.

Terms of Sale: Cash sales account for approximately 95% of total volume, this percentage including instalment sales, which are financed by a bank, without recourse.
Suburban receives full cash payments from the bank as soon as the latter has approved
credit for the account. The remaining 5% of sales are on a deferred payment plan, payments being scheduled up to a period of three months, with notes on certain sales being
secured by a chattel mortgage on automobiles. This paper is carried by Suburban.

Exhibit 2 (Continued)

COMPARATIVE FINANCIAL STATEMENTS

	Jan. 31, 1949	Jan. 31, 1950	Jan. 31, 1951
Cash......................................	$ 121,305	$ 130,361	$ 157,402
Accounts receivable.....................	49,628	49,128	86,598
Inventory..............................	1,291,778	1,293,516	1,347,799
Total current assets...............	$1,462,711	$1,473,005	$1,591,799
Equipment, fixtures.....................	132,574	144,712	129,578
Prepaid and deferred...................	22,005	29,775	24,048
Total assets.....................	$1,617,290	$1,647,492	$1,745,425
Due banks.............................	$ 345,000	$ 345,000	$ 345,000
Accounts payable.......................	285,963	323,615	291,062
Reserve for taxes.......................	120,518	96,295	101,835
Television service contract................	......	44,759	75,183
Customers' deposits......................	......	14,778	19,864
Total current liabilities.............	751,481	824,447	832,944
Reserve unrealized profit on instalment sales............................	51,633	41,700	57,524
Common stock........................	433,838	400,833	394,422
Surplus................................	380,338	380,512	460,535
Total liabilities...................	$1,617,290	$1,647,492	$1,745,425
Net sales..............................	$6,800,228	$7,304,935	$8,292,551
Net profit*...........................	......	......	......
Dividends*............................	......	......	......

* Not made public.

GENERAL COMMENTS

Management has declined to furnish complete operating particulars, but points out that during fiscal year ended January 31, 1951, company realized satisfactory profit from operations. This profit was offset to a large extent through inventory writedowns.

Financial condition at January 31, 1951, continues to show relatively large current debt as the result of transacting a sizable volume in relation to net working capital, but at the same time the figures reflect a favorable improvement over the preceding year.

Notwithstanding the fact that company trades quite actively in relation to the net investment, it has been able to finance operations and to meet maturing obligations in a satisfactory manner by reason of the fact that fully 95% of sales are on a cash or close to cash basis, plus the fact that substantial bank lines are utilized in order to enable the company to carry representative lines of merchandise at each of its stores. During periods of lower than average inventories (which usually occur in the early months of the calendar year), bank loans are rotated in order to give each bank a full cleanup. During the remaining months of the year, full use is made of borrowing facilities at all of the company's banks.

Television service contracts payable, amounting to $75,183 at January 31, 1951, are liquidated at monthly intervals during the life of each service contract, which runs for a period of one year.

Exhibit 2 (Continued)

Comparative Financial Statements

GENERAL COMMENTS

Management has declined to furnish complete operating particulars, but points out that during fiscal year ended January 31, 1951, company realized satisfactory profit from operations. This profit was offset to a large extent through inventory writedowns.

Financial condition at January 31, 1951, continues to show relatively large current debt as the result of transacting a sizable volume in relation to net working capital, but at the same time the figures reflect a favorable improvement over the preceding year.

Notwithstanding the fact that the company trades quite actively in relation to the net investment, it has been able to finance operations and to meet maturing obligations in a satisfactory manner by reason of the fact that fully 95% of sales are on a cash or close to cash basis, plus the fact that substantial bank lines are utilized in order to enable the company to carry representative lines of merchandise at each of its stores. During periods of lower-than-average inventories (which usually occur in the early months of the calendar year), bank loans are rotated in order to give each bank a full cleanup. During the remaining months of the year, full use is made of borrowing facilities at all of the company's banks.

Television service contracts payable, amounting to $75,183 at January 31, 1951, are liquidated at monthly intervals during the life of each service contract, which runs for a period of one year.

Reserve for unrealized profit on instalment sales, $57,524, is a surplus reserve transferable to earned surplus on a percentage basis, upon collection of each monthly payment on respective instalment basis.

BANKING RELATIONS

Accounts are maintained at three local banks. Satisfactory average balances are reported. Accommodation is granted on corporate note, endorsed by Sidney G. Snider. In addition, one of the banks also discounts customers' paper on a nonrecourse basis. Active use is made of loan facilities, but each of the banks was given a full cleanup during the current year.

Exhibit 2 (Continued)

CREDIT INTERCHANGE BUREAUS
OF THE
NATIONAL ASSOCIATION OF CREDIT MEN

Central Offices
512 Arcade. Bldg.
St. Louis 1, Mo.

Report on SUBURBAN AUTO STORES CORP.

Los Angeles, California
South Flower Street
Los Angeles County

March 16, 1952

Business Classification	How Long Sold	Date of Last Sale	Highest Recent Credit	Now Owing Including Notes	Past Due Including Notes	Terms of Sale	Paying Record Discounts	Pays When Due	Days Slow	Comments
SOUTHERN CALIF.										
220-2										
AutoA	yrs.	1-52	12,310	5,900		2-10 EOM		x		
Hdwe.	yrs.	12-51	1,855	712	712	2-10-30			30	Slower
Inds.	1 yr.	12-51	26,475	12,575		60-1-10	x			
Tool	yrs.	1-52	175			2-10-30		x		
I & S	2 yrs.	1-52	19,400	7,300		Special		x		
Elec.	yrs.	11-51	28,940			2-10-30		x	30	
Elec.	yrs.	12-51	1,940	1,940	1,940	2-10-30			45	
AutoA	10-51	1-52	1,058			2-10	x			
Chem.	yrs.	12-51	838	838		2-10px		x		
Rdo.	yrs.	12-51	8,125			2-10 EOM	x			
Equip.	6-51	11-51	3,084	1,550	1,550	3-5px			60	
Tex.	yrs.	10-51	24,600	18,600	16,500	2-10 EOM			90	
NORTH & CENTRAL CALIF.										
221-14										
AutoA	yrs.	1-52	28,375	28,375	500	2-10 EOM		x	30	First time slow
Elec.	10-51	12-51	940			5-10-30	x			
Hdwe.	yrs.	10-51	19,529	19,529		2-10-30			30	
Plstc.	yrs.	12-51	7,500	7,500		2-10px		x		
Rbr.	yrs.	1-52	22,478	22,478		Regular		x		

Account						Terms			Days	Note
ARIZONA										
222–12										
Chem.	yrs.	9–51	250			2–10px		x	30	
Elec.	yrs.	11–51	24,490			2–10–30		x	45	
Equip.	6–51	1–52	2,845	2,845	2,845	2–10px				
ROCKY MTS.										
223–106										
Chem.	yrs.	11–51	28,464	28,464	6,464	2–10–30			60	
AutoA	yrs.	10–51	21,495	21,475	21,475	2–10–30			90	Slower
Elec.	1–52	1–52	7,050			2–10–30	x			First sale
I & S	yrs.	1–52	22,310			2–10 EOM		x		
Inds.	yrs.	11–51	27,400			Special		x		
CHICAGO										
223–18										
Elec.	yrs.	12–51	490	490	490	2–10 EOM		x	45	
Hdwe.	yrs.	1–52	26,400	12,400		2–10–30		x		
Hdwe.	yrs.	1–52	9,410	9,410		2–10–30		x	45	
Equip.	6 mos.	9–51	3,000				x			
Tool	yrs.	1–52	18,650	18,650		2–10–30		x		
CLEVELAND										
223–28										
Elec.	12–51	1–52	5,100	5,100	5,100	2–10–30		x	30–60	
Chem.	yrs.	9–51	3,400			2–10–30	x			
TOLEDO										
223–19										
Rbr.	yrs.	12–51	23,540	18,500	12,500	Regular		x	90	
Rbr.	yrs.	1–52	7,500	7,500		2–10px				
NEW YORK–										
PHILADELPHIA										
224–225										
Elec.	1–51	12–51	16,538	8,538	3,540	2–10–30			45	
Chem.	yrs.	1–52	250				x			
Tex.	yrs.	1–52	1,812	800				x		
Hdwe.	yrs.	12–51	6,540			2–10–30	x			
BU 95 LM										

Inconco Corporation

Paul Howe, member of the board of directors of Inconco Corporation, a large diversified manufacturing company, recently submitted to Jerome Drummond, president, a letter (Exhibit 1) expressing dissatisfaction with the cash flow forecast that was sent to the board in connection with its study of possible long-range plans (Exhibit 2). Mr. Howe suggested a form for a statement which he thought better able to provide the board with the data needed for making policy decisions at the board level so far as future flows of funds were concerned. The suggested statement is shown as Exhibit 3.

Mr. Howe, a stockholder of Inconco for 13 years, recently had been elected to the board of directors. As he attended the first few meetings of the board, Mr. Howe observed that although the company's income forecasts were satisfactory, there was considerable discussion and obviously a problem about the adequacy of the internally generated funds. The idea was accepted that sometime in the next few years public financing would be necessary, but there certainly was no agreement on the amount or on the form the financing should take. There also was a running debate on the subject of the desirability of increasing the cash dividend on the common stock, which had been $2.80 per share for several years.

The cash flow statements used merely grouped flows by sources and uses, with no distinction made among the groups of flows connected with operations, taxes, assets (that is, nonoperating sources and uses), and financing. Mr. Howe noted that these categories encompassed the four major areas of policy decision making. He remarked to Anthony Burbow, a fellow board member, after the attempt at the February meeting to use the prepared information in connection with the declaration of the quarterly dividend, "you probably noticed: they gave us an after-dividend figure [retained earnings], which assumes the policy that management recommends!" The policy being recommended was that of paying common stock dividends amounting to 50% of earnings after preferred stock dividends, a change from the existing scheme.

The current cash flow statement (Exhibit 2) contained actual figures for 1969, and projected figures for the years 1970–74.

Certain other information was made available to the directors at the same time as the cash flow forecast. The supplementary schedules were: (1) a schedule showing planned capital investments by divisions of the company, and (2) a forecast income statement showing only sales and net income after taxes. In fact, in order to obtain the detailed income information and interest cost information required to obtain funds provided by operations in the new format (Exhibit 3), Mr. Howe had to request the details. The adjustments made to operating income as reported were mainly those which in the revised format were appropriately treated under "financing."

Mr. Howe's objective was to have the firm's financial information portrayed in such a way that answers to the following questions would become obvious:

1. What amounts, if any, would remain of the internally generated funds after necessary expenditures for capital investment?
2. What amounts had to be expended for interest and dividend payments?
3. Was the debt limit as set forth in the bond indenture (35% of net tangible assets) being exceeded, or close to being exceeded? Was the Inconco debt limit policy of 33⅓% of net tangible assets now, or was it projected to be, close to being exceeded?

Mr. Howe was confident that his rearrangement accomplished these purposes. He knew the other directors would want a specific explanation of his arrangement, including how it was derived from the usual data, and why the new format was superior to the old. He was looking forward to explaining the concept in detail at the next board meeting. Now, with the February 4 meeting two days away, he wondered if anything further could be done to improve the new cash flow statement format.

Exhibit 1

Date: January 23, 1970
To: Jerome Drummond
From: Paul Howe
Dear Jerry:

You remember when we discussed my coming on the board, I said that I might have some suggestions about the kind of financial planning material we get. Now I'm ready. I've studied what was done and here are my ideas. I'd like to talk this over with you.

Except for the ending figures, beginning with "Net Change in Cash," the format we have been using is most uninformative. Many important details lying behind the figure for "retained earnings" are missing. I refer to the amounts of interest payments, lease payments, and dividends. Each of these, especially the last, is subject to policy decisions. I am especially troubled by this at this time because we are looking forward into a period of much higher interest costs.

You recall that in our meeting January 7, it required several minutes to ascertain the balance of earnings after taxes and dividends from supporting schedules. This illustrates why I am attempting to group pertinent information by the types of decisions we are asked to make.

I am enclosing a table made in the new format I am suggesting. It was derived from the Consolidated Cash Flow 1969–74 form that Mr. Gassle sent us, dated November 13, 1969. [The material enclosed is shown as Exhibit 3.] Certain supplementary figures were obtained from supporting schedules, and Mr. Gassle furnished further details.

The format I am suggesting groups the items affecting cash according to functional headings:

Operations—the result of marketing and production decisions.
Tax flows—the result of decisions concerning tax policy.
Asset accounts—the results of investment and disinvestment decisions.
Funds profile—the combined effect of the above, that is, the effect of all flows except those related to financing.
Financing—the result of past and present financial decisions.

From the new format, one can easily draw such conclusions as:

From 1971 onward, the operations of the company can supply the cash needed for investment.

By 1973 these operations in addition can cover, approximately, the interest and dividend requirements scheduled.

By matching each dollar of reinvested earnings with debt up to the 35% limit, new debt or lease capacity is created as follows:

1969	$22.0	1972	$37.0
1970	26.5	1973	42.4
1971	30.7	1974	46.7

It is obvious from the figures of the *funds provided by financing* and the *closing cash position* that the company's borrowing needs are greater than this. They must be supplied from current liabilities, by a change in the restrictive ratio, by a revision somewhere in the capital investment figures in the table, or by lowered dividends. Our dividend policy is said to be 50% of net earnings although, as you know, we have not changed the cash payout for the last six years.

When one turns to possible revision of policy, the organization of this work sheet really begins to pay off.

I'm sending this to you personally. I'd like your comments. If you agree, we can go to the board with this.

Sincerely,
Paul

Exhibit 2

INCONCO CORPORATION

Consolidated Cash Flow, Actual 1969, Projected 1970–74

(in millions)

	1969	1970	1971	1972	1973	1974
CASH SOURCES						
New debt financing	$ 10.2	$ …	$ …	$ …	$ …	$ …
Depreciation	68.5	73.5	71.2	70.1	67.8	66.7
Sale of stock to existing options	1.9	3.7	1.8	1.4	0.3	0.2
Assets sold	28.3	5.7	5.7	5.7	5.7	5.7
Deferred taxes	1.2	…	…	…	…	…
Increase in current tax liability	8.4	(18.9)	2.0	4.7	3.7	2.9
Retained earnings	40.8	49.2	57.0	68.7	78.8	86.7
Tax recovery, assets sold	7.5	1.9	…	…	…	…
Substitution of land for cash to pension fund	3.5	…	…	…	…	…
Total sources	$ 170.3	$ 115.1	$ 137.7	$ 150.6	$ 156.3	$ 162.2
CASH USES						
Capital expenditures	$(204.6)	$(201.1)	$(156.2)	$(136.3)	$(125.4)	$(123.4)
Less: Externally financed						
Leases	17.3	28.3	13.6	8.7	8.2	8.8
International Division	8.7	26.2	17.9	10.7	9.2	7.7
New product—Phase I	7.7	7.2	…	…	…	…
Phase II	9.7					
NET CAPITAL EXPENDITURES	$(161.2)	$(139.4)	$(124.7)	$(116.9)	$(108.0)	$(106.9)
Long-term debt retired	(14.9)	(10.6)	(15.5)	(15.7)	(13.4)	(12.5)
Working capital increase, excluding cash	(11.8)	(22.4)	(37.2)	(41.2)	(34.8)	(36.4)
Acquisition for cash	(10.8)	…	…	…	…	…
Total uses	$(198.7)	$(172.4)	$(177.4)	$(173.8)	$(156.2)	$(155.8)
NET CHANGE OF CASH						
Opening cash	$ 75.1	$ 46.7	$ (10.6)	$ (50.3)	$ (73.5)	$ (73.4)
Change during year	(28.4)	(57.3)	(39.7)	(23.2)	0.1	6.4
Closing cash	$ 46.7	$ (10.6)	$ (50.3)	$ (73.5)	$ (73.4)	$ (67.0)
Bank balance required	(24.0)	(24.0)	(24.0)	(24.0)	(24.0)	(24.0)
INVESTING OR BORROWING POSITION	$ 22.7	$ (34.6)	$ (74.3)	$ (97.5)	$ (97.4)	$ (91.0)

Exhibit 3

INCONCO CORPORATION

Consolidated Funds Flow, 1969–74

Based on figures dated November 13, 1969

(in millions)

KEY: *Sources*—Appear without parentheses; *Uses*—Appear in parentheses.

	1969	1970	1971	1972	1973	1974
OPERATIONS						
Operating income before investment credit....	$162.1	$228.1	$245.3	$294.4	$338.9	$370.5
Depreciation eliminated....	68.5	73.5	71.2	70.1	67.8	66.7
Interest and lease payments transferred below....	15.0	16.6	16.0	15.5	14.9	14.2
Other expenses....	....	(18.5)	(20.6)	(21.0)	(22.2)	(23.7)
FUNDS PROVIDED BY OPERATIONS (BT)....	$245.6	$299.7	$312.5	$359.0	$397.4	$427.7
TAX FLOWS						
Tax exposure: operations*....	($127.7)	($164.8)	($157.8)	($181.3)	($200.7)	($216.0)
Tax shield: depreciation*....	35.6	40.7	36.0	35.5	34.4	33.8
Investment credit....	7.3	7.1	5.7	5.3	4.9	4.9
Increase in current tax liability....	9.6†	(18.9)	2.0	4.7	3.7	2.9
Tax recovery: assets sold....	7.5	1.9	....	....	....	....
FUNDS REQUIRED BY TAXES....	($ 67.7)	($134.0)	($114.1)	($135.8)	($157.7)	($174.4)
ASSET ACCOUNTS						
Working capital increase, excluding cash....	($ 11.8)	($ 22.4)	($ 37.2)	($ 41.2)	($ 34.8)	($ 36.4)
Capital expenditures....	(215.4)‡	(201.1)	(156.2)	(136.3)	(125.4)	(123.4)
Assets sold....	28.3	5.7	5.7	5.7	5.7	5.7
Substitution of land for cash to pension fund....	3.5	....	....	....	....	....
FUNDS REQUIRED FOR INVESTMENTS....	($195.4)	($217.8)	($187.7)	($171.8)	($154.5)	($154.1)
FUNDS PROFILE BEFORE FINANCING....	($ 17.5)	($ 52.1)	$ 10.7	$ 51.4	$ 85.2	$ 99.2

FINANCING

FUNDS REQUIRED BY FINANCING					
Interest and lease payments............	($ 15.0)	($ 16.6)	($ 16.0)	($ 15.5)	($ 14.2)
Tax shield on interest and lease payments.....	7.8	9.1	8.1	7.8	7.2
Preferred dividends.............	(3.3)	(3.3)	(3.3)	(3.3)	(3.3)
Common dividends§.............	(41.0)	(49.2)	(57.0)	(68.7)	(86.7)
Subtotal................	($ 51.5)	($ 60.0)	($ 68.2)	($ 79.7)	($ 97.0)
Long-term debt retired.........	(14.9)	(10.6)	(15.5)	(15.7)	(12.5)
TOTAL, FUNDS REQUIRED BY FINANCING.....	($ 66.4)	($ 70.6)	($ 83.7)	($ 95.4)	($109.5)
FUNDS PROVIDED BY FINANCING					
New debt financing............	$ 10.2	...	...	...	...
Leases................	17.3	$ 28.3	$ 13.6	$ 8.7	$ 8.8
International division...........	8.7	26.2	17.9	10.7	7.7
New plant mortgage:					
Phase I................	7.7	...	...	...	...
Phase II................	9.7	7.2	...	...	...
Sale of stock to existing options......	1.9	3.7	1.8	1.4	0.2
TOTAL, FUNDS PROVIDED BY FINANCING.....	$ 55.5	$ 65.4	$ 33.3	$ 20.8	$ 16.7
NET CHANGE IN CASH...........	($ 28.4)	($ 57.3)	($ 39.7)	($ 23.2)	$ 0.1
OPENING CASH.............	75.1	22.7	(34.6)	(74.3)	(97.5)
LESS: BALANCE REQUIRED...........	(24.0)	...	...	...	...
CLOSING CASH POSITION...........	$ 22.7	($ 34.6)	($ 74.3)	($ 97.5)	($ 91.0)

* Tax exposure is the average corporate income tax rate times the revenue to be treated as income; tax shield is the tax rate times an item treated as expense.
† Includes deferred taxes of $1.2 million.
‡ Includes acquisition of Amerigo & Sons for $10.8 million.
§ Proposed policy was to pay a cash dividend to the common stockholders of 50% of earnings after taxes and preferred dividends.

Big City Trust Company

"Dick, Monday morning I'm flying out to Halley, Nebraska, to spend a couple of days with the people at the Auto-Drive Company. I hope to be able to come away with a fairly intimate feeling for the company's future. From what my friends in the automobile industry tell me, these people are about to perfect their Auto-Drive, a sort of automatic pilot for cars. Installed in a car, the pilot makes it impossible for the car to run off the road or into another car.

"When they get the Auto-Drive into cars, if it's accepted at all, the company will take off. Just think of the lives that would be saved! I'll bet consumers will insist that it be put in every car! If it looks good, I surely want the pension funds managed by Big City Trust to buy Auto-Drive common now."

Mr. Samuel Cooper, a senior trust officer at Big City Trust Company, enthusiastically addressed Mr. Richard Brainard, an analyst in the trust department. "I just wonder how much the stock can grow, though. It seems to me that the way Auto-Drive chooses to finance this growth in sales will be very important. If it has to issue a lot of new stock, much of the benefit of expanded earnings may be dissipated by the added shares. I wonder whether the methods used by other glamour companies, such as Xerox and Polaroid, to finance their growth would throw some light on the options open to Auto-Drive. In fact, before I fly out to Nebraska, I'd like to have the facts on just those two companies fresh in my mind. Dick, could you gather the financial statements for Xerox and Polaroid and summarize for me what their growth has meant in terms of funds requirements and how they have met these needs in the past four or five years?"

To prepare his analysis of how Polaroid and Xerox had acquired and used their resources, Dick Brainard gathered the material shown in Exhibits 1–8.

Exhibit 1

XEROX CORPORATION

Balance Sheets December 31, 1960 and 1964

(dollar figures in thousands)

ASSETS	1960	1964	Net Change 1960–64
Cash..	$ 1,779	$ 5,868	$+ 4,089
Accounts receivable..........................	5,536	35,400	+ 29,864
Inventories.................................	5,966	22,860	+ 16,894
Other current assets.........................	1,276	21,809	+ 20,533
Total current assets....................	$14,557	$ 85,937	$+ 71,380
Investments................................	1,376	25,556	+ 24,180
Property, plant and equipment*...............	38,520	262,678	+224,158
Less: Depreciation.........................	(9,241)	(92,628)	(+ 83,387)
Net property, plant and equipment.......	$29,279	$170,050	$+140,771
Intangible assets...........................	10,643	36,346	+ 25,703
Other assets...............................	572	2,658	+ 2,086
Total assets..........................	$56,427	$320,547	$+264,120
LIABILITIES			
Accounts payable...........................	$ 1,907	$ 6,099	$+ 4,192
Notes payable, bank........................	3,500	4,600	+ 1,100
Accrued liabilities..........................	3,574	42,531	+ 38,957
Other current liabilities.....................	2,117	7,780	+ 5,663
Total current liabilities.................	$11,098	$ 61,010	$+ 49,912
Deferred income tax........................	—	5,712	+ 5,712
Long-term debt............................	4,666	102,514	+ 97,848
Due for patents processes (in stock and cash)....	11,018	22,435	+ 11,417
Deferred executive compensation..............	949	1,608	+ 659
Rental income—prepaid.....................	353	—	− 353
Total liabilities.......................	$28,084	$193,279	$+165,195
Cumulative preferred stock..................	1,880	—	− 1,880
Common stock.............................	4,676	20,519†	+ 15,843
Paid-in surplus‡...........................	13,218	34,774	+ 21,556
Earned surplus§...........................	8,569	71,975	+ 63,406
Total equity........................	$28,343	$127,268	$+ 98,925
Total liabilities and equity............	$56,427	$320,547	$+264,120

* Includes leased machines valued in 1960 and 1964 at $18 million and $85 million.

† Of the increase of the common stock account $15,256 thousand is due to a transfer from "Paid-in surplus" of that amount to effect a change of each previously issued share of $1.25 par value into 5 shares of $1 par value.

After adjustment for the 5 for 1 split in 1963 there were 18,004,575 shares outstanding on December 31, 1960, and 20,518,956 on December 31, 1964.

During the period new shares were issued for the following purposes (adjusted/for split): (a) Conversion of debentures—717,254; (b) Acquisition of other companies—483,435; (c) Payment for patents—437,500; (d) Employee stock options—176,592.

‡ See Exhibit 3.

§ See Exhibit 4.

Exhibit 2

XEROX CORPORATION

Income Statements for 1960, 1964, and for the Period from 12/31/60–12/31/64
(dollar figures in thousands)

	1960	1964	Total 1961–64
Operating revenues			
Rentals, service on royalties.....................	$10,841	$184,157	$394,990
Net sales.....................................	26,233	83,870	225,078
Total operating revenues....................	$37,074	$268,027	$620,068
Costs and expenses			
Costs of sales and other operating expenses.........	17,777	88,314	218,718
Selling, service, administrative, and general expenses..	12,376	88,866	199,396
Profit-sharing, retirement, and pension plans........	516	10,264	21,480
Total costs and expenses....................	$30,670	$187,444	$439,594
Operating income...............................	$ 6,404	$ 80,583	$180,474
Other income...................................	54	440	1,210
Other deductions			
Interest.......................................	$ 253	$ 3,934	$ 9,276
Other...	189	381	2,145
Total other deductions......................	$ 442	$ 4,315	$ 11,421
Income before income taxes......................	$ 6,016	$ 76,707	$170,264
Income taxes...................................	3,418	38,177	89,323
Net income....................................	$ 2,598	$ 38,530	$ 80,941

Exhibit 3

XEROX CORPORATION

Statement of Additional Paid-in Surplus, 12/31/60–12/31/64
(Dollar Figures in Thousands)

Balance 12/31/60...	$13,218
Plus:	
Excess of par value of shares issued........................	36,812
	$50,030
Less:	
Transfer to common stock accounts as a result of change of each of previously issued shares of $1.25 par value into 5 shares of $1 par value...	15,256
Balance 12/31/64..	$34,774

Exhibit 4

XEROX CORPORATION

Statement of Earned Surplus, 12/31/60–12/31/64

(dollar figures in thousands)

Balance 12/31/60	$ 8,569
Plus:	
Net income	80,941
Credits to earned surplus	380
	$89,890
Less:	
Debits to earned surplus	$ 468
Dividends on preferred stock	34
Dividends on common stock	17,413
	$17,915
Balance 12/31/64	$71,975

Exhibit 5

POLAROID CORPORATION

Balance Sheets, December 31, 1960 and 1964

(dollar figures in thousands)

ASSETS	1960	1964	Net Change 1960–64
Cash	$11,864	$ 41,062	$+29,198
Receivables	26,222	37,557	+11,335
Inventories	13,980	13,177	− 803
Other current assets	379	834	+ 455
Total current assets	$52,445	$ 92,630	$+40,185
Properties, buildings and equipment	27,421	51,075	+23,654
Less: Depreciation	(9,639)	(20,747)	(+11,108)
Net property, buildings and equipment	$17,782	$ 30,328	$+12,546
Investment	277	146	− 131
Total assets	$70,504	$123,104	$+52,600
LIABILITIES			
Payables	$10,731	$ 11,204	$+ 473
Provision for taxes	7,089	14,212	+ 7,123
Total liabilities	$17,820	$ 25,416	$+ 7,596
Cumulative first preferred stock	900	—	− 900
Cumulative second preferred stock	35	—	− 35
Common stock*	3,871	15,750	+11,879
Paid-in surplus†	14,414	16,359	+ 1,945
Retained earnings‡	33,464	65,579	+32,115
Total equity	$52,684	$ 97,688	$+45,004
Total liabilities and equity	$70,504	$123,104	$+52,600

* Stock split 4 for 1 in 1964. Further increases in "Common stock" due to exercising of stock options.
† See Exhibit 7.
‡ See Exhibit 8.

Exhibit 6

POLAROID CORPORATION

Income Statements for 1960, 1964, and for the Period
12/31/60–12/31/64

(dollar figures in thousands)

	1960	1964	Total 1961–64
Net sales and other income.........	$99,446	$139,350	$468,026
Cost of goods sold.................	$50,304	$ 65,235	$231,125
Selling, administrative, distribution, research, and engineering expenses	27,039	32,761	119,932
Depreciation and amortization......	2,871	5,240	16,780
Total expenses..............	$80,214	$103,236	$367,837
Earnings before taxes.............	$19,232	$ 36,114	$100,189
Taxes on income.................	10,420	17,791	52,571
Net earnings after taxes...........	$ 8,812	$ 18,323	$ 47,618

Exhibit 7

POLAROID CORPORATION

Statement of Additional Paid-in Surplus for the Period
12/31/60–12/31/64

(dollar figures in thousands)

Balance 1/1/61.....................................	$14,414
Plus:	
Proceeds in excess of par value from stock options exercised..	1,877
Other proceeds......................................	68
Balance 12/31/64...................................	$16,359

Exhibit 8

POLAROID CORPORATION

Statement of Retained Earnings for the Period
12/31/60–12/31/64

(dollar figures in thousands)

Balance 1/1/61.....................................	$33,464
Plus:	
Net income..	47,618
Prior year's tax adjustments (1961).....................	131
	$81,213
Less:	
Premium on redemption of preferred stock (1963)........	331
Amount transferred to "Common Stock" to effect stock split (1964)..	11,814
Preferred dividends (1961–63)........................	156
Common stock dividends.............................	3,333
	$15,634
Balance 12/31/64...................................	$65,579

Sprague Machine Tool Company

On September 20, 1951, Mr. Harry Greenwood, vice president of the Wolverine National Bank of Detroit, was examining the company's credit file on Sprague Machine Tool Company, a customer located in a nearby small city. Renewal of a $350,000 loan made to that company was to be considered by the loan committee the next day, and Mr. Greenwood was reviewing what had happened since the bank had taken on Sprague's account, so that he could decide what action he should recommend to the committee. The note had originally been a 9-month loan made in December, 1950, but the Sprague management was requesting a 90-day extension.

Since its establishment in 1900, Sprague had successfully weathered the cyclical fluctuations characteristic of the machine tool manufacturing business. Its peak production had been achieved during World War II, sales reaching $7,300,000 in 1943. From that year, however, sales had declined, reaching a low of $1,765,000 in 1947, and the sales volume had been below $3 million in each subsequent year through 1948. Sprague had come out of World War II with a strong working capital position; with volume reduced in subsequent years, it had had no need to borrow prior to December, 1950.

Mr. Greenwood recalled that in December, 1950, Mr. Robert G. Murray, president of Sprague, requested a loan of $350,000 to assist in purchasing the stock interests of several dissident stockholders. While Sprague Machine Tool Company at that time had some excess cash over that required for normal operations, even more cash was required for the stock purchase, and Mr. Murray had, therefore, requested the Wolverine National Bank to lend Sprague Machine Tool Company $350,000 for a period of 9 months. To justify the credit, Mr. Murray had submitted a monthly forecast of shipments for 1951 (Exhibit 1) and a balance sheet dated November 30, 1950 (shown in the first column of Exhibit 2). The

Wolverine National Bank had agreed to make the loan, and in December, 1950, the company had retired 24,300 shares of its $10 par value stock purchased from its stockholders at an aggregate cost of $936,100. After this, there remained several hundred stockholders.

After the loan was made, Mr. Murray regularly sent the bank profit and loss statements and balance sheets. Mr. Greenwood selected the figures given on Exhibits 2 and 3 for use in his analysis.

The company manufactured machine tools which were sold to several metalworking industries but principally to automobile manufacturers and some aircraft manufacturers. These products were largely made to order; their sales prices ranged from $20,000 to $500,000 per installation. Sprague's selling terms were 30 days net. Occasionally, a customer placing a large order would make Sprague an advance payment to help finance the construction of the machines involved, which covered periods up to 5 or 6 months for some of the more complex types of machines. Upon completion and shipment of orders against which advances had been obtained, Sprague deducted the amount of the advance from the amount billed the customer.

On September 19, 1951, Mr. Greenwood had received a letter from Mr. Murray requesting a 90-day extension of Sprague Machine Tool Company's note. Mr. Murray's letter commented at some length on the company's financial condition and stated that the management expected to be able to pay off the note in full within 90 days. Mr. Murray's letter is set forth in full as Exhibit 4.

Exhibit 1

Shipments at Selling Price
(dollar figures in thousands)

1951	As Forecast December, 1950	Actual	As Forecast September, 1951
Jan.	$434	$287	
Feb.	624	224	
Mar.	545	622	
Apr.	351	522	
May	431	291	
June	493	540	
July	496	241	
Aug.	599	169	
Total	$3,973	$2,896	
Sept.	433		$721
Oct.	449		435
Nov.	437		468
Dec.	766		655

Exhibit 2

SPRAGUE MACHINE TOOL COMPANY

Balance Sheets

(dollar figures in thousands)

	11/30/50	12/31/50	3/31/51	6/30/51	7/31/51	8/31/51
Cash	$ 855	$ 155	$ 214	$ 507	$ 652	$ 602
Accounts receivable, net	415	664	657	631	423	228
Inventories	867	883	1,158	1,092	1,208	1,588
Total current assets	$2,137	$1,702	$2,029	$2,230	$2,283	$2,418
Fixed assets	$1,301	$1,301	$1,301	$1,302	$1,302	$1,308
Less: Reserve for depreciation	998	1,002	1,011	1,018	1,018	1,022
Net fixed assets	$ 303	$ 299	$ 290	$ 284	$ 284	$ 286
Prepaid expenses	21	20	13	8	8	14
Total assets	$2,461	$2,021	$2,332	$2,522	$2,575	$2,718
Notes payable—bank	$ 116	$ 350	$ 350	$ 350	$ 350	$ 350
Accounts payable	140	117	227	133	207	316
Accruals	138	249	283	179	148	137
Reserve for federal taxes*—1950	138.	154	108	63	63	63
—1951		...	112	218	242	277
Customer advance payments	280	280	280	522	522	522
Total current liabilities	$ 674	$1,150	$1,360	$1,465	$1,532	$1,665
Common stock	380	137	137	137	137	137
Surplus	1,407	734	835	920	906	916
Total liabilities	$2,461	$2,021	$2,332	$2,522	$2,575	$2,718

* 1950 federal income taxes payable in 1951: 30% of total on each of March 15 and June 15; 20% of total on each of September 15 and December 15. 1951 federal income taxes payable in 1952: 35% of total on each of March 15 and June 15; 15% of total on each of September 15 and December 15.

Exhibit 3

SPRAGUE MACHINE TOOL COMPANY

Income Statements

(dollar figures in thousands)

	Year Ended 12/31/50	1950 Dec.	1951 Jan.	Feb.	Mar.	Apr.	May	June	July	Aug.	Eight Months Ended 8/31/51
Net sales*	$2,618	$517	$287	$224	$622	$522	$291	$540	$241	$169	$2,896
Cost of sales*	1,684	374	158	123	454	379	189	399	170	92	1,964
Gross profit	$ 934	$143	$129	$101	$168	$143	$102	$141	$ 71	$ 77	$ 932
Selling and administration expenses	564	107	49	32	97	83	47	68	40	31	447
Net profit before taxes	$ 370	$ 36	$ 80	$ 69	$ 71	$ 60	$ 55	$ 73	$ 31	$ 46	$ 485
Provision for federal and state taxes	154	16	41	35	36	29	28	46	24	36	275
Net profit	$ 216	$ 20	$ 39	$ 34	$ 35	$ 31	$ 27	$ 27	$ 7	$ 10	$ 210
Dividends paid	$ 14	....	$ 7	....	....	....	....	....	$ 21	....	$ 28

* Includes depreciation charges of $28,000 in 1950, $4,000 in December, and $3,000 per month in 1951.

Exhibit 4

Dearborn, Michigan

September 18, 1951

Mr. Harry Greenwood, Vice President
Wolverine National Bank
Detroit, Michigan

Dear Mr. Greenwood:

I enclose the company's August 31 financial statements. While our cash balance currently is $602,000, you will note that we have an obligation to a customer for cash advances of $522,000, and we expect to ship this order over the next 2 months. With respect to our note for $350,000 due September 25, we request that you renew our loan for another 90 days. At the end of that period, as you can see for yourself, we expect to be able to have enough cash on hand to retire our obligation in full.

For the past month or more, we have been producing at capacity and expect to continue at that rate through the end of the year. On August 31, our backlog of unfilled orders amounted to about $5,500,000. Our shipment schedule has been upset, particularly the last month or two, because we have had to wait on our suppliers for shipment of electrical control mechanisms; at August 31, we had seven machines with an accumulated cost of about $440,000 completed except for the installation of these electrical components. The components were finally received last week and will enable us to complete a number of machines in the next few days. The remainder of our work in process will probably stay at present levels for the foreseeable future because of our capacity rate of production. Our finished goods inventories are negligible at all times, since we ship machines within a day of completion.

We bought raw materials beyond our current needs in July and August to be assured of completing our orders scheduled to be shipped by December 31. Our purchases were $220,000 in July and $330,000 in August. We have, therefore, accumulated about $140,-000 worth of scarcer components above our normal raw material inventories. The extra $140,000 will be used up by the end of the year, bringing our raw material inventories back to normal levels for capacity production. Because we have bought ahead this way, we expect to cut our purchases to about $200,000 a month in each of the four remaining months of 1951.

Our revised shipment estimates are as follows:

	(At Selling Prices)
September	$ 721,000
October	435,000
November	468,000
December	655,000
	$2,279,000

The shipment estimates include the $700,000 order for the Giant Automobile Company. We are now scheduled to ship against this order as follows: September $280,000, October $280,000, November $140,000. Since we obtained a $522,000 advance from Giant on this order, we will be due nothing on these shipments until their $522,000 credit with us is exhausted.

You will probably note the decline in our accrued expenses. As I mentioned to you last month when you visited us, we have been paying off commissions due our two principal salesmen (who are also large stockholders in the company). Last year when we needed funds to redeem part of our capital stock, these men agreed to defer their commissions until the funds could more easily be spared. In August, we paid off the last of these back commissions. This has been the principal cause of the decline in this item, which normally does not change much from month to month. Our outlay each month for all expenses other than materials should be around $136,000. This assumes that accruals will stay about the same as on August 31.

The business which we expect to ship in the next 4 months is on our books on profitable terms. While our profit, as you know, varies with the item involved, our engineering estimates indicate we will probably make a net profit (before taxes) of about 15% of sales on these items. Unfortunately, we shall be working mostly for Uncle Sam—we have

Exhibit 4 (Continued)

already exceeded our excess profits tax credit and as a result our profits earned during the next four months will be taxed at 77% (normal tax plus excess profits tax).

We have spent very little on new equipment in the last 8 months. We will avoid buying new equipment in the next 4 months, unless breakdowns make it necessary to replace existing equipment.

Our profits for the year to date have been quite satisfactory, and toward the end of December we plan to pay a dividend to our stockholders. Our dividend disbursements in 1951 have been quite modest so far, and we want to be sure that those stockholders who stood by us last December have no cause to regret their action. Under the circumstances, we feel that a $50,000 dividend payable in December is the least we can do in view of our high earnings.

If there is anything further you need to know, please do not hesitate to write or phone.

Sincerely yours,
ROBERT G. MURRAY
President

Brown Marine Supply Company (1)

It was mid-August, 1967. Nathaniel Brown put down the telephone and sat for a moment in thought, then rose and walked to the window where he stood looking out over the harbor. His cashier, Michael Stone, had called with the message that the company's cash balance had fallen below $2,000. Mr. Stone had called attention to the outstanding accounts payable to his suppliers that would fall due at the end of the week, and expressed a fear that collections from customers during the week would not produce sufficient cash to make it possible to pay these accounts when due. It seemed to Mr. Brown that while he was consistently making profits, he was getting shorter and shorter of cash. The company's shortage of cash was particularly disturbing in light of Mr. Brown's proposed project to broaden the company's activities through the construction of additional waterfront facilities. This expansion would cost the company approximately $280,000.

Mr. Brown decided that his first step must be to walk across to the local bank where the Brown Marine Supply Company's deposits were maintained and try to arrange an increase in the company's existing $10,000 borrowing limit, which was already being fully used. Bank borrowing had risen to $10,000 during the summer of 1966 and had not been reduced since. Mr. Brown believed that he might be able to get the bank to increase this limit to $50,000, a "round figure" which he guessed would be large enough to solve the cash problem for at least two years. He believed that he would be able to obtain the funds needed, since the company's sales performance remained excellent and 1967 would certainly be a record year, but he very much disliked to admit that such a crisis had been allowed to develop. The next step, once the immediate action had been taken, must be to work out how the company had gotten itself into this mess.

The Brown Marine Supply Company had been founded by Mr. Brown at the beginning of the 1965 boating season and had been successful from the start. Excellent premises had been available for lease,[1] and Mr. Brown's long experience as a salesman for a large boat distributor and many contacts in the trade had made it possible for him to obtain a number of valuable franchises. Although the boat business was highly seasonal, Brown Marine's location on the Southeast Coast ensured that the seasonal variation was less marked than it would have been in, for instance, a New England sailing center. Nevertheless, the company's sales were largely concentrated in the 8-month period, March through October.

Sales had been $150,000 in the last 6 months of 1965 and $430,000 in 1966. Now, in mid-August, 1967, Mr. Brown estimated that sales revenue for the current year would be about $575,000. Modest profits had been recorded right from the beginning, and profits should increase very considerably if the estimate of 1967 volume proved correct.

Despite growing sales and continued profitable operation, however, the company always seemed to be short of cash and on a number of recent occasions had been criticized by its trade suppliers for failing to pay bills on time. One major boat hull manufacturer had indicated that if any more of its bills were not met within the stated terms of sale, all future shipments would be placed on a C.O.D. basis. Mr. Brown was dismayed to note that the bills falling due in the coming week included one from this supplier. Brown Marine also held an exclusive Southeast Coast franchise for a line of inboard-outboard engines made by a major Scandinavian manufacturer. Purchase of these engines was on the basis of 30-day drafts attached to the bill of lading and therefore payable 30 days from shipping date. As the shipment time from Europe frequently exceeded 30 days, Brown Marine often had to pay for these items before they had been received. Mr. Brown was also conscious that the company was failing to take advantage of prompt-payment discounts. Purchases of boats, engines, and equipment were generally on terms of 2% 10 days, net 30 days.

Mr. Brown knew that one potential way to make more funds available to supplement or reduce bank borrowing was to speed up collections from customers. The nature of Brown Marine's business, however, made it difficult to do so. Approximately 15% of Brown Marine's sales were made to individual boat owners. The rest were to small local boat dealers, usually one-man businesses which were typically undercapitalized. Brown Marine's terms of sale allowed 5% discount for payment within 10 days, but very few customers paid within this period. Many customers' accounts were weeks or even months overdue, and Brown Marine's accounts receivable early in the season averaged 55 days' to 60 days' sales. Competition in the recreational boating field was intense and still increasing, and small dealers who were refused extended credit might easily take

---

[1] The premises were leased for an initial period of 5 years at an annual rental of $27,000 with an assurance that the lease would be renewable at the end of that period.

their business to distributors of competitive lines whose credit terms were more liberal. Manufacturers of the products for which Brown Marine held distribution franchises insisted that its orders from dealer customers should be filled promptly even though the latter had not paid for previous orders.

While the need to provide extended credit terms to dealers seemed to be a major factor in his company's current financial embarrassment, Mr. Brown suspected that this was not the only problem area. He wondered what else might be going wrong, and how he should go about locating the trouble. He wondered if he was receiving all the information that was needed to manage his finances efficiently.

Before commencing operations, Mr. Brown had employed a certified public accountant of his acquaintance to set up a simple set of management controls, consisting of simple cost and expense budgets and a break-even analysis. According to these controls the company should have been profitable if costs were kept within budgeted figures and annual sales revenues exceeded $342,000. In fact, sales had comfortably exceeded this figure in 1966, and the operation had been profitable (Exhibit 2). Sales promised to exceed the break-even level more handsomely in 1967. Mr. Brown wondered how it arose that he was consistently making profits but getting shorter and shorter of cash. He questioned whether some basic error had crept into the break-even calculation.

The current crisis was additionally disturbing in that it seemed to suggest that plans Mr. Brown had been making to broaden the company's activities might have to be shelved. A waterfront site close to the company's leased premises had recently been placed on the market, and Mr. Brown had obtained an option to purchase it. The site would provide ample room for the construction of a yacht service center, with slipways, quayside refueling facilities, and additional workshops, as well as for a new showroom and office building to replace the currently leased building when the lease expired in 1970. The site would cost $200,000, with a further $80,000 expenditure for immediate construction and development work. Mr. Brown had been assuming on the basis of his break-even analysis that 1967 levels of sales would produce profits of approximately $30,000 a year, and the projected property development would generate an additional $10,000 a year of net earnings through fuel sales and additional servicing on overhaul operations.

Mr. Brown picked up the telephone and called Michael Stone: "Mike, I think we had better put our heads together about this financial situation. Bring all our past financial statements, and I want you to get out some figures for me for the current season so far. I want to know how we have stood at the end of every month—say, from April to the end of last month. Make a note of how much we have sold in the month, what our inventories were at the month-end, how much we owed to suppliers, how much our customers owed us, and what our cash balances were. When you have that, come and see me and we'll see if we can work out what is going on here."

The financial statements that Mr. Stone compiled appear as Exhibits 1–4.

Exhibit 1

BROWN MARINE SUPPLY COMPANY

Balance Sheet as of December 31, 1966

ASSETS

Cash and deposits	$121,274
Accounts receivable	65,993
Inventories at cost	42,579
Total current assets	$229,846
Equipment and fixtures	34,285
Total assets	$264,131

LIABILITIES AND PROPRIETORSHIP

Notes payable to bank	$ 10,000
Accounts payable	88,270
Total current liabilities	$ 98,270
Proprietorship account	165,861
Total liabilities and proprietorship	$264,131

Exhibit 2

BROWN MARINE SUPPLY COMPANY

Operating Statement for 8 Months Ended December 31, 1965,
Year Ended December 31, 1966, and 3 Months Ended March 31, 1967

(dollar figures in thousands)

	May–December 1965	Year Ended December 31, 1966	January–March 1967
Sales, net of discounts	$ 274	$ 430	$ 104
Cost of sales	(202)	(328)	(73)
Gross profit	$ 72	$ 102	$ 31
Operating, sales, and administrative expenses*	(62)	(84)	(27)
Net profit†	$ 10	$ 18	$ 4
Owner's withdrawals	(8)	(12)	(3)
Change in proprietorship account	$ 2	$ 6	$ 1

* Including rental payments on lease.
† Brown Marine Supply Company was taxed as an unincorporated business. Profits were considered the personal income of Mr. Brown, who paid personal income taxes on them. Mr. Brown anticipated that his withdrawals, which were in addition to his salary of $12,000 a year, would provide the necessary funds.

Exhibit 3

BROWN MARINE SUPPLY COMPANY
Monthly Operating Data, April–July 1967

	April	May	June	July	April–July	
Sales	$ 78,104	$ 92,215	$ 112,771	$ 105,482	$ 388,572	100.6%
Sales discounts allowed	(478)	(570)	(743)	(530)	(2,321)	(0.6)
Net sales	$ 77,626	$ 91,645	$ 112,028	$ 104,952	$ 386,251	100.0%
Cost of goods sold (expense)	(60,510)	(69,282)	(85,721)	(80,867)	(296,380)	(76.7)
Operating expenses requiring funds						
Wages and salaries	(7,660)	(8,844)	(9,875)	(9,250)	(35,629)	(9.2)
Other	(320)	(345)	(275)	(410)	(1,350)	(0.3)
Total expenses	$(68,490)	$(78,471)	$(95,871)	$(90,527)	$(333,359)	(86.3)%
Funds provided by operations	$ 9,136	$ 13,174	$ 16,157	$ 14,425	$ 52,892	13.7%
Interest and lease expense	(2,600)	(2,600)	(2,600)	(2,600)	(10,400)	(2.7)
Net funds provided	$ 6,536	$ 10,574	$ 13,557	$ 11,825	$ 42,492	11.0%
Depreciation expense	(285)	(285)	(285)	(285)	(1,140)	(0.3)
Net profit	$ 6,251	$ 10,289	$ 13,272	$ 11,540	$ 41,352	10.7%

Exhibit 4

BROWN MARINE SUPPLY COMPANY

Month-end Balance Sheets, March–July 1967

	March 31	April 30	May 31	June 30	July 31
ASSETS					
Cash.......................	$110,152	$ 73,584	$ 48,228	$ 19,284	$ 2,758
Accounts receivable...........	53,202	108,802	148,214	194,296	211,059
Inventories...................	34,964	40,254	53,112	59,846	65,204
Total current assets......	$198,318	$222,640	$249,554	$273,426	$279,021
Equipment and fixtures........	33,430	33,145	32,860	32,575	32,290
Total assets...........	$231,748	$255,785	$282,414	$306,001	$311,311
LIABILITIES					
Notes payable................	$ 10,000	$ 10,000	$ 10,000	$ 10,000	$ 10,000
Accounts payable.............	55,380	73,166	89,506	99,821	93,591
Total current liabilities...	$ 65,380	$ 83,166	$ 99,506	$109,821	$103,591
Proprietorship account.........	166,368	172,619	182,908	196,180	207,720
Total liabilities and pro-prietorship...........	$231,748	$255,785	$282,414	$306,001	$311,311

Brown Marine Supply Company (2)

Russell Deacon, a recently graduated MBA, lived in the town in which Brown Marine was located. He had first met Mr. Brown in the early summer of 1966 when he purchased a small racing sailboat from Brown Marine. In August, 1967, he was spending a vacation in his hometown before taking up a job with a major manufacturing company. Shortly after the events related in Brown Marine Supply Company (1), Mr. Deacon called at the Brown Marine showrooms to talk about the possibility of trading to a larger sailboat. Mr. Brown himself was in the showroom, and asked what Mr. Deacon had been doing since their last meeting.

On hearing that Mr. Deacon's studies had included two courses in financial management, Mr. Brown smiled and said: "You are just the man I need. How would you like to try out your theory on a real business problem? I seem to have a fine case of financial mismanagement on my hands right now, and I'm not sure what to do about it. How about giving me a few hours of consulting and I'll give you a great deal on that sailboat!"

Mr. Deacon decided that the assignment might be an interesting one and arranged to call on Mr. Brown on the very next wet or windless day.

Three days later Mr. Deacon and Mr. Brown lunched together and talked for two hours afterwards. Mr. Brown outlined the company's history and explained some of the more important aspects of the boat business: terms of trade, the distributor-dealer relationship, and the competitive position. He then described the situation in which the company now found itself. A crisis had developed during the previous week when the cash balance was found to have fallen to less than $2,000. Mr. Brown had approached the company's bank with a request that his borrowing limit be raised from the existing figure of $10,000 (fully utilized) to $50,000, ("a good round figure, which seemed to give us something in reserve to see us through the rest of the season"). The manager of the bank, although less than enthusiastic, had agreed that the company's rate of growth in sales was very impressive. At the beginning of the present week, he had telephoned to say that the bank's credit committee had authorized an increase of Brown Marine's loan limit to $30,000, subject to the restriction that the company must supply the bank with quarterly financial statements and quarterly schedules of the aging of receivables. The total $30,000 credit would be granted at an interest rate of 7%.

Mr. Brown showed Mr. Deacon the month-by-month operating and balance sheet information for the past four months prepared during the previous week (Exhibits 3 and 4 of Brown Marine Supply Company (1), and commented: "These figures are very interesting, especially the month-end figures for cash and accounts receivable and such. I've a feeling that the key to what is going on is right here. I'm no accountant, but I seem to see a definite pattern developing. My cash balance goes steadily down, my inventories go steadily up, and both payables and receivables are increasing very rapidly. The same picture appears every month. What troubles me, Russ, is that I don't see how I can do business without this happening, and yet if it goes on happening, I'm going to be running back to the bank for more money every few months. The operating figures tell me that I'm making money, and I know I'm over the break-even point, but I look like I'm going deeper and deeper into debt."

Mr. Deacon, after looking at the figures for some minutes, said: "You're right in thinking that the answer to what is happening is right here in these figures. I think I can do a couple of things for you. I'll show you the information in a form that illustrates rather more clearly what is going on. Then I'll demonstrate how you can use this format to look ahead and see problems coming rather than just to look for explanations when the problem is already here.

"The trouble with your break-even analysis is that it is based on concepts of earnings and profits that are used by accountants in preparing financial statements but are really no help at all in determining whether or not you will run out of cash. Take the concept of sales. Accountants recognize a sale when a boat leaves your showroom and are not concerned for this purpose whether you get immediate cash payment or have to give 12 months' credit. It makes a difference to you, though. If you had unlimited financial resources, the break-even concept would be fine. You could simply say that the boat was sold, that the money would be received some time, and that the sale therefore represented a profit. The fact is, though, that you are short of cash. And you can't pay your bills with what your customers owe you; only with what they pay you.

"The factor that is missing from the kind of analysis you have been doing is the timing of cash settlements. You need a form of analysis that tells you not what theoretical profit you are going to record in a given period but what is going to happen to your cash balance. Therefore, we have to take account of all the events that will increase or decrease cash. This includes items that do not appear in the income statement at all, such as repayment of bank debt. We need to know the amounts involved and the time the event will take place. For our purposes there is a very real difference between cash sales and credit sales, for instance. Cash sales produce an inflow of cash now. This idea of flows or movements of cash in or out of the company at definite points in time is the basis of the kind of analysis I am talking about, and we call this approach 'cash flow analysis' or 'cash flow forecasting.'

"I can show you what such a procedure will tell you by picturing the history of recent months in this way. Then, if you like it, we can try to forecast the future in the same manner. Just let me have recent balance sheets and income statements and I'll get to work."

When Mr. Deacon had been provided with the information he had requested, he sat down in a corner of Mr. Brown's office to draw up his analysis of cash flows in the last four months. After some time he explained his findings to Mr. Brown, pointing out that his cash flow analysis (Exhibit 1) provided a complete explanation of the company's cash shortage on a single sheet of paper. It did this by taking relevant information from both the income statement and the balance sheet; recognizing transactions only at the point in time at which they were settled in cash; and eliminating any noncash items, such as depreciation and amortization, that appeared in the income statement.

The analysis indicated the limitations of the break-even approach in which Mr. Brown had originally placed so much trust. Mr. Deacon pointed out that in June, when sales had been furthest above the break-even point, the accounting system had indicated a record net profit of over $13,000, but cash reserves had fallen during the month and had also fallen drastically in the following month.

Mr. Deacon explained what was really happening in the company. Sales were at record levels but were predominantly credit sales on generous terms to small dealers, who were themselves short of cash at this stage in the year. Rising sales, therefore, did not produce any corresponding immediate cash inflow. The balance sheet data showed inventory rising as sales increased, but although this was certainly a contributory factor, the cash flow analysis indicated that the major problem was in the relationship between sales, receipts from sales, and payments to suppliers. The liberal credit given to customers was not matched by equally liberal credit from suppliers. The normal credit terms given by suppliers required settlement in 30 days. Thus, any increase in purchases in one month resulted in larger outflows of cash to suppliers in the following month than could be covered by collections of the proceeds of sales of the goods purchased.

Mr. Deacon indicated that in his opinion the analysis showed that Mr. Brown should make more use of the inventory floor plan schemes through which suppliers offered extended credit. Two of Brown Marine's major boat suppliers offered such schemes. Under their terms, 10% of the manufacturer's price of boats being purchased for stock rather than against a firm customer order would be paid in cash on delivery and the distributor would sign a note for the balance of the sum due at an 8% interest rate. These notes were payable in equal monthly instalments over a period of one year. When a boat financed on such a note was sold, however, the terms of the note were automatically modified to whatever terms the distributor had given to the customer, and the distributor transferred immediately all payments received from his customer. Brown Marine had made little use of these floor plans, despite the fact that 40% in dollar value of the boats and equipment bought by the company could have been obtained on these terms.

When he was confident that Mr. Brown understood the figures used in the analysis and the sources from which they had been obtained, Mr. Deacon continued his explanation. He said that the real value of this type of analysis was not in showing what had already happened, but in forecasting what was likely to happen to cash balances in a future period on the basis of any particular set of plans and assumptions.

Mr. Brown commented: "Well, now this is really getting interesting. I mentioned that I have been planning some extensions around here, and I have an option on the site I want to use. The last couple of weeks have made me wonder whether perhaps I should drop the whole idea. Can we use your analysis to see if I can afford to go ahead with the new developments?" (Page 643 of Brown Marine Supply Company (1) details the expenditures involved in the expansion project.) The $200,000 cost of the site would be due in November and the $80,000 expenditure for construction in March of the following year.

Mr. Deacon replied: "Yes, provided that you are willing to do some guesstimating and to make some assumptions about cost-volume relationships. In fact, we can go a step further. We can see whether your plans are practicable under your present policies and then go through the calculations again on the assumption that you are making full use of the inventory floor plans and see what difference that makes.[1]

"Why don't you start by estimating as well as you can what your sales are likely to be month-by-month to the end of 1968?"

By the end of the afternoon, Mr. Brown had produced a monthly sales forecast for the 17 months (Exhibit 2). He was convinced that it would be reasonable to assume that cost of sales, and wage, salary, and miscellaneous cost would maintain approximately the same relationship to sales that had existed in recent months. Cost of goods sold was expected to remain at approximately 77% of net sales and variable operating expenses at about 3%. Approximately $6,500 of monthly operating ex-

---

[1] Floor plan loans would be available only on new purchases.

penses, excluding $285 of depreciation, were period costs, which would not respond to changing sales. Monthly lease and interest payments were also fixed. They would rise to $2,725 per month because of the terms of the new bank loan.

The assumption to be made about collection of receivables was obviously a most critical one. After considerable discussion Mr. Brown decided that a realistic estimate was that credit sales made in the summer season (April through August) would require an average of 9 weeks' credit, and that off-season sales would be paid in an average of five weeks.[2] He expected cash sales to fall slightly in relation to credit sales, down to approximately 8% of total sales.

He decided that he would continue to use his bank line of credit of $30,000 to the full but would not try to increase it. Although at times the company had lagged behind in its payments to suppliers, Mr. Brown wanted to pay within the 30-day limit in the future. (Accounts payable at July 31 were $93,591.) He told Mr. Deacon that at the start of the 1968 summer season he would need to spend about $8,000 on new fixtures and showroom redecoration and that the bills for this would be payable in June. No other special expenses were expected, since no capital investments were planned other than the new site development already referred to.

Mr. Deacon first worked out a forecast of sales, purchases, and collections made by the company over the next 17 months. These results are shown in Exhibit 2. This task took Mr. Deacon a considerable amount of time. He then started to build these assumptions into a cash flow forecast that would indicate what might be expected to happen to the company's cash balances during the remainder of 1967 and the whole of 1968.[3] He wondered as he was making the forecast how much reliance he should place in the various estimates and whether he should repeat the forecast with different assumptions about some of the more critical variables.

---

[2] At the end of July, the total accounts receivable were $211,000, of which approximately $117,000 were over 30 days and slightly more than $20,000 were over 60 days.

[3] In making his forecast, Mr. Deacon assumed that Mr. Brown would make no owner's withdrawals until he saw the forecasted cash on hand.

Exhibit 1

BROWN MARINE SUPPLY COMPANY

Cash Flow Analysis, April–July, 1967

	April	May	June	July	April–July
Funds provided by operations.	$ 9,136	$ 13,174	$ 16,157	$ 14,425	$ 52,892
Changes in inventories.	(5,290)	(12,858)	(6,734)	(5,358)	(30,240)
Funds profile.	$ 3,846	$ 316	$ 9,423	$ 9,067	$ 22,652
Financing					
Changes in accounts receivable.	$(55,600)	$(39,412)	$(46,082)	$ (16,763)	$(157,857)
Changes in accounts payable.	17,786	16,340	10,315	(6,230)	38,211
Interest and lease expense	(2,600)	(2,600)	(2,600)	(2,600)	(10,400)
Monthly changes in cash.	$(36,568)	$(25,356)	$(28,944)	$ (16,526)	$(107,394)
Cumulative changes in cash.	$(36,568)	$(61,924)	$(90,868)	$(107,394)	

Exhibit 2

Forecasts of Net Sales, Purchases, and Collections, 1967–68

	Net Sales	Cash Sales (8%)	Credit Sales	Collections of Credit Sales	Purchases
August, 1967.........	$ 88,000	$ 7,000	$ 81,000	$ 94,000	$ 65,000
September............	60,000	5,000	55,000	96,000	42,000
October..............	45,000	4,000	41,000	132,000	28,000
November............	35,000	3,000	32,000	48,000	21,000
December............	30,000	2,000	28,000	44,000	18,000
January, 1968........	30,000	2,000	28,000	29,000	15,000
February............	30,000	2,000	28,000	28,000	25,000
March...............	55,000	4,000	51,000	21,000	48,000
April................	85,000	7,000	78,000	14,000	71,000
May.................	100,000	8,000	92,000	51,000	88,000
June.................	120,000	10,000	110,000	59,000	105,000
July.................	110,000	9,000	101,000	89,000	85,000
August..............	90,000	7,000	83,000	106,000	62,000
September...........	70,000	6,000	64,000	103,000	48,000
October.............	50,000	4,000	46,000	140,000	32,000
November...........	40,000	3,000	37,000	55,000	22,000
December...........	40,000	3,000	37,000	51,000	20,000

The Estella Five-Year Plan

Early in October, 1963, John Walton, an outside director of Digital Engineering Company (DENCO), was reviewing a "Five-Year Capital and Financing Plan" for the company sent him by Mr. Estella, DENCO's treasurer. Mr. Estella intended to discuss the plan at a forthcoming board meeting. Presumably, if the plan and the premises on which it was drawn were endorsed by the board, it would greatly influence the financial policies and indeed the total development of the firm in the coming years.

Mr. Walton had worked in the financial department of Giant Electric Company for some years and currently served as treasurer. As the board member most experienced in financial matters, he knew that other members of the board would be keenly interested in his comments on the Estella Plan. This likelihood was heightened by the fact that Mr. Walton had been somewhat outspokenly critical of what he had termed "hand-to-mouth financial planning" in the company in the recent past. Presumably, the Estella Plan (Exhibit 1) was at least in part a response to this criticism.

After some study, Mr. Walton identified several questions as important ones for his further consideration and resolution. Among these were the following:

1. In view of the uneven growth in sales, inventory, and receivables and earnings in the past, was Mr. Estella's use of averages for his projections a valid and useful approach?
2. How valid and useful was the assumption that a capitalization equal to 40% of annual sales would meet the company's needs?
3. What were the implications of the assumption that further equity financing should be deferred until bank debt/equity fell to a 24%–16% relationship? What advantages and what hazards were involved if this approach were accepted as a financial policy guideline?

4. What were the main points that Mr. Estella was trying to get across to his associates in management and the board? Should he, Mr. Walton, accept or challenge Mr. Estella's ideas?

DIGITAL ENGINEERING COMPANY—BACKGROUND

DENCO was founded in 1953 in Pittsburgh by a group of four young electrical engineers. The founders were subsequently joined by three executives with demonstrated business skill and an ability to work with the founders of the company. As an incentive to attract these men to the organization, the new executives were given stock options. They had exercised the options, and the seven men held approximately equal shares of DENCO. In late 1963 the group still retained ownership of 51.5% of the common stock. Mr. Joseph Grace was president, and Mr. Thomas Estella, one of the founding engineers, was serving as treasurer. DENCO's management seemed to be highly regarded by their customers and banks and was considered to have technical depth and breadth. In addition to Mr. Walton, the board of directors included two outside members, a prominent and respected figure in the Pittsburgh financial world and a senior executive of a major engineering company.

DENCO designed, developed, manufactured, and marketed digital equipment, including components, subassemblies, and memory subsystems. Units of these types were often called "modules," a collective term for the devices from which digital computing equipment is built. The modules were sold to customers who wished to build their digital systems. DENCO's modular product line, which accounted for 71% of the company's fiscal 1962 sales, put the company in competition with both the large end-use system manufacturers and with the smaller, specialized component firms. DENCO, however, had been one of the first companies to offer a comprehensive line of standard, high-quality modules at prices reflecting mass production savings. DENCO's product line had been gradually expanded from one product to several proprietary lines which were produced primarily for off-the-shelf sale.

In addition to producing component parts, DENCO designed and manufactured custom products, including both components and systems for data processing, control, and other applications. These developments were undertaken as the result of management's initiative as well as under contract for other firms. In 1961, for example, DENCO introduced its first general computer, the DENCO 10. It was a relatively small and inexpensive unit designed to be a component in a variety of larger systems and used in data processing and scientific computer applications. This unit did not receive a very enthusiastic market reception, but an advanced version (the DENCO 20) was given favorable reports and was selling well. During fiscal 1962, DENCO's systems accounted for only 29% of sales. For the fiscal year ending November 2, 1963, however, computers were expected to amount to 9%, special-purpose systems to 29%, and modules and related products to 62% of DENCO's sales.

Management expected the sales of systems to continue to grow relative to the growth in module sales. It was, in fact, this trend that was contributing significantly to DENCO's needs for funds. Material and work-in-process inventory requirements for systems were substantially larger in proportion to sales than those for the modular product line. These requirements were already having an effect on DENCO's cash position, as is indicated by the company's backlog figures. Early in 1963 the total backlog amounted to $2.3 million. Toward the end of the year the size of the backlog had risen to $6.5 million, of which $4 million represented orders for DENCO's computers. (Exhibits 2 and 3 include recent financial statements.)

A significant characteristic of DENCO's market was that a large proportion of its components and systems was sold either directly or indirectly to the U.S. government. In fiscal 1962, 87% of DENCO's shipments had ultimately been delivered to the government, and most of these sales were made under competitive bid contracts subject to renegotiation. DENCO's deliveries through fiscal 1961 had been reviewed and cleared, however, and management had reported to the shareholders that they believed no refunds would be required on profits earned in fiscal 1962.

DENCO began early to develop a field sales force. By late 1963 it sold entirely through its own sales force operating out of 11 offices spread over the country. Overseas sales were made through independent manufacturers' representatives.

DENCO's success thus appeared to have depended on a combination of research and development skills, which were required to design new products and improve old ones, on its ability to produce these units efficiently, and on a field sales force which could help develop customer applications for DENCO's products. Moreover, since the value of the modules in inventory could be drastically reduced as the result of a sudden change in technology, accurate product forecasting and production control was essential.

DENCO's main office was located in its Pittsburgh facility, which consisted of two modern buildings containing 90,000 square feet of space. The plant was rented under a long-term lease requiring annual rental payments of $185,000. Warehouse space was leased nearby for an additional $4,000 a year. DENCO also leased production facilities in California and in Cleveland. The California plant totaled 7,500 square feet and cost $14,400 a year. The lease had recently been renewed through 1968. The Cleveland subsidiary was located in a new building of 10,000 square feet to which an addition of 10,000 square feet was being constructed. After completion of the addition, rentals under the long-term lease would amount to $25,000. DENCO also was committed to annual rentals of $8,500 for its sales offices throughout the country and to equipment rental charges of $12,800 a month.

Financing to Date

DENCO had traditionally handled all its banking through the Triangle National Bank of Pittsburgh, a medium-sized bank with a reputation for aggressive competition. One of Pittsburgh's largest banks and a large New York bank had both been calling on DENCO with the thought that it would just be a matter of time before DENCO would need to increase its banking relationships.

During most of 1962 and early 1963, DENCO's financial managers were working with an issue of common stock. Early in May of 1962, it had appeared that funds were needed most urgently, and plans had been made to push the stock issue ahead regardless of market conditions. In July the stock issue had been called off because of the market break in late May. DENCO had arranged to satisfy its needs temporarily by borrowing from Triangle against the security of its receivables (85%, without notification to the customers) and of its inventory (50%). Triangle had told DENCO officers that, given the existing equity base, the maximum loan possible without notification was $1.5 million.

Messrs. Grace and Estella expressed annoyance at this limitation, but the New York bank had indicated that in their opinion Triangle was being extremely generous. It pointed out it was unlikely that DENCO customer relations would be hurt if notification proved necessary but suggested that management consider a private placement of convertible debentures. If this alternative turned out to be unattractive, the New York bank had said that it might be willing to consider a joint loan with Triangle. Their offer was not explored more thoroughly because in February, 1963, DENCO was able to sell 130,000 shares of common stock at $8 a share to net $958,750. (DENCO's stock subsequently sold as low as $5⅝. By October, 1963, the price had recovered to $13.)

Despite the February addition of equity capital, DENCO's need for additional funds remained great. By October, 1963, its loan from Triangle was up almost to that bank's legal loan limit of $3 million, and Triangle had proposed that the New York bank take a one-third participation in Triangle's loan to DENCO. DENCO had been borrowing $2.3 million from Triangle on an unsecured line, and Triangle had predicted that DENCO's loan requirements would increase to $4 million or $4.5 million by the end of 1964. DENCO was already planning for another equity issue for early 1964.

Exhibit 1

Five-Year Capital and Financing Plan: 1963–68, Prepared by Mr. Estella, Treasurer

Permanent *new* capital requirements for DENCO depend almost entirely on growth vs. retained profits. Our growth has been rapid—48% per year compounded since 1957, 44% since 1959, 60% since 1961. Our net profits after taxes since 1958 have averaged 2.9% of sales on a straight average basis and 2.7% on a cumulative basis. Profits have not increased our capital rapidly enough to keep up with requirements, resulting in the necessary sale of stock in 1960 and again in 1963.

At the end of this fiscal year, 1963, our net worth will be about 2.3 meg.,* and our fiscal year's shipments about 12 meg. This 19% (capital of sales) is a reasonable amount of capital on which DENCO can presently operate. The planning figure I use is 20%. Our bank loan will be about equal to our net worth (the sum of the two equals 40% of sales). New capital must be raised and received by DENCO within a few months of the point at which our net worth dips below 16% of shipments. (Thus, notes would average 24% of shipments, and 150% of capital.)

The return on the (20%) capital is:

 a) 3% net profit after taxes—3 × 5 = 15% return
 b) 4% net profit after taxes—4 × 5 = 20% return
 c) 5% net profit after taxes—5 × 5 = 25% return

The accompanying table shows a 5-year projection by 6-month periods of shipments at a 40% growth rate per year compound, the (3%) profit-generated capital, and the outside financing required.

In 5 years, shipments grow from 11.5 meg. to 62.3 meg., and net worth from 2.3 meg. to 12.6 meg. Outside capital of 1.5 meg. will be required by November, 1965, and an additional 3.5 meg. by April, 1968. Each financing will require about 12% additional stock.

Earnings per share grow from $0.178 per *6 months* to $0.758 per share, and stock market price (at 45 times 6 months' earnings) from $8.01/share to $34.11/share—an increase of 33.3% per year compound.

Note that, even though profits may *average* 3%, capital will have to be raised sooner (or later) than November, 1965, depending on individual yearly profits and growth. For example, if fiscal year 1964 had 40% growth but 0 profit, *1.2 meg.* of capital would be required during the last half of 1964.

 * NOTE: "Meg.," equals "million."

Exhibit 1 (Continued)

Denco Capital Requirements—Five Years

Six Months to Fiscal Year

	Fiscal Year Nov. 1963	Six Months to Fiscal Year		Six Months to Fiscal Year		Six Months to Fiscal Year		Six Months to Fiscal Year		Six Months to Fiscal Year	
		Apr. 1964	Nov. 1964	Apr. 1965	Nov. 1965	Apr. 1966	Nov. 1966	Apr. 1967	Nov. 1967	Apr. 1968	Nov. 1968
Shipments—six months ending ($ meg.)	6.2	7.4	8.7	10.4	12.2	14.6	17.1	20.4	24.0	28.6	33.7
Shipments—one year ending ($ meg.)	11.5	13.6	16.1	19.1	22.6	26.8	31.7	37.5	44.4	52.6	62.0
Net profit—six months ending (3%) ($ meg.)	0.18	0.22	0.26	0.31	0.37	.44	.51	.61	.72	.86	1.01
Net worth (with added earnings) ($ meg.)	2.30	2.52	2.78	3.09	3.46	3.90	4.41	5.02	5.74	6.60	7.61
Net worth shipments	20.0%	18.5%	17.3%	16.2%	15.3%						
Additional capital (net) ($ meg.)					1.50					3.50	
Net worth—revised ($ meg.)					4.96	5.40	5.91	6.52	7.24	11.60	12.61
Net worth (R)/shipments					21.9%	20.1%	18.6%	17.4%	16.3%	22.1%	20.2%
Shares outstanding (meg.)	1.010	1.010	1.010	1.010	1.132	1.135*	1.135	1.135	1.135	1.273	1.333*
Earnings per share—6 months ($)	0.178	0.218	0.257	0.307	0.327	0.388	0.449	0.537	0.634	.676	.758
Market price/share (45 × 6 months earnings) ($)	8.01	9.81	11.56	13.82	14.72	17.46	20.21	24.16	28.53	30.40	34.11
% stock for additional capital					11.9%					12.2%	

* Stock options (0.03 exercised).

Exhibit 1 (Continued)

It is extremely interesting to note the relationship to net profit of additional capital, earnings per share, and market price per share.

Net Profit as % of Sales	5-Year Cumulative Profit ($ Meg.)	Net Worth Nov. 1968 (No Added Capital)	Additional Capital Required ($ Meg.)	Nov. 1968 6-Months' Earnings ($ Meg.)	Shares Outstanding Nov. 1968 (Meg.)	Nov. 1968 6 Months' Earnings Per Share ($)	Nov. 1968 Stock Price Per Share ($)
1	1.77	4.07	8.5	0.34	2.200	0.154	8.00
2	3.54	5.84	6.8	0.67	1.650	0.406	10.25
3	5.31	7.61	5.0	1.01	1.333	0.758	34.11
4	7.08	9.38	3.2	1.35	1.192	1.133	51.00
5	8.85	11.15	1.5	1.68	1.115	1.507	67.80
6	10.62	12.92	0.0	2.02	1.070	1.887	85.05

Obviously, the higher the profit rate, the less dilution of stock, and the doubly high leverage on stock price. The stock prices per share are based purely on 45 times 6 months' earnings. The consistently demonstrated average earnings will determine the basic stock price. The *potential* stock price in November, 1968 is high if the growth is achieved with low earnings. However, it would take several years after that to demonstrate different earnings.

For reference, growth at 20%, 30%, 40%, and 50% compound rates with 3% net profit results as follows:

Growth Rate per Year (Percent)	Shipments Fiscal Year 1968 ($ Meg.)	5-Year Cumulative Profit ($ Meg.)	Net Worth Nov. 1968 (No Added Capital) ($ Meg.)	Additional Capital Required ($ Meg.)	Nov. 1968 6-Months' Earnings ($ Meg.)	Shares* Outstanding Nov. 1968 (Meg.)	Nov. 1968 6 Months' Earnings Per Share ($)	Nov. 1968 Stock Price Per Share ($)
20	28.7	3.09	5.39	0.4	0.45	1.104	.408	18.36
30	42.9	4.07	6.37	2.3	0.69	1.225	.563	25.33
40	62.3	5.31	7.61	5.0	1.01	1.333	.758	34.11
50	87.8	6.86	9.16	8.6	1.45	1.431	1.013	45.59

To reach the proper operating end point of capital in the above cases, we have sold 3%, 14%, 24%, and 34% more of DENCO stock. However, the November, 1968 stock price per share more than adequately reflects the added investment. By far the best possible operation is to generate profit at a rate (5%–6%) proper to sustain internal growth without added capital.

* Additional capital raised at the average of (**$8.00**/share and the November, 1968 market price/share) less applicable expenses.

Exhibit 2

DIGITAL ENGINEERING COMPANY

Balance Sheets

(dollar figures in thousands)

	Oct. 31 1959	Oct. 27 1960	Oct. 28 1961	Nov. 3 1962	Actual—36 weeks to July 13, 1963	Projected—52 weeks to Nov. 2, 1963
ASSETS						
Cash..........	$ 34	$ 227	$ 84	$ 38	$ 96	$ 70
Accounts receivable..........	507	453	918	1,706	1,950	1,963
Inventories..........	455	613	905	1,603	2,167	3,408
Total current assets....	$ 996	$1,302	$1,907	$3,348	$4,213	$5,441
Fixed assets..........	103	110	145	189	238	250
Other assets..........	21	37	55	28	213	190
Total assets..........	$1,117	$1,453	$2,107	$3,566	$4,662	$5,881
LIABILITIES AND NET WORTH						
Due banks..........	$ 332	$ 444	$ 701	$1,470	$1,450	$2,200
Accounts payable..........	96	129	246	395	592	650
Accrued expenses..........	133	121	283	325	...	...
Accrued taxes..........	157	8	45	321	441	666
Advances on uncompleted contracts....	31	...				
Total current liabilities....	$ 749	$ 702	$1,275	$2,512	$2,483	$3,516
Common stock and capital surplus....	70	656	720	652	1,590	1,590
Retained earnings..........	298	95	112	402	589	775
Net worth..........	$ 368	$ 751	$ 832	$1,054	$2,179	$2,365
Total liabilities and net worth....	$1,117	$1,453	$2,107	$3,566	$4,662	$5,881

Note: These statements have not been adjusted retroactively for a merger in 1961 or to allow for stock splits, stock dividends, etc.

Exhibit 3

DIGITAL ENGINEERING COMPANY

Consolidated Income Statements

(dollar figures in thousands)

Fiscal year ended:

	Oct. 31 1959	Oct. 29 1960	Oct. 28 1961	Nov. 3 1962	Actual—36 weeks ending July 13, 1963	Projected—52 weeks ending Nov. 2, 1963
Net sales...............	$2,870	$ 3,084	$4,812	$8,669	$6,363	$11,100
Cost of sales............	1,794	2,022	3,276	5,155	3,918	6,321
Research, development....	190	344	431	894	600	1,100
Total cost of sales.....	$1,985	$ 2,366	$3,707	$6,049	$4,518	$ 7,421
Gross profit............	$ 885	$ 718	$1,105	$2,621	$2,345	$ 3,679
Selling, administrative, and general expense......	594	905	988	1,936	1,913	2,814
Interest expense.........	9	25	36	76		
Operating income (loss)......	$ 282	$ (12)	$ 81	$ 608	$ 432	$ 865
Other deductions, including profit sharing........	1	4	2	42	30	60
Income (loss) before taxes....	$ 281	$ (17)	$ 79	$ 567	$ 402	$ 805
Provision for taxes......	136	2	36	277	209	426
Net income (loss).......	$ 145	$ (19)	$ 43	$ 290	$ 193	$ 379
Shares outstanding (000's)...	779	901	895	880		
Net income (loss) per share....	$0.186	$(0.021)	$0.048	$0.33		

Note: These statements have been adjusted retroactively for a merger in 1961 and for stocks splits and stock dividends, etc.

Illuminated Tubes Company

"Howard, it looks now as though they're really going to strike the set makers. Leonard Moore, head of purchasing over at Television Corporation of America (TCA), called me this morning. He said the union people walked out of the bargaining session last night. The way everyone's mad at everyone else, this could be a long, bitter strike. And I'm afraid we stand to lose more than anyone else. With our new rectangular color tube nobody can touch us. If sales kept on as they have recently, we could be the top picture tube maker in a couple of months. This strike couldn't have come at a worse time!"

On April 1, 1965, the day before an expected strike of the North American Electrical Workers against all the major television set manufacturers, Mr. Robert Morse, executive vice president of Illuminated Tubes Company (IT), expressed his irritation to an assistant, Howard Jones. In April, 1965, IT was one of three principal producers of color television picture tubes. (One of the others was also a major set manufacturer.) All of IT's sales were to the set makers for use in new sets. Since 1963 IT had increased its share of the market from 25% to 35%. IT's competitors had 50% and 15% of the market.

"There's just one thing that will save us," Mr. Morse continued. "We've got to hope that the set makers will try hard to settle early, in order not to miss out on this current sales boom. If they hold out long, the Japanese might improve their color sets and flood the market. If that happened, lost sales would be permanently lost, not just postponed.

"When I spoke to Len Moore, he said that as of the end of this week he'd have to temporarily cancel TCA's open order for color picture tubes. I'm sure we can expect the same word from the other makers, too, before the day is out. That means for the duration of the strike there will be virtually no sales at all. We're certainly going to have to reconsider our production plans.

"The big question in my mind is, how long will the strike last? If it doesn't go too long and no foreign sets enter the market, as soon as the set manufacturers can start producing again they'll really want to push to make up lost sales. If that's the case, we're going to have to have the tubes ready, or we'll lose any chance of improving our market share. In fact, since we're operating near capacity now, if the set makers push up volume and we don't have the inventory, we could actually lose some of our market share. Our competitors still have a good deal of unused capacity.

"I'd like to continue operating at full capacity for other reasons, too. It can be very expensive to lay workers off. I'd hate to think of trying to get back to capacity if we had to recruit and train new glass workers. These people are pretty skilled, and there are other jobs in the glass industry. If our workers did not wait to be rehired by us, we'd have to look for new people.

"Then too, shutting down would hurt relations with our suppliers. We're the only customer some of them have, and if we shut down they might go out of business for good. We have a 30-day supply of materials on hand now and another 30 days' worth on order. We could cancel the outstanding orders, but there would be considerable expense in doing so in terms of financial penalties and damaged supplier relations."

"All you say sounds reasonable," Mr. Jones interjected, "so much so that I'm not sure there's any choice. The risks and costs of shutting down are too great; we've got to keep producing!"

"Howard, you're right, we've got to, but I'm not sure we can, or at least I'm not sure how long we can. That's why I said the length of the strike is crucial. I don't know how long an inventory buildup our finances can stand.

"Of course, if we were really in straitened circumstances, we might be able to borrow from our banks, but I shouldn't want to depend on that. We could never be sure until we actually needed it how much money we could get. Besides, by borrowing we might use up our last reserve of financial strength to meet possible future difficulties. In making our decisions, I think we'd better not consider borrowing money. Let's leave borrowing for when we really need it.

"Look, here are financial statements (Exhibits 1 and 2) for the last 2 years as well as for the quarter just ended. I wish you would try to figure how our cash position and overall financial position would be affected by continued operations. If we were to continue to operate at full capacity, see what would happen if the strike lasted 1, 2, or 3 months. Also, for those same time periods, see what our financial position would look like if we were to shut down immediately. Why don't you also determine our balance sheet position one month after the strike ends, after accounts receivable have had a chance to build up again? To begin, you can use these rough profit and loss statements I've worked up for a month's operations (Exhibit 3); as long as the strike lasts, one month will look pretty much like the next. As you can see, I've forecast continued selling and administrative expenditures. Since strikes get settled, I can't see firing salesmen and secretaries and ruining the organization we've so painfully built up.

"Besides salary payments we can expect a cash drain from income tax payments of about $100,000 in April and $600,000 in June. However, we'll be able to claim a tax refund from the government equal to about half of our operating loss. I don't know how quickly the government will credit us with the cash, though. Until we check with our tax lawyers, we had better not count this tax loss as a source of funds."

With a sense of urgency, Howard Jones began to peruse IT's financial statements. Besides the suggestions Mr. Morse had made, he realized that if the strike lasted 3 months, the situation might be made more difficult by special cash needs in July. On July 1, $200,000 of the long-term debt would come due. In addition, it had also been the custom of IT's board to declare a dividend payable on the 15th of January, April, July, and October; for the last two quarters, IT had paid 25 cents a share. For his first projections he decided to assume that both the debt payments and dividends would be paid.

Exhibit 1

ILLUMINATED TUBES COMPANY

Balance Sheets, as of December 31, 1963 and 1964, and March 31, 1965

(dollar figures in thousands)

ASSETS		December 31, 1963		December 31, 1964		March 31, 1965
Cash...................		$ 2,012		$ 1,994		$ 1,718
Accounts receivable........		1,543		1,829		2,128
Inventory						
Raw materials..........$	319		$ 372		$ 431	
Goods in process........	191		233		238	
Finished goods..........	337		391		409	
Total inventory.....		847		996		1,078
Total current assets..		$ 4,402		$ 4,819		$ 4,924
Plant and equipment.......$11,263			$12,741		$13,256	
Less: Depreciation.......	2,010		2,792		3,082	
Plant and equip- ment, net.........		$ 9,253		$ 9,949		$10,174
Total assets.........		$13,655		$14,768		$15,098
LIABILITIES AND NET WORTH						
Taxes payable.............		$ 830		$ 1,010		$ 1,050
Accounts payable and accruals...............		992		1,242		1,285
Dividends payable........		150		250		250
Other current liabilities.....		429		372		220
Total current liabilities........		$ 2,401		$ 2,874		$ 2,805
Long-term debt..........		2,700		2,300		2,300
Total liabilities......		$ 5,101		$ 5,174		$ 5,105
Common stock, $5 par.....		5,000		5,000		5,000
Paid-in capital...........		2,659		2,659		2,659
Retained earnings........		895		1,935		2,334
		$13,655		$14,768		$15,098

Exhibit 2

ILLUMINATED TUBES COMPANY

Income Statements, Years Ended December 31, 1963 and 1964, and 3 months
Ended March 31, 1965

(dollar figures in thousands)

	Year Ended December 31, 1963		*Year Ended December 31, 1964*		*3 Months Ended March 31, 1965*	
Net sales...............		$17,743		$21,175		$5,942
Cost of sales						
Materials..............$3,921			$4,734		$1,321	
Direct labor........... 3,038			4,104		1,236	
Other................. 3,025			3,162		720	
Total cost of sales..		9,984		12,000		3,277
Gross margin......		$ 7,759		$ 9,175		$2,665
Selling and administrative expenses*.............		4,424		5,000		1,413
Operating profit....		$ 3,335		$ 4,175		$1,252
Income tax.............		1,734		2,088		599
Net income........		$ 1,601		$ 2,087		$ 653

* Includes depreciation:
   $ 875 thousand in 1963
   $1,036 thousand in 1964
   $ 341 thousand for the first 3 months of 1965.

Exhibit 3

Projected Monthly Income Statements for Illuminated Tubes Company
(dollar figures in thousands)

	During Strike		*After Strike*	
	If Tubes Are Produced	*If Factory Shuts Down*	*If Tubes Were Produced for Inventory*	*No Finished Goods Inventory Buildup*
Sales....................	...	...	$2,500*	$2,000*
Cost of sales†				
Materials..............	...	...	$ 560	$ 450
Direct labor...........	...	...	520	420
Other.................	...	$300	310	300
Total cost of sales...	...	$300	$1,390	$1,170
Gross margin...........	...	($300)	$1,110	$ 830
Selling and administrative expenses‡.............	$400	400	400	400
Operating profit..........	($400)	($700)	$ 710	$ 430
Income tax.............	(200)	(350)	350	210
Net income..............	($200)	($350)	$ 360	$ 220

* Assumes that sales with large finished goods inventories are 25% greater than they would be were
there no significant finished goods inventory to sell from.
   † Approximately $3.6 million of cost of sales at an annual rate is fixed no matter what volume is pro-
duced. If IT produces tubes for inventory, this $3.6 million is charged to inventory and is not an expense.
If nothing is produced, the $3.6 million cannot be charged to inventory and must be expensed.
   ‡ Includes $100 thousand of depreciation.

The Case of the Unidentified Investment Projects

Imagine a corporate investment committee faced with a very unusual problem. Eight different proposals have been presented for approval and they are similar in only one respect: the initial capital outlay required in each case is $160,000. In all other respects, including the expected stream of financial benefits, they are very different. The financial details are shown in Exhibit 1.

The company in question does not have the capital that would permit it to do all eight projects ($1,280,000) even if it wanted to, and so it must decide its order of preference among these alternatives. You are asked to do the analysis necessary to enable the company to rank the projects from the point of view of financial benefit alone.

In approaching this problem consider the following questions:

1. Before doing any calculations, can you determine simply by inspection of Exhibit 1 what the ranking should be? If you cannot rank from one through eight by inspection, can you identify some projects that are clearly preferable to some others?
2. What methods for calculating a ranking can be employed which will provide useful information to the company?
3. What are the results which follow from using these methods of analysis? Do the ranking results differ from one method to another? Can you explain why the differences occur?
4. How would you rank the ranking methods—which would you prefer to use? Why?
5. What kinds of real investment opportunities could have the cash flow characteristics of the several projects shown in Exhibit 1?
6. How did your analytical results come out in comparison to your "eyeball" analysis of question 1?

Exhibit 1

Investment Proposals Providing a Range of Cash Flow Benefits

				Project				
	1	*2*	*3*	*4*	*5*	*6*	*7*	*8*
Initial investment..............	$160,000	$160,000	$160,000	$160,000	$160,000	$160,000	$160,000	$160,000
Resulting change in after-tax cash flows								
Year 1....................	$103,000	$ 18,800	$ 83,000	$ 32,000	$ 25,000	$ (19,000)	$ 12,000	$171,000*
2....................	59,000*	18,800	72,000	24,000	26,000	(7,000)	44,000	
3....................	24,000	18,800	37,000*	24,000	27,000	9,000	69,000	
4....................			12,000	24,000	28,000	26,000	47,000*	
5....................			7,000	24,000	28,000	53,000	38,000	
6....................				24,000	29,000*	72,000	24,000	
7....................				24,000*	29,000	47,000*	(42,000)	
8....................		18,800*		104,000	30,000	36,000		
9....................					30,000	102,000		
10....................					84,000			
11....................								
12....................								
13....................								
14....................								
15....................		18,800						
Sum of cash flow benefits.....	$186,000	$282,000	$211,000	$280,000	$336,000	$319,000	$192,000	$171,000
Excess over initial investment...	$ 26,000	$122,000	$ 51,000	$120,000	$176,000	$159,000	$ 32,000	$ 11,000

* Asterisk indicates year in which payback is accomplished.

The Zenith Steel Company, Inc.

In October, 1961, Zenith Steel Company, one of the nation's larger steel manufacturers, had just experienced its worst quarter since the first quarter of 1956. For the first 9 months of 1961, Zenith's net profit of $14.4 million ran 58% below 1960 for the same period as a result of a sales drop of 5%. With a 9-month net profit of just $0.45 per share, Zenith was headed for its worst year since 1956 and was unlikely to cover the 1960 dividend of $0.80 (Exhibit 1).

By comparison with results reported by its major competitor, Blakely Steel, Zenith's situation was even worse. Blakely Steel reported 9-month sales of $2.1 billion, up 2.8% over 1960, and net profits of $102 million, down a comparatively mild 11%. However, even though investors tended to compare the two companies, their situations were different. Zenith relied much more than Blakely Steel on sales of light-gauge steel products (66% in 1960 vs. 43% for Blakely Steel). Light-gauge products constituted a large proportion of the steel requirements of the automotive and container industries and of other consumer goods manufacturers.

The Pittsburgh Division of Zenith was comprised of semifinishing mills where the first rolling operations were performed on the ingots and plate, and sheet and strip mills where the slabs were further processed into finished light-gauge steel sheets and plates. The main customers of the Pittsburgh Division were the automobile manufacturers.

Conditions in the automotive industry were not good, as the management at the Pittsburgh, Pennsylvania, headquarters of the Pittsburgh Division of Zenith Steel well knew. Continued pressure from customers for lower prices backed by potential European competition, coupled with rising costs, were narrowing margins. In addition, not only had motor vehicle production dropped 17% in 1961 but also the compact cars accounted for 33% of domestic production in 1961 as compared to 13% in 1959, thus lowering still further the steel tonnage used in production.

669

Although historically the Pittsburgh Division had been a sizable profit producer, 1960 had been a subnormal profit year and the failure of the Pittsburgh Division to move back into a high-profit position was a matter of grave corporate concern. In view of the bleak prospects for profit performance in the near future, the decentralized management of the various divisions had been instructed to determine and institute programs of immediate cost reduction and profit improvement.

Mr. C. C. Johnston, executive assistant to the vice president and general manager of the Pittsburgh Division, was in addition manager of management services. In this role, he had discussed with George Ray, manager of the business systems staff, the need for prompt improvement in profits and had asked Ray to look at the operations of his department and report back with recommendations. (Exhibit 2 shows the organization of the Pittsburgh Division.)

The business systems staff provided data processing services and management consulting services on systems and procedures to the three profit centers of the Pittsburgh Division. Service functions such as those provided by business systems were budgeted on the basis of estimated usage and costs. Per-hour charges were then calculated to cover these costs. Any profit or loss incurred by the department was credited or charged to the profit centers in proportion to their billings at the end of the year.

Therefore, the only way Ray could affect profits directly was to reduce the cost of his services. The major expenditures of his department were rental for the IBM 705 system and wages of the technical and administrative staff. Over $690,000 was forecast for machine rental in 1962, out of $1,250,000 estimated total expenditures for his organization. Ray knew that this equipment could be purchased for approximately $2 million. He also knew that under Zenith's system of corporate financing, funds were made available to the various divisions from time to time on a loan basis by corporate headquarters. The current charge to the division for such a loan was $3\frac{1}{2}\%$ per annum. He decided to call in John Steele, the resident IBM representative, to discuss the possibility of purchase of all or some part of the 705 system.

The possibility of buying IBM equipment had been considered briefly in 1957. When the original equipment had been installed in 1955, IBM did not offer their equipment for sale. However, in January, 1956, the Justice Department obtained from IBM a consent decree requiring IBM to set prices on its products and offer them for sale. At that time, Ray's predecessor had decided that the capabilities of the then existing system would not be sufficient for even the short-term future and that purchase would not be advantageous.

At the time of his visit in response to Ray's call, Steele left some literature on rent-or-buy analysis with Ray and promised to send him a detailed breakdown of installed and ordered equipment with rental and purchase figures (Exhibits 3 and 4).

Various detailed studies of anticipated needs for data processing services over the next five years had been completed the previous summer. As a result of these studies, the computer had recently been converted to a new high-speed tape system capable of reading and writing 62,500 characters per second as contrasted to the 15,000 characters per second capability of the old system. With this new system, anticipated needs through 1965 were expected to be met easily on a two-shift basis. Both Ray and Steele thought that these studies were realistic and that, barring some major, unanticipated change, the present system would provide the most economical means of providing the services required.

Ray did not think that physical obsolescence would be a problem for at least five years. The original 705 Model I had been installed in July, 1956, updated to a Model II in 1957 and the present Model III installed in July, 1960. It was also thought that there was very little chance of upgrading the 705 further. The internal rate of the machine would not allow a faster tape drive, and in fact the 705 had now been superseded by the 7080 and was no longer in production. The 7080 was much too big for Zenith, and the additional annual rental of $180,000 made it too costly to be considered. In fact, it would require approximately double the anticipated requirements for 1965 to be economical. There had been some talk that IBM might develop an intermediate machine to fill the gap between the 705 and 7080, but there was no definite information on this.

Since its installation in 1956, the 705 system had involved an annual expenditure of 35–40 man-years of engineering at a cost of approximately $10,000 per man-year in developing new computer programs. It was estimated that conversion of existing programs would take anywhere from 50–75 man-years. Therefore, Ray felt that even if new equipment were available today, it would take approximately a year to appraise and analyze the equipment and reach a positive decision. At this point it would take an additional two years to convert existing programs. The various procedures and systems in use could not be halted for conversion, and parallel data processing units (the old and the new) would most likely have to be run until all programs were converted and "debugged." In other words, present equipment would be needed for at least three years.

In addition, the recent study indicated that the conversion to faster tape provided sufficient capacity to handle anticipated needs over at least the next five years. While modifications to computing equipment were being made constantly, Ray felt that machine capability was well ahead of man's ability to utilize it and that it would require changes of a very major nature to warrant the substantial costs of conversion. In Ray's opinion, even though the lease could be canceled on 30 days' notice, the practicalities of the situation meant that Zenith was "locked in" for at least three years.

When Ray received Steele's figures, he determined that $2,033,283 would be the cost of the required equipment including sales and excise taxes. In order to help him in his analysis, he gathered together some other figures from present costs and projected costs over the next five years. Estimated rental costs based on projected requirements would be: 1962—$690,000; 1963—$710,000; 1964—$724,000; 1965—$745,000; and 1966—$760,000.

These rental charges included certain expenses that would have to be continued even if the equipment were purchased. Ray then listed these:

1. Certain items of tab equipment (not included in Exhibit 4) would not be purchased and would involve rental charges of $44,767 in 1962 and $28,572 each year thereafter.
2. Maintenance cost was estimated at $66,792 in 1962; $69,529 in 1963; $74,943 in 1964; $79,619 in 1965; and $83,753 in 1966. These maintenance charges were based on present contractual rates. They were based on the number of hours the equipment was used and included all labor and parts. Any change in rates would most likely be reflected in rental charges as well.
3. IBM's rental charges included insurance on the equipment. Ray estimated that this insurance could be purchased by Zenith Steel for $7,000 per year.

If it was necessary to change models during the next five years, Ray was sure that some allowance would be received for their present system. IBM put out a schedule of trade-in allowances which could change at any time but had been in effect for several years. According to this schedule, the following allowances would be made after varying periods from the installation date: 1 year—60% of original cost; 2 years—48%; 3 years —36%; 4 years—24%; 5 years—15%; 6 years—7½%.

With this information in hand, Ray believed he was in a position to proceed to organize the material and prepare a presentation for Mr. Johnston.

Exhibit 1

Selected Financial Data

(thousands of dollars)

	1960	1959	1958	1957	1956	1955
Net sales.	1,320,119	1,289,693	1,279,597	1,356,105	1,020,629	972,659
Profit after taxes.	53,364	58,014	40,472	49,041	2,357	28,892
Preferred dividends.	1,100	1,162	1,212	1,266	1,275	1,283
Common dividends.	28,001	24,406	22,944	22,656	22,460	22,193
Profit per common share.	1.50	1.64	1.43	1.41	.03	.83
Dividends per common share. . . .	.80	.70	.65	.65	.65	.65
Book value per common share. . . .	17.88	17.13	16.18	15.39	14.57	15.16
Market price of common on NYSE (range).	77–66	74¾–47⅝	50¼–37½	46⅜–35⅜	44½–34⅜	56¼–35⅞

Exhibit 2

Pittsburgh Division

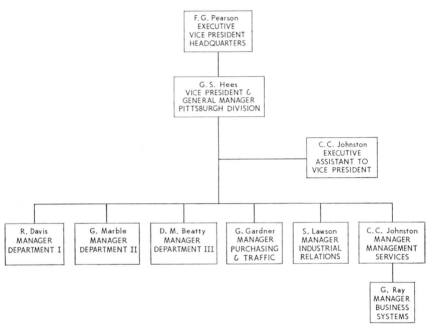

Exhibit 3

Excerpts from IBM General Information Manual—A Rent-or-Buy Analysis

Basic Concepts of the Rent-or-Buy Problem

The question of whether to rent or buy IBM data processing machines or systems can be analyzed in the same manner that the value (or rate of return) of other business investment opportunities is examined. Since the business need for the equipment has been generated by data handling requirements, the only problem remaining is whether purchase or rental is the best financial policy. Companies utilize different approaches in analyzing this kind of problem. The most common techniques are:

> The payout method.
> The average annual savings method.
> The present-value method.

The payout method determines the number of years required to simply recover the principal of an investment while earning a zero rate of return. This method overemphasizes the "short-payment" investments.

In the "average annual savings" method the total savings are calculated (accumulated rentals less purchase expenses) from a capital investment and then an average of these savings is made over the expected life of the investment. This average savings is divided by the initial investment to yield a rate of return. Because all savings are averaged, two shortcomings become apparent:

1. The savings are considered to occur at the middle of the investment life, and the time value of money is not considered.
2. This averaging process does not distinguish between investments having the most return in the early years and those having the most return in the later years.

Exhibit 3 (Continued)

The present-value method (sometimes called the investors method) is more inclusive because it not only considers the time distribution of an irregular pattern of savings accruing in the future but it also evaluates the rate of return that the business is continually earning upon the unrecovered balance of the original investment.

The Concept of Present Value

The Time Value of Money. It is almost axiomatic that a dollar received 10 years from today is not worth as much as a dollar possessed today. Ignoring the effects of inflation and deflation, the truth of this statement arises from the existence of interest rates. To finance the purchase of plant and equipment by borrowing money requires the payment of interest for the use of this money. Even if money does not have to be borrowed to finance these purchases, but available funds are used, interest as a cost must be considered just as much as if it had been paid out. "In this situation, interest is a cost in the sense of an opportunity foregone, an economic sacrifice of a possible income that might have been obtained by investment elsewhere."[1]

The Effect of Interest on "Present Value." The fact that a dollar received tomorrow is worth less than a dollar today is best explained by an illustrative example:

Suppose $100 is deposited in a savings bank account which pays 3% interest compounded annually. At the end of the first year, this would amount to $103 ($100 plus 3% × 100) and at the end of the second year, $106.09 ($103 plus 3% × $103). This example could be continued indefinitely; it illustrates the fact that investing money at some interest rate causes a dollar to be worth more at some future date than it is worth at present. This example can be turned around to show that $106.09 two years from now is worth only $100 today (discounted at 3% annually). Thus, it can be said that the "present value" of $106.09 two years from now is only $100. The amount of money S which a person would receive at the end of n periods of time if that person deposited P dollars in a bank which paid a compound interest rate of $i\%$ is given by the following equation:

$$S = P(1 + i)^n$$

Thus, P is the amount of money that would have to be invested today at compound interest rate of $i\%$ in order to have an amount S in n periods.

In all cases where the interest rate is more than zero, S is always greater than P. This means that the present value of any sum of money to be received in the future is always less than some future sum of money, provided interest can be obtained on that money.

Avoided Costs Are Economically Equivalent to Income

It is also true that not having to pay out a given sum is equivalent to the receipt of income. An example may help to illustrate the validity of this principle. Suppose one arranged with his landlord to pay him an amount equal to 11 months' rent at the beginning of the year instead of paying him 1 month's rent 12 times throughout the year. The landlord might agree to this even though, at first glance, it appeared that he was losing 1 month's rent. Actually, if he did agree, it would be because he could invest the lump sum at an interest rate which would yield him a sum at the end of the year equal to or greater than 12 months' rent received throughout the year. From the tenant's point of view, the payment of the lump sum at the beginning of the year is the price he was willing to pay to avoid having to pay out a stream of 12 monthly sums. This would be the same as if the choice open to the tenant were the payment of a lump sum in return for *receiving* an income stream of 12 monthly sums.

The Costs and Savings to a Purchaser

The user of IBM data processing equipment incurs the following costs if a decision is made to buy rather than to rent the equipment:

a) The purchase price.
b) The federal manufacturer's excise tax on the purchase price.
c) The local sales taxes.
d) Personal property taxes.
e) Insurance premiums.

[1] E. D. Grant, *Principles of Engineering Economy* (3d ed., New York: Ronald Press Co. 1950), p. 72.

Exhibit 3 (Continued)

f) State and federal capital gains taxes where applicable.
g) Maintenance charges.

There are also those elements which represent savings or avoided costs (equivalent to income) and which partially offset the purchaser's cash expenditure:

a) Tax savings due to depreciation for federal and state income tax purposes.
b) The salvage value in dollars at the end of the useful life of the equipment.
c) The monthly rental charges.
d) The federal manufacturer's excise tax on the monthly rental charges.
e) Local use taxes.

Exhibit 4

Summary of Equipment in Total 705 Installation

Machine and Serial no.	Description	Monthly Charge*	Purchase Price at Time of Installation	Age as of 1/1/62 (Months)	Purchase Prices Jan. 1, 1962
705 System					
705–20033	CPU	$17,370	$ 860,150	17	$ 738,301.15
727–23763	Tape Unit	550	18,200	38	12,436.61
727–23764	Tape Unit	550	18,200	38	12,436.61
729–20437	Tape Unit	900	41,250	6	39,187.50
729–20440	Tape Unit	900	41,250	6	39,187.50
729–20441	Tape Unit	900	41,250	6	39,187.50
729–20445	Tape Unit	900	41,250	6	39,187.50
729–20448	Tape Unit	900	41,250	6	39,187.50
729–20449	Tape Unit	900	41,250	6	39,187.50
729–20450	Tape Unit	900	41,250	6	39,187.50
729–20451	Tape Unit	900	41,250	6	39,187.50
729–20452	Tape Unit	900	41,250	6	39,187.50
729–61015	Tape Unit	900	41,250	6	39,187.50
734–10011	Magnetic Drum	2,300	90,000	65	41,250.00
744–10011	Drum Control	500	21,500	65	9,854.00
745–20034	Power Supply	1,500	100,000	17	85,834.00
754–10064	Tape Control	1,500	78,000	38	53,299.74
782–20033	Console	1,100	58,000	17	49,783.72
721–11012	Tape Control	3,000	105,000	6	99,750.00
		$37,370	$1,761,550		$1,494,820.83

Exhibit 4 (Continued)

Machine and Serial no.	Description	Monthly Charge*	Purchase Price at Time of Installation	Age as of 1/1/62 (Months)	Purchase Prices Jan. 1, 1962
1401 Model C-3 System					
1401–20154	CPU	$ 3,560	$ 162,135	8	$ 151,327.08
1402–20026	Reader-Punch	550	30,000	8	28,000.20
1403–10466	Printer	775	34,000	8	31,733.56
729–72144	Tape Unit	700	36,000	8	33,600.24
729–72220	Tape Unit	700	36,000	8	33,600.24
		$ 6,285	$ 298,135		$ 278,261.32
1401 Model D-11 System†					*Purchase Prices May, 1962*
1401	CPU	$ 1,945	$ 126,000‡		$ 126,000.00
1403	Printer	775	34,000‡		34,000.00
7330	Tape Unit	450	22,000‡		22,000.00
		$ 3,170	$ 182,000‡		$ 182,000.00
Total of all units		$46,825	$2,241,685		$1,955,082.15

* Monthly charge based on 176 hours of use. Each additional hour billed at 40% of monthly charge divided by 176.
† Scheduled for delivery May, 1962.
‡ Subject to change prior to delivery.

Liberty Petroleum Company

In the fall of 1965 the officers of Liberty Petroleum Company were considering what price to bid for a large tract of timberland in southern Georgia. The proposed acquisition involved a considerable amount of cash as well as a major commitment in a field of endeavor that was relatively new to Liberty.

For years an important integrated oil company, Liberty in the late 1950's began a program of diversification into many agricultural and industrial chemical fields. The company had grown steadily throughout its history but especially so in the early 1960's as the demand for its products increased greatly. Annual sales for the year 1965 were expected to amount to about $360 million and total assets to about $550 million. Net profits would be about $45 million, and the return on invested capital 11.5%.[1]

Diversification Program

In the course of its diversification program, Liberty purchased a major interest in Duride Corporation in 1963. Duride was a producer of natural glues and resins for the plywood industry and for the particle-board and pulp and paper industry. Its plant was located in northern California, but at the time of acquisition by Liberty, the Duride management was in the process of constructing an additional plant in the Southeast to supply the rapidly growing southern pine plywood industry. The Liberty executives felt that Duride was a natural extension of its petrochemical diversification activities, since Duride consumed both phenol and urea, which

---

[1] "Invested capital" (or "capitalization") is usually the difference between total assets and current liabilities. If the amounts are large, intangible assets may be deducted, and portions of the current debt that are expected to "roll over" may be added.

679

Liberty was already producing, as well as formaldehyde, which Liberty planned to develop.

In late 1964, under the direction of the president, a group of officers began to analyze the merits of diversification into the forest products industry, primarily the plywood manufacturing field. Such diversification would embody a "wood fiber and chemicals" concept, which was rapidly coming to the fore in industry literature. According to industry sources, the chemical value in forest products such as plywood, particle-board, and other types of building materials would in a very short period of time be at least equal to the value of the fiber content. Liberty was already supplying certain basic raw materials for plywood and particle-board through its interest in Duride. It appeared that through this means Liberty would continue to be in a position to supply the various plastic coatings and lamination materials that in future years would occupy a prominent role in the fabrication of such building products. The acquisition of a plywood company by an oil company would not be unprecedented. One of Liberty's competitors, a large midwestern oil company, had made a similar move the previous year.

Liberty, therefore, entered the forest products field by the acquisition of United Plywood Company, a customer of Duride. United Plywood was one of the country's largest plywood manufacturers, with four plants in the Pacific Northwest and one in Georgia, the latter a part of the rapidly growing pine plywood industry in the South. Despite limited financial resources, United Plywood had been one of the first companies to undertake an expansion program in the South. Many of its stronger competitors had subsequently followed. The Liberty executives had been impressed by the youthful and aggressive management of United Plywood and had felt that if these people had the capital availability which Liberty could provide, and which United Plywood lacked, the company could experience considerable growth.

The Duncan Timberlands

United Plywood's southern pine plywood mill was adjacent to the timber reserves owned by the Duncan family in southern Georgia. The Duncan family owned roughly 100,000 acres of prime pine timberland in the area and in the early 1960's had begun looking for a way to realize on the value of its properties. Hence, when United Plywood came into the South in 1963 investigating raw material supplies for a plywood plant, the association between United Plywood and the Duncan timberlands had been a natural one. In late 1964 United Plywood was awarded a contract for the right to the sawtimber growth on the Duncan properties for a period of 15 years, amounting to between 12 and 18 million board feet per year. United Plywood also made similar contracts with several smaller landowners in the area.

When discussing long-range plans with officers of United Plywood in the latter part of 1965, the president of Liberty learned that the Duncan family would soon sell its property for reasons of estate planning. Since the Liberty officers had already considered the possibility of a greater commitment in forest products, it appeared logical for them to consider the acquisition of the Duncan timber products, adjacent to United Plywood's southern mill. In addition, it appeared that the Duncan properties might also have some interest to Liberty from a mineral standpoint, although no surveys of this possibility had been made.

The Liberty officers felt that they must reach a decision quickly, because of the competition for timberlands. Further evaluation of the possible acquisition became the task of Mr. Henry Jonas, the assistant treasurer of Liberty.

It was understood that the Duncan family would sell for cash. The figure of $18 million had been mentioned. During the preceding 12 to 18 months, timber properties in the South had been selling for values regarded by people in the industry as quite exorbitant. High prices were being paid by companies whose managements felt that they must have a position in southern pine timber if they were to remain a factor in their industry. They were paying what might be termed "insurance" values for large tracts of property. Although the Liberty officers were aware of this type of competition for large properties, certain circumstances indicated to them that Liberty might be able to purchase timberlands for what the Liberty management would consider a more "realistic" price than $18 million.

The dominant circumstance was that United Plywood held the right to the sawtimber growth on the Duncan property, and this right was accompanied by a very favorable stumpage or sawtimber price, since the contract had been entered into before the increase in values had been established. To a third-party purchaser looking for a southern pine timber position for either plywood or pulp and paper manufacture, this circumstance meant, first, that the growth from the property would be unavailable to it during the first 15 years of its ownership, because the growth was already committed to the United Plywood mill. In other words, the property must be held for the first 15 years simply as a passive investment. Second, even if the third-party purchaser was willing to hold the property during that period simply as an investment, the capitalized earnings value it could afford to pay for the property would be rather modest because of the low price at which the timber was committed to United Plywood.

Liberty's valuation of the property, of course, would also be inhibited by this circumstance. Since Liberty owned United Plywood, it actually would achieve indirectly the benefit of the advantageous price itself.

With these thoughts in mind, the executives of Liberty retained the forestry consulting firm of Jackson & Jackson, Natchez, Mississippi, to prepare a valuation of the Duncan properties. It was agreed that the analysis should proceed from cash flow estimates and not accounting data. Thus, it would be necessary to determine the after-tax cash flows expected in each of the years to be studied. In addition, since the cash flows would be affected by the assumptions made (because of the tax shields developed from depletion expenses, which were based on cost), it was decided to explore the results from purchase prices of $10, $15, $18, and $20 million.

Method of Valuation

The valuation might be sensitive to two factors in the environment. The first was the pattern of sawtimber and pulpwood selling prices to be assumed for the sales from the property in the future years after the expiration of the 15-year contract. It was finally decided to test the valuation under three pricing patterns, the low, medium, and upper price projections. These levels were based on historical records and the judgment of the consultants.

The second environmental factor to which the valuation might be sensitive was the timber-cutting pattern under which the property would be managed. One cutting pattern would involve the assumption of sustained-yield management, wherein the cut from the property would be limited to the annual growth from the property. Based upon accepted rules of thumb regarding restocking and sales price, the value of the property at the end of 30 years would be $14,592,870, which was taken as the terminal value for the analysis. This figure was expected to approximate the book value of the property at that time.

A second cutting pattern was an accelerated cut, wherein the property would actually be cut at a rate exceeding the annual growth, thereby gradually depleting the property. This assumption would be studied to see whether an acceleration of timber revenues would have an effect on the present values of the property significant enough to give the technique serious consideration. The study was especially important given the severe reduction in terminal value with the use of an accelerated cut. A happy medium had to be found regarding the degree of acceleration, however, so that the property would retain some value to the plywood mills as a long-term source of raw material supply. For example, it would have been possible to assume a cut that within a few years would leave the forest lands producing only pulpwood and yielding no sawtimber at all for the plywood mills. Such a result would have been somewhat in conflict with the original reason for purchasing the properties. At the end of 30 years this cutting method would leave mostly pulpwood, with an estimated final value for the property of $7,714,634.

To summarize the first steps of the analysis, it was decided to analyze the property under three different price conditions, two different cutting pattern conditions, and four purchase price assumptions. This required working out 24 different detailed cash flow calculations. Jackson & Jackson were instructed to make the calculations of value before giving effect to any method of financing that might be chosen for the project. They thus prepared an all-equity cash flow analysis based upon the stated assumptions.

The analysis began with an estimate of potential cash receipts for each of 30 years under the 24 sets of assumptions. The estimate involved assumptions as to the amount of lumber to be taken from the land and the prices to be paid for various grades of timber. That is, the expected yields of pine pulpwood, pine sawtimber, hardwood pulpwood, and hardwood sawtimber for each of the 30 years were multiplied by the prices assumed to be applicable to those items and years.

The consultants next estimated the various expenses associated with management of the timberland. These included the costs of surveying, administration, and sales, as well as the capitalized cost for planting and the equipment necessary to maintain the property as a continuing source of timber supply. Estimates were made for each of the 30 years so as to determine an inflow-outflow relationship between sales and expenses.

Since tax regulations made provision for depletion of natural resources, the final segment of the consultants' report concerned detailed projections of future inventory and depletion accounts. These projections, too, were made for a 30-year period on an annual basis so that a yearly federal tax figure could be estimated, given the applicable 25% tax rate. This permitted determination of the net annual cash throw-off on an all-equity basis.

Discounted cash flow rates of return on investment were then calculated by computer for each of the 24 combinations of purchase price, cutting pattern, and selling price. Graphic summaries of the results are presented in Exhibits 1 and 2. Exhibit 1 illustrates the rates of return associated with the various purchase prices under the assumption of a sustained cut at three different price levels. Exhibit 2 is similar except for the assumption that an accelerated rate of cut would be utilized on the property.

Financing

After studying the all-equity charts, the Liberty executives decided that the most reasonable set of assumptions was that of a sustained-yield cut and a medium price level. Since Liberty used 7.5% as the cost of its invested capital, the purchase obviously was not feasible at the asking price of $18 million. The internal rate of return at that price was 4.8%. In fact, a price slightly under $12 million was indicated. This amount would surely be unsatisfactory to the Duncans.

Upon hearing of this decision, the consultants suggested that the rate of return on Liberty's investment might be increased by the use of a loan secured by the value of the timberlands. Another client of theirs had recently obtained from a large insurance company a 15-year 5.4% direct reduction mortgage loan of 50% of the purchase price of a similar property. The consultants therefore were authorized to explore the effects of using debt to finance half of the $18 million asking price of the Duncan property.

The consultants' analysis then proceeded to adjust the all-equity flows for the effect of $9 million of debt financing, thus reducing Liberty's equity investment to $9 million. It was assumed, on the basis of the recent loan made by the insurance company, that the principal amount of the financing was to be amortized over 15 years. In essence, then, the all-equity cash flows derived were reduced by the sum of the annual principal payments on the investment and the after-tax cost of the interest payments. It was then possible to relate the after-financing cash flow to the amount of the purchase price not financed, in terms of the discounted cash flow rate of return on equity (the amount considered to be at Liberty's risk).

Exhibit 3 indicates the effect of this analysis and the rate of return anticipated from the resulting flows. The irregularity in the cash flows, which may be observed in column (1), resulted from the care with which the estimates were made. These estimates reflected changing patterns in the kinds of wood cut, and the use of accelerated depreciation following periodic replacements of plant items as needed. They were accepted by the Liberty officers as being realistic for the analysis of the property.

Analysis of the results from column (4) of Exhibit 3 showed that this method of financing did not produce a sufficient return from the proposed project, because the internal rate of return was 5.4%. A member of the consulting group then commented that some of their clients felt that assigning a portion of the cash flow to the repayment of the financing did not accurately reflect the nature of the timber property involved. Implicit in retiring the loan was the assumption that the debt capacity of the project was declining. Presumably, given the initial existence of the debt capacity and the use of a sustained-yield cutting scheme, the debt capacity would not fall, and the project could be refinanced as needed.

The consultants argued that use of a conventional approach to leverage had locked the analysis into an assumption that was no more applicable to the project than any other wrong assumption, such as one concerning price level or cutting pattern. The asset was one that would not depreciate over time but, if anything, would appreciate over time. Not only were large, well-stocked tracts of timber such as this one becoming increasingly scarce but, in fact, the trees themselves were growing at a rate that would increase the total inventory of fiber over the long term. It seemed that under these circumstances the debt capacity of the project was going to increase rather than decrease.

With these thoughts in mind, the consultants developed a second approach to leverage for presentation to the Liberty management. This approach reflected the financing of the project by what might be called "perpetually outstanding debt." The flows from the all-equity analysis were reduced only by the after-tax cost of the interest payments on the outstanding debt. The principal amount of the financing was assumed to be paid back out of the salvage value derived from the project in year 30 when the calculation was arbitrarily terminated. The net effect of this approach, of course, was to leave a much larger cash flow available for payout and a higher rate of return on the equity portion of the investment. The results are shown in column (6) of Exhibit 3, from which an internal rate of return of 6.6% was computed. While less than 7.5%, it was within the bounds of possibility, in Mr. Jonas' opinion.

Finally, the consultants pointed out that if continuous compounding was used, instead of the end-of-year compounding that had been the practice of the Liberty management, the internal rate of return would rise to 6.8%. (See Exhibit 4 for a summary of the rates mentioned above.)

It was Mr. Jonas' task to appraise the work of the consultants, selecting the figures that he decided were based on appropriate assumptions, and even making alterations if they were justified. He would then prepare for the committee of senior officers his recommendations as to the price the company should consider the absolute maximum, citing the necessary evidence to justify his conclusions.

Although discounted cash flow calculations had been presented to this committee before, the ideas about the use of debt were novel to its members; so Mr. Jonas knew that his choice would have to be explained very clearly. In particular, he anticipated that there would be questioning concerning the terminal values chosen.

Exhibit 1

Sustained-Yield Cut

(rates of return associated with various purchase prices
and three pricing patterns)

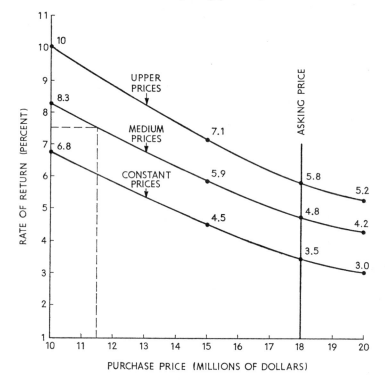

PURCHASE PRICE (MILLIONS OF DOLLARS)

Exhibit 2

Accelerated-Yield Cut

(rates of return associated with various purchase prices
and three pricing patterns)

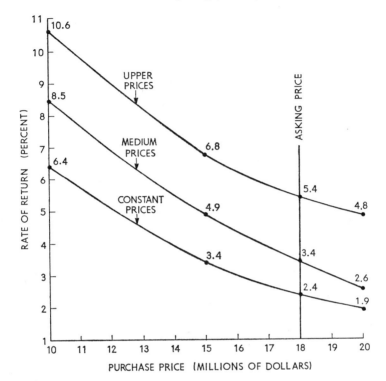

Exhibit 3

All-Equity Cash Flows Related to $18 Million Price and Adjustments Caused by Possible Debt Programs
(tabulated figures in thousands)

| Year | (1) All Equity Cash Flows | $9 Million Loan, Payment of $890,000 Annually | | | $9 Million Loan, Constant | |
		(2) Applied to Principal	(3) Interest after 48% Tax	(4) Adjusted Cash Flows	(5) Interest After 48% Tax	(6) Adjusted Cash Flows
1......	$ 439	$(405)	$(253)	$ (218)	$(253)	$ 186
2......	657	(426)	(241)	(11)		404
3......	732	(450)	(229)	53		480
4......	805	(474)	(217)	115		553
5......	855	(499)	(203)	152		602
6......	928	(526)	(189)	212		676
7......	624	(555)	(175)	(106)		371
8......	740	(585)	(159)	(4)		487
9......	804	(616)	(143)	45		551
10......	869	(650)	(125)	94		617
11......	916	(685)	(107)	125		664
12......	1,167	(722)	(88)	357		914
13......	1,285	(761)	(68)	457		1,032
14......	843	(802)	(46)	(5)		590
15......	805	(845)	(24)	(64)		552
16......	1,237	...	...	1,237		984
17......	824	...	...	824		571
18......	587	...	...	587		334
19......	754	...	...	754		502
20......	1,437	...	...	1,437		1,184
21......	1,328	...	...	1,328		1,075
22......	1,372	...	...	1,372		1,119
23......	1,366	...	...	1,366		1,114
24......	1,361	...	...	1,361		1,108
25......	1,356	...	...	1,356		1,102
26......	1,139	...	...	1,139		886
27......	1,090	...	...	1,090		837
28......	1,086	...	...	1,086		833
29......	1,083	...	...	1,083		830
30......	1,035	...	...	1,035	(253)	782
Terminal Value 30......	$14,593	...	...	$14,593	...	$5,593
Rate of return..........	4.8%	...	...	5.4%	...	6.6%

Exhibit 4

Tabulation of Rates of Return and Net Present Values from Exhibit 3

Financing Method	Rate of Return	Net Present Value at 7.5%
All equity.........................	4.8%	$11,981,299
Amortized debt....................	5.4	5,523,890
Perpetual debt		
Annual discounting..............	6.6	7,968,699
Continuous discounting...........	6.8	8,219,682

Molecular Compounds Corporation*

The Molecular Compounds Corporation (MOCOM) manufactured a wide variety of products in the chemical field and related areas, ranging from industrial chemicals through consumer goods. During the 1950's MOCOM's sales had grown over 60%, reaching a level in excess of $700 million in 1962. Net income had withstood the pressures of competition within the chemical industry, with the result that per share earnings had also risen about 60% during this time. This rise occurred despite additional profit erosion caused by increased depreciation charges and higher allocations for research and development. The corporate executive group was extremely anxious to match or exceed this growth record in the decade from 1960 to 1970. Toward this end, it had instructed the Central Financial and Planning Staff to reevaluate the methods of financial analysis to insure that adequate investments were being made.

The fundamental objective of the company's current capital budgeting process was to maximize corporate growth and especially the growth of earnings per share. This objective would permit the payment of a fair and, it was hoped, growing dividend to stockholders; and, subject to the vagaries of the stock market, it would create conditions favorable for significant capital appreciation.

Developments in the chemical industry had contributed to executive concern about MOCOM's growth prospects. Recently, a number of successful, large firms (for example, Standard Oil Company [New Jersey], Goodyear Tire and Rubber Company, W. R. Grace and Company, and the Borden Company) had entered the field and had aggressively sought to share in the chemical and allied products market, which had sales of $30 billion in 1961. There were already 10 firms, primarily in chemicals, with sales of over $300 million and numerous smaller firms with signifi-

*Abridged.

cant sales in narrower segments of the market. Each of these firms was tending to diversify further. Some of the substantial postwar expansion had led to overcapacity. All this meant increased competition among giants for available demand. In particular, price cutting in established products had squeezed margins considerably without generating much new volume. Sales and earnings also seemed likely to become more volatile, especially as foreign competition became more important. The greatest hope for the achievement of corporate goals was seen in the development and rapid exploitation of new products (including product improvement).

At the same time, the industry was becoming increasingly mature. Some segments still retained the dynamic growth patterns that had been evident during the introduction of petrochemicals and plastics. However, more firms were spending more on research to achieve a strong position in these fields, and existing competitive advantages were proving more tenuous. In total, the balance had shifted toward a higher proportion of products with limited prospects for growing demand.

These factors led MOCOM's top management to conclude that it would be necessary to secure full and effective utilization of available capital resources if the firm was to achieve continued rapid growth. The increased size and complexity of MOCOM's operations, however, made such an objective all the more difficult to achieve. A recent drop in the amount of capital expenditures submitted for approval had thus been the cause of considerable concern.

Partially because of these considerations, the members of MOCOM's Central Financial and Planning Staff were considering a revision in the company's budgeting procedure in early 1962. In their judgment, the most significant revision would eliminate the 12% (after-tax) minimum return on investment criterion or "cutoff" rate. This rate had been used to evaluate all projects since the existing procedures had been introduced in the middle 1950's. The essence of the argument for elimination of the rate was that the existing system was overstructured. For example, some executives argued that a cutoff rate tended to discourage submission of low-return but relatively riskless projects in which MOCOM could profitably invest. In short, the elimination of the artificial restraint of a cutoff rate might encourage operating personnel to submit any project that appeared worthwhile.

Other members of the Planning Staff, however, thought that a cutoff rate (preferably 12%, but certainly no lower than 6% or 7%) was essential as a management tool. They believed that with no formal guideline the divisions would create their own rules and procedures, many of which would be more stringent than the 12% rate currently set by the corporation. There remained, however, considerable disagreement as to just what cutoff rate should be used and how it should be administered in order to stimulate satisfactory growth.

Decentralized Management

MOCOM was organized into 11 autonomous divisions. Each division was self-supporting and contained its own staff groups, including a Financial and Planning Staff. Division executives were held responsible for planning the course of their divisions and for operating them successfully. Although plans and problems were discussed regularly with headquarters personnel, central management's greatest influence arose through performance appraisal. Performance was evaluated by a number of financial methods as well as by less formal factors. Top corporate management considered, for example, a division's return on investment (operating income, less an allocation for corporate overhead and for depreciation on the division's assets, divided by the sum of gross fixed investment and gross working capital), its operating percentages (income as a percentage of sales, etc.), and growth trends.

Through these evaluations, top management communicated its desires and criticisms in ways, sometimes subtle, that appeared to have a profound effect upon divisional attitudes and orientations. While unquestionably misinterpretations and other misunderstandings arose, top management considered that this planning system worked more successfully than would a more formal set of policies, goals, and operating directives. Nevertheless, the influence of performance evaluations on subsequent actions was a cause for modest concern because of the difficulty of comparing actual success against relative differences in available opportunities.

Any adjustments in the capital budgeting process would have to take existing division-headquarters relationships into account.

Existing Capital Budgeting Procedures

Although each division was responsible for generating projects, all divisions were expected to abide by the 12% cutoff rate, which was applied by the divisional financial analyst following procedures set by the Central Financial and Planning Staff. Projects below that rate were actively discouraged and usually rejected, even though they required less than $150,000 and could consequently be approved by division management without central management review.

About 40% of the corporation's total capital expenditures were included in the division budgets and were not reviewed by headquarters, although this percentage varied from division to division. Only projects requiring an investment of more than $150,000 were forwarded to the Central Financial and Planning Staff, which reviewed the request on behalf of the Capital Budget Review Committee. This committee, consisting of the corporation's president, the executive vice president, two divisional managers (including the originator of a project under discussion), and two Central Staff vice presidents, gave final[1] approval to projects in excess of the size divisional management could approve. In addition, if any project smaller than $150,000 and returning less than 12% seemed particularly attractive, division management could request the Capital Budget Review Committee to waive the cutoff requirement.

The 12% cutoff rate had been selected after an extensive investigation by the Central Financial and Planning Staff, which considered a wide variety of possibly relevant considerations. The four most important were:

1. *Growth expectations.* Over the previous 50 years the company's earnings per share had increased 7% to 8% a year. It was assumed that the stockholders expected that this rate of growth would be maintained and in addition that a dividend yield of at least 3% would be provided. A combination of these two figures (dividends per share divided by market price, plus "growth") yielded a cost of equity capital of 10% or 11%. Twelve percent was selected to allow a slight margin for error in the budgeting process.

2. *Cost of capital.* From an actual balance sheet, a weighted average cost of capital, including debt (estimated interest charges) and equity (estimated earnings per share/market price), was calculated (see Exhibit 2). This measurement turned out to be substantially lower than 12%.

3. *Industry standards.* Cutoff rates used by other companies in MOCOM's industries were investigated and found to be roughly around 12%.

4. *Feasibility.* Management believed that the 12% rate was quite practical, since it would not generate more projects than the firm could absorb. As there seemed to be no sound, rigorous basis for making the necessary final judgment, a 12% cutoff rate (after taxes) was accepted because it seemed about right.

The corporation also had installed a standard method of computing return on investment. After experimentation with several financial measures, management chose a net after-tax present-value technique. In this measurement present-valued cash outflows were subtracted from present-valued cash inflows (including an estimate for recovery) to arrive at a net present-value figure. From alternative investments, the one showing the highest net present value was selected, all other factors being equivalent. Other measurements, such as internal rate of return (that rate which makes the net present value equal to zero), after-tax return on gross investment, payback years in present-value dollar terms, and profits as a percentage of sales, were used as supplementary guides.

Forecasts were sometimes measured on an expected value basis. Division Planning Staff personnel were supposed to consider various

---

[1] In certain instances approval by the board of directors was also required.

alternative outcomes and calculated related cash flows. They then assigned probabilities to the flows and used the probabilities as weights to obtain an expected present-value figure. This adjustment was used to correct the "most likely" estimate when skewed probability distributions were observed.

Problems with the Existing System

The Central Financial and Planning Staff acted as consultants to the divisions in their planning and capital budget preparation, in addition to reporting to the corporate headquarters and providing the reports, plans, and analyses top management needed. Many of the analysts had worked in one or another of the divisions before they transferred to the Central Staff group. The members of the Staff thus considered themselves fairly familiar with the attitudes of the divisions and with the informal methods that existed on local levels to supplement the formal capital budgeting procedure.

As a result of their visits and work in the field, the Central Planning Staff began to suspect that the existing capital budgeting system was possibly choking off investments at the extremes of the opportunity spectrum. At the least, the planning group believed that too few low-risk, low-return and too few high-risk, high-return projects were being submitted to the Capital Budget Review Committee. For example, very few projects were ever submitted that were as low as the cutoff rate of 12%. The average internal return rate seemed to be between 17% and 20% on low-risk projects and went up much higher for any request that had a major risk associated with it.

Moreover, the Capital Budget Review Committee rarely rejected a project. "When one is rejected," an executive of the Central Staff remarked, "you can hear the anguished cries through the whole building." Some members of the financial and planning group considered this situation evidence that few borderline projects were being submitted for top-level consideration. As a consequence top corporate management was unable to exercise significant influence on the allocation of funds within the company. "It's not the obvious investments that top management should consider," commented one analyst, "since anyone can decide these. They should be concerned with the marginal projects which are at present being screened out all along the line."

While it was less clear-cut, there was also evidence that very few projects were being rejected at lower echelons. This condition further suggested that only those projects which were relatively certain to receive final approval were even flowing into the beginning of the decisional pipeline. The criteria used by the divisions to screen possible attractive opportunities were not always known, but they appeared to be, often-times, more cautious than top management wished. The negative decisions, then, were commonly made at the source of the idea, at a level in the organization quite removed from direct communication with the Capital Budget Review Committee.

Equally important, screening criteria at intermediate levels were known to differ from division to division and probably from person to person. For example, a number of executives were known to use a cutoff rate of 15% based upon after-tax return on gross investment (a cutoff criterion used within the company prior to 1956) in evaluation of projects. Unquestionably, other standards were employed wherever they seemed appropriate to individuals.

In composite, these negative decisions were probably quite significant. First of all, some executives were afraid that MOCOM might be underspending relative to its ability. MOCOM's top management believed that the company had sufficient sources of funds to support a substantial increase in the rate of plant expenditures. The company's debt-to-capitalization ratio ranged between 25% and 30%, well below levels considered safe. Management believed that the firm could borrow nearly $100 million more at favorable interest terms. This potential source of funds, combined with a large after-tax income and a substantial depreciation throwoff, practically ensured that even extremely large capital budgets could be sustained over a number of years without recourse to common stock financing. Indeed, in recent years internally generated funds alone had proved adequate to meet normal dividend and capital expenditure demands for funds.

There was good evidence that many favorable opportunities were never submitted. For example, the question of the effectiveness of the capital budgeting system was raised in a dramatic way in 1960, when the limit on projects that could be included in division budgets changed from $75,000 to $150,000. The number of projects included in the division budgets increased substantially, and it appeared that the dollar volume of projects requiring investments of between $100,000 and $150,000 would be about four times its previous level.

Top management's influence on the strategic balance of overall expenditures was limited. While they might suggest directions for expansion or encourage increased outlays for certain divisions, top executives were perforce limited to selecting from projects submitted. Their lack of familiarity with the specific details of projects lost in the screening process made it difficult for them to offer suggestions.

Finally, several types of projects were clearly being overlooked. One category included very safe projects promising a return of between 5% or 6% and 12%. These investments typically were in the cost reduction area and generally promised to continue producing savings long after the nominal 15 years used in calculating the economic value of the project. For example, this type of project would include such installations as power plants, plants for producing basic materials, and improvements in basic heavy equipment. An increase in outlays for these projects might tend to dampen existing cyclical earnings swings.

There seemed to be an equal lack of projects at the other extreme, the high-risk and high-return ventures. In this category were new products which faced great uncertainties in the market but which, if they succeeded, could provide MOCOM with handsome profits.

The problem with the high-risk projects, as the financial and planning group saw it, was the extent of the risk to the division or plant managers. "It is hard to get a division manager," noted one of the Central Staff analysts, "to commit himself and his division to a project which requires new assets equal to a major percent of the assets he has allocated to him at present. The risk [probability of success or failure] to him and to his division is the same as the risk to the corporation, but the extent of the risk [the seriousness of failure] is greater. If he guesses wrong and the project is a dud, he's got to do some explaining to show why his return on assets has dropped. But the potential returns are so great that the company could afford to have a bunch of duds for each one which pans out and still come off ahead." In essence, the planning staff believed that the utility curves of the division managers were quite different from the utility curve of the corporation as a whole. At lower organizational levels, this problem appeared even more severe.

Exhibit 1

Market Price, Earnings and Dividends per Share
1947–March, 1962

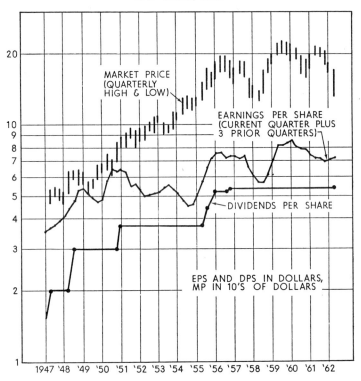

Exhibit 2

Earnings-Price Ratio
1947–March, 1962

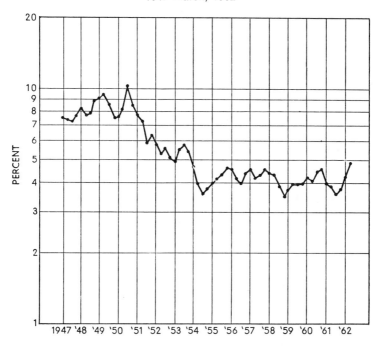

Storkline Shops

In early January, 1958, Mr. Barnes, the president of a small bank in Houston, Texas, was reviewing the latest loan request from Storkline Shops, a chain of retail stores specializing in maternity clothes and accessories, Mr. Barnes had handled the Storkline account since Mr. Richard Klein, owner and president of the business, first approached the bank in August, 1955, requesting $15,000 to finance the fall seasonal needs. The initial loan request had been granted, and since that time the firm had experienced a persistent and increasing need for funds. This need had been met in part by the bank; and in early January, 1958, the proprietorship was borrowing $30,000. From the granting of the initial request to the present time, Storkline Shops had been steadily in debt to the bank. Mr. Klein's most recent request was for an additional $10,000 to finance "unexpected inventory requirements" in the coming weeks. Before reaching a decision on this latest request, Mr. Barnes wanted to review developments in the account since it was opened in August, 1955.

Establishment of Storkline Shops—August, 1954

Mr. Klein founded Storkline Shops in the fall of 1954 with an initial investment of $15,000. Though he had no direct experience in the retailing of women's clothing and accessories, he had extensive experience in the merchandising and distribution of various other consumer goods. This experience, at both retail and wholesale levels, was gained with numerous companies throughout the Southwest. Deciding to enter a retail business of his own, he surveyed the many available alternatives and selected the maternity clothes line because he believed there was a unique and unfilled demand for a specialty shop in this field.

Mr. Klein started his business by opening three shops in the Houston area. Within the next 6 months, he added five more shops, one in Houston

698

and four in other large Texas cities. Mr. Klein performed all the buying for his shops by visits to eastern fashion shows. He also planned all the merchandising, pricing, and advertising programs for the chain as a whole, as well as working out in detail the specific interior design and merchandising plans for each shop location. Each shop was staffed by one or two women, selected by the owner himself for their experience, appearance, and sales ability. Storkline shops owned no store locations; each store was leased on a 2- to 3-year basis at annual rentals averaging about $3,300.

As was typical in the ladies' ready-to-wear business, sales mounted seasonally during the spring and during the fall. Sales were on a cash-and-carry basis, and there was little investment in fixed assets. The main investment of the business was in retail inventory; a broad line of clothing and accessories had to be maintained to service the seasonal buying habits and changing fashion requirements of customers. In preparation for peak selling seasons, retail inventories were usually built up by March 15 and September 30 of each year. Mr. Klein also carried a line of accessories in his chain of stores, with such items amounting to approximately 15% of retail sales and inventory value. Most maternity garment makers sold to Storkline on terms 8/10 E.O.M. or a negotiated net price due 10 days E.O.M. Accessories were typically purchased on terms ranging from 2/10, net 30 to 8/10, net 30.[1]

The Initial Loan—August, 1955

In his initial request for a loan in August, 1955, Mr. Klein reported that his operations were very satisfactory for the first 6 months of 1955 and submitted to the bank his most recent operating statement and balance sheet (see Exhibits 1 and 2). The early operations were attributable primarily to the first three Houston stores, as the other stores had been in operation for only 2 or 3 months. In addition to his proprietorship in Storkline Shops, Mr. Klein owned a building in the Houston area with a market value of $60,000, against which he had a mortgage of $40,000. He also had other miscellaneous assets of an approximate value of $15,000. Mr. Klein emphasized the unique appeal of a maternity wear specialty shop and the limited competition in this line of retailing. After some study, Mr. Barnes decided that his bank could accommodate the

---

[1] Terms of 2/10 net 30 mean that if the bill is paid within 10 days from the date of the invoice, a deduction of 2% is allowed from the face of the bill. The bill becomes due 30 days from the date of the invoice or shipment. E.O.M. means that all shipments are subject to the stated terms as if made at the end of the month. In some lines of trade, especially dry goods and apparel, the end of the month is considered to be the 25th day of the month in which the invoice is dated. Where no net credit term is stated, as in 8/10 E.O.M., the discount amounts to a trade discount (T. N. Beckman and R. S. Foster, *Credits and Collections: Management and Theory* [8th ed.; New York: McGraw-Hill Book Co., 1969], pp. 259, 264, 265).

young and growing organization and granted the company a $15,000 loan, with the understanding that it was to be repaid by the end of 1955. Recognizing Mr. Klein's aggressiveness and zest for expansion, Mr. Barnes obtained his assurance that he would open no new outlets without first consulting the bank.

Developments during the First 6 Months of 1956

On a visit to the bank in January, 1956, Mr. Klein brought with him the company's financial statements for the full year 1955 (see Exhibits 1 and 2). Mr. Klein explained that the year-end inventory was $8,000 greater than anticipated, because sales in November and December had not been up to expectations. Looking ahead to the first half of 1956, Mr. Klein expected that sales would reach $223,000, earnings before drawings and taxes would be $35,000, and the inventory would peak in March at about $75,000 and be reduced to $29,000 by June 30. Though the loan balance as of the end of the year had remained at $15,000, as shown in Exhibit 3, it was paid down to $10,000 on January 2. In order to pay personal income taxes coming due, Mr. Klein requested renewal of the $10,000 and that an additional $10,000 be loaned to the proprietorship. Based on his 6-month estimates, Mr. Klein felt there would be no problem in paying all indebtedness by June 30. Mr. Barnes granted this loan request with the understanding that a cleanup would be accomplished as planned.

During the following month, Mr. Klein again visited the bank and requested an added $5,000. The proprietor of Storkline Shops reported that he had opened an additional Houston store during the latter part of January and was interested in another location in a Dallas suburb. He wanted the added $5,000 to purchase the inventory presently stocked at this suburban location and to take over operation of the shop. Mr. Klein said that his earlier estimate of net profits for the last 6 months of 1956 now appeared very conservative. The request for an additional $5,000 was granted, but Mr. Barnes cautioned that the notes had to be paid by June 30 and no new shops were to be added until figures for the first half of the year were available.

Developments during the Last 6 Months of 1956

By late July the chain of stores and locations had increased to 13 with an aggregate annual lease expense on these locations amounting to approximately $39,000. In a visit to the bank during July, Mr. Klein stated that the minimum basic inventory to support the present sales level of his company amounted to about $50,000. Though the business was unable to clean up its bank debt by June 30, it had been able to meet $9,000 of a $10,000 note, and thus had reduced the loan balance to $16,000 by June 30 (Exhibit 3).

Financial statements for the first 6 months of operations in 1956 were received by the bank in mid-September (see Exhibits 1 and 2). Shortly afterward, Mr. Klein requested a renewal of the $16,000 loan and asked for an additional $9,000 to finance the rising seasonal inventory, which he estimated would reach $75,000 at the end of September (see Exhibit 2). He reported that profits before drawings for July through October were running some $5,000 to $8,000 per month. Mr. Barnes granted the request for additional funds on a promise that a cleanup would be made before December 31.

Developments during the First 6 Months of 1957

In early January, 1957, Mr. Klein again visited the bank, bringing an estimated balance sheet as of the end of 1956. Though his inventory had been up to about $87,000 at the end of October, Mr. Klein believed he had reduced it to about $56,000 by the end of the year. A year-end audit was currently under way in each store. Though he had been unable to clean up his bank debt, as earlier arranged, Mr. Klein pointed out that his profits had been better than expected and that net working capital had increased since June 30 by $18,000. Mr. Klein also volunteered information about the small manufacturing operation he had started in late 1956 in order to reduce his cost of purchases. The proprietor said that he was doing his own design and cutting work but that sewing was being contracted with a local concern. Mr. Klein estimated that during the fall of 1956, his manufacturing operation netted about $3,700 before drawings and taxes. The proprietor said he planned to manufacture only for the retail side of his business and that he hoped to provide perhaps three fifths of his retail needs for spring sales from this source. Since he was doing this manufacturing, he would need to borrow earlier than would have been necessary with a purely retail operation. As a result, the proprietor wanted to renew the outstanding $10,000 note and to borrow an additional $10,000 to finance the purchases of the piece goods inventory. Since Mr. Klein had continued to generate a growing profit, Mr. Barnes granted this request for funds.

In mid-February, 1957, the bank received the operating and financial statements for 1956 (see Exhibits 1 and 2), accompanied by a memo from Mr. Klein that he had opened up three new locations, one in Houston and two in suburban areas of other Texas cities, bringing the total number of locations to 16. After discussing the 1956 results with Mr. Barnes a few days later at lunch, Mr. Klein asked for an additional $15,000 to finance peak inventory needs for the spring season. He reported that his present inventory amounted to about $80,000, of which $50,000 was in staple retail merchandise. The added $15,000 would bring borrowings to a new high of $35,000 (see Exhibit 3), but Mr. Klein believed this amount was required to get over the seasonal hump. With the agreement that all notes would be repaid by June 30, the request was granted.

In mid-April Mr. Klein called to report that his 3-month operations to March 31 had been very successful; sales had been $155,000, and profits before drawings and taxes were $11,700. Of this profit, $2,000 was from retail operations and $9,700 from manufacturing. Retail sales for the coming 3 months were estimated at $180,000, which, in combination with tight control of purchases, would draw down retail inventory to $60,000 by June 30. Upon inquiry, Mr. Klein said that his present inventory amounted to $101,000, of which $17,000 was in piece goods (see Exhibit 2). Mr. Klein said that he still believed there would be a cleanup of his notes by June 30, 1957, as agreed to earlier.

Developments during the Last 6 Months of 1957

In July, 1957, Mr. Barnes noted that Storkline had reduced its notes only to $15,000 at midyear (see Exhibit 3). In discussing the plans for the fall season with Mr. Klein in early September, Mr. Barnes learned that the company had now expanded to 18 locations and that operations for the fall season were mounting. Retail sales for August had reached about $40,000; and for September and October together, Mr. Klein expected volume to reach $100,000. Mr. Klein said he was also selling manufactured products to a few select outside customers. Mr. Klein expected his retail inventory to peak by the end of August, and a request for an additional $5,000 was granted. Financial statements for the 7 months ending July 31 were recorded during this visit (see Exhibits 1 and 2).

In mid-October the bank received a financial statement as of September 30, indicating inventory had mounted to $130,900, of which $98,600 was in retail goods (see Exhibit 2). Mr. Klein appended a note to this statement, stating that he expected his retail inventory to be reduced to $65,000 by the end of the year.

In talking with Mr. Barnes in mid-December, Mr. Klein argued that a $65,000 minimum inventory level was unrealistic for the present size of his business. Mr. Klein considered a more appropriate figure to be in the vicinity of $90,000. During this visit, Mr. Klein requested an additional $10,000 loan to finance the acquisition of piece goods inventory for the manufacturing operations and early purchasing for spring retail needs. Mr. Klein emphasized how very profitable the manufacturing operations were becoming and considered this part of his business to have special promise. Storkline's proprietor assured Mr. Barnes that the $10,000 note, bringing the company's indebtedness to $30,000, would be adequate for seasonal requirements, and the request was granted.

The Latest Request—January, 1958

In mid-January, 1958, Mr. Klein brought to the bank a report of his 5-month operations since August 31, 1957, and a year-end balance sheet (see Exhibits 1 and 2). In discussing future operations, Mr. Klein predicted that the manufacturing side of the business would have sales of $300,000 during the first 6 months of 1958. Storkline's spring line was being very well received, and many additional customers were actively interested in purchasing the line. He said he was now manufacturing 60% of his own requirements, in addition to selling to a few leading department stores and chains. He added that he was able to do a much larger volume in the manufacturing side of the business than at present but that in compliance with the bank's suggestion he was moving slowly in accepting orders from outside concerns. He further reported that although national retail sales of maternity clothes during 1957 had dropped some 20% from the 1956 level, Storkline Shops had maintained sales at the 1956 level. Because of the exceptional progress since the beginning of his business in 1954, and the cooperation the bank had given him throughout that period, Mr. Klein hoped that the bank would be pleased to meet his current needs. In this regard, the proprietor wanted an additional $10,000 to finance payment of some maturing bills for piece goods.[2] Mr. Klein believed that he would have no difficulty in completely liquidating his bank debt by midsummer. Whereas in previous years his profits had depended heavily upon the retail side of the business, Mr. Klein pointed out the keen buyer interest and lucrative profits being generated in the designing and manufacturing operation. He said in parting that the added credit would very much improve his ability to repay all notes by midsummer. Since total loans of $40,000 would permit expansion of the highly profitable manufacturing operations, Mr. Klein thought that the cash generated from these operations in the next 6 months would be more than enough to liquidate all bank debts.

[2] Garment makers usually purchased piece goods on terms of 2/10 E.O.M. or on the basis of a negotiated price due net 60.

Exhibit 1

Operating Data for Selected Periods
(dollar figures in thousands)

	1955		1956		First 7 Months 1957		Last 5 Months 1957	
	First 6 Months	12 Months	First 6 Months	12 Months	Retail	Manufacturing	Retail	Manufacturing
Net sales............	$107.5	$260.1	$199.0	$425.7	$283.0	$96.0†	$231.1	$117.0‡
Cost of goods sold........	58.0	135.0	107.2	226.1	n.a.	n.a.	115.0	75.0
Gross profit............	49.5	125.1	91.8	199.6	n.a.	n.a.	116.1	42.0
Operating expenses........	37.2	97.1	77.7	163.4	n.a.	n.a.	85.1	17.0
Includes: Depreciation........	n.a.	3.4	n.a.	6.9	n.a.	n.a.	n.a.	n.a.
Store rentals........	n.a.	15.2	n.a.	37.5	30.4	...	26.0	...
Net profit........	12.3	28.0	14.1	36.2	13.8	17.4	31.0	25.0
Withdrawals during period........	6.2	8.5	6.2	18.5	$20.3	...	$3.0	...
Reinvestment of withdrawals, end of period..	6.0	1.0	0.1	13.1	...	...	...	...

† $3,000 to outside customers in the first 7 months of 1957.
‡ $47,000 to outside customers in the last 5 months of 1957.

Exhibit 2

STORKLINE SHOPS

Selected Balance Sheets

(dollar figures in thousands)

ASSETS	Audited 6/30/55	Audited 12/31/55	Audited 6/30/56	Estimated 9/30/56	Audited 12/31/56	Estimated 4/15/57	Audited 7/31/57	Estimated 9/30/57	Estimated 12/31/57
Cash	$ 4.6	$ 8.6	$10.9	$16.0	$ 4.4	$ 6.0	$ 8.4	$ 14.0	$ 8.0
Accounts receivable	...	...	...	...	2.8	...	2.2	8.3	30.1
Inventory									
Retail	27.0	48.2	57.9	75.0	64.5	84.0	77.2	99.9	105.0
Piece goods	...	...	...	...	1.0	17.0	25.0	31.0	41.0*
Current assets	$31.6	$56.8	$68.8	$91.0	$ 72.7	$107.0	$112.8	$153.2	$184.1
Machinery, fixtures, equipment (net)	13.6	17.7	20.7	n.a.	30.6	n.a.	32.3	31.2	35.0
Miscellaneous assets	2.1	2.7	7.7	n.a.	4.1	n.a.	4.1	4.3	2.1
Total assets	$47.3	$77.2	$97.2	n.a.	$107.4	n.a.	$149.2	$188.7	$221.1
LIABILITIES									
Notes payable—bank	...	15.0	16.0	25.0	10.0	35.0	15.0	20.0	30.0
Notes payable—others	3.1	1.1	2.6	...	1.7	...	...	...	...
Accounts payable	10.7	11.0	22.2	26.0	15.1	22.0	35.2	42.6	40.1
Accruals	2.7	4.9	3.2	2.0	4.5	3.0	12.0	14.5	11.0
Current liabilities	$16.5	$32.0	$44.0	$53.0	$ 31.3	$ 60.0	$ 62.2	$ 77.1	$ 81.1
Net worth	30.8	45.2	53.2	n.a.	76.1	n.a.	87.0	111.6	140.0
Total liabilities	$47.3	$77.2	$97.2	n.a.	$107.4	n.a.	$149.2	$188.7	$221.1
Data received and recorded by the bank	8/16/55	1/25/56	9/13/56	9/21/56	2/17/57	4/18/57	9/2/57	10/11/57	1/13/58

* Includes $15,000 finished goods held by manufacturing operation against firm orders.

Exhibit 3

Record of Balance of Notes Payable—Bank
(end of month)
(dollar figures in thousands)

	1955	1956	1957		1955	1956	1957
January	—	$20	$20	July	—	$16	$15
February	—	25	35	August	$11	16	15
March	—	25	35	September	15	25	20
April	—	25	35	October	15	25	20
May	—	25	25	November	15	16	20
June	—	16	25	December	15	10	30

Plowman Poultry Farm

On March 1, 1966, the board of directors of the First National Bank of Westhaven was reviewing an application for extension of a $10,000 line of credit to Mr. Roger Plowman. Because Mr. Plowman already owed the bank $6,000, Mr. H. W. Barclay, executive vice president and chief loan officer of the bank, was presenting to the board a detailed account of the events leading up to this second loan request.

The First National Bank of Westhaven was founded in 1909 by a group of Westhaven businessmen who felt the need of a local bank to meet the community's banking needs. For the first 50 years of the bank's operations, however, it remained a small, conservatively oriented institution, and a substantial part of the community's banking needs continued to be serviced by banks in neighboring towns. In 1959 the directors of the bank asked Mr. H. W. Barclay, a former employee who had left four years earlier to become associated with a bank in Connecticut, to rejoin the Westhaven bank as chief executive officer. Mr. Barclay had agreed to return and had almost immediately initiated a new, more liberal lending policy—including the introduction of instalment credit loans. By 1965 the bank's outstanding loans of $3 million were double the 1959 volume, and the loan portfolio was split about equally between business and personal loans.

It was Mr. Barclay's conviction that loan requests should be considered only from people living within the Westhaven area. For one thing, he felt that it was only within this limited area that he could maintain a sufficient familiarity with the community and its people to make intelligent decisions on loan applications. Then, too, he believed that he would not be acting in the best interests of the bank's predominantly local depositors if he made loans outside the community as long as there were opportunities within the area which would directly benefit the depositors.

The town of Westhaven, located 25 miles south of Boston, had a population of 10,000; it also serviced the needs of two small, adjoining communities—Easthaven and Chesterton—whose populations approximated 3,000 each. Local industry included an assembly plant of a large manufacturer of machine tools—employing 800—and a number of small, locally owned enterprises. Many of the community's wage earners commuted to jobs in neighboring areas—particularly along heavily industrialized Route 128—and in Boston proper.

Mr. Plowman had first approached the bank for credit for his poultry farm operation in January, 1965, when he sought $6,000 to purchase some new equipment and some additional geese and to make other improvements around the farm. The bank was already acquainted with Plowman at that time, since he had obtained several small loans during the preceding 3 years to finance inventories in his tinsmith business.

Mr. Barclay knew that Plowman, 45, had moved to Easthaven in 1952 and had worked as a tinsmith in the local area with some success. His business involved the custom fabrication of stovepipe, storage tanks, metal ducts for heating systems, and the like. Mr. Barclay estimated Plowman's yearly earnings at $6,500. Shortly after coming to Easthaven, Plowman had met and married Cora Diamond, 43, a teacher in the local school system, and together they had purchased a run-down farm in the community with the intention of renovating it and putting it on a profitable basis. The couple had no children, and both continued to pursue their former occupations, working the farm in their spare time. Mr. Barclay estimated that Mrs. Plowman contributed $5,500 to the yearly income of the family.

In early 1963 Plowman heard that raising geese was a profitable part-time undertaking. He had investigated the possibilities and found that among geese farmers it was the practice to purchase a small "brood" flock for the production of fertilized eggs, which were then incubated, hatched into goslings, raised to maturity, and slaughtered for meat. He had also learned that brood flocks were sold in "units" of two female geese and one gander and that they had very long, productive lives running to as much as 50 years. Thus, one did not replenish his brood stock every two or three years as was the practice among chicken and turkey farmers. Because brood geese were very expensive, Mr. Plowman had purchased a flock of only 51 in 1963. During the next two years, he had gone about developing a local market for geese and, with a little advertising, had soon gained a reputation for producing large, plump, tasty birds.

During his January, 1965, visit, Plowman had explained that if the bank granted him a loan of approximately $6,000, he would use the money to purchase a new farm truck, a plucking machine, a packaging machine, additional geese for his brood flock, and materials for the construction of additional goose shelters on the farm. It was his intention to increase his 1965 production to 400 birds with these improved facilities, and he felt confident that, should the loan be granted, he would be able to repay at least a part of it by the end of that same year.

Mr. Barclay had decided to present the loan application to the board with a favorable recommendation for several reasons. First, he was impressed by Plowman himself. He appeared to be a clean-cut, energetic fellow who had already demonstrated to the bank his sense of responsibility by the promptness with which he had met his repayment schedules on earlier loans. The bank had checked on Plowman through its regional credit bureau and had turned up no unfavorable reports. The balance sheet which Plowman had drawn up for the bank (see Exhibit 1) showed a net worth in excess of the loan being requested, and Mr. Barclay had learned that the unencumbered Plowman farm was worth substantially more in the current market than the $6,000 for which it was carried on the balance sheet. Finally, Mr. Plowman had already demonstrated his competence in raising geese during the past two years, and the revenues from this operation, in addition to the earnings which both Mr. and Mrs. Plowman drew from their full-time occupations, gave the family a substantial combined income.

The bank's board of directors had agreed with Mr. Barclay's analysis of the application and had voted to grant Mr. Plowman the $6,000 loan. The loan was made in the form of a 3-month renewable note at 6% interest signed by both Mr. and Mrs. Plowman. The bank took a lien on both the equipment purchased and the flock of brood geese, which would number 140 when Plowman had purchased the additional birds he planned. It was the understanding of the bank that a good portion of the loan would be repaid during 1965, when the marketable geese had been slaughtered and sold.

At the end of each 3 months during 1965, Mr. Plowman came in to renew his note with the bank, but on each occasion he reported that he was unable to make any repayment on the note at that time. In January, 1966, Plowman again visited Mr. Barclay at the bank to renew his note, and it was then that he made the request that the bank grant him an additional $10,000 line of credit. He explained during this visit that he had not found it possible to make the profits he had anticipated at his present small-scale level of operations. Having purchased the new equipment and additional geese for his brood flock, he now felt that he was ready to expand his flock and thus reap the economies of large-scale operation. He proposed to increase his annual goose production from 400 to 5,800 birds. He pointed out that while the local market was not large enough to accommodate this many birds, the commission merchant who handled the wholesale distribution of geese in the Boston area had expressed confidence in being able to sell without difficulty the larger flock of geese which Plowman proposed to raise.

Mr. Plowman went on to explain that he had made a tentative agreement with a local feed company to advance to him on credit the necessary grain to feed the growing goslings and was now seeking money from the bank to finance the other operating expenses associated with the enlarged venture. He had compiled a month-by-month cash budget for Mr. Barclay (see Exhibit 2) and estimated his cash needs at about $10,000. He had also drawn up a projection of estimated revenues and profits (see Exhibit 3) and had estimated the latter at $17,000 for the first year's operations. Mr. Barclay had agreed to consider the additional loan request and had asked that a meeting be arranged between the representative of the co-operating feed company, the Boston commission merchant, Mr. Plowman, and himself.

At the meeting, which was held over a lunch in Boston, Mr. Barclay learned that another feed company which Plowman had first approached had dismissed his proposal as too risky. It had pointed to the demonstrated volatility in the chicken and turkey markets, particularly in the past year, and said that it felt no assurance that the goose market would be any less erratic. Mr. Carl Boyer, a leading Boston commission merchant who was present at the meeting, had described the demand for geese as much more stable, however. There were, he said, a large group of families of middle-European extraction in the Boston area who incorporated roast goose into their festive celebration of Thanksgiving, Christmas, and Easter. It had been his experience that these people were much less likely to substitute other poultry or meats in the place of geese than were other groups. He did point out, however, that the demand for geese was closely tied to the holiday season—with the greatest number being consumed at Christmas—and that unless the geese were ready when the holiday arrived, it would be very difficult to dispose of them in the nonholiday market. He went on to explain that most of the geese now consumed in the Boston area were being supplied from several western states, and he expressed a desire to obtain a source of geese which was both close and dependable. He added that he would be willing to give Mr. Plowman a written guarantee for the purchase of all of his 1966 geese production at prevailing prices if delivered to him in time for the holiday market.

Mr. Plowman had then outlined his plans for undertaking the production of the larger flock. He explained that in the hatching and growing of geese, timing was crucial. Full-grown geese were voracious eaters and thus, to prevent them from eating up potential profits, it was important that they be slaughtered as soon as they reached maturity. Geese farmers therefore planned the incubation and hatching of their eggs on a schedule which would bring batches of geese to maturity only in quantities which they could manage to slaughter, eviscerate, and package immediately. Plowman planned to contract with several commercial hatcheries to incubate the eggs produced by his brood flock on a time schedule which would permit the hatching and delivery to him of approximately 500 goslings each week for about 12 weeks, beginning on April 1. The first batch would then reach maturity by the beginning of October, and he was sure that, with his new equipment and some extra workers, he could handle the slaughter, eviscerating, dressing, and packaging of 500 geese weekly. He added that once the geese had been packaged and quick-frozen, they would be shipped to the Quincy Market Cold Storage and Warehouse Company in Boston for storage until the holiday season arrived. The commission merchant, Mr. Boyer, would then transfer the birds to his own place of business as they were needed and would forward the receipts of their sale (less his commission of $0.01½ per pound) to Mr. Plowman.

The feed company's representative, in outlining his firm's position, had made it clear to Mr. Plowman that its tentative agreement to advance the necessary feed on credit—he estimated it would amount to approximately $10,000 worth—was contingent upon the bank's willingness to finance Plowman's cash needs during the growing period. He also indicated that the feed company would want some sort of security from Plowman in exchange for its extension of credit.

When Mr. Barclay had asked the feed company representative and Mr. Boyer for their estimate of potential profits to Mr. Plowman from the first year's operations, both had felt that the minimum return would be $10,000 after all expenses.

At the close of the meeting, Mr. Barclay had asked Mr. Plowman to send the bank an up-to-date statement of his assets and liabilities. Several days later, Mr. Plowman had appeared at the bank with a detailed inventory of his assets (see Exhibit 4). Upon glancing down the list, Mr. Barclay had noted that there were two farms listed as assets instead of one which had appeared on his 1964 balance sheet. Mr. Plowman explained that in late 1965 he had taken advantage of an opportunity to purchase 90 acres of land and some buildings located about a half mile from his first farm and that he planned to house some of his geese at the new location beginning in 1966. When Mr. Barclay asked him how he had financed the purchase, Mr. Plowman explained that he had made a down payment of $3,000 and had obtained a mortgage for the balance of the $14,000 purchase price, using both farms as security. In answer to Mr. Barclay's queries about other debts he now owed, Mr. Plowman stated that his only liability was $250 which was due to a supplier of sheet metal for his tinsmith business.

In concluding his recount of the Plowman loan application to the bank's board of directors, Mr. Barclay stressed the point that should the board decide to grant the $10,000 loan request, adequate safeguards must be included in the terms of the loan to ensure that the bank would be repaid before Mr. Plowman was permitted to make any further additions to his capital assets.

Exhibit 1

PLOWMAN POULTRY FARM

Net Worth as of May 31, 1964

Cash............................	$ 300	Accounts payable.............	$ 372
Accounts receivable............	835		
Total current assets.....	$1,135	Net worth....................	8,863
Land (80 acres) and buildings...	6,000		
Tools..........................	1,000		
Truck..........................	1,100		
Total.................	$9,235	Total.................	$9,235

Exhibit 2

PLOWMAN POULTRY FARM

Cash Budget for 1966 Growing Period

	April	May	June	July	Aug.	Sept.	Oct.
Goose feed for breeders	$ 80	$ 100	$ 80	$ 80	$ 100	$ 80	$ 80
Gas and oil for truck	60	100	80	40	50	40	40
Utilities, miscellaneous	120	120	120	90	90	80	90
Notes due to bank	100			100			
Goslings ordered:							
Connecticut Hatchery: 2,500 ordered @ $1 each; ½ needed for down payment	1,250						
Plymouth Hatchery: 1,000 ordered @ $1.25 each; no down payment needed	.....						
New Hampshire Hatchery: 1,000 ordered @ $1 each; no down payment needed	.....						
Goslings delivered	825	1,750	925				
Farm worker	240	240	300	240	240	300	240
Fencing		500					
Cry-o-vac bags for 5,500 geese @ $0.03 each				165			
Four extra workers for dressing and eviscerating							864
Monthly cash needs	$2,675	$2,810	$1,505	$ 715	$ 480	$ 500	$1,314
Cumulative cash needs	2,675	5,485	6,990	7,705	8,185	8,685	9,999

Note: Large gas and oil expenses are necessary to make trips to hatcheries.

Exhibit 3

Estimate of revenues and profits from the 1966 growing year:

All geese will be oven-ready and packaged. They will weigh between 10 and 15 pounds and will average 12 pounds per bird. It is expected that they will bring between $0.57 and $0.60 per pound at wholesale. Carl Boyer and Company will be the marketing agents.

5,000	Geese	1966 Holiday Season..............	$0.57/lb.	$34,200
250	Geese	S. S. Pierce Co., Inc...............	.60/lb.	1,800
250	Geese	S. W. Theise 1280 Commonwealth Ave. Allston, Mass.......	.57/lb.	1,710

Retail at Farm:

In 1965 we sold 150 and we expect to double it in 1966, as we have so many repeat orders for next year already.

300	Geese	$0.70/lb.	2,520
	Total...		$40,230

By-product: Goose Feathers:

2,900	Grey Toulouse	Will yield ½ lb. body feathers per bird...................................	2,537
2,900	White Embden	Will yield ½ lb. body feathers per bird...................................	2,973
	Total for feathers...		5,510
	Total business.......................................		$45,740

Estimated profit:

5,800 birds @ $2 per bird...		11,600
Yield for feathers..		5,510
Approximate net profit..		$17,110

Note: Geese are very hardy—mortality is about 1 percent.

Exhibit 4

Inventory of Assets, January 1, 1966

No.	Item	Estimated Value
5...........	A. H. Wood Brooders	$ 297.50
5...........	Kitson Waterers (with hose and clamps)	66.00
8...........	Fountains	6.00
220........	Feet of plastic pipe with fittings and washers	37.62
4...........	Kitson floats	7.36
5...........	Ashcans	26.05
4...........	Heavy-duty aprons	6.27
6........	Knives	5.95
1...........	Semiscalder (galvanized electric—40 gallons)	155.65
1...........	McClintock cutter	3.75
500........	Pliofilm bags	8.50
1...........	20 gal. tank for wax	106.15
250........	Cedar fence posts	200.00
14..........	Rolls of wire	102.12
½..........	Roll parchment paper	3.84
500........	Glassine bags	1.38
41..........	Range feeders	301.74
31..........	Waterers	51.42
6...........	Wire egg baskets @ $1.25	7.50
1...........	High-powered egg candler	4.00
	Tools	670.00
5...........	Sheet metal	15.00
	Fabricated pipe and elbows	100.00
	Furniture, rugs, bedding, etc.	2,442.00
	Clothing	1,245.00
	Jewelry	550.00
	Cameras, books, television, etc.	555.00
	Dishes and glassware	750.00
2...........	Farms 87 and 90 acres $6,000 and $14,000	20,000.00
	(not including 7 house lots $1,200–$1,500 each)	8,000.00
4...........	Thermometers	2.70
2...........	Infrared 250 bulbs	2.20
6...........	Directional signs with arrows	106.00
4...........	Large round tubs	6.81
500........	Goose folders	12.50
2...........	300 gal. tanks for water	50.00
1...........	Gasoline water pump	122.44
56..........	Loads of gravel for road	396.00
16..........	Turkey crates	64.08
250........	Burlap bags	25.00
	Uncured feathers	350.00
	Picker	220.00
	Refrigerator	335.00
	20 cubic ft. deep freeze—cost $1,200	350.00
3...........	Rolls wire fencing	15.75
	Petersime Incubator #7—cost $1,390	675.00
130........	White Embden geese, $15.00	1,950.00
	International Harvester pickup, 1963 (new motor job)	850.00
1...........	Kenmore vacuum cleaner	109.50
24..........	Cement blocks	6.00
	Miscellaneous equipment	$ 434.39
		$42,209.33

Long Beach Electronics Company, Inc.

On September 19, 1962, Mr. Roy Johnson, an assistant vice president of the Community National Bank of Long Beach, California, was considering the position he should adopt on the request of Long Beach Electronics Company, Inc. (LBEC) for additional funds. The following day, Mr. Arthur Smith, LBEC's treasurer, was due at the bank at Mr. Johnson's invitation to discuss the company's prospects and financial requirements for the coming year. A week earlier, Mr. Smith had explained that he expected at least a 20% sales increase in fiscal 1963, provided Community National was willing to increase the existing $200,000 short-term credit by no less than $25,000 and perhaps as much as $50,000.

Mr. Johnson had only recently taken on the LBEC account, along with several other loan situations, after the promotion of one of his colleagues, Mr. Jack Ray. In order to get an overall understanding of the situation, he had scanned the material in the company's credit folder and had talked briefly with Mr. Smith. As he prepared to examine the LBEC loan situation in greater depth, Mr. Johnson planned to consider particularly carefully his predecessor's repeatedly expressed view that, ultimately, the bank would be forced to take a firm position against further credit extensions to a company which he considered undercapitalized. While Mr. Ray acknowledged that such action would almost certainly choke off the company's rapid growth and might even place LBEC in a disadvantageous position vis-à-vis equally rapidly growing competitors, he had stressed his conviction that sound banking practice precluded the indefinite substitution of bank debt for equity in a growing company. Mr. Johnson wondered whether the time to take such a firm position had arrived.

Company Background

LBEC had been incorporated in 1932 as La Salle Radio Co., Inc., owned equally by Mr. James La Salle and Mr. Howard Fiske. Through World War II, the company had functioned primarily as a retailer of radios, radio tubes, and parts, and related electrical equipment, with sales being made to the general public and to a growing number of individuals interested in radio as a hobby. With the purchase of Mr. La Salle's ownership interest by Mr. Smith late in 1946, the complexion of the company, whose annual sales had hitherto never succeeded $100,000, began to change. By 1962 sales to the general public accounted for a very minor portion of the company's revenues, which now were derived primarily from the industrial distribution of nationally known lines of such electrical and electronic parts and supplies as semiconductors, vacuum tubes, capacitors, and laboratory test equipment. LBEC's 1962 industrial catalog listed more than 25,000 individual items within 12 broad product lines. Sales were made to both very large and very small electronic and aerospace companies in the greater Los Angeles area on the customary terms of 2% 10 net 30 days.

LBEC's president, Mr. Fiske, 53, took an especial interest in the areas of purchasing and inventory control. Prior to founding the company in 1932, Mr. Fiske had been a purchasing agent for a medium-sized electrical parts producer. Mr. Smith, 60, had the title of treasurer but was active in general management and sales as well as in finance. In addition to their investment in LBEC, both men had some assets outside LBEC. Mr. Fiske's liquid savings, the equity in his home, and the cash surrender value of his life insurance were estimated to total $75,000. A June, 1962, statement showed Mr. Smith's "outside" net worth as approximately $100,000 in marketable securities, savings, equity in his home and one other piece of property, and cash surrender value of his life insurance. LBEC carried $100,000 worth of "key man" life insurance on each of the partners under a program instituted in 1954. Community National's files contained a notation by Mr. Ray that the amount of insurance currently carried would be inadequate for full payout of one of the two ownership interests.

LBEC's year-end figures were audited by Harold Wadsworth & Co., a small but very reliable firm of CPA's. The firm also assisted in the compilation of quarterly financial figures. In addition, Mr. Harold Wadsworth, the senior partner, was frequently consulted by Mr. Fiske and Mr. Smith on major financial decisions.

Bank Relationship

The borrowing relationship between LBEC and Community National began in 1952 with a $2,500, 30-day loan to help the company finance an unexpected and very temporary inventory buildup. Following the prompt repayment of this initial loan, the company began to borrow regularly from the bank in relatively small but ever-increasing amounts as working capital needs outstripped its cash generation ability. Borrowing by LBEC took the form of 90-day renewable notes up to a maximum amount established on a yearly basis by the bank. Borrowings were guaranteed by Mr. Smith and Mr. Fiske. The interest rate was usually $1\frac{1}{2}\%$ above prime, and in 1962 was 6%.

In early 1955 LBEC asked Community National to participate in the financing of the construction of a new warehouse on land adjacent to the company's existing facilities. Title to the new $90,000 property ($30,000 for land and $60,000 for the building) would be held by a wholly owned LBEC subsidiary, Long Beach Realty Co., to which LBEC would pay rent sufficient for maintenance, taxes, interest, other expenses, and debt retirement. After considerable negotiation, Mr. Fiske and Mr. Smith agreed to invest an additional $22,500 in the form of subordinated debt in LBEC, whereupon Community National agreed to a $45,000, 10-year 6% mortgage loan to Long Beach Realty Co., which had only a nominal capitalization, and to lend $22,500 at 5% on a 5-year term basis to LBEC. Both the mortgage and the term loan were fully guaranteed by Messrs. Fiske and Smith. The bank also agreed to continue to make short-term advances to LBEC, over and above the $22,500 term loan, as necessary.

Through fiscal 1959, the total amount owed to Community National by LBEC never exceeded $30,000 (see Exhibit 1). In the fall of 1959, however, Mr. Smith had advised that the company might require as much as $90,000 of additional bank financing during fiscal 1960. Mr. Smith attributed this need to two factors. First, LBEC's sales had increased steadily in the past several years to slightly less than $1 million in 1959 (see Exhibit 2) and Mr. Smith anticipated a further growth to as much as $3 to $4 million annual volume within the next 4 to 5 years. Second, the prices quoted by electronics parts distributors within the greater Los Angeles area for any given item tended to fall within a relatively narrow range, since most industrial customers, particularly the larger companies, obtained quotations periodically from a number of sources in order to obtain the lowest possible price. With virtual price equality among distributors, then, individual suppliers were forced to compete primarily on the basis of prompt delivery and were therefore required to maintain large inventories. Recently, LBEC's management had completed an exhaustive study of the relative profitability of each of the 20 product lines traditionally carried by the company, and the decision had been made to concentrate exclusively on the 12 most profitable lines. Nevertheless, Mr. Smith stated, given a continuation and very probable intensification of present competitive pressures, LBEC would almost certainly be forced to increase its inventory investment substantially, perhaps by as much as $50,000.

Mr. Smith had explained to the bank that, despite the very technical nature of the material involved, the danger of inventory obsolescence was relatively slight. As he explained LBEC's arrangements, most suppliers would either take back inventory at cost price if it had not moved for 6 months or would take it back at any time if twice as much new inventory, in dollar terms, was ordered at the same time. Mr. Smith explained that it was always possible to follow the latter approach by ordering fast-moving items. The small part of the inventory not covered by these arrangements did occasionally show losses, but Mr. Smith pointed out that LBEC obtained considerable public relations value from its policy of giving away such merchandise to radio enthusiasts and hobbyists.

After careful consideration of Mr. Smith's presentation, Community National had agreed to increase the company's borrowing line, not to $120,000 but to $90,000, on the basis of a year-end fiscal 1959 net worth of slightly more than $175,000 and an approximately equivalent amount in working capital. At the same time, Mr. Smith acknowledged the importance of making some paydown of the loan. In view of his expectation that the concentration on the more profitable product lines would boost the company's profit from approximately $15,000 in 1958 and 1959 to a $40,000 to $50,000 level within the next year or so, he agreed to a bank proposal that at the end of 6 months (i.e., in March, 1960) the outstanding bank debt would be put on a demand basis with equal monthly instalments sufficient to pay out the loan over a 3-year period.

In actuality, despite a close watch over expenses, the anticipated profit level failed to materialize, and LBEC was not able to begin a payout of the loan. Since the loan limit of $90,000 was insufficient to permit LBEC to take account of purchase discounts, Community National agreed in December, 1960, to allow the company to borrow an additional $25,000. At this time, the bank indicated its willingness to continue lending to LBEC on 90-day renewable notes, reviewing the situation periodically, with the understanding that the company would not be in a position to go out of debt for several years.

Late in 1961 LBEC approached Community National with a twofold loan request. In a memorandum to the bank, Mr. Smith explained that for the past several months, LBEC had been stretching its trade payables in order to support a sudden bulge in its receivables. He reported that it had become the custom in the trade to carry customers' accounts beyond the formal credit terms, and LBEC was reluctantly following this practice in order to remain fully competitive with other distributors in the area. Accordingly, LBEC was losing substantial income by passing discounts. As an example, Mr. Smith pointed to approximately $40,000 in bills outstanding on which $700 in discounts could have been earned had they been paid on the December 10 discount date. In addition, concluded Mr. Smith, overdue payables presently amounted to $60,000, of which $10,000 were over 30 days past due, so that LBEC's credit rating was in danger of serious deterioration.

Mr. Smith also explained that the big expansion in volume since 1955 was seriously taxing LBEC's existing warehouse space, and if adequate financing could be arranged, he and Mr. Fiske would construct a $70,000 addition to the existing facility in the spring of 1962. Mr. Smith wondered if it might not be possible to combine this expansion with LBEC's continuing working capital problem and to arrange a $150,000, 10-year term loan to Long Beach Realty Co. This would let Long Beach Realty repay the outstanding balance of the original $45,000 mortgage to Community National, construct the new facility, and still, according to Mr. Smith's calculations, advance approximately $40,000 to LBEC. As security, Long Beach Realty Co. could offer the original building, which had recently been assigned an "available market value" of $110,000 and a "reasonable market value" of $70,000 by an independent appraiser, plus the $70,000 addition, or a possible total value of $180,000. According to Mr. Smith, a major insurance company had expressed a willingness to consider such a term loan, incorporating an 18- to 24-month delay in the initiation of sinking fund repayments.

In view of LBEC's pressing working capital needs and in anticipation of more permanent financing, Community National agreed on January 6, 1962, to increase the company's borrowing capacity by $60,000 to $175,000. Shortly thereafter, the insurance company decided against a term loan. However, a regional business development corporation expressed an interest in the situation provided Community National was willing to participate in the credit. After a week of intensive study and negotiation, the bank agreed to participate equally with respect to both amount and maturity in a $100,000, 10-year 6% first mortgage on the property, and the business development corporation agreed to supply alone an additional $50,000, secured by a second mortgage on the property.

Shortly after the new facility was started, construction costs spurted because of the need to protect the building's foundation against an unsuspected structural fault in the underlying rock. By the time the "$70,000 facility" was completed in April, 1962, it had cost well over $95,000. Accordingly, the amount which Long Beach Realty could advance to LBEC dwindled from the original figure of $40,000 to roughly $15,000. At a May meeting with representatives of Community National and the regional business development corporation, it was decided to retain the $15,000 of "excess" funds in the Long Beach Realty corporate entity to provide a reserve against any future contingencies arising out of the rock fault. At the same meeting, Community National agreed to increase LBEC's borrowing capacity by an additional $25,000 to $200,000 to alleviate the company's continuing cash shortage.

Mr. Johnson's Preliminary Impressions

As he scanned the material in the company's credit folder, Mr. Johnson noted that his predecessor, Mr. Ray, had repeatedly cautioned Mr. Smith that ultimately the bank would be forced to a firm position of "this much credit—no more!" with LBEC. In an August, 1962, meeting, for instance, Mr. Ray had pointed out that while working capital had grown over the past 5 years, the company's indebtedness had more than tripled, and that this was as far as Community National would like to see it go. Putting it another way, Mr. Ray had explained to Mr. Smith that, in 1958, LBEC's indebtedness was $124,000 and working capital was $149,000. At that time, only $0.25 would have had to be realized on each dollar of inventory in order to repay the company's total indebtedness. At the end of fiscal 1962, however, total indebtedness was $360,000 and net working capital was only $226,000. At this time, $0.47 would have to be realized for each dollar of inventory in order to liquidate total indebtedness.

Mr. Smith and Mr. Ray had explored the possibility of an additional equity investment in the company, in the form of either common stock or subordinated debt. Mr. Smith had explained that he and Mr. Fiske had agreed upon equal ownership interests in LBEC. While Mr. Smith was willing to contribute additional equity, Mr. Fiske was not yet in a position to do so, primarily as a result of having incurred exceptionally heavy medical expenses during his wife's recent serious illness. With Mr. Fiske unable to convert any of his remaining personal assets at the present time, an equity contribution by Mr. Smith would result in an imbalance in the ownership interests and would almost certainly cause personal friction between the two men.

In recognition of the bank's cooperation over the years, both Mr. Smith and Mr. Fiske were willing to discuss with a well-known investment banking firm the possibility of raising additional equity through a small public offering. At the meeting Mr. Smith had explained that the 1962 income statement contained a number of nonrecurring expenses caused by the installation of the enlarged warehouse operation, rearrangement of the inventory, and the establishment of an improved system of inventory control. Mr. Smith was fully confident that 1963 and succeeding years would see a net profit of well over $50,000 on a 10% to 20% sales increase. Noting these expectations and LBEC's rather erratic earnings record during recent years, the investment banker had strongly advised that any public offering be postponed for several years in order to give LBEC an opportunity to establish a favorable earnings trend.

After this meeting, Mr. Smith had acknowledged the bank's reasonableness in terms of conservative loan policy but had urged Mr. Ray to go along with the existing loan, pointing out that the company's receivables were from such high-quality names as Lockheed and General Dynamics and that operations had been moderately profitable for a number of years. During one conversation Mr. Smith mentioned that, on the basis of recent experience, he was confident that a large Los Angeles bank would be happy to take over the entire loan, but that this was the last thing he wanted after so many years of harmonious relations with Community National. Mr. Ray had acknowledged that the bank valued highly the fine relationship through the years with the company and with Mr. Fiske and Mr. Smith personally, but stressed again that LBEC must realize that sound banking practice precluded the indefinite substitution of bank debt for equity in a growing company.

Mr. Johnson noted that for the past several years corporate and personal balances arising from the loan to LBEC had averaged as follows:

Year	Average Balance
1962	$28,300 (8 months)
1961	26,600
1960	18,500

In order to sharpen his thinking on this problem, Mr. Johnson gathered some financial data from published sources, primarily *Standard & Poor's Corporation Records*, on companies which appeared to be roughly comparable to LBEC (see Exhibit 3). While he did not expect to find any definitive answers to his own problem in the financial statistics of other companies, he hoped to gain some clues on the question of a reasonable debt limit for a company such as LBEC.

Exhibit 1

LONG BEACH ELECTRONICS COMPANY, INC.

Comparative Balance Sheets
as of July 31, 1957–62
(dollar figures in thousands)

ASSETS	1957	1958	1959	1960	1961	1962
Cash	$ 2	$ 12	$ 6	$ 11	$ 20	$ 17
Accounts receivable (net)	79	71	79	105	135	159
Inventory	153	168	200	285	316	394
Other	1	1	1	2	3	7
Total current assets	235	252	286	403	474	577
Furniture and equipment (net)	9	8	7	9	11	11
Cash value life insurance	6	8	11	15	20	25
Loans to subsidiary	34	18	14	11	11	8
Total assets	$284	$286	$318	$438	$516	$621

LIABILITIES						
Accounts payable	$ 68	$ 64	$ 71	$114	$113	$113
Due banks	18	18	30	65	115	200
Accrued taxes	16	10	11	26	28	24
Other accruals	11	11	8	10	12	13
Total current liabilities	113	103	120	215	268	350
Notes to banks	9	4	—	—	—	—
Due officers*	15	17	21	18	13	10
Total liabilities	$137	$124	$141	$233	$281	$360
Capital stock	15	15	15	15	15	15
Earned surplus	132	147	162	190	220	246
Total capital	147	162	177	205	235	261
Total liabilities and capital	$284	$286	$318	$438	$516	$621

* Subordinated to bank debt in event of bankruptcy.

Exhibit 2

LONG BEACH ELECTRONICS COMPANY, INC.

Summary Income Statements (Years Ended July 31)

(dollar figures in thousands)

	1957	1958	1959	1960	1961	1962
Sales						
Industrial........................	$778	$745	$ 963	$1,117	$1,289	$1,567
Service..........................	39	37	28	24	27	13
Retail...........................	77	77	95	110	100	83
Total sales......................	894	859	1,086	1,251	1,416	1,663
Cost of sales*...................	677	647	842	948	1,059	1,269
Gross profit.....................	217	212	244	303	357	394
Expenses						
Selling..........................	$ 76	$ 84	$ 103	$ 122	$ 139	$ 158
Administrative†..................	67	66	75	82	110	131
Operating.......................	40	39	43	50	55	60
Total expenses..................	183	189	221	254	304	349
Profit before taxes..............	34	23	23	49	53	45
Taxes...........................	13	8	8	21	23	19
Net profit.......................	$ 21	$ 15	$ 15	$ 28	$ 30	$ 26
* Beginning Inventory	$ 152	$ 153	$ 168	$ 200	$ 285	$ 316
Purchases	678	662	874	1,033	1,090	1,347
Ending inventory	153	168	200	285	316	394
Average inventory	152	161	184	242	300	355
† Including executive salaries totaling	$ 36	$ 36	$ 38	$ 40	$ 46	$ 46

Exhibit 3

Comparison Sheet

(dollar figures in thousands)

	Bell Electronic Corporation		Gem Electronic Distributors, Inc.		Harvey Radio Company		Lafayette Radio Electronics Co.	
	1961	1962	1961	1962	1961	1962	1961	1962
Sales	$4,406	$4,854	$3,110	$3,638	$3,755	$3,920	$21,209	$22,442
Net income	274	281	127	183	183	210	711	608
Bank debt								
Short-term	630	675	144	45	2	2	1,122	2,970
Long-term	76	1,125	.....	.....	49	47	2,166	1,799
Total	$ 706	$1,800	$ 144	$ 45	$ 51	$ 49	$ 3,288	$ 4,769
Debt								
Current liabilities*	1,883	1,301	791	464	417	540	2,942	5,008
Long-term	75	1,125	.....	.....	49	47	2,166	1,799
Total	$1,958	$2,426	$ 791	$ 464	$ 466	$ 587	$ 5,108	$ 6,807
Net worth	1,237	1,333	437	996	1,125	1,335	3,183	4,212
Bank debt/net worth	57%	135%	34%	4%	4%	4%	103%	113%
Total debt/net worth	158%	182%	185%	44%	41%	44%	161%	162%

* Including short-term bank debt.

NOTES:

Bell Electronic Corp.: Company and subsidiaries distribute electronic parts and components made by others. Products include more than 25,000 items: semiconductors, tubes . . . transformers; connectors; cables; relays; . . . test equipment; and precision gears. Sales are made to more than 3,500 industrial and institutional customers who use products mainly for defense contracts. Company located in Southern California area. . . .

Gem Electronic Distributors, Inc.: Company markets a wide line of electronic components; parts and equipment . . . all made by others. It carries more than 30,000 items purchased from 160 suppliers for each of which it is an authorized or franchised dealer. . . . Company operates in New York City area.

Harvey Radio Co., Inc.: Company and subsidiaries market in New York City and upstate New York electronic components, parts, supplies, and equipment made by others. . . . About half of sales are to industrial customers and the remainder to retail customers.

Lafayette Radio Electronics Co.: Company and its subsidiaries distribute an extensive line of electronic parts and equipment and high fidelity sound components. . . . Company located primarily in the Northeast.

Custom Plastics, Inc.

In the last week of July, 1956, Mr. Stanley Ebanson, vice president and loan officer of the Tradesman National Bank of Milwaukee, was introduced to Mr. Charles Miller, newly elected president of Custom Plastics, Inc. Mr. Miller, who with an investment group had purchased control of Custom Plastics 2 months earlier, was requesting short-term credit accommodation for the company from the Tradesman Bank. Though Custom Plastics was an old and reputable firm in the custom molding field, the company had suffered financial difficulties since 1953. In view of the company's continuing management and operating problems, the former owners accepted the offer of Mr. Miller's group to acquire immediate control of the company and pay out the former owners over a 5-year period. The company had been extended short-term bank credit for many years by the Manufacturers Bank; but by mutual agreement between the former owners, Mr. Miller, and the officers of the Manufacturers Bank, the new president was to arrange the company's short-term credit needs with a new financial institution as soon as possible.

Custom Plastics was a manufacturer of custom molded plastic products. Manufacturing facilities were located in Milwaukee, Wisconsin, where the company leased a four-story plant for $50,000 per year, the current lease to expire in 1958. The company employed about 300 personnel and currently was operating on a two-shift basis. Custom Plastics was equipped with a complete line of molding machines, both compression and injection, capable of producing items of all sizes and shapes typically required by an industrial customer. Though the machinery was old and less efficient than new equipment on the market, the management believed the company's technical and engineering skills were of greater importance to profitable operation.

As was typical for a custom molder, Custom Plastics helped design a plastic product, obtained the specially cut mold from a local toolmaker, and manufactured the end product in its own molding machines. The company had a wide reputation for its ability successfully to undertake tricky mold design and product manufacturing assignments. The full cost of mold design and purchase was borne by the customer and paid to Custom Plastics in the initial purchases of the special plastic item. Custom Plastics was fully responsible for the quality of a finished plastic component, and most customers had rigid inspection procedures and quality standards. To obtain physical custody of a mold, the customer was required under a "mold contract" to pay Custom Plastics an additional 30% over the reimbursement price previously agreed to and paid Custom Plastics in the initial purchases.

In 1952 the company entered the plastic dinnerware business under a design and brand name licensing agreement with a nationally known designer. The line of dinnerware provided about 20% of the total sales volume in 1955. Two separate sales forces were maintained to contact the company's 175 customers, no one of which accounted for more than 10% of the company's volume. On the other hand, the list of the company's 15 most important customers in 1954 accounted for over half of that year's volume and included large, nationally known manufacturing, service, and retail distribution companies, each with a top credit rating.

Having been founded in 1905, Custom Plastics had "grown up" with the plastics industry and over the years had established a reputation for quality and service. Except during the depression years, the financial position of the company had always been healthy and operations profitable. Ownership was concentrated in the Saunders family; the senior member of the family had been active in the company management until the late 1940's. Though in many years a high proportion of earnings was paid out in dividends, the owners had retained adequate working capital and had established a substantial equity in the business as of the end of 1952.

During 1952 the production manager died; in his long association with the company, this man had become a key figure in the control and profitability of the manufacturing process. In his absence, cost control procedures were relaxed, and cost estimates and pricing decisions were less firmly based on adequate information. In an effort to lessen the impact of pricing decisions based on underestimated costs, material specifications were sidestepped, and some customers began to reject and return merchandise. At the same time, the coordination between engineering and production personnel began to weaken. Finally, productivity and morale among the employees reached a low point after a profit participation plan promised them over the years was withdrawn from consideration in mid-1953. This incident, in combination with generally deteriorating morale conditions in the plant, led to a 4-month strike in the early part of 1954 and continued management-labor friction thereafter.

As a result of these management and operating complications taking effect in 1953, the company's net profit before federal income tax fell from $238,000 in 1952 to a loss of $91,000 in 1953 (Exhibit 1). In 1954 the company suffered heavy losses due to a large reduction in revenues and excessive costs due to the strike and the heavy, unexpected returns of merchandise. At the time, however, the magnitude of these losses was not clearly known because of faulty accounting procedures in effect at the company.

During this period, financial strain developed, and the company began to rely heavily on trade and bank credit. Since the late 1940's the company had been borrowing from the Manufacturers Bank moderate amounts, $10,000–$50,000, on unsecured notes to finance working capital needs arising from slight seasonality or unusually large orders. As the unfavorable operating results and the heavy demand for funds developed in late 1953, the management arranged a line of credit with the bank, pledging as security the company's accounts receivable in bulk. The bank agreed to loan up to 90% of the receivables balance. During the same year, added reliance was placed on trade credit, with trade payables increasing from $85,000 at the end of 1952 to $205,000 at the end of 1953 (Exhibit 2). Of this amount, $107,000, which was payable to five important suppliers, was placed on a deferred basis in early 1954 and secured by a chattel mortgage on certain machinery and equipment. Repayment of these notes in 18 monthly instalments with interest at $4\frac{1}{2}\%$ was to commence in January, 1956. These financing arrangements permitted the company to remain current on new material purchases during 1954 and early 1955.

Owing to turnover in management personnel and almost complete loss of accounting and manufacturing cost control, the extent of the losses taking place in 1954 and early 1955 was not fully recognized until mid-1955. Upon the recommendation of the Manufacturers Bank, the owners of the business discharged the accounting manager and replaced him with an experienced CPA. After a thorough audit, losses before taxes in 1954 were calculated to have been $495,000, of which some $150,000 had been obscured by a failure to reflect returns and allowances as deductions from outstanding accounts receivable and from the period's sales. Losses for the first 4 months of 1955 were estimated at $85,000 before taxes.

When the scope of unprofitable operations became clear, the owners of the company decided to sell their interest in Custom Plastics rather than attempt its rehabilitation. This decision was stimulated, at least in part, by the vigorous suggestion of the bank, and by the recommendation of the five trade-note creditors, whose prospects of receiving payment on schedule seemed dim. While the owners were looking for a buyer, losses mounted to $109,000 before taxes by the end of 1955 (Exhibit 1). Working capital was squeezed to a minimum, and cash was drawn down to below $5,000. By the end of 1955 the Saunders family had invested an additional $53,000 in the company on unsecured notes, with the hope of tiding operations over until a buyer with an acceptable plan of purchase could be located. As the Saunders family wanted to withdraw entirely from the operations of the company, it expected a prospective buyer to pay out these notes as a part of the purchase plan. The deferred notes due trade creditors starting January, 1956, were renegotiated in late 1955 to postpone the payment schedule 6 months. At the same time, it again was becoming difficult to pay for current purchases.

Based on the unfavorable disclosures in 1955 regarding the company's receivables, the Manufacturers Bank asked Custom Plastics to pledge the cash surrender value of life insurance on certain officers and to give a chattel mortgage on the machinery not mortgaged to trade creditors as additional security behind its loan. In addition, the bank raised the interest rate from 5% to 6% on its loan and required the Saunders family to subordinate the company debt held by them to the bank obligations. Also, the bank became much more selective in the receivables against which it would lend, accepting only receivables under 60 days of age of the better credit risks. Finally, the bank hinted to Mr. Saunders that it would terminate its credit to the firm unless a prospective buyer of the business would be willing to bring substantial new equity funds into the company. Upon the completion of transfer of ownership to the new owners, the bank considered its obligation to the Saunders family and the company had been fulfilled and thought a fresh look by a new creditor might be beneficial to all parties.

In early 1956 Mr. Charles Miller, the president of Louisville Desk Company, a small but prosperous manufacturer of metal furniture, became acquainted with Custom Plastics' situation and went to Milwaukee to investigate the company. Mr. Miller had a varied background in investment banking and light industry and with the aid of a group of friends had purchased the Louisville Desk Company in 1948. Though this company had a record of unprofitable operations and poor future prospects, Mr. Miller quickly revived the organization, reorganized its management, shifted product emphasis, and within a few years had built it into a quite successful small enterprise. Having completed this task, he sold his interest in the company at a substantial capital gain and was again looking for a "sick" company to purchase and rehabilitate.

Through the early months of 1956, Mr. Miller investigated the Custom Plastics operation rather thoroughly. Convinced that the company's former profitability could be restored under new ownership and management, he arranged in May, 1956, to buy the company, with payment over a 5-year period. The Miller syndicate first purchased $150,000 of newly issued debentures, convertible into a new and second series of common stock. These debentures were secured by a second mortgage on all machinery and by an assignment of the company's mold contracts. Notes payable to the former owners of $53,000 were retired with cash received from the sale of the first $50,000 in new debentures. The existing and first series of common stock was placed in a voting trust with syndicate members as trustees. In each of the next 5 years, 15% of the company's after-tax profits in each year were to be used to repurchase this stock for cancellation, with the proceeds going to the former owners. Any stock not repurchased by the fifth year was automatically transferred to the company and canceled. Furthermore, the total of the five annual repurchase transactions was limited to $98,000. In summary, the obligation under this agreement was contingent upon profits and limited in aggregate amount and period of liability. The monthly balance sheet and operating statements of the company throughout the period of and following the negotiations are shown in Exhibits 3 and 4.

Though Mr. Miller brought additional funds into the Custom Plastics business and presented a plan for regaining profitable operations, the Manufacturers Bank decided to terminate its lending relationship with the company. Upon assumption of control of Custom Plastics, Mr. Miller had quickly organized a board of directors from among prominent Milwaukee businessmen, one of whom was the treasurer of an equipment manufacturer in Milwaukee. This new director was very much impressed with the plans and managerial skill of Mr. Miller, and he offered his assistance to Mr. Miller in finding new credit accommodations for the company. As his company was an important depositor at the Tradesman National Bank and had a long and successful relationship there, the new director introduced Mr. Miller to Mr. Stanley Ebanson, a vice president and loan officer at this bank.

At a meeting with Mr. Ebanson in early August, 1956, Mr. Miller outlined his program for rehabilitating Custom Plastics. In order to utilize the full capacity of the machinery and to push operations well above a break-even level, Mr. Miller believed that sales volume had to be increased quickly. Mr. Miller thought break-even operations currently would result at a sales level of $200,000 per month; and to surpass this level, he intended to push aggressively for new business as well as regain the confidence and orders of lost customers. Though the backlog of orders stood at about $400,000, it consisted of many older and less profitable orders which had been deferred by the previous management in order to process the more profitable, cash-generating orders. Many customers, promised delivery in March, had not received shipment in July, and Mr. Miller considered it vital that this work receive first priority. To encourage salesmen to push profitable new projects, the president was offering bonuses for selected types of orders. In addition, he was personally trouble-shooting problems of rejections and returns which were causing direct losses and poor customer relations. Finally, selective price increases were being made to some customers who had been receiving merchandise on unreasonably good terms.

The second part of Mr. Miller's program was designed to increase the company's gross margin. Whereas the company's margin had been running from 10% to 14%, the industry range was 15% to 18%. The margin on the dinnerware line was about 23%. In reviewing the manufacturing costs. Mr. Miller was especially concerned with the low worker productivity at Custom Plastics. He intended gradually to put in a piecework system wherever possible, and some incentives had already been installed and well received by the employees. To assume much of the direct control of manufacturing operations which he was presently handling, the new president had just hired an able and experienced production manager from a competing molding firm. This new man would be expected to work quickly in expediting old orders, accurately estimating costs on new business and making sound pricing recommendations, increasing labor and machinery productivity and worker morale, and reducing wastage of raw materials.

Mr. Miller expected that operations in July and August would probably show a loss, due primarily to the backlog of unattractive orders which he had inherited. He believed September and October would be break-even months, and profits could be expected in October and thereafter. The new president said that if sales of $200,000 to $250,000 per month could be reached and gross margins increased as planned, the earnings of the company could be restored to 1951–52 levels. He hoped to have his accounting people make a more thorough cost study of the industrial versus the dinnerware lines; his own tentative studies indicated the profits from the dinnerware line were being offset by the losses in the industrial line. Mr. Miller pointed out also that the company had a federal income tax loss carry-over in the next 4 years of over $500,000 and that no taxes would have to be paid on earnings in this amount made during that period.

In light of these plans, Mr. Miller asked the Tradesman Bank to loan Custom Plastics 80% on net receivables up to a loan limit of $200,000. The company would pledge these assets, maintain accurate aging records, adequately provide for returns and adjustments, screen new credit with care (but with full knowledge of the need for additional business), and present the bank with timely monthly reports of the condition of receivables and the month's operating results. Mr. Miller planned to redeem the cash proceeds of the life insurance to supplement working capital. Pointing out the substantial investment he and his associates already had placed in Custom Plastics, Mr. Miller said he would not consider personally endorsing the company's bank indebtedness. The president added that the company's five main trade creditors were confident of the company's future, because they agreed again to defer their notes, now totaling $98,000, and accept repayment at about $5,000 per month (including interest) beginning in September and extending for 22 months.

Mr. Ebanson was impressed with Mr. Miller's seeming insight into the problems at Custom Plastics. From the Louisville banker who was closely familiar with Mr. Miller's handling of the Louisville Desk situation, Mr.

Ebanson received a strong recommendation of the new president of Custom Plastics. Mr. Miller was described as unimpeachable in integrity, venturesome in spirit, able to accomplish plans and deal with emergencies, and frank and open in his relations with creditors. Also, the associates of Mr. Miller were reputable businessmen, well-known in their separate communities and fields. Finally, although money and credit conditions were currently tight, the Tradesman Bank was actively interested in seeking new customers and establishing relationships which would prove attractive in the long run.

As Mr. Miller would want to know in a day or so whether the Tradesman Bank would be able to meet the company's loan request, Mr. Ebanson set about immediately to evaluate the company's financial needs and the basis, if any, upon which the Tradesman Bank would be willing to accommodate Custom Plastics.

Exhibit 1

CUSTOM PLASTICS, INC.

Operating Statements, 1951–55

(dollar figures in thousands)

	1951	1952	1953	1954	1955
Gross sales	$2,051	$2,335	$2,306	$1,687	n.a.
Returns and allowances	$137	$168	$ 50	$239	n.a.
Amortization of dies	22	48	3	2	n.a.
Discounts	17	19	14	15	n.a.
	176	235	67	256	
Net sales	$1,875	$2,100	$2,239	$1,431	$1,944
Materials	$601	$477	$692	$556	n.a.
Direct labor	372	462	513	385	n.a.
Indirect labor	223	261	328	278	n.a.
Overhead	278	318	366	316	n.a.
	1,474	1,518	1,899	1,535	
Gross profit	$ 401	$ 582	$ 340	$ (104)	182
Officers' salaries	$ 53	$110	$115	$111	n.a.
Sales salaries and commissions	130	119	192	192	n.a.
Other general and administrative	92	133	169	106	n.a.
	275	362	476	409	300
Operating profit	$ 126	$ 220	$ (136)	$ (513)	$ (118)
Other income—net	33	18	45	18	9
Net profit before tax	$ 159	$ 238	$ (91)	$ (495)	$ (109)
Federal income tax	34	165	(90)	(75)	n.a.
Net profit after tax	$ 125	$ 73*	$ (1)	$ (420)	n.a.

* After renegotiation.

Exhibit 2

CUSTOM PLASTICS, INC.

Balance Sheets as of December 31

(dollar figures in thousands)

ASSETS	1950	1951	1952	1953*	1955*
Cash	$ 59	$ 52	$163	$116	$ 3
Accounts receivable	114	164	199	321	198
Inventory	201	271	219	265	192
Total current assets	$374	$487	$581	$702	$393
Machinery and equipment, net	146	131	117	129	94
Cash value life insurance	28	29	30	31	34
Miscellaneous receivables	4	6	18	25	6
Secret process	27	27	27	27	...
Total fixed assets	$205	$193	$192	$212	$134
Total assets	$579	$680	$773	$914	$527

LIABILITIES					
Notes payable—banks	$ 45	$ 25	...	$125	$212
Notes payable—equipment	8	...	...	...	...
Notes payable—vendors	...	...	...	...	63
Accounts payable	124	70	$ 85	205	172
Accrued taxes	...	50	75	67	...
Other accruals	30	44	58	60	75
Total current liabilities	$207	$189	$218	$457	$522
Notes payable—equipment	...	...	...	...	7
Notes payable—vendors	...	...	...	...	44
Notes payable—officers	...	...	...	...	53
Total long-term liabilities	...	...	...	...	$104
Common stock	$263	$263	$263	$263	263
Earned surplus	109	228	292	193	(362)
Total net worth	$372	$491	$555	$456	$ (99)
Total liabilities	$579	$680	$773	$913	$527

* No data available for 1954.

Exhibit 3

CUSTOM PLASTICS, INC.

Monthly Operating Statements, 1956

(dollar figures in thousands)

	Jan.	Feb.	Mar.	April	May	June
Net sales	$140	$191	$200	$192	$195	$173
Material	n.a.	n.a.	n.a.	n.a.	68	60
Direct labor	n.a.	n.a.	n.a.	n.a.	43	38
Indirect labor	n.a.	n.a.	n.a.	n.a.	34	32
Overhead	n.a.	n.a.	n.a.	n.a.	29	28
Cost of sales	$127	$157	$168	$167	$174	$158
Gross profit	$ 13	$ 34	$ 32	$ 25	$ 21	$ 15
Officers' salaries	n.a.	n.a.	n.a.	n.a.	3	5
Other general and administrative	n.a.	n.a.	n.a.	n.a.	19	21
Operating expense	$ 25	$ 22	$ 23	$ 23	$ 22	$ 26
Operating profit	(12)	12	9	2	(1)	(11)
Other income—net	3	1	2	1	6	2
Net profit before tax	(9)	13	11	3	5	(9)

Exhibit 4

CUSTOM PLASTICS, INC.
Month End Balance Sheets, 1956
(dollar figures in thousands)

ASSETS

	Feb. 29	March 31	April 30	May 29	June 30
Cash	$ 1	$ 6	$ 5	$ 9	$ 26
Accounts receivable	198	224	178	162	160
Inventory	186	209	222	238	230
Current assets	$385	$439	$405	$409	$416
Machinery and equipment, net	89	87	90	89	89
Cash value life insurance	34	34	34	34	34
Prepaid expenses	31	34	35	23	30
Fixed assets	$154	$155	$159	$146	$153
Total assets	$539	$594	$564	$555	$569

LIABILITIES

	Feb. 29	March 31	April 30	May 29	June 30
Notes payable—bank	$176	$202	$156	$128	$111
Notes payable—vendors	63	58	83	83	56
Accounts payable	184	204	203	172	131
Other accruals	97	102	118	102	77
Customer advances	16	18	20	7	...
Current liabilities	$536	$584	$580	$492	$375
Debentures	...	...	...	50	150
Notes payable—officers	54	53	53	...	...
Notes payable—vendors	38	35	6	31	74
Notes payable—equipment	6	6	6	6	6
Long-term liabilities	$ 98	$ 94	$ 65	$ 87	$230
Common stock	263	263	263	263	263
Earned surplus	(358)	(347)	(344)	(287)	(299)
Net worth	$(95)	$(84)	$(81)	$(24)	$(36)
Total liabilities	$539	$594	$564	$555	$569

BREAKDOWN AND AGING OF ACCOUNTS RECEIVABLE—JUNE 30, 1956

Type	Amounts	Current	Last Month	Previous Month	Prior Months
Industrial	$113	$ 79	$24	$ 8	$ 2
Dinnerware	47	27	7	3	10
	$160	$106	$31	$11	$12

Terms: Industrial... 1%—10; net 30
Dinnerware... 2%—E.O.M.

Digital Engineering Company

Late in October, 1963, the Triangle National Bank of Pittsburgh invited Mr. Jackson Carl, vice president of Gotham National Bank, to commit Gotham to a one-third participation in a $4.5 million credit line Triangle wished to make available to Digital Engineering Company (DENCO) of Pittsburgh, Pennsylvania. Mr. Carl, a member of Gotham's new Advanced Technologies Division, had been calling on DENCO since the fall of 1960 to solicit an account and to offer Gotham's services when DENCO decided to establish a banking relationship with a New York bank. The information below describes DENCO and lists the events leading up to Triangle's offer.

Digital Engineering Company

DENCO was founded in 1953 in Pittsburgh by a group of four young electrical engineers. The founders were subsequently joined by three executives with demonstrated business skill and an ability to work with the founders of the company. As an incentive to attract these men to the organization, the new executives were given the opportunity to invest in the company. They had exercised the options, and the seven men held approximately equal shares of DENCO. In late 1963 the group still retained ownership of 51.5% of the common stock. Mr. Carl understood that the management was highly regarded by their customers and by Triangle and was considered to have technical depth and breadth. The board of directors included two outside members, a prominent and respected figure in the Pittsburgh financial world and a senior executive of a major engineering company.

DENCO designed, developed, manufactured, and marketed digital equipment including components, subassemblies, and memory subsystems. (A more detailed product list is given in Exhibit 1.) Units of these types were often called "modules," a collective term for the devices from which digital computing equipment is built. The modules were sold to customers who wished to build their own digital systems. DENCO's modular product line, which accounted for 71% of the company's fiscal 1962 sales, put the company in competition with both the large end-use system manufacturers and with the smaller, specialized component firms. DENCO, however, had been one of the first companies to offer a comprehensive line of standard, high-quality modules at prices reflecting mass production savings. DENCO's product line had been gradually expanded from one product to several proprietary lines which were produced primarily for off-the-shelf sale.

In addition to producing standard component parts, DENCO designed and manufactured custom products, including both components and systems for data processing, control, and other applications. These developments were undertaken as the result of management's initiative as well as under contract for other firms. In 1961, for example, DENCO introduced its first general computer, the DENCO 10. It was a relatively small and inexpensive unit designed to be a component in a variety of larger systems and used in data processing and scientific computer applications. This unit did not receive a very enthusiastic market reception, but an advanced version (the DENCO 20) was given favorable reports and was selling well. During fiscal 1962 DENCO's systems only accounted for 29% of sales. For the fiscal year ending November 2, 1963, however, computers were expected to amount to 9%, special-purpose systems to 29%, and modules and related products to 62% of DENCO's sales.

Management expected the sales of systems to continue to grow relative to the growth in module sales. It was, in fact, this trend that was contributing significantly to DENCO's needs for funds. Material and work-in-process inventory requirements for systems were substantially larger in proportion to sales than those for the modular product lines. These requirements were already having an effect on DENCO's cash position, as is indicated by the company's backlog figures. Early in 1963 the total backlog amounted to $2.3 million. Toward the end of the year the size of the backlog had risen to $6.5 million, of which $4 million represented orders for DENCO's computers. (Exhibits 2 and 3 present recent financial statements.)

A significant characteristic of DENCO's market was that a large proportion of its components and systems was sold either directly or indirectly to the United States government. In fiscal 1962, 87% of DENCO's shipments had ultimately been delivered to the government, and most of these sales were made under competitive bid contracts subject to renegotiation. DENCO's deliveries through fiscal 1961 had been reviewed and cleared, however, and management had reported to the shareholders that they believed no refunds would be required on profits earned in fiscal 1962.

DENCO began early to develop a field sales force. By late 1963 it sold entirely through its own sales force operating out of 11 offices spread over the country. Overseas sales were made through independent manufacturers' representatives.

DENCO's success thus appeared to have depended on a combination of research and development skills, which were required to design new products and improve old ones, on its ability to produce these units efficiently, and on a field sales force which could help develop customer applications for DENCO's products. Moreover, since the value of the modules in inventory could be drastically reduced as the result of a sudden change in technology, accurate product forecasting and production control was essential.

DENCO's main office was located in its Pittsburgh facility, which consisted of two modern buildings containing 90,000 square feet of space. The plant was rented under a long-term lease requiring annual rental payments of $185,000. Warehouse space was leased nearby for an additional $4,000 a year. DENCO also leased production facilities in California and in Cleveland. The California plant totaled 7,500 square feet and cost $14,400 a year. The lease had recently been renewed through 1968. The Cleveland subsidiary was located in a new building of 10,000 square feet, to which an addition of 10,000 square feet was being constructed. After completion of the addition, rentals under the long-term lease would amount to $25,000. DENCO also was committed to annual rentals of $8,500 for its sales offices throughout the country and to equipment rental charges of $12,800 a month.

Gotham's Relationship with DENCO

In the fall of 1960 a vice president in Gotham's trust department who had responsibility for several particularly aggressive portfolios, purchased 25% of a $400,000 private placement of DENCO common stock. Mr. Carl learned at that time that DENCO's management had established close and friendly relationships with the trust department vice president. Shortly thereafter Mr. Carl called at DENCO to introduce himself to Mr. Joseph Grace, DENCO's president, and to Mr. Thomas Estella, one of the founding engineers who had served as treasurer. DENCO's officers were very pleased to see Mr. Carl and noted that they appreciated Gotham's participation in the recent placement. Mr. Carl outlined the services Gotham could offer DENCO. Mr. Grace was particularly interested in the help the bank could give DENCO's efforts to expand its international sales efforts. Mr. Carl promised to put the appropriate department of the bank in touch with Mr. Grace and DENCO's international sales manager.

When the conversation turned to banking relationships, Mr. Grace's comments indicated that he was quite loyal to DENCO's existing bank of account, the Triangle National Bank of Pittsburgh (Triangle), a medium-sized bank with a reputation for aggressive competition. Representatives of one of Pittsburgh's largest banks had been calling on DENCO, but Mr. Grace saw no reason to change his relationship with Triangle. Representatives of no other New York bank had visited the company.

Before leaving Pittsburgh, in the course of a routine visit to Triangle, Mr. Carl called on Mr. Edward Dickens, vice president at Triangle, who supervised the DENCO account. Mr. Dickens had gained a reputation for his imaginative and aggressive lending to smaller electronic companies in western Pennsylvania. Having known of this reputation, Mr. Carl thought it would be a useful learning experience if he could arrange an opportunity to work with Mr. Dickens on a joint loan. It appeared that DENCO might eventually provide such an opportunity. In addition, Gotham maintained a valued correspondent relationship with Triangle, and Mr. Carl thought it might help strengthen this if he were to indicate Gotham's willingness to join Triangle in a loan to DENCO when such participation might be required.

Mr. Dickens was quite unenthusiastic about Mr. Carl's interest in DENCO. He said he believed it was too early for DENCO to increase its banking relationships.

During 1961 and 1962, Mr. Carl, who considered DENCO an attractive potential account, continued to call on DENCO's management from time to time. During his visits he was impressed with the plant and with DENCO's personnel. The plant looked busy but efficient, and morale appeared high. DENCO continued to grow rapidly, and Mr. Carl thought it just a matter of time before DENCO's capital requirements would exceed Triangle's ability to meet them.

At each visit Mr. Carl was cordially received, but Mr. Grace and Mr. Estella never decided the appropriate time had come for DENCO to establish a new banking account. Nevertheless, Mr. Carl arranged for Gotham to provide DENCO with introductions and help in the European market, and Gotham also took over from a Pittsburgh bank a $10,000 loan to Mr. Grace. From time to time Mr. Carl suggested to DENCO's management that it would undoubtedly be advantageous to establish a New York banking relationship well in advance of the time DENCO needed additional bank resources.

During most of 1962 and early 1963, DENCO's financial managers were working with an issue of common stock. Mr. Carl learned of DENCO's preliminary plans in January, 1962. Early in May of 1962, he was told that funds were needed most urgently and that the stock issue would be pushed ahead regardless of market conditions. In July Mr. Carl found that the stock issue had been called off because of the market break in late May. DENCO had arranged to satisfy its needs temporarily by borrowing from Triangle against the security of its receivables (85% without notification to the customers) and of its inventory (50%). Triangle had told DENCO officers that, given the existing equity base, the maximum loan possible without notification was $1.5 million.

Messrs. Grace and Estella expressed annoyance at this limitation, but Mr. Carl indicated that in his opinion Triangle was being extremely generous. He pointed out that it was unlikely that DENCO customer relations would be hurt if notification proved necessary. He suggested that management consider a private placement of convertible debentures. If even this alternative turned out to be unattractive, Mr. Carl said, Gotham might be willing to consider a joint loan with Triangle. His offer was not explored more thoroughly because in February, 1963, DENCO was able to sell 130,000 shares of common stock at $8 a share to net $958,750. (DENCO's stock subsequently sold as low as $5⅝. By October, 1963, the price had recovered to $13.)

Proposed Participation with Triangle

Despite the February addition of equity capital, DENCO's need for additional funds remained great. By October, 1963, its loan from Triangle was up almost to that bank's legal loan limit of $3 million. It was at this point that Mr. Dickens of Triangle came to New York to propose that Gotham take a one-third participation in Triangle's loan to DENCO. DENCO currently was borrowing $2.3 million from Triangle on an unsecured line. Mr. Dickens predicted that DENCO's loan requirements would increase to $4 million or $4.5 million by the end of 1964. In support of the loan participation request, Mr. Dickens supplied Mr. Carl with two documents prepared by Mr. Estella for DENCO's directors. The first was a 5-year plan outlining DENCO's capital requirements and proposing a financial plan.[1] Mr. Dickens noted that DENCO was planning another equity issue for early 1964. The other report was Mr. Estella's forecast for the fiscal year ending November 2, 1963 (Exhibit 4).

Mr. Dickens proposed that Triangle would remain DENCO's principal bank of account and supervise the loan. Both banks would receive compensating balances of 15%. The interest rate would be 5½%, which compared favorably with the current prime rate of 4½% and an average rate of 5% on short-term business loans.

In the course of considering Mr. Dickens' request, Mr. Carl called the Gotham vice president (in the trust department) who had originally purchased the DENCO stock, a member of the investment research staff who was familiar with the company and the industry, and a partner of DENCO's investment banking firm. The reports these men gave Mr. Carl were as favorable as he thought he could expect on a small company

---

[1] For this plan please refer to Exhibit 1 of the earlier case in this book, "The Estella Five-Year Plan."

competing with IBM, General Electric, and other giants of the industry. DENCO appeared to have surpassed the performance of a number of smaller firms in its competitive area, and the consensus was that the company could expect a period of rapid growth.

Even so, Mr. Carl doubted that the bank would be adequately rewarded in the near term for the time and risk involved in accepting a participation in Triangle's loan to DENCO. The longer-range possibilities of DENCO's growth, the opportunity to work with Mr. Dickens and Triangle, and the chance to gain entry to and experience in the area of DENCO's business appeared to offset some of the immediate problems of lending to the company.

Exhibit 1

Summary of Products of Digital Engineering Company

Proprietary Products

Modules.   Digital circuit modules are produced for inventory and sold from catalog specifications at list prices. Modules are packaged digital circuits which can perform decision, storage, control, and other functions. They form the basic building blocks for digital systems. DENCO's initial vacuum units sold satisfactorily and were replaced in 1957 with a new line of transistorized components. In 1962 DENCO offered three major lines of second-generation modules.

Memories.   Two types of memory units are produced, which store information for later use in a computer system.

Input Devices.   DENCO manufactures and sells two types of input devices. An input device feeds information into digital equipment. One type is useful in situations where precise positional information is required, such as in any machine tool control system. The other type is used for applications when information is inserted manually into digital systems, such as by means of a keyboard.

Systems

DENCO designs and builds a variety of special-purpose systems to fulfill requirements which cannot be met as effectively by commercially available general-purpose computers. A special system provides one or more special advantages, such as lower initial cost, lower operating cost, easier maintenance, higher speed, smaller size, and less power. DENCO's special systems are used in space research and rocketry, such as in the Mariner probes of Venus, for navigational and positioning applications, such as for airborne telescopes, and for signal processing, data converting, communications testing, and general use.

Source: Prospectus of February, 1963.

Exhibit 2

DIGITAL ENGINEERING COMPANY

Balance Sheets

(dollar figures in thousands)

	Oct. 31 1959	Oct. 27 1960	Oct. 28 1961	Nov. 3 1962
ASSETS				
Cash.................................	$ 34	$ 227	$ 84	$ 38
Accounts receivable.....................	507	453	918	1,706
Inventories...........................	455	622	905	1,603
Total current assets...............	$ 996	$1,302	$1,907	$3,348
Fixed assets...........................	103	110	145	189
Other assets...........................	21	41	55	28
Total assets.....................	$1,117	$1,453	$2,107	$3,566
LIABILITIES AND NET WORTH				
Due banks............................	$ 332	$ 444	$ 701	$1,470
Accounts payable.......................	96	129	246	395
Accrued expenses.......................	164	121	283	325
Accrued taxes..........................	157	8	45	321
Total current liabilities............	$ 749	$ 702	$1,275	$2,512
Common stock and capital surplus........	70	656	720	652
Retained earnings......................	298	95	112	402
Net worth....................	$ 368	$ 751	$ 832	$1,054
Total liabilities and net worth.......	$1,117	$1,453	$2,107	$3,566

Exhibit 3

DIGITAL ENGINEERING COMPANY

Consolidated Income Statements

(dollar figures in thousands)

	Fiscal year ended:			
	Oct. 31 1959	Oct. 29 1960	Oct. 28 1961	Nov. 3 1962
Net sales.............................	$2,870	$ 3,084	$4,812	$8,669
Cost of sales........................	1,794	2,022	3,276	5,155
Research, development................	190	344	431	894
Total cost of sales................	$1,985	$ 2,366	$3,707	$6,049
Gross profit..........................	$ 885	$ 718	$1,105	$2,621
Selling, administrative and general expense............................	594	905	988	1,936
Interest expense.......................	9	25	36	76
Operating income (loss).................	$ 282	$ (12)	$ 81	$ 608
Other deductions, including profit sharing...........................	1	4	2	42
Income (loss) before taxes...............	$ 281	$ (17)	$ 79	$ 567
Provision for taxes.....................	136	2	36	277
Net income (loss)......................	$ 145	$ (19)	$ 43	$ 290
Shares outstanding (000's)..............	779	904	895	880
Net income (loss) per share.............	$0.186	$(0.021)	$0.048	$ 0.33

Exhibit 4

DIGITAL ENGINEERING COMPANY

Forecast of Financial Statements for the
Fiscal Year Ending November 2, 1963
(dollar figures in thousands)

Balance Sheet

	(Consolidated) Actual—36 Weeks to July 13, 1963	Projected—52 Weeks to November 2, 1963
ASSETS		
Quick assets................................	$2,046	$2,033
Inventory...................................	2,167	3,408
Total current assets....................	$4,213	$5,441
Fixed assets................................	236	250
Other assets................................	213	190
Total assets..........................	$4,662	$5,881
LIABILITIES		
Notes.......................................	$1,450	$2,200
Accrued taxes..............................	441	666
Accounts payable and other.................	592	650
Total current liabilities.................	$2,483	$3,516
Capital stock & paid-in surplus...............	1,590	1,590
Retained earnings..........................	589	775
Total capitalization....................	$2,179	$2,365
Total liabilities......................	$4,662	$5,881

Income Statement

	36 Weeks ending July 13, 1963	52 Weeks ending November 2, 1963
Sales.......................................	$6,863	$11,100
Cost of sales...............................	4,518	7,421
Gross profit................................	$2,345	$ 3,679
Selling & administrative expense..............	1,913	2,814
Operating profit............................	$ 432	$ 865
Taxes.......................................	239	486
	$ 193	$ 379

The Dunning Cabinet Company

On September 3, 1950, Mr. Dunning, 68-year-old president and sole owner of The Dunning Cabinet Company, called on Mr. Vines, vice president and loan officer of the Jefferson National Bank of Richmond, Virginia, to discuss the renegotiation of a $140,000 term loan arranged in March, 1950, to finance the expansion of the Dunning company's plant capacity.

The Dunning Cabinet Company, located in Roanoke, Virginia, manufactured wooden television cabinets against firm orders on hand. It was not a large producer and was best suited for production runs of about 5,000 units. Its high-priced, quality cabinets were sold to large manufacturers of television sets for their console models.

The Jefferson National Bank, a medium-sized bank with a legal loan limit of $1 million, was actively attempting to build a reputation as a progressive bank. To help achieve this goal, the bank's loan officers were encouraged to use originality, whenever the risks did not seem insurmountable, in arranging suitable credit for companies that showed promise of developing into good accounts. It was hoped that by extending credit to companies in situations where other banks might be hesitant in offering support, sound bank-customer relationships would be established that would prove beneficial to the bank over the long run.

In March, 1950, Mr. Dunning was contemplating a $140,000 addition to the company's single-story plant which would double its production capacity. The company's customers were pressing for production many times the operating capacity of a $1 million annual sales volume. In the period from January 21, 1950, to March 15, 1950, orders totaling $3.7 million from six major television set manufacturers were declined. These represented initial orders only; and Mr. Dunning estimated that if these orders had been accepted, repeat business would have easily tripled these initial orders.

743

When Mr. Dunning visited the small Roanoke bank where the company had maintained its account since 1932, he was informed that a $140,000 loan was above the bank's legal limit. Although the loan officer of the local bank expressed his willingness to introduce Mr. Dunning to a loan officer at a large metropolitan bank in Washington, D.C., Mr. Dunning preferred to see Mr. Vines, whom he had known casually for several years. When he went to the Jefferson National Bank on March 17, 1950, to discuss the required loan, Mr. Dunning brought the balance sheets and income statements reproduced in Exhibits 1 and 2.

While at the bank, Mr. Dunning told Mr. Vines that the company had always operated profitably since its founding in 1932 and that it had never failed to have a substantial backlog of firm orders from at least one radio or television set manufacturer during its entire history. Mr. Dunning thought that the company's trade reputation was excellent and that with adequate production facilities the Dunning company could easily double its sales volume. Since a number of the company's expenses, such as sales and administration, were fixed, he believed that the proposed expansion would more than double profits and would pay for itself within a little more than a year's time. He foresaw no problems in doubling plant capacity, for there appeared to be an ample supply of skilled woodworking labor in the Roanoke area. However, to finance the plant expansion, Mr. Dunning estimated the company would require a 2-year loan of $140,000. He also thought additional funds would be needed to increase the working capital to a level that would support the expected increase in sales volume.

Subsequent to Mr. Dunning's visit, Mr. Vines made several checks with television manufacturers regarding Dunning's trade reputation. A typical response was: "We feel very close to Dunning and think highly of them. They are reliable in their dealings, and they make a high-quality, high-price article that cannot be obtained in the mass production cabinets usually put out by larger woodworking concerns. Our purchasing department is highly pleased with Dunning's performance, and as long as we need cabinets, we will give Dunning consideration." These sources also confirmed newspaper articles which predicted that television sales would continue to grow in the foreseeable future. The Dunning company's previous bank of account, which was not a correspondent bank of Jefferson, informed Mr. Vines that the company in recent years maintained a moderate five-figure bank account and properly attended to small seasonal loans which were required occasionally.

In reviewing the balance sheet and income statements provided, Mr. Vines noted that the company had nearly doubled its sales volume within the last 3 years without creating financial imbalance. Whereas only $12,000 principal repayments were required on the $78,000 first mortgage on the company's plant, the outstanding balance had been reduced by $24,000 in 1949. On the whole, Mr. Vines was impressed with Mr. Dunning as an individual, and an examination of the company's financial development in recent years strengthened his confidence.

When Mr. Vines visited the Dunning plant in late March, 1950, he noted that the production process was orderly and inventories appeared well controlled. He was favorably impressed with several younger officers he met during his tour.

On March 30, 1950, Mr. Vines completed a 2½-year term loan agreement for $140,000 with the Dunning company. In addition, a $160,000, 4%, open line of credit was extended to cover increased working capital requirements. When the loan agreement was signed, Mr. Vines briefly discussed the covenants of the term loan with Mr. Dunning.

Bearing interest of 4½%, the term loan was to be repaid in quarterly amounts of $16,000 beginning February 28, 1951, with the final maturity on February 28, 1953. Prepayments without penalty were permitted in whole or in part at any time prior to final maturity date and would be applied against instalments due in inverse order. However, there was a ¼% penalty fee if the loan was repaid by means of outside financing. The positive and negative covenants of the term loan agreement are set forth below:

Positive: The company agrees to . . .
1. Maintain net working capital of greater than $100,000 after excluding the current portion of the term loan from current liabilities.
2. Supply the bank with monthly balance sheets and income statements.

Negative: The company will not without prior permission from the bank . . .
1. Merge; consolidate; sell; or lease any asset.
2. Create a pledge or mortgage against any asset with the exception of the present $78,000 first mortgage on the "old" plant.
3. Replace or acquire more fixed assets in any year than can be purchased from the annual depreciation allowance, except for the proposed plant expansion totaling $140,000.
4. Pay dividends.
5. Purchase securities other than U.S. government bonds.
6. Repurchase the company's capital stock.
7. Increase the salaries of the company's officers.

Subsequent to the signing of the loan agreement, Mr. Vines received the monthly financial statements reproduced in Exhibit 3. As developments in the account seemed normal, he found no reason to inquire further about Dunning's progress. On August 31 he had noted that $80,000 of the term loan had been borrowed by the company but that its deposit balance exceeded $60,000.

On September 3, 1950, Mr. Dunning came to the bank to inform Mr. Vines of a change in the company's expansion plans. Instead of rebuilding the plant for a total capacity of $2 million sales volume, the enlarged plant would increase production capacity to an annual sales volume of $3,500,000. This change, Mr. Dunning explained, had been forced by increased pressure from the company's customers for more cabinets. Construction was well under way, and Mr. Dunning expected the new plant to be completed by the end of 1950. He said that $53,000 of the building program had been paid but that construction costs were now estimated at $470,000. Because the $140,000 term loan was inadequate to meet the new requirements, Mr. Dunning requested that the bank negotiate a new loan for $400,000 to replace the original loan.

Sales during the first 6 months of 1950 had been $679,000, with profits before taxes equal to $123,000. In July, despite closing the plant for a 2-week vacation, sales had amounted to $83,000, and Mr. Dunning estimated August volume was $138,000. Sales for the last 4 months of 1950 were estimated at $700,000. Of this amount, he had accepted firm orders as follows:

$$
\begin{array}{lr}
\text{September} & \$146,000 \\
\text{October} & 232,000 \\
\text{November} & 171,000 \\
\text{December} & 28,000 \\
\end{array}
$$

By the end of September he expected to be fully committed for the remainder of 1950. Sales in 1951 were expected to approximate the plant's capacity of $3,500,000. Although a portion of the new plant was already in operation, Mr. Dunning was still turning down orders at the rate of $800,000 per month.

Mr. Dunning estimated that profits before taxes would continue at the level of 18%, the actual results for the first 6 months of 1950. Income taxes payable in 1951 were estimated at 42%. He anticipated the unused $160,000 line of credit extended by the bank would adequately cover the expected increase in working capital requirements.

Mr. Vines was shocked at the action taken by Mr. Dunning, particularly in view of the fixed asset covenant in the original term loan. When asked about this restriction, Mr. Dunning said he had forgotten about it. Mr. Vines replied that such negligence was certainly not conducive to good bank-customer relations. However, he reluctantly agreed to consider a new term loan agreement.

When Mr. Vines inquired about the effect on the company's business of the Korean conflict, which had begun in June, Mr. Dunning said that it did not appear likely there would be any major cutback in television production. If there was a cutback, however, he was not much concerned, since the company had had sufficient woodworking business to operate the plant 24 hours a day during the last war. Mr. Dunning expected to do as well during the Korean War if it became necessary to convert to war production in the future.

After Mr. Dunning had left, Mr. Vines phoned several of Dunning's customers to determine the company's outlook. A typical response was: "We consider Dunning an important supplier of high-quality cabinets. They are fine people to deal with; and if war or another unexpected economic development does not interfere with production of television sets, we expect our orders with Dunning will undoubtedly run higher in 1951. However, they are not one of our major suppliers due to their inability to produce in volume. In the event of an all-out war necessitating a cutback or discontinuance in television production and a resumption of war orders requiring woodworking jobs, Dunning will receive consideration."

With this information at hand, Mr. Vines began reviewing Dunning's financial requirements to determine whether the bank should grant the request for a $400,000 term loan.

Exhibit 1

THE DUNNING CABINET COMPANY

Selected Balance Sheets

(dollar figures in thousands)

ASSETS	December 31, 1947	December 31, 1948	December 31, 1949	February 28, 1950*
Cash...........................	$ 19	$ 22	$ 25	$ 40
Accounts receivable...............	62	30	62	56
Inventory.......................	114	144	147	98
Total current assets.........	$195	$196	$234	$194
Plant and equipment (net).........	210	254	279	285
Other assets.....................	6	3	6	6
Total assets...............	$411	$453	$519	$485
LIABILITIES				
Accounts payable.................	$ 14	$ 33	$ 53	$ 18
Taxes payable....................	53	22	43	43
Accrued payables.................	22	39	30	17
Total current liabilities......	$ 89	$ 94	$126	$ 78
Mortgage........................	108	108	84	78
Common stock (800 shares—				
par value $25).................	20	20	20	20
Surplus.........................	194	231	289	309
Total liabilities and net worth..................	$411	$453	$519	$485

* Unaudited.

Exhibit 2

THE DUNNING CABINET COMPANY

Income Statements

(dollar figures in thousands)

	1946	1947	1948	1949	Jan. and Feb. 1950
Sales..........................	$505.0	$716.2	$778.5	$981.9	$181.4
Cost of goods sold*............	338.9	499.5	598.4	754.2	
Gross profit...................	$166.1	$216.7	$180.1	$227.7	
Operating expenses............	89.4	91.0	121.8	123.5	
Operating profit..............	$ 76.7	$125.7	$ 58.3	$104.2	
Other income (net)............	0.6	2.9	2.1	0.8	
Profit before taxes............	$ 77.3	$128.6	$ 60.4	$105.0	20.0
Taxes......................	32.3	53.2	21.8	43.2	
Net profit....................	45.0	75.4	38.6	61.8	
Dividends....................	0	0	2.0	4.0	

```
* Includes depreciation of:
  1946........$12,000
  1947........ 13,000
  1948........ 15,000
  1949........ 15,000
```

Exhibit 3

THE DUNNING CABINET COMPANY

Selected Unaudited Balance Sheets

(dollar figures in thousands)

ASSETS	March 31, 1950	April 30, 1950	May 31, 1950	June 30, 1950	July 31, 1950
Cash..........................	$ 25.8	$ 25.6	$ 22.2	$ 10.7	$ 18.2
Accounts receivable............	102.6	114.3	106.4	60.3	73.6
Finished goods.................	10.3	10.1	2.2	1.9	1.8
Work-in-process...............	20.8	19.7	22.4	120.1	138.5
Raw materials.................	48.9	85.4	111.4	42.3	37.5
Supplies......................	4.3	3.9	9.5	11.3	14.3
Total current assets......	$212.7	$259.0	$274.1	$246.6	$283.9
Net plant and equipment........	282.9	290.4	293.8	316.7	331.5
Other assets..................	5.3	7.2	6.8	6.6	6.5
Total assets.............	$500.9	$556.6	$574.7	$569.9	$621.9
LIABILITIES					
Accounts payable...............	$ 29.5	$ 39.0	$ 45.1	$ 27.5	$ 23.7
Taxes payable.................	26.4	26.4	26.4	17.6	17.6
Accrued payables..............	17.6	18.6	24.0	20.4	20.2
Total current liabilities....	$ 73.5	$ 84.0	$ 95.5	$ 65.5	$ 61.5
Mortgage.....................	78.0	78.0	72.0	72.0	72.0
Term loan....................					40.0
Common stock—(800 shares—par value $25)...............	20.0	20.0	20.0	20.0	20.0
Surplus.......................	329.4	374.6	387.2	412.4	428.4
	$500.9	$556.6	$574.7	$569.9	$621.9
Sales.........................	$108.0	$143.8	$ 96.9	$148.8	$ 83.0
Profit before taxes.............	20.2	45.2	12.6	25.2	16.0

Central Broadcasting Company

On the morning of June 29, 1961, Mr. Toby Stone was reviewing the highlights of his tour through the operating departments of Cook County National Bank, a large multifaceted Chicago bank aggressively competing for corporate deposits and loans on a national scale. Mr. Stone was currently working in the credit department, the final phase of his training program. He remembered with particular pleasure several projects of the past year which had required him to draw on research and writing skills and insights he had gained during graduate work in business administration.

One of these assignments had been a comprehensive study of the radio-television broadcasting industry undertaken at the request of Mr. Albert Roth, a senior lending officer. Mr. Roth believed that many sound loan situations in the industry were being overlooked or turned down by the banking community because traditional yardsticks were used to measure debt capacity and because bankers had not adequately analyzed key elements in this relatively young industry. Mr. Stone knew that the few bank loans made to broadcasting companies were on a patently conservative basis and hoped that his study would enable Cook County National Bank to pioneer in more aggressive lending to this industry.

While Mr. Stone was speculating on how long he would remain in the credit department before permanent assignment, Mr. Roth approached his desk. "Toby, you're the expert on radio–TV loans; I've got an interesting situation here I'd like your opinion on. Central Broadcasting Company (CBC) wants to borrow $23.5 million to finance the purchase of KMOC and KMOC–TV in Kansas City, and radio station WSUB here in Chicago. As the lead bank, First Cincinnati Trust has agreed to take $7 million of the $16 million bank portion of the loan and has asked us to take $6 million. I believe they are trying to place the remaining $3 million at a New York bank. Several insurance companies have indicated a possible interest in taking the $7.5 million long-term segment of the loan.

"I haven't checked the figures yet, but the principals are well connected and highly regarded. As you'll see in the file, there are collateral business possibilities here. Incidentally, our good neighbors at the Loop National turned this one down.

"Whether or not you think this loan is do-able, I hope you'll take this as an opportunity to dig deeper into this situation and come up with some guidelines we can use in evaluating future broadcasting credits. How much can you lend to a company with good cash flows but a negative tangible net worth? Specifically, how much would you be willing to lend CBC against their current operations and proposed purchases, and on what basis?

"I have a luncheon meeting tomorrow with Mr. Carter of First Cincinnati, so I'd like to have your report by 10 A.M."

THE BROADCASTING INDUSTRY

In the course of his recent study, Mr. Stone had gathered a variety of facts about the broadcasting industry. By December, 1960, there were 530 TV stations and 3,688 radio stations operating in 226 metropolitan markets. The TV industry had grown rapidly in the middle Fifties from 122 stations in 1952 to 501 stations in 1957; however, in the following few years the total had shown only a nominal increase. This leveling trend was due to several factors:

1. Uhf stations, which operated on channels 14–83, had not fared well. Whereas 40% of TV sets produced in 1953 were equipped to receive uhf channels, only 15% were so equipped in 1960. The number of uhf stations operating in 1960 was 91, down from 121 in 1953.
2. The Federal Communications Commission was increasingly reluctant to grant coveted vhf licenses in the face of opposition from stations serving the area where the applicant planned to broadcast and in light of adequate coverage in most areas.
3. The industry was approaching saturation. Of the 226 metropolitan markets, 84 were served by three or more stations, 21 by four or more. Since there were only three major networks, it had become increasingly difficult for an applicant to show that the approval of his license would be "in the public interest," a phrase the FCC used often in defining its responsibilities.

The number of radio stations in operation had shown a similar leveling trend. This was believed attributable more to declining opportunities for profit, resulting from competition from TV and other media, than to difficulty in obtaining licenses to operate.

Profitability

Data collected by Mr. Stone, which showed a wide difference in profit performance of TV stations versus radio stations, are given in Exhibit 1.

Total TV sales and earnings had more than doubled between 1954 and 1960, while the number of stations had increased by only 29%. During the same period the number of radio stations had increased by 38%, and although sales kept pace, aggregate earnings stabilized at a relatively low level.

In both the radio and the TV industries, profits varied over a wide range between stations. Return on equity figures were available only for a few publicly owned companies, but Mr. Stone gathered from a variety of sources that in many cases profits had been quite substantial. Unlike public utilities, broadcasting companies were not restricted by the government as to rates or profits.

Operations

Mr. Stone believed that broadcasting could be characterized as the business of selling to advertisers the markets reached by the stations' transmitting facilities. Advertising revenues were attracted in two ways. Some revenues came through the national networks, which sold programs such as "Bonanza" (or in the case of radio, "Mary Noble, Backstage Wife") to the agencies of national advertisers, then passed along approximately 25% of the revenue to those of their affiliated stations that contracted to broadcast the program. The stations also received revenue directly from national and local advertisers, which sponsored nonnetwork programming such as a film series ("Playboy Penthouse," for example), a cartoon series, or a movie. The rights to broadcast these films were purchased by each station from independent producers. National and local advertisements were also aired during station breaks and locally produced programs.

A recent industry breakdown of these revenues was as follows:

	TV	*Radio*
Network	21%	6%
National	55	31
Local	24	63

Profitability was affected to an unusually great extent by variations in revenues, since the direct costs associated with incremental revenues were minor, consisting primarily of sales commissions. Network hourly rates were fixed by agreement between the station and the network and were generally subject to change by the network; national spot and local rates were determined by each station and publicly quoted in its rate card. Network and national spot revenues were relatively stable and were to some extent beyond the control of the station sales manager. Local sales were less stable, and while a heavy percentage of local revenues may have been a sign of good sales effort, it was also considered an indication that cash flows and profits were vulnerable.

Local and national spot rates were based on independent estimates of population and number of sets in use in the service area of the station and were affected by appraisals made by various rating agencies of the number of sets tuned into the station. The basis for determining rates was quite consistent across the country, and in the TV industry rates had increased from time to time as a result of the effectiveness of TV as an advertising medium.

Mr. Stone was impressed with the prime importance of network affiliation to a TV station; the network was a major source of revenue and an important factor in the station's relative popularity in its market area. The affiliation was a freely negotiated arm's-length transaction subject to cancellation by either party.

Each station was required to have its license renewed every 3 years by the FCC. Although this was normally a formality, the FCC had on rare occasions refused to renew licenses because of programming or other actions "not in the public interest."

Purchases of Broadcasting Stations

Transfers of existing licenses were subject to the approval of the FCC, but approval was routinely granted. As a result of the great profitability of TV stations and the limited number of new licenses being granted, the price of successful stations had risen substantially above cost. Thus many recently acquired stations had a high intangible value on the asset side of their balance sheets, frequently entitled "Network Affiliation Contracts." These intangibles were not depreciable for tax purposes.

CENTRAL BROADCASTING COMPANY

CBC began operations in the fall of 1954 with the purchase of TV station WTLO in Toledo. In August, 1957, CBC was purchased outright by a group of businessmen headed by Mr. Simon J. Becker, who became the new president, bringing with him an experienced management team.

Mr. Becker had been active in radio since 1935 and in TV since 1946 and was widely regarded as one of the most capable executives in the broadcasting industry. He had excellent connections with the National Broadcasting Company, and was very close to First Cincinnati Trust Company, a bank with which Cook County National Bank had been trying for years to establish an important correspondent relationship but with little success. His business associates, some of whom had their offices in Chicago, were successful men with ample personal bank accounts and a variety of business interests. In a recent discussion with Mr. Roth, Mr. Becker had talked about his plans for CBC:

As you know, because they are not regulated as to return on equity, broadcasting companies under capable management have a unique opportunity to be quite profitable compared with the average manufacturing enterprise. We feel that we can purchase stations and, through our know-how and experience, add profits to existing revenues by cutting operating costs and bring in new business to increase profits even further. Since advertising outlays by major corporations are projected to reach all-time highs in 1962, the outlook for CBC looks really promising.

When Mr. Roth had asked him about possible clouds on the horizon, Mr. Becker had replied, "Despite well-publicized problems[1] of the mass communications industry, we do not feel threatened by any particular legislation or disruption of any existing business relationship. We feel that our principal future problem is the economy itself since advertising budgets are subject to rapid reappraisals."

Of his plans for future acquisitions, Mr. Becker had said, "It's definitely a seller's market. The scramble for stations for the past 10 years has bid prices up to the point where good stations at any price are now hard to find."

Acquisitions

Shortly after the acquisition of CBC by Mr. Becker's group, CBC purchased TV station WCAP in Champaign, Illinois. As reflected in CBC's December 31, 1958, balance sheet (included in Exhibit 2), the cost of these properties ($2.6 million) plus working capital needs were financed by $2.8 million equity and $1.4 million bank debt.

In early 1959 CBC purchased WCNO–AM and WCNO–TV in Cincinnati at prices of $1.0 million and $4.0 million respectively. This purchase and the additional working capital requirements were financed by a term loan of $6 million and subordinated debentures of $1.5 million. The loan, from First Cincinnati Trust, called for repayment in quarterly instalments of $125,000 for 4 years with a $4 million balloon. All the cash flows stemming from depreciation, amortization of intangibles, and earnings in excess of $500,000 a year were to be applied to the balloon portion of the loan. The $1.5 million subordinated debentures, held privately, were due on April 15, 1964. Warrants attached to the debentures entitled the holders to purchase 214,286 common shares at $7 a share until that date. Thus by the end of 1959, CBC had succeeded in obtaining debt-equity leverage of almost 3 to 1.

Under Mr. Becker's leadership significant improvement was shown for each property (see Exhibit 3). Both revenues and operating margins of each station were boosted. According to Mr. Carter of First Cincinnati Trust, CBC's performance had exceeded the detailed cash flow projections submitted by Mr. Becker prior to the 1959 term loan.

These results, in conjunction with the rising market for broadcasting properties, caused the market value of CBC stations (as appraised by an

---

[1] Among the vocal critics of television programming practices was the newly appointed head of the Federal Communications Commission, Newton Minow, who labeled TV programming "a vast wasteland."

industry expert at the request of Mr. Carter) to be substantially in excess of book value, as shown in the accompanying table.

	Cost	Market Value, 1961
WTLO, Toledo	$1,000,000	$ 9,000,000
WCAP, Champaign	1,600,000	6,500,000
WCNO–TV, Cincinnati	5,000,000	10,000,000
WCNO–AM, Cincinnati	1,000,000	2,000,000
	$8,600,000	$27,500,000

Condition of Stations

The appraisal of CBC properties certified that all broadcasting towers and equipment were up to date, in good condition, and equipped for color, and that CBC's film contracts were in good condition and not immediately subject to unusual decline in value. CBC's fund flows resulting from earned depreciation would not be needed for capital expenditures, which in the case of less well-equipped stations could be major. Installation of color transmitting facilities, for example, often required an outlay of over $250,000. Film contracts consisted of film series, usually bought a year in advance, for 39 shows plus 13 reruns; cartoons, for which the normal contracts ran for a period of 4 years; and films, which were purchased up to 5 years in advance. Outstanding film contracts could be a negative factor in the appraisal of a TV station if they were judged to be overvalued, too large, or for too long a maturity.

Markets

In a ranking of the 226 metropolitan markets by size in *TV Factbook*, a leading trade publication, markets served by CBC stations were rated as follows:

Cincinnati	16th
Toledo	39th
Champaign–Decatur–Springfield	65th

According to census estimates, these areas promised better than average growth potential. In each of the three areas, CBC was considered to be more aggressive than its competitors and gaining on them. Currently, WCNO–TV was ahead of two Cincinnati competitors; WCNO–AM was fourth of seven; WCAP was even with two competing stations in Champaign; and WTLO was second of three in Toledo.

Sources of Revenues

Long an advocate of concentrating sales effort on national rather than local advertisers, Mr. Becker regarded the distinctive mix of CBC's revenues shown in the accompanying table as lending an element of stability to his operations:

| | *Sources of CBC Revenues* | |
	TV	*Radio*
Network	21%	1%
National	61	64
Local	18	35

The Loan Proposal

After reading the CBC credit file, Mr. Stone turned to Mr. Roth's memorandum describing the proposed loan and the attached cash flow projections submitted by CBC. The $16 million bank portion of the $23.5 million loan was divided into two parts: $12 million at $5\frac{1}{4}\%$ payable to November 15, 1967, in 12 semiannual instalments of $1 million each; and a $4 million, $5\frac{1}{2}\%$ balloon due January 1, 1968. Under the proposed terms, each year 75% of the total cash generated from depreciation, amortization, and earnings in excess of $2 million would be applied to the balloon until fully paid. The $7.5 million, $5\frac{3}{4}\%$ long-term portion of the loan was to be payable in semiannual instalments of $1 million due May 15, 1969, to May 15, 1972, with the balance of $500,000 due on November 15, 1972. This portion of the loan was to be issued with warrants to purchase 75,000 common shares at $20 per share until November 15, 1972.

The loan proceeds were to be used as follows:

To purchase KMOC and KMOC–TV in Kansas City	$14 million
To purchase radio station WSUB in Chicago	5 million
To repay the outstanding balance of the 1959 term loan	4.5 million

KMOC and KMOC–TV

Stations KMOC and KMOC–TV had begun operations on September 30, 1958. Despite unimpressive management and a mediocre rating as compared with competition in the Kansas City area, the stations showed an operating profit of over $1.2 million for the year ended May 31, 1961. In addition to the normal improvements they could expect to attain, CBC executives saw two special plus factors in the Kansas City situation. First, competition, though fairly competent, was notably unaggressive. Second, the market reached by Kansas City stations was underrated at present; the forthcoming 1961 market appraisal by the American Research Bureau was expected to move Kansas City from 29th to 22nd in the ranking of metropolitan markets, which would allow an upward adjustment of rate cards. Exhibit 4 shows KMOC–TV's 1960 operating results as compared with those of KCM, the larger of its two competitors.

WSUB

WSUB, a station located on the northwest fringe of Chicago, had had for years the image of a suburban station, although its signal covered the Chicago metropolitan area. Becker planned to compete vigorously with the major midtown radio stations by means of aggressive rock-and-roll programming and saw an opportunity thereby to add substantially to local advertising revenues.

Cash Flow Projections

CBC's 6-year projections are presented in Exhibit 5. Mr. Stone noted that according to the projections, the balloon portion of the bank loan would be retired at the beginning of 1967, and that if the "Cash Retained" by CBC were applied to the balloon, it could be retired shortly after the end of 1965.

Mr. Stone's Report

For the purpose of evaluating the CBC credit and generalizing his analysis to cover a range of broadcasting credits, Mr. Stone decided to use a checklist he had roughed out during his study of the broadcasting industry. As he started to write his report, he noted that the pro forma balance sheet submitted by CBC showed a debt to stated equity ratio of about 6:1 (see Exhibit 2). That, he mused, would raise a few eyebrows around the bank.

Mr. Stone's report is presented in Appendix A (page 760).

Exhibit 1

Trends in the U.S. Broadcasting Industry, 1954–60
(dollar figures in millions)

	Number of Stations	Total Revenues	Total Expenses	Pretax Earnings
TV:				
1954	410	$ 593.0	$ 502.7	$ 90.3
1955	437	744.7	594.5	150.2
1956	475	896.9	707.3	189.6
1957	501	943.2	783.2	160.0
1958	514	1,030.0	858.1	171.9
1959	521	1,163.9	941.6	222.3
1960	530	1,268.6	1,024.5	244.1
Radio:				
1954	2,598	$ 449.5	$ 407.7	$ 41.8
1955	2,742	453.4	407.4	46.0
1956	2,966	480.6	431.4	49.2
1957	3,164	517.9	463.3	54.6
1958	3,290	523.1	485.8	37.3
1959	3,528	560.0	517.6	42.4
1960	3,688	597.7	551.8	45.9

Exhibit 2

CENTRAL BROADCASTING COMPANY

Condensed Balance Sheets, as of December 31

(dollar figures in thousands)

	1958	1959	1960	1961 Pro Forma, after Proposed Acquisitions and Financing
Cash.........................	$ 173	$ 506	$ 1,313	$ 1,804
Receivables..................	342	874	1,228	1,260
Inventory....................	28	71	58	107
Film contracts...............	172	433	416	957
Total current assets.....	$ 715	$ 1,884	$ 3,015	$ 4,128
Fixed assets..................	2,294	4,844	4,362	7,779
Prepaid expenses.............	85	147	155	176
Film contracts...............	326	968	770	2,132
Network affiliation contracts...	641	3,860	3,860	17,933
Total assets............	$4,061	$11,703	$12,162	$32,148
Payables and accruals.........	$ 505	$ 552	$ 541	$ 1,163
Federal taxes................	...	...	686	935
Current term debt............	635	1,131	1,332	2,807
Total current liabilities..	$1,140	$ 1,683	$ 2,559	$ 4,905
Term debt...................	794	6,011	4,793	21,966
Subordinated debt...........	...	1,500	1,500	1,500
Common stock...............	1,150	1,150	1,150	1,150
Capital surplus..............	1,634	1,634	1,634	1,634
Earned surplus..............	(657)	(275)	526	993
Total liabilities........	$4,061	$11,703	$12,162	$32,148

Exhibit 3

Selected Station Operating Results
(dollar figures in thousands)

Station and Year	Gross Sales	Net Sales*	Operating Profit	Percent to Gross Sales
WCAP:				
1955...............	$ 640	$ 548	$ 99	15.5
1956...............	928	789	232	25.0
1957†..............	549	473	(59)	. . .
1958...............	735	631	17	2.3
1959...............	1,056	894	228	21.6
1960...............	1,398	1,187	483	34.5
WTLO:				
1955...............	$ 477	$ 416	$ (173)	. . .
1956...............	1,102	940	126	11.4
1957†..............	1,533	1,314	332	21.7
1958...............	2,141	1,773	751	35.1
1959...............	2,127	1,752	599	28.1
1960...............	2,277	1,869	737	32.4
WCNO–TV:				
1958...............	$1,939	$1,587	$ 870	44.9
1959†..............	2,474	1,984	1,147	46.4
1960...............	3,951	3,131	1,900	48.1
WCNO–AM:				
1958...............	$ 476	$ 352	$ 170	35.7
1959†..............	411	310	(6)	. . .
1960...............	795	607	195	24.5

* After agency commissions.
† Year acquired by CBC.

Exhibit 4

Operating Results of Kansas City TV Stations, 1960

	KMOC-TV	KCM-TV
Gross revenue....................	$2,960,000	$4,674,000
Agency and representatives........	468,000	842,000
Net revenue.....................	$2,492,000	$3,832,000
Operating expense...............	1,718,000	2,094,000
Operating profit.................	$ 774,000	$1,738,000

Exhibit 5

CENTRAL BROADCASTING COMPANY

Cash Flow Projections
(dollar figures in thousands)

	(12 months to 5/31/61) Actual	1962	1963	1964	1965	1966	1967
Net revenue:							
CBC	$ 6,795	$ 7,300	$ 7,850	$ 8,436			
WSUB	1,321	1,523	1,774	1,903			
KMOC-TV	2,492	2,930	4,386	4,646			
KMOC	687	1,020					
Total	$11,295	$12,773	$14,010	$14,985			
Operating expenses:							
CBC	$ 3,580	$ 3,800	$ 3,990	$ 4,190			
WSUB	969	915	960	1,008			
KMOC-TV	1,559	1,740	2,200	2,200			
KMOC	402	490					
Total	$ 6,510	$ 6,945	$ 7,150	$ 7,398			
Operating profit:							
CBC	$ 3,215	$ 3,500	$ 3,860	$ 4,246			
WSUB	352	608	814	895			
KMOC-TV	933	1,190	2,186	2,446			
KMOC	285	530					
Total	$ 4,785	$ 5,828	$ 6,860	$ 7,587	$ 7,587	$ 7,587	$ 7,587
Other deductions:							
Corporate expense	$ 503	$ 570	$ 630	$ 675	$ 675	$ 675	$ 675
Depreciation	916	1,414	1,321	911	911	911	911
Interest	421	1,349	1,249	1,082	959	859	759
Total	$ 1,840	$ 3,333	$ 3,200	$ 2,668	$ 2,545	$ 2,445	$ 2,345
Profit before taxes	$ 2,945	$ 2,495	$ 3,660	$ 4,919	$ 5,042	$ 5,142	$ 5,242
Income tax (54.64%)	1,451	1,363	2,000	2,688	2,755	2,810	2,864
Net profit	$ 1,494	$ 1,132	$ 1,660	$ 2,231	$ 2,287	$ 2,332	$ 2,378
Add: Depreciation	916	1,414	1,321	911	911	911	911
Cash available	$ 2,410	$ 2,546	$ 2,981	$ 3,142	$ 3,198	$ 3,243	$ 3,289
Payments on loan:							
Fixed		$ 2,000	$ 2,000	$ 2,000	$ 2,000	$ 2,000	$ 2,000
75% of remaining cash available		410	736	857	898	934	165*
Cash retained		$ 136	$ 245	$ 285	$ 300	$ 309	$1,124
Beginning loan balance‡		$25,000‡	$22,590‡	$19,854	$15,497	$12,599	$9,665
Payments		2,410	2,736	4,357†	2,898	2,934	2,165
Ending loan balance		$22,590	$19,854	$15,497	$12,599	$9,665	$7,500

* Balance of balloon portion of term debt due banks.

† Assumes that $1,500,000 subordinated debentures due 1964 would be offset by exercise of attached warrants, entitling holders to purchase 214,286 common shares at $7 per share, which expired on due date. Current market for CBC stock (1,168,223 shares outstanding) was 22¾.

‡ Includes $1.5 million subordinated debentures.

APPENDIX A

Memorandum

To: Mr. Albert V. Roth

Re: Central Broadcasting Company

I have taken the CBC situation as an opportunity to go deeper into the thinking that lies behind credit evaluations in this type of business. The television checklist is an attempt to break down the general conclusion on a TV credit into its various components, and develop a method of looking at and evaluating these components individually, rather than relying on a general "feel" for the situation.

Inasmuch as the $23.5 million loan request comes within CBC's debt capacity as determined by use of the checklist, I recommend that CCNB agree to participate in this loan.

Toby M. Stone
Credit Department

June 30, 1961

Guidelines for Lending to the Broadcasting Industry

The following checklist was prepared to clarify and substantiate the financial analysis of the CBC loan. However, the overall purpose of the analysis is to determine standards for establishing the minimum amount of equity required in the ownership of any broadcasting properties, or more exactly, the maximum amount of bank debt that can be put into any television broadcasting situation with a reasonable amount of risk.

The guidelines are the result of an attempt to form a summary checklist of significant factors which must be taken into consideration in evaluating the creditworthiness of a loan to the owner, or prospective owner, of a television station or group of stations. It is an attempt to formalize the thinking and underlying considerations which make up the final analysis and mathematically come up with a guideline figure which will approximate the amount that can be safely loaned against the properties involved. This should help to provide uniformity and consistency to these evaluations. However, it should be emphasized that this system, which involved the use of a confidence index, is no more than a weighted average use of probabilities, and the results of the analysis will be no better than the individual evaluations which go into the final figure.

It is most important to recognize that this procedure is primarily designed to insure that the lending officer will: (1) consider *all* the factors appropriate to the loan, and (2) keep these factors in their *proper perspective*.

Establishment of Base Figure

To establish the base figure against which the loan will be made, it is necessary to have as accurate an appraisal as possible made of the company, so that the equity base may be restated and a revalued figure for the net worth of the company established. Balance sheet figures in this business *have very little meaning*, unless the property has been recently traded or purchased. Consequently, if the book value of the stations owned is considerably less than their market value, the stations must be realistically reevaluated and placed on the balance sheet at a conservative figure for their current market value. In some cases the stations may even be overvalued on the balance sheet, and in these cases their value must be discounted and the best estimate of their worth used. In this manner the equity of the corporation will be restated, and it is this "Restated Asset Base" that will be used in the subsequent calculations. It is against this figure that the composite ratio will be applied, thus making the composite ratio a form of a debt/equity ratio. CBC's Restated Asset Base will be $27.5 million, the market value of presently owned properties, plus $19 million, the purchase price of the stations being acquired, or a total of $46.5 million.

Use of Composite Ratio

The final composite ratio is determined from the checklist by utilizing the accompanying explanations for each category to assist in applying a reasonable confidence index. The maximum composite ratio that could possibly be obtained is .66 which in effect would allow a 2 to 1 debt/equity ratio. This would appear to be the farthest the bank should extend itself in any loan of this nature. However, to reach this ratio, it would be necessary for the lending officer to have 100% confidence in each aspect of the analysis; consequently, the officer may find it is extremely difficult to justify even a 1 to 1 debt/equity ratio. The use of these guidelines prevents the lender from completely discounting or overlooking the significant aspects of the credit and, it is hoped, will guide him to a more realistic evaluation of the situation.

If the figure reached by the lending officer in making this analysis is satisfactory to him, the checklist will then provide a detailed and inclusive means of substantiating his conclusions.

EXPLANATION OF CHECKLIST FACTORS

(The remainder of Mr. Stone's report covered material presented in the body of the case.)

Exhibit A-1

Guidelines for Lending to the Television Broadcasting Business
(television checklist)

Central Broadcasting Company Loan Proposal	Column I Weight Factor*	Column II Confidence Index† 0–100%	Column I × Column II
Cash flow			
1. Reliability			
Historic figures (available used).........	6	80%	4.8
Degree of optimism...................	5	60	3.0
Depreciation—Tax estimated (basis for)...	5	90	4.5
Capital expenditures estimates (Height of tower, color facilities, condition and quality of broadcasting equipment)........	5	90	4.5
2. Length of payout.....................	10	30	3.0
Cash Flow Subtotal................	31		19.8
Management			
1. Track record in industry and supporting personnel...........................	6	100	6.0
2. General reputation, integrity, etc.........	4	100	4.0
Markets			
1. Size......................................	5	90	4.5
2. Growth potential.......................	5	70	3.5
Network Affiliations and License.............	7	90	6.3
1. Number of stations in market (also overlap)			
2. Number of stations owned			
3. Station position in market and strength of other stations			
4. Ownership of license and history			
Outside Influences........................	8	100	8.0
Balances			
Other relationships			
New business potential			
Interest rate			
Film Contracts—if significant minus (up to minus 5)			
Composite Ratio..........................	66		52.1
Restated Asset Base × Composite Ratio = Debt Capacity ($46,500,000) × (52.1)/ 100 = $24,227,000.			

* Subject to modifications based on experience and the dictates of common sense, these weight factors should be applicable to *any* broadcasting loan.

† These percentages apply only to CBC and reflect the author's judgment based on available information.

Ampro Europe

Late in October, 1966, Mr. Andrew Riley, a vice president and head of the Overseas Credit Analysis Department of the Gotham National Bank of New York (Gotham), faced a decision relative to the protective covenants that he should recommend in a proposed term loan to Ampro Electra S.A., the Belgian subsidiary of a valued American customer of the bank. Officers of Gotham's Brussels branch had vigorously warned that insistence on certain proposed terms would play into the hands of less démanding Belgian banks and quite possibly cause Gotham to lose a desirable loan and customer relationship. On the other hand, Mr. Riley had a responsibility for helping to implement the credit policy of the bank and to assess the inherent soundness of the proposed loan arrangement, even though final approval of the credit would rest with European District officers in the New York head office. Further, he had been among a group of officers in the bank who espoused and had strongly articulated the view that Gotham should push vigorously to improve lending practice overseas and that Gotham's term lending abroad should fully incorporate the skills and experience of the bank developed over more than 30 years of term lending to American businesses in the United States. Further, Mr. Riley felt a real challenge to his professional craftsmanship in fitting the terms of the credit to the specific circumstances of the borrower and in anticipating problems and pitfalls in the credit arrangement over time.

Consideration of the Ampro Electra S.A. credit had begun a month earlier, when Mr. David Graham, vice president and treasurer of Ampro Corporation of Peoria, Illinois, met with Mr. Benjamin Sloane, assistant vice president and an officer in the European District of Gotham National, to discuss the possibility of a $1.6 million loan arrangement for Ampro's various European subsidiaries. "As you know," Mr. Graham remarked, "our European companies have been going great guns ever since they started up in 1958. Their profits have been excellent but they need money badly to support their growth. We've been hoping Gotham could help out."

Based on recently completed 5-year cash projections for Ampro's European subsidiaries, the loan request was received with enthusiasm by Gotham's officers, who regarded Mr. Graham's request as a positive indication that Ampro Corporation intended to do most of its future banking business with Gotham. After several years of solicitation by Gotham's Midwestern District, Ampro had opened a small account in November, 1964. Shortly thereafter, Gotham's Tokyo branch made available a $300,000, 3-year term loan to Ampro's Japanese subsidiary, after which the parent company increased its balances in its Gotham home office account to about $100,000. This new opportunity to extend financing to European subsidiaries was therefore welcome. However, Mr. Graham made it clear that the parent company would be unable to give its guarantee on the loan due to restrictive covenants in its indenture agreement with a large insurance company. Mr. Graham explained that the company preferred not to ask the insurance company for a modification to the indenture terms at that time; nor, he added, was it assured one could be obtained were it requested. Mr. Graham said that he would supply the bank with consolidating statements so that the creditworthiness of the borrowing companies could be evaluated.

As Mr. Graham prepared to leave the bank, he said, "This has been a most productive meeting. Incidentally, we like our subsidiaries to retain a good deal of autonomy in their financial arrangements. I wonder if it would be appropriate for one of your branches to do the negotiating and place the loan, provided one actually goes through."

"Our Brussels branch would be the right one to handle it," Mr. Sloane replied, "and all it takes is a cable to find out. We'll let you know as soon as possible."

Next day, the following cable was sent to Mr. Richard Gibbons at Gotham's Brussels branch:

To GIBBONS
GOTHAM NATIONAL BANK
BRUSSELS
BELGIUM

RE AMPRO CORPORATION EUROPEAN SUBSIDIARIES STOP WE ARE TRYING TO WORK OUT A CREDIT, WHICH MIGHT CALL FOR YOUR BRANCH TO LEND THE EQUIVALENT OF $1.6 MILLION FOR 5 YEARS AMORTIZED OVER LAST THREE YEARS STOP CAN YOU HANDLE THIS AMOUNT STOP WHAT DO YOU THINK THE RATE MIGHT BE STOP PLEASE CABLE

A day later a reply arrived from Brussels:

DELIGHTED WITH PROSPECT OF WORKING WITH AMPRO STOP NO PROBLEM IN OUR HANDLING PROPOSED LOAN WHICH CAN BE

DONE ON TWO BASES STOP FIRST COMMA LOAN CAN BE SET UP ON A FLUCTUATING RATE BASIS AT BN + 0.5 PERCENT COMMA PRESENTLY 7.5 PERCENT PER ANNUM ON UNUSED BALANCE WHICH STARTS TO RUN IMMEDIATELY UPON SIGNING OF LOAN AGREEMENT STOP SECOND COMMA CREDIT CAN BE EXTENDED WITH SNCI FORMAT CALLING FOR A FIXED RATE OF 7.10 DIS-COUNTED ANNUALLY IN ADVANCE COMMA EQUIVALENT TO A TRUE RATE OF 7.65 STOP WHILE WE WOULD PREFER FIRST FOR-MULA COMMA WE ARE PERFECTLY WILLING TO HANDLE IT WITH SNCI FORMAT COMMA AND FEEL CLIENT SHOULD BE GIVEN CHOICE SINCE WE WISH TO AVOID HAVING AMPRO LEARN OF FIXED RATE ALTERNATIVE FROM A COMPETING BANK STOP SNCI FORMAT HAS BEEN RECENTLY ALTERED TO CALL FOR A COMMIT-MENT COMMISSION COMMA WHICH STARTS TO RUN THREE MONTHS AFTER SIGNING OF LOAN AGREEMENT COMMA CALLING FOR PAYMENT OF 0.25 PERCENT PER ANNUM ON UNUSED BAL-ANCE IF CUSTOMER PROVIDES US WITH FIXED TAKEDOWN SCHEDULE STOP IF SUBSEQUENTLY THERE IS A DEVIATION FROM THIS SCHEDULE COMMITMENT COMMISSION IS INCREASED TO 0.75 PERCENT PER ANNUM STOP IF FIXED TAKEDOWN SCHEDULE IS NOT PROVIDED COMMA COMMITMENT COMMISSION WOULD BE 0.25 PERCENT PER ANNUM ON UNUSED BALANCE STOP PLEASE ADVISE IF YOU NEED ADDITIONAL DETAILS STOP REGARDS

GIBBONS

Gotham's Overseas Term Lending

Although Gotham's overseas branches managed most of their lending autonomously, it was not unusual for the head office to perform credit analyses in overseas lending situations which presented certain problems or where time was a factor.

Help in such cases came from head office personnel specially trained in the intricacies of credit analysis and closely attuned to the current lending policies as shaped by senior management of the bank.

The officers of the various foreign branches were deeply involved in the process of negotiation with foreign borrowers and the administration of the loans, but the required financial analysis and tailoring of loan terms, etc., were sometimes accomplished in the head office. No loan was ever made, however, unless the local branch management concurred in the recommendations received from New York.

In the Ampro proposal, Mr. Sloane decided that the head office would analyze the credit, decide whether a loan should be made and if so, propose appropriate terms. Based on the guidelines established in New York, the branch officers, if they concurred, would then proceed with local negotiations with the financial managers of Ampro's European subsidiaries.

Mr. Andrew Riley, a Gotham vice president who headed the bank's

Overseas Credit Analysis Department, was asked to evaluate the credit-worthiness of the Ampro subsidiaries and to draw up a loan proposal which might be mutually satisfactory to the bank and the company.

Company Background

Ampro Corporation (USA) was a leading American manufacturer of connectors used by electric power companies and by producers of electric and electronic equipment. Most of its products were used as parts of generation equipment, electrical switchboards, connection boxes, and motors. The company was established in 1924 and had its home offices in Peoria, Illinois. Parent company sales and earnings had more than doubled in the 10 years ending in 1965. In that year profits of $3.5 million were realized on sales of $58 million.

In the years following the late 1950's, Ampro expanded rapidly overseas, both in sales volume and number of manufacturing subsidiaries and affiliates. By 1966 the company was established in Europe, Canada, Australia, Japan, Great Britain, Brazil, and Mexico. In Europe, Ampro operated a manufacturing plant in Brussels, Ampro Electra S.A., which produced a portion of the Ampro line both for local sale and for distribution through six other sales subsidiaries, each separately constituted and wholly owned by the parent company:

Ampro Elektra A.G., Zurich, Switzerland
Ampro Elektra GmbH, Cologne, West Germany
Ampro S.A., Paris, France
Ampro SpA, Milan, Italy
Ampro Iberica S.A., Barcelona, Spain
Ampro Svenska AB, Stockholm, Sweden

A part of Ampro's European sales represented exports from the United States, but most of the Ampro products sold by the European subsidiaries were made in Brussels by Ampro Electra S.A. Collectively, the seven subsidiaries were referred to as Ampro Europe.

Through Gotham's Brussels branch, Mr. Riley learned that Ampro Electra S.A., in Brussels, was organized in 1959 with limited capital amounting to about $500,000. In addition to electrical connectors, the Brussels plant, which was a modern structure, also made electric motors and small appliances. Employees numbered about 75 workers and 8 clerks. A Belgian credit agency reported that there were some start-up difficulties but that the company subsequently operated quite effectively. Its bankers considered Ampro Electra S.A. "good for its engagements," as one report stated, and made no unfavorable comment on the way payments were made. Another credit agency reported that payables were met promptly.

Mr. Riley referred to a recent balance sheet of Ampro Europe and

Ampro Electra S.A., sent to the bank by Mr. Graham (see Exhibit 1). The accompanying sales and profit figures were also available.

Ampro Europe
($000)

	1962	1963	1964	1965
Sales......................	2,728	2,730	3,600	4,209
Net profit (after taxes)........	240	171	273	292

Net profits had averaged 7.4% of sales during the past four years, he noted. The amount owed to the parent company ($2,009,000) represented purchases ($634,000), patents ($1,125,000) and direct loans ($250,-000). The bank debt of $850,000 was owed to Caisse d'Epargne, a Belgian bank ($350,000), and Great America Trust ($500,000).

Most of Ampro Europe's sales were made to electric utilities, many of which were government owned. Presumably the receivables were quite good, although the collection period of 83 days seemed a long one.

Ampro Electra S.A. was clearly the most substantial subsidiary, having 85% of the total assets. It held most of the group's fixed assets and was the borrower of nearly all of Ampro Europe's debt. The sales of the six companies in the group were financed through advances from Ampro Electra S.A. and inventory and accounts receivable were their major assets.

Early in October, 1966, Mr. Graham forwarded consolidated financial projections of Ampro Europe through 1972 (Exhibits 2 and 3). Exhibit 2 presents consolidated *pro forma* balance sheets, and Exhibit 3 shows actual and projected sales and profit figures.

Mr. Riley noted that the company projections provided for a $1.6 million term loan from Gotham, as well as liquidation of the Great America Trust loan by 1967. Ampro Europe expected to slowly repay the loan from Caisse d'Epargne over the next 10 years. According to the projections, Ampro Europe would take down $1 million of the Gotham loan by the end of 1966, and the remaining $600,000 in 1967. In the letter which accompanied the projections, Mr. Graham stated that proceeds of the proposed Gotham loan would serve to repay the parent company $134,000 on purchases and $250,000 on patents, as well as provide about $1.2 million for proposed capital expenditures.

Mr. Graham also wrote:

These projections were prepared by our people in Brussels and were based on a number of assumptions. The most important of these is that sales will grow at a 19.6% compound growth rate and that net profit on sales will compound at 13.6% (after an assumed Belgian tax rate of 40%). Although both of these figures are higher than historic rates, our people feel that they are being conservative. Accounts receivable have been assumed to remain at 23% of sales, and accounts payable at 11%, both historically based. Inventories were based on an assumed future turnover of three times per year, a not unrealistic assumption, based on past experience. One further item is of importance, the matter of dividends. Our agreement with Ampro Europe is such that none of the companies will pay dividends to the parent, with one exception. For legal reasons, it would be impractical if our German company, Ampro Elektra GmbH, did not pay dividends. Therefore, we have assumed that dividends equal to that company's projected earnings will be remitted to Ampro (USA) on the accompanying schedule.

1966	$ 86,000
1967	88,000
1968	128,000
1969	156,000
1970	180,000
1971	200,000
1972	220,000

The Emerging Loan Proposal

After evaluating the information he had received from Ampro, Mr. Riley was still undecided about what direction his recommendation should take. He was impressed with the performance of Ampro Europe, but there were important ambiguities in the situation. Clearly, the operating and financial ties between Ampro (USA), Ampro Electra S.A., and the Ampro Europe group were consequential. Yet the absence of a parent guarantee for the subsidiaries' debts forced a focus on the immediate entity, Ampro Electra S.A., which would be the obligator.

Further, the seven Ampro Europe companies operated in many respects as an economic and financial unit. However, each was a separate and distinct legal entity owned by the American parent and incorporated under the laws of the country in which it operated. Although the financial statements were consolidated in a single currency, dollars, the individual companies, of course, operated in local currencies, and it was not certain that the currencies would continue over the years to be readily convertible and transferable between countries. It would certainly be desirable if ways could be devised to insure that the consolidated cash flow of all the seven companies were positioned in support of the loan repayment by Ampro Electra S.A.

Within a few days, Mr. Riley recommended favorable action on the loan proposal and submitted a list of conditions precedent to granting it, which are included in Exhibit 4. The "go-ahead" was cabled to Gotham's Brussels branch, followed a day or two later by a summary of the recommended terms of the loan. Mr. Gibbons of the Brussels branch responded immediately by cable:

RE YOUR OCTOBER 20 LETTER AMPRO CORP. OUR RECENT EXPERIENCE WITH [several specific companies] MAKES IT PAINFULLY

CLEAR THAT THE BELGIAN BANKS ARE QUITE PREPARED TO UNDERCUT OUR CREDIT STANDARD IN ORDER TO GAIN BUSINESS STOP WE FEEL THAT CREDIT PROPOSAL AS PRESENTLY STRUCTURED WITH FORMIDABLE ARRAY OF CONDITIONS AND RESTRICTIVE COVENANTS IS WIDE OPEN TO COUNTERPROPOSAL BY THE GÉNÉRALE WHICH COULD RESULT IN COMPLETE LOSS TO US OF THIS ATTRACTIVE BUSINESS STOP . . . FEEL IT IS MOST IMPORTANT YOU EMPHATICALLY PLACE DANGER OF INSISTENCE ON THESE TERMS BEFORE RESPONSIBLE DISTRICT OFFICERS STOP FOR YOUR GUIDANCE WE FEEL DIVIDEND PAYOUT RESTRICTION COUPLED WITH SIMPLE SUBORDINATION AMPRO DEBT TO PARENT RESULTING IN EFFECTIVE NET WORTH OF OVER DOLLARS 3MM AGAINST TERM DEBT DOLLARS 2.47MM WITH CURRENT RATIO 3:1 SHOULD BASICALLY SUFFICE STOP THIS TOGETHER WITH STRONG MANAGEMENT BACKED BY HEALTHY HISTORICAL TRENDS AND FAVORABLE FORECASTS SHOULD ELIMINATE NECESSITY MANY RESTRICTIVE CONDITIONS STOP PLEASE KEEP US CLOSELY ADVISED

GIBBONS

Mention of the "Générale" in the cable referred to the Société Générale de Banque, which was a large Belgian commercial bank. Mr. Gibbons' cable was amplified a few days later by a letter from Walter Gerard, the branch's assistant manager:

This will refer to our recent exchange on the subject of future finance for the European Ampro group and particularly to our letter with enclosures dated October 20th and our recent cable.

It seems important from the start to establish that we, as well as Head Office, are delighted at the possibilities which this Ampro financing package gives us of coming into their operations with a major portion of their business both in the States and here in Europe. We are, in taking over from Great America Trust here in Brussels, offered a most important role at a crucial time in the development of the company. It seems to us, however, that we would be closing our eyes to reality if, in this highly competitive market, we put forward proposals in connection with this financing which appeared to the company to be excessive and overrestrictive. This is particularly true in the situation where the sole other bank is the Société Générale de Banque, whose competitiveness, particularly in the field of extension of credit, has been very clearly indicated to us in recent term financing negotiations (with several specific companies). Furthermore, we are in this case dealing with a profitable company enjoying good management and in an important expansionary phase.

Some of the covenants called for in the summary of terms included with Ben Sloane's letter appear particularly likely to offer an opportunity to the local management, should they wish to avail themselves of it, to prove to Mr. Graham that they could succeed in negotiating better terms with a Belgian bank. A lack of flexibility in our "package" might upset the Ampro European management and conceivably even jeopardize their desire to work with us. On the other hand, we realize the need to take into consideration the fact of the local company's thinness on the capital side and the fact that part of this package is required to finance current receivables.

There is no doubt that such prohibitions as number four in the "list of conditions precedent to granting the loan," are particularly restrictive in the context of European corporate financing customs, for, as you know, the discounting of trade paper constitutes a valuable source of cheaper financing for companies and the present difference in rate would be around 2% between this and their term finance. Would it not be safer, if we precluded them from "any other debt for borrowed money, including liabilities resulting from the discount of trade paper with recourse," to include in our own facilities a sufficient segment—say, $500,000—to be used either for the discount of such paper (or similar short-term credit) or as part of term borrowing depending on the company's needs. It seems to us also that the prohibition of the subsidiaries comprising "Ampro Europe" from engaging in any activities other than acting as sales agents and distributors for Ampro product is too sweepingly restrictive. It would, for instance, preclude the company from undertaking manufacturing operations through its other European subsidiaries at any time during the life of our loan. On the other hand, a call for subordination of debts owing from the European companies for patents, loans, and purchases would appear to us to constitute a sound and sensible major basis for this credit extension.

In your discussions with responsible officers in the Midwestern District and preferably before the arrival here of David Graham, vice president and treasurer, Ampro Corporation, in two weeks, we would appreciate your emphasizing the importance of our being able to present a competitive front in discussing this term finance. A cable indication of any modifications to the approach outlined in Head Office's recent discussion, referred to above, would be very helpful to us so that we know exactly what face to put on for our meeting with David Graham.

The following day Mr. Riley gathered a group of men from his own department along with interested officers from other departments to discuss the Brussels reaction. He opened by asking, "Well, how far do we let Brussels go on their own? We really should respond as soon as we can to their problem."

"As I see it, Andy, our Brussels people want to at least do away with conditions number 4 and number 5 as you have them outlined in the loan term summary," remarked Norton Frazier, a member of the Overseas Credit Analysis group.

"Right," said Mr. Riley.

"Well, I don't like to be a wet blanket, Andy, but I rather like the idea of keeping them both in," Mr. Frazier replied. "After all, it's very common in term loans to restrict further borrowing, and I can see every justification of doing it this time. In addition, there is quite a bit of merit to the idea of restricting the sales subsidiaries from engaging in other types of business. And, if something important comes up, they can always turn to us for a modification of the terms."

"Well, I disagree," said Jim Cotter, who was an officer in the bank's Midwestern District. "I worked hard, as did a number of other district officers, to court Ampro Corporation. I'd hate to lose the chance of becoming their prime bank just because we bound up a loan agreement too tightly. I don't see much advantage to either covenant, and for that matter, feel we could relax a couple of the other provisions, such as the working capital requirement."

"I'm not sure we can make a decision here," remarked Ken Stoughton who was in the European group. "The branch is close to the situation. It's clear to me that Ampro Electra's management is shopping for the best deal. I believe that Ampro's subsidiaries are fairly free to choose whatever financing arrangements they like, and in this case, we can do little at the head office that will help. I'm all in favor of deferring the entire matter to Dick Gibbons, in Brussels. He knows what he's doing."

These and other divergent opinions brought Mr. Riley no closer to a decision, but he felt that they did bring out a number of pertinent factors. As he walked back to his desk, he realized he should be prepared to advise Mr. Sloane of his recommendation some time that day.

Exhibit 1

AMPRO EUROPE
Balance Sheets as of 12/31/65
(thousand of U.S. dollars)

	Ampro Europe	Ampro Electra S.A.
ASSETS		
Current assets		
Cash	$ 403	$ 177
Accounts receivable	976	514
Inventory	1649	1037
Other current assets	241	60
Total	$3269	$1788
Net fixed assets	953	884
Other assets	23	761*
Intangibles	1076	1031
Total assets	$5321	$4464
LIABILITIES AND NET WORTH		
Current liabilities		
Accounts payable and accruals	$ 578	$ 396
Reserve for taxes	85	92
Other current liabilities	5	. . .
Total	$ 668	$ 488
Long-term debt (banks)	$ 850	$ 847
Due Ampro (USA)	2009	1995
Total liabilities	$3527	$3330
Net worth	1784	1134
Total liabilities and net worth	$5321	$4464

* Advances to subsidiaries of Ampro (USA).

Exhibit 2

AMPRO EUROPE

Consolidated Pro Forma Balance Sheet

($000)

	(Actual)	(Projected)						
ASSETS	12/31/65	12/31/66	12/31/67	12/31/68	12/31/69	12/31/70	12/31/71	12/31/72
Cash	403	566	576	804	1,111	1,523	1,954	2,272
Accounts receivable	976	1,260	1,530	1,800	2,100	2,400	2,800	3,160
Inventory	1,649	2,000	2,200	2,600	3,000	3,500	4,000	4,600
Other current assets	241	276	284	312	344	368	396	426
Current assets	3,269	4,102	4,515	5,366	6,335	6,513	8,843	10,128
Fixed assets	1,100	2,086	3,054	3,370	3,726	3,982	4,300	4,765
Less: Accumulated depreciation	(147)	(429)	(738)	(1,115)	(1,520)	(1,935)	(2,375)	(2,835)
Net fixed assets	953	1,657	2,316	2,255	2,206	2,047	1,925	1,930
Other assets	23	26	28	30	32	34	38	42
Intangible assets	1,076	966	856	753	656	562	469	275
Total assets	5,321	6,751	7,790	8,554	9,449	10,434	11,582	12,805
LIABILITIES AND NET WORTH								
Accounts payable and accruals	578	744	786	920	1,070	1,180	1,360	1,510
Provision for taxes	85	107	148	177	217	266	301	373
Other current liabilities	5	6	7	8	10	12	14	16
Current liabilities	668	857	941	1,105	1,297	1,458	1,675	1,899
Gotham term loan	...	1,000	1,600	1,450	1,250	950	550	...
Caisse d'Epargne	350	546	495	443	367	291	215	139
Great America Trust Term loan	500	250	...	...	...	...	...	...
Due parent co. (Ampro, USA) on purchases	634	500	500	500	500	500	500	500
Loan	250	250	250	250	250	250	250	250
On patents	1,125	1,000	875	750	625	500	375	250
Net worth	1,794	2,348	3,129	4,056	5,160	6,485	8,017	9,767
Total liabilities and net worth	5,321	6,751	7,790	8,554	9,449	10,434	11,582	12,805

Exhibit 3

Sales and Profitability

($000)

	Actual							Projected			
	1962	*1963*	*1964*	*1965*	*1966*	*1967*	*1968*	*1969*	*1970*	*1971*	*1972*
Sales	2,728	2,780	3,600	4,209	5,470	6,654	7,818	9,114	10,532	12,074	13,764
% Increase		0	32.0	17.0	37.0	21.6	17.5	16.6	15.6	14.6	14.6
Actual compound growth rate		16.0%									
Projected compound growth rate								19.6%			
Net profit (after tax)	240	171	273	292	640	869	1,055	1,260	1,505	1,732	1,970
% Increase		−29.0	60.0	7.0	125.0	36.0	21.4	19.2	19.5	15.1	13.7
Actual compound growth rate		13%									
Projected compound growth rate								36%			
Net profit as % of sales	8.8	6.3	7.6	6.9	11.7	13.0	13.5	13.8	14.3	14.3	14.3
Average Actual		7.4%									
Average Projected								13.6%			

Exhibit 4

Proposed Summary of Loan Terms

Borrower: Ampro Electra S.A., Malines, Belgium
Amount: $1.6 million (B.F. equivalent)
Lender: Gotham Brussels
Availability: To December 31, 1967, with takedowns in multiples of $100,000
(BF equivalent) upon at least seven days' notice.
Repayment: Quarterly each 3/31, 6/30, 9/30, 12/31:

$$
\begin{array}{ll}
\$ \ 37,500 & \text{beginning } 3/31/68 \\
50,000 & \text{beginning } 3/31/69 \\
75,000 & \text{beginning } 3/31/70 \\
100,000 & \text{beginning } 3/31/71 \\
137,500 & \text{beginning } 3/31/71
\end{array}
$$

Prepayment: 1. *Mandatory*—annually 50% of net profits in excess of $600,000 on a noncumulative basis commencing in 1968 to be applied in inverse order of maturity.
2. *Optional*—at any time in inverse order of maturity.
Commitment Fee: ½% p.a. on the unused portion.
Interest: 8% p.a.
Information: 1. Within 90 days of fiscal year-end, consolidated and consolidating balance sheets and profit and loss statements audited by an independent accounting firm acceptable to the bank.
2. Quarterly, within 45 days, similar statements signed by a duly authorized officer of the company.
3. Quarterly, within 45 days, a certification by the company that no default, under the terms contained herein exists.
Conditions Precedent to Granting the Loan Ampro (USA)
1. Will maintain 100% ownership of the following subsidiaries comprising "Ampro Europe":
> Ampro Electra S.A.
> Ampro Elektra A.G.
> Ampro S.A.
> Ampro Elektra GmbH
> Ampro SpA
> Ampro Svenska AB
> Ampro Iberica S.A.

2. Covenants that on a consolidated basis "Ampro Europe," as defined in No. 1 above, will maintain net current assets of at least the equivalent of $2.5MM, and after 1/1/70 $4MM, or current assets in excess of current liabilities by a ratio of 2.5:1, whichever results in the higher net current asset figure. Current assets and current liabilities shall be computed in accordance with generally accepted accounting principles in the United States. Current liabilities shall include the current portion of long-term debt, the current portion of debt due Ampro (USA) for patents, and the liability resulting from the discount of trade paper with recourse.
3. Covenants that on a consolidated basis "Ampro Europe," as defined in No. 1 above, will maintain a ratio of total indebtedness (inclusive of trade obligations) to the Borrowing Base (net worth plus subordinated debt) of not more than 1:1 commencing 1/1/68.
4. Will prohibit "Ampro Europe" from incurring any other debt for borrowed money, including liabilities resulting from the discount of trade paper with recourse.
5. Will prohibit the subsidiaries comprising "Ampro Europe"

Exhibit 4 (Continued)

from engaging in any activities other than acting as sales agents and distributors for Ampro products.

6. Will prohibit the remittance of any cash dividends from the subsidiaries comprising "Ampro Europe" except from Ampro Elektra GmbH from whom dividends shall in no case exceed cumulative net earnings of that subsidiary since 12/31/65.

7. Agrees to subordinate to our loan debts owing to it from the Borrower for Patents ($1,125,000), for Loans ($250,000), and for Purchases ($500,000).

Covenants, Negative:

1. No other debt for borrowed money inclusive of deferred payment obligations.

2. No cash dividends or other capital distributions or retirements.

3. No merger or consolidation.

4. No sale of assets.

5. No sale and leaseback.

6. No new mortgages, new pledges or other encumbrance on assets.

Shannon Corporation

In May, 1966, Grace Gardner, financial vice president of the Shannon Corporation, was considering two proposals for permanent financing. The reason for Mrs. Gardner's study of external financing alternatives was that the firm had recently spent over $1 million to purchase a block of its own common stock and now needed to replenish funds.

The Shannon Corporation produced jams, jellies, and preserves. The main office and plant were located in Detroit, Michigan; a second manufacturing plant was located in Toledo, Ohio; and the newest plant had been established at Cincinnati, Ohio, in 1964. The firm was named for the family of the president's wife, which now owned 37% of the common stock outstanding. The income statement for the fiscal year ended March 31, 1966, appears as Exhibit 1.

Early in May the board of directors of Shannon had approved the purchase by the company of 307,024 shares of its own common stock in order to settle an estate. The book value per share was $2.20 March 31, and the price paid by the company was $3.97. Sven Christiansen, president of Shannon, was aware that book value was often paid in retirements of this type, where the stock had no market. However, in this case he was forced to pay more because of competitive bidding for control.

The shares purchased amounted to 19% of the outstanding common stock, and the number of shares outstanding was reduced to 1,285,011. The purchase had been temporarily financed by a $1.2 million 90-day loan from a Detroit bank, which also financed Shannon's large seasonal needs. The bank had indicated a willingness to extend the note if necessary, but Mr. Christiansen wished to arrange the permanent financing as soon as possible.

The capitalization of Shannon as of March 31, 1966, before the transaction referred to above, is shown in Exhibit 2. It consisted of a note, a 6% mortgage on the Cincinnati plant, preferred and common stock. The 5-

year note for $260,000 had originally been issued in connection with the renovation of the Toledo plant. The contractor for the renovation had quoted a price to be paid in 1968. The mortgage was being amortized at the rate of $120,000 a year, payable at the end of each year, with a balloon payment of $600,000 in fiscal 1970. The preferred stock outstanding amounted to $892,210. The firm had been retiring the preferred stock, by use of the call provision, as circumstances allowed and had reduced the number of shares outstanding by 26% in the two most recent fiscal years.

Mrs. Gardner had contemplated borrowing $2.0 million from an insurance company to repay the short-term loan and build up working capital. A proposal to lend this amount at 6% was being considered by the Midstate Insurance Company. This proposal, the terms of which had been suggested by Midstate, would require annual payments of $250,000 beginning at the end of fiscal 1967, the maintenance of working capital of $3.0 million, and the restriction of cash dividends on all classes of capital stock to 50% of net income earned subsequent to March 31, 1966. Some $770,000 of the proceeds would be used to assist in raising the working capital to the required level. In the event the debt financing was obtained, the recently acquired stock would be placed in the treasury to be utilized ultimately in connection with an expansion program.

As an alternative, Mr. Christiansen had found a party interested in a private placement of 300,000 shares of the repurchased common stock at a price of $4.15 a share. This would result in net receipts by the firm of $4 a share after expenses, and the arrangements could be completed within the next few weeks. The party was not interested in participating in control of Shannon, a matter which had been of some concern to Mr. Christiansen. Mrs. Gardner knew that Shannon, already one of the most highly levered firms in the industry, would at some time in the next 5 years require additional equity financing.

When Mrs. Gardner had met the vice president of Midstate at a recent social event, he had asked for a funds flow forecast that would show the effect of the loan repayment schedule on the funds available for use in the business. He expressed concern over the note due in 1968 and the balloon terminal mortgage payment in 1970. In preparation to answer this request Mrs. Gardner began a projection of funds flow for the next 5 years, shown in Exhibit 3.

The competitive situation in the industry was stable. New processing techniques and machinery were emerging from the development phase with cost-cutting potential which was allowed for in the projections. Exhibit 3 is a projection of flows after the repurchase of shares, assuming a short-term loan of $1.2 million for 2 months, but making no allowance for permanent financing.

As a result of expected cost reductions, and of expected sales increases of about 3% a year, earnings after taxes but before financing charges were expected to increase by 15% a year. Needed investment in working capital (noncash) and fixed assets, which had been $829,000 in 1966, was projected to grow at the rate of 5% a year. The significant exception was 1969, when $3.3 million would be needed to provide for both the projected growth and a purchase of property under the terms of a lease agreement. Depreciation would continue at about $570,000 a year except for 1970, when it was expected to jump to about $820,000. Thus the book value of the assets would increase some 250% in five years. A gradual increase was planned in the per-share cash dividends to common stock in order to increase the stock's attractiveness to investors in anticipation of an eventual public offering. From 16% in 1966, this ratio would rise in annual 1% increments to 21% in 1971. These expectations are reflected in Exhibit 4, with no allowance for permanent financing.

Mrs. Gardner had noted that on May 6 the common stock of a leading producer of jams and jellies, the J. M. Smucker Company, was trading at about 15 times the earnings of the fiscal year ended April 30, 1965, with the final quarter expected earnings to be confirmed. Furthermore, Smucker common normally traded at 18–22 times earnings. This caused her to wonder whether the $4 price per common share that would be received under the equity alternative adequately reflected Shannon's current earnings per share, much less the anticipated earnings growth.

Exhibit 1

SHANNON CORPORATION

Income Statement for the Fiscal Year Ended March 31, 1966
(in thousands)

Net sales...		$32,614
Costs and expenses		
Cost of sales......................................	($18,255)	
Selling and delivery expenses........................	(9,486)	
Administrative expenses............................	(2,272)	
Depreciation and amortization......................	(567)	
		(30,580)
Earned before interest and taxes......................		$ 2,034
Interest...		(66)
Income before income taxes...........................		$ 1,968
Provision for income taxes (48.2%)....................		(949)
Net income..		$ 1,019
Earnings per common share (1,592,035 shares)...........		$ 0.61*

    * After allowance for preferred dividend.

Exhibit 2

SHANNON CORPORATION

Statement of Financial Position

(in thousands)

	March 31, 1966	Pro Forma March 31, 1966*
Net assets employed in the business		
Current assets		
Cash and marketable securities...............	$ 782	$ 764
Receivables, less allowance for doubtful		
accounts...............................	1,396	1,396
Inventories...............................	1,488	1,488
Prepaid expenses.........................	73	73
Total current assets...................	$3,739	$3,721
Current liabilities		
Accounts payable.........................	$ 841	$ 841
Accrued liabilities.........................	509	509
Federal and state income taxes..............	275	275
90-day note payable.......................		1,200
Total current liabilities................	$1,625	$2,825
Working capital............................	$2,114	$ 896
Property, plant and equipment................	$8,921	$8,921
Accumulated depreciation and amorti-		
zation................................	5,157	5,157
Net property, plant and equipment......	$3,764	$3,764
Total assets less current liabilities..........	$5,878	$4,660
Less: Deferred federal income tax........	$ 261	$ 261
Net assets employed in the business........	$5,617	$4,399
Sources from which assets were provided		
Note......................................	$ 260	$ 260
Mortgage.................................	960	960
Long-term debt...........................	$1,220	$1,220
Preferred stock, 5% cumulative, $10 par........	$ 892	$ 892
Common stock, $1 par......................	$1,592	$1,592
Capital in excess of par value..................	541	541
Retained earnings..........................	1,372	1,372
Less treasury stock.........................		(1,218)
Common stock equity......................	$3,505	$2,287
Total sources from which assets were		
provided..............................	$5,617	$4,399

* Showing impact of share purchase and temporary financing.

Exhibit 3

SHANNON CORPORATION

Cash Forecasts, 1966–71, Fiscal Years Ending March 31

(dollar figures in thousands)

	Actual 1966	1967	1968	1969	1970	1971
Earnings before interest and taxes	$2,034	$2,340	$2,690	$3,090	$3,555	$4,090
Depreciation eliminated	567	570	570	570	820	820
Funds provided by operations	$2,601	$2,910	$3,260	$3,660	$4,375	$4,910
Tax exposure*	(1,254)	(1,455)	(1,630)	(1,830)	(2,188)	(2,455)
Tax shield, depreciation	273	285	285	285	410	410
Funds provided by operations, after tax	$1,620	$1,740	$1,915	$2,115	$2,598	$2,865
Capital investment	(829)	(870)	(914)	(3,300)	(1,008)	(1,058)
Funds Profile	$ 791	$ 870	$1,001	($1,185)	$1,590	$1,807
Financial Payments						
Interest, net of tax shield	(33)†	(31)‡	(25)	(22)	(18)	. . .
Debt repayments	(1,320)	(120)	(380)	(120)	(600)	. . .
Preferred stock dividends	(45)	(45)	(45)	(45)	(45)	(45)
Common stock dividends	(159)	(186)	(230)	(281)	(343)	(420)
Cash Excess or Shortage	($ 766)	$ 488	$ 321	($1,653)	$ 584	$1,342

* Rate 50% after 1966.

† Including $1,012, less the tax shield, of nonmortgage interest.

‡ Including $8,334, less the tax shield, of the $1,200,000 temporary stock purchase financing for an assumed two months.

Exhibit 4

SHANNON CORPORATION
Earnings and Dividend Estimates
(figures in thousands, except per share)

	Actual 1966	1967	1968	1969	1970	1971
Funds provided by operations, after tax	$1,620					
Depreciation	(567)					
Interest, net of tax shield	(33)			*Details Not Entered*		
Preferred dividends	(45)					
	$ 974	$1,094	$1,275	$1,478	$1,715	$2,000
Net earnings available for common						
Earned per share*	$ 0.76	$ 0.85	$ 0.99	$ 1.15	$ 1.33	$ 1.56
Dividend per share	$ 0.10	$ 0.15	$ 0.18	$ 0.22	$ 0.27	$ 0.33

*1,285,011 shares.

Piedmont Garden Apartments

"Look, Tom, we've kicked this thing around long enough. Bill Mosby called again last night and said that O'Donnell is after him to show the properties to some other prospects he has stirred up. Mosby thinks he can hold O'Donnell off for three or four days more but not much longer. Mosby is reasonably confident that he'll take $375,000 in cash. Why don't you and Jay come over early tomorrow morning. We will lock ourselves in my study until we can decide how attractive an opportunity this really is for us and whether we should call Mosby to put in a $375,000 offer. If we decide to make the offer and O'Donnell accepts it, we could probably plan to pass papers as of the 1st of January." With these words David Hill, a Philadelphia businessman, concluded a conversation with a friend, Thomas Jackson, with whom he and a mutual friend, Jay Early, had been considering the purchase of the equity interest in a garden apartment complex in Chapel Hill, North Carolina.

After concluding the telephone call, Mr. Hill turned to the task of organizing his own analysis of the investment opportunity. If they were to go forward with the investment, it would be the first venture into income real estate for two of the three men. For many years Mr. Jackson had operated a 28-unit apartment inherited from his father.

Mr. Hill's interest in the investment opportunity dated back to a conversation in June, 1969, with William Mosby, an old friend who had left a corporate job in New York to return to his original home in Charlotte, North Carolina, and to undertake to build up his own business as a real estate broker. Mr. Mosby had spoken with enthusiasm about the real estate investment opportunities in the Charlotte area. His comments had keenly interested Mr. Hill, who explained that he was anxious to work out a tax-sheltered investment. Mr. Mosby responded that uncertainties stemming from proposals for tax reform, which were currently under active consideration in Congress, had slowed down transactions in real estate primarily motivated by tax-saving considerations. However, he noted that he did have one very sound listing that he thought might interest Mr. Hill, even though the tax benefits promised to be moderate.

A few days later Mr. Mosby had sent on some summary data concerning the investment opportunity, a garden apartment complex in Chapel Hill, North Carolina, known as Piedmont Garden Apartments. Mr. Hill had been moderately interested and a few weeks later had flown to Charlotte to visit the property in Chapel Hill with Mr. Mosby. Subsequently, he had decided to invite Mr. Jackson, who he knew was favorably inclined toward real estate, to join him in considering the investment. The two subsequently brought in a third party, Mr. Early. In ensuing weeks, each of Mr. Hill's two prospective associates had also visited Chapel Hill. As their interest grew, the three had hired a local real estate dealer to inspect the property and add his advice.

The inquiry revealed that Piedmont Garden Apartments had been built in 1967 by a syndicate headed by a Charlotte architect, Richard O'Donnell. Mr. O'Donnell, with associates, had developed several such properties in the Charlotte area in recent years. Apparently, it was his practice to establish the properties as fully rented, going businesses and then to offer them for sale at prices that represented a capitalization of the revenue-producing capabilities of the project. Presumably the price being asked for Piedmont Garden Apartments was well above its construction cost to the O'Donnell group.

Piedmont Garden Apartments was located not far from the center of Chapel Hill, which was 9 miles southwest of Durham, North Carolina, on the Southern Railway. Chapel Hill had been incorporated in 1851 and operated in 1969 under a city manager type of government. It was located within Orange County, which in turn fell within the Standard Metropolitan Statistical area of Durham. The respective populations in 1960 and year-end 1969 were as shown in the accompanying table.

	1960	Year-end 1969	% Increase from 1960
Durham SMSA	154,965	188,786	21.8%
Orange County	42,970	57,424	33.6%
Chapel Hill	12,573	20,068	59.6%

Note: Chapel Hill population figures do not include some 16,000 students at the University of North Carolina.

Although there was no industry in the town, Chapel Hill had grown substantially in recent years. A large part of its growth was directly traceable to the growth of the University of North Carolina located there. Exhibit 1 presents additional information on Chapel Hill and its growth pattern.

The university offered courses leading to the Master's degree in 54 fields, and the D.D.S., M.D., D.P.H. and Ed.D. degrees. There were approximately 16,000 students enrolled in the various programs in 1969. In presenting the opportunity, Mr. Mosby had stressed the high probability that the university would continue to grow in future years. Moreover, much of the growth was expected in the graduate schools, particularly the schools of law, business administration, and medicine.

Currently, dormitory space was barely adequate for the existing college population, and dormitory construction was not expected to keep pace with the university expansion. The university had built two small apartment buildings for married students, but most married students found apartments in and around Chapel Hill or even in Durham. Piedmont Garden Apartments was one of three apartment complexes located near the center of town and within a mile of the university. Persons approaching Piedmont Garden Apartments from the university or from downtown Chapel Hill passed through a moderately attractive but aging section of town characterized by older homes and few small apartments. Piedmont Garden Apartments themselves were in an area bounded on two sides by smaller but pleasant homes and on the other two sides by homes that were rather seedy and rundown in appearance. The builders had partially screened the apartment complex from the rundown area by the use of several hundred feet of high cedar fence, but the view from the upper floors of the apartments on two sides of the project was not attractive.

On the whole, however, Mr. Hill and his associates had been impressed by the appearance of the apartment buildings. The complex was made up of eight $2\frac{1}{2}$- and 3-story apartment buildings of contemporary design. The architect had taken advantage of a sloping lot so that only the third-floor apartments had walk-up stairways. Each of the 127 apartments had its own entrance. The lower-level apartments had covered patio entrances; the apartments on the other two levels had entrances in front on the upper ground level and balconies on the other, downhill, side. A heated swimming pool, operated from early April until late October, was popular with the tenants. Blacktopped parking areas were provided within the project, and the number of parking places appeared adequate.

The builders had succeeded in leaving a number of native dogwood, oak, and maple trees on the project, and the expansive lawn areas were reasonably attractive. However, little additional landscaping had been undertaken. Mr. Hill had been negatively impressed by the arrangements for trash disposal. Six large metal containers, called "Dempster Dumpsters," were sited around the project. Tenants dumped trash into these, and city garbage trucks came in three times a week to empty the containers. Although apparently a necessary component of the city's garbage disposal methods, these containers struck the visitors as decidedly unattractive. Also creating a negative impression was the rundown condition of a children's playground, the red clay exposed by paths cut across several banks, and the rather cluttered patios of several apartments.

Mr. Hill had given considerable thought to the problem of future management of the project. It appeared possible to get a local firm to undertake the management of the apartments on a continuing basis. The usual charges for such comprehensive services were 5% or 6% of the gross revenues of the project.

The current onsite managers reported that they had experienced little difficulty in filling up the apartments. About half of the renters had some connection with the university, as either students or employees. Annual leases were required, with deposits to cover damage or unusual wear and tear on the apartments. Most of the student tenants were married, and a number had small children. About 10 apartments were rented to unmarried male students. Usually three or four such students shared a three-bedroom apartment, and the managers reported that they had given little or no trouble. The heavy university orientation, however, had contributed to a rather substantial annual turnover of tenants. The local managers estimated that 50 to 60 of the apartments turned over each year. Most of the leases expired during the summer months.

As of mid-October, 1969, there was only one vacant apartment, and it was expected to be rented very soon. Altogether, the prices and facilities at Piedmont Garden Apartments appeared competitive with those of other projects in the area.

The original rent roll of the project was $220,092. In March, 1969, a new increased rent schedule was introduced to apply to all apartments with leases expiring after June 30, 1969. In September the rents were being billed at a rate of $234,444 a year. When all the proposed increases became effective, the gross annual rate would move up to $244,860. The original and new rent schedules are shown in Exhibit 2.

The purchase price of $375,000 to the O'Donnell group assumed that the purchase would be made subject to outstanding mortgage loans on the property, which would amount to $1,078,353.67 on December 31, 1969. The total mortgage debt was made up of three separate loans from Metropolitan Life Insurance Company. The loans carried an effective composite interest rate slightly above 6.2%. The total annual debt service requirements on the mortgages amounted to $95,775. The loans had been written for a 20-year term with constant annual payments of 8.25% or 9.00% of the original loan amount. These payments would leave a loan balance at maturity of about $157,000.

The project buildings were constructed on two parcels of leased land. The leases had a term of 99 years running from 1965. Through 1985, the annual rent was fixed at $8,976.

Mr. Mosby, the real estate broker, had pointed to the 6.2% interest rate as an especially attractive feature. He noted that interest rates had increased sharply since these loans had been negotiated. Current commitments for apartment projects were being made at rates of 8½% or 9%, giving the owners of Piedmont Garden Apartments a competitive advantage over subsequent high-rate projects. The new buyers would incur no personal liability under the mortgage loans, which would apply only to the properties themselves.

A part of the local consultant's assignment was the task of reviewing the financial statements for 1968 and making appropriate projections for the new owners. In explaining his projections (Exhibits 3 and 4), the consultant stressed the sensitivity of the overall results to vacancy experience. He explained that his 5% vacancy allowance was a relatively standard figure for circumstances where supply and demand conditions were favorable to the owners. He hoped that the 5% figure would prove high, but the higher-than-average tenant turnover rate experienced to date necessarily created some vacancies, even though normally short, when turnover occurred.

The consultant further argued that a very low vacancy rate indicated that the rental schedule was unnecessarily low. He commented on the outlook for rentals as follows: "The rental market in Chapel Hill is strong. Although several projects are presently in the planning or construction phases, they will not, in my opinion, soften the market. Rather they will help fill an existing demand. I personally inspected five other projects and was able to obtain information on four others. Generally the rents at Piedmont Garden Apartments are competitive, although the quality of construction is somewhat inferior to that of some of the newer outlying projects." Mr. Hill had felt some uneasiness about the long-term competitive outlook and the possibility of overbuilding in the area. This was partly a response to the rather universal enthusiasm he had found in Chapel Hill for the prospects of growth of the university and the area. Such unanimity of optimism suggested the very real possibility of overbuilding. If overbuilding resulted, the owners of new apartment houses being completed would experience intense financial pressure to get their units rented. In response, both Mr. Mosby and the consultant had stressed the strong position of well-situated existing units under current conditions of increasing construction and financing costs.

The consultant noted that the 1968 maintenance figures were low because the property was new and many of the appliances were still under a manufacturer's warranty. As the property aged, more breakdowns in appliances, especially dishwashers, disposals, and air-conditioning compressor units were to be anticipated. The consultant urged that the investors anticipate upgrading the capabilities of the onsite maintenance man hired by the project so that he could do some of the appliance repair work as well as other routine maintenance. Further, the consultant argued that the "bottom of the line" quality of the appliances suggested higher-than-average maintenance expense. Moreover, it was necessary to redecorate apartments on turnover of tenants, and the higher-than-average turnover rates would raise the redecorating maintenance outlay. There had been considerable discussion among the potential investors about the level of maintenance that should be anticipated.

The management fees projected by the consultant were based on an estimate of 5% of gross income for a professional management firm plus provision of a three-bedroom apartment for a resident manager. The resident manager's salary would be paid by the professional management firm. This amount appeared reasonable to all. In fact, it seemed likely that the allowances for accounting and legal fees and office expense might prove high if the management firm did a good job. Among the normal responsibilities of property management firms was the provision of full accounting reports.

Overall, the consultant had not attempted to defend his expense projections in great detail. "You can be sure O'Donnell has kept expenses at rock bottom so that he would have some good figures to sell. On the other hand, the biggest outlays are for land rent and mortgage payments, and these are fixed for years to come. If inflation pushes up utility and other costs, you ought to be able to at least pass these increases on to the tenants in the form of higher rentals. In fact, if inflation continues, it will boost costs for development of new properties. They will have to get higher rentals to justify their higher costs, and this should give well-located and well-run existing projects a protective cost-price umbrella."

The investors had sharply questioned the consultant's emphasis on the cash flow return figures rather than the accounting income projections of Exhibit 4. Specifically, they questioned the validity of return figures that contained nothing for depreciation. As one had argued, "Certainly the appliances are going to wear out. We shall have to be replacing disposals and so forth before long. The parking lot will have to be repaved. And these buildings certainly won't last indefinitely. How can we sensibly ignore depreciation?"

"That's true," the consultant had replied. "But a well-maintained property doesn't suffer rapid physical deterioration. The real hooker is inflation. Plenty of properties built in 1950 are worth more now than they cost then. Building costs have been going up lately at 10% or 15% a year. The building trades are highly unionized even here in North Carolina. Perhaps the cost spiral will slow down or radical new building methods will be developed, so that costs will be less for a given space and quality factor, but I'm inclined to bet on continued cost inflation.[1]

"Besides, the net cash flow projections are after amortization. Even in year one you would be paying down the mortgage by $30,000 and the paydown accelerates over time. If the income holds up and costs of building continue to increase, you can probably get a rewrite of the mortgage in 6 or 8 years and get all of your original investment out by increasing

---

[1] Researching this subject further, Mr. Hill found the following construction cost index for apartments, hotels, and office buildings, prepared by the Boeckh Division of the American Appraisal Company. This index did not reflect the additional higher cost of financing.

(1957–59 = 100)

1964	114.6	1967	130.7
1965	118.5	1968	139.9
1966	123.2	Sept. 1969	154.4

the amount of the mortgage. In the trade we call that 'mortgaging out.' Of course the new mortgage would probably be written at higher interest rates, and the new higher amortization schedule would cut into your net cash flow after the rewrite. But at that point, with your cash investment fully recovered, any net cash flow from the business would be pure gravy for you. Or you may want to sell after 5 or 10 years when your interest and depreciation tax shields have gotten smaller and you're experiencing heavier taxable income."

Exhibit 5 presents a list of yields available in alternative investments as of October 20, 1969. Mr. Hill had jotted them down for comparative purposes in considering the Piedmont Garden Apartments proposal.

Mr. Hill and his associates had discussed at some length the question of how each could get out of his investment in Piedmont Garden Apartments should his circumstances or inclinations change. Each believed he could reasonably lock up $125,000 in a relatively illiquid investment but recognized that illness, death, or other major change could lead to a need to liquidate the investment. The investors had considered the advisability of a legal buy-sell agreement under which the remaining investors would have first refusal of existing associates' interests. They had tentatively decided not to enter into such a binding legal arrangement but rather to consider each morally obligated to offer his interest first to the remaining associates. Moreover, they had agreed to settle by majority action any policy issues that might arise.

Each of the partners currently enjoyed taxable income sufficient to make his marginal taxable income subject to a tax rate of 50% or more. Each anticipated that his earning power and tax liability would stay at the same or higher levels for at least 10 years, but of course this was not assured. None was really dependent on investment income to meet current living expenses.

Preliminary discussions between Mr. Hill and counsel for his firm suggested that the investors would fare best on taxes by avoiding corporate ownership of the property. Instead, they planned to hold the property as "tenants in common." For tax purposes each investor would treat his investment much as if he were a general partner in a partnership.

Mr. Hill was concerned about possible personal exposure to liability suits under a noncorporate form. He and his associates had agreed to carry liability insurance, and the local consultant had insisted that an annual premium of $4,000 would adequately cover liability as well as fire and other physical damage hazards to the property. Each of the potential investors expected to have to liquidate some investments in order to raise $125,000 in cash by January 1. Currently the stock market had shown continued weakness, and Mr. Hill was not especially eager to sell any of his holdings at what he regarded as moderately depressed levels. However, he had some securities that could be sold without major tax liability.

Exhibit 1

The Greater Chapel Hill Area Growth Pattern

Preface: Economic and population forecasting is, at best, an inexact science in which the prognosticator is often wrong. When past trends are stable and constant, projections of the future can be quite accurate. The depression of the 1930's and World War II both had adverse effects on the growth of U.N.C. and Chapel Hill. The past decade, however, reflects a steady pattern of growth and development.

The projections in this report are based on this recent consistent trend. There are several factors that will have a definite influence on these figures:

1. The anticipated growth of the University and Division of Health Affairs.
2. The industrial potential of Orange County.
3. The retirement attraction of Chapel Hill.
4. The impact of the Research Triangle.

[refers to three universities in the area]

Population:	Town	U.N.C.	Carrboro	Chapel Hill Township
1940............	3,654	4,098	....	13,765
1950............	9,177	6,864	....	22,374
1960............	12,573	8,592	....	25,165
1970............	20,068	16,775	3,385	40,076
1975 (Est.).......	33,500	18,804	5,500	57,804
1980 (Est.).......	37,000–44,000	23,000–24,000	8,000–10,000	68,000–85,000

Automobiles in Township (Estimated):
    1950—6,720; 1960—9,441; 1970—15,850; 1980—34,900
Assessed Valuation of Chapel Hill (Based on 70% Real Value):
    1940—$3,567,093; 1950—$7,074,366; 1960—$28,486,519; 1965—$50,000,000; 1966—$57,678,395; 1967—$61,832,200; 1968—$76,695,882; 1969—$92,008,391
Number of Households in Chapel Hill:
    1955—4,621; 1960—5,755; 1966—7,713; 1967—8,247; 1968—9,000; 1969—9,250; 1970—10,148

Residential Construction in Greater Chapel Hill—Carrboro:

	Homes	Apartments
1960........................	157	26
1961........................	226	28
1963........................	153	169
1964........................	285	350
1965........................	277	193
1967........................	117	399
1968........................	57	806
1969........................	104	63
1970........................	129	125

Effective Buying Income and Cash Income Breakdown for Orange County:

Buying Income	Net Dollars	Per Capita	Per Household
1965..............	102,025,000	2,148	8,502
1966..............	109,999,000	2,277	9,016
1967..............	120,669,000	2,447	9,731
1968..............	122,504,000	2,532	10,521
1969..............	161,566,000	2,532	11,298

Note: Per-household buying income for Chapel Hill estimated at slightly over $17,126, the highest in North Carolina.

Exhibit 1 (Continued)

Percentage Household by Income Groups:

	(A) 0–2,999	(B) 3,000–4,999	(C) 5,000–7,999	(D) 8,000–9,999	(E) 10,000 Plus
1965	23.7	19.2	28.0	11.2	17.9
1966	26.1	19.8	24.3	10.2	19.6
1967	23.9	17.6	24.3	10.4	23.8
1968	22.8	16.2	24.1	10.2	26.7
1969	23.9	12.6	17.4	7.6	38.5

For a number of years, Chapel Hill has been rated in the top five cities of North Carolina in per capita income.

Census figures for 1960 revealed that Chapel Hill leads the state in the highest median family income ($7,547 annually), percentage of persons employed in white-collar work, percent of persons age 25 and over having 4 years high school education, and percentage of persons 14 to 17 in school.

Source: Compiled by the Chapel Hill–Carrboro Chamber of Commerce, September, 1970.

Exhibit 2

Rent Schedules

Type	No. of Units	Rate Original	Rate New
1 BR with storage	18	$125.50	$135.00
2 BR—top floor	22	142.50	159.00
2 BR—middle floor	22	138.50	155.00
2 BR—storage	9	142.50	159.00
2 BR—ground floor	1	135.00	150.00
3 BR—top floor	13	158.50	178.00
3 BR—middle floor	13	154.50	174.00
3 BR—ground floor	3	147.50	165.00
2 BR—no windows	1	125.00	125.00
	102		
1 BR with storage	2	134.50	145.00
2 BR—top floor	5	152.50	170.00
2 BR—middle floor	5	143.50	160.00
2 BR—storage	1	152.50	170.00
2 BR—ground floor	1	144.50	162.00
3 BR—top floor	4	168.50	188.00
3 BR—middle floor	4	160.00	180.00
3 BR—ground floor	3	162.50	182.00
	25		
Total	127		

Exhibit 3

PIEDMONT GARDEN APARTMENTS
Projections of Cash Flow

	Present Owners, 1968 Statement	Adjusted 1969	With Full Rent Increase
Gross rentals if fully rented.............	$220,342	$236,500	$244,900
Vacancy.............................	8,940*	11,800†	12,200
	$211,402	$224,700	$232,700
Other income (coin laundry concession)...	1,271	1,200	1,200
Total income........................	$212,673	$225,900	$233,900
Expenses:			
Ground rental......................	8,976	8,976	
Property taxes......................	18,781	20,600	
Insurance..........................	7,263	4,000	
Utilities—gas.......................	10,577	10,600	
Utilities—water and sewer............	3,816	3,800	
TV cable...........................	2,596	2,800	
Electricity—project..................	924	1,000	
Repairs and maintenance.............	7,591	14,850	
Lawn service.......................	2,166	2,600	
Payroll (maintenance man)...........	5,312	10,000	
Snow and trash removal..............	495	300	
Office expense......................	1,708	1,500	
Accounting and legal................	2,700	1,700	
Management fees...................	13,273	14,200	
Miscellaneous......................	281	1,000	
Total........................	$ 86,459	$ 97,926	$ 97,926
Cash flow before amortization...........	126,214	127,974	135,974
Mortgage interest and amortization......	95,775	95,775	95,775
Net cash flow.......................	$ 30,439	$ 32,199	$ 40,199

* Actual.
† At 5%.

Exhibit 4

PIEDMONT GARDEN APARTMENTS
Projection of Depreciation and Taxable Income

Balance of mortgages as of 12/31/69..................	$1,078,354
Cash payment.....................................	375,000
Total cost of property.......................	$1,453,354
Cost attributable to buildings.....................	1,353,354
Cost attributable to equipment.....................	100,000

Using 150% declining balance depreciation:
Building 33⅓ years life—150% declining balance
Equipment 10 years straight line

Year	Cash Flow	Approximate Amortization	Total Income before Taxes & Depreciation	Depreciation	Taxable Income
1..............	$30,000	$30,000	$60,000	$77,700	$(17,700)
2..............	40,000	32,000	72,000	74,300	(2,300)
3..............	40,000	34,200	74,200	71,000	3,200
4..............	40,000	36,500	76,500	68,000	8,500

Exhibit 5

PIEDMONT GARDEN APARTMENTS

Alternative Investment Returns Available as of October, 1969

Moody's municipal bond yield average (tax-exempt)
    Ten-year state
        Aaa...................................... 5.53%
        Aa....................................... 5.64
Long-term Treasury issues...................... 6.02
Ten-year index of yields on U.S. Treasury issues... 6.62
Corporate bond yield averages
    Average corporation........................ 7.74
    Aaa....................................... 7.35
    Aa.. 7.54
    A... 7.82
    Baa....................................... 8.23

Source: *Moody's Bond Survey*, October 27, 1969.

Nautilus, Inc.

"The problem in this industry is that you just have to take a long-term view of things. You have to be actively engaged in finding a solution to what may be the problem-after-next long before you have finished implementing the solution to the major current one. The growth potential in this field is enormous but so are the headaches. Our sales growth last year caught us completely by surprise, and we are into the bank for $1 million of short-term money. If our new stock offering works out, we shall have taken care of that problem, but I am already worrying about how we can finance the investments I know we shall have to make in 1971—and in 1973—and in 1977. And all my figures may be underestimates. According to my projection our sales in 1977 could be just 10 times what we expect them to be this year, and some of the decisions we have to make right now are going to control whether that potential is realized."

Background

In May, 1968, the speaker, Paul Godwin, was the financial vice president of Nautilus, Inc., a small manufacturing company located in a small Texas city. The company had been started in early 1963 by two engineers, Guy Olson and Laurence Crawford, to produce improved types of undersea free-diving equipment, a field in which both men had had previous work experience. Each had contributed his entire savings to the venture: $15,000 from Mr. Olson and $25,000 from Mr. Crawford. The initial capitalization consisted of 8,000 shares, $5 par, which the founders held in proportion to their cash contributions: Mr. Olson, 3,000 shares and Mr. Crawford, 5,000.

The firm's first products, a powerful spotlight for underwater use and an electrically powered propulsion unit, had been marketed in the spring of 1964 and had been immediately successful. Mr. Godwin, a friend of

Mr. Olson's, had joined the company at this time as business manager and had invested his own savings of $16,000 in the company. In view of the progress already made by the company in developing two products to the point of production feasibility, it was agreed that Mr. Godwin should buy into the company at a price of $8 per $5-par share, giving him a holding of 2,000 shares.

Believing that the most promising area of development was likely to be in underwater communications and electronics applications, the founders hired three more engineers in the fall of 1964 to work in this field. Two government contracts were also obtained at this time.

The company continued to be successful, and sales grew from $400,000 in 1964 to $2.6 million in 1966. The most serious problems encountered were financial ones. Although the venture was clearly undercapitalized, the founders were very unwilling to sell any equity interest in the company at that time. The task of finding funds to support the expansion fell to Mr. Godwin. The government research contracts, for study into problems of life-support during prolonged submersion in underwater laboratory structures, provided a useful flow of payments; but extensive use had also to be made of secured bank borrowing and supplier credit. All earnings were retained in the company, the three stockholders paying themselves modest salaries and no dividends.

The financial problems reached crisis proportions during 1967. The company had anticipated continued growth in both its existing sales lines and its contract work. Projections for 1967, however, did not include expectations of large sales from new products. In midyear a range of special-purpose trawl devices for the collection of marine botanical and biological specimens from the seabed were announced and received some publicity in academic journals. The new products generated immediate interest. By August, 1967, demand for both the new and some of the older products was considerably in excess of supply. It became apparent that 1967 revenues would reach $4 million. More workpeople were hurriedly recruited, and an additional factory building was leased. The need to finance additional wage bills, lease payments, and inventories of raw materials and subcomponents presented a very serious problem, forcing Mr. Godwin to call upon the company's banking connection for assistance.

The company had since its inception made use of a medium-sized commercial bank located nearby.[1] The original line of credit granted had been secured by notes endorsed by the two founders and by the assignment of accounts receivable. As the organization began to demonstrate its competence and to attain profitable operation, the requirement for endorsement had been dropped and the bank had steadily increased its loan as Nautilus' operations expanded. The need for additional funds in late 1967, however, was far greater than anything the company had yet experienced. Mr. Godwin met a number of times with the bank's vice

---

[1] In Texas, branch banking is not allowed.

president in charge of loans, and ultimately with its president. The bank officers, though very unhappy about the situation, decided to continue their support of the company, and by the end of 1967 Nautilus' short-term indebtedness to the bank approached $1 million.[2]

The president of the bank made it very clear that he considered this a rescue operation and that he would insist on the replacement of this short-term indebtedness by long-term funds as quickly as possible. He urged that the company should increase the equity portion of its capitalization and suggested that the record sales in the past year would make it possible to sell stock at an attractive price. He offered to introduce Mr. Godwin to an investment banking house in Houston with which his own bank maintained an excellent relationship. Mr. Godwin expressed interest in this proposal and undertook to discuss the matter with Mr. Olson and Mr. Crawford.

The founders of Nautilus quickly faced up to the realities of the situation and agreed that the reluctance to sell any part of their equity in the firm might have to be abandoned if the current rate of growth was to be maintained. They held a first meeting with representatives of the investment bank, Parker, Marsh and Charleton, one week later.

After analyzing the financial and operating data supplied by the company, the leader of the banking team, Mr. Marsh, outlined a possible offering of stock to the public. He advised that in order to retire the short-term debt, provide a basis for some longer-term borrowing, and support further growth in the next few years, it would be necessary to sell enough stock to produce proceeds of about $2 million for the company. Mr. Marsh suggested that 500,000 shares of new common stock should be authorized, of which 300,000 shares would go to the founders and Mr. Godwin in exchange for their present shares and in proportion to them. Of the remainder, 150,000 shares would be offered to the public at a price of $15 a share.[3] The issue would be underwritten by a syndicate headed by Parker, Marsh and Charleton at a spread of 10%, making the net proceeds to the company $2,025,000. He advised the company to set aside $100,000 to cover the legal and other costs of the issue.

Mr. Marsh also requested that a seat be created on the board of directors for a member of his firm and stated that the firm would press for the initiation of cash dividends on the common shares, at a level of approximately 50% of net earnings, after a few years. He explained that he and his partners dealt with many investors who insisted on the prospect of dividend income as well as capital gains. If this source of money could not be tapped, the stock would not sell for $15 per share, in his opinion.[4]

---

[2] The balance sheet and income statement for 1967 are provided in Exhibits 1 and 2.

[3] On the basis of 1967 net profits and a total of 450,000 shares issued, this price was approximately 23 times current earnings, after tax.

[4] The directors could not promise publicly to declare dividends in the future, but they might be permitted to say that dividends would be considered. This would be in contrast with many new firms, which state that there is no intention to consider dividends.

The company executives met with Mr. Marsh on several more occasions during the following month. Mr. Olson and Mr. Crawford, in spite of their reluctance to sell any stock to outsiders, were eventually convinced that such a move was inevitable. They agreed that a stock issue of 150,000 shares should be offered to the public at a price of $15, as Mr. Marsh had suggested. Parker, Marsh and Charleton gave a firm agreement to act as underwriters for the offering. The offer was to be made in July, 1968. The bankers would use their best efforts to distribute the shares in lots not greater than 200 shares to one investor, thus creating the basis for trading in the "after market."

Mr. Godwin's Position in May, 1968

In mid-May, 1968, Mr. Godwin was reviewing the company's financial situation. The decision to implement Mr. Marsh's proposed new equity financing had been taken, and the necessary legal and accounting work had begun. The bank had expressed its willingness to continue its existing short-term loans until the funds from the sales of stock became available. Thus, no immediate problem existed. The continuing financial crisis of the past year had been a very disturbing experience, however, and Mr. Godwin wanted to ensure that future needs for funds were anticipated and plans to meet these needs were formulated before another such crisis could arise. He realized that he would have to turn much more of his attention to forecasting the company's financial requirements and that the starting point for any such planning must be an estimate of future company growth.

Mr. Godwin was by no means certain that he agreed with Mr. Marsh's suggestion that a cash dividend should be introduced on the common stock. Mr. Marsh had argued that notwithstanding rapid growth in revenues over the past two years, the company was still little known and could not yet be considered to have an established "track record." Often new issues, after a period of popularity, subsided into a dull "thin" market with very few shares traded. It was his opinion that the inauguration of a cash dividend policy would make the investing public recognize that the company had "matured," and bid for the stock more actively.

Mr. Godwin believed that three powerful counterarguments might be advanced. He felt that any investor who bought stock in a small company in a relatively new industry such as this one was probably more interested in long-term capital gains than in dividend income. In the second place, he knew that Mr. Olson, Mr. Crawford, and he himself did not need such income. Their tax liability positions gave them good reason to prefer to see the funds left in the company rather than paid out in cash dividends. Any cash dividends received by the principals were very likely to be reinvested in the company, in fact, so that in their case the only benefit from the proposed dividend policy would be to the government. Finally, and most seriously, he believed that it would be a grave mistake to make any decision about cash dividends without first examining the company's future needs for cash and trying to determine the consequences of a cash dividend policy for the company's subsequent new financing and future rate of growth. Mr. Godwin decided that the problem was sufficiently important and complex to justify obtaining outside assistance and that the company should use the services of a consultant.

Building the Planning Structure

During the spring of 1967 Mr. Godwin had attended an executive development program at a major business school, and had developed cordial relations with a number of professors at the school. He was aware that many faculty members undertook consulting assignments and decided to invite Professor Martin Ross, who had taught financial management on the program, to consult with Nautilus, Inc., during the summer months. A long-distance telephone conversation in May, 1968, followed by a backup letter outlining the situation, convinced Professor Ross that the project might be both interesting and a useful source of new teaching material. It was arranged that he would make his first visit to the company early in June.

Mr. Godwin and Professor Ross decided at their first meeting that the initial requirement was to try to determine what the company's growth rate might be over the planning period if no financial constraints existed: that is, in circumstances in which the factors limiting growth were the time required to develop new products and new research strength, and the development of market demand for these products and capabilities, but *not* the need for funds to finance additional working capital, plant, equipment, or other facilities. They decided that the professor's first step should be to talk to all those people in the organization whose knowledge and responsibilities qualified them to contribute to the formulation of such an estimate. During the next few weeks Professor Ross discussed his requirements with Mr. Olson, Mr. Crawford, the marketing manager, project leaders and other scientists, and representatives of the government agencies for whom much of the research and development work was being performed.

An initial problem was the choice of a planning horizon. Forecasts of market demand for even existing products could not be made with any confidence more than 2 or 3 years into the future. On the other hand, some of the projects on which the research groups were currently working would not begin to produce revenues until the mid-1970's. Many long-lead-time, high-technology projects had recently been undertaken, particularly in the areas of "artificial gill" and thin-membrane breathing devices, low-frequency underwater radio transmission, and undersea transportation. Although it was extremely difficult to estimate the size and timing of revenues from these projects, it was expected that they would represent a major part of the company's activities. The representatives of government agencies were confident that their budgets for the general area of oceanography research and development would be rapidly increased in the next decade; but they found it difficult to forecast the proportions of these budgets that would be devoted to hardware purchases, hardware development, and long-term theoretical research.

The consultant finally decided, nevertheless, that the long-lead-time nature of many of the firm's activities dictated a relatively long planning horizon and that a 10-year period would be the most meaningful one despite the uncertainty that must attach to the figures estimated for the later years in the planning period. He regarded his work as a study of feasibility rather than an actual forecast.

The sales figures gathered by Professor Ross from his various sources and combined by him to form the top line of his forecast (see Exhibit 3) revealed that the company's growth potential over the coming decade was very great. Mr. Godwin later commented on the projection: "These figures force us to think in terms of a growth rate that I would probably never have considered. Of course, I know they are not accurate, especially for the later years. But even if the margin of error proves to be as much as plus-or-minus 25%, the exercise has been a very valuable one. We were tending to feel that the equity financing we expect next month would really get us off the hook and give us a big enough base for our expansion for some years to come. But if we face up to the challenge of these figures, well, we are going to need a lot more cash quite soon."

Having estimated total revenues for every year of the planning period, the consultant's next step was to forecast net earnings in each year. He decided that it was unrealistic to try to forecast profit margins for individual products. The alternative chosen was to assume a ratio of earnings before interest and taxes (E.B.I.T.) to total revenues. In the 1967 financial year, this had been approximately 15%. A moderate improvement upon this figure was expected, however, when new facilities were in full operation and higher volumes had been achieved. Making allowance on this basis, he estimated that the company should be able to produce net before-tax earnings of at least 16% of revenues, and used this basis as background for the before-tax figures given in Exhibit 3.

In determining the company's needs for new funds during the planning period, Professor Ross decided to try to obtain estimates of actual costs for new capital investments but to estimate additional working capital requirements as a ratio of working capital to net sales based on the company's past experience. The capital investment figures were based on existing expansion plans and studies and discussion with the company's research, engineering, and production executives. The assumption underlying the calculation of new working capital requirements was that the working capital exclusive of cash would approximate 28% of net sales, as had been the case in recent weeks.

Professor Ross, in estimating depreciation charges, used the double declining balance method, consistent with the company's practice.[5] It was now possible to complete the schedule given as Exhibit 3, which was an attempt to present the company's inflows and outflows of funds over a 10-year period, exclusive of all matters related to financing. Since there was a negative cash change for each period, it was clear that the very rapid expansion of the company would not be feasible without the introduction of new funds. Of course, the company was about to receive $1.9 million, approximately, from the sale of shares. But about $1 million of this was to be used to pay off the bank. Obviously, the net new funds provided would be consumed early in 1970.

The president of the commercial bank serving Nautilus, Inc., had indicated his opinion that the company should in the future ensure that the equity should constitute at least two thirds of the company's total capitalization.[6] Mr. Godwin asked Professor Ross to assume that the company would consistently use debt up to but not in excess of this limit. Calculating from the figures in the balance sheet of Exhibit 2, and the estimated earnings of 1968, Professor Ross found that $1,578,000 new debt could be created.[7] Some of it, doubtless, would be based on receivables, and the rest would be in a form still undecided.

Continuing the one-third debt assumption, and assuming a 6% before-tax cost on borrowed money, Professor Ross prepared Exhibit 4, which showed that by reinvesting earnings and borrowing up to one third of the capitalization the company would experience cash shortages in 1971 and 1972.

Professor Ross pointed out to Mr. Godwin that the shortages in 1971 and 1972 could be covered by reducing the net working capital balance from 28% to 25%, and it was decided to assume that this temporary change could be made. Nevertheless, it was observed that there were signals of possible financial stringency within 3 years.

The obvious next step was to make a similar projection using the same estimates of revenues, earnings, and expenditures but assuming a consistent cash dividend policy of paying out 50% of net after-tax earnings beginning in 1973, after the cash shortage had disappeared. The result

---

[5] Since Professor Ross worked from a detailed property schedule, the user of this case cannot check his figures.

[6] Capitalization is defined as the total of all assets, less the current liabilities. That is, it is the total of the long-term debts and all the accounts belonging to the stockholder interest.

[7]
Equity 12/31/67.............................	$1,306
Added by stock sale..........................	2,000
Added by net after-tax earnings, 1968............	402
Equity 12/31/68.............................	$3,708
Permissible debt—one third of total capitalization (one half of equity)..............	$1,854
Long-term debt 12/31/67......................	276
Net debt possible............................	$1,578

is given as Exhibit 5(a). Little explanation of this projection is required. The line showing the cumulative excess (deficit) in cash if no new equity financing were undertaken indicates an increasing deficit. That is, the introduction of a cash dividend policy would mean that the company could only attain its maximum potential growth rate if further funds from external financing were introduced. The professor calculated the extent of the new equity financing that would be required, making full allowance for the increase in debt capacity that would accompany any injection of equity funds. The result is summarized in Exhibit 5(b). After the $2 million stock issue planned for 1968 it would become necessary to raise at least $1 million of new equity in 1973, $2 million in 1974, $2.5 million in 1976, and $1 million in 1977.

No one could predict, of course, whether the financial markets would accept the proposed issues or, if they did, at what price per share. Mr. Godwin believed that the policy reflected in Exhibit 5(b) could not be accepted as a feasible alternative by the founders of the company.

The choice facing the company's directors was not confined to the two courses of action already explored: either abandoning the cash dividend proposal or paying cash dividends and accepting the need for continuing new equity financing. A third possibility was to adopt the cash dividend policy from 1973 on, decide not to undertake new equity financing, and accept a lower rate of growth in revenues and earnings. Professor Ross made a projection based on this policy also. He continued to assume that debt would be used to the limit of the one-third capitalization rule, and reasoned that the funds available for new working capital and capital investment in any period would depend on the funds retained from operations in the previous period plus new debt capacity created by the retention of earnings. The available investment and working capital funds would in turn determine the permissible expansion in sales. By assuming an approximately linear relationship between sales and the fixed asset base necessary to produce those sales, it was possible to construct a formula to predict total revenues in each period. Professor Ross observed the amounts proposed in Exhibit 3 and saw that the relation of the increase in sales to the total of the increases in working capital and other investments was approximately 1.2 to 1 in the period 1973–77.

The sales projections produced by this formula are shown in Exhibit 6. They indicate a slower growth rate such that by 1977 the company's revenues would reach approximately $42 million instead of the estimated maximum possible figure of $55 million which might be attained under conditions of continuing capital adequacy. Net earnings at the slower growth rate would increase to $3,164,000 in 1977 instead of the $4,096,-000 forecast in Exhibit 4.

A major problem remained, and Professor Ross felt that he must make it clear to the Nautilus executives that it was their responsibility to decide upon what grounds this problem should be resolved. He was certain that the interests and inclinations of Mr. Olson, Mr. Crawford, and Mr. Godwin would be best served by the adoption of a policy of maximum growth, no cash payout, and no further equity financing in the foreseeable future. But from mid-1968 onwards, a minimum of 33% of the stock of the Nautilus company would be in the hands of outside investors. The professor felt that some account of the interests of this group should be taken in deciding on a financial policy. Some of these new owners would no doubt value cash dividends more highly than did the company's founders. He realized, also, that Mr. Godwin and his colleagues were reluctant to undertake continued new equity financing largely because of the possible dilution in their control of the company, and that other owners might well have no such objections so long as any future stock offerings could be made at a share price that did not dilute existing earnings per share. Similarly, the outside investors might be expected to attach less value to revenue growth in absolute terms than did the inside group.

The alternative policy of cash dividends, no new equity financing, and limited growth might be acceptable to these outsiders if it resulted in a pattern of cash dividends plus capital appreciation per share in excess of the values offered by the other policies. Professor Ross realized that to obtain a solution to this problem it would be necessary to make some sweeping assumptions about the future prices of Nautilus common stock and about the needs and characteristics of the investors who might be expected to purchase the stock at the coming public stock offering.

Professor Ross was also beginning to question whether the company's commercial bankers were being both ungenerous and ultraconservative. The bank had urged that debt should not make up more than 33⅓% of total capitalization and that a significant part of the proceeds of the new equity financing should be used to reduce the existing short-term bank notes. It occurred to him that if the bank accepted a higher debt ratio of, perhaps, 45%, or was willing to continue to provide a line of credit outside the debt ratio, then it would be possible for the company to pay cash dividends, to avoid new equity financing, and to enjoy a growth in revenues close to the maximum rate shown in Exhibit 3. He wondered if one of the company officers should approach the bank to discuss these possibilities, or even begin to look for another banking relationship.

Professor Ross and Mr. Godwin realized that they must very soon discuss the company's financial strategies with Mr. Olson and Mr. Crawford. They wondered what their recommendations should be.

Exhibit 1

NAUTILUS, INC.

Income Statement for the Year Ended December 31, 1967
(in thousands)

Net sales revenues.............................	$3,850	100.0%
Cost of sales*.................................	(3,270)	(84.9)
Gross profit................................	$ 580	15.1%
Interest expense..............................	(42)	(1.1)
Other expenses...............................	(17)	(0.4)
Net income before taxes......................	$ 521	13.5%
Federal income tax...........................	(232)	(6.0)
Net income................................	$ 289	7.5%
Retained earnings at beginning of period.........	$ 961	
Add: Net income...........................	289	
Total..................................	$1,250	
Earnings per common share....................	$28.90	

* Including depreciation charges of $58,400.

Exhibit 2

NAUTILUS, INC.

Balance Sheet as of December 31, 1967
(in thousands)

ASSETS

Current assets	
Cash..	$ 32
Accounts receivable...................................	1,833
Inventories..	1,964
Prepaid expenses.....................................	38
Total current assets.............................	$3,867
Fixed assets	
Plant, equipment, and leasehold improvements...........	971
Less: Accumulated depreciation......................	187
Net fixed assets...................................	784
Total assets..................................	$4,651

LIABILITIES AND NET WORTH

Current liabilities	
Notes payable to bank................................	$ 984
Accounts payable....................................	1,241
Unliquidated progress payments.......................	382
Taxes payable and accruals...........................	462
Total current liabilities.........................	$3,069
Mortgages payable...................................	135
Loans from officers..................................	141
Common stock (10,000 shares @ $5 par)	
and capital surplus...............................	56
Retained earnings...................................	1,250
Total liabilities and net worth...................	$4,651

Exhibit 3

NAUTILUS, INC.

Sales, Earnings, and Cash Flow Projection Exclusive of Financial Burdens

(in thousands)

	1968	1969	1970	1971	1972	1973	1974	1975	1976	1977
Net sales	$5,500	$8,750	$14,000	$20,000	$26,000	$30,000	$35,000	$40,000	$47,000	$55,000
Before-tax operating cash potential	$1,090*	$1,745	$2,435	$3,515	$4,580	$5,380	$6,210	$7,170	$8,380	$9,770
Tax exposure (50%)	(545)	(872)	(1,217)	(1,757)	(2,290)	(2,690)	(3,105)	(3,585)	(4,190)	(4,885)
Depreciation tax shield	105	172	97	157	210	290	305	385	430	485
Internally generated funds	$ 650	$1,045	$1,315	$1,915	$2,500	$2,980	$3,410	$3,970	$4,620	$5,370
Increase in working capital	(460)	(900)	(1,450)	(1,700)	(1,700)	(1,100)	(1,400)	(1,400)	(2,000)	(2,200)
Other investments	(810)	(1,145)	(1,295)	(1,515)	(1,520)	(2,380)	(2,710)	(2,970)	(4,360)	(3,570)
Funds profile, annual	$ (620)	$(1,000)	$(1,430)	$(1,300)	$ (720)	$ (500)	$ (700)	$ (400)	$(1,740)	$ (400)
After-tax earnings before financial charges	$ 440†	$ 700	$ 1,120	$ 1,600	$ 2,080	$ 2,400	$ 2,800	$ 3,200	$ 3,760	$ 4,400

* Sample of calculation to reach figures on this line:

E.B.I.T. (16% of net sales)	$ 880
Depreciation eliminated	210
Before-tax operating cash potential	$1,090

† Sample of calculation to reach the figures on this line:

Internally generated funds	$650
Depreciation expense	210
After-tax earnings before financial charges	$440

Exhibit 4

NAUTILUS, INC.
Cash Flow Projections Assuming a Two-Thirds Equity Position in Total Capitalization
(in thousands)

	1968	1969	1970	1971	1972	1973	1974	1975	1976	1977
Funds profile, annual	$ (620)	$(1,000)	$(1,430)	$(1,300)	$ (720)	$ (500)	$ (700)	$ (400)	$(1,740)	$ (400)
New equity financing, net	1,925									
Repayment of bank loan	(1,000)									
New debt to maintain 33⅓% ratio	1,578	322§	528	759	988	1,134	1,316	1,497	1,754	2,048
Interest (6%) on all debt*	(76)†	(111)	(130)	(162)	(208)	(267)	(335)	(414)	(504)	(609)
Tax shield from interest	38	56	65	81	104	134	168	207	252	305
Change in cash, annual	$1,845	$ (733)	$ (967)	$ (622)	$ 164	$ 501	$ 449	$ 890	$ (238)	$1,344
Cumulative change	1,845	1,112	145	(477)	(313)	188	637	1,527	1,289	2,633
Net earnings after tax	$ 402‡	$ 645	$ 1,055	$ 1,519	$1,976	$2,267	$2,633	$2,993	$ 3,508	$4,096

* Interest computed on debt as at the end of the previous year.

† On $1,000 bank loan, mortgage, and loans from officers.

‡ Sample of calculation to reach figures on this line:

After-tax earnings before financial charges		$440
Interest expense	$(76)	
Tax shield, interest	38	(38)
		$402

§ Sample of calculation to reach figures on this line:

Equity at end of previous year	$3,708
Net earnings, after tax, current year	645
Equity at end of current year	$4,353
Permissible debt, current year	$2,176
Debt at end of previous year	1,854
New debt	$ 322

Exhibit 5(a)

NAUTILUS, INC.

Cash Flow Projection, Assuming 50% Cash Dividend After 1972
(in thousands)

	1973	1974	1975	1976	1977
Funds profile, annual..............	$(500)	$(700)	$(400)	$(1,740)	$(400)
Cash dividend, 50%..............	(1,133)	(1,325)	(1,515)	(1,783)	(2,090)
New debt at 33⅓% ratio..........	567	663	757	892	1,045
Interest (6%) on all debt..........	(267)	(301)	(341)	(386)	(440)
Tax shield from interest...........	134	151	171	193	220
Change in cash...................	$(1,199)	$(1,512)	$(1,328)	$(2,824)	$(1,665)
Cash deficit, beginning of period...	(313)				
Cumulative change................	(1,512)	(3,024)	(4,352)	(7,176)	(8,841)
Net earnings after tax.............	$ 2,267	$ 2,650	$ 3,030	$ 3,567	$ 4,180

Exhibit 5(b)

NAUTILUS, INC.

Cash Flow Projection, Assuming 50% Dividend Payout and Further Equity as Needed
(in thousands)

	1973	1974	1975	1976	1977
Funds profile, annual..............	$(500)	$(700)	$(400)	$(1,740)	$(400)
Cash dividend, 50%..............	(1,133)	(1,317)	(1,492)	(1,761)	(2,049)
New equity.....................	1,000	2,000	—	2,500	1,000
New debt at 33⅓% ratio..........	1,067	1,659	747	2,131	1,525
Interest (6%) on all debt..........	(267)	(331)	(431)	(475)	(603)
Tax shield from interest...........	134	166	216	238	302
Change in cash...................	$ 301	$ 1,477	$(1,360)	$ 893	$(225)
Cash deficit, beginning of period....	(313)				
Cumulative change..............	(12)	1,465	105	998	773
Net earnings after tax.............	$ 2,267	$ 2,635	$ 2,985	$ 3,523	$ 4,099

Exhibit 6

NAUTILUS, INC.

Maximum Sales Revenues Realizable with 50% Dividend Payout after 1972,
33⅓% Debt Ratio, and No Equity Financing after 1968

(in thousands)

	1973	1974	1975	1976	1977
Sales revenue	$30,000	$32,362	$35,290	$38,603	$42,173
Before-tax operating cash potential	$ 5,380	$ 5,788	$ 6,416	$ 6,976	$ 7,648
Tax exposure (50%)	(2,690)	(2,894)	(3,208)	(3,488)	(3,824)
Depreciation tax shield	290	305	385	400	450
Internally generated funds, after tax	$ 2,980	$ 3,199	$ 3,593	$ 3,888	$ 4,274
New debt at 33⅓% ratio	567	610	664	725	791
Interest on all debt at 6%*	(267)	(301)	(338)	(378)	(421)
Tax shield from interest	134	151	169	189	211
Cash dividend	(1,133)	(1,219)	(1,327)	(1,449)	(1,582)
Cash deficit, beginning of period	(313)				
Funds available to finance expansion in next period	$ 1,968	$ 2,440	$ 2,761	$ 2,975	$ 3,273
Factor	1.2	1.2	1.2	1.2	1.2
Incremental sales in next period	2,362	2,928	3,313	3,570	3,928
Total sales in next period	$32,362	$35,290	$38,603	$42,173	$46,101
Net earnings after tax	$ 2,267	$ 2,439	$ 2,654	$ 2,899	$ 3,164

* Interest computed on debt at the end of the previous year.

SCM Corporation *

In October, 1965, Mr. Paul Elicker, vice president and treasurer of SCM Corporation, was considering possible changes in SCM's dividend policy. He knew that this topic would be discussed at the December meeting of the board of directors, and he wanted to be adequately prepared to make a sound recommendation on this matter to Mr. Mead, president of SCM, and to the board of directors.

Earlier in October, Mr. Elicker had received a comprehensive report on dividend policy for SCM from the Corporate Services Division of Irving Trust Company. This report recommended that SCM resume paying cash dividends in December and eliminate its stock dividend at the same time. After reviewing this recommendation, Mr. Elicker had asked Mr. Anthony H. Meyer of Irving Trust Company for his opinion about the implications of deferring the resumption of cash dividend payments until a later time. Part of Mr. Meyer's reply is reproduced in Exhibit 3.

SCM's business had been founded in 1903 to manufacture and sell typewriters. In the early 1950's, the company, then known as the Smith-Corona Typewriter Company, had two main product lines. Office typewriters were expected to provide a fairly stable earnings base regardless of swings in the business cycle. Portable typewriters were thought to be more subject to consumer whims and economic conditions, and thus were expected to contribute to the company's profits primarily during periods of prosperity. On a cash basis, sales of office typewriters (with relatively short collection periods) were expected to provide a steady net inflow of cash throughout the year. Portables, on the other hand, were subject to a pronounced seasonal sales pattern (which required a seasonal buildup of inventories) and were sold through dealers who were often slow in paying SCM for the typewriters (necessitating a seasonal swing in receivables).

---

* Abridged.

Because of the stability of the office typewriter line, and because many of the 300,000 shares of common stock then outstanding were held by a family group who had special dividend interests, the company had adopted what it considered to be a fairly liberal cash dividend policy in the early 1950's. For example, the dividend pay-out ratio ranged from 36% to 64% in the 1951–53 period.

During the 1950's, however, manual office typewriter sales proved to be unstable for SCM, and as IBM electric typewriters began to command an increasing share of the office typewriter market, SCM's manual typewriter line began to generate large losses. Sales of portable typewriters grew rapidly during this period and proved to be relatively insensitive to general business conditions. While SCM's share of the market for portables increased from 30% in 1953 to 35% in 1960, this growth of sales plus the seasonal pattern of inventories and receivables for this line created a growing need for funds at a time when losses on office typewriters were also consuming funds. By the late 1950's, these developments had created a severe cash shortage.

Despite the cash squeeze and the necessity for additional debt financing in the late 1950's, cash dividends continued to be paid. Earnings declined to $0.30 per share in fiscal 1959, but SCM maintained its dividend payment of $0.85 per share in the hope that earnings would improve in the following year. In addition, the company planned to force conversion of its outstanding convertible debentures in fiscal 1959 to strengthen its equity base in anticipation of future debt financing, and an adverse market price reaction to a dividend cut could have made it impossible to force conversion of the debentures. In fiscal 1960, however, when SCM reported a loss of $0.24 per share, the directors voted—in a close vote—to eliminate the cash dividend payment entirely. Modest earnings of $301,747 (or $0.16 per share) were reported in fiscal 1961, but special charges and writeoffs of $2,398,000 were made directly to Earned Surplus.

SCM's management had begun taking steps in the late 1950's to improve the company's long-range prospects. The acquisition of Kleinschmidt Laboratories (1956) and Marchant Company (1958) added teletype equipment and calculators to the product line, and by 1965 other product lines, such as office supplies, photocopy machines, peripheral data processing equipment, electronic calculators, adding machines, and accounting machines, had been developed or acquired.

This restructuring of SCM's business began to show results in fiscal 1962 as earnings improved to $2,592,000 ($1.35 per share), and a 2% stock dividend was declared shortly after the close of this year. Management's rationale for the 2% stock dividend was that it should enable stockholders to benefit from the improving earnings outlook. Cash dividends were not considered appropriate at that time because of the company's continuing cash squeeze.

Earnings in 1963 and 1964 were somewhat below the 1962 level, but stock dividends of 3% were declared in each of these years. In fiscal 1965, earnings had increased to $3,815,477 ($1.47 per share), and management was very optimistic about the outlook for SCM's photocopy equipment, particularly a new model of the Coronastat electrostatic office copier scheduled for introduction in fiscal 1968. The directors had discussed resuming cash dividend payments during fiscal 1965; but the company's cash needs were still considerable, and additional external financing was planned to raise additional cash. As a result of the optimistic earnings outlook during a period of continuing cash stringency, the directors declared a 5% stock dividend during fiscal 1965.

As Mr. Elicker turned to the question of dividends in October, he had certain additional data available for consideration. SCM's annual report for fiscal 1965 had recently been sent to stockholders, so Mr. Elicker knew that investors were aware of the company's improved situation. (Exhibits 1 and 2 contain financial data about the company.) The cash situation was still tight in view of SCM's projected need for funds, but he felt that the worst part of the cash squeeze was past. (Exhibit 3 shows an historical record of sources and uses of funds; Exhibit 4 is the company's forecast of sources and uses of funds for a 4-year period, based upon the assumption that SCM adopts Irving Trust Company's recommendation of a $0.10 cash dividend per quarter.)

Mr. Elicker's own research had suggested that "glamour companies" which paid modest cash dividends might have higher price-earnings ratios than those in the nondividend-paying group, but he was not sure whether the apparent difference in P/E ratios was due to dividend policy differences or to other factors. It was possible, but not certain, that a cash dividend might help maintain the current high market price of SCM's stock or push it up even further.

Since external financing was contemplated in the future, Mr. Elicker desired to take legitimate steps to create a better and more solid market value for the common stock. On the other hand, SCM had not paid a cash dividend for 5 years, the image of the company had changed significantly during that time, and SCM's stock was actively traded. The market price had risen from $25¾ to $51⅝ during September, and the shares had been trading in late October between $44 and $52 per share. Consequently, Mr. Elicker doubted if SCM's present shareholders really cared very much about cash dividends.

Since Mr. Elicker expected dividend policy to be a main topic for discussion at the December directors' meeting, he planned to review the material again and then decide what type of dividend action he would recommend. If he decided that resumption of cash dividends was desirable, he would have to decide on a recommendation about the amount of the cash dividend as well as whether a stock dividend should also be declared.

Exhibit 1

SCM CORPORATION

Consolidated Balance Sheet
(dollar figures in millions)

ASSETS

	June 30, 1964	June 30, 1965
Current assets		
Cash.	$ 1.2	$ 2.1
Accounts receivable.	25.0	28.0
Inventories.	41.2	41.5
Total current assets.	$67.4	$71.6
Fixed assets, net.	22.5	23.9
Other assets.	1.8	1.4
Total.	$91.7	$96.9

LIABILITIES

Current liabilities.	$18.0	$20.7
Long-term debt.	23.3	21.9
Deferred income taxes.	.5	1.4
Stockholders' equity.	49.9	52.9
Total.	$91.7	$96.9

Notes:

1. Under the provisions of the long-term debt, approximately $2.5 million of retained earnings was available for cash dividends at June 30, 1965.

2. In June, 1965, the company announced that it would redeem for cash any shares of its convertible preferred stock still outstanding on July 8, 1965. As a result of this announcement, over 99% of the outstanding preferred stock was converted into common stock in June and early July.

3. At June 30, 1965, 2,694,178 shares of common stock were issued and outstanding, and an additional 235,445 shares were reserved (and subsequently issued) for conversion of the preferred stock.

Exhibit 2

SCM CORPORATION

Eight-Year Statistical Summary
(fiscal years ended June 30)

	1958	*1959*	*1960*	*1961*	*1962*	*1963*	*1964*	*1965*
Net sales (in thousands)*	$87,146	$90,411	$93,359	$96,476	$103,165	$117,343	$124,704	$149,657
Net income (loss) (in thousands)	2,244	482	(455)	302	2,592	1,656	2,437	3,815
Earnings per common share*	1.22	0.23	(0.21)	0.14	1.21	0.57	0.83	1.47
Dividends paid on common stock:								
Cash dividends per share	0.77	0.75	...	...	...	...	...	...
Stock dividends	...	...	...	...	2%	3%	3%	5%
Market price of common stock (calendar years)†	$13¼–20¼	$11–19½	$9⅞–16¼	$10¾–26⅞	$8⅞–24⅞	$9⅛–15	$12½–19⅛	$15⅞–52½
Price-earnings ratio‡								
SCM Corporation	14.5	66.3	...	13.4	13.9	21.2	19.0	23.3
Dow-Jones Industrials	18.2	18.3	19.4	21.5	17.3	17.2	17.8	16.8

* The year 1965 on average shares outstanding after stock dividend; prior years adjusted for subsequent stock dividends.
† Range for year to October 25, 1965.
‡ Based on mid-point of year's price range.

Exhibit 3

SCM CORPORATION
Source and Use of Funds
(years ended June 30 in millions)

	1958	1959	1960	1961	1962	1963	1964	1965
Beginning cash balance	2.4	4.2	4.0	3.2	3.2	2.3	3.9	1.0
Add:								
Income after taxes*	2.2	0.5	(0.5)	0.3	2.6	1.7	2.4	3.8
Depreciation	1.2	1.6	2.0	2.0	2.3	2.7	2.4	2.5
Borrowings from (repayments to) banks	(3.1)	(6.7)	7.4	2.4	0.9	(10.7)	0.5	1.6
Other increases (decreases) in current liabilities	1.0	(2.0)	(0.5)	1.5	1.7	(0.1)	1.9	1.9
Debentures	4.2	7.4	...	...	...	...	...	...
Other long-term debt	9.7	6.0	...	...	...	...	...	...
Increases (decreases) in stockholders' equity	0.2	4.9†	(1.7)†‡	(2.0)§	(0.6)**	11.4††	0.1	(0.1)
Total available	17.8	15.9	10.7	7.4	10.1	7.3	11.2	10.9
Less:								
Increase (decrease) in accounts receivable	5.0	(4.0)	3.0	0.6	1.1	1.0	1.1	3.0
Increase (decrease) in inventories	1.0	4.8	(0.2)	2.8	2.2	(0.9)	4.8	0.3
Capital expenditures*	6.2	3.7	3.0	2.5	2.2	1.4	2.8	3.8
Long-term debt repayments	...	4.9†	1.5	1.1	2.6	1.4	1.5	1.4
Other increases (decreases) in assets	...	1.0	0.2	(2.8)||	(0.3)	0.1	(0.7)	(0.4)
Cash dividends paid	1.4	1.5	...	...	...	0.4‡‡	0.7‡‡	0.7‡‡
Total cash employed	13.6	11.9	7.5	4.2	7.8	3.4	10.2	8.8
Ending cash balance	4.2	4.0	3.2	3.2	2.3	3.9	1.0	1.9
Interest expense—long term debt*	1.2	1.5	2.0	2.2	2.0	1.7	1.4	1.6

* Casewriter's estimate, based upon analysis of published financial statements.
† Increase in equity in 1959 represents conversion of outstanding 6% convertible subordinated debentures into 229,128 shares of common stock. An equivalent reduction in long-term debt is included in "debt repayments" for 1959.
‡ Net special charges to retained earnings amounted to $1,737,349 in 1960, and represented provision for nonrecurring costs and write-downs of assets (less estimated reduction in U.S. income taxes).
§ Reduction in equity in 1961 was due to special charges to retained earnings ($2,144,850), less proceeds from issuance of common stock for acquisitions and stock options.
|| Includes write-offs and sales of assets.
** Due primarily to change in accounting method in one corporate division.
†† Represents net proceeds from sale of $12,002,200 (par value) 5½% convertible preferred stock, after issuance and distribution expenses of $561,050.
‡‡ Dividends paid on 5½% convertible preferred stock.

Exhibit 4

SCM CORPORATION

Source and Use of Funds Forecast
(years ended June 30 in millions)

	1966	1967	1968	1969	Total
Beginning cash balance....................	$ 2.1	$ 4.8	$ 4.7	$ 5.0	$ 2.1
Add:					
Income after taxes*.....................	8.6	10.9	11.9	18.7	50.1
Depreciation..........................	2.1	5.6	8.1	10.4	26.2
Borrowings—banks and payables.........	15.5	4.3	(20.5)	5.5	4.8
Debentures............................	. . .	. . .	33.0	. . .	33.0
Other long-term debt...................	. . .	10.0	. . .	. . .	10.0
Increase in equity†.....................	1.9	5.5	. . .	. . .	7.4
Total available.....................	$30.2	$41.1	$37.2	$39.6	$133.6
Less:					
Increase in accounts receivable...........	$ 6.0	$ 5.3	$ 5.7	$ 7.5	$ 24.5
Increase in inventories..................	6.1	7.5	8.0	10.5	32.1
Increase in lease inventories.............	1.3	6.7	7.7	9.2	24.9
Capital expenditures....................	5.0	8.5	6.7	3.9	24.1
Debt repayments†.....................	3.0	6.9	1.9	1.9	13.7
Other increases in assets................	3.4	0.2	0.8	0.2	4.6
Cash dividend‡........................	0.6	1.3	1.4	1.4	4.7
Total cash employed................	$25.4	$36.4	$32.2	$34.6	$128.6
Ending cash balance.....................	$ 4.8	$ 4.7	$ 5.0	$ 5.0	$ 5.0
Interest on long-term debt at 7%§.........	$ 1.4	$ 1.6	$ 3.1	$ 4.2	$ 10.3

* The reader may assume an income tax rate of 50% in his study of this exhibit.

† Increases in equity in 1966 and 1967 represent anticipated conversion of $7,441,900 of outstanding 5¼% convertible subordinated debentures for 377,378 shares of common stock. An equivalent reduction in long-term debt is included in "debt repayments" for 1966 and 1967.

‡ Assuming dividends of $0.10 per quarter (two quarters in fiscal 1966) on outstanding shares (including shares issued for conversion of convertible preferred stock in fiscal 1966 and shares expected to be issued for conversion of the 5¼% convertible subordinated debentures in fiscal 1966 and 1967).

§ Casewriter's estimate.

Exhibit 5

IRVING TRUST COMPANY

One Wall Street

New York, N.Y. 10015

Anthony H. Meyer
Assistant Vice President

Telephone: LL3–3283

October 20, 1965

Mr. Paul Elicker
Vice President and Treasurer
SCM Corporation
410 Park Avenue
New York, New York

Dear Paul:

You asked me to comment on our dividend policy recommendations for SCM with respect to what the results might be if you decide to defer the resumption of cash dividends for the time being.

Short range, we would not expect any very significant reaction. As we stated in our report, SCM's shareholders at this point are not likely to be dividend oriented. Even if they were, no reasonable dividend would provide a yield of any consequence.

However, you'll recall that Mr. Mead's remarks at the New York Society of Security Analysts last summer implied that the time to resume dividends was not too far distant. The market may be looking for a dividend declaration, not for yield but as an expression of management's confidence in the future, and may expect it to come when the stock dividend is usually declared. To avoid any possible adverse reaction, SCM should make it clear if dividends are deferred that this decision is in no way a reflection of management's thinking about earnings prospects.

We would also have to recommend that you pay a stock dividend again this year if you don't reinstitute a cash payout. Again we are considering short-range market effect. As you know we don't believe there are any permanent market effects from stock dividends, but you could get an unfavorable temporary reaction by taking no dividend action whatever in December.

Long range, we are back in never-never land because of the difficulty of relating payout policy to price-earnings ratio. We do believe that the ultimate effect of a regular cash dividend policy is to enhance a stock's investment quality, thereby broadening its ownership base and improving both its price-earnings ratio and its price stability. If SCM defers the resumption of cash dividends, it is doing no more than deferring the time when it begins to acquire the improved investment quality a regular dividend record would give it.

If current cash needs merit a higher priority than enhancing your image a bit sooner, we would see no serious objection to delaying the dividend. At the same time, we would hate to see a "cash needs" argument marshaled against dividends year after year. There is a positive value to a cash dividend record, even if the dividend is modest. On the other side of the coin, the difference between retaining 75% of earnings and retaining them all is relatively minor in terms of helping to meet SCM's capital needs.

You sometimes hear people say that dividends can't matter for growth companies because there are nondividend-paying growth companies whose stocks sell at very fancy earnings multiples. What this argument overlooks is that there is no way of knowing where these stocks would sell if they did pay a dividend. . . .

. . . .

I hope some of these thoughts will be useful to you. Let me know if we can do anything more.

With best regards,

Sincerely,
/s/Tony

The Prudential Insurance Company of America

Introduction

In January, 1962, Mr. David Lloyd, an investment analyst in the Minneapolis office of The Prudential Insurance Company of America, was attempting to draw up a set of loan terms for a prospective new borrowing customer, Alliance Dairy Company. Alliance had asked for a loan of $340,000 on a long-term basis to help finance the construction of new plant facilities.

Alliance Dairy Company

Alliance Dairy Company was incorporated in Illinois in 1950, as Alliance Cooperative Dairy Company, to process and distribute dairy products at wholesale to independent member grocers. Initially, milk and butter were sold to 59 customers in Urbana, Illinois. The dairy's sales volume had grown steadily, aided by the broadening of its product line to include ice cream, cottage cheese, and a variety of other dairy products and by the addition of new member-customers. Alliance had been first in its area to use bulk tank milk pickup from its dairy farm suppliers and to supply milk to its customers in half-gallon containers.

By 1962 Alliance distributed its products over an area within a 50-mile radius of Urbana with a population of 440,000. Its 165 independent grocer customers were at the same time stockholders, since each was required to purchase shares of Alliance's common stock. This stock served as collateral for payables due Alliance. Milk was purchased directly from about 80 dairy farmers, collected by Alliance tank trucks, and processed at the Alliance plant.

Alliance was the second largest of the 35 dairy processing firms operating in the Urbana area, with 11% of the milk products business. Foremost Dairies, which had recently moved a milk-processing facility from
Urbana to Stoneham—60 miles away—was Alliance's largest competitor,
with 18% of the area business. Two other dairies each had about 10%
of the market.

Alliance's net income was subject to the usual corporate income taxes,
but under current tax regulations, rebates distributed to stockholders on
the basis of their patronage were deductible as a business expense. To
minimize its tax liability, therefore, the dairy made a practice of rebating
all net proceeds from operations which were not needed to operate the
business. Working capital needs were small, since accounts receivable
were settled weekly and payments to dairy farmers for raw milk were
made on a twice-monthly basis. (See Exhibits 1 and 2 for comparative
financial data.)

Although Alliance enjoyed a reputation as an aggressively and skillfully operated business, its management in recent years had been increasingly dissatisfied with its antiquated milk-processing plant, which was
both inefficient and limited in capacity. In November, 1960, therefore,
the owner-patrons of Alliance had voted to build and equip a new bulk
milk-processing and storage plant of sufficient capacity to permit continued expansion of operations. The old plant building was expected to
have little value in a resale, but some of the equipment being used there
could be transferred to the new facility. Because Alliance did not have
sufficient funds available to finance the undertaking, the membership
agreed to have an overcharge levied on them for milk and ice cream purchased from the dairy, beginning in December, 1960. In this way it was
expected that $200,000 could be raised during the next year to help
finance part of the $950,000 undertaking. The overcharge was to be re-
turned to the owner-patrons in the form of preferred stock.

Soon after the membership had voted in favor of the surcharge, Alliance's commercial bank, the Peoples National Bank of Urbana, agreed
to provide construction credit up to $150,000 to permit the building
operation to be started immediately. In addition, it had agreed to supply
$160,000 of the permanent financing needed and to assist Alliance in
locating the $380,000 additional long-term funds required to complete
the financing of the project, which would be finished by September,
1962. Alliance's management hoped to obtain an 8- to 10-year loan on
terms which would not unduly burden them with constricting covenants
and which recognized the somewhat distinctive nature of its operations
and financing.

The Prudential Insurance Company of America

The Commercial and Industrial Loan Department of Prudential had
been established in 1956 to extend financing to small companies whose

capital needs had heretofore been considered too modest to warrant the time and attention of institutional lenders. By the end of 1961 the department had loans outstanding of $428 million and had been allocated $130 million in new funds to invest in 1962. This allocation provided strong incentive to accommodate as many loan requests as it could, within reason. In as many applications as possible the department sought to answer the question, "HOW can the loan be made?" rather than "CAN it be made?" The department had been organized into eight regional offices, each staffed with from two to six representatives. These offices initiated all departmental loan proposals and competed aggressively with other lending institutions for the business in their areas. Once a regional office had satisfied itself as to the soundness of a loan opportunity, it forwarded the pertinent financial data, along with tentative loan terms, to Prudential's home office in Newark, New Jersey, where it was reviewed by the loan officers there. The corporate office could deny further consideration of a loan proposal sent in by one of the regional offices but could not on its own authority grant a loan. If it judged that the proposal merited it, the pertinent data and recommended loan terms were summarized for presentation to Prudential's Finance Committee, which made the final decision on all loan proposals.

When Mr. Lloyd had first been asked by the Peoples National Bank to consider the Alliance loan request, several questions had arisen in his mind. Noting that the owner-patrons had voted to levy on themselves a surcharge on each half gallon of milk purchased from Alliance, Mr. Lloyd had queried what would prevent some or all of these owner-patrons from switching to competitive suppliers. Several inquiries about this convinced Mr. Lloyd that customer loyalty to Alliance had been strong. An executive of a competing dairy expressed the opinion that because of the dual role as owner and customer, it was practically impossible for other dairy processors to compete with Alliance for its customers' business. When Mr. Lloyd talked to the loan officer at the Peoples National Bank, he was told that the bank, in a move to demonstrate to Prudential its confidence in Alliance, was prepared to increase its participation in the long-term financing from $160,000 to $200,000, its legal lending limit. Thus, the size of the loan being requested from Prudential was reduced by $40,000 to $340,000. The bank had also agreed to accept security and repayment guarantees on a pro rata basis with the insurance company.

Mr. Lloyd had also raised questions about the reliability of Alliance's source of raw milk. Alliance's management conceded that there had been some dissatisfaction among the local dairy farmers over the price received for milk they produced for Alliance and other dairy processors. Management did not believe, however, that there was a serious possibility of a disruption in the supply of milk.

Having determined that the loan opportunity was worthy of further consideration and that if satisfactory terms could be worked out, a 6% interest rate would be appropriate, Mr. Lloyd turned to the task of composing a set of covenants which would protect Prudential adequately yet not unduly restrict Alliance. He knew that several other institutional lenders had expressed preliminary interest in the dairy's capital needs and that if the proposed terms were unsatisfactory to Alliance, it might attempt to obtain financing from one of Prudential's competitors. To aid him, Mr. Lloyd had Prudential's manual of guidelines for framing loan covenants, excerpts from which are presented in Exhibit 3.

Exhibit 1

ALLIANCE DAIRY COMPANY

Comparative Operating Data—Years Ending November 30

(dollar figures in thousands)

	1952	1953	1954	1955	1956	1957	1958	1959	1960	1961
Gross sales	$646	$744	$823	$991	$1,209	$1,331	$1,499	$1,873	$2,352	$2,640
Less: Cost of sales	570	650	717	873	1,059	1,135	1,254	1,567	1,914	2,043
Gross margin	76	94	106	118	150	196	245	306	438	597
Less: Selling, general and administrative expense (excluding depreciation)	38	56	73	83	97	126	158	189	259	309
Operating profit before depreciation	38	38	33	35	53	70	87	117	179	288
Less: Depreciation and amortization	5	7	8	12	17	19	21	27	34	36
Interest expense	3	1	0	1	5	4	3	2	3	4
Retained overcharges paid in cash or in stock	0	9	9	5	10	28	39	74	127	221
Plus: Other income	2	0	0	0	2	0	2	7	9	3
Taxable income	32	21	16	17	23	19	26	21	24	30
Less: Income tax paid	5	5	4	5	7	6	8	6	7	11
Net income after tax	27	16	12	12	16	13	18	15	17	19
Less: Preferred dividends	1	0	1	0	1	0	1	1	4	16
Common dividends	0	0	0	0	1	1	0	0	0	0
Net income after dividends	26	16	11	12	14	12	17	14	13	3
Previous earned surplus	(12)	14	30	41	53	67	79	96	110	123
Earned surplus at end of year	14	30	41	53	67	79	86	110	123	126

Exhibit 2

ALLIANCE DAIRY COMPANY
Comparative Balance Sheets—as of November 30
(dollar figures in thousands)

ASSETS	1952	1953	1954	1955	1956	1957	1958	1959	1960	1961
Cash	$ 8	$ 7	$ 20	$ 17	$ 27	$ 42	$ 59	$ 47	$183	$ 61
Accounts receivable	23	17	30	30	36	19	34	52	87	96
Inventory (lower of cost or market)	24	28	34	32	40	47	55	83	73	84
Prepaid expenses	2	1	2	2	2	3	3	3	7	9
Total current assets	$ 57	$ 53	$ 86	$ 81	$105	$111	$152	$185	$350	$ 250
Net plant	62	59	61	152	169	172	173	192	237	224
Construction in process	0	0	0	0	0	0	0	0	0	576
Bulk milk tanks	0	0	0	0	0	3	23	75	70	63
Miscellaneous assets	0	4	4	11	13	13	14	12	18	0
Total assets	$119	$116	$151	$244	$287	$299	$362	$464	$675	$1,113

LIABILITIES	1952	1953	1954	1955	1956	1957	1958	1959	1960	1961
Notes payable	40	14	0	20	25	0	0	0	0	0
Accounts payable and accrued	36	33	61	70	77	77	91	139	94	159
Reserve for income tax	5	5	4	5	7	6	8	6	7	11
Debt due within one year	0	0	0	0	0	0	0	28	32	28
Total current liabilities	$ 81	$ 52	$ 65	$ 95	$109	$ 83	$ 99	$173	$133	$ 198
Deferred income	0	0	0	2	2	1	0	0	3	2
Funded debt	0	0	0	44	50	50	46	22	45	179
Deposits for purchase of stock	0	3	6	11	15	14	52	56	62	97
Preferred stock	10	10	10	10	10	10	10	10	181	373
Common stock	14	21	29	29	34	62	59	93	128	138
Surplus	14	30	41	53	67	79	96	110	123	126
Total liabilities and equity	$119	$116	$151	$244	$287	$299	$362	$464	$675	$1,113

Exhibit 3

Excerpts from Manual on Framing Loan Covenants

1. Maturity—Generally 10 years to 15 years. The long-term predictable nature of life insurance policy claims has demanded that we take a long-term point of view toward investments.
2. Interest Rate—The interest rate should be related to the current money market. It should be borne in mind that direct placements usually command a higher rate than public offerings because of the elimination of substantial costs associated with public financing, and that our rates reflect the inherently greater risk associated with the smaller industrial concern, too small for public financing.
3. Price—At 100, except in very unusual circumstances.
4. Standby Fee—One half of 1 percent to 1 percent per year.
5. Security—A mortgage or pledge of collateral gives The Prudential a preferred position with respect to the company's assets covered by the lien or pledge and may be desirable even though value alone would not justify the loan. In some instances, very attractive real estate may justify the investment where credit is borderline.
6. Concurrent Financing and Participations—Normally Prudential will purchase the entire issue; however, we will be happy to cooperate with the other lending institutions either on a *"pari passu"* basis, or in the later maturities where commercial banks are involved, providing we are not placed in a subordinate position at any time during the life of the loan.
7. Principal Payments—Generally, principal payments should be made in even thousands of dollars, in a constant amount, and payable on a semiannual or annual basis. Balloons or delays in the start of the principal payments may be applied in meeting special problems and in those instances where justified.
8. Optional Prepayments—Optional prepayments should be held to a minimum. However, the right to repay, at any time, at 100, in whole but not in part, if Prudential refuses consent to additional funded debt, shall be considered a standard provision. Such additional debt need not be offered to The Prudential, but the borrower must have a bona fide offer from another source. This provision does not apply if the borrower seeks merely to replace the Prudential loan.

   Where there is a participating lender, it is important that funds are not permitted to be paid out to the detriment of our position by reason of more liberal prepayment options than are granted by our terms.
9. Financial Statements and Audits—The loan terms will also include standard provisions for submission of annual audits, four quarterly interim financial statements and "Certificates of No Default."

Negative Covenants:

10. Working Capital Tests.
    a) Default level—The default level is based on the pro forma working capital and gives The Prudential protection against a continuing deterioration in the balance sheet. A high default level set close to pro forma level is usually desirable for the following reason: The fact that a company may be borrowing the money for working capital shows that it needs working capital at the pro forma level; if the company grows as expected, it will need *more* rather than *less* working capital; and except for operating losses and debt retirements, reductions in working capital are controllable and limited to capital expenditure and restrictive payments.
    b) Dividend Test—A working capital minimum as a dividend test is generally used in those rare situations when a realistic default level cannot be obtained.
11. Dividends and Other Restrictive Payments—The primary purpose of this covenant is to protect Prudential against excess payout of earnings, to insure maintenance of net worth, and to provide the wherewithal for future company growth. Limitation on restrictive payments depends on the types of credits involved. A mathematical evaluation of the disposition of the earnings should be made, taking into account requirements for (a) debt repayment, (b) restricted payments, and (c) retention for reasonable growth.

    The covenant should provide that restrictive payments be limited to a percent-

Exhibit 3 (Continued)

age of the net earnings available for distribution to stockholders. Where the company is small or the funded debt heavy, the percentage should, of course, be smaller than that permitted for the stronger companies. On larger and stronger credits, and companies which are publicly held, it is sometimes necessary to permit a dollar cushion or to defer application of the dividend test for one year in order to permit the borrower to build up a reasonable amount of retained earnings available for dividends.

"Stockholders compensation" may be eliminated entirely from the restricted payment clause where the company is essentially publicly held. Where the company is not publicly held and such control is deemed necessary, a fixed dollar limit on compensation should ordinarily be incorporated in a separate covenant, but may alternatively be included in restricted payments.

Normally, preferred dividends, if not too large, are permitted regardless of the operation of the dividend formula, but such payments should be included in computations of surplus available for common dividends.

12. Funded Debt—Additional funded debt is prohibited without consent of The Prudential. This is a basic requirement except for finance companies and other highly specialized situations. The Prudential prefers use of this outright prohibition to the formula approach used by other lenders, due to the difficulty in developing a formula which would give The Prudential adequate protection in the average industrial case and still leave the borrower with any significant freedom. Debt fully subordinated as to principal and interest, with principal and interest payable only under the dividend formula, may be issued.

13. Current Debt—It is important that no creditor be placed in a preferred position over The Prudential. Normally, if current debt is secured, it is secured by a pledge of the company's current assets; other general creditors, including The Prudential, would therefore have no recourse to the company's most liquid assets.

     a) Maximum Limitation—The maximum amount of unsecured and unendorsed current borrowings permitted should generally reflect the company's present and reasonably expectable seasonal requirements.

     b) The borrower is generally required to be completely free of bank loans for 90 consecutive days in either the fiscal or calendar year.

14. Discounting or Sale of Receivables with Recourse—The sale of receivables with recourse or discounting is prohibited except in unusual circumstances, since it is another form of current borrowing in which the purchaser of the receivables has the right of selection to the highest quality assets against general creditors including The Prudential. Moreover, this is usually an expensive way of borrowing. An exception may be made in the case of instalment receivables with appropriate safeguards.

15. Loans, Advances and Investments—Except for U.S. Governments, these are usually limited to a moderate dollar amount depending on individual circumstances. This provision prevents investments in unrelated ventures by acquisition-minded management, without the consent of The Prudential. Prime commercial paper maturing within one year from date of acquisition is excluded from this restriction.

16. Mergers, Consolidations or Sale of a Substantial Part of Assets—All of these actions are to be prohibited except where subsidiaries are absorbed by the parent or each other. These provisions protect The Prudential against loss of corporate identity and disposition of important earning assets. It may be necessary, however, to give more leeway to larger, more established concerns with adequate management depth.

17. Subsidiaries—Consolidated subsidiaries are to be only United States or Canadian companies wholly, or very nearly wholly owned. If a minority equity is substantial, there is a possibility of difficulty in any transfer of assets to the parent to meet its financial requirements. Any borrowings by a subsidiary other than from the parent company are prohibited since a creditor of a subsidiary would have a prior claim on the subsidiary's assets over a creditor of the parent.

18. Lease Rentals—A maximum dollar limit is to be placed on lease rentals involving real estate and major production equipment where such facilities are essential for the successful operation of the business. Short-term leases up to 3-year duration ordinarily should be excluded from the lease rental limitation. The limitation is

Exhibit 3 (Continued)

usually an amount reasonably in excess of present rentals. Rentals are another fixed operating charge of a company and should be kept within reason. The Prudential expects, however, to have a voice in any substantial expansion program involving large increases in rental obligations. Retail chain operations are a special situation, to be considered on an individual case basis.

19. Sale-and-Leaseback Transactions—Sale and leaseback of presently owned property or those to be financed with the proceeds of our loan are to be prohibited. These transactions are simply another form of a fixed obligation which does not appear on the company's financial statement. No prohibition is normally required on future acquired properties. Our protection in this instance will be a dollar limitation on rents. In purchase agreements which tightly restrict lease obligations, the covenant may be eliminated.

Other Covenants:

20. Closely Held Businesses—Small, closely held businesses present problems due to their size and ownership which must be anticipated by the investor. For this reason, it is desirable to include such covenants as:

   a) Hazard Insurance—As small companies particularly could be underinsured, it is desirable to require that adequate hazard insurance be carried and, in particular, use and occupancy, along with customary extended fire insurance. Otherwise, a severe loss could have disastrous financial consequences.

   b) Management Clauses—In cases where a company is particularly thin in management, dominated by one individual or dependent on the continuation of an important franchise or customer, The Prudential should have the right to mature the debt if that officer ceases being active in management. Likewise, if the company loses a key contract which we considered vital to the company's earning power at the time the loan was approved.

   c) Life Insurance on Officers—Life insurance on officers is important where one or a few men appear vital to the success of a business. Such insurance may also help in those cases where there are special problems arising out of death of a controlling or substantial stockholder in companies which are closely held. Note, however, we do not require that the insurance be taken with The Prudential.

   d) Control of transactions with stockholders and affiliated concerns.

21. Special Provisions Involving Bank Participations:

   a) It is desirable, particularly on borderline cases in which a bank is closely identified with the company, for The Prudential to share in the bank's right of offset applicable to the bank's long-term loan on a pro rata basis. This right of offset gives the bank the right to apply the company's deposits in that bank to a liquidation of the company's indebtedness to the bank in the event of default.

   b) Optional prepayments should be made pro rata to the bank and to The Prudential.

Oren Weaving Company, Inc.

The balance sheet of the Oren Weaving Company, Inc., a family-owned corporation that manufactured synthetic and woolen cloth, as of June 28, 1964 (shown as the first column in Exhibit 1), contained several items reflecting the fact that the corporation had been reorganized under Chapter XI of the Bankruptcy Act and discharged on that date.

The income statements in Exhibit 2 show that the company's operations after its discharge from bankruptcy were very successful. By December, 1965, it was possible to predict accurately the results for the fiscal year ended January 31, 1966, and to forecast with confidence the result of operations for the ensuing fiscal year, as shown in the last column of Exhibit 2.

The abrupt "turnaround" in the company's affairs occurred in part because two extremely unsuccessful divisions had been liquidated during the bankruptcy proceeding, but it came about also because of the successful introduction, at first on an exclusive basis, of a process of "bonding" two fabrics of different nature together to make a product that was new to the stylists. It was felt that the bonded fabric would continue in large demand indefinitely, but as the process was not patented, competition could be expected to cut gross margins by the 1967 selling season.

The high level of demand for synthetic and woolen products during the recent months had also produced profitable conditions throughout the industry.

The general situation in the industry was seen as follows:

A strong market for synthetic fibers and textiles is being matched by price strength for the leading companies' stocks. Earnings increases will be good in 1966, but most companies will probably be unable to match their tremendous percentages of gain of recent years. . . .

There is a partnership here between the makers of synthetics (or raw materials for them), and the weavers of textiles. Between them, they are achieving changes which are encouraging for the long term, as they point to a lessening of cyclical fluctuations which often were violent in the past. . . .

. . . .

While cyclical variations will be unavoidable, all this is reason to remain optimistic about these groups. Projected population patterns also brighten their prospects.[1]

The balance sheet of the company at the beginning of November, 1965, the latest available to the officers in early December, showed not only that many of the debts that had emerged from the bankruptcy had been settled but also that the company had a strong position in liquid funds. Pro forma statements for later dates confirmed this trend. Mr. David Oren, Jr., treasurer of the Oren Weaving Company, therefore believed that some rearrangement of the remaining debt contracts was both possible and desirable, to allow the company to adopt policies suitable to a profitable, financially strong concern.

The pertinent terms of the various debt arrangements in force at the end of December, 1965, are summarized below. First are described those arrangements that might be classified as in the ordinary course of business, and second, those inherited from the reorganization.

Factoring

The company maintained a factoring arrangement with the firm that also acted as its exclusive sales agent. This firm, located in New York City, had worked with the Oren Weaving Company for many years. It received commissions for furnishing styling advice and on the sales developed, and also was paid 0.75% of each receivable handled. The latter charge was considered reasonable by the officers of the Oren company, as the factor's service relieved it of all costs usually created by handling customer credits.

The factoring arrangement provided that the Oren company could draw 90% of the amount of any account booked, with an interest charge on these drawings which varied with the general level of interest rates. The remaining 10% was available at the end of the credit period granted to the debtor, whether he had paid or not. In December, 1965, as for the preceding 2 years, the rate used on the drawings was 5.75%; but at his last interview with the factoring firm, Mr. Oren, Jr., had learned that he could expect an increase to 6.75% in 1966.

On the other hand, the factor had never pressed the Oren company to use its available funds, and there had been times in the past when the financial portion of the factoring arrangement had been unused. This had not been the case, however, since the reorganization.

---

[1] *Moody's Stock Survey*, Vol. 57 (December 27, 1965), p. 310.

Trade Accounts Payable—Taxes Payable

These were accounts due from current operations, on normal terms, and payments were being made promptly. The company began the 1966 fiscal year with an unused loss carry-forward of about $1,527,500 applicable to offset taxable income, so the amounts shown as taxes payable on November 3 and January 31 were exclusively for state and local obligations.

Other Current Liabilities

These included the usual accrued expenses and, in November and January, an amount of about $66,000 for a liability due to the company's pension trust immediately after the end of the fiscal year.

Chapter XI Debt

The November 3 balance of $16,600 was the remainder of the obligation created to settle "all other unsecured debts, as proved or allowed, including those scheduled as undisputed, and including those arising from the rejection of executory contracts." Of the original debts of this class, none above $300 was settled in full, according to the plan. The $16,600 was payable before the end of calendar 1965.

Equipment Purchase Obligations

This debt was incurred for machinery purchased on conditional sales contracts. The 1965 balance of about $20,000 had become a current liability. Mr. Oren, Sr., considered the plant well equipped and efficient. He expected that large amounts for new fixed assets would not be needed for at least 5 years. In fact, production could be substantially increased by more intensive use of shifts, and the plant had excess floor space where new capacity, as needed, could be installed. But in the longer run, it would be necessary to replace much of the equipment as it was made obsolete by changes known to be on the drawing boards.

Mortgage Payable

This debt was held by an insurance company. It was secured by a first mortgage on the company's real property in North Carolina. The debt, undisturbed by the reorganization, scheduled monthly payments for principal and interest averaging about $775 in 1965 and 1966. The interest rate was 5.5%. Maturity fell in 1977. Prepayment was not mentioned in the loan agreement.

Term Loan

This loan, from a bank in a neighboring city introduced to the Oren company by its New York bank during the reorganization proceedings, was arranged as part of the reorganization plan, although it was not taken down until August, 1964. Originally $350,000, the loan was at 6%, and was payable in quarterly instalments of $13,800 (principal and interest) beginning January 1, 1965. Prepayment was not mentioned in the loan agreement, but one prepayment, applied to the most remote payments, had been allowed without comment. The loan was currently scheduled to be paid off during 1971.

The Oren company had not actively used the new banking relationship, but it did try to maintain an average deposit balance of 20% of the loan with the bank, as it had been advised to do by its New York bankers. There had been no talks between officers of this bank and the Oren officers, since the prepayment referred to, but the bank had been sent semi-annual reports, as required by the loan agreement.

Loan without Interest

For many years the Oren company's only bank connection, other than local payroll accounts, had been with the Hudson Trust Company, one of the largest commercial banks in New York City. This bank had supported the Oren company with loans for seasonal purposes and had made a term loan in the early 1960's to assist the purchase of the divisions that later were liquidated during the reorganization. The interest rates charged had usually been "0.5% over prime" on short-term loans, and the rate on the term loan was 1% over the prime rate at the time the loan was arranged. In December, 1965, the prime rate was 5%, and it was expected to go higher.

At the end of the reorganization, the Oren company owed $1,040,988 to the Hudson Trust Company on account of the defaulted term loan, accrued interest on this loan, and a frozen short-term loan with its accrued interest. The bank agreed to the deferred payment of this sum, without any interest, on the following terms. It had been insistent, although only informally through conversations with the Orens, that it expected average balances of 20% of the loan. Any drawdown for seasonal or other needs should be offset at other dates.

The schedule of minimum payments of the loan began on July 1, 1965, with $40,000. Quarterly payments of $14,218.80 would be due beginning October 1, 1965. Additionally, the company promised to pay, at times to be chosen by it:

$106.6 thousand by July 1, 1967
42.4 thousand by July 1, 1969
146.5 thousand by July 1, 1971
146.5 thousand by July 1, 1973
47.2 thousand by July 1, 1974

According to this schedule the loan would be extinguished on July 1, 1974. (Discounted values of this schedule as of January 1, 1966, assuming payments of the above additional sums at the latest possible dates, have been computed by the case writer and appear in Exhibit 3.) If, however, 50% of net profits after all taxes from June 30, 1965 to July 1, 1967 should exceed the payments already made, the total payment was to be increased to this sum on July 1, 1967. Similar calculations and payments were to apply to each succeeding 2-year period.

No provision had been made to permit more rapid payment of this loan, but in an interview early in December, 1965, Mr. Oren, Jr., learned from the bank vice president who handled the account that the bank would be interested in a proposition to settle the remaining indebtedness for "about $800,000 depending on the exact date."[2] Mr. Oren left the interview feeling that a partial payment would also be welcomed.

Collateral

The first mortgage has already been mentioned. The factoring arrangement was for the purchase of approved accounts without recourse to the company. The factor also held a security interest in all other accounts receivable of the company and in any interest the company might have in merchandise delivered to customers on account. These were normal arrangements in most factoring contracts. In addition, at the time the Oren company was discharged from bankruptcy, the factor had obtained a security interest in all the inventories of the company, to apply until the company had earned $275,000 after taxes in a fiscal year, and total indebtedness (including factor's advances) had fallen below $2 million.

The term loan was secured by a second mortgage on the real estate and a chattel mortgage on all machinery and equipment, including after-acquired property of the same kind. This pledge was to be discharged after the final settlement of the interest-free loan, described above, from the Hudson Trust Company.

Restrictive Provisions of Loans

The interest-free loan was unsecured but contained the following restrictive covenants. The term loan also contained the same clauses in the exact same wording as the interest-free loan.

1. Net Operating Loss. A net operating loss (before tax adjustments) in excess of $100,000 in either of the fiscal years commencing in 1965 and 1966 shall be an event of default except that a net operating profit in the first year can be used as offset in computing the extent of the net loss in the second year.
2. Working Capital. To be maintained at not less than $1 million; or

---

[2] If the loan was retired at a discount, the saving would become part of the taxable income of the Oren Weaving Company.

an amount that is $275,000 less than Oren's working capital at June 28, 1964 (Exhibit 1), whichever is less.

3. Accounts Receivable. Oren must not have outstanding at its own risk (i.e., not accepted by the factor) more than $90,000 of accounts receivable at any one time. (But Oren was not required to draw against the factored accounts before they were collected.)

4. Total Debt. Must be kept at or below $2 million, exclusive of factoring.

5. Real and Personal Property Leasing. Aggregate rental payment obligations must not exceed $80,000 per fiscal year without prior written consent. (The company had no long-term leases in force at December, 1965.)

6. Dividends. Except for stock dividends in its own stock, Oren shall not pay dividends or distribute assets to its stockholders, except that when and if net worth exceeds $1,735,393 (150% of the net worth at June 28, 1964) such payments may be made but not to exceed in any one year $7,000 or 20% of net earnings after taxes, whichever is less.

7. Capital Investments. No more than $5,000 per single expenditure; aggregate expenditures, net of cash received from retirements, must not exceed 50% of depreciation accumulated since June 28, 1964.

8. Investments. Oren shall not invest in securities or obligations of any person, firm, etc. other than short-term U.S. government or time certificates of deposit issued by banks.

9. Loans to Others. Oren shall make no loans or incur contingent liabilities by way of guaranty or otherwise for the obligations of others unless first approved by the directors representing the banks.

10. Salaries. No changes in salaries of the officers are to be made by Oren or any subsidiary unless approved by the Salary Committee of the board of directors. (There had been no changes in salary levels since the bankruptcy proceedings were started in 1963.)

11. Voting of Shares. The family shareholders had agreed to vote their shares so as to elect to the board one representative of each lending bank, so long as the term loan or the interest-free loan remained outstanding. These directors constituted a majority of the Salary Committee.

As Mr. David Oren, Jr., the treasurer of the corporation, discussed the situation with his father in December, 1965, it appeared that the time was fast approaching when a financial policy suitable to a prosperous company should be established. The father was particularly anxious to be rid of "the residue of the bankruptcy," and suggested concentrating all efforts on the reduction of the interest-free loan. He pointed out that this loan, appearing in credit agency reports, probably hurt the company's commercial credit. The son, however, argued that one seldom has the use of $1 million without cost, and thought that the interest-free loan should be regarded as an opportunity instead of a source of shame. He remarked that every supplier was giving the Oren company normal trade terms. There was disagreement also about how much debt should be carried on a long-term basis by a small company in the textile industry. The father was willing to accept the mortgage debt but preferred to have all other debt financing retired and to use the factor's services to the full. Finally, both the Orens were aware of pressure from other members of the family (who held the remaining 40% of the shares) for the commencement of dividend payments as soon as warranted. One of the younger shareholders, a law student, had recently suggested that his shares be repurchased, instead.

Exhibit 1

OREN WEAVING COMPANY, INC.

Balance Sheets as of June 28, 1964 and November 3, 1965
and Estimated Balance Sheet as of January 30, 1966
(dollar figures in thousands)

	June 28, 1964	November 3, 1965	Pro Forma January 31, 1966
ASSETS			
Cash on hand and U.S. notes.............	$ 392.6	$ 380.6	$ 905.2
Factored accounts*......................			
Cash available........................	280.9	560.9	350.0
Required 10% equity..................	198.4	137.8	201.6
Inventories.............................	· 1,332.1	1,268.6	1,228.3
Prepaid expenses.......................	36.2	26.8	24.2
Nonfactored receivables.................	82.3	3.2	52.1
Total current assets...............	$2,322.5	$2,377.9	$2,761.4
Fixed assets.............................	3,899.8	3,795.8	3,726.2
Reserve for depreciation................	(2,561.8)	(2,720.2)	(2,743.5)
Net fixed assets......................	$1,338.0	$1,075.6	$ 982.7
Other assets............................	7.4	3.5	3.5
Cash value of life insurance†..............	42.3	46.3	46.3
Total assets......................	$3,710.2	$3,503.3	$3,793.9
LIABILITIES AND EQUITY			
Customers' deposits......................	$ 11.9	$ 5.3	$ 5.8
Trade accounts payable..................	71.6	243.1	195.1
Taxes payable...........................	81.5	88.5	52.5
Other current liabilities...................	62.3	125.7	93.5
Current portion, debt arrangements........	7.5	121.4	121.4
Chapter XI debt........................	1,054.1	16.6	. . .
Total current liabilities.............	$1,288.9	$ 600.6	$ 468.3
Noncurrent portions of liabilities			
Equipment purchase obligations.........	88.9	. . .	. . .
Mortgage payable.....................	134.5	121.9	120.5
Term loan.............................	. . .	208.6	196.6
Loan without interest..................	1,041.0	929.9	915.7
Total liabilities....................	$2,553.3	$1,861.0	$1,701.1
Common stock and surplus...............	1,156.9	1,642.3	2,092.8
Total liabilities and equity........	$3,710.2	$3,503.3	$3,793.9
Net working capital.....................	$1,033.6	$1,777.3	$2,293.1

* The total of factored accounts can be obtained by multiplying the required equity by 10.
† Cash value of $150,000 on the life of David Oren, Sr.

Exhibit 2

OREN WEAVING COMPANY, INC.

Income Statements, Fiscal Year 1964–65 and Estimated Income Statements,
Fiscal Years 1965–66 and 1966–67
(dollar figures in thousands)

	Year ended January 31, 1965	Pro forma Year ended January 31, 1966	Pro forma Year ended January 31, 1967
Sales	$6,483.8	$8,508.3	$9,500
Cost of sales	(5,677.7)	(6,688.3)	(7,300)
Gross profit	$ 806.1	$1,820.0	$2,200
Marketing expense	(227.2)	(452.6)	(450)
Administrative expenses	(260.1)	(294.3)	(280)
Provision for profit sharing	. . .	(78.8)	(90)
Total	$ (487.3)	$ (825.7)	$ (820)
Operating profit	$ 318.8	$ 994.4	$1,380
Interest cost	(12.9)	(29.1)	(25)
Factoring cost	(101.2)	(176.9)	(200)
Purchase discounts	*	38.3	40
Gain or (loss) on sale of assets	14.7	(22.0)	. . .
Other income	4.4	1.9	. . .
Total	$ (95.0)	$ (187.8)	$ (185)
Net profit	$ 223.8	$ 806.5	$1,195
Provision for income tax	. . .	. . .	(335)
Profit after tax	$ 223.8†	$ 806.5	$ 860
Depreciation included	$ 222.8	$ 185.0	$ 160.0

* Deducted in cost of sales.
† Approximately $115,000 earned after June 28, 1964.

Exhibit 3

Discounted Value of Payment Schedule, Interest-Free Loan, as of January 1, 1966
(face amount $972,550)

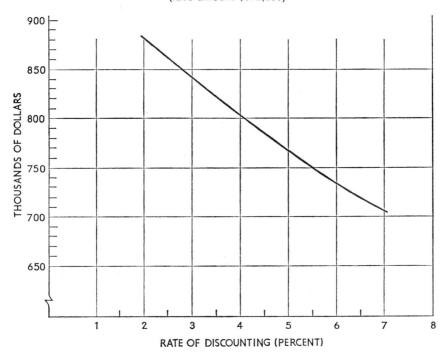

Sun Stores, Inc.*

In November, 1957, Mr. David Stevens, an associate with the investment banking firm of Hanson and Company, was reviewing his analysis of alternative securities which Sun Stores, Inc., might sell in order to obtain $3.5 million as a second step in financing its 3-year expansion program. Mr. Stevens was expected to recommend a specific security issue to the management of Sun Stores, for their choice.

Sun Stores, Inc., operated 146 retail stores in Iowa, Missouri, Nebraska, Kansas, Wyoming, and Colorado, with about 15% of these stores concentrated in and around Kansas City, Missouri. In addition to these "corporate" stores, the company sold at wholesale to 419 independently owned, franchised "agency" stores. Total sales of the company exceeded $150 million in fiscal 1957, representing a gain of 25% over the previous year's sales volume. The company had experienced a steady growth during the past 5 years, as earnings more than doubled, and the stockholders' equity in the company increased by nearly 60%.

Anticipating further expansion, Sun Stores had projected its external funds needs over the 3-year period starting in March, 1957, at $6.9 million, and Hanson and Company estimated that the cost of raising these funds would require an additional $400,000, making the total new funds requirement $7.3 million. After deducting the $3 million of recently sold debentures, the company planned to obtain $3.5 million by February 28, 1959,[1] and the remaining $800,000 in fiscal 1960. The following table summarizes this financing program:

---

* Abridged.

[1] Unless otherwise noted, all references to years are in terms of Sun Stores' fiscal periods ending about February 28. Thus "1958" refers to the fiscal year ending March 1, 1958.

External requirements of expansion program	$6,900,000
Cost of raising funds	400,000
Total funds requirements	$7,300,000
To be met as follows:	
Fiscal 1958	3,000,000
Fiscal 1959	3,500,000
Fiscal 1960	800,000
	$7,300,000

This program, and the methods to be used in obtaining the funds, had been developed by Sun Stores and Hanson and Company after careful analysis of the company's financial needs. In March, 1957, the decision was made to obtain the 1958 requirements through a term loan. Hanson and Company prepared the selling memorandum and assisted in the negotiations that culminated in the placing of $3 million of unsecured notes with seven institutional investors in October, 1957. The second-stage financing to raise the $3.5 million needed in fiscal 1959 was to utilize an equity-type security, and the final $800,000 would be raised with a term bank loan. With the initial financing successfully completed, Sun's management turned its attention to the second phase and requested Hanson and Company to appraise three equity-type securities for obtaining the $3.5 million—convertible subordinated debentures, convertible preferred stock, and common stock.

To assist him in his analysis, Mr. Stevens first developed a tabulation of the annual costs to the company of each of these securities, using assumed interest and dividend rates of $5\frac{1}{2}\%$ for the convertible debentures and $5\frac{3}{4}\%$ for the convertible preferred stock (Exhibit 1). Next, after assuming selling or conversion prices for each of the issues, he projected the number of additional common shares that would ultimately be required (Exhibit 2). With these tabulations, he then summed up the principal advantages and disadvantages he saw in each of the three types of securities:

CONVERTIBLE SUBORDINATED DEBENTURES

Advantages:

1. Convertible debentures, although a relatively new security, were currently a "fashionable" instrument for financing rapidly growing companies and had recently received favorable comment in the financial press.
2. Subordinated convertible debentures are viewed by institutions as enlarging the base for private senior borrowing almost to the same extent capital stock financing does.
3. Both dilution of per share earnings and added dividend costs are minimized (Exhibit 1). Conversion would probably not take place prior to the expected dramatic earnings increase during fiscal 1960. And even then, conversion may be gradual in consequence of acts or policy decisions initiated by management. Furthermore, once the debentures are selling substantially above conversion parity, the company would be in a position to force conversion by a call for redemption.
4. Prior to conversion, net interest cost (after 54% tax saving) would be about half of the dividend cost under the convertible preferred and common stock plans.
5. The announcement of convertible debenture financing for the expansion program should not cause any significant decline in the market price of the common stock, because such debentures would be convertible at a premium above the existing

market price of the common stock. Also, it is realized that conversion usually takes place when earnings per share and the stock price have risen substantially above existing levels. As a consequence, the present stockholders' current position would not be impaired.

6. The number of additional shares involved would be less than under the common stock plan (Exhibit 1).
7. There is a reasonable chance that the debentures will be partially converted during fiscal 1960.

Disadvantages:

1. Until the debentures are converted, the company will tend to be limited to the issuance of senior debt to obtain additional financing at a reasonable price.

CONVERTIBLE PREFERRED STOCK

Advantages:

1. Similar to the subordinated debenture, the conversion price assigned to the preferred stock would represent a premium over the prevailing market price at the time of the offering. Thus, if the preferred stock were converted, the company could view the transaction as a means of selling common stock above the prevailing market price, whereas direct sale of common stock would involve a price below the present market (Exhibit 2).
2. Preferred stock would be an addition to equity, whereas convertible subordinated debentures are viewed by Moody's and Standard and Poor's as part of overall debt in rating public issues of senior debt.

Disadvantages:

1. It is more expensive than the debenture issue, as previously noted.
2. Although dividend payments can be deferred in times of financial stress, they represent an obligation of the company which must be paid in full before any resumption of dividends to the common stock.
3. As is true with a convertible debenture, a convertible preferred stock tends to limit the company's choice of subsequent financing to senior obligations until the preferred is converted.

COMMON STOCK

Advantages:

1. Sun stock is currently selling at about 1.5 times its book value. If common stock were offered, the new investor would be putting funds into the company directly and immediately at a premium over the funds invested previously by stockholders.
2. It is the safest medium. In future financing, the management would be freer to choose a medium other than senior debt.
3. Common stock financing would immediately broaden the market for Sun stock by the very fact of the issuance of 125,000 additional shares. This would be the first underwritten distribution of the common stock through a national syndicate.

Disadvantages:

1. An issue of common stock would reduce 1958 earnings per share immediately (Exhibits 1 and 2), and would drive down the market price of the outstanding common stock to, say, 27 or 28.
2. Earnings per share during subsequent fiscal years would be about 12% lower than they would be if a comparable issue of convertible debentures or preferred were outstanding.

The $3\frac{7}{8}\%$ notes of 1966, which were sold in 1951, and the recently sold $5\frac{1}{2}\%$ notes of 1972 had been placed privately with institutional investors, and Sun's management had been pleased with the success of these issues. Regarding the present financing, Mr. Stevens estimated that the cost of a private placement would be about $61,000 or 1.75% of the principal amount of the issue, whereas a public offering would cost about $103,000. However, the interest rate on a private placement of notes would probably be about 0.25% higher than on a similar public offering, and a privately placed preferred would also require a similarly higher dividend rate.

Mr. Stevens believed that a private placement was especially suited for the smaller, lesser-known companies, and for this reason it might be the best method for Sun to use in obtaining its funds. On the other hand, both the earnings and the equity of the company had doubled since 1954, and this performance suggested that a public issue of the company's securities might be well received in the financial markets.

The success of any offering would be influenced to some extent by the current trends in the stock market. In recent weeks the market seemed to be showing signs of recovering from the decline that began in late July. On July 12, the Dow-Jones Industrial Average had reached 520.77, which was just a fraction less than its all-time peak, and then started to fall sharply. In the face of this general market decline, market prices of many food store shares had shown a moderate increase (Exhibit 3). Recent comments by various market observers suggested even more than normal uncertainty regarding the future action of the market. The currently unsettled market conditions raised questions as to how a public offering of any type of Sun Stores security would be received by the financial community.

Also inherent in the problem of choosing and selling the security, Mr. Stevens believed, was the question of whether Sun Stores' common stock should be listed on a national security exchange. The company's stock was presently traded over-the-counter, and its relatively small trading volume had been a continuing obstacle in broadening the ownership, and consequently the knowledge, of Sun Stores. Mr. Stevens decided, however, that action on this question could be deferred for the present. Although listing might conceivably encourage a broader distribution of Sun's common stock, and thus bring the Sun name to a larger number of potential investors, Mr. Stevens believed that this could be accomplished equally well by the active support of some of the leading over-the-counter wire houses. These firms, which maintained positions in unlisted securities, were able to create active markets by virtue of their close communications with brokers and dealers throughout the country.

Exhibit 1

Annual Cost of $3.5 Million New Capital and Projected Earnings per Share, 1958–60

	Convertible Subordinated Debentures		Convertible Preferred Stock		Common Stock
	Before Conversion	After Conversion	Before Conversion	After Conversion	
Face interest rate.................	5½%		5¾%		
Face interest or dividend cost (thousands)...	$193	$147*	$201	$147*	$175*
Less: Tax saving on interest (54%) (thousands)...	104	....	....	....	....
Net cost after taxes (thousands)...	$ 89	$147	$201	$147	$175
Net rate of cost...	2.53%	4.20%	5.75%	4.20%	5.00%
Net cost per present common share†...	15¢	46¢	33¢	46¢	53¢
Cash outlay by company					
Net interest or dividend cost (as above) (thousands)...	$ 89	$147	$201	$147	$175
Plus sinking fund (thousands)...	175‡	....	70§	....	....
	$264	$147	$271	$147	$175
Company estimates of future earnings per common share	*Excluding Impact of New Financing*				
Fiscal 1958...	$3.11**	$2.96	$2.65	$2.78	$2.65	$2.58
Fiscal 1959...	3.53**	3.38	3.01	3.20	3.01	2.93
Fiscal 1960...	4.84**	4.69	4.14	4.51	4.14	4.02

* Based on present dividend rate of $1.40 per share and conversion or offering prices as estimated in Exhibit 2.
† Based on 609,000 shares outstanding and $3.11 earned per share if no financing takes place.
‡ No sinking fund for first 10 years.
§ No sinking fund for first 5 years.
** Numbers in this column exclude the changes due to new financing. In subsequent columns, the numbers are after the deduction of the annual interest or the preferred dividend on the new financing appropriate to the choice indicated.

Exhibit 2

Pro Forma Addition to
Number of Shares Outstanding

	Convertible Debentures or Preferred	*Common Stock*
Amount of issue........................	$3,500,000	$3,500,000
Conversion or offering price.............	33⅓*	28†
Number of shares to be issued...........	105,000	125,000
Number of shares now outstanding.......	609,000	609,000
Number of shares, pro forma.............	714,000	734,000
Additional shares as percent of total......	14.7%	17.0%

* Assuming 11% premium over current market price of 30.
† Assuming spot offering at market price of 28—a discount of 6% from the current market price of 30.

Exhibit 3

Indexes of Dow-Jones Industrial Averages and 10 Leading
Food Chain Stock Prices, January–November, 1957

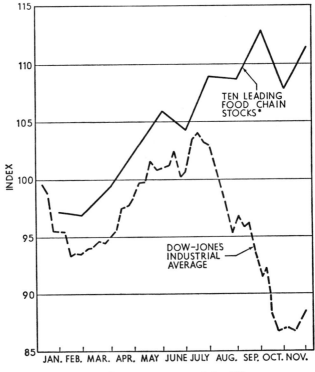

* 1. American Stores	6. Jewel Tea
2. First National Stores	7. Kroger
3. Food Fair Stores	8. National Tea
4. Grand Union	9. Safeway
5. Great A & P Tea Co.	10. Colonial Stores

Boxer Corporation

In April, 1966, the management of the Boxer Corporation, a manufacturer of kraft paper, corrugated board, and boxes, all of which were widely used for commercial purposes, was considering whether under the circumstances it should continue to appropriate funds for the purchase and subsequent retirement of the preferred stocks of the company. If such a policy were continued, the management would be required to decide whether it should continue purchasing shares in small lots from time to time or whether it should call both issues of the outstanding preferred stocks at the redemption prices. In either case the company would need to obtain funds to provide for the acquisition of the shares.

As will appear below, the treasurer of the company had explored possibilities of financing and had developed an offer of a refunding issue of 20-year debenture bonds to raise a maximum of $6 million.

Balance sheets for the years 1963–65 and the current position at March 31, 1966, will be found in Exhibit 1. Exhibit 2 contains a summary of income figures and dividend payments from 1956 through 1965, and Exhibit 3 gives more detailed earnings statements for the years 1963–65. A change in the efficiency of operation will be noted. In 1963 the company had made a careful study of its production costs and sales margins and subsequently had made substantial changes in policy, the results of which were reflected in the increased rate of earnings in 1964. It was believed that this increase in efficiency could be maintained in future years. On such a basis, the management felt that at an annual sales volume of $15 million, net profits would be adequate to provide not only for preferred dividends but also for dividends of at least $0.30 a share on the common stock. Plans in regard to the financial needs of the next few years had been made in 1963 on the assumption that an annual sales volume of $15 million was a practical goal, at least in the immediate future. There would be no need to force sales, by cutting margins, to reach higher totals.

The company maintained principal banking relationships with two large city banks and had been told regularly by them that its credit was so strong that the seasonal loans requested were well within the limit that the company would be able to borrow. The company also had been able to obtain occasional temporary loans to permit the purchase of blocks of its own stock. These loans had been repaid, when due, out of earnings.

The high volume of business activity in the 1960's led to an increased volume of orders for the standard products of the company. Some novelty lines with low margins were cut out, but demands for special types of containers developed so rapidly that sales for 1965 were approximately $18.6 million. During the first 3 months of 1966 the sales of the Boxer Corporation were $5,456,000, an increase of $1,272,000 over the same period in 1965. Unfilled orders at April 1 totaled $4,104,000. It was estimated that the year's sales would exceed $20.5 million. The rate of net profits on sales, which was 9.9% before taxes and 5.1% after taxes in 1965, was maintained in the first quarter of 1966, and management expected to earn about the same rate for the rest of the year. The director of marketing believed that sales in 1967 and 1968 would probably total about $20 million and $21 million, respectively.

Pending a determination of policy, the treasurer did not include in his budget any provisions for the continued purchase of shares of the company, as had been a recent policy.

The treasurer talked with investment bankers about refunding the two types of preferred stock outstanding with an issue of 20-year debenture bonds. It was understood that a $6 million issue of bonds with a 5¾% coupon could be sold to net the company the par price. The bonds would have a sinking fund requiring annual retirement of $200,000 principal, beginning in 1971. Although further details had not been worked out, the bankers had stated that three provisions would have to be included in the indenture: (1) that all debt, current and fixed, should not exceed 200% of the current assets; (2) that the company could not mortgage any property while any of the bonds were outstanding; (3) that the bonds would be callable in whole or in part at 105% of the public issue price, except that the call would not be permitted for the purpose of refunding at a rate lower than 5¾%.

The 8% first preferred stock and the common stock of the company were listed on an organized exchange and were widely held, although infrequently traded. The 7% preferred stock was unlisted and had been almost completely inactive since 1963.

Through occasional public tender offers, the company had begun to acquire shares of various classes of its stock in the open market as part of a plan to simplify its capital structure and reduce its outstanding capitalization by the retirement of the stock so purchased. Exhibit 4 tabulates the number of shares of the various classes of stock retired and the average prices paid in the years 1964 and 1965. No purchases of any class of stock had been made to date in 1966.

By April, 1, 1966, it was clear that few, if any, more shares of the 7% preferred stock could be obtained without call. Small blocks of shares of the 8% first preferred stock continued to come on the market from time to time, principally from trust accounts and estates liquidating some of their investments. The only quotation so far recorded in 1966 was in the week of March 19, at $123 a share. The number of shares traded in this week was 10.

The provisions of the capital stock issues are summarized in Exhibit 5.

Because of the heavy burden of the preferred dividends, the company had not made any payments to the common stockholders since 1954. The management was anxious to clear the way for dividends on the common stock in the immediate future. Further purchases of common shares did not seem advisable in view of the need to conserve cash.

Exhibit 1

BOXER CORPORATION

Balance Sheets as of December 31, 1963–65, and Current Position,
March 31, 1966
(in thousands)

	1963	1964	1965	March 31, 1966
ASSETS				
Current Assets:				
Cash and deposits...................	$ 1,013	$ 1,893	$ 801	$ 723
U.S. government securities...........	60	150	150	50
Accounts receivable.................	2,466	2,264	2,907	1,953
Inventories*.......................	2,647	2,735	3,532	4,136
Total current assets..............	$ 6,186	$ 7,042	$ 7,390	$6,862
Investment in subsidiaries, etc.†........	855	855	350	
Land†..............................	226	198	438	
Buildings, machinery, equipment†.......	$10,624	$10,683	$11,031	
Less: Allowance for depreciation.......	6,920	7,240	7,677	
	$ 3,704	$ 3,443	$ 3,354	
Deferred charges and supplies..........	283	237	374	
Total assets....................	$11,254	$11,775	$11,906	
LIABILITIES AND CAPITAL				
Current Liabilities:				
Accounts payable...................	$ 510	$ 555	981	$ 838
Accruals........................	253	303	707	756
Estimated income tax liability........	666	961	1,031	816
Total current liabilities..........	$ 1,429	$ 1,819	$ 2,719	$2,410
8% first preferred stock, $100 par.......	$ 4,584	$ 4,584	$ 4,584	
Less: Par value in treasury..........		83	736	‡
	$ 4,584	$ 4,501	$ 3,848	
7% preferred stock, $100 par..........	$ 183	$ 183	$ 183	
Less: Par value in treasury..........		98	171	‡
	$ 183	$ 85	$ 12	
Common stock, $5.00 par..............	$ 2,120	$ 2,120	$ 2,120	
Less: Par value in treasury..........		52	58	‡
	$ 2,120	$ 2,068	$ 2,062	
Difference between par value and cost of treasury stock.....................		(149)	(298)	
Earned surplus......................	2,938	3,451	3,563	
Total liabilities and capital.....	$11,254	$11,775	$11,906	

* Lower of cost or market.
† Cost.
‡ No shares were purchased or retired after December 31, 1965.

Exhibit 2

BOXER CORPORATION

Summary Income Statements for Years Ended December 31, 1956–65
(in thousands)

Year	Sales	Net Income before Taxes	Tax Rate	Net Income after Taxes
1956	$ 9,516	$ (899)^d	..	$(561)^{d*}
1957	9,356	111	38%	69
1958	11,897	839	38	520
1959	12,471	924	38	573
1960	14,073	1,398	47	741
1961	15,085	1,400	62	532
1962	13,377	171	52	82
1963	14,991	850	52	408
1964	15,049	1,774	50	887
1965	18,577	1,831	48	952

* After tax loss carry-back.
^{d} Deficit.

Exhibit 3

BOXER CORPORATION

Income Statements for Years Ended December 31, 1963–65, and
Dividends Paid in First Quarter of 1966
(in thousands)

	1963	1964	1965	1st Quarter 1966
Sales	$14,991	$15,049	$18,577	$5,456
Cost of goods sold*	9,448	9,039	11,976	
	$ 5,543	$ 6,010	$ 6,601	Figures not yet available
Selling and administrative expense*	4,600	4,203	4,798	
	$ 943	$ 1,807	$ 1,803	
Other income	(14)	(8)	(57)	
Other expense	107	41	29	
Net income before income tax	$ 850	$ 1,774	$ 1,831	
Estimated federal income tax	$ 442(52%)	887(50%)	879(48%)	
Net income available for dividends	$ 408	$ 887	$ 952	
Dividends paid:†				
8% first preferred stock	$ 367	$ 365	$ 332	$ 77
7% preferred stock	55	9	3	0.2
Total dividends paid	$ 379	$ 374	$ 335	$ 77.2
Income transferred to surplus	29	513	617	

* Depreciation expenses included as follows:
  1963 . . . . $408,000
  1964 435,000
  1965 552,000
† 8% first preferred stock, average number of shares outstanding:
  1956–63 . . . . 45,840 shares
  1964 45,425
  1965 41,745
7% preferred stock, average number of shares outstanding:
  1956–63 . . . . 1,830 shares
  1964 1,340
  1965 485

Exhibit 4

Acquisitions by the Company of Its Own Stock, 1964 and 1965

Class of Stock	Number of Shares Acquired	Total Par Values Acquired	Average Cost per Share	Total Cost
1964:				
1. 8% first preferred......	830	$ 83,000	$ 96.91	$ 80,435
2. 7% preferred..........	980	98,000	80.15	78,900
Total preferred......		$181,000		$159,335
3. Common.............	10,400	52,000	21.40	222,560
				$381,895
1965:				
1. 8% first preferred......	6,530	$653,000	118.75	$775,438
2. 7% preferred..........	730	73,000	111.93	81,709
Total preferred......		$726,000		$857,147
3. Common.............	1,240	6,200	19.40	24,056
				$881,203

Exhibit 5

Certain Provisions of Outstanding Capital Stock, April 1, 1965

	8% First Preferred Stock, Par $100	7% Preferred Stock, Par $100	Common Stock Par $5
Actually outstanding	38,480 shares	120 shares	412,400 shares
Redemption provisions	Callable on 90 days' notice at $150 and accumulated dividends. Not redeemable in part, (38,480 × $150 = $5,772,000).	Callable on 90 days' notice at $115 and accumulated dividends. Not redeemable in part, (120 × $115 = $13,800).	None
Voting power	Obtains 10 votes per share whenever dividends are $12 or more in arrears and also the right to elect two thirds of the board of directors. Otherwise, does not vote.	None	One vote per share
Dividend priority	8%, senior to all other classes, fully cumulative (8% of $3,848,000 = $307,840).	Junior to first preferred, senior to all others. 7% fully cumulative (7% of $12,000 = $840).	Dividends may not be paid unless remaining surplus would amount to at least 1 year's dividend requirement on both preferred stocks.
Dividend record	No arrearages	No arrearages	No dividend since 1954.

General Public Utilities Corporation

The Dividend Decision

In January, 1968, Mr. William Kuhns, president of General Public Utilities Corporation (GPU), was considering both the merit of a new dividend policy and the wisdom of inviting shareholder participation in deciding whether or not to adopt the policy. The dividend proposal which Mr. Kuhns was analyzing would eliminate three of the company's four quarterly cash dividends and substitute in their place stock dividends with a market value equal to the eliminated cash dividends. A large increase in the capital requirements of GPU prompted Mr. Kuhns to consider this policy in lieu of raising equity capital through rights offerings to GPU's shareholders.

Prior Financing of Capital Needs

Over the period 1959 through 1967, GPU issued common stock in 1960 and 1966. In each case, the shares were sold through rights offerings,[1] and the amount of new stock issued represented about 5% of the number of shares previously outstanding. Rights for over 50% of the shares in each instance were exercised by the individuals who initially received them.

Over the same 9-year period, the percentage of long-term debt in GPU's capital structure grew from 51.5% to 60.2% while preferred stock shrank from 9.9% to 5.4% (Exhibit 1). GPU had been able to provide the capital needed to support growth in customer electric power require-

---

[1] For an explanation of rights offerings, see this text, p. 509.

ments mainly through a combination of internal cash throw-off and long-term debt additions. In 1967 the company began taking on significant amounts of short-term debt in addition to its traditional long-term borrowings. The Securities and Exchange Commission[2] gave the company authority to borrow up to $75 million by issuing commercial paper, and the company had sufficient bank lines of credit to give it a short-term borrowing capacity (including commercial paper) up to $150 million. So long as GPU wished to maintain a capital structure consisting of 60% debt, 5% preferred stock, and 35% common equity, the corporation had to limit long-term debt additions to 170% of earnings retentions (i.e., $0.60/0.35 = 1.70$).

According to Mr. George Schneider, financial vice president of GPU, a 60% long-term debt fraction was close to the limit which industry lenders and regulatory authorities would allow. Furthermore, certain states required that long-term debt be held below 60% of total capitalization if the securities of the company were to qualify as legal investments for savings banks and other regulated financial institutions. While there was no formal regulation to establish this debt ceiling, few public utilities attempted to exceed it. A move in the direction toward higher debt utilization could endanger a utility's bond rating (causing the interest rate to be higher on all of its future debt issues) and/or invite additional regulation at the state and federal governmental levels.

Growing Capital Demands for the Industry

Mr. Schneider outlined the reasons for a sudden surge in the capital-raising burden facing the electric utility industry in the future.

While the electric utilities as a group have been able to get by with occasional small stock issues in the past, in the immediate future and out as far as 3 to 5 years, we all face a dramatic acceleration in the needs for capital to finance our growth. This expansion in the need for capital has come about for six reasons.

First, and perhaps most importantly, the rate of growth in electric power consumption is accelerating. Take "all-electric"[3] homes as an example. These homes use almost five times as much electric power as comparable homes without this feature. Construction of "all-electric" homes is increasing substantially.

Second, the electric utility industry is becoming even more capital intensive than it has been in the past. The construction cost of a nuclear-powered generating plant lies between $160 and $180 per kilowatt of installed capacity versus $135 per kilowatt for a fossil-fired[4] plant.

---

[2] The SEC held this authority under the Public Utility Holding Company Act of 1935.

[3] All-electric homes were built and sold with many electrical appliances, including an oven, range, water heater, and furnace, incorporated into the original home design.

[4] A fossil-fired plant burns fossil fuel such as coal, oil, or gas in the process of generating electric power.

Third, since the failure of the Northeast power grid at the end of 1965,[5] there has been a good deal of pressure for additional spending on redundant facilities to enhance system reliability.

Fourth, the utilities face longer lead times in constructing power-generating facilities than they did 8 or 10 years ago. There used to be a 4-year lead time on plant construction. Now it's 6 years. Since we make progress payments equal to 90% of the project's total price, a longer lead time substantially increases the size of our "plant under construction" account.

Fifth, inflation has eroded the purchasing power of the dollar so that we're paying more for a unit of power-generating capacity than we were 10 years ago.

Finally, expenditures for beautification such as wire-burying within cities adds substantially to our needs for capital.

The Future Capital Expenditures of GPU

Mr. Kuhns spoke specifically of the capital-raising burden in terms of its impact on GPU.

Relating capital requirements more specifically to GPU, in the late 1950s and early 1960s, we expended an average of $80 million per year for new facilities. As late as 1964 we spent only $90 million. From 1968 through 1970, our capital spending will be in excess of $200 million annually, and at this time I cannot really foresee much of a letup after 1970.

GPU's capital requirements made it clear to us that given our current dividend policy the company would have to raise additional equity capital through annual rights offerings to our shareholders for at least the next few years. Coincidentally, it appeared that the amount of equity financing required each year would approximate three-quarters of the cash dividends which the company expected to pay out to its shareholders.

Exhibit 2 shows projections of GPU's sources and uses of funds through 1972. Since the elimination of three quarters of GPU's cash dividend would permit the company to meet its capital needs without resorting to additional annual equity financing, (line 20 vs. line 35 of Exhibit 2) the company began to seriously examine the feasibility of a dividend policy which would make this earnings retention possible.

Meeting the Shareholders' Needs for Cash

The officers of GPU were sure that many of the company's shareholders preferred regular cash income. Any new GPU dividend plan would thus have to deal effectively with the shareholders' demands for regular cash payments. The company felt that this demand could be met if *stock*

---

[5] Early in the evening of November 9, 1965, a massive electric power failure threw most of the Eastern Seaboard of the United States and Canada into darkness. The blackout stretched from Toronto to Washington and lasted for more than 10 hours in some affected areas.

dividends equal in market value to the projected *cash* dividends were paid for the first three quarters of each year. By simply checking an IBM card, GPU shareholders would be able to specify anew each quarter whether they wished to sell their stock dividend for cash or receive certificates representing the number of GPU shares paid out as a dividend. Shareholders could round a fractional interest to a full share by either selling or buying the necessary fractional share. GPU was willing to absorb all transaction expenses (except brokerage commissions equal to about $33 per 100 shares) involved in selling dividend shares for cash.

A Comparison—the Old Plan vs. the New Plan

When compared with a cash dividend pay-out ratio equal to 68% of earnings—coupled with an annual rights offering—the stock dividend alternative plus one quarterly cash dividend presented substantial tax savings to the investor (Exhibit 3).

A shareholder in the 20% federal income tax bracket[6] who normally *exercised* his rights would receive $312 after taxes per 1,000 shares of GPU owned if the stock dividend plan were adopted, an increase of $234 over the $78 which would be received if the old cash dividend plan were continued. (See Basis A of Exhibit 3.)

The shareholder in the same tax bracket who normally *sold* his rights would receive $1,519 after taxes per 1,000 shares of GPU owned if the stock dividend plan were adopted, an increase of $117 over the $1,402 which would be received if the old cash dividend plan were continued.

Exhibit 4 shows that for shareholders in higher federal income tax brackets, the favorable impact of the stock dividend plan would be substantially greater. A shareholder in the 70% tax bracket would increase his after-tax cash receipts by more than $500 regardless of his usual practice regarding the decision to exercise or sell his rights.

Comparative Cost of Administering the Plan

The benefits of the stock dividend plan to the shareholders of GPU were fairly clear. In terms of the cost to the corporation, bank charges for each quarterly cash dividend payment were roughly $25,000. A single rights offering would cost the company about $450,000. A combination of four quarterly cash dividends plus one rights offering would thus cost the company $550,000. The stock dividends would cost roughly $175,000 each. The combination of three quarterly stock dividends and one cash dividend would thus cost GPU approximately $550,000. On balance then, the cost to GPU of either plan would be about the same so long as GPU anticipated a rights offering each year.

---

[6] As of 1967, the minimum marginal federal income tax rate for a married taxpayer was 14%. For taxable income between $4,000 and $8,000, the rate rose to 19%. For taxable income over $200,000, the marginal rate rose as high as 70%.

Some Possible Drawbacks in the Stock Dividend Plan

GPU's dividend proposal was quite attractive from the standpoint of cash flow to any shareholder subject to income taxes. It was neutral from the standpoint of GPU's corporate administrative costs. Finally, the plan did have some drawbacks at both the shareholder and corporate levels. For example, GPU's officers were uncertain about the period of years during which heavy earnings retentions might be necessary. Comparatively speaking, quarterly stock dividends would be very expensive to administer unless the company faced an equally costly annual rights offering. Should GPU's capital requirements stabilize in the early 1970's, the company would rapidly increase the equity percentage in its overall capital structure under the stock dividend plan. Mr. Kuhns mentioned that another large utility had frozen the level of its per share cash dividend in 1952 to conserve cash for a large capital expenditure program. The utility in question had 35% equity in its capital structure in 1952. By 1962 the reduced cash pay-out coupled with stable capital expenditures had raised their equity percentage to 50% of total capital, and the frozen-dividend plan was finally abandoned. Mr. Kuhns did not want to make a fundamental change in GPU's dividend policy unless it could be justified by long-term benefits.

Other potential problem areas were evident in the new dividend policy proposal.

First, if a shareholder received cash in lieu of fractions of a share in a stock dividend, according to law these cash payments would be taxable to the recipients as ordinary income. A holder of 60 or less GPU shares would probably receive less than a single share in each quarterly stock dividend distribution. If this small holder wished to sell this fractional share, the cash received would have to be treated as ordinary income. The small GPU stockholder would thus gain no tax-saving benefit from the stock dividend plan and would in fact have to bear a small charge for selling the fractional share. This charge would have been avoided with a straight cash dividend. Only about 4% of GPU's stock was held in lots of less than 60 shares (Exhibit 5), so this drawback of the dividend plan did not appear to be a serious problem. However, some of the large holdings registered in the names of brokers might have been actually owned by a large number of small holders.

Second, since GPU would be establishing a convenient marketing mechanism for shareholders with the stock dividend plan, the company might have to maintain an effective registration statement continuously with the SEC on the theory that this was an indirect form of marketing shares of GPU. While this would not be a serious drawback (most mutual funds were in perpetual registration), it was inconvenient in that it would limit what GPU's management could report to the financial press regarding earnings projections or favorable company developments.

Finally, the most troublesome problem involving the proposed new dividend plan might arise with respect to shares held by estates and trusts. A conflict with regard to stock dividends could arise when the income beneficiary of a trust was not the same person as the beneficiary of trust principal (the remainderman). In such a situation, stock dividend shares were regarded as a distribution of principal in some states, such as Massachusetts, while in other states, such as New York and Pennsylvania, they were treated as income. Where banks expected a conflict of interest between the income beneficiary and the remainderman, they might resolve the problem by selling their shares of GPU stock. GPU's officers were uncertain about how much selling pressure this problem might engender. The normal volume of GPU shares traded annually on the New York Stock Exchange totaled about 1.5 million shares. GPU's officers felt that if an extra million shares of selling pressure arose over a 1-year period, under normal circumstances the company's stock might have to decline 5% or more in order to attract the required number of new buyers.

If any such selling should develop, however, GPU's officers felt that the beneficial aspects of the new dividend plan might encourage new buyers to take up the extra available stock without any reduction in market price. While GPU's managers examined the company's stockholder list to determine the number of shares held in trust accounts at Massachusetts banks, they had no way of knowing how many of these shares were held in trusts where the income beneficiary and the remainderman were different persons (Exhibit 5). In addition, they had no way of knowing the amount of buying interest which the new dividend plan might engender among existing GPU shareholders or investors as yet unknown to the company.

Checking Shareholder Reactions

Before making a decision on the new dividend plan, the officers of GPU felt that it might be useful on an informal basis to explore with some interested parties the acceptability of the new dividend proposal. GPU's officers were particularly concerned that some of the company's shares held by Massachusetts banks might have to be sold if the new dividend proposal were adopted. GPU's management was reluctant to make contact with Massachusetts bankers, however, since if the company were to do so, GPU's entire stockholder group would have to be simultaneously informed that the proposal was under consideration. A new ruling by the New York Stock Exchange Board of Governors[7] had made

---

[7] Part of the text of the NYSE ruling follows:

"Negotiations leading to acquisitions and mergers, stock splits, the making of arrangements preparatory to an exchange or tender offer, changes in dividend rates or earnings, calls for redemption, new contracts, products, or discoveries, are the type of developments where the risk of untimely and inadvertent disclosure of corporate plans is most likely to occur. Frequently, these matters require discussion and study by corporate officials before

such disclosure necessary even though in the past companies often sought out the opinions of major shareholders and others outside the management group—without such disclosure—before making financial policy changes.

If the shareholders were informed of the proposal, a logical extension of this action might be to ask the shareholders to vote on the matter. Since dividend policy had traditionally been determined at the level of the board of directors, Mr. Kuhns was somewhat wary of setting a new precedent by involving the shareholders in the dividend policy question.

Required Decisions

In January, 1968, Mr. Kuhns thus faced the twin problem of (1) deciding whether the benefits of the proposed dividend plan were sufficiently attractive to merit an attempt to put them into practice, and (2) deciding whether or not to involve the shareholder group in the making of his decision.

---

final decisions can be made. Accordingly, extreme care must be used in order to keep the information on a confidential basis.

. . . .

"At some point it usually becomes necessary to involve persons other than top management of the company or companies to conduct preliminary studies or assist in other preparations for contemplated transactions, e.g., business appraisals, tentative financing arrangements, attitude of large outside holders, availability of major blocks of stock, engineering studies, market analyses and surveys, etc. Experience has shown that maintaining security at this point is virtually impossible. Accordingly, fairness requires that the company make an immediate public announcement as soon as confidential disclosures relating to such important matters are made to 'outsiders.'"

Exhibit 1

Selected Income and Balance Sheet Items for GPU, 1959–67

INCOME ITEMS	1959	1960	1961	1962	1963	1964	1965	1966	1967
Revenues ($ millions)	196.0	204.8	214.3	227.2	240.0	253.2	270.0	289.3	310.9
Net profit after taxes ($ millions)	33.1	35.1	36.5	40.7	41.6	44.1	46.4	48.7	51.9
Common shares outstanding (millions)	22.6	23.7	23.8	23.8	23.8	23.8	23.8	23.9	24.8
Earning per share ($)	1.46	1.48	1.53	1.71	1.75	1.85	1.95	2.04	2.09
Dividends per share ($)	1.05	1.09	1.13	1.15	1.22	1.30	1.37	1.42	1.52
Average share price in year ($)	24.20	24.20	30.30	29.70	33.30	35.90	37.20	31.10	29.70
Average P/E ratio in year	16.5	16.3	19.8	17.4	19.0	19.4	19.1	15.2	14.2
Average dividend yield in year (%)	4.4	4.5	3.7	3.7	3.6	3.6	3.7	4.6	5.1
BALANCE SHEET ITEMS									
Current assets ($ millions)	55.1	45.8	47.1	60.2	59.8	62.4	60.4	62.4	75.4
Property, plant and equipment ($ millions)	859.8	832.0	886.5	933.4	982.7	1,042.6	1,117.2	1,241.9	1,365.3
Other assets ($ millions)	21.0	53.0	52.9	82.0	77.3	72.3	66.5	60.6	68.9
Total assets ($ millions)	935.9	930.8	986.5	1,076.0	1,120.0	1,177.3	1,244.1	1,364.9	1,509.6
Current liabilities ($ millions)	55.3	45.7	51.1	57.1	75.0	71.2	52.6	54.2	50.6
Long-term debt ($ millions)	437.6	442.6	480.9	522.4	534.8	576.8	654.9	732.2	862.0
Preferred stock ($ millions)	84.2	84.2	84.2	84.2	84.2	83.7	79.7	77.5	77.5
Common equity ($ millions)	328.6	341.9	354.0	394.7	407.2	420.3	434.3	477.2	491.5
Other liabilities ($ millions)	30.2	16.4	16.3	17.6	18.8	25.3	22.6	23.8	28.0
Total liabilities ($ millions)	935.9	930.8	986.5	1,076.0	1,120.0	1,177.3	1,244.1	1,364.9	1,509.6
L.T. debt/Total capital (%)	51.5	50.9	52.2	52.2	52.0	53.4	56.0	56.8	60.2
Preferred/Total capital (%)	9.9	9.7	9.2	8.4	8.2	7.7	6.8	6.1	5.4
Common/Total capital (%)	38.6	39.4	38.6	39.4	39.8	38.9	37.2	37.1	34.4
	100.0	100.0	100.0	100.0	100.0	100.0	100.0	100.0	100.0

Exhibit 2. Estimated Funds Flow, 196?–72 ($ Millions)

	Actual 1967	1968	1969	1970	1971	1972
Pro forma:						
1. Use of funds						
2. Additions to plant including investments						
3. in nuclear fuel....	176.5	203.1	250.9	246.3	235.0	235.0
4. Working capital additions and						
5. other uses....	13.6	4.0	4.0	4.0	4.0	4.0
6. Total funds applied....	190.1	207.1	254.9	250.3	239.0	239.0
New dividend plan:						
11. Sources of funds						
12. Net income plus tax deferrals[1]	55.3	59.8	64.6	69.8	75.5	81.5
13. Less: Dividends (17%)[2]	37.6	10.2	11.0	11.9	12.9	13.8
14. Income retained....	17.7	49.6	53.6	57.9	62.6	67.7
15. Depreciation....	37.8	40.7	46.1	51.0	56.0	61.0
16. Total internal cash generation....	55.5	90.3	99.7	108.9	118.6	128.7
17. Additions to short-term debt....	27.8	24.4	55.3	34.0	4.2	(15.3)
18. Additions to long-term debt[3]....	106.8	85.3	92.3	99.1	107.2	116.0
19. Additions to preferred stock[3]....	-0-	7.1	7.6	8.3	9.0	9.6
20. Extra equity capital needed....	-0-	-0-	-0-	-0-	-0-	-0-
21. Total funds available....	190.1	207.1	254.9	250.3	239.0	239.0
Old dividend plan:						
26. Sources of funds						
27. Net income plus tax deferrals[1]	55.3	59.8	64.6	69.8	75.5	81.5
28. Less: Dividends (68%)[2]	37.6	40.0	44.0	47.5	51.3	55.5
29. Income retained....	17.7	19.8	20.6	22.3	24.2	26.0
30. Depreciation....	37.8	40.7	46.1	51.0	56.0	61.0
31. Total internal cash generation....	55.5	60.5	66.7	73.3	80.2	87.0
32. Additions to short-term debt....	27.8	24.4	55.3	34.0	4.2	(15.3)
33. Additions to long-term debt[3]....	106.8	85.3	92.3	99.1	107.2	116.0
34. Additions to preferred stock[3]....	-0-	7.1	7.6	8.3	9.0	9.6
35. Extra equity capital needed....	-0-	29.8	33.0	35.6	38.4	41.7
36. Total funds available....	190.1	207.1	254.9	250.3	239.0	239.0

[1] Assumes that net income plus tax deferrals would increase about 8% each year over the base year 1967.

[2] GPU's annual dividend payments had historically amounted to 68% of reported earnings and tax deferrals. Under the proposed stock dividend plan, one quarter of this amount (17%) of earnings and tax deferrals would be paid out in cash. An amount equivalent to 51% of earnings and tax deferrals would be declared in the form of a stock dividend.

[3] Assuming a capital structure with 35% common equity, 5% preferred stock and 60% debt, long-term debt additions equal to 0.60/0.35 = 1.70 times retained earnings could be made each year. Preferred stock additions equal to 0.5/0.35 = 0.143 times retained earnings could also be made annually.

Source: The company was unable to provide and/or substantiate data relating to income and/or dividend projections due to SEC regulation. GPU had a security in registration when the case was being prepared. Projections were thus made by the casewriter.

Exhibit 3

I. Cash Effects of New Dividend Policy on Holder of 1,000 GPU Shares
(000 omitted)

	Shares	Price per Share	Cash Dividend	Stock Dividend	20% Income Tax	Net Receipts Stockholder
Basis A—Shareholder Maintains Position by Exercising Rights or Accumulating Stock Dividends						
Old dividend plan (use rights offering)						
Cash dividend received	1,000	$ 1.56	$1,560.00		$312.00	$1,248.00
Cash outlay to exercise rights	50	$23.40 (a)				(1,170.00)
Total	1,050					$ 78.00
New stock dividend plan						
Cash dividend received	1,000	0.39	$ 390.00		$ 78.00	$ 312.00
Stock dividend accumulated	43⅓	$27.00		$1,170.00		
Total	1,043⅓					$ 312.00
Basis B—Shareholder Does Not Subscribe to Rights Offering or Sells Stock Dividend						
Old dividend plan (use rights offering)						
Cash dividend received	1,000	$ 1.56	$1,560.00		$312.00	$1,248.00
Proceeds from sale of rights	50	$ 3.43 (f)	171.50		17.15	154.35
Total	1,000		$1,731.50		$329.15	$1,402.35
New stock dividend plan						
Cash dividend received	1,000	$ 0.39	$ 390.00		$ 78.00	$ 312.00
Proceeds from sale of stock dividend		$ 1.17 (c), (e)		$1,170.00	117.00	1,053.00
Proceeds from sale of additional shares	(6⅓)	$27.00 (b), (c), (d), (e)		171.50	17.15	154.35
Total	993⅓				$212.15	$1,519.35

II. Cash Effects of New Dividend Policy on GPU as a Corporate Entity
(000 omitted)

	Shares (000)	Stock Dividend (000)	(Disbursements) (000)
Basis A: Old dividend plan (use rights offering)			
Cash dividend received..................	24,805 @ $ 1.56		$(38,696)
Cash outlay to exercise rights..........	1,240 @ $23.40		29,016
Total.....	26,045		$ (9,680)
New stock dividend plan			
Cash dividend received.................	24,805 @ $ 0.39		$ (9,680)
Stock dividend accumulated............	1,075	$29,016	—
Total.....	25,880		$ (9,680)

(a) Assumes market value of common stock equals $27 and that one right is issued for each share of common stock held. One thousand rights entitle their owner to purchase 50 shares of GPU common stock at $23.40/share. The 1000 rights received by the GPU shareholder would thus have a total value equal to approximately 50 × ($27 − $23.40) = $180.

(b) Additional holdings are sold to maintain same equity position as under a rights offering wherein the rights are sold. In other words:

	Total Shares (000)	Shareholder's Holdings	Shareholder Equity
Initial..........	24,805	1,000	0.00403%
Rights offering........	26,045	1,050	.00403
Sell rights........	26,045	1,000	.00384
Initial..........	24,805	1,000	.00403
Stock dividend........	25,880	1,043⅓	.00403
Sell stock........	25,880	1,000	.00386
Sell additional shares......	25,880	993⅔	.00384

(c) Assumes stock has a cost basis for tax purposes of zero, the most conservative possible assumption.

(d) Under the stock dividend plan, the GPU shares retained by the shareholder would continue to have a zero tax basis. With cash dividends, the shareholder who exercised his rights would slowly build up a small tax basis for his stock. For this reason, the calculations assume that the shareholder does not sell his GPU holdings during his lifetime.

(e) All calculations assume that the GPU shareholder has owned his shares for at least 6 months and that capital gains are therefore taxed at reduced rates.

(f) The ex-rights price of the common stock should be [($27 × 20) − $23.40]/21 = $26.83. The proceeds from the sale of the rights would thus be 50 × ($26.83 − $23.40).

Exhibit 4

Increased Cash in Hand to Shareholder if Stock Dividend
Plan Were Adopted when Compared to Existing Dividend
Policy

Shareholder's Marginal Income Tax Bracket	Extra Cash per 1,000 GPU Shares Owned	
	Basis A*	Basis B†
20%....................	$234	$117
30.....................	351	176
40.....................	468	234
50.....................	585	293
60.....................	702	410
70.....................	819	527

* Basis A—assumes that the shareholder would (1) subscribe to the
rights offering under the old dividend plan or (2) accumulate his stock dividends under the new plan. Either action would leave his percentage equity
interest in GPU intact.

† Basis B—assumes that the shareholder would (1) sell his rights under
the old dividend plan or (2) sell his stock dividend and a small number of
his common shares under the new plan. Either action would reduce slightly
his percentage equity interest in GPU.

Exhibit 5(a)

Common Shareholders of GPU at December 31, 1967

Size of Holdings	No. Holders	%	No. Shares	%
1 to 20 shares.................	17,089	22	153,775	1
21 to 60 shares................	17,328	22	679,113	3
61 to 100 shares...............	11,152	14	949,203	4
101 to 300 shares..............	23,820	30	4,072,560	16
301 to 1,000 shares............	7,469	10	3,680,096	15
1,001 shares & over............	1,853	2	15,270,349	61
Totals.................	78,711	100	24,805,096	100

Exhibit 5(b)

GENERAL PUBLIC UTILITIES
CORPORATION
Institutional Holders of GPU Common
Stock
(millions of shares)

Bank trust departments	
Pennsylvania..................	3.0
New York.....................	2.9
Massachusetts.................	1.6
Other states..................	2.1
Mutual funds....................	1.5
Insurance companies.............	1.0
Pension funds....................	.2
Total....................	12.3

Note: Some shares held by bank trust departments and insurance companies were beneficially
owned by pension funds.

Extone Chemicals, Inc.*

The decision, taken June 24, 1963, by the board of directors of Extone Chemicals, Inc., to instruct the treasurer to buy up to 60,000 shares of its common stock marked an important change in the policy of the company. Although shares had previously been purchased in annual amounts ranging from 14,000 to 25,000 shares, these purchases had been roughly equal in magnitude to the number of shares required to be issued to meet obligations under the restricted stock option plans approved by the stockholders from time to time. There had been no intention to acquire treasury stock for any other reason, and the board had previously rejected all suggestions for additional purchases. There was a strong undercurrent of feeling on the board that such purchasing "smelled of manipulation by insiders" for their benefit. Holders of stock options, for instance, might be such beneficiaries.

The new policy was announced to the stockholders in the annual report covering the fiscal year ended June 30, 1963, which was mailed so as to reach the holders on August 26, 1963, in the following words:

Stock Purchase

During July, the company acquired 10,780 shares of its common stock which are being held in the Treasury. These purchases are part of a program to reacquire shares previously issued in connection with an acquisition. The Board of Directors, because of this and other considerations, has authorized the purchase of up to 60,000 shares of the company's common stock in the open market, but there is no assurance that this number of shares will in fact be purchased. The Board of Directors, however, may in the future approve the purchase of shares in addition to those for which purchase has been authorized.

It was the opinion of counsel for the company that this decision did not require stockholder approval; so no formal motion on the subject was

---

* Abridged.

put before the annual stockholders' meeting that took place September 17.

Although there had been considerable discussion of the desirability of the new policy, and opinions among directors and officers were not unanimous, there is no need to record the differences here, because all the arguments were revived in the spring of 1964, when the recommendation to continue with further stock purchases was under discussion.

Recent Events in Company History

With the exception of a small rise in 1961, the earnings available for the common stock of Extone Chemicals, Inc., had declined steadily from the all-time high of $4.70 a share[1] in the fiscal year 1958–59 to $2.61 in the fiscal year 1961–62. A sharp recovery, to $3.97 a share in the fiscal year 1962–63, gave rise to the expectation that the company had removed the drains on its profitability that, in the opinion of the management, had been due to the operations of certain unprofitable divisions, whose liquidation was well under way by the spring of 1963.

In the early 1950's, Extone Chemicals, which already manufactured a broad line of specialized chemicals, had extended its interests into certain mechanical and electronics fields. The new lines were by-products of research work in the Extone laboratories. They soon proved to be outside the management's main competence, however, and were not profitable. In recent years, therefore, on the advice of the president and other officers, the board of directors had decided that the company should concentrate on specialized areas of chemistry, where Extone Chemicals had proven strength. Accordingly, while new and profitable products were being introduced into these divisions of the business through company research, there were liquidations, both piecemeal and by the sale of operating units, of other activities.

The Middlesex division, acquired through the issuance of 60,000 shares of Extone common stock in the fiscal year 1959–60, was sold as a unit for cash in the fiscal year 1962–63.

The annual report of the fiscal year 1962–63 stated:

. . . orderly liquidation [of the electronics division] . . . is now in progress. . . . As a result of the liquidation, substantial cash will be available for reinvestment in other areas in our business which promise greater return on our capital.

Other liquidations took place and were planned so that by the end of the fiscal year 1963–64 Extone Chemicals was expected to have sold all its units in the mechanical and electronics divisions and to have entirely completed the program of disinvestment that had been decided upon.

Dividends, established at the rate of $2.50 a share in the fiscal year 1959–60, were maintained at this rate according to a policy several times stated to the stockholders in annual reports:

---

[1] All per-share figures used in this case have been adjusted for all stock splits occurring in the period.

Extone Chemicals, Inc., has followed a policy of paying consistent, regular dividends on its common stock. After a regular rate has been established, it has never been reduced. At the same time, the company has endeavored to diversify and expand mainly through the use of retained earnings. The amount of this reinvestment has varied from year to year, but has averaged 37% of earnings for the last 10 years.

Viewing the response of the market price of the stock to declining earnings, and considering the company's future needs, the financial officers of the company had decided to continue the announced dividend policy, to plan on an average dividend payout of 50%, and to emphasize the creation of earnings per share as the primary objective of financial policy in the stockholders' interest. Investment bankers advising the company endorsed these decisions but emphasized that a steady increase of dividend in proportion to growth seemed to be given high value by investors in the stocks of the chemical industry. Pertinent data on the common stock for the last 5 fiscal years, together with estimates for the year ending June 30, 1964, are given in Exhibit 1.

Despite the dividends paid and the considerable sums spent on capital investment, and as a result of the retention of earnings and the program of disinvestment, Extone Chemicals became possessed of a high level of liquid resources during the fiscal years under discussion in this case. The condition is indicated by the figures in the following table, which include also the comptroller's estimate for the end of the next fiscal year (figures in thousands, taken from consolidated balance sheets):

	1959	1960	1961	1962	1963	1964*
Net working capital...	$ 84,131	$ 71,691	$ 70,313	$ 76,575	$ 85,478	$ 83,900
Cash...............	17,436	14,603	12,039	12,833	14,358	12,000
Short-term investments............	11,557	...	...	...	35,053	42,200
Sales volume.........	524,158	516,305	552,492	524,545	502,988	518,400

* Estimated.

Stock Acquisition Policy, 1963

During the fiscal year 1962–63 Mr. Prouse, the financial vice president, had instructed the treasurer, Mr. Blaine, to undertake a program of investing surplus funds. The program had produced an average return of 4% before income taxes. Impressed by the relatively low level of this return, and recognizing that the company's policy of expanding in its chosen fields of concentration would not require funds shortly, the financial officers succeeded, over some opposition, in persuading first the president, then the Finance Committee of the board, and finally a majority of the board of directors to approve, as a first step to be followed by more thorough study, the reacquisition of 60,000 shares, an amount equal to the shares that had been issued in the Middlesex acquisition. Consequently, the announcement was made to stockholders in 1963, and the purchasing was subsequently carried out by the treasurer (who dealt with several brokerage firms personally) under the following conditions, which had been voted by the board of directors after review by counsel:

1. No purchase price should exceed $83 a share.
2. Purchases on the New York Stock Exchange should not be in excess of one third of the daily volume, or 30% of the monthly volume, of sales, and should be at a price within the range of trading on the exchange. [A study of volume records for the previous 2 fiscal years showed a daily average of 1,800 to 2,300 shares traded. The investment banking firm with which the financial officers had consulted on the details of the proposed operation had recommended the 30% limit as one which had served well in a number of situations where buyers wished to accumulate stock in a way that would not attract the attention of specialists or other traders.]
3. Purchases of secondary offerings of blocks of stock should be exempt from the volume limitation.

Purchasing began at the beginning of July, 1963, and continued almost daily until the middle of February, 1964. Seldom (except for taking advantage of a few secondary offerings) did a daily purchase reach 450 shares. The total cost of the 60,000 shares was $4,624,800 at the average price of $77.08 a share. The treasurer was satisfied that his purchases could have had no noticeable effect on the general movements of the market price of Extone stock. Market prices by months for the period January, 1962–April, 1964 appear in Exhibit 2, compared with the Standard and Poor's stock price indexes for 11 chemical companies (excluding Du Pont). These data are charted in Exhibit 3.

There was an easy flow of ideas in the Extone Chemicals organization, and those which had to do with financial policy questions came to Mr. Prouse or Mr. Blaine. These officers were acquainted not only with the formally adopted policies of the board of directors but also with underlying attitudes, since Mr. Prouse was secretary of the board's Finance Committee, and Mr. Blaine attended meetings to present the most recent financial results. Using such background, they could make choices about which ideas were worth pursuing, and which had no chance of survival.

For example, when the purchase of 60,000 shares neared completion in February, 1964, Mr. Blaine once more pointed out to Mr. Prouse that the liquid position of Extone Chemicals continued to be very generous, and that short-term forecasts were for a further increase in cash items on hand. With Mr. Prouse's approval, he instructed his assistant, Mr. Gibson, to prepare a report discussing the amounts involved and the alternatives to be considered. Mr. Gibson was specifically instructed to consider the desirability of calling the company's preferred stock for redemption, as this alternative had been suggested by certain directors when the matter had been under discussion in the spring of 1963, and it was to be expected that the proposal would be raised once more.

The 5% cumulative preferred stock, with a par value of $21,261,400, had been issued in 1928. Dividends on this stock had never been in arrears. It had been deemed advisable in 1928 to set a high call price, $115 a share, to aid in making the offer attractive. Thus, with $115 a share required to eliminate a dividend of $5 a share, this alternative investment of $24,450,610 could be said to offer a return of 4.35%, after income taxes. Another measure of the consequence of retiring the preferred stock was to say that it would increase the earnings on the common stock outstanding in February, 1964 (approximately 3,285,500 shares) by $0.17 a share, a number obtained by deducting from the amount of the preferred dividend ($1,063,070) 2% of $24,450,000, or $489,000, to represent the after-tax income from surplus fund investments.

The development of comparable figures for the alternative of expending $24,450,000 on the purchase and retirement of common shares proved more difficult for Mr. Gibson because of the anticipated growth of the company.

After study of the record of market prices for the stock in recent months, and giving consideration to the continued gain in earnings (7% higher in the last 6 months of 1963 than in the same period of 1962), and consultation with Mr. Blaine, Mr. Gibson decided that an average purchase price of $89½ a share could be assumed, if the buying was undertaken promptly. Higher prices were expected for later years. Under this assumption, 273,184 shares would be purchased, relieving the company of $682,296 in dividends at the current rate.

In the fiscal year 1962–63, earnings available for common shares were $13,252,677. Deducting 2% of $24,450,000, or $489,000, to represent the after-tax income from the investment of surplus funds, and rounding, Mr. Gibson obtained $12,764,000. He then prepared the following comparison:

$$\frac{\text{1962–63 Earnings}}{\text{February, 1964 Number of Shares}} = \frac{\$13,252,677}{3,285,500} = \$4.03 \text{ per share} .$$

$$\frac{\text{1962–63 Earnings, Adjusted}}{\text{Reduced Number of Shares}} = \frac{\$12,764,000}{3,012,316} = \$4.24 \text{ per share} .$$

As the earnings of Extone Chemicals were expected to grow, Mr. Gibson performed a similar calculation for increases in operating earnings of 15%, 30%, and 45%.[2]

_____

[2] AUTHOR'S NOTE: Actually, forecasts made by the comptroller's department were available that permitted Mr. Gibson to put dates on the occurrence of these amounts of growth. They have been omitted here, in order not to reveal the planning factors of the company.

Operating earnings	F/Y 62–63	+15%	+30%	+45%
E.P.S. 3,285,500 shares	$4.03	$4.62	$5.20	$5.78
E.P.S. 3,012,316 shares	4.24	4.87	5.51	6.14
Gain from repurchase of 273,184 shares	$0.21	$0.25	$0.31	$0.36

Knowing Mr. Prouse's interest in the computation of "return-on-investment" figures, Mr. Gibson then proceeded as follows. He computed the amount of earnings, after taxes, necessary to make $4.24 earned per share on 3,285,500 shares. The product of these numbers was $13,930,520, a quantity $1,166,520 greater than the $12,764,000 actually earned. He related this number, $1,166,520, to $24,450,000 to obtain the rate of 4.8% after taxes. From a similar computation, he found an indicated rate of return of 6.8%, after operating earnings had increased by 45%.

Upon reviewing the study made by Mr. Gibson, Mr. Blaine concluded that the purchase of common stock would be preferable to the retirement of the preferred issue. The figures showed a small immediate advantage both in earnings per share and in rate of return for the policy, and the advantage would become greater as the earnings of Extone Chemicals grew larger. Mr. Blaine also was well aware of the steady growth in stock repurchases by corporations generally.

Mr. Blaine felt that as much as $34 million could be used (379,888 shares at $89½), after considering forecasts of future funds flows as well as the existing amount of temporary investments, even after allowing $12 million for cash to support operations. He noted that, even at the rate of 450 shares purchased per day, it would take a long time to accomplish the desired result, and he therefore gave favorable consideration to acquiring the shares through an invitation to the shareholders to tender them to the company.

The investment bankers advising the company had reported that few companies had chosen to ask for tenders as a means of acquiring shares but that the practice was by no means unknown. Their advice, however, was against the practice because: (1) A tender offer was unusual, and therefore would attract comment and, perhaps, unfavorable gossip, especially in view of recent publicity given to the sale of several parts of the business. (2) It required setting a price, which was not an easy operation, though possible. The price would certainly have to be higher than market, to attract the volume of shares desired. But at the price offered, the desired quantity might not be obtained. Offerings of too few or too many shares might produce unfavorable comment. (3) Although the company and its advisers would offer a price that was an appraisal of the current market situation, there was no way to avoid having some shareholders interpret it as an official statement of the "value" of their stock—with misunderstandings and complaints to follow, whichever way the market value might move. (Usually, tender offers were followed by increases, because the normal supply to the market was absorbed.)

Nevertheless, Mr. Blaine was favorably disposed toward the use of tenders. His reasons included: (1) The transaction could be completed quickly, as contrasted with the long time needed by purchasing small quantities in the open market. If it affected price, its effect would soon be over. (2) It would create immediately the full effect on earnings per share. (3) It gave the maximum assurance of full disclosure to share-holders, since each listed owner would receive a description of the offer directly from the company and could hardly avoid considering the matter.

Mr. Blaine knew that some companies made use of tender offers. For example, in March he noted in *The Wall Street Journal* an invitation from Thompson Ramo Wooldridge, Inc., to its stockholders to tender shares. The announcement of the invitation is reproduced in Exhibit 4. The invitation had had the desired results.

When Mr. Blaine discussed the matter with Mr. Prouse, however, he learned that the board of directors would surely be unfavorable to the idea of using tenders. In addition to the reasons given by the investment bankers, Mr. Prouse emphasized that: (1) A sudden distribution of a very large quantity of funds scarcely fitted the image of the dynamic company that Extone Chemicals was, in fact. (2) A number of investing institutions held large blocks of Extone stock, and the tender scheme would offer them too easy an opportunity to take capital gains on their entire holding. (3) Also, once the invitation was issued, there was no flexibility, as to either price or quantity of shares. Extone Chemicals was actively following a policy leading to acquisitions, and therefore might wish to revise its stock repurchase policy in one way or another. (4) A single tender offer might be considered, but the method did not offer a basis for any continuing policy. (The rumor of a tender offer usually caused price increases, and so no inference of a policy of repeated tenders could be permitted.)

At the same time as the studies on repurchase of stock were under way, Extone Chemicals arranged to purchase a company that would make an important addition to its line of chemical specialties. The purchase was to be accomplished by issuing to the sellers 264,000 shares of Extone common stock. This transaction emphasized in Mr. Prouse's and Mr. Blaine's minds the importance of having on hand a substantial number of treasury shares to permit acquisitions without any immediate dilution. They also felt that it would be desirable to put the pending acquisition "on a cash basis" at current levels in the stock market. In this case, as in several that were under consideration, the terms of exchange depended on the market values of the shares of the two companies. With Extone stock selling at low price-earnings multiples, it was hard to find desirable acquisitions that did not seem high priced, in terms of dilution.

With such information at hand, Mr. Blaine prepared a formal recommendation to Mr. Prouse that the board of directors be asked to approve further acquisitions in the manner previously used. In his memorandum, Mr. Blaine said:

I would certainly recommend that we continue the rules relating to the volume of daily purchasing and the range within which purchases should be made.

I would not like to see a definite maximum set and I definitely do not recommend that any further notification of our intention to purchase should be given to stockholders. Such an announcement would give all and sundry definite knowledge of our intention to purchase and might also in some way be construed as support of the market.

The purchase program could be said to be a mechanism by which we could reacquire equity capital formerly directed to the mechanical and electronics phases of our business, allowing it to be redirected to chemicals without seriously penalizing our stockholders.

As he prepared to draft his own recommendation to be presented to higher officers, Mr. Prouse recalled certain negative views that had been argued in the previous year. Most, if not all of them, could be expected once more, and he wanted to consider how they could be compromised or overcome in order to obtain the repurchase policy, which he favored strongly. These negative views were:

1. It was desirable to retire the preferred stock, which was an obsolete and expensive kind of financing. If necessary, it should be retired by refunding into some sort of debt.

2. Although both the long-term debt and the preferred stock contracts contained the same maximum for long-term debt of $50 million (and Extone Chemicals was currently obligated for about $43,875,000), the preferred stock was held by many owners. It would be hard, therefore, to get the restriction in the preferred contract changed. The debt contract containing this restriction, on the other hand, was held by one insurance company, which was expected to be reasonable about changes. (The company's debt ratio was not "out of line" in the industry.)

3. The price of the common stock was above book value, and it was unfair to the remaining shareholders to reduce their book values by the proposed repurchases.

4. The board ought not to approve repurchases unless a new statement of intent, similar to the 1963 statement specifying the number of shares to be acquired, was made before any purchases began. Directors with this opinion believed that any purchases, no matter how carefully made, would inevitably affect market prices if they were continued over many days, as would be the case for the current proposal. Therefore, they wanted as explicit a statement as possible, and they wanted it renewed each time the board of directors authorized a new number of shares to be purchased. One of these directors went so far as to propose that the nature of the restrictions on the treasurer's buying should also be made public.

An opinion of company counsel was obtained, that the 1963 announcement met all legal requirements for publicity, so long as similar quantities and methods of purchase were involved. If, however, more than 5% of the shares were to be retired, an announcement in advance of any buying would remove any question of inadequate disclosure under SEC rulings.

The studies and discussions described above, which had begun in February, 1964, lasted until early May. At this date, the end of the fiscal year was approaching. Earnings per share for the year 1963–64 were estimated at $4.39 on the 3,513,416 shares outstanding. The directors would next meet early in June, and the text of the annual report would be open to changes until early in July.

Exhibit 1

Data on Common Stock, for Years Ended June 30, 1959–64

	6/30 1959	*6/30 1960*	*6/30 1961*	*6/30 1962*	*6/30 1963*	*6/30 1964**
Net earnings for common stock	$15,082,172	$9,991,474	$11,256,374	$8,686,417	$13,252,677	$15,435,000
Number of common shares, end of year†	3,208,816	3,289,477	3,314,563	3,328,995	3,341,206	3,513,416
Earned per share†	$4.70	$3.04	$3.40	$2.61	$3.97	$4.39
Dividends per share†	$2.20	$2.425	$2.50	$2.50	$2.50	$2.50
Percentage of common stock earnings paid out	46.8%	79.8%	73.5%	95.8%	63.0%	56.9%
	CALENDAR YEARS					
	1959	*1960*	*1961*	*1962*	*1963*	*Jan.-Apr. 1964*
Market prices						
High	$83⅝	$69¾	$80¾	$70⅝	$89	$88¼
Low	$61¼	$49¾	$64⅝	$44¾	$65⅜	$75
Standard & Poor's weekly stock price indexes for 11 chemical companies, excluding Du Pont (1941–43 = 10). Average of weekly indexes	45.76	42.77	44.68	35.44	39.94	45.92

* Estimated.
† Adjusted for all stock splits.

Exhibit 2

Monthly High and Low Market Prices of Common Stock, 1962–April, 1964

	1962		*1963*		*1964*		*Standard & Poor's Stock Price Index for Chemical Companies* (1941–43 = 10)*		
	Low	*High*	*Low*	*High*	*Low*	*High*	*1962*	*1963*	*1964*
January	60⅝	70⅝	65⅜	70⅞	79⅝	84⅛	41.41	37.95	45.16
February	60⅞	63½	66⅝	71⅜	76½	81¾	41.59	38.28	45.17
March	60⅜	66⅝	69¾	73¾	79⅛	88¼	40.19	38.05	46.09
April	58⅜	62½	73⅛	79⅛	75	86¼	37.91	39.94	47.24
May	44¾	61¼	71⅜	77⅝			34.86	40.54	
June	50	57¾	71⅞	77⅞			30.61	39.80	
July	46⅛	53⅛	67½	75			30.45	38.83	
August	49	57	71⅞	81¼			31.33	39.73	
September	53⅛	59⅜	76½	85⅛			32.05	40.81	
October	52⅛	57	82	89			32.07	40.49	
November	55¼	64⅜	75	83⅛			36.05	41.21	
December	63¼	67⅛	80¾	84⅞			36.76	43.63	

* Composite of 11 stocks, excluding Du Pont. Monthly averages of weekly indexes.

Exhibit 3

Share Value Indices

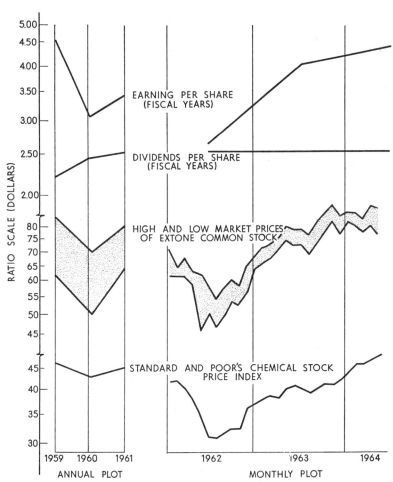

Exhibit 4

A Typical Invitation to Tender Shares

THOMPSON RAMO WOOLDRIDGE INC.

INVITATION TO TENDER 250,000 SHARES

of Common Stock at $56 Per Share

By letter dated March 2, 1964, the company has invited its shareholders to tender 250,000 shares of its Common Stock, at a price of $56 per share. The company will pay any Federal and. State Transfer Taxes involved in its purchase of shares.

The invitation to tender will expire at 3:30 pm., EST, on March 17, 1964 unless extended for a period of not more than ten days. The company reserves the right to purchase more or less than 250,000 shares, but in no event less than 100,000 shares.

All tenders are invited in accordance with the terms and conditions specified in the formal invitation to tender and accompanying tender form mailed to shareholders of record.

To accept this invitation, shareholders should send the prescribed letter of transmittal accompanied by their stock certificates to:

> The National City Bank of Cleveland
> Corporate Trust Department
> 623 Euclid Avenue
> Cleveland, Ohio 44101

> or

> Morgan Guaranty Trust Company of New York
> Corporate Trust Division
> 23 Wall Street
> New York, New York 10015

Additional copies of the invitation to tender and tender form may be obtained from either of such banks, or by writing to or telephoning the undersigned at 23555 Euclid Avenue, Cleveland, Ohio 44117 — Phone: Area Code 216, 383-2257.

THOMPSON RAMO WOOLDRIDGE INC.
P. W. Schuette, Secretary

Upstate Canning Company, Inc.

During the period following his graduation from a business school in 1950, Mr. Nelson Shields had attempted to prepare himself for the opportunity of becoming the manager and sole or part owner of a company with real growth possibilities. Because he lacked financial resources, he had sought employment which offered substantial immediate income as well as managerial experience which would be useful in later years. This search led him successively through positions in three distinctly different businesses, in each of which experience was largely concentrated in the sales and sales management areas. By 1956 he had accumulated personal savings of $15,000, which, added to some family money placed at his disposal, gave him an investment fund of $35,000.

At this point, Mr. Shields had begun an active search for opportunities to purchase an existing business. In the course of the year he looked into about 25 possibilities which came to his attention. Some of these were quickly rejected; others involved the expenditure of considerable time and some money before a negative decision was reached. While looking for business possibilities, Shields also sought to develop contacts with business and professional men who might be induced to invest equity capital in an attractive opportunity, should one be found requiring more capital than he possessed. By the end of 1956 Mr. Shields was still investigating business leads, but with no real prospect in sight. Meanwhile, the pressure to settle on a business was increasing. Shields had given up employment in October in order to devote full time to his search, and he realized that he could not afford many months of unemployment without eating into the sum set aside for investment.

In February of 1957 a business broker telephoned Shields to advise him that a small cannery had just come up for sale. The property consisted of two plants, equipped for the canning of fruits and vegetables, which were located close to the source of supply in rural towns in New York

State. The business, known as the Upstate Canning Company, Inc., was owned and managed by Mr. A. C. Fordham. Mr. Fordham's health was uncertain and, at 55, he had decided to sell out because he had no relatives to take his place in the business. The broker urged Shields to investigate this opportunity because it looked as though it might fit his circumstances.

Mr. Shields immediately set out to learn what he could about the fruit and vegetable canning industry in general and this business in particular. The broker arranged a meeting with Mr. Fordham; and from this and subsequent meetings and telephone conversations, Mr. Shields assembled a picture of the business.

In general, Mr. Fordham was very cooperative in providing the information requested from him. He was reluctant, however, to disclose the financial details of operations for the 3 years prior to 1956. During 1952 Fordham had brought in a general manager on a 3-year employment contract as a means of easing himself out of the day-to-day responsibilities of the business. The new man had not worked out well, and sales and profits had suffered as a result. Upon the termination of this contract, Fordham had again assumed full management responsibilities, and results in 1956 improved substantially over those of 1953, 1954, and 1955. Fordham argued that these years were not representative of the earnings potential of the business and that 1956 should be taken as the most accurate measure of its possibilities. From what Shields had been able to find out about the business from other sources, he was inclined to accept Fordham's explanation and to base his estimates on the figures for 1956.

The physical plants of the business appeared to be in very good condition. The two buildings had been kept in excellent repair, and the canning equipment was modern. The combined plants and equipment had recently been appraised for insurance purposes, and their value had been placed at $200,000. Shields was assured that no major repairs would be necessary over the next few years.

Mr. Fordham had been accustomed to operating the plants only during the limited harvest season for the fruits and vegetables which he canned. The season lasted for 4 months, from July through October, with August and September normally accounting for two thirds of the company's total production. At times, Fordham had considered stretching out the production period with other canning operations, but he had never taken any action on the idea. During the 1956 season, Upstate had produced canned fruits and vegetables with a total value of $850,000 (valued at Upstate's selling price). This production represented only about 50% of combined productive capacity of the plants during the production season. Excess capacity was attributed to the substantial expansion of facilities which had been undertaken to meet wartime demands.

The vegetables and fruits canned by Upstate were bought on a contract basis from farmers in the surrounding area; farmers were paid cash on delivery on the basis of prevailing market prices at the time of delivery. The quantities canned by Upstate varied to some extent with the crop conditions from year to year; normally, output could be increased considerably, however, by noncontract purchases, if good marketing opportunities existed. The production process was almost entirely mechanical, and the towns and surrounding areas offered an ample supply of seasonal labor sufficiently skilled to perform the various operations in the plant. Labor was paid on a weekly basis.

The products of the Upstate Canning Company were marketed primarily under the Upstate brand through jobbers. It was the normal practice to sell the entire season's pack before the next canning season began, so that little inventory would be carried over from one year to the next. Sales tended to be concentrated during and immediately following the production period. Fordham indicated that about 50% of the pack would normally be sold by the end of the canning season (October) and 70% by the end of December. The balance of sales was customarily spread rather evenly over the remaining months through June.

Mr. Shields was particularly attracted by the marketing opportunities of the business. It was his impression that Fordham had not been aggressive in sales promotion—that much better use could be made of the company's productive capacity. Shields believed that he could greatly increase the scale of operations by undertaking an active but relatively inexpensive sales program. He had in mind direct sales to supermarket chains of both Upstate and private brands, to be obtained largely through his own efforts with no significant increase in present selling costs.

Relying on these expectations, Shields prepared a 5-year sales program (see Exhibit 1) which he planned to use as the basis of his estimates of profits and working capital requirements. He was informed by Fordham that collections on accounts receivable caused little trouble in this business; bad-debt losses were rare, and accounts were normally collected within 30 days. Shields expected that the planned expansion would not affect this collection period and might even improve it, because he would be increasing direct sales to large accounts.

In examining the cost aspects of the business, Shields soon became aware of the high proportion of variable costs. The principal items were the fruits and vegetables and other ingredients, cans, and direct labor. As previously indicated, fruits and vegetables were bought on a cash basis, labor was paid weekly at fixed hourly rates, and cans and "other ingredients" were purchased on normal terms of 2/10, net 30 days. The details of revenues and costs for 1956 are shown in Exhibits 2 and 3.

As negotiations proceeded, it became evident that Fordham was anxious to sell the business as soon as possible. The new crop season was coming on; and Fordham felt that if he were to operate the business for another year, it would soon be necessary to sign contracts with farmers for the year's production. After 3 weeks, during which Shields was gathering and studying information and talking to bankers, can company officials, government agencies, and others, Fordham came forward with a specific proposal for the sale of the business (see Exhibit 4).

The plan anticipated that Shields would organize a new company and purchase certain Upstate assets, namely, its plant and equipment, a small amount of finished goods inventory, and the right to use the Upstate brand names. Current assets (other than the inventory mentioned above) and liabilities of the old company would not pass to the new company. It was apparent from the plan that Fordham had guessed that Shields had very limited resources and, accordingly, had provided for an instalment purchase of Upstate assets through the gradual redemption of $300,000 of income bonds to be issued to Fordham. By this time, Shields had become convinced that this business was sufficiently promising to justify a full and detailed study of Fordham's proposal.

Before accepting Fordham's proposal or making a counterproposal, it was necessary for Shields to determine how the new company was to be financed. His best lead for additional equity capital was a professional man who had indicated that he was prepared to invest as much as $100,000 if the right opportunity came along. This man was 50 years of age, and his investment goal appeared to be that of capital appreciation over the years rather than immediate income.

Shields was determined that the plan for the new company would include a means by which he could become the owner of 51% of the voting stock as soon as possible. More specifically, he hoped to obtain control within 5 years, and hence was intent on arranging a compensation plan for himself as manager which would enable him to accomplish this objective. Shield's plan, as tentatively formulated, provided for a basic salary of $15,000 plus 5% of profits before taxes; these figures took account of his estimate that roughly 60% of his annual income would be absorbed by living expenses and tax payments. His plan also included an option to buy enough additional shares—either new shares to be issued by the company or outstanding shares held by his associate(s)—to raise Shields' holdings to 51% of all outstanding voting stock. It was clear, however, that the exact details of the final plan would have to be worked out with the other shareholder or shareholders before arrangements could be completed with Fordham.

As part of his program to assure an adequate supply of capital, Mr. Shields obtained an introduction, through a mutual friend, to one of the officers of a medium-sized bank in a nearby city. This officer indicated that it was the bank's normal policy to avoid substantial loans to new enterprises, but that exceptions were occasionally made where there was adequate security. Canning operations were important to the surrounding area, and he suggested that the bank might consider a secured loan to the new company if it looked promising on closer examination. From further conversation, Shields concluded that the best possibility would be a loan of up to 75% of the cost of finished goods inventory under a field warehousing arrangement. The cost of this kind of financing, including field warehousing expenses, which would not otherwise have been incurred, would be about 6% per annum. In addition to the bank loan, Shields also believed that it might be possible to stretch the payment period on cans to 60 days without creating serious credit problems.

In considering the preliminary calculations, Shields planned to make a detailed study of the year 1957–58 and to use this as a basis for approximating the necessary figures for the fiscal years 1958–59 through 1961–62. He had in mind a fiscal year beginning July 1.

Shields was aware that the next move was up to him. As he saw it, there were three obvious courses of action: (1) accept Fordham's proposal as presented; (2) reject the proposal and look for another business; (3) propose a compromise plan which would have a reasonable prospect of meeting the objectives of all interested parties.

Exhibit 1

Planned Sales Volume, 1957–62

1957–58.....................	$ 850,000
1958–59.....................	1,050,000
1959–60.....................	1,250,000
1960–61.....................	1,450,000
1961–62.....................	1,650,000

Exhibit 2

UPSTATE CANNING COMPANY, INC.

Income Statement for Year Ended Dec. 31, 1956
(dollar figures in thousands)

	Amount	Percent of Sales
Sales (net after returns and allowances).................	$850	100%
Less: Cost of goods sold		
Beginning inventory, Jan. 1, 1956................$257		
Add: Cost of goods manufactured................ 630		
$887		
Less: Ending inventory, December 31, 1956............ 254	633	74
Gross profit on sales....................................	$217	
Less: Selling and administrative expense		
Selling and delivery............................$ 64		8
Administrative and general (including salary to		
Fordham of $20,000)........................ 56	120	7
Profit before taxes.....................................	$ 97	
Less: Federal income tax*.............................	45	5
Net profit after taxes..................................	$ 52	6

* Federal income tax is computed on the basis of 30% of the first $25,000 of taxable income plus 52% of income in excess of $25,000. For companies of this size the tax is payable in the succeeding fiscal year as follows: 50% on the 15th day of the 3d month following the end of the tax year and 50% on the 15th day of the 6th month following.

Exhibit 3

UPSTATE CANNING COMPANY, INC.
Statement of Cost of Goods Manufactured for
Year Ended Dec. 31, 1956
(dollar figures in thousands)

	Amount		*Percent of Total Cost of Goods Manufactured*
Direct costs			
Vegetables and fruit..............................	$232		
Labor..	138		
Cans...	112		
Other ingredients................................	36	$518	82%
Variable overhead			
Fuel oil..	$ 17		
Electricity and water.............................	7		
Factory supplies..................................	5		
Payroll taxes.....................................	7		
Truck and auto expenses...........................	2		
Gas and oil.......................................	5	43	7
Fixed overhead			
Repairs and maintenance..........................	$ 18		
Insurance..	12		
Property taxes....................................	10		
Depreciation—plant and equipment..................	24		
Machinery rental.................................	5	$ 69	11
Total cost of goods manufactured.....................		$630	100%

Exhibit 4

Initial Proposal by Mr. Fordham for the Purchase of Certain Assets of
the Upstate Canning Company, Inc., by Mr. Shields and Associate(s)

1. New corporation to be formed with capitalization of $400,000 and with a capital structure as follows:
   a) $100,000 of common stock, $1 par, one vote per share, to be issued to Shields and associate(s) for $100,000 cash. Cash to be retained in new corporation.
   b) $300,000 of income bonds due on June 1, 1967; 3% interest per annum, payable semiannually (June 1 and December 1) if and when earned, cumulative, to be issued to Fordham in exchange for all plant and equipment of Upstate Canning Company, $50,000 of salable finished goods inventory, and the right to use the brand names of the Upstate Canning Company. (Prior to the exchange, the Upstate Canning Company will be liquidated and the assets distributed to Fordham as sole owner.)
2. Repayment provisions of income bonds:
   a) Company to repurchase $50,000 of income bonds on or before June 1, 1958.
   b) In succeeding years, company to repurchase income bonds equivalent in par value to 50% of the net profit after taxes, provided that the amount in any year will be no less than $15,000. The $15,000 will be due on June 1, and any balance within 30 days after the close of the fiscal year.
   c) Company to have the option of purchasing any amount of income bonds in excess of the minimum requirements according to a schedule of discounted prices as follows: in the first year at 80% of par, in the second year at 82½% of par, in the third year at 85% of par, and so on.
3. No fixed assets to be sold or encumbered in any way without the consent of the income bondholders.
4. Control of the company to be divided equally between the income bondholders and the common shareholders until the income bonds have been completely retired. Each group will elect two directors to a four-man board.
5. Fordham to act as chairman of the board and receive compensation for whatever time he spends on operating matters, beyond board meetings, on a basis to be determined in further negotiations.
6. Shields to act as president and general manager.
7. New company to be incorporated and assets of Upstate to be acquired on or about June 1, 1957. In the meantime, it is to be understood that Fordham and Shields will work together in negotiating contracts with farmers and arranging for an orderly transfer of ownership.

Head Ski Company, Inc.

In late February, 1960, Mr. Thomas Long, a partner in the Baltimore investment banking firm of Robert Garrett & Sons,[1] was nearing a decision on the price at which Robert Garrett would offer to underwrite and sell publicly a certain number of shares of the common stock of the Head Ski Company (HEAD). Since December, 1959, Mr. Long had been negotiating with Mr. Howard Head, president and chief stockholder of HEAD, in an attempt to arrive at the most suitable plan for the first public offering of that company's stock. The proposed offering would total approximately $280,000. Since the size of the offering was less than $300,000, HEAD would be exempt from a complete and costly Securities and Exchange Commission registration requirement. The company desired to raise approximately $162,000 in net proceeds (after underwriting commissions) to supplement existing working capital. In addition, certain selling stockholders wished to raise $90,000 in net proceeds through a secondary offering; thus, the proposed new issue would include both a corporate and a secondary offering of HEAD's common stock. It was Mr. Long's responsibility to determine the number of new shares to be issued by the company, the number of shares to be sold by the selling stockholders, and the price at which Robert Garrett & Sons would be willing to underwrite and offer to the public the Head company stock.

The Company

The Head Ski Company was founded in Baltimore, Maryland, in 1947 by Mr. Howard Head, then 32 years old, and was operated as an individual proprietorship until 1953. Between 1947 and 1950 Mr. Head concentrated on the development of a ski radically different from the

---

[1] In this case, names of officers of Robert Garrett & Sons have been disguised.

traditional hickory skis in wide use at that time. By 1950 the Head ski had been developed—a composite design of aluminum alloy, plastic, steel, and wood. Head skis were placed on the market during the 1950 winter skiing season. Their acceptance was immediate; sales rose from 300 pairs in the 1950–51 skiing season to 8,000 pairs in 1954–55 and 33,000 in 1958–59. During this period the demand for Head skis consistently outstripped the company's production capabilities. By 1959 Head skis had developed a wide reputation in the United States, Canada, and abroad as strong, lightweight, and easily maneuverable skis, suitable for experts as well as beginners. Mr. Head estimated that sales during the 1959–60 season would approximate 40,000 pairs of skis.

HEAD currently manufactured and sold two models—the "Standard," retailed at $89.50, and the "Vector," which sold for $107.50. The Vector model was introduced in 1959 for use by more experienced skiers. With the increased interest in racing arising out of the 1960 Winter Olympics, HEAD accelerated its work on the development of an international racing ski. Three Olympic skiers visited the company after the winter games to assist on this project and won several international races on Head skis late in the 1960 skiing season. Mr. Head thought that a product line which included a racing ski as well as the Standard and Vector models would enable Head to serve most classes of skiers.

Currently, the company employed 140 people in a new 27,000-square-foot plant constructed in 1959 near Baltimore; the new facilities would accommodate an annual production level of up to 160,000 pairs of skis. Although Mr. Head had designed the original Head ski, the company currently employed six engineers and technicians who assisted Mr. Head in the research and development of new products and in refinement of existing products. Sixty-five percent of present sales were made in the United States and Canada through 500 franchised dealers selected for their wide experience in the sale of skis and ski equipment. One distributor in Switzerland accounted for 30% of HEAD's total sales; this dealer had established subdistributorships for sales throughout Western Europe. The remaining 5% of the company's sales were to other countries outside of Europe and North America. HEAD rigidly enforced the retail prices on its Standard and Vector model skis in order to eliminate the possible unfavorable aspects of price cutting on its product line.

The competition for Head skis came from the manufacturers of traditional hickory skis and the makers of other metal-plastic composite skis. Traditional hickory skis had for many years enjoyed popularity in the inexpensive ski field and as special-purpose racing skis. The volume of sales achieved by HEAD, however, indicated that the Head design was continuing to overtake major parts of the hickory ski market. The success of the Head design had also promoted the establishment of a number of manufacturers of metal-plastic composite skis both in the United States and abroad. Mr. Head had patented certain aspects of the Head ski, but his patent protection could not prevent the development of slightly different competitive designs. This competition, however, had not prevented HEAD from selling all the skis it could produce prior to the move to its new plant in 1959. Mr. Head estimated that the second largest metal ski manufacturer produced approximately 20% of HEAD's volume and that the volume of all such manufacturers was approximately 50% of that of HEAD.

Financial History

The company was incorporated in 1953; at that time Mr. Head was issued 900 shares of cumulative preferred stock and 825 shares of common stock in exchange for assets valued at $90,825. Later in 1953 the requirements for additional working capital to finance expanding production levels resulted in the addition of $60,075 in equity funds through the private sale of 600 shares of cumulative preferred stock and 675 shares of common. In 1955, $7,500 was raised through the private sale of 50 shares of cumulative preferred stock and a like amount of common stock. These capital additions represented the extent of equity financing in HEAD's growth from 1947 to early 1960. As of April 25, 1959, HEAD's capital stock consisted of 1,550 shares of cumulative preferred and 1,550 shares of common stock. Changes in the company's capital accounts between April, 1959, and January, 1960, reflected the retirement of the preferred with accumulated dividends and the no par value common stock in exchange for new shares of $1.50 par value common stock (Exhibit 1). Currently, Mr. Head owned 57.6% of HEAD's outstanding common stock.

Other than by the additions to equity capital between 1953 and 1955, HEAD's growth had been financed entirely out of retained earnings and short-term bank borrowings. By the nature of its business, HEAD's sales and heavy shipments out of inventory began in August and September, reached peak levels in October and November, and declined gradually to the end of its shipping season in early March. In the past a substantial portion of the company's seasonal cash requirements had been provided through an unsecured line of credit from a Baltimore bank. Borrowing normally began in August, peaked in December, and declined thereafter to complete payout by the end of March. Because of its rapid growth in sales, HEAD's credit line had increased each year since 1953 and reached a high of $450,000 in December, 1959; at that time the company's accounts receivable totaled $690,000 and inventories $263,000.

With sales showing no tendency to level off, Mr. Head anticipated that the company's need for bank credit would continue to increase. Earnings retention during the next few years appeared insufficient to meet expected increases in working capital requirements, and he estimated that the company would require credit accommodations of between $700,000 and

$750,000 within the next 2 or 3 years. In early December, 1959, when HEAD's borrowing had reached $450,000, its bank had stated that that level represented the reasonable maximum credit the bank would be willing to extend on the basis of the company's net worth. HEAD's net worth was then slightly over $500,000, and the bank had been following a policy of placing an upper limit on the company's credit of slightly less than its net worth. At that time HEAD's banker suggested that additional equity capital would not only strengthen the company's working capital position but also provide a larger equity base, and one upon which the bank would be willing to increase its maximum credit line to the company.

The Proposed Common Stock Offering

It was on the basis of the preceding considerations tι at Mr. Head approached Mr. Long of Robert Garrett & Sons early in December, 1959. The two men quickly agreed that the sale of common stock would provide the most practical method of raising additional capital. The alternative of raising debt capital was clearly undesirable in view of HEAD's seasonal borrowing requirements and was considered inappropriate in view of the need for larger amounts of permanent capital. Mr. Head was also averse to selling preferred stock, since the company had just recently retired the 1,550 shares of preferred that had been outstanding since 1956. Mr. Head was receptive to Mr. Long's suggestion that a public offering of HEAD's stock would satisfy the objectives of raising new capital and would also facilitate, for the first time, a trading market in the company's stock. The two previous stock sales, in 1953 and 1955, had been private sales to a limited number of investors who had not traded actively in the stock. Between December, 1959, and February, 1960, negotiations between Mr. Head and Mr. Long were continued on the assumption that HEAD's new capital would be raised through a public stock offering underwritten by Robert Garrett & Sons.

A preliminary consideration in establishing the size of the proposed offering was the amount of capital that HEAD would need in order to raise its borrowing capacity from $450,000 to the $700,000–$750,000 range. The company's net worth of $534,000 on January 2, 1960 (Exhibits 2 and 5) reflected an addition to retained earnings from net profits since April 25, 1959, of $62,500. Mr. Head estimated that total net earnings for the year ended April 30, 1960, would approximate $75,000. This would be lower than the $95,000 earned in 1959, despite an increase in sales, because HEAD had experienced nonrecurring expenses associated with the move to its new plant and with the development of the Vector model ski. Since HEAD paid no dividends on its outstanding common stock, estimated earnings of $75,000 for fiscal 1960 would produce a net worth on April 30, 1960, of approximately $546,000 (exclusive of the proposed offering). In discussing these projections with the company's commercial bank, Mr. Head was informed that the addition of between $160,000 and $170,000 in equity funds would enable the bank to increase HEAD's line of credit to a maximum of $700,000.

Mr. Head and Mr. Long next discussed the possibility of including a secondary offering by the existing stockholders in the proposed new issue. This appeared to be an attractive opportunity in light of the relatively small amount of capital required by the company for corporate use. A secondary offering would increase the size of the issue and make more shares available for sale; it was hoped that such a plan would stimulate increased trading activity in the stock among a wider group of investors.

An important consideration relative to a combined corporate and secondary offering involved the expense to HEAD of registering a new issue with the SEC. Mr. Head desired to keep this expense as small as possible. Under the terms of the Securities Act of 1933, a public security offering was exempt from full registration requirements if the aggregate amount of the issue offered to the public did not exceed $300,000. Mr. Long estimated that such an exemption in the case of HEAD's proposed offering would save the company between $5,000 and $10,000. According to HEAD's legal advisers, an additional consideration under such a partially exempt registration was that a secondary offering would be limited to $100,000.

On the basis of the preceding factors, Mr. Head and Mr. Long decided to limit the combined corporate and secondary offering to less than $300,000. Tentative agreement was also reached on a 10% underwriting commission to Robert Garrett & Sons as compensation for accepting the responsibility of buying and then reselling HEAD's stock to security dealers and to the public. With these stipulations as guidelines, the two men were able to define within fairly narrow limits those portions of the proceeds from the proposed issue to be allocated to the company, to the selling shareholders, and to underwriting commissions. The size of the issue would be approximately $280,000; $162,000 would represent net proceeds to the company, $90,000 would go to the selling shareholders, and $28,000 would represent the 10% underwriting commission.

By late February, 1960, the remaining issue of major importance concerned Mr. Long's recommendation to Mr. Head as to the price at which Robert Garrett & Sons would offer to sell HEAD's stock to the public. The determination of the offering price would enable Mr. Long to calculate the number of new shares to be offered by the company and the shares to be sold by the selling shareholders in arriving at the total offering price of $280,000. Mr. Head had contacted the company's major stockholders, and each had agreed to sell the same percentage of his stock ownership as the percentages sold by the other members in arriving at the gross figure of $100,000 under the secondary offering. Conceivably, Mr. Head's ownership in the company could fall below 50% after the proposed new issue, depending upon the offering price of the stock. The offering price would, in turn, determine the number of shares to be sold by Mr. Head as part of the secondary offering and the dilution in his stock ownership resulting from the new corporate issue. Mr. Head did not consider such a possibility a major drawback to the proposed offering; he indicated that he would continue to receive the backing of the present stockholders and that the combined holdings of this group would represent well over 50% of the stock outstanding subsequent to the issue. (Exhibit 3 describes HEAD's common stock and the rights associated therein.)

An important factor relative to Mr. Long's pricing recommendation to Mr. Head concerned HEAD's past earnings record (Exhibits 4 and 5). Potential investors would, as one method of evaluation, concern themselves with the offering price of HEAD's stock in relation to the company's past earnings per share. In order accurately to reflect HEAD's earnings relative to the proposed offering, Mr. Long realized that the company's past per share earnings would have to be adjusted downward on the basis of the larger number of common stock shares that would be outstanding subsequent to the offering. An additional consideration concerned the company's dividend policy; Mr. Head desired to continue the policy of reinvesting all earnings in order to strengthen the company's working capital position in anticipation of increased sales and production levels. Mr. Long did not feel that such a policy would have an adverse effect upon the marketability of HEAD's stock, however, since the reinvestment of all earnings had become an accepted policy of many companies which were expanding rapidly and whose stock was actively traded.

To aid him in his pricing decision, Mr. Long had compiled comparative financial and descriptive data on selected companies in the recreational and amusement fields (Exhibits 6, 7, and 8). None of these companies concentrated solely on the manufacture and sale of skis since, to Mr. Long's knowledge, all such companies were either privately owned or were subsidiaries of larger, publicly owned corporations. Mr. Long had also compiled published statements regarding the future prospects for the amusement industry (Exhibit 9).

A corollary consideration in Mr. Long's pricing recommendation concerned the present conditions in the capital stock markets. The number of relatively small companies issuing stock publicly for the first time had shown a marked increase since the fall of 1959. According to many underwriting firms and security dealers, this had produced an oversupply of stocks in the new issues market, promoting lower prices for the stocks of many companies in relation to their past earnings records. On the other hand, Mr. Head anticipated that HEAD's new issue would generate considerably more investor appeal than the moderate interest expressed in some current new issues. He thought that many owners of Head skis would be potential buyers of HEAD's stock; this, coupled with the relatively small supply of stock anticipated in the proposed offering, would, he hoped, stimulate an active buying interest in the issue.

If Robert Garrett & Sons was accepted as HEAD's underwriter, it was Mr. Long's intention to distribute the stock to security dealers for resale to the public in those areas of the country where interest in skiing was most pronounced; specifically, he would allocate approximately half of the stock to dealers in California and Colorado and the remainder to dealers along the East Coast. The offering would be scheduled for early April, 1960, and would be traded in the over-the-counter market. Under the terms of the proposed underwriting agreement, the selling stockholders would be restricted from selling additional stock for a period of one year from the date of the issue. During that period, then, the trading activity in HEAD's stock would be confined to the number of shares offered through the underwriting.

Mr. Long's most important objective in his recommendation to Mr. Head was the determination of that price for HEAD's stock that would result in the highest proceeds and lowest dilution in earnings per share to the company and the selling shareholders, consistent with a price that would stimulate active and continued investor appeal. He would consider the issue successful if the stock rose to a premium of one or two points above the offering price in the trading market after the offering. If HEAD continued to grow at its present rate, the company might wish to return to the equity markets in the future; a successful offering at this time would certainly make it easier for HEAD to consider future public offerings of common stock.

Exhibit 1

HEAD SKI COMPANY, INC.
Net Worth and Capital Stock Outstanding
April 30, 1955—January 2, 1960

	4/30/55	4/30/56	4/30/57	4/26/58	4/25/59	6/10/59	1/2/60
Net worth:							
Common stock	$ 1,500	$ 4,000	$ 4,000	$ 4,000	$ 4,000	$158,400	$167,400
Preferred stock—5% cumulative	149,400	154,400	154,400	154,400	154,400	...	...
Surplus	63,051	154,075	135,077	207,841	302,731	n.a.	366,340
Total	$213,951	$312,475	$293,477	$366,241	$461,131	n.a.	$533,740
Preferred stock dividends earned but not declared	$ 15,375	$ 23,062	$ 30,812	$ 38,562	$ 46,312	...	...
Capital stock outstanding (number of shares):							
No par value common	1,500	1,550	1,550	1,550	1,550	...	...
No par value new common	...	...	...	...	...	74,400*	...
$1.50 par value common	...	...	...	...	...	...	111,600†
No par value preferred	1,500	1,550	1,550	1,550	1,550	...	...

* 74,400 no par shares new common stock outstanding following issuance of (1) 13 shares for each share of preferred stock and accumulated dividend arrearages thereon and (2) 35 shares for each share of old common stock.

† 111,600 shares of $1.50 par value common stock outstanding following issuance of 1½ shares of $1.50 par value common for each one share of nopar value common.

Exhibit 2

HEAD SKI COMPANY, INC.

Balance Sheet* as at January 2, 1960

(unaudited)

ASSETS

Current assets:

Cash in bank and on hand	$ 64,107	
Trade acceptances	17,054	
Accounts receivable (net)	543,315	
Inventories (see Note A)†	316,251	
Prepaid expenses and other	$ 33,341	
Total current assets		$ 974,068

Fixed assets:

Machinery and equipment	$211,477		
Less: Depreciation to date	100,847	$110,630	
Other	$ 40,472		
Less: Depreciation and amortization to date	16,195	24,277	
Building	$261,476		
Less: Depreciation to date	10,644	250,832	
Total fixed assets			385,739

Other assets:

Cash surrender value—life insurance (see Note B)†	$ 36,918	
Miscellaneous	26,306	63,223
Total assets		$1,423,031

LIABILITIES AND NET WORTH

Current liabilities:

Vouchers payable	$206,839		
Notes payable	300,000		
Mortgage payable—current portion (see Note C)†	8,820		
Customers' advance payments	14,153		
Estimated federal and state income taxes payable	63,388		
Other	94,911		
Total current liabilities			$ 688,111

Long-term debt:

Mortgage payable—noncurrent portion (see Note C)†		201,180
Total liabilities		$ 889,291

Commitments and contingent liabilities (see Note D)†

Net worth:

Common stock, $1.50 par value, authorized, 200,000 shares; issued and outstanding, 111,600 shares	$167,400	
Retained earnings	366,340	
Total net worth		533,740
Total liabilities and net worth		$1,423,031

* Figures are rounded and therefore may not add to totals.
† The notes to financial statements (see Exhibit 5) are an integral part hereof.

Exhibit 3

HEAD SKI COMPANY, INC.

Description of Common Stock, as of February, 1960

Prior to June 10, 1959, the authorized capital stock of the company consisted of 1,550 shares without par value of preferred stock and 1,550 shares without par value of common stock, all of which shares were issued and outstanding. By amendments of the charter and stock splits since that date, these shares have all been reclassified into the now outstanding 111,600 shares of the par value of $1.50 per share of common stock of the company; and the authorized capital stock has been increased to the present 200,000 shares of common stock, all of one class.

All shareholders will participate equally, share for share, in any dividends which may be paid or on liquidation. On all matters of voting, each shareholder is entitled to one vote for each share of stock standing in his name. Cumulative voting for directors is not provided for by the charter or by the bylaws, and the shares have noncumulative voting rights; that is, the holders of more than 50% of the shares voting for the election of directors can elect 100% of the directors if they choose to do so; and in such event, the holders of the remaining less than 50% of the shares voting for the election of directors will not be able to elect any person or persons to the board of directors. The holders of the common stock have under the charter of the company no pre-emptive rights.

Exhibit 4

HEAD SKI COMPANY, INC.

Statements of Income for the Periods Indicated Below
(unaudited)

	Fiscal Year Ended April 30, 1957	52 Weeks Ended April 26, 1958	52 Weeks Ended April 25, 1959	36 Weeks Ended January 2, 1960
Sales	$1,076,652	$1,315,063	$1,613,872	$1,514,181
Less: Cost of sales	800,190	919,762	1,122,578	1,085,095
Gross profit	$ 276,462	$ 395,301	$ 491,294	$ 429,086
Less: Expenses:				
Selling expenses	$ 76,848	$ 101,187	$ 109,305	$ 97,800
Administrative expenses	77,809	92,751	107,405	91,614
Corporate expenses	26,951	39,987	77,459	113,870
Total expenses	$ 181,608	$ 233,926	$ 294,168	$ 303,284
Net profit before income taxes	$ 94,854	$ 161,375	$ 197,126	$ 125,802
Federal and state income taxes	49,988	88,611	102,236	63,388
Net profit after income taxes (see Note E)*	$ 44,866	$ 72,764	$ 94,890	$ 62,414
Earnings per share (based upon 111,600 shares outstanding on January 2, 1960, giving retroactive effect to recapitalization)	$0.40	$0.65	$0.85	$0.56

* The notes to financial statements (see Exhibit 5) are an integral part hereof.

Exhibit 5

HEAD SKI COMPANY, INC.
Notes to Financial Statements

Note A—Inventories

Inventories are valued at lower of cost or market and are detailed below:

Finished goods	$ 75,985
Goods in process	98,259
Raw materials	125,127
Manufacturing supplies	16,880
Total	$316,251

Note B—Cash Surrender Value of Life Insurance

The company is the owner and beneficiary of life insurance contracts in the face amount of $500,000 on the life of its president, Howard Head. The cash surrender value of these policies was $36,918 on January 2, 1960.

Insurance owned by the corporation on the life of its president, with maturity value of $50,000 and cash surrender value of $3,463 at January 2, 1960, has been pledged as additional security for the mortgage loan payable to Loyola Federal Savings and Loan Association.

Insurance owned by the corporation on the life of its president, with maturity values of $400,000 and aggregate cash surrender value of $28,581 at January 2, 1960, is held by a trustee pursuant to the terms of a stock redemption contract between the company and its president. The company is permitted by this contract to exercise various rights with respect to such policies, including the right to borrow and the right to change beneficiaries. The company is obligated to purchase only as much of the president's stock as the insurance proceeds can buy. Shares which are subject to the agreement are in the custody of the trustee. The president has limited rights to withdraw some of his shares from the trustee, thereby removing these shares from the effects of the contract.

Note C—Mortgage Payable

The company plant at Timonium, Maryland, and a life insurance contract owned by the company are pledged to secure a 6% mortgage loan payable in monthly instalments to Loyola Federal Savings and Loan Association. The last monthly payment will be due on December 1, 1974.

Note D—Long-Term Leases, Commitments, Contingent Liabilities

The company, prior to moving into its present facilities, occupied premises at 1507 Roland Heights Avenue in Baltimore under a lease which will expire on March 31, 1964. The rental under such lease is $7,520 per annum. The company has subleased said premises for the remaining term of the lease at an annual rental of $7,800.

Land upon which the company has constructed its plant is leased for twenty years beginning on September 1, 1959, at an annual rental of $7,200, subject to reduction until certain utilities and grading have been supplied by the lessor, and subject to an increase of $1,152 per acre in the annual rental to the extent that a portion of the leased tract, consisting of 1.562 acres and reserved for storm drainage, is made available for company use. The lease gives the company options to renew for three successive 20-year terms followed by a final term of 19 years. In addition, the company has the option to purchase the land at any time during the last 15 years of the initial 20-year term of the lease at a price of $25,000 per acre of land not reserved for Baltimore County storm drainage less the sum of $12,500. If the present reservation for storm drainage purposes is not changed, upon exercise of the purchase option the company would acquire 6.25 acres, not subject to storm drainage use, for a price of $143,750.

Skis sold by the company bear a guaranty for one year from the retailer's sales date. The financial statements make no provision for the contingent liabilities created by such guaranties, since the extent of such liability is indeterminate and, in the opinion of the company's officials, based upon past experience, is not considered material.

Exhibit 5 (Continued)

Note E—Statements of Income and Retained Earnings

Examination indicates a correction is needed to the company's opening inventory for the 36-week fiscal period ended January 2, 1960, and here reported. Inventories as of April 25, 1959, were undervalued by $38,850. As a consequence, net profit after income taxes for the fiscal period April 26, 1959, to January 2, 1960, includes $11,888 which was earned prior to April 26, 1959, and which is computed as follows:

Increase in current-period income because of inventory undervaluation...	$38,850
Less: Increase in current-period profit sharing and incentive bonus expenses as result of above increase.................................	12,781
Increase in net profits before income taxes....................	$26,069
Less: Income taxes on above income.......................	14,182
Increase in net profits after taxes..................................	$11,888

During the fiscal period April 26, 1959, to January 2, 1960, depreciation charges amounted to $47,117, and the following extraordinary expenses were incurred and charged off:

Expenses of moving plant from Baltimore to Timonium (included in corporate expenses)..	$20,896
Contribution to Winter Olympic Ski Team (included in administrative expenses)...	2,500
Total..	$23,396

Testing and research expenses are included in corporate expenses. For the 52 weeks ended April 25, 1959, these expenses amounted to $28,417. Because of increased experimentation, research, and product development, testing and research expenses aggregated $36,147 for the 36 weeks ended January 2, 1960.

Because of increased borrowings, including interest paid on construction loans, interest expense for the 36 weeks ended January 2, 1960, was $19,471, as compared with $11,068 for the 52 weeks ended April 25, 1959. Interest expense is included in corporate expenses.

Exhibit 6

Comparative Stock Pricing and Financial Data on Selected Companies (February 26, 1960)

	Head Ski Company, Inc.	MCA, Inc.	Shake-speare Company	Higbie Mfg. Company	A. G. Spalding & Bros., Inc.	Milton Bradley Co.	Murray Ohio Mfg. Co.	U.S. Play-ing Card Co.	Brunswick-Balke-Collender Co.	Outboard Marine Corp.
Fiscal year end	4/25	12/31	7/31	7/31	7/31	12/31	12/31	12/31	12/31	9/30
Latest complete year	4/25/59	12/31/59	7/31/59	7/31/59	7/31/59	12/31/59	12/31/59	12/31/59	12/31/59	9/30/59
Sales (000)	$ 1,614	$ 56,929	$ 14,954	$ 7,748	$ 14,954	$ 12,336	$ 33,178	$ 21,547	$ 275,100	$ 171,569
Net income (000)	95	5,186	1,378	593	1,378	746	1,243	2,204	26,859	13,785
Net income/sales	5.9%	9.1%	9.2%	7.7%	9.2%	6.1%	3.8%	10.2%	9.7%	8.0%
Net income/net worth	20.5%	17.8%	10.6%	11.2%	8.2%	18.6%	10.0%	15.6%	26.6%	16.8%
Earnings per share:										
1959	$0.85	$1.28	$2.85	$1.64	$1.35	$6.87	$4.23	$1.43	$3.42	$1.76
1958	0.65	1.18	2.73	0.74	1.21	3.02	2.74	1.40	2.13	1.16
1957	0.40	0.12	2.59	0.98	0.79	2.38	2.12	1.22	1.38	1.67
1956	0.82	0.74	2.00	0.96	1.32	2.60	2.28	1.18	0.77	1.69
1955	0.22	0.61	2.38	1.10	1.05	2.06	3.42	1.10	0.32	1.23
1959 versus 5-year average	143%	130%	114%	151%	118%	202%	142%	113%	213%	117%
Market priceᵖ	...	25	28½ᵇ	15¾	23⅝	57ᵇ	31½	32⅜	58⅝	34¼
Price/earnings:										
1959	...	19.5	10.0	9.6	17.5	8.3	7.5	22.6	17.2	19.5
5-year average, 1955–59	...	25.4	11.4	14.4	20.6	16.8	10.6	25.6	36.5	22.6
Current cash dividend rate	...	$ 0.00	$ 1.80	$ 0.60	$ 0.00	$ 0.95	$ 2.00	$ 1.25	$ 0.53	$ 0.80
Current cash yield	...	0.00%	6.3%	3.8%	0.00%	1.7%	6.3%	3.9%	0.9%	2.3%
Market price/net tangible assets per share (Common)ⁿ	...	366%	128%ᵉ	168%ᵉ	118%ᵉ	167%	174%	353%	460%	330%
Common shares:										
Total outstanding	111,600	3,996,000	483,000	363,000	855,000	106,000	294,000	1,540,000	7,823,000	7,854,000
Recent offering	...	400,000	...	...	...	...	...	...	...	...
Date of offering	...	10/8/59	...	...	...	...	...	...	...	...
Offering price	...	$17.50	...	...	...	...	...	...	...	...
Traded	...	NYSE	O.C.	ASE	NYSE	O.C.	ASE	NYSE	NYSE	NYSE

p = Closing quotations February 26, 1960.
b = Bid prices.
n = Based on capitalization 12/31/59.
e = Estimated.

Exhibit 7

Comparative Financial Data on Selected Companies

(dollar figures in thousands)

Balance Sheet Analysis	Head Ski Company, Inc. 1/2/60	MCA, Inc. 12/31/59	Shakespeare Co. 7/31/59	Outboard Marine Corp. 9/30/59
ASSETS				
Cash	$ 64	$ 2,753	$ 2,579	$ 15,518
Marketable securities	......	2,407	2,384	5,424
Accounts receivable (net)	539	4,592	1,642	14,049
Inventories	316	18,786	3,280	37,468
Other current assets	55	354	128	......
Total current assets	$ 974	$28,892	$10,013	$ 72,459
Land, buildings, etc.	$ 514	$17,537	$ 5,160	$ 62,804
Depreciation	128	3,122	2,278	22,394
Net property	$ 386	$14,415	$ 2,882	$ 40,410
Unamortized assets	......	25,093	......	......
Other assets	63	2,123	106	6,432
Total assets	$1,423	$70,523	$13,001	$119,301
LIABILITIES AND CAPITAL				
Notes payable	$ 300	$ 3,000	$	$ 3,500
Accounts payable	207	6,915	428	6,672
Federal income taxes	63	4,020	1,203	998
Accruals and other	118	4,241	669	5,899
Total current liabilities	$ 688	$18,176	$ 2,300	$ 17,069
Contracts or notes payable, other long-term debt	$ 201	$23,232	$	$ 20,779
Preferred stock	......	1,799	......	......
Common stock	167	7,476	2,417	2,356
Retained earnings and surplus	367	19,840	8,284	79,097
Total liabilities and capital	$1,423	$70,523	$13,001	$119,301

Head Ski Company, Inc.

Year	Sales	Increase over Previous Year
1959	$1,614	23%
1958	1,315	22%
1957	1,077	28%
1956	839	294%
1955	213	.....

Year	Net Earnings	Increase over Previous Year
1959	$ 95	30%
1958	73	62%
1957	45	(51%)
1956	91	264%
1955	25	.....

MCA, Inc.

Year	Sales	Increase over Previous Year
1959	$56,929	20%
1958	47,473	22%
1957	38,878	24%
1956	31,392	31%
1955	23,895	.....

Year	Net Earnings	Increase over Previous Year
1959	$ 5,106	20%
1958	4,328	5%
1957	4,121	49%
1956	2,758	21%
1955	2,286	.....

Shakespeare Co.

Year	Sales	Increase over Previous Year
1959	$14,954	7%
1958	13,962	(1%)
1957	14,099	13%
1956	12,456	3%
1955	12,112	.....

Year	Net Earnings	Increase over Previous Year
1959	$ 1,378	4%
1958	1,320	5%
1957	1,253	29%
1956	969	(16%)
1955	1,154	.....

Outboard Marine Corp.

Year	Sales	Increase over Previous Year
1959	$171,569	8%
1958	158,713	6%
1957	150,476	23%
1956	122,045	42%
1955	85,856	.....

Year	Net Earnings	Increase over Previous Year
1959	$ 13,785	52%
1958	9,095	(30%)
1957	13,071	8%
1956	12,098	54%
1955	7,864	.....

Exhibit 8

HEAD SKI COMPANY, INC.

Descriptions of Companies Listed in Exhibits 6 and 7

Music Corporation of America, Inc. (MCA), produced television film series and distributed these films throughout the United States and to foreign countries. The company also acted as agents for artists in the entertainment business. On October 8, 1959, MCA's common stock became publicly owned through an issue of 400,000 shares at $17.50 a share.

The *Shakespeare Company* manufactured and sold steel tubing and fishing reels. Over 50% of the company's operations were devoted to the manufacture of small-diameter welded steel tubing, of which 80% was sold to the automobile industry. Fishing reels represented between 35% and 40% of the company's business.

A. G. Spalding & Bros., Inc., was a well-known manufacturer of a varied line of sporting goods.

Milton Bradley Company manufactured school materials, display booths, and a varied line of additional amusements, toys, and novelties.

The *Murray Ohio Manufacturing Company* manufactured a complete line of juvenile automobiles, bicycles, wagons, scooters, etc. In 1957, over 45% of the company's sales were to Sears Roebuck & Co.

U.S. Playing Card Company manufactured and sold all types of playing cards.

Brunswick-Balke-Collender Company was the largest manufacturer of bowling equipment in the United States. The company also manufactured and sold school furniture, sports equipment, nonpharmaceutical laboratory supplies, and various defense products.

Outboard Marine Corporation was the largest domestic producer of outboard motors. The company also manufactured power lawn mowers, chain saws, and similar types of equipment.

Exhibit 9

Selected Comments on the Amusement Industry*

All indications point to the greatest boom in the history of the amusement industry over the next decade and longer. . . .

Factors are:

. . . current projections for a 41% rise in the number of persons between 15 and 29 years old in the 1960–70 period. . . .

. . . the substantial increase in consumer income anticipated in coming years. . . .

. . . the growing amount of leisure time enjoyed by the average working man.

Current indications suggest the largest relative gains in sales and earnings will be experienced by those segments of the entertainment industry in which individuals are involved as participants rather than as spectators. . . .

. . . Total spending on sporting goods in 1959 is expected to rise roughly 8% to a new peak of $1.97 billion. . . .

* Standard and Poor's Corporation, *Industry Surveys: Amusements*, May 21, 1959.

Wizard Corporation

On December 27, 1961, David Prescott, president of Cutter & Dunlop, Inc., of Lynn, Massachusetts, was negotiating to acquire the assets and business of the Wizard Corporation of Framingham, Massachusetts. James Gruber, president and sole owner of the Wizard Corporation, had found Mr. Prescott's first three offers unacceptable, and negotiations had reached the point where Mr. Prescott was certain that his next bid must be final. He was also aware that any commitment resulting from the negotiations would have to be approved by both the board of directors of Cutter & Dunlop and two thirds of its stockholders.

History of Cutter & Dunlop

Cutter & Dunlop was incorporated on March 27, 1951, to succeed a partnership formed in 1946 by James Cutter and Foster Dunlop. The company designed, developed, and manufactured measuring instruments and miniature assembly lighting and control equipment. Virtually all of Cutter & Dunlop's products were proprietary items developed internally. Profits were volatile, and sizable losses were recorded in 1955 and 1957. In early 1958 David Prescott, production manager of Inca Camera Corporation, purchased Mr. Cutter's interest and became executive vice president of Cutter & Dunlop. He was elected president the following year. For the year ended December 31, 1960, Mr. Prescott received a salary of $15,000, and Mr. Dunlop received $10,000. Otherwise, no employee of the company received remuneration in excess of four figures. Under Mr. Prescott's leadership Cutter & Dunlop completely revised operating policies and procedures. In addition to a cost-cutting program, the president started a research and development program aimed at servicing the needs of the electronics and miniaturization industries. By the end of 1960, despite heavy research expenditures, the company had

893

achieved record-breaking sales and profits. Exhibits 1 and 2 present balance sheets and profit and loss statements for the years 1958–60.

Much of this success was attributable to customer acceptance of the company's new line of optical comparators and projectors. These products were measuring devices which, with the use of light and optics, permitted gauging to very close tolerances. They were also used as quality control instruments, as devices for assembling intricate and minute parts, and as a means of monitoring parts in process. An optical comparator might be described as a microscope in which a magnified image of a part is reflected on a screen marked with a precise measuring scale to test the conformity of the manufactured product to established standards.

As an adjunct to precision measuring and control equipment, Cutter & Dunlop had also developed optically ground and polished lenses coupled with high-intensity fluorescent lamps to provide a wide, uniformly illuminated magnified area for examination of precision parts. Like the optical comparators and projectors, these products were designed for industries requiring a concentrated source of localized lighting.

The company's largest customers, for all products, were major optical manufacturers and missile and electronics firms. Cutter & Dunlop's sales for the year ended December 31, 1960, were divided among its products as follows:

Comparators and projectors............	35.8%
Lighting aids........................	63.9
Special designing and consulting........	0.3
	100.0%

Management believed that most of the company's future growth would come from expansion of its interest in optical instrumentation rather than from lighting aids.

In Mr. Prescott's opinion, the continued success of Cutter & Dunlop depended upon the company's ability to strengthen its marketing facilities in order to capitalize fully on several new products: a large-screen machine tool projector, an audiovisual projector, and a projection microscope. The markets for these products were considered by management to be almost insatiable.

The company had no collective bargaining agreements with any union and had never had a strike. Production facilities, leased for $3,600 a year, consisted of 12,000 square feet of space on the first, third, and part of the fourth floors of a factory building located in Lynn, Massachusetts. Housed in these quarters Cutter & Dunlop had a well-equipped general machine shop capable of producing most of its products. The remainder were subcontracted to several local job shops.

In June, 1961, Cutter & Dunlop successfully sold 100,000 shares of common stock to the public at $3 a share through Crane Bros., an investment banking firm of New York. The issue was quickly oversubscribed, and trading opened at $6 a share. After underwriting commissions and expenses, the company netted $242,000. As additional compensation, Cutter & Dunlop granted the underwriter a 5-year option to purchase 20,000 shares of the company's common stock at $3 a share, exercisable 13 months after the date of the public offering.

A monthly history of the market price of Cutter & Dunlop stock appears below:

Bid and Asked Prices of Cutter & Dunlop Shares
by Month for the Period June to December 15, 1961

Month	Bid	Asked
June	6	7
July	8½	9
August	7	7½
September	6½	7
October	5½	6
November	6	6½
December 15	6	6½

Following the public offering, Cutter & Dunlop's shareholder distribution appeared as follows:

	Number of Shares	Percentage of Total
David Prescott	43,700	16.7%
Nancy Prescott	85,100	32.6
Foster Dunlop	27,600	10.6
Employees of company	4,600	1.8
Public investors	100,000	38.3
Total shares issued and outstanding	261,000	100.0%
Total shares authorized	300,000	

In addition to Mr. Prescott, the board of directors of Cutter & Dunlop included Peter Mann, a senior partner of the law firm of Wellington, Creme, and Mann, counsel for the company; Clarence Bedash, treasurer of the company; and Basil Haliday, a friend of Mr. Prescott's and sales manager of Filter Corporation of America. Mr. Mann and Mr. Bedash each held 200 shares of Cutter & Dunlop stock. Mr. Haliday was not a stockholder.

Proposal of Merger

In early November, Roger Crane, a partner of Crane Bros., telephoned to Frederick Ingalls, a prominent tax consultant in the Boston area. Over the past several years Mr. Ingalls had built a reputation for his ability in finding and negotiating mergers and acquisitions for several small "scientific" companies. Mr. Crane explained that he was very anxious to have Cutter & Dunlop acquire a small but profitable optical company or a manufacturer of miniature electronic components. Mr. Prescott had mentioned, on his previous visit to Crane Bros. in New York, that his company would be interested in acquiring a firm in one of these two industries. The banker continued by saying that heavy start-up production costs and promotional expenses related to new products, plus a poor year for the economy in general, had prevented Cutter & Dunlop from realizing its profit forecasts. Even though 1961 would probably be a record sales year, the currently high market price of the shares indicated that investors were expecting a more favorable profit report for the current period than would actually appear. A merger at this time would be considered a constructive step in offsetting the interruption of the company's growth trend. A flood of new orders suggested that the company would meet its 1962 sales and profit goals and might even exceed forecasts.

Mr. Ingalls replied, "At the moment I have nothing in mind, but I will talk to David Prescott personally if an attractive situation comes up." The following week Mr. Ingalls telephoned Mr. Prescott and briefly described the Wizard Corporation, the owner of which wanted to merge with an aggressive, publicly held company. When Mr. Prescott expressed an interest in the situation, Mr. Ingalls offered to arrange a meeting between the management of both organizations. If progress was made, he would assist in the negotiations and act as an intermediary between the two parties. In return, he expected a customary finder's fee of 5%, in cash or stock, whichever was the vehicle used by the participants to consummate the merger. In the event that the proposed merger fell through, Mr. Ingalls did not expect any compensation for the time or effort expended in bringing the parties together. Mr. Prescott agreed to these terms.

History of the Wizard Corporation

The Wizard Corporation was founded as a sole proprietorship by James Gruber in 1955 and was incorporated in 1959. The company designed and manufactured precision components of a miniature nature for the electronics, missile, electrical appliance, and related industries. Before forming his own business, Mr. Gruber had been production manager of the Munster Watch Company. He had been associated with this organization for over 20 years, working up from skilled machinist to production manager with a yearly salary of $18,000. Nevertheless, the desire to be his own boss led Mr. Gruber to establish a company engaged in the fabrication of small metal products. The initial capital he ventured was $40,000, a substantial part of his life savings.

The Wizard Corporation quickly made substantial progress in penetrating the precision parts market, which was growing rapidly in eastern Massachusetts. Sales in 1959 and 1960 were $127,000 and $362,000, respectively. Profits were difficult to judge because the business filed its corporate tax returns on a cash rather than an accrual basis.

The Wizard Corporation employed 40 full-time people, of whom 32 were skilled machinists and 8 were supervisory and clerical help. Over the past year and a half the company had been running two 10-hour shifts. Mr. Gruber expected to continue this high rate of production well through 1962.

Mr. Gruber commented, "I believe our growth rate over the next 5 years will level off to 10% a year. Profit margins will remain at their current levels. For 1962 we have conservatively estimated sales at $450,000. Since I bring in 95% of the business, selling expenses are kept at a minimum. We have sales representatives on a commission basis, but they are ineffective. The secret of our success is that we hold overhead down. Wizard's market is very competitive but, because of our skill in manufacturing, we can do jobs others turn down. I have the best machinists in the country and pay top wages."

The Wizard Corporation was nonunion and had never had a strike. The company rented 15,000 square feet of a factory building on a long-term lease for $800 a month. There was adequate space for expansion.

Merger Negotiations

A history follows of the events leading up to the final merger talks between the two companies:

November 17—Mr. Prescott, Mr. Roger Crane, and Mr. Ingalls visited the Wizard Corporation. Mr. Gruber escorted the group around the plant and showed them some finished products. He told them that the company was currently highly profitable, still expanding, and in a strong competitive position as a result of its unique production ability.

November 21—Mr. Gruber visited Cutter & Dunlop. Mr. Prescott carefully showed him the plant and demonstrated several of the company's optical instruments. He also detailed his plans for expansion over the next 5 years.

December 3—Mr. Ingalls met with Mr. Prescott. The finder indicated that Mr. Gruber had checked references on Cutter & Dunlop and was pleased with the results. Mr. Prescott had also investigated the Wizard Corporation and found that Mr. Gruber had the reputation of being a tough competitor, a top salesman, and well liked by the trade. Mr. Prescott said, "Arrange another meeting for the day after tomorrow and we will talk numbers."

December 5—Mr. Prescott and Mr. Morganstern, Cutter & Dunlop's accountant, handed Mr. Gruber the financial statements and estimates appearing in Exhibits 1, 2, and 3. Mr. Morganstern said that the Wizard Corporation's statements, being prepared on a cash and not an accrual basis, were unacceptable for valuation purposes in their existing form. Although Mr. Prescott desired financial statements for the Wizard Corporation since its incorporation, the costs of reauditing the books was considered by Mr. Gruber prohibitive. After a 2-hour bargaining session Mr. Gruber agreed to let Mr. Morganstern examine the company's statements for the last year and draw up a 1961 balance sheet and profit and loss statement. The cost of these financial statements to the Wizard Corporation was estimated at $2,500. Mr. Prescott expected that he could accurately value the Wizard Corporation from the financial data prepared by the accountant.

Mr. Prescott also said, "If we can agree on valuation, I should be interested in acquiring all the stock of the Wizard Corporation. We should then operate the company as a division of Cutter & Dunlop. The staff and management would be completely retained." Mr. Gruber nodded in approval and added, "What I really want is to be left alone to run my own show."

December 17—Mr. Morganstern delivered the financial and operating statements appearing in Exhibits 4, 5, and 6. The accountant pointed out that on Mr. Gruber's sales estimate for 1962 of $450,000, net profits on an accrual basis should reach $50,000. Mr. Gruber later confirmed this figure. After carefully examining the statements, Mr. Prescott mapped out in detail the advantages of the merger.

1. The Wizard Corporation had the production "know-how" and capacity, without reducing external sales, to manufacture the precision parts that Cutter & Dunlop was now purchasing from outside sources for use in its optical comparators. Mr. Prescott estimated that he could give the Wizard Corporation $100,000 worth of business in 1962.
2. The Wizard Corporation had access to an empty building that provided more than adequate physical room for expansion of both companies. Cutter & Dunlop could avoid moving its complete plant and facilities to larger quarters, since this additional space adjoining the Wizard plant could be rented for the manufacture of several of Cutter & Dunlop's products.
3. The Wizard Corporation had certain machinery and equipment costing about $50,000, which Cutter & Dunlop needed in order to manufacture precision parts for its new line of audiovisual projectors.
4. Since both companies called upon many of the same customers, some sales economy might result.
5. And, lastly, several of the Wizard Corporation's customers were potential customers of Cutter & Dunlop. Mr. Prescott believed that his sales force might be in a stronger selling position if the company was already a supplier. Sharing knowledge of potential customers could prove valuable in increasing sales of both companies.

In Mr. Prescott's opinion, the only disadvantage of the proposed merger was the possibility that the two managements might not function together harmoniously. He thought, "Of course, only time will tell. We are basically a scientific organization, working hand in hand with young men of proved managerial capacity. Our staff is proud of its educational and engineering accomplishments. Jim Gruber's operation, when you trim the fat off, is a highly efficient job shop with no really sophisticated engineering talents. Some friction could develop even if Wizard remains autonomous. In the last analysis, however, Jim Gruber's influence will be in direct proportion to the terms of the deal."

Mr. Prescott next telephoned Mr. Ingalls to inquire whether he knew how much money and what kind of arrangement Mr. Gruber desired. The finder replied that the Wizard Corporation could be acquired for 125,000 shares of Cutter & Dunlop stock. Since the market that morning quoted the shares at 6 bid, 6½ asked, Mr. Prescott deduced that Mr. Gruber valued his company at about $750,000.

December 18—Mr. Prescott decided to start negotiations by offering exactly half of the number of shares the finder indicated would be acceptable to Mr. Gruber. He therefore formally offered 62,500 shares of Cutter & Dunlop stock for all the stock of the Wizard Corporation.

December 19—Mr. Gruber turned the offer down. To protect his interests he asked for 128,000 shares, the same number as those held by the Prescott family.

December 20—Mr. Prescott talked with Roger Crane, who strongly urged that Cutter & Dunlop acquire the Wizard Corporation. He further suggested that Mr. Prescott offer a cash deal, since stock might dilute earnings per share.

December 22—Mr. Prescott offered Mr. Gruber $250,000 in cash, believing that if it was accepted, the cash from the combined companies plus a bank loan would be adequate to meet the purchase price. Mr. Gruber refused to consider a straight cash transaction because of the capital gains tax, which would have to be paid immediately.

Mr. Prescott again conferred with Roger Crane, who suggested that, both for the sake of control and to avoid dilution, Cutter & Dunlop offer Mr. Gruber cash and stock over a period of years. This type of payment would lessen taxes.

December 23—Mr. Prescott offered Mr. Gruber a combination of stock and cash: each year over the next 5 years Mr. Gruber would receive 4,000 shares of Cutter & Dunlop stock and $60,000 cash.

December 24—Mr. Gruber refused the last offer and indicated that unless Mr. Prescott took a more realistic view of the value of his company, negotiations would end at once. During this talk with Mr. Gruber, Mr. Prescott realized that one area of substantial difference between them was the determination of real earnings. Mr. Prescott, thinking in terms of the profit and loss statements, had decided upon $40,000 net earnings as the point of valuation. Mr. Gruber, on the other hand, believed that $100,000 was a truer figure, contending that depreciation and his own salary of $39,600 should also be included in arriving at the profitability of the company. When Mr. Prescott inquired whether Mr. Gruber expected to draw this salary in the event of a merger, he said, "I will sign a 5-year employment contract at a fixed salary of $29,000. Also, even though our fixed equipment is in excellent condition, it has been largely written down. A careful examination of the machinery should indicate that it could not be replaced for less than $100,000."

December 26—Mr. Prescott and Mr. Ingalls met in conference. When asked about the bargaining strengths of the two parties, the finder remarked, "The Wizard Corporation has been offered merger opportunities by two medium-size electronics companies. Although Mr. Gruber has tentatively turned both offers down, they indicate that he is placing an attractive package on the market. Last month he talked with a local underwriter, Wieler & Co., which valued the company at $1.5 million. Harold Wieler wished to sell one third of the company to the public for $500,000 on a best-efforts basis to net the Wizard Corporation $400,000. Mr. Gruber felt that the commissions were exorbitant and also questioned the ability of the investment banker to sell the issue. He said further that if he were to merge or to 'go public,' he wanted to do so immediately. Considering the backlog of registration statements filed with the Securities and Exchange Commission, it is likely that a public offering by the Wizard Corporation may be held up by red tape for a period of 6 months."

Mr. Ingalls appeared unwilling to reveal any additional information about the alternative offers to the Wizard Corporation, and Mr. Prescott was unable to learn any more through other means.

"Looking at your side of the coin," Mr. Ingalls continued, "Cutter & Dunlop's strength is that you are a growth company in a glamorous industry. I have never heard of another company of your size that can boast of such management and scientific abilities as Cutter & Dunlop employs. Jim knows this and fully realizes that Cutter & Dunlop may some day blossom into a large, successful company. In other words, Jim is willing to gamble his strong balance sheet position of today for a piece of the future.

"Also, an exchange of stock with Cutter & Dunlop would simplify estate valuation for the Gruber family in the event of death. Jim is a married man in his middle 50's, with two teen-aged sons. He believes that his estate would be in a stronger and more liquid position if it held stock in a publicly traded company."

Later that afternoon Mr. Prescott telephoned Roger Crane to discuss the situation. The banker pointed out that common stocks of publicly traded companies similar to the Wizard Corporation were then selling at approximately 15 times earnings. He also said, "By merging with Wizard you will be increasing the size of Cutter & Dunlop's capitalization as well as its assets and earning power. The larger Cutter & Dunlop becomes, by either internal or external means, the more solid the company will appear to investors. I should then expect the market price of the shares to be less volatile than in the past."

On several occasions Mr. Prescott had examined his company's transfer records and had been disturbed by the heavy trading volume in Cutter & Dunlop securities. Crane Bros. estimated that a total of 200,000 shares, or twice the number of shares sold to the public, had changed hands in the 6-month period following the public offering. To counteract this speculative fervor, Mr. Prescott had recently employed a public relations firm, C. D. LaVine & Co., to establish a stockholder relations program. Mr. LaVine suggested, however, that Cutter & Dunlop wait until 1962 before taking an active interest in this area so that company publicity would be concurrent with an improved profit picture.

Mr. Crane thought that the marketplace would probably place the same price-earnings multiple on the combined companies as it did on Cutter & Dunlop alone. This, in the banker's opinion, would create a strong upward pressure on the shares and would put the company in a stronger position to negotiate other acquisitions. Mr. Crane was anxious for Mr. Prescott to complete the merger immediately so that the Wizard Corporation's earnings could be consolidated with Cutter & Dunlop's for the year ending December 31, 1961. In this way, the profit and loss statement for the combined companies would appear in the annual report and in the newspapers.

Exhibit 1

CUTTER & DUNLOP, INC.

Balance Sheets as of December 31, 1958–1960, and November 30, 1961

ASSETS	12/31 1958	12/31 1959	12/31 1960	11/30 1961
Current assets				
Cash..................................	$ 6,192	$ 2,191	$ 9,724	$129,795
Accounts receivable....................	40,102	59,394	55,375	63,834
Inventory.............................	55,453	93,838	110,891	141,170
Prepaid expenses and deposits...........	4,092	1,980	1,932	24,058
Advances—officers and employees........	456	983	89	176
Due from officers......................	...	...	8,938	16,015
Total current assets.................	$106,295	$158,386	$186,949	$375,048
Machinery and equipment (net)...........	19,979	19,894	24,556	47,563
Total assets.......................	$126,274	$178,280	$211,505	$422,611

LIABILITIES AND CAPITAL	12/31 1958	12/31 1959	12/31 1960	11/30 1961
Current liabilities				
Notes payable.........................	$ 25,000	$ 15,507	$ 25,000	$ ...
Accounts payable......................	11,239	57,916	24,009	21,244
Advance on contracts..................	400	3,201	...	...
Accrued salaries, wages, and commissions..	8,031	9,715	9,581	7,231
Withheld and accrued taxes.............	3,175	5,258	9,894	8,642
Reserve for federal taxes................	...	...	12,000	4,406
Deposits on projectors..................	1,100	1,100	1,100	1,100
Loans payable—officers................	746	312	...	...
Due to officers........................	...	...	2,245	117
Total current liabilities..............	$ 49,691	$ 93,009	$ 83,829	$ 42,740
Capital				
Common stock, no par value*...........	60,200	60,200	60,200	301,947
Surplus..............................	16,383	25,071	67,476	77,924
Total liabilities and capital..........	$126,274	$178,280	$211,505	$422,611
Book value per share—based on 261,000 shares	$0.29	$0.33	$0.49	$1.46

* 1,400 shares outstanding, 1958–60. In March, 1961, authorized common stock was increased to 300,000 shares, and the 1,400 outstanding shares were exchanged for 161,000 shares. In June, 1961, 100,000 common shares were sold to the public; upon completion of the offering there were 261,000 shares issued and outstanding. In addition, Crane Bros. was granted five-year warrants to purchase 20,000 shares of authorized but heretofore unissued common stock.

Exhibit 2

CUTTER & DUNLOP, INC.

Profit and Loss Statements for Years Ended December 31, 1958–60

	1958	1959	1960
Net sales	$287,985	$372,785	$629,759
Cost of goods manufactured and sold	194,393	272,760	425,765
Gross profit	$ 93,592	$100,025	$203,994
Selling and administrative expenses	93,672	90,619	144,065
Operating profit (loss)	$ (80)	$ 9,406	$ 59,929
Total other income (charges)	(783)	482	(524)
Net income (loss) before taxes	$ (863)	$ 9,888	$ 59,405
Income taxes	500	1,200	17,000
Net income (loss) after taxes	$ (1,363)	$ 8,688	$ 42,405
Earnings per share—based on 261,000 shares	—	$0.03	$0.16

Exhibit 3

CUTTER & DUNLOP, INC.

Estimated Profit and Loss Statements for Years Ended December 31, 1961–63

	1961*	1962*	1963*
Net sales	$795,000	$1,740,000	$2,845,000
Cost of goods manufactured and sold	505,000	1,068,000	1,720,000
Gross profit	$290,000	$ 672,000	$1,125,000
Selling and administrative expenses	190,000	450,000	670,000
Net income before taxes	$100,000	$ 222,000	$ 455,000
Provision for state and federal taxes	35,000	122,000	252,000
Net income	$ 65,000	$ 100,000	$ 203,000
Depreciation	$ 5,400	$ 6,100	$ 5,600
Earnings per share—based on 261,000 shares	$0.25	$0.38	$0.78

* Estimates prepared in April, 1961.

Exhibit 4

WIZARD CORPORATION

Estimated Balance Sheet as of December 31, 1961, Based on Actual Balance Sheet as of December 15, 1961

ASSETS

Current assets

Cash		$ 75,405
Accounts receivable		93,053
Due from employees		1,022
Due from officer		170
Prepaid expenses		6,094
Total current assets		$175,744

Fixed assets

Cost		$106,675
Less accumulated depreciation		55,142
Net fixed assets		$ 51,533
Total assets		$227,277

LIABILITIES AND CAPITAL

Current liabilities

Accounts payable		$ 444
Notes payable (Note 1)		12,784
Accrued payroll		2,600
Accrued and withheld taxes		14,977
Federal income taxes (Note 2)		46,436
Total current liabilities		$ 77,241

Deferred notes payable (Note 1)		5,894

Capital:

Common stock (no par value)—115 shares outstanding		15,300
Surplus		128,842
Total liabilities and capital		$227,277

NOTE 1—Machinery and equipment in the amount of $87,115 was pledged to secure notes payable in the amount of $18,678 on conditional sales contracts.

NOTE 2—The Wizard Corporation had filed its corporate state and federal returns on a cash basis since its inception on February 5, 1959. At this report, date, there had been no examination by either the state or the federal taxing authorities. If at some future time, within the statutory period, the taxing authorities, upon examination, did not concur with the basis used by the corporation in filing its returns, there might be possible additional state and federal assessments of approximately $55,000.

Exhibit 5

WIZARD CORPORATION

Estimated Profit and Loss Statement for the Year Ending December 31, 1961,
Based on Actual Results up to December 15, 1961

		Percentage of Sales
Net sales	$423,160	100%
Cost of goods manufactured and sold:		
Raw materials	$20,652	4.9
Direct labor	84,790	20.0
Subcontract	68,740	16.2
Shop burden	97,033	23.0
Total cost of goods manufactured and sold	$271,215	64.1
Gross profit on sales	$151,945	35.9
General, selling, and administrative expenses	77,959	18.4
Total income	$ 73,986	17.5
Other charges (net)	(1,003)	(0.2)
Net income before federal taxes	$ 72,983	17.3
Provision for federal taxes	32,452	7.7
Net income after taxes	$ 40,531	9.6%
Depreciation	$ 19,520	4.6%

Exhibit 6

Estimated Schedule of Shop Burden, General, Selling, and Administrative Expenses
of Wizard Corporation for the Year Ended December 31, 1961*

		Percentage of Sales
Shop burden		
Supervisory salaries	$25,400	6.0%
Depreciation—machinery and equipment	18,753	4.4
Mill supplies	12,075	2.8
Product inspection	9,139	2.2
Rent	7,641	1.8
Tooling	7,554	1.8
Insurance	4,973	1.2
Payroll taxes	4,585	1.1
Maintenance and repairs	2,934	0.7
Production clerk	1,986	0.5
Light, heat, and power	1,547	0.4
Amortization—lease improvements	446	0.1
Total shop burden	$97,033	23.0%
General, selling, and administrative expenses		
Officers' salaries	$39,600	9.4%
Professional fees	10,525	2.5
Promotion, travel, and entertainment	7,777	1.8
Taxes	6,701	1.6
Office salaries	3,795	0.9
General and office expenses	2,500	0.6
Commissions	2,352	0.6
Motor vehicle expenses	1,575	0.4
Telephone	1,234	0.3
Postage and express	1,133	0.2
Depreciation—motor vehicle	607	0.1
Depreciation—office equipment	160	—
Total general, selling, and administrative expenses	$77,959	18.4%
Other income (charges)		
Interest expense	$ (3,020)	(0.7)%
Sales discounts	(2,690)	(0.6)
Interest income	2,362	0.6
Sale of scrap	1,446	0.3
Rental income	550	0.1
Miscellaneous	349	0.1
Total other charges	$ (1,003)	(0.2)%

* Based on actual results for the period ended December 15, 1961.

Norwest Construction Holdings, Limited

On September 15, 1964 Norwest Construction Holdings, Limited, made its first public offering of ordinary shares to the investing community, thus changing its legal status from a private to a public company. The immediate effect of this act was to reduce the proportion of the stock held by the founder and his immediate family from 100% to 74%.[1] Although not fully realized at the time, the act of "going public" was to have a profound impact on the future of the company.

The Early Years: 1923–64

Norwest Construction was formed in Liverpool, England, in 1923 by four young business associates with an investment of £1,000 and their time, evenings and on weekends. Seeing the profit that could be made in the business of their employer—that of laying underground telephone cables—they decided to seek small contracts on their own. It soon developed that these men had to choose between their regular jobs and the new business, and two dropped out within a very short time. By 1938 one man remained with the new business, Mr. N. H. Le Mare, and it is with Mr. Le Mare, therefore, that the early history of the company is principally identified.

Mr. Le Mare had begun his working career as a seagoing engineer but came ashore for family reasons to work in the office of a construction company. It was here that he began to develop the skill of preparing a contract bid, a key contribution to the success of the new business. Recognizing the competitive advantage that would result from a careful and systematic analysis of past experience, Mr. Le Mare began to keep his

---

[1] At this time, the minimum proportion required to be held by the general public was 25%. Following changes in taxation, the figure is now 35%.

"Big Book"—detailed cost data on the important elements of every completed contract showing where money was lost or profit made so that future contract bids would reflect an increasingly thorough knowledge of the job to be done and an increasingly accurate idea of the costs involved.

Over the years before World War II, Norwest Construction achieved a substantial expansion of its operations both as to overall volume and variety of construction work undertaken. It was an industry which was inherently unstable, partly because of the year-to-year fluctuations in the underlying demand for building and related services and partly because of the somewhat random selection of contracts falling to any one firm. In a conscious effort to even out the work load, provide continuous employment for key personnel, and spread overhead costs, Norwest moved into water and gas main laying, drainage, small-bridge work, reinforced concrete, and piling. Expanding entirely from within, the company gradually extended the range of its competence and its grasp for new opportunity. In view of the depressed economic circumstances of the 1930's, it is significant that the company always made a profit—though in 1935 that profit totaled only £53. By 1939 the profit was up to £14,800.

The war years shifted the work of the company as the priorities of defense took over. A major undertaking was the construction of a large jetty in Liverpool harbor, a contract of a scale and technical complexity never before undertaken by Norwest. The company gained substantially in experience and profits (average profit of 1941–43 was £24,000) but found by the end of the war that it had lost a large part of its peacetime contract business and also a large part of its work force to military service. A new start had to be made. Profits in 1944 were £5,700; 1945, £8,000; and 1946, £14,000.

In the postwar period, Norwest resumed the activity of main laying for the Post Office but sought new directions for balance and expansion. Between 1946 and 1948 the company did a considerable amount of site preparation for prefabricated postwar housing. Under the urging of Mr. Baucher, a nephew of Mr. Le Mare who had come to the company as a young man in 1930, the company reentered the business of water and gas main laying which had been a small and unprofitable activity before the war. This turned out to be of growing importance and profitability beginning in the later 1940's. When the prefabricated housing phased out, Norwest moved into some selective building construction, such as churches and pubs, though not on a large scale.

The effect of all this activity was manifested in substantial growth in the volume of business and profitability as seen in the following figures on trading profit (before taxes):

1946	£14,000	1952–53	£ 71,191
1947	25,535	1953–54	61,804
1948–49	57,524	1954–55	54,967
1949–50	26,208	1955–56	92,556
1950–51	15,060	1956–57	128,053
1951–52	65,042	1957–58	70,000

In 1958, at the urging of N. H. Le Mare's son, Mr. D. B. Le Mare, who had entered the business in 1946 after war service, the company took its first step to enter the field of speculative housing construction. This was a whole new area for Norwest involving new risks and new skills. Favorable building sites had to be acquired and houses built in advance of known demand. The move had been opposed by the founder on the grounds that speculative housing construction did not have a universally good reputation and that to move into this area might damage the company's reputation in its traditional business. In spite of this reluctance, however, the company went ahead. The first couple of years were not really successful financially, but beginning about 1960, with the help of an experienced man brought in from another company, this area not only increased in volume but also became profitable.

Thus, by 1964 substantial changes had taken place in the nature and scope of Norwest Construction business, and the record, particularly in recent years, was one which could be a source of satisfaction to the owners. Some statistics for 1960 to 1964 are given in the accompanying table.

	1960	1961	1962 (In £000)	1963	1964
Trading					
Turnover...............	3,886	4,048	4,870	4,534	5,741
Consolidated profit before					
taxes................	48	67	128	213	250
Net profit after tax........	36	42	68	130	118
Funds employed					
Total equity capital.......	406	425	496	599	686
Loans..................	171	155	156	135	180
Bank overdrafts..........	342	372	346	330	451
Total funds employed..	955	1,024	1,099	1,175	1,509

This expansion had been obtained only by a full utilization of the company's financial resources. However, this was not the primary reason why the decision to become a public company was taken.

The Decision to "Go Public" (1964)

Over the many years of fortune and misfortune, including a serious economic depression and a major war, Mr. N. H. Le Mare had managed to retain 100% ownership of Norwest Construction. A major element of the satisfaction he derived from life was that of being in undisputed control of his own activities and deriving a full measure of the financial results of his own effort. As he reached normal retirement age, but with no thought of retiring, Mr. Le Mare began to give some thought to his ultimate departure. His first step was to transfer some of the stock in the company to his children and grandchildren. However, the major ownership remained in the name of himself and his wife. By 1960 Mr. Le Mare was 72 years of age, and he was becoming increasingly concerned about the problem of cash for death duties in the event of the death of himself or his wife.

With all of his assets tied up in Norwest Construction, there appeared to Mr. Le Mare to be only one solution to the problem—turn Norwest into a public company and sell some of his stock to outside shareholders. This was a hard step to take, but it was finally faced up to in 1964. This was an ideal time to go public because of the strong growth in turnover and in earnings over the preceding 5 years, a record of performance which was essential to attract outside investors to a "new," small, and relatively unknown company. The company could also point to a diversity of activities which promised greater stability:

	Percent
Laying of underground telephone and electric cables	23
Laying of gas, water, and oil pipelines	14
Civil engineering—bridges, drainage, etc.	23
Building—factories, offices, and schools	22
Private housing and estate development	12
Plant hire and other	6
Total	100

Once the decision was made, the steps toward becoming a public company moved forward smoothly. Norwest Construction Holdings, Limited, which had been incorporated as a private company in 1962 became a public company on September 15, 1964. Prior to this date, application was made to the Liverpool and Manchester Stock Exchanges for permission to deal in, and for quotation of, the company's preference and ordinary shares. As a public company, Norwest had a capital structure consisting of £300,000 of 7½% Redeemable, cumulative preference shares, £1 each and £525,000 of ordinary shares of 5s each. The public offering of stock was arranged in London through the Industrial and Commercial Finance Corporation, Limited,[2] which on September 15 announced the sale of 150,000 preference shares and 412,500 ordinary shares. This sale reduced the ownership of Mr. N. H. Le Mare and his family to 74.4% of the ordinary shares. The I.C.F.C. retained 5.4% of the ordinary shares.

As previously stated, this change in the character of the company was made reluctantly on the part of its founder. The immediate pressure which overcame this reluctance was the threat of estate taxation and liquidation.

---

[2] The I.C.F.C. is owned by the Bank of England, the English Clearing Banks, and the Scottish Banks. It was organized to serve small- and medium-sized businesses in the British Isles in cases where the traditional facilities provided by banking institutions and the stock exchanges were not easily available.

On the other hand, changes had been occurring within the company which in the long run may have forced the change in any case. The growth of the postwar period was beyond the capacity of self-financing through retained earnings. The family had no fortune beyond that tied up in the business, so that the entire burden of excess capital needs fell on commercial bank borrowing. So far this had been adequate. However, the company was now expanding in directions which required a much higher investment per unit of turnover—notably the private housing industry. This trend had been quite apparent to Mr. G. L. Clegg, the company's financial director, but knowing of the strong personal considerations which governed the question of ownership, he felt unwilling to exert any pressure designed to hasten public ownership.

Growth by Acquisition, 1965

The first action of management which was to test the financial resources of the new company came in March, 1965. Mr. D. B. Le Mare was now joint managing director with Mr. Baucher and his father was now chairman. On a chance social contact, one weekend, Mr. D. B. Le Mare discovered that a friend in the building business was going up to London the next Monday to arrange for the sale of his business. Mr. Le Mare immediately raised the question as to why he should not give Norwest a chance to make an offer, and the friend agreed to consider this provided they acted quickly. The immediate attraction of the company was a substantial holding of first-class land. In consultation with Mr. Clegg, D. B. Le Mare quickly reviewed the financial position of Roberts and Sloss, Limited, and by Monday noon was prepared to accept the owner's asking price of £550,000. The acquisition was based on net asset value, and the problems raised in negotiation related primarily to the effects of taxation on the deal. The fact that first-class management was being acquired was not fully appreciated at the time. The deal was made on the basis of 250,000 Norwest ordinary shares and £341,000 in cash. The cash portion of the transaction required the cooperation of Norwest's bank in raising its overdraft limit.

Thus, the first acquisition was an unpremeditated one and was made possible by the fact of being able to use new ordinary shares as a substitute for cash or a debt contract. This could not have taken place 6 months earlier. As it happened, the deal took place during a vacation absence of Mr. N. H. Le Mare and came to him as a complete surprise— but as an accomplished fact. The date of the purchase was March 25, 1965. The balance sheet at the fiscal year-end, March 31, 1965 showed the family investment in ordinary shares reduced to 65.4%.

The acquisition of Roberts and Sloss marked a realization of the full implications of the decision to become a public company. It did so in two respects. The first was the effect of acquisition on the growth rate of turnover, earnings, and earnings per share—the sudden lift from financial consolidation of two companies as contrasted with the more gradual response from internal growth in the investment base. The second was the recognition that Norwest was now a part of a much larger pool of capital. It was no longer restricted to the limits of the Le Mare family and its borrowing power but could now tap the London debt and equity market. As a follow-up to the Roberts and Sloss acquisition and in anticipation of further expansion, Norwest in October, 1965, made a public offering of £800,000 of 7¼% debenture stock (1985–90 at £98½). With the proceeds it paid off an I.C.F.C. loan of £225,000, reduced bank overdrafts, and added to working capital. Public capital was beginning to flow.

Now for the first time Norwest began to search actively for companies to acquire as a definite part of its strategy of growth. In this approach, Mr. D. B. Le Mare and Mr. Clegg played the central role. From the beginning the search was confined to businesses in the construction industry engaged in the same or related activities and located within the British Isles. The first step extended activities in the area of construction equipment rental and sales. This was the purchase of 34% of the share capital of Joseph Thompson (Liverpool), Limited, for which Norwest gave 150,000 ordinary shares. This company was well known to Norwest and was short of capital for further expansion. At the time Norwest was anxious to expand its interest in plant hire, which it considered a "growth" area—a decision vindicated by events. Although negotiations were protracted, there were no real problems before, or after, the deal was completed. As the only acquisition during the fiscal year ended March 31, 1966, this reduced the Le Mare family interest in stock of Norwest to 60%.

While no acquisition was effected during the 1966–67 fiscal year, negotiations were proceeding for the purchase of Walter Holme and Sons, Limited, a business specializing in timber engineering and timber construction. The decision to negotiate was based on the fact that "Holme" was a well-known specialist in its own field, a particular line of activity which held out great promise for the future. The principal shareholders of "Holme" were another private limited company which lacked finance necessary for further expansion. The difficulties were (1) the valuation of "Holme" and (2) the complete secrecy in which the negotiations were shrouded. Negotiations broke down on two occasions on price and were reopened on the basis of a new formula. The secrecy inhibited any proper assessment of current trading or middle management.

During the year prior to acquisition, this company had a profit of £51,000 which was expected to increase to £55,000 the next year. Norwest acquired all of the share capital of Walter Holme for 275,000 of its ordinary shares valued at 20s per share. At about the same time, the company sold a small block of 25,000 shares to its Group Pension fund at a price of 25s per share. These actions together with the sale of a small amount of stock by the Le Mare family reduced their ownership to less than 52%. The management was now at a second critical "hurdle." Having given up 100% control to become a public company, they were now at the point where an additional acquisition would mean giving up an absolute majority of voting power.

This issue was strongly argued at top levels. While the debate was going on, a potential acquisition was passed over because it would have reduced the family ownership below 50%. Events later proved that this company would have been an excellent buy. In the end the viewpoint in favor of continued growth through acquisition prevailed. The argument was made and finally accepted that effective control could be exercised by a dominant shareholder so long as the remaining shares were dispersed. As of May 31, 1967, the rest of the stock was held partly by pension funds and limited companies (21.7%) and partly by private individuals (20.1%). The largest single shareholding outside of the Le Mare family was 4% held by I.C.F.C.

The next move was not long in coming. During 1967 the purchase of a second housing development company, Eric Entwistle, Limited, was successfully negotiated. This company specialized in housing and had a good stock of land in a geographical area complementary to the current Norwest Group operations. Having quickly established "net asset" basis, the negotiations presented few problems. Full ownership was obtained for 200,000 shares of Norwest valued at 36s. (Certain of the properties acquired were subsequently sold to the staff pension fund for £90,000.) Now, for the first time in the 44 years since the company was founded, the Le Mare family was a minority shareholder.

Throughout this period and during 1968, the company had been expanding not only because of acquisitions but also because of internal growth in the parent and in the newly acquired companies. For the fiscal year ended March 31, 1968, turnover was up to £12,823,000 compared with £8,745,000 in fiscal 1967 and £6,985,000 in fiscal 1966. In 1968 and early 1969 this growth could no longer be financed through retained earnings, bank overdrafts, and other loans. In May, 1968, the company had a rights issue of ordinary shares on a one-for-five basis—608,000 ordinary shares sold at 35s per share. The net proceeds of approximately £1,040,000 were used to reduce bank overdrafts.

However, these funds were not enough, and by the end of 1968 Norwest was planning another public offering. The new offering made on February 7, 1969, took a new form. The issue was of £2 million 6% convertible unsecured loan stock 1984 (at par). This loan stock was offered to ordinary shareholders at the rate of £1 of loan stock for every two shares of ordinary stock held. The loan stock was convertible into fully paid ordinary shares in any of the years 1975–84 inclusive at a rate of 41 ordinary shares (5s par) for each £100 of loan stock (equivalent to a price of 48s 9d per ordinary share). The reasons for the issue as stated in the prospectus of February 7 were as follows:

Turnover of the Group in 1966–67 amounted to £8.7 million, in 1967–68 to £12.8 million and it is anticipated that turnover for the current year will be approximately £16 million. Your directors expect that the present Group will continue to expand and as in the past intend to take advantage of favorable opportunities for making acquisitions.

The proceeds of the rights issue of ordinary shares made last May, approximately £1 million, were employed principally in providing additional working capital, development land, and plant for this continued expansion; since that date, trade investments have also been increased by £226,817 and mortgages reduced by a net amount of £197,249.

In the opinion of your directors the net proceeds of the current issue, estimated at £1,947,000, together with the bank facilities available, will provide adequate working capital for its anticipated requirements.

The net proceeds of the issue will be applied initially in repaying the bank borrowings of the Group which at 24th January, 1969, totaled £1,169,332.

During 1968 other events of significance occurred. One was the acquisition of a plant hire company in Belfast for 40,000 shares valued at 45s per share (£90,000). The attraction of Versatile Plant, Ltd., was the opportunity to extend Group plant hire operations to Northern Ireland. The management was small but had an excellent growth record (which has continued). The vendor was selling for tax reasons, and apart from some argument on price, the negotiations were straightforward. This business was expected to contribute £20,000 to Group profit in 1968–69. Another event of a different nature was the decision by Mr. N. H. Le Mare, chairman, to liquidate a substantial part of his shareholdings, reducing the shares he beneficially owned from 313,468 to 150,000.

The record of these acquisitions as outlined in summary form in this case suggest a picture of successful negotiation which is not wholly accurate. In fact, many negotiations failed. Most of those which broke down did so either on price or because management proved to be of indifferent quality and with little growth prospect. Many approaches were quickly turned down because the company was too small or because it was operating in parts of the market where, in Norwest's judgment, profit was difficult to earn. In all cases it was a rule of negotiation that the acquisition must not reduce earnings per share.

1969—Perspective and Outlook

In early 1969 the management of Norwest was at a stage where it could look back on 4 years of rapid growth in which acquisition had played a key role and assess the results of that policy. (See Exhibits 1, 2, and 3 for financial performance data.) Not every acquisition that had been made was considered to have been an unqualified success. In many cases there was a time pressure to act on the basis of incomplete information. When acquiring in the same industry, there was a natural reluctance on the part of the business being acquired to reveal all its secrets in the event that the negotiations broke down. In some cases it was part of the bargaining strategy to give as little information as possible and even to deliberately mislead. In some cases the desired information was not available because it did not exist. Norwest had learned to be much more wary. It had also learned negotiating skills and had a clearer idea of the minimum information it wanted in order to make a decision.

Over these years Norwest had developed an explicit acquisition program related to a formal set of targets and a 5-year budget of expenditure. Targets were expressed in terms of a 5-year turnover, and profit objective and the acquisition program reflected the specific industry areas in which growth was desired. Management was now keenly aware that continued growth was reflected in a rising market price for the stock and that each new acquisition had required fewer shares per £100 of value. Rising market values for the ordinary shares were primarily related to a rising earnings per share and to the "image" of the company in the stock market as it became better known and more clearly identified as a growth company in the mind of the general investor. The company image took tangible form in the price-earnings ratio, which responded both to company performance and to general market reaction. Recently Norwest stock had been the beneficiary of the market interest in natural gas exploration and development, including pipeline construction. (See Exhibit 4 for the record of market value for Norwest ordinary shares.)

Norwest management had come to believe that its plan for rapid growth through acquisition was a rational move in direction and timing so far as the British construction industry was concerned. Norwest was convinced that rationalization of the industry demanded fewer and larger construction companies as the industry became more capital intensive and economies of scale opened up. As the management looked forward from 1969 it was aware that this period of rationalization would not continue indefinitely. New acquisition opportunities with high growth potential for Norwest were becoming harder to find. As Norwest grew larger, it was now looking for larger companies to acquire, if only for the reason of reducing the very heavy burden of investigation and negotiation which fell primarily on Mr. D. B. Le Mare and Mr. Clegg. It was also focusing on companies which would expand the company's areas of activity in complementary construction work. The company had remained in the building and civil engineering industry, but its horizons were broadening. For example, management had been keeping a careful eye on plastic materials and their effect on traditional construction practice.

Against this background and with the Le Mare family ownership now reduced to 30%, Norwest was now, in the spring of 1969, contemplating its next possible acquisition. The company under discussion was the biggest bite Norwest had ever considered. It was about one half the size of Norwest in turnover and profit. This company was family owned, and its owners could be expected to retain the Norwest stock it received and take an active interest in Norwest. If the business was acquired on a basis roughly proportional to its earnings, it was likely that the former owners of the acquired company would have a share of Norwest stock as large as or larger than that of the Le Mare family. The acquisition was under active consideration.

Exhibit 1

NORWEST CONSTRUCTION HOLDINGS, LIMITED

Group Profit and Loss Account for the Year Ended March 31, 1968.

	1968		1967	
	£	£	£	£
Sales and value of work carried out............		12,822,736		8,745,345
Group trading profit.......................		903,063		605,860
Less: Interest charges....................		132,196		91,711
Group profit before taxation................		770,867		514,149
Taxation................................		332,666		207,608
Group profit after taxation.................		438,201		306,541
Allocated as follows:				
Dividends paid and proposed-gross preference.........................		22,500		22,500
Ordinary:				
Interim of 6% on 2.5 million shares........			37,500	
Final of 10½ on 2.5 million shares.........			65,625	
Interim of 7½% on 2.8 million shares...................	52,500			
Final of 10% on 3,040,000 shares.	76,000	128,500		103,125
		151,000		125,625
Retained in group				
Revenue reserve-unappropriated profit				
Holding company...........	16,205		52,607	
Subsidiaries...............	270,996		122,227	
	287,201		174,834	
Capital reserves of subsidiaries...	—		6,082	
		287,201		180,916
		£438,201		£306,541

Exhibit 2

NORWEST CONSTRUCTION HOLDINGS, LIMITED

Group Balance Sheet as at March 31, 1968

	1968		1967	
	£	£	£	£
CAPITAL EMPLOYED				
Preference shares....................		300,000		300,000
Ordinary shares....................	750,000		625,000	
Reserves.........................	1,569,067		983,994	
Funds attributable to ordinary share-holders.........................		2,319,067		1,608,994
Outside shareholders' interest in sub-sidiary company.................		1,000		1,000
Loan capital.......................		1,402,278		1,159,089
Deferred taxation..................		178,226		78,988
Investment grants suspense account...		155,861		62,211
		£4,356,432		£3,210,282
REPRESENTED BY				
Fixed assets.......................	1,414,749		1,141,322	
Trade investments.................	129,611		124,000	
		1,544,360		1,265,322
Current assets				
Development land................	2,445,106		1,683,659	
Stocks and work in progress........	2,602,317		1,503,228	
Debtors and payments in advance...	2,458,510		1,470,584	
Balance at bank and cash in hand....	37,304		10,360	
	7,543,237		4,667,831	
Current liabilities				
Creditors, accrued charges and liabili-ties for reinstatements...........	2,509,085		1,885,589	
Bank overdrafts..................	1,532,015		386,554	
Taxation........................	608,440		379,478	
Proposed ordinary final dividend gross.........................	76,000		65,625	
Preference dividend accrued gross...	5,625		5,625	
Net current assets................	4,731,165		2,722,871	
		2,812,072		1,944,960
		£4,356,432		£3,210,282

Exhibit 3

Group Financial Summary for Norwest Construction Holdings
(£000)

	Year ending March 31					
	1963	1964	1965	1966	1967	1968
Funds employed:						
Preference capital..............	50	100	300	300	300	300
Equity capital and reserves.......	599	686	1,105	1,410	1,609	2,319
Minority shareholder's interest....				1	1	1
Future taxation..............	61	92	288	124	79	178
Investment grants suspense account...................					62	156
Loans......................	135	180	255	970	1,159	1,402
Total capital employed:	845	1,058	1,918	2,805	3,210	4,356
Bank overdrafts................	330	451	554	449	387	1,532
Total funds employed........	1,175	1,509	2,472	3,254	3,597	5,888
Trading:						
Turnover.....................	4,534	5,741	6,654	6,985	8,745	12,823
Depreciation..................	112	154	194	265	332	388
Loan and bank interest...........	28	32	38	73	92	132
Consolidated profit before taxation.	213	250	337	412	514	771
Taxation.....................	83	132	116	124	208	333
Net profit after tax..............	130	118	218	288	306	438

Exhibit 4

Graph of Monthly Share Prices in Shillings, 1964–68

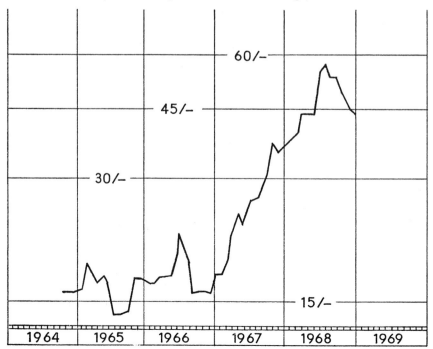

Cerarts Company

On September 23, 1965, Mr. Robert Applington, Cleveland partner of the New York investment banking firm, Mason, Brown & Company, Inc., discussed the future of the Cerarts Company with Mr. William Strong, its president. "Will, ever since I met you 7 or 8 years ago I've been amazed with what you've done with an idea as simple as a clay mug with a college seal on it. Now, I think both you and I recognize that Cerarts is coming of age. Sales and profits are up, but from what I can judge you have some problems too. Correct me if I'm wrong, now—not having seen any financial statements I can only infer that your needs for both working capital and plant and equipment are becoming significant. So far you haven't sold stock, and to my knowledge, haven't got any term money. If my guess is right you must be sorely in need of funds!

"Not only should you think of your company, though; you ought to consider your own and your family's interests. To be a bit blunt, if you or Steve Adler were to die tomorrow—or next year—how would the estate tax be met? It might be pretty hard to get a good price for the stock of a privately held company under distress conditions.

"Will, Mason, Brown doesn't normally handle small underwritings, but we *are* interested in establishing new relationships. And as I said, you interested me particularly because you've grown so fast, and with your resourcefulness and imagination I think you'll continue to grow.

"I understand another underwriter offered you a lot to sell your stock in 1962. Well, we wouldn't have touched a speculation like that. Then it was a speculation. Now it's less of one.

"While you may not be ready to sell Cerarts shares right now, I'm guessing you'll want to before long. If Mason, Brown were to underwrite such an issue, I think we could help prepare you for this step. You'll probably need some more interim financing and perhaps some other advice too. You're a great businessman, Will, but you haven't the experience in the securities markets we have. Mason, Brown's a specialist and we could help you get the best price possible for your stock when you choose to sell."

Mr. Strong, who had joined Mr. Applington for lunch at the latter's request, replied, "Bob, if you fellows can consistently do a job as good as you did analyzing our needs you certainly can help us. You're almost completely right in the inferences you've drawn. You couldn't have known that the company owns sufficient life insurance on Steve's and my life to obviate the estate tax problem. Otherwise, the problems you suggested are there. We recently forecasted sales and profits increases of about 20% annually for the next 5 years. We haven't projected the resultant funds needs, but they'll certainly be considerable. Right now we've about extended our bank borrowing to the limit what with chattel mortgages, receivables financing, and an open credit line besides [see Exhibit 2]. We've wondered what we'd do from here. We could probably finance plant and equipment purchases of $50,000–$100,000 a year with 4- to 5-year bank money. This plus our seasonal lines can keep us going, but we won't grow on it.

"In talking about our expansion plans, Steve Adler, our executive vice president, and I have listed some long-term sources of funds that might be worth our attention. I'll send the list to you with some financial statements when I get back to the office. I don't mind telling you though, when I contemplate negotiating with a life insurance company for a term loan or think about selling stock I feel like a lamb in a den of wolves! I'm pretty confident in dealing with the bank; we've had a long, close relationship with them. On the other hand, I'd like to have someone like you to rely on if we sell stock.

"If you can come up with a plan that I'm convinced is sound, I'd be glad to take Mason, Brown on as financial consultants with the understanding that when the time's ripe you would help us get some long-term funds.

"Before you take us up on this though, I want you to know something about Steve's and my personal feelings. I started this company after the war with an idea and tremendous desire to be my own boss—to have things my own way most of the time. Well, the ideas are different now, but I still like to run things. That's why I'm leery of a merger. Some companies let a subsidiary manage itself, but I'm afraid of being swallowed up by a giant.

"Ever since we began to make money and make ourselves felt, a lot of friends have been after me to sell them a piece of Cerarts stock. I'm certain we could peddle $500,000 worth in Cleveland alone. That's precisely what I don't want to do! There's a great danger that an issue like that of limited size would be bid up to a price all out of proportion to what it's really worth. Then if the market fell out of bed, friends of mine would be hurt.

"You remember, just the same thing happened to Cleveland Instruments a few years back. Nate Simmons, Cleveland Instruments' president was a friend of mine. He told me later that after that he felt like crossing the street to avoid meeting friends when he saw them coming.

"If sometime Cerarts is big enough to sell its stock nationally, then I think we'd have a deal. Ideally, I'd like to make an arrangement where no stock was sold in Cleveland. However, I wonder when we'll ever be big enough for something like that. We'll have sales of $7 million in a few years, but I'm not even sure that's big enough."

The following Monday Mr. Applington, the investment banker, telephoned Mr. Strong, "Will, this morning's mail brought in all the material you promised me. Let's see, besides your note I've got financial statements, forecasts, and the list of financing alternatives [see Exhibits 1 through 7]. I guess that's all there's supposed to be, isn't it?

"I hope all this turns out to be as interesting as what you told me at lunch last Thursday. I've thought a lot about your problems since then; I'm intrigued with the nuances introduced by the mixture of your own private goals and the corporate needs of Cerarts. I think maybe Mason, Brown will be able to show you how useful we can be as a financial consultant and perhaps, underwriter.

"Before going much further in charting a course of action, though, I have to gauge the importance to you and Steve of finding an immediate solution to the problem of diversifying your personal assets. I know you're both anxious about being so dependent on your equity in Cerarts, but would you consider foregoing a secondary offering of your stock if we could find a cheaper source of long-term funds for Cerarts than new equity? The reason I ask is that I'm afraid by itself a secondary offering of Cerarts would be so small as to be very expensive in terms of underwriting and selling costs. However, if you're pretty definite in wanting to sell some of your shares in the near future, we ought to be more inclined than otherwise toward an issue of new shares to spread the costs. Before you decide finally though, let me send you a book which will outline the problems small companies face in going public [see Exhibit 8]."

Mr. William Strong attempted to explain what he and Steve Adler, the other owner, were seeking, "Bob, neither Steve nor I are so old that we expect to die soon. Besides, as I told you the other day, the company owns enough insurance on our lives to buy back the Cerarts shares from our estates thus providing plenty of cash for estate taxes.

"However for each of us this stock is a major part, if not all, of our net worth. It strikes us as pretty risky having all our eggs in one basket like that. In addition, Steve and I've identified in ourselves a curious turn toward conservatism away from taking the risks that made us successful. We're less of entrepreneurs today than we used to be. Now that we've built up some wealth and with it a certain standard of living, we're reluctant to give it up; now what we seem to want to do is conserve what we've got. I'm afraid Cerarts suffers from this. We've passed up some new-product possibilities because they seemed risky at the time. Looking back, I believe Cerarts has missed good profit opportunities as a consequence. If we were to become less dependent on Cerarts, we might become more freewheeling, and Cerarts could prosper even more than it has.

"From this you can probably judge that while there's no necessity that we sell our Cerarts shares (neither of us will probably need the cash in the near future), there are a lot of good reasons to have a secondary offering."

Advantages of the Cerarts Company

With a greater understanding of the needs and desires of Cerarts' owners, Mr. Applington wanted to begin outlining a plan which would meet both the financial needs of the company and the requirements of its owners. Combining what he had known for a long time and what he had uncovered since his luncheon with Mr. Strong, Mr. Applington thought he understood a great deal of Cerarts' history, its products, and its methods of operation.

From 1947 to 1965 Cerarts had developed from selling only glazed ceramic mugs with a college seal imprinted on the side to where it offered mugs, ashtrays, china sets—in fact anything which was ceramic and on which a special decoration could be placed. Mr. Adler, Cerarts' executive vice president, had told Mr. Applington, "We're not the only maker of mugs. We do make the best mug and give the fastest delivery, but we also get a better price than the others do. However, competition keeps a constant pressure on us to keep our prices down.

"In the face of this pressure I think our biggest asset is our sales force. They've been trained to find out what a customer can use that we might be able to make. Then we design it for them. The result is we're not much more than a job shop, but even so we have a skilled group of employees who can make a good profit on these small runs. A couple of years ago a salesman was talking to a friend who was planning an exhibit for his company at a major trade show. The friend wanted to know how he could make fairgoers really carry home the company's name in their minds. Well, the salesman suggested that Cerarts could design an attractive ashtray with the company's name and motto decorating the surface. Simple, but it worked! By giving away these inexpensive ashtrays, this company easily persuaded visitors to the show to carry the company's message right into their offices and homes! Now all sorts of messages are conveyed in this way. We're also beginning to create special fancy gifts that corporations can give to important customers among others.

"Besides developing original ideas, Cerarts competes by offering a very good deal for the price. None of our competitors is as fully integrated as we. We sell, design, do all the production and then ship. Others waste both time and money shipping to subcontractors for designing or for glazing and then having the goods shipped back to the plant. Ceramic ware isn't light, so a significant expense is involved. Time is wasted, too, which seriously affects their ability to deliver quickly. Consequently, our competitors have to make major compromises with quality to meet our prices. Unless someone wants to invest in the full range of equipment involved and approach our capacity, we'll probably remain the lowest cost producer relative to the level of quality we offer."

Early History of the Cerarts Company

Mr. Applington had long been familiar with the origins of the Cerarts Company. When he had first been introduced to Mr. Strong, friends had related to him how Mr. Strong had first developed the idea of selling decorated mugs in his college days at The Ohio State University in the late 1930's. At that time he had asked a local manufacturer to produce a few mugs with the Ohio State seal, which he promptly sold to acquaintances. Then and there he had concluded that he had a good idea which he could exploit. However, Mr. Strong had decided he needed a wide range of business experience before risking his capital and his idea in his own new business. It was not until 1946, after several advertising and promotion jobs, that the Cerarts Company had been started. From the outset the operation had been profitable. Both profits and sales had increased steadily in the 1960's when there had been a slight leveling off (see Exhibit 5).

Growth had been accompanied by problems, however; Cerarts' financial statements (see Exhibits 2 and 3), reflected the degree to which the company had had to extend itself to finance its expansion. Fearing the impositions of minority shareholders, Mr. Strong and his original partner, Mr. Adler, had sold no stock to outsiders. In 1965 Mr. Strong owned about 61% of the stock, Mr. Adler 33%, and several key employees the remaining 6%. In all cases stockholders and their estates were committed to sell their stock back to the company at book value if they left Cerarts.[1] With no additional equity other than retained earnings Cerarts had resorted to extensive bank financing.

Compounding the need for financing was a pronounced seasonal pattern to Cerarts' sales and receipts. A large portion of Cerarts' sales were made to schools and to college bookstores for the opening of school in the fall. To maintain level production, inventory was customarily built up from the beginning of each year. Many customers had agreed to receive orders well before their autumn selling period provided that Cerarts would

---

[1] The insurance Cerarts owned on the lives of Mr. Strong and Mr. Adler would be used to repurchase their stock.

give them a September billing date.[2] As a result inventories did not build up too far before being converted to accounts receivable, which then mounted until August or September. Exhibit 4 reflects Cerarts' seasonal buildup of working capital.

Financial Requirements of Cerarts

Mr. Applington recognized that unless Cerarts' seasonal fluctuations in working capital were modified, the company would continue to require short-term financing as well as increasing amounts of permanent capital. Cerarts' management had decided that it had either to maintain level production or add more plant and equipment to meet peak levels of demand. It had been determined that the former course would involve less risk of obsolescence of machinery and be less costly to finance. To meet the combined requirements of inventories, accounts receivables, and shipping receivables, Cerarts had a $250,000 open line of credit with its bank, the City State Bank of Cleveland.

In addition to short-term needs, Mr. Strong expected Cerarts would require permanent funds for both working capital and plant and equipment to achieve its forecasted rate of growth. At Mr. Strong's request, Cerarts' accountant had drawn up for Mr. Applington some preliminary estimates of the asset requirements to support the company's sales growth (Exhibit 6). With these estimates and the sales forecasts (Exhibit 5), Mr. Applington felt confident that the approximate future financing requirements could be established. Besides these fairly predictable requirements, Mr. Applington knew that Mr. Strong was at that time considering an acquisition which would cost nearly $500,000, and he was certain that Mr. Strong would like to have available sufficient reserves of financial strength to take advantage of other opportunities as they might develop. Therefore, Mr. Applington wanted to consider financing acquisitions as well as internal expansion. Exhibit 7 is a list of alternative sources of funds Cerarts' owners had considered before meeting Mr. Applington.

Problems of Cerarts' Owners

Since the owners' estates would be made liquid from the proceeds of the sale of their Cerarts stock back to the company, the only obvious service Mr. Applington felt Mason, Brown could do for Mr. Strong and Mr. Adler would be to help them diversify their personal portfolios. However, because both owners were advancing in age (in 1965 they were in their early 50's), the cost of sufficient term insurance to repurchase their nearly $750,000 of equity in Cerarts (at book value) was becoming increasingly high.[3] He reasoned that if the owners' portfolios were diver-

---

[2] Cerarts generally sold to its customers on terms of 1/10 net 30.

[3] At their present ages this amounted to nearly $13,000 a year.

sified through public sale of Cerarts stock, their estates would probably be able to meet estate taxes without recourse to selling stock back to the company. As a result Cerarts would be saved the major expense of insurance premiums, an expense not deductible for purposes of federal income taxes. Therefore, Mr. Applington considered recommending that Cerarts drop its life insurance in the event the owners sold some of their stock in Cerarts.

Alternatives

Mr. Applington believed that eventually the Cerarts Company would "go public" through either a primary or secondary offering or through a combination of the two. As a result of this conclusion, two major issues remained in Mr. Applington's mind. First, when would Cerarts be ready for a successful offering? Second, how should Mason, Brown advise Cerarts to prepare itself for the eventual sale of its stock? He thought that the sources of interim financing and the image the company continued to create for itself would be relevant to the reception Cerarts stock would eventually receive in the marketplace. With respect to Cerarts' corporate image, Mr. Applington realized that the policy the company pursued on growth especially through acquisition, would be important. While new acquisitions might increase the dynamic appearance of the company in the interim before it went public, there were risks involved too. First, new operations might take a while to be effectively integrated with Cerarts' existing organization creating a drag on earnings in the meantime. Then too, financing would be difficult, especially if Mr. Strong and Mr. Adler wished to avoid dilution of their control of Cerarts. With all these considerations in mind, Mr. Applington wondered how he should advise Cerarts and what sort of price he might be able to promise its owners.

Exhibit 1

Letter Sent from Mr. Strong to Mr. Applington with
Material Shown in Exhibits 2 through 7

CERARTS COMPANY
239 Pilgrim Parkway
Cleveland, Ohio

September 24, 1965

Mr. Robert K. Applington
Mason, Brown & Co., Inc.
6 Williams Street
Cleveland, Ohio

Dear Bob:

I've enclosed the materials I promised you yesterday. In addition, I have included the *pro forma* balance sheets that I asked my accountant, Bill Abrams, to rough out assuming our predicted rate of growth is achieved. Besides the financial statements and forecasts I've enclosed a list of financing alternatives for Cerarts that Steve and I recently drew up. I don't know if it's complete but it's a start.

I also checked on the offering by Walter A. Jones & Co. to sell our stock. It was even richer than I told you. In March 1962 they offered us $1.3 million in cash for 70% of Cerarts' stock. You remember that earlier in '62 the new issues market was booming and "education" companies were being bought at all sorts of high price earnings multiples. However, we felt it wasn't in the company's best interests to introduce outside shareholders at that time.

/s/ Will Strong
President

Enc. 6

Exhibit 2

CERARTS COMPANY
Quarterly Balance Sheets,* December 31, 1963–December 31, 1964

ASSETS	Dec. 31, 1963	Mar. 31, 1964	June 30, 1964	Aug. 31, 1964	Sept. 30, 1964	Dec. 31, 1964
Cash	$ 20	$ 22	$ 22	$ 27	$ 39	$ 63
Accounts receivable (net)	477	354	500	1,083	811	383
Inventory	364	340	454	380	380	459
Total current assets	$ 861	$ 716	$ 976	$1,490	$1,230	$ 905
Net property, plant and equipment	449	443	470	468	463	445
Other assets	3	3	4	4	4	14
Total assets	$1,313	$1,162	$1,450	$1,962	$1,697	$1,364
LIABILITIES						
Accounts payable	$ 103	$ 93	$ 92	$ 131	$ 134	$ 97
Notes payable, unsecured	175	175	235	60	...	...
Notes payable, secured by receivables	241	238	250	536	344	186
Accrued income taxes	49	53	5	76	86	61
Dividends payable	2	...	...	...	...	2
Other current liabilities	64	80	145	222	181	135
Total current liabilities	$ 634	$ 639	$ 727	$1,025	$ 745	$ 481
Chattel mortgages	...	...	115	115	115	85
Total liabilities	$ 634	$ 639	$ 842	$1,140	$ 860	$ 566
Capital stock	$ 204	$ 204	$ 204	$ 204	$ 204	$ 204
Capital surplus	21	21	21	21	21	21
Earned surplus	454	298	383	597	612	573
Total equity	$ 679	$ 523	$ 608	$ 822	$ 837	$ 798
Total liabilities and equity	$1,313	$1,162	$1,450	$1,962	$1,697	$1,364

* The August 31, 1964 balance sheet is also included to reflect the maximum need for funds.

Exhibit 3

CERARTS COMPANY

Income Statements, Years Ending December 31, 1963 and 1964

	1963	1964
Gross sales	$2,907,859	$3,086,278
Returns, etc.	127,738	124,776
Net sales	$2,780,121	$2,961,502
Cost of goods sold	1,665,886	1,764,947
Gross profit	$1,114,235	$1,196,555
Selling expense	555,023	595,176
General & administrative expense*	372,362	376,740
Net income from operations	$ 186,850	$ 224,639
Other income	30,584	18,748
	$ 217,434	$ 243,387
Other expense	75,018	53,779
Net income before taxes	$ 142,416	$ 189,608
Income taxes	43,597	70,071
Net income	$ 98,819	$ 119,537
Dividends	$ 2,007	$ 2,039

* Executive salaries were considered normal for a company of this size.

Exhibit 4

Monthly Record of Orders Received, Shipments,
Net Income and Collections, 1964
($ figures in thousands)

	Orders Received	Shipments (Gross Sales)	Net Income	Collections
January	$ 148	$ 129	$(50)	$ 221
February	189	135	(52)	137
March	258	140	(54)	167
April	311	195	(17)	169
May	444	245	12	174
June	372	349	90	301
July	291	462	137	188
August	206	544	76	235
September	317	266	17	538
October	222	295	7	525
November	180	179	(24)	319
December	185	147	(22)	205
Total	$3,123	$3,086	$120	$3,179

Exhibit 5

Historical Annual Sales and Net Income 1948–64
Forecast Annual Sales and Net Income 1965–69
($ figures in thousands)

		Net Income	
Actual:	*Sales*	*Dollars*	*as % of Sales*
1948...................	$ 140	$ 1	0.9%
1949...................	207	4	2.1
1950...................	300	19	6.5
1951...................	263	1	0.5
1952...................	295	10	3.3
1953...................	421	8	2.0
1954...................	602		
1955...................	756	18	2.4
1956...................	930	10	1.0
1957...................	1,066	10	0.9
1958...................	1,318	21	1.6
1959...................	1,681	24	1.4
1960...................	2,238	103	4.6
1961...................	2,742	135	4.9
1962...................	2,848	106	3.7
1963...................	2,908	99	3.4
1964...................	3,086	120	3.9
Forecast:			
1965...................	$3,550	$140	3.9%
1966...................	4,275	190	4.4
1967...................	5,350	250	4.7
1968...................	6,390	320	5.0
1969...................	7,090	355	5.0

Exhibit 6

CERARTS COMPANY
Projected Balance Sheet

	1967 Sales $5 Million		1969 Sales $7 Million	
	Aug. 31	*Dec. 31*	*Aug. 31*	*Dec. 31*
Cash..........................	$ 50	$ 50	$ 75	$ 75
Accounts receivable				
33% of sales in August...............	1,670		2,330	
12% of sales in December............		600		840
Inventory				
13% in August.....................	650		910	
15% in December..................		750		1,050
Net plant and equipment...............	750	750	1,050	1,050
Other assets.........................	10	10	15	15
Total Assets....................	$3,130	$2,160	$4,380	$3,030
Accounts payable				
5% of sales in August................	250		350	
4% of sales in December.............		200		280
Other current liabilities				
7% in August......................	350		490	
5% in December...................		250		350
Existing capital and surplus.............	800	800	800	800
Profits retained from 1965 and 1966.......	330	330	330	330
Profits retained from 1967 and 1968.......			570	570
Total liabilities and equity.......	$2,730	$1,580	$2,540	$2,330
To be financed*......................	$1,400	$ 580	$1,840	$ 700

* These estimates exclude any funds required for acquisitions.

Assumptions used in balance sheet forecast:

1. Cash, accounts receivable, inventory, accounts payable, and other current liabilities are anticipated to maintain their current relationship with sales volume.
2. Net plant and equipment levels are expected to grow proportionately with sales—$600,000 increase will provide sufficient capacity for the anticipated sales of $7 million.
3. Earnings as forecasted in Exhibit 5 will be achieved and retained—no dividends will be paid.

Exhibit 7

Alternative Sources of Long-Term Funds for the Cerarts Company as Set Forth by Mr. Strong

A. Sale of stock publicly.
1. Local general public distribution.
    a) Would probably be significant demand among owners' friends.
    b) Risk alienating these friends if the market breaks.
2. Limited local distribution to a small number of "moneyed" people.
    a) Might sell to a limited number of people who would not trade the stock and would not bid up the price inordinately.
    b) These people could be expected to see the real value of Cerarts and pay about two times book value.
    c) Role of such minority investors in management uncertain.
    d) Because of relative ease of communicating with a few people and because of their sophistication Cerarts stock might be sold to them before it was ready for a national market.
3. National distribution.
    a) Would achieve wide distribution obviating problem of major minority shareholders.
    b) Unclear how soon Cerarts could be sold nationally if at all.
4. Small offering of less than $300,000.
    a) Avoid requirement of registering with the SEC and consequent publishing of financial statements.
    b) Might be inadequate to support financing needs.
    c) Might be expensive to sell such a small issue.
B. Merger.
1. Fear losing control of operations to the acquiring company.
2. Might receive a more marketable common stock or cash. If stock were received this might be the one way by which Cerarts' owners could avoid paying a major capital gains levy.
C. Private placement of debt with an insurance company.
1. Might be able to sell $500,000 to $1 million of debentures maturing in 5–10 years
2. Fear rate would be over 6%.
3. Not all this money would be needed immediately so that Cerarts would have redundant assets for some period.
4. The longer the loan the more attractive because debt service is less. High debt service would encumber Cerarts' growth.
D. Bank term loans.
1. More flexible than insurance company loans. With its good bank relationships Cerarts could probably tailor the loan to its requirements.
2. Short term (4–5 years) implies burdensome debt-servicing requirements.
E. More capital from present owners.
1. Only W. Strong has appreciable net worth besides his Cerarts assets.
2. This would amplify rather than mitigate the problem of concentration of owners' assets.

Exhibit 8

Costs of Going Public*

The cost of going public varies considerably depending on the size and quality of the issue, the underwriter, market conditions and other factors. With small issues the cost is proportionately higher than with large issues. This is because almost every underwriting, regardless of size, involves certain fixed costs and the smaller the issue the larger the proportion of fixed cost to proceeds. The principal elements of cost to the issuing corporation of going public are underwriting commissions and the fees of attorneys, accountants, and other specialists who may have to cooperate in the operation. Other costs include the SEC registration fee, federal issue and transfer taxes and printing expenses.

The underwriter's commissions or "spread" are deducted from the proceeds of the issue. Thus, suppose a public offering of 150,000 shares was made at $2.00 per share yielding gross proceeds of $300,000. Underwriting commissions of $0.30 per share would amount to $45,000 (15% of the total issue) and would provide net proceeds to the issuing company in the amount of $255,000.

The spread involved with high-grade issues is generally considerably smaller than in the case of issues with more speculative character. Where the common stock of a closely held corporation is offered to the public for the first time and involves great selling efforts, the spread may be as high as 20% of the proceeds of the offering. Where spreads reach this level, corporations may seek alternate methods of financing, particularly where they regard the price at which the common is proposed to be offered to the public as inadequate.

* Gerald J. Robinson, *Going Public* (New York, C. Boardman & Company, 1961).

TABLE A
Present Value of $1

Periods until Payment	1%	2%	2½%	3%	4%	5%	6%	8%	10%	12%	14%	15%	16%	18%	20%	22%	24%	25%	26%	30%	40%	50%
1	0.990	0.980	0.976	0.971	0.962	0.952	0.943	0.926	0.909	0.893	0.877	0.870	0.862	0.847	0.833	0.820	0.806	0.800	0.794	0.769	0.714	0.667
2	0.980	0.961	0.952	0.943	0.925	0.907	0.890	0.857	0.826	0.797	0.769	0.756	0.743	0.718	0.694	0.672	0.650	0.640	0.630	0.592	0.510	0.444
3	0.971	0.942	0.929	0.915	0.889	0.864	0.840	0.794	0.751	0.712	0.675	0.658	0.641	0.609	0.579	0.551	0.524	0.512	0.500	0.455	0.364	0.296
4	0.961	0.924	0.906	0.888	0.855	0.823	0.792	0.735	0.683	0.636	0.592	0.572	0.552	0.516	0.482	0.451	0.423	0.410	0.397	0.350	0.260	0.198
5	0.951	0.906	0.884	0.863	0.822	0.784	0.747	0.681	0.621	0.567	0.519	0.497	0.476	0.437	0.402	0.370	0.341	0.328	0.315	0.269	0.186	0.132
6	0.942	0.888	0.862	0.837	0.790	0.746	0.705	0.630	0.564	0.507	0.456	0.432	0.410	0.370	0.335	0.303	0.275	0.262	0.250	0.207	0.133	0.088
7	0.933	0.871	0.841	0.813	0.760	0.711	0.665	0.583	0.513	0.452	0.400	0.376	0.354	0.314	0.279	0.249	0.222	0.210	0.198	0.159	0.095	0.059
8	0.923	0.853	0.821	0.789	0.731	0.677	0.627	0.540	0.467	0.404	0.351	0.327	0.305	0.266	0.233	0.204	0.179	0.168	0.157	0.123	0.068	0.039
9	0.914	0.837	0.801	0.766	0.703	0.645	0.592	0.500	0.424	0.361	0.308	0.284	0.263	0.225	0.194	0.167	0.144	0.134	0.125	0.094	0.048	0.026
10	0.905	0.820	0.781	0.744	0.676	0.614	0.558	0.463	0.386	0.322	0.270	0.247	0.227	0.191	0.162	0.137	0.116	0.107	0.099	0.073	0.035	0.017
11	0.896	0.804	0.762	0.722	0.650	0.585	0.527	0.429	0.350	0.287	0.237	0.215	0.195	0.162	0.135	0.112	0.094	0.086	0.079	0.056	0.025	0.012
12	0.887	0.788	0.744	0.701	0.625	0.557	0.497	0.397	0.319	0.257	0.208	0.187	0.168	0.137	0.112	0.092	0.076	0.069	0.062	0.043	0.018	0.008
13	0.879	0.773	0.725	0.681	0.601	0.530	0.469	0.368	0.290	0.229	0.182	0.163	0.145	0.116	0.093	0.075	0.061	0.055	0.050	0.033	0.013	0.005
14	0.870	0.758	0.708	0.661	0.577	0.505	0.442	0.340	0.263	0.205	0.160	0.141	0.125	0.099	0.078	0.062	0.049	0.044	0.039	0.025	0.009	0.003
15	0.861	0.743	0.690	0.642	0.555	0.481	0.417	0.315	0.239	0.183	0.140	0.123	0.108	0.084	0.065	0.051	0.040	0.035	0.031	0.020	0.006	0.002
16	0.853	0.728	0.674	0.623	0.534	0.458	0.394	0.292	0.218	0.163	0.123	0.107	0.093	0.071	0.054	0.042	0.032	0.028	0.025	0.015	0.005	0.002
17	0.844	0.714	0.657	0.605	0.513	0.436	0.371	0.270	0.198	0.146	0.108	0.093	0.080	0.060	0.045	0.034	0.026	0.023	0.020	0.012	0.003	0.001
18	0.836	0.700	0.641	0.587	0.494	0.416	0.350	0.250	0.180	0.130	0.095	0.081	0.069	0.051	0.038	0.028	0.021	0.018	0.016	0.009	0.002	0.001
19	0.828	0.686	0.626	0.570	0.475	0.396	0.331	0.232	0.164	0.116	0.083	0.070	0.060	0.043	0.031	0.023	0.017	0.014	0.012	0.007	0.002	
20	0.820	0.673	0.610	0.554	0.456	0.377	0.312	0.215	0.149	0.104	0.073	0.061	0.051	0.037	0.026	0.019	0.014	0.012	0.010	0.005	0.001	
21	0.811	0.660	0.595	0.538	0.439	0.359	0.294	0.199	0.135	0.093	0.064	0.053	0.044	0.031	0.022	0.015	0.011	0.009	0.008	0.004	0.001	
22	0.803	0.647	0.581	0.522	0.422	0.342	0.278	0.184	0.123	0.083	0.056	0.046	0.038	0.026	0.018	0.013	0.009	0.007	0.006	0.003	0.001	
23	0.795	0.634	0.567	0.507	0.406	0.326	0.262	0.170	0.112	0.074	0.049	0.040	0.033	0.022	0.015	0.010	0.007	0.006	0.005	0.002		
24	0.788	0.622	0.553	0.492	0.390	0.310	0.247	0.158	0.102	0.066	0.043	0.035	0.028	0.019	0.013	0.008	0.006	0.005	0.004	0.002		
25	0.780	0.610	0.539	0.478	0.375	0.295	0.233	0.146	0.092	0.059	0.038	0.030	0.024	0.016	0.010	0.007	0.005	0.004	0.003	0.001		
26	0.772	0.598	0.526	0.464	0.361	0.281	0.220	0.135	0.084	0.053	0.033	0.026	0.021	0.014	0.009	0.006	0.004	0.003	0.002	0.001		
27	0.764	0.586	0.513	0.450	0.347	0.268	0.207	0.125	0.076	0.047	0.029	0.023	0.018	0.011	0.007	0.005	0.003	0.002	0.002	0.001		
28	0.757	0.574	0.501	0.437	0.333	0.255	0.196	0.116	0.069	0.042	0.026	0.020	0.016	0.010	0.006	0.004	0.002	0.002	0.002	0.001		
29	0.749	0.563	0.489	0.424	0.321	0.243	0.185	0.107	0.063	0.037	0.022	0.017	0.014	0.008	0.005	0.003	0.002	0.002	0.001			
30	0.742	0.552	0.477	0.412	0.308	0.231	0.174	0.099	0.057	0.033	0.020	0.015	0.012	0.007	0.004	0.003	0.002	0.001	0.001			
40	0.672	0.453	0.372	0.307	0.208	0.142	0.097	0.046	0.022	0.011	0.005	0.004	0.003	0.001	0.001							
50	0.608	0.372	0.291	0.228	0.141	0.087	0.054	0.021	0.009	0.003	0.001	0.001	0.001									

SOURCE: Jerome Bracken and Charles J. Christenson, *Tables for Use in Analyzing Business Decisions* (Homewood, Ill.: Richard D. Irwin, Inc., 1965), except for the data on 2½%, the source for which is *Mathematical Tables from Handbook of Chemistry and Physics* (6th ed.; Cleveland: Chemical Rubber Publishing Co. 1938).

AUTHORS NOTE: These values are obtained by compounding at the end of each period. Other tables use different schemes of compounding, without changing the magnitudes greatly.

TABLE B

Present Value of $1 Received Annually

Periods to Be Paid	1%	2%	2½%	3%	4%	5%	6%	8%	10%	12%	14%	15%	16%	18%	20%	22%	24%	25%	26%	30%	40%	50%
1	0.990	0.980	0.976	0.971	0.962	0.952	0.943	0.926	0.909	0.893	0.877	0.870	0.862	0.847	0.833	0.820	0.806	0.800	0.794	0.769	0.714	0.667
2	1.970	1.942	1.927	1.914	1.886	1.859	1.833	1.783	1.736	1.690	1.647	1.626	1.605	1.566	1.528	1.492	1.457	1.440	1.424	1.361	1.224	1.111
3	2.941	2.884	2.856	2.829	2.775	2.723	2.673	2.577	2.487	2.402	2.322	2.283	2.246	2.174	2.106	2.042	1.981	1.952	1.923	1.816	1.589	1.407
4	3.902	3.808	3.762	3.717	3.630	3.546	3.465	3.312	3.170	3.037	2.914	2.855	2.798	2.690	2.589	2.494	2.404	2.362	2.320	2.166	1.849	1.605
5	4.853	4.713	4.646	4.580	4.452	4.330	4.212	3.993	3.791	3.605	3.433	3.352	3.274	3.127	2.991	2.864	2.745	2.689	2.635	2.436	2.035	1.737
6	5.795	5.601	5.508	5.417	5.242	5.076	4.917	4.623	4.355	4.111	3.889	3.784	3.685	3.498	3.326	3.167	3.020	2.951	2.885	2.643	2.168	1.824
7	6.728	6.472	6.349	6.230	6.002	5.786	5.582	5.206	4.868	4.564	4.288	4.160	4.039	3.812	3.605	3.416	3.242	3.161	3.083	2.802	2.263	1.883
8	7.652	7.325	7.170	7.020	6.733	6.463	6.210	5.747	5.335	4.968	4.639	4.487	4.344	4.078	3.837	3.619	3.421	3.329	3.241	2.925	2.331	1.922
9	8.566	8.162	7.971	7.786	7.435	7.108	6.802	6.247	5.759	5.328	4.946	4.772	4.607	4.303	4.031	3.786	3.566	3.463	3.366	3.019	2.379	1.948
10	9.471	8.983	8.752	8.530	8.111	7.722	7.360	6.710	6.145	5.650	5.216	5.019	4.833	4.494	4.192	3.923	3.682	3.571	3.465	3.092	2.414	1.965
11	10.368	9.787	9.514	9.253	8.760	8.306	7.887	7.139	6.495	5.938	5.453	5.234	5.029	4.656	4.327	4.035	3.776	3.656	3.544	3.147	2.438	1.977
12	11.255	10.575	10.258	9.954	9.385	8.863	8.384	7.536	6.814	6.194	5.660	5.421	5.197	4.793	4.439	4.127	3.851	3.725	3.606	3.190	2.456	1.985
13	12.134	11.348	10.983	10.635	9.986	9.394	8.853	7.904	7.103	6.424	5.842	5.583	5.342	4.910	4.533	4.203	3.912	3.780	3.656	3.223	2.468	1.990
14	13.004	12.106	11.691	11.296	10.563	9.899	9.295	8.244	7.367	6.628	6.002	5.724	5.468	5.008	4.611	4.265	3.962	3.824	3.695	3.249	2.478	1.993
15	13.865	12.849	12.381	11.938	11.118	10.380	9.712	8.559	7.606	6.811	6.142	5.847	5.576	5.092	4.676	4.315	4.001	3.859	3.726	3.268	2.484	1.995
16	14.718	13.578	13.055	12.561	11.652	10.838	10.106	8.851	7.824	6.974	6.265	5.954	5.668	5.162	4.730	4.357	4.033	3.887	3.751	3.283	2.488	1.997
17	15.562	14.292	13.712	13.166	12.166	11.274	10.477	9.122	8.022	7.120	6.373	6.047	5.749	5.222	4.775	4.391	4.059	3.910	3.771	3.295	2.492	1.998
18	16.398	14.992	14.353	13.754	12.659	11.690	10.828	9.372	8.201	7.250	6.467	6.128	5.818	5.273	4.812	4.419	4.080	3.928	3.786	3.304	2.494	1.999
19	17.226	15.678	14.979	14.324	13.134	12.085	11.158	9.604	8.365	7.366	6.550	6.198	5.878	5.316	4.844	4.442	4.097	3.942	3.799	3.311	2.496	1.999
20	18.046	16.351	15.589	14.877	13.590	12.462	11.470	9.818	8.514	7.469	6.623	6.259	5.929	5.353	4.870	4.460	4.110	3.954	3.808	3.316	2.497	1.999
21	18.857	17.011	16.185	15.415	14.029	12.821	11.764	10.017	8.649	7.562	6.687	6.312	5.973	5.384	4.891	4.476	4.121	3.963	3.816	3.320	2.498	2.000
22	19.660	17.658	16.765	15.937	14.451	13.163	12.042	10.201	8.772	7.645	6.743	6.359	6.011	5.410	4.909	4.488	4.130	3.970	3.822	3.323	2.498	2.000
23	20.456	18.292	17.332	16.444	14.857	13.489	12.303	10.371	8.883	7.718	6.792	6.399	6.044	5.432	4.924	4.499	4.137	3.976	3.827	3.325	2.499	2.000
24	21.243	18.914	17.885	16.936	15.247	13.799	12.550	10.529	8.985	7.784	6.835	6.434	6.073	5.451	4.937	4.507	4.143	3.981	3.831	3.327	2.499	2.000
25	22.023	19.523	18.424	17.413	15.622	14.094	12.783	10.675	9.077	7.843	6.873	6.464	6.097	5.467	4.948	4.514	4.147	3.985	3.834	3.329	2.499	2.000
26	22.795	20.121	18.951	17.877	15.983	14.375	13.003	10.810	9.161	7.896	6.906	6.491	6.118	5.480	4.956	4.520	4.151	3.988	3.837	3.330	2.500	2.000
27	23.560	20.707	19.464	18.327	16.330	14.643	13.211	10.935	9.237	7.943	6.935	6.514	6.136	5.492	4.964	4.524	4.154	3.990	3.839	3.331	2.500	2.000
28	24.316	21.281	19.965	18.764	16.663	14.898	13.406	11.051	9.307	7.984	6.961	6.534	6.152	5.502	4.970	4.528	4.157	3.992	3.840	3.331	2.500	2.000
29	25.066	21.844	20.454	19.188	16.984	15.141	13.591	11.158	9.370	8.022	6.983	6.551	6.166	5.510	4.975	4.531	4.159	3.994	3.841	3.332	2.500	2.000
30	25.808	22.396	20.930	19.600	17.292	15.372	13.765	11.258	9.427	8.055	7.003	6.566	6.177	5.517	4.979	4.534	4.160	3.995	3.842	3.332	2.500	2.000
40	32.835	27.355	25.103	23.115	19.793	17.159	15.046	11.925	9.779	8.244	7.105	6.642	6.234	5.548	4.997	4.544	4.166	3.999	3.846	3.333	2.500	2.000
50	39.196	31.424	28.362	25.730	21.482	18.256	15.762	12.233	9.915	8.304	7.133	6.660	6.246	5.554	4.999	4.545	4.167	4.000	3.846	3.333	2.500	2.000

Source: Jerome Bracken and Charles J. Christenson, *Tables for Use in Analyzing Business Decisions* (Homewood, Ill.: Richard D. Irwin, Inc., 1965), except for the data on 2½%, the source for which is *Mathematical Tables from Handbook of Chemistry and Physics* (6th ed.; Cleveland: Chemical Rubber Publishing Co., 1938).

Authors Note: These values are obtained by compounding at the end of each period. Other tables use different schemes of compounding, without changing the magnitudes greatly.

Tax Table

To be used in connection with cases in this book. This is not a complete statement of applicable rates, and it should not be used as a reference for general purposes. For example, the table of payment dates assumes that the taxpayer is on a calendar year basis, and special payment dates for small taxpayers are not detailed.

Income Years	Rate	Income Years	Rate
1954–1963	52.0%	1968–1969	52.8%
1964	50.0%	1970	49.2%
1965–1967	48.0%	1971	48.0%

In each case the rate breaks down into a normal tax of 30% on taxable income less than $25,000, and a surtax on the balance of taxable income to make up the rate shown in the table above.

Domestic corporations must deposit income and estimated taxes in a Federal Reserve Bank or an authorized commercial bank by the due date. The schedule of due dates is as follows (for companies that are on a calendar year basis):

| | Percentage Paid Each Due Date | | | | | | | |
| | Income Year* | | | | Following Year† | | | |
Year	Apr. 15	June 15	Sept. 15	Dec. 15	Mar. 15	June 15	Sept. 15	Dec. 15
1957.........	—	—	15%	15%	35%	35%	—	—
1958.........	—	—	20	20	30	30	—	—
1959.........	—	—	25	25	25	25	—	—
1960.........	—	—	25	25	25	25	—	—
1961.........	—	—	25	25	25	25	—	—
1962.........	—	—	25	25	25	25	—	—
1963.........	—	—	25	25	25	25	—	—
1964.........	1%	1%	25	25	24	24	—	—
1965.........	4	4	25	25	21	21	—	—
1966.........	12	12	25	25	13	13	—	—
1967 and sub- sequent years......	25	25	25	25	—	—	—	—

* These are percentages of the estimated tax liability on income of the current year.
† These are percentages of the tax liability on income of the previous year.
Sources: Derived from *Prentice-Hall Federal Taxes* (Englewood Cliffs, N.J.: Prentice-Hall, Inc., 1965) and *Prentice-Hall Federal Tax Course 1971.*

INDEXES

Index of Cases

American Motors Financial 594
Ampro Europe 762

Big City Trust Company 630
Boxer Corporation 839
Brown Marine Supply Company (1) 641
Brown Marine Supply Company (2) 647

Case of the Unidentified Industries, The 585
Case of the Unidentified Investment Projects, The 667
Central Broadcasting Company 749
Cerarts Company 918
Custom Plastics, Inc. 725

Digital Engineering Company 735
Dunning Cabinet Company, The 743

Estella Five-Year Plan, The 654
Extone Chemicals, Inc. 857

General Public Utilities Corporation 845

Head Ski Company, Inc. 877

Illuminated Tubes Company 663
Inconco Corporation 624

Liberty Petroleum Company 679
Long Beach Electronics Company, Inc. 716

Molecular Compounds Corporation 689

Nautilus, Inc. 793
Norwest Construction Holdings, Limited 906

O. M. Scott & Sons Company, The 599
Oren Weaving Company, Inc. 824

Piedmont Garden Apartments 782
Plowman Poultry Farm 707
Prudential Insurance Company of America, The 815

SCM Corporation 807
Shannon Corporation 775
Shin Mitsubishi Financial 588
Sprague Machine Tool Company 635
Storkline Shops 698
Sun Stores, Inc. 833

Union Paint and Varnish Company 614
Upstate Canning Company, Inc. 870

Wizard Corporation 893

Zenith Steel Company, Inc., The   669

Index

A

Abbott Laboratories, 456–57
Absolute priority rule, in reorganization, 577
Acceleration of principal; *see* Maturity, accelerated
Accounting methods
  and earnings per share, 546, 548
  for mergers, 545–46, 548
  for stock dividends, 481–82
Accounts receivable; *see also* Receivables
  accounting for, 63–64
  as security for loans, 254–55, 271, 273–76
  protection from risk in, 274–75
Accrued expenses
  defined, 207
  as source of funds, 206–7
Accrued income taxes, as source of funds, 207–8
Acid test ratio, 121
Acquisition, defined, 539–40
Acquisitions, 541–45; *see also* Mergers
  conglomerate, 546–48
Affirmative covenant, 381
After-acquired property clause, 443, 448
Agency basis, in securities issues, 319, 328, 330–31
Aging schedules, 62–63, 122, 206
Allied Chemical Corp., 444
Allied Crude Vegetable Oil Refining Corporation, 280–81
Allis-Chalmers Manufacturing Co., 341 n
Allocation of value, to securities, 452
Amalgamation, 539
Amerada Hess Corporation, 458
American Airlines, 422–23
American Cement Corporation, 442

American Express Company, 281
American Express Field Warehousing Corporation, 280
American Institute of Certified Public Accountants
  Accounting Principles Board of, 392, 425 n, 481 n, 545–46
American Metal Climax, Inc., 68
American Stock Exchange, 338–39, 496
American Telephone and Telegraph Company
  Employees Stock Plan, 331
  money position of, 79–80
  securities issues, 80, 297, 330, 468
  stock split, 480–81, 483
Amortization
  of intangible assets, 86
  of loans, 163–64
Annuities, discounting, 161–63
Arbitraging, 342
Arrearages, in preferred dividends, 360, 380–82, 435, 460–61
Assessed value, 550
Assets; *see also* Fixed assets *and* Inventories
  productive use of, 14, 16–18
  ratio analysis of, 117–20, 123
  return on investment in; *see* Return on investment, in assets
  of U.S. manufacturing corporations, 10–12
Atlantic Acceptance Corporation, Ltd., 78
Atlantic Richfield, 468

B

Bad debts, 47, 49, 56–58, 63, 65
  reserve for, 63
Balance sheet, ratios from, 353–54, 365–66

Balance sheet projections, 129, 135–39, 141
  procedure, 135–39
Balloon maturity, 238, 348
Bank of America National Trust and Savings Association, 215, 256 n
Bank credit
  contrasted with trade credit, 219
  importance of, 210–13
  for small businesses, 212–13, 240–41, 524,
    527–28
Bank deposits
  balance requirements, 70, 72–73, 229–30,
    241, 252
  demand (checking), 69–75, 213–14, 216
    check collection, 69–71, 81–82
  float, 69–71, 80, 526
  interest on, 73–75
  savings, 216
  time, 69, 216
Bank relationships, 54, 69–73, 82, 85, 225,
    237, 248, 252–53 n
  credit negotiations, 229–31
  line of credit, 84–85, 226–27
  for term loans, 237, 244–46, 248
Banker's acceptance, 46, 76, 259–61
Banker's spread, 321, 332–36
Bankruptcy, 60–61, 373–75, 563–64, 571–
    82; see also Failure and Insolvency
  creditor categories, 60, 435, 581
  defined, 564
  involuntary, 564
  legal action for, 564
  lessor's position in, 422
  without liquidation, 270, 571–79
    arrangement proceedings, 571–74
    reorganization, 571, 574–79
  minority creditors in, 573, 576
  priority of claims in, 60, 270, 272, 374–
    75, 447, 574, 577, 581
    absolute priority rule, 577
  secured lenders' status in, 270, 272, 374,
    447, 581
  statistics, 580, 581
  subordinated claims in, 288
  trustee, 575–76
  voluntary, 564
Bankruptcy Act, 564, 571–80, 582
  Chapter X (reorganization), 571–72,
    574–81
  Chapter XI (arrangement), 571–74
  Chapters X and XI compared, 571–72
Banks; see Commercial banks; Mutual
  savings banks; National banks; and
  State banks
Barack, Peter J., 488 n, 563 n
Beckman, T. N., 48 n
Beneficial Finance Co., 457–58
"Best efforts" in security selling, 322, 329
Bethlehem Steel Corporation, 188
Block sales of securities, 341, 342, 558

Blue-sky laws, 500
Blum, Walter J., 577 n
Bogen, Jules I., 299 n
Bond certificate, 346–47
Bond purchase, capital budgeting for, 149,
    151–53, 155–56
Bond valuation, time adjustment, 149
Bond value tables, 186
Bonds
  basic promises in, 346–47, 472
  burden (service, cash drain), defined,
    348
  call provision, 445–47, 455, 483
  convertible, 450, 454–56, 483
  cost of capital, 185–88, 350
  debenture, 288, 444, 450, 459
  in default, 347 n, 380, 422, 435, 443–44
  funds flows, 348, 350–54
  income bond, 434, 459
  indenture, 346–47, 446, 506–8
  maturity of, 4, 347–48, 472–73
  mortgage, 447–49
  new issues of, 296, 316–18, 320, 323, 329,
    333; see also New issues of securi-
    ties
  private placement of, 317–18, 418
  rating of, 187–88, 377
  in recapitalization, 472–75
  refunding of, 146, 348, 472–75
  risk position of, 374–76, 383, 435, 439–41
  serial, 441
  sinking fund for, 187, 347–48, 439–41,
    473
  subordinated, 288, 434, 450, 459
  tax implications of, 349–50
Book value, 194, 545, 554–57, 559, 564
  accounting practices, 545, 554–55, 557
  defined, 550, 554
Bosland, C. C., 559
Braniff Airways, Inc., 438–39
Brigham, Eugene F., 178 n
Brittain, John A., 414
Burden
  of debt, 348–53, 395, 472–75
    measures of significance, 350–53
  defined, as service, cash drain, 348
  of lease, 421–22, 425–26, 432–33
  of preferred stock, 360–62
  related to risk, 376–77, 395–96
  tax implications of, 349–50
  of total fixed charges, 362, 377
Burden coverage ratios, 352–53, 361–62,
    395, 432
Business development corporations, 261,
    533–34
Business turnover, 517, 563, 565

C

Call provision, 442–43, 445–47, 453, 455,
    473–75, 483

Capital assets, defined, 86

Capital budget, defined, 145

Capital budgeting, 91, chaps. 8, 9, 10; *see also* Cash flows; Forecasting funds flows; *and* Funds flows
  alternative projects, 149–50, 155–56, 162–63, 165–66, 183–84
  asset costs, 149
  cash flow forecasting, 150, 153–54
  cash flows
    effect of investment on, 150–51, 153–54
    schedule, 150, 153
  criteria for ranking projects; *see* Investment priorities
  forecast for, 392
  mathematics of, 156–64
  and taxation, 153, 155
  terminal values, 152–53
  time adjustment, 149, 152–53, 156–64, 167, 173, 175–76

Capital expenditure, described, 145–46

Capital gains, 406–8, 454–55, 458, 467, 477
  as cost of capital, 190–91

Capitalization, 365–66
  defined, 123, 365

Capitalization rate, 553–54

Capitalized earnings, 550–54
  estimate of, 551–53

Capitalizing asset costs, defined, 146

Captive finance companies, 46, 259

Carborundum Company, 95 n

Case problems, objectives and use of, 7–8

Cash budget; *see* Cash flows, forecasting *and* Forecasting funds flows

Cash flows
  analysis of, 149, 172
  associated with
    debt, 238, 350, 395–96
    depreciation, 93–96
    inventories, 31–32, 34–36
    leasing, 90, 92, 427–32
    payables, 132–34, 206
    receivables, 36, 63–64, 131, 134
    sales, 35–36, 131–33, 139
    tax payments, 208
    work in process, 34
  forecasting, 129–35, 139–40; *see also* Forecasting funds flows
  for capital budgeting, 150, 153–54
  described, 129–30
  to improve money position, 82–83
  limitations of, 137, 139–41
  for loan payments, 230, 238–39, 247
  and investment alternatives, 149–50
  net (cash throwoff), 238–39, 247
  operational, 112–13, 234, 238–39

Cash throwoff, 238–39, 247

CD's; *see* Certificate, of deposit

Certificates
  of deposit (CD), 74–77, 252
  of incorporation, 539

Chattel mortgage, 282–83, 449

Check collection, 69–71, 81–82

Chrysler Corporation, subscription rights issued, 329–30

Ciaccio, Jack N., 212 n

C.I.T. Financial Corporation (C.I.T.), 254, 256 n

Cities Service, 468

Citizens and Southern National Bank, 256 n

Citizens Utilities Company, 461

Closed-end mutual funds, 307 n

Closely held corporations, 287, 404

Coefficient of variation, 178

Collateral trust bond, 449

Collateral value, 550

Collection agencies, 60

Comaker on loans, 286–87

Combustion Engineering, Inc., 258

Commercial banks
  branch banking, 215
  commitment to lend, 227
  demand (checking) accounts, 69–75, 213–14, 216
  discounting notes, 228
  government regulation of, 214–15, 225
  income of, 216–17
  investments, 216–18, 309–10
  line of credit, 85, 226–27
  loan policies of, 214, 222–27
  loans; *see also* Term loans
    continuing renewal of, 223–24
    interest rates on, 216–18, 228
    negotiation of, 230–32
    procedures for, 226–30
    rejection of, 231–32
    restrictions on, 215, 225
    risk in, 218–19
    security used in, 267–68
    self-liquidating (STISL), 220–23
    short-term, 220–28
    volume of, 210–12
  as profit-making business, 215–16
  risk-taking, 218–20, 225
  savings deposits, 216
  trust accounts, 305, 309–10

Commercial Credit Company, 254–56

Commercial paper
  described, 75–76, 250, 252–53
  notes discounted, 252, 273
  rating of, 250, 252
    "prime" name, 250, 252
  as source of short-term funds, 250, 252
  volume used, 250–52

Common stock
  certificate, 354–55
  classified, 379, 460–61, 469
  cost of capital, 189–92, 194

Common stock—*Cont.*
  described, 354–56, 358
  dilution of ownership, 382, 384, 419, 444,
    454, 456, 461–62, 467, 476
  direct sales to personnel, 331, 332, 467
  dividend cover, 357
  dividend income, 189–90
  dividends; *see* Dividend policy *and* Divi-
    dends
  earnings and dividends, 189–92, 356–58
  earnings per share, 190–91, 356–57
  flexibility of management with, 355, 358,
    360
  funds flow, 356–58
  new issues, 296, 329–33, 335; *see also*
    New issues of securities
    cost of, 318, 332, 335–36
  nonvoting, 379–80, 469
  over-the-counter trading in, 340
  repurchase of shares, 484–87
    reasons for, 485–86
  risk position of, 359, 374–76, 378, 383,
    451
  subscription rights, 316, 329–30, 445,
    462–468, 476, 509–10
  voting power, 379, 382–84, 387, 442, 468–
    69, 476
  wealth of owners of, 406–08, 412
Commonwealth Edison Company of Chi-
    cago, 16
Compensating balances, 73, 218 n, 229–30,
    241
Competitive bidding for underwriting, 319–
    20, 323, 326–28, 508–09
Composition in insolvency, 569–70, 573
Compounding a single sum, 156–60
  compound amount, 157
Compromise settlements, 60–61, 569–71
Condemnation value, 550
Conditional sales contracts, 46, 283
Conditions of supply, 28
Conditions precedent in loan agreements,
    240
Conglomerate corporation
  described, 546
  effect of formation on earnings per share,
    547–48
  financial strategy of, 547–48
Consolidation, defined, 539
Continental Baking Company, 454–56
Contingent payments, 453–54, 459–60
Contractual burden
  defined, 351
  in financial planning, 393
Control of a corporation
  bondholders' power, 381
  and debt-equity mix, 381–84
  defined, 364–65, 379, 381
  minority, 380–81
  modifications in, 468–69

Control of a corporation—*Cont.*
  risks to, 380–81, 382, 444, 461–62
  through take-over bids, 495–96
  through terms of security issues, 379,
    381–83, 468–69
  through voting power, 379–80, 382, 384,
    442, 468–69, 511–12
  proxy, 493–95
Controller, 6
Convertibility, 454–58, 483–84
  of bonds, 450, 454–56, 483
  of preferred stock, 454, 456–58, 478,
    483–84
  in mergers, 457–58
  tax implications of, 457, 474, 477
Corporation charter, 488
Cost of capital, 30, 81, 398–99, 473–75
  average standard, 192–96
  for bonds, 185–88, 350
  calculations of, 185–95, 398–99
  for common stock, 189–92, 194
    capital gains, 189–92
    dividends, 189–92, 398–99
  and debt-equity mix, 192–96, 377–78,
    398–99, 411, 511
  defined, 185
  historical behavior of, 398–99
  opportunity cost, 198–99
  for preferred stock, 188–89
  retained earnings, 195–96
  short-term financing, 398
  by size of issue, 333–35
  as standard for investment priority, 195
  alternatives to, 196–99
Cox, Edwin B., 489 n
Credit
  as source of funds, 203–8
  sources of, 203–8; *see also* Bank credit;
    Commercial   banks;   *and*   Trade
    credit
Credit applications to banks, 230–32
  analyzed for term loans, 236–37
Credit cards, 64
Credit department
  collection problems, 59–61
    compromise settlement, 60–61, 569
  functions of, 46, 51, 54–60
Credit information
  credit reports, 54–55
  ratings, 51–54
  sources of, 51–56, 72
Credit losses; *see* Bad debts
Credit policies, 47–51
Credit reporting organizations, 51–56
Credit risk
  evaluation of, 56–59
    Four C's of Credit, 56
    by value of added business, 58–59
Creditors' committee, 61, 570
Crenshaw, Gordon L., 486

Crown Cork International Corporation, 461
Cumulative free cash, 394
Cumulative preferred dividends, 359, 404, 460
Cumulative voting, 380
Current ratio, 120–21, 438
  defined, 120
  use in analysis, 120–21
Customer prepayments
  as financial aid, 257–58

D

Day's purchases outstanding, 206
DCF (Discounted cash flow rate), 169
"Death Sentence Act"; see Public Utility Holding Company Act of 1935
Debenture, 444, 450
  subordinated, 288, 450, 459
Debt
  cost of, 350
  ratios; see Ratios
  secured position of, 374–75
  subordination of, 287–88, 444, 450
Debt capacity, 396–97, 401, 410–11
Debt coverage, ratios, 352–53
Debt-equity obligations, 403
Debt-equity proportions, 15–16, 122–24, 353–54, 364–66, 373–84, 419, 444, 472; see also Securities, balance of types of
  in cost of capital, 192–96, 377–78, 398–99, 441, 511
  debt-level-norms, 378–79, 401
  by industries, 379
  ratios, 123, 353–54, 365–66, 369–70, 379–80
  in return on capital, 15–16, 118–19, 367–73
  and risk, 15, 375–77, 395–98
  SEC standards for, 505–08, 510, 511
  tax implications of, 192–93, 511
Debt service; see Burden
Deere & Company, 46
Default
  on bond, 347 n, 380, 422, 435, 443–44
  defined, 435
  on lease, 422
  priority of claims in, 435, 447–51
  technical, 435–36
Deficiency judgment, 270
Depreciation
  accelerated, 95 n, 173
  accounting, 93–97, 392
  for tax purposes, 93–96, 98–99, 389, 392
  declining balance, 96–97
  funds flows, 93–99, 114, 389
  straight-line, 94–97, 173, 392
  as tax shield, 93–96, 98–99, 389, 392
Development credit corporations, 261
Dickerson, O. D., 566 n

Dilution of equity, 382, 384, 419, 445, 454, 456, 461–62, 467
  immediate, 461–62
  protecting value against, 462–68
  and voting power, 382, 384
Directors, 4–5, 246, 355
  dividend policy decisions, 4, 355, 358, 402–3, 405–6, 414
  election of, 379–80, 387
Discount
  for cash payments, 48–50, 204–5
  on securities, 185
Discounted cash flow rate (DCF), 169
Discounted value, defined, 158
Discounting
  acceptances, 261
  an annuity, 161–63
  in investment project analysis, 157–63, 167–69
  notes, 228, 252, 273
  a single sum, 157–60
Dividend cover, 357–58
Dividend meeting, 405
Dividend policy
  capital budget restraint on, 410–11, 413
  continuity in, 406, 413–15
  decision making, 355, 358, 402–3, 405–6, 414
  defined, 405
  distribution procedures, 405
  earned surplus used, 403
  and growth rate, 407–8, 410–13
  and market price, 408–9, 413
  restrictions on, 403–4, 437
  retained earnings alternative, 113–14, 405–7, 410–13
  after stock dividend or split, 483
  stockholders' position, 406–10
  the M.M. hypothesis, 407–8
  and taxation, 404, 408, 412
  time lag in, 414–15
Dividend yield, 357–58, 398–99
  defined, 409
Dividends
  on common stock, 398–99
  as cost of capital, 188–92
  described, 402–3
  as funds flow, 114, 356, 361
  per share, 356–58
  on preferred stock, 358–63, 404
  regular and extra, 406
  stock, 403, 481–83
  after stock splits, 480–81
  tax implications of, 350
  in valuation, 554
Dodd, David L., 470 n
Donaldson, Gordon, 387, 400
Dow Chemical Company, 78 n
Draft, 259–60

Dun & Bradstreet, Inc., 51–55, 68, 250, 517, 563–67
  credit rating, 52–54
  failure studies, 517, 563–67
  Reference Book, 51–53

E

Earned surplus; *see* Retained earnings
Earnings
  and burden coverage, 395
  capitalized, 550–54
  coverage, 188
  forecasting, 389–92, 552
  growth rate of, 407–08
Earnings
  before interest, lease payments and taxes (E.B.L.I.T.), 432
  before interest and taxes (E.B.I.T.), 352, 367, 372, 388, 432
    range-of-earnings chart, 372, 385
  per share, 190–91, 357–58, 371–73, 546–47
  yield (E/P), 189, 357–58
Eastern Gas and Fuel Associates, 342
E.B.I.L.T.; *see* Earnings, before interest lease payments, and taxes (E.B.I.L.T.)
E.B.I.T.; *see* Earnings, before interest and taxes (E.B.I.T)
Economic order quantity (EOQ), 29 n
Economic (productive) life, of an investment, 150, 154
Endorsement of loans, 273, 286–87
Equal and ratable security clause, 444
Equipment
  instalment purchase of, 273, 283
  investment in, 167–68
  leasing of, 167–68
  as security for borrowing, 269, 273, 282–84
Equipment trust certificates, 269, 283–84, 423
Equity, defined, 123
Erie Forge & Steel Corporation, 440
Erie Railroad, market price of securities, 375–76
Ex-dividend date, 405
Executive stock options, 467
Export-Import Bank of the U.S. (Exim-bank), 264–65

F

Factoring, 64, 255–57, 276
  active firms listed, 256 n
Failure; *see also* Bankruptcy *and* Insolvency
  causes of, 348, 566–68
  defined, 563–64
  management's role in, 582
  in new and small businesses, 517–18
  statistics of, 517, 565, 567

Fair market value, 550, 558
Federal Deposit Insurance Corporation (FDIC), 214–15, 498
Federal Home Loan Banks, 298
Federal Power Commission, 328
Federal Reserve Banks, 70
Federal Reserve Board, 74–75
Federal Reserve System
  limitation on speculative credit, 500
  member banks, 214
    loans by, 211–13, 267–68, 276–77, 284, 286
  Regulation U of Board of Governors, 286 n
  studies
    of bank lending, 211–13, 223 n, 267–68, 276–77
    of credit rejection, 231–32
    of small business financing, 526
Federal Savings and Loan Associations, 299
Federal Trade Commission (FTC), merger study, 540–41
FIFO, 31 n
Finance companies
  affiliates of suppliers, 46, 259, 283
  business (commercial), 254–55
  captive, 46, 259, 283
  described, 253–54
  factoring, 255–57
  loans by, 254–55, 268, 276
    on instalment notes, 254, 283
  personal (consumer), 254
  sales financing, 254, 283
  source of short-term credit, 75, 253–56
Finance function in business, 3–5
  organization to carry out, 5–7
Financial analysis, 110–26
  factors in, 110–11
  by ratios, 115–26
Financial objective, 12–13, 17, 146–47, 452
Financial officer, 5–6
  and credit policies, 46–47, 61, 63
  defined, 6
  and forecasting, 127, 131, 134–35, 140
  and inventory management, 18, 24, 27, 37, 40–41
  relations with management group, 6, 7, 27, 37, 40, 46–47, 75, 127, 140
  responsibilities of, 5–7, 13, 16, 18, 46, 66, 68, 75, 127, 246, 385
Financial policy, federal regulation of, 502–12
Financial programs, analysis of, 387–96
  for earnings, 389, 391–92
  financial specification, 393–95
  funds profile, 390, 392
  operating funds flow, 388
  for solvency, 387–88, 390, 392, 394, 396

Financial specification, 393–95
Financial statements, analysis of, 110–15
Finished goods; see also Inventories
  cash flows, 35–36
  investment in, 17, 24, 34–36
First Boston Corporation, 330, 342
First National Bank of Boston, 256 n
First National Bank of New York, 225
First National City Bank of New York, 74,
  256 n
Fitchburg Paper Company, 478
Fixed assets
  cost of, 91–92, 99
  defined, 86
  funds flows, 91–99
  investment in, 86–91, 96, 98–103, 136
    alternatives to purchasing, 87, 90, 92
    by American business, 99–102
    and liquidity position, 90–91, 102
    ratio analysis of, 102–3
    return on investment in, 90, 92–93, 102–3
  as security for loans 282–85
Flexibility in capital structure, 355, 358,
  360, 400–1, 446, 449, 458, 473
Float, 69–71, 82, 536
Floating charge, 450
Floating lien, on inventory, 281–82
Forbes magazine, 80
Ford, Henry, 35
Ford Foundation, The, 78 n, 321
Ford Motor Company, 297, 321
Forecasting funds flows, 127–42; see also
  Capital budgeting and Cash flows
  advantages of, 82–83, 127–29
  cash budgets, 129–30
  by cash flow forecast, 129–35, 139–41
    weaknesses of, 137, 139–41
  long-range, 141–42, 552
  for new business, 518
  operational, 388–389
  payments, 132–34, 136
  profit budgets, 130–31
  by projected balance sheets, 129, 135–39,
    141
  sales, 35–36, 131–32
Foreclosure, 285
Foreign trade, 259–61, 264–65
Fortune's 500, 16
Foster, R. S., 48 n
Foulke, R. A., 48 n
Franklin, Benjamin, 72
Friend, Irwin, 502 n
Frozen loans, 222, 224
Full disclosure; see Securities and Exchange Commission, full disclosure
  policy
Funding, 473–75
  defined, 471

Funds
  defined, 7, 112
  in the finance function, 3–5, 18, 21, 114–
    15
  forecasting need for, 127–42
  provided by operations (FPO), 92–94,
    96, 112–14, 351–52, 388–89, 452
  sources of, 12, 107–8, 112–16, 203–8
Funds flows, 10, 12, 21, 71, 112, 452
  analysis of, 112–16, 350–53, 356–58
  forecasting; see Forecasting funds flows
  related to, bonds, 348, 350–54, 474–75
    common stock, 356–58
    depreciation, 93–99, 114, 389
    fixed assets, 91–99
    operations, 91–93, 96–99, 112–14, 352–
      53, 388–91, 452
    preferred stock, 361–62, 474–75
    tax payments, 93, 155, 208, 389, 474
  statements of, 112
Funds profile, 392–93, 414, 415

G

Gant, D. R., 422 n
General Baking Company, 404 n
General Electric Company, 484
General Motors Corporation, 68, 484, 494
General Telephone Company of California,
  473–75
Ghana, corporate law in, 484 n
Gillette Company, The, 16
Glass-Steagall Act, 488
Going-concern value, 550
Gordon, Myron J., 408, 409
Grace, W. R., and Company, Inc., 450
Graham, Benjamin, 470 n
Great Northern Railway Company, 379
Gross margin, 117
Growth, internal versus external, 538, 542,
  547
Growth rate
  in earnings per share, 190–91, 370–71
  objectives, 542, 547
Guaranty of loans, 286–87
"Guideline lives," 95, 427
Guthart, Leo A., 484 n, 485–86

H

Hammond Organ Company, 258
Handy and Harmon, Inc., 29 n
Heller, W. E., and Company, 256 n
Hertz, David B., 179 n
Holding companies, public utility, 503–4
Horizon, for project life, 154–55
Household Finance Corporation, 254
Hunt, Pearson, 370 n, 487 n
Hurdle (cutoff) rate, 155, 166, 169–70, 172,
  180–81, 184, 195–96
  multiple, 180–81

I

IBM, 555
Implicit rate of interest, 169
Income, 364, 367–73
  defined, 364, 413
Income bond, 434, 459
Incorporation
  certificate of, 539
  charter, 488
  state laws on, 488
Indenture (bond), 346–47, 446, 506–8
  trustee, 346, 347
Individuals as investors
  census of shareholders, 313
  dividend-interest income of, 314
  financial savings, 297, 299, 301, 312
  stock holdings, 312–14
Inland Steel Company, 447–48
Insolvency; *see also* Bankruptcy *and* Liquidation
  without bankruptcy, 568–71
    arrangement, 569
    composition, 569–70, 573
    creditors' committee, 570
  creditors' attitude toward, 569–71
  defined, 350, 373, 563–64
  prevention of, 568–69, 579
Instalment credit; *see also* Finance companies
  on asset purchases, 282–83
  bank loans for, 224, 283
  conditional sales contract, 46, 283
  consumer financing, 45–46, 254
Instalment notes, loans on, 283
Institutional Investor Study, 502
Institutional investors, 298, 311–12, 316, 489
  listed, 299–300
Insurance companies; *see also* Life insurance companies
  equity participation in small business, 524
Insurance companies
  property-liability as investors in securities, 304, 442, 448 n
Intangible assets, 86
Interest rates
  on bonds, 440, 453
  implicit, 169
  on secured loans, 276, 284, 286
  on short-term loans, 216–18, 228
  on term loans, 240–41, 247–48
Intermediate-term credit, 224; *see also* Term loans
Internal rate of return (IRR), 167–69, 185–86, 428
  on leasing, 167–69, 428
International Paper Company, 91

Interstate Commerce Commission, 328, 459, 490
Intrinsic (investment) value, 550, 558
Inventories, 21–41
  analysis of, 37–40
  borrowing against, methods of, 279–82
  carrying costs, 17, 29–31
  cash flows, 31–32, 34–36
  day's sales, 25, 30, 38
  finished goods, 24–26, 32–36
  investment in, 10, 22, 24–25, 29–41
    control of, 29, 38–41
  obsolescence, 36
  optimum levels, 25–34, 41
  raw materials, 17, 24–32
  risks, 36–37
  sales ratios, 25, 30, 37–39, 64, 119–20, 136
  as security for loans, 254–55, 276–82
  supplies, 21
  turnover, 23–24, 38–41
  warehousing of, 279–81
  work in process, 24–26, 32–34
Invested capital, defined, 365
Investment
  defined, 150
  effect on cash flow, 150–51, 153–54, 167
  initial, defined, 150
Investment Advisors Act of 1940, 489 n
Investment analysis
  basic quantities in, 150–56
  defined, 147
  by incremental effect
    on cash flow, 148–49, 153, 167
    on value of business, 148
  standards, 155, 166, 195–99
Investment bankers
  on agency basis, 319, 328, 330–31
  "best efforts," 322, 329
  distribution of new issues, 318–31
  functions of, 318–20, 323, 328, 330–31, 341–42
  private placements, 319, 330–31
  secondary offerings, 342
  syndicates, 320–23, 326, 342
  underwriting
    by competitive bidding, 319–20, 323, 326–28, 508–9
    costs of, 321, 333–36, 509
    negotiated, 319–22, 328
    standby, 319, 330, 336
Investment Bankers Association of America, 342
Investment companies, 307–8
Investment Company Act of 1940, 489 n, 501 n
Investment Company Amendments Act of 1970, 501
Investment decisions, objectives of, 146–47, 197–99

Investment opportunity analysis, choice of alternatives, 149–50, 155–56, 162–63, 165–66, 183–84, 196–99; *see also* Investment priorities
Investment opportunity cost, 198
Investment priorities, 165–76
  hurdle (cutoff) rate, 155, 166, 169–70, 172, 180–81, 184, 195–96
  multiple, 180–81
  ranking by
    cost of capital, 180, 195–99
    discounting, 157–63, 167–69
    effect on reported income, 172–73
    internal rate of return, 166–69
    payback, 173, 175–76, 180
    present value, 158, 169–72
    profitability, 170, 172, 175
    return on investment, 155–56, 162–93, 166–69, 173, 184
    risk probability, 175–82, 196
    standards for determining, 166, 169, 183–84, 195
Investors
  institutional, 299–300, 311–12, 316, 489
  noninstitutional, 297–98, 312–14, 316
  objectives of, 417–18
Investors Mutual, Inc., 307 n
IRR; *see* Internal rate of return
Iselin, William, & Company, Inc., 256 n
Issuer of securities
  bargaining with investors, 417–19, 478–79
  defined, 490

J

Jamieson, A. B., 220 n

K

Kawaja, Michael, 566 n
Kendall Company, 445
Kentucky Power Company
  SEC case of, 506
Kohler, Eric L., 86 n

L

Lanston, Aubrey G., & Co., Inc., 342
Lawrence Warehouse Company, 279 n
Lead bank (agent), 234
Lease
  financial
    characteristics of, 421–22, 433
    contractual relationships in, 422–23
  net, 421
Leasing
  accounting methods for, 421–22, 425
  burden, 421–22, 425–26, 432–33
  cash flows in, 92, 427–32
  compared with debt financing, 422, 424–26, 428–32

Leasing—*Cont.*
  compared with ownership, 87, 92, 167–68, 421–24, 426, 428–32
  costs of, 427–32
  internal rate of return, 167–69
  tax advantages of, 426–28, 430, 431, 433
  terminal values in, 426–28, 431–32
Lehman Brothers, Inc., 318, 323
Letter of credit, 46, 260
Level payments, of long-term loans, 163–64
Leverage, defined, 367; *see also* Trading on the equity
Lewellen, Wilbur G., 192 n
Life insurance, as security for loan, 286
Life insurance companies
  assets of, 302–3
  as investors in securities, 300, 302–4, 316, 524
  term loans by, 241–43, 246
LIFO, 31 n
Line of credit, 85, 226–27
Ling-Temco-Vought, Inc., 438
Lintner, John, 414–15
Liquidating dividend, 544, 582
Liquidation, 565–66, 569, 575, 579–82
  creditors' attitude toward, 569, 571
  creditors' position in, 60, 447–51, 581–82
  defined, 565–66
  distribution of assets in, 364, 373–74, 580–81
  referee, 580–81
Liquidation values, 550, 556, 559
Liquidity position, 71–73, 79–85
  reserves, 71–72, 79, 84–85
Listing, on stock exchanges, 338
Litton Industries, Inc., 478
Loans; *see also* Commercial banks, loans; Term loans
  level payment of, 163–64
  line of bank credit for, 85, 226–28
  negotiating, 229–32
  from private lenders, 257
  procedures for, 226–29
  on promissory note, 228–29, 250
  security for; *see* Security for loans
  self-liquidating, 220–23, 233
  short-term, 220–28, 233
    continuing renewal of, 223–24, 242
    revolving credit, 224
Loeb, Rhoades & Co., 342
Loss, Louis, 495 n, 496 n, 501 n, 505 n, 507 n
Loughlin, McHugh, 212 n
Louisiana Land & Exploration Co., 458

M

McGee, Hugh H., 239 n
McGraw-Hill Publishing Company, Inc., 101 n, 102 n
McLean, Gordon A., 309

Maguire, John P., and Company, Inc., 256 n
Maintenance and replacement fund, 441
Manufacturing; see U.S. industrial corporations
Market value (price), 189–93, 378, 550–59
   affected by
      rate of return, 189–92, 552–53
      retained earnings, 406–7
      risk, 374–76, 378, 553–54
   described, 550, 557
   in valuation, 408–9, 550, 557–59
Marketability, of securities, 396–97
Marketable securities; see Money assets
Martin, William M., Jr., 526 n
Massachusetts Business Development Corporation, 261, 534
Maturity
   accelerated, 234, 243, 347–48, 380, 435–36, 438
   of bonds, 4, 347–48, 472–73
   of term loans, 234, 244
Mead Johnson & Company, 469
Meinhard-Commercial Corporation, 256 n
Merger, defined, 539–40
Merger movement, 540–41
Mergers
   accounting methods in, 543, 545–46
   conglomerate, 546–48
   convertible preferred used in, 458–59
   effect on earnings per share, 547–48
   minority interests in, 539, 544
   procedures, 539, 543–46
      asset purchase, 544–45
      stock purchase, 543–45
   reasons for, 541–42
   state corporation laws on, 539, 543
   statutory, 539–40, 543
   with subsidiary, 539, 543–44
   valuation in, 544, 548–59
Merrill Lynch, Pierce, Fenner & Smith, Inc., 342
MESBIC, 532
Michigan Consolidated Gas Company, 449
Michigan Electric Company, 441
Mid-America Pipeline Company, 458, 468
Military suppliers, government aid to, 265–66, 268
Miller, Merton H., 378 n, 407
Miller, Norman C., 280 n
Minnesota Mining and Manufacturing Company, 78 n
Minority Enterprise Small Business Investment Companies (MESBIC), 532
"M.M." hypothesis, of dividend policy, 407–8
Model Business Corporation Act, 403
Modigliani, Franco, 378 n, 407
Modigliani-Miller hypothesis of dividend policy ("M.M."), 407–8

Modigliani-Miller thesis of market value, 378
Money assets
   defined, 68–69
   functions of, 69–73
   income-producing, 73–79, 85
   management of, 68–85
   mobilization of, 81–82
   operational requirements of, 69–71, 83–84
   precautionary reserves, 84–85
   risks, 74–75, 85
Money market banks, 217
Money position, 66–68, 79–85
   defined, 66
Moody's Industrial Manual, 187, 404 n
Moody's Investor Service, ratings, 187–88
Morgan Stanley & Company, 320, 327 n, 342
Mortgage
   bonds, 447–49
   chattel, 282–83, 449
   on homes, 224, 298
   on plant and real estate, 284–85, 374, 447–48
Municipal securities
   dealers in, 340
   defined, 299, 340
   tax-exemption, 299, 309–10
Mutual funds, 307–8, 311
   closed-end, 307 n
   open-end, 307
Mutual savings banks, 213–14, 310
Myers, Stewart C., 409

N

National Association of Securities Dealers (NASD), 341, 497, 499
National Aviation Corporation, subscription rights, 463–66
National banks, 214–15
National Credit Office (NCO), 250, 252
National Lead Company, 78 n
National Quotation Bureau, 340–41
National Stock Exchange, 338–39
Near-cash investments, 66, 121; see also Money assets
Negative pledge (covenant), 270, 381, 443, 469
Negotiated credit, 212
Net income, 349
New business; see also Small business
   bank credit, 213
   conservation of funds, 536
   disadvantages of, 518–22
   failures, 517–18
   financial problems of, 518–20, 536–37
   securities, choice of, 385–86
   sources of funds, 519–20, 522–26
New Deal, 488

New England Gas and Electric Association, SEC case of, 506
New issues of securities
  costs of sale, 318, 332–37, 525
  direct sale to special groups, 331–32, 467
  federal regulation of, 489–92
  marketability of, 396–97
  price stabilization, 322
  private placements, 316–18, 330–32, 336–37, 418
    advantages of, 317–18, 418
    defined, 316
  public offerings, 316, 319–29, 418
    defined, 316
  rights; see Preemptive right; Rights offerings
  sales statistics, 295–97
  subscription rights, 316, 329–30, 462–64, 467, 476, 509–10
  timing of, 397–98
  types of transactions in, 316–19
New York State
  aid to small business, 533
  corporation law, 539
New York Stock Exchange, 311, 315, 329, 337–39, 479, 496–97
  "Census of Shareownership," 313, 489
  institutional problems of, 497–98
  listing requirements of, 338, 469
  Rule 325 (net capital), 497
  value of securities traded, 338–39, 496
Nonprofit institutions, investments by, 310–11
Nonunderwritten public issues, 328
Northeast Airlines, Inc., 425
Notes
  on credit sales, 45
  discounting, 228, 252, 273
  promissory, 228–29, 250, 273
Notice filing, concerning security, 272

O

Off-the-balance-sheet financing, 421–22, 425
Open-account selling, 45–46
Open-end clause in mortgage, 449
Open-end mutual funds, 307
Operating budget, defined, 145
Opportunity rate in capital budgeting, 155–56, 190
Over-the-counter markets (OTC), 339–41, 498–99
Overdrafts, 277
Oversubscription privilege ("second bite"), 467

P

Partnership, taxation of, 208
Payables
  aging schedules, 122, 206
  analyzing changes in, 205–6
Payables—*Cont.*
  forecasting, 132–34, 136
  policy of company, 121–22, 136, 205–6
  ratio analysis, 121–22, 206
  as sources of funds, 203–8, 536
Payback criterion, 173, 175–76, 180
Payout ratio, 191, 357–58
Penn Central Transportation Company, bankruptcy, 78, 250, 252
Pennzoil Offshore Gas Operators, 456
Pension funds
  private, 304–6, 309, 311
  public, 306, 316
Perpetual debt, policy of, 348
Personal trusts, 309–10
Pfeffer, Irving, 566 n
Pink Sheets, 340–41
Pinkerton's, Inc., survey on inventory losses, 29 n
Plant and equipment; see Fixed assets
Pooling-of-interest accounting, 545–46
Preemptive right
  of common stock, 316, 329–30, 445, 462–68, 476, 509
  described, 445, 462–64, 467, 476
  and market price
    cum-rights, ex-rights, 463–66
    formulas, 465–66
  in public utilities, 509–10
  subscription price, 463–64
  valuation of, 465–67
Preferred stock, 358–60, 362–63
  bonds compared with, 358, 360, 511
  burden coverage, 360–62
  callable, 442–43, 473, 483
  certificate, 358
  and common stock, 359–60, 419, 460, 510
  convertible, 454, 456–58, 478, 483–84
  dividends
    in arrears, 360, 380–82, 435, 460
    cumulative, 359, 404, 460
    as fixed charge, 361, 374–75, 453, 511
  funds flow, 361–62, 474–75
  new issues, 296, 323, 329, 333; see also New issues of securities
  participating, 459–60
  priority rights, 359–60, 374–75, 383, 450–51
  protective provisions, 381–82, 403, 510
  in public utilities, SEC policy for, 510–12
  sinking fund, 361, 363, 441–43
  straight, 359
  tax implications of, 361, 474, 477, 511
  voting power, 379n, 380, 381–83, 460, 469, 511–12
  yield ratio, 359
Premium over face value, 146, 185, 473–74
Prepayment of term loans, 239
Present value, 158–64, 169–72, 551
  defined, 158

Present value—*Cont.*
  as standard in capital budgeting, 158, 169–72
Price-earnings ratio, 189–93, 357, 399
  in conglomerates, 547–48
Primary distribution, 297–98, 315–32
Prime bank rate, 217–18, 240
Privileged subscriptions, 329, 462–68; *see also* Preemptive right *and* Warrants, stock purchase
Probability curves, 177
Prochnow, H. V., 221 n
Procurement lead time, 28
Profit budgets, 130–31
Profitability index, 170, 172
Progress payments, to government suppliers, 265–66
Promissory note, 228–29, 250, 273; *see also* Commercial paper
Prospectus, 321, 322, 491
Protective covenants, 381–82; *see also* Protective provisions
Protective liquidity, 83–85
Protective provisions, 381–82, 403–4, 434–35
  against additional obligations, 434, 443–45, 448
  for bonds, 381, 403, 435–36, 439–41
  against changes in business, 436
  for common stock, 445–47, 476
  for debt, 437–39, 443–44
  against diversion of assets, 436–37
  dividend restrictions, 437
  equal and ratable security clause, 444
  against financial degeneration, 437–38
  for preferred stock, 381–82, 403–4, 441–42, 444–45, 510
  in technical default, 435–38
  for term loans, 236, 240, 246–47, 425, 443
Proxy
  control by, 379, 380, 493–95
  fights, 494–95
  SEC rules for, 493–95
  solicitations, 493–94
Public utility companies, 16, 23, 42, 67, 79, 87
  concentration of control, by holding companies, 503–4
  cost of capital, 508–9
  debt-equity balance in, 505–8, 510–12
  "fair return," 79
  federal regulation of, 328, 503–13
Public Utility Holding Company Act of 1935, 328, 489 n, 501, 503–4, 506, 508–10, 513
Puget Sound Power and Light Company, 188
Purchase method of accounting, 545–46
Purchase warrants (rights), 329

Purchasing Week survey of inventory costs, 29–30, 36

R

Range-of-earnings charts, 372, 385
Rate of return; *see also* Return on investment
  ratios, 14, 118–19, 190, 409
  and risk, 553–54
  as standard for investment, 166, 169, 173
Ratings of securities, Moody's, 187–88
Ratios
  of asset use, 13–14, 116, 119–20, 123
  of burden coverage, 352–53, 361–62, 395, 432
  capitalization, 123, 353–54, 358, 365–66, 369–70, 395
  common stock
    dividend cover (payout), 357–58
    dividend yield, 357–58, 409
    earnings yield, 189, 357–58
  "days' purchases outstanding," 206
  "days' sales outstanding," 61–62, 119–20
  debt-assets, 122–24
  debt and equity, 123, 353–54, 365–66, 369–70, 379–80, 432
  of debt coverage, 352–53
  inventories-sales, 25, 30, 38–39, 64, 119–20, 136
  liquidity, 81, 116, 120–22
    acid test, 121
    current, 120–21, 438
    money assets-current liabilities, 80–81
    net quick, 121, 438
  payables—purchases, 121–22, 206
  preferred stock, yield, 359
  price-earnings, 189–93, 357, 399, 409
  profitability, 116–19, 170, 172
    assets—profit, 118–19
    equity capital—assets, 118–19
    sales—expense, 117
    sales—profits, 116–17
  rate of return, 14, 118–19, 190, 409
  receivables—assets, 42–44
  receivables—sales, 43–44, 49, 61–62, 119–20, 135–36
  related to risk, 178
  times burden covered, 352–53, 362
  times burden earned, 352–53, 362
  times interest earned, 352, 362
  use in financial analysis, 116, 124–26
Raw materials
  cash flow, 31–32
  defined, 24 n
  investment in, 24–25
RCA Corporation, cost of capital, 186–89, 191–94
Real Estate Investment Trusts (REIT), 322–23

Real Estate Investment Trusts—*Cont.*
time schedule for underwriting, 323, 324–26
Real property, 270
Recapitalization, 471, 475–87
of bonds; *see* Refunding
by conversion, 483–84
defined, 471, 475
dissenting stockholders in, 476
examples of, 477–78
preferred stock in, 477–78, 483
tax implications of, 474, 477
voluntary, 475
Receivables
accounting for, 63–64
aging schedules, 62–63
analysis of, 60–63, 119–20, 135–36
borrowing against, 256, 273–76
collection period, 43–45, 63–65
collection problems, 59–61
credit policies, 47–51
discounts, 48–50
factoring, 64, 255–57
forms of, 45–46, 259–61
instalment payments, 45–46
investment in, 10–12, 42–44, 49, 50, 61–62
determinants of level of, 47–51, 61, 64–65
open account sales, 45–46
risk, 49, 56–59
as security for bank loans, 271, 273–76
terms of sale, 47–50
Reconstruction   Finance   Corporation
(RFC), 262, 264, 268
Record date, 405
Redemption privilege, 473, 510–11
Redundant assets, 556
Refinancing, defined, 471
Refunding, 146, 348, 348 n, 472–75
after call, 473–75
defined, 471
funds flows in, 474–75
at maturity, 471–73
of term loans, 244
Registration statement, 320, 321, 326 n,
490–91, 493
Rental; *see also* Lease *and* Leasing
accounting methods for, 421–22, 425
of assets, 87, 421, 423, 425
by small business, 423, 528, 534
Reorganization, 573–79
under Bankruptcy Act, (chap. 10), 573–78
creditors' position in, 270, 574, 576
"fair and equitable," 577, 579
"feasibility" of, 577–79
procedures, 574–79
Reproduction value, 550, 555
Repurchase of securities, 473, 484–87
Residual value; *see* Terminal values

Retailers
inventories, 22–23
receivables, 42–43, 45–46; *see also* Instalment credit
trade credit, 204
Retained earnings
costs, 195–96
described, 366
as dividend alternative, 405–7, 410–13
in growth companies, 405, 411–13
as source of funds, 366, 402, 406–7
tax considerations, 404, 408, 412
Return on capital, 14, 15–16, 367–73, 551
debt, 452–53
effect of debt-equity mix, 15–16, 118–19, 367–73
equity, 14, 15–16, 367–73
calculation of, 15–16
ratios, 118–19, 190, 409
fixed payment commitments, 452–53
rate of
on common equity, 15, 190, 368–71
related to risk, 15–16, 439–40, 453, 553–54
Return on investment (ROI)
in assets, 13–18, 68, 90, 92–93, 102–3, 117–19
calculation of, 14
maximizing, 13–14, 17
ratios, 14, 103, 118–19
defined, 13
as measure of performance, 13, 18, 172
owners'; *see* Return on capital, equity
as standard for priority, 155–56, 166, 169, 173, 184
Revenue Expenditure and Control Act, 529
Revolving credit, 224
Rights offerings, described, 329, 464–67, 509; *see also* Preemptive right *and* Warrants
Risk
analysis of, 176–82, 395–96, 434–39
by computer model, 179–80, 395
and burden, 376–77, 395–96
and cost of capital, 180, 196, 377–78
and debt-ownership mix, 15, 375–77, 395–98
defined, 434
distribution among security types, 374–77, 443–51
and earnings, 553–54
and interest rates, 218, 439–40
in inventory investment, 36–37
and market price, 374–76, 378
probability distribution, 177–79
standard deviation, 178
in term loans, 236, 240
Risk bearing, 181–82, 396, 401
by banks, 218–20, 225
by investors, 219–20, 396, 418

Risk bearing—*Cont.*
by management, 410
"utility junction," 182
Robichek, Alexander A., 409
Rogers, Dean E., 238 n
ROI; *see* Return on Investment
Royal McBee Corporation, 478

S

Safeway Stores, Incorporated, 16
St. Regis Paper Company, 442
Salad oil swindle, 280–81
Sale and leaseback, 424
Sales forecasts, 35–36, 131–32, 135–36
Salomon Bros., survey of bond issues, 454–55
San Francisco National Bank, 78
Savings and loan associations, 213–14, 298–99, 310
SBIC; *see* Small business investment companies
Schwartz, Eli, 378 n
Sears, Roebuck and Company, 46
Seasonal datings, 259
SEC v. *Texas Gulf Sulphur Co.*, 499
Second mortgage, 448
Secondary markets, 315–16, 337–42, 490
Secured loans; *see also* Security for loans
from banks, 224, 229, 267–68, 275–77
Securities
allocation of value to, 452
balance of types of; *see also* Debt-equity
proportions
debt capacity, 396–97, 401, 410–11
decisions on, 385–87, 395–401, 472
in new business, 386
points of view on, 386–87
basic types of, 122–23, 345–46, 363, 364, 383, 384, 419
earnings relationships among, 419
federal regulation, of new issues, 489–92; *see also* Securities and Exchange Commission
fixed payment commitments, 361, 374–75, 452–53; *see also* Burden
issues of; *see* New issues of securities
as legal contracts, changing terms of, 476–77
modified types of, 419, 469–70
Securities Act of 1933, 489–92, 494
Securities Acts Amendments of 1964, 501
Securities and Exchange Commission, 335, 338, 419, 545
authority of, 419, 489–90, 503–4
and competitive bidding, 328, 508–9
full disclosure policy, 425, 484–85, 490–96, 503, 548
stop order, 491
informational requirements, 244–45, 320–21, 490, 493

Securities and Exchange Commission—*Cont.*
on insolvency, 572, 578
margin limitations, 500
proxy rules, 493–95
public utility regulation, 503–13
registration requirements, 490–93
on repurchase of shares, 484–85
Rule U–50, 328
Statement of Policy (public utility), 506–13
stock exchange regulations, 496–98
studies and investigations, 501–2, 525
Securities dealers, 341–42, 498–99
Securities Exchange Act of 1934, 489, 492–93, 495–500
Williams bill amendments to, 495–96
Securities exchanges; *see* New York Stock
Exchange *and* Securities Markets, stock exchanges
Securities Investor Protection Corporation (SIPC), 498
Securities markets
federal regulation, 488–89, 492–93, 496–98, 502–3
of primary distribution in, 489–92
of trading, 492–93, 498–500
functions of firms in, 341–42
margin rules, 500
over-the-counter (OTC), 339–41, 498–99
securities traded, 340–41
primary distribution in, 297–98, 315–32, 489–92
for secondary distribution, 315–16, 337–42, 492–93, 496–97
stock exchanges, 315, 337–39, 496–98
institutional problems in, 497–98
Security for loans, 224, 229, 267–89, 374, 443, 447–50
advantages of using, 268–70
assets used as, 270–73, 443–44, 447–49
equipment, 282–84
inventory, 276–82
plant, 284–85, 447–48
receivables, 256, 273–76
securities, 286
cosigners, 286–87
disadvantages of giving, 289
legislation on, 271–73
life insurance, 286
pledge of specific assets, 282, 374, 443, 447
Security Banknote Company, 459
Seiden, Martin H., study of credit, 48 n, 52
Shapiro, Eli, 409
Short-term credit; *see also* Commercial
banks, loans *and* Trade credit
commercial paper, 75, 250–53
from finance companies, 75, 253–56
sources listed, 249

Short-term investment media, 75–79
Short-term self-liquidating loans (STISL), 220–23
Sinking fund
  as burden, 348, 361, 363
  contingent, 440
  for debt contracts (bonds), 187, 347–48, 439–41, 473, 507
  for preferred stock, 361, 363, 441–43
Size of companies, percentage distribution by employment class, 520
Small business, 517–37
  cost of capital, 333–35, 525
  financial management in, 518–22, 526
  fixed assets of, 534–36
  government aid to, 261–64, 526–34
    state and local, 261, 533–34
  leases, 423, 528
  as percentage of total companies, 520–21
  sources of funds, 521–34
    banks, 212–13, 240–41, 524, 527–28
    debt financing, 212–13, 521, 525–26
    equity financing, 297, 524–26, 530–31
    SBA loans, 527–30
    term loans, 240–41, 524
    trade credit, 204, 519, 524, 536
    taxation, 208, 533
Small Business Act (1953), 263–64
Small Business Administration, 264, 527–33
  loans, 241, 262–64, 268, 527–30
  loss experience, 263, 530
  services of, 264, 527
Small Business Investment Act (1958), 527, 530
  Amendments of 1966 and 1967, 531–32
Small Business Investment Companies, National Association of, 532
Small business investment companies (SBIC), 241, 264, 527, 528–32
  problems of, 531–32
Smith, Adam, 220–21 n, 231
Sources of funds
  alternative choices, 241, 244
  classified list of, 107–8
  internal, defined, 293, 295, 402
Sources and uses of funds
  analysis of, 113–16, 293–96
  statements of, 112–16
  statistics for corporations, 294, 296
Southland Paper Mills, Inc., 318
Sperry Rand Corporation, 469
Spiegel, Inc., 457–58
Spontaneous sources of credit, 203–8
Spread (price), 185
Stabilization, of price, 322, 558
Standard deviation, 178
Standard Oil Company (New Jersey), 68, 484
Standby underwriting, 319, 330, 336
State banks, 214

State governments
  aid to small businesses, 261, 533–34
  borrowing, 299
State legislation
  on corporations, 488
  on dividend payment, 403
  on mergers, 539
  on recapitalization, 476
  on secured lending, 271–73
  on securities transactions, 501, 513
STISL loans; see Short-term self-liquidating loans
Stock dividends, 403, 481–83
  "fair value" of, 481 n
Stock exchanges; see Securities markets
Stock split, 464, 479–83
  accounting procedure, 481–82
  and market price, 464, 479–80
  reverse, 479
Stockholders
  census of, 313, 489
  dissenting, 476, 539
  expectations of, 189–92, 197, 354–55, 358, 387, 483
  management's responsibility to, 197–99, 355, 358, 387, 419, 452
  wealth of, 406–8, 412
Stop order, 491
Streater Corporation, 478
Subcontracting, to specialized manufacturers, 87, 90
Subordinated debenture, 288, 450, 454–56, 459
Subordinated income bond, 434
Subordination of debt claims, 287–88, 444, 450
Subscription rights, 316, 329–30, 445, 462–64, 467, 476, 509–10
Supplies, defined, 21
Syndicates of bankers, 320–23, 326, 342
  "several basis" purchase, 326 n

T

Take-over bids, 495–96
Talcott, James, Inc., 256 n
Tampa Electric, 468
Tax carry-back and -forward, 208
Tax exposure
  after-tax–before-tax formula, 351–53
  defined, 350, 352
Tax Reform Act of 1969, 96
Tax shield
  on debt, 349–52, 474
  defined, 94, 350
  depreciation, 93–96, 98–99, 389, 392, 428, 430–31
  on leasing, 426–28, 430, 431, 433
Taxation
  before-tax–after-tax computation, 155–56, 351–53

Taxation—*Cont.*
  and bonds, 349–53, 417, 459, 474
  and capital budgeting, 153
  costs excluded from, 93–96, 98–99, 349–
    50
  and dividends, 350, 361, 417, 459, 474,
    477
  as funds flow, 93, 155, 389, 474
  income taxes, accrued, 207–8
  in mergers, 543
  of personal income, 309–10, 404
  on retained earnings, 404, 408, 412
  of small business, 208, 533
Temporary National Economic Committee,
    merger study, 540–41
Tender offer
  for stock, 486, 495–96, 544
Term lending, development of, 233–35
Term loans
  analysis of applications for, 236–37
  borrower's position, 241–45
  costs to borrower, 240–42, 247
  described, 224, 233–34
  interest rates, 240–41, 247–48
  from life insurance companies, 241–43,
    246
  negotiating, 234, 245–48
    agent (lead) bank, 234
  from pension funds, 241–42
  protective provisions, 236, 240, 246–47
  repayment of, 230, 233–34, 238–39, 244,
    247
  risks to lender, 236–37, 240
  "taking down," 243
  volume of, 235
Terminal values
  of investments, 152–53, 190
  in leases, 426–28, 431–32
Terms of sale, 47–50, 275
Texas Company, 446
Textile Banking Company, Inc., 256 n
"Thin market," 558
Time adjustment
  in capital budgeting, 149, 152–53, 156–64,
    167, 173, 175–76
  in leasing, 431
  procedures, 156–60
Trade credit
  defined, 42
  delayed payments, 205–6
  for new business, 204, 519, 524
  normal, 203–5
  policy of company, 47–51
  risk and profit, 219
  for small business, 519, 524, 536
  as source of funds, 203–5, 211, 273, 519,
    524, 536
  special terms of, 258–59
Trading on the equity, 192, 367–73, 433
  defined, 367, 369

Trading—*Cont.*
  effect on return on common equity, 368–
    70
Trans World Airlines, Inc., 449
Treasurer, 6
Tri-Continental Corporation, 307 n
Trust Company of Georgia, The, 256 n
Trust Indenture Act of 1939, 489 n, 506
Trust receipts, for inventory as security,
    281
Trustee, in insolvency, reorganization, or
    liquidation, 570, 575–76, 580–81
Two-name paper, 273

U

Uncertainty, as factor in financial policy,
    4, 154, 236, 373, 408, 413, 434
Underwriting; *see* Investment bankers
Underwriting spread, 321, 332–36
Uniform Commercial Code, 272, 282
Uniroyal, Inc., 450
Unit, for purchase of mixed securities,
    458, 468
United Aircraft Corporation, 258
United California Bank, 256 n
U.S. Comptroller of the Currency, national
    bank supervision by, 214
U.S. Department of Commerce, study of
    bank loans, 212
U.S. government
  aid to small business, 262–64
  as source of funds, 261–66, 268
U.S. government obligations, income yield,
    78
  investment in, 12, 66–67, 74, 75–76, 217–
    18, 298, 309–10
  issue of, 298–99
  traded over-the-counter, 132
U.S. industrial corporations
  accrued expenses, 207
  accrued income taxes, 208
  composite balance sheets, 10–12
  current ratios of, 81
  five hundred largest, return on invest-
    ment, 16
  inventories, 10, 22–26
  investments, in assets, 10–11, 87–89, 96,
    98–102
    in government securities, 66–67
    in money assets, 66–67, 81
    in receivables, 10–12, 42–44, 48, 64
  return on investment, 16
  sources of funds, 12, 203–4, 293, 295
  trade credit, 203–4
U.S. Plywood-Champion Papers, Inc., 437
U.S. Revenue Code on retained earnings,
    404
U.S. Steel Corporation, recapitalization
    with bonds, 477–78

Universal Leaf Tobacco Company, 486
Utility function, 182

V

Valuation
  by asset approaches, 550, 554–57
    accounting practices, 545–46, 548
  book value in, 550, 554–57, 559, 564
  by capitalized earnings, 550–54, 559, 578–79
    capitalization rate, 553–54
    estimate of earnings, 551–53
  concept of, 548–50
  in liquidation, 550, 556, 559
  by market value (price), 408–9, 550, 557–59
  in mergers, 544, 548–49, 559
  model for, 409, 412
  negotiation of, 559
  redundant assets, 556
  in reorganization, 578–79
  reproduction value in, 550, 555
  situations demanding, 476, 544, 549–50
Value
  added by manufacture, 33
  types of, 550
Van Horne, James C., 178 n
Virginia–Carolina Chemical Corporation, 460
Voting power
  cumulative, 380
  dilution of, 382, 384
  of equity investors, 379–84, 442, 460, 468–69, 511–12

W

Wall Street Journal, The, 457, 466
Walter, James E., 408, 412

Warehousing
  field, 279–80
  public, 279
  receipts, as loan security, 279–80
Warrants, stock purchase, 329, 458, 467–68
Westinghouse Electric Corporation
  bond issue, 346–54, 356, 361–62, 377
    burden of debt, 351–53
    taxation on, 349–50
  capital structure, 365–66, 383–84
  control, 381–82
  debt-equity ratio, 353–54
  preferred stock, 359–62
  return on capital, 367–73
  trading on the equity, 367–73
Weston, J. Fred., 178 n
Wharton School of Finance and Commerce, study of the securities market, 501
Wheat Report, 1969, 502
White, William L., 192 n
Wholesalers
  inventories, 22–23
  receivables, 42, 48
  trade credit, 42, 204
Woolworth, F. W., Company, 440
Work in process
  cash flows, 34
  investment in, 24–25, 32–34
Working capital, 21
  in new business, 518–19
  in small business, 535–36

Y

Yield, to investors, 359, 398–99
Yield ratio, 359

This book has been set in 11 point and 10 point Bodoni Book with Garamond Bold #3, leaded 1 point. Part numbers and titles are in Helvetica Bold and Helvetica Medium. Chapter numbers and titles are in Helvetica and Helvetica Medium. The size of the type page is 27 by 46½ picas.